habituation v. dishabituation
mental repres
object permanence
3 dimensions of temperament
internal working model

Introducing the Interactive Companion Website for:

- ## *Infants, Children, and Adolescents, 4/e*
- ## *Infants and Children: Prenatal Through Middle Childhood, 4/e*

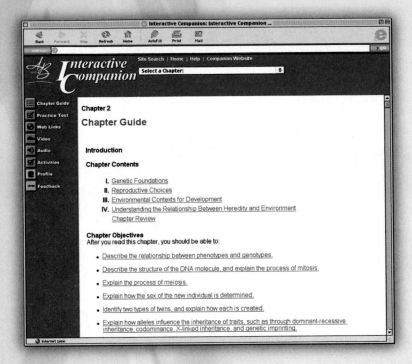

Learning has reached a whole new level with the Interactive Companion Website — by encouraging you to apply what you've learned through audio and video clips, Websites, activities and practice tests.

With the purchase of Berk's *Infants, Children, and Adolescents, 4/e,* or *Infants and Children: Prenatal Through Middle Childhood, 4/e,* you'll get access to this PIN-code protected Website FREE of charge.
The Allyn & Bacon Interactive Companion Website represents an exciting new study tool that uses the latest in multimedia to review, enrich, and expand on key concepts presented in its companion textbook.

Using chapter headings as its organizing structure, the Interactive Companion helps you apply what you've learned by presenting you with hundreds of links to audio and video clips, Websites, activities, and practice tests. The Weblinks are annotated with brief descriptions that help you understand the value and purpose of them in the context of the chapter.

Everything you need is right here at your fingertips!

ACTIVATE YOUR PIN.

How will you benefit from using the Interactive Companion Website?

✓ **Provides you with frequent feedback on your learning progress to perform better on tests.**

✓ **Offers highly interactive ways for you to engage with the textbook content.**

✓ **Adds variety to course materials and helps you study more effectively.**

✓ **Helps you think critically about the information presented to you in the textbook and on the Website.**

✓ **Gives you access to the latest information related to the textbook topics via the Web.**

> *A major advantage of the Website is that it allows students to connect with a wealth of learning support any time and any place. Professors can create a vast array of assignments and projects, knowing that all students — those in dorms and those commuting from home miles away, those with easy access to libraries and those who are more isolated — have the resources to complete the assignments and projects.*
>
> *Anita Woolfolk*
> *Educational Psychology Professor*
> *The Ohio State University*

Easy navigation that lets you study the way you want!

- Contents
- Practice Test
- Web Links
- Video
- Audio
- Activities
- Profile
- Feedback

1. **Chapter learning objectives are linked to the various topic areas,** allowing you to go directly from what you need to learn in the chapter to the media assets that will help you learn this information.

2. **Every chapter ends with…**

   A **Key Term Activity** presented as a flash-card exercise, allowing you to reinforce your mastery of important concepts.

   A **Practice Test** that promotes self-monitoring, a key element of successful learning.

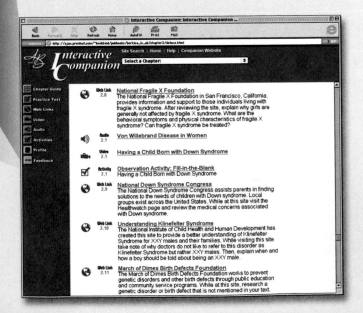

Interactive ways to prepare for that in-class exam and research paper!

Practice Test

Click on a **"Practice Test"** icon, and you'll be able to test your understanding of the chapter material by completing a self-scoring practice test. You'll receive immediate results from your test, allowing you to review your weak areas in preparation for the actual in-class exam.

> *I think it's great. You can take practice tests so that when you really get tested, you already know what to expect. I think it really contributes to your learning.*
> **Gloria, age 27**

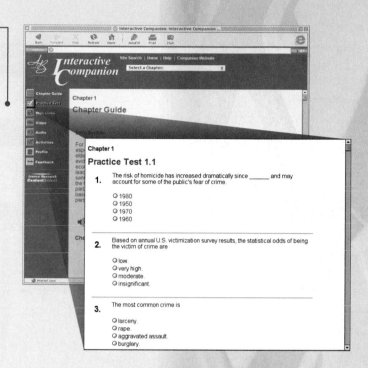

Weblinks

With the benefit of an Internet connection, by clicking on the **"Weblinks"** icon, you'll jump to current Websites that provide you with additional information about the specific topics you're studying. Weblinks are continuously monitored and updated by Allyn & Bacon, so you'll always have the most current sites to access. This is a great resource for you to utilize when writing a research paper!

> *These Weblinks help me find quality Internet resources for the types of assignments required for class.*
> **Debra, age 22**

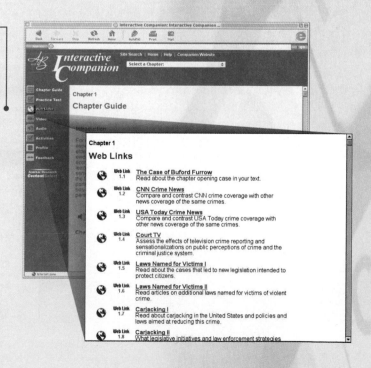

Information comes alive when you see it and hear it!

Video

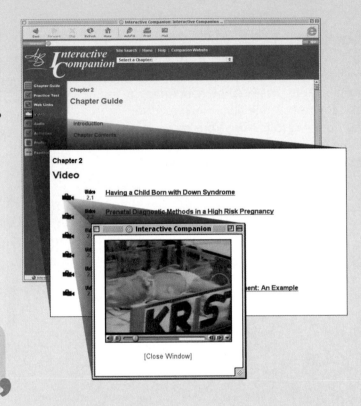

Click on a **"Video"** icon, and you'll be captivated by the **sights and sounds of video segments directly related to the material you just read.** Your textbook author filmed all of these segments as a special complement to this book.

> " The audio, feedback, and videos help me understand each chapter.
> **Janel, age 40** "

Audio

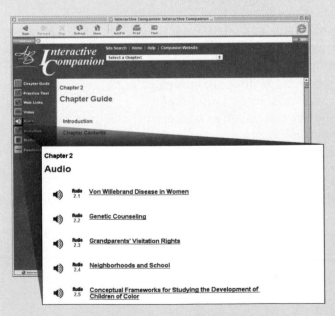

Click on an **"Audio"** icon, and concepts in the book will be explained to you. **Often the "voice" will add background information or give examples that extend material in the chapter.**

Activities give you more opportunities to test your level of understanding!

Activities

Click on an **"Activities"** icon, and you can complete interesting activities directly related to the information presented in the textbook. **You'll be asked to research, discuss, think critically, and more!**

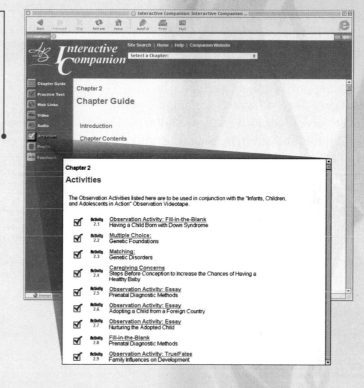

> "*I enjoyed using the Website! The matching games and the vocabulary terms helped me the most.*
> **Andy, age 18**"

Profile

By entering your profile on the site, you can avoid retyping it every time you need to submit homework. Once saved, the information will appear automatically whenever it's required.

Feedback

We are always looking to improve and expand on the information and technology we offer you. If you have any suggestions, questions or technical difficulties, please contact us through the feedback feature on the site.

More online resources to help you get a better grade!

ContentSelect for Psychology

The task of writing a research paper just got much less daunting!

NEW from Allyn & Bacon — customized discipline-specific online research collections. Each database contains 25,000+ articles, which include content from top tier academic publications and journals. Sophisticated keyword search coupled with a simple and easy-to-use interface will give you a competitive course advantage by providing you with a relevant and flexible research tool. You no longer have to spend hours culling through irrelevant results from other less sophisticated databases! This incredible research tool is FREE for six months, and can be accessed from the password-protected Web site available with this textbook. For more details visit: **www.ablongman.com/techsolutions**

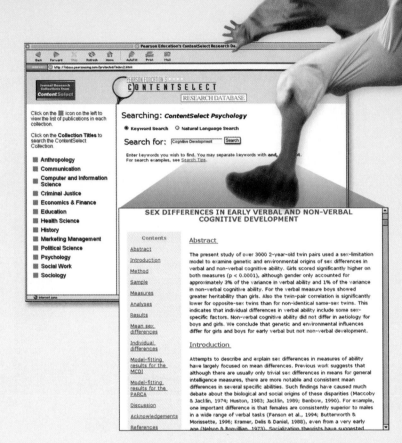

This powerful research tool will cut down on the amount of time you spend finding relevant information for your research papers.

Everything you need is right here at your fingertips!

ACTIVATE YOUR PIN.

Allyn & Bacon
A Pearson Education Company

Web: www.ablongman.com

Fax: (617) 848-7490

Tel: (800) 852-8024

Bookmark **www.ablongman.com/psychology** today & visit often to see what's NEW and available in the discipline of psychology!

www.ablongman.com/techsolutions

We're committed to helping instructors with their technology needs! Let us help you piece it together!

Infants, Children, and Adolescents

FOURTH EDITION

LAURA E. BERK

ILLINOIS STATE UNIVERSITY

ALLYN AND BACON

BOSTON   LONDON   TORONTO   SYDNEY   TOKYO   SINGAPORE

**IN LOVING MEMORY OF MY COUSINS,
ESTHER AND WALTER LENTSCHNER**

Executive Editor: Carolyn O. Merrill
Development Editor: Susan Messer
Series Editorial Assistants: Lara Zeises and Jonathan Bender
Senior Marketing Manager: Caroline Croley
Composition Buyer: Linda Cox
Manufacturing Buyer: Megan Cochran
Senior Production Editor: Elizabeth Gale Napolitano
Cover Coordinator: Linda Knowles
Photo Researcher: Sarah Evertson, ImageQuest
Copyeditor: Betty Barr
Text Design: Seventeenth Street Studios
Electronic Composition: Schneck-DePippo Graphics

Copyright © 2002, 1999, 1996, 1993 by Allyn & Bacon
75 Arlington Street, Suite 300
Boston, MA 02116

Internet: *www.ablongman.com*

Portions of this book are also published under the title
Infants and Children: Prenatal Through Middle Childhood, Fourth Edition, by Laura E. Berk, copyright © 2002, 1999, 1994 by Allyn & Bacon.

Library of Congress Cataloging-in-Publication Data

Berk, Laura E.
    Infants, children, and adolescents / Laura E. Berk. — 4th ed.
      p. cm.
    Includes bibliographical references and index.
    ISBN 0-205-33606-X (alk. paper)
    1. Child development. 2. Infants—Development. 3. Adolescence. I. Title.

RJ131.B387 2001
305.231—dc21   2001037305

Printed in the United States of America

10 9 8 7 6 5 4 3 2 VHP 05 04 03 02

Laura E. Berk is a distinguished professor of psychology at Illinois State University, where she teaches child development to both undergraduate and graduate students. She received her bachelor's degree in psychology from the University of California, Berkeley, and her master's and doctoral degrees in early childhood development and education from the University of Chicago. She has been a visiting scholar at Cornell University, UCLA, Stanford University, and the University of South Australia. Berk has published widely on the effects of school environments on children's development and, more recently, on the development of private speech in typically developing children and in children with learning and behavior problems. Her research has been funded by the U.S. Office of Education and the National Institute of Child Health and Development. It has appeared in many prominent journals, including *Child Development, Developmental Psychology, Merrill-Palmer Quarterly, Journal of Abnormal Child Psychology, Development and Psychopathology,* and *Early Childhood Research Quarterly.* Her empirical studies have attracted the attention of the general public, leading to contributions to *Psychology Today* and *Scientific American.* Berk has served as research editor for *Young Children* and consulting editor for *Early Childhood Research Quarterly.* She is the author of the chapter on the extracurriculum for the *Handbook of Research on Curriculum* and of the chapter on development for *The Many Faces of Psychological Research in the Twenty-First Century.* Her books include *Private Speech: From Social Interaction to Self-Regulation, Scaffolding Children's Learning: Vygotsky and Early Childhood Education,* and *Landscapes of Development: An Anthology of Readings.* In addition to *Infants, Children, and Adolescents,* she is author of the two best-selling texts *Child Development* and *Development Through the Lifespan.* Her recently released book for parents and teachers is titled *Awakening Children's Minds: How Parents and Teachers Can Make a Difference.*

Laura Berk with sons Peter and David

Brief Contents

List of Features

Contents

I THEORY AND RESEARCH IN CHILD DEVELOPMENT

II FOUNDATIONS OF DEVELOPMENT

IV EARLY CHILDHOOD: TWO TO SIX YEARS

V MIDDLE CHILDHOOD: SIX TO ELEVEN YEARS

11 PHYSICAL DEVELOPMENT IN MIDDLE CHILDHOOD

12 COGNITIVE DEVELOPMENT IN MIDDLE CHILDHOOD

Preface for Instructors

My decision to write *Infants, Children, and Adolescents* was inspired by a wealth of professional and personal experiences. First and foremost were the interests and needs of hundreds of students of child development with whom I have worked in thirty years of college teaching. I aimed for a text that is intellectually stimulating, that provides depth as well as breadth of coverage, that portrays the complexities of child development with clarity and excitement, and that is relevant and useful in building a bridge from theory and research to children's everyday lives. Instructor and student enthusiasm for the book not only has been among my greatest sources of pride and satisfaction, but also has inspired me to rethink and improve each edition.

The decade since *Infants, Children, and Adolescents* first appeared has been a period of unprecedented expansion and change in theory and research. This fourth edition ushers in the new millennium with a wealth of new content and teaching tools:

- *Increased attention is granted to multiple levels of the environment in which the child develops.* The contemporary move toward viewing the child's thoughts, feelings, and behavior as an integrated whole, affected by a wide array of influences in biology, social context, and culture, has motivated developmental researchers to strengthen their links with other fields of psychology and other disciplines. Topics and findings included in the text increasingly reflect the contributions of educational psychology, social psychology, health psychology, clinical psychology, neuropsychology, biology, pediatrics, sociology, anthropology, and other fields.

- *Diverse pathways of change are highlighted.* Investigators have reached broad consensus that variations in biological makeup, everyday tasks, and the people who support children in mastery of those tasks lead to wide individual differences in children's skills. This edition pays more attention to variability in development and recent theories, including ecological, sociocultural, and dynamic systems, that attempt to explain it.

- *The complex, bidirectional relationship between biology and environment is given greater emphasis.* Accumulating evidence on development of the brain, motor skills, cognitive competencies, temperament, and developmental problems underscores the way biological factors share power with experience. The interconnection between biology and environment is revisited throughout the text narrative and in a Biology and Environment feature with new and updated topics.

- *The link between theory, research, and applications—a theme of this book since its inception—is strengthened.* As researchers intensify their efforts to generate findings that can be applied to real-life situations, I have placed greater weight on social policy issues and sound theory- and research-based practices.

- *The educational context of development becomes a stronger focus.* The home, school, and community are featured as vital educational contexts in which the child develops. Research on effective teaching practices appears in many chapters and in the new Educational Concerns tables and Social Issues: Education boxes.

- *The role of active student learning is made more explicit.* "Ask Yourself" questions at the end of each major section have been expanded to promote four approaches to engaging actively with the subject matter—Review, Apply, Connect, and Reflect. This feature assists students in reflecting on what they have read from multiple vantage points.

TEXT PHILOSOPHY

The basic approach of this book has been shaped by my own professional and personal history as a teacher, researcher, and parent. It consists of seven philosophical ingredients that I regard as essential for students to emerge from a course with a thorough understanding of child development:

1. An understanding of major theories and the strengths and shortcomings of each. The first chapter begins by emphasizing that only knowledge of multiple theories can do justice to the richness of child development. As I take up each age sector and domain of development, I present a variety of theoretical perspectives, indicate how each highlights previously overlooked contributions to development, and discuss research that has been used to evaluate them. Consideration of contrasting theories also serves as the context for an even-handed analysis of many controversial issues throughout the text.

2. An appreciation of research strategies for investigating child development. To evaluate theories, students must have a firm grounding in research methods and designs. In addition to a special section in Chapter 1 covering research strategies, throughout the book numerous studies are discussed in sufficient detail for students to use what they have learned to critically assess the findings, conclusions, and implications of research.

3. Knowledge of both the sequence of child development and the processes that underlie it. Students are provided with a description of the organized sequence of development, along with a discussion of processes of change. An understanding of process—how complex interactions of biological and environmental events produce development—has been the focus of most recent research. Accordingly, the text reflects this emphasis. But new information about the timetable of change has also emerged. In many ways, children have proven far more competent than they were believed to be in the past. Current evidence on the timing and sequence of development, along with its implications for process, is presented throughout the book.

4. An appreciation of the impact of context and culture on child development. A wealth of research indicates that children live in rich physical and social contexts that affect all aspects of development. In each chapter, the student travels to distant parts of the world as I review a growing body of cross-cultural evidence. The text narrative also discusses many findings on socioeconomically and ethnically diverse children, and children with varying abilities and disabilities. Besides highlighting the role of immediate settings, such as family, neighborhood, and school, I make a concerted effort to underscore the impact of larger social structures—societal values, laws, and government programs—on children's well-being.

5. An understanding of the joint contributions of biology and environment to development. The field recognizes more powerfully than ever before the interaction of hereditary/constitutional and environmental factors—that these contributions to development combine in complex ways and cannot be separated in a simple manner. Numerous examples of how biological dispositions can be maintained as well as transformed by social contexts are presented throughout the book.

6. A sense of the interdependency of all domains of development—physical, cognitive, emotional, and social. Every chapter takes an integrated approach to understanding children. I show how physical, cognitive, emotional, and social development are interwoven. Within the text narrative and in the "Ask Yourself . . . Connect" questions, students are referred to other sections of the book to deepen their grasp of relationships between various aspects of change.

7. An appreciation of the interrelatedness of theory, research, and applications. Throughout this book, I emphasize that theories of child development and the research stimulated by them provide the foundation for sound, effective practices with children. The link between theory, research, and applications is reinforced by an organizational format in which theory and research are presented first, followed by implications for practice. In addition, a current focus in the field—harnessing child development knowledge to shape social policies that support children's needs—is reflected in every chapter. The text addresses the current condition of children in the United States and around the world and shows how theory and research have sparked successful interventions.

TEXT ORGANIZATION

I have chosen a chronological organization for this text. The chronological approach has the advantage of enabling students to get to know children of a given age period very well. It also eases the task of integrating the various aspects of development. At the same time, a chronologically organized book requires that theories covering several age periods be presented piecemeal. This creates a challenge for students, who must link the various parts together. To assist with this task, I remind students of important earlier achievements before discussing new developments. Also, chapters devoted to the same topic (for example, Cognitive Development in Early Childhood, Cognitive Development in Middle Childhood) follow similarly organized patterns, making it easier for students to draw connections across age periods and construct a continuous vision of developmental change.

NEW COVERAGE IN THE FOURTH EDITION

In this edition, I continue to represent a rapidly transforming contemporary literature with theory and research from more than 1,500 new citations. To make room for new coverage, I have condensed and reorganized some topics and eliminated others that are no longer as crucial in view of new evidence. The following is a sampling of major content changes, organized by chapter (a more complete description of changes can be found in the Instructor's Resource Manual that accompanies the text):

■ **CHAPTER 1**
■ New sections describing major periods and domains of development at the beginning of the chapter. ■ Revised section on basic issues on which major theories take a stand. ■ Expanded discussion of applications of information-processing research. ■ Enhanced section on development as a dynamic system. ■ New sections on psychophysiological methods as well as methods for studying culture, illustrated in a new Cultural Influences box on immigrant youth.

■ **CHAPTER 2**
■ Increased attention to the complexity of genetic influences, including a revised and updated Biology and Environment box on the Human Genome Project. ■ New section on environmental influences on gene expression,

including discussion of epigenesis. ■ Updated section on environmental contexts for development, with special attention to family and neighborhood influences. ■ New Biology and Environment box on uncoupling genetic–environmental correlations for mental illness and antisocial behavior.

■ **CHAPTER 3**

■ Updated research on the relationship of family size to development. ■ Enhanced and updated discussion of teratogens, with special attention to the consequences of illegal drugs, alcohol, radiation, environmental pollutants, and infectious disease for brain development. ■ New Social Issues: Health box on the prenatal environment and health in later life.

■ **CHAPTER 4**

■ Expanded and updated sections on social support, interventions, and complications during labor and delivery; maternal bonding; and capacities of the newborn. ■ New Biology and Environment box on factors that control the timing of birth. ■ Updated Social Issues: Health box, including current international data on infant mortality and paid maternity and paternity leave policies.

■ **CHAPTER 5**

■ New case examples, including the story of Grace, a 16-month-old toddler born in Cambodia and adopted by American parents. ■ Enhanced discussion of brain development, including synaptic pruning, lateralization, plasticity, and sensitive periods, with implications for appropriate infant and toddler stimulation. ■ New research on development of vision, including pattern and face perception and perception of object unity. ■ New Biology and Environment box on development of infants with severe visual impairments.

■ **CHAPTER 6**

■ New research on infants' reasoning about the physical world, including object permanence and physical causality. ■ New research on development of vision, including pattern and face perception and perception of object unity. ■ Updated findings on development of representation, memory, and categorization. ■ Expanded treatment of the social context of early cognitive development. ■ Updated research on specialization of brain areas for language, with emphasis on the role of language-learning experiences in lateralization. ■ New section on a sensitive period for language development. ■ New Biology and Environment box on parent–child interaction and cognitive development of deaf children.

■ **CHAPTER 7**

■ Application of the dynamic systems perspective to early emotional development. ■ Cross-cultural evidence on

development of stranger anxiety. ■ Enhanced consideration of the development of emotional self-regulation, including cultural variations. ■ Expanded discussion of dimensions of temperament, stability of temperament, and cultural influences on the development of temperament. ■ Updated consideration of the role of infant temperament and caregiving in attachment security. ■ New findings on disorganized/disoriented attachment. ■ Updated Social Issues box on child care and attachment security, including findings from the NICHD Study of Early Child Care.

■ **CHAPTER 8**

■ New evidence on lateralization and handedness. ■ Revised and updated Biology and Environment box on treating short children with growth hormone. ■ Expanded discussion of environmental influences on preschoolers' eating behaviors. ■ Updated statistics on child health indicators, including nutrition, immunization, and infectious disease. ■ New Social Issues: Health box on otitis media and development. ■ Expanded discussion of prevention strategies of unintentional injuries. ■ Updated consideration of development of drawing and writing.

■ **CHAPTER 9**

■ Revised section on preschoolers' understanding of symbol–real world relations. ■ New research on reasoning by analogy, causal reasoning, and categorization. ■ Revised section evaluating Vygotsky's theory. ■ New section on problem solving, covering overlapping-waves theory of strategy development. ■ New Cultural Influences box on young children's daily life in a Yucatec Mayan village, illustrating diversity in preschool cognitive development. ■ Updated discussion of the young child's theory of mind. ■ Updated discussion of literacy and mathematical development. ■ New evidence on outcomes associated with child-centered versus academic preschools. ■ New evidence on language development, including vocabulary, grammar, and conversational skills.

■ **CHAPTER 10**

■ New Cultural Influences box on implications of cultural variations in personal storytelling for preschoolers' self-concepts. ■ New evidence on understanding of intentions and emotions, emotional self-regulation, and self-conscious emotions. ■ Updated section on empathy, including the distinction between empathy and sympathy. ■ New findings on cultural variations in peer sociability and on friendships as social supports during the transition to school. ■ New section on social problem solving. ■ Revised and updated section on television and aggression. ■ New research on morality, with special attention to distinctions between moral imperatives, social conventions, and matters of personal choice. ■

Expanded discussion of cultural variations in child-rearing styles. ■ Updated section on child maltreatment.

■ **CHAPTER 11**
■ Current findings on development of myopia. ■ Updated and expanded discussion of childhood obesity. ■ Updated Social Issues: Education box on children's understanding of health and illness. ■ Expanded consideration of sex differences in motor skills and adult-organized youth sports.

■ **CHAPTER 12**
■ Updated research on cognitive inhibition, planning, and early reading development. ■ Enhanced consideration of culture, language styles, and mental test performance. ■ Updated research on dynamic testing. ■ Expanded consideration of gains in communication skills. ■ Revised and updated sections on bilingual development and bilingual education. ■ New Social Issues: Education box on school readiness, academic redshirting, and early retention. ■ Enhanced discussion of school grouping practices, cooperative learning, and inclusion. ■ Updated section on gifted children, with special attention to the distinction between talent and creativity.

■ **CHAPTER 13**
■ Enhanced consideration of self-concept and self-esteem, including cultural variations. ■ Expanded treatment of self-conscious emotions, emotional understanding, and emotional self-regulation. ■ Updated consideration of school-age children's grasp of linkages between moral rules and social conventions. ■ Expanded discussion of peer groups. ■ New evidence on peer acceptance, including two subtypes of popular children. ■ Updated Biology and Environment box on bullies and their victims. ■ Updated discussion of development of gender stereotypes, including girls' tendency to discount their academic talent. ■ New section on never-married, single-parent families. ■ Updated section on divorce, with special attention to long-term consequences. ■ Enhanced attention to age differences in children's adjustment to blended families. ■ Updated section on child care for school-age children. ■ Inclusion of findings on school-based violence prevention programs.

■ **CHAPTER 14**
■ New findings on the link between the emotional quality of childhood experiences and timing of puberty. ■ New section on implications of adolescents' tendency to stay up late for their learning, mood, and behavior. ■ Updated research on parent–child relationships and anorexia nervosa and bulimia nervosa. ■ New evidence on sexual activity, adolescent parenthood, and pregnancy prevention. ■ Updated findings on substance use and abuse. ■ New Biology and Environment box on intergenerational continuity in adolescent parenthood.

■ **CHAPTER 15**
■ New evidence on the development of propositional thought and scientific reasoning. ■ Updated coverage of sex differences in mathematical and spatial abilities. ■ New research on language development, including understanding of figurative language. ■ Current research on school transitions, family and peer influences on academic achievement, and drop-out prevention strategies. ■ New Social Issues: Education box on highly achieving, optimistic African American high school students. ■ Updated research on the school-to-work transition.

■ **CHAPTER 16**
■ Updated research on self-concept and self-esteem, including profiles of separate self-esteems. ■ Enhanced discussion of identity development, including a new section on the role of close friends. ■ Updated Cultural Influences box on ethnic identity. ■ Expanded treatment of sex differences in moral reasoning, including cross-cultural research. ■ Enhanced discussion of influences on moral reasoning, including a new section on the role of personality and a revised section on the impact of culture. ■ New Social Issues: Education box on development of civic responsibility. ■ Expanded treatment of adolescent sibling relationships. ■ Enhanced discussion of adolescent friendships, including stability of friendships and significance of other-sex friends. ■ Special emphasis on personal and contextual factors that contribute to adolescent problem behavior, as illustrated by depression, suicide, and delinquency.

INSTRUCTOR'S SUPPLEMENTS

A variety of teaching tools are available to assist instructors in organizing lectures, planning demonstrations and examinations, and ensuring student comprehension.

■ **INSTRUCTOR'S RESOURCE MANUAL (IRM)**
Prepared by Sara Harris and Laura E. Berk, Illinois State University, this thoroughly revised IRM contains additional material to enrich your class presentations. For each chapter, the IRM provides a Chapter-at-a-Glance grid, Brief Chapter Summary, Learning Objectives, detailed Lecture Outline, Lecture Extensions, Learning Activities, "Ask Yourself" questions with answers, Suggested Readings, Transparencies listing, and Media Materials.

■ **TEST BANK**
Prepared by Gabrielle Principe, Cornell University, and Karla Gingerich, Colorado State University, the test bank contains over 2,000 multiple-choice questions, each of which is cross-referenced to a Learning Objective, page-referenced to chapter content, and classified by type (factual, applied, or conceptual); essay questions; and premade tests.

■ **COMPUTERIZED TEST BANK**

This computerized version of the test bank is available in Windows and Macintosh formats using ESATEST III, the best-selling test generation software.

■ **TRANSPARENCIES**

Two hundred full-color transparencies taken from the text and other sources are available on adoption of the text.

■ *SEASONS OF LIFE* **VIDEO SERIES**

Illustrating the text's interdisciplinary focus, this five-video series explores a multitude of biological, psychological, and social influences on development. Nearly 75 psychologists, biologists, sociologists, and anthropologists present theory, methods, and research. Student Activities are provided in the IRM to help you integrate *Seasons of Life* into your course. Your publisher's representative can provide you with details on class enrollment restrictions.

■ **FILMS FOR THE HUMANITIES & SCIENCES: CHILD DEVELOPMENT VIDEO**

Complementing the text's linkage of theory and research to application, this revised video features high-interest segments on topics such as genetic counseling, fetal alcohol syndrome, the child's theory of mind, and adolescent depression. The IRM provides synopses and Discussion Questions for each segment.

■ **"INFANTS, CHILDREN, AND ADOLESCENTS IN ACTION" OBSERVATION PROGRAM**

I have revised and expanded this real-life videotape, containing a wealth of observation segments that illustrate the many theories, concepts, and milestones of child development. An Observation Guide helps students use the video in conjunction with the textbook, deepening their understanding of the material and applying what they have learned to everyday life. The videotape and Observation Guide are free to instructors who adopt the text and are available to students at a discount when packaged with the text.

■ **POWERPOINT™ CD-ROM**

A PowerPoint™ CD-ROM contains outlines of key points and illustrations from each chapter, as well as an electronic version of the Instructor's Resource Manual, making it easy to customize content.

■ **WEBSITE**

www.ablongman.com/berk

Designed for students and faculty of child and human development classes, this website includes current links and information about development, Online Practice Tests, a Teaching Aids section, Websketches (extensions of the stories illustrating development in the text), and a variety of additional features. With the purchase of a new text, your students will receive a PIN code that provides them with access to a robust Interactive Companion site that encourages interactive learning by providing many activities that have been specially created for this edition and access to Content Select, which provides online access to journal articles from most major journals.

■ **COURSE MANAGEMENT**

CourseCompass™ is a dynamic, interactive online course management tool powered by Blackboard.™ This exciting product allows you to teach with text-specific content in an easy-to-use customizable format.

ACKNOWLEDGMENTS

The dedicated contributions of a great many individuals helped make this book a reality and contributed to refinements and improvements in this fourth edition. An impressive cast of reviewers provided many helpful suggestions, constructive criticisms, and encouragement and enthusiasm for the organization and content of the text. I am grateful to each one of them.

■ **REVIEWERS OF THE OF THE FIRST THROUGH THIRD EDITIONS**

Mark B. Alcorn, University of Northern Colorado
Kathleen Bey, Palm Beach Community College
Donald Bowers, Community College of Philadelphia
Michele Y. Breault, Truman State University
Jerry Bruce, Sam Houston State College
Joseph J. Campos, University of California, Berkeley
Nancy Taylor Coghill, University of Southwest Louisiana
Diane Brothers Cook, Gainesville College
Jennifer Cook, Kent State University
Roswell Cox, Berea College
Zoe Ann Davidson, Alabama A & M University
Sheridan DeWolf, Grossmont College
Constance DiMaria-Kross, Union County College
Kathleen Fite, Southwest Texas State University
Trisha Folds-Bennett, College of Charleston
Vivian Harper, San Joaquin Delta College
Janice Hartgrove-Freile, North Harris Community College
Vernon Haynes, Youngstown State University
Bert Hayslip, Jr., University of North Texas
Paula Hillmann, University of Wisconsin, Waukesha
Malia Huchendorf, Normandale Community College
Clementine Hansley Hurt, Radford University
John S. Klein, Castleton State College
Eugene Krebs, California State University, Fresno
Carole Kremer, Hudson Valley Community College
Gary W. Ladd, University of Illinois, Urbana-Champaign
Linda Lavine, State University of New York at Cortland
Gail Lee, Jersey City State College
Judith R. Levine, State University of New York at
    Farmingdale

Frank Manis, University of Southern California
Mary Ann McLaughlin, Clarion University of Pennsylvania
Cloe Merrill, Weber State University
Rich Metzger, University of Tennessee at Chattanooga
Jennifer Trapp Myers, University of Michigan
Peter V. Oliver, University of Hartford
Virginia Parsons, Carroll College
Alan Russell, Flinders University
Tizrah Schutzengel, Bergen Community College
Johnna Shapiro, Illinois Wesleyan University
Gregory Smith, Dickinson College
Thomas Spencer, San Francisco State University
Carolyn Spies, Bloomfield College
Connie Steele, University of Tennessee, Knoxville
Janet Strayer, Simon Fraser University
Marcia Summers, Ball State University
Judith Ward, Central Connecticut State University
Shawn Ward, Le Moyne College
Alida Westman, Eastern Michigan University
Sue Williams, Southwest Texas State University
Deborah Winters, New Mexico State University
Connie K. Varnhagen, University of Alberta

■ **REVIEWERS OF THE FOURTH EDITION**

Armin W. Arndt, Eastern Washington University
Lanthan D. Camblin, University of Cincinnati
Linda A. Camras, DePaul University
Bronwyn Fees, Kansas State University
Lisa Huffman, Ball State University
Claire Kopp, Claremont Graduate School
Annie McManus, Parkland College
Karla Miley, Black Hawk College
Virginia Navarro, University of Missouri, St. Louis
Joe M. Price, San Diego State University
Mary Kay Reed, York College of Pennsylvania
Kathy Stansbury, University of New Mexico
Belinda Wholeben, Rockford College

In addition, I thank the following individuals for responding to a survey that provided vital feedback for the new edition:

Megan E. Bradley, Frostburg State University
Edward J. Bujdos, Albion College
Diane Clark, Shippensburg University
Andrea Clements, East Tennessee State University
Jeffrey Coldren, Youngstown State University
Diane Cook, Gainesville College
Ron Craig, Edinboro University of Pennsylvania
Valerie Dargan, University of Maryland, College Park
Claire Etaugh, Bradley University
Kathy Fite, Southwest Texas State University
Janice Hartgrove-Freile, North Harris College
Rick Holigrocki, University of Indianapolis
Don Holmlund, College of Marin County

Dennis Karpowitz, University of Kansas
Jacqueline Kikuchi, University of Rhode Island
Pat Kolasa, University of Nebraska at Omaha
Ann Kruger, Georgia State University
Gary W. Ladd, University of Illinois – Urbana
Judith Levine, SUNY Farmingdale
Amy Malkus, Washington State University
Martin Marino, Atlantic Cape Community College
Deborah Margolis, Boston College
Kathryn A. Markell, Cardinal Stritch University
Jamie Nekich, University of Idaho
Deanna Nekovei, Texas A & M University
Brenda Perry-Hawkins, Coastal Carolina Community College
Joe M. Price, San Diego State University
Jack P. Shilkret, Anne Arundel Community College
Reggie Smith, Salem Community College
Diana Volk, Cleveland State University
Shawn L. Ward, Le Moyne College
Alida Westman, Eastern Michigan University
Marlene S. Winter, Carlow College

Colleagues and graduate students at Illinois State University aided my research and contributed significantly to the text's supplements. Richard Payne, Department of Political Science, Illinois State University, is a kind and devoted friend with whom I have shared many profitable discussions about the writing process, the condition of children and families, and other topics and significantly influenced by perspective on child development and social policy. JoDe Paladino's outstanding, dedicated work in helping conduct literature searches, secure library materials, and revise the Study Guide has been invaluable. Dorothy Welty-Rodriguez helped plan the revised Observation Video, collaborated with me on its accompanying Observation Guide, and assisted with preparation of website materials and other media supports. Sara Harris joined me in preparing a thoroughly revised Instructor's Resource Manual, bringing to this task enthusiasm, imagination, depth of knowledge, and impressive writing skill.

The supplement package also benefited from the talents and diligence of several other individuals. Gabrielle Principe of Cornell University and Karla Gingerich of Colorado State University revised the Test Bank with great concern for clarity and accuracy. Many thanks, also, to Elizabeth Kenny for a superb job in coordinating the preparation of the supplement package and to Kelly Perkins for her wonderful coordination of filming for the Observation Video.

I have been fortunate to work with an exceptionally capable editorial team at Allyn and Bacon. It has been a privilege to author this book under the sponsorship of Executive Editor Carolyn Merrill. When I first met Carolyn, she told me that she was a "woman of action," and she has been true to her word. Her enthusiasm, organizational skills, and fielding of potential difficulties contributed to a smooth and timely revision process. Her genuine interest in child development sparked many fruitful discussions that influenced my approach to preparing sections of the book as well as its pedagogical features. Carolyn graciously took time to provide life histories of Caitlin, Grace, and Timmy, the three new characters whose experiences and development illustrate Infancy and Toddlerhood, Chapters 5–7.

I would like to express a heartfelt thank you to Joyce Nilsen, Director of Marketing, and Caroline Croley, Marketing Manager of Psychology, for the outstanding work they have done in marketing my texts. Each has made sure that accurate and clear information about my books and their ancillaries reached Allyn and Bacon's sales force and that the needs of prospective and current adopters were met. Marcie Melia, Field Marketing Specialist, has also devoted much time and energy to marketing activities, and I greatly appreciate the lovely social occasions she has planned and the kind greetings she sends from time to time, despite her very busy schedule.

Susan Messer undertook the development activities for the book. It is difficult to find words that do justice to her contributions. Susan worked closely with me as I wrote each chapter, making sure that every thought and concept would be precisely expressed and well developed. Her keen writing and editing skills and prompt and patient responses to my concerns and queries have enhanced every aspect of this edition. It has been a pleasure to get to know Susan during the past year.

Liz Napolitano, Senior Production Editor, managed the complex production tasks that resulted in a beautiful fourth edition. I am grateful for her competence, flexibility, efficiency, and thoughtfulness, and I look forward to a continuing partnership with her in future editions of my texts. I thank Sarah Evertson for obtaining the exceptional photographs that so aptly illustrate the text narrative. Lara Zeises and Jonathan Bender, Editorial Assistants, arranged for manuscript reviews and attended to a wide variety of pressing, last-minute details.

A final word of gratitude goes to my family, whose love, patience, and understanding have enabled me to be wife, mother, teacher, researcher, and text author at the same time. My sons, David and Peter, grew up with my child development texts, passing from childhood to adolescence and then to young adulthood as successive editions were written. David has a special connection with the books' subject matter as an elementary school teacher. Peter is embarking on a career in law as the book goes to press. Both continue to enrich my understanding through reflections on events and progress in their own lives. My husband, Ken, willingly made room for yet another time-consuming endeavor in our life together and communicated his belief in its importance in a great many unspoken, caring ways.

ABOUT THE CHAPTER OPENING ART

I would like to extend grateful acknowledgments to the International Museum of Children's Art, Oslo, Norway; Queensland University of Technology; and the International Child Art Foundation, Washington, DC; for the exceptional chapter opening artwork. A new participant to this edition, the International Child Art Foundation provided the opening artwork for Chapters 1, 3, 5, 11, 12, 13, 14, 15, and 16. To celebrate the year 2000, the International Child Art Foundation sponsored an international art contest, ChildArt 2000. Children from around the world submitted drawings based on the theme, "My World in the Year 2000." The artwork for the openers was created by ChildArt 2000 contest finalists. The winners traveled to Washington, DC, to collaborate on the beautiful mural shown in Chapter 1.

A Personal Note to Students

My thirty years of teaching child development have brought me in contact with thousands of students like you—students with diverse college majors, future goals, interests, and needs. Some are affiliated with my own department, psychology, but many come from other child-related fields—education, sociology, anthropology, family studies, and biology, to name just a few. Each semester, my students' aspirations are as varied as their fields of study. Many look toward careers in applied work with children—teaching, caregiving, nursing, counseling, social work, school psychology, and program administration. Some plan to teach child development, and a few want to do research. Most hope someday to have children, whereas others are already parents who come with a desire to better understand and rear their own youngsters. And almost all arrive with a deep curiosity about how they themselves developed from tiny infants into the complex human beings they are today.

My goal in preparing this fourth edition of *Infants, Children, and Adolescents* is to provide a textbook that meets the instructional goals of your course as well as your personal needs. To achieve these objectives, I have grounded this book in a carefully selected body of classic and current research

brought to life with stories and vignettes about children and families, many of whom I have known personally. In addition, the text highlights the interactive contributions biology and environment make to the developing child, explains how the research process helps solve real-world problems, emphasizes the broader social and educational contexts in which the child develops, and pays special attention to policy issues that are crucial for safeguarding children's well-being in today's world. I have also provided a unique pedagogical program that will assist you in mastering information, integrating various aspects of development, critically examining controversial issues, reflecting on your own childhood experiences, and applying what you have learned.

PEDAGOGICAL FEATURES

Maintaining a highly accessible writing style—one that is lucid and engaging without being simplistic—continues to be one of this text's goals. I will frequently speak directly to you and encourage you to relate what you read to your own life. In doing so, I hope to make the study of child development involving and pleasurable.

■ **Stories and Vignettes About Children.** To help you construct a clear image of development and to enliven the text narrative, each chronological age division is unified by case examples woven throughout that set of chapters. For example, within the infancy and toddlerhood section, we'll look in on three children, observe dramatic changes and striking individual differences, and address the impact of family background, child-rearing practices, and parents' and children's life experiences on development. Besides a set of main characters, many additional vignettes offer vivid examples of development and diversity among children. Student response to this feature has been so positive that I have enhanced it. Caitlin, Grace, and Timmy, whom you'll meet in Chapters 5 to 7, are new to this edition.

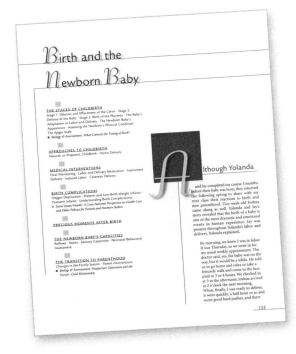

■ **Chapter Introductions and End-of-Chapter Summaries.** To provide a helpful preview of what you are about to read, I include an outline and overview of chapter content in each chapter introduction. Especially comprehensive end-of-chapter summaries, organized according to the major divisions of each chapter and highlighting important terms, will remind you of key points in the text discussion. Review questions are included in the summaries to encourage active study.

■ **Ask Yourself . . .** Active engagement with the subject matter is supported by study questions at the end of each major section. Four types of questions prompt you to think about the subject matter in diverse ways: *Review* questions help you recall and comprehend information you have just read; *Apply* questions encourage you to apply your knowledge to controversial issues and problems faced by parents, teachers, and children; *Connect* questions help you build an image of the whole child by integrating what you have learned across age periods and domains of development; and *Reflect* questions make the study of child development personally meaningful by asking you to reflect on your own development and that of others you know well.

■ **Boxes.** Four types of boxes accentuate the philosophical themes of this book:

■ *Cultural Influences* boxes underscore the impact of culture on all aspects of development. They include Immigrant Youth: Amazing Adaptation; Young Children's Daily Life in a Yucatec Mayan Village; Cultural Variations in Personal Storytelling: Implications for Early Self-Concept; and Identity Development Among Ethnic Minority Adolescents.

■ *Biology and Environment* boxes present a balanced, interconnected view of key biological and environmental influences on development. Examples include Uncoupling Genetic–Environmental Correlations for Mental Illness and Antisocial Behavior; Factors that Control the Timing of Birth; Development of Infants with Severe Visual Impairments; Parent–Child Interaction and Cognitive Development of Deaf Children; and Intergenerational Continuity in Adolescent Parenthood.

■ *Social Issues* boxes discuss the condition of children around the world and emphasize the need for sensitive social policies and interventions to ensure their well-being. This edition includes two types: **Social Issues: Health** boxes address values and practices relevant to children's physical and mental health. Examples include The Prenatal Environment and Health in Later Life; Otitis Media and Development; Children's Eyewitness Testimony; and Like Mother, Like Child: Intergenerational Continuity in Adolescent Parenthood. **Social Issues: Education** boxes focus on home, school, and community influences on children's learning. They include: When Are Children Ready for School? Academic Redshirting and Early Retention; Dispositions Toward Collective Struggle: Highly Achieving, Optimistic African-American High School Students; and Development of Civic Responsibility

Caregiving Concerns and Educational Concerns Tables.
To accentuate the relationship of theory and research to practice, two types of tables provide easily accessible practical advice. **Caregiving Concerns** tables emphasize caring for, protecting, and supporting children's physical, emotional, and social well-being. They include Ways Couples Can Ease the Transition to Parenthood, Keeping Infants and Toddlers Safe, and Adult Practices that Support Healthy Identity Development. **Educational Concerns** tables focus on effective teaching strategies. Examples include Signs of Developmentally Appropriate Child Care, Enhancing Make-Believe Play in Early Childhood, Signs of High-Quality Education in Elementary School, and Factors that Support High Achievement During Adolescence.

Milestones Tables. A Milestones table appears at the end of each chronological age division of the text. These tables summarize major physical, cognitive, language, and emotional and social developments of each age span. Entries in the Milestones tables are page-referenced to the text narrative to facilitate study and review.

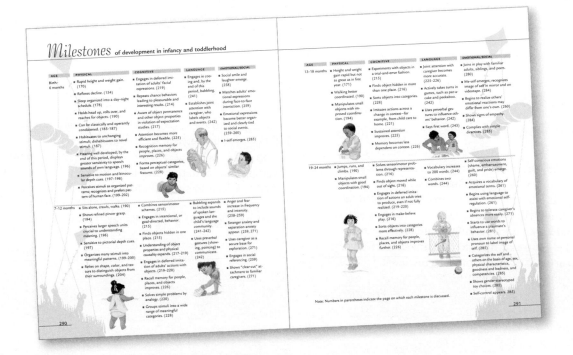

- **Additional Tables, Illustrations, and Photographs.** Additional tables are liberally included to help you grasp essential points in the text discussion, extend information on a topic, and consider applications. The many full-color illustrations throughout the book depict important theories, methods, and research findings. In this edition, the photo program has been extended. Each photo has been carefully selected to portray the text discussion and to represent the diversity of children around the world.

- **Marginal Glossary, End-of-Chapter Term List, and End-of-Book Glossary.** Mastery of terms that make up the central vocabulary of the field is promoted through a marginal glossary, an end-of-chapter term list, and an end-of-book Glossary. Important terms and concepts also appear in boldface type in the text narrative.

- **FYI . . . For Further Information and Help.** Students in my classes frequently ask where they can go to find out more about high-interest topics or to seek help in areas related to their own lives. To meet this need, I have included an annotated section at the end of each chapter that provides the names, phone numbers, and website addresses of organizations that disseminate information about child development and offer special services.

STUDY AIDS

Beyond the study aids found in the textbook, Allyn and Bacon offers a number of supplements for students. Ask your instructor or your bookstore about their availability.

- **Study Guide.** Prepared by JoDe Paladino and Laura E. Berk, Illinois State University, this helpful guide offers Chapter Summaries, Learning Objectives, Study Questions organized according to major headings in the text, "Ask Yourself" questions, Suggested Readings, Crossword Puzzles for mastering important terms, and multiple-choice Self-Tests.

- **Practice Tests.** Twenty multiple-choice items per chapter plus an answer key with justifications are drawn from the test bank to assist you in preparing for course exams.

- **Websites.** Visit *http://www.ablongman.com/berk*, a companion website that offers multiple-choice online practice tests. In addition, with the purchase of a new textbook, you gain access via a PIN code to a robust website that encourages interactive learning by providing a wealth of activities that have been specially created for this textbook. Also provided are many links to relevant sites and access to top journal articles to assist you with research.

I hope your experience learning about child development will be as rewarding as I have found it over the years. I would like to know what you think about both the field of child development and this book. I welcome your comments; please feel free to send them to me at Department of Psychology, Box 4620, Illinois State University, Normal, IL 61790, or in care of the publisher, who will forward them to me.

—Laura E. Berk

Infants, Children, and Adolescents

"My World in the Year 2000" Mural

Washington, DC

Children from all corners of the globe gathered to create this spectacular image of their world. The resulting mural reminds us that child development is complex, fascinating, diverse, and mystifying. Chapter 1 will introduce you to a multiplicity of ways of thinking about and studying children.

History, Theory, and Research Strategies

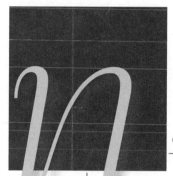

ot long ago, I left my Midwestern home to live for a year near the small city in northern California where I spent my childhood years. One morning, I visited the neighborhood where I grew up—a place I had not seen since I was 12 years old.

I stood at the entrance to my old schoolyard. Buildings and grounds that looked large to me as a child now seemed strangely small. I peered through the window of my first-grade classroom. The desks were no longer arranged in rows but grouped in intimate clusters. A computer rested against the far wall, near the spot where I once sat.

I walked my old route home from school, the distance shrunken by my larger stride. I stopped in front of my best friend Kathryn's house, where we once drew sidewalk pictures, crossed the street to play kickball, produced plays for neighborhood audiences in the garage, and traded marbles and stamps in the backyard. In place of the small shop where I had purchased penny candy stood a neighborhood child-care center, filled with the voices and vigorous activity of toddlers and preschoolers.

As I walked, I reflected on early experiences that contributed to who and what I am today—weekends helping my father in his downtown clothing shop, the year my mother studied to become a high school teacher, moments of companionship and rivalry with my sister and brother, Sunday outings to museums and the seashore, and visits to my grandmother's house, where I became someone extra special.

As I passed the homes of my childhood friends, I thought of what I knew about their present lives. Kathryn, star pupil and president of our sixth-grade class—today a successful corporate lawyer and mother of two children. Shy, withdrawn Phil, cruelly teased because of his cleft lip—now owner of a thriving chain of hardware stores and member of the city council. Julio, immigrant from Mexico who joined our class in third grade—today director of an elementary school bilingual education program and single parent of an adopted Mexican boy. And finally, my next-door neighbor Rick, who picked fights at recess, struggled with reading, repeated fourth grade, dropped out of high school, and (so I heard) moved from one job to another over the following 10 years.

As you begin this course in child development, perhaps you, too, wonder about some of the same questions that crossed my mind during that nostalgic neighborhood walk:

- How is the infant and young child's perception of the world the same as the adult's, and how is it different?

- Why do some of us, like Kathryn and Rick, retain the same styles of responding that characterized us as children, whereas others, like Phil, change in essential ways?

- How did Julio, transplanted to a foreign culture at 8 years of age, master its language and customs and succeed in its society, yet still strongly identify with his ethnic community?

- What determines the features that humans have in common and those that make each of us unique—in physical characteristics, mental capacities, interests, and behaviors?

- In what ways are children's home, school, and neighborhood experiences the same today as they were in generations past, and in what ways are they different? How does generational change—employed mothers, child care, divorce, smaller families, and new technologies—affect children's characteristics and skills?

These are central questions addressed by **child development**, a field of study devoted to understanding all aspects of human constancy and change from conception through adolescence. Child development is part of a larger discipline known as *developmental psychology,* or in its interdisciplinary sense, *human development,* which includes all changes we experience throughout the lifespan. Great diversity characterizes the interests and concerns of the thousands of investigators who study child development. But all have a single goal in common: the desire to describe and identify those factors that influence the consistencies and transformations in young people during the first two decades of life.

The Field of Child Development

ook again at the questions just listed, and you will see that they are not just of scientific interest. Each has *applied,* or practical, importance as well. In fact, scientific curiosity is just one factor that led child development to become the exciting field of study it is today. Research about development has also been stimulated by social pressures to better the lives of children. For example, the beginning of public education in the early part of the twentieth century led to a demand for knowledge about what and how to teach children of different ages. Pediatricians' interest in improving children's health

child development
A field of study devoted to understanding all aspects of human constancy and change from conception through adolescence.

required an understanding of physical growth and nutrition. The social service profession's desire to treat children's anxieties and behavior problems required information about personality and social development. And parents have continually asked for advice about child-rearing practices and experiences that would promote the well-being of their child.

Our large storehouse of information about child development is *interdisciplinary*. It has grown through the combined efforts of people from many fields. Because of the need for solutions to everyday problems concerning children, academic scientists from psychology, sociology, anthropology, and biology joined forces in research with professionals from a variety of applied fields, including education, family studies, medicine, public health, and social service, to name just a few. Today, the field of child development is a melting pot of contributions. Its body of knowledge is not just scientifically important but relevant and useful.

PERIODS OF DEVELOPMENT

How can we divide the dramatic changes that occur during childhood and adolescence into phases that are sensible and manageable? To solve this dilemma, researchers usually segment the first two decades of life into the following five age periods, according to which I have organized this book. Each period brings with it new capacities and social expectations that serve as important transitions in major theories.

- *The prenatal period: from conception to birth.* This 9-month period is the most rapid phase of change, during which a one-celled organism is transformed into a human baby with remarkable capacities for adjusting to life in the surrounding world.

- *Infancy and toddlerhood: from birth to 2 years.* This period brings dramatic changes in the body and brain that support the emergence of a wide array of motor, perceptual, and intellectual capacities; the beginnings of language; and first intimate ties to others.

- *Early childhood: from 2 to 6 years.* During this period, the body becomes longer and leaner, motor skills are refined, and children become more self-controlled and self-sufficient. Make-believe play blossoms and supports every aspect of psychological development. Thought and language expand at an astounding pace, a sense of morality becomes evident, and children establish ties with peers.

- *Middle childhood: from 6 to 11 years.* These are the school years, a phase in which children learn about the wider world and master new responsibilities that increasingly resemble those they will perform as adults. Improved athletic abilities, participation in organized games with rules, more logical thought processes, mastery of basic literacy skills, and advances in understanding the self, morality, and friendship are hallmarks of this phase.

- *Adolescence: from 11 to 20 years.* This period is the bridge between childhood and adulthood. Puberty leads to an adult-sized body and sexual maturity. Thought becomes abstract and idealistic, and school achievement becomes more serious as young people prepare for the world of work. Defining personal values and goals and establishing autonomy from the family are major concerns of this phase.

DOMAINS OF DEVELOPMENT

In addition to age periods, development is often divided into three broad domains, or aspects, which make the vast, interdisciplinary study of human constancy and change more orderly and convenient:

- *Physical development*—changes in body size, proportions, appearance, and the functioning of various body systems; brain development; perceptual and motor capacities; and physical health

Child development is so dramatic that researchers divide it into age periods. These brothers and sisters illustrate, clockwise from bottom, toddlerhood, early childhood (age 4), middle childhood (age 6), and middle childhood (age 8).

prenatal period
infancy + toddlerhood
early childhood
middle childhood
adolescence

■ *Cognitive development*—development of a wide variety of thought processes and intellectual abilities, including attention, memory, academic and everyday knowledge, problem solving, imagination, creativity, and the uniquely human capacity to represent the world through language

■ *Emotional and social development*—development of emotional communication, self-understanding, ability to manage one's own feelings, knowledge about other people, interpersonal skills, friendships, intimate relationships, and moral reasoning and behavior

Turn to the Contents of this book on page xiv and review its chapter titles. Notice that within each period of development, we will consider the domains of development in the order just listed. Yet we must keep in mind that the domains are not really distinct. Instead, they combine in an integrated, holistic fashion to yield the living, growing child. Furthermore, each domain influences and is influenced by the others. For example, in Chapter 5, we will see that new motor capacities, such as reaching, sitting, crawling, and walking (physical), contribute greatly to infants' understanding of their surroundings (cognitive). When babies think and act more competently, adults begin to stimulate them more with games, language, and expressions of delight at their new achievements (emotional and social). These enriched experiences, in turn, promote all aspects of development.

Although each chapter focuses on a particular domain, you will encounter instances of the interwoven nature of all domains on almost every page of this book. Also, look for the *Ask Yourself* boxes at the end of major sections. In those boxes, I have included *Review* questions, which help you recall and think about information you have just read; *Apply* questions, which encourage you to apply your knowledge to controversial issues and problems faced by parents, teachers, and children; *Connect* questions, which help you form a coherent, unified picture of child development; and *Reflect* questions, which invite you to reflect on your own development and that of people you know well. The four types of questions are designed to promote active engagement with the subject matter. By answering them, I hope to deepen your understanding and inspire new insights.

With this introduction in mind, let's turn to some basic issues that have captivated, puzzled, and divided child development theorists. Then our discussion will trace the emergence of the field and survey major theories. (We will return to each contemporary theory in greater detail in later chapters of this book.)

Basic Issues

Before scientific study of the child, questions about children were answered by turning to common sense, opinion, and belief. Research on children did not begin until the early part of the twentieth century. Gradually it led to the construction of theories of child development, to which professionals and parents could turn for understanding and guidance.

For our purposes, we can define a **theory** as an orderly, integrated set of statements that describes, explains, and predicts behavior. For example, a good theory of infant–caregiver attachment would (1) *describe* the behaviors of babies around 6 to 8 months of age as they seek the affection and comfort of a familiar adult, (2) *explain* why infants have this strong desire to bond with a caregiver, and (3) *predict* what might happen if babies do not develop this close emotional bond.

Theories are vital tools in child development (and any other scientific endeavor) for two reasons. First, they provide organizing frameworks for our observations of children. In other words, they *guide and give meaning to* what we see. Second, theories that are verified by research often serve as a sound basis for practical action. Once a theory helps us *understand*

theory
An orderly, integrated set of statements that describes, explains, and predicts behavior.

development, we are in a much better position to *know what to do* to improve the welfare and treatment of children.

As we will see later, theories are influenced by the cultural values and belief systems of their times. But theories differ in one important way from mere opinion and belief: A theory's continued existence depends on *scientific verification* (Scarr, 1985). This means that the theory must be tested by using a fair set of research procedures agreed on by the scientific community.

The field of child development contains many theories with very different ideas about what children are like and how they develop. The study of child development provides no ultimate truth because investigators do not always agree on the meaning of what they see. In addition, children are complex beings; they grow physically, cognitively, emotionally, and socially. As yet, no single theory has been able to explain all these aspects. Finally, the existence of many theories helps advance knowledge, since researchers are continually trying to support, contradict, and integrate these different points of view.

Although there are many theories, we can easily organize them, since almost all take a stand on three basic issues about child development. To help you remember these controversial issues, they are briefly summarized in Table 1.1. Let's take a close look at each.

Theories help us understand development and improve the welfare and treatment of children. For example, theories have contributed to new approaches to education that emphasize exploration, discovery, and collaboration. Teachers grant children far more choice and decision-making power than in earlier times, when children sat at desks and followed directions for most of the day.

CONTINUOUS OR DISCONTINUOUS DEVELOPMENT?

Recently, the mother of 16-month-old Angelo reported to me with amazement that her young son had pushed a toy car across the living room floor while making a motorlike sound, "Brmmmm, brmmmm," for the first time. When he hit a nearby wall with a bang, Angelo let go of the car, exclaimed, "C'ash," and laughed heartily.

"How come Angelo can pretend, but he couldn't a few months ago?" queried his mother. "And I wonder what 'Brmmmm, brmmmm' and 'Crash!' mean to Angelo? Is his understanding of motorlike sounds and collision similar to mine?"

Angelo's mother has raised a puzzling issue about development: How can we best describe the differences in capacities and behavior between small infants, young children, adolescents, and adults? As Figure 1.1 on page 8 illustrates, major theories recognize two possibilities.

On one hand, babies and preschoolers may respond to the world in much the same way as adults. The difference between the immature and mature being may simply involve amount or complexity of behavior. For example, little Angelo's thinking might be just as logical and well organized as our own. Perhaps (as his mother reports) he can sort objects into simple categories, recognize whether there are more of one kind than another, and remember where he left his favorite toy at child care the week before. Angelo's only limitation may be that he cannot perform these skills with as much information and precision as we can. If

TABLE 1.1

Basic Issues in Child Development

ISSUE	QUESTIONS RAISED ABOUT DEVELOPMENT
Continuous or discontinuous development?	Is child development a matter of cumulative adding on of skills and behaviors, or does it involve qualitative, stagewise changes? Do *both* continuous and discontinuous changes characterize development?
One course of development or many?	Does one course of development characterize all children, or are there many possible courses, depending on the contexts—unique combinations of genetic and environmental circumstances—that children experience? Does development have *both* universal features and features unique to the individual and his or her contexts?
Nature or nurture as more important?	Are genetic or environmental factors more important determinants of development? If *both* nature and nurture play major roles, how do they work together? To what extent do early experiences establish lifelong patterns of behavior? Can later experiences overcome early negative effects?

FIGURE 1.1

Is development continuous or discontinuous? (a) Some theorists believe that development is a smooth, continuous process. Children gradually add more of the same types of skills. (b) Other theorists think that development takes place in discontinuous stages. Children change rapidly as they step up to a new level of development and then change very little for a while. With each step, the child interprets and responds to the world in a qualitatively different way.

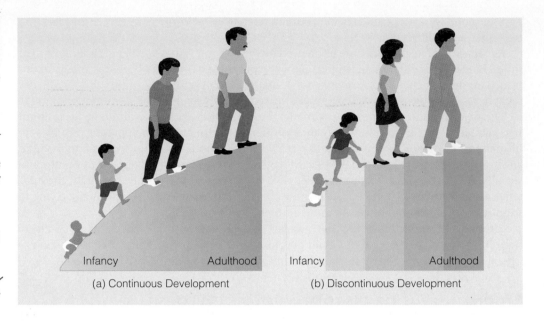

(a) Continuous Development   (b) Discontinuous Development

Handwritten margin notes:
continuous v. discontinuous development

discontinuous—new ways emerge @ specific times.

continuous development
A view that regards development as a cumulative process that consists of gradually adding on more of the same types of skills that were there to begin with.

discontinuous development
A view in which new ways of understanding and responding to the world emerge at specific times.

stage
A qualitative change in thinking, feeling, and behaving that characterizes a specific period of development.

contexts
Unique combinations of genetic and environmental circumstances that can result in markedly different paths of development.

this is so, then Angelo's development must be **continuous**—a cumulative process that consists of gradually adding more of the same types of skills that were there to begin with.

On the other hand, Angelo may have ways of thinking, feeling, and behaving that must be understood on their own terms—ones quite different from our own. If so, then development is a **discontinuous** process, in which new ways of understanding and responding to the world emerge at specific times. From this perspective, Angelo is not yet able to organize objects or remember and interpret experiences in the same way as adults. Instead, he will move through a series of developmental steps, each of which has unique features, until he reaches the highest level of human functioning.

Theories that accept the discontinuous perspective regard development as taking place in **stages**—qualitative changes in thinking, feeling, and behaving that characterize specific periods of development. In stage theories, development is much like climbing a staircase, with each step corresponding to a more mature, reorganized way of functioning than the one that came before. The stage concept also assumes that children undergo periods of rapid transformation as they step up from one stage to the next, followed by plateaus during which they stand solidly within a stage. In other words, change is fairly sudden rather than gradual and ongoing.

Does development actually take place in a neat, orderly sequence of stages? For now, let's note that this is a very ambitious assumption that has not gone unchallenged. We will review some influential stage theories later in this chapter.

ONE COURSE OF DEVELOPMENT OR MANY?

Stages are always assumed to be universal across children and cultures. That is, because children have similar brains and bodies and live in stimulating environments, stage theorists believe that children everywhere follow the same sequence of development. For example, in the domain of cognition, a stage theorist might try to identify the common influences that lead children to represent their world through language and make-believe play in early childhood; think more logically and systematically in middle childhood; and reason abstractly in adolescence.

At the same time, the field of child development is becoming increasingly aware that children grow up in distinct **contexts;** that is, each child experiences unique combinations of genetic and environmental circumstances. For example, a shy child, who is genetically prone to be socially fearful, develops in very different contexts from those of a sociable agemate who readily seeks out other people (Rubin & Coplan, 1998). Children in non-Western village societies encounter experiences in their families and communities that differ sharply from those encountered by children in large Western cities. These different circumstances can result in markedly different cognitive capacities, social skills, and feelings about the self and others (Shweder et al., 1998).

As we will see, contemporary theorists regard the contexts that lead to different paths of development as many-layered and complex. They include immediate settings in which children spend their days, such as home, child-care center, school, and neighborhood, as well as circumstances more remote from children's everyday lives—community resources, societal values and priorities, and historical time period. Finally, a special interest in culture has led child development researchers to be more conscious than ever before of diversity in development.

NATURE OR NURTURE AS MORE IMPORTANT?

In addition to describing the course of child development, each theory takes a stand on a major question about its underlying causes: Are genetic or environmental factors more important? This is the age-old **nature–nurture controversy.** By *nature*, we mean inborn biological givens—the hereditary information we receive from our parents at the moment of conception that signals the body to grow and affects all our characteristics and skills. By *nurture,* we mean the complex forces of the physical and social world that influence our biological makeup and psychological experiences before and after birth.

Although all theories grant at least some role to both nature and nurture, they vary in the emphasis placed on each. For example, consider the following questions: Is the older child's ability to think in more complex ways largely the result of an inborn timetable of growth? Or is it primarily influenced by stimulation from parents and teachers? Do children acquire language because they are genetically predisposed to do so or because parents intensively tutor them from an early age? And what accounts for the vast individual differences among children—in height, weight, physical coordination, intelligence, personality, and social skills? Is nature or nurture more responsible?

The stances theories take on nature versus nurture affect their explanations of individual differences. Some theorists emphasize *stability*—that children who are high or low in a characteristic (such as verbal ability, anxiety, or sociability) will remain so at later ages. These theorists typically stress the importance of *heredity,* or nature. If they regard environment as important, they generally point to *early experiences* as establishing a lifelong pattern of behavior. Powerful negative events in the first few years, they argue, cannot be fully overcome by later, more positive ones (Bowlby, 1980; Sroufe, Egeland, & Kreutzer, 1990). Other theorists are more optimistic. They believe that *change* is possible if new experiences, or nurture, support it (Masten & Coatsworth, 1998; Sampson & Laub, 1993).

Throughout this book, we will see that investigators disagree, often sharply, on the question of *stability or change.* The answers they provide are of great applied significance. If you believe that development is largely due to nature, then providing children with experiences aimed at stimulating change would seem to be of little value. If, on the other hand, you are convinced of the supreme importance of early experience, then you would intervene as soon as possible, offering high-quality stimulation and support to ensure that children develop at their best. Finally, if you think that environment is profoundly influential throughout development, you would extend high-quality experiences into later years. In addition, you would provide assistance any time children or adolescents face difficulties, believing that they can recover from early negative events with the help of favorable life circumstances.

A BALANCED POINT OF VIEW

So far, we have discussed the basic issues of child development in terms of extremes, with views emphasizing one side or the other. As we trace the unfolding of the field of child development in the rest of this chapter, you will see that the positions of many theories have softened. Modern ones, especially, recognize the merits of both sides. Some theorists believe that both continuous and discontinuous changes characterize development and alternate with one another. And some acknowledge that development can have both universal features and features unique to the individual and his or her contexts. Furthermore, researchers have

nature–nurture controversy Disagreement among theorists about whether genetic or environmental factors are more important determinants of development and behavior.

[handwritten margin notes:]
children grow up in different environments.

Stability & early experiences are influential in development.

Biology & ENVIRONMENT

RESILIENT CHILDREN

John and his best friend, Gary, grew up in a run-down, crime-ridden, inner-city neighborhood. By age 10, each had experienced years of family conflict followed by parental divorce. Reared for the rest of childhood and adolescence in mother-headed households, John and Gary rarely saw their fathers. Both achieved poorly, dropped out of high school, and were in and out of trouble with the police.

Then John and Gary's paths of development diverged. By age 30, John had fathered two children with women he never married, had spent time in prison, was unemployed, and drank alcohol heavily. In contrast, Gary had returned to finish high school, had studied auto mechanics at a community college, and became manager of a gas station and repair shop. Married with two children, he had saved his earnings and bought a home. He was happy, healthy, and well adapted to life.

A wealth of evidence shows that environmental risks—poverty, negative family interactions, and parental divorce, job loss, mental illness, and drug abuse—predispose children to future problems (Masten & Coatsworth, 1998). Why did Gary "beat the odds" and come through unscathed?

New evidence on *resiliency*—the ability to spring back from adversity—is receiving increasing attention because investigators want to find ways to protect young people from the damaging effects of stressful life conditions (Cicchetti & Garmezy, 1993). Resiliency research was inspired by several long-term studies on the relationship of life stressors in childhood to competence and adjustment in adolescence and adulthood (Garmezy, 1993; Rutter, 1987; Werner & Smith, 1992). In each study, some children were shielded from negative outcomes, whereas others had lasting problems. Three broad factors seemed to offer protection from the damaging effects of stressful life events.

PERSONAL CHARACTERISTICS

A child's genetically influenced characteristics can reduce exposure to risk or lead to experiences that compensate for early stressful events. Temperament is particularly powerful. Children with calm, easy-going, sociable dispositions who are willing to take initiative have a special capacity to adapt to change and elicit positive responses from others. Children who are emotionally reactive and irritable often strain the patience of people around them (Milgram & Palti, 1993; Smith & Prior, 1995). For example, both John and Gary moved several times during their childhoods. Each time, John became anxious and angry, picking arguments with his parents, siblings, and peers. In contrast, Gary was sad to leave his home but soon looked forward to making new friends and exploring the new neighborhood. Intellectual ability is another protective factor (Masten et al., 1999). It increases the chances of rewarding experiences in school that may offset the impact of a stressful home life.

A WARM PARENTAL RELATIONSHIP

A close relationship with at least one parent who provides affection and assistance and introduces order and organization into the child's life fosters resiliency. But note that this factor (as well as the next one) is not independent of children's personal characteristics. Children who are relaxed, socially responsive, and able to deal with change are easier to rear and more likely to enjoy positive relationships with parents and other people. At the same time, some children may develop more attractive dispositions as a result of parental warmth and attention (Smith & Prior, 1995; Wyman et al., 1999).

SOCIAL SUPPORT OUTSIDE THE IMMEDIATE FAMILY

A person outside the immediate family—perhaps a grandparent, teacher, or close friend—who forms a special relationship with the child can promote resiliency. Gary may have overcome the effects of a stressful home life because of the support he received in adolescence from his grandfather, who listened to Gary's concerns and helped him solve problems constructively. In addition, Gary's grandfather had a stable marriage and work life and handled stressors skillfully. Consequently, he served as a model of effective coping (Zimmerman & Arunkumar, 1994).

Research on resiliency highlights the complex connections between heredity and environment. Armed with positive characteristics—which may stem from innate endowment, favorable rearing experiences, or both—children can take action to reduce stressful situations. Nevertheless, when many risks pile up, they are increasingly difficult to overcome (Quyen et al., 1998). Therefore, effective interventions need to reduce risks and enhance relationships at home, in school, and in the community. This means attending to both the person and the environment—building the child's capacity as well as fixing problems.

ALAN HICKS/STONE

This child's special relationship with her grandfather provides the social support she needs to cope with stress and solve problems constructively. A warm tie with a person outside the immediate family can promote resiliency.

moved away from asking which is more important, heredity or environment (de Waal, 1999). Instead, they want to know precisely *how nature and nurture work together* to influence the child's traits and capacities.

Finally, as you will discover in later parts of this book, the relative impact of early and later experiences varies greatly from one domain of development to another and even (as the Biology and Environment box on the previous page indicates) across individuals! Because of the complex network of factors contributing to human change and the challenge of isolating the effects of each, many theoretical points of view have gathered research support. Although debate continues, this circumstance has also sparked more balanced visions of child development.

now, there is more of a focus on the duality of nature & nurture.

Ask YOURSELF...

review   Why are there many theories of how children develop? Cite three basic issues on which almost all theories take a stand.

apply   A school counselor advises a parent, "Don't worry about your teenager's argumentative behavior. It shows that she understands the world differently than she did as a young child." What stance is the counselor taking on the issue of continuous or discontinuous development? Explain.

connect   Provide an example of how one domain of development (physical, cognitive, or emotional/social) can affect development in another domain.

reflect   Cite an aspect of your development that differs from a parent's or a grandparent's when he or she was your age. How might contexts explain this difference?

Historical Foundations

Modern theories of child development result from centuries of change in Western cultural values, philosophical thinking about children, and scientific progress. To understand the field as it exists today, we must return to its early beginnings—to influences that long preceded scientific child study. We will see that many early ideas about children linger on as important forces in current theory and research.

MEDIEVAL TIMES

In medieval Europe (the sixth through the fifteenth centuries), childhood was not viewed as a separate phase of the life cycle. The idea accepted by many theories today, that the child's nature is unique and different from that of youths and adults, was much less common then. Instead, once children emerged from infancy, they were regarded as miniature adults, a view called **preformationism** (Ariès, 1962). This attitude is reflected in the art, entertainment, and language of the times. Look carefully at medieval paintings, and you will see children depicted as miniature adults. Before the sixteenth century, toys and games were not designed to amuse children but were for all people. And age, so central to modern personal identity, was unimportant. People did not refer to it in conversation, and it was not recorded in family and civil records until the fifteenth and sixteenth centuries.

Nevertheless, faint glimmerings of the idea that children are unique emerged during medieval times. Some laws recognized that children needed protection from people who

In this medieval painting, young children are depicted as miniature adults. Their dress and expressions resemble those of their elders. Through the fifteenth century, little emphasis was placed on childhood as a unique phase of the life cycle.

preformationism
Medieval view of the child as a miniature adult.

might mistreat them, and medical literature provided special instructions for their care. But even with some awareness of the vulnerability of children, no theories described the uniqueness of childhood or separate developmental periods (Borstelmann, 1983).

THE REFORMATION

In the sixteenth century, a revised image of childhood sprang from the Puritan belief in original sin. According to Puritan doctrine, children were born evil and stubborn and had to be civilized (Ariès, 1962; Shahar, 1990). Harsh, restrictive child-rearing practices were recommended to tame the depraved child. Children were dressed in stiff, uncomfortable clothing that held them in adultlike postures, and disobedient pupils were routinely beaten by their schoolmasters. Although punitiveness was the prevailing child-rearing philosophy, love and affection for their children prevented most Puritan parents from exercising extremely repressive measures (Moran & Vinovskis, 1986).

As the Puritans emigrated from England to the United States, they brought the belief that child rearing was one of their most important obligations. Although they continued to regard the child's soul as tainted by original sin, they tried to promote reason in their sons and daughters so they would be able to separate right from wrong (Clarke-Stewart, 1998). The Puritans were the first to devise special reading materials for children that instructed them in religious and moral ideals. As they trained their children in self-reliance and self-control, Puritan parents gradually adopted a moderate balance between discipline and indulgence, severity and permissiveness.

PHILOSOPHIES OF THE ENLIGHTENMENT

The seventeenth-century Enlightenment brought new philosophies of reason and emphasized ideals of human dignity and respect. Conceptions of childhood appeared that were more humane than those of centuries past.

■ **JOHN LOCKE.** John Locke (1632–1704), a leading British philosopher, viewed the child as a **tabula rasa.** Translated from Latin, this means a "blank slate." According to this idea, children are, to begin with, nothing at all, and all kinds of experiences can shape their characters. Locke (1690/1892) described parents as rational tutors who can mold the child in any way they wish, through careful instruction, effective example, and rewards for good behavior. He was ahead of his time in recommending child-rearing practices that present-day research supports. For example, Locke suggested that parents not reward children with money or sweets but rather with praise and approval. He also opposed physical punishment: "The child repeatedly beaten in school cannot look upon books and teachers without experiencing fear and anger." Locke's philosophy led to a change from harshness toward children to kindness and compassion.

Look carefully at Locke's ideas, and you will see that he took a firm stand on each of the basic issues we discussed earlier in this chapter. Locke regarded development as *continuous;* adultlike behaviors are gradually built up through the warm, consistent teachings of parents. Furthermore, Locke's view of the child as a tabula rasa led him to champion *nurture*—the power of the environment to determine whether children become good or bad, bright or dull, kind or selfish. And his faith in nurture suggests the possibility of *many courses of development* and of *change at later ages* due to new experiences.

Finally, Locke's philosophy characterizes children as passive—as doing little to influence their own destiny, which is written on blank slates by others. This vision has been discarded. All contemporary theories view children as active, purposeful beings who make sense of their world and contribute substantially to their own development.

■ **JEAN JACQUES ROUSSEAU.** In the eighteenth century, the French philosopher Jean Jacques Rousseau (1712–1778) introduced a new theory. Children, Rousseau (1762/1955) thought,

tabula rasa
Locke's view of the child as a blank slate whose character is shaped by experience.

are not blank slates and empty containers to be filled by adult instruction. Instead, they are **noble savages,** naturally endowed with a sense of right and wrong and an innate plan for orderly, healthy growth. Unlike Locke, Rousseau believed children's built-in moral sense and unique ways of thinking and feeling would only be harmed by adult training. His was a permissive philosophy in which the adult should be receptive to the child's needs at each of four stages of development: infancy, childhood, late childhood, and adolescence.

Rousseau's philosophy includes two vitally important concepts that are found in contemporary theories. The first is the concept of *stage,* which we discussed earlier. The second is the concept of **maturation,** which refers to a genetically determined, naturally unfolding course of growth. If you accept the notion that children mature through a sequence of stages, then they cannot be preformed, miniature adults. Instead, they are unique and different from adults, and their development is determined by their own inner nature. Unlike Locke, Rousseau saw children as determining their own destinies. And he viewed development as *a discontinuous, stagewise* process that follows a *single, unified course* mapped out by *nature.*

DARWIN'S THEORY OF EVOLUTION

A century after Rousseau, another ancestor of modern child study—this time, of its scientific foundations—emerged. In the mid-nineteenth century, Charles Darwin (1809–1882), a British naturalist, joined an expedition to distant parts of the world, where he made careful observations of fossils and animal and plant life. Darwin (1859/1936) noticed the infinite variation among species. He also saw that within a species, no two individuals are exactly alike. From these observations, he constructed his famous theory of evolution.

The theory emphasized two related principles: *natural selection* and *survival of the fittest.* Darwin explained that certain species survived in particular parts of the world because they had characteristics that fit with, or were adapted to, their surroundings. Other species died off because they were not as well suited to their environments. Individuals within a species who best met the survival requirements of the environment lived long enough to reproduce and pass their more favorable characteristics to future generations. Darwin's emphasis on the adaptive value of physical characteristics and behavior eventually found its way into important twentieth-century theories.

During his explorations, Darwin discovered that the early prenatal growth of many species was strikingly similar. This suggested that all species, including human beings, descended from a few common ancestors. Other scientists concluded from Darwin's observation that the human child, from conception to maturity, followed the same developmental plan as the evolution of the human species. Although this belief eventually proved inaccurate, efforts to chart parallels between child growth and human evolution prompted researchers to make careful observations of all aspects of children's behavior. Out of these first attempts to document an idea about development, the science of child study was born.

SCIENTIFIC BEGINNINGS

Scientific child study evolved quickly during the early part of the twentieth century. As we will see in the following sections, rudimentary observations of individual children were soon followed by improved methods and theories. Each advance contributed to the firm foundation on which the field rests today.

■ **THE BABY BIOGRAPHIES.** Imagine yourself as a forerunner in the field of child development, confronted with studying children for the first time. How might you go about this challenging task? Scientists of the late nineteenth and early twentieth centuries did what most of us would probably do in their place—they selected a child of their own or of a close relative. Then they jotted down day-by-day descriptions and impressions of the youngster's behavior, beginning in infancy. By the early twentieth century, dozens of these baby biographies had been

noble savage
Rousseau's view of the child as naturally endowed with a sense of right and wrong and an innate plan for orderly, healthy growth.

maturation
A genetically determined, naturally unfolding course of growth.

[Handwritten margin notes:]
Rousseau's theories emphasized discontinuous development, nature, & stagewise processes.

saw parents as intervening beings.

Early theories of child development sparked a parenting-advice literature, which today fills shelf after shelf in public libraries and bookstores. This woman prepares for parenthood by reading about what to expect in the first year of her baby's life.

Hall said children develop due to genetic predeterminants.

normative approach
An approach in which age-related averages are computed to represent typical development.

published. In the following excerpt, the author of one of these works reflects on the birth of her young niece, whose growth she followed during the first year of life:

> Its first act is a cry, not of wrath, . . . nor a shout of joy, . . . but a snuffling, and then a long, thin, tearless á—á, with the timbre of a Scotch bagpipe, purely automatic, but of discomfort. With this monotonous and dismal cry, with its red, shriveled, parboiled skin . . . , squinting, cross-eyed, pot-bellied, and bow-legged, it is not strange that, if the mother . . . has not come to love her child before birth, there is a brief interval occasionally dangerous to the child before the maternal instinct is fully aroused.
>
> It cannot be denied that this unflattering description is fair enough, and our baby was no handsomer than the rest of her kind. . . . Yet she did not lack admirers. I have never noticed that women (even those who are not mothers) mind a few little aesthetic defects, . . . with so many counterbalancing charms in the little warm, soft, living thing. (Shinn, 1900, pp. 20–21)

Can you tell from this passage why the baby biographies have sometimes been upheld as examples of how *not* to study children? These first investigators tended to be emotionally invested in the infants they observed, and they seldom began with a clear idea of what they wanted to find out about the child. Not surprisingly, many of the records made were eventually discarded as biased. However, we must keep in mind that the baby biographers were like explorers first setting foot on alien soil. When a field is new, we cannot expect its theories and methods to be well formulated.

Nevertheless, the baby biographies were clearly a step in the right direction. In fact, two nineteenth-century theorists, Darwin (1877) and German biologist William Preyer (1882/1888), contributed to these early records of children's behavior. Preyer, especially, set high standards for making observations, recording what he saw immediately and checking the accuracy of his notes against those of a second observer (Cairns, 1998). These are the same high standards today's researchers use when observing children. As the result of the biographers' pioneering efforts, in succeeding decades the child became a common focus of scientific research.

■ **THE NORMATIVE PERIOD OF CHILD STUDY.** G. Stanley Hall (1846–1924), one of the most influential American psychologists of the early twentieth century, is generally regarded as the founder of the child study movement (Dixon & Lerner, 1999). Inspired by Darwin's work, Hall and his well-known student Arnold Gesell (1880–1961) developed theories based on evolutionary ideas. These early leaders regarded child development as a genetically determined series of events that unfolds automatically, much like a blooming flower (Gesell, 1933; Hall, 1904).

Hall and Gesell are remembered less for their one-sided theories than for their intensive efforts to describe all aspects of child development. Aware of the limitations of the baby biographies, Hall set out to collect a sound body of objective facts about children. This goal launched the **normative** approach to child study. In a normative investigation, measures of behavior are taken on large numbers of children. Then age-related averages are computed to represent typical development. Using this method, Hall constructed elaborate questionnaires asking children of different ages almost everything they could tell about themselves—interests, fears, imaginary playmates, dreams, friendships, everyday knowledge, and more (White, 1992).

In the same fashion, Gesell collected detailed normative information on the motor achievements, social behaviors, and personality characteristics of infants and children. He hoped to relieve parents' anxieties by informing them of what to expect at each age. If, as he believed, the timetable of development is the product of millions of years of evolution, then children are naturally knowledgeable about their needs. His child-rearing advice, in the tradition of Rousseau, was a permissive approach that recommended sensitivity and responsiveness to children's cues (Thelen & Adolph, 1992). Gesell's books were widely read. Along with Benjamin Spock's famous *Baby and Child Care,* they became part of a rapidly expanding child development literature for parents.

■ **THE MENTAL TESTING MOVEMENT.** While Hall and Gesell were developing their theories and methods in the United States, French psychologist Alfred Binet (1857–1911) also took a normative approach to child development, but for a different reason. In the early 1900s, Binet and his colleague Theodore Simon were asked by Paris school officials to find a way to identify children with learning problems who needed to be placed in special classes. The first successful intelligence test, which they constructed for this purpose, grew out of practical educational concerns.

Previous attempts to create a useful test of intelligence had met with little success. But Binet's effort was unique in that he began with a well-developed theory. In contrast to earlier views, which reduced intelligence to simple elements of reaction time and sensitivity to physical stimuli, Binet captured the complexity of children's thinking (Siegler, 1992). He defined intelligence as good judgment, planning, and critical reflection. Then he selected test questions that directly measured these abilities, creating a series of age-graded items that permitted him to compare children's intellectual progress.

[handwritten margin note:] To Binet, intelligence was good judgment, planning, & critical reflection.

In 1916, at Stanford University, Binet's test was translated into English and adapted for use with American children. It became known as the *Stanford-Binet Intelligence Scale*. Besides providing a score that could successfully predict school achievement, the Binet test sparked tremendous interest in individual differences in development. The mental testing movement was in motion. Comparisons of the intelligence test scores of children who vary in sex, ethnicity, birth order, family background, and other characteristics became a major focus of research. Intelligence tests also rose quickly to the forefront of the controversy over nature versus nurture that continues today.

[handwritten:] nurture ↑   nature ↑

Ask YOURSELF...

review
reflect

Suppose we could arrange a debate between John Locke and Jean Jacques Rousseau on the nature–nurture controversy. Summarize the argument that each historical figure is likely to present.

Find out if your parents read Gesell, Spock, or other parenting-advice books when you were growing up. What questions about child rearing most concerned them? Do you think today's parents of young children have concerns that are different from those of your parents? Explain.

Mid-Twentieth-Century Theories

In the mid-twentieth century, the field of child development expanded. Specialized societies were founded, and research journals were launched. As child development attracted increasing interest, a variety of theories emerged, each of which continues to have followers today. In these theories, the European concern with the child's inner thoughts and feelings contrasts sharply with the focus of American academic psychology on scientific precision and concrete, observable behavior.

THE PSYCHOANALYTIC PERSPECTIVE

By the 1930s and 1940s, many parents whose children suffered from serious emotional stress and behavior problems sought help from psychiatrists and social workers. The earlier normative movement had answered the question, What are children like? But to treat children's difficulties, child guidance professionals had to address the question, How and why did

TABLE 1.2

Freud's Psychosexual Stages

PSYCHOSEXUAL STAGE	APPROXIMATE AGE	DESCRIPTION
Oral	Birth–1 year	The new ego directs the baby's sucking activities toward breast or bottle. If oral needs are not met appropriately, the individual may develop such habits as thumb sucking, fingernail biting, and pencil chewing in childhood and overeating and smoking later in life.
Anal	1–3 years	Young toddlers and preschoolers enjoy holding and releasing urine and feces. Toilet training becomes a major issue between parent and child. If parents insist that children be trained before they are ready or make too few demands, conflicts about anal control may appear in the form of extreme orderliness and cleanliness or messiness and disorder.
Phallic	3–6 years	Id impulses transfer to the genitals, and the child finds pleasure in genital stimulation. Freud's Oedipus conflict for boys and Electra conflict for girls arise, and young children feel a sexual desire for the other-sex parent. To avoid punishment, they give up this desire and, instead, adopt the same-sex parent's characteristics and values. As a result, the superego is formed. The relations between id, ego, and superego established at this time determine the individual's basic personality.
Latency	6–11 years	Sexual instincts die down, and the superego develops further. The child acquires new social values from adults outside the family and from play with same-sex peers.
Genital	Adolescence	Puberty causes the sexual impulses of the phallic stage to reappear. If development has been successful during earlier stages, it leads to mature sexuality, marriage, and the birth and rearing of children.

children become the way they are? They turned for help to the **psychoanalytic perspective** because of its emphasis on understanding the unique developmental history of each child.

According to the psychoanalytic approach, children move through a series of stages in which they confront conflicts between biological drives and social expectations. The way these conflicts are resolved determines the person's ability to learn, to get along with others, and to cope with anxiety. Although many individuals contributed to the psychoanalytic perspective, two have been especially influential: Sigmund Freud, founder of the psychoanalytic movement, and Erik Erikson.

■ **FREUD'S THEORY.** Freud (1856–1939), a Viennese physician, saw patients in his practice with a variety of symptoms, such as hallucinations, fears, and paralyses, that appeared to have no physical basis. Seeking a cure for these troubled adults, Freud found that their symptoms could be relieved by having patients talk freely about painful events of their childhoods. Using this "talking cure," he carefully examined the unconscious motivations of his patients. Startling the straightlaced Victorian society in which he lived, Freud concluded that infants and children are sexual beings. On the basis of adult remembrances, Freud constructed his **psychosexual theory** of development. It emphasizes that how parents manage their child's sexual and aggressive drives in the first few years of life is crucial for healthy personality development.

Three Parts of the Personality.   In Freud's theory, three parts of the personality—id, ego, and superego—become integrated during a sequence of five stages (summarized in Table 1.2). The *id*, the largest portion of the mind, is the source of basic biological needs and desires. The *ego*—the conscious, rational part of personality—emerges in early infancy to redirect the id's impulses so they are discharged in acceptable ways. For example, aided by the ego, the hungry baby of a few months of age stops crying when he sees his mother warm a bottle or unfasten her clothing for breast-feeding. And the more competent preschooler goes into the kitchen and gets a snack on her own.

psychoanalytic perspective
An approach to personality development introduced by Freud that assumes children move through a series of stages in which they confront conflicts between biological drives and social expectations. The way these conflicts are resolved determines psychological adjustment.

psychosexual theory
Freud's theory, which emphasizes that how parents manage children's sexual and aggressive drives in the first few years of life is crucial for healthy personality development.

Between 3 and 6 years of age, the *superego,* or conscience, develops from interactions with parents, who insist that children conform to the values of society. Now the ego faces the increasingly complex task of reconciling the demands of the id, the external world, and conscience (Freud, 1923/1974). For example, when the ego is tempted to gratify an id impulse by hitting a playmate to get an attractive toy, the superego may warn that such behavior is wrong. The ego must decide which of the two forces (id or superego) will win this inner struggle or work out a reasonable compromise, such as asking for a turn with the toy. According to Freud, the relations established between id, ego, and superego during the preschool years determine the individual's basic personality.

Psychosexual Development. Freud (1938/1973) believed that over the course of childhood, sexual impulses shift their focus from the oral to the anal to the genital regions of the body. In each stage, parents walk a fine line between permitting too much or too little gratification of their child's basic needs. If parents strike an appropriate balance, then children grow into well-adjusted adults with the capacity for mature sexual behavior, investment in family life, and rearing of the next generation.

Freud's psychosexual theory highlighted the importance of family relationships and early experiences for children's development. But Freud's perspective was eventually criticized for several reasons. First, the theory overemphasized the influence of sexual feelings in development. Second, because the theory was based on the problems of sexually repressed, well-to-do adults, it did not apply in cultures differing from nineteenth-century Victorian society. Finally, Freud's ideas were called into question because he did not study children directly.

■ **ERIKSON'S THEORY.** Several of Freud's followers took what was useful from his theory and stretched and rearranged it to improve on his vision. The most important of these neo-Freudians for the field of child development was Erik Erikson (1902–1994).

Although Erikson (1950) accepted Freud's psychosexual framework, he expanded the picture of development at each stage. In his **psychosocial theory,** Erikson emphasized that the ego does not just mediate between id impulses and superego demands. It is also a positive force in development. At each stage, it acquires attitudes and skills that make the individual an active, contributing member of society. A basic psychological conflict, which is resolved along a continuum from positive to negative, determines healthy or maladaptive outcomes at each stage. As Table 1.3 on page 18 shows, Erikson's first five stages parallel Freud's stages, but Erikson added three adult stages. He was one of the first to recognize the lifespan nature of development.

Finally, unlike Freud, Erikson pointed out that normal development must be understood in relation to each culture's life situation. For example, among the Yurok Indians (a tribe of fishermen and acorn gatherers on the northwest coast of the United States), babies are deprived of breast-feeding for the first 10 days after birth and instead are fed a thin soup from a small shell. At age 6 months, infants are abruptly weaned—an event enforced, if necessary, by having the mother leave for a few days. These experiences, from our cultural vantage point, might seem cruel. But Erikson explained that the Yurok live in a world in which salmon fill the river just once a year, a circumstance that requires the development of considerable self-restraint for survival. In this way, he showed that child rearing can be understood only by making reference to the competencies valued and needed by the child's society.

Erik Erikson expanded Freud's theory, emphasizing the psychosocial outcomes of development. At each stage, a major psychological conflict is resolved. If the outcome is positive, individuals acquire attitudes and skills that permit them to contribute constructively to society.

■ **CONTRIBUTIONS AND LIMITATIONS OF PSYCHOANALYTIC THEORY.** A special strength of the psychoanalytic perspective is its emphasis on the individual's unique life history as worthy of study and understanding (Emde, 1992). Consistent with this view, psychoanalytic theorists accept the clinical method, which synthesizes information from a variety of sources into a detailed picture of the personality of a single child. (We will discuss the clinical method further toward the end of this chapter.) Psychoanalytic theory has also inspired a wealth of research on many aspects of emotional and social development, including infant–caregiver attachment, aggression, sibling relationships, child-rearing practices, morality, gender roles, and adolescent identity.

psychosocial theory
Erikson's theory, which emphasizes that at each Freudian stage, individuals not only develop a unique personality, but also acquire attitudes and skills that help them become active, contributing members of their society.

TABLE 1.3

Erikson's Psychosocial Stages, with Corresponding Psychosexual Stages Indicated

PSYCHOSOCIAL STAGE	PERIOD OF DEVELOPMENT	DESCRIPTION
Basic trust versus mistrust (Oral)	Birth–1 year	From warm, responsive care, infants gain a sense of trust, or confidence, that the world is good. Mistrust occurs when infants have to wait too long for comfort and are handled harshly.
Autonomy versus shame and doubt (Anal)	1–3 years	Using new mental and motor skills, children want to choose and decide for themselves. Autonomy is fostered when parents permit reasonable free choice and do not force or shame the child.
Initiative versus guilt (Phallic)	3–6 years	Through make-believe play, children experiment with the kind of person they can become. Initiative—a sense of ambition and responsibility—develops when parents support their child's new sense of purpose. The danger is that parents will demand too much self-control, which leads to overcontrol, meaning too much guilt.
Industry versus inferiority (Latency)	6–11 years	At school, children develop the capacity to work and cooperate with others. Inferiority develops when negative experiences at home, at school, or with peers lead to feelings of incompetence.
Identity versus identity confusion (Genital)	Adolescence	The adolescent tries to answer the question, Who am I, and what is my place in society? Self-chosen values and vocational goals lead to a lasting personal identity. The negative outcome is confusion about future adult roles.
Intimacy versus isolation	Young adulthood	Young people work on establishing intimate ties to others. Because of earlier disappointments, some individuals cannot form close relationships and remain isolated.
Generativity versus stagnation	Middle adulthood	Generativity means giving to the next generation through child rearing, caring for other people, or productive work. The person who fails in these ways feels an absence of meaningful accomplishment.
Integrity versus despair	Old age	In this final stage, individuals reflect on the kind of person they have been. Integrity results from feeling that life was worth living as it happened. Old people who are dissatisfied with their lives fear death.

Despite its extensive contributions, the psychoanalytic perspective is no longer in the mainstream of child development research (Cairns, 1998). Psychoanalytic theorists may have become isolated from the rest of the field because they were so strongly committed to the clinical approach that they failed to consider other methods. In addition, many psychoanalytic ideas, such as psychosexual stages and ego functioning, are so vague that they are difficult or impossible to test empirically (Thomas, 2000; Westen & Gabbard, 1999). Nevertheless, Erikson's broad outline of psychosocial change captures the essence of personality development during childhood and adolescence. Consequently, we will return to it in later chapters.

BEHAVIORISM AND SOCIAL LEARNING THEORY

As psychoanalytic theory gained prominence, child study was also influenced by a very different perspective: **behaviorism,** a tradition consistent with Locke's image of the tabula rasa. American behaviorism began with the work of psychologist John Watson (1878–1958) in the early twentieth century. Watson wanted to create an objective science of psychology. Unlike psychoanalytic theorists, he believed in studying directly observable events—stimuli and responses—rather than the unseen workings of the mind (Horowitz, 1992).

■ **TRADITIONAL BEHAVIORISM.** Watson was inspired by the studies of animal learning carried out by famous Russian physiologist Ivan Pavlov. Pavlov knew that dogs release saliva

behaviorism
An approach that views directly observable events—stimuli and responses—as the appropriate focus of study and the development of behavior as taking place through classical and operant conditioning.

social learning theory
An approach that emphasizes the role of modeling, or observational learning, in the development of behavior. Its most recent revision stresses the importance of thinking in social learning and is called *social-cognitive theory.*

as an innate reflex when they are given food. But he noticed that his dogs were salivating before they tasted any food—when they saw the trainer who usually fed them. The dogs, Pavlov reasoned, must have learned to associate a neutral stimulus (the trainer) with another stimulus (food) that produces a reflexive response (salivation). As a result of this association, the neutral stimulus by itself could bring about the response. Anxious to test this idea, Pavlov successfully taught dogs to salivate at the sound of a bell by pairing it with the presentation of food. He had discovered *classical conditioning.*

Watson wanted to find out if classical conditioning could be applied to children's behavior. In a historic experiment, he taught Albert, an 11-month-old infant, to fear a neutral stimulus—a soft white rat—by presenting it several times with a sharp, loud sound, which naturally scared the baby. Little Albert, who at first had reached out eagerly to touch the furry rat, soon cried and turned his head away when he caught sight of it (Watson & Raynor, 1920). In fact, Albert's fear was so intense that researchers eventually questioned the ethics of studies like this one. On the basis of findings like these, Watson concluded that environment is the supreme force in development. According to the traditional behaviorist view, the child is a passive being whom adults can mold by carefully controlling stimulus–response associations. And development is a continuous process, consisting of a gradual increase with age in the number and strength of these associations.

> Watson believed the environment to be the most important force in development.

After Watson, American behaviorism developed along several lines. The first was Clark Hull's *drive reduction theory.* According to this view, children continually act to satisfy physiological needs and reduce states of tension. As *primary drives* of hunger, thirst, and sex are met, stimuli associated with them become *secondary,* or *learned, drives.* For example, a Hullian theorist believes that infants prefer the closeness and attention of adults who have given them food and relieved their discomfort. To ensure these adults' affection, children will acquire all sorts of responses that the adults desire of them—politeness, honesty, patience, persistence, obedience, and more.

> behaviorism – child is molded

Another form of behaviorism was B. F. Skinner's (1904–1990) *operant conditioning theory.* Skinner rejected Hull's idea that primary drive reduction is the only way to get children to learn. According to Skinner, a child's behavior can be increased by following it with a wide variety of *reinforcers* besides food and drink, such as praise, a friendly smile, or a new toy. A behavior can also be decreased through *punishment,* such as withdrawal of privileges, parental disapproval, or being sent to one's room. As a result of Skinner's work, operant conditioning became a broadly applied learning principle in child psychology. We will consider these conditioning principles more fully when we explore the infant's learning capacities in Chapter 5.

> Skinner – reinforce behavior w/ praise.

■ **SOCIAL LEARNING THEORY.** Psychologists quickly became interested in whether behaviorism might more directly and effectively explain the development of children's social behavior than did the less precise concepts of psychoanalytic theory. This sparked the emergence of **social learning theory.** Social learning theorists accepted and built on the principles of conditioning and reinforcement, offering expanded views of how children and adults acquire new responses. By the 1950s, social learning theory had become a major force in child development research.

Several kinds of social learning theory emerged. The most influential was devised by Albert Bandura and his colleagues. Bandura (1977) demonstrated that *modeling,* otherwise known as *imitation* or *observational learning,* is an important basis for children's behavior. He recognized that children acquire many favorable and unfavorable responses by watching and listening to people around them. The baby who claps her hands after her mother does so, the child who angrily hits a playmate in the same way that he has been punished at home, and the teenager who wears the same clothes and hairstyle as her friends at school are all displaying observational learning.

Bandura's work continues to influence much research on children's social development. However, like the field of child development as a whole, today his

His father's encouragement, praise, and modeling of persistence has helped this boy develop a sense of self-efficacy—belief in his own ability and characteristics—that leads him to enjoy challenging tasks and persist in the face of difficulty.

© BILL LAI/THE IMAGE WORKS

theory stresses the importance of *cognition,* or thinking. Bandura has shown that children's ability to listen, remember, and abstract general rules from complex sets of observed behavior affects their imitation and learning. In fact, the most recent revision of Bandura's (1986, 1989, 1992) theory places such strong emphasis on how children think about themselves and other people that he calls it a *social-cognitive* rather than a social learning approach.

According to this view, children gradually become more selective in what they imitate. From watching others engage in self-praise and self-blame and through feedback about the worth of their own actions, children develop *personal standards* for behavior and a *sense of self-efficacy*—the belief that their own abilities and characteristics will help them succeed. These cognitions guide responses in particular situations (Bandura, 1997). For example, imagine a parent who often remarks, "I'm glad I kept working on that task, even though it was hard," who explains the value of persistence to her child, and who encourages it by saying, "I know you can do that homework very well!" As a result, the child starts to view himself as hardworking and high achieving and, from the many people available in the environment, selects models with these characteristics to copy.

Applied behavior analysis seeks to improve.

■ **CONTRIBUTIONS AND LIMITATIONS OF BEHAVIORISM AND SOCIAL LEARNING THEORY.** Like psychoanalytic theory, behaviorism and social learning theory have had a major applied impact. Yet the techniques used are decidedly different. **Applied behavior analysis** refers to procedures that combine conditioning and modeling to eliminate undesirable behaviors and increase desirable responses. It has been used to relieve a wide range of serious developmental problems, such as persistent aggression, language delays, and extreme fears (Pierce & Epling, 1995; Wolpe & Plaud, 1997). But it is also effective in dealing with common, everyday difficulties, including poor time management; unwanted habits, such as nail biting and smoking; and anxiety over such recurrent events as test taking, public speaking, and medical and dental treatments. In one study, preschoolers' anxious reactions at the dentist were reduced when the children received small toys (reinforcers) for answering questions about a story read to them while the dentist worked. Because the children could not listen to the story and kick and cry at the same time, their disruptive behaviors subsided (Stark et al., 1989).

Nevertheless, modeling and reinforcement do not provide a complete account of development (Horowitz, 1987). We will see in later sections that many theorists believe that behaviorism offers too narrow a view of important environmental influences. These extend beyond immediate reinforcements and modeled behaviors to the richness of children's physical and social worlds. Finally, behaviorism and social learning theory have been criticized for underestimating children's contributions to their own development. In emphasizing cognition, Bandura is unique among theorists whose work grew out of the behaviorist tradition in granting children an active role in their own learning.

PIAGET'S COGNITIVE-DEVELOPMENTAL THEORY

If one individual has influenced the modern field of child development more than any other, it is Swiss cognitive theorist Jean Piaget (1896–1980). American investigators had been aware of Piaget's work since 1930. However, they did not grant it much attention until the 1960s, mainly because Piaget's ideas and methods of studying children were very much at odds with behaviorism, which dominated mid-twentieth-century American psychology (Zigler & Gilman, 1998). Piaget did not believe that knowledge was imposed on a passive, reinforced child. According to his **cognitive-developmental theory,** children actively construct knowledge as they manipulate and explore their world, and their cognitive development takes place in stages.

■ **PIAGET'S STAGES.** Piaget's view of development was greatly influenced by his early training in biology. Central to his theory is the biological concept of *adaptation* (Piaget,

YVES DE BRAINE/BLACK STAR

Through careful observations of and clinical interviews with children, Jean Piaget developed his comprehensive theory of cognitive development. His work has inspired more research on children than any other single theory.

applied behavior analysis Procedures that combine reinforcement and modeling to eliminate undesirable behaviors and increase desirable responses.

cognitive-developmental theory An approach introduced by Piaget that views children as actively constructing knowledge as they manipulate and explore their world, and cognitive development as taking place in stages.

ERIKA STONE

TOM MCCARTHY/PICTOR

According to Piaget's theory, at first schemes are motor action patterns. As this 1-year-old takes apart, bangs, and drops these nesting cups, she discovers that her movements have predictable effects on objects and that objects influence one another in regular ways.

In Piaget's preoperational stage, preschool children represent their earlier sensorimotor discoveries with symbols. Language and make-believe play develop rapidly. These 4-year-olds create an imaginative play scene with dress-up clothes and the assistance of a cooperative family pet.

The mind forms itself in such a way to fit the external world.

1971). Just as the structures of the body are adapted to fit with the environment, so the structures of the mind develop during childhood to better fit with, or represent, the external world. In infancy and early childhood, children's understanding is very different from adults'. For example, Piaget believed that young babies do not realize that an object hidden from view—a favorite toy or even the mother—continues to exist. He also concluded that preschoolers' thinking is full of faulty logic. Children younger than age 7 commonly say that the amount of milk or lemonade changes when it is poured into a differently shaped container. According to Piaget, children eventually revise these incorrect ideas in their ongoing efforts to achieve an *equilibrium,* or balance, between internal structures and information they encounter in their everyday worlds. *balance b/w internal + external*

TIM DAVIS/PHOTO RESEARCHERS, INC.

In Piaget's theory, children move through four broad stages of development, each of which is characterized by a qualitatively distinct way of thinking. Table 1.4 on page 22 provides a brief description of Piaget's stages. In the *sensorimotor stage,* cognitive development begins with the baby's use of the senses and movements to explore the world. These action patterns evolve into the symbolic but illogical thinking of the preschooler in the *preoperational stage.* Then cognition is transformed into the more organized reasoning of the school-age child in the *concrete operational stage.* Finally, in the *formal operational stage,* thought becomes the complex, abstract reasoning system of the adolescent and adult.

■ **PIAGET'S METHODS OF STUDY.** Piaget devised special methods for investigating how children think. In the early part of his career, he carefully observed his three infant children and also presented them with everyday problems, such as an attractive object that could be grasped, mouthed, kicked, or searched for when hidden from view. From their reactions, Piaget derived his ideas about cognitive changes that take place during the first 2 years.

In studying childhood and adolescent thought, Piaget took advantage of children's ability to describe their thinking. He adapted the clinical method of psychoanalysis, conducting open-ended *clinical interviews* in which a child's initial response to a task served as the basis for the next question he would ask. We will look at an example of a Piagetian clinical interview, as well as the strengths and weaknesses of this technique, when we discuss research methods later in this chapter.

In Piaget's concrete operational stage, school-age children think in an organized and logical fashion about concrete objects. This 8-year-old boy understands that the hamster on one side of the balance scale is just as heavy as the metal weights on the other, even though the two types of objects look and feel quite different from each other.

TABLE 1.4

Piaget's Stages of Cognitive Development

STAGE	PERIOD OF DEVELOPMENT	DESCRIPTION
Sensorimotor	Birth–2 years	Infants "think" by acting on the world with their eyes, ears, hands, and mouth. As a result, they invent ways of solving sensorimotor problems, such as pulling a lever to hear the sound of a music box, finding hidden toys, and putting objects in and taking them out of containers.
Preoperational	2–7 years	Preschool children use symbols to represent their earlier sensorimotor discoveries. Development of language and make-believe play takes place. However, thinking lacks the logic of the two remaining stages.
Concrete operational	7–11 years	Children's reasoning becomes logical. School-age children understand that a certain amount of lemonade or play dough remains the same even after its appearance changes. They also organize objects into hierarchies of classes and subclasses. However, thinking falls short of adult intelligence. It is not yet abstract.
Formal operational	11 years and older	The capacity for abstraction permits adolescents to reason with symbols that do not refer to objects in the real world, as in advanced mathematics. They can also think of all possible outcomes in a scientific problem, not just the most obvious ones.

■ **CONTRIBUTIONS AND LIMITATIONS OF PIAGET'S THEORY.** Piaget's cognitive-developmental perspective convinced the field that children are active learners whose minds consist of rich structures of knowledge. Besides investigating children's understanding of the physical world, Piaget explored their reasoning about the social world. As we will see in later chapters, his stages have sparked a wealth of research on children's conceptions of themselves, other people, and human relationships. Practically speaking, Piaget's theory encouraged the development of educational programs that emphasize children's discovery learning and direct contact with the environment.

Despite Piaget's overwhelming contribution to child development and education, in recent years his theory has been challenged. New evidence indicates that Piaget underestimated the competencies of infants and preschoolers. We will see in later chapters that when young children are given tasks scaled down in difficulty, their understanding appears closer to that of the older child and adult than Piaget believed. This discovery has led many investigators to conclude that the maturity of children's thinking may depend on their familiarity with the investigator's task and the kind of knowledge sampled. Finally, many studies show that children's performance on Piagetian problems can be improved with training. This finding raises questions about his assumption that discovery learning, rather than adult teaching, is the best way to foster development.

Today, the field of child development is divided over its loyalty to Piaget's ideas. Those who continue to find merit in Piaget's approach accept a modified view of his cognitive stages—one in which changes in children's thinking take place much more gradually than Piaget believed (Bidell & Fischer, 1992; Case, 1992, 1998). Others have given up the idea of cognitive stages in favor of a continuous approach to development—information processing, which we will take up in the next section.

In Piaget's formal operational stage, adolescents can think logically and abstractly. These high school students solve a complex scientific problem by thinking of all possible outcomes, not just the most obvious. Then they systematically test each possibility to see if it occurs in the real world.

Ask YOURSELF...

review   New theories often become prominent because they overcome the limitations of existing theories. What aspect of behaviorism made it attractive to critics of psychoanalytic theory? How does Piaget's theory respond to a major limitation of behaviorism?

apply   A 4-year-old becomes frightened of the dark and refuses to go to sleep at night. How would a psychoanalyst and a behaviorist differ in their views of how this problem developed?

connect   Although social learning theory focuses on social development and Piaget's theory on cognitive development, they have enhanced our understanding of other domains as well. Mention an additional domain of development addressed by each theory.

Recent Theoretical Perspectives

New ways of understanding the child are constantly emerging—questioning, building on, and enhancing the discoveries of earlier theories. Today, a burst of fresh approaches and research emphases, including information processing, ethology, Vygotsky's sociocultural theory, Bronfenbrenner's ecological systems theory, and the dynamic systems perspective, are broadening our understanding of children's development.

INFORMATION PROCESSING

During the 1970s, child development researchers became disenchanted with behaviorism as a complete account of children's learning and were also disappointed in their efforts to fully verify Piaget's ideas. They turned to new trends in the field of cognitive psychology for ways to understand the development of children's thinking. Today, a leading perspective is **information processing,** a general approach that emerged with the design of digital computers that use mathematically specified steps to solve problems. These systems suggested to psychologists that the human mind might also be viewed as a symbol-manipulating system through which information flows (Klahr & MacWhinney, 1998). From presentation to the senses at *input* to behavioral responses at *output,* information is actively coded, transformed, and organized.

Information-processing researchers often use flowcharts to map the precise steps individuals use to solve problems and complete tasks, much like the plans devised by programmers to get computers to perform a series of "mental operations." Let's look at an example to clarify the usefulness of this approach. The top of Figure 1.2 on page 24 shows the strategies that Andrea, an academically successful 8-year-old, used to complete a two-digit addition problem with a carrying operation. The bottom of the figure displays the faulty procedure of Jody, who arrived at the wrong answer. The flowchart approach ensures that models of child and adult thinking will be very clear. For example, by comparing the two procedures shown in Figure 1.2 , we know exactly what is necessary for effective problem solving and where Jody went wrong in searching for a solution. As a result, we can pinpoint Jody's difficulties and design an intervention to help her improve her reasoning.

A wide variety of information-processing models exist. Some (like the one in Figure 1.2) are fairly narrow in that they track children's mastery of one or a few tasks. Others describe the human information-processing system as a whole (Atkinson & Shiffrin, 1968; Lockhart & Craik, 1990). These general models are used as guides for asking questions about broad age changes in children's thinking. For example, does a child's ability to search the environment for information needed to solve a problem become more organized and planful with age?

information processing
An approach that views the human mind as a symbol-manipulating system through which information flows and regards cognitive development as a continuous process.

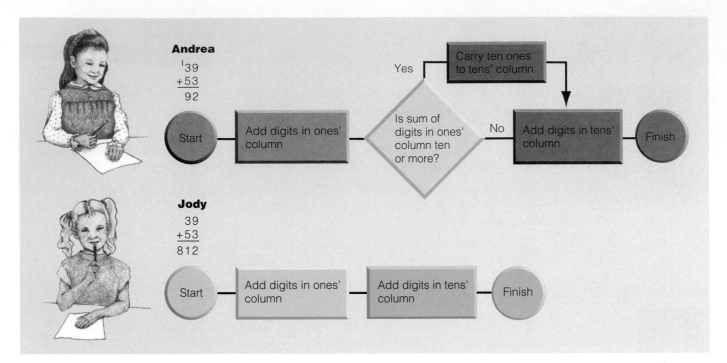

FIGURE 1.2

Information-processing flow-charts showing the steps that two 8-year-olds used to solve a math problem. In this two-digit addition problem requiring a carrying operation, Andrea's procedure is correct, whereas Jody's results in a wrong answer. Research shows that children like Jody, who use incorrect procedures and do not realize that their answers are way out of range, benefit from teaching that points out effective strategies and that requires them to explain and justify their solution techniques.

info processing
continuous
stages
active kids

How much new information can preschoolers hold in memory compared with older children and adults? To what extent does a child's current knowledge influence her ability to learn more?

The information-processing approach is also being used to clarify the processing of social information. For example, flowcharts exist that track the steps children use to solve social problems (such as how to enter an ongoing play group) and acquire gender-linked preferences and behaviors (Crick & Dodge, 1994; Ruble & Martin, 1998). If we can identify how social problem solving and gender stereotyping arise in childhood, then we are in a good position to design interventions that promote more favorable social development.

Like Piaget's theory, the information-processing approach regards children as active, sense-making beings who modify their own thinking in response to environmental demands (Klahr & MacWhinney, 1998). But unlike Piaget's theory, there are no stages of development. Rather, the thought processes studied—perception, attention, memory, categorization of information, planning, problem solving, and comprehension of written and spoken prose— are assumed to be similar at all ages but present to a lesser extent in children. Therefore, the view of development is one of continuous increase rather than abrupt, stagewise change.

A great strength of the information-processing approach is its commitment to careful, rigorous research methods to investigate cognition. Because it has provided precise accounts of how children of different ages engage in many aspects of thinking, its findings have important educational implications (Geary, 1994; Siegler, 1998). For example, children like Jody, who do not notice that their answer to a math problem is way out of range, benefit from teaching that points out effective strategies and requires them to explain and justify their solution procedures (McClain, Cobb, & Bowers, 1998). Too often, such children have tried to memorize a strategy without understanding why it works, so they apply it incorrectly.

The greatest shortcoming of the information-processing approach stems from its central strength: Although good at analyzing thinking into its components, it has difficulty putting them back together into a comprehensive theory of development. In addition, aspects of children's cognition that are not linear and logical, such as imagination and creativity, are all but ignored by this approach (Lutz & Sternberg, 1999). Furthermore, much information-processing research has been conducted in artificial, laboratory situations. Consequently, critics complain that it isolates children's thinking from important features of real-life learning sit-

Konrad Lorenz was one of the founders of ethology and a keen observer of animal behavior. He developed the concept of imprinting. Here, young geese who were separated from their mother and placed in the company of Lorenz during an early, critical period show that they have imprinted on him. They follow him about as he swims through the water, a response that promotes survival.

uations. Recently, investigators have addressed this concern by focusing on more realistic materials and activities. Today, they study children's conversations, stories, memory for everyday events, and (as Figure 1.2 illustrates) strategies for performing academic tasks.

A major advantage of having many theories is that they encourage one another to attend to previously neglected dimensions of children's lives. A unique feature of the final four perspectives we will discuss is the emphasis they place on *contexts* for development—the way children's genetic heritage combines with diverse environmental circumstances to affect pathways of change. The first of these views, ethology, emphasizes that human capacities have been shaped by a long evolutionary history during which our brains and bodies adapted to their surroundings.

ETHOLOGY

Ethology is concerned with the adaptive, or survival, value of behavior and its evolutionary history (Dewsbury, 1992; Hinde, 1989). It was first applied to research on children in the 1960s but has become even more influential today. The origins of ethology can be traced to the work of Darwin. Two European zoologists, Konrad Lorenz and Niko Tinbergen, laid its modern foundations.

Watching the behaviors of diverse animal species in their natural habitats, Lorenz and Tinbergen observed behavior patterns that promote survival. The best known of these is *imprinting,* the early following behavior of certain baby birds that ensures that the young will stay close to the mother and be fed and protected from danger. Imprinting takes place during an early, restricted period of development. If the mother goose is not present during this time, but an object resembling her in important features is, young goslings may imprint on it instead (Lorenz, 1952).

Observations of imprinting led to a major concept that has been widely applied in child development: the *critical period.* It refers to a time during which the child is biologically prepared to acquire certain capacities but needs the support of an appropriately stimulating environment. Many researchers have conducted studies to find out whether complex cognitive and social behaviors must be learned during certain time periods. For example, if children are deprived of adequate food or physical and social stimulation during the early years of life, will their intelligence be impaired? If language is not mastered during the preschool years, is the child's capacity to acquire it reduced?

As we address these and other similar questions in later chapters, we will discover that the term *sensitive period* offers a better account of human development than does the strict notion of a critical period (Bornstein, 1989). A **sensitive period** is a time that is optimal for certain capacities to emerge and in which the individual is especially responsive to environmental

ethology
An approach concerned with the adaptive, or survival, value of behavior and its evolutionary history.

sensitive period
A time that is optimal for certain capacities to emerge and in which the individual is especially responsive to environmental influences.

sensitive period—time needed for certain capacities to emerge.

influences. However, its boundaries are less well defined than are those of a critical period. Development may occur later, but it is harder to induce at that time.

Inspired by observations of imprinting, British psychoanalyst John Bowlby (1969) applied ethological theory to the understanding of the human infant–caregiver relationship. (He argued that babies' attachment behaviors, such as smiling, babbling, grasping, and crying, are built-in social signals that encourage the parent to approach, care for, and interact with the baby. By keeping the mother near, these behaviors help ensure that the baby will be fed, protected from danger, and provided with the stimulation and affection necessary for healthy growth.)

The development of attachment in human infants is a lengthy process involving changes in psychological structures that lead the baby to form a deep affectional tie with the caregiver (Bretherton, 1992). As we will see in Chapter 7, it is far more complex than imprinting in baby birds. But for now, note how the ethological view of attachment, which emphasizes the role of innate infant signals, differs sharply from the behaviorist drive-reduction explanation we mentioned earlier—that the baby's desire for closeness to the mother is a learned response based on feeding.

Observations by ethologists have shown that many aspects of children's social behavior, including emotional expressions, aggression, cooperation, and social play, resemble those of our primate relatives. Today, efforts are also under way to apply an evolutionary perspective to children's cognition (Bjorklund, 1997; Siegler, 1996). Researchers are returning to the central question posed by Piaget: How must children think to adapt to the environments in which they find themselves? We will explore some new answers in later chapters.

Although ethology emphasizes the genetic and biological roots of development, learning is also considered important because it lends flexibility and greater adaptiveness to behavior. The interests of ethologists are broad. They want to understand the entire organism–environment system (Hinde, 1989; Miller, 1993). The next contextual perspective we will discuss, Vyogtsky's sociocultural theory, serves as an excellent complement to ethology, since it highlights the social and cultural aspects of children's experiences.

VYGOTSKY'S SOCIOCULTURAL THEORY

The field of child development research has recently seen a dramatic increase in studies addressing the cultural context of children's lives. Investigations that make comparisons across cultures, and between ethnic groups within cultures, provide insight into whether theories apply to all children or are limited to particular environmental conditions. As a result, cross-cultural and multicultural research helps us untangle the contributions of genetic and environmental factors to the timing, order of appearance, and diversity of children's behaviors (Greenfield, 1994).

In the past, researchers focused on broad cultural differences in development—for example, whether children in one culture are more advanced in motor development or do better on intellectual tasks than do children in another. However, this approach can lead us to conclude incorrectly that one culture is superior in enhancing development, whereas another is deficient. In addition, it does not help us understand the precise experiences that contribute to cultural differences in children's behavior.

Today, more research is examining the relationship of *culturally specific practices* to child development. The contributions of Russian psychologist Lev Vygotsky (1896–1934) have played a major role in this trend. Vygotsky's (1934/1987) perspective is called **sociocultural theory.** It focuses on how *culture*—the values, beliefs, customs, and skills of a social group—is transmitted to the next generation. According to Vygotsky, *social interaction*—in particular, cooperative dialogues between children and more knowledgeable members of society—is necessary for children to acquire the ways of thinking and behaving that make up a community's culture (Wertsch & Tulviste, 1992). Vygotsky believed that as adults and more-expert peers help children master culturally meaningful activities, the communication between them becomes part of children's thinking. Once children internalize the essential

According to Lev Vygotsky, many cognitive processes and skills are socially transferred from more knowledgeable members of society to children. Vygotsky's sociocultural theory helps us understand the wide cultural variation in cognitive competencies. Vygotsky is pictured here with his daughter.

sociocultural theory
Vygotsky's theory, in which children acquire the ways of thinking and behaving that make up a community's culture through cooperative dialogues with more knowledgeable members of society.

ecological systems theory
Bronfenbrenner's approach, which views the child as developing within a complex system of relationships affected by multiple levels of the environment, from immediate settings of family and school to broad cultural values and programs.

[handwritten margin note:] Bowlby believed babies had inborn behaviors that spurred the mother to rxt. to the child.

features of these dialogues, they use the language within them to guide their own actions and acquire new skills (Berk, 2001). The young child instructing herself while working a puzzle or tying her shoes has started to produce the same kind of guiding comments that an adult previously used to help her master important tasks.

Vygotsky's theory has been especially influential in the study of children's cognition. But Vygotsky's approach to cognitive development is quite different from Piaget's. Recall that Piaget did not regard direct teaching by adults as vital for cognitive development. Instead, he emphasized children's active, independent efforts to make sense of their world. Vygotsky agreed with Piaget that children are active, constructive beings. But unlike Piaget, he viewed cognitive development as a *socially mediated process*—as dependent on the support that adults and more-expert peers provide as children try new tasks. Finally, Vygotsky did not believe that all children move through the same sequence of stages. Instead, he proposed that as soon as children acquire language, their enhanced ability to communicate with others leads to continuous changes in thought and behavior that can vary greatly from culture to culture.

A major finding of cross-cultural research is that cultures select different tasks for children's learning. In line with Vygotsky's theory, the assistance granted children as they master these tasks leads to knowledge and skills essential for success in a particular culture (Rogoff & Chavajay, 1995). For example, among the Zinacanteco Indians of southern Mexico, young girls become expert weavers of complex garments through the informal guidance of adults (Childs & Greenfield, 1982). In Brazil and other developing nations, child candy sellers with little or no schooling develop sophisticated mathematical abilities as the result of buying candy from wholesalers, pricing it in collaboration with adults and experienced peers, and bargaining with customers on city streets (Saxe, 1988).

Vygotsky's theory, and the research stimulated by it, reveal that children in every culture develop unique strengths. A cultural perspective reminds us that the majority of child development researchers reside in the United States, and their findings are based on only a small minority of humankind. We cannot assume that the developmental sequences observed in our own children are "natural" or that the experiences fostering them are "ideal" without looking around the world.

At the same time, Vygotsky's emphasis on culture and social experience led him to neglect biological contributions to development. Although he recognized the importance of heredity and brain growth, he said little about their role in cognitive change. Furthermore, Vygotsky's focus on social transmission of knowledge meant that he placed less emphasis than did other theorists on children's capacity to shape their own development. Contemporary followers of Vygotsky grant the individual and society more balanced roles (Rogoff, 1998; Wertsch & Tulviste, 1992).

ECOLOGICAL SYSTEMS THEORY

Urie Bronfenbrenner, an American psychologist, is responsible for an approach to child development that has risen to the forefront of the field over the past two decades because it offers the most differentiated and complete account of contextual influences on children's development. **Ecological systems theory** views the child as developing within a complex *system* of relationships affected by multiple levels of the surrounding environment. Since the child's heredity joins with environmental forces to mold development, Bronfenbrenner (1998) recently characterized his perspective as a *bioecological model*.

Before Bronfenbrenner's (1979, 1989, 1993) theory, most researchers viewed the environment fairly narrowly—as limited to events and conditions immediately surrounding the child. As Figure 1.3 on page 28 shows, Bronfenbrenner expanded this view by envisioning the

This Burmese child candy seller solves arithmetic problems involving currency values through everyday street vending activities. His mathematical skills illustrate how culture and social experience influence cognitive development.

URIE BRONFENBRENNER, CORNELL UNIVERSITY

Urie Bronfenbrenner is the originator of ecological systems theory. According to this view, the child's heredity joins with multiple levels of the surrounding environment— from immediate settings to cultural values, laws, customs and resources—to mold development. Together, these forces affect children's activity patterns and relationships and, in turn, their physical attributes, personalities, and capacities.

Bronfenbrenner took into account other aspects of the children's environment, aside from the immediate one.

FIGURE 1.3

Structure of the environment in ecological systems theory. The *microsystem* includes relations between the developing person and the immediate environment; the *mesosystem,* connections among immediate settings; the *exosystem,* social settings that affect but do not contain the child; and the *macrosystem,* the values, laws, customs, and resources of the culture that affect activities and interactions at all inner layers. The *chronosystem* (not pictured) is not a specific context. Instead, it refers to the dynamic, ever-changing nature of the child's environment.

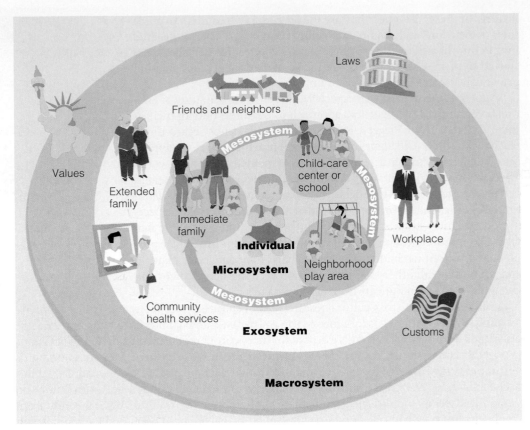

microsystem
In ecological systems theory, the activities and interaction patterns in the child's immediate surroundings.

mesosystem
In ecological systems theory, connections between children's immediate settings.

Relationships are bidirectional.

environment as a series of nested structures that includes but extends beyond home, school, and neighborhood settings in which children spend their everyday lives.

■ **THE MICROSYSTEM.** The innermost level of the environment is the **microsystem,** which refers to activities and interaction patterns in the child's immediate surroundings. Bronfenbrenner emphasizes that to understand child development at this level, we must keep in mind that all relationships are *bidirectional.* That is, adults affect children's behavior, but children's genetically and socially influenced characteristics—their physical attributes, personalities, and capacities—also affect adults' behavior. For example, a friendly, attentive child is likely to evoke positive, patient reactions from parents, whereas a distractible youngster is more likely to receive restriction and punishment. When these reciprocal interactions occur often over time, they have an enduring impact on development (Bronfenbrenner, 1995; Collins et al., 2000).

Third parties also affect whether parent–child (or other two-person) relationships enhance or undermine development. If other individuals in the setting are supportive, then the quality of relationships is enhanced. For example, when parents encourage one another in their child-rearing roles, each engages in more effective parenting (Cowan, Powell, & Cowan, 1998). In contrast, marital conflict is associated with inconsistent discipline and hostile reactions toward children. In response, children typically become hostile, and their adjustment suffers (Hetherington, Bridges, & Insabella, 1998).

■ **THE MESOSYSTEM.** For children to develop at their best, child-rearing supports must also exist in the larger environment. The second level in Bronfenbrenner's theory is the **mesosystem.** It encompasses connections between microsystems, such as home, school, neighborhood, and child-care center, that foster children's development. For example, a child's academic progress depends not just on activities that take place in classrooms but also on parent involvement in school life and the extent to which academic learning is carried over into the home (Connors & Epstein, 1996). Similarly, parent–child interaction is likely to be affected by the child's relationships with caregivers at child care, and vice versa. Parent–child and caregiver–child relationships are each likely to support development when there are links, in the form of visits and exchange of information, between home and child-care setting.

■ **THE EXOSYSTEM.** The **exosystem** refers to social settings that do not contain children but that affect their experiences in immediate settings. These may be formal organizations, such as the parents' workplace or health and welfare services in the community. For example, work settings can help parents in their child-rearing roles and, indirectly, enhance development by offering flexible work schedules, paid maternity and paternity leave, and sick leave for parents whose children are ill. Exosystem supports can also be informal, such as parents' social networks—friends and extended-family members who provide advice, companionship, and even financial assistance. Research confirms the negative impact of a breakdown in exosystem activities. Families who are socially isolated because they have few personal or community-based ties or who are affected by unemployment show increased rates of conflict and child abuse (Emery & Laumann-Billings, 1998).

■ **THE MACROSYSTEM.** The outermost level of Bronfenbrenner's model, the **macrosystem**, consists of cultural values, laws, customs, and resources. The priority that the macrosystem gives to children's needs affects the support they receive at inner levels of the environment. For example, in countries that require high-quality standards for child care and workplace benefits for employed parents, children are more likely to have favorable experiences in their immediate settings. As we will see in greater detail in later chapters, although most Western nations have such programs in place, they are not yet widely available in the United States (Children's Defense Fund, 2000; Kamerman, 1993).

■ **AN EVER-CHANGING SYSTEM.** According to Bronfenbrenner, we must keep in mind that the environment is not a static force that affects people in a uniform way. Instead, it is ever-changing. Important life events, such as the birth of a sibling, entering school, moving to a new neighborhood, or parents' divorce, modify existing relationships between children and their environments, producing new conditions that affect development. In addition, the timing of environmental change affects its impact. The arrival of a new sibling has very different consequences for a homebound toddler than for a school-age child with many relationships and activities beyond the family.

Bronfenbrenner refers to the temporal dimension of his model as the **chronosystem** (the prefix *chrono-* means "time"). Changes in life events can be imposed on the child, as in the examples just given. But they can also arise from within the child, since as children get older they select, modify, and create many of their own settings and experiences. How they do so depends on their physical, intellectual, and personality characteristics and the opportunities available to them. Therefore, in ecological systems theory, development is neither controlled by environmental circumstances nor driven by inner dispositions. Instead, children are both products and producers of their environments in a network of interdependent effects. Notice how our discussion of resilient children on page 10 illustrates this idea. We will see many more examples in later chapters of this book.

NEW DIRECTIONS: DEVELOPMENT AS A DYNAMIC SYSTEM

Today, researchers recognize both consistency and variability in children's development. But instead of merely describing consistencies, they want to do a better job of explaining variation.

A new wave of theorists has adopted a **dynamic systems perspective** on development (Fischer & Bidell, 1998; Thelen & Smith, 1998; Wachs, 2000). According to this view, the

exosystem
In ecological systems theory, settings that do not contain children but that affect their experiences in immediate settings. Examples are parents' workplace and health and welfare services in the community, as well as parents' social networks.

macrosystem
In ecological systems theory, cultural values, laws, customs, and resources that influence experiences and interactions at inner levels of the environment.

chronosystem
In ecological systems theory, temporal changes in children's environments, which produce new conditions that affect development. These changes can be imposed externally or arise from within the child.

dynamic systems perspective
A view that regards the child's mind, body, and physical and social worlds as a dynamic, integrated system. A change in any part of the system leads the child to reorganize his or her behavior so the various components of the system work together again but in a more complex and effective way.

FIGURE 1.4

The dynamic systems view of development. Rather than envisioning a single line of stagewise or continuous change (refer to Figure 1.1 on page 8), dynamic systems theorists conceive of development as a web of fibers branching out in many directions. Each strand in the web represents a potential area of skill within the major domains of development—physical, cognitive, and emotional/social. The differing directions of the strands signify possible variations in paths and outcomes as the child masters skills necessary to participate in diverse contexts. The interconnections of the strands within the vertical windows portray stagelike changes—periods of major transformation in which various skills work together as a functioning whole. As the web expands, skills become more numerous, complex, and effective. (Adapted from Fischer & Bidell, 1998.)

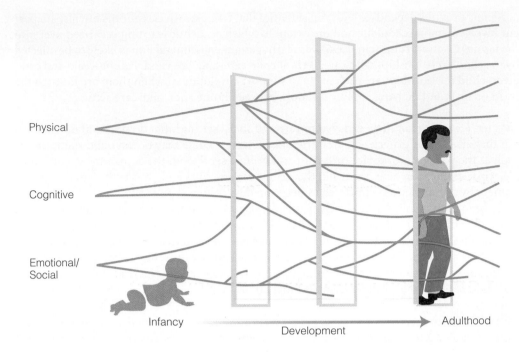

Although these children are about the same age, they vary widely in competencies. The dynamic systems perspective aims to explain this variation by examining how the child's mind, body, and physical and social worlds form an integrated system that guides mastery of new skills.

child's mind, body, and physical and social worlds form an *integrated system* that guides mastery of new skills. The system is *dynamic,* or constantly in motion. A change in any part of it—from brain maturation to physical and social surroundings—disrupts the current organism–environment relationship. When this happens, the child actively reorganizes his or her behavior so the various components of the system work together again but in a more complex and effective way.

Dynamic systems theorists acknowledge that a common human genetic heritage and basic regularities in children's physical and social worlds yield certain universal, broad outlines of development. But biological makeup, everyday tasks, and the people who support children in mastery of those tasks vary greatly, leading to wide individual differences in specific skills. Even when children master the same skills, such as walking, talking, or adding and subtracting, they often do so in unique ways. And because children build competencies by engaging in real activities in real contexts, different skills vary in maturity within the same child. From this perspective, development cannot be characterized as a single line of change.

As Figure 1.4 shows, it is more like a web of fibers branching out in many directions, each of which represents a different skill area that may undergo continuous and stagewise transformations (Fischer & Bidell, 1998).

The dynamic systems view has been inspired by similar ideas in other scientific disciplines, especially biology and physics (Thelen & Smith, 1994, 1998). In addition, it draws on information processing and contextual theories—ethology, sociocultural theory, and ecological systems theory. At present, dynamic systems research is in its early stages. The perspective has largely been applied to children's motor and cognitive skills, but some investigators believe it might help explain emotional and social development as well (Lewis, 1995b). As the field of child development enters the twenty-first century, researchers are analyzing development in all its complexity in search of an all-encompassing approach to understanding change.

review   *What features of Vygotsky's sociocultural theory distinguish it from Piaget's cognitive-developmental theory?*

apply   *Return to the Biology and Environment box on page 10. How does the story of John and Gary illustrate bidirectional influences within the microsystem, as described in ecological systems theory?*

reflect   *To illustrate the chronosystem in ecological systems theory, select an influential event from your childhood, such as a move to a new neighborhood, a class with an inspiring teacher, or parental divorce or remarriage. How did the event affect you? How might its impact have differed had you been 5 years younger? How about 5 years older?*

Comparing Child Development Theories

In the preceding sections, we reviewed theoretical perspectives that are major forces in child development research. They differ in many respects. First, they focus on different domains of development. Some, such as the psychoanalytic perspective and ethology, emphasize children's emotional and social development. Others, such as Piaget's cognitive-developmental theory, information processing, and Vygotsky's sociocultural theory, stress important changes in children's thinking. The remaining approaches—behaviorism, social learning theory, ecological systems theory, and the dynamic systems perspective—discuss factors assumed to affect many aspects of children's functioning.

Second, every theory contains a point of view about child development. As we conclude our review of theoretical perspectives, take a moment to identify the stand that each theory takes on the three controversial issues presented at the beginning of this chapter. Then check your own analysis of theories against Table 1.5 on page 32. If you had difficulty classifying any of them, return to the relevant section of this chapter and reread the description of that theory.

Finally, we have seen that theories have strengths and weaknesses. This may remind you of an important point made earlier in this chapter—that no theory provides a complete account of development. Perhaps you found that you were attracted to some theories, but you had doubts about others. As you read more about child development research in later chapters of this book, you may find it useful to keep a notebook in which you test your own theoretical likes and dislikes against the evidence. Don't be surprised if you revise your ideas many times, just as theorists have done throughout this century. By the end of the course, you will have built your own personal perspective on child development. It might turn out to be a blend of several theories, since each viewpoint we have discussed has contributed in important ways to what we know about children. And, like the field of child development as a whole, you will be left with some unanswered questions. I hope they will motivate you to continue your quest to understand children in the years to come.

Studying the Child

In every science, theories, like those we've just reviewed, guide the collection of information, its interpretation, and its application to everyday life. In fact, research usually begins with a *hypothesis*, or prediction, drawn directly from a theory. But theories and hypotheses are only the beginning of the many activities that result in sound research on child development. Conducting research according to scientifically

TABLE 1.5

Stances of Major Theories on Basic Issues in Child Development

THEORY	CONTINUOUS OR DISCONTINUOUS DEVELOPMENT?	ONE COURSE OF DEVELOPMENT OR MANY?	NATURE OR NURTURE AS MORE IMPORTANT?
Psychoanalytic perspective	*Discontinuous:* Psychosexual and psychosocial development takes place in stages.	*One course:* Stages are assumed to be universal.	*Both nature and nurture:* Innate impulses are channeled and controlled through child-rearing experiences. *Early experiences* set the course of later development.
Behaviorism and social learning theory	*Continuous:* Development involves an increase in learned behaviors.	*Many possible courses:* Behaviors reinforced and modeled may vary from child to child.	*Emphasis on nurture:* Development results from conditioning and modeling. *Both early and later experiences* are important.
Piaget's cognitive-developmental theory	*Discontinuous:* Cognitive development takes place in stages.	*One course:* Stages are assumed to be universal.	*Both nature and nurture:* Development occurs as the brain matures and children exercise their innate drive to discover reality in a generally stimulating environment. *Both early and later experiences* are important.
Information processing	*Continuous:* Children gradually improve in perception, attention, memory, and problem-solving skills.	*One course:* Changes studied characterize most or all children.	*Both nature and nurture:* Children are active, sense-making beings who modify their thinking as the brain matures and they confront new environmental demands. *Both early and later experiences* are important.
Ethology	*Both continuous and discontinuous:* Children gradually develop a wider range of adaptive behaviors. Sensitive periods occur, in which qualitatively distinct capacities emerge fairly suddenly.	*One course:* Adaptive behaviors and sensitive periods apply to all members of a species.	*Both nature and nurture:* Behaviors are the result of evolution, but an appropriately stimulating environment is necessary to elicit them. *Early experiences* set the course of later development.
Vygotsky's sociocultural theory	*Continuous:* Through interaction with more expert members of society, children gradually acquire culturally adaptive skills.	*Many possible courses:* Socially mediated changes in thought and behavior vary from culture to culture.	*Both nature and nurture:* Heredity, brain growth, and dialogues with more expert members of society jointly contribute to development. *Both early and later experiences* are important.
Ecological systems theory	*Not specified.*	*Many possible courses:* Children's characteristics join with environmental forces at multiple levels to mold development in unique ways.	*Both nature and nurture:* Children's characteristics and the reactions of others affect each other in a bidirectional fashion. Layers of the environment influence child-rearing experiences. *Both early and later experiences* are important.
Dynamic systems perspective	*Both continuous and discontinuous:* Change in the system is always ongoing. Stagelike transformations occur as various parts of the system join together to work as a functioning whole.	*Many possible courses:* Biological makeup, everyday tasks, and social experiences vary, yielding wide individual differences in specific skills.	*Both nature and nurture:* The child's mind, body, and physical and social surroundings form an integrated system that guides mastery of new skills. *Both early and later experiences* are important.

accepted procedures involves many important steps and choices. Investigators must decide which participants, and how many, to include. Then they must figure out what the participants will be asked to do and when, where, and how many times each will have to be seen. Finally, they must examine relationships and draw conclusions from their data.

In the following sections, we look at research strategies commonly used to study children. We begin with *research methods*—the specific activities of participants, such as taking tests, answering questionnaires, responding to interviews, or being observed. Then we turn to *research designs*—overall plans for research studies that permit the best possible test of the investigator's hypothesis. Finally, we discuss special ethical issues involved in doing research on children.

At this point, you may be wondering, Why learn about research strategies? Why not leave these matters to research specialists and concentrate on what is already known about the child and how this knowledge can be applied? There are two reasons. First, each of us must be wise and critical consumers of knowledge, not naive sponges who soak up facts about children. A basic appreciation of the strengths and weaknesses of research strategies becomes important in separating dependable information from misleading results. Second, individuals who work directly with children—psychologists, teachers, doctors, nurses, social workers, and others—may carry out research studies, either on their own or with an experienced investigator. At other times, they may have to provide information on how well their goals for children are being realized to justify continued financial support for their programs and activities. Under these circumstances, an understanding of research strategies becomes essential, practical knowledge.

COMMON METHODS OF GATHERING INFORMATION

How does a researcher choose a basic approach to gathering information about children? Common methods in the field of child development include systematic observation, self-reports, psychophysiological measures, clinical or case studies of a single child, and ethnographies of the life circumstances of a specific group of children. As you read about these methods, you may find it helpful to refer to Table 1.6 on page 34, which summarizes the strengths and limitations of each.

■ SYSTEMATIC OBSERVATION. Observations of the behavior of children, and of adults who are important in their lives, can be made in different ways. One approach is to go into the field, or natural environment, and observe the behavior of interest, a method called **naturalistic observation.**

A study of preschoolers' responses to their peers' distress provides a good example of this technique (Farver & Branstetter, 1994). Observing 3- and 4-year-olds in child-care centers, the researchers recorded each instance of a child crying and the reactions of nearby children—whether they ignored, watched curiously, commented on the child's unhappiness, scolded or teased, shared, helped, or expressed sympathy. Caregiver behaviors, such as explaining why a child was crying, mediating conflict, or offering comfort, were noted to see if adult sensitivity was related to children's caring responses. A strong relationship emerged. The great strength of naturalistic observation in studies like this one is that investigators can see directly the everyday behaviors they hope to explain (Miller, 1998).

Naturalistic observation also has a major limitation: Not all individuals have the same opportunity to display a particular behavior in everyday life. In the study just mentioned, some children may have witnessed a child crying more often than did others or been exposed to more cues for positive social responses from caregivers. For this reason, they might have displayed more compassion.

Researchers commonly deal with this difficulty by making **structured observations** in a laboratory. In this approach, the investigator sets up a situation that evokes the behavior of interest so that every participant has an equal opportunity to display the response. In one study, children's comforting behavior was observed by seeing how they reacted to a tape

MICHAEL NEWMAN/PHOTOEDIT

In naturalistic observation, the researcher goes into the field and records the behavior of interest. This observer might be recording children's attention, activity preferences, emotional expressions, or social contacts. Although she can see directly the everyday behaviors of interest, not all children have the same opportunity to display a particular behavior in everyday life.

naturalistic observation
A method in which the researcher goes into the natural environment to observe the behavior of interest.

structured observation
A method in which the investigator sets up a situation that evokes the behavior of interest and observes it in a laboratory.

TABLE 1.6

Strengths and Limitations of Common Information-Gathering Methods

METHOD	DESCRIPTION	STRENGTHS	LIMITATIONS
Systematic Observation			
Naturalistic observation	Observation of behavior in natural contexts	Reflects participants' everyday behaviors.	Cannot control conditions under which participants are observed.
Structured observation	Observation of behavior in a laboratory, where conditions are the same for all participants	Grants each participant an equal opportunity to display the behavior of interest.	May not yield observations typical of participants' behavior in everyday life.
Self-Reports			
Clinical interview	Flexible interviewing procedure in which the investigator obtains a complete account of the participant's thoughts	Comes as close as possible to the way participants think in everyday life; great breadth and depth of information can be obtained in a short time.	May not result in accurate reporting of information; flexible procedure makes comparing individuals' responses difficult.
Structured interview, questionnaires, and tests	Self-report instruments in which each participant is asked the same questions in the same way	Permits comparisons of participants' responses and efficient data collection and scoring.	Does not yield the same depth of information as a clinical interview; responses are still subject to inaccurate reporting.
Psychophysiological Methods	Methods that measure the relationship between physiological processes and behavior	Reveals which central nervous system structures contribute to development and individual differences in certain competencies. Helps identify the perceptions, thoughts, and emotions of infants and young children, who cannot report them clearly.	Cannot reveal with certainty how an individual processes stimuli. Many factors besides those of interest to the researcher can influence a physiological response.
Clinical Method (Case Study)	A full picture of a single individual's psychological functioning, obtained by combining interviews, observations, test scores, and sometimes psychophysiological assessments	Provides rich, descriptive insights into processes of development.	May be biased by researcher's theoretical preferences; findings cannot be applied to individuals other than the participant.
Ethnography	Participant observation of a culture or distinct social group; by making extensive field notes, the researcher tries to capture the culture's unique values and social processes	Provides a more complete and accurate description than can be derived from a single observational visit, interview, or questionnaire.	May be biased by researcher's values and theoretical preferences; findings cannot be applied to individuals and settings other than the ones studied.

recording of a baby crying in the next room. Using an intercom, children could either talk to the baby or push a button so they did not have to listen (Eisenberg et al., 1993). Notice how structured observation gives investigators more control over the research situation. But its great disadvantage is that people do not necessarily behave in the laboratory as they do in everyday life.

The procedures used to collect systematic observations vary considerably, depending on the purpose of the research. Some investigators need to describe the entire stream of behavior—everything said and done over a certain time period. The goal of one of my own studies was to find out how sensitive, responsive, and verbally stimulating caregivers were when they interacted with children in child-care centers (Berk, 1985). In this case, everything each caregiver said and did—even the amount of time she spent away from the children, taking coffee breaks and talking on the phone—was important. In other studies, only one or a few kinds of behavior are of interest, so preserving the entire behavior stream is unnecessary. In these instances, researchers record only certain events or mark off behaviors on checklists.

Systematic observation provides invaluable information on how children and adults behave, but it tells us little about the reasoning behind their responses. For this kind of information, researchers must turn to another type of method: self-reports.

TONY FREEMAN/PHOTOEDIT

Using the clinical interview, this researcher asks a mother to describe her child's development. The method permits large amounts of information to be gathered in a fairly brief period. A major drawback of this method is that participants do not always report information accurately.

■ **SELF-REPORTS: INTERVIEWS AND QUESTIONNAIRES.** Self-reports are instruments that ask participants to answer questions about their perceptions, thoughts, abilities, feelings, attitudes, beliefs, and past experiences. They range from relatively unstructured clinical interviews—the method used by Piaget to study children's thinking—to highly structured interviews, questionnaires, and tests.

Let's look at an example of a **clinical interview** in which Piaget questioned a 5-year-old child about his understanding of dreams. Notice how Piaget used a flexible, conversational style to encourage the child to expand his ideas.

> Where does the dream come from?—*I think you sleep so well that you dream.*—Does it come from us or from outside?—*From outside.*—When you are in bed and you dream, where is the dream?—*In my bed, under the blanket. I don't really know. If it was in my stomach, the bones would be in the way and I shouldn't see it.*—Is the dream there when you sleep?—*Yes, it is in the bed beside me . . .* —You see the dream when you are in the room, but if I were in the room, too, should I see it?—*No, grownups don't ever dream.*—Can two people ever have the same dream?—*No, never.*—When the dream is in the room, is it near you?—*Yes, there!* (pointing to 30 cm. in front of his eyes). (Piaget, 1926/1930, pp. 97–98)

The clinical interview has two major strengths. First, it permits people to display their thoughts in terms that are as close as possible to the way they think in everyday life. Second, the clinical interview can provide a large amount of information in a fairly brief period. For example, in an hour-long session, we can obtain a wide range of child-rearing information from a parent—much more than we could capture by observing parent–child interaction for the same amount of time.

A major limitation of the clinical interview has to do with the accuracy with which people report their thoughts, feelings, and experiences. Some participants, desiring to please the interviewer, may make up answers. When asked about past events, they may have trouble recalling exactly what happened. And because the clinical interview depends on verbal ability and expressiveness, it may underestimate the capacities of individuals who have difficulty putting their thoughts into words.

The clinical interview has also been criticized because of its flexibility. When questions are phrased differently for each participant, differences in responses may be due to the manner of interviewing rather than to real differences in the way people think about a certain topic. **Structured interviews,** in which each participant is asked the same questions in the same way, can eliminate this problem. In addition, these techniques are much more efficient. Answers are briefer, and researchers can obtain written responses from an entire class of

clinical interview
A method in which the researcher uses a flexible, conversational style to probe for the participant's point of view.

structured interview
A method in which each participant is asked the same questions in the same way.

children or group of parents at the same time. Also, when structured interviews use multiple-choice, yes/no, and true/false formats, as is done on many tests and questionnaires, responses can be tabulated by machine. However, we must keep in mind that these approaches do not yield the same depth of information as a clinical interview, and they can still be affected by inaccurate reporting.

■ **PSYCHOPHYSIOLOGICAL METHODS.** Researchers' desire to uncover the biological bases of children's cognitive and emotional responses has led to the use of **psychophysiological methods,** which measure the relationship between physiological processes and behavior. Investigators who rely on these methods want to find out which central nervous system structures contribute to development and individual differences. Psychophysiological methods also can help identify the perceptions, thoughts, and emotions of infants and young children, who cannot describe their psychological experiences clearly.

Involuntary activities of the autonomic nervous system—changes in heart rate, blood pressure, respiration, and pupil dilation—are among the most commonly used physiological measures because of their sensitivity to psychological state. For example, heart rate can be used to infer whether an infant is staring blankly at a stimulus (heart rate is stable) or attending to and processing information (heart rate slows during concentration) (Izard et al., 1991; Porges, 1991). Heart rate variations are also linked to certain emotional expressions, such as interest, anger, and sadness (Fox & Card, 1998). And as Chapter 7 will reveal, distinct patterns of autonomic activity are related to aspects of temperament, such as shyness and sociability (Kagan, 1992, 1998).

Autonomic indicators of cognition and emotion have been enriched by measures of brain functioning. In an *electroencephalogram (EEG),* researchers tape electrodes to the scalp to record the electrical activity of the brain. EEG waves are linked to different states of arousal, from deep sleep to alert wakefulness, permitting researchers to see how these states change with age. EEG patterns also vary with infants' and children's emotional states—whether they are upbeat and happy or sad and distressed (Jones et al., 1997). At times, investigators study *event-related potentials (ERPs),* or EEG waves that accompany particular events. For example, a unique wave pattern appears when infants older than 4 months of age are re-exposed to a stimulus they saw earlier. This reaction seems to reflect babies' active efforts to search their memories (Nelson, 1993).

Functional brain-imaging techniques, which yield three-dimensional pictures of brain activity, provide the most precise information on which brain regions are specialized for certain functions, such as language or emotion. *Functional magnetic resonance imaging (fMRI)* is the most promising of these methods, since it does not depend on X-ray photography, which requires injection of radioactive substances. Instead, when a child is shown a stimulus, changes in blood flow within the brain are detected magnetically, producing a computerized image of active areas. Currently, researchers are using fMRI to study age-related changes in brain organization and the brain functioning of children with serious learning and emotional problems (Gaillard et al., 2000; Georgiewa et al., 1999; Rivkin, 2000).

Despite their virtues, psychophysiological methods have limitations. First, interpreting the results involves a high degree of inference. Even though a stimulus produces a consistent pattern of autonomic or brain activity, researchers cannot be sure that an infant or child has processed it in a certain way. Second, many factors can influence a physiological response—hunger, boredom, fatigue, or fear of the laboratory equipment and situation. fMRI, for example, involves confinement to a small space and operation of noisy equipment. Preparing children by taking them through a simulated fMRI procedure before actual brain scanning greatly reduces their fear (Rosenberg et al., 1997). Without such efforts, detecting correspondences between physiological and psychological reactions is difficult or impossible.

■ **THE CLINICAL, OR CASE STUDY, METHOD.** Earlier in this chapter, we discussed the **clinical method** (sometimes called the **case study** approach) as an outgrowth of psychoanalytic theory, which stressed the importance of understanding the individual. Recall that the clinical method brings together a wide range of information on a child, including interviews, observations, test scores, and sometimes psychophysiological measures (Haynes, 1991). The

[Handwritten margin note: Psychophy. methods are used to pinpoint areas of the brain involved in specific f(x)s.]

psychophysiological methods
Methods that measure the relationship between physiological processes and behavior. Among the most common are measures of autonomic nervous system activity (such as heart rate and respiration) and brain functioning (such as the EEG and fMRI).

clinical, or case study, method
A method in which the researcher attempts to understand the unique individual child by combining interview data, observations, test scores, and sometimes psychophysiological measures.

AP/WIDE WORLD PHOTOS

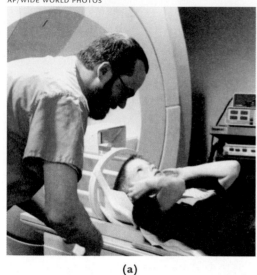

(a)

B. J. CASEY/UPMC

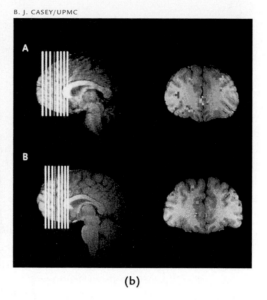

(b)

In functional magnetic resonance imaging (fMRI), the child looks up at a stimulus, and changes in blood flow within brain tissue are detected magnetically (a). The result is a computerized image of activated areas (b), permitting study of age-related changes in brain organization and the brain functioning of children with serious learning and emotional problems.

aim is to obtain as complete a picture as possible of a child's psychological functioning and the experiences that led up to it.

In one investigation, researchers wanted to find out what contributes to the accomplishments of *prodigies*—extremely gifted children who before age 10 attain the competence of an adult in a particular field (Feldman & Goldsmith, 1991). Consider Adam, a boy who read, wrote, and composed musical pieces before he was out of diapers. By age 4, Adam was intensively involved in mastering human symbol systems—BASIC for the computer, French, German, Russian, Sanskrit, Greek, ancient hieroglyphs, music, and mathematics. At age 8, he composed a symphony. Adam's parents provided a home rich in stimulation and raised him with affection, firmness, and humor. They searched for schools in which he could develop his abilities while forming rewarding social relationships.

Because prodigies are scarce and vary widely in their special abilities, it is risky to study all of them in the same way. Consequently, the clinical method is well suited to investigating such children. To explore the possibility of common themes in development, researchers can examine other similar cases as they accumulate (Gardner, 1998a). For example, could Adam have realized his abilities without high motivation and parents and teachers who sensitively nurtured his talents? Probably not, since a burning desire to achieve, a loving family life, parental encouragement and expectation for hard work, and outstanding teachers are evident in the lives of diverse prodigies.

Parents + other role models must nurture the children: interests of their children.

The clinical method yields case narratives rich in descriptive detail that offer valuable insights into the multiplicity of factors that affect development. Nevertheless, like all other methods, it has drawbacks. Information often is collected unsystematically and subjectively, permitting too much leeway for researchers' theoretical preferences to bias their interpretations. In addition, investigators cannot assume that their conclusions apply to anyone other than the child studied. Even when patterns emerge across several cases, it is wise to try to confirm them with other research methods.

■ **METHODS FOR STUDYING CULTURE.** To study the impact of culture, researchers adjust the methods just considered or tap procedures specially devised for cross-cultural and multicultural research. Which approach they choose depends on their research goals (Triandis, 1995, 1998).

Sometimes researchers are interested in characteristics believed to be universal but that vary in degree from one culture to the next. These investigators might ask, Do parents demand greater maturity from young children in some societies than in others? How strong are gender stereotypes in different nations? In each instance, several cultural groups must be compared, and all participants must be questioned or observed in the same way. Therefore,

Cultural INFLUENCES

IMMIGRANT YOUTHS: AMAZING ADAPTATION

During the past quarter-century, a rising tide of immigrants has come to the United States, fleeing war and persecution in their homelands or otherwise seeking better life chances. Today, nearly 20 percent of the U.S. youth population has foreign-born parents; almost 30 percent of these youths are foreign born themselves (Fuligni, 1998b). They are ethnically diverse; most are from Asian and Latin American countries, such as Korea, the Philippines, Vietnam, Cuba, El Salvador, and Mexico.

ACADEMIC ACHIEVEMENT AND ADJUSTMENT

Although educators and laypeople often assume that the transition to a new country has a negative impact on psychological well-being, recent evidence reveals that children of immigrant parents adapt amazingly well. Students who are first generation (foreign born) and second generation (American born with immigrant parents) achieve in school as well as or better than do students of native-born

parents. Their success is evident in many academic subjects, including English, even though they are likely to come from non-English-speaking homes (Fuligni, 1997; Rumbaut, 1997).

Findings on psychological adjustment resemble those on achievement. Compared with their agemates, adolescents from immigrant families are less likely to commit delinquent and violent acts, to use drugs and alcohol, and to have sex at an early age. They are also in better health—less likely to be obese and to have missed school because of illness. And in terms of self-esteem, they feel as positively about themselves as do young people with native-born parents and report less emotional distress. These successes do not depend on having extensive time to adjust to a new way of life. The school performance and psychological well-being of immigrant high school students who recently arrived in the United States is as high as—and sometimes higher than—that of students who came at younger ages (Fuligni, 1997, 1998; Rumbaut, 1997).

The outcomes just described are strongest for Asian youths, less dramatic for Hispanic adolescents (Fuligni, 1997; Kao & Tienda, 1995). Variations in parents' education and income account for these ethnic differences. Still, even first- and second-generation youths from ethnic groups that face considerable economic hardship (such as Mexican and Southeast Asian) are remarkably successful (Harris, 2000; Kao, 2000). Factors other than income are responsible.

FAMILY AND COMMUNITY INFLUENCES

Ethnographies of immigrant populations reveal that uniformly, parents express the belief that education is the surest way to improve life chances. Consequently, they place a high value on their children's academic achievement (Suarez-Orozco & Suarez-Orozco, 1995; Zhou & Bankston, 1998). Aware of the challenges their children face, immigrant parents underscore the importance of trying hard. They remind their children that educational opportunities were not available in

---

ethnography
A method in which the researcher attempts to understand the unique values and social processes of a culture or a distinct social group by living with its members and taking field notes for an extended period of time.

researchers draw on the self-report and observational procedures we have already considered, adapting them through translation so they can be understood in each cultural context. For example, to study cultural variation in parenting attitudes, the same questionnaire, asking for ratings on such items as "If my child gets into trouble, I expect him or her to handle the problem mostly by himself or herself," is given to all participants (Chen et al., 1998).

At other times, researchers want to uncover the *cultural meanings* of children's and adults' behaviors by becoming as familiar as possible with their way of life (Shweder et al., 1998). To achieve this goal, researchers rely on a method borrowed from the field of anthropology—**ethnography.** Like the clinical method, ethnographic research is a descriptive, qualitative technique. But instead of aiming to understand a single individual, it is directed toward understanding a culture or a distinct social group (Jessor, 1996; Shweder, 1996).

The ethnographic method achieves its goals through *participant observation.* Typically, the researcher lives with the cultural community for months or years, participating in its daily life. Extensive field notes are gathered, consisting of a mix of observations, self-reports from members of the culture, and careful interpretations by the investigator. Later, these notes are put together into a description of the community that tries to capture its unique values and social processes.

their native countries and, as a result, they themselves are often limited to menial jobs.

Adolescents from immigrant families internalize their parents' valuing of education, endorsing it more strongly than do agemates with American-born parents (Fuligni, 1997). Because minority ethnicities usually stress allegiance to family and community over individual goals, first- and second-generation young people feel a strong sense of obligation to their parents (Fuligni et al., 1999). They view school success as one of the most important ways they can repay their parents for the hardships they endured in coming to a new land. Both family relationships and school achievement protect these youths from risky behaviors, such as delinquency, early pregnancy, and drug use (refer to the Biology and Environment box on resiliency on page 10).

Immigrant parents typically develop close ties to an ethnic community. It exerts additional control through a high consensus on values and constant monitoring of young peoples'

whereabouts and activities. Consider Versailles Village, a low-income Vietnamese neighborhood in New Orleans, where the overwhelming majority of high school students say that obedience to parents and working hard are very important (Zhou & Bankston, 1998). A local educational association promotes achievement by offering after-school homework tutoring sessions and English- and Vietnamese-language classes. Almost 70 percent of Vietnamese adolescents enroll, and attendance is positively related to school performance.

The comments of these Vietnamese teenagers capture the power of family and community forces:

Thuy Trang, age 14, middle-school Student of the Year: "When my parents first immigrated from Vietnam, they spent every waking hour working hard to support a family. They have sacrificed for me, and I am willing to do anything for them."

This family recently immigrated to the United States from Ecuador. Ethnographic research shows that immigrant parents typically place a high value on academic achievement and emphasize family and community goals over individual goals. Their children, who feel a strong sense of obligation to meet their parents' expectations, achieve as well as or better than native-born agemates, and they are less likely to commit antisocial acts.

Elizabeth, age 16, straight-A student, like her two older sisters: "My parents know pretty much all the kids in the neighborhood. . . . Everybody here knows everybody else. It's hard to get away with much." (Zhou & Bankston, 1998, pp. 93, 130)

The ethnographic method assumes that by entering into close contact with a social group, researchers can understand the beliefs and behaviors of its members more accurately, in a way not possible with an observational visit, interview, or questionnaire. In some ethnographies, investigators focus on many aspects of children's experience, as one researcher did in describing what it is like to grow up in a small American town (Peshkin, 1978). In other instances, the research is limited to one or a few settings, such as home, school, or neighborhood life (LeVine et al., 1994; Peshkin, 1997; Valdés, 1998). Researchers interested in cultural comparisons may supplement traditional self-report and observational methods with ethnography if they suspect that unique meanings underlie cultural differences, as the Cultural Influences box above reveals.

Ethnographers strive to minimize their influence on the culture they are studying by becoming part of it. Nevertheless, at times their presence does alter the situation. And, as with clinical research, investigators' cultural values and theoretical commitments sometimes lead them to observe selectively or misinterpret what they see. Finally, the findings of ethnographic studies cannot be assumed to apply to people and settings other than those in which the research was conducted (Hammersley, 1992).

Ask **YOURSELF...**

review   *What strengths and limitations do the clinical method and ethnography have in common?*

apply   *A researcher wants to study the thoughts and feelings of children who have experienced their parents' divorce. Which method is best suited for investigating this question? Why?*

connect   *Refer to the Cultural Influences box on pages 38–39. What explains the close link between academic success and positive psychological adjustment among first- and second-generation immigrant youths?*

GENERAL RESEARCH DESIGNS

In deciding on a research design, investigators choose a way of setting up a study that permits them to test their hypotheses with the greatest certainty possible. Two main designs are used in all research on human behavior: correlational and experimental.

■ **CORRELATIONAL DESIGN.** In a **correlational design,** researchers gather information on individuals, generally in natural life circumstances—their homes, child-care centers, schools, and neighborhoods—without altering their experiences in any way. Suppose we want to answer these questions: Do mothers' styles of interacting with their children have any bearing on children's intelligence? Does attending a child-care center promote children's friendliness with peers? How do child abuse and neglect affect children's feelings about themselves and relationships with peers? In these and many other instances, it is either very difficult or ethically impossible to arrange and control the conditions of interest.

The correlational design offers a way of looking at relationships between children's experiences or characteristics and their behavior or development. But correlational studies have one major limitation: We cannot infer cause and effect. For example, if we find that mothers' interaction does correlate with children's intelligence, we would not know whether mothers' behavior actually *causes* intellectual differences among children. In fact, the opposite is certainly possible. The behaviors of highly intelligent children may be so attractive that they cause parents to interact more favorably. Or a third variable that we did not even consider, such as amount of noise and distraction in the home, may be causing both maternal interaction and children's intelligence to change together in the same direction.

In correlational studies, and in other types of research designs, investigators often examine relationships by using a **correlation coefficient,** a number that describes how two measures, or variables, are associated with one another. We will encounter the correlation coefficient in discussing research findings throughout this book. So let's look at what it is and how it is interpreted. A correlation coefficient can range in value from +1.00 to −1.00. The *magnitude, or size, of the number* shows the *strength of the relationship.* A zero correlation indicates no relationship, but the closer the value is to +1.00 or −1.00, the stronger the relationship. For instance, a correlation of −.78 is high, −.52 is moderate, and −.18 is low. Note, however that correlations of +.52 and −.52 are equally strong. The *sign of the number* refers to the *direction of the relationship.* A positive sign (+) means that as one variable *increases,* the other also *increases.* A negative sign (−) indicates that as one variable *increases,* the other *decreases.*

Let's take some examples to illustrate how a correlation coefficient works. In one study, a researcher found that a measure of maternal language stimulation at 13 months was positively correlated with the size of children's vocabularies at 20 months, at +.50 (Tamis-LeMonda & Bornstein, 1994). This is a moderate correlation, which indicates that the more mothers spoke to their infants, the more advanced their children were in spoken language during the second year of life. In another study, a researcher reported that the extent to which mothers ignored

correlational design
A research design in which the researcher gathers information without altering participants' experiences and examines relationships between variables. Does not permit inferences about cause and effect.

correlation coefficient
A number, ranging from +1.00 to −1.00, that describes the strength and direction of the relationship between two variables.

their 10-month-olds' bids for attention was negatively correlated with children's willingness to comply with parental demands 1 year later—at −.46 for boys and −.36 for girls (Martin, 1981). These moderate correlations reveal that the more mothers ignored their babies, the less cooperative their children were during the second year of life.

Both investigations found a relationship between maternal behavior in the first year and children's behavior in the second year. Although the researchers suspected that maternal behavior affected children's responses, in neither study could they be sure about cause and effect. However, finding a relationship in a correlational study suggests that tracking down its cause—with a more powerful experimental strategy, if possible—would be worthwhile.

■ EXPERIMENTAL DESIGN. Unlike correlational studies, an **experimental design** permits inferences about cause and effect. In an experiment, the events and behaviors of interest are divided into two types: independent and dependent variables. The **independent variable** is the one anticipated by the investigator to cause changes in another variable. The **dependent variable** is the one the investigator expects to be influenced by the independent variable. Inferences about cause-and-effect relationships are possible because the researcher directly *controls* or *manipulates* changes in the independent variable. This is done by exposing participants to two or more treatment conditions and comparing their performance on measures of the dependent variable.

In one *laboratory experiment,* researchers explored the impact of adults' angry interactions on children's adjustment (El-Sheikh, Cummings, & Reiter, 1996). They hypothesized that the way angry encounters end (independent variable) affects children's emotional reactions (dependent variable). Four- and 5-year-olds were brought one at a time to a laboratory, accompanied by their mothers. One group was exposed to an *unresolved-anger treatment,* in which two adult actors entered the room and argued but did not work out their disagreements. The other group witnessed a *resolved-anger treatment,* in which the adults ended their disputes by apologizing and compromising. As Figure 1.5 shows, during a follow-up adult conflict, more children in the resolved-anger treatment showed a decline in distress, as measured by anxious facial expressions, freezing in place, and seeking closeness to their mothers. The experiment revealed that anger resolution can reduce the stressful impact of adult conflict on children.

In experimental studies, investigators must take special precautions to control for participants' characteristics that could reduce the accuracy of their findings. For example, in the study just described, if a greater number of children from homes high in parental conflict happened to end up in the unresolved-anger treatment, we could not tell whether the independent variable or children's background characteristics produced the results. *Random assignment* of participants to treatment conditions offers protection against this problem. By using an evenhanded procedure, such as drawing numbers out of a hat or flipping a coin, the experimenter increases the chances that children's characteristics will be equally distributed across treatment groups.

Sometimes researchers combine random assignment with another technique called *matching.* In this procedure, participants are measured before the experiment on the factor in question—in our example, parental conflict. Then children from homes high and low in parental conflict are assigned in equal numbers to each treatment condition. In this way, the experimental groups are deliberately matched, or made equivalent, on characteristics that are likely to distort the results.

■ MODIFIED EXPERIMENTAL DESIGNS: FIELD AND NATURAL EXPERIMENTS. Most experiments are conducted in laboratories, where researchers can achieve the maximum possible control over treatment conditions. But, as we have already indicated, findings obtained in laboratories may not apply to everyday situations. The ideal solution to this problem is to do experiments in the field as a complement to laboratory investigations. In *field experiments,* investigators capitalize on rare opportunities to randomly assign people to treatment conditions in natural settings. In the experiment we just considered, for example, we can conclude that the emotional climate established by adults affects children's behavior in the laboratory. But does it also do so in daily life?

Another study helps answer this question (Yarrow, Scott, & Waxler, 1973). This time, the research was carried out in a child-care center. A caregiver deliberately interacted differently

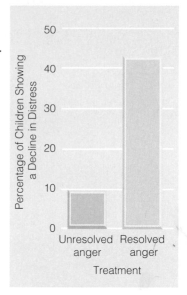

FIGURE 1.5

Does the way adults end their angry encounters affect children's emotional reactions? A laboratory experiment showed that when adults resolve their disputes by apologizing and compromising, children are more likely to decline in distress when witnessing subsequent adult conflicts than when adults leave their arguments unresolved. Notice in this graph that only 10 percent of children in the unresolved-anger treatment declined in distress (see bar on left), whereas 42 percent of children in the resolved-anger treatment did so (see bar on right). (Adapted from El-Sheikh, Cummings, & Reiter, 1996.)

experimental design
A research design in which the investigator randomly assigns participants to treatment conditions. Permits inferences about cause and effect.

independent variable
The variable the researcher expects to cause changes in another variable in an experiment.

dependent variable
The variable the researcher expects to be influenced by the independent variable in an experiment.

with two groups of preschoolers. In one condition (the *nurturant treatment*), she modeled many instances of warmth and helpfulness. In the second condition (the *control,* since it involved no treatment), she behaved as usual, with no special emphasis on concern for others. Two weeks later, the researchers created several situations that called for helpfulness. For example, a visiting mother asked each child to watch her baby for a few moments. The baby's toys had fallen out of the playpen, and the investigators recorded whether or not each child returned the toys to the baby. Children exposed to the nurturant treatment behaved in a much more helpful way than did those in the control condition.

Researchers cannot always randomly assign participants and manipulate conditions in the real world, as these investigators were able to do. Sometimes researchers can compromise by conducting *natural experiments.* Treatments that already exist, such as different family environments, schools, child-care centers, and preschool programs, are compared. These studies differ from correlational research only in that groups of participants are carefully chosen to ensure that their characteristics are as much alike as possible. In this way, investigators rule out alternative explanations for their treatment effects as best they can. But despite these efforts, natural experiments are unable to achieve the precision and rigor of true experimental research.

To help you compare the correlational and experimental designs we have discussed, Table 1.7 summarizes their strengths and limitations. It also includes an overview of designs for studying development, to which we now turn.

DESIGNS FOR STUDYING DEVELOPMENT

Scientists interested in child development require information about the way research participants change over time. To answer questions about development, they must extend correlational and experimental approaches to include measurements at different ages. Longitudinal and cross-sectional designs are special *developmental* research strategies. In each, age comparisons form the basis of the research plan.

■ **THE LONGITUDINAL DESIGN.** In a **longitudinal design,** participants are studied repeatedly at different ages, and changes are noted as the participants mature. The time spanned may be relatively short (a few months to several years) or very long (a decade or even a lifetime).

The longitudinal approach has two major strengths. First, since it tracks the performance of each person over time, researchers can identify common patterns of development as well as individual differences in the paths children follow to maturity. Second, longitudinal studies permit investigators to examine relationships between early and later events and behaviors. Let's take an example to illustrate these ideas.

A group of researchers wondered whether children who display extreme personality styles—either angry and explosive or shy and withdrawn—retain the same dispositions when they become adults. In addition, they wanted to know what kinds of experiences promote stability or change in personality and what consequences explosiveness and shyness have for long-term adjustment. To answer these questions, the researchers delved into the archives of the Guidance Study, a well-known longitudinal investigation initiated in 1928 at the University of California, Berkeley, and continued over several decades (Caspi, Elder, & Bem, 1987, 1988).

Results revealed that the two personality styles were only moderately stable. Between ages 8 and 30, a good number of individuals remained the same, whereas others changed substantially. When stability did occur, it appeared to be due to a "snowballing effect," in which children evoked responses from adults and peers that acted to maintain their dispositions (Caspi, 1998). In other words, explosive youngsters were likely to be treated with anger and hostility (to which they reacted with even greater unruliness), whereas shy children were apt to be ignored.

Persistence of extreme personality styles affected many areas of adult adjustment, but these outcomes were different for males and females. For men, the results of early explosiveness were most apparent in their work lives, in the form of conflicts with supervisors, frequent job changes, and unemployment. Since few women in this sample of an earlier generation worked after marriage, their family lives were most affected. Explosive girls grew up

longitudinal design
A research design in which participants are studied repeatedly at different ages.

TABLE 1.7

Strengths and Limitations of Research Designs

DESIGN	DESCRIPTION	STRENGTHS	LIMITATIONS
General			
Correlational	The investigator obtains information on already existing groups, without altering participants' experiences.	Permits study of relationships between variables.	Does not permit inferences about cause-and-effect relationships.
Experimental	The investigator manipulates an independent variable and looks at its effect on a dependent variable; can be conducted in the laboratory or in the natural environment.	Permits inferences about cause-and-effect relationships.	When conducted in the laboratory, findings may not apply to the real world. When conducted in the field, control is usually weaker, and results may be due to variables other than the treatment.
Developmental			
Longitudinal	The investigator studies the same group of participants repeatedly at different ages.	Permits study of common patterns and individual differences in development and relationships between early and later events and behaviors.	Age-related changes may be distorted because of dropout and test-wiseness of participants and cohort effects.
Cross-sectional	The investigator studies groups of participants differing in age at the same point in time.	More efficient than the longitudinal design.	Does not permit study of individual developmental trends. Age differences may be distorted because of cohort effects.
Longitudinal-sequential	The investigator selects two or more groups of participants born in different years and studies them repeatedly at different ages.	Permits both longitudinal and cross-sectional comparisons; reveals existence of cohort effects.	May have the same problems as longitudinal and cross-sectional strategies, but the design helps identify cohort effects.
Microgenetic	The investigator presents children with a novel task and follows their mastery over a series of closely spaced sessions.	Offers unique insights into the process of development.	Requires intensive study of participants' moment-by-moment behaviors; the time required for participants to change is difficult to anticipate; practice effects may distort developmental trends.

to be hotheaded wives and parents who were especially prone to divorce. Sex differences in the long-term consequences of shyness were even greater. Men who had been withdrawn in childhood were delayed in marrying, becoming fathers, and developing stable careers. Because a withdrawn, unassertive style was socially acceptable for females, women who had shy personalities showed no special adjustment problems.

■ **PROBLEMS IN CONDUCTING LONGITUDINAL RESEARCH.** Despite their many strengths, longitudinal investigations pose a number of problems. Participants may move away or drop out of the research for other reasons. This often leads to *biased samples* that no longer represent the populations to whom researchers want to generalize their findings. Also, from repeated study, people may become "test-wise." Their performance may improve as a result of *practice effects*—better test-taking skills—not because of factors associated with development.

The most widely discussed threat to the accuracy of longitudinal findings is cultural-historical change, or what are commonly called **cohort effects.** Longitudinal studies examine the development of *cohorts*—children born in the same time period who are influenced by a particular set of cultural and historical conditions. Results based on one cohort may not apply to children growing up at other times. For example, children's intelligence test performance has risen since the middle of the twentieth century and is still rising (Flynn, 1996, 1999). Gains in nutrition, the stimulating quality of schooling and daily life, and parents' attitudes toward fostering children's mental development may be involved. And in the study of personality styles described in the preceding section, we might ask whether the sex differences obtained are still true, in view of recent changes in gender roles in our society.

■ **THE CROSS-SECTIONAL DESIGN.** The length of time it takes for many behaviors to change, even in limited longitudinal studies, has led researchers to turn to a more convenient strategy for studying development. In the **cross-sectional design,** groups of people differing in age are studied at the same point in time.

An investigation in which children in grades 3, 6, 9, and 12 filled out a questionnaire asking about their sibling relationships offers a good illustration (Buhrmester & Furman, 1990). Findings revealed that sibling interaction was characterized by greater equality and less power assertion with age. Also, feelings of sibling companionship declined during adolescence. The researchers thought that several factors contributed to these age differences. As later-born children become more competent and independent, they no longer need and are probably less willing to accept direction from older siblings. In addition, as adolescents move from psychological dependence on the family to greater involvement with peers, they may have less time and emotional need to invest in their siblings These intriguing ideas about the impact of development on sibling relationships, as we will see in Chapter 16, have been confirmed in subsequent research.

■ **PROBLEMS IN CONDUCTING CROSS-SECTIONAL RESEARCH.** The cross-sectional design is a very efficient strategy for describing age-related trends. But evidence about change at the level at which it actually occurs—the individual—is not available (Kraemer et al., 2000). For example, in the cross-sectional study of sibling relationships just discussed, comparisons are limited to age-group averages. We cannot tell if important individual differences exist. Indeed, longitudinal findings reveal that children vary considerably in the changing quality of their sibling relationships, many becoming more distant but some becoming increasingly supportive and intimate in adolescence (Dunn, Slomkowski, & Beardsall, 1994).

Cross-sectional studies, especially those that cover a wide age span, have another problem. Like longitudinal research, they can be threatened by cohort effects. For example, comparisons of 5-year-old cohorts and 15-year-old cohorts—groups of children born and reared in different years—may not really reveal age-related changes. Instead, they may reflect unique experiences associated with the different time periods in which the age groups were growing up.

■ **IMPROVING DEVELOPMENTAL DESIGNS.** Researchers have devised ways of building on the strengths and minimizing the weaknesses of longitudinal and cross-sectional approaches. Several modified developmental designs have resulted.

Combining Longitudinal and Cross-sectional Designs. Researchers merge longitudinal and cross-sectional strategies in the **longitudinal-sequential design.** It is called *sequential* because it is composed of two or more age groups of participants, each of which is followed longitudinally. For example, suppose we select three samples—sixth, seventh, and eighth graders—and track them for two years. That is, we observe each sample this year and next year, as follows: Sample 1 from grades 6 to 7, Sample 2 from grades 7 to 8, and Sample 3 from grades 8 to 9.

cohort effects
The effects of cultural-historical change on the accuracy of findings: Children born in a particular time period are influenced by a particular set of cultural and historical conditions.

cross-sectional design
A research design in which groups of people differing in age are studied at the same point in time.

longitudinal-sequential design
A research design with both longitudinal and cross-sectional components in which groups of participants born in different years are followed over time.

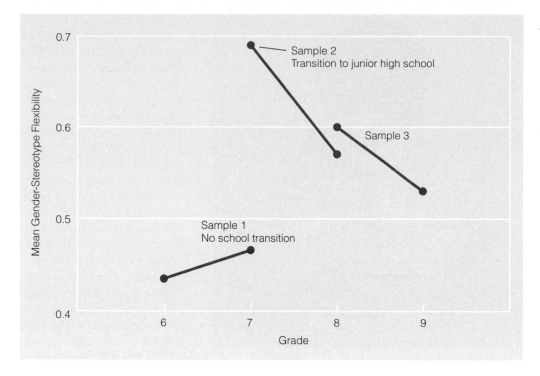

FIGURE 1.6

A longitudinal-sequential study of the development of gender-stereotyped beliefs during adolescence. Three samples were followed longitudinally from one school year to the next. To test for cohort effects, the researchers compared Sample 1 with Sample 2 at grade 7 and Sample 2 with Sample 3 at grade 8. The scores of Samples 1 and 2 did not match! The reason, the investigators discovered from additional evidence, was that a cohort effect—transition to junior high school—prompts a temporary rise in gender-stereotype flexibility. Because the scores of Samples 2 and 3 were similar at grade 8, the researchers were confident that gender-stereotype flexibility declines sharply in the years following transition to junior high school. (Adapted from Alfieri, Ruble, & Higgins, 1996.)

The design has three advantages: (1) It permits researchers to find out whether cohort effects are operating by comparing children of the same age (or grade in school) who were born in different years. Using our example, we can compare children from different samples at grades 7 and 8. If they do not differ, then we can rule out cohort effects. (2) It is possible to do both longitudinal and cross-sectional comparisons. If outcomes are similar in both, then we can be especially confident about our findings. (3) The design is efficient. In our example, we can find out about change over a 4-year period by following each cohort for just 2 years.

A study of adolescents' gender-stereotyped beliefs included the longitudinal-sequential features just described (Alfieri, Ruble, & Higgins, 1996). The researchers focused on stereotype flexibility—young people's willingness to say that "masculine" traits (such as *strong*) and "feminine" traits (such as *gentle*) characterize both males and females. As Figure 1.6 reveals, Samples 2 and 3 showed a sharp longitudinal decline in stereotype flexibility and had similar scores when measured at grade 8. But Sample 1, on reaching seventh grade, showed far less flexibility than did seventh graders in Sample 2.

The reason, the researchers discovered, was that Sample 1 had remained in the same school from sixth to seventh grade, whereas Samples 2 and 3 had moved from an elementary to a junior high school. Entry into junior high sparked a temporary rise in gender-stereotype flexibility for Samples 2 and 3, perhaps because they were exposed to a wide range of older peers, some of whom challenged stereotypes. Over time, stereotype flexibility decreases as teenagers feel pressure to conform to traditional gender roles—a topic we will take up in Chapter 16.

Examining Microcosms of Development. Notice how, in the examples of developmental research we have discussed, observations of children are fairly widely spaced. When we observe once a year or every few years, we can describe development, but we have little opportunity to capture the processes that produce change. A modification of the longitudinal approach, called the **microgenetic design,** is becoming more popular because it offers unique insights into how development takes place. In microgenetic studies, researchers present children with a novel task and follow their mastery over a series of closely spaced sessions (Kuhn, 1995; Siegler & Crowley, 1991, 1992). Within this "microcosm" of development, they see how change occurs.

microgenetic design
A research design in which researchers present children with a novel task and follow their mastery over a series of closely spaced sessions.

What strategies does this child use to solve puzzles, and how does she become proficient at puzzle-solving? Since a microgenetic design permits researchers to follow children's mastery of a challenging task, from the time change begins until it stabilizes, it is uniquely suited to answering these questions.

The microgenetic design is especially useful for studying cognitive development. For example, researchers can examine the strategies children use to acquire new knowledge in reading, mathematics, and science (Kuhn et al., 1995; Siegler, 1996). As we will see in Chapter 5, the microgenetic design has also been used to trace infants' mastery of motor skills.

Nevertheless, microgenetic studies are very difficult to carry out. Researchers must pore over hours of videotaped records, analyzing each participant's behavior many times. In addition, the time required for children to change is hard to anticipate. It depends on a careful match between the child's capabilities and the demands of the task (Siegler & Crowley, 1991). Finally, as in other longitudinal research, practice effects can distort microgenetic findings. But when researchers overcome these challenges, they reap the benefits of seeing development as it takes place.

ETHICS IN RESEARCH ON CHILDREN

Research into human behavior creates ethical issues because, unfortunately, the quest for scientific knowledge can sometimes exploit people. When children take part in research, the ethical concerns are especially complex. Children are more vulnerable than adults to physical and psychological harm. In addition, immaturity makes it difficult or impossible for children to evaluate for themselves what participation in research will mean. For these reasons, special ethical guidelines for research on children have been developed by the federal government, by funding agencies, and by research-oriented associations such as the American Psychological Association (1992) and the Society for Research in Child Development (1993).

Table 1.8 presents a summary of children's basic research rights drawn from these guidelines. Once you have examined them, read the following research situations, each of which poses a serious ethical dilemma. What precautions do you think should be taken in each instance? Is either so threatening to children's well-being that it should not be carried out?

- To study children's willingness to separate from their caregivers, an investigator decides to ask mothers of 1- and 2-year-olds to leave their youngsters alone for a brief time period in an unfamiliar playroom. The researcher knows that under these circumstances, some children become very upset.

- In a study of moral development, a researcher wants to assess children's ability to resist temptation by videotaping their behavior without their knowledge. Seven-year-olds are promised an attractive prize for solving some very difficult puzzles. They are also told not to look at a classmate's correct solutions, which are deliberately placed at the back of the room. If the researcher has to tell children ahead of time that cheating is being studied or that their behavior is being closely monitored, she will destroy the purpose of her study.

TABLE 1.8

Children's Research Rights

RESEARCH RIGHT	DESCRIPTION
Protection from harm	Children have the right to be protected from physical or psychological harm in research. If in doubt about the harmful effects of research, investigators should seek the opinion of others. When harm seems possible, investigators should find other means for obtaining the desired information or abandon the research.
Informed consent	All research participants, including children, have the right to have explained to them, in language appropriate to their level of understanding, all aspects of the research that may affect their willingness to participate. When children are participants, informed consent of parents as well as others who act on the child's behalf (such as school officials) should be obtained, preferably in writing. Children, and the adults responsible for them, have the right to discontinue participation in the research at any time.
Privacy	Children have the right to concealment of their identity on all information collected in the course of research. They also have this right with respect to written reports and any informal discussions about the research.
Knowledge of results	Children have the right to be informed of the results of research in language that is appropriate to their level of understanding.
Beneficial treatments	If experimental treatments believed to be beneficial are under investigation, children in control groups have the right to alternative beneficial treatments if they are available.

Sources: American Psychological Association, 1992; Society for Research in Child Development, 1993.

Did you find it difficult to decide on the best course of action in these examples? Virtually every committee that has worked on developing ethical principles for research has concluded that the conflicts raised by studies like these cannot be resolved with simple right-or-wrong answers. The ultimate responsibility for the ethical integrity of research lies with the investigator.

However, researchers are advised or, in the case of federally funded research, required to seek advice from others. Special committees for this purpose exist in colleges, universities, and other institutions. These committees balance the costs of the research to participants in terms of time, stress, and inconvenience against its value for advancing knowledge and improving conditions of life. If any risks to the safety and welfare of participants outweigh the worth of the research, then priority is always given to the interests of the research participants.

The ethical principle of *informed consent* requires special interpretation when research participants are children. Investigators must take into account the competence of youngsters of different ages to make choices about their own participation. Parental consent is meant to protect the safety of children whose ability to make these decisions is not yet fully mature. Besides parental consent, researchers should obtain the agreement of other individuals who act on children's behalf, such as institutional officials when research is conducted in schools, child-care centers, or hospitals. This is especially important when research includes special groups of children, such as abused youngsters, whose parents may not always represent their best interests (Fisher, 1993; Thompson, 1990b).

For children 7 years and older, their own informed consent should be obtained in addition to parental consent. Around age 7, changes in children's thinking permit them to better understand basic scientific principles and the needs of others. Researchers should respect and enhance these new capacities by providing school-age children with a full explanation of research activities in language they can understand (Fisher, 1993). Extra care must be taken when telling children that the information they provide will be kept confidential and that they can end their participation at any time. Children may not understand, and sometimes do not believe, these promises (Abramovitch et al., 1995; Ondrusek, Abramovitch, & Koren, 1998).

Finally, young children rely on a basic faith in adults to feel secure in unfamiliar situations. For this reason, some types of research may be particularly disturbing to them. All ethical guidelines advise that special precautions be taken in the use of deception and concealment, as occurs when researchers observe children from behind one-way mirrors, give them false feedback about their performance, or do not tell them the truth regarding what the research is about. When these procedures are used with adults, *debriefing,* in which the experimenter provides a full account and justification of the activities, occurs after the research session is over. Debriefing should also take place with children, but it often does not work as well. Despite explanations, children may come away from the research situation with their belief in the honesty of adults undermined. Ethical standards permit deception in research with children if investigators satisfy institutional committees that such practices are necessary. Nevertheless, since deception may have serious emotional consequences for some youngsters, many child development specialists believe that its use is always unethical and that researchers should come up with other research strategies when children are involved (Cooke, 1982).

review   *Explain how cohort effects can distort the findings of both longitudinal and cross-sectional studies.*

apply   *A researcher compares children who went to summer leadership camps with children who attended athletic camps. She finds that those who attended leadership camps are friendlier. Should the investigator tell parents that sending children to leadership camps will cause them to be more sociable? Why or why not?*

connect   *Can researchers enhance children's cognitive, emotional, and social development by fully explaining research activities and rights to them, in language they can understand? Explain.*

reflect   *Suppose a researcher asks you to enroll your baby in a 10-year longitudinal study. What factors would lead you to agree and stay involved? Do your answers shed light on why longitudinal studies often have biased samples? Explain.*

Summary

THE FIELD OF CHILD DEVELOPMENT

What is the field of child development, and what factors stimulated its expansion?

- **Child development** is the study of human constancy and change from conception through adolescence. It is part of a larger field known as developmental psychology, or human development, which includes the entire lifespan. Research on child development has been stimulated by both scientific curiosity and social pressures to better the lives of children. Knowledge of child development is interdisciplinary; it has grown through the combined efforts of people from many fields.

How can we divide child development into sensible, manageable periods and domains?

- Usually, researchers segment child development into five periods, which serve as important transitions in major theories: (1) the prenatal period; (2) infancy and toddlerhood; (3) early childhood; (4) middle childhood; and (5) adolescence.

- Development is often further divided into three domains: (1) physical development, (2) cognitive development, and (3) emotional and social development. These domains are not really distinct; they combine in an integrated, holistic fashion.

BASIC ISSUES

Identify three basic issues on which child development theories take a stand.

- Child development **theories** can be organized according to the stand they take on three controversial issues: (1) Is development a **continuous** process, or does it follow a series of **discontinuous stages**? (2) Does one general course of development characterize all children, or do many possible courses exist, depending on the **contexts** in which children grow up? (3) Is development primarily determined by **nature** or **nurture**?

HISTORICAL FOUNDATIONS

Describe major historical influences on modern theories of child development.

- Modern theories of child development have roots extending far back into the past. In medieval times, children were thought of as miniature adults, a view called **preformationism.** By the sixteenth and seventeenth centuries, childhood was viewed as a distinct phase of the life cycle. However, the Puritan conception of original sin led to a harsh philosophy of child rearing.

- The Enlightenment brought new ideas favoring more humane treatment of children. Locke's notion of the **tabula rasa** provided the basis for twentieth-century behaviorism, and Rousseau's idea of the **noble savage** foreshadowed the concepts of stage and **maturation.** A century later, Darwin's theory of evolution stimulated scientific child study.

- Efforts to observe the child directly began in the late nineteenth and early twentieth centuries with the baby biographies. Soon after, Hall and Gesell introduced the **normative approach,** which produced a large body of descriptive facts about children. Binet and Simon constructed the first successful intelligence test, which initiated the mental testing movement.

MID-TWENTIETH-CENTURY THEORIES

What theories influenced child development research in the mid-twentieth century?

- In the 1930s and 1940s, child guidance professionals turned to the **psychoanalytic perspective** for help in understanding children with emotional problems. In Freud's **psychosexual theory,** children move through five stages, during which three portions of the personality—id, ego, and superego—become integrated. Erikson's **psychosocial theory** builds on Freud's theory by emphasizing the development of culturally relevant attitudes and skills and the lifespan nature of development.

- Academic psychology also influenced child study. From **behaviorism** and **social learning theory** came the principles of conditioning and modeling and practical procedures of **applied behavior analysis** with children.

- In contrast to behaviorism, Piaget's **cognitive-developmental theory** emphasizes that children actively construct knowledge as they manipulate and explore their world. According to Piaget, children move through four stages, beginning with the baby's sensorimotor action patterns and ending with the elaborate, abstract reasoning system of the adolescent. Piaget's work has stimulated a wealth of research on children's thinking and encouraged educational programs that emphasize discovery learning.

RECENT THEORETICAL PERSPECTIVES

Describe recent theoretical perspectives on child development.

- **Information processing** views the mind as a complex, symbol-manipulating system, operating much like a computer. This approach helps investigators achieve a detailed understanding of what children of different ages do when faced with tasks and problems.

- Four theories place special emphasis on contexts for development. **Ethology** stresses the evolutionary origins and adaptive value of behavior and inspired the **sensitive period** concept.

- Vygotsky's **sociocultural theory** has enhanced our understanding of cultural influences, especially in the area of cognitive development. Through cooperative dialogues with more mature members of society, children acquire culturally relevant knowledge and skills.

- In **ecological systems theory,** nested layers of the environment—**microsystem, mesosystem, exosystem,** and **macrosystem**—

are seen as major influences on children's well-being. The **chronosystem** represents the dynamic, ever-changing nature of children and their experiences.

■ Inspired by ideas in other sciences and recent perspectives in child development, a new wave of theorists has adopted a **dynamic systems perspective.** They want to account for wide variation in development.

COMPARING CHILD DEVELOPMENT THEORIES

Identify the stand taken by each major theory on the basic issues of child development.

■ Theoretical perspectives that are major forces in child development research vary in their focus on different domains of development, in their strengths and weaknesses, and in their views of the nature of development. (For a full summary, see Table 1.5 on page 32.)

STUDYING THE CHILD

Describe research methods commonly used to gather information on children.

■ **Naturalistic observations,** gathered in children's everyday environments, permit researchers to see directly the everyday behaviors they hope to explain. In contrast, **structured observations** take place in laboratories, where every participant has an equal opportunity to display the behaviors of interest.

■ Self-report methods, such as the **clinical interview,** can be flexible and open-ended. Alternatively, **structured interviews** and questionnaires permit efficient administration and scoring.

■ **Psychophysiological methods** measure the relation between physiological

processes and behavior. They help researchers uncover the biological bases of children's perceptual, cognitive, and emotional responses.

■ Investigators rely on the **clinical,** or **case study,** method to obtain in-depth understanding of a child. It involves synthesizing a wide range of information, including interviews, observations, test scores, and sometimes psychophysiological measures.

■ A growing interest in the impact of culture has prompted researchers to adapt observational and self-report methods to permit direct comparisons of cultures. To uncover the cultural meanings of children's and adults' behaviors, researchers rely on **ethnography.** It uses participant observation to capture the unique values and social processes of a culture or distinct social group.

Distinguish correlational and experimental research designs, noting the strengths and limitations of each.

■ The **correlational design** examines relationships between variables as they happen to occur, without any intervention. The **correlation coefficient** is often used to measure the association between variables. Correlational studies do not permit statements about cause and effect. However, their use is justified when it is difficult or impossible to control the variables of interest.

■ An **experimental design** permits inferences about cause and effect. Researchers randomly assign participants to treatment conditions and manipulate an **independent variable.** Then they determine what impact this manipulation has on a **dependent variable.** To achieve high degrees of control, most experiments are conducted in laboratories, but their findings may not apply to everyday life. Field and natural experiments compare treatments in natural environments.

Describe designs for studying development, noting the strengths and limitations of each.

■ The **longitudinal design** permits study of common patterns as well as individual differences in development and the relationship between early and later events and behaviors. Among problems researchers face in conducting longitudinal research are biased samples, practice effects, and **cohort effects.** The **cross-sectional design** offers an efficient approach to investigating development. However, it is limited to comparisons of age group averages. Findings of cross-sectional research also can be distorted by **cohort effects,** especially when they cover a wide age span.

■ Modified developmental designs overcome some of the limitations of longitudinal and cross-sectional research. By combining the two approaches in the **longitudinal-sequential design,** investigators can test for cohort effects. In the **microgenetic design,** researchers track change as it occurs for unique insights into processes of development.

What special ethical concerns arise in doing research on children?

■ Because of their immaturity, children are especially vulnerable to harm and often cannot evaluate the risks and benefits of research. Ethical guidelines and special committees that weight the risks and benefits of research help ensure that children's research rights are protected. Besides consent from parents and others who work on children's behalf, researchers should seek the informed consent of children 7 years and older for research participation. The use of deception in research with children is especially risky since it may undermine their basic faith in the trustworthiness of adults.

important terms and concepts

applied behavior analysis (p. 20)
behaviorism (p. 18)
child development (p. 4)
chronosystem (p. 29)
clinical interview (p. 35)
clinical, or case study, method (p. 36)
cognitive-developmental theory
  (p. 20)
cohort effects (p. 44)
contexts (p. 8)
continuous development (p. 8)
correlation coefficient (p. 40)
correlational design (p. 40)
cross-sectional design (p. 44)
dependent variable (p. 41)
discontinuous development (p. 8)

dynamic systems perspective (p. 29)
ecological systems theory (p. 26)
ethnography (p. 38)
ethology (p. 25)
exosystem (p. 29)
experimental design (p. 41)
independent variable (p. 41)
information processing (p. 23)
longitudinal design (p. 42)
longitudinal-sequential design (p. 44)
macrosystem (p. 29)
maturation (p. 13)
mesosystem (p. 28)
microgenetic design (p. 45)
microsystem (p. 28)
naturalistic observation (p. 33)

nature–nurture controversy (p. 9)
noble savage (p. 13)
normative approach (p. 14)
preformationism (p. 11)
psychoanalytic perspective (p. 16)
psychophysiological methods (p. 36)
psychosexual theory (p. 16)
psychosocial theory (p. 17)
sensitive period (p. 25)
social learning theory (p. 18)
sociocultural theory (p. 26)
stage (p. 8)
structured interview (p. 35)
structured observation (p. 33)
tabula rasa (p. 12)
theory (p. 6)

"Returning Home From Work"

Thao Phuong Vu

10 years, Vietnam

This portrayal of daily life in a Vietnamese village captures the multiplicity of factors—within the child and in the surrounding environment—that influence development. Chapter 2 will introduce you to this complex blend of genetic, family, school, neighborhood, community, and societal forces.

Biological and Environmental Foundations

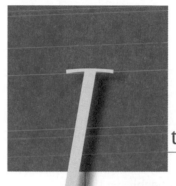

"It's a girl,"

announces the doctor, who holds up the squalling little creature while her new parents gaze with amazement at their miraculous creation. "A girl! We've named her Sarah!" exclaims the proud father to eager relatives waiting by the telephone for word about their new family member. As we join these parents in thinking about how this wondrous being came into existence and imagining her future, we are struck by many questions. How could this well-formed baby, equipped with everything necessary for life outside the womb, have developed from the union of two tiny cells? What ensures that Sarah will, in due time, roll over, reach for objects, walk, talk, make friends, imagine, and create—just like every other normal child born before her? Why is she a girl and not a boy, dark-haired rather than blond, calm and cuddly instead of wiry and energetic? What difference will it make that Sarah is given a name and place in one family, community, nation, and culture rather than another?

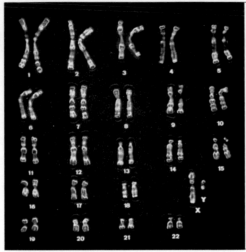
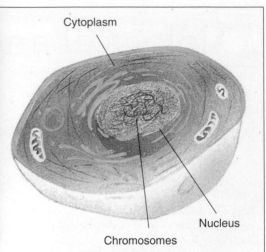

FIGURE 2.1

A karyotype, or photograph, of human chromosomes. The 46 chromosomes shown on the left were isolated from a human cell, stained, greatly magnified, and arranged in pairs according to decreasing size of the upper "arm" of each chromosome. Note the twenty-third pair, XY. The cell donor is a male. In a female, the twenty-third pair would be XX. (CNRI/Science Photo Library/Photo Researchers)

phenotype
The individual's physical and behavioral characteristics, which are determined by both genetic and environmental factors.

genotype
The genetic makeup of an individual.

chromosomes
Rodlike structures in the cell nucleus that store and transmit genetic information.

deoxyribonucleic acid (DNA)
Long, double-stranded molecules that make up chromosomes.

gene
A segment of a DNA molecule that contains hereditary instructions.

mitosis
The process of cell duplication, in which each new cell receives an exact copy of the original chromosomes.

gametes
Human sperm and ova, which contain half as many chromosomes as a regular body cell.

meiosis
The process of cell division through which gametes are formed and in which the number of chromosomes in each cell is halved.

crossing over
During meiosis, the exchange of genes between chromosomes next to each other.

To answer these questions, this chapter takes a close look at the foundations of development: heredity and environment. Because nature has prepared us for survival, all humans have many features in common. Yet a brief period of time spent in the company of any child and his or her family reveals that each human being is unique.

Take a moment to jot down the most obvious similarities in physical characteristics and behavior for several sets of children and parents you know well. Did you find that one child shows combined features of both parents, another resembles just one parent, whereas still a third is not like either parent? These directly observable characteristics are called **phenotypes.** They depend in part on the individual's **genotype**—the complex blend of genetic information that determines our species and influences all our unique characteristics. Throughout life, phenotypes are also affected by the person's experiences.

We begin our discussion of development at the moment of conception, an event that establishes the hereditary makeup of the new individual. In the first section of this chapter, we review basic genetic principles that help explain our similarities and differences in appearance and behavior. Next, we turn to aspects of the environment that play powerful roles in children's lives.

As our discussion proceeds, you will quickly see that both nature and nurture affect all aspects of development. In fact, some findings and conclusions may surprise you. For example, many people believe that when children inherit unfavorable characteristics, not much can be done to help them. Others are convinced that when environments are harmful, the damage done to children can easily be corrected. We will see that neither of these assumptions is true. In the final section of this chapter, we take up the question of how nature and nurture *work together* to shape the course of development.

Genetic Foundations

Each of us is made up of trillions of units called *cells.* Inside every cell is a control center, or *nucleus.* When cells are chemically stained and viewed through a powerful microscope, rodlike structures called **chromosomes** are visible in the nucleus. Chromosomes store and transmit genetic information. Their number varies from species to species—48 for chimpanzees, 64 for horses, 40 for mice, and 46 for human beings.

Chromosomes come in matching pairs (an exception is the XY pair in males, which we will discuss shortly). Each member of a pair corresponds to the other in size, shape, and the traits they regulate. One is inherited from the mother and one from the father. Therefore, in humans, we speak of 23 *pairs* of chromosomes residing in each human cell (see Figure 2.1).

THE GENETIC CODE

Chromosomes are made up of a chemical substance called **deoxyribonucleic acid, or DNA.** As Figure 2.2 shows, DNA is a long, double-stranded molecule that looks like a twisted ladder. Notice that each rung of the ladder consists of a specific pair of chemical substances called *bases,* joined together between the two sides. Although the bases always pair up in the same way across the ladder rungs—A with T and C with G—they can occur in any order along its sides. It is this sequence of base pairs that provides genetic instructions. A **gene** is a segment of DNA along the length of the chromosome. Genes can be of different lengths—from about 2 thousand to 2 million ladder rungs long (Genome International Sequencing Consortium, 2001). An estimated 30,000 to 35,000 genes lie along the human chromosomes.

Genes accomplish their task by sending instructions for making a rich assortment of proteins to the *cytoplasm,* the area surrounding the nucleus of the cell. Proteins, which trigger chemical reactions throughout the body, are the biological foundation on which our characteristics and capacities are built.

A unique feature of DNA is that it can duplicate itself. This special ability makes it possible for a single cell, formed at conception, to develop into a complex human being composed of a great many cells. This process of cell duplication is called **mitosis.** In mitosis, the DNA ladder splits down the middle, opening somewhat like a zipper (refer again to Figure 2.2). Then each base pairs up with a new mate from the area surrounding the nucleus of the cell. Notice how this process creates two identical DNA ladders, each containing one new side and one old side. During mitosis, each chromosome copies itself. As a result, each new body cell contains the same number of chromosomes and the identical genetic information.

THE SEX CELLS

New individuals are created when two special cells called **gametes,** or sex cells—the sperm and ovum—combine. A gamete contains only 23 chromosomes, half as many as a regular body cell. Gametes are formed through a cell division process called **meiosis,** which halves the number of chromosomes normally present in body cells.

Meiosis takes place according to the steps in Figure 2.3 on page 56. First, chromosomes pair up within a cell, and each one copies itself. Then a special event called **crossing over** takes place. In crossing over, chromosomes next to each other break at one or more points along their length and exchange segments, so that genes from one are replaced by genes from another. This shuffling of genes in crossing over creates new hereditary combinations. Next, the paired chromosomes separate into different cells, but chance determines which member of each pair will gather with others and eventually end up in the same gamete. Finally, in the last phase of meiosis, each chromosome leaves its partner and becomes part of a gamete containing 23 chromosomes instead of the usual 46.

In the male, four sperm are produced when meiosis is complete. Also, the cells from which sperm arise are produced continuously throughout life. For this reason, a healthy man can father a child at any age after sexual maturity. In the female, gamete production results in just one ovum. In addition, the female is born with all her ova already present in her ovaries, and she can bear children for only three to four decades. Most women stop ovulating between the ages of 45 and 53. Still, there are plenty of ova. About 1 to 2 million are present at birth, 40,000 remain at

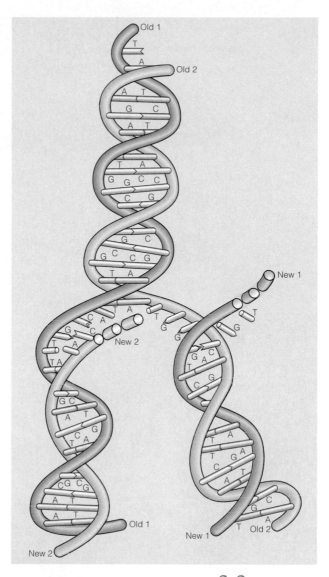

FIGURE 2.2

DNA's ladderlike structure. This figure shows that the pairings of bases across the rungs of the ladder are very specific: adenine (A) always appears with thymine (T), and cytosine (C) always appears with guanine (G). Here, the DNA ladder duplicates by splitting down the middle of its ladder rungs. Each free base picks up a new complementary partner from the area surrounding the cell nucleus.

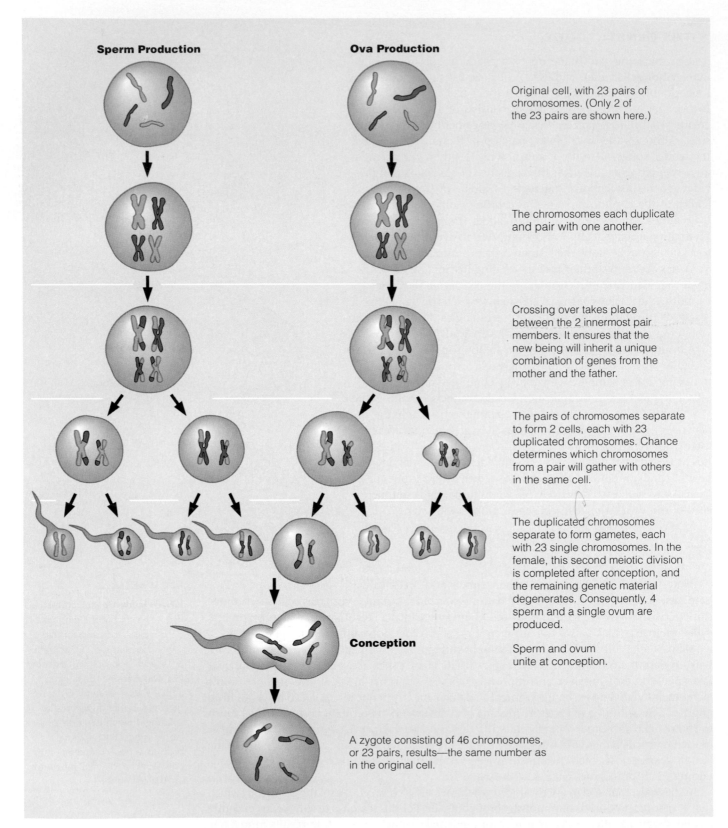

Sperm Production

Ova Production

Original cell, with 23 pairs of chromosomes. (Only 2 of the 23 pairs are shown here.)

The chromosomes each duplicate and pair with one another.

Crossing over takes place between the 2 innermost pair members. It ensures that the new being will inherit a unique combination of genes from the mother and the father.

The pairs of chromosomes separate to form 2 cells, each with 23 duplicated chromosomes. Chance determines which chromosomes from a pair will gather with others in the same cell.

The duplicated chromosomes separate to form gametes, each with 23 single chromosomes. In the female, this second meiotic division is completed after conception, and the remaining genetic material degenerates. Consequently, 4 sperm and a single ovum are produced.

Conception

Sperm and ovum unite at conception.

A zygote consisting of 46 chromosomes, or 23 pairs, results—the same number as in the original cell.

FIGURE 2.3

The cell division process of meiosis, leading to gamete formation. (Here, original cells are depicted with 2 rather than the full complement of 23 pairs.) Meiosis creates gametes with only half the usual number of chromosomes. When sperm and ovum unite at conception, the first cell of the new individual (the zygote) has the correct, full number of chromosomes.

adolescence, and approximately 350 to 450 will mature during a woman's child-bearing years (Moore & Persaud, 1998).

Look again at the steps of meiosis displayed in Figure 2.3, and notice how they ensure that a constant quantity of genetic material (46 chromosomes in each cell) is transmitted from one generation to the next. When sperm and ovum unite at conception, the cell that results, called a **zygote,** will again have 46 chromosomes.

Can you also see how meiosis leads to variability among offspring? Crossing over and random sorting of each member of a chromosome pair into separate gametes mean that the chances of offspring of the same two parents being genetically the same is extremely slim—about 1 in 700 trillion (Gould & Keeton, 1997). Therefore, meiosis helps us understand why siblings differ from each other, even though they also have features in common, since their genotypes come from a common pool of parental genes. The genetic variability produced by meiosis is important in an evolutionary sense. It increases the chances that at least some members of a species will be able to cope with ever-changing environments and survive.

REG PARKER/FPG INTERNATIONAL

These identical, or monozygotic, twins were created when a duplicating zygote separated into two clusters of cells, and two individuals with the same genetic makeup developed. Identical twins look alike, and as we will see later in this chapter, tend to resemble each other in a variety of psychological characteristics.

BOY OR GIRL?

Using special microscopic techniques, we can distinguish the 23 pairs of chromosomes in each human cell from one another. Twenty-two of them are matching pairs, called **autosomes.** They are numbered by geneticists from longest (1) to shortest (22) (refer back to Figure 2.1 on page 54). The twenty-third pair consists of **sex chromosomes.** In females, this pair is called XX; in males, it is called XY. The X is a relatively large chromosome, whereas the Y is short and carries less genetic material. When gametes form in males, the X and Y chromosomes separate into different sperm cells. In females, all gametes carry an X chromosome. The sex of the new organism is determined by whether an X-bearing or a Y-bearing sperm fertilizes the ovum. In fact, scientists have isolated a single gene on the Y chromosome that triggers male sexual development by switching on the production of male sex hormones. When that gene is absent, the fetus that develops is female (Goodfellow & Lovell, 1993).

MULTIPLE BIRTHS

Ruth and Peter, a couple I know well, tried for several years to have a child, without success. When Ruth reached age 33, her doctor prescribed a fertility drug, and twins—Jeannie and Jason—were born. Jeannie and Jason are **fraternal,** or **dizygotic, twins,** the most common type of multiple birth. The drug that Ruth took caused two ova to be released from her ovaries, and both were fertilized. Therefore, Jeannie and Jason are genetically no more alike than ordinary siblings. Older maternal age (up to 35 to 39 years) and fertility drugs are major causes of multiple births—factors responsible for the dramatic rise in twinning since the 1970s (Bortolus et al., 1999). As Table 2.1 on page 58 shows, other genetic and environmental factors are also involved.

Twins can be created in another way. Sometimes a zygote that has started to duplicate separates into two clusters of cells that develop into two individuals. These are called **identical,** or **monozygotic, twins** because they have the same genetic makeup. The frequency of identical twins is unrelated to the factors listed in Table 2.1. It is the same around the world—about 3 of every 1,000 births (Tong, Caddy, & Short, 1997). Animal research has uncovered a variety of environmental influences that prompt this type of twinning, including temperature changes, variation in oxygen levels, and late fertilization of the ovum.

During their early years, children of single births often are healthier and develop more rapidly than twins (Mogford-Bevan, 1999). Jeannie and Jason were born early (as are most twins)—3 weeks before Ruth's due date (Powers & Wampler, 1996). As we will see in Chapter 4, like other premature infants, they required special care after birth. When the twins came home from the hospital, Ruth and Peter had to divide time between them. Perhaps because neither baby got quite as much attention as the average single infant, Jeannie and

zygote
The newly fertilized cell formed by the union of sperm and ovum at conception.

autosomes
The 22 matching chromosome pairs in each human cell.

sex chromosomes
The twenty-third pair of chromosomes, which determines the sex of the child—in females, called XX; in males, called XY.

fraternal, or **dizygotic, twins**
Twins resulting from the release and fertilization of two ova. They are genetically no more alike than ordinary siblings.

identical, or **monozygotic, twins**
Twins that result when a zygote, during the early stages of cell duplication, divides in two. They have the same genetic makeup.

TABLE 2.1

Maternal Factors Linked to Fraternal Twinning

FACTOR	DESCRIPTION
Ethnicity	Occurs in 4 per 1,000 births among Asians, 8 per 1,000 births among whites, 12 to 16 per 1,000 births among blacks[a]
Family history of twinning	Occurs more often among women whose mothers and sisters gave birth to fraternal twins
Age	Rises with maternal age, peaking between 35 and 39 years, and then rapidly falls
Nutrition	Occurs less often among women with poor diets; occurs more often among women who are tall and overweight or of normal weight as opposed to slight body build
Number of births	Is more likely with each additional birth
Fertility drugs and in vitro fertilization	Is more likely with fertility hormones and in vitro fertilization (see page 68), which also increase the chances of triplets to quintuplets

[a]Worldwide rates, not including multiple births resulting from use of fertility drugs.
Source: Bortolus et al., 1999; Mange & Mange, 1998.

Jason walked and talked several months later than other children their age, although both caught up in development by middle childhood.

PATTERNS OF GENETIC INHERITANCE

Jeannie has her parents' dark, straight hair, whereas Jason is curly-haired and blond. Patterns of genetic inheritance—the way genes from each parent interact—explain these outcomes. Recall that except for the XY pair in males, all chromosomes come in corresponding pairs. Two forms of each gene occur at the same place on the autosomes, one inherited from the mother and one from the father. Each form of a gene is called an **allele.** If the alleles from both parents are alike, the child is **homozygous** and will display the inherited trait. If the alleles are different, the child is **heterozygous,** and relationships between alleles determine the trait that will appear.

■ **DOMINANT–RECESSIVE RELATIONSHIPS.** In many heterozygous pairings, only one allele affects the child's characteristics. It is called *dominant;* the second allele, which has no effect, is called *recessive.* Hair color is an example of **dominant–recessive inheritance.** The allele for dark hair is dominant (we can represent it with a capital *D*), whereas the one for blond hair is recessive (symbolized by a lowercase *b*). Children who inherit either a homozygous pair of dominant alleles (*DD*) or a heterozygous pair (*Db*) will be dark-haired, even though their genetic makeup differs. Blond hair (like Jason's) can result only from having two recessive alleles (*bb*). Still, heterozygous individuals with just one recessive allele (*Db*) can pass that trait to their children. Therefore, they are called **carriers** of the trait.

In dominant–recessive inheritance, if we know the genetic makeup of the parents, we can predict the percentage of children in a family who are likely to display a trait or be carriers of it. Figure 2.4 shows the pattern of inheritance for hair color. Note that for Jason to be blond, both Peter and Ruth must carry a recessive allele (*b*). The figure also indicates that if Peter and Ruth decide to have more children, most are likely to be dark-haired, like Jeannie.

Some human characteristics and disorders that follow the rules of dominant–recessive inheritance are given in Table 2.2 on the following page and Table 2.3 on pages 60–61. As you can see, many disabilities and diseases are the product of

FIGURE 2.4

Dominant–recessive model of inheritance as illustrated by hair color. By looking at the possible combinations of the parents' genes, we can predict that 25 percent of their children are likely to inherit two dominant genes for dark hair; 50 percent are likely to receive one dominant and one recessive gene, resulting in dark hair; and 25 percent are likely to receive two recessive genes for blond hair.

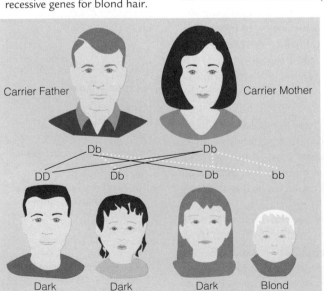

recessive alleles. One of the most frequently occurring recessive disorders is *phenylketonuria,* or *PKU.* It affects the way the body breaks down proteins contained in many foods, such as cow's milk, bread, eggs, and fish. Infants born with two recessive alleles lack an enzyme that converts one of the basic amino acids that make up proteins (phenylalanine) into a by-product essential for body functioning (tyrosine). Without this enzyme, phenylalanine quickly builds to toxic levels that damage the central nervous system. Recent evidence suggests that phenylalanine disrupts the chemical transmission of neural messages and inhibits the formation of *myelin,* the fatty sheath coating neural fibers that improves message transfer (Dyer, 1999). Around 3 to 5 months of age, infants with untreated PKU start to lose interest in their surroundings. By 1 year, they are permanently retarded.

Despite its potentially damaging effects, PKU provides an excellent illustration of the fact that inheriting unfavorable genes does not always lead to an untreatable condition. All U.S. states and Canadian provinces require that each newborn be given a blood test for PKU. If the disease is found, treatment involves placing the baby on a diet low in phenylalanine. Children who receive this treatment show delayed development of higher-order cognitive skills, such as planning and problem solving, in infancy and early childhood because even small amounts of phenylalanine interfere with brain functioning (Diamond et al., 1997; Pietz et al., 1998). But as long as dietary treatment begins early and continues, children with PKU usually attain an average level of intelligence and have a normal lifespan (Eisenberg, 1999).

PKU also illustrates that single genes often affect more than one trait. Due to their inability to convert phenylalanine into tyrosine (which is responsible for pigmentation), children with PKU usually have light hair and blue eyes. Furthermore, children vary in the degree to which phenylalanine accumulates in their tissues and in the extent to which they respond to treatment. This is due to the action of **modifier genes,** which enhance or dilute the effects of other genes.

As Table 2.3 suggests, only rarely are serious diseases due to dominant alleles. Think about why this is so. Children who inherited the dominant allele would always develop the disorder. They would seldom live long enough to reproduce, and the harmful dominant allele would be eliminated from the family's heredity in a single generation. Some dominant disorders, however, do persist. One of them is *Huntington disease,* a condition in which the central nervous system degenerates. Why has this disorder endured in some families? Its symptoms usually do not appear until age 35 or later, after the person has passed the dominant gene to his or her children.

■ **CODOMINANCE.** In some heterozygous circumstances, the dominant–recessive relationship does not hold completely. Instead, we see **codominance,** a pattern of inheritance in which both alleles influence the person's characteristics.

The *sickle cell trait,* a heterozygous condition present in many black Africans, provides an example. *Sickle cell anemia* (see Table 2.3) occurs in full form when a child inherits two recessive alleles. They cause the usually round red blood cells to become sickle (or crescent-moon) shaped, a response that is especially great under low oxygen conditions—for example, at high altitudes or after intense physical exertion. The sickled cells clog the blood vessels and block the flow of blood, causing intense pain, swelling, and tissue damage. About 50 percent of affected people survive to age 40, only 1 percent to age 60 (Ashley-Koch, Yang, & Olney, 2000). Heterozygous individuals are protected from the disease under most circumstances. However,

TABLE 2.2

Examples of Dominant and Recessive Characteristics

DOMINANT	RECESSIVE
Dark hair	Blond hair
Normal hair	Pattern baldness
Curly hair	Straight hair
Nonred hair	Red hair
Facial dimples	No dimples
Normal hearing	Some forms of deafness
Normal vision	Nearsightedness
Farsightedness	Normal vision
Normal vision	Congenital eye cataracts
Normally pigmented skin	Albinism
Double-jointedness	Normal joints
Type A blood	Type O blood
Type B blood	Type O blood
Rh-positive blood	Rh-negative blood

Note: Many normal characteristics that were previously thought to result from dominant–recessive inheritance, such as eye color, are now regarded as due to multiple genes. For the characteristics listed here, most experts agree that the simple dominant–recessive relationship holds.
Source: McKusick, 1998.

allele
Each of two forms of a gene located at the same place on the autosomes.

homozygous
Having two identical alleles at the same place on a pair of chromosomes.

heterozygous
Having two different alleles at the same place on a pair of chromosomes.

dominant–recessive inheritance
A pattern of inheritance in which, under heterozygous conditions, the influence of only one allele is apparent.

carrier
A heterozygous individual who can pass a recessive trait to his or her children.

modifier genes
Genes that can enhance or dilute the effects of other genes.

codominance
A pattern of inheritance in which both alleles in a heterozygous combination are expressed.

TABLE 2.3

Examples of Dominant and Recessive Diseases

DISEASE	DESCRIPTION	MODE OF INHERITANCE	INCIDENCE	TREATMENT	PRENATAL DIAGNOSIS	CARRIER IDENTIFICATION[a]
Autosomal Diseases						
Cooley's anemia	Pale appearance, retarded physical growth, and lethargic behavior begin in infancy.	Recessive	1 in 500 births to parents of Mediterranean descent	Frequent blood transfusions. Death from complications usually occurs by adolescence.	Yes	Yes
Cystic fibrosis	Lungs, liver, and pancreas secrete large amounts of thick mucus, leading to breathing and digestive difficulties.	Recessive	1 in 2,000 to 2,500 Caucasian births; 1 in 16,000 African-American births	Bronchial drainage, prompt treatment of respiratory infections, dietary management. Advances in medical care allow survival with good life quality into adulthood.	Yes	Yes
Phenylketonuria (PKU)	Inability to neutralize the harmful amino acid phenylalanine, contained in many proteins, causes severe central nervous system damage in the first year of life.	Recessive	1 in 8,000 births	Placing the child on a special diet results in average intelligence and normal lifespan. Subtle difficulties with planning and problem solving are often present.	Yes	Yes
Sickle cell anemia	Abnormal sickling of red blood cells causes oxygen deprivation, pain, swelling, and tissue damage. Anemia and susceptibility to infections, especially pneumonia, occur.	Recessive	1 in 500 African-American births	Blood transfusions, painkillers, prompt treatment of infections. There is no known cure; 50 percent die by age 40.	Yes	Yes
Tay-Sachs disease	Central nervous system degeneration, with onset at about 6 months, leads to poor muscle tone, blindness, deafness, and convulsions.	Recessive	1 in 3,600 births to Jews of European descent	None. Death occurs by 3 to 4 years of age.	Yes	Yes

when they experience oxygen deprivation, the single recessive allele asserts itself, and a temporary, mild form of the illness occurs.

The sickle cell allele is common among black Africans for a special reason. Carriers of it are more resistant to malaria than are individuals with two alleles for normal red blood cells. In Africa, where malaria is common, these carriers have survived and reproduced more frequently than others, leading the gene to be maintained in the black population. In regions of the world where the risk of malaria is low, the frequency of the gene is declining—for exam-

TABLE 2.3 CONTINUED

DISEASE	DESCRIPTION	MODE OF INHERITANCE	INCIDENCE	TREATMENT	PRENATAL DIAGNOSIS	CARRIER IDENTIFICATION[a]
Huntington disease	Central nervous system degeneration leads to muscular coordination difficulties, mental deterioration, and personality changes. Symptoms usually do not appear until age 35 or later.	Dominant	1 in 18,000 to 25,000 American births	None. Death occurs 10 to 20 years after symptom onset.	Yes	Not applicable
Marfan syndrome	Disease results in tall, slender build; thin, elongated arms and legs; heart defects; and eye abnormalities, especially of the lens. Excessive lengthening of the body results in a variety of skeletal defects.	Dominant	1 in 20,000 births	Correction of heart and eye defects is sometimes possible. Death from heart failure in young adulthood is common.	Yes	Not applicable

X-Linked Diseases

DISEASE	DESCRIPTION	MODE OF INHERITANCE	INCIDENCE	TREATMENT	PRENATAL DIAGNOSIS	CARRIER IDENTIFICATION[a]
Duchenne muscular dystrophy	This degenerative muscle disease causes abnormal gait, loss of ability to walk between 7 and 13 years of age.	Recessive	1 in 3,000 to 5,000 male births	None. Death from respiratory infection or weakening of the heart muscle usually occurs in adolescence.	Yes	Yes
Hemophilia	Blood fails to clot normally. Can lead to severe internal bleeding and tissue damage.	Recessive	1 in 4,000 to 7,000 male births	Blood transfusions; safety precautions to prevent injury.	Yes	Yes
Diabetes insipidus	This form of diabetes present at birth is caused by insufficient production of the hormone vasopressin. Results in excessive thirst and urination. Dehydration can cause central nervous system damage.	Recessive	1 in 2,500 male births	Hormone replacement.	Yes	Yes

[a]Carrier status detectable in prospective parents through blood test or genetic analyses.

Sources: Behrman, Kliegman, & Arvin, 1996; Gott, 1998; Grody, 1999; Knoers et al., 1993; McKusick, 1998; Schulman & Black, 1997.

ple, only 8 percent of African Americans carry it, compared to 20 percent of black Africans (Mange & Mange, 1998).

■ X-LINKED INHERITANCE. Males and females have an equal chance of inheriting recessive disorders carried on the autosomes, such as PKU and sickle cell anemia. But when a harmful allele is carried on the X chromosome, **X-linked inheritance** applies. Males are more likely to be affected because their sex chromosomes do not match. In females, any recessive

X-linked inheritance
A pattern of inheritance in which a recessive gene is carried on the X chromosome. Males are more likely to be affected.

in girls   disease carried on 1 X Chromosome is masked by other X chromosome

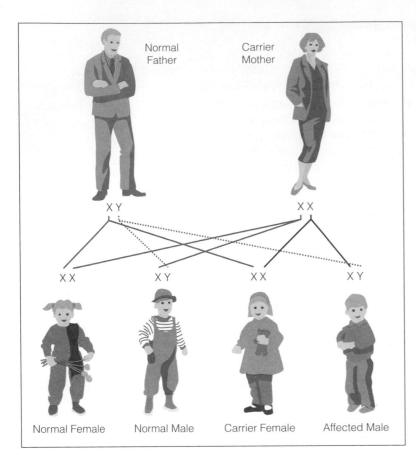

FIGURE 2.5

X-linked inheritance. In the example shown here, the allele on the father's X chromosome is normal. The mother has one normal and one abnormal recessive allele on her X chromosomes. By looking at the possible combinations of the parents' alleles, we can predict that 50 percent of male children will have the disorder and 50 percent of female children will be carriers of it.

genetic imprinting
A pattern of inheritance in which alleles are imprinted, or chemically marked, in such a way that one pair member is activated, regardless of its makeup.

mutation
A sudden but permanent change in a segment of DNA.

polygenic inheritance
A pattern of inheritance in which many genes determine a characteristic.

allele on one X chromosome has a good chance of being suppressed by a dominant allele on the other X. But the Y chromosome is only about one-third as long and therefore lacks many corresponding alleles to override those on the X.

Red–green color blindness (a condition in which individuals cannot tell the difference between shades of red and green) is one example of an X-linked recessive trait. It affects males twice as often as it does females (Mange & Mange, 1998). In one 3-year-old boy I know, the problem was discovered when he had difficulty learning the names of colors at preschool. The boy's maternal grandfather was also color blind. Although his mother was unaffected, she was a carrier who had passed an X chromosome with the recessive allele to her son. Refer again to Table 2.3 and review the diseases that are X-linked. A well-known example is hemophilia, a disorder in which the blood fails to clot normally. Figure 2.5 shows its greater likelihood of inheritance by male children whose mothers carry the abnormal allele.

Besides X-linked disorders, many sex differences reveal the male to be at a disadvantage. Rates of miscarriage, infant and childhood deaths, and birth defects are greater for males. Learning disabilities, behavior disorders, and mental retardation are also more common among boys (Halpern, 1997). It is possible that these sex differences can be traced to the genetic code. The female, with two X chromosomes, benefits from a greater variety of genes. Nature, however, seems to have adjusted for the male's disadvantage. Worldwide, about 106 boys are born for every 100 girls, and judging from miscarriage and abortion statistics, a still greater number of boys appear to be conceived (Pyeritz, 1998).

Nevertheless, in recent decades the proportion of male births has declined in many industrialized countries, including Canada, Denmark, Germany, Finland, the Netherlands, Norway, and the United States (Davis, Gottlieb, & Stampnitzky, 1998). Some researchers blame increased occupational and community exposure to pesticides for a reduction in sperm counts overall, especially Y-bearing sperm. In addition, many surviving Y-bearing sperm are damaged, heightening the rates of miscarriage, infant deaths, and birth defects among males.

■ **GENETIC IMPRINTING.** More than 1,000 human characteristics follow the rules of dominant–recessive and codominant inheritance (McKusick, 1998). In these cases, regardless of which parent contributes a gene to the new individual, the gene responds in the same way. Geneticists, however, have identified some exceptions governed by a newly discovered mode of inheritance. In **genetic imprinting**, alleles are *imprinted*, or chemically *marked*, in such a way that one pair member (either the mother's or the father's) is activated, regardless of its makeup. The imprint is often temporary: it may be erased in the next generation, and it may not occur in all individuals (Everman & Cassidy, 2000).

Imprinting helps us understand the confusion in genetic inheritance for some disorders. For example, children are more likely to develop diabetes if their father, rather than their mother, suffers from it. And people with asthma or hay fever tend to have mothers, not fathers, with the illness. Scientists do not yet know what causes this parent-specific genetic transmission. At times, it reveals itself in heartbreaking ways. Imprinting is involved in several childhood cancers and in *Prader-Willi syndrome*, a disorder with symptoms of mental retardation and severe obesity (Couper & Couper, 2000). It may also explain why Huntington disease, when inherited from the father, tends to emerge at an earlier age and progress more rapidly (Navarrete, Martinez, & Salamanca, 1994).

In these examples, genetic imprinting affects traits carried on the autosomes. It can also operate on the sex chromosomes, as *fragile X syndrome* reveals. In this disorder, an abnormal repetition of a sequence of DNA bases occurs in a special spot on the X chromosome, damaging a particular gene. Fragile X syndrome is the most common inherited cause of mild to moderate mental retardation. It has also been linked to 2 to 3 percent of cases of infantile autism, a serious emotional disorder of early childhood involving bizarre, self-stimulating behavior and delayed or absent language and communication (Mazzocco, 2000). Research reveals that the defective gene at the fragile site is expressed only when it is passed from mother to child (Ashley-Koch et al., 1998).

■ **MUTATION.** How are harmful genes created in the first place? The answer is **mutation,** a sudden but permanent change in a segment of DNA. A mutation may affect only one or two genes, or it may involve many genes, as is the case for the chromosomal disorders we will discuss shortly. Some mutations occur spontaneously, simply by chance. Others are caused by a wide variety of hazardous environmental agents that enter our food supply or are present in the air we breathe.

Although nonionizing forms of radiation—electromagnetic waves and microwaves—have no demonstrated impact on DNA, ionizing (high-energy) radiation is an established cause of mutation. Women who receive repeated doses before conception are more likely to miscarry or give birth to children with hereditary defects. Genetic abnormalities, such as physical malformations and childhood cancer, are also higher when fathers are exposed to ionizing radiation in their occupations (Brent, 1999). Does this mean that routine chest and dental X-rays are dangerous to future generations? Research indicates that infrequent and mild exposure does not cause genetic damage, but high doses over a long period of time result in genetic abnormalities.

Although only 3 percent of pregnancies result in the birth of a baby with a hereditary abnormality, these children account for about 40 percent of childhood deaths and 5 to 10 percent of childhood hospital admissions (Shiloh, 1996). As these figures reveal, progress in preventing and treating genetic diseases still lags far behind that of non-genetic diseases. However, as we will see shortly, great strides are being made.

■ **POLYGENIC INHERITANCE.** So far, we have discussed patterns of inheritance in which people either display a particular trait or do not. These cut-and-dried individual differences are much easier to trace to their genetic origins than are characteristics that vary continuously among people. Many traits of interest to child development specialists, such as height, weight, intelligence, and personality, are of this second type. People are not just tall or short, bright or dull, outgoing or shy. Instead, they show gradations between these extremes. Continuous traits like these are due to **polygenic inheritance,** in which many genes determine the characteristic in question. Polygenic inheritance is complex, and much about it is still unknown. In the final section of this chapter, we will pay special attention to this form of genetic transmission by examining ways that researchers infer the influence of heredity on human attributes when knowledge of precise patterns of inheritance is unavailable.

CHROMOSOMAL ABNORMALITIES

Besides problems associated with inheriting harmful alleles, abnormalities of the chromosomes cause serious developmental problems. Most chromosomal defects result from mistakes during meiosis, when the ovum and sperm are formed. A chromosome pair does not separate properly, or part of a chromosome breaks off. Since these errors involve far more DNA than do problems caused by single genes, they usually produce disorders with many physical and mental symptoms.

■ **DOWN SYNDROME.** The most common chromosomal disorder, occurring in 1 out of every 800 live births, is *Down syndrome.* In 95 percent of cases, it results from a failure of the twenty-first pair of chromosomes to separate during meiosis, so the new individual inherits

Polygenic inheritance - lots of genes determine the trait in q.

© 2000 LAURA DWIGHT

The facial features of the 9-year-old boy on the left are typical of Down syndrome. Although his intellectual development is impaired, this child is doing well because he is growing up in a stimulating home where his special needs are met and he is loved and accepted. Here he collaborates with his normally developing 4-year-old brother in making won ton dumplings.

TABLE 2.4

Risk of Giving Birth to a Down Syndrome Child by Maternal Age

MATERNAL AGE	RISK
20	1 in 1,900 births
25	1 in 1,200
30	1 in 900
33	1 in 600
36	1 in 280
39	1 in 130
42	1 in 65
45	1 in 30
48	1 in 15

Note: The risk of giving birth to a Down syndrome baby after age 35 has increased slightly over the past 20 years, due to improved medical interventions during pregnancy and consequent greater likelihood of a Down syndrome fetus surviving to be liveborn.

Source: Adapted from Halliday et al., 1995; Meyers et al., 1997.

three of these chromosomes rather than the normal two. For this reason, Down syndrome is sometimes called *trisomy 21*. In other, less frequent forms, an extra broken piece of a twenty-first chromosome is present. Or an error occurs during the early stages of mitosis, causing some but not all body cells to have the defective chromosomal makeup (called a *mosaic* pattern). In these instances, since less genetic material is involved, symptoms of the disorder are less extreme (Hodapp, 1996; Muller et al., 2000).

The consequences of Down syndrome include mental retardation, speech problems, limited vocabulary, and slow motor development. Affected individuals also have distinct physical features—a short, stocky build, a flattened face, a protruding tongue, almond-shaped eyes, and an unusual crease running across the palm of the hand. In addition, infants with Down syndrome often are born with eye cataracts and heart and intestinal defects. Because of medical advances, fewer individuals with Down syndrome die early than was the case in the past. Many survive into their sixties and beyond (Selikowitz, 1997).

Infants with Down syndrome are more difficult to care for than are normal infants. Their facial deformities often lead to breathing and feeding difficulties. Also, they smile less readily, show poorer eye-to-eye contact, and explore objects less persistently. When parents take extra steps to encourage them to become engaged in their surroundings, Down syndrome children develop more favorably (Harris, Kasari, & Sigman, 1996). They also benefit from infant and preschool intervention programs, although emotional, social, and motor skills improve more than intellectual performance (Hines & Bennett, 1996). Thus, even though Down syndrome is a genetic disorder, environmental factors affect how well these children fare.

As Table 2.4 shows, the risk of a Down syndrome baby rises dramatically with maternal age. Why is this so? Geneticists believe that the ova, present in the woman's body since her own prenatal period, weaken over time because of the aging process or increased exposure to harmful environmental agents. As a result, chromosomes do not separate properly as they complete the process of meiosis. The mother's gamete, however, is not always the cause of a Down syndrome child. In about 5 to 10 percent of cases, the extra genetic material originates with the father. However, Down syndrome and other chromosomal abnormalities are not related to advanced paternal age (Savage et al., 1998; Stoll et al., 1998). In these instances, the mutation occurs for other unknown reasons.

■ **ABNORMALITIES OF THE SEX CHROMOSOMES.** Disorders of the autosomes other than Down syndrome usually disrupt development so severely that miscarriage occurs. When such babies are born, they rarely survive beyond early childhood. In contrast, abnormalities of the sex chromosomes usually lead to fewer problems. In fact, sex chromosome disorders often are not recognized until adolescence when, in some deviations, puberty is delayed. The most common problems involve the presence of an extra chromosome (either X or Y) or the absence of one X chromosome in females.

A variety of myths about individuals with sex chromosome disorders exist. For example, as Table 2.5 reveals, males with *XYY syndrome* are not necessarily more aggressive and antisocial than XY males. And most children with sex chromosome disorders do not suffer from mental retardation (Netley, 1986; Stewart, 1982). Instead, their intellectual problems usually are very specific. Verbal difficulties—for example, with reading and vocabulary—are common among girls with *triple X syndrome* and boys with *Klinefelter syndrome,* both of whom inherit an extra X chromosome. In contrast, girls with *Turner syndrome,* who are missing an X, have trouble with spatial relationships—for example, drawing pictures, telling right from left, following travel directions, and noticing changes in facial expressions (Money, 1993; Romans et al., 1997; Temple & Carney, 1995). These findings tell us that adding to or subtracting from the usual number of X chromosomes results in particular intellectual deficits. At present, geneticists do not know why.

TABLE 2.5

Sex Chromosomal Disorders

DISORDER	DESCRIPTION	INCIDENCE	TREATMENT
XYY syndrome	Extra Y chromosome. Above-average height, large teeth, and sometimes severe acne. Intelligence, male sexual development, and fertility are normal.	1 in 1,000 male births	No special treatment necessary.
Triple X syndrome (XXX)	Extra X chromosome. Tallness and impaired verbal intelligence. Female sexual development and fertility are normal.	1 in 500 to 1,250 female births	Special education to treat verbal ability problems.
Klinefelter syndrome (XXY)	Extra X chromosome. Tallness, body fat distribution resembling females, incomplete development of sex characteristics at puberty, sterility, and impaired verbal intelligence.	1 in 900 male births	Hormone therapy at puberty to stimulate development of sex characteristics; special education to treat verbal ability problems.
Turner syndrome (XO)	Missing X chromosome. Short stature, webbed neck, incomplete development of sex characteristics at puberty, sterility, and impaired spatial intelligence.	1 in 2,500 to 8,000 female births	Hormone therapy in childhood to stimulate physical growth and at puberty to promote development of sex characteristics; special education to treat spatial ability problems.

Sources: Money, 1993; Moore & Persaud, 1993; Netley, 1986; Pennington et al., 1982; Ratcliffe, Pan, & McKie, 1992; Rovet et al., 1996; Schiavi et al., 1984.

review   *Explain the genetic origins of PKU and Down syndrome. Cite evidence indicating that both heredity and environment contribute to the development of children with these disorders.*

apply   *Gilbert and Jan are planning to have children. Gilbert's genetic makeup is homozygous for dark hair. Jan's is homozygous for blond hair. What proportion of their children are likely to be dark-haired? Explain.*

connect   *Parents of children with genetic disorders, such as Down syndrome, often face increased stresses. Referring back to our discussion of ecological systems theory in Chapter 1 (see pages 27–29), explain why this is so. What factors, within and beyond the family, can help such parents support their child's development?*

Reproductive Choices

Two years after they married, Ted and Marianne gave birth to their first child. Kendra appeared to be a healthy and lively infant, but by 4 months her growth had slowed. Diagnosed as having Tay-Sachs disease (see Table 2.3), Kendra died at 2 years of age. Ted and Marianne were devastated by Kendra's death. Although they did not want to bear another infant who would endure such suffering, they badly wanted a child. When Ted and Marianne took walks in the neighborhood, they saw children in strollers, and tears came to their eyes. They began to avoid family get-togethers, where little nieces and nephews were constant reminders of the void in their lives.

TABLE 2.6

Prenatal Diagnostic Methods

METHOD	DESCRIPTION
Amniocentesis	The most widely used technique. A hollow needle is inserted through the abdominal wall to obtain a sample of fluid in the uterus. Cells are examined for genetic defects. Can be performed by 11 to 14 weeks after conception but is safest after 15 weeks; 1 to 2 more weeks are required for test results. Entails small risk of miscarriage.
Chorionic villus sampling	A procedure that can be used if results are desired or needed very early in pregnancy. A thin tube is inserted into the uterus through the vagina or a hollow needle is inserted through the abdominal wall. A small plug of tissue is removed from the end of one or more chorionic villi, the hairlike projections on the membrane surrounding the developing organism. Cells are examined for genetic defects. Can be performed at 6 to 8 weeks after conception, and results are available within 24 hours. Entails a slightly greater risk of miscarriage than does amniocentesis. Also associated with a small risk of limb deformities, which increases the earlier the procedure is performed.
Fetoscopy	A small tube with a light source at one end is inserted into the uterus to inspect the fetus for defects of the limbs and face. Also allows a sample of fetal blood to be obtained, permitting diagnosis of such disorders as hemophilia and sickle cell anemia, as well as neural defects (see below). Usually performed between 15 and 18 weeks after conception, although can be done as early as 5 weeks. Entails some risk of miscarriage.
Ultrasound	High-frequency sound waves are beamed at the uterus; their reflection is translated into a picture on a videoscreen that reveals the size, shape, and placement of the fetus. By itself, permits assessment of fetal age, detection of multiple pregnancies, and identification of gross physical defects. Also used to guide amniocentesis, chorionic villus sampling, and fetoscopy. When used five or more times, may increase the chances of low birth weight.
Maternal blood analysis	By the second month of pregnancy, some of the developing organism's cells enter the maternal bloodstream. An elevated level of alpha-fetoprotein may indicate kidney disease, abnormal closure of the esophagus, or neural tube defects, such as anencephaly (absence of most of the brain) and spina bifida (bulging of the spinal cord from the spinal column). Isolated cells can be examined for genetic defects, such as Down syndrome.
Preimplantation genetic diagnosis	After in vitro fertilization and duplication of the zygote into a cluster of about eight cells, one cell is removed and examined for hereditary defects. Only if that cell is free of detectable genetic disorders is the fertilized ovum implanted in the woman's uterus.

Sources: Eiben et al., 1997; Lissens & Sermon, 1997; Moore & Persaud, 1998; Newnham et al., 1993; Quintero, Puder, & Cotton, 1993; Wapner, 1997; Willner, 1998.

In the past, many couples with genetic disorders in their families chose not to have children rather than risk the birth of an abnormal baby. Today, genetic counseling and prenatal diagnosis help people make informed decisions about conceiving, carrying a pregnancy to term, or adopting a child.

GENETIC COUNSELING

Genetic counseling is a communication process designed to help couples assess their chances of giving birth to a baby with a hereditary disorder and choose the best course of action in view of risks and family goals (Shiloh, 1996). Individuals likely to seek counseling are those who have had difficulties bearing children, such as repeated miscarriages, or who know that genetic problems exist in their families. In addition, women who delay childbearing past age 35 are candidates for genetic counseling. After this time, the overall rate of chromosomal abnormalities rises sharply, from 1 in 190 to as many as 1 in 10 pregnancies at age 48 (Meyers et al., 1997).

If a family history of mental retardation, physical defects, or inherited diseases exists, the genetic counselor interviews the couple and prepares a *pedigree*, a picture of the family tree in which affected relatives are identified. The pedigree is used to estimate the likelihood that parents will have an abnormal child, using the same genetic principles we discussed earlier

genetic counseling
A communication process designed to help couples assess their chances of giving birth to a baby with a hereditary disorder and choose the best course of action in view of risks and family goals.

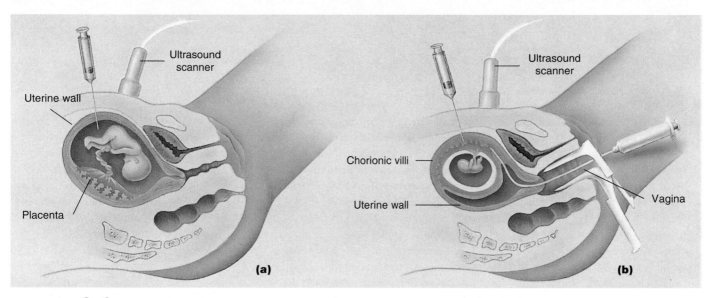

FIGURE 2.6

Amniocentesis and chorionic villi sampling. Today, more than 250 defects and diseases can be detected before birth using these two procedures. (a) In amniocentesis, a hollow needle is inserted through the abdominal wall into the uterus from 11 to 14 weeks after conception. Fluid is withdrawn and fetal cells are cultured, a process that takes about 2 weeks. (b) Chorionic villus sampling can be performed much earlier in pregnancy, at 6 to 8 weeks after conception, and results are available within 24 hours. Two approaches to obtaining a sample of chorionic villi are shown: inserting a thin tube through the vagina into the uterus and inserting a needle through the abdominal wall. In both amniocentesis and chorionic villus sampling, an ultrasound scanner is used for guidance. (From K. L. Moore & T. V. N. Persaud, 1998, *Before We Are Born,* 5th ed., Philadelphia: Saunders, p. 115. Adapted by permission of the publisher and author.)

in this chapter. In the case of many disorders, blood tests or genetic analyses can reveal whether the parent is a carrier of the harmful gene. Turn back to pages 60–61, and you will see that carrier detection is possible for nearly all the diseases listed in Table 2.3. A carrier test has been developed for fragile X syndrome as well (Ryynänen et al., 1995).

When all the relevant information is in, the genetic counselor helps people consider appropriate options. These include "taking a chance" and conceiving, choosing from among a variety of reproductive technologies (see the Social Issues: Health box on pages 68–69), or adopting a child.

PRENATAL DIAGNOSIS AND FETAL MEDICINE

If couples who might bear an abnormal child decide to conceive, several **prenatal diagnostic methods**—medical procedures that permit detection of developmental problems before birth—are available (see Table 2.6). Women of advanced maternal age are prime candidates for *amniocentesis* or *chorionic villus sampling* (see Figure 2.6). Except for *ultrasound* and *maternal blood analysis,* prenatal diagnosis should not be used routinely, since other methods have some chance of injuring the developing organism (Steele et al., 1996).

Improvements in prenatal diagnosis have led to new advances in fetal medicine. Today, some medical problems are being treated before birth. For example, by inserting a needle into the uterus, doctors can administer drugs to the fetus. Surgery has been performed to repair such problems as heart and lung malformations, urinary tract obstructions, and neural defects. Recently, a fetus with a hereditary immune deficiency received a bone marrow transplant from his father that succeeded in creating a normally functioning immune system (Flake et al., 1996).

Nevertheless, these techniques frequently result in complications, the most common being premature labor and miscarriage (James, 1998). Yet when parents are told that their unborn child has a serious defect, they may be willing to try almost any option, even if there is only a slim chance of success. How can health professionals help parents make informed

prenatal diagnostic methods Medical procedures that permit detection of developmental problems before birth.

Social ISSUES: HEALTH
THE PROS AND CONS OF REPRODUCTIVE TECHNOLOGIES

Some couples decide not to risk pregnancy because of a history of genetic disease. And many others—in fact, one-sixth of all couples who try to conceive—discover that they are sterile. Today, increasing numbers of individuals are turning to alternative methods of conception—technologies that, although fulfilling the wish of parenthood, have become the subject of heated debate.

DONOR INSEMINATION AND IN VITRO FERTILIZATION

For several decades, *donor insemination*—injection of sperm from an anonymous man into a woman—has been used to overcome male reproductive difficulties. In recent years, it has also permitted women without a heterosexual partner to bear children. In the United States alone, thirty thousand children are conceived through donor insemination each year (Nachtigall et al., 1997).

In vitro fertilization is another reproductive technology that has become increasingly common. Since the first "test tube" baby was born in England in 1978, many thousands of infants have been created this way. With in vitro fertilization, hormones are given to a woman, stimulating ripening of several ova. These are removed surgically and placed in a dish of nutrients, to which sperm are added. Once an ovum is fertilized and begins to duplicate into several cells, it is injected into the mother's uterus where, she hopes, it will implant and develop.

In vitro fertilization is successful for 20 percent of those who try it. By mixing and matching gametes, pregnancies can be brought about when either or both partners have a reproductive problem. Fertilized ova and sperm can even be frozen and stored in embryo banks for use at some future time, thereby guaranteeing healthy zygotes should age or illness lead to fertility problems (Ahaja et al., 1997).

Children conceived through these methods may be genetically unrelated to one or both of their parents. In addition, most parents who have used in vitro fertilization do not tell their children about their origins, although health professionals now encourage them to do so (Nachtigall et al., 1998). Does lack of genetic ties or secrecy surrounding these techniques interfere with parent–child relationships? Parenting is actually somewhat warmer for children conceived through in vitro fertilization or donor insemination. And such children are just as well adjusted as those who were easily conceived (Chan, Raboy, & Patterson, 1998; Golombok et al., 1995). A strong desire for parenthood among couples who have experienced reproductive problems seems to enhance family functioning.

Although donor insemination and in vitro fertilization have many benefits, serious questions have arisen about their use. Many states have no legal guidelines for these procedures. As a result, donors are not always screened for genetic or sexually transmitted diseases. In addition, few American doctors keep records of donor characteristics. Yet the resulting children may someday want to know their genetic background or need to know for medical reasons (Nachtigall, 1993).

SURROGATE MOTHERHOOD

A more controversial form of medically assisted conception is *surrogate motherhood*. Typically in this procedure, sperm from a man whose wife is infertile are used to inseminate a woman, called a surrogate, who is paid a fee for her childbearing services. In return, the surrogate agrees to turn the baby over to the man (who is the natural father). The child is then adopted by his wife.

Although most of these arrangements proceed smoothly, those that end up in court highlight serious risks for all concerned. In one case, both parties rejected the infant with severe disabilities that resulted from the pregnancy. In several others, the surrogate mother changed her mind and wanted to keep the baby. These children came into the world in the midst of family conflict that threatened to last for years.

Since surrogacy favors the wealthy as contractors for infants and the less economically advantaged as surrogates, it may promote exploitation of financially needy women (Sureau, 1997). In addition, most surrogates already have children of their own, who may be deeply affected by the pregnancy. Knowledge that their mother would give away a baby for profit may cause these children to worry about the security of their own family circumstances.

NEW REPRODUCTIVE FRONTIERS

Reproductive technologies are evolving faster than societies can weigh the ethics of these procedures. Doctors have used donor ova from younger women in combination with in vitro fertilization to help post-menopausal women become pregnant. Most recipients are in their forties, but a 62-year-old has given birth in Italy and a 63-year-old in the United States (Beck, 1994; Kalb, 1997). Even though candidates for postmenopausal-assisted childbirth are selected on the basis of good health, serious questions arise about bringing children into the world whose parents may not live to see them reach adulthood. Based on U.S. life expectancy data, 1 in 3 mothers and 1 in 2 fathers having a baby at age 55 will die before their child enters college (U.S. Bureau of the Census, 2000).

Currently, experts are debating other reproductive options. At donor banks, customers can select ova or sperm on the basis of physical characteristics and even the IQ of potential donors. Some worry that this practice is a dangerous step toward selective breeding of the human species. Researchers have delivered baby mice using the transplanted ovaries of aborted fetuses (Hashimoto, Noguchi, & Nakatsuji, 1992). If the same procedure were eventually applied to human

beings, it would create babies whose genetic mothers had never been born.

Finally, scientists have successfully cloned (made multiple copies of) fertilized ova in sheep, cattle, and monkeys, and they are working on effective ways to do so in humans. By providing extra ova for injection, cloning might improve the success rate of in vitro fertilization. It might also offer an unlimited source of human cells that could be directed to differentiate into a wide variety of organs for transplant therapy (Trounson & Pera, 1998). But human cloning also opens the possibility of mass producing genetically identical people. Therefore, it is widely condemned (Fasouliotis & Schenker, 2000).

Although new reproductive technologies permit many barren couples to rear healthy newborn babies, laws are needed to regulate these procedures. In Australia, New Zealand, and Sweden, individuals conceived with donated gametes have a right to infor-

mation about their genetic origins (Daniels & Lewis, 1996). Pressure from those working in the field of assisted reproduction may soon lead to a similar policy in the United States.

In the case of surrogate motherhood, the ethical problems are so complex that 18 U.S. states have sharply restricted the practice, and Australia, Canada, and many European nations have banned it, arguing that the status of a baby should not be a matter of commercial arrangement, and that a part of the body should not be rented or sold (McGee, 1997). France, Great Britain, and Italy have prohibited in vitro fertilization for women past menopause (Andrews & Elster, 2000). At present, nothing is known about the psychological consequences of being a product of these procedures. Research on how such children grow up, including what they know and how they feel about their origins, is important for weighing the pros and cons of these techniques.

Fourteen years after menopause, 63-year-old Arceli Keh gave birth to a baby using a donor ovum that was fertilized in vitro with her 61-year-old husband's sperm and injected into her uterus. Will baby Cynthia's parents live to see her reach adulthood? Postmenopausal childbearing is highly controversial.

NATIONAL ENQUIRER

Biology & ENVIRONMENT

THE HUMAN GENOME PROJECT

Begun in 1990, the Human Genome Project is an ambitious, international research program aimed at deciphering the chemical makeup of human genetic material (genome) and identifying all 30,000 to 35,000 human genes. Its main goals are to provide powerful new approaches for understanding human evolution and the development of genetic disorders so they can be prevented and treated. An additional goal is to examine the ethical, legal, and social implications of genetic technologies and to educate the public about them.

The research is an enormous undertaking. The human genome contains 3.2 billion chemical building blocks, or base pairs—enough to fill one thousand 1000-page telephone books if each base pair were represented by a single letter. Given the size of the project, researchers had to develop methods for DNA analysis that could process large amounts of information relatively quickly and accurately. Even with these procedures, scientists worked for more than a decade before they accomplished their first goal in

June 2000: mapping the sequence of all human base pairs.

APPLICATIONS

The sequence map produced by the Human Genome Project is a first step toward a much bigger challenge: "annotating" the entire genome—identifying all its genes and their functions in terms of how they code for proteins in the cell cytoplasm and, from there, affect human traits (Butler & Smaglik, 2000). Since valuable information about human genes can be obtained by comparing them with corresponding genes in other species, mapping and annotating is also being carried out on other organisms, including the mouse, the rat, the fruit fly, the roundworm, yeast, and the common intestinal bacterium E. coli. Armed with this information, scientists hope to understand each of the estimated four thousand human disorders—those due to single genes and those that result from a complex interplay of multiple genes and environmental factors, including heart disease, many forms of cancer, and mental illnesses, such as depression and alcoholism. As of the year 2001,

more than 22,000 genes had been identified, including those involved in several hundred diseases, including cystic fibrosis, Huntington disease, Duchenne muscular dystrophy, Marfan syndrome, and some forms of cancer (Genome International Sequencing Consortium, 2001).

Discovery of disease-associated genes is leading to rapid advances in genetic counseling and prenatal diagnosis as additional tests for detecting abnormal genes become available. The Human Genome Project is also providing the basis for a new, molecular medicine. Gene-based treatments are being developed for hereditary disorders, cancer, and AIDS. Among these experimental procedures is *gene splicing*— delivering DNA carrying a functional gene to the patient's cells, thereby correcting a genetic abnormality.

Although inserting a gene into its proper place in a patient's genome is an immense challenge, one successful experiment reveals its potential. Four-year-old Ashanthi and 9-year-old Cynthia, each born with an inherited defect of the immune system, had experienced one life-threatening infection after another until researchers found a way to

---

decisions about fetal surgery? One suggestion is to consult an independent counselor—a doctor or nurse who understands the risks but is not involved in doing research on or performing the procedure (Harrison, 1993).

Advances in *genetic engineering* also offer new hope for correcting hereditary defects. Genetic repair of the prenatal organism—once inconceivable—is a goal of today's genetic engineers. As part of the Human Genome Project, researchers are finding the precise location of thousands of genes for specific traits and using this information to identify abnormal conditions with greater accuracy and to devise gene-based treatments. To find out about the project's progress, refer to the Biology and Environment box above.

THE ALTERNATIVE OF ADOPTION

Adults who cannot have children, who are likely to pass along a genetic disorder, or who are older and single but want a family are turning to adoption in increasing numbers. Adoption agencies try to find parents of the same ethnic and religious background as the child.

inject a normal, disease-fighting gene into their white blood cells. Because the body constantly replaces these cells, the procedure is not a cure; it must be repeated regularly. But today, Ashanthi and Cynthia are leading healthy, active lives (Bodmer & McKie, 1997).

ETHICAL, LEGAL, AND SOCIAL CONCERNS

As the Human Genome Project transforms biological research and medical practice, it has sparked concerns about how its tools will be applied. A major controversy involves testing children and adults who are at risk for genetic diseases but who do not yet show symptoms. Delay between the availability of diagnostic tests and effective intervention means that affected people must live with the anxiety of a future illness they cannot prevent. And some have encountered discrimination because of their heredity; they have lost their health insurance and even their jobs. Yet another concern is inadvertent alteration of the human genome as a result of gene therapy.

Currently, guidelines and laws ensuring responsible use of genetic technologies are being drawn up. Experts in medical ethics recommend that genetic testing be offered only to individuals at high risk for a disorder who undergo extensive education and counseling before the test and close medical and psychological follow-up if they test positive. In the United States, it is now illegal to discriminate in the workplace or to deny health insurance on the basis of genetic information when a person has not been diagnosed with a condition related to that information (Haddad et al., 1999). Procedures are also being developed for ensuring genetic privacy and for testing the safety and effectiveness of gene-based treatments before their application (Yang, Flake, & Adzick, 1999).

The Human Genome Project is making invaluable contributions to our knowledge of the hereditary basis of human biology and disease—information that offers great promise for improving human health. As its discoveries become broadly available to the scientific community, investigators continue to debate the best ways to protect the public interest while reaping the project's monumental rewards.

A researcher participating in the Human Genome Project examines a visual image of the sequence of bases in a particular region of a chromosome. Recently completed sequence mapping of all human DNA bases permits meaningful interpretation of sequence variations between people, which can reveal who is healthy and who is susceptible to or stricken by certain diseases.

Where possible, they also try to choose parents who are the age of most natural parents. Because the availability of healthy babies has declined (since fewer young unwed mothers give up their babies than in the past), more people are adopting from foreign countries or taking children who are older or who have developmental problems.

Selection of adoptive parents is important, since sometimes adoptive relationships do not work out. The risk of adoption failure is greatest for children adopted at older ages and for children with disabilities, but the failure rate is not high. More than 85 percent do well in their adoptive homes. Of those who do not, 9 out of 10 are successfully placed with new parents, most of whom report high satisfaction with the adoptive experience (Glidden & Pursley, 1989; Rosenthal, 1992).

Still, adopted children and adolescents—whether born in a foreign country or the country of their adoptive parents—have more learning and emotional difficulties than do other children (Peters, Atkins, & McKay, 1999). There are many possible reasons for this trend. The biological mother may have been unable to care for the child because of problems believed to be partly genetic, such as alcoholism or severe depression, and she may have passed this

FIGURE 2.7

FIGURE 2.7

Percentage of 15-year-olds with high maladjustment scores who were adopted, placed in foster homes, or returned to their biological mothers shortly after birth, in a Swedish longitudinal study. All adolescents had been candidates for adoption when they were born. Compared with the other two groups, adopted young people were rated by teachers as having far fewer problems, including anxiety, withdrawal, aggression, inability to concentrate, peer difficulties, and poor school motivation. (Adapted from Bohman & Sigvardsson, 1990.)

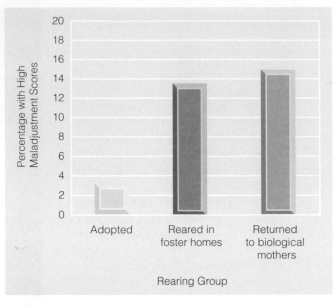

tendency to her offspring. Or perhaps she experienced stress, poor diet, or inadequate medical care during pregnancy—factors that can affect the child (as we will see in Chapter 3). Furthermore, children adopted after infancy often have a history of conflict-ridden family relationships and lack of parental affection. Finally, adoptive parents and children, who are genetically unrelated, are less alike in intelligence and personality than are biological relatives—differences that may threaten family harmony.

But despite these risks, most adopted children fare well. In a Swedish longitudinal study, researchers followed more than 600 infant adoption candidates into adolescence. Some were adopted shortly after birth; some were reared in foster homes; and some were reared by their biological mothers, who changed their minds about giving them up. As Figure 2.7 shows, adoptees developed much more favorably than did children growing up in foster families or returned to their birth mothers (Bohman & Sigvardsson, 1990).

By adolescence, adoptees' lives often are complicated by unresolved curiosity about their roots. Some have difficulty accepting the possibility that they may never know their birth parents. Others worry about what they would do if their birth parents suddenly reappeared (Grotevant & Kohler, 1999; Schaffer & Kral, 1988). Despite concerns about their origins, most adoptees appear well adjusted as adults. And as long as their parents took steps to help them learn about their heritage in childhood, transracially or transculturally adopted young people generally develop identities that are healthy blends of their birth and rearing backgrounds (Simon, Altstein, & Melli, 1994).

As we conclude our discussion of reproductive choices, perhaps you are wondering how things turned out for Ted and Marianne. Through genetic counseling, Marianne discovered a history of Tay-Sachs disease on her mother's side of the family. Ted had a distant cousin who had died of the disorder. The genetic counselor explained that the chances of giving birth to another affected baby were 1 in 4. Ted and Marianne took the risk. Their son, Douglas, is now 12 years old. Although Douglas is a carrier of the recessive allele, he is a normal, healthy boy. In a few years, Ted and Marianne will tell Douglas about his genetic history and explain the importance of genetic counseling and testing before he has children of his own. Consult the Caregiving Concerns table on the following page for steps that prospective parents can take before conception to increase their chances of having a healthy baby.

This transracially adopted African-American baby plays with her Caucasian older sisters. Will she develop an identity that is a healthy blend of her birth and rearing backgrounds? The answer depends on the extent to which her adoptive parents expose her to her African-American heritage.

© JIM PICKERELL/STOCK BOSTON

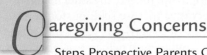aregiving Concerns

Steps Prospective Parents Can Take before Conception to Increase the Chances of Having a Healthy Baby

SUGGESTION	RATIONALE
Arrange for a physical exam.	A physical exam before conception permits detection of diseases and other medical problems that might reduce fertility, be difficult to treat after the onset of pregnancy, or affect the developing organism.
Reduce or eliminate toxins under your control.	Since the developing organism is highly sensitive to damaging environmental agents during the early weeks of pregnancy (see Chapter 3), couples trying to conceive should avoid drugs, alcohol, cigarette smoke, radiation, pollution, chemical substances in the home and workplace, and infectious diseases. Furthermore, stay away from ionizing radiation and some industrial chemicals, which are known to cause mutations.
Consider your genetic makeup.	Find out if anyone in your family has had a child with a genetic disease or disability. If so, seek genetic counseling before conception.
Consult a physician after 12 months of unsuccessful efforts at conception.	Long periods of infertility may be due to undiagnosed spontaneous abortions, which can be caused by genetic defects in either partner. If a physical exam reveals a healthy reproductive system, seek genetic counseling.

 **YOURSELF...**

review   *Describe the ethical pros and cons of fetal surgery, surrogate motherhood, postmenopausal-assisted childbearing, and the detection of abnormal genes made possible by the Human Genome Project.*

apply   *A woman over age 35 has just learned that she is pregnant. Although she would like to find out as soon as possible whether her child has a chromosomal disorder, she wants to minimize the risk of injury to the developing organism. Which prenatal diagnostic method is she likely to choose?*

reflect   *Put yourself in the place of a woman who is a carrier of fragile X syndrome but who wants to have children. Would you become pregnant, adopt, use a surrogate mother, or give up your desire for parenthood? Explain. If you became pregnant, would you opt for prenatal diagnosis? Why or why not?*

Environmental Contexts for Development

Just as complex as the heredity that sets the stage for development is the surrounding environment—a many-layered set of influences that combine to help or hinder physical and psychological well-being. Take a moment to think back to your own childhood, and jot down a brief description of events and people you regard as having a significant impact on your development. When I ask my students to do this, most items on their lists involve their families. This emphasis is not surprising, since the family is the first and longest-lasting context for development. But other settings turn out to be important as well. Friends, neighbors, school, workplace, scouting troops, religious organizations, and successes and disappointments at school generally make the top ten.

Think back to Bronfenbrenner's ecological systems theory, discussed in Chapter 1. It emphasizes that environments extending beyond the microsystem, or the immediate settings just mentioned, powerfully affect development. Indeed, my students rarely mention one very important context. Its impact is so pervasive that we seldom stop to think about it in our daily lives. This is the broad social climate of society—its values and programs that support and protect children's development. All families need help in rearing their children—through safe neighborhoods, well-equipped parks and playgrounds, good schools, affordable health services, and high-quality child care and other services that permit them to meet both work and family responsibilities. And some families, because of poverty or special tragedies, need considerably more help than others.

In the following sections, we take up these environmental contexts. Since they affect every age and aspect of change, we will return to them in later chapters. For now, our discussion emphasizes that besides heredity, environments can enhance or create risks for development. And when a vulnerable child—a youngster with physical or psychological problems—is exposed to unfavorable environmental contexts, development can be seriously threatened.

THE FAMILY

In power and breadth of influence, no context for development equals the family. The family introduces children to the physical world through the opportunities it provides for play and exploration of objects. It also creates unique bonds between people. The attachments children form with parents and siblings usually last a lifetime, and they serve as models for relationships in the wider world of neighborhood, school, and community. Within the family, children acquire language, an abundance of useful information and skills, an understanding of themselves and other people, and moral and cultural values. And at all ages, children and adolescents turn to family members for assistance and pleasurable interaction. Warm, gratifying family ties predict psychological well-being throughout development. In contrast, isolation or alienation from the family is often associated with developmental problems (Parke & Buriel, 1998).

Contemporary researchers view the family as a network of interdependent relationships. Recall from ecological systems theory that *bidirectional influences* exist in which the behaviors of each family member affect those of others (Bronfenbrenner, 1989, 1995). The very term *system* implies that the responses of all family members are related. These system influences operate in both *direct* and *indirect* ways.

LAWRENCE MIGDALE/STONE

The family is a network of interdependent relationships; each person influences the behavior of others, in both direct and indirect ways. The positive mealtime atmosphere in this family is the result of many forces, including parents who respond to children with warmth and patience, grandparents who support parents in their child-rearing roles, and children who have developed cooperative dispositions.

■ **DIRECT INFLUENCES.** Recently, as I passed through the checkout counter at the supermarket, I witnessed the following two episodes, in which parents and children directly affected each other:

■ Little Danny stood next to tempting rows of candy as his mom lifted groceries from the cart onto the counter. "Pleeeeease, can I have it, Mom?" begged Danny, holding up a large package of bubble gum. "Do you have a dollar? Just one?"

"No, not today," his mother answered. "Remember, we picked out your special cereal. That's what I need the dollar for." Danny's mother handed him the cereal while gently taking the bubble gum from his hand and returning it to the shelf. "Here, let's pay the man," she said, as she lifted Danny into the empty grocery cart where he could see the cash register.

■ Three-year-old Meg sat in the cart while her mom transferred groceries to the counter. Meg turned around, grabbed a bunch of bananas, and started to pull them apart.

"Stop it, Meg!" shouted her mom, who snatched the bananas from Meg's hand. Meg reached for a chocolate bar from a nearby shelf while her mother wrote the check. "Meg, how many times have I told you, DON'T TOUCH!" Loosening the candy from Meg's tight little grip, Meg's mother slapped her hand. Meg's face turned red with anger as she began to wail. "Keep this up, and you'll get it when we get home," threatened Meg's mom as they left the store.

These observations fit with a wealth of research on the family system. Many studies show that when parents are warm but patient (like Danny's mom), children tend to comply with their requests. And when children cooperate, their parents are likely to be warm and gentle in the future. In contrast, parents who discipline with harshness and impatience (like Meg's mom) have children who refuse and rebel. And because children's misbehavior is stressful for parents, they may increase their use of punishment, leading to more unruliness by the child (Dodge, Pettit, & Bates, 1994; Patterson, Reid, & Dishion, 1992). In these examples, the behavior of one family member helps sustain a form of interaction in another that either promotes or undermines children's well-being.

■ **INDIRECT INFLUENCES.** The impact of family relationships on child development becomes even more complicated when we consider that interaction between any two members is affected by others present in the setting. Bronfenbrenner calls these indirect influences the effect of *third parties* (see Chapter 1, page 28). Researchers have become intensely interested in how a range of relationships—mother with father, parent with sibling, grandparent with parent—modifies the child's direct experiences in the family.

Third parties can serve as effective supports for child development or, alternatively, they can undermine children's well-being. For example, when parents' marital relationship is warm and considerate, mothers and fathers praise and stimulate their children more and nag and scold them less. In contrast, when a marriage is tense and hostile, parents are likely to express anger, criticize, and punish (Erel & Burman, 1995; Harold & Conger, 1997). Yet even when arguments between their parents strain children's adjustment, other family members may help restore effective interaction. Grandparents are a case in point. They can promote children's development in many ways—both directly, by responding warmly to the child, and indirectly, by providing parents with child-rearing advice, models of child-rearing skill, and even financial assistance (Drew, Richard, & Smith, 1998). Of course, like any indirect influence, grandparents can sometimes be harmful. When quarrelsome relations exist between parents and grandparents, parent–child communication may suffer.

■ **ADAPTING TO CHANGE.** Think back to the *chronosystem* in Bronfenbrenner's theory (see page 29). The interplay of forces within the family must constantly adapt to the development of its members, since each changes throughout the lifespan.

For example, as children acquire new skills, parents adjust the way they treat their more competent youngsters. When you next have a chance, notice the way that a parent relates to a tiny baby as opposed to a walking, talking toddler. During the first few months of life, much time is spent feeding, changing, bathing, and cuddling the infant. Within a year, things change dramatically. The 1-year-old points, shows, names objects, and makes his way through the household cupboards. In response, parents devote less time to physical care and more to talking, playing games, and disciplining (Biringen et al., 1995; Campos, Kermoian, & Zumbahlen, 1992). These new ways of interacting encourage the child's expanding motor, cognitive, and social skills.

Parents' development affects children as well. In Chapter 14, we will see that the mild increase in parent–child conflict that often occurs in early adolescence is not solely due to teenagers' striving for independence and desire to explore new values and goals. Most parents of adolescents have reached middle age and are reconsidering their own commitments. They are very conscious that their youngsters will soon leave home and establish their own lives (Grotevant, 1998). Consequently, while the adolescent presses for greater autonomy, the parent may press for more togetherness. This imbalance promotes friction that parent and teenager gradually resolve by accommodating to changes in one another (Collins, 1997). Indeed, no social unit other than the family is required to adjust to such vast changes in its members.

Historical time period also contributes to a dynamic family system. In recent decades, high rates of divorce, participation of women in the workforce, and postponement of parenthood have contributed to a smaller family size and a greater number of single parents, remarried parents, employed mothers, and dual-earner families. Clearly, families in industrialized nations have become more diverse than ever before. In later chapters we will take up this wide variation in family forms, emphasizing how each affects family relationships and, ultimately, children's development.

Despite the family's flexible and changing nature, child development specialists have discovered some general rules about good parenting. As we will see in later chapters, parental *responsiveness* is consistently associated with better development. In infancy, responsive parents sensitively adapt their caregiving to the needs of their baby. They hold the infant tenderly, wait until she is ready for the next spoonful of food, and gaze into her eyes, smile, and talk softly when she indicates she is ready for social stimulation. Babies who receive such care are likely to develop into especially competent toddlers and preschoolers, both cognitively and socially (Crockenberg & Leerkes, 2000; Thompson, 1998).

During childhood and adolescence, responsive parents communicate in a warm, affectionate manner and listen patiently to their youngster's point of view. And when they combine this sensitivity with another crucial feature of effective parenting—*reasonable demands for mature behavior*—their children tend to be socially responsible and achieve well in school (Baumrind, 1971, 1991). In fact, research examining parenting in more than 180 societies indicates that a warm but moderately demanding style is common around the world (Rohner & Rohner, 1981).

Nevertheless, consistent differences in parenting practices do exist. In Chapter 10 we will see that the balance of parental warmth and control often varies with ethnicity—in ways that reflect cultural values and family life circumstances (Parke & Buriel, 1998). And in the United States and other Western nations, a major source of variation in parenting is socioeconomic status.

SOCIOECONOMIC STATUS AND FAMILY FUNCTIONING

People in industrialized nations are stratified on the basis of what they do at work and how much they earn for doing it—factors that determine their social position and economic well-being. Researchers assess a family's standing on this continuum through an index called **socioeconomic status (SES)**. It combines three interrelated, but not completely overlapping, variables: (1) years of education and (2) the prestige of and skill required by one's job, both of which measure social status; and (3) income, which measures economic status. As SES rises and falls, parents and children face changing circumstances that profoundly affect family functioning.

SES is linked to timing of parenthood and family size. People in skilled and semiskilled manual occupations (for example, machinists, truck drivers, and custodians) tend to become parents earlier and to have more children than do people in white-collar and professional occupations. The two groups also differ in child-rearing values and expectations. For example, when asked about personal qualities they desire for their children, lower-SES parents tend to place greater emphasis on external characteristics, such as obedience, neatness, and cleanliness. In contrast, higher-SES parents emphasize psychological traits, such as curiosity, happiness, and self-direction.

These differences are reflected in family interaction. Lower-SES fathers focus on their provider role and devote less time to parenting, whereas higher-SES fathers often share in housework and child-rearing responsibilities (although their commitment rarely equals that of mothers). Furthermore, higher-SES parents talk to and stimulate their infants more and grant them greater freedom to explore. When their children are older, higher-SES parents use more explanations and verbal praise. In contrast, commands, such as "You do that because I told you to," as well as criticism and physical punishment occur more often in low-SES households (Dodge, Pettit, & Bates, 1994; Hoff-Ginsberg & Tardiff, 1995).

The life conditions of families help explain these findings. Lower-SES parents often feel a sense of powerlessness and lack of influence in their relationships beyond the home. For example, at work they must obey the rules of others in positions of power and authority. When they get home, their parent–child interaction seems to duplicate these experiences, only with them in the authority roles. Higher-SES parents have a greater sense of control over their own lives. At work, they are used to making independent decisions and convincing others of their point of view. At home, they teach these skills to their children (Greenberger, O'Neil, & Nagel, 1994).

socioeconomic status (SES) A measure of a family's social position and economic well-being that combines three interrelated, but not completely overlapping, variables: (1) years of education and (2) the prestige of and skill required by one's job, both of which measure social status; and (3) income, which measures economic status.

Education also contributes to SES differences in child rearing. Higher-SES parents' interest in verbal stimulation and nurturing inner traits is supported by years of schooling, during which they learned to think about abstract, subjective ideas (Uribe, LeVine, & LeVine, 1994). Furthermore, the greater economic security of higher-SES parents frees them from having to worry about making ends meet on a daily basis. They can devote more time, energy, and material resources to furthering their own and their children's psychological characteristics.

As early as the second year of life, SES is positively correlated with cognitive and language development. Throughout childhood and adolescence, higher-SES children do better in school, and they attain higher levels of education (Brody, 1997; Walker et al., 1994). Researchers believe that differences in parenting practices have much to do with these outcomes.

THE IMPACT OF POVERTY

When families slip into poverty, effective parenting and children's development are seriously threatened. Shirley Brice Heath (1990), an anthropologist who has spent many years studying children and families of poverty, describes the case of Zinnia Mae, who grew up in Trackton, a close-knit black community located in a small southeastern American city. As unemployment struck Trackton in the 1980s and citizens moved away, 16-year-old Zinnia Mae caught a ride to Atlanta. Two years later, Heath visited her there. By then, Zinnia Mae was the mother of three children—a 16-month-old daughter named Donna and 2-month-old twin boys. She had moved into high-rise public housing.

Each of Zinnia Mae's days was much the same. She watched TV and talked with girlfriends on the phone. The children had only one set meal (breakfast) and otherwise ate whenever they were hungry or bored. Their play space was limited to the living room sofa and a mattress on the floor. Toys consisted of scraps of a blanket, spoons and food cartons, a small rubber ball, a few plastic cars, and a roller skate abandoned in the building. Zinnia Mae's most frequent words were, "I'm so tired." She worried about how to get papers to the welfare office, where to find a baby-sitter so she could go to the laundry or grocery, and what she would do if she located the twins' father, who had stopped sending money. She rarely had enough energy to spend time with her children.

Over the past 30 years, economic changes in the United States have caused the poverty rate to climb substantially; it has dropped only slightly in recent years. Today, nearly 36 million people—14 percent of the population—are affected. Those hit hardest are parents under age 25 with young children and elderly people who live alone. Poverty is also magnified among ethnic minorities and women. For example, 19 percent of American children are poor, a rate that climbs to 34 percent for Hispanic children, 37 percent for African-American children, and 32 percent for Native-American children. For single mothers with preschool children, the poverty rate is over 60 percent (National Center for Children in Poverty, 2000; U.S. Bureau of the Census, 2000). Joblessness, a high divorce rate, a high rate of adolescent parenthood, and (as we will see later) inadequate government programs to meet family needs are responsible for these disheartening statistics. The child poverty rate is higher than that of any other age group—a circumstance that is particularly worrisome because the earlier poverty begins and the longer it lasts, the more devastating its effects on physical and mental health and school achievement (McLeod & Shanahan, 1996; Zigler & Hall, 2000).

The constant stresses that accompany poverty gradually weaken the family system. Poor families have many daily hassles—bills to pay, the car breaking down, loss of welfare and unemployment payments, something stolen from the house, to name just a few. When daily crises arise, parents become depressed, irritable, and distracted; hostile interactions increase; and children's development suffers (McLoyd, 1998). These outcomes are especially severe in families that must live in poor housing and dangerous neighborhoods—conditions that make everyday existence even more difficult while reducing social supports that assist in coping with economic hardship (Duncan, Brooks-Gunn, & Klebanov, 1994; McLoyd et al., 1994).

Homelessness in the United States has risen over the past two decades. Families like this one travel from place to place in search of employment and a safe and secure place to live. Because of constant stress and few social supports, homeless children are usually behind in development, have frequent health problems, and show poor psychological adjustment.

TONY FREEMAN/PHOTOEDIT

Besides poverty, another problem—one that was quite uncommon 20 years ago—has reduced the life chances of poverty-stricken children in the United States: homelessness. On any given night, approximately 700,000 people have no place to live (Wright, 1999). Nearly 40 percent of America's homeless population is made up of families, and 1 in every 4 homeless individuals is a child. The rise in family homelessness is due to a number of factors, the most important of which are an inflationary rise in rents and a dramatic decline in the availability of government-supported low-cost housing (National Coalition for the Homeless, 1999a, 1999b).

Most homeless families consist of women with children younger than age 5. Besides health problems (which affect most homeless people), homeless children suffer from delays in motor, language, cognitive, and social development and from serious emotional stress (Oberg, Bryant, & Bach, 1995). Practically no homeless children attend preschool, and an estimated 25 to 30 percent who are old enough do not go to public school. School-age children who are enrolled achieve less well than other poverty-stricken children due to frequent absences and health and emotional difficulties (National Law Center on Homelessness and Poverty, 1997; Vostanis, Grattan, & Cumella, 1997).

BEYOND THE FAMILY: NEIGHBORHOODS, SCHOOLS, TOWNS, AND CITIES

In ecological systems theory, the mesosystem and the exosystem underscore that ties between family and community are vital for children's well-being. From our discussion of child poverty, perhaps you can see why this is so. In poverty-stricken urban areas, community life usually is disrupted. Families move often, parks and playgrounds are in disarray, and community centers providing organized leisure activities do not exist (Wilson, 1991). Research indicates that child abuse and neglect are greatest where residents are dissatisfied with their community, describing it as a socially isolated place to live. In contrast, when family ties to the community are strong—as indicated by regular church attendance and frequent contact with friends and relatives—family stress and child adjustment problems are reduced (Garbarino & Kostelny, 1993).

■ **NEIGHBORHOODS.** Let's take a closer look at the functions that communities serve in the lives of children by beginning with the neighborhood. What were your childhood experiences like in the yards, streets, and parks surrounding your home? How did you spend your time, whom did you get to know, and how important were these moments to you?

The resources offered by neighborhoods play an important part in children's development. In one study, the more varied children's neighborhood experiences—group memberships (such as scouting and 4-H), contact with adults of their grandparents' generation, visits to parents' workplace, and places to go off by themselves or with friends (a treehouse, a fort, or a neighbor's garage)—the better their emotional and social adjustment (Bryant, 1985).

Neighborhood resources, however, have a greater impact on young people growing up in economically disadvantaged neighborhoods than they do in well-to-do ones (McLeod & Shanahan, 1996). Affluent families are not as dependent on their immediate surroundings for social support, education, and leisure pursuits. They can afford to reach beyond the streets near their homes, transporting their children to lessons and entertainment and, if necessary, to better-quality schools in distant parts of the community (Elliott et al., 1996). In low-income neighborhoods, after-school programs that substitute for lack of resources by providing enrichment activities are associated with improved school performance and psychological adjustment in middle childhood (Posner & Vandell, 1994; Vandell & Posner, 1999). Neighborhood organiza-

The resources neighborhoods offer are important for development and well-being at all ages. Here, East Indian residents of a Los Angeles neighborhood gather at a city park for the Festival of Lights, celebrated by Hindus all over the world. The opportunity to share this feast of joy and socialize in a relaxed, safe atmosphere fosters warm bonds with neighbors and social support.

A. RAMEY/WOODFIN CAMP & ASSOCIATES

tions and informal social activities predict many aspects of adolescents' psychological well-being, including self-confidence, school performance, and educational aspirations (Gonzales et al., 1996).

In areas riddled with unemployment, crime, and population turnover, social ties that link families to one another and to other institutions are weak or absent, since relationships are constantly changing. Consequently, informal social controls—adults who keep an eye on children's play activities and who intervene when they see young people skipping school or behaving antisocially—disintegrate, giving rise to substance abuse and delinquent gangs. In unstable, poverty-stricken neighborhoods, stronger parental supervision and control are needed to prevent children from becoming involved in antisocial activities. When lack of neighborhood organization combines with little or no parent involvement, youth antisocial activity is especially high (Elliott et al., 1996; Sampson, 2000).

■ SCHOOLS. Unlike the informal worlds of family and neighborhood, school is a formal institution designed to transmit knowledge and skills that children need to become productive members of their society. Children spend many long hours in school—6 hours a day, 5 days a week, 36 weeks a year—totaling, altogether, about 15,000 hours by graduation from high school. In fact, today, many children younger than 5 years of age attend child-care centers and preschools that are "school-like," so the impact of schooling begins earlier and is even more powerful than these figures suggest.

Schools themselves are complex social systems that affect many aspects of development. Schools differ in the quality of their physical environments—size of the student body, number of children per class, and how much space is available for work and play. They also vary in their educational philosophies—whether teachers regard children as passive learners to be molded by adult instruction; as active, curious beings who determine their own learning; or as collaborative partners assisted by more expert cultural members, who guide their mastery of new skills. Finally, social life varies from school to school—for example, in the degree to which pupils are cooperative or competitive; in the extent to which children of different abilities, SES, and ethnic backgrounds spend time together; and in whether classrooms, hallways, and play yards are safe, humane settings or riddled with violence. We will discuss each of these aspects of schooling in later chapters.

Regular contact between families and teachers—an aspect of the mesosystem in ecological systems theory—supports development at all ages. Parents who are involved in school activities and who attend parent–teacher conferences have children and adolescents who show superior academic achievement (Connors & Epstein, 1996; Grolnick & Slowiaczek, 1994). Phone calls and visits to school are common among higher-SES parents, whose backgrounds and values are similar to those of teachers. In contrast, low-SES and ethnic minority parents often feel uncomfortable about coming to school (Delgado-Gaitan, 1994; Heath, 1989). Contact between parents and teachers is also more frequent in small towns, where most citizens know each other and schools serve as centers of community life (Peshkin, 1994). School staff must take extra steps with low-income, poverty-stricken, and ethnic minority families and in large urban areas to build supportive family–school ties.

When these efforts lead to cultures of good parenting and teaching, they deliver an extra boost to children's well-being. For example, when many parents in a neighborhood are highly involved in adolescents' school life, the impact on academic achievement is magnified (Darling & Steinberg, 1997). When excellent education becomes a team effort of teachers, school administrators, and community members, its effects on learning are stronger and reach many more children (Brown, 1997; Tharp, 1993).

■ TOWNS AND CITIES. Besides enhanced family–school contact, other aspects of life are different for children growing up in small towns rather than large cities. A well-known study examined the kinds of community settings children entered and the roles they played in a Midwestern town with a population of 700 (Barker, 1955). For example, children were granted important responsibilities—stocking shelves at Kane's Grocery Store, playing in the town

1999 © JOURNAL-COURIER/STEVE WARMOWSKI/THE IMAGE WORKS

Compared with their city-reared counterparts, children growing up in small towns are more often granted important responsibilities and are more actively involved in the community. This 9-year-old regularly milks cows on her family's dairy farm.

band, and operating the snow plow when help was short. They did so alongside adults, who taught them the skills they needed to become responsible community members.

Of course, children in small towns cannot visit aquariums, take rides on subways and buses, enjoy a variety of ethnic foods, or attend professional baseball games and orchestra concerts on a regular basis. The variety of settings is somewhat reduced compared to large cities. In small towns, however, children are more actively involved in the community. In addition, public places in small towns are relatively safe and secure. Streets and people are familiar, and responsible adults are present in almost all settings to monitor children's activities—a situation hard to match in today's urban environments.

Think back to the case of Zinnia Mae and her three young children, described on page 77. In her high-rise urban housing project, community life was especially undermined. Typically, high-rises are heavily populated with young, single mothers who are separated from family, friends, and neighborhoods in which they once felt a sense of cultural identity and belonging. They report intense feelings of loneliness in the small, cramped apartments. At Heath's (1990) request, Zinnia Mae agreed to tape-record her interactions with her children over a 2-year period. In 500 hours of tape, Zinnia Mae started a conversation with Donna and the boys (other than simple directions or questions about what the children were doing) only 18 times. Cut off from community ties, Zinnia Mae found it difficult to join in activities with her children. The result was a barren, understimulating early environment—one very different from the home and community in which Zinnia Mae had grown up.

THE CULTURAL CONTEXT

Our discussion in Chapter 1 emphasized that child development can only be fully understood within its larger cultural context. In the following sections, we expand on this important theme by taking up the macrosystem's role in children's development. First, we discuss ways that cultural values and practices affect environmental contexts for development. Second, we consider how healthy development depends on laws and government programs that shield children from harm and foster their well-being.

■ **CULTURAL VALUES AND PRACTICES.** Cultures shape family interaction, school experiences, and community settings beyond the home—in short, all aspects of the child's daily life. Many of us remain blind to aspects of our own cultural heritage until we see them in relation to the practices of others.

Each semester, I ask my students to think about the question, Who should be responsible for rearing young children? Here are some typical answers: "If parents decide to have a baby, then they should be ready to care for it." "Most people are not happy about others intruding into family life." These statements reflect a widely held opinion in the United States—that the care and rearing of young children, and paying for that care, are the duty of parents, and only parents (Rickel & Becker, 1997; Scarr, 1996). This view has a long history—one in which independence, self-reliance, and the privacy of family life emerged as primary American values. It is one reason, among others, that the American public has been slow to endorse publicly supported benefits for all families, such as health insurance and high-quality child care. America's valuing of an autonomous family also has contributed to the large number of families that remain poverty stricken despite the fact that their members are gainfully employed. These families are not poor enough to qualify for American public-assistance programs (Chase-Lansdale & Vinovskis, 1995; Zigler & Hall, 2000).

[handwritten margin note: In America, family viewed as a private domain.]

Cultural INFLUENCES

THE AFRICAN-AMERICAN EXTENDED FAMILY

The African-American extended family can be traced to the African heritage of most black Americans. In many African societies, newly married couples do not start their own households. Instead, they live with a large extended family, which assists its members with all aspects of daily life. This tradition of maintaining a broad network of kinship ties traveled to the United States during the period of slavery. Since then, it has served as a protective shield against the destructive impact of poverty and racial prejudice on African-American family life (McAdoo, 1993). Today, more black than white adults have relatives other than their own children living in the same household. African-American parents also see more kin during the week and perceive them as more important figures in their lives, respecting the advice of relatives and caring deeply about what they think is important (Wilson et al., 1995).

By providing emotional support and sharing income and essential resources, the African-American extended family helps reduce the stress of poverty and single parenthood. In addition, extended-family members often help with child rearing (Pearson et al., 1990). The presence of grandmothers in the households of many African-American teenagers and their infants protects babies from the negative influence of an overwhelmed and inexperienced mother. Furthermore, black adolescent mothers living in extended families are more likely to complete high school and get a job and less likely to be on welfare than are mothers living on their own—factors that in turn benefit children's well-being (Trent & Harlan, 1994).

For single mothers who were very young at the time of their child's birth, extended-family living continues to be associated with more positive mother–child interaction during the preschool years. For older single mothers, establishing an independent household with the help of nearby relatives is related to improved child rearing. Perhaps this arrangement permits the more mature mother who has developed effective parenting skills to implement them (Chase-Lansdale, Brooks-Gunn, & Zamsky, 1994). In families rearing adolescents, kinship support increases the likelihood of effective parenting, which is related to adolescents' self-reliance, emotional well-being, and reduced delinquency (Taylor & Roberts, 1995).

Finally, the extended family plays an important role in transmitting African-American culture. Compared with nuclear family households (which include only parents and their children), extended-family arrangements place more emphasis on cooperation and moral and religious values. And older black adults, such as grandparents and great-grandparents, regard educating children about their African heritage as especially important (Tolson & Wilson, 1990). These influences strengthen family bonds, protect children's development, and increase the chances that the extended-family lifestyle will carry over to the next generation.

LAWRENCE MIGDALE/STONE

Strong bonds with extended-family members protect the development of many African-American children growing up under conditions of poverty and single parenthood. This family gathers for Kwanzaa, a holiday celebrated between December 26 and January 1 by Africans and African descendants throughout the world. In Swahili, *matunda ya kwanzaa* means "first fruits." Kwanzaa rituals are derived from African harvest celebrations.

Although many Americans value independence and privacy, cooperative family structures can be found in the United States. In large industrialized nations like ours, not all citizens share the same values. **Subcultures** exist—groups of people with beliefs and customs that differ from those of the larger culture. The values and practices of some ethnic minority groups help protect their members from the harmful effects of poverty. A case in point is the African-American family. As the Cultural Influences box above indicates, the black cultural tradition of **extended-family households,** in which parent and child live with one or more

subculture
A group of people with beliefs and customs that differ from those of the larger culture.

extended-family household
A household in which parent and child live with one or more adult relatives.

adult relatives, is a vital feature of black family life that has enabled its members to survive despite a long history of prejudice and economic deprivation. Active and involved extended families also characterize Asian-American, Native-American, and Hispanic subcultures (Harrison et al., 1994).

Consider our discussion so far, and you will see that it reflects a broad dimension on which cultures and subcultures differ: the extent to which *collectivism versus individualism* is emphasized. In **collectivist societies,** people define themselves as part of a group and stress group over individual goals. In **individualistic societies,** people think of themselves as separate entities and are largely concerned with their own personal needs (Triandis, 1995). Although individualism tends to increase as cultures become more complex, cross-national differences remain. The United States is more individualistic than most other industrialized nations. As we will see in the next section, collectivist versus individualistic values have a powerful impact on a nation's approach to protecting children's development and well-being.

■ **PUBLIC POLICIES AND CHILD DEVELOPMENT.** When widespread social problems arise, such as poverty, homelessness, hunger, and disease, nations attempt to solve them by developing **public policies**—laws and government programs designed to improve the condition of children and families. For example, when poverty increases and families become homeless, a country might decide to build more low-cost housing, raise the minimum wage, and increase welfare benefits. When reports indicate that many children are not achieving well in school, federal and state governments might grant more tax money to school districts and make sure that help reaches the children who need it most.

The United States is among the wealthiest of nations and has the broadest knowledge base for intervening effectively in children's lives. Still, American public policies safeguarding children and youths have lagged behind those in other developed nations. As Table 2.7 reveals, the United States does not rank among the top countries on any key measure of children's health and well-being.

The problems of American children and youths extend beyond the indicators in the table. For example, although some 70 countries provide at least 12 weeks of paid employment leave for childbirth and parenting, the United States guarantees only 6 weeks of unpaid leave. Fifteen percent of American children have no health insurance, making them the largest segment of the uninsured population (Children's Defense Fund, 2000). National standards and funding to guarantee high-quality child care are nonexistent; according to recent evidence, much American child care is substandard (Cost, Quality, and Outcomes Study Team, 1995; Vandell, Dadisman, & Gallagher, 2000). In families affected by divorce, weak enforcement of child support payments heightens poverty in mother-headed families. By the time American young people finish high school, many do not have the educational and vocational preparation they need to contribute fully to society. And about 11 percent of adolescents leave high school without a diploma (U.S. Department of Education, 2000). If they do not return to finish their education, they are at risk for lifelong poverty.

Why have attempts to help children and youths been more difficult to realize in the United States than in other industrialized nations? A complex set of political and economic forces is involved. As noted earlier, the American ideals of self-reliance and privacy have made government hesitant to become involved in family matters. In addition, there is less consensus among Americans than European citizens on issues of child and family policy. Finally, good social programs are expensive, and they must compete for a fair share of a country's economic resources. Children can easily remain unrecognized in this process, since they cannot vote or speak out to protect their own interests, as adult citizens do (Zigler & Finn-Stevenson, 1999). Instead, they must rely on the good will of others to become an important government priority.

■ **CONTEMPORARY PROGRESS IN MEETING CHILDREN'S NEEDS.** Public policies aimed at fostering children's development can be justified on two important grounds. The first is that children are the future—the parents, workers, and citizens of tomorrow. Investing in children can yield valuable returns to a nation's quality of life. In contrast, failure to

[Handwritten margin note: U.S. lags behind in programs aimed @ positive childhood development.]

collectivist societies
Societies in which people define themselves as part of a group and stress group over individual goals.

individualistic societies
Societies in which people think of themselves as separate entities and are largely concerned with their own personal needs.

public policies
Laws and government programs designed to improve current conditions.

TABLE 2.7

How Does the United States Compare to Other Nations on Indicators of Child Health and Well-Being?

INDICATOR	U.S. RANK	SOME COUNTRIES THE UNITED STATES TRAILS
Childhood poverty[a]	8th (among 8 industrialized nations considered)	Australia, Canada, Germany, Great Britain, Norway, Sweden, Switzerland
Infant deaths in the first year of life	21st (worldwide)	Hong Kong, Ireland, Singapore, Spain
Low-birth-weight newborns	20th (worldwide)	Bulgaria, Egypt, Greece, Iran, Jordan, Kuwait, Paraguay, Romania, Saudi Arabia
Teenage pregnancy rate	11th (among 11 industrialized nations considered)	Australia, Canada, Czech Republic, France, New Zealand, Sweden
Percentage of young children immunized against measles	43rd (worldwide)	Chile, Czechoslovakia, Jordan, Poland, Romania
Expenditures on education as percentage of gross domestic product[b]	14th (among 16 industrialized nations considered)	Canada, France, Great Britain, the Netherlands, Sweden

[a]The U.S. child poverty rate of nearly 20 percent is more than twice that of any of these nations. For example, the rate is 9 percent in Australia, 9.3 percent in Canada, 4.6 percent in France, and 1.6 percent in Sweden.

[b]Gross domestic product is the value of all goods and services produced by a nation during a specified time period. It serves as an overall measure of a nation's wealth.

Sources: Bellamy, 2000; Central Intelligence Agency, 1999; Children's Defense Fund, 2000; Guyer et al., 1999; Harris, 1996; Sivard, 1996.

invest in children can result in "economic inefficiency, loss of productivity, shortages in needed skills, high health care costs, growing prison costs, and a nation that will be less safe, less caring, and less free" (Hernandez, 1994, p. 20).

Second, child-oriented policies can be justified on humanitarian grounds—children's basic rights as human beings. In 1989, the United Nations' General Assembly drew up the *Convention on the Rights of the Child,* an international treaty written in the form of a legal agreement among nations. It commits each cooperating country to work toward guaranteeing environments that foster children's development, protect them from harm, and enhance their community participation and self-determination. The Caregiving Concerns table on page 84 provides a sample of children's rights as articulated in the Convention. An international committee of experts monitors participating nations' progress toward reaching the Convention's goals. Although the United States played a key role in drawing up the Convention, it is one of the very few countries in the world whose legislature has not yet ratified it. American individualism has stood in the way; opponents maintain that the Convention's provisions will shift the burden of child rearing from the family to the state (Levesque, 1996).

To be sure, a wide variety of government-sponsored child and family programs do exist in the United States, and we will see many examples in later chapters. But they are largely crisis oriented, aimed at handling the most severe family difficulties rather than preventing problems before they happen. Furthermore, funding for these efforts has waxed and waned and been seriously threatened at various times. In most cases, only a minority of needy children and youths are helped (Harris, 1996; McLoyd, 1998).

Nevertheless, new policy initiatives promise to improve the status of American children. Extra federal dollars have been allocated to upgrade the quality of child care and to cover costs for low-income employed parents (although the amount granted is still far short of the need). A recent federal law facilitates payroll deductions from the paycheck of a noncustodial parent who fails to make child support payments. Furthermore, public health insurance coverage for low-income pregnant women and their children has recently expanded. And all medically

*C*aregiving Concerns

A Sampling from the U.N. Convention on the Rights of the Child

CATEGORY OF RIGHTS	EXAMPLES
Protection from harm	Protection from all forms of abuse and neglect
	Protection from participation in armed conflict
Survival and development	The highest attainable standard of health
	A standard of living adequate for physical, mental, spiritual, moral, and social development
	A happy, understanding, and loving family environment
	Free and compulsory education that develops physical abilities, the intellect, personality, and respect for one's cultural identity, one's homeland, other civilizations, and the environment
	Rest, leisure, and age-appropriate play and recreational activities; participation in cultural activities and the arts
Community participation and self-determination	Freedom to seek, receive, and impart information and ideas of all kinds, subject to respect for the rights of others, public health, and morals
	Freedom to express personal opinions in all matters affecting the child
	Protection against interference with privacy and family life
	Freedom of thought, conscience, and religion, subject to appropriate parental guidance and national law

uninsured children are now guaranteed free vaccinations (still, as Table 2.7 shows, the U.S. immunization rate falls behind that of many other nations) (Children's Defense Fund, 2000).

Child-related professional organizations are exerting strong leadership to advance child and family policies. For example, in the absence of federal guidelines for high-quality child care, the National Association for the Education of Young Children (NAEYC, a 103,000-member organization of early childhood educators) established a voluntary accreditation system for preschools and child-care centers. It grants special professional recognition to programs that meet its rigorous standards of quality. We can hope that such efforts will inspire the nation as a whole.

In 1973, Marion Wright Edelman founded the Children's Defense Fund, a private, nonprofit organization that provides a strong, effective voice for American children, who cannot vote, lobby, or speak for themselves. Edelman continues to serve as president of the Children's Defense Fund today.

WESTENBERGER/LIAISON AGENCY

Finally, child development specialists are joining with concerned citizens to become advocates for children's causes. One of the most vigorous groups is the Children's Defense Fund (CDF), a private nonprofit agency founded by Marion Wright Edelman in 1973. It engages in research, public education, legal action, drafting of legislation, congressional testimony, and community organizing. Each year, CDF publishes *The State of America's Children*, which provides a comprehensive analysis of the current condition of children, government-sponsored programs serving them, and proposals for improving child and family programs. As efforts like these continue, there is every reason to expect responsiveness to the needs of children and families to increase.

review   Links between family and community are essential for children's well-being. Provide examples and research findings from our discussion that support this idea.

apply   Check your local newspaper for a week and one or two national news magazines to see how many and what kinds of articles appear on the condition of children and families. Why is it important for researchers to communicate with the general public about children's needs?

connect   How does poverty affect functioning of the family system, thereby risking children's development in all domains?

reflect   Do you agree with the widespread American sentiment that government should not intrude in family life? Explain.

Understanding the Relationship Between Heredity and Environment

Throughout this chapter, we have discussed a wide variety of hereditary and environmental influences, each of which has the power to alter the course of development. Yet children born into the same family (and who therefore share genes and environments) often are quite different in characteristics. We also know that some children are affected more than others by their homes, neighborhoods, and communities. Cases exist in which a child provided with all the advantages in life does poorly, whereas a second child exposed to the worst of rearing conditions does well. How do scientists explain the impact of heredity and environment when they seem to work in so many different ways?

Behavioral genetics is a field devoted to uncovering the contributions of nature and nurture to this great diversity in human traits and abilities. All behavioral geneticists agree that both heredity and environment influence every aspect of development. But for polygenic traits (due to many genes) such as intelligence and personality, scientists are a long way from knowing the precise hereditary influences involved. Geneticists must study the impact of genes on these characteristics indirectly, and the nature–nurture controversy remains unresolved because researchers do not agree on how heredity and environment influence these complex traits.

Some believe that it is useful and possible to answer the question of *how much* each factor contributes to differences among children. A second group regards this question as neither useful nor answerable. These investigators believe that heredity and environment do not make separate contributions to behavior. Instead, they are always related, and the real question we need to explore is how they work together. Let's consider each of these positions in turn.

THE QUESTION, "HOW MUCH?"

Behavioral geneticists use two methods—heritability estimates and concordance rates—to infer the role of heredity in complex human characteristics. Let's look closely at the information these procedures yield, along with their limitations.

■ **HERITABILITY.** **Heritability estimates** measure the extent to which individual differences in complex traits in a specific population are due to genetic factors. Researchers have

[handwritten margin notes:]

Behavioral genetics studies the relation b/w NATURE and NURTURE.

How much do nature + nurture contribute? How do these factors interact?

behavioral genetics
A field devoted to uncovering the contributions of nature and nurture to individual differences in human traits and abilities.

heritability estimate
A statistic that measures the extent to which individual differences in complex traits in a specific population are due to genetic factors.

obtained heritabilities for intelligence and a variety of personality characteristics. We will take a brief look at their findings here, returning to them in later chapters, when we consider these topics in greater detail. Heritability estimates are obtained from **kinship studies,** which compare the characteristics of family members. The most common type of kinship study compares identical twins, who share all their genes, with fraternal twins, who share only some. If people who are genetically more alike are also more similar in intelligence and personality, then the researcher assumes that heredity plays an important role.

Kinship studies of intelligence provide some of the most controversial findings in the field of child development. Some experts claim a strong role for heredity, whereas others believe that genetic factors are barely involved. Currently, most researchers support a moderate role for heredity. When many twin studies are examined, correlations between the intelligence test scores of identical twins are consistently higher than those of fraternal twins. In a summary based on more than 13,000 twin pairs, the average correlation was .86 for identical twins and .55 for fraternal twins (Scarr, 1997).

Researchers use a complex statistical procedure to compare these correlations, arriving at a heritability estimate ranging from 0 to 1.00. The value for intelligence is about .50 for child and adolescent twin samples in Western industrialized nations. This indicates that differences in genetic makeup can explain half the variation in intelligence (Plomin, 1994a). The intelligence of adopted children is more strongly related to the scores of their biological parents than to those of their adoptive parents, offering further support for the role of heredity (Horn, 1983; Scarr & Weinberg, 1983).

Heritability research on identical and fraternal twins also reveals that genetic factors are important in personality. In fact, for personality traits that have been studied a great deal, such as sociability, emotional expressiveness, and activity level, heritability estimates are at about the same moderate level as that reported for intelligence (Braungart et al., 1992; Loehlin, 1992).

■ CONCORDANCE. A second measure that has been used to infer the contribution of heredity to complex characteristics is the **concordance rate.** It refers to the percentage of instances in which both twins show a trait when it is present in one twin. Researchers typically use concordance to study the contribution of heredity to emotional and behavioral disorders that can be judged as either present or absent.

A concordance rate ranges from 0 to 100 percent. A score of 0 indicates that if one twin has the trait, the other twin never has it. A score of 100 means that if one twin has the trait, the other one always has it. When a concordance rate is much higher for identical twins than for fraternal twins, then heredity is believed to play a major role. As Figure 2.8 reveals, twin studies of schizophrenia (a disorder involving delusions and hallucinations, difficulty distinguishing fantasy from reality, and irrational and inappropriate behaviors) and severe depression show this pattern of findings. Look carefully at the figure, and you will see that the influence of heredity on antisocial behavior and criminality, although apparent, is less strong. In that case, the difference between concordance rates for identical and fraternal twins is smaller (Plomin, 1994a). Once again, adoption studies lend support to these results. Biological relatives of adoptees with a history of schizophrenia, depression, and criminality are more likely to share the disorder than are adoptive relatives (Bock & Goode, 1996; Loehlin, Willerman, & Horn, 1988).

heredity plays a moderate role

FIGURE 2.8

Concordance rates for schizophrenia, severe depression, and antisocial behavior and criminality. Heredity plays some role in schizophrenia and is even more influential in severe depression, since the concordance rate is much higher for identical than for fraternal twins. Heredity contributes less to antisocial behavior and criminality, since the difference in concordance rates for identical and fraternal twins is smaller. (From Gottesman, 1991; Gottesman, Carey, & Hanson, 1983; McGuffin & Sargeant, 1991.)

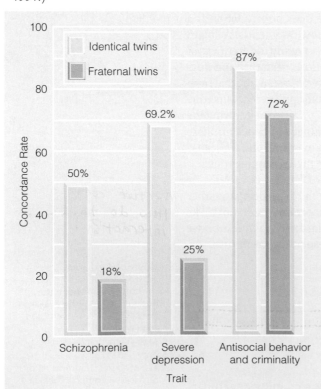

Taken together, concordance and adoption research suggests that the tendency for schizophrenia, depression, and criminality to run in families is partly due to genetic factors. However, we also know that environment is involved, since the concordance rate for identical twins would have to be 100 percent if heredity were the only influence operating. Already we have seen that environmental stresses, such as poverty, family conflict, and a disorganized home and neighborhood life, often are associated with emotional and behavioral problems. You will encounter many more examples of this relationship throughout this book.

■ **LIMITATIONS OF HERITABILITY AND CONCORDANCE.** Although heritability estimates and concordance rates provide evidence that genetic factors contribute to complex human characteristics, questions have been raised about their accuracy. Both measures are heavily influenced by the range of environments to which twin pairs are exposed. For example, identical twins reared together under highly similar conditions have more strongly correlated intelligence test scores than do those reared apart in very different environments. When the former are used to compute heritability estimates, the higher correlation causes the importance of heredity to be overestimated (Hoffman, 1994).

To overcome this difficulty, researchers try to find twins who have been reared apart in adoptive families. But few separated twin pairs are available for study, and when they are, social service agencies often place them in advantaged homes that are alike in many ways (Eisenberg, 1998a). Because the environments of most twin pairs do not represent the broad range of environments found in the general population, it often is difficult to generalize heritability and concordance findings to the population as a whole.

Heritability estimates are controversial measures because they can easily be misapplied. For example, high heritabilities have been used to suggest that ethnic differences in intelligence, such as the poorer performance of black children in relation to white children, have a genetic basis (Jensen, 1969, 1985, 1998). Yet this line of reasoning is widely regarded as incorrect. Heritabilities computed on mostly white twin samples do not tell us what is responsible for test score differences between ethnic groups. We have already seen that large economic and cultural differences are involved. In Chapter 12, we will discuss research indicating that when black children are adopted into economically advantaged homes at an early age, their scores are well above average and substantially higher than those of children growing up in impoverished families.

Perhaps the most serious criticism of heritability estimates and concordance rates has to do with their usefulness. Although they tell us that heredity is undoubtedly involved in complex traits, they give us no precise information about how these traits develop or how children might respond when exposed to environments designed to help them develop as far as possible (Bronfenbrenner & Ceci, 1994; Wachs, 1999). Indeed, research shows that the heritability of intelligence is higher in advantaged homes and communities, which permit children to actualize their genetic endowment. In disadvantaged environments, children are prevented from realizing their potential. Consequently, enhancing their experiences through

Identical twins Bob and Bob were separated by adoption shortly after birth and not reunited until adulthood. The two Bobs discovered they were alike in many ways. Both hold bachelor's degrees in engineering, are married to teachers named Brenda, wear glasses, have mustaches, smoke pipes, and are volunteer firemen. The study of identical twins reared apart reveals that heredity contributes to many psychological characteristics. Nevertheless, not all separated twins match up as well as this pair, and generalizing from twin evidence to the population is controversial.

kinship studies
Studies comparing the characteristics of family members to determine the importance of heredity in complex human characteristics.

concordance rate
The percentage of instances in which both members of a twin pair show a trait when it is present in one pair member. Used to study the contribution of heredity to emotional and behavioral disorders that can be judged as either present or absent.

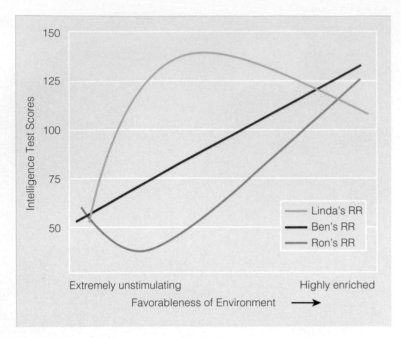

FIGURE 2.9

Intellectual ranges of reaction (RR) for three children in environments that vary from extremely unstimulating to highly enriched. Each child, due to his or her genetic makeup, responds differently as quality of the environment changes. Ben's intelligence increases steadily, Linda's rises sharply and then falls off, and Ron's begins to increase only after the environment becomes modestly stimulating. (Adapted from Wahlsten, 1994.)

ROR— person has a unique rxn. 2 environment b/c of thin genetic makeup.

range of reaction
Each person's unique, genetically determined response to a range of environmental conditions.

canalization
The tendency of heredity to restrict the development of some characteristics to just one or a few outcomes.

interventions (such as parent education and high-quality preschool or child care) has a greater impact on development (Bronfenbrenner & Morris, 1998; Scarr, 1998).

According to one group of experts, heritability estimates have too many problems to yield any firm conclusions about the relative strength of genetic and environmental influences on development (Collins et al., 2000). In response to critics, investigators who conduct heritability research argue that their studies are a first step. As more evidence accumulates to show that heredity underlies important human characteristics, scientists can begin to ask better questions—about which genes are involved, how they affect development, and how environmental factors modify their impact.

THE QUESTION, "HOW?"

According to a second perspective, heredity and environment cannot be divided into separate influences. Instead, behavior results from a dynamic interplay between these two forces. How do heredity and environment work together to affect development? Several important concepts shed light on this question.

■ **REACTION RANGE.** The first of these ideas is **range of reaction** (Gottesman, 1963). It emphasizes that each person responds to the environment in a unique way because of his or her genetic makeup. Let's explore this idea in Figure 2.9. Reaction range can apply to any characteristic; here it is illustrated for intelligence. Notice that when environments vary from extremely unstimulating to highly enriched, Ben's intelligence increases steadily, Linda's rises sharply and then falls off, and Ron's begins to increase only after the environment becomes modestly stimulating.

Reaction range highlights two important points about the relationship between heredity and environment. First, it shows that because each of us has a unique genetic makeup, we respond quite differently to the same environment. Look carefully at Figure 2.9, and notice how a poor environment results in similarly low scores for all three children. But Linda is by far the best-performing child when environments provide an intermediate level of stimulation. And when environments are highly enriched, Ben does best, followed by Ron, both of whom now exceed Linda. Second, sometimes different genetic–environmental combinations can lead to the same result! For example, if Linda is reared in a minimally stimulating environment, her score will be about 100—average for children in general. Ben and Ron can also obtain this score, but to do so they must grow up in a fairly enriched home.

The concept of range of reaction tells us that children differ in their range of possible responses to the environment. And it illustrates the meaning of the phrase *heredity and environment interact*, since it shows that unique blends of heredity and environment lead to both similarities and differences in behavior (Wahlsten, 1994).

■ **CANALIZATION.** The concept of canalization provides another way of understanding how heredity and environment combine. **Canalization** is the tendency of heredity to restrict the development of some characteristics to just one or a few outcomes. A behavior that is strongly canalized follows a genetically set growth plan, and only strong environmental forces can change it (Waddington, 1957). For example, infant perceptual and motor development seems to be strongly canalized, since all normal human babies eventually roll over, reach for objects, sit up, crawl, and walk. It takes extreme conditions to modify these behaviors or cause them not to appear. In contrast, intelligence and personality are less strongly canalized, since they vary much more with changes in the environment. When we look at the kinds of behaviors that are constrained by heredity, we can see that canalization is highly adaptive. Through it, nature ensures that children will develop certain basic capacities under a wide range of rearing conditions, thereby promoting survival.

Recently, scientists expanded the notion of canalization to include environmental influences. We now know that environments can also limit development (Gottlieb, 1996). For example, when children experience harmful environments early in life, later experiences may have limited capacity to change characteristics (such as intelligence) that were quite flexible to begin with. In Chapter 3, we will see that this is the case for babies exposed prenatally to high levels of alcohol and radiation. And later in this book, we will find that it is also true for children who spend many years living in extremely deprived homes and institutions (Turkheimer & Gottesman, 1991).

JIM SMITH/PHOTO RESEARCHERS, INC.

Using the concept of canalization, we learn that genes restrict the development of some characteristics more than others. And over time, even very flexible behaviors can become fixed and canalized, depending on children's experiences.

■ GENETIC–ENVIRONMENTAL CORRELA-TION. Nature and nurture work together in still another way. Several investigators point out that a major problem in trying to separate heredity and environment is that they are often correlated (Plomin, 1994a; Scarr & McCartney, 1983). According to the concept of **genetic–environmental correlation,** our genes influence the environments to which we are exposed. The way this happens changes with development.

Passive and Evocative Correlation. At younger ages, two types of genetic–environmental correlations are common. The first is called *passive* correlation because the child has no control over it. Early on, parents provide environments that are influenced by their own heredity. For example, parents who are good athletes are likely to emphasize outdoor activities and enroll their children in swimming and gymnastics lessons. Besides getting exposed to an "athletic environment," the children may have inherited their parents' athletic ability. As a result, they are likely to become good athletes for both genetic and environmental reasons.

The second type of genetic–environmental correlation is *evocative.* Children evoke responses from others that are influenced by the child's heredity, and these responses strengthen the child's original style of responding. For example, an active, friendly baby is likely to receive more social stimulation from those around her than is a passive, quiet infant. And a cooperative, attentive preschooler will probably receive more patient and sensitive interactions from parents than will an inattentive, distractible child.

Active Correlation. At older ages, *active* genetic–environmental correlation becomes common. As children extend their experiences beyond the immediate family to school,

This mother is an accomplished musician who exposes her son to a stimulating musical environment. In addition, the boy may have inherited his mother's talent for music. When heredity and environment are correlated, they jointly foster the same capacities, and the influence of one cannot be separated from the influence of the other.

genetic–environmental correlation
The idea that heredity influences the environments to which individuals are exposed.

Biology & ENVIRONMENT

UNCOUPLING GENETIC–ENVIRONMENTAL CORRELATIONS FOR MENTAL ILLNESS AND ANTISOCIAL BEHAVIOR

Diagnosed with schizophrenia, Lars's and Sven's biological mothers had such difficulty functioning in everyday life that each gave up her infant son for adoption. Lars had the misfortune of being placed with adoptive parents who, like his biological mother, were mentally ill. His home life was chaotic, and his parents were punitive and neglectful. Sven's adoptive parents, in contrast, were psychologically healthy and reared him with love, patience, and consistency.

Lars displays a commonly observed genetic–environmental correlation: a predisposition for schizophrenia coupled with maladaptive parenting. Will he be more likely than Sven, whose adoption *uncoupled* this adverse genotype–environment link, to develop mental illness? In a large Finnish adoption study, researchers followed up on nearly 200 adopted children of schizophrenic mothers in adulthood (Tienari et al., 1994). Those (like Sven) who were reared by healthy adoptive parents showed little mental illness—no more than did a control group with healthy biological and adoptive parents. In contrast, psychological impairments piled up in adoptees (like Lars) with disturbed biological and adoptive parents. These children were considerably more likely to develop mental illness than were controls whose biological parents were healthy but who were be-

ing reared by severely disturbed adoptive parents.

Similar findings emerged in several American and Swedish adoption studies addressing genetic and environmental contributions to antisocial behavior (Bohman, 1996; Yates, Cadoret, & Troughton, 1999). As Figure 2.10 shows, adopted infants whose biological mothers were imprisoned criminal offenders displayed a high rate of antisocial behavior in adolescence only when reared in adverse homes, as indicated by adoptive parents or siblings with severe adjustment problems. In families free of psychological disturbance, adoptees with a predisposition to criminality did not differ from adoptees without this genetic background.

In sum, the chances that genes for psychological disorder will be expressed are far greater when child rearing is maladaptive. Healthy-functioning families seem to promote healthy development in children, despite a genetic risk associated with mental illness or criminality in a biological parent.

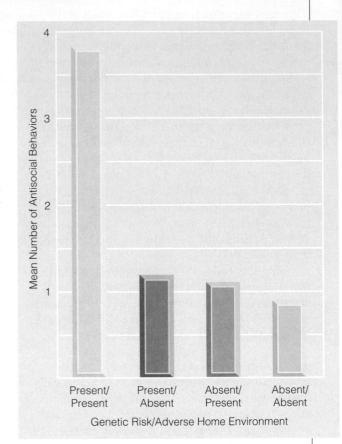

FIGURE 2.10

Mean number of antisocial behaviors of adoptees varying in genetic and home environment risk for criminality. Adolescent adoptees at genetic risk for criminality displayed a high rate of antisocial behavior only when reared in adverse home environments. When reared in favorable homes, they did not differ from adoptees at no genetic risk. (Adapted from Cadoret, Cain, & Crowe, 1983.)

neighborhood, and community and are given the freedom to make more of their own choices, they play an increasingly active role in seeking out environments that fit with their genetic tendencies. The well-coordinated, muscular child spends more time at after-school sports, the musically talented youngster joins the school orchestra and practices his violin, and the intellectually curious child is a familiar patron at her local library.

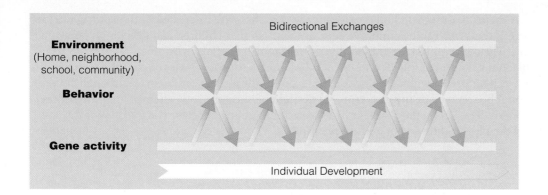

FIGURE 2.11

The epigenetic framework. Development takes place through ongoing, bidirectional exchanges between heredity and all levels of the environment. Genes affect children's behavior and experiences; their experiences and behavior also affect gene expression. (Adapted from Gottlieb, 2000.)

This tendency to actively choose environments that complement our heredity is called **niche-picking** (Scarr & McCartney, 1983). Infants and young children cannot do much niche-picking, since adults select environments for them. In contrast, older children and adolescents are much more in charge of their own environments. The niche-picking idea explains why pairs of identical twins reared apart during childhood and later reunited may find, to their great surprise, that they have similar hobbies, food preferences, friendship choices, and vocations—a trend that is especially evident when twins' environmental opportunities are similar (Bouchard et al., 1990; Plomin, 1994). Niche-picking also helps us understand some curious longitudinal findings indicating that identical twins become somewhat more similar and fraternal twins and adopted siblings less alike in intelligence from infancy to adolescence (Loehlin, Horn, & Willerman, 1997). The influence of heredity and environment is not constant but changes over time. With age, genetic factors may become more important in determining the environments we experience and choose for ourselves.

■ **ENVIRONMENTAL INFLUENCES ON GENE EXPRESSION.** Some theorists consider genetic–environmental correlation to be entirely driven by genetics (Harris, 1998; Rowe, 1994). They argue that this makes sense because children's genetic makeup causes them to receive, evoke, or seek experiences that actualize their inborn tendencies. Other theorists object to this simplistic analysis. Although genetic–environmental correlation is well documented, heredity does not dictate children's experiences in a rigid way. As the Biology and Environment box on the previous page illustrates, parents and other caring adults can *uncouple* adverse genetic–environmental correlations. They often provide children with experiences that modify the expression of heredity, yielding favorable outcomes.

The relationship between heredity and environment is not a one-way street, from genes to environment to behavior. Rather, like other system influences considered in this and the previous chapter, it is *bidirectional*: Genes affect children's behavior and experiences, but their experiences and behavior also affect gene expression (Gottlieb, 2000). Stimulation—both *internal* to the child (activity within the cytoplasm of the cell, hormones released into the bloodstream) and *external* to the child (home, neighborhood, school, and community)—triggers gene activity.

Researchers call this view of the relationship between heredity and environment the *epigenetic* framework (Gottlieb, 1992, 1998). It is depicted in Figure 2.11. **Epigenesis** means development of the individual resulting from ongoing, bidirectional exchanges between heredity and all levels of the environment. To cite just one illustration, granting a baby a healthy diet increases brain growth, which translates into new connections and faster message transfer between nerve cells and, in turn, transformed gene expression. This series of interactions opens the door to new gene–environment exchanges—for example, advanced exploration of objects and interaction with caregivers, which further enhance brain growth and gene expression. These ongoing bidirectional influences foster cognitive and social development. Can you provide additional examples of epigenesis?

niche-picking
A type of genetic–environmental correlation in which individuals actively choose environments that complement their heredity.

epigenesis
Development of the individual resulting from ongoing, bidirectional exchanges between heredity and all levels of the environment.

A major reason that child development researchers are interested in the nature–nurture issue is that they want to improve environments so that children can develop as far as possible. The concepts of range of reaction, canalization, genetic–environmental correlation, and epigenesis remind us that development is best understood as a series of complex transactions between nature and nurture. Environments can modify genetic influences, although children cannot be changed in any way we might desire. The success of any attempt to improve development depends on the characteristics we want to change, the genetic makeup of the child, and the type and timing of our intervention.

Ask YOURSELF...

review
Why did one group of experts conclude that heritability estimates have too many problems to yield firm conclusions about the relative strength of genetic and environmental influences on development?

apply
Bianca's parents are both accomplished musicians. Bianca began taking piano lessons when she was 4 years old and was accompanying her school choir by age 10. When she reached adolescence, she asked her parents if she could attend a special music high school. Explain how genetic–environmental correlation promoted Bianca's talent.

connect
The discussion of range of reaction on page 88 illustrates genetic–environmental interaction for intelligence—that unique blends of heredity and environment lead to both similarities and differences in behavior. How do the findings shown in Figure 2.10 in the Biology and Environment box on page 90 depict this idea for antisocial behavior?

reflect
What aspects of your own adolescent and adult development—for example, interests, hobbies, college major, and vocational choice—are probably due to niche-picking? Explain.

Summary

GENETIC FOUNDATIONS

What are genes, and how are they transmitted from one generation to the next?

- Each individual's **phenotype,** or directly observable characteristics, is a product of both **genotype** and environment. **Chromosomes,** rodlike structures within the cell nucleus, contain our hereditary endowment. Along their length are **genes,** segments of **DNA** that make us distinctly human and influence our development and characteristics.

- **Gametes,** or sex cells, are produced through the process of cell division known as **meiosis. Crossing over** and independent assortment of chromosomes ensure that each gamete receives a unique set of genes from each parent. Once sperm and ovum unite, the resulting **zygote** starts to develop into a complex human being through cell duplication, or **mitosis.**

- If the fertilizing sperm carries an X chromosome, the child will be a girl; if it contains a Y chromosome, a boy will be born. **Fraternal,** or **dizygotic, twins** result when two ova are released from the mother's ovaries and each is fertilized. In contrast, **identical,** or **monozygotic, twins** develop when a zygote divides in two during the early stages of cell duplication.

Describe various patterns of genetic inheritance.

- **Dominant–recessive** and **codominant** relationships are patterns of inheritance that apply to many traits controlled by single genes. In dominant–recessive inheritance, **heterozygous** individuals with one recessive **allele** are **carriers** of the recessive trait. **Modifier genes** enhance or dilute the effects of other genes.

- When recessive disorders are **X-linked** (carried on the X chromosome), males are more likely to be affected. **Genetic imprinting** is a pattern of inheritance in which one parent's allele is activated, regardless of its makeup.

- Unfavorable genes arise from **mutations,** which can occur spontaneously or be induced by hazardous environmental agents.

- Human traits that vary continuously, such as intelligence and personality, are **polygenic,** or influenced by many genes. Since the genetic principles involved are unknown, scientists must study the influence of heredity on these characteristics indirectly.

Cite major chromosomal abnormalities, and explain how they occur.

- Most chromosomal abnormalities are due to errors in meiosis. The most common chromosomal disorder is Down syndrome, which results in physical defects and mental retardation. Disorders of the **sex chromosomes**—XYY, triple X, Klinefelter, and Turner syndromes—are milder than defects of the **autosomes.**

REPRODUCTIVE CHOICES

What procedures can assist prospective parents in having healthy children?

- **Genetic counseling** helps couples at risk for giving birth to children with genetic abnormalities consider appropriate reproductive options. **Prenatal diagnostic methods** make early detection of genetic problems possible. Although reproductive technologies, such as donor insemination, in vitro fertilization, surrogate motherhood, and postmenopausal-assisted childbirth, permit many barren individuals to become parents, they raise serious legal and ethical concerns.

- Many parents who cannot conceive or who have a high likelihood of transmitting a genetic disorder decide to adopt. Although adopted children have more learning and emotional problems than children in general, in the long run most fare quite well.

ENVIRONMENTAL CONTEXTS FOR DEVELOPMENT

Describe family functioning from the perspective of ecological systems theory, along with aspects of the environment that support family well-being and children's development.

- Just as complex as heredity are the environments in which children grow up. The family is the child's first and foremost context for development. Ecological systems theory emphasizes that the behaviors of each family member affect those of others in both direct and indirect ways. The family system is also dynamic, constantly adjusting to the development of its members and to societal change.

- Two aspects of parenting promote effective development at all ages: (1) responsiveness, and (2) reasonable demands for mature behavior. Although warm, moderately demanding child rearing is a common pattern around the world, it is affected by ethnicity and **socioeconomic status (SES).** Effective parenting, along with all aspects of children's development, is seriously undermined by poverty and homelessness.

- Children profit from supportive ties between the family and the surrounding environment. Neighborhoods that provide constructive leisure activities, high-quality schools that communicate often with parents, and communities that promote children's active participation alongside adults enhance child development.

- The values and life conditions of cultures and **subcultures** mold the environments in which children grow up. **Extended-family households,** in which parent and child live with one or more adult relatives, are common among ethnic minorities. They protect children's development under conditions of high life stress.

- In the complex world in which we live, children's well-being depends on favorable **public policies.** Effective social programs are influenced by many factors, including

Summary (continued)

cultural values that stress **collectivism** over **individualism,** a nation's economic resources, and organizations and individuals that work for children's causes.

UNDERSTANDING THE RELATIONSHIP BETWEEN HEREDITY AND ENVIRONMENT

Explain the various ways heredity and environment may combine to influence complex traits.

■ **Behavioral genetics** is a field devoted to uncovering the contributions of nature and nurture to complex traits. Some researchers believe that it is useful and possible to determine "how much" each factor contributes to individual differences. These investigators compute **heritability estimates** and **concordance rates** from **kinship studies.** Although these measures show that genetic factors contribute to such traits as intelligence and personality, questions have been raised about their accuracy and usefulness.

■ Other scientists believe that the important question is "how" heredity and environment work together. The concepts of **range of reaction, canalization, genetic–environmental correlation, niche-picking,** and **epigenesis** remind us that development is best understood as a series of complex exchanges between nature and nurture.

*I*mportant terms and concepts

allele (p. 59)
autosomes (p. 57)
behavioral genetics (p. 85)
canalization (p. 88)
carrier (p. 59)
chromosomes (p. 54)
codominance (p. 59)
collectivist societies (p. 82)
concordance rate (p. 87)
crossing over (p. 54)
deoxyribonucleic acid (DNA) (p. 54)
dominant–recessive inheritance (p. 59)
extended-family household (p. 81)
epigenesis (p. 91)

fraternal, or dizygotic, twins (p. 57)
gametes (p. 54)
gene (p. 54)
genetic counseling (p. 66)
genetic imprinting (p. 62)
genetic–environmental correlation (p. 89)
genotype (p. 54)
heritability estimate (p. 85)
heterozygous (p. 59)
homozygous (p. 59)
identical, or monozygotic, twins (p. 57)
individualistic societies (p. 82)
kinship studies (p. 87)

meiosis (p. 54)
mitosis (p. 54)
modifier genes (p. 59)
mutation (p. 62)
niche-picking (p. 91)
phenotype (p. 54)
polygenic inheritance (p. 62)
prenatal diagnostic methods (p. 67)
public policies (p. 82)
range of reaction (p. 88)
sex chromosomes (p. 57)
socioeconomic status (SES) (p. 76)
subculture (p. 81)
X-linked inheritance (p. 61)
zygote (p. 57)

. . . for further information and help

Consult the companion website for this book, where you will find additional weblinks and associated learning activities:
www.ablongman.com/berk

GENETICS AND GENETIC DISORDERS

Human Genome Project
www.ornl.gov/hgmis

Provides comprehensive information about the international Human Genome Project, including project goals and current status.

March of Dimes Birth Defects Foundation
www.modimes.org

Works to prevent genetic disorders and other birth defects through public education and community service programs.

National PKU News Organization
www.pkunews.org

Provides up-to-date, accurate news and information to families and professionals dealing with phenylketonuria (PKU).

Sickle Cell Association
www.sicklecell-texas.org

Provides information to individuals affected by sickle cell disease and related blood disorders.

National Down Syndrome Congress
www.nsdccenter.org

Assists parents in finding solutions to the needs of children with Down syndrome.

INFERTILITY

Resolve, Inc.
www.resolve.org

Developed by the National Infertility Association; offers counseling, referral, and support to persons with fertility problems.

ADOPTION

Adopt: Assistance Information Support
www.adopting.org

Provides assistance, information, and support on diverse aspects of adoption, including children from other countries and children with special needs.

PUBLIC POLICY

Children's Defense Fund
www.childrensdefense.org

An active child-advocacy organization. Provides information on the condition of American children and government-sponsored programs serving them.

National Center for Children in Poverty
cpmcnet.columbia.edu/dept/nccp

Aims to reduce the number of young children living in poverty by disseminating information about early education and maternal and child health and by proposing new initiatives to lawmakers.

National Coalition for the Homeless
www.nationalhomeless.org

A network of citizens and service providers committed to ending homelessness through public education, public policy advocacy, and grassroots organizing. Provides updated information on various aspects of homelessness, including homeless families with children and homeless youths.

"The Gift of Life"

Lotfieh Mohamed El Masri

11 years, Lebanon

This painting captures the physical and psychological bonds that form as expectant parents await the arrival of a new being. How is the one-celled organism gradually transformed into a baby with the human capacity to play, dream, and create? What factors support or undermine this earliest phase of development? Chapter 3 provides answers to this question.

Prenatal Development

After months of wondering if the time in their lives was right, Yolanda and Jay decided to have a baby. I met them one fall in my child development class, when Yolanda was just 2 months pregnant. Both were full of questions: "How does the baby grow before birth? When is each organ formed? Has its heart begun to beat? Can it hear, feel, or sense our presence?" Already, Yolanda and Jay had scanned the shelves of the public library and local bookstores, picking up a dozen or more sources on pregnancy, childbirth, and caring for the newborn.

Most of all, Yolanda and Jay wanted to do everything possible to make sure their baby would be born healthy. At first, they believed that the uterus completely shielded the developing organism from any dangers in the environment. All babies born with problems, they thought, had unfavorable genes. After browsing through several pregnancy books, Yolanda and Jay realized they were wrong. Yolanda started to wonder about

Three generations of women—expectant mother, grandmother, and great grandmother—anticipate a future baby. Compared with a generation or two ago, adults today are far more likely to have made well-reasoned choices about whether, when, and how to have children.

her diet and whether she should keep up her daily aerobics routine. And she asked me whether an aspirin for a headache, a sleeping pill before bedtime, a glass of wine at dinner, or a few cups of coffee during study hours might be harmful.

In this chapter we answer Yolanda and Jay's questions, along with a great many more that scientists have asked about the events before birth. We begin our discussion during the time period before pregnancy with these puzzling questions: Why is it that generation after generation, most couples who fall in love and marry want to become parents? And how do they decide whether to have just one child or more than one?

Then we trace prenatal development—the 9-month period before birth. Our discussion pays special attention to environmental supports that are necessary for healthy growth, as well as damaging influences that threaten the child's health and survival. Finally, we look at how couples prepare psychologically for the arrival of the baby and start to forge a new sense of self as mother or father.

Motivations For Parenthood

s part of her semester project for my class, Yolanda interviewed her grandmother, asking why she had wanted children and how she settled on a particular family size. Yolanda's grandmother, whose children were born in the 1940s, replied,

We didn't think much about whether or not to have children in those days. We just had them—everybody did. It would have seemed odd not to! I was 22 years old when I had the first of my four children, and I had four because—well, I wouldn't have had just one since we all thought children needed brothers and sisters, and only children could end up spoiled and selfish. Life is more interesting with children, you know. And now that we're older, we've got family we can depend on and grandchildren to enjoy.

WHY HAVE CHILDREN?

In some ways, the reasons for wanting children given by Yolanda's grandmother are like those of contemporary parents. In other ways, they are very different. In the past, the issue of whether to have children was, for many adults, "a biological given or unavoidable cultural demand" (Michaels, 1988, p. 23). Today, in Western industrialized nations, it is a matter of true individual choice. Effective birth control techniques permit adults to avoid having children in most instances. And changing social values allow people to remain childless with much less fear of social criticism and rejection than was the case a generation or two ago.

When American couples are asked about their desire to have children, they mention a variety of advantages and disadvantages, which are listed in Table 3.1. Although some ethnic and regional differences exist, reasons for having children that are most important to all

TABLE 3.1

Advantages and Disadvantages of Parenthood Mentioned by American Couples

ADVANTAGES	DISADVANTAGES
Giving and receiving warmth and affection	Loss of freedom, being tied down
Experiencing the stimulation and fun that children add to life	Financial strain
Being accepted as a responsible and mature member of the community	Family–work conflict—not enough time to meet both child-rearing and job responsibilities
Experiencing new growth and learning opportunities that add meaning to life	Interference with mother's employment opportunities and career progress
Having someone carry on after one's own death	Worries over children's health, safety, and well-being
Gaining a sense of accomplishment and creativity from helping children grow	Risks of bringing up children in a world plagued by crime, war, and pollution
Learning to become less selfish and to sacrifice	Reduced time to spend with husband or wife
Having offspring who help with parents' work or add their own income to the family's resources	Loss of privacy
	Fear that children will turn out badly, through no fault of one's own

Source: Cowan & Cowan, 2000.

groups include the desire for a warm, affectionate relationship and the stimulation and fun that children provide. Also frequently mentioned are growth and learning experiences that children bring into the lives of adults, the desire to have someone carry on after one's own death, and feelings of accomplishment and creativity that come from helping children grow (Cowan & Cowan, 2000; Michaels, 1988).

Most young adults are also aware that having children means years of extra burdens and responsibilities. When asked about the disadvantages of parenthood, they mention "loss of freedom" most often, followed by "financial strain." Indeed, the cost of child rearing is a major factor in modern family planning. According to a conservative government estimate, today's new parents will spend about $260,000 to rear a child from birth through 4 years of college (U.S. Department of Labor, 2000). Finally, many adults worry greatly about family–work conflict—not having enough time to meet both child-rearing and job responsibilities (Hochschild, 1997).

Greater freedom to choose whether, when, and how to have children (see the discussion of reproductive choices in Chapter 2) makes modern family planning more challenging than it was in Yolanda's grandmother's day. As each partner expects to have equal say, childbearing often becomes a matter of delicate negotiation (Cowan & Cowan, 2000). Yet careful weighing of the pros and cons of having children means that many more couples are making informed and personally meaningful decisions—a trend that should increase the chances that they are ready for parenthood and will find it an enriching experience.

HOW LARGE A FAMILY?

In contrast to her grandmother, Yolanda plans to have no more than two children. And she and Jay are talking about whether to limit their family to a single child. In 1960, the average number of children in an American family was 3.1. Today, it is 1.8, a downward trend expected to continue. In other developed countries, the birthrate is even lower—for example, 1.7 in Australia; 1.6 in Austria,

Health counselors explain birth control options to mothers in rural Madagascar. Family planning combined with education helps limit rising birthrates in developing countries. Smaller families mean an enhanced quality of life for both mothers and children.

© PETER BARKER/PANOS PICTURES

Social

ISSUES: EDUCATION

A GLOBAL PERSPECTIVE ON FAMILY PLANNING

Approximately one-fifth of the world's population—one billion people—live in extreme poverty, the majority in slums and shantytowns of developing countries. If current trends in population growth continue, the number of poor will quadruple within the next 60 to 70 years (United Nations, 1998). Poverty and rapid population growth are intertwined: Poverty leads to high birthrates, and rising birthrates heighten poverty and deprivation. Why is this so?

There are many reasons. First, in poor regions of the world where child death rates are high, parents have more children to compensate for the fact that some will certainly die. Second, lack of status, education, and opportunities for women, characteristic of most non-industrialized societies, restrict life choices to early marriage and prolonged childbearing. Third, in regions with few basic services and labor-saving technologies, families often depend on children to help in the fields and at home. Fourth, poverty is associated with the absence of family planning services, which causes birthrates to remain high

even when people begin to realize the advantages of smaller families (Bulatao, 1998). And finally, lack of hope in the future is a major obstacle to life planning in general and family planning in particular.

As a country's population grows, poverty worsens. The labor force expands more quickly than available work, and a new generation of unemployed or underemployed parents emerges. Basic resources, including food, water, land, and fuel, are in shorter supply, and health and educational services are increasingly strained. As a result, overcrowding in urban areas—along with malnutrition, disease, illiteracy, and hopelessness—spreads. A circuit forms through which poverty and high birthrates perpetuate one another.

Two interrelated strategies are especially effective for intervening in this cycle:

- Emphasizing education and literacy, particularly for girls. Years of schooling is a powerful predictor of small family size. Because women with more education have better life op-

portunities, they are more likely to marry at a later age and take advantage of family planning services. As a result, they have fewer, more widely spaced, and healthier children (Caldwell, 1999).

- Making family planning services available to all who want them, in ways that are compatible with each country's cultural and religious traditions. Over the past 40 years, the proportion of married women in the developing world using birth control has increased from 10 to 50 percent, contributing to an overall decline in birthrate in developing countries from 6.1 to 3.3 (United Nations, 1998).

Still, the unmet need for family planning remains high. About 100 million women in developing countries want to limit family size or increase spacing between births (DaVanzo & Adamson, 2000). Yet those with weak reading skills or who are illiterate have difficulty accessing family planning information. Their knowledge about effective birth control is often limited or incorrect

Flourishing careers for women and effective birth control rates are reasons for lower kid rates.

Canada, Great Britain, and Sweden; 1.5 in the Netherlands and Japan; and 1.3 in Germany (Bellamy, 2000; Pearce, Cantisani, & Laihonen, 1999). In addition to more effective birth control, a major reason for this decline is that many women are reaping the economic and personal rewards of a career. A family size of one or two children is more compatible with a woman's decision to divide her energies between family and work.

Children benefit from growing up in small families. Parents who have fewer children are more patient and less punitive. They also have more time to devote to each child's activities, schoolwork, and other special needs. Furthermore, in smaller families, siblings are more likely to be widely spaced (born more than 2 years apart), which adds to the attention and resources parents can invest in each child. Together, these findings may account for the fact that children who grow up in small families are healthier, have somewhat higher intelligence test scores, do better in school, and attain higher levels of education (Powell & Steelman, 1993).

(Gazmararian, Parker, & Baker, 1999). Hence, they have many unintended pregnancies. As Figure 3.1 shows, the world's population continues to increase at an astounding rate because of high birthrates in poverty-stricken, developing countries. Population growth in sub-Saharan Africa is much greater than in Asia and Latin America. In Nigeria, for example, the average woman will give birth to 6.5 children in her lifetime.

Education combined with family planning leads to substantial declines in birthrates and resulting improvements in quality of life for both mothers and children. These benefits carry over to future generations.

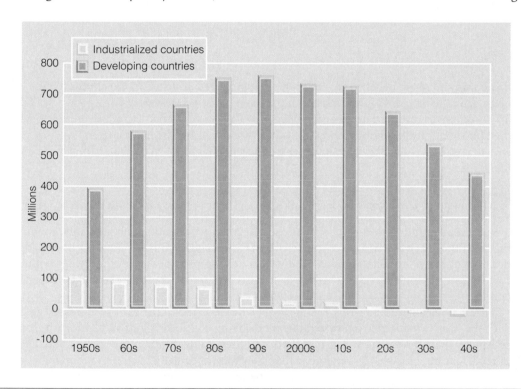

FIGURE 3.1

Population increases by decade in industrialized and developing countries, projected through the first half of the twenty-first century. Although birthrates are declining, the downward trend is very recent for developing nations. The world's population is still growing, with almost all this growth concentrated in developing countries. In the 2030s, the population in industrialized countries will start to decrease, whereas that of developing nations will continue to swell by more than 500 million people. (From DaVanzo & Adamson, 2000.)

However, recall from Chapter 1 that a correlation between family size and children's characteristics does not tell us for sure about causation. Large families are usually less well off economically than smaller ones. Factors associated with low income—crowded housing, inadequate nutrition, and poorly educated and stressed parents—may contribute to the negative relationship between family size and children's well-being. Indeed, evidence supports this idea. Parents with lower intelligence test scores (many of whom are poorly educated) tend to have larger families (Rodgers et al., 2000). And when children of bright, stimulating, economically advantaged parents grow up in large families, unfavorable outcomes associated with large family size are eliminated (Guo & VanWey, 1999). As the Social Issues box above indicates, education and family planning are closely linked. Both are vital for improving children's quality of life, especially in poverty-stricken regions of the world.

Is Yolanda's grandmother right: Are parents who have just one child likely to end up with a spoiled, selfish youngster? As we will see in Chapter 13, a great deal of research challenges

TABLE 3.2

Advantages and Disadvantages of a One-Child Family

ADVANTAGES		DISADVANTAGES	
Mentioned by Parents	Mentioned by Children	Mentioned by Parents	Mentioned by Children
Having time to pursue one's own interests and career	Having no sibling rivalry	Walking a "tightrope" between healthy attention and overindulgence	Not getting to experience the closeness of a sibling relationship
Less financial pressure	Having more privacy		
	Enjoying greater affluence	Having only one chance to "make good" as a parent	Feeling too much pressure from parents to succeed
Not having to worry about "playing favorites" among children	Having a closer parent–child relationship	Being left childless in case of the child's death	Having no one to help care for parents when they get old

Source: Hawke & Knox, 1978.

this commonly held belief. Only children are just as well adjusted as are children with siblings. Still, the one-child family has both pros and cons, as does every family lifestyle. Table 3.2 summarizes results of a survey in which only children and their parents were asked what they liked and disliked about living in a single-child family. The list is a useful one for parents to consider when deciding how many children would best fit their personal and family life plans.

FIGURE 3.2

First births to American women of different ages in 1970 and 1998. The birthrate decreased during this period for women 20 to 24 years of age, whereas it increased for women 25 years and older. For women in their thirties, the birthrate more than doubled. (Adapted from U.S. Department of Health and Human Services, 2000i; Ventura, 1989.)

IS THERE A BEST TIME DURING ADULTHOOD TO HAVE A CHILD?

Yolanda's grandmother had her first child in her early twenties. Yolanda is pregnant for the first time at age 28. Many people believe that women giving birth in their twenties is ideal, not only because the risk of having a baby with a chromosomal disorder increases with age (see Chapter 2) but also because younger parents have more energy to keep up with active children.

However, as Figure 3.2 reveals, first births to women in their thirties have increased greatly over the past two decades. Many people are delaying childbearing until their education is complete, their careers are well established, and they know they can support a child. Older parents may be somewhat less energetic than they were at earlier ages, but they are financially better off and emotionally more mature. For these reasons, they may be better able to invest in parenting.

Nevertheless, reproductive capacity does decline with age. Fertility problems among women increase from age 15 to 50, with a sharp rise in the mid-thirties. Between ages 25 and 34, nearly 14 percent of women are affected, a figure that climbs to 26 percent for 35- to 44-year-olds (U.S. Department of Health and Human Services, 1999a). Age also affects male reproductive capacity. Amount of semen and concentration of sperm in each ejaculation gradually decline after age 30 (Ford et al., 2000). Although there is no best time during adulthood to begin parenthood, individuals who decide to put off childbirth until well into their thirties or early forties risk having fewer children than they desire or none at all.

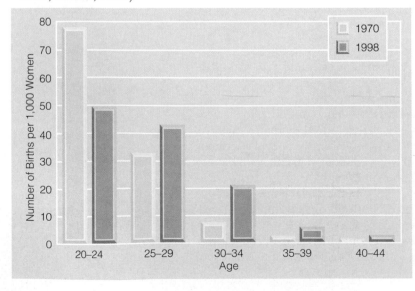

review   *Why are poverty and limited education linked to large family size? What are the consequences of a high birthrate for children's development and a nation's future?*

apply   *Rhonda and Mark are career-oriented, 35-year-old parents of an only child. They are thinking about having a second baby. What factors should they keep in mind as they decide whether to add to their family at this time in their lives?*

reflect   *Return to Table 3.1 on page 99, which lists advantages and disadvantages of parenthood. Which are most important and which are least important to you? What is your ideal family size? Explain.*

Prenatal Development

The sperm and ovum that unite to form the new individual are uniquely suited for the task of reproduction. The ovum is a tiny sphere, measuring $1/175$ inch in diameter, that is barely visible to the naked eye as a dot the size of a period at the end of this sentence. But in its microscopic world, it is a giant—the largest cell in the human body. The ovum's size makes it a perfect target for the much smaller sperm, which measure only $1/500$ inch.

CONCEPTION

About once every 28 days, in the middle of a woman's menstrual cycle, an ovum bursts from one of her *ovaries,* two walnut-sized organs located deep inside her abdomen (see Figure 3.3 on page 104). Surrounded by thousands of nurse cells that will feed and protect it along its path, the ovum is drawn into one of two *fallopian tubes*—long, thin structures that lead to the hollow, soft-lined uterus. While the ovum is traveling, the spot on the ovary from which it was released, now called the *corpus luteum,* begins to secrete hormones that prepare the lining of the uterus to receive a fertilized ovum. If pregnancy does not occur, the corpus luteum shrinks, and the lining of the uterus is discarded 2 weeks later with menstruation.

The male produces sperm in vast numbers—an average of 300 million a day—in the *testes,* two glands located in the *scrotum,* sacs that lie just behind the penis. In the final process of maturation, each sperm develops a tail that permits it to swim long distances, upstream in the female reproductive tract, through the *cervix* (opening of the uterus), and into the *fallopian tube,* where fertilization usually takes place. The journey is difficult, and many sperm die. Only 300 to 500 reach the ovum, if one happens to be present. Sperm live for up to 6 days and can lie in wait for the ovum, which survives for only 1 day after being released into the fallopian tube. However, most conceptions result from intercourse during a 3-day period—on the day of or during the 2 days preceding ovulation (Wilcox, Weinberg, & Baird, 1995).

With conception, the story of prenatal development begins to unfold. The vast changes that take place during the 38 weeks of pregnancy are usually divided into three phases: (1) the period of the zygote, (2) the period of the embryo, and (3) the period of the fetus. As we look at what happens in each, you may find it useful to refer to Table 3.3 on page 105, which summarizes major milestones of prenatal development.

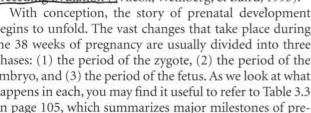

In this photo taken with the aid of a powerful microscope, sperm penetrate the surface of the enormous-looking ovum, the largest cell in the human body. When one sperm is successful at fertilizing the ovum, the resulting zygote will begin duplicating into the new organism.

JACK BURNS/ACE/PHOTOTAKE

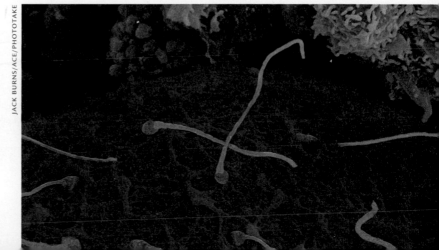

Period of the zygote: seventh to ninth day. The fertilized ovum duplicates at an increasingly rapid rate, forming a hollow ball of cells, or blastocyst, by the fourth day after fertilization. Here the blastocyst, magnified thousands of times, burrows into the uterine lining between the seventh and ninth day.

THE PERIOD OF THE ZYGOTE

The period of the zygote lasts about 2 weeks, from fertilization until the tiny mass of cells drifts down and out of the fallopian tube and attaches itself to the wall of the uterus. The zygote's first cell duplication is long and drawn out; it is not complete until about 30 hours after conception. Gradually, new cells are added at a faster rate. By the fourth day, 60 to 70 cells exist that form a hollow, fluid-filled ball called a **blastocyst** (refer again to Figure 3.3). The cells on the inside, called the **embryonic disk,** will become the new organism; the thin outer ring of cells, termed the **trophoblast,** will become the structures that provide the organism with protective covering and nourishment.

■ **IMPLANTATION.** Sometime between the seventh and ninth days, **implantation** occurs: the blastocyst burrows deep into the uterine lining. Surrounded by the woman's nourishing blood, it starts to grow in earnest. At first, the trophoblast (protective outer layer) multiplies fastest. It forms a membrane, called the **amnion,** that encloses the developing organism in

blastocyst
The zygote 4 days after fertilization, when the tiny mass of cells forms a hollow, fluid-filled ball.

embryonic disk
A small cluster of cells on the inside of the blastocyst, from which the new organism will develop.

trophoblast
The thin outer ring of cells of the blastocyst, which will become the structures that provide protective covering and nourishment to the new organism.

implantation
Attachment of the blastocyst to the uterine lining 7 to 9 days after fertilization.

amnion
The inner membrane that forms a protective covering around the prenatal organism.

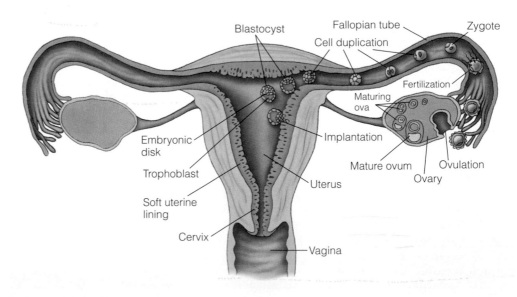

FIGURE 3.3

Journey of the ovum to the uterus. Once every 28 days, an ovum matures, is released from one of the woman's ovaries, and is drawn into the fallopian tube. After fertilization, it begins to duplicate, at first slowly and then more rapidly. By the fourth day, it forms a hollow, fluid-filled ball called a blastocyst. The inner cells, or embryonic disk, will become the new organism; the outer cells, or trophoblast, will provide protective covering. At the end of the first week, the blastocyst begins to implant in the uterine lining. (Adapted from K. L. Moore & T. V. N. Persaud, 1998, *Before We Are Born,* 5th ed., Philadelphia: Saunders, p. 44. Reprinted by permission of the publisher and author.)

Zygote: 1–2 weeks
embryo: 3–8 weeks
fetus ≐ 9–38 weeks

TABLE 3.3

Major Milestones of Prenatal Development

TRIMESTER	PERIOD	WEEKS	LENGTH AND WEIGHT	MAJOR EVENTS
First	Zygote	1		The one-celled zygote multiplies and forms a blastocyst.
		2		The blastocyst burrows into the uterine lining. Structures that feed and protect the developing organism begin to form—amnion, chorion, yolk sac, placenta, and umbilical cord.
	Embryo	3–4	¼ inch	A primitive brain and spinal cord appear. Heart, muscles, backbone, ribs, and digestive tract begin to develop.
	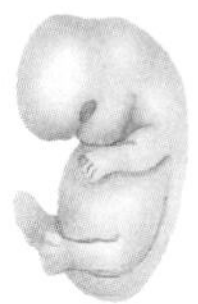	5–8	1 inch; ⅟₇ ounce	Many external body structures (face, arms, legs, toes, fingers) and internal organs form. The sense of touch begins to develop, and the embryo can move.
	Fetus 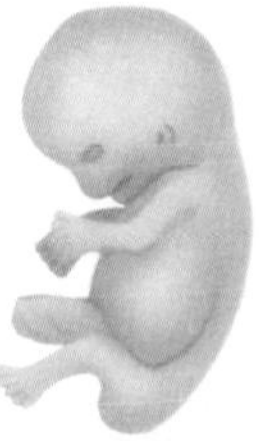	9–12	3 inches; less than 1 ounce	Rapid increase in size begins. Nervous system, organs, and muscles become organized and connected, and new behavioral capacities (kicking, thumb sucking, mouth opening, and rehearsal of breathing) appear. External genitals are well formed, and the fetus's sex is evident.
Second	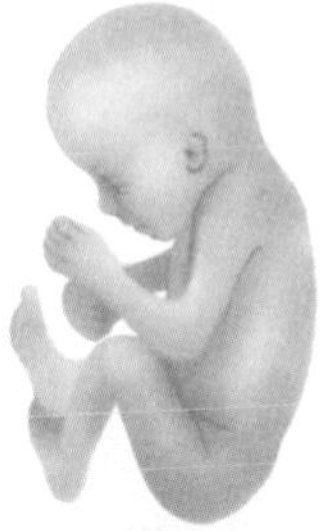	13–24	12 inches; 1.8 pounds	The fetus continues to enlarge rapidly. In the middle of this period, fetal movements can be felt by the mother. Vernix and lanugo keep the fetus's skin from chapping in the amniotic fluid. All the neurons that will ever be produced in the brain are present by 24 weeks. Eyes are sensitive to light, and the fetus reacts to sound.
Third	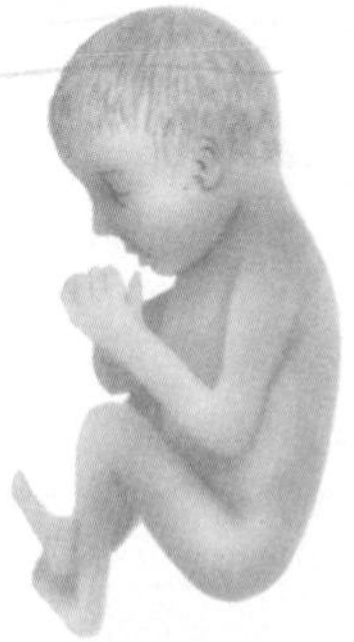	25–38	20 inches; 7.5 pounds	The fetus has a chance of survival if born during this time. Size increases. Lungs mature. Rapid brain development causes sensory and behavioral capacities to expand. In the middle of this period, a layer of fat is added under the skin. Antibodies are transmitted from mother to fetus to protect against disease. Most fetuses rotate into an upside-down position in preparation for birth.

Sources: Moore & Persaud, 1998; Nilsson & Hamberger, 1990.

amniotic fluid. The amnion helps keep the temperature of the prenatal world constant and provides a cushion against any jolts caused by the woman's movement. A *yolk sac* also appears. It produces blood cells until the developing liver, spleen, and bone marrow are mature enough to take over this function (Moore & Persaud, 1998).

The events of these first 2 weeks are delicate and uncertain. As many as 30 percent of zygotes do not make it through this phase. In some, the sperm and ovum do not join properly.

amniotic fluid
The fluid that fills the amnion, helping to keep temperature constant and to provide a cushion against jolts caused by the mother's movement.

FIGURE 3.4

Cross-section of the uterus showing detail of the placenta. The fetus's blood flows from the umbilical cord arteries into the chorionic villi and returns via the umbilical cord vein. The mother's blood circulates in spaces surrounding the chorionic villi. A membrane between the two blood supplies permits food and oxygen to be delivered and waste products to be carried away. The two blood supplies do not mix directly. The umbilical arteries carry oxygen-poor blood (shown in blue) to the placenta, and the umbilical vein carries oxygen-rich blood (shown in red) to the fetus. (Adapted from K. L. Moore and T. V. N. Persaud, 1998, *Before We Are Born,* 5th ed., Philadelphia: Saunders, p. 128. Reprinted by permission of the publisher and the author.)

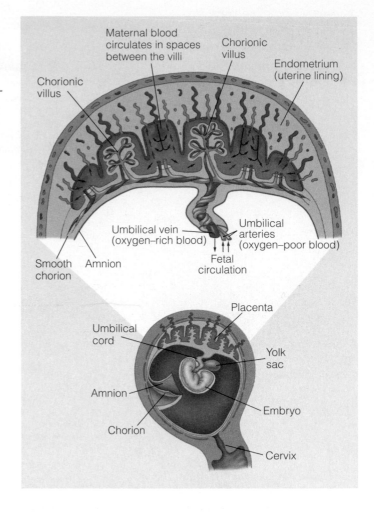

In others, for some unknown reason, cell duplication never begins. By preventing implantation in these cases, nature eliminates most prenatal abnormalities in the very earliest stages of development (Sadler, 1995).

■ **THE PLACENTA AND UMBILICAL CORD.** By the end of the second week, cells of the trophoblast form another protective membrane—the chorion, which surrounds the amnion. From the **chorion,** tiny fingerlike *villi,* or blood vessels, begin to emerge.[1] As these villi burrow into the uterine wall, a special organ called the **placenta** starts to develop. By bringing the mother's and the embryo's blood close together, the placenta will permit food and oxygen to reach the developing organism and waste products to be carried away. A membrane forms that allows these substances to be exchanged but prevents the mother's and the embryo's blood from mixing directly (see Figure 3.4).

The placenta is connected to the developing organism by the **umbilical cord.** In the period of the zygote, it first appears as a primitive body stalk, but during the course of pregnancy, it grows to a length of 1 to 3 feet. The umbilical cord contains one large vein that delivers blood loaded with nutrients and two arteries that remove waste products. The force of blood flowing through the cord keeps it firm, much like a garden hose, so it seldom tangles while the embryo, like a space-walking astronaut, floats freely in its fluid-filled chamber (Moore & Persaud, 1998).

---

[1]Recall from Chapter 2 that *chorionic villus sampling* is the prenatal diagnostic method that can be performed earliest, by 6 to 8 weeks after conception. In this procedure, tissues from the ends of the villi are removed and examined for genetic abnormalities.

chorion
The outer membrane that forms a protective covering around the prenatal organism. It sends out tiny, fingerlike villi, from which the placenta begins to develop.

placenta
The organ that separates the mother's bloodstream from the embryo or fetal bloodstream but permits exchange of nutrients and waste products.

umbilical cord
The long cord connecting the prenatal organism to the placenta; it delivers nutrients and removes waste products.

Beginning
of ears

Brain

Will become
eyes

Will become
the jaw

Heart

Lower limb
buds will
become legs

Upper limb
buds will
become arms

Beginning of
muscles and
backbone

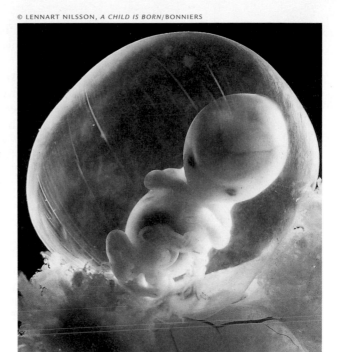

Period of the embryo: fourth week. In actual size, this 4-week-old embryo is only ¼ inch long, but many body structures have begun to form.

Period of the embryo: seventh week. The embryo's posture is more upright. Body structures—eyes, nose, arms, legs, and internal organs—are more distinct. An embryo of this age responds to touch. It also can move, although at less than one inch long and an ounce in weight, it is still too tiny to be felt by the mother.

By the end of the period of the zygote, the developing organism has found food and shelter. Already, it is a very complex being. These dramatic beginnings take place before most mothers know they are pregnant.

THE PERIOD OF THE EMBRYO

The period of the **embryo** lasts from implantation through the eighth week of pregnancy. During these brief 6 weeks, the most rapid prenatal changes take place, as the groundwork for all body structures and internal organs is laid down. Because all parts of the body are forming, the embryo is especially vulnerable to interference with healthy development. But a short time span of embryonic growth helps limit opportunities for serious harm.

embryonic disk:
ectoderm
mesoderm
endoderm

■ **LAST HALF OF THE FIRST MONTH.** In the first week of this period, the embryonic disk forms three layers of cells: (1) the *ectoderm,* which will become the nervous system and skin; (2) the *mesoderm,* from which will develop the muscles, skeleton, circulatory system, and other internal organs; and (3) the *endoderm,* which will become the digestive system, lungs, urinary tract, and glands. These three layers give rise to all parts of the body.

At first, the nervous system develops fastest. The ectoderm folds over to form a **neural tube,** or primitive spinal cord. At 3½ weeks, the top swells to form a brain. Production of *neurons* (nerve cells that store and transmit information) begins deep inside the neural tube. Once formed, neurons travel along tiny threads to their permanent locations, where they will form the major parts of the brain (Nelson & Bosquet, 2000).

While the nervous system is developing, the heart begins to pump blood through the embryo's circulatory system, and muscles, backbone, ribs, and digestive tract start to

embryo
The prenatal organism from 2 to 8 weeks after conception, during which time the foundations of all body structures and internal organs are laid down.

neural tube
The primitive spinal cord that develops from the ectoderm, the top of which swells to form the brain.

appear. At the end of the first month, the curled embryo consists of millions of organized groups of cells with specific functions, although it is only one-fourth inch long.

■ **THE SECOND MONTH.** In the second month, growth continues rapidly. The eyes, ears, nose, jaw, and neck form. Tiny buds become arms, legs, fingers, and toes. Internal organs are more distinct: the intestines grow, the heart develops separate chambers, and the liver and spleen take over production of blood cells so that the yolk sac is no longer needed. Changing body proportions cause the embryo's posture to become more upright. Now 1 inch long and one-seventh of an ounce in weight, the embryo can already sense its world. It responds to touch, particularly in the mouth area and on the soles of the feet. And it can move, although its tiny flutters are still too light to be felt by the mother (Nilsson & Hamberger, 1990).

THE PERIOD OF THE FETUS

Lasting until the end of pregnancy, the period of the **fetus** is the "growth and finishing" phase. During this longest prenatal period, the developing organism begins to increase rapidly in size. The rate of body growth is extraordinary, especially from the ninth to the twentieth week (Moore & Persaud, 1998).

■ **THE THIRD MONTH.** In the third month, the organs, muscles, and nervous system start to become organized and connected. The brain signals, and in response, the fetus kicks, bends its arms, forms a fist, curls its toes, opens its mouth, and even sucks its thumb. The tiny lungs begin to expand and contract in an early rehearsal of breathing movements (Joseph, 2000). By the twelfth week, the external genitals are well formed, and the sex of the fetus is evident. Using ultrasound, Yolanda's doctor could see that she would have a boy (although Yolanda and Jay asked not to be told the fetus's sex). Other finishing touches appear, such as fingernails, toenails, tooth buds, and eyelids that open and close. The heartbeat is now stronger and can be heard through a stethoscope.

Prenatal development is sometimes divided into **trimesters,** or three equal periods of time. At the end of the third month, the first trimester is complete. Two more must pass before the fetus is fully prepared to survive outside the womb.

■ **THE SECOND TRIMESTER.** By the middle of the second trimester, between 17 and 20 weeks, the new being has grown large enough that the mother can feel its movements. If we could look inside the uterus, we would find the fetus completely covered with a white cheeselike substance called **vernix.** It protects the skin from chapping during the long months spent in the amniotic fluid. A white, downy covering called **lanugo** also appears over the entire body, helping the vernix stick to the skin.

At the end of the second trimester, many organs are quite well developed. And a major milestone is reached in brain development, in that most neurons are in place; few will be produced after this time. However, *glial cells*, which support and feed the neurons, continue to increase at a rapid rate throughout the remaining months of pregnancy, as well as after birth.

Brain growth means new behavioral capacities. The 20-week-old fetus can be stimulated as well as irritated by sound. And if a doctor has reason to look inside the uterus using fetoscopy (see Chapter 2, page 66), fetuses try to shield their eyes from the light with their hands, indicating that the sense of sight has begun to emerge (Nilsson & Hamberger, 1990). Still, a fetus born at this time cannot survive. Its lungs are quite immature, and the brain has not yet developed enough to control breathing movements and body temperature.

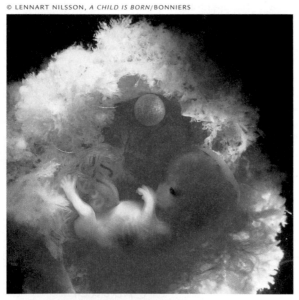

Period of the fetus: eleventh week. The organism increases rapidly in size, and body structures are completed. At 11 weeks, the brain and muscles are better connected. The fetus can kick, bend its arms, open and close its hands and mouth, and suck its thumb. Notice the yolk sac, which shrinks as pregnancy advances. The internal organs have taken over its function of producing blood cells.

© LENNART NILSSON, *A CHILD IS BORN*/BONNIERS

© LENNART NILSSON, *A CHILD IS BORN*/BONNIERS

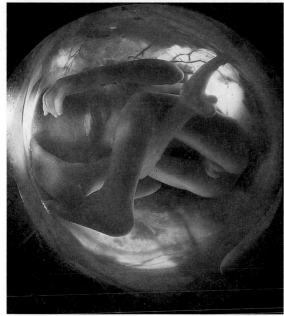

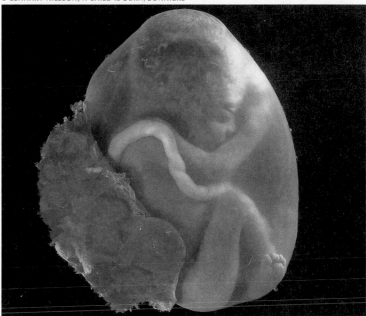

Period of the fetus: twenty-second week. This fetus is almost a foot long and weighs slightly more than a pound. Its movements can be felt easily by the mother and other family members who place a hand on her abdomen. The fetus has reached the age of viability; if born, it has a slim chance of surviving.

Period of the fetus: thirty-sixth week. This fetus fills the uterus. To support its need for nourishment, the umbilical cord and placenta have grown large. Notice the vernix (cheeselike substance) on the skin, which protects it from chapping. The fetus has accumulated a layer of fat to assist with temperature regulation after birth. In 2 more weeks, it would be full term.

■ **THE THIRD TRIMESTER.** During the final trimester, a fetus born early has a chance for survival outside the womb. The point at which the baby can first survive is called the **age of viability.** It occurs sometime between 22 and 26 weeks (Moore & Persaud, 1998). If born between the seventh and eighth months, a baby would still have trouble breathing, and oxygen assistance would be necessary. Although the respiratory center of the brain is now mature, tiny air sacs in the lungs are not yet ready to inflate and exchange carbon dioxide for oxygen.

The brain continues to make great strides during the last 3 months. The *cerebral cortex,* the most highly evolved part of our brain and the seat of human intelligence, enlarges (see Figure 3.5 on page 111). As neurological organization improves, the fetus spends more time awake. At 20 weeks, the fetal heart rate reveals no periods of alertness. But by 28 weeks, fetuses are awake about 11 percent of the time, a figure that rises to 16 percent just before birth (DiPietro et al., 1996a). And from the vigor of its movements and its daily cycles of activity and rest, the fetus takes on the beginnings of a personality (see the Biology and Environment box on page 110).

The third trimester also brings greater responsiveness to external stimulation. Around 24 weeks, fetuses can first feel pain, so after this time painkillers should be used in any surgical procedures (Royal College of Obstetricians and Gynecologists, 1997). When Yolanda turned on an electric mixer, the fetus reacted with a forceful startle. By 28 weeks, fetuses blink their eyes in reaction to nearby sounds (DiPietro et al., 1996a; Kisilevsky & Low, 1998). And in the last weeks of pregnancy, they learn to prefer the tone and rhythm of their mother's voice. In one clever study, mothers were asked to read aloud Dr. Seuss's lively book *The Cat in the Hat* to their unborn babies for the last 6 weeks of pregnancy. After birth, their infants were given a chance to suck on nipples that turned on recordings of the mother reading this book or different rhyming stories. The infants sucked hardest to hear *The Cat in the Hat,* the sound they had come to know while still in the womb (DeCasper & Spence, 1986).

fetus
The prenatal organism from the beginning of the third month to the end of pregnancy, during which time completion of body structures and dramatic growth in size takes place.

trimesters
Three equal time periods in prenatal development, each of which lasts 3 months.

vernix
A white, cheeselike substance that covers the fetus and prevents the skin from chapping due to constant exposure to amniotic fluid.

lanugo
A white, downy hair that covers the entire body of the fetus, helping the vernix stick to the skin.

age of viability
The age at which the fetus can first survive if born early. Occurs sometime between 22 and 26 weeks.

Biology & ENVIRONMENT

TEMPERAMENT IN THE WOMB

As Yolanda, in her seventh month of pregnancy, rested one afternoon, she felt several bursts of fetal activity, interspersed with quiet periods. "Hey, little one," she whispered, looking down at her large abdomen as it bulged after a foot kick, "you're on the move again. You always do this when I try to take a nap!" Then Yolanda wondered, "Can the fetus's behavior tell us anything about what he or she will be like after birth?"

Yolanda's question is at the heart of current efforts to determine whether individual differences in temperament have genetic origins. The earlier temperamental traits can be identified, the greater the likelihood that heredity contributes to those traits. Until recently, limited access to the fetus made it hard to study the relationship between fetal measures and temperament after birth. Today, sophisticated equipment for monitoring fetal responses permits researchers to address this issue.

In the most extensive study to date, 31 volunteer women, whose newborns were delivered healthy and full term, were monitored periodically during the prenatal period, from 20 weeks to just before birth (DiPietro et al., 1996b). During each session, the mothers lay quietly while a variety of fetal measures, including heart rate and activity level, were recorded. Then, at 3 and 6 months after birth, the mothers were asked to rate various aspects of their baby's temperament, including fussiness, adaptability to new persons and situations, activity level, and regularity of eating and sleeping.

Findings revealed that the pattern of fetal activity in the last few weeks of pregnancy was the best predictor of infant temperament. Fetuses (like Yolanda's) who cycled between quiet and active periods tended to become calm babies with predictable sleep–waking schedules. In contrast, fetuses who were highly active for long

stretches were more likely to become difficult, unpredictable babies—fussy, especially when confronted with new people and situations; irregular in eating and sleeping habits; constantly wriggling and squirming; and waking often during the night (see Figure 3.6).

But we must keep in mind that these links between prenatal measures and infant characteristics are only modest. In Chapter 7, we will see that sensitive care can modify a difficult baby's temperamental style. Furthermore, researchers have yet to determine whether fetal activity predicts *actual* infant behavior, not just *maternal judgments* of that behavior.

But if the relationships just described hold up, then parents whose fetuses are very active can prepare for extra caregiving challenges. Recognizing that their baby may have a fussy, difficult disposition, they can take extra steps to provide a sympathetic environment as soon as the baby is born.

FIGURE 3.6

Temperament scores 6 months after birth of highly active fetuses versus other fetuses. Fetuses who were very active in the last weeks of pregnancy developed into 6-month-old babies who were fussier, less adaptable to new people and situations, more irregular in eating and sleeping, and more active, as judged by their mothers. They also woke more often at night (not shown in the graph). (Adapted from DiPietro et al., 1996b.)

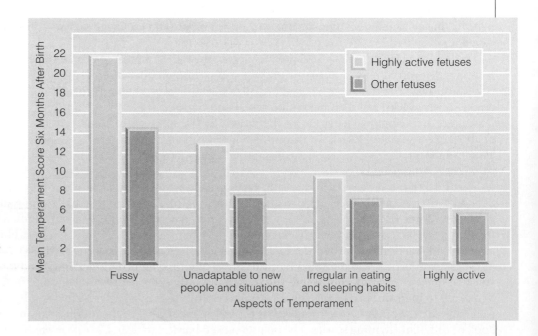

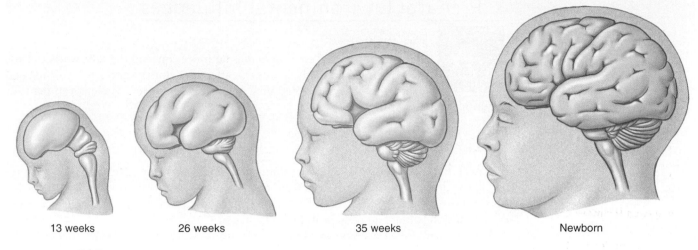

13 weeks   26 weeks   35 weeks   Newborn

FIGURE 3.5

Growth of the brain during the prenatal period, shown one-half actual size. The *cerebral cortex,* the outer layer of gray matter, is responsible for higher brain functions, including sensation, voluntary movement, and thought. At 13 weeks, its surface is smooth. By 26 weeks (beginning of the third trimester), grooves and convolutions start to appear. These permit a dramatic increase in surface area without extensive increase in head size. As a result, maximum prenatal brain growth takes place while still permitting the full-term baby's head to pass through the birth canal. As cortical folds become more apparent (35 weeks), fetal sensory and behavioral capacities expand. The fetus spends more time awake, responds to external stimulation, and moves more vigorously (although less often as it fills the uterus). It also learns to prefer familiar sounds, such as the tone and rhythm of the mother's voice. (Adapted from Moore, Persaud, & Shiota, 1994.)

Brain development + physical growth contribute to a decline in movement.

During the final 3 months, the fetus gains more than 5 pounds and grows 7 inches. As it fills the uterus, it gradually moves less often. In addition, brain development, which enables the organism to inhibit behavior, may also contribute to a decline in physical activity (DiPietro et al., 1996a).

In the eighth month, a layer of fat is added under the skin to assist with temperature regulation. The fetus also receives antibodies from the mother's blood to protect against illnesses, since the newborn's own immune system will not work well until several months after birth. In the last weeks, most fetuses assume an upside-down position, partly because of the shape of the uterus and partly because of gravity: the head is heavier than the feet. Growth slows, and birth is about to take place.

Ask YOURSELF...

review   *Why is the period of the embryo regarded as the most dramatic prenatal phase? Why is the period of the fetus called the "growth and finishing" phase?*

apply   *Amy, who is 2 months pregnant, wonders how the developing organism is being fed and what parts of the body have formed. "I don't look pregnant yet. Does that mean that not much development has taken place?" she asks. How would you respond to Amy?*

connect   *How does brain development relate to fetal behavior? What implications do individual differences in fetal behavior have for the baby's temperament after birth?*

Prenatal Environmental Influences

Although the prenatal environment is far more constant than the world outside the womb, a great many factors can affect the embryo and fetus. Yolanda and Jay learned that they could do a great deal to create a safe environment for development before birth.

TERATOGENS

The term **teratogen** refers to any environmental agent that causes damage during the prenatal period. It comes from the Greek word *teras,* meaning "malformation" or "monstrosity." This label was selected because scientists first learned about harmful prenatal influences from cases in which babies had been profoundly damaged.

Yet the harm done by teratogens is not always simple and straightforward. It depends on the following factors:

- *Dose.* We will see as we discuss particular teratogens that larger doses over longer time periods usually have more negative effects.

- *Heredity.* The genetic makeup of the mother and the developing organism plays an important role. Some individuals are better able to withstand harmful environments.

- *Other negative influences.* The presence of several negative factors at once, such as poor nutrition, lack of medical care, and additional teratogens, can worsen the impact of a single harmful agent.

- *Age of the prenatal organism.* The effects of teratogens vary with the age of the organism at time of exposure.

We can best understand this last idea if we think of prenatal development in terms of the *sensitive period* concept introduced in Chapter 1. Recall that a sensitive period is a limited time span in which a part of the body or a behavior is biologically prepared to develop rapidly. During that time, it is especially vulnerable to its surroundings. If the environment is harmful, then damage occurs, and recovery is difficult and sometimes impossible.

Figure 3.7 summarizes sensitive periods during prenatal development. Look carefully at it, and you will see that some parts of the body, such as the brain and eye, have long sensitive periods that extend throughout the prenatal phase. Other sensitive periods, such as those for the limbs and palate, are much shorter. Figure 3.7 also indicates that we can make some general statements about the timing of harmful influences. In the period of the zygote, before implantation, teratogens rarely have any impact. If they do, the tiny mass of cells is usually so completely damaged that it dies. The embryonic period is the time when serious defects are most likely to occur, since the foundations for all body parts are being laid down. During the fetal period, damage caused by teratogens is usually minor. However, some organs, such as the brain, eye, and genitals, can still be strongly affected.

The effects of teratogens are not limited to immediate physical damage. Although deformities of the body are easy to notice, some health effects may not show up for decades (see the Social Issues: Health box on pages 114–115). Psychological consequences also may be delayed and result, indirectly, from physical damage. For example, a defect resulting from drugs the mother took during pregnancy can change the reactions of others to the child as well as the child's ability to move about the environment. Over time, parent–child interaction, peer relations, and opportunities to explore may suffer. These experiences, in turn, can have far-reaching consequences for cognitive, emotional, and social development (Friedman, 1996).

Notice how an important idea about development discussed in earlier chapters is at work here—that of *bidirectional influences* between child and environment. Now let's take a look at what scientists have discovered about a variety of teratogens.

teratogen
Any environmental agent that causes damage during the prenatal period.

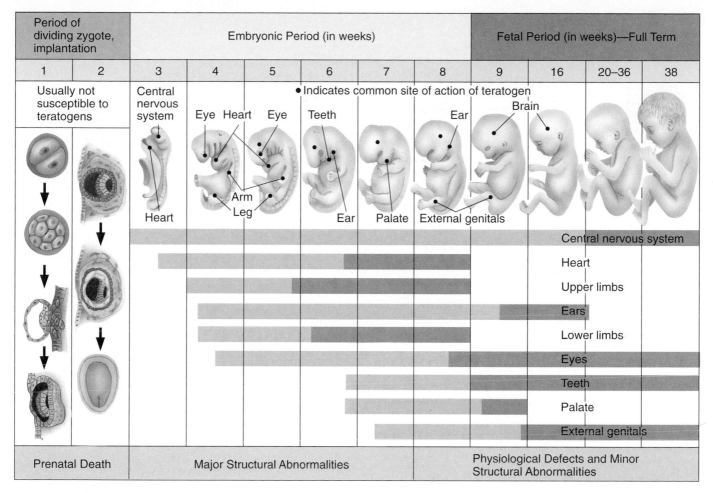

FIGURE 3.7

Sensitive periods in prenatal development. Each organ or structure has a sensitive period, during which its development may be disturbed. Gray horizontal lines indicate highly sensitive periods. Pink horizontal lines indicate periods that are somewhat less sensitive to teratogens, although damage can occur. (From K. L. Moore & T. V. N. Persaud, 1998, *Before We Are Born,* 5th ed., Philadelphia: Saunders, p. 166. Reprinted by permission of the publisher and the author.)

■ **PRESCRIPTION AND NONPRESCRIPTION DRUGS.** In the early 1960s, the world learned a tragic lesson about drugs and prenatal development. At that time, a sedative called **thalidomide** was widely available in Canada, Europe, and South America. When taken by mothers 4 to 6 weeks after conception, thalidomide produced gross deformities of the embryo's developing arms and legs and, less frequently, damage to the ears, heart, kidneys, and genitals. About 7,000 infants worldwide were affected (Moore & Persaud, 1998). As children exposed to thalidomide grew older, many scored below average in intelligence. Perhaps the drug damaged the central nervous system directly. Or the child-rearing conditions of these severely deformed youngsters may have impaired their intellectual development (Vorhees & Mollnow, 1987).

Another medication, a synthetic hormone called *diethylstilbestrol (DES),* was widely prescribed between 1945 and 1970 to prevent miscarriages. As daughters of these mothers reached adolescence and young adulthood, they showed unusually high rates of cancer of the vagina and malformations of the uterus. When they tried to have children, their pregnancies more often resulted in prematurity, low birth weight, and miscarriage than those of non-DES-exposed women. Young men showed an increased risk of genital abnormalities and cancer of the testes (Giusti, Iwamoto, & Hatch, 1995; Palmlund, 1996).

thalidomide
A sedative widely available in Europe, Canada, and South America in the early 1960s. When taken by mothers between the fourth and sixth weeks after conception, it produced gross deformities of the embryo's arms and legs.

Social ISSUES : HEALTH

THE PRENATAL ENVIRONMENT AND HEALTH IN LATER LIFE

When Michael entered the world 55 years ago, 6 weeks premature and weighing only 4 pounds, the doctor delivering him wasn't sure he would make it. Michael not only survived but enjoyed good health until his mid-forties, when, during a routine medical checkup, he was diagnosed with high blood pressure and adult-onset diabetes. Michael wasn't overweight, didn't smoke, and didn't eat high-fat foods—risk factors for these conditions. Nor did the illnesses run in his family. Could the roots of Michael's health problems date back to his prenatal development? Increasing evidence suggests that prenatal environmental factors—ones not toxic (like tobacco or alcohol) but rather fairly subtle, such as the flow of nutrients and hormones across the placenta—can affect an individual's health decades later (Wheeler, Barker, & O'Brien, 1999).

LOW BIRTH WEIGHT AND HEART DISEASE, STROKE, AND DIABETES

Carefully controlled animal experiments reveal that a poorly nourished, underweight fetus experiences changes in body structure and function that result in cardiovascular disease in adulthood (Dennison et al., 1997). To explore this relationship in humans, researchers tapped public records, gathering the birth weights of every male baby born in two areas of England between 1907 and 1930—more than 13,000 cases. Then, for those who had died, the cause of death was obtained. Men weighing less than 5 pounds at birth had a 50 percent greater chance of dying of heart disease and stroke, after SES and a variety of other health risks were controlled. The birth weight–cardiovascular disease connection was strongest for men whose weight-to-length ratio at birth was very low—a sign of prenatal growth stunting (Martyn, Barker, & Osmond, 1996).

In other large-scales studies, a consistent link between low birth weight and heart disease, stroke, and diabetes in middle adulthood has emerged—for both sexes and in several countries, including Finland, India, Jamaica, and the United States (Fall et al., 1998; Forsén et al., 2000; Rich-Edwards et al., 1997, 1999). Smallness itself does not cause later health problems; rather, researchers believe that complex, associated factors are involved.

Some speculate that a poorly nourished fetus diverts large amounts of blood to the brain, causing organs in the abdomen, such as the liver and kidney (involved in controlling cholesterol and blood pressure), to be undersized (Barker, 1999). The result is heightened later risk for heart disease and stroke. In the case of diabetes, inadequate prenatal nutrition may permanently impair functioning of the pancreas, leading glucose intolerance to rise as the person ages (Rich-Edwards et al., 1999). Yet another hypothesis, supported by both animal and human research, is that the malfunctioning placentas of some expectant mothers permit high levels of stress hormones to reach the fetus. These hormones retard fetal growth, increase fetal blood pressure, and promote hyperglycemia (excess blood sugar), predisposing the developing person to later disease (Benediktsson et al., 1997).

HIGH BIRTH WEIGHT AND BREAST CANCER

The other prenatal growth extreme—high birth weight—is related to breast cancer, the most common malignancy in adult women (Potischman & Troisi, 1999). In one study, the mothers of 589 nurses with invasive breast cancer and 1,569 nurses who did not have breast cancer were asked to provide their daughter's birth weight, family health history (such as relatives diag-

---

[handwritten margin note: Drugs w/ small molecules can enter the placenta & affect the baby"]

Any drug taken by the mother that has a molecule small enough to penetrate the placental barrier can enter the embryonic or fetal bloodstream. Despite the bitter lesson of thalidomide, many pregnant women continue to take over-the-counter drugs without consulting their doctors. Aspirin is one of the most common. Several studies suggest that repeated use of aspirin is linked to low birth weight, infant death around the time of birth, poorer motor development, and lower intelligence test scores in early childhood (Barr et al., 1990; Streissguth et al., 1987). Other research, however, fails to confirm these findings (see, for example, Hauth et al., 1995).

Coffee, tea, cola, and cocoa contain another frequently consumed drug, caffeine. Heavy caffeine intake (more than 3 cups of coffee per day) is associated with low birth weight, prematurity, miscarriage, and newborn withdrawal symptoms, such as irritability and vomiting

nosed with breast cancer), and pre-natal and early life exposures (for example, smoking during pregnancy). The nurses themselves provided information on adult health. After other risk factors were controlled, high birth weight—especially more than 8.7 pounds—emerged as a clear predictor of breast cancer (see Figure 3.8). Researchers think that the culprit is excessive maternal estrogen during pregnancy, which promotes large fetal size and also

alters beginning breast tissue so that it may respond to estrogen in adulthood by becoming malignant (Michels et al., 1996).

PREVENTION

The prenatal development–later-life illness relationships emerging in research are not inevitable. Rather, prenatal environmental conditions *influence* adult health, and the steps we take to protect our health can prevent

prenatal risks from becoming reality. Researchers advise that children and adults who were low birth weight get regular medical checkups and attend to diet, weight, fitness, and stress—controllable factors that contribute to heart disease and adult-onset diabetes. And high-birth-weight women should be conscientious about breast self-exams and mammograms, which permit breast cancer to be detected early and, in many instances, cured.

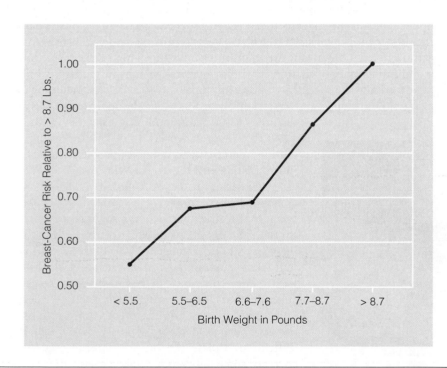

FIGURE 3.8

Relationship of birth weight to breast-cancer risk in adulthood. In a study of 589 nurses with invasive breast cancer and 1,569 nurses who did not have breast cancer, high birth weight predicted breast cancer incidence after many other prenatal and postnatal health risks were controlled. The breast-cancer risk was especially high for women whose birth weight was greater than 8.7 pounds. (Adapted from Michels et al., 1996.)

(Eskenazi, 1993; Fernandes, 1998). Some researchers report dose-related effects: the more caffeine consumed, the greater the likelihood of negative outcomes (Eskenazi et al., 1999; Fortier, Marcoux, & Beaulac-Baillargeon, 1993).

Because children's lives are involved, we must take findings like these quite seriously. At the same time, we cannot be sure that these drugs actually cause the problems just mentioned. Imagine how difficult it is to study the effects of many substances on the unborn! Often mothers take more than one kind of drug. If the prenatal organism is injured, it is hard to tell which drug might be responsible or if other factors correlated with drug taking are really at fault (LaGasse, Seifer, & Lester, 1999). Until we have more information, the safest course of action is the one that Yolanda took: Cut down on or avoid these drugs entirely.

hard to determine what + whether drugs contribute to prenatal abnormalities

■ **ILLEGAL DRUGS.** The use of highly addictive mood-altering drugs, such as cocaine and heroin, has become more widespread, especially in poverty-stricken inner-city areas, where drugs provide a temporary escape from a daily life of hopelessness. The number of "cocaine babies" born in the United States has reached crisis levels in recent years. About 100,000 to 375,000 infants are affected annually, a figure that is rising (Cornelius et al., 1999; Landry & Whitney, 1996).

Babies born to users of cocaine, heroin, or methadone (a less addictive drug used to wean people away from heroin) are at risk for a wide variety of problems, including prematurity, low birth weight, physical defects, breathing difficulties, and death around the time of birth (Datta-Bhutada, Johnson, & Rosen, 1998; Walker, Rosenberg, & Balaban-Gil, 1999). In addition, these infants arrive drug addicted. They often are feverish and irritable at birth and have trouble sleeping, and their cries are abnormally shrill and piercing—a common symptom among stressed newborns (Friedman, 1996; Martin et al., 1996). When mothers with many problems of their own must take care of these babies, who are difficult to calm down, cuddle, and feed, behavior problems are likely to persist.

Throughout the first year, heroin- and methadone-exposed infants are less attentive to the environment, and their motor development is slow. After infancy, some children get better, whereas others remain jittery and inattentive. The kind of parenting these youngsters receive may explain why problems last for some but not for others (Cosden, Peerson, & Elliott, 1997).

Growing evidence on cocaine suggests that large numbers of prenatally exposed babies have lasting difficulties. Cocaine constricts the blood vessels, causing oxygen delivered to the developing organism to fall dramatically for 15 minutes following a high dose. It also alters the production and functioning of neurons and the chemical balance in the fetus's brain. These effects may contribute to a specific set of cocaine-linked physical defects, including eye, bone, genital, urinary tract, kidney, and heart deformities, as well as brain hemorrhages and seizures (Espy, Kaufmann, & Glisky, 1999; Mayes, 1999; Plessinger & Woods, 1998). Motor, visual, attention, memory, and language problems appear in infancy and persist into the preschool years (Mayes et al., 1996; Richardson et al., 1996).

Babies born to mothers who smoke crack (a cheap form of cocaine that delivers high doses quickly through the lungs) seem worst off in terms of low birth weight and damage to the central nervous system (Bender et al., 1995; Richardson et al., 1996). Fathers may contribute to these outcomes. Research suggests that cocaine can attach itself to sperm, "hitchhike" its way into the zygote, and cause birth defects (Yazigi, Odem, & Polakoski, 1991). Still, it is difficult to isolate the precise damage caused by cocaine, since users often take several drugs and engage in other high-risk behaviors. The joint impact of these factors along with poor caregiving may be responsible for negative outcomes and lead the development of many cocaine-exposed infants to worsen over time (Alessandri, Bendersky, & Lewis, 1998; Chasnoff et al., 1998).

Another illegal drug, marijuana, is used more widely than heroin and cocaine. Studies examining its relationship to low birth weight and prematurity reveal mixed findings (Fried, 1993). Several researchers have linked prenatal marijuana exposure to smaller head size (a measure of brain growth), newborn startle reactions, disturbed sleep, and inattention in infancy and childhood (Dahl et al., 1995; Fried, Watkinson, & Gray, 1998; Lester & Dreher, 1989). In one study, the reduced head sizes of children born to heavy marijuana users persisted into adolescence (Fried, Watkinson, & Gray, 1999). Overall, however, long-term effects of marijuana have not been established.

CHUCK NACKE/WOODFIN CAMP & ASSOCIATES

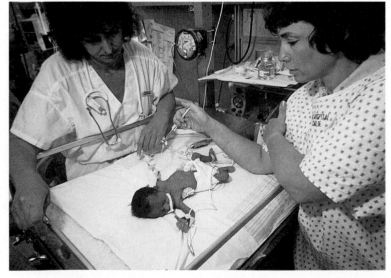

This baby, whose mother took crack during pregnancy, was born many weeks before his due date. He breathes with the aid of a respirator. His central nervous system may be damaged. Researchers are not yet sure if these outcomes are caused by crack or by the many other high-risk behaviors of drug users.

■ **TOBACCO.** Although smoking has declined in Western nations, an estimated 24 percent of American women of childbearing age are regular cigarette users. Many women quit around the time they become pregnant. Still, about 12 percent of expectant mothers smoke regularly (Ebrahim et al., 2000).

The most well-known effect of smoking during pregnancy is low birth weight. But the likelihood of other serious consequences, such as miscarriage, prematurity, impaired heart rate and breathing during sleep, infant death, and cancer later in childhood, is also increased (Franco et al., 2000; Walker, Rosenberg, & Balaban-Gil, 1999). The more cigarettes a mother smokes, the greater the chances that her baby will be affected. If a pregnant woman decides to stop smoking at any time, even during the last trimester, she can help her baby. She immediately reduces the chances that the infant will be born underweight and suffer from future problems (Ahlsten, Cnattingius, & Lindmark, 1993; Groff et al., 1997).

Even when a baby of a smoking mother appears to be born in good physical condition, slight behavioral abnormalities may threaten the child's development. Newborns of smoking mothers are less attentive to sounds and display more muscle tension (Fried & Makin, 1987). An unresponsive, restless baby may not evoke the kind of interaction from adults that promotes healthy psychological development. Some studies report that prenatally exposed youngsters have shorter attention spans, poorer mental test scores, and more behavior problems in childhood and adolescence, even after many other factors have been controlled (Millberger et al., 1998; Trasti et al., 1999; Weissman et al., 1999). Other researchers have not confirmed these findings, so lasting effects remain uncertain (Barr et al., 1990; Streissguth et al., 1989).

Exactly how can smoking harm the fetus? Nicotine, the addictive substance in tobacco, constricts blood vessels, lessens blood flow to the uterus, and causes the placenta to grow abnormally. This reduces the transfer of nutrients, so the fetus gains weight poorly. Also, nicotine raises the concentration of carbon monoxide in the bloodstreams of both mother and fetus. Carbon monoxide displaces oxygen from red blood cells. It damages the central nervous system and reduces birth weight in the fetuses of laboratory animals. Similar effects may occur in humans (Friedman, 1996).

From one-third to one-half of nonsmoking pregnant women are "passive smokers" because their husbands, relatives, or co-workers use cigarettes. Passive smoking is also related to low birth weight, infant death, and possible long-term impairments in attention and learning (Dejin-Karlsson et al., 1998; Makin, Fried, & Watkinson, 1991). Consequently, Jay made a special effort to give up cigarettes when Yolanda became pregnant.

■ **ALCOHOL.** In a moving story, Michael Dorris (1989), a Dartmouth University anthropology professor, described what it was like to raise his adopted son Adam, whose biological mother drank heavily throughout pregnancy and died of alcohol poisoning shortly after his birth. A Sioux Indian, Adam was 3 years old when he came into Dorris's life. He was short and underweight and had a vocabulary of only 20 words. Although he ate well, Adam grew slowly and remained painfully thin. He was prone to infection and had repeated brain seizures. His vocabulary did not expand like that of normal preschoolers. When he was 7, special testing revealed that Adam's intelligence was below average. At age 12, he could not add, subtract, or identify the town in which he lived.

Fetal alcohol syndrome (FAS) is the scientific name for Adam's condition. Mental retardation; impaired motor coordination, attention, memory, and language; and overactivity are typical of children with the disorder. Distinct physical symptoms also accompany it, including slow physical growth and a specific pattern of facial abnormalities: widely spaced eyes; short eyelid openings; a small, upturned nose; a thin upper lip; and a small head, indicating that the brain has not developed fully. Other defects—of the eyes, ears, nose, throat, heart, genitals, urinary tract, or immune system—may also be present.

In all babies born with FAS, the mother drank heavily through most or all of her pregnancy. In a related condition, known as **fetal alcohol effects (FAE),** individuals display only some of these abnormalities. Usually, their mothers drank alcohol in smaller quantities. The

The mother of the severely retarded boy above drank heavily during pregnancy. His widely spaced eyes, thin upper lip, and short eyelid openings are typical of fetal alcohol syndrome. The adolescent girl below also has these physical symptoms. The brain damage alcohol caused before she was born is permanent. It has made learning in school and adapting to everyday challenges extremely difficult.

fetal alcohol syndrome (FAS)
A set of defects that results when women consume large amounts of alcohol during most or all of pregnancy. Includes mental retardation, slow physical growth, and facial abnormalities.

fetal alcohol effects (FAE)
The condition of children who display some but not all of the defects of fetal alcohol syndrome. Usually their mothers drank alcohol in smaller quantities during pregnancy.

particular defects of FAE children vary with timing and length of alcohol exposure during pregnancy (Goodlet & Johnson, 1999; Mattson et al., 1998).

Even when provided with enriched diets, FAS babies fail to catch up in physical size during infancy or childhood. Mental impairment is also permanent: In his teens and twenties, Adam's intelligence remained below average, and he had trouble concentrating and keeping a routine job. He also suffered from poor judgment. For example, he would buy something and not wait for change, or he would wander off in the middle of a task. The more alcohol consumed by a woman during pregnancy, the poorer the child's motor coordination, speed of information processing, reasoning, and intelligence and achievement test scores during the preschool and school years (Aronson, Hagberg, & Gillberg, 1997; Hunt et al., 1995; Jacobson et al., 1993). In adolescence, FAS is associated with poor school performance, trouble with the law, inappropriate sexual behavior, alcohol and drug abuse, and lasting mental health problems (Streissguth et al., 1999). Adolescents with FAS who managed to escape mental retardation still have serious cognitive impairments, including deficits in attention, memory, planning, and spatial abilities (Olson et al., 1998).

How does alcohol produce its devastating effects? First, it interferes with cell duplication and migration in the primitive neural tube. Psychophysiological measures, such as fMRI and EEGs, reveal structural damage and abnormalities in brain functioning, including electrical and chemical activity involved in transferring messages from one part of the brain to another (Guerri, 1998; Roebuck, Mattson, & Riley, 1999). Second, the body uses large quantities of oxygen to metabolize alcohol. A pregnant woman's heavy drinking draws away oxygen that the developing organism needs for cell growth.

Like heroin and cocaine, alcohol abuse is higher in poverty-stricken sectors of the population (Streissguth, 1997). On the reservation where Adam was born, many children show symptoms of prenatal alcohol exposure. Unfortunately, when girls with FAS or FAE later become pregnant, the poor judgment caused by the syndrome often prevents them from understanding why they should avoid alcohol themselves. Thus, the tragic cycle is likely to repeat itself in the next generation.

How much alcohol is safe during pregnancy? One study linked as little as 2 ounces of alcohol a day, taken very early in pregnancy, to FAS-like facial features (Astley et al., 1992). But recall that other factors—both genetic and environmental—can make some fetuses more vulnerable to teratogenic effects. Therefore, a precise dividing line between safe and dangerous drinking levels cannot be established, and it is best for pregnant women to avoid alcohol entirely.

■ **RADIATION.** In Chapter 2, we saw that ionizing radiation can cause mutation, damaging the DNA in ova and sperm. When mothers are exposed to radiation during pregnancy, additional harm can come to the embryo or fetus. Defects due to radiation were tragically apparent in the children born to pregnant Japanese women who survived the bombing of Hiroshima and Nagasaki during World War II. Similar abnormalities surfaced in the 9 months following the 1986 Chernobyl, Ukraine, nuclear power plant accident. After each disaster, the incidence of miscarriage, babies born with underdeveloped brains or physical deformities, and infants displaying slow physical growth rose dramatically (Schull & Otake, 1999; Terestchenko, Lyaginskaya, & Burtzeva, 1991).

Even when a radiation-exposed baby seems normal, problems may appear later. For example, even low-level radiation, as the result of industrial leakage or medical X-rays, can increase the risk of childhood cancer (Fattibene et al., 1999). In middle childhood, prenatally exposed Chernobyl children showed abnormal EEG brain-wave activity, lower intelligence test scores, and rates of language and emotional disorders two to three times greater than those of nonexposed Russian children. Furthermore, Chernobyl children's parents were highly anxious, due to forced evacuation from their homes and worries about living in irradiated areas.

This child's mother was just a few weeks pregnant during the Chernobyl nuclear power plant disaster. Radiation exposure probably is responsible for his limb deformities. He also is at risk for low intelligence and language and emotional disorders.

CHARLTON-BOURDILLON/LIAISON AGENCY

The more tension parents reported, the poorer their children's emotional functioning (Kolo-minsky, Igumnov, & Drozdovitch, 1999; Loganovskaja & Loganovsky, 1999). Stressful rearing conditions seemed to combine with the damaging effects of prenatal radiation to impair children's development.

■ **ENVIRONMENTAL POLLUTION.** Yolanda and Jay like to refinish antique furniture in their garage, and Jay is an enthusiastic grower of fruit trees in the backyard. When Yolanda became pregnant, they postponed work on several pieces of furniture, and Jay did not spray the fruit trees in the fall and spring of that year. Continuing to do so, they learned, might expose Yolanda and the embryo or fetus to chemical levels thousands of times greater than judged safe by the federal government. An astounding number of potentially dangerous chemicals are released into the environment in industrialized nations. In the United States, more than 100,000 are in common use, and 1,000 new ones are introduced each year (Samuels & Samuels, 1996).

Mercury is an established teratogen. In the 1950s, an industrial plant released waste containing high levels of mercury into a bay providing food and water for the town of Minimata, Japan. Many children born at the time displayed physical deformities, mental retardation, abnormal speech, difficulty in chewing and swallowing, and uncoordinated movements. Autopsies of those who died revealed widespread brain damage (Vorhees & Mollnow, 1987).

Another teratogen, *lead,* is present in paint flaking off the walls of old buildings and in certain materials used in industrial occupations. High levels of lead exposure are consistently related to prematurity, low birth weight, brain damage, and a wide variety of physical defects (Dye-White, 1986). Even low levels of prenatal lead exposure seem to be dangerous. Affected babies show slightly poorer mental development during the first 2 years (Bellinger et al., 1987).

For many years, *polychlorinated biphenyls (PCBs)* were used to insulate electrical equipment, until research showed that (like mercury) they found their way into waterways and entered the food supply. In Taiwan, prenatal exposure to very high levels of PCBs in rice oil resulted in low birth weight, discolored skin, deformities of the gums and nails, EEG brain-wave abnormalities, and delayed cognitive development (Chen & Hsu, 1994; Chen et al., 1994).

Steady, low-level PCB exposure is also harmful. Newborn babies of women who frequently ate PCB-contaminated Great Lakes fish had slightly lower than average birth weights, smaller heads (suggesting brain damage), more intense physiological reactions to stress, and less interest in their surroundings than did infants whose mothers ate little or no fish (Jacobson et al., 1984; Stewart et al., 2000). Follow-ups later in the first year and in early childhood revealed persisting memory difficulties and lower verbal intelligence (Jacobson, 1998; Jacobson et al., 1992).

■ **MATERNAL DISEASE.** On her first prenatal visit, Yolanda's doctor asked if she and Jay had already had measles, mumps, and chicken pox, as well as other illnesses. In addition, Yolanda was checked for the presence of several infections, and for good reason. As you can see in Table 3.4 on page 120, certain diseases during pregnancy are major causes of miscarriage and birth defects.

Viruses. Five percent of women catch a virus of some sort while pregnant. Most of these illnesses, such as the common cold and various strains of the flu, appear to have no impact on the embryo or fetus. However, a few can result in extensive damage.

The best known of these is **rubella** (3-day or German measles). In the mid-1960s, a worldwide epidemic of rubella led to the birth of more than 20,000 American babies with serious defects. Consistent with the sensitive-period concept, the greatest damage occurs when rubella strikes during the embryonic period. More than 50 percent of infants whose mothers become ill during that time show heart defects; eye cataracts; deafness; genital, urinary, and intestinal abnormalities; and mental retardation. Infection during the fetal period is less harmful, but low birth weight, hearing loss, and bone defects may still occur (Eberhart-Phillips, Frederick, & Baron, 1993).

rubella
Three-day German measles. Causes a wide variety of prenatal abnormalities, especially when it strikes during the embryonic period.

TABLE 3.4

Effects of Some Infectious Diseases During Pregnancy

DISEASE	MISCARRIAGE	PHYSICAL MALFORMATIONS	MENTAL RETARDATION	LOW BIRTH WEIGHT AND PREMATURITY
Viral				
Acquired immune deficiency syndrome (AIDS)	o	?	+	?
Chicken pox	o	+	+	+
Cytomegalovirus	+	+	+	+
Herpes simplex 2 (genital herpes)	+	+	+	+
Mumps	+	?	o	o
Rubella (German measles)	+	+	+	+
Bacterial				
Syphilis	+	+	+	?
Tuberculosis	+	?	+	+
Parasitic				
Malaria	+	o	o	+
Toxoplasmosis	+	+	+	+

+ = established finding, o = no present evidence, ? = possible effect that is not clearly established.

Sources: Behrman, Kliegman, & Jenson, 2000; Chatkupt et al., 1989; Cohen, 1993; Peckham & Logan, 1993; Qazi et al., 1988; Samson, 1988; Sever, 1983; Vorhees, 1986.

Since 1966, infants and young children have been routinely vaccinated against rubella, so the number of prenatal cases today is much less than it was a generation ago. Still, 10 to 20 percent of American women of childbearing age lack the rubella antibody, so new outbreaks of the disease are still possible (Lee et al., 1992).

The *human immunodeficiency virus (HIV)*, which can lead to **acquired immune deficiency syndrome (AIDS)**, a disease that destroys the immune system, has infected increasing numbers of women over the past decade. Currently, 13 percent of AIDS victims in the United States and more than 50 percent in Africa are women. When they become pregnant, they pass the deadly virus to the developing organism 20 to 30 percent of the time (Nourse & Butler, 1998).

In older children and adults, AIDS symptoms take years to emerge; in infants, the disease progresses rapidly. By 6 months, weight loss, diarrhea, and repeated respiratory illnesses are common. The virus also causes brain damage, as indicated by seizures, a gradual loss in brain weight, and delayed mental and motor development. Most prenatal AIDS babies survive for only 5 to 8 months after the appearance of these symptoms (Parks, 1996). The antiviral drug zidovudine (ZDV) reduces prenatal AIDS transmission by as much as 95 percent, even in women with advanced disease (Lindgren et al., 1999; Steihm et al., 1999). ZDV is responsible for a dramatic decline in prenatally acquired AIDS in he United States, with no harmful consequences of drug treatment for children (Culnane et al., 1999).

As Table 3.4 reveals, the developing organism is especially sensitive to the family of herpes viruses, for which no vaccine or treatment exists. Among these, *cytomegalovirus* (the most frequent prenatal infection, transmitted through respiratory or sexual contact) and *herpes simplex 2* (which is sexually transmitted) are especially dangerous. In both, the virus invades the mother's genital tract. Babies can be infected either during pregnancy or at birth.

Bacterial and Parasitic Diseases. Table 3.4 also includes several bacterial and parasitic diseases. Among the most common is **toxoplasmosis,** caused by a parasite found in many animals. Pregnant women may become infected from eating raw or undercooked meat or from contact

acquired immune deficiency syndrome (AIDS)
A relatively new viral infection that destroys the immune system and is spread through transfer of body fluids from one person to another. It can be transmitted prenatally.

toxoplasmosis
A parasitic disease caused by eating raw or undercooked meat or coming in contact with the feces of infected cats. During the first trimester, it leads to eye and brain damage.

with the feces of infected cats. About 40 percent of women who have the disease transmit it to the developing organism. If it strikes during the first trimester, it is likely to cause eye and brain damage. Later infection is linked to mild visual and cognitive impairments (Peckham & Logan, 1993). Expectant mothers can avoid toxoplasmosis by making sure that the meat they eat is well cooked, having pet cats checked for the disease, and turning over care of litter boxes to other family members. Outdoor areas that cats may frequent also should be avoided.

OTHER MATERNAL FACTORS

Besides avoiding teratogens, expectant parents can support the developing organism in other ways. Regular exercise, good nutrition, and emotional well-being of the mother are crucially important. Blood type differences between mother and fetus can create preventable difficulties. Finally, many expectant parents wonder how a mother's age and previous births affect the course of pregnancy. We examine each factor in the following sections.

■ **EXERCISE.** Yolanda continued her half-hour of aerobics three times a week into the third trimester, although her doctor cautioned against bouncing, jolting, and jogging movements that might subject the fetus to too many shocks and startles. In healthy, physically fit women, regular moderate exercise, such as walking, swimming, biking, and aerobics, is related to increased birth weight (Hatch et al., 1993). However, very frequent, vigorous exercise (working up a sweat four or more times a week) predicts the opposite outcome—lower birth weight than in healthy, non-exercising controls (Bell, Palma, & Lumley, 1995; Pivarnik, 1998). Hospital-sponsored childbirth education programs frequently offer exercise classes and suggest appropriate routines that help prepare for labor and delivery. Exercises that strengthen the back, abdominal, pelvic, and thigh muscles are emphasized, since the growing fetus places some strain on these parts of the body.

During the last trimester, when the abdomen grows very large, mothers have difficulty moving freely and often must cut back on exercise. In most cases, a mother who has remained fit during the earlier months experiences fewer physical discomforts, such as back pain, upward pressure on the chest, and difficulty breathing.

Pregnant women with health problems, such as circulatory difficulties or a history of miscarriages, should consult their doctors about fitness routines. For these mothers, exercise (especially the wrong kind) can endanger the pregnancy.

■ **NUTRITION.** Children grow more rapidly during the prenatal period than at any other phase of development. During this time, they depend totally on the mother for nutrients to support their growth. A healthy diet, consisting of a gradual increase in calories—an extra 100 calories a day in the first trimester, 265 in the second, and 430 in the third—resulting in a weight gain of 25 to 30 pounds (10 to 13.5 kilograms), helps ensure the health of mother and baby (Reifsnider & Gill, 2000).

Consequences of Prenatal Malnutrition. During World War II, a severe famine occurred in the Netherlands, giving scientists a rare opportunity to study the impact of nutrition on prenatal development. Findings revealed that the sensitive-period concept operates with nutrition, just as it does with the teratogens discussed earlier in this chapter. Women affected by the famine during the first trimester were more likely to have miscarriages or give birth to babies with physical defects. When women were past the first trimester, fetuses were more likely to survive, but many were born underweight and had small heads (Stein et al., 1975).

This government clinic in Kenya prevents early malnutrition by promoting a proper diet for pregnant women and young children, including breast-feeding in infancy (see Chapter 5, pages 181–182).

BETTY PRESS/WOODFIN CAMP & ASSOCIATES

We now know that prenatal malnutrition can damage the central nervous system. Autopsies of malnourished babies who died at or shortly after birth reveal fewer brain cells and a brain weight that is as much as 36 percent below average. The poorer the mother's diet, the greater the loss in brain weight, especially if malnutrition occurred during the last trimester. During that time, the brain is growing rapidly, and a maternal diet high in all the basic nutrients is necessary for it to reach its full potential (Morgane et al., 1993). An inadequate diet during pregnancy can distort the structure of other organs, including the liver, kidney, and pancreas, thereby increasing the risk of heart disease, stroke, and diabetes in adulthood (refer again to the Social Issues: Health box on pages 114–115).

Prenatally malnourished babies enter the world with serious problems. They frequently catch respiratory illnesses, since poor nutrition suppresses development of the immune system (Chandra, 1991). In addition, these infants are irritable and unresponsive to stimulation. Like drug-addicted newborns, they have a high-pitched cry that is particularly distressing to their caregivers. In poverty-stricken families, these effects quickly combine with a stressful home life. With age, low intelligence test scores and serious learning problems become more apparent (Pollitt, 1996).

Prevention and Treatment. Many studies show that providing pregnant women with adequate food has a substantial impact on the health of their newborn babies. Yet the growth demands of the prenatal period require more than just increasing the quantity of a typical diet. Finding ways to optimize maternal nutrition through vitamin–mineral enrichment as early as possible is also crucial.

For example, folic acid can prevent abnormalities of the neural tube, such as anencephaly and spina bifida (see Table 2.6 on page 66). In a study of nearly 2,000 women in seven countries who had previously given birth to a baby with a neural tube defect, half were randomly selected to receive a daily folic acid supplement around the time of conception and half received a mixture of other vitamins or no supplement. As Figure 3.9 reveals, the folic acid group showed 72 percent fewer neural tube defects (MCR Vitamin Study Research Group, 1991). In addition, adequate folate intake during the last 10 weeks of pregnancy cuts in half the risk of premature delivery and low birth weight (Scholl, Heidiger, & Belsky, 1996). Because of these findings, the U.S. Public Health Service recommends that all women of childbearing age consume at least 0.4 but not more than 1 milligram of folic acid per day (since excessive intake can be harmful). Currently, bread, flour, rice, pasta, and other grain products are being fortified with folic acid (Lewis et al., 1998).

Other vitamins and minerals also have established benefits. Enriching women's diets with calcium helps prevent maternal high blood pressure and premature births (Repke, 1992). Adequate magnesium and zinc reduce the risk of many prenatal and birth complications (Facchinetti et al., 1992; Jameson, 1993; Spätling & Spätling, 1988). Fortifying table salt with iodine virtually eradicates cretinism—a common cause of mental retardation and stunted growth in many parts of the world (Dunn, 1993). And taking vitamin C early in pregnancy promotes growth of the placenta and adequate birth weight (Mathews, Yudkin, & Neil, 1999). Nevertheless, a supplement program should complement, not replace, efforts to improve maternal diets during pregnancy. For women who do not get enough food or an adequate variety of foods, multivitamin tablets are a necessary, but not sufficient, intervention.

When poor nutrition continues throughout pregnancy, infants often require more than dietary enrichment. Their tired, restless behavior leads mothers to be less sensitive and stimulating. In response, babies become even more passive and withdrawn. Successful interventions must break this cycle of apathetic mother–baby interaction. Some do so by teaching parents how to interact effectively with their infants, whereas others focus on stimulating infants to promote active engagement with their physical and social surroundings (Grantham-McGregor et al., 1994; Zeskind & Ramey, 1978, 1981).

Although prenatal malnutrition is highest in poverty-stricken regions of the world, it is not limited to developing countries. Each year, 80,000 to 120,000 American infants are born

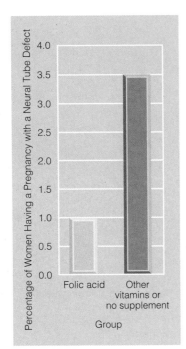

FIGURE 3.9

Percentage of pregnancies with a neural tube defect in folic-acid-supplemented women versus others. Folic acid taken around the time of conception dramatically reduced the incidence of neural tube defects—a finding confirmed by other large-scale studies. Note, however, that folic acid did not eliminate all neural tube defects. These abnormalities, like many others, have multiple origins in the embryo's genetic disposition and factors in the environment. (Adapted from MCR Vitamin Study Research Group, 1991.)

seriously undernourished. Although the federal government provides food packages to low-income pregnant women through its Special Supplemental Food Program for Women, Infants, and Children, funding is limited, and only 70 percent of those eligible are served (Children's Defense Fund, 2000).

Finally, the diets of some economically advantaged expectant mothers are inadequate. In the United States, where thinness is the feminine ideal, women often feel uneasy about gaining weight during pregnancy, and they may limit their food intake. When they do, they risk their infant's development in all the ways just described.

■ **EMOTIONAL STRESS.** When women experience severe emotional stress during pregnancy, their babies are at risk for a wide variety of difficulties. Intense anxiety is associated with a higher rate of miscarriage, prematurity, low birth weight, and newborn irritability, respiratory illness, and digestive disturbances. It is also related to certain physical defects, such as cleft lip and palate, heart deformities, and pyloric stenosis (tightening of the infant's stomach outlet, which must be treated surgically) (Carmichael & Shaw, 2000; Hoffman & Hatch, 1996).

How can maternal stress affect the developing organism? To understand this process, think back to how your own body felt the last time you were under considerable stress. When we experience fear and anxiety, stimulant hormones are released into our bloodstream. These cause us to be "poised for action." Large amounts of blood are sent to parts of the body involved in the defensive response—the brain, the heart, and muscles in the arms, legs, and trunk. Blood flow to other organs, including the uterus, is reduced. As a result, the fetus is deprived of a full supply of oxygen and nutrients. Stress hormones also cross the placenta, leading the fetus's heart rate and activity to rise dramatically. In addition, stress weakens the immune system, making pregnant women more susceptible to infectious disease (Cohen & Williamson, 1991; Monk et al., 2000). Finally, women who experience long-term anxiety are more likely to smoke, drink, eat poorly, and engage in other behaviors that harm the embryo and fetus.

But women under severe emotional stress do not always give birth to babies with problems. The risks are greatly reduced when mothers have husbands, other family members, and friends who offer support (Nuckolls, Cassel, & Kaplan, 1972). The link between social support and positive pregnancy outcomes is particularly strong for low-income women (Hoffman & Hatch, 1996). These results suggest that enhancing supportive social networks for mothers during pregnancy can help prevent prenatal complications.

■ **RH BLOOD INCOMPATIBILITY.** When inherited blood types of mother and fetus differ, the incompatibility can result in serious problems. The most common cause of these difficulties involves a blood protein called the **Rh factor.** When the mother is Rh-negative (lacks the protein) and the father is Rh-positive (has the protein), the baby may inherit the father's Rh-positive blood type. (Recall from Table 2.2 on page 59 that Rh-positive blood is dominant and Rh-negative blood is recessive, so the chances are good that a baby will be Rh-positive.)

During the third trimester and at the time of birth, some maternal and fetal blood cells usually cross the placenta, in small enough amounts to be quite safe. But if even a little of the baby's Rh-positive blood passes into a mother's Rh-negative bloodstream, she begins to form antibodies to the foreign Rh protein. If these enter the baby's system, they destroy red blood cells, reducing the supply of oxygen. Mental retardation, damage to the heart muscle, and infant death can occur.

Since it takes time for the mother to produce Rh antibodies, first-born children are rarely affected. The danger increases with each additional pregnancy. Fortunately, the harmful effects of Rh incompatibility can be prevented in most cases. After the birth of each Rh-positive baby, Rh-negative mothers are routinely given a vaccine to prevent the buildup of antibodies. In emergency cases, blood transfusions can be performed immediately after delivery or, if necessary, even before birth.

Rh factor
A protein that, when present in the fetus's blood but not in the mother's, can cause the mother to build up antibodies. If these return to the fetus's system, they destroy red blood cells, reducing the oxygen supply to organs and tissues.

■ **MATERNAL AGE AND PREVIOUS BIRTHS.** Earlier I mentioned that women who delay having children until their thirties or forties face a greater risk of infertility, miscarriage, and babies born with chromosomal defects. Are other pregnancy problems more common for older mothers?

For many years, scientists thought that aging of the mother's reproductive organs increased the likelihood of a wide variety of pregnancy complications. Recently, this idea has been questioned. When women without serious health difficulties are considered, those in their forties experience about the same rate of prenatal and birth problems as do those in their twenties (Bianco et al., 1996; Cnattingius et al., 1992; Prysak, Lorenz, & Kisly, 1995).

In the case of teenage mothers, does physical immaturity cause prenatal problems? Again, research indicates that it does not. A teenager's body is large enough and strong enough to support pregnancy. In fact, as we will see in Chapter 14, nature tries to ensure that once a girl can conceive, she is physically ready to carry and give birth to a baby. Infants of teenagers are born with a higher rate of problems for quite different reasons. Many pregnant adolescents do not have access to medical care or are afraid to seek it. In addition, most pregnant teenagers come from low-income backgrounds, where stress, poor nutrition, and health problems are common (Coley & Chase-Lansdale, 1998).

RON LEVY/PHOTOTAKE

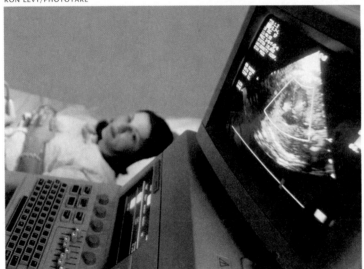

During a routine prenatal visit, a doctor uses ultrasound to evaluate the development of the fetus. All pregnant women need early and regular prenatal care—to protect their own health and the health of their babies.

THE IMPORTANCE OF PRENATAL HEALTH CARE

Yolanda had her first prenatal appointment 3 weeks after her first missed menstrual period. After that, she visited the doctor's office once a month until she was 7 months pregnant, then twice during the eighth month. As birth grew near, Yolanda's appointments increased to once a week. The doctor kept track of her general health, weight gain, and the capacity of her uterus and cervix to support the fetus. The fetus's growth was also carefully monitored. During these visits, Yolanda had plenty of opportunity to ask questions, pick up literature in the waiting room, get to know the person who would deliver her baby, and plan the birth experience she and Jay desired.

Yolanda's pregnancy, like most others, was free of complications. But unexpected difficulties can arise, especially if mothers have health problems to begin with. For example, women with diabetes need careful monitoring. Extra sugar in the diabetic mother's bloodstream causes the fetus to grow larger than average, although it is physically less mature than the fetus of a nondiabetic mother. As a result, birth problems are common. Another complication, **toxemia** (or *eclampsia*), in which blood pressure increases sharply and the face, hands, and feet swell in the second half of pregnancy, is experienced by 5 to 10 percent of pregnant women. The cause of toxemia is unknown. If untreated, it can cause convulsions in the mother and fetal death. Usually, hospitalization, bed rest, and drugs can lower blood pressure to a safe level. If not, the baby must be delivered at once (Carlson, Eisenstat, & Ziporyn, 1996).

Unfortunately, 18 percent of pregnant women in the United States wait until after the first trimester to seek prenatal care, and 4 percent delay until the end of pregnancy or never get any at all. Most of these mothers are adolescents, unmarried, or poverty stricken. Their infants are far more likely to be born underweight and to die before birth or during the first year of life than are the babies of mothers who receive early medical attention (Children's Defense Fund, 2000).

Why do these mothers delay going to the doctor? One frequent reason is lack of health insurance. Financial problems are a major barrier to early prenatal care (Beckmann, Buford,

toxemia
An illness of the last half of pregnancy, in which the mother's blood pressure increases sharply and her face, hands, and feet swell. If untreated, it can cause convulsions in the mother and death of the fetus. Also called *eclampsia*.

Caregiving Concerns

Do's and Don'ts for a Healthy Pregnancy

DO	DON'T
Do make sure that you have been vaccinated against infectious diseases dangerous to the embryo and fetus, such as rubella, before you get pregnant. Most vaccinations are not safe during pregnancy.	Don't take any drugs without consulting your doctor.
Do see a doctor as soon as you suspect that you are pregnant—within a few weeks after a missed menstrual period.	Don't smoke. If you have already smoked during part of your pregnancy, cut down or (better yet) quit. If other members of your family are smokers, ask them to quit or smoke outside.
Do continue to get regular medical checkups throughout pregnancy.	Don't drink alcohol from the time you decide to get pregnant. If you find it difficult to give up alcohol, ask for help from your doctor, local family service agency, or nearest chapter of Alcoholics Anonymous.
Do obtain literature from your doctor, local library, and bookstore about prenatal development and care. Ask questions about anything you do not understand.	
Do eat a well-balanced diet and take vitamin–mineral supplements as prescribed by your doctor. On the average, a woman should increase her intake by 100 calories a day in the first trimester, 265 in the second, and 430 in the third. Gain 25 to 30 pounds gradually.	Don't engage in activities that might expose your embryo or fetus to environmental hazards, such as radiation or chemical pollutants. If you work in an occupation that involves these agents, ask for a safer assignment or a leave of absence.
Do keep physically fit through mild exercise. If possible, join a special exercise class for expectant mothers.	
Do avoid emotional stress. If you are a single parent, find a relative or friend on whom you can count for emotional support.	Don't engage in activities that might expose your embryo or fetus to harmful infectious diseases, such as toxoplasmosis.
Do get plenty of rest. An overtired mother is at risk for pregnancy complications.	Don't choose pregnancy as a time to go on a diet.
Do enroll in a prenatal and childbirth education class along with your partner. When parents know what to expect, the 9 months before birth can be one of the most joyful times of life.	Don't gain too much weight during pregnancy. A very large weight gain is associated with complications.

& Witt, 2000). Although the very poorest of these mothers are eligible for government-sponsored health services, many low-income women do not qualify. In Europe, where affordable health care is universally available, the percentage of late-care pregnancies and maternal and infant health problems are greatly reduced. Some countries offer special financial incentives. For example, in France, every expectant mother who maintains a regular schedule of prenatal visits throughout pregnancy receives a monetary allowance (Buekens et al., 1993).

Besides financial hardship, some mothers have other reasons for not seeking prenatal care. When researchers asked women who first went to the doctor late in pregnancy why they waited so long, they mentioned a wide variety of obstacles. These included situational barriers, such as difficulty finding a doctor, difficulty getting an appointment, long waiting time during the visit, and lack of transportation. The women also mentioned many personal barriers—psychological stress, the demands of taking care of young children, ambivalence about the pregnancy, family crises, and lack of belief in the benefits of prenatal care (Maloni et al., 1996; Rogers & Shiff, 1996). Many were also engaging in high-risk behaviors, such as smoking and drug abuse. These women, who had no medical attention for most of their pregnancies, were among those who needed it most!

Clearly, public education about the importance of early and sustained prenatal care for all pregnant women is badly needed in the United States. The Caregiving Concerns table above provides a summary of "do's and don'ts" for a healthy pregnancy, based on our discussion of the prenatal environment.

Ask YOURSELF...

review   Why is it difficult to determine the effects of many environmental agents, such as drugs and pollution, on the embryo and fetus?

apply   Trixie has just learned that she is pregnant. Since she has always been healthy and feels good right now, she cannot understand why the doctor wants her to come in for checkups so often. Why is early and regular prenatal care important for Trixie?

connect   List teratogens and other maternal factors that affect brain development during the prenatal period. Why is the central nervous system often affected when the prenatal environment is compromised?

reflect   A recent survey reported that only 7 percent of American women of childbearing age are aware that taking a daily folic acid supplement around the time of conception reduces neural tube defects (U.S. Department of Health and Human Services, 1999b). Were you aware of this finding? If you could publicize five environmental influences in a campaign aimed at safeguarding prenatal development, which ones would you choose, and why?

Preparing for Parenthood

Although we have discussed a great many ways that development can be thrown off course during the prenatal period, over 90 percent of pregnancies in industrialized nations result in normal newborn babies. For most expectant parents, the prenatal period is not a time of medical hazard. Instead, it is a period of major life change accompanied by excitement, anticipation, and looking inward. The 9 months before birth not only permit the fetus to grow but also give men and women time to develop a new sense of themselves as mothers and fathers.

This period of psychological preparation is vital. Many young people say they do not feel ready to deal with the demands and responsibilities of parenthood (Cowan & Cowan, 2000). How effectively individuals construct a new parental identity during pregnancy has important consequences for the parent–infant relationship. A great many factors contribute to the personal adjustments that take place.

SEEKING INFORMATION

We know most about how mothers adapt to the psychological challenges of pregnancy, although some evidence suggests that fathers use many of the same techniques (Colman & Colman, 1991). One common strategy is to seek information, as Yolanda and Jay did when they read books on pregnancy and childbirth and enrolled in my class. In fact, expectant mothers regard books as an extremely valuable source of information, rating them as second in importance only to their doctors. And the more a pregnant woman seeks information— by reading, accessing relevant websites, asking friends, consulting her own mother, or attending a prenatal class—the more confident she tends to feel about her own ability to be a good mother (Cowan & Cowan, 2000; Deutsch et al., 1988).

THE BABY BECOMES A REALITY

At the beginning of pregnancy, the baby seems far off in the future. Except for a missed period and some morning sickness (nausea that most women experience during the first trimester), the woman's body has not changed much. But gradually, her abdomen enlarges,

and the baby starts to become a reality. A major turning point occurs when expectant parents are presented with concrete proof that a fetus is, indeed, developing inside the uterus. For Yolanda and Jay, this happened 13 weeks into the pregnancy, when their doctor showed them an ultrasound image of the fetus. As Jay described this experience, "We saw it, these little hands and feet waving and kicking. It had the cord and everything. It's really a baby in there!" Sensing the fetus's movements for the first time can be just as thrilling. Of course, the mother feels these "kicks" first, but soon after, the father (and siblings) can participate by touching her abdomen.

Parents get to know the fetus as an individual through these signs of life. And both may form an emotional attachment to the new being, dream about the future parent–infant relationship, and talk about names. In a Swedish study, the stronger mothers' and fathers' attachment to their fetus, the more positively parents related to each other and to their baby after birth, and the more positive the baby's mood at 8 months of age (White et al., 1999).

MODELS OF EFFECTIVE PARENTHOOD

As pregnancy proceeds, expectant parents think about important models of parenthood in their own lives—for a woman, her mother, and for a man, his father. When men and women have had good relationships with their own parents, they are more likely to develop positive images of themselves as parents during pregnancy (Deutsch et al., 1988). These images, in turn, predict favorable relationships with children during infancy and early childhood (Cowan et al., 1994; Fonagy, Steele, & Steele, 1991; Klitzing et al., 1999).

If their own parental relationships are mixed or negative, expectant mothers and fathers may have trouble building a healthy picture of themselves as parents. Some adults handle this problem constructively, by seeking other examples of effective parenthood. One father named Roger shared these thoughts with his wife and several expectant couples who met regularly with a counselor to talk about their concerns during pregnancy:

> I rethink past experiences with my father and my family and am aware of how I was raised. I just think I don't want to do that again, I want to change that; I don't want to be like my father in that way. I wish there had been more connection and closeness and a lot more respect for who I was. For me, my father-in-law combines spontaneity, sincerity, and warmth. He is a mix of empathy and warmth plus stepping back and being objective that I want to be as a father. (Colman & Colman, 1991, p. 148)

Like Roger, many people come to terms with negative experiences in their own childhood, recognize that other options are available to them as parents, and build healthier and happier relationships with their children (Cox et al., 1992). Roger achieved this understanding after he participated in a special intervention program for expectant mothers and fathers. Couples who take part in such programs feel better about themselves and their marital relationships, regard the demands of caring for the new baby as less stressful, and adapt more easily when family problems arise (Cowan & Cowan, 1997).

PRACTICAL CONCERNS

When women first learn that they are pregnant, they often wonder how long they will be able to continue their usual activities. Culture has a major impact on answers to this question. In the United States, women in good health often work and travel until the very end of their pregnancies, without any apparent harm to the fetus. And as long as the pregnancy has gone well, American health professionals advise that sexual intercourse can be continued until 2 to 4 weeks before the estimated birth date (Reilly, 2000).

As this couple shares the thrill of sensing the fetus's movements, parenthood starts to become a reality. Mother and father get to know the fetus as an individual. They may become emotionally attached to the new being and dream about the future parent–infant relationship.

In contrast, when a Japanese woman learns that she is pregnant, she changes her daily life considerably, out of a belief that this is necessary to protect the health of her baby. Nancy Engel (1989), an American nurse, described her experience of becoming pregnant for the first time while living in Japan:

> When I announced my pregnancy it was assumed that I would quit my teaching position and drop out of language school. My teacher told me that language study was stressful, and the increased [hormone levels] it caused were harmful to the baby. Similarly, I was advised that the noise of train travel, typing, or using a sewing machine should be avoided. My colleagues at college … were particularly concerned when I revealed plans to go to Thailand on vacation during the fourth month. They told me that airplane travel would cause miscarriage, and they cited numerous examples.… My doctor assumed that I would not engage in sexual activity, to ensure a healthy newborn. (p. 83)

As the seventh or eighth month of pregnancy approaches, the Japanese woman returns to her mother's home, where she rests until birth and recuperates for several months afterward.

Although Engel could not accept these practices for herself, she realized that they were based on cultural values that hold the maternal role in high esteem and place the safety of the infant first. This investment in the child's well-being makes Japan an excellent place to have a baby. It has one of the lowest rates of pregnancy and birth complications in the world (Bellamy, 2000).

THE PARENTAL RELATIONSHIP

The most important preparation for parenthood takes place in the context of the parents' relationship. Expectant couples who are unhappy in their marriages during pregnancy continue to be dissatisfied after the baby is born (Cowan & Cowan, 2000). Deciding to have a baby in hopes of improving a troubled relationship is a serious mistake. Pregnancy adds to rather than subtracts from family conflict if a marriage is in danger of falling apart (Belsky & Kelly, 1994).

When a couple's relationship is faring well and both partners want and planned for the baby, the excitement of a first pregnancy may bring husband and wife closer. At the same time, pregnancy does change a marriage. Expectant parents must adjust their established roles to make room for children. In addition, each partner is likely to develop new expectations of the other. Women look for greater demonstrations of affection, interest in the pregnancy, and help with household chores. They see these behaviors as important signs of continued acceptance of themselves, the pregnancy, and the baby to come. Similarly, men are particularly sensitive to expressions of warmth from their partner. These reassure them of a central place in the new mother's emotional life after the baby is born (Cowan & Cowan, 2000).

When a relationship rests on a solid foundation of love and respect, parents are well equipped for the challenges of pregnancy. They are also prepared to handle the much more demanding family changes that will take place as soon as the baby is born.

Ask YOURSELF…

apply   *Muriel, who is expecting her first child, recalls her own mother as cold and distant. Muriel is worried about whether she will be effective at caring for her new baby. What factors during pregnancy are related to maternal behavior?*

reflect   *Find out how your mother and your grandmothers managed regular activities, such as work and travel, during pregnancy. How were their daily lives different from those of contemporary pregnant women?*

Summary

MOTIVATIONS FOR PARENTHOOD

How has decision making about childbearing changed over the past 30 years, and what are the consequences for child rearing and child development?

- Today, adults in Western industrialized nations have greater freedom to choose whether, when, and how to have children, and they are more likely to weigh the advantages and disadvantages of becoming parents. Parents are also having smaller families, a trend that grants children more parental attention and that has positive consequences for children's development.

- When couples limit their families to just one child, their children are just as well adjusted socially as are children with siblings. Many adults are waiting until later in their lives to have children, when their careers are well established and they are emotionally more mature.

PRENATAL DEVELOPMENT

List the three phases of prenatal development, and describe the major milestones of each.

- The first prenatal phase, the period of the zygote, lasts about 2 weeks, from fertilization until the **blastocyst** becomes deeply **implanted** in the uterine lining. During this time, structures that will support prenatal growth begin to form. The **embryonic disk** is surrounded by the **trophoblast,** which forms structures that protect and nourish the organism. The **amnion** fills with **amniotic fluid** to regulate temperature and cushion against the mother's movements. From the **chorion,** villi emerge that burrow into the uterine wall, and the **placenta** starts to develop. The developing organism is connected to the placenta by the **umbilical cord.**

- The period of the **embryo** lasts from 2 to 8 weeks, during which the foundations for all body structures are laid down. In the first week of this period, the **neural tube** forms, and the nervous system starts to develop. Other organs follow and grow rapidly. At the end of this phase, the embryo responds to touch and can move.

- The period of the **fetus,** lasting until the end of pregnancy, involves a dramatic increase in body size and completion of physical structures. It is the longest prenatal phase and includes the second and third **trimesters.** By the middle of the second trimester, the mother can feel movement. The fetus becomes covered with **vernix,** which protects the skin from chapping. White, downy hair called **lanugo** helps the vernix stick to the skin. At the end of the second trimester, production of neurons in the brain is complete.

- The **age of viability** occurs at the beginning of the final trimester, sometime between 22 and 26 weeks. The brain continues to develop rapidly, and new sensory and behavioral capacities emerge. Gradually the lungs mature, the fetus fills the uterus, and birth is near.

PRENATAL ENVIRONMENTAL INFLUENCES

What are teratogens, and what factors influence their impact?

- **Teratogens** are environmental agents that cause damage during the prenatal period. Their effects conform to the sensitive period concept. The developing organism is especially vulnerable during the embryonic period, since all essential body structures emerge rapidly.

- The impact of teratogens varies, due to amount and length of exposure, the genetic makeup of mother and fetus, the presence or absence of other harmful agents, and the age of the organism at time of exposure. The effects of teratogens are not limited to immediate physical damage. Serious health and psychological consequences may appear later in development. Some psychological outcomes are indirectly caused by physical defects through bidirectional exchanges between child and environment.

List agents known or suspected of being teratogens, and discuss evidence supporting the harmful impact of each.

- Drugs, cigarettes, alcohol, radiation, environmental pollution, and infectious diseases are teratogens that can endanger the developing organism. **Thalidomide,** a sedative widely available in the early 1960s, showed without a doubt that drugs could cross the placenta and cause serious damage. Babies whose mothers took heroin, methadone, or cocaine during pregnancy have withdrawal symptoms after birth and are jittery and inattentive. Cocaine is especially risky, since it is associated with physical defects and central nervous system damage.

- Infants of parents who use tobacco are often born underweight and may have attention, learning, and behavior problems in early childhood. When mothers consume alcohol in large quantities, **fetal alcohol syndrome (FAS),** a disorder involving mental retardation, poor attention, overactivity, slow physical growth, and facial abnormalities, often results. Smaller amounts of alcohol may lead to some of these problems—a condition known as **fetal alcohol effects (FAE).**

- High levels of radiation, mercury, lead, and PCBs lead to physical malformations and severe brain damage. Low-level exposure has also been linked to diverse impairments. For radiation, these include language and emotional disorders. For PCB exposure, more intense physiological reactions to stress, reduced interest in the environment, and memory difficulties are involved.

- Among infectious diseases, **rubella** causes a wide variety of abnormalities, which vary with its time of occurrence during pregnancy. The human immunodeficiency virus (HIV), responsible for **acquired immune deficiency syndrome (AIDS),**

Summary (continued)

can be transmitted prenatally and results in brain damage, delayed development, and early death. **Toxoplasmosis** in the first trimester may lead to eye and brain damage.

Describe the impact of other maternal factors on prenatal development.

■ In healthy, physically fit women, regular moderate exercise contributes to an expectant woman's general health and readiness for childbirth and is related to increased birth weight. However, very "vigorous exercise results in lower birth weight. When the mother's diet is inadequate, low birth weight and damage to the brain and other organs are major concerns.

■ Severe emotional stress is linked to many pregnancy complications, although its impact can be reduced by providing the mother with emotional support.

■ When the mother's blood is Rh-negative, or lacks the **Rh factor,** and the fetus's blood is Rh-positive, special precautions must be taken to ensure that antibodies to the Rh protein do not pass from mother to fetus.

■ Aside from the risk of chromosomal abnormalities in older women, maternal age is not a major cause of prenatal problems. Instead, poor health and environmental risks associated with poverty are the strongest predictors of pregnancy complications.

Why is early and regular health care vital during the prenatal period?

■ Unexpected difficulties, such as **toxemia,** can arise, especially when pregnant mothers have health problems to begin with. Prenatal care is especially crucial for women unlikely to seek it—in particular, those who are young, single, or poverty stricken.

PREPARING FOR PARENTHOOD

What factors contribute to preparation for parenthood during the prenatal period?

■ Pregnancy is an important period of psychological transition. Mothers and fathers prepare for their new role by seeking information from books and other sources. Ultrasound images, fetal movements, and the mother's enlarging abdomen lead the baby to become a reality, and parents may form an emotional attachment to the new being. They also rely on effective models of parenthood to build images of themselves as mothers and fathers.

■ The most important preparation for parenthood takes place in the context of the couple's relationship. During the 9 months preceding birth, parents adjust their various roles and their expectations of each other as they prepare to welcome the baby into the family.

Important terms and concepts

acquired immune deficiency syndrome (AIDS) (p. 120)
age of viability (p. 109)
amnion (p. 104)
amniotic fluid (p. 105)
blastocyst (p. 104)
chorion (p. 106)
embryo (p. 107)
embryonic disk (p. 104)

fetal alcohol effects (FAE) (p. 117)
fetal alcohol syndrome (FAS) (p. 117)
fetus (p. 109)
implantation (p. 104)
lanugo (p. 109)
neural tube (p. 107)
placenta (p. 106)
Rh factor (p. 123)
rubella (p. 119)

teratogen (p. 112)
thalidomide (p. 113)
toxemia (p. 124)
toxoplasmosis (p. 120)
trimesters (p. 109)
trophoblast (p. 104)
umbilical cord (p. 106)
vernix (p. 109)

. . . for further information and help

Consult the companion website for this book, where you will find additional weblinks and associated learning activities: www.ablongman.com/berk

PRENATAL HEALTH

National Center for Education in Maternal and Child Health
www.ncemch.georgetown.edu

Government-sponsored agency that provides information on all aspects of maternal and child health.

Childbirth.org
www.childbirth.org

Offers a wealth of information on all aspects of childbirth.

BIRTH DEFECTS

National Easter Seal Society for Crippled Children and Adults
www.easter-seals.org

Provides information on birth defects. Works with other agencies to help individuals with disabilities.

National Information Center for Children and Youth with Disabilities
www.nichcy.org

Provides information to parents and educators on services for children with disabilities.

March of Dimes Birth Defects Foundation
www.modimes.org

Works to prevent birth defects through public education and community service programs.

National Organization on Fetal Alcohol Syndrome
www.nofas.org

Seeks to raise public awareness of fetal alcohol syndrome, stimulate prevention efforts, and provide information on intervention.

Alcoholics Anonymous
www.alcoholics-anonymous.org

An international organization aimed at helping people recover from alcoholism. Local chapters exist in many countries.

Parents Helping Parents
www.php.com

Offers a wide variety of services and educational programs to help parents rear children with special needs, including those with birth defects.

"Mexican Mother"

Cyntia Arrieta Rodriguez

11 years, Mexico

This idyllic scene suggests a birth that went smoothly and an infant who has successfully made the transition to life outside the womb with the support of a loving parent. Chapter 4 explores the birth process and the marvelous competencies of newborn babies.

Birth and the Newborn Baby

Although Yolanda and Jay completed my course 3 months before their baby was born, they returned the following spring to share with my next class their reactions to birth and new parenthood. Two-week-old Joshua came along as well. Yolanda and Jay's story revealed that the birth of a baby is one of the most dramatic and emotional events in human experience. Jay was present throughout Yolanda's labor and delivery. Yolanda explained,

> By morning, we knew I was in labor. It was Thursday, so we went in for my usual weekly appointment. The doctor said, yes, the baby was on the way, but it would be a while. He told us to go home and relax or take a leisurely walk and come to the hospital in 3 or 4 hours. We checked in at 3 in the afternoon; Joshua arrived at 2 o'clock the next morning. When, finally, I was ready to deliver, it went quickly; a half hour or so and some good hard pushes, and there

he was! His body had stuff all over it, his face was red and puffy, and his head was mis-shapen, but I thought, "Oh! he's beautiful. I can't believe he's really here!"

Jay was also elated by Joshua's birth. "I wanted to support Yolanda and to experience as much as I could. It was awesome, indescribable," he said, holding little Joshua over his shoulder and patting and kissing him gently.

In this chapter we explore the experience of childbirth, from both the parents' and the baby's points of view. As recently as 30 years ago, the birth process was treated more like an illness than a natural part of life. Today, women in industrialized nations have many choices about where and how they give birth, and hospitals go to great lengths to make the arrival of a new baby a rewarding, family-centered event.

Joshua reaped the benefits of Yolanda and Jay's careful attention to his needs during pregnancy. He was strong, alert, and healthy at birth. Nevertheless, the birth process does not always go smoothly. We will pay special attention to the problems of infants who are born underweight or too early. Our discussion will also examine the pros and cons of medical interventions, such as pain-relieving drugs and surgical deliveries, designed to ease a difficult birth and protect the health of mother and baby.

Finally, Yolanda and Jay spoke candidly about how, since Joshua's arrival, life at home had changed. "It's exciting and wonderful," reflected Yolanda, "but the adjustments are enormous. I wasn't quite prepared for the intensity of Joshua's 24-hour-a-day demands." In the last part of this chapter, we take a close look at the remarkable ability of newborn babies to adapt to the external world and to communicate their needs. We also consider how parents adjust to the realities of everyday life with a new baby.

The Stages of Childbirth

It is not surprising that childbirth is often referred to as *labor*. It is the hardest physical work that a woman may ever do. As the Biology and Environment box on pages 136–137 explains, a complex series of hormonal changes initiates the process. Yolanda's whole system, which for 9 months supported and protected Joshua's growth, now turned toward a new goal: getting him safely out of the uterus.

The events that lead to childbirth begin slowly in the ninth month of pregnancy and gradually pick up speed. Several signs indicate that labor is near:

- Yolanda felt the upper part of her uterus contract once in a while. These contractions are often called *false labor* or *prelabor,* since they remain brief and unpredictable for several weeks.

- About 2 weeks before birth, an event called *lightening* occurred; Joshua's head dropped low into the uterus. Yolanda's cervix had begun to soften in preparation for delivery and no longer supported Joshua's weight so easily.

- A sure sign that labor is only hours or days away is the *bloody show*. As the cervix opens more, the plug of mucus that sealed it during pregnancy is released, producing a reddish discharge (Samuels & Samuels, 1996). Soon after, contractions of the uterus become more frequent, and mother and baby have entered the first of three stages of labor (see Figure 4.1).

STAGE 1: DILATION AND EFFACEMENT OF THE CERVIX

Stage 1 is the longest, lasting an average of 12 to 14 hours with a first baby and 4 to 6 hours with later births. **Dilation and effacement of the cervix** take place—that is, uterine contractions gradually become more frequent and powerful, causing the cervix to open (dilate) and thin (efface), forming a clear channel from the uterus into the birth canal, or

dilation and effacement of the cervix
Widening and thinning of the cervix during the first stage of labor.

Stage 1

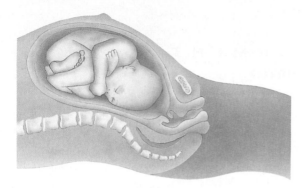

(a) Dilation and Effacement of the Cervix

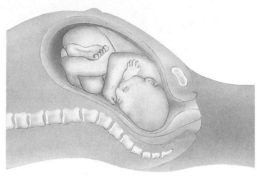

(b) Transition

Stage 2

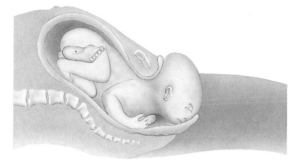

(c) Pushing

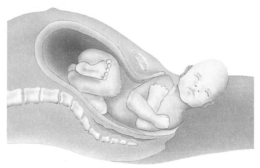

(d) Birth of the Baby

Stage 3

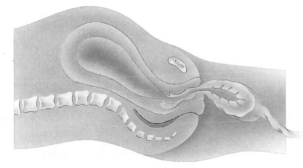

(e) Delivery of the Placenta

FIGURE 4.1

The three stages of labor. Stage 1: (a) Contractions of the uterus cause the cervix to open and thin. (b) Transition is reached when the frequency and strength of the contractions are at their peak and the cervix opens completely. Stage 2: (c) The mother pushes with each contraction, forcing the baby down the birth canal, and the head appears. (d) Near the end of Stage 2, the shoulders emerge and are followed quickly by the rest of the baby's body. Stage 3: (e) With a few final pushes, the placenta is delivered.

vagina. Uterine contractions that open the cervix are forceful and regular, starting out 10 to 20 minutes apart and lasting about 15 to 20 seconds. Gradually, they get closer together, occurring every 2 to 3 minutes. In addition, they become more powerful, continuing for as long as 60 seconds.

During this stage, Yolanda could do nothing to speed up the process. Jay held her hand, provided sips of juice and water, and helped her get comfortable. Throughout the first few hours, Yolanda walked, stood, or sat upright. As the contractions became more intense, she leaned against pillows or lay on her side.

The climax of Stage 1 is a brief period called **transition,** in which the frequency and strength of contractions are at their peak and the cervix opens completely. Although transition is the most uncomfortable part of childbirth, it is especially important that the mother relax. If she tenses or bears down with her muscles before the cervix is completely dilated and effaced, she may bruise the cervix and slow the progress of labor.

transition
Climax of the first stage of labor, in which the frequency and strength of contractions are at their peak and the cervix opens completely.

Biology & ENVIRONMENT

WHAT CONTROLS THE TIMING OF BIRTH?

Only in the past decade has animal and human research begun to uncover the precise biological changes that control the timing of birth. Through most of pregnancy, the placenta secretes high levels of the hormone *progesterone,* which keeps the uterus relaxed and the cervix firm and inflexible, so it remains tightly closed and capable of supporting the growing fetus. But the placenta also secretes *estrogen,* which rises during pregnancy and counters the effects of progesterone in three ways:

- by producing a protein called *connexin,* which links uterine muscle cells to one another so they contract in a coordinated fashion;
- by making the uterine muscle sensitive to *oxytocin,* a hormone released from the brain that induces contractions; and

- by stimulating the placenta to release *prostaglandins,* hormones that soften the cervix so it will dilate during labor.

What switches on the production of estrogen and leads it to overwhelm progesterone? Researchers began to suspect that another placental hormone called *corticotropin-releasing hormone (CRH)* is involved when they found that mothers who go into premature labor have higher blood levels

FIGURE 4.2

Release of CRH by the placenta in relation to timing of birth. CRH levels in the blood of 500 women were measured repeatedly as their pregnancies progressed. As early as the 16th to 20th week after conception, CRH concentration predicted who would deliver prematurely, who would deliver on time, and who would deliver late. (From Smith, R., "The Timing of Birth," *Scientific American,* 280(3), 68–75. Copyright © 1999 by Scientific American, Inc. All rights reserved. Reprinted by permission.)

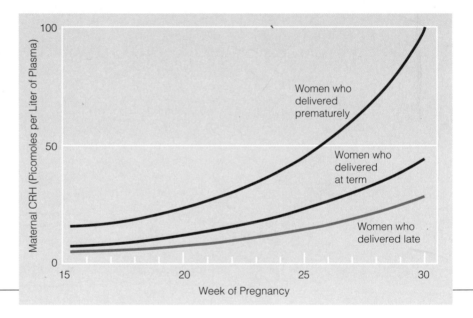

STAGE 2: DELIVERY OF THE BABY

In Stage 2, which lasts about 50 minutes for a first baby and 20 minutes in later births, the infant is born. Strong contractions of the uterus continue, but the mother also feels a natural urge to squeeze and push with her abdominal muscles. As she does so with each contraction, she forces the baby down and out.

Yolanda dozed lightly between contractions. As each new wave came, "I pushed with all my might," she said. In the meantime, the doctor performed an **episiotomy,** or small incision that increases the size of the vaginal opening, permitting the baby to pass without tearing the mother's tissues.

When the doctor announced that the baby's head was *crowning*—the vaginal opening had stretched around the entire head—Yolanda felt renewed energy; she knew that soon the baby would arrive. Quickly, with several more pushes, Joshua's forehead, nose, and chin emerged, then his upper body and trunk. The doctor held him up, wet with amniotic fluid and still attached to the umbilical cord. Air rushed into his lungs, and Joshua cried. When the umbilical cord stopped pulsing, it was clamped and cut. Joshua was placed on Yolanda's chest,

episiotomy
A small incision made during childbirth to increase the size of the vaginal opening.

© AFP/CORBIS

Thousands of Muslim women pray in Jerusalem's old city during Friday noon prayer of the month of Ramadan, a time of daily fasting from dawn to sunset. Pregnant women may postpone the fast to a later time—an exception that recognizes food deprivation as a threat to the mother's and baby's health. Fasting may precipitate early birth by causing the fetus to produce an excess of cortisol, a stress hormone. Cortisol initiates a rise in corticotropin-releasing hormone (CRH), which, in turn, triggers increased estrogen production, required for labor.

of CRH than do other women in the same week of pregnancy (see Figure 4.2) (McLean et al., 1995). In fact, CRH levels measured as early as the 16th to 20th week are good predictors of whether a woman will give birth early, on time, or past her due date.

How does CRH work? When it reaches a high enough level, it leads the fetal adrenal glands (located on top of each kidney) to produce *cortisol,* a stress hormone that clears the infants' lungs of fluid so they are ready to breathe air. Cortisol, in turn, further stimulates CRH production, which triggers estrogen secretion in the placenta, resulting in the rapid estrogen rise required for labor (Emanuel et al., 1994; Smith, 1999). Notice how the "CRH–cortisol circuit" helps ensure that labor will occur only when the fetus is ready to survive outside the womb.

What causes the placenta to make CRH, and what affects how much is produced? Researchers are still trying to answer to this question. The genetic makeup of CRH-producing cells may lead CRH to rise too early in some women, resulting in prematurity. Another potential influence is maternal nutrition. Food deprivation precipitates early birth in some mammals; the same effect may operate in humans. In support of this possibility, an Israeli study reported that pregnant Jewish women observing the day-long fast of Yom Kippur showed a sharp rise in delivery rates during the last 6 hours of the fast and the day after. This increase was not observed in non-Jewish women living in the same region or in Jewish women observing the harvest holiday of Succot, celebrated with a special meal (Wiser et al., 1997). Perhaps even brief periods of inadequate nutrition can activate the fetal stress system, which prompts excess production of CRH.

In sum, a complex hormonal system, initiated by CRH and involving both mother and fetus, controls the timing of birth. New knowledge about birth timing is leading to more effective prevention of prematurity—a major cause of infant death and disability. Already, studies show that CRH production can be chemically inhibited and, in turn, delay birth in sheep (Smith, 1999). If tests of CRH inhibitors in nonhuman primates prove safe and effective, then trials in human mothers are not far off.

where she and Jay could see, touch, and gently talk to him. Then he was wrapped snugly to help with temperature regulation.

STAGE 3: BIRTH OF THE PLACENTA

Stage 3 brings labor to an end with a few final contractions and pushes. These cause the placenta to separate from the wall of the uterus and be delivered in about 5 to 10 minutes. Yolanda and Jay were surprised at the large size of the thick 1½-pound red-gray organ that had taken care of Joshua's basic needs for the previous 9 months.

THE BABY'S ADAPTATION TO LABOR AND DELIVERY

At first glance, labor and delivery seem like a dangerous ordeal for the baby. The strong contractions of Yolanda's uterus exposed Joshua's head to a great deal of pressure, and they squeezed the placenta and the umbilical cord repeatedly. Each time, Joshua's supply of oxygen was temporarily reduced.

TABLE 4.1
The Apgar Scale

SIGN[a]	SCORE		
	0	1	2
Heart rate	No heartbeat	Under 100 beats per minute	100 to 140 beats per minute
Respiratory effort	No breathing for 60 seconds	Irregular, shallow breathing	Strong breathing and crying
Reflex irritability (sneezing, coughing, and grimacing)	No response	Weak reflexive response	Strong reflexive response
Muscle tone	Completely limp	Weak movements of arms and legs	Strong movements of arms and legs
Color	Blue body, arms, and legs	Body pink with blue arms and legs	Body, arms, and legs completely pink

[a]To remember these signs, you may find it helpful to use a technique in which the original labels are reordered and renamed as follows: color = **A**ppearance, heart rate = **P**ulse, reflex irritability = **G**rimace, muscle tone = **A**ctivity, and respiratory effort = **R**espiration. Together, the first letters of the new labels spell **Apgar**.

Source: Apgar, 1953.

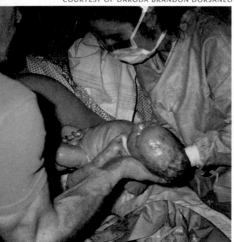

COURTESY OF DAKODA BRANDON DORSANEO

This newborn is held by his mother's birthing coach (on the left) and midwife (on the right) just after delivery. The umbilical cord has not yet been cut. The baby's head is molded from being squeezed through the birth canal for many hours. As the infant takes his first breaths, his body turns from blue to pink. He is wide awake and ready to get to know his new surroundings.

Apgar Scale
A rating used to assess the newborn baby's physical condition immediately after birth.

Fortunately, healthy babies are well equipped to withstand the trauma of childbirth. The force of the contractions causes the infant to produce high levels of stress hormones. Recall from Chapter 3 that during pregnancy, the effects of maternal stress can endanger the baby. In contrast, during childbirth, the infant's production of stress hormones is adaptive. It helps the baby withstand oxygen deprivation by sending a rich supply of blood to the brain and heart. In addition, it prepares the baby to breathe effectively by causing the lungs to absorb any remaining fluid and by expanding the bronchial tubes (passages leading to the lungs). Finally, stress hormones arouse the infant into alertness at birth. Joshua was born wide awake, ready to interact with the surrounding world (Lagercrantz & Slotkin, 1986).

THE NEWBORN BABY'S APPEARANCE

What do babies look like after birth? Jay smiled when my students asked this question. "Yolanda and I are probably the only people in the world who thought Joshua was beautiful!" The average newborn is 20 inches long and 7½ pounds in weight; boys tend to be slightly longer and heavier than girls. Body proportions contribute to the baby's strange appearance. The head is very large in comparison to the trunk and legs, which are short and bowed. Proportionally, if your head were as large as that of a newborn infant, you would be balancing something about the size of a watermelon between your shoulders! As we will see in later chapters, the combination of a big head (with its well-developed brain) and a small body means that human infants learn quickly in the first few months of life. But unlike most mammals, they cannot get around on their own until much later.

Even though newborn babies may not match the idealized image many parents created in their minds during pregnancy, some features do make them attractive. Their round faces, chubby cheeks, large foreheads, and big eyes make adults feel like picking them up and cuddling them (Berman, 1980; Lorenz, 1943).

ASSESSING THE NEWBORN'S PHYSICAL CONDITION: THE APGAR SCALE

Infants who have difficulty making the transition to life outside the uterus must be given special help at once. To quickly assess the newborn's physical condition, doctors and nurses use the **Apgar Scale.** As Table 4.1 shows, a rating of 0, 1, or 2 on each of five characteristics is made at 1 and 5 minutes after birth. A combined Apgar score of 7 or better indicates that the infant is in good physical condition. If the score is between 4 and 6, the baby requires assistance in establishing breathing and other vital signs. If the score is 3 or below, the infant is in serious danger, and emergency medical attention is needed. Two Apgar ratings are given, since some babies have trouble adjusting at first but do quite well after a few minutes (Apgar, 1953).

Color is the least dependable of the Apgar ratings. Dark-skinned babies like Joshua cannot be judged easily for pinkness and blueness. However, all newborns can be rated for a rosy glow that results from the flow of oxygen through body tissues once the baby starts to breathe, since skin tone is usually lighter at birth than the baby's inherited pigmentation.

Ask **YOURSELF...**

review   *Name and briefly describe the three stages of labor.*

apply   *On seeing her newborn baby for the first time, Caroline exclaimed, "Why is she so out of proportion?" What observations prompted Caroline to ask this question? Explain why her baby's appearance is adaptive.*

connect   *How do findings on the timing of birth illustrate bidirectional influences between mother and fetus? How do they illustrate the roles of both nature and nurture?*

Approaches to Childbirth

Childbirth practices, like other aspects of family life, are molded by the society of which mother and baby are a part. In many village and tribal cultures, expectant mothers are well acquainted with the childbirth process. For example, the Jarara of South America and the Pukapukans of the Pacific Islands treat birth as a vital part of daily life. The Jarara mother gives birth in full view of the entire community, including small children. The Pukapukan girl is so familiar with the events of labor and delivery that she can frequently be seen playing at it. Using a coconut to represent the baby, she stuffs it inside her dress, imitates the mother's pushing, and lets the nut fall at the proper moment. In most nonindustrialized cultures, women are assisted during the birth process. Among the Mayans of the Yucatán, the mother leans against the body of a woman called the "head helper," who supports her weight and breathes with her during each contraction (Jordan, 1993; Mead & Newton, 1967).

In large Western nations, childbirth has changed dramatically over the centuries. Before the late 1800s, birth took place at home and was a family-centered event. The industrial revolution brought greater crowding to cities along with new health problems, so childbirth moved from home to hospital, where the health of mothers and babies could be protected. Once doctors assumed responsibility for childbirth, women's knowledge of it declined, and relatives and friends were no longer welcome to participate (Borst, 1995).

By the 1950s and 1960s, women started to question medical procedures that had become routine during labor and delivery. Many felt that frequent use of strong drugs and delivery instruments had robbed them of a precious experience and were often not necessary or safe for the baby. Gradually, a natural childbirth movement arose in Europe and spread to the United States. Its purpose was to make hospital birth as comfortable and rewarding for mothers as possible. Today, most hospitals offer birth centers that are family centered and homelike. *Freestanding birth centers* also exist. They operate independently of hospitals and encourage early contact between parents and baby but offer less backup medical care. And a small but growing number of American women are rejecting institutional birth by choosing to have their babies at home.

Let's take a closer look at two childbirth approaches that have gained popularity in recent years: natural childbirth and home delivery.

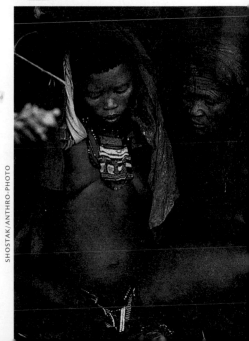

Among the !Kung of Botswana, Africa, a mother gives birth in a sitting position, and she is surrounded by women who encourage and help her.

SHOSTAK/ANTHRO-PHOTO

NATURAL, OR PREPARED, CHILDBIRTH

Yolanda and Jay chose **natural, or prepared, childbirth.** Although many natural childbirth techniques exist, all try to overcome the idea that birth is a painful ordeal that requires extensive medical intervention. Most programs draw on methods developed by Grantly Dick-Read (1959) in England and Fernand Lamaze (1958) in France. These physicians recognized that cultural attitudes had taught women to fear the birth experience. An anxious, frightened woman in labor tenses her muscles, turning the mild pain that sometimes accompanies strong contractions into a great deal of pain.

Yolanda and Jay enrolled in a typical natural childbirth program offered by a hospital birth center. The program consisted of three ingredients:

- *Information about labor and delivery.* Yolanda and Jay attended classes in which they learned about the anatomy and physiology of labor and delivery. Knowledge about the birth process reduces a mother's fear.

- *Relaxation and breathing techniques.* During each class, Yolanda practiced relaxation and breathing exercises aimed at counteracting any pain she might feel during uterine contractions.

- *Labor coach.* Jay learned how to help Yolanda during childbirth—by reminding her to relax and breathe, massaging her back, supporting her body during labor and delivery, and offering encouragement and affection.

Studies comparing mothers who experience natural childbirth with those who do not reveal many benefits. Because mothers feel more in control of labor and delivery, their attitudes toward the childbirth experience are more positive (Mackey, 1995; Waldenström, 1999). They also feel less pain. As a result, they require less medication—very little or none at all (Hetherington, 1990).

■ **SOCIAL SUPPORT AND NATURAL CHILDBIRTH.** Social support is important to the success of natural childbirth techniques. In Guatemalan and American hospitals that routinely isolated patients during childbirth, some mothers were randomly assigned a trained companion who stayed with them throughout labor and delivery, talking to them, holding their hands, and rubbing their backs to promote relaxation. These mothers had fewer birth complications, and their labors were several hours shorter than those of women who did not have supportive companionship. Guatemalan mothers who received support also interacted more positively with their babies during the first half-hour after delivery, talking, smiling, and gently stroking (Kennell et al., 1991; Sosa et al., 1980).

The continuous rather than intermittent support of a trained companion during labor and delivery strengthens these outcomes. It is particularly helpful during a first childbirth, when mothers are more anxious (DiMatteo & Kahn, 1997; Scott, Berkowitz, & Klaus, 1999). Finally, this aspect of natural childbirth makes Western hospital birth customs more acceptable to women from parts of the world where assistance from family and community members is the norm (Granot et al., 1996).

FIGURE 4.3

Sitting position often used for delivery in a birth center or at home. It facilitates pushing during the second stage of labor; increases blood flow to the placenta, which grants the baby a richer supply of oxygen; and permits the mother to see the delivery, enabling her to track the effectiveness of each contraction.

■ **POSITIONS FOR DELIVERY.** When natural childbirth is combined with delivery in a birth center or at home, mothers often give birth in the upright, sitting position shown in Figure 4.3 rather than lying flat on their backs with their feet in stirrups (which is the traditional hospital delivery room practice). In Europe, women often are encouraged to give birth on their sides because it reduces the need for an episiotomy, since pressure of the baby's head against the vaginal opening is less intense (Bobak, Jensen, & Zalar, 1989).

Research findings favor the sitting position. When mothers are upright, labor is shortened because pushing is easier and more effective. The baby benefits from a richer supply of oxygen because blood flow to the placenta is increased. Furthermore, since the mother can see the delivery, she can track the effectiveness of each contraction in pushing the baby out of the birth canal (Kelly, Terry, & Naglieri, 1999). This helps her work with the doctor or midwife to ensure that the baby's head and shoulders emerge slowly, which reduces the chances of tearing the vaginal opening.

HOME DELIVERY

Home birth has always been popular in certain industrialized nations, such as England, the Netherlands, and Sweden. The number of American women choosing to have their babies at home has increased in recent years, although it remains small, at about 1 percent (Curtin & Park, 1999). These mothers want birth to be an important part of family life. In addition, most want to avoid unnecessary medical procedures. And they also want greater control over their own care and that of their babies than most hospitals permit (Wickham, 1999). Although some home births are attended by doctors, many more are handled by *certified nurse-midwives* who have degrees in nursing and additional training in childbirth management.

The joys and perils of home delivery are well illustrated by the story that Don, who painted my house as I worked on this book, related to me. "Our first child was delivered in the hospital," he said. "Even though I was present, Kathy and I found the atmosphere to be rigid and insensitive. We wanted a warmer, more personal birth environment." With the coaching of a nurse-midwife, Don delivered their second child, Cindy, at their farmhouse, three miles out of town.

Three years later, when Kathy went into labor with Marnie, a heavy snowstorm prevented the midwife from reaching the house on time. Don delivered the baby alone, but the birth was difficult. Marnie failed to breathe for several minutes; with great effort, Don managed to revive her. The frightening memory of Marnie's limp, blue body convinced Don and Kathy to return to the hospital to have their last child. By then, the hospital's birth practices had changed, and the event was a rewarding one for both parents.

Don and Kathy's experience raises the question of whether it is just as safe to give birth at home as in a hospital. For healthy women who are assisted by a well-trained doctor or midwife, it seems so, since complications rarely occur (Olsen, 1997). However, if attendants are not carefully trained and prepared to handle emergencies, the rate of infant death is high (Mehlmadrona & Madrona, 1997). When mothers are at risk for any kind of complication, the appropriate place for labor and delivery is the hospital, where life-saving treatment is available.

© SUZANNE ARMS

About to give birth at home, this mother discusses the progress of her labor with the midwife while her husband and their older child look on. Mothers who choose home birth want to make the experience an important part of family life, avoid unnecessary medical procedures, and exercise greater control over their own care and that of their babies.

Medical Interventions

Medical interventions during childbirth occur in both industrialized and non-industrialized cultures. For example, some preliterate tribal and village societies have discovered labor-inducing drugs and developed surgical techniques to deliver babies (Jordan, 1993). Yet, more so than anywhere else in the world, childbirth in the United States is a medically monitored and controlled event. What medical techniques are doctors likely to use during labor and delivery? When are they justified, and what dangers do they pose to mothers and babies? These are questions we take up in the following sections.

FETAL MONITORING

Fetal monitors are electronic instruments that track the baby's heart rate during labor. An abnormal heartbeat pattern may indicate that the baby is in distress due to lack of oxygen and needs to be delivered immediately. Fetal monitors are required in almost all American hospitals and used in 83 percent of American births (Curtin & Park, 1999). Two types are common. The most popular is strapped across the mother's abdomen throughout labor. A second, more accurate method involves threading a recording device through the cervix and placing it directly under the baby's scalp.

natural, or prepared, childbirth
An approach designed to reduce pain and medical intervention and to make childbirth a rewarding experience for parents.

fetal monitors
Electronic instruments that track the baby's heart rate during labor.

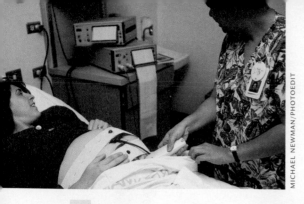

MICHAEL NEWMAN/PHOTOEDIT

Throughout labor, this mother has an external fetal monitor, which records fetal heart rate using ultrasound, attached to her abdomen. When mothers have a history of pregnancy and birth complications, fetal monitoring saves many lives. But it also may lead to an increase in unnecessary cesarean (surgical) deliveries. Also, some women complain that the monitors are uncomfortable and restrict their freedom of movement.

FIGURE 4.4

Instrument delivery. (a) The pressure that must be applied to pull the infant from the birth canal with *forceps* involves risk of injury to the baby's head. (b) An alternative method, the *vacuum extractor,* is less likely than forceps to injure the mother. However, it is just as risky for the infant; scalp injuries are common.

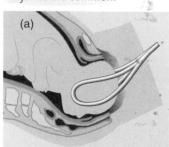
(a)

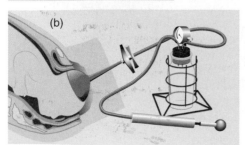
(b)

Fetal monitoring is a safe medical procedure that has saved the lives of many babies in high-risk situations. Nevertheless, the practice is controversial. Fetal monitoring does not reduce the already low rates of infant brain damage and death in mothers who have had healthy pregnancies. Most infants have some heartbeat irregularities during labor, and critics worry that fetal monitors identify many babies as in danger who, in fact, are not (Berkus et al., 1999; Haggerty, 1999). Monitoring is linked to an increase in the number of emergency cesarean (surgical) deliveries, a practice we will discuss shortly. In addition, some women complain that the devices are uncomfortable, prevent them from moving easily, and interfere with the normal course of labor.

Still, fetal monitors will probably continue to be used routinely, even though they might not be necessary in most cases. Today, doctors can be sued for malpractice if an infant dies or is born with problems and they cannot show that they did everything possible to protect the baby (Chez, 1997).

LABOR AND DELIVERY MEDICATION

Some form of medication is used in 80 to 95 percent of births in the United States (Glosten, 1998). **Analgesics** are drugs used to relieve pain. When given during labor, the dose is usually mild and intended to help a mother relax. **Anesthetics** are a stronger type of painkiller that blocks sensation. A regional anesthetic may be injected into the spinal column to numb the lower half of the body.

Although pain-relieving drugs enable doctors to perform essential life-saving medical interventions, they can cause problems when used routinely. Anesthetics weaken uterine contractions during the first stage of labor and interfere with the mother's ability to feel contractions and push during the second stage. As a result, labor is prolonged (Alexander et al., 1998). In addition, since labor and delivery medication rapidly crosses the placenta, the newborn baby may be sleepy and withdrawn, suck poorly during feedings, and be irritable when awake (Emory, Schlackman, & Fiano, 1996).

Does the use of medication during childbirth have a lasting impact on physical and mental development? Some researchers claim so (Brackbill, McManus, & Woodward, 1985), but their findings have been challenged (Golub, 1996). Anesthesia may be related to other risk factors that could account for the long-term consequences in some studies, and more research is needed to sort out these effects. In the meantime, the negative impact of these drugs on the early infant–mother relationship supports the current trend to limit their use.

INSTRUMENT DELIVERY

Forceps, metal clamps placed around the baby's head to pull the infant from the birth canal, have been used since the sixteenth century to speed up delivery (see Figure 4.4). A more recent instrument, the **vacuum extractor,** consists of a plastic cup (placed on the baby's head) attached to a suction tube. Instrument delivery is appropriate if the mother's pushing during the second stage of labor does not move the baby through the birth canal in a reasonable period of time.

In the United States, forceps are used in nearly 4 percent of births, vacuum extractors in 8 percent, yielding an instrument delivery rate of 12 percent. In contrast, instruments are used in less than 5 percent of births in Europe (National Center for Health Statistics, 2000). These figures suggest that instruments may be applied too freely in American hospitals.

When a doctor uses forceps to pull the baby through most or all of the birth canal, deliveries are associated with higher rates of brain damage. As a result, forceps are seldom used this way today. Low-forceps delivery (carried out when the baby is most of the way through the vagina) is not associated with poorer intellectual functioning in childhood and adolescence (Wesley, van den Berg, & Reece, 1993). Still, some risk of injury to the baby's head and to the mother's tissues remains. Vacuum extractors are less likely to tear the mother's tissues than are forceps, but the chances of harming the infant are just as great (Johanson et al., 1993). For these reasons, neither method should be used when the mother can be encouraged to deliver normally and there is no special reason to hurry the birth.

INDUCED LABOR

An **induced labor** is one that is started artificially, usually by breaking the amnion, or bag of waters (an event that typically occurs naturally in the first stage of labor), and giving the mother synthetic oxytocin, a hormone that stimulates contractions. In the United States, slightly more than 18 percent of labors are induced, a figure that has doubled over the past decade (Curtin, 1999).

Inducing labor is justified when continuing the pregnancy threatens the well-being of mother or baby. Too often, though, labors are induced for the doctor's or the patient's convenience. In a healthy mother, the onset of labor should not be scheduled like her doctor's appointment. An induced labor often proceeds differently from a naturally occurring one. Contractions are longer, harder, and closer together, increasing the possibility of inadequate oxygen supply to the baby. In addition, mothers often find it more difficult to stay in control of an induced labor, even when they have been coached in natural childbirth techniques. As a result, labor and delivery medication is likely to be used in larger amounts, and the chances of instrument delivery are greater (Brindley & Sokol, 1988).

Occasionally, induction is performed before the mother is physically ready to give birth, and the procedure fails. When this happens, a cesarean delivery is necessary. The rate of cesareans is more than twice as great in induced labors as in spontaneous labors (Seyb et al., 1999). The placental hormone CRH (turn back to the Biology and Environment box on pages 136–137) helps predict the success of induction procedures. Mothers with high levels of CRH are more likely to respond well than are those whose CRH levels are low (Smith, 1999).

CESAREAN DELIVERY

A **cesarean delivery** is a surgical birth; the doctor makes an incision in the mother's abdomen and lifts the baby out of the uterus. It received its name from the belief that Roman emperor Julius Caesar was born this way.

Thirty years ago cesarean delivery was rare in the United States, performed in only 3 percent of births, when the life of mother or baby was in danger. Since then, the cesarean rate has climbed, reaching 24 percent in 1994 and dropping slightly to 21 percent in 1999. Still, it is the highest in the world, surpassing Canada, the second-ranked nation at 18 percent (Canadian Institute for Health Information, 2000; U.S. Bureau of the Census, 2000). Some countries, such as Japan and the Netherlands, have cesarean rates of less than 7 percent (Samuels & Samuels, 1996). Yet these nations, as we will see shortly, have considerably lower infant death rates than does the United States.

Cesareans have always been warranted by medical emergencies, such as Rh incompatibility, premature separation of the placenta from the uterus, or serious maternal illness or infection (for example, the herpes simplex 2 virus, which can infect the baby during a vaginal delivery). However, surgical delivery is not always needed in other instances. For example, although the most common reason for a cesarean is a previous cesarean, the technique used today—a small horizontal cut in the lower part of the uterus—makes a vaginal birth safe in subsequent pregnancies (Korte, 1997).

In contrast, when babies are **breech position,** or turned so that the buttocks or feet would be delivered first (about 1 in every 25 births), cesareans often are justified. The breech position increases the possibility that the umbilical cord may be squeezed as the large head moves through the birth canal, depriving the infant of oxygen. Head injuries are also more likely during a breech birth (Koo, Dekker, & van Geijn, 1998). But the infant's exact position (which can be felt by the doctor) makes a difference. Certain breech babies fare just as well with a normal delivery as they do with a cesarean (Ismail et al., 1999). Sometimes the doctor can gently turn the baby into a head-down position during the early part of labor.

Because many unnecessary cesareans are performed in the United States, pregnant women should ask questions about the procedure when choosing a doctor. When a mother does have a cesarean, she and her baby need extra support. The operation itself is quite safe, but it requires

analgesic
A mild pain-relieving drug.

anesthetic
A strong painkilling drug that blocks sensation.

forceps
Metal clamps placed around the baby's head, used to pull the infant from the birth canal.

vacuum extractor
A plastic cup attached to a suction tube, used to help deliver the baby.

induced labor
A labor started artificially by breaking the amnion and giving the mother a hormone that stimulates contractions.

cesarean delivery
A surgical delivery in which the doctor makes an incision in the mother's abdomen and lifts the baby out of the uterus.

breech position
A position of the baby in the uterus that would cause the buttocks or feet to be delivered first.

more time for recovery. Since anesthesia may have crossed the placenta, cesarean newborns are more likely to be sleepy and unresponsive and to have breathing difficulties (Cox & Schwartz, 1990). These factors can negatively affect the early mother–infant relationship.

Ask YOURSELF...

review   *Describe the ingredients and benefits of natural childbirth. What aspect contributes greatly to favorable outcomes, and why?*

apply   *Sharon, a heavy smoker, has just arrived at the hospital in labor. Which one of the medical interventions discussed in the preceding sections is her doctor justified in using? (For help in answering this question, return to the discussion of prenatal effects of tobacco in Chapter 3, page 117.)*

connect   *Use of any one medical intervention during labor increases the chances that others will also be used. Provide as many examples as you can to illustrate this idea.*

reflect   *If you were an expectant parent, would you choose home birth? Why or why not?*

Birth Complications

We have seen that some babies—in particular, those whose mothers are in poor health, do not receive good medical care, or have a history of pregnancy problems—are especially likely to experience birth complications. Inadequate oxygen, a pregnancy that ends too early, and a baby who is born underweight are serious risks to development that we have touched on many times. A baby remaining in the uterus too long is yet another risk. Let's look at the impact of each complication on later development.

OXYGEN DEPRIVATION

Some years ago, I got to know 2-year-old Melinda and her mother, Judy, both of whom participated in a special program for infants with disabilities at our laboratory school. Melinda has **cerebral palsy,** which is a general term for a variety of problems that result from brain damage before, during, or just after birth. Difficulties in muscle coordination are always involved, such as a clumsy walk, uncontrolled movements, and unclear speech. The disorder can range from very mild tremors to severe crippling and mental retardation. One out of every 500 children born in the United States has cerebral palsy. Ten percent of these youngsters experienced **anoxia,** or inadequate oxygen supply, during labor and delivery (Anslow, 1998).

Melinda walks with a halting, lumbering gait and has difficulty keeping her balance. "Some mothers don't know how the palsy happened," confided Judy, "but I do. I got pregnant accidentally, and my boyfriend didn't want to have anything to do with it. I was frightened and alone most of the time. I arrived at the hospital at the last minute. Melinda was breech, and the cord was wrapped around her neck."

Squeezing of the umbilical cord, as in Melinda's case, is one cause of anoxia. Another cause is *placenta abruptio,* or premature separation of the placenta, a life-threatening event with a high rate of infant death (Ananth et al., 1999). Although the reasons for placenta abruptio are not well understood, teratogens that cause abnormal development of the placenta, such as cigarette smoking, are strongly related to it (Handler et al., 1994). Just as serious is *placenta previa,* a condition caused by implantation of the blastocyst low in the uterus so the placenta covers the cervical opening. As the cervix dilates and effaces in the third trimester, part of the

cerebral palsy
A general term for a variety of problems, all of which involve muscle coordination, that result from brain damage before, during, or just after birth.

anoxia
Inadequate oxygen supply.

placenta may detach (Chamberlain & Steer, 1999). When hemorrhaging from placenta abruptio or placenta previa is severe, an emergency cesarean must be performed.

In still other instances, the birth seems to go along all right, but the baby fails to start breathing within a few minutes. Healthy newborns can survive periods of little or no oxygen longer than adults can; they reduce their metabolic rate, thereby conserving the limited oxygen available. Nevertheless, brain damage is likely if regular breathing is delayed more than 10 minutes (Parer, 1998). Can you think of other possible causes of oxygen deprivation that you learned about as you studied prenatal development and birth?

How do children who experience anoxia during labor and delivery fare as they get older? Although they often are behind their agemates in intellectual and motor progress in early childhood, by elementary school most catch up in development (Corah et al., 1965; Raz, Shah, & Sander, 1996). In the fetus and newborn baby, damage to inner brain structures involved in control of body movement usually occurs first; the cerebral cortex can better withstand oxygen deprivation. This helps explain why Melinda's physical disability was permanent, but otherwise she did well.

Cell death in an injured brain can continue for weeks or months, however, so researchers are experimenting with ways to prevent this ongoing damage. Placing a device around the head that cools the brain by several degrees and administering growth factors (substances naturally produced by the brain to promote recovery from injury) are effective in newborn rats, pigs, and sheep. The techniques show promise for human babies as well (Gunn, 2000; Robertson & Edwards, 1998).

When problems do persist, the anoxia was probably extreme. Perhaps it was caused by prenatal insult to the baby's respiratory system, or it may have happened because the infant's lungs were not yet mature enough to breathe. For example, infants born more than 6 weeks early commonly have **respiratory distress syndrome** (otherwise known as *hyaline membrane disease*). Their tiny lungs are so poorly developed that the air sacs collapse, causing serious breathing difficulties. Today, mechanical ventilators keep many such infants alive. In spite of these measures, some babies suffer permanent damage from lack of oxygen, and in other cases their delicate lungs are harmed by the treatment itself (Vohr & Garcia-Coll, 1988). Respiratory distress syndrome is only one of many risks for babies born too soon, as we will see in the following section.

PRETERM AND LOW-BIRTH-WEIGHT INFANTS

Janet, almost 6 months pregnant, and her husband, Rick, boarded a flight in Hartford, Connecticut, on their way to a vacation in Hawaii. During a stopover in San Francisco, Janet told Rick she was bleeding. They realized she was in trouble. Rushed to a hospital, she gave birth to Keith, who weighed less than 1½ pounds. Delivered 23 weeks after conception, he had barely reached the age of viability (see Chapter 3, page 109).

During Keith's first month, he experienced one crisis after another, all of which are common in very premature infants. Three days after birth, an ultrasound scan suggested that fragile blood vessels feeding Keith's brain had hemorrhaged, a complication that can cause brain damage. Within three weeks, Keith had surgery to close a valve in his heart that seals automatically in full-term babies. Keith's immature immune system made infections difficult to contain. Repeated illnesses and the drugs used to treat them caused permanent hearing loss. He also had respiratory distress syndrome and was attached to a ventilator. Soon there was evidence of lung damage, and Keith's vision was threatened because of constant exposure to oxygen. It took more than 3 months of hospitalization for Keith's rough course of complications and treatment to ease.

Babies born 3 weeks or more before the end of a full 38-week pregnancy or who weigh less than 5½ pounds (2,500 grams) have for many years been referred to as "premature." A wealth of research indicates that premature babies are at risk for many problems. Birth weight is the best available predictor of infant survival and healthy development. Many newborns who weigh less than 3⅓ pounds (1,500 grams) experience difficulties that are not overcome, an effect that becomes stronger as birth weight decreases (Minde, 2000; Palta et al., 2000). Frequent

♯ Stopping point ♯

SIMON FRASER/PRINCESS MARY HOSPITAL/
SCIENCE PHOTO LIBRARY/PHOTO RESEARCHERS, INC.

This baby was born 13 weeks before her due date and weighs little more than 2 pounds. Since her lungs are too immature to function independently, she breathes with the aid of a respirator. Her survival and development are seriously at risk.

respiratory distress syndrome
A disorder of preterm infants in which the lungs are so immature that the air sacs collapse, causing serious breathing difficulties. Also know as *hyaline membrane disease.*

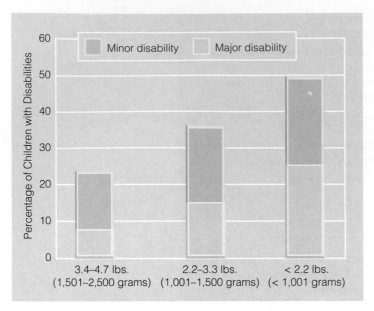

FIGURE 4.5

Incidence of major and minor disabilities by birth weight, obtained from studies of low-birth-weight children at school age. *Major disabilities* include cerebral palsy, mental retardation, and vision and hearing impairments. *Minor disabilities* include intelligence slightly below average, learning disabilities (usually in reading, spelling, and math), mild difficulties in motor control, and behavior problems (including poor attention and impulse control, aggressiveness, noncompliance, depression, passivity, anxiety, and difficulty separating from parents at school age). (Adapted from D'Agostino & Clifford, 1998.)

preterm
Infants born several weeks or more before their due date. Although small in size, their weight may still be appropriate for the time they spent in the uterus.

small for date
Infants whose birth weight is below normal when length of pregnancy is taken into account.

illness, inattention, overactivity, language delays, low intelligence test scores, deficits in motor coordination and school learning, and poor emotional adjustment are some of the difficulties that extend into the childhood years (Hack et al., 1994, 1995; Mayes & Bornstein, 1997).

About 1 in 16 infants in the United States is born underweight. The problem can strike unexpectedly, as it did for Janet and Rick. But it is highest among low-income pregnant women, especially ethnic minorities (Ventura et al., 2000). These mothers, as indicated in Chapter 3, are more likely to be undernourished and exposed to other harmful environmental influences—factors strongly linked to low birth weight. In addition, they often do not receive the prenatal care necessary to protect their vulnerable babies.

Recall from Chapter 2 that prematurity is also common among twins. Twins usually are born about 3 weeks early, and because of restricted space inside the uterus, they gain less weight after the twentieth week of pregnancy than do singletons.

■ **PRETERM VERSUS SMALL FOR DATE.** Although low-birth-weight infants face many obstacles to healthy development, individual differences exist in how well they do. Most go on to lead normal lives; half of those who weighed only a couple of pounds at birth have no disability (see Figure 4.5). To better understand why some babies do better than others, researchers have divided them into two groups. The first is called **preterm.** These infants are born several weeks or more before their due date. Although small in size, their weight may still be appropriate for the amount of time they spent in the uterus. The second group is called **small for date.** These babies are below their expected weight when length of the pregnancy is taken into account. Some small-for-date infants are actually full term. Others are preterm infants who are especially underweight.

Of the two types of babies, small-for-date infants usually have more serious problems. During the first year, they are more likely to die, catch infections, and show evidence of brain damage. By middle childhood, they have lower intelligence test scores, are less attentive, achieve more poorly in school, and are socially immature (Minde, 2000; Schothorst & van Engeland, 1996). Small-for-date infants probably experienced inadequate nutrition before birth. Perhaps their mothers did not eat properly, the placenta did not function normally, or the babies themselves had defects that prevented them from growing as they should.

■ **CONSEQUENCES FOR CAREGIVING.** Imagine a scrawny, thin-skinned infant whose body is only a little larger than the size of your hand. You try to play with the baby by stroking and talking softly, but he is sleepy and unresponsive. When you feed him, he sucks poorly. He is usually irritable during the short, unpredictable periods in which he is awake.

The appearance and behavior of preterm babies can lead parents to be less sensitive and responsive in caring for them. Compared to full-term infants, preterm babies—especially those who are very ill at birth—are less often held close, touched, and talked to gently. At times, mothers of these infants are overly stimulating and intrusive, engaging in interfering pokes and verbal commands in an effort to obtain a higher level of response from a baby who is a passive, unrewarding social partner (Barratt, Roach, & Leavitt, 1996).

Some parents may step up these intrusive acts when ungratifying infant behavior continues. This may explain why preterm babies as a group are at risk for child abuse. When these infants are born to isolated, poverty-stricken mothers who have difficulty managing their own lives and cannot provide good nutrition, health care, and parenting, the chances for unfavorable outcomes increase (Bacharach & Baumeister, 1998). In contrast, parents with stable life circumstances and social supports usually can overcome the stresses of caring for a preterm infant. In these cases, even sick preterm babies have a good chance of catching up in development by middle childhood (Liaw & Brooks-Gunn, 1993).

These findings suggest that how well preterm babies develop has a great deal to do with the parent–child relationship. Consequently, interventions directed at supporting both sides of this emotional tie have a better chance of helping these infants recover.

■ **INTERVENTIONS FOR PRETERM INFANTS.** A preterm baby is cared for in a special plexiglass-enclosed bed called an isolette. Temperature is carefully controlled, since these infants cannot yet regulate their own body temperature effectively. Air is filtered before it enters the isolette to help protect the baby from infection. When a preterm infant is fed through a stomach tube, breathes with the aid of a respirator, and receives medication through an intravenous needle, the isolette can be very isolating indeed! Physical needs that otherwise would lead to close contact with adults are met mechanically.

Special Infant Stimulation. At one time doctors believed that stimulating such a fragile baby could be harmful. Now we know that in proper doses, certain kinds of stimulation can help preterm infants develop. In some intensive care nurseries, preterm babies can be seen rocking in suspended hammocks or lying on waterbeds designed to replace the gentle motion they would have received while still in the mother's uterus. Other forms of stimulation have also been used—for example, an attractive mobile or a tape recording of a heartbeat, soft music, or the mother's voice. Many studies show that these experiences promote faster weight gain, more predictable sleep patterns, and greater alertness during the weeks after birth (Beckwith & Sigman, 1995; Marshall-Baker, Lickliter, & Cooper, 1998; Standley, 1998).

Touch is an especially important form of stimulation. In baby animals, touching the skin releases certain brain chemicals that support physical growth—effects believed to occur in humans as well (Field, 1998). In one study, preterm infants who were gently massaged several times each day in the hospital gained weight faster and, at the end of the first year, were advanced in mental and motor development over preterm babies not given this stimulation (Field et al., 1986).

In developing countries where hospitalization is not always possible, skin-to-skin "kangaroo care," in which the preterm infant is tucked between the mother's breasts and peers over the top of her clothing, is encouraged. The technique is used often in Europe and the United States as a supplement to hospital intensive care. It fosters oxygenation of the baby's body, temperature regulation, improved sleep and feeding, and infant survival. In addition, mothers practicing kangaroo care feel more confident about handling and meeting other needs of their preterm infants (Gale & VandenBerg, 1998; Hamelin & Ramachandran, 1993).

Some very small or sick babies are too weak for much stimulation. The noise, bright lights, and constant medical monitoring of the intensive care nursery are already quite overwhelming. And like full-term infants, preterm infants differ in how excited and irritable they get when exposed to sights and sounds (Korner, 1996). Doctors and nurses must carefully adjust the amount and kind of stimulation to fit the baby's individual needs.

Training Parents in Infant Caregiving Skills. When effective stimulation helps preterm babies develop, parents are likely to feel encouraged and interact with the baby more effectively. Interventions that support the parenting side of this relationship generally teach parents about the infant's characteristics and promote caregiving skills.

For parents with the economic and personal resources to care for a preterm infant, just a few sessions of coaching in recognizing and responding to the baby's needs are helpful. Infants of mothers randomly selected to receive this training during home visits in the months after hospital discharge, compared to infants of mothers who were not, gained steadily in mental test performance over the childhood years until their scores equaled those of full-term youngsters (Achenbach et al., 1990).

When preterm infants live in stressed, low-income households, long-term, intensive intervention is required. In the Infant Health and Development Project, preterm babies born into poverty received a comprehensive intervention that combined medical follow-up, weekly parent training sessions, and cognitively stimulating child care from 1 to 3 years of age. As Figure 4.6 shows, compared with controls receiving only medical follow-up, nearly four times as many intervention children were within normal range in intelligence, psychological adjustment, and

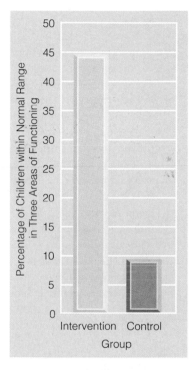

FIGURE 4.6

Percentage of preterm infants born into poverty and assigned to either an intensive intervention or a control group who were developing normally at age 3. Children who experienced the intervention, consisting of medical follow-up, parent training, and cognitively stimulating child care, were nearly four times more likely than medical-follow-up-only controls to be within normal range in intelligence, psychological adjustment, and physical growth. Without continued intervention, however, these gains are not sustained. (Adapted from Bradley et al., 1994.)

Social

ISSUES: HEALTH

A CROSS-NATIONAL PERSPECTIVE ON HEALTH CARE AND OTHER POLICIES FOR PARENTS AND NEWBORN BABIES

Infant mortality is an index used around the world to assess the overall health of a nation's children. It refers to the number of deaths in the first year of life per 1,000 live births. Although the United States has the most up-to-date health care technology in the world, it has made less progress than many other countries in reducing infant deaths. Over the past three decades, it has slipped in the international rankings, from seventh in the 1950s to twenty-first in the year 2000. Members of America's poor ethnic minorities, African-American babies especially, are at greatest risk. Black infants are more than twice as likely as white infants to die in the first year of life. Their infant mortality rate is about the same as in developing nations with poor economies, such as Trinidad and Tobago (Bellamy, 2000; Children's Defense Fund, 2000).

Neonatal mortality, the rate of death within the first month of life, accounts for 67 percent of the high infant death rate in the United States. Two factors are largely responsible for neonatal mortality. The first is serious physical defects, most of which cannot

be prevented. The percentage of babies born with physical defects is about the same in all ethnic and income groups. The second leading cause of neonatal mortality is low birth weight, which is largely preventable. Black babies are more than four times more likely to die because they are born early and under-weight than are white infants. On an international scale, the number of underweight babies born in the United States is alarmingly high—higher than in 22 other countries (Bellamy, 2000).

Experts agree that widespread poverty and weak health care programs for mothers and young children are largely responsible for these trends. Each country in Figure 4.7 that outranks the United States in infant survival provides all its citizens with government-sponsored health care benefits. And each takes extra steps to make sure that pregnant mothers and babies have access to good nutrition, high-quality medical care, and social and economic supports that promote effective parenting.

For example, all Western European nations guarantee women a certain number of prenatal visits at very low or no cost. After a baby is born, a health

professional routinely visits the home to provide counseling about infant care and to arrange continuing medical services. Home assistance is especially extensive in the Netherlands. For a token fee, each mother is granted a specially trained maternity helper, who assists with infant care, shopping, housekeeping, meal preparation, and the care of other children during the days after delivery (Kamerman, 1993).

Paid, job-protected employment leave is another vital societal intervention for new parents. It is widely available in industrialized nations, where it typically ranges from 2 to 12 months. In Sweden, a couple has the right to a short, paid birth leave of a few days for fathers plus 15 months of paid leave to share between them. Canada's policy is similar, permitting a mother or father to remain at home with the baby for up to 12 months. Even less-developed nations offer paid employment leave. For example, in the People's Republic of China, a new mother is granted 3 months at full pay. Furthermore, many countries supplement basic paid leave. In Germany, for example, after a fully paid 3-month leave, a parent can take 2 more years at a

---

infant mortality
The number of deaths in the first year of life per 1,000 live births.

neonatal mortality
The number of deaths in the first month of life per 1,000 live births.

physical growth at age 3 (Bradley et al, 1994). In addition, mothers in the intervention group were more affectionate and more often encouraged play and cognitive mastery in their children—a reason their 3-year-olds may have been developing so favorably (McCarton, 1998).

Yet by age 5, the intervention children had lost ground. And by age 8, the development of intervention and control children who had been very low birth weight no longer differed (Brooks-Gunn et al., 1994; McCarton et al., 1997). To sustain gains in very vulnerable children, high-quality intervention must continue well beyond age 3—even into the school years. And special strategies may be necessary to achieve lasting changes in children with the lowest birth weights, for whom birth trauma was particularly severe (Berlin et al., 1998).

What happened to Keith, the very sick baby you met at the beginning of this section? Because of advanced medical technology and new ways of helping parents, many preterm infants survive and eventually catch up in development, but Keith was not one of the lucky ones. Even with the best care, all but a few babies born as early and as low birth weight as

modest flat rate and a third year at no pay (Hyde, 1995; Kamerman, 2000). Yet in the United States, the federal government mandates *only 12 weeks of*

unpaid leave for employees in businesses with at least 50 workers.

When a family is stressed by a baby's arrival, short employment

leaves of 6 weeks or less (the norm in the United States) are linked to maternal anxiety and depression and negative interactions with the baby. Longer leaves of 12 weeks or more predict favorable maternal mental health and sensitive, responsive caregiving (Clark et al., 1997; Hyde et al., 1995). Single women and their babies are most hurt by the absence of a national paid leave policy. These mothers are usually the sole source of support for their families and can least afford to take time from their jobs.

In countries with low infant mortality rates, expectant mothers need not wonder how or where they will get health care and other resources to support their baby's development. The powerful impact of universal, high-quality medical and social services on maternal and infant well-being provides strong justification for implementing similar programs in the United States.

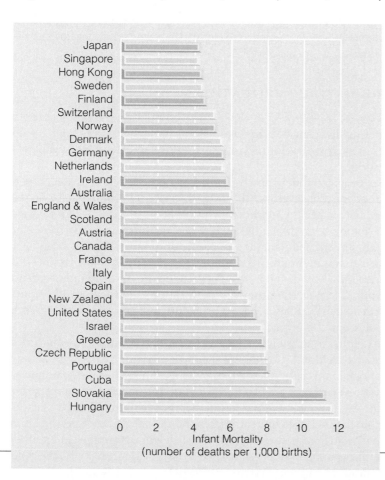

FIGURE 4.7

Infant mortality in 28 nations. Despite its advanced health care technology, the United Sates ranks poorly. It is twenty-first in the world, with a death rate of 8 infants per 1,000 births. (Adapted from March of Dimes, 2000.)

Keith either die or end up with serious disabilities (Howard, Williams, & Port, 1999). Six months after he was born, Keith died without ever having left the hospital.

Keith's premature birth was unavoidable, but the high rate of underweight babies in the United States—one of the worst in the industrialized world—could be greatly reduced by improving the health and social conditions described in the Social Issues: Health box aobve. Fortunately, today we can save many preterm babies, but an even better course of action would be to prevent this serious threat to infant survival and development before it happens.

POSTTERM INFANTS

The normal length of pregnancy is 38 weeks. Infants born after 42 weeks are **postterm.** About 5 percent fall into this category (Shea, Wilcox, & Little, 1998). Most of these late-arriving newborns are quite normal. However, a small number start to lose weight at the end

postterm
Infants who spend a longer-than-average time in the uterus—more than 42 weeks.

© STEVE PERCY/PANOS PICTURES

In Munyak, Uzbekistan, nearly 1 in every 5 babies is postterm and therefore at elevated risk for oxygen deprivation and head injuries during labor and delivery. This Uzbekistani mother and child are hospitalized because they suffer from severe anemia—another consequence of widespread pollution. Some pollutants, such as nitrate, interfere with the oxygen-carrying capacity of blood.

of pregnancy because the placenta no longer functions properly. As the baby becomes more overdue, the amount of amniotic fluid drops sharply, increasing the chances that the infant's movements in the uterus will squeeze the umbilical cord. Also, since postterm infants are larger, they may have difficulty moving through the birth canal. All these factors increase the possibility of oxygen deprivation and head injuries (Rosen & Dickenson, 1992).

Since the likelihood of birth complications and infant death rises steeply as a pregnancy continues past 42 weeks, doctors usually induce labor in these mothers (Wilcox & Skjaerven, 1992). Once born, most postterm babies do well. Their mental development may be slightly behind during infancy and early childhood, but it generally evens out by school entry (Shime, 1988).

The causes of postterm delivery are still a mystery. Low SES is linked to it, as is exposure to environmental pollution. In Munyak, the most polluted city in Uzbekistan (a country in west-central Asia), 18 percent of all births occurred after 42 weeks—considerably more than in other nearby cities. Postterm births also increased in the Ukraine after the Chernobyl nuclear power plant disaster (Kulakov et al., 1993). Certain environmental agents may disrupt the balance of hormones responsible for the onset of labor.

UNDERSTANDING BIRTH COMPLICATIONS

In the preceding sections, we considered a variety of birth complications. Now let's try to put the evidence together. Can any general principles help us understand how infants who survive a traumatic birth are likely to develop? A landmark study carried out in Hawaii provides answers to this question.

In 1955, Emmy Werner began to follow nearly 700 infants on the island of Kauai who experienced either mild, moderate, or severe birth complications. Each was matched, on the basis of SES and ethnicity, with a healthy newborn (Werner & Smith, 1982). Findings revealed that the likelihood of long-term difficulties increased if birth trauma was severe. But among mildly to moderately stressed children, the best predictor of how well they did in later years was the quality of their home environments. Children growing up in stable families did almost as well on measures of intelligence and psychological adjustment as did those with no birth problems. Those exposed to poverty, family disorganization, and mentally ill parents often developed serious learning difficulties, behavior problems, and emotional disturbance during childhood and adolescence.

The Kauai study tells us that as long as birth injuries are not overwhelming, a supportive home environment can restore children's growth. But the most intriguing cases in this study were the handful of exceptions to this rule. A few children with both serious birth complications and troubled families grew into competent adults who fared as well as controls in career attainment and psychological adjustment. Werner found that these children relied on factors outside the family and within themselves to overcome stress. Some had attractive personalities that caused them to receive positive responses from relatives, neighbors, and peers. In other cases, a grandparent, aunt, uncle, or baby-sitter established a warm relationship with the child and provided the needed emotional support (Werner, 1989, 1993; Werner & Smith, 1992).

Do these outcomes remind you of the characteristics of resilient children, discussed in Chapter 1? The Kauai study reveals that the impact of early mild to moderate biological risks often wanes as children's personal characteristics and social experiences increasingly contribute to their functioning—an outcome consistent with other similar investigations. For example, when researchers matched birth records of more than 300,000 children born in Florida between 1985 and 1990 with their school kindergarten records, a birth weight of less than 3½ pounds (1,500 grams) was the strongest predictor of placement in special education. When birth weight exceeded 3½ pounds, family factors—having a mother who was poverty stricken, who had not gotten prenatal care, who had less than a high school education, or who was single—were 5 to 10 times more effective in predicting special educational placement than was birth weight (Resnick et al., 1999).

In sum, when the overall balance of life events tips toward the favorable side, children with serious birth problems can develop successfully. When negative factors outweigh positive ones, even a sturdy newborn can become a lifelong casualty.

review   Sensitive care can help preterm infants recover, but unfortunately they are less likely to receive such care than are full-term newborns. Explain why.

apply   Cecilia and Adena each gave birth to a baby 7 weeks preterm and weighing only 3 pounds. Cecilia did not finish high school and is single and on welfare. Adena and her husband graduated from college and earn a good income. Plan an intervention program appropriate for helping each baby develop favorably.

connect   List factors discussed in this chapter and in Chapter 3 that increase the chances that an infant will be born underweight. How many of these factors could be prevented by better health care for mothers and babies?

reflect   Many people question the advisability of extraordinary medical measures to save extremely low-birth-weight babies (less than 1½ pounds or 1,000 grams), since most who survive develop serious physical, cognitive, and emotional problems. Do you agree or disagree? Explain.

Precious Moments After Birth

Yolanda and Jay's account of Joshua's birth revealed that the time spent holding and touching him right after delivery was filled with intense emotion. A mother given her infant at this time will usually stroke the baby gently, look into the infant's eyes, and talk softly (Klaus & Kennell, 1982). Fathers respond similarly. Most are overjoyed at the birth of the baby; characterize the experience as "awesome," "indescribable," or "unforgettable"; and display intense interest in their newborn child (Bader, 1995; Rose, 2000). Regardless of SES or participation in childbirth classes, fathers touch, look at, talk to, and kiss their newborn infants just as much as mothers do. When they hold the baby, sometimes they exceed mothers in stimulation and affection (Parke & Tinsley, 1981).

Immediately after birth, many nonhuman animals engage in specific caregiving behaviors that are critical for survival of the young. For example, a mother cat licks her newborn kittens and then encircles them with her body (Schneirla, Rosenblatt, & Tobach, 1963). Rats, sheep, and goats engage in similar licking behaviors. But if the mother is separated from her young during the period following delivery, her responsiveness declines until finally she rejects the infant (Poindron & Le Neindre, 1980; Rosenblatt & Lehrman, 1963).

Do human parents also require close physical contact in the hours after birth for **bonding,** or feelings of affection and concern for the infant, to develop? Current evidence indicates that the human parent–infant relationship does not depend on a precise, early period of togetherness. Some parents report sudden, deep feelings of affection on first holding their babies. For others, these emotions emerge gradually (Lamb, 1994). In adoptive parents, a warm, affectionate relationship can develop even if the child enters the family months or years after birth (Dontas et al., 1985; Hodges & Tizard, 1989). Human bonding is a complex process that depends on many factors, not just what happens during a short sensitive period.

Still, contact with the baby after birth might be one of several factors that helps build a good parent–infant relationship. Research shows that mothers learn to discriminate their own newborn baby from other infants on the basis of touch, smell, and sight (a photograph) after as little as one hour of contact (Kaitz et al., 1987, 1988, 1993a, 1993b). This early recognition probably facilitates responsiveness to the infant. Also, mothers with close and continuous proximity to their newborns report thinking often about the baby's safety and well-being. These concerns intensify with brief separations, but they drop sharply with prolonged separation and potential loss of the baby—for example, when a very low-birth-weight newborn must remain in an intensive care nursery and might not survive (Feldman et al., 1999).

ERIKA STONE

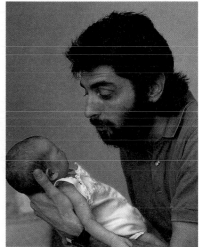

This father displays intense interest in and involvement with his newborn child. Parents typically express their elation at the baby's arrival by stroking the infant gently, looking into the baby's eyes, and talking softly.

bonding
Parents' feelings of affection and concern for the newborn baby.

Clearly, early contact supports maternal feelings of caring and affection. Realizing this, today hospitals offer an arrangement called **rooming in,** in which the infant stays in the mother's hospital room all or most of the time. If parents choose not to take advantage of this option or cannot do so for medical reasons, there is no evidence that their competence as caregivers will be compromised or that the baby will suffer emotionally (Lamb, 1994).

The Newborn Baby's Capacities

As recently as the mid-twentieth century, scientists considered the newborn baby to be a passive, disorganized being who could see, hear, feel, and do very little. Today we know that this image is wrong. Newborn babies have a remarkable set of capacities that are crucial for survival and for evoking attention and care from parents. In relating to the physical and social world, babies are active from the very start.

REFLEXES

A **reflex** is an inborn, automatic response to a particular form of stimulation. Reflexes are the newborn baby's most obvious organized patterns of behavior. Human infants come into the world with dozens of them. As Jay placed Joshua on a table in my classroom, we saw several. When Jay bumped the side of the table, Joshua reacted by flinging his arms wide and bringing them back toward his body. As Yolanda stroked Joshua's cheek, he turned his head in her direction. When she put her finger in Joshua's palm, he grabbed on tightly. Look at Table 4.2 and see if you can name the newborn reflexes that Joshua displayed. Then let's consider the meaning and purpose of these curious behaviors.

■ **ADAPTIVE VALUE OF REFLEXES.** Some reflexes have survival value. The rooting reflex helps a breast-fed baby find the mother's nipple. And if sucking were not automatic, our species would be unlikely to survive for a single generation! The swimming reflex helps a baby who is accidentally dropped into a body of water stay afloat, increasing the chances of retrieval by the caregiver.

Other reflexes probably helped babies survive during our evolutionary past. For example, the Moro or "embracing" reflex is believed to have helped infants cling to their mothers when they were carried about all day. If the baby happened to lose support, the reflex caused the infant to embrace and, along with the grasp reflex (so strong during the first week that it can support the baby's entire weight), regain its hold on the mother's body (Kessen, 1967; Prechtl, 1958).

Several reflexes help parents and infants establish gratifying interaction. A baby who searches for and successfully finds the nipple, sucks easily during feedings, and grasps when her hand is touched encourages parents to respond lovingly and feel competent as caregivers.

Reflexes can also help parents comfort the baby, since they permit infants to control distress and amount of stimulation. For example, on short trips with Joshua to the grocery store, Yolanda brought along a pacifier. If he became fussy, sucking helped quiet him until she could feed, change, or hold and rock him.

The next time you have a chance to watch a young baby nursing, look carefully. You will see that the baby's sucking behavior is highly organized. Bursts of sucks are separated by pauses, a style of feeding that is unique to the human species. Notice what most mothers do during the baby's pause: they jiggle the infant to encourage more sucking. In response, newborn babies learn to expect and wait for their mother's jiggle. This early sequence of interaction during

In the Moro reflex, loss of support or a sudden loud sound causes the baby to arch her back, extend her arms outward, and then bring them in toward her body.

MIMI FORSYTH/MONKMEYER PRESS

TABLE 4.2

Some Newborn Reflexes

REFLEX	STIMULATION	RESPONSE	AGE OF DISAPPEARANCE	FUNCTION
Eye blink	Shine bright light at eyes or clap hands near head	Infant quickly closes eyelids	Permanent reflex	Protects infant from strong stimulation
Rooting	Stroke cheek near corner of mouth	Head turns toward source of stimulation	3 weeks (becomes voluntary head turning at this time)	Helps infant find the nipple
Sucking	Place finger in infant's mouth	Infant sucks finger rhythmically	Permanent reflex	Permits feeding
Swimming	Place infant face down in pool of water	Baby paddles and kicks in swimming motion	4–6 months	Helps infant survive if dropped into body of water
Moro	Hold infant horizontally on back and let head drop slightly, or produce a sudden loud sound against surface supporting infant	Infant makes an "embracing" motion by arching back, extending legs, throwing arms outward, and then bringing them in toward the body	6 months	In human evolutionary past, may have helped infant cling to mother
Palmar grasp	Place finger in infant's hand and press against palm	Spontaneous grasp of adult's finger	3–4 months	Prepares infant for voluntary grasping
Tonic neck	Turn baby's head to one side while lying awake on back	Infant lies in a "fencing position." One arm is extended in front of eyes on side to which head is turned, other arm is flexed	4 months	May prepare infant for voluntary reaching
Stepping	Hold infant under arms and permit bare feet to touch a flat surface	Infant lifts one foot after another in stepping response	2 months	Prepares infant for voluntary walking
Babinski	Stroke sole of foot from toe toward heel	Toes fan out and curl as foot twists in	8–12 months	Unknown

Sources: Knobloch & Pasamanick, 1974; Prechtl & Beintema, 1965.

feeding resembles the turn taking of human conversation (Kaye & Wells, 1980). Using the primitive sucking reflex, the young baby participates as an active, cooperative partner.

■ **REFLEXES AND THE DEVELOPMENT OF MOTOR SKILLS.** A few reflexes form the basis for complex motor skills that will develop later. For example, the tonic neck reflex may prepare the baby for voluntary reaching. When infants lie on their backs in this "fencing position," they naturally gaze at the hand in front of their eyes. The reflex may encourage them to combine vision with arm movements and, eventually, reach for objects (Knobloch & Pasamanick, 1974).

The stepping reflex looks like a primitive walking response. In infants who gain weight quickly in the weeks after birth, the stepping reflex drops out because thigh and calf muscles are not strong enough to lift the baby's increasingly chubby legs. However, if the lower part of the infant's body is dipped in water, the reflex reappears, since the buoyancy of the water lightens the load on the baby's muscles (Thelen, Fisher, & Ridley-Johnson, 1984). When the stepping reflex is exercised regularly, babies display more spontaneous stepping movements and are likely to walk several weeks earlier than if it is not practiced (Zelazo, 1983; Zelazo et al., 1993). However, there is no special need for parents to get their infants to use the stepping reflex, since all normal babies walk in due time.

[handwritten note: sucking is like convo since babies wait for mom's jiggling to resume sucking.]

rooming in
An arrangement in which the newborn baby stays in the mother's hospital room all or most of the time.

reflex
An inborn, automatic response to a particular form of stimulation.

TABLE 4.3

Infant States of Arousal

STATE	DESCRIPTION	DAILY DURATION IN NEWBORN
Regular sleep	The infant rests fully and shows little or no body activity. The eyelids are closed, no eye movements occur, the face is relaxed, and breathing is slow and regular.	8–9 hours
Irregular sleep	Gentle limb movements, occasional stirring, and facial grimacing occur. Although the eyelids are closed, occasional rapid eye movements can be seen beneath them. Breathing is irregular.	8–9 hours
Drowsiness	The infant is either falling asleep or waking up. The body is less active than in irregular sleep but more active than in regular sleep. The eyes open and close; when open, they have a glazed look. Breathing is even but somewhat faster than in regular sleep.	Varies
Quiet alertness	The infant's body is relatively inactive, with eyes open and attentive. Breathing is even.	2–3 hours
Waking activity and crying	The infant shows frequent bursts of uncoordinated body activity. Breathing is very irregular. Face may be relaxed or tense and wrinkled. Crying may occur.	1–4 hours

Source: Wolff, 1966.

LAURA DWIGHT

When held upright under the arms, newborn babies show reflexive stepping movements.

This baby shows the Babinski reflex. When an adult strokes the sole of the foot, the toes fan out. Then they curl as the foot twists in.

■ **THE IMPORTANCE OF ASSESSING NEWBORN REFLEXES.** Look at Table 4.2 again, and you will see that most newborn reflexes disappear during the first 6 months of life. Researchers believe that this is due to a gradual increase in voluntary control over behavior as the cerebral cortex develops.

Pediatricians test reflexes carefully, especially if a newborn has experienced birth trauma, since reflexes can reveal the health of the baby's nervous system. In brain-damaged infants, reflexes may be weak or absent or, in some cases, exaggerated and overly rigid. Brain damage may also be indicated when reflexes persist past the age at which they should normally disappear. However, some individual differences in reflexive responses are not cause for concern. Newborn reflexes must be observed along with other characteristics to accurately distinguish normal from abnormal central nervous system functioning (Touwen, 1984).

STATES

Throughout the day and night, newborn infants move in and out of five **states of arousal**, or degrees of sleep and wakefulness, described in Table 4.3. During the first month, these states alternate frequently. Quiet alertness is the most fleeting. It usually moves quickly toward fussing and crying. Much to the relief of their fatigued parents, newborns spend the greatest amount of time asleep—on the average, about 16 to 18 hours a day.

However, striking individual differences in daily rhythms exist that affect parents' attitudes toward and interactions with the baby. A few infants sleep for long periods at an early age, increasing the rest their parents get and the energy they have for sensitive, responsive care. Other babies cry a great deal, and their parents must exert great effort to soothe them. If they do not succeed, parents may feel less competent and positive toward their infant. Babies who spend more time alert are likely to receive more social stimulation. And

INNERVISIONS

since this state provides opportunities to explore the environment, infants who favor it may have a slight advantage in cognitive development (Moss et al., 1988).

Of the five states listed in Table 4.3, the two extremes—sleep and crying—have been of greatest interest to researchers. Each tells us something about normal and abnormal early development.

■ **SLEEP.** One day, Yolanda and Jay watched Joshua while he slept and wondered why his eyelids and body twitched and his rate of breathing varied, speeding up at some points and slowing down at others. "Is this how babies are supposed to sleep?" they asked, somewhat worried. "Indeed, it is," I responded.

Sleep is made up of at least two states. Yolanda and Jay happened to observe irregular, or **rapid-eye-movement (REM), sleep.** The expression "sleeping like a baby" was probably not meant to describe this state! During REM sleep, electrical brain-wave activity, measured with an EEG, is remarkably similar to that of the waking state. The eyes dart beneath the lids; heart rate, blood pressure, and breathing are uneven; and slight body movements occur. In contrast, during regular, or **non-rapid-eye-movement (NREM), sleep,** the body is almost motionless, and heart rate, breathing, and brain-wave activity are slow and regular.

Like children and adults, newborns alternate between REM and NREM sleep. However, they spend far more time in the REM state than they ever will again. REM sleep accounts for 50 percent of the newborn baby's sleep time. By 3 to 5 years of age, it has declined to an adultlike level of 20 percent (Louis et al., 1997).

Why do young infants spend so much time in REM sleep? In older children and adults, the REM state is associated with dreaming. Babies probably do not dream, at least not in the same way we do. Young infants are believed to have a special need for the stimulation of REM sleep because they spend little time in an alert state, when they can get input from the environment. REM sleep seems to be a way in which the brain stimulates itself (Roffwarg, Muzio, & Dement, 1966). Sleep researchers believe that this stimulation is vital for growth of the central nervous system. In support of this idea, the percentage of REM sleep is especially great in the fetus and in preterm babies, who are even less able to take advantage of external stimulation than are full-term newborns (DiPietro et al., 1996a; Sahni et al., 1995).

Whereas the brain-wave activity of REM sleep safeguards the central nervous system, rapid eye movements protect the health of the eye. During the waking state, eye movements cause the vitreous (gelatin-like substance within the eye) to circulate, thereby delivering oxygen to parts of the eye that do not have their own blood supply. During sleep, when the eye and the vitreous are still, visual structures are at risk for anoxia. As the brain cycles through REM-sleep periods, rapid eye movements stir up the vitreous, ensuring that the eye is fully oxygenated (Blumberg & Lucas, 1996).

Because the normal sleep behavior of the newborn baby is organized and patterned, observations of sleep states can help identify central nervous system abnormalities. In infants who are brain damaged or who have experienced serious birth trauma, disturbed REM–NREM sleep cycles often are present. Babies with poor sleep organization are likely to be behaviorally disorganized and, therefore, to have difficulty learning while awake and eliciting caregiver interactions that enhance their development (Groome et al., 1997; Halpern, MacLean, & Baumeister, 1995).

■ **CRYING.** Crying is the first way that babies communicate, letting parents know that they need food, comfort, and stimulation. During the weeks after birth, all babies seem to have some fussy periods when they are difficult to console. But most of the time, the nature of the cry, combined with the experiences that led up to it, helps guide parents toward its cause. The baby's cry is actually a complex stimulus that varies in intensity, from a whimper to a message of all-out distress (Gustafson & Harris, 1990). As early as the first few weeks of life, infants can be identified by the unique vocal "signature" of their cry, which helps parents locate their baby from a distance (Gustafson, Green, & Cleland, 1994).

Newborn infants usually cry because of physical needs. Hunger is the most common cause, but young infants may also cry in response to temperature change when undressed, a

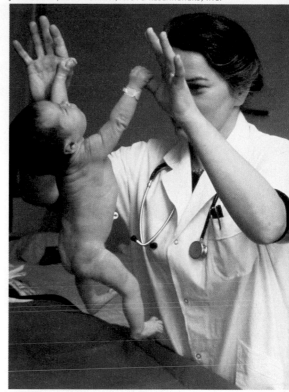

J. DA CUNHA/PETIT FORMAT/PHOTO RESEARCHERS, INC.

The palmar grasp reflex is so strong during the first week after birth that many infants can use it to support their entire weight.

states of arousal
Different degrees of sleep and wakefulness.

rapid-eye-movement (REM) sleep
An "irregular" sleep state in which brain-wave activity is similar to that of the waking state; eyes dart beneath the lids; heart rate, blood pressure, and breathing are uneven; and slight body movements occur.

non-rapid-eye-movement (NREM) sleep
A "regular" sleep state in which the body is quiet and heart rate, breathing, and brain-wave activity are slow and regular.

ROSANNE OLSON/STONE

To soothe her crying infant, this mother holds her baby upright against her gently moving body. This technique encourages infants to become quietly alert and attentive to the environment.

sudden noise, or a painful stimulus. Newborn crying can also be caused by the sound of another crying baby (Dondi, Simion, & Caltran, 1999). Some researchers believe that this response reflects an inborn capacity to react to the suffering of others.

The next time you hear an infant cry, notice your own mental and physical reaction. The sound stimulates strong feelings of arousal and discomfort in just about anyone—men and women, parents and nonparents (Boukydis & Burgess, 1982; Murray, 1985). This powerful response is probably innately programmed in all human beings to make sure that babies receive the care and protection they need to survive.

Although parents do not always interpret their baby's cry correctly, experience quickly improves their accuracy. Fortunately, as the Caregiving Concerns table below indicates, there are many ways to soothe a crying baby when feeding and diaper changing do not work. The technique Western parents usually try first, lifting the baby to the shoulder, is most effective. Among the Quechua, who live in the cold, high-altitude desert regions of Peru, young babies are dressed in several layers of clothing and blankets. Then a cloth belt is tightly wound around the body, over which are placed additional blankets that cover the head and face and serve as a carrying cloth. The result—a nearly sealed, warm pouch placed on the mother's back that moves rhythmically as she walks—reduces crying and promotes sleep. As a result, the baby conserves energy for early growth in the harsh Peruvian highlands (Tronick, Thomas, & Daltabuit, 1994).

Like reflexes and sleep patterns, the infant's cry offers a clue to central nervous system distress. The cries of brain-damaged babies and those who have experienced prenatal and birth complications are often shrill and piercing (Boukydis & Lester, 1998; Lester, Boukydis, & Zachariah, 1992). Even newborns with a fairly common problem—*colic*, or persistent cry-

  Caregiving Concerns

Ways to Soothe a Crying Newborn

METHOD	EXPLANATION
Lift the baby to the shoulder and rock or walk.	This provides a combination of physical contact, upright posture, and motion. It is the most effective soothing technique, causing young infants to become quietly alert.
Swaddle the baby.	Restricting movement and increasing warmth often soothes an infant.
Offer a pacifier, preferably sweetened with a sugar solution.	Sucking helps babies control their own level of arousal. Sucking a sweetened pacifier relieves pain and quiets a crying infant.
Talk softly or play rhythmic sounds.	Continuous, monotonous, rhythmic sounds, such as a clock ticking, a fan whirring, or peaceful music, are more effective than intermittent sounds.
Take the baby for a short car ride or a walk in a baby carriage; swing the baby in a cradle.	Gentle, rhythmic motion of any kind helps lull the baby to sleep.
Massage the baby's body.	Stroke the baby's torso and limbs with continuous, gentle motions. This technique is used in some non-Western cultures to relax the baby's muscles.
Combine several methods just listed.	Stimulating several of the baby's senses at once is often more effective than stimulating only one.
If these methods do not work, let the baby cry for a short period.	Occasionally, a baby responds well to just being put down and will, after a few minutes, fall asleep.

Sources: Blass, 1999; Campos, 1989; Field, 1998; Lester, 1985; Reisman, 1987.

TABLE 4.4

The Newborn Baby's Sensory Capacities

SENSE	FUNCTIONING IN THE NEWBORN
Touch	Responsive to touch, temperature change, and pain
Taste	Prefers sweetness; can distinguish sweet, salty, sour, and bitter tastes; readily learns to like a taste that at first evoked either a negative or a neutral response
Smell	Reacts to the smell of certain foods in the same way as adults; can identify the location of an odor and turn away from unpleasant odors; prefers the smell of own mother's amniotic fluid and the lactating breast (if breast fed, can distinguish own mother's breast odor)
Hearing	Prefers complex sounds to pure tones; can distinguish some sound patterns; recognizes differences among almost all human speech sounds; turns in the general direction of a sound; prefers high-pitched, expressive voices with rising intonation, sound of own mother's voice over an unfamiliar woman's voice, and sound of native language as opposed to a foreign language
Vision	Least developed sense at birth; infant has limited focusing ability and visual acuity; scans visual field and attempts to track moving objects; looks at single features rather than entire object; color vision not yet well developed

ing—tend to have high-pitched, harsh, and turbulent-sounding cries (Zeskind & Barr, 1997). Although the cause of colic is unknown, some researchers believe it is due to disturbed brain regulation of sleeping–waking cycles (Papousek & Papousek, 1996).

Most parents try to respond to a sick baby's call for help with extra care and attention, but sometimes the cry is so unpleasant and the infant so difficult to soothe that parents become frustrated, resentful, and angry. Preterm and ill babies are more likely to be abused by their parents than are healthy infants. Often these parents mention a high-pitched, grating cry as one factor that caused them to lose control and harm the baby (Frodi, 1985).

SENSORY CAPACITIES

On his visit to my class, Joshua looked wide-eyed at my bright pink blouse and turned to the sound of his mother's voice. During feedings, he lets Yolanda know by the way he sucks that he prefers the taste of breast milk to a bottle of plain water. Clearly, Joshua has some well-developed sensory capacities. In the following sections, we explore the newborn baby's responsiveness to touch, taste, smell, sound, and visual stimulation. Table 4.4 summarizes these remarkable abilities.

■ TOUCH. Our discussion of preterm infants revealed that touch helps stimulate early physical growth. And as we will see in Chapter 7, touch is important for emotional development as well. Therefore, it is not surprising that sensitivity to touch is well developed at birth. The reflexes listed in Table 4.2 reveal that the newborn baby responds to touch, especially around the mouth, palms, and soles of the feet. During the prenatal period, these areas, along with the genitals, are the first to become sensitive to touch (Humphrey, 1978).

Reactions to temperature change are also present at birth. When Yolanda and Jay undress Joshua, he often expresses his discomfort by crying and becoming

Similar to women in the Zambian culture, this mother of Bhutan—a small country in the Himalaya Mountains—carries her baby about all day, providing close physical contact and a rich variety of stimulation.

JEFFREY AARONSON/NETWORK ASPEN

more active. Newborn babies are more sensitive to stimuli that are colder than body temperature than to those that are warmer (Humphrey, 1978).

At birth, infants are quite sensitive to pain. If male newborns are circumcised, anesthetic is sometimes not used because of the risk of giving pain-relieving drugs to a very young infant. Babies often respond with an intense, high-pitched, stressful cry and a dramatic rise in heart rate, blood pressure, palm sweating, pupil dilation, and muscle tension (Jorgensen, 1999). Recent research establishing the safety of certain local anesthetics for newborns promises to ease the stress of these procedures. Offering a nipple that delivers a sugar solution is also helpful; it quickly reduces crying and discomfort in young babies, preterm and full term alike (Overgaard & Knudsen, 1999; Smith & Blass, 1996).

Permitting a newborn to endure severe pain can affect later behavior. Compared with their anesthetized counterparts, newborns not given a local anesthetic during circumcision react more intensely to routine vaccination at 4 to 6 months of age (Taddio et al., 1997).

■ **TASTE.** All babies come into the world with the ability to communicate their taste preferences to caregivers. When given a sweet liquid instead of water, Joshua uses longer sucks with fewer pauses to savor the taste of his favorite food (Crook & Lipsitt, 1976). In contrast, he is either indifferent to or rejects salty water (Mennella & Beauchamp, 1998). Newborns also reveal their taste preferences through facial expressions. Like adults they relax their facial muscles in response to sweetness, purse their lips when the taste is sour, and show a distinct archlike mouth opening when it is bitter (Rosenstein & Oster, 1990; Steiner, 1979).

These reactions are important for survival, since (as we will see in Chapter 5) the food that is ideally suited to support the infant's early growth is the sweet-tasting milk of the mother's breast. Nevertheless, newborns can readily learn to like a taste that at first evoked either a neutral or negative response. For example, babies allergic to cow's milk formula who are given a soy or other vegetable-based substitute (typically very strong and bitter-tasting) soon prefer it to regular formula. A taste previously disliked can come to be preferred when it is paired with relief of hunger (Harris, 1997). By four months of age, babies react positively to the salty taste, a change that may prepare them to accept solid foods (Beauchamp et al., 1994).

■ **SMELL.** Like taste, the newborn baby's responsiveness to the smell of certain foods is similar to that of adults, suggesting that some odor preferences are innate. For example, the smell of bananas or chocolate causes a relaxed, pleasant facial expression, whereas the odor of rotten eggs makes the infant frown (Steiner, 1979). Newborns can also identify the location of an odor and, if it is unpleasant, defend themselves by turning their heads in the other direction (Reiser, Yonas, & Wikner, 1976).

In many mammals, the sense of smell plays an important role in eating and in protecting the young from predators by helping mothers and babies recognize each other. Although smell is less well developed in humans, traces of its survival value remain. Newborns given a choice between the smell of their own mother's amniotic fluid and that of another mother spend more time oriented toward the familiar fluid (Marlier, Schaal, & Soussignan, 1998) The smell of the mother's amniotic fluid is comforting; babies exposed to it cry less than do babies who are not (Varendi et al., 1998).

Immediately after birth, babies placed face down between their mother's breasts spontaneously latch on to a nipple and begin sucking within an hour. If one breast is washed to remove its natural scent, most newborns grasp the unwashed breast, indicating that they are guided by smell (Porter & Winberg, 1999). At 4 days of age, breast-fed babies prefer the smell of their own mother's breast to that of an unfamiliar lactating woman (Cernoch & Porter, 1985). Bottle-fed babies orient to the smell of any lactating woman over the smells of formula or a nonlactating woman (Marlier & Schaal, 1997; Porter et al., 1992).

Newborn infants' dual attraction to the odors of their mother and of the lactating breast helps them locate an appropriate food source. In the process, they find safety and security and begin to distinguish their caregiver from other people.

■ **HEARING.** Newborn infants can hear a wide variety of sounds, but they are more responsive to some than to others. For example, they prefer complex sounds, such as noises and voices, to pure tones (Bench et al., 1976). In the first days of life, infants can already tell the difference between a few sound patterns—a series of tones arranged in ascending versus descending order; utterances with two versus three syllables; the stress patterns of words, such as *ma*-ma versus ma-*ma*; and happy-sounding speech as opposed to speech with angry, sad, or neutral emotional qualities (Bijeljac-Babic, Bertoncini, & Mehler, 1993; Mastropieri & Turkewitz, 1999; Sansavini, Bertoncini, & Giovanelli, 1997).

Tiny infants are especially sensitive to the sounds of human speech, and they come into the world prepared to respond to the sounds of any human language. Young infants can make fine-grained distinctions among many speech sounds—"ba" and "ga," "ma" and "na," and the short vowel sounds "a" and "i," to name just a few. For example, when given a nipple that turns on the "ba" sound, babies suck vigorously for a period of time, and then sucking slows down as the novelty wears off. When the sound switches to "ga," sucking picks up, indicating that infants detect this subtle difference. Using this method, researchers have found only a few speech sounds that newborns cannot discriminate. Their ability to perceive sounds not found in their own language is more precise than an adult's (Jusczyk, 1995). These capacities reveal that the baby is marvelously prepared for the awesome task of acquiring language.

Responsiveness to sound supports the newborn baby's exploration of the environment. Infants as young as 3 days turn their eyes and head in the general direction of a sound. The ability to identify the precise location of a sound improves greatly over the first 6 months and shows further gains into the second year (Litovsky & Ashmead, 1997).

Listen carefully to yourself the next time you talk to a young baby. You will probably speak in a high-pitched, expressive voice and use a rising tone at the ends of phrases and sentences. Adults probably communicate this way with infants because they notice that babies are more attentive when they do so. Indeed, newborns prefer speech with these characteristics (Aslin, Jusczyk, & Pisoni, 1998). They will also suck more on a nipple to hear a recording of their own mother's voice than that of an unfamiliar woman, and to hear their native language as opposed to a foreign language (Moon, Cooper, & Fifer, 1993; Spence & DeCasper, 1987). These preferences may have developed from hearing the muffled sounds of the mother's voice before birth.

■ **VISION.** Vision is the least mature of the newborn baby's senses. Visual centers in the brain are not yet fully formed, nor are structures in the eye. For example, muscles of the *lens*, the part of the eye that permits us to adjust our focus to varying distances, are weak. Also, cells in the *retina*, the membrane lining the inside of the eye that captures light and transforms it into messages that are sent to the brain, are not as mature or densely packed as they will be in several months (Banks & Bennett, 1988). Furthermore, the optic nerve and other pathways that relay these messages, along with cells in the cortex that receive them, will not be adultlike for several years (Hickey & Peduzzi, 1987).

Because of these factors, newborn babies cannot focus their eyes well, and their **visual acuity,** or fineness of discrimination, is limited. At birth, infants perceive objects at a distance of 20 feet about as clearly as adults do at 600 feet (Courage & Adams, 1990). In addition, unlike adults (who see nearby objects most clearly), newborn babies see equally unclearly across a wide range of distances (Banks, 1980). As a result, images such as the parent's face, even from close up, look much like the blur shown in Figure 4.8.

Although newborn infants cannot yet see well, they actively explore their environment by scanning it for interesting sights and tracking moving objects. However, their eye movements are slow and inaccurate (Hofsten & Rosander, 1998). Joshua's captivation with my pink blouse reveals that he is attracted to bright objects. Nevertheless, once newborns focus on an object, they tend to look only at a single feature—for example, the corner of a triangle instead of the entire shape. Although newborn babies prefer to look at colored rather

(a) Newborn View

(b) Adult View

FIGURE 4.8

View of the human face by the newborn and the adult. The newborn baby's limited focusing ability and poor visual acuity lead the mother's face, even when viewed from close up, to look much like the fuzzy image in part (a) rather than the clear image in part (b).

visual acuity
Fineness of visual discrimination.

than gray stimuli, they are not yet good at discriminating colors. It will take a month or two for color vision to improve (Adams & Courage, 1998; Teller, 1998).

NEONATAL BEHAVIORAL ASSESSMENT

The many capacities described in the preceding sections have been put together into tests that permit doctors, nurses, and researchers to assess the behavior of the infant during the newborn period. The most widely used of these tests, T. Berry Brazelton's **Neonatal Behavioral Assessment Scale (NBAS),** evaluates the baby's reflexes, state changes, responsiveness to physical and social stimuli, and other reactions (Brazelton & Nugent, 1995).

The NBAS has been given to many infants around the world. As a result, researchers have learned a great deal about individual and cultural differences in newborn behavior and how child-rearing practices can maintain or change a baby's reactions. For example, NBAS scores of Asian and Native-American babies reveal that they are less irritable than Caucasian infants. Mothers in these cultures often encourage their babies' calm dispositions through swaddling, close physical contact, and nursing at the first signs of discomfort (Chisholm, 1989; Murrett-Wagstaff & Moore, 1989). In contrast, the poor NBAS scores of undernourished infants in Zambia, Africa, are quickly changed by the way their mothers care for them. The Zambian mother carries her baby about on her hip all day, providing a rich variety of sensory stimulation. As a result, by 1 week, a once unresponsive newborn has been transformed into an alert, contented baby (Brazelton, Koslowski, & Tronick, 1976).

Can you tell from these examples why a single NBAS score is not a good predictor of later development? Since newborn behavior and parenting styles combine to shape development, *changes in NBAS scores* over the first week or two of life (rather than a single score) provide the best estimate of the baby's ability to recover from the stress of birth. NBAS "recovery curves" predict intelligence with moderate success well into the preschool years (Brazelton, Nugent, & Lester, 1987).

The NBAS has also been used to help parents get to know their infants. In some hospitals, health professionals discuss with or demonstrate to parents the newborn capacities assessed by the NBAS. Parents of both preterm and full-term newborns who participate in these programs interact more confidently and sensitively with their babies (Eiden & Reifman, 1996). In one study, Brazilian mothers who experienced a 50-minute NBAS-based discussion a few days after delivery were more likely than controls receiving only health-care information to establish eye contact, smile, vocalize, and soothe in response to infant signals a month later (Wendland-Carro, Piccinini, & Millar, 1999). Although lasting effects on development have not been demonstrated, NBAS interventions are useful in helping the parent–infant relationship get off to a good start.

Neonatal Behavioral Assessment Scale (NBAS)
A test developed to assess the behavior of the infant during the newborn period.

Ask **YOURSELF...**

review   *What functions does REM sleep serve in young infants? When newborn babies are awake, about how much time do they spend crying? Can sleep and crying tell us anything about the health of the newborn's central nervous system? Explain.*

apply   *Jackie, who had a difficult birth, observes her 2-day-old daughter, Kelly, being given the NBAS. Kelly scores poorly on many items. Jackie wonders if this means that Kelly will not develop normally. How would you respond to Jackie's concern?*

connect   *How do the diverse capacities of newborn babies contribute to their first social relationships? Provide as many examples as you can.*

The Transition to Parenthood

The early weeks after a new baby enters the family are full of profound changes. The mother needs to recover from childbirth and adjust to massive hormone shifts in her body. If she is breast-feeding, energies must be devoted to working out this intimate relationship. The father needs to become a part of the new threesome while supporting the mother in her recovery. At times, he may feel jealous of the baby, who constantly demands and gets his wife's attention. And as we will see in Chapter 7, in families with other children, siblings—especially those who are young and first born—understandably feel displaced. They often react with jealousy and anger.

While all this is going on, the tiny infant is assertive about his urgent physical needs, demanding to be fed, changed, and comforted at odd times of the day and night. The family schedule becomes irregular and uncertain. Yolanda spoke candidly about the changes she and Jay experienced:

> When we brought Joshua home, we had to deal with the realities of our new responsibility. Joshua seemed so small and helpless, and we worried about whether we would be able to take proper care of him. It took us 20 minutes to change the first diaper. I rarely feel rested because I'm up two to four times every night, and I spend a good part of my waking hours trying to anticipate Joshua's rhythms and needs. If Jay weren't so willing to help by holding and walking Joshua, I think I'd find it much harder.

CHANGES IN THE FAMILY SYSTEM

The demands of new parenthood—disrupted sleep schedules, less time for husband and wife to devote to each other, and new financial responsibilities—often lead to a mild decline in marital happiness. In addition, entry of the baby into the family usually causes the roles of husband and wife to become more traditional (Cowan & Cowan, 2000; Huston & Vangelisti, 1995). This is true even for couples like Yolanda and Jay, who are strongly committed to gender equality and used to sharing household tasks. Yolanda took a leave of absence from work, whereas Jay's career continued just as it had before. As a result, Yolanda spent much more time at home with the baby, whereas Jay focused more on his provider role.

This movement toward traditional roles is hardest on new mothers who have been involved in their careers. The larger the difference in men's and women's responsibilities, the greater the rise in conflict and decline in marital satisfaction and mental health after childbirth, especially for women (Hawkins et al., 1993; Levy-Shiff,

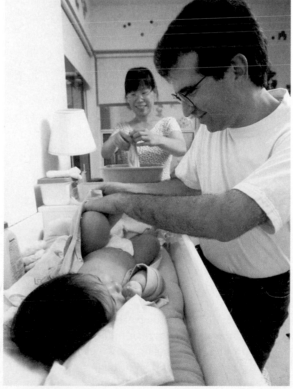

© GRANTPIX/PHOTO RESEARCHERS, INC.

The demands of new parenthood often lead to a mild decline in marital happiness. Sharing child-care responsibilities can protect the marital relationship and enhance the quality of infant care. By participating, this father feels "included," prevents the mother from being overwhelmed by child-care burdens, and frees up time for partners to spend together.

Biology & ENVIRONMENT

POSTPARTUM DEPRESSION AND THE PARENT–CHILD RELATIONSHIP

For as many as 50 to 80 percent of first-time mothers, the excitement of the baby's arrival gives way to an emotional letdown during the first week after delivery known as the *postpartum* (or after-birth) *blues.* The blues are temporary. They die down as new mothers adjust to hormonal changes following childbirth, gain confidence in caring for the baby, and are reassured by their husbands, family members, and friends. However, as many as 10 percent of women do not bounce back so easily. They experience **postpartum depression,** mild to severe feelings of sadness and withdrawal that continue for weeks or months.

During Stella's pregnancy, her husband Kyle's lack of interest in the baby caused her to worry that having a child might be a mistake. Shortly after Lucy was born, Stella's mood plunged. She was anxious and weepy, overwhelmed by Lucy's needs, and angry that she no longer had control over her own schedule. When Stella approached Kyle about her own fatigue and his unwillingness to help with the baby, he snapped that she overreacted to every move he made. Stella's friends, who did not have children, stopped by once to see Lucy and did not call again. Although Stella's genetic makeup may have predisposed her to postpartum depression, social and cultural factors play vital roles in the disorder (Cooper & Murray, 1998).

Stella's depressed mood quickly affected her baby. In the weeks after birth, infants of depressed mothers sleep poorly, are less attentive and responsive to their surroundings, and show continuously elevated stress-hormone levels (Field, 1998). As Lucy spent more time alert, Stella rarely smiled and talked to her. Lucy responded to Stella's sad, vacant gaze by turning away, crying, and often looking sad or angry herself (Campbell, Cohen, & Meyers, 1995; Murray & Cooper, 1997). Each time this happened, Stella felt guilty and inadequate, and her depression deepened. By 6 months of age, Lucy displayed emotional symptoms common in babies of depressed mothers—a negative, irritable mood and attachment difficulties (Teti et al., 1995).

When maternal depression persists, the parent–child relationship worsens. Depressed parents use inconsistent discipline—sometimes lax, at other times too forceful—a pattern that reflects their disengaged as well as hostile behavior (Zahn-Waxler et al., 1990). As we will see in later chapters, children who experience these maladaptive parenting practices often have serious adjustment difficulties. To avoid their parent's insensitivity, they sometimes withdraw into a depressive mood themselves. Or they may mimic their parent's anger and become impulsive and antisocial (Conger, Patterson, & Ge, 1995; Murray et al., 1999).

Over time, the parenting behaviors just described lead children to develop a negative world view—one in which they perceive their parents and other people as threatening. Children who constantly feel in danger are likely to become overly aroused in stressful situations, easily losing control in the face of cognitive and social challenges (Cummings & Davies, 1994). Depressed parents are also more likely to have unhappy marriages, which worsen as the depression persists. Repeated exposure to parental arguments sensitizes children to conflict, increasing their distress and aggression (Cummings & Zahn-Waxler, 1992). Although children of depressed parents may inherit a tendency to develop emotional and behavior problems, quality of parenting is a major factor in their adjustment.

To prevent maternal depression from harming children, early treatment is vital. Stella described her tearfulness, fatigue, and inability to comfort Lucy to her doctor. He referred her to a special program for depressed mothers and their babies. A counselor worked with the family for several months, helping Stella and Kyle with their marital problems and encouraging them to be more sensitive and patient with Lucy. At times, antidepressant medication is prescribed. In most cases of postpartum depression, short-term treatment is successful (Cooper & Murray, 1997; Steinberg & Bellavance, 1999). When mothers do not respond easily to treatment, a warm relationship with the father or another caregiver can safeguard children's development.

---

postpartum depression
Feelings of sadness and withdrawal that appear shortly after childbirth and that continue for weeks or months.

1994). Overall, women experience a more difficult transition to parenthood than do men. (See the Biology and Environment box above).

Postponing childbearing until the late twenties or thirties, as Yolanda and Jay did, eases the transition to parenthood. Waiting permits couples to pursue occupational goals, build financial security, and gain life experience (Taniguchi, 1999). Under these circumstances, men are more enthusiastic about becoming fathers and therefore more willing to participate. And women whose careers are well under way are more likely to encourage their husbands to share housework and child care (Coltrane, 1990).

Men who view themselves as especially caring show less decline in marital satisfaction after the birth of a baby, probably because they are better at meeting the needs of their wives and infants. The father's involvement may increase his understanding of the challenges a mother faces in coping with a new baby, reduce his feelings of being an "outsider," and free up time for partners to spend together. It may also heighten a woman's favorable evaluation of her husband's competence at and motivation to engage in infant care—attitudes that predict continuing paternal involvement (Beitel & Parke, 1998). Finally, fathers' participation in infant care enhances the marital relationship because women tend to see it as a loving act toward themselves (Bird, 1999; Levy-Shiff, 1994).

PARENT INTERVENTIONS

The Caregiving Concerns table below lists strategies couples can use to ease the transition to parenthood. Also, special interventions exist to foster parents' adjustment. For those who are not at high risk for problems, couples' groups led by counselors are highly effective (Cowan & Cowan, 1995). In one program, first-time expectant couples gathered once a week for 6 months to discuss their dreams for the family and changes in relationships sparked by the baby's arrival. Eighteen months after the program ended, participating fathers reported being more involved with their child than did fathers in a no-intervention condition. Perhaps because of fathers'

Caregiving Concerns

How Couples Can Ease the Transition to Parenthood

STRATEGY	DESCRIPTION
Devise a plan for sharing household tasks.	As soon as possible, discuss division of household responsibilities. Decide who does a particular chore based on who has the needed skill and time, not gender. Schedule regular times to reevaluate your plan to fit changing family circumstances.
Begin sharing child care right after the baby's arrival.	For fathers, strive to spend equal time with the baby early. For mothers, refrain from imposing your standards on your partner. Instead, share the role of "child-rearing expert" by discussing parenting values and concerns often. Attend a new-parenthood course together.
Talk over conflicts about decision making and responsibilities.	Face conflict through communication. Clarify your feelings and needs and express them to your partner. Listen and try to understand your partner's point of view. Then be willing to negotiate and compromise.
Establish a balance between work and parenting.	Critically evaluate the time you devote to work in view of new parenthood. If it is too much, try to cut back.
Press for workplace and public policies that assist parents in rearing children.	Difficulties faced by new parents are partly due to lack of workplace and societal supports. Encourage your employer to provide benefits that help combine work and family roles, such as paid employment leave; flexible work hours; and on-site high-quality, affordable day care. Communicate with lawmakers and other citizens about improving policies for children and families.

caregiving assistance, participating mothers maintained their prebirth satisfaction with family and work roles. Three years after the birth, the marriages of all participating couples were still intact and just as happy as they had been before parenthood. In contrast, 15 percent of couples receiving no intervention had divorced (Cowan & Cowan, 1997, 2000).

For high-risk parents struggling with poverty or the birth of a child with disabilities, interventions must be more intensive. Programs in which a trained intervener visits the home and focuses on enhancing social support and the parent–child relationship have resulted in improved parent–infant interaction and benefits for children's cognitive and social development up to 5 years after the intervention (Meisels, Dichtelmiller, & Liaw, 1993).

When couples try to support each other's needs, the stress caused by the birth of a baby remains manageable. Nevertheless, as one pair of counselors who have worked with many new parents point out, "As long as children are dependent on their parents, those parents find themselves preoccupied with thoughts of their children. This does not keep them from enjoying other aspects of their lives, but it does mean that they never return to being quite the same people they were before they became parents" (Colman & Colman, 1991, p. 198).

Ask YOURSELF...

review   *Explain how persisting postpartum depression seriously impairs children's development.*

connect   *Louise has just given birth to her first child. Because her husband works long hours and is seldom available to help, she feels overwhelmed by the pressures of caring for a new baby. Why does Louise's 4-week maternity leave pose a risk to her mental health? (Hint: Consult the Social Issues: Health box on pages 148–149.)*

reflect   *If you are a parent, what was the transition to parenthood like for you? What factors eased the stress of this major life change? What factors made it more difficult? If you are not a parent, pose these questions to someone you know who recently became a parent.*

Summary

THE STAGES OF CHILDBIRTH

Describe the three stages of childbirth, the baby's adaptation to labor and delivery, and the newborn baby's appearance.

- In the first stage of childbirth, **dilation and effacement of the cervix** occur as uterine contractions increase in strength and frequency. This stage culminates in **transition,** a brief period in which contractions are strongest and closest together and the cervix opens completely. In the second stage, the mother feels an urge to bear down with her abdominal muscles, and the baby is born. Often an **episiotomy** is performed to permit the baby to pass without tearing the mother's tissues. In the final stage, the placenta is delivered.

- During labor, infants produce high levels of stress hormones, which help them withstand oxygen deprivation, clear the lungs for breathing, and arouse them into alertness at birth. Newborn infants have large heads, small bodies, and facial features that make adults feel like picking them up and cuddling them. The **Apgar Scale** is used to assess the newborn baby's physical condition at birth.

APPROACHES TO CHILDBIRTH

Describe natural childbirth and home delivery, noting benefits and concerns associated with each.

- **Natural, or prepared, childbirth** involves classes in which expectant mothers and their partners learn about labor and delivery, relaxation and breathing techniques to counteract pain, and coaching during childbirth. The method helps reduce stress and pain during labor and delivery. As a result, most mothers require little or no medication, and they feel more positive about the birth experience.

- Social support, a vital part of natural childbirth, reduces the length of labor and the incidence of birth complications. When mothers give birth in a sitting position, labor is also shortened.

- Home birth reduces unnecessary medical procedures and permits mothers to exercise greater control over their own care and that of their babies. As long as mothers are healthy and assisted by a well-trained doctor or midwife, giving birth at home is just as safe to as giving birth in a hospital.

MEDICAL INTERVENTIONS

List common medical interventions during childbirth, circumstances that justify their use, and any dangers associated with each.

- Medical interventions during childbirth are more common in the United States than anywhere else in the world. When women have a history of pregnancy and birth complications, **fetal monitors** help save the lives of many babies. However, when used routinely, they may identify infants as in danger who, in fact, are not. Fetal monitoring is linked to an increase in cesarean delivery.

- **Analgesics** and **anesthetics** are necessary in complicated deliveries. When given in large doses, anesthetics prolong labor and increase the likelihood of an instrument delivery. They also produce a depressed state in the newborn that affects the early mother–infant relationship. **Forceps** or **vacuum extractors** are appropriate if the mother's pushing does not move the infant through the birth canal in a reasonable period of time, but they can cause head injuries.

- Since **induced labors** are more difficult than naturally occurring ones, they should be scheduled only when continuing the pregnancy threatens the well-being of mother or baby, not for reasons of convenience. **Cesarean deliveries** are justified in cases of medical emergency and serious maternal illness and sometimes when babies are in **breech position.** Many unnecessary cesareans are performed in the United States.

BIRTH COMPLICATIONS

What risks are associated with oxygen deprivation, preterm and low birth weight, and postterm birth, and what factors can help infants who survive a traumatic birth?

- Although most births proceed normally, serious complications can occur. A major cause of **cerebral palsy** is lack of oxygen during labor and delivery. As long as **anoxia** is not extreme, most oxygen-deprived newborns catch up in development by the school years. **Respiratory distress syndrome,** which can cause permanent damage due to immaturity of the lungs and resulting oxygen deprivation, is common in infants born more than 6 weeks early.

- The incidence of premature births is high among low-income pregnant women and mothers of twins. Compared with **preterm** babies, whose weight is appropriate for time spent in the uterus, **small-for-date** infants are more likely to develop poorly. The fragile appearance and unresponsive, irritable behavior of preterm infants can lead parents to be less sensitive and responsive in caring for them.

- Some interventions provide special stimulation through gentle motion, attractive mobiles, soothing sounds, and massage in the intensive care nursery. Others teach parents how to care for and interact with their babies. Parents with stable life circumstances and social supports need only a few sessions of coaching in caring for a preterm baby to help their child develop favorably. When preterm infants live in stressed, low-income households, long-term, intensive intervention is required. A major cause of **neonatal** and **infant mortality** is low birth weight.

- The longer a **postterm** infant remains in the uterus, the greater the risk for birth complications. Therefore, doctors usually induce labor in mothers whose pregnancies have continued for more than 42 weeks.

Summary (continued)

■ When babies experience birth trauma, favorable personal characteristics, a supportive family environment, or relationships with other caring adults can help restore their growth. Even infants with serious birth complications can recover with the help of positive life events.

PRECIOUS MOMENTS AFTER BIRTH

Is close parent–infant contact shortly after birth necessary for bonding?

■ Human parents do not require close physical contact with the baby immediately after birth for **bonding** and effective parenting to occur. Nevertheless, early contact supports maternal feelings of caring and affection. Hospital practices that promote parent–infant closeness, such as **rooming in,** may help parents build a good relationship with their newborn.

THE NEWBORN BABY'S CAPACITIES

Describe the newborn baby's reflexes and states of arousal, including sleep characteristics and ways to soothe a crying baby.

■ **Reflexes** are the newborn baby's most obvious organized patterns of behavior. Some have survival value, others help parents and infants establish gratifying interaction, and still others provide the foundation for voluntary motor skills.

■ Although newborns move in and out of five **states of arousal,** they spend most of their time asleep. Sleep consists of at least two states: **rapid-eye-movement (REM) sleep** and **non-rapid-eye movement (NREM) sleep.** REM sleep is greater during the newborn period than at any later age. It provides young infants with the stimulation essential for central nervous system development. Rapid eye movements ensure that structures of the eye remain oxygenated during sleep.

■ A crying baby stimulates strong feelings of discomfort in nearby adults. The intensity of the cry and the experiences that led up to it help parents identify what is wrong. Once feeding and diaper changing have been tried, lifting the baby to the shoulder and rocking or walking is the most effective soothing technique. Many other soothing methods, including swaddling, offering a pacifier, and talking softly, are helpful.

Describe the newborn baby's sensory capacities.

■ The senses of touch, taste, smell, and sound are well developed at birth. Newborns are sensitive to pain, prefer sweet tastes and smells, and orient toward the odor of their own mother's amniotic fluid and the lactating breast. Already they can distinguish a few sound patterns, as well as almost all speech sounds in human languages. They are especially responsive to high-pitched expressive voices, their own mother's voice, and speech in their native language as opposed to a foreign language.

■ Vision is the least mature of the newborn's senses. At birth, focusing ability and **visual acuity** are limited. In exploring the visual field, newborn babies are attracted to bright objects, but they limit their looking to single features. Newborn babies have difficulty discriminating colors.

Why is neonatal behavioral assessment useful?

■ The most widely used instrument for assessing the behavior of the newborn infant is Brazelton's **Neonatal Behavioral Assessment Scale (NBAS).** The NBAS has helped researchers understand individual and cultural differences in newborn behavior. Sometimes it is used to teach parents about their baby's capacities, which can help parents interact more confidently and sensitively.

THE TRANSITION TO PARENTHOOD

Describe typical changes in the family after the birth of a new baby.

■ The new baby's arrival is exciting but stressful. The demands of new parenthood often lead to a mild decline in marital happiness, and family roles become more traditional.

■ About 10 percent of women experience **postpartum depression.** If not treated early, it can have serious consequences for children's development.

■ When parents are low risk, couples' groups involving discussion of changing family relationships can ease the transition to parenthood. High-risk parents struggling with poverty or the birth of a baby with disabilities benefit from intensive home interventions focusing on enhancing social support and parent–infant interaction.

Important terms and concepts

analgesic (p. 143)
anesthetic (p. 143)
anoxia (p. 144)
Apgar Scale (p. 138)
bonding (p. 151)
breech position (p. 143)
cerebral palsy (p. 144)
cesarean delivery (p. 143)
dilation and effacement of the
    cervix (p. 134)
episiotomy (p. 136)
fetal monitors (p. 141)

forceps (p. 143)
induced labor (p. 143)
infant mortality (p. 148)
natural, or prepared, childbirth
    (p. 141)
Neonatal Behavioral Assessment
    Scale (NBAS) (p. 160)
neonatal mortality (p. 148)
non-rapid-eye-movement (NREM)
    sleep (p. 155)
postpartum depression (p. 162)
postterm (p. 149)

preterm (p. 146)
rapid-eye-movement (REM)
    sleep (p. 155)
reflex (p. 153)
respiratory distress syndrome
    (p. 145)
rooming in (p. 153)
small for date (p. 146)
states of arousal (p. 155)
transition (p. 135)
vacuum extractor (p. 143)
visual acuity (p. 159)

fyi . . . for further information and help

Consult the companion website for this book, where you will find additional weblinks and associated learning activities:
www.ablongman.com/berk

GENERAL CHILDBIRTH INFORMATION

Childbirth.Org
www.childbirth.org

Through an informative website, offers a wealth of information on all aspects of childbirth.

NATURAL CHILDBIRTH

Lamaze International
www.lamaze-childbirth.com

Trains and certifies instructors in the Lamaze method of natural childbirth. Provides information to expectant parents.

American Academy of Husband-Coached Childbirth
www.bradleybirth.com

Certifies instructors in the Bradley method of natural childbirth, which emphasizes coaching by the husband.

MIDWIVES

American College of Nurse-Midwives
www.acnm.org

Certifies nurse-midwives and provides referrals to expectant parents.

CESAREAN DELIVERY

International Cesarean Awareness Network
www.childbirth.org/section/ICAN.html

Provides information on cesarean birth, including avoiding unnecessary cesareans and vaginal birth after a cesarean.

CEREBRAL PALSY

United Cerebral Palsy Association
www.ucpa.org

Provides assistance to people with cerebral palsy and their families. Local and state chapters offer medical, therapeutic, and social services.

"My World in the Year 2000"

Giada Kuka

10 years, Albania

The delighted expressions and animated behavior of children in this scene suggest a strong drive to explore, understand, and gain control of their world. During the first year, infants grow quickly, move on their own, explore their surroundings more effectively, and make sense of complicated sights and sounds. Chapter 5 traces these awesome achievements.

Physical Development in Infancy and Toddlerhood

On a brilliant June morning, 16-month-old Caitlin emerged from her front door, ready for the short drive to the child-care home where she spent her weekdays while her mother, Carolyn, and her father, David, worked. Clutching a teddy bear in one hand and her mother's arm with the other, Caitlin descended the steps. "One! Two! Threeeee!" Carolyn counted as she helped Caitlin down, mother and daughter laughing after each giant step.

"How much she's changed!" Carolyn thought to herself, looking at the child who, not long ago, had been a newborn cradled in her arms. With her first steps, Caitlin had passed from *infancy* to *toddlerhood*—a period spanning the second year of life. At first, Caitlin did, indeed, "toddle" with an awkward gait, rocking from side to side and tipping over frequently. But her face reflected the thrill of being upright and conquering a new skill.

As they walked toward the car, Carolyn and Caitlin caught sight of 3-year-old Eli and his father, Kevin, in the neighboring yard. Eli dashed toward them, holding a bright yellow envelope. Carolyn bent down, opened the envelope, and took out a card. It read, "Into the world, into our hearts, into our home. Announcing the arrival of Grace Ann. Born: Cambodia. Age: 16 months."

"Caitlin," Carolyn said excitedly, "Eli's sister is finally here!" Caitlin watched as Carolyn turned toward Kevin and Eli. "This is wonderful news! When can we see her?"

"Let's wait a few days," Kevin replied soberly. "Monica's taken Grace to the doctor this morning. She's underweight, malnourished, and exhausted from the long journey." Kevin described Monica's first night with Grace in a hotel room in Phnom Penh before they flew to the United States. Grace lay on the bed, passive, withdrawn, and fearful. Eventually she fell asleep, clutching crackers in both hands.

Carolyn felt a tug at her sleeve. Caitlin was impatient. Off they drove to child care, where Vanessa had just dropped off her 18-month-old son, Timmy. Within moments, Caitlin and Timmy were in the sandbox, shoveling sand into plastic cups and buckets with the help of their caregiver, Ginette.

A few weeks later, Grace joined Caitlin and Timmy at Ginette's child-care home. Although still tiny and unable to crawl or walk, she had grown taller and heavier, and her sad, vacant gaze had given way to an alert expression, a ready smile, and an enthusiastic desire to imitate and explore. When Caitlin headed for the sandbox, Grace stretched out her arms, asking Ginette to carry her there, too. Soon Grace was pulling herself up at every opportunity. Finally, at age 18 months, she walked!

This chapter traces physical growth during the first 2 years—one of the most remarkable and busiest times of development. We will see how rapid changes in the infant's body and brain support rapid learning and new motor skills and perceptual capacities. Caitlin, Grace, and Timmy will join us along the way, to illustrate individual differences and environmental influences on physical development.

Body Growth

The next time you have a chance, briefly observe several infants and toddlers while walking in your neighborhood or at a nearby shopping center. You will see that their capabilities differ vastly. One reason for the change in what children can do over the first 2 years is that their bodies change enormously—faster than at any other time after birth.

CHANGES IN BODY SIZE

As Figure 5.1 shows, by the end of the first year a typical infant's height is 50 percent greater than it was at birth, and by 2 years of age it is 75 percent greater. Weight shows similar dramatic gains. By 5 months of age, birth weight has doubled, at 1 year it has tripled, and at 2 years it has quadrupled.

Rather than steady gains, infants and toddlers grow in little spurts. In one study, children followed over the first 21 months of life went for periods of 7 to 63 days with no growth and then added as much as a half-inch in a 24-hour period! Almost always, parents described their babies as irritable, restless, and very hungry on the day before the spurt (Lampl, 1993; Lampl, Veldhuis, & Johnson, 1992).

As in all aspects of development, differences among children in body size exist. In infancy, girls are slightly shorter and lighter than boys. This small sex difference continues throughout early and middle childhood and will be greatly magnified at adolescence. Ethnic differences in body size are apparent as well. Look again at Figure 5.1, and you will see that at 18 months, Grace, a Cambodian-American child, is below the growth norms (height and weight averages for children her age). Although early malnutrition contributed to Grace's small size, even after substantial catch-up she remained below North American averages, a trend typi-

A 1-year-old and two 18-month-olds play at the park, with the assistance of a 4-year-old. Children grow quickly during infancy and toddlerhood—faster than at any other times of life. Height increases by 75 percent, and weight quadruples. In the second year, body proportions become less top heavy as the trunk and legs catch up with the head and chest.

© DION OGUST/THE IMAGE WORKS

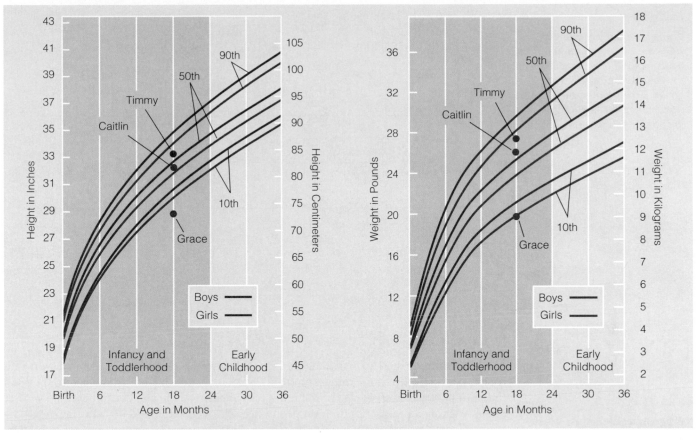

FIGURE 5.1

FIGURE 5.1

Gains in height and weight during infancy and toddlerhood among North American children. The steep rise in these growth curves shows that children grow rapidly from birth to 2 years. At the same time, wide individual differences in body size exist. Infants and toddlers who fall at the 50th percentile are average in height and weight. Those who fall at the 90th percentile are taller and heavier than 90 percent of their agemates. Those who fall at the 10th percentile are taller and heavier than only 10 percent of their peers. Notice that girls are slightly shorter and lighter than boys. As children move into early childhood, rate of growth slows.

cal for Asian children. In contrast, Timmy is slightly above average, as African-American children tend to be (Tanner, 1990).

CHANGES IN BODY PROPORTIONS

As the child's overall size increases, parts of the body grow at different rates. Two growth patterns describe these changes in body proportions. The first, called the **cephalocaudal trend,** is depicted in Figure 5.2. Translated from Latin, it means "head to tail." Recall from Chapter 3 that during the prenatal period, the head develops first from the primitive embryonic disk, followed by the lower part of the body. After birth, the head and chest continue to have a growth advantage, but the baby's trunk and legs gradually pick up speed. At birth, the head takes up one-fourth of total body length, the legs only one-third. Notice how the lower portion of the body catches up. By age 2, the head accounts for only one-fifth and the legs for nearly one-half of total body length.

The second pattern is the **proximodistal trend,** meaning that growth proceeds, literally, from "near to far," or from the center of the body outward. In the prenatal period, the head, chest, and trunk grew first, followed by the arms and legs, and finally by the hands and feet. During infancy and childhood, the arms and legs continue to grow somewhat ahead of the hands and feet. As we will see later, motor development follows these same developmental trends.

cephalocaudal trend
An organized pattern of physical growth and motor control that proceeds from head to tail.

proximodistal trend
An organized pattern of physical growth and motor control that proceeds from the center of the body outward.

FIGURE 5.2

Changes in body proportions from the early prenatal period to adulthood. This figure illustrates the cephalocaudal trend of physical growth. The head gradually becomes smaller, and the legs longer, in proportion to the rest of the body.

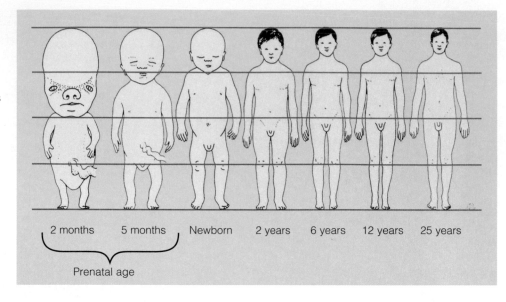

2 months   5 months   Newborn   2 years   6 years   12 years   25 years

Prenatal age

FIGURE 5.3

Diagram of a long bone showing upper and lower epiphyses. Cartilage cells are produced at the growth plates of the epiphyses and gradually harden into bone. (From J. M. Tanner, *Foetus into Man* [2nd ed.], Cambridge, MA: Harvard University Press, p. 32. Copyright © 1990 by J. M. Tanner. All rights reserved. Reprinted by permission of the publisher and author.)

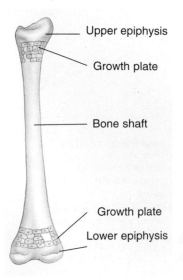

Upper epiphysis

Growth plate

Bone shaft

Growth plate

Lower epiphysis

CHANGES IN MUSCLE–FAT MAKEUP

One of the most obvious changes in infants' appearance is their transformation into round, plump babies by the middle of the first year. Body fat (most of which lies just beneath the skin) begins to increase in the last few weeks of prenatal life and continues to do so after birth, reaching a peak at about 9 months of age. This very early rise in "baby fat" helps the small infant keep a constant body temperature. Then, during the second year, most toddlers start to slim down, a trend that continues into middle childhood (Tanner, 1990).

Muscle tissue grows according to a different plan. It increases very slowly during infancy and childhood and will not reach a peak until adolescence. Babies are not very muscular creatures, and their strength and physical coordination are limited.

As with body size, slight differences exist between boys and girls in muscle–fat makeup. From the beginning, girls have a higher ratio of fat to muscle than do boys, a difference that will increase in middle childhood and become very large during adolescence (Malina & Bouchard, 1991).

SKELETAL GROWTH

Children of the same age differ in *rate* of physical growth; some make faster progress toward a mature body size than others. We cannot tell how quickly a child's physical growth is moving along just by looking at current body size. For example, Timmy is larger and heavier than Caitlin and Grace, but he is not physically more mature. In a moment, you will see why.

■ GENERAL SKELETAL GROWTH. The best way of estimating a child's physical maturity is to use **skeletal age,** a measure of development of the bones of the body. The embryonic skeleton is first formed out of soft, pliable tissue called *cartilage.* Then, beginning in the sixth week of pregnancy, cartilage cells harden into bone, a gradual process that continues throughout childhood and adolescence (Moore & Persaud, 1998).

Once bones have taken on their basic shape, special growth centers called **epiphyses** appear just before birth (see Figure 5.3). In the long bones of the body, the epiphyses emerge at the two extreme ends of each bone. As growth continues, the epiphyses get thinner and disappear. When this occurs, no more bone growth is possible. Skeletal age can be estimated by X-raying the bones and seeing how many epiphyses there are and the extent to which their growth plates are fused. These X-rays are compared with norms established for bone maturity based on large numbers of children (Malina & Bouchard, 1991).

When the skeletal ages of infants and children are examined, they reveal that African-American children tend to be slightly ahead of Caucasian-American children at all ages. And girls are considerably ahead of boys—the reason Timmy's skeletal age lags behind that of Caitlin and Grace. At birth, the sexes differ by about 4 to 6 weeks, a gap that widens over infancy and childhood and is responsible for the fact that girls reach their full body size several years before boys (Humphrey, 1998). Girls are advanced in development of other organs as well. Their greater physical maturity may contribute to their greater resistance to harmful environmental influences throughout development. As pointed out in Chapter 2, girls experience fewer developmental problems than do boys, and infant and childhood mortality for girls is also lower.

■ **GROWTH OF THE SKULL.** Doctors routinely measure children's head size between birth and 2 years of age. Skull growth is especially rapid during the first 2 years because of large increases in brain size. At birth, the bones of the skull are separated by six gaps, or "soft spots," called **fontanels** (see Figure 5.4). The gaps permit the bones to overlap as the large head of the baby passes through the mother's narrow birth canal. You can easily feel the largest gap, the anterior fontanel, at the top of a baby's skull. It is slightly more than an inch across. It gradually shrinks and is filled in during the second year. The other fontanels are smaller and close more quickly. As the skull bones come in contact with one another, they form *sutures,* or seams. These permit the skull to expand easily as the brain grows. The sutures disappear completely in adolescence, when skull growth is complete.

APPEARANCE OF TEETH

On the average, an African-American baby's first tooth appears at about 4 months, a Caucasian baby's around 6 months, although there are wide individual differences. Timmy's first tooth erupted when he was 2 months old; a few infants do not get their first tooth until 1 year of age. After the first tooth erupts, new ones appear every month or two. By age 2, the average child has 20 teeth (Ranly, 1998). Dental development provides a rough clue to overall rate of skeletal development. A child who gets teeth early is likely to be advanced in physical maturity.

Although increased irritability, sleeplessness, ear rubbing, facial rash, and mild fever are associated with teething, 65 percent of teething infants show no symptoms. So before parents conclude that signs of illness are due to teething, other possible causes should be ruled out (Macknin et al., 2000). Around the time the teeth appear, antibodies received from the mother during the prenatal period decline. As a result, infants are somewhat less resistant to infection, although breast-feeding affords extra immunity.

Brain Development

At birth, the brain is nearer than any other physical structure to its adult size, and it continues to develop at an astounding pace throughout infancy and toddlerhood. We can best understand brain growth by looking at it from two vantage points: (1) the microscopic level of individual brain cells, and (2) the larger level of the cerebral cortex, the most complex brain structure and the one responsible for the highly developed intelligence of our species.

DEVELOPMENT OF NEURONS

The human brain has 100 to 200 billion **neurons,** or nerve cells, that store and transmit information, many of which have thousands of direct connections with other neurons. Neurons differ from other body cells in that they are not tightly packed together. They have tiny gaps, or **synapses,** between them where fibers from different neurons come close together but

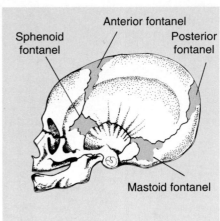

FIGURE 5.4

The skull at birth, showing the fontanels and sutures. The fontanels gradually close during the first 2 years, forming sutures that permit the skull to expand easily as the brain grows. (From *Human Growth and Development Throughout Life*, by P.M. Hill and P. Humphrey, © 1989. Reprinted with permission of Delmar, a division of Thomson Learning.)

skeletal age
An estimate of physical maturity based on development of the bones of the body.

epiphyses
Growth centers in the bones where new cartilage cells are produced and gradually harden.

fontanels
Six soft spots that separate the bones of the skull at birth.

neurons
Nerve cells that store and transmit information.

synapses
The gaps between neurons, across which chemical messages are sent.

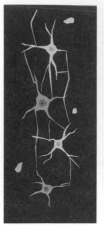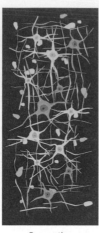

Birth   6 months   2 years

FIGURE 5.5

Development of neurons.
Growth of neural fibers takes place rapidly from birth to 2 years. During this time, new synapses form at an astounding pace, supporting the emergence of many new capacities. Stimulation is vitally important for maintaining and increasing this complex communication network. (Reprinted by permission of the publisher from *The Postnatal Development of the Human Cerebral Cortex*, Vol. I–III, by Jesse LeRoy Conel, Cambridge, Mass.: Harvard University Press. Copyright ©1939, 1975 by the President and Fellows of Harvard College.)

synaptic pruning
Loss of connective fibers by seldom-stimulated neurons, thereby returning them to an uncommitted state so they can support the development of future skills.

glial cells
Cells that are responsible for myelinization.

myelinization
A process in which neural fibers are coated with an insulating fatty sheath (called myelin) that improves the efficiency of message transfer.

do not touch. Neurons release chemicals that cross the synapse, sending messages to one another.

The basic story of brain growth concerns how neurons develop and form this elaborate communication system. Recall from Chapter 3 that neurons are produced in the primitive neural tube of the embryo. From there, they migrate to form the major parts of the brain. By the end of the second trimester of pregnancy, production of neurons is largely complete.

Once neurons are in place, they establish their unique functions by extending their fibers to form synaptic connections with neighboring cells. As Figure 5.5 shows, during infancy and toddlerhood, growth of neural fibers and synapses increases at an astounding pace (Huttenlocher, 1994; Moore & Persaud, 1998). Because developing neurons require space for these connective structures, a surprising aspect of brain growth is that many surrounding neurons die during the peak period of synaptic growth in any brain area. Fortunately, during the prenatal period, an excess of neurons is produced—far more than the brain will ever need (Diamond & Hopson, 1999).

As neurons form connections, *stimulation* becomes vital in their survival. Neurons that are stimulated by input from the surrounding environment continue to establish new synapses, forming increasingly elaborate systems of communication that support more complex abilities. Neurons seldom stimulated soon lose their synapses, a process called **synaptic pruning.** At first, stimulation leads to an overabundance of synapses, many of which serve identical functions, thereby ensuring that the child will acquire the motor, cognitive, and social skills that members of our species need to survive. Synaptic pruning returns neurons not needed at the moment to an uncommitted state so they can support the development of future skills (Johnson, 1998). Notice how appropriate stimulation of the child's brain is crucial during periods in which the formation of synapses is at its peak (Eisenberg, 1999; Greenough et al., 1993).

Perhaps you are wondering, if few neurons are produced after the prenatal period, what causes the dramatic increase in brain size during the first 2 years? About half the brain's volume is made up of **glial cells,** which do not carry messages. Instead, they are responsible for **myelinization,** the coating of neural fibers with an insulting fatty sheath (called *myelin*) that improves the efficiency of message transfer. Glial cells multiply dramatically from the fourth month of pregnancy through the second year of life, after which their production slows down (Casaer, 1993). Dramatic increase in neural fibers and myelinization are responsible for the rapid gain in overall size of the brain. At birth, the brain is nearly 30 percent of its adult weight; by the time toddlerhood is complete, it reaches 70 percent (Thatcher et al., 1996).

DEVELOPMENT OF THE CEREBRAL CORTEX

The **cerebral cortex** surrounds the rest of the brain, much like a half-shelled walnut. It is the largest, most complex brain structure, accounting for 85 percent of the brain's weight and containing the greatest number of neurons and synapses. The cerebral cortex is the last part of the brain to stop growing. For this reason, it is believed to be much more sensitive to environmental influences for a longer period of time than any other part of the brain.

■ **REGIONS OF THE CORTEX.** As Figure 5.6 shows, different regions of the cerebral cortex have specific functions, such as receiving information from the senses, instructing the body to move, and thinking. The order in which cortical regions develop corresponds to the order in which various capacities emerge in the infant and growing child. For example, a burst of synaptic growth in the auditory and visual cortexes (refer to Figure 5.6) occurs from 3 to 4 months until the end of the first year—a period of dramatic gains in auditory and visual perception. Among the areas responsible for body movement, neurons that control the head, arms, and chest form connections before those that control the trunk and legs. (Can you name this growth trend?) As the Social Issues: Health box on page 176 indicates, problems in early cortical functioning, which prevent some babies from learning certain life-saving motor responses, may lead to sudden infant death syndrome, a major cause of infant mortality.

Among the last regions of the cortex to myelinate and form synaptic connections are the *frontal lobes,* which are responsible for thought and consciousness. From age 2 months on, this area functions more effectively. It shows especially rapid gains between 2 and 6 years of age and continues its growth for years, well into the second and third decades of life (Huttenlocher & Dabholkar, 1997; Johnson, 1998; Thompson et al., 2000).

■ LATERALIZATION AND PLASTICITY OF THE CORTEX.

The cortex has two *hemispheres*—left and right. The hemispheres do not have precisely the same functions. Some tasks are done mostly by one hemisphere and some by the other. For example, each hemisphere receives sensory information from and controls only one side of the body—the one opposite to it.[1] For most of us, the left hemisphere is responsible for verbal abilities (such as spoken and written language) and positive emotion (for example, joy). The right hemisphere handles spatial abilities (judging distances, reading maps, and recognizing geometric shapes) and negative emotion (such as distress) (Banish & Heller, 1998; Nelson & Bosquet, 2000). This pattern may be reversed in left-handed people, but more often, the cortex of left-handers is less clearly specialized than that of right-handers.

Specialization of the two hemispheres is called **lateralization.** A lateralized brain is adaptive because it permits a greater variety of abilities than if both sides of the cortex served exactly the same functions. Researchers are interested in when brain lateralization occurs because they want to know more about **brain plasticity.** In a highly *plastic* cortex, many areas are not yet committed to specific functions. If a part of the brain is damaged, other parts can take over the tasks it would have handled. But once the hemispheres lateralize, damage to a specific region means that the abilities it controls will be lost forever.

At birth, the hemispheres have already begun to specialize. For example, most newborns favor the right side of the body in their head position and reflexive reactions (Grattan et al., 1992; Rönnqvist & Hopkins, 1998). Most also show greater EEG brain-wave activity in the left hemisphere while listening to speech sounds. In contrast, the right hemisphere reacts more strongly to nonspeech sounds as well as to stimuli (such as a sour-tasting fluid) that evoke negative emotion (Davidson, 1994; Fox & Davidson, 1986).

Nevertheless, dramatic evidence for early brain plasticity comes from research on brain-damaged children. In a large sample of preschoolers with a wide variety of brain injuries sustained in the first year of life, deficits in language and spatial abilities were milder than those observed in brain-injured adults. And by age 5, cognitive impairments had largely disappeared (Stiles, 1998, 2000). As the children gained perceptual, cognitive, and motor experiences, other stimulated cortical structures compensated for the damaged areas, regardless of the site of injury.

Additional findings indicate mild deficits in general intelligence in children with early brain injuries—the price they seem to pay for massive brain reorganization. But their IQs are near normal, and verbal and spatial abilities are intact (Bates et al., 1998, 1999). In contrast, older children and adults have only a limited capacity to recover functions following brain injury (Chugani, 1994; Johnson, 1998).

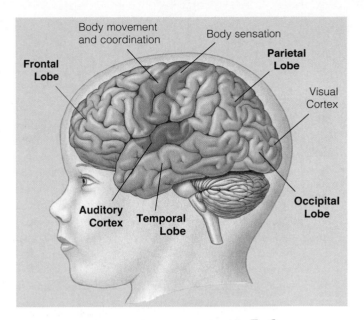

Body movement and coordination — Body sensation — **Frontal Lobe** — **Parietal Lobe** — Visual Cortex — **Auditory Cortex** — **Temporal Lobe** — **Occipital Lobe**

FIGURE 5.6

The left side of the human brain, showing the cerebral cortex. The cortex is divided into different lobes, each of which contains a variety of regions with specific functions. Some major ones are labeled here.

cerebral cortex
The largest, most complex structure of the human brain, and the one responsible for the highly developed intelligence of the human species. Surrounds the rest of the brain, much like a half-shelled walnut.

lateralization
Specialization of functions of the two hemispheres of the cerebral cortex.

brain plasticity
The ability of other parts of the brain to take over functions of damaged regions. Disappears when hemispheres of the cerebral cortex lateralize.

---

[1]The eyes are an exception. Messages from the right half of each retina go to the left hemisphere; messages from the left half of each retina go to the right hemisphere. Thus, visual information from *both* eyes is received by *both* hemispheres.

Social

ISSUES: HEALTH

THE MYSTERIOUS TRAGEDY OF SUDDEN INFANT DEATH SYNDROME

Millie awoke with a start one morning and looked at the clock. It was 7:30, and Sasha had missed her night waking and early morning feeding. Wondering if she was all right, Millie and her husband Stuart tiptoed into the room. Sasha lay still, curled up under her blanket. She had died silently during her sleep.

Sasha was a victim of **sudden infant death syndrome (SIDS),** the unexpected death, usually during the night, of an infant younger than 1 year of age that remains unexplained after thorough investigation. In industrialized nations, SIDS is the leading cause of infant mortality between 1 week and 12 months of age. It accounts for over one-third of these deaths in the United States (MacDorman & Atkinson, 1999).

Although the precise cause of SIDS is not known, its victims usually show physical problems from the very beginning. Early medical records of SIDS babies reveal higher rates of prematurity and low birth weight, poor Apgar scores, and limp muscle tone. Abnormal heart rate and respiration and disturbances in sleep–waking activity are also involved (Leach et al., 1999; Malloy & Hoffman, 1995). At the time of death, many SIDS babies have a mild respiratory infection (Kohlendorfer, Kiechl, & Sperl, 1998). This seems to increase the chances of respiratory failure in an already vulnerable baby.

One hypothesis about the cause of SIDS is that problems in brain functioning prevent these infants from learning how to respond when their survival is threatened—for example, when respiration is suddenly interrupted (Horne et al., 2000; Panigrahy et al., 1997). Between 1 and 4 months of age, when SIDS is most likely, reflexes decline and are replaced by voluntary, learned responses. Respiratory and muscular weaknesses may stop SIDS babies from acquiring behaviors that replace defensive reflexes. As a result, when breathing difficulties occur during sleep, the infants do not wake up, shift their position, or cry out for help. Instead, they simply give in to oxygen deprivation and death.

In an effort to reduce the occurrence of SIDS, researchers are studying environmental factors related to it. Maternal cigarette smoking, both during and after pregnancy, as well as smoking by other caregivers strongly predicts the disorder. Babies exposed to cigarette smoke have more respiratory infections and are 2 to 3 times more likely to die of SIDS than are non-exposed infants (Dwyer, Ponsonby, & Couper, 1999; Dybing & Sanner, 1999). Prenatal abuse of drugs that depress central nervous system functioning (opiates and barbiturates) increases the risk of SIDS tenfold (Kandall et al., 1993).

SIDS babies are also more likely to sleep on their stomachs than their

backs and are often wrapped very warmly in clothing and blankets (Kleeman et al., 1999). Researchers think that smoke, depressant drugs, sleeping on the stomach, and excessive body warmth place a strain on the respiratory control system in the brain. In an at-risk baby, the respiratory center may stop functioning. In other cases, healthy babies sleeping face down in soft bedding may die from continually breathing their own exhaled breath.

Quitting smoking, changing an infant's sleeping position, and removing a few bedclothes can reduce the incidence of SIDS. For example, if women refrained from smoking while pregnant, an estimated 30 percent of SIDS would be prevented. Public education campaigns that discourage parents from putting babies down on their stomachs have led to dramatic reductions in SIDS in many countries, including Australia, Denmark, Great Britain, New Zealand, Sweden, and the United States (American Academy of Pediatrics, 2000; Schlaud et al., 1999).

When SIDS does occur, surviving family members require a great deal of help to overcome their grief. As Millie commented 6 months after Sasha's death, "It's the worst crisis we've ever been through. What's helped us most are the comforting words of parents in our support group who've experienced the same tragedy."

---

sudden infant death syndrome (SIDS)
The unexpected death, usually during the night, of an infant younger than 1 year of age that remains unexplained after thorough investigation.

Another illustration of how early experience can mold brain organization comes from studies of deaf adults who, as infants and children, learned to communicate through sign language. EEG brain-wave recordings reveal that compared with hearing adults, these individuals depend more on the right hemisphere for language processing (Mills, Coffey-Corina, & Neville, 1994). Also, toddlers advanced in language development show greater left-hemispheric specialization than do their more slowly developing agemates. This shows that the very process of acquiring language promotes lateralization (Bates, 1999; Mills, Coffey-Corina, & Neville, 1993, 1997). We will discuss further cortical areas specialized for language when we take up language development in Chapter 6.

During the first few years, the brain is more plastic than at any later time of life, perhaps because many of its synapses are not yet established. And although the cortex is programmed from the start for hemispheric specialization, experience greatly influences the rate and success of this genetic program.

SENSITIVE PERIODS IN BRAIN DEVELOPMENT

Recall that stimulation of the brain is vital during periods in which it is growing most rapidly—when formation of synapses is at a peak. The existence of sensitive periods in development of the cerebral cortex has been amply demonstrated in studies of animals exposed to extreme forms of sensory deprivation. For example, there seems to be a time when rich and varied visual experiences must occur for the visual centers of the brain to develop normally. If a month-old kitten is deprived of light for as brief a time as 3 or 4 days, these areas of the brain degenerate. If the kitten is kept in the dark for as long as 2 months, the damage is permanent. Enriched versus deprived early environments also affect overall brain growth. When animals reared as pets are compared with animals reared in isolation, the brains of the pets are heavier and thicker (Greenough & Black, 1992).

Because we cannot ethically expose children to such experiments, researchers interested in identifying sensitive periods for human brain development must rely on less direct evidence. They have found some close parallels with the animal evidence just described. For example, without early corrective surgery, babies born with strabismus (a condition in which one eye does not focus because of muscle weakness) show permanent impairments in depth perception, which depends on blending visual images from both eyes (Birch, 1993).

■ **BRAIN GROWTH SPURTS.** Focusing on the cerebral cortex as a whole, investigators have identified intermittent brain growth spurts, based on gains in brain weight and skull size as well as changes in neural activity, as measured by the EEG and fMRI. For example, several surges in frontal-lobe activity, which gradually spread to other cortical regions, occur during the first 2 years of life: at 3 to 4 months, when infants typically reach for objects; around 8 months, when they begin to crawl and search for hidden objects; around 12 months, when they walk and display more advanced object-search behaviors; and between $1\frac{1}{2}$ and 2 years, when language flourishes (Bell & Fox, 1994, 1998; Fischer & Bidell, 1998). Between ages 3 and 6, frontal-lobe areas devoted to planning and organizing actions show a dramatic increase in activity—a period when children become better at using language to guide their behavior (Thompson & Nelson, 2001). Later frontal-lobe activity spurts, at ages 9, 12, 15, and 18 to 20, may reflect the emergence and refinement of abstract thought (Fischer & Rose, 1995).

Massive production of synapses may underlie brain growth spurts in the first 2 years. Development of more complex and efficient neural networks, due to synaptic pruning, myelinization, and longer-distance connections between the frontal lobes and other cortical regions, may account for the later ones. Researchers are convinced that what "wires" a child's brain during each of these periods is experience. But they still have many questions to answer about just how brain and behavioral development might best be supported during each growth spurt.

■ **APPROPRIATE STIMULATION.** The evidence we do have confirms that the brain is particularly spongelike during the first few years of life; children learn new skills rapidly. As we will see later in this chapter and in chapters to come, understimulating infants and young children by depriving them of rich and varied experiences available in caring family environments—the world over—impairs their development. The more extreme and longer lasting the early deprivation, the harder it is to overcome with later enrichment.

In one study, researchers followed a large sample of children transferred between birth and 2 years of age from barren, neglectful Romanian orphanages and homes to adoptive families in Great Britain (Rutter et al., 1998). On arrival, most were malnourished, prone to infection, and impaired in all domains of psychological development. By age 4, physical catch-up for almost all the children was dramatic. Although cognitive catch-up was also impressive, it was not as great for those adopted after 6 months of age. These children scored

This 12-month-old, growing up in the Santa Clara pueblo community of New Mexico, has climbed on a chair to beat the ceremonial drum she has seen her father play during festival dances. Her more advanced actions on objects suggest that she might be in the midst of a brain growth spurt. Rich and varied stimulation in caring family environments best supports early brain growth.

©NITA WINTER/THE IMAGE WORKS

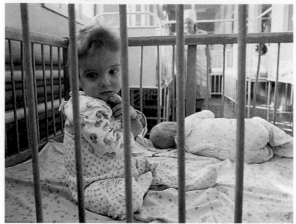

B. BISSON/CORBIS SYGMA

These Romanian institutionalized babies, orphaned shortly after birth, spend their days confined to a crib, with little adult contact and stimulation. The longer they remain in a barren environment, the more they will withdraw and wither.

lower in IQ than did Romanian and British children adopted in the first 6 months of life. That Romanian children adopted before age 6 months were similar in preschool IQ to British adoptees suggests complete recovery from severe early deprivation.

Did Grace remain behind in development, like the later-adopted Romanian children just described? Her progress was more favorable. Kevin and Monica had also adopted Eli from Cambodia. Two years later, they sent a photo and letter to the Cambodian orphanage that had arranged his adoption, describing Eli as a bright, happy child. One day, an orphanage caregiver showed Eli's biological mother the photo. The next day, she tearfully asked that her 14-month-old daughter be sent to join her brother. Two months later, Kevin and Monica adopted Grace. Although Grace's early environment was very deprived, her biological mother's loving care may have prevented irreversible damage to her brain. By age 18 months, Grace scored as well as the average American child her age in mental test performance. Of course, we do not know how she might have progressed had she received sufficient food and stimulation from the very beginning.

Besides impoverished environments, ones that overwhelm children with expectations beyond their current capacities fail to capitalize on the brain's potential. In recent years, expensive early learning centers have sprung up, in which infants are trained with letter and number flash cards and slightly older toddlers are given a full curriculum of reading, math, science, art, gym, and more. The tremendous growth in synapses during infancy and toddlerhood does not mean that teaching of culturally specific knowledge and skills should begin at this time. To the contrary, no sensitive periods for this kind of learning have been identified (Bruer, 1999). Academic, artistic, and athletic mastery do not occur easily in the first few years, but they do during childhood, adolescence, and adulthood, as the brain gradually undergoes synaptic pruning (Spelke, 1999).

Trying to prime infants and toddlers with stimulation for which they are not ready can cause them to withdraw, thereby threatening their interest in learning and creating conditions much like stimulus deprivation! In addition, when such programs do not produce young geniuses, they lead to disappointed parents who may view their children as failures at a very tender age.

CHANGING STATES OF AROUSAL

Rapid brain growth leads the organization of sleep and wakefulness to change substantially between birth and 2 years, and fussiness and crying also decline. Recall from Chapter 4 that the newborn baby takes round-the-clock naps that total about 16 hours. The decline in total sleep time during the first 2 years is not great; the average 2-year-old still needs 12 to 13 hours. The greatest change is that short periods of sleep and wakefulness are put together (Whitney & Thoman, 1994). Although from birth babies sleep more at night than during the day, this pattern increases with age. Infants gradually remain awake for longer daytime periods and need fewer naps—by the second year, only one or two (Blum & Carey, 1996).

Although these changing arousal patterns are due to brain development, they are affected by the social environment. In the United States and most Western nations, parents usually succeed in getting their babies to sleep through the night around 4 months of age by offering an evening feeding before putting them down in a separate, quiet room. In this way, they push young infants to the limits of their neurological capacities. Not until the middle of the first year is the secretion of melatonin, a hormone within the brain that promotes drowsiness, much greater at night than during the day (Sadeh, 1997).

As the Cultural Influences box on the following page reveals, the practice of isolating infants to promote sleep is rare elsewhere in the world. When babies sleep with their parents, their average sleep period remains constant at 3 hours, from 1 to 8 months of age. Only at the end of the first year, as REM sleep (the state that usually prompts waking) declines, do infants move in the direction of an adultlike sleep–waking schedule (Ficca et al., 1999).

Cultural INFLUENCES

CULTURAL VARIATION IN INFANT SLEEPING ARRANGEMENTS

While awaiting the birth of a new baby, American middle-SES parents typically furnish a room as the infant's sleeping quarters. At first, young babies may sleep in a bassinet or cradle in the parents' bedroom for reasons of convenience, but most are moved by 3 to 6 months of age. Many adults in the United States regard this nighttime separation of baby from parent as perfectly natural, and child-rearing advice from experts has strongly encouraged it. The most recent edition of Benjamin Spock's *Baby and Child Care* recommends that babies be moved out of their parents' room early in the first year, explaining, "Otherwise, there is a chance that they may become dependent on this arrangement" (Spock & Parker, 1998, p. 102).

Yet parent–infant "cosleeping" is common around the globe, in industrialized and nonindustrialized countries alike. Japanese children usually lie next to their mothers throughout infancy and early childhood and continue to sleep with a parent or other family member until adolescence (Takahashi, 1990). Cosleeping is also frequent in some American subcultures. African-American children are more likely than Caucasian-American children to fall asleep with parents and to remain with them for part or all of the night (Lozoff et al., 1995). Appalachian children of eastern Kentucky typically sleep with their parents for the first 2 years of life (Abbott, 1992). Among the Maya of

rural Guatemala, mother–infant cosleeping is interrupted only by the birth of a new baby, at which time the older child is moved beside the father or to another bed in the same room (Morelli et al., 1992).

Available household space plays a minor role in infant sleeping arrangements. Instead, cultural values—specifically, *collectivism versus individualism* (see Chapter 2, page 82)—are much more important. In one study, researchers interviewed American middle-SES mothers and Guatemalan Mayan mothers about their sleeping practices. American mothers conveyed an individualistic perspective, mentioning the importance of early independence training, preventing bad habits, and protecting their own privacy. In contrast, Mayan mothers stressed a collectivist perspective, explaining that cosleeping builds a close parent–child bond, which is necessary for children to learn the ways of people around them. When told that American infants sleep by themselves, Mayan mothers reacted with shock and disbelief, stating that it would be painful for them to leave their babies alone at night (Morelli et al., 1992).

Infant sleeping practices affect other aspects of family life. Sleep problems are not an issue for Mayan parents. Babies doze off in the midst of ongoing social activities and are carried to bed by their mothers. In the United States, getting young children ready for bed often requires an elaborate ritual that takes a good part of the evening. Per-

haps bedtime struggles, so common in American homes but rare elsewhere in the world, are related to the stress young children feel when they are required to fall asleep without assistance (Latz, Wolf, & Lozoff, 1999). The few Caucasian-American parents who permit cosleeping tend to feel uncomfortable about the practice (Lozoff, Askew, & Wolff, 1996).

Infant sleeping arrangements, like other parenting practices, are meant to foster culturally valued characteristics in the young. American middle-SES parents view babies as dependent beings who must be urged toward independence, and so they usually require them to sleep alone. In contrast, Japanese, Mayan, and Appalachian parents regard young infants as separate beings who need to establish an interdependent relationship with the community to survive.

Perhaps because cosleeping is rare in the United States, American parents who practice it sometimes fail to take appropriate safety precautions. Suffocation due to entrapment in soft covers, wedging between the mattress and other parts of the bed, and overlying by an adult are responsible for about 500 deaths of children under age 2 annually (Nakamura, Wind, & Danello, 1999). In countries where cosleeping is widespread, parents and infants often sleep on hard surfaces, such as floor mats and wooden planks, which minimize these dangers (Nelson, Schiefenhoevel, & Haimerl, 2000).

STEPHEN L. RAYMER/NATIONAL GEOGRAPHIC IMAGE COLLECTION

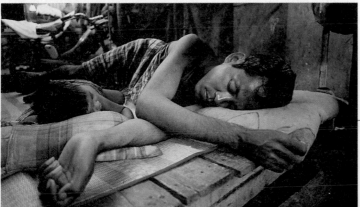

This Cambodian father and child sleep together—a practice common in their culture and around the globe. When children fall asleep with their parents, sleep problems are rare during the early years. And many parents who practice cosleeping believe that it helps build a close parent–child bond.

Even after infants sleep through the night, they continue to wake at night occasionally for the next few years. In studies carried out in Great Britain, Israel, and the United States, about 30 percent of children between ages 1 and 4 awoke during the night at least once a week (Beltramini & Hertzig, 1983; Johnson, 1991; Scher et al., 1995). Night wakings peaked between 18 months and 2 years and then declined. As Chapter 7 will reveal, the emotional and social challenges of this period—ability to range farther from the familiar caregiver and awareness of the self as separate from others—often prompt anxiety in toddlers, evident in increased clinginess and disturbed sleep. When parents offer comfort and support, these behaviors soon subside.

Ask YOURSELF...

review   How does stimulation affect early brain development? Cite evidence at the level of neurons and at the level of the cerebral cortex.

apply   When Joey was born, the doctor found that his anterior fontanel had started to close prematurely. Joey had surgery to open the fontanel when he was 3 months old. From what you know about the function of the fontanels, why was early surgery necessary?

connect   Suppose you were offered two cognitive enrichment programs for your 1-year-old. The first emphasizes gentle talking and touching, exposure to a wide variety of interesting sights and sounds, and simple, pleasurable social games, such as pat-a-cake and peekaboo. The second program teaches words and numbers and includes French and classical-music lessons. On the basis of findings on brain development, which program would you choose, and why?

reflect   What is your attitude toward parent–infant cosleeping? Is it influenced by your cultural background? Explain.

Factors Affecting Early Physical Growth

P hysical growth, like other aspects of development, results from the continuous and complex interplay between heredity and environment. Caitlin, who has tall parents, is likely to be tall herself. As we will see in the following sections, in addition to genetic makeup, nutrition, relative freedom from disease, and emotional well-being affect early physical growth.

HEREDITY

Since identical twins are much more alike in body size than are fraternal twins, we know that heredity is important in physical growth. When diet and health are adequate, height and rate of physical growth (as measured by skeletal age) are largely determined by heredity. In fact, as long as negative environmental influences such as poor nutrition or illness are not severe, children and adolescents typically show *catch-up growth*—a return to a genetically determined growth path. After her adoption, Grace grew rapidly; by age 2, she was nearly average in size by Cambodian standards. Physical growth is a strongly canalized process (see Chapter 2, pages 88–89).

Genetic makeup also affects body weight, since the weights of adopted children correlate more strongly with those of their biological than adoptive parents (Stunkard et al., 1986). However, as far as weight is concerned, environment—in particular, nutrition—plays an especially important role.

NUTRITION

Good nutrition is important at any time of development, but it is especially crucial in infancy because the baby's brain and body are growing so rapidly. Pound for pound, a young baby's energy needs are twice those of an adult. Twenty-five percent of the infant's total caloric intake is devoted to growth, and babies need extra calories to keep rapidly developing organs of the body functioning properly (Pipes, 1996).

Babies not only need enough food, they need the right kind of food. In early infancy, breast milk is especially suited to their needs, and bottled formulas try to imitate it. Later, infants require well-balanced solid foods. If a baby's diet is deficient in either quantity or quality, growth can be permanently stunted.

■ **BREAST- VERSUS BOTTLE-FEEDING.** For thousands of years, all babies were fed the ultimate human health food: breast milk. Only within the past hundred years has bottle-feeding been available. As formulas became easier to prepare, breast-feeding declined from the 1940s into the 1970s, when more than 75 percent of American infants were bottle-fed. Partly as a result of the natural childbirth movement (see Chapter 4), breast-feeding became more common, especially among well-educated, middle-SES women. Today, nearly two-thirds of American mothers breast-feed, although most do so for only a few months (U.S. Department of Health and Human Services, 2000i).

The Caregiving Concerns table on page 182 summarizes the major nutritional and health advantages of breast-feeding. Because of these benefits, breast-fed babies in poverty-stricken regions of the world are much less likely to be malnourished and 6 to 14 times more likely to survive the first year of life. Breast-feeding exclusively for the first 6 months would save the lives of one million infants annually. And breast-feeding for just a few weeks would offer some protection against respiratory and intestinal infections that are devastating to young children in developing countries. Furthermore, because a mother is less likely to get pregnant while she is nursing, breast-feeding helps increase spacing between siblings, a major factor in reducing infant and childhood deaths in economically depressed populations (Darnton-Hill & Coyne, 1998). (Note, however, that breast-feeding is not a reliable method of birth control.)

Yet many mothers in the developing world do not know about the benefits of breast-feeding. Consequently, they give their babies low-grade nutrients, such as rice water, highly diluted cow's and goat's milk, or commercial formula. These foods often lead to illness because they are contaminated due to poor sanitation. The United Nations has encouraged all hospitals and maternity units in developing countries to promote breast-feeding as long as mothers do not have viral or bacterial infections (such as HIV or tuberculosis) that can be transmitted to the baby. Today, most developing countries have banned the practice of giving free or subsidized formula to any new mother who desires it.

In industrialized nations, most women who choose breast-feeding find it emotionally satisfying, but it is not for everyone. Some mothers simply do not like it or are embarrassed by it. A few others, for physiological reasons, do not produce enough milk. Occasionally, medical reasons—such as illness or treatment with certain drugs—prevent a mother from nursing (Kuhn & Stein, 1997).

Breast milk is so easily digestible that a breast-fed infant becomes hungry quite often—every $1\frac{1}{2}$ to 2 hours in comparison to every 3 or 4 hours for a bottle-fed baby. This makes breast-feeding inconvenient for many employed women. Not surprisingly, mothers who return to work sooner wean their babies from the breast earlier (Roe et al., 1999). However, a mother who cannot be with her baby all the time can still breast-feed or combine it with bottle-feeding. For example, Carolyn returned to her job

Breast-feeding is especially important in developing countries, where infants are at risk for malnutrition, infectious disease, and early death due to widespread poverty. This baby of Rajasthan, India, is likely to grow normally during the first year because his mother decided to breast-feed.

JANE SCHREIRMAN/PHOTO RESEARCHERS, INC.

Caregiving Concerns

Nutritional and Health Advantages of Breast-Feeding

ADVANTAGE	DESCRIPTION
Correct balance of fat and protein	Compared with the milk of other mammals, human milk is higher in fat and lower in protein. This balance, as well as the unique proteins and fats contained in human milk, is ideal for a rapidly myelinating nervous system.
Nutritional completeness	A mother who breast-feeds need not add other foods to her infant's diet until the baby is 6 months old. The milks of all mammals are low in iron, but the iron contained in breast milk is easily absorbed by the baby's system.
Protection against disease	Through breast-feeding, antibodies and other infection-fighting agents are transferred from mother to child. As a result, breast-fed babies have far fewer respiratory and intestinal illnesses and allergic reactions than do bottle-fed infants. Components of human milk that protect against disease can be added to formula, but breast-feeding provides superior immunity.
Protection against faulty jaw development and tooth decay	Breast-feeding helps avoid malocclusion, a condition in which the upper and lower jaws do not meet properly that worsens with extensive sucking on an artificial nipple. Bottle-feeding also promotes tooth decay when formula or juice remains in the mouths of infants who continue to suck a bottle after falling asleep.
Digestibility	Since breast-fed babies have a different kind of bacteria growing in their intestines than do bottle-fed infants, they rarely become constipated or have diarrhea.
Smoother transition to solid foods	Breast-fed infants accept new solid foods more easily than do bottle-fed infants, perhaps because of their greater experience with a variety of flavors, which pass from the maternal diet into the mother's milk.

Sources: Bruerd & Jones, 1996; Pickering et al., 1998; Raisler, 1999; Sullivan & Birch, 1994.

part time when Caitlin was 12 weeks old. Each morning, she pumped her milk into a bottle for later feeding by Caitlin's caregiver.

The same technique can be used for infants who are hospitalized. Preterm infants, especially, benefit from the antibodies and easy digestibility of breast milk. The breast milk produced for a preterm baby differs from that produced for a full-term infant. It is higher in protein and certain minerals and specially adapted to the preterm infant's growth needs (Gross, Geller, & Tomarelli, 1981).

Some women who cannot or do not want to breast-feed worry that they are depriving their baby of an experience essential for healthy psychological development. Yet breast- and bottle-fed children in industrialized nations do not differ in emotional adjustment (Fergusson & Woodward, 1999). Regardless of the feeding method a mother chooses, she can respond promptly to her hungry baby and hold and stroke the infant gently—aspects of feeding that foster emotional security. Many studies reveal a slight but consistent advantage for breast-fed children and adolescents in mental test performance after many factors are controlled (Anderson, Johnstone, & Remley, 1999). Notice in the Caregiving Concerns table above that breast milk provides nutrients ideally suited for early rapid brain development.

■ ARE CHUBBY BABIES AT RISK FOR LATER OVERWEIGHT AND OBESITY? Timmy was an enthusiastic eater from early infancy. He nursed vigorously and gained weight quickly. By 5 months, he began reaching for solid food from his mother's plate. Vanessa wondered: Was she overfeeding Timmy and increasing his chances of being permanently overweight?

Only a slight correlation exists between fatness in infancy and obesity at older ages (Roche, 1981). Most chubby infants thin out during toddlerhood and the preschool years, as weight gain slows and they become more active. Infants and toddlers can eat nutritious foods freely, without risk of becoming overweight.

When infants first eat solid foods, iron-fortified cereal mixed with whole milk satisfies their needs. Between 6 and 12 months, mashed and minced fruits, vegetables, starches, and meats should be added. Around 1 year, most infants have enough teeth to make the transition to chopped table foods.

How can concerned parents prevent their infants from becoming overweight children and adults? One way is to encourage good eating habits. Candy, soft drinks, sweetened juices, French fries, and other high-calorie foods loaded with sugar, salt, and saturated fats should be avoided. When given such foods regularly, young children start to prefer them (Birch & Fisher, 1995). Physical exercise also guards against excessive weight gain. Once toddlers learn to walk, climb, and run, parents should encourage their natural delight at being able to control their bodies by providing opportunities for energetic play.

MALNUTRITION

Osita is an Ethiopian 2-year-old whose mother has never had to worry about his gaining too much weight. When she weaned him at 1 year, he had little to eat besides starchy rice flour cakes. Soon his belly enlarged, his feet swelled, his hair fell out, and a rash appeared on his skin. His bright-eyed curiosity vanished, and he became irritable and listless.

In developing countries and war-torn areas where food resources are limited, malnutrition is widespread. Recent evidence indicates that 40 to 60 percent of the world's children do not get enough to eat (Bellamy, 1998). Among the 4 to 7 percent who are severely affected, malnutrition leads to two dietary diseases: marasmus and kwashiorkor.

Marasmus is a wasted condition of the body caused by a diet low in all essential nutrients. It usually appears in the first year of life when a baby's mother is too malnourished to produce enough breast milk and bottle-feeding is also inadequate. Her starving baby becomes painfully thin and is in danger of dying.

Osita has **kwashiorkor**, caused by an unbalanced diet very low in protein. Kwashiorkor usually strikes after weaning, between 1 and 3 years of age. It is common in areas of the world where children get just enough calories from starchy foods, but protein resources are scarce. The child's body responds by breaking down its own protein reserves, leading to the swelling and other symptoms that Osita experienced.

Children who survive these extreme forms of malnutrition grow to be smaller in all body dimensions (Galler, Ramsey, & Solimano, 1985a). In addition, the brain is seriously affected. One long-term study of marasmic children revealed that an improved diet led to some catch-up growth in height, but the children failed to catch up in head size (Stoch et al., 1982). The malnutrition probably interfered with myelinization, causing a permanent loss in brain weight. By middle childhood, these children score low on intelligence and achievement tests, show poor fine motor coordination, and have difficulty paying attention in school (Galler et al., 1984, 1990; Galler, Ramsey, & Solimano, 1985b).

Recall from our discussion of prenatal malnutrition in Chapter 3 that the passivity and irritability of malnourished children worsen the impact of poor diet. These behaviors may appear even when protein-calorie deprivation is only mild to moderate. They also accompany *iron-deficiency anemia*—a condition common among poverty-stricken infants and children that interferes with many central nervous system processes. Withdrawal and listlessness reduce the nutritionally deprived child's ability to pay attention, explore, and evoke sensitive caregiving from parents, whose lives are already disrupted by poverty and stressful living conditions (Lozoff et al., 1998; Sigman & Whaley, 1998). For this reason, interventions for malnourished children must improve the family situation as well as the child's nutrition.

Even better are efforts at prevention—providing food and medical care before the effects of early malnutrition are allowed to run their course. Research in Guatemala, where dietary deficiencies are common, underscores the importance of early nutritional intervention. Children receiving food supplements prenatally and during the first 2 years of life scored higher

The swollen abdomen and listless behavior of this Honduran child are classic symptoms of kwashiorkor, a nutritional illness that results from a diet very low in protein.

marasmus
A disease usually appearing in the first year of life that is caused by a diet low in all essential nutrients. Leads to a wasted condition of the body.

kwashiorkor
A disease usually appearing after weaning, between 1 and 3 years of age, that is caused by a diet low in protein. Symptoms include an enlarged belly, swollen feet, hair loss, skin rash, and irritable, listless behavior.

on a variety of mental tests in adolescence than did children not given supplements until after their second birthday (Pollitt et al., 1993). Other longitudinal findings from Egypt, Kenya, and Mexico reveal that quality of food (protein, vitamin, and mineral content) is far more important than quantity in contributing to the favorable outcomes just described (Sigman, 1995; Watkins & Pollitt, 1998).

Malnutrition is not confined to developing countries. Recent surveys indicate that over 12 percent of children in the United States go to bed hungry. Although few of these children have marasmus or kwashiorkor, their physical growth and ability to learn in school are still affected (Children's Defense Fund, 2000; Wachs, 1995). Malnutrition is clearly a national and international crisis—one of the most serious problems confronting the human species today.

EMOTIONAL WELL-BEING

We are not used to thinking of affection and stimulation as necessary for healthy physical growth, but they are just as vital to infants as food. **Nonorganic failure to thrive** is a growth disorder resulting from lack of parental love that is usually present by 18 months of age. Infants who have it show all the signs of marasmus—their bodies look wasted, and they are withdrawn and apathetic. But no organic (or biological) cause for the baby's failure to grow can be found. The baby is offered enough food and does not have a serious illness.

Lana, an observant nurse at a public health clinic, became concerned about 8-month-old Melanie, who was three pounds lighter than she had been at her last checkup. Her mother claimed to feed her often and could not understand why she did not grow. Lana noted Melanie's behavior. Unlike most infants her age, she did not mind separating from her mother. Lana tried offering Melanie a toy, but she showed little interest. Instead, she anxiously kept her eyes on adults in the room. When Lana smiled and tried to look into Melanie's eyes, she turned her head away (Black et al., 1994; Leonard, Rhymes, & Solnit, 1986).

Family circumstances surrounding failure to thrive help explain these typical reactions. During feeding, diaper changing, and play, Melanie's mother sometimes acted cold and distant, at other times impatient and hostile (Hagekull, Bohlin, & Rydell, 1997). Melanie tried to protect herself by keeping track of her mother's whereabouts and, when her mother approached, avoiding her gaze. Often an unhappy marriage and parental psychological disturbance contribute to these serious caregiving problems (Drotar, Pallotta, & Eckerle, 1994; Duniz et al., 1996). Melanie's alcoholic father was out of work, and her parents argued constantly. Melanie's mother had little energy to meet the psychological needs of Melanie and her other three children. Sometimes the baby is irritable and displays abnormal feeding behaviors, such as poor sucking or vomiting, that stress the parent–child relationship further (Wooster, 1999).

When treated early, by helping parents or placing the baby in a caring foster home, failure-to-thrive infants show quick catch-up growth. But if the disorder is not corrected in infancy, most children remain small and show lasting cognitive and emotional difficulties (Heffner & Kelley, 1994).

nonorganic failure to thrive A growth disorder usually present by 18 months of age that is caused by lack of affection and stimulation.

Ask YOURSELF...

review Explain why breast-feeding offers babies protection against disease and early death in poverty-stricken regions of the world.

apply Ten-month-old Shaun is below average in height and painfully thin. He has one of two serious growth disorders. Name them, and indicate what clues you would look for to tell which one Shaun has.

connect How are bidirectional influences between parent and child involved in the impact of malnutrition on psychological development? After her adoption, how did those influences change for Grace, leading to rapid gains in intellectual development?

Learning Capacities

Learning refers to changes in behavior as the result of experience. Healthy, well-nourished babies come into the world with built-in learning capacities that permit them to profit from experience. Infants are capable of two basic forms of learning, which were introduced in Chapter 1: classical and operant conditioning. They also learn through their natural preference for novel stimulation. Finally, young babies have a remarkable ability to learn by observing others; shortly after birth, they can imitate the facial expressions and gestures of adults.

CLASSICAL CONDITIONING

Newborn reflexes, discussed in Chapter 4, make **classical conditioning** possible in the young infant. In this form of learning, a neutral stimulus is paired with a stimulus that leads to a reflexive response. Once the baby's nervous system makes the connection between the two stimuli, the new stimulus produces the behavior by itself.

Recall from Chapter 1 that Russian physiologist Ivan Pavlov first demonstrated classical conditioning in his research with dogs (see page 19). Classical conditioning is of great value to human infants, as well as other animals, because it helps them recognize which events usually occur together in the everyday world. As a result, they can anticipate what is about to happen next, and the environment becomes more orderly and predictable (Rovee-Collier, 1987). Let's take a closer look at the steps of classical conditioning.

As Carolyn settled down in the rocking chair to nurse Caitlin, she often gently stroked Caitlin's forehead. Soon Carolyn noticed that each time Caitlin's forehead was stroked, she made active sucking movements. Caitlin had been classically conditioned. Here is how it happened (see Figure 5.7 on page 186):

- Before learning takes place, an **unconditioned stimulus (UCS)** must consistently produce a reflexive, or **unconditioned, response (UCR)**. In Caitlin's case, the stimulus of sweet breast milk (UCS) resulted in sucking (UCR).

- To produce learning, a *neutral stimulus* that does not lead to the reflex is presented at about the same time as the UCS. Ideally, the neutral stimulus should occur just before the UCS. Carolyn stroked Caitlin's forehead as each nursing period began. Therefore, the stroking (neutral stimulus) was paired with the taste of milk (UCS).

- If learning has occurred, the neutral stimulus by itself produces the reflexive response. The neutral stimulus is then called a **conditioned stimulus (CS),** and the response it elicits is called a **conditioned response (CR).** We know that Caitlin has been classically conditioned because stroking her forehead outside the feeding situation (CS) results in sucking (CR).

If the CS is presented alone enough times, without being paired with the UCS, the CR will no longer occur. In other words, if Carolyn strokes Caitlin's forehead again and again without feeding her, Caitlin will gradually stop sucking in response to stroking. This is referred to as **extinction.**

Young infants can be classically conditioned most easily when the association between two stimuli has survival value. Caitlin learned quickly in the feeding situation, since learning which stimuli regularly accompany feeding improves the infant's ability to get food and survive (Blass, Ganchrow, & Steiner, 1984). In contrast, some responses are very difficult to condition in young babies. Fear is one of them. Until infants have the motor skills to escape unpleasant events, they do not have a biological need to form these associations. But between 8 and 12 months, fear is easy to condition, as seen in the famous example of little Albert, conditioned by John Watson to withdraw and cry at the sight of a furry white rat. Return to Chapter 1, page 19, to review this well-known experiment. Then test your knowledge of classical conditioning

classical conditioning
A form of learning that involves associating a neutral stimulus with a stimulus that leads to a reflexive response.

unconditioned stimulus (UCS)
In classical conditioning, a stimulus that leads to a reflexive response.

unconditioned response (UCR)
In classical conditioning, a reflexive response that is produced by an unconditioned stimulus (UCS).

conditioned stimulus (CS)
In classical conditioning, a neutral stimulus that, through pairing with an unconditioned stimulus (UCS), leads to a new response (CR).

conditioned response (CR)
In classical conditioning, an originally reflexive response that is produced by a conditioned stimulus (CS).

extinction
In classical conditioning, decline of the conditioned response (CR) as a result of presenting the conditioned stimulus (CS) enough times without the unconditioned stimulus (UCS).

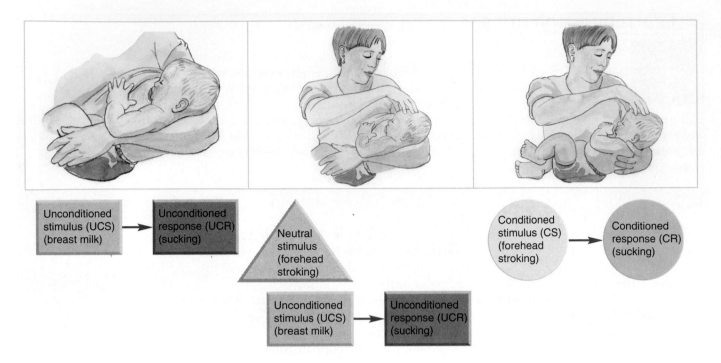

FIGURE 5.7

The steps of classical conditioning. The example here shows how Caitlin's mother classically conditioned her to make sucking movements by stroking her forehead at the beginning of feedings.

operant conditioning
A form of learning in which a spontaneous behavior is followed by a stimulus that changes the probability that the behavior will occur again.

reinforcer
In operant conditioning, a stimulus that increases the occurrence of a response.

punishment
In operant conditioning, a stimulus (removal of a desirable one or presentation of an unpleasant one) that decreases the occurrence of a response.

by identifying the UCS, UCR, CS, and CR in Watson's study. In Chapter 7, we will discuss the development of fear, as well as other emotional reactions, in detail.

OPERANT CONDITIONING

In classical conditioning, babies build expectations about stimulus events in the environment, but their behavior does not influence the stimuli that occur. **Operant conditioning** is quite different. In this form of learning, infants act (or operate) on the environment, and stimuli that follow their behavior change the probability that the behavior will occur again.

Recall from Chapter 4 that newborn babies take longer sucks with fewer pauses when a nipple delivers sweet liquid as opposed to plain water. When given a salty fluid, they shorten their sucks or stop sucking entirely. When you read about this research, you were actually studying operant conditioning. A stimulus that increases the occurrence of a response is called a **reinforcer.** Removing a desirable stimulus or presenting an unpleasant one to decrease the occurrence of a response is called **punishment.** In the example just described, sweet liquid *reinforces* the sucking response, whereas salty fluid *punishes* it.

Because the young infant can control only a few behaviors, successful operant conditioning in the early weeks of life is limited to sucking and head-turning responses. However, many stimuli besides food can serve as reinforcers. For example, researchers have created special laboratory conditions in which the baby's rate of sucking on a nipple produces a variety of interesting sights and sounds. Newborns will suck faster to see visual designs or hear music and human voices (Floccia, Christophe, & Bertoncini, 1997). Even preterm babies will seek reinforcing stimulation. In one study, they increased their contact with a soft teddy bear that "breathed" quietly at a rate reflecting the infant's respiration, whereas they decreased their contact with a nonbreathing bear (Thoman & Ingersoll, 1993). As these findings suggest, operant conditioning has become a powerful tool for finding out what stimuli babies can perceive and which ones they prefer.

As infants get older, operant conditioning expands to include a wider range of responses and stimuli. For example, researchers have hung special mobiles over the cribs of 2- to 6-month-olds. When the baby's foot is attached to the mobile with a long cord, the infant can, by kicking, make the mobile turn. Under these conditions, it takes only a few minutes for infants to start kicking vigorously (Rovee-Collier, 1999; Shields & Rovee-Collier, 1992). As Chapter 6 will

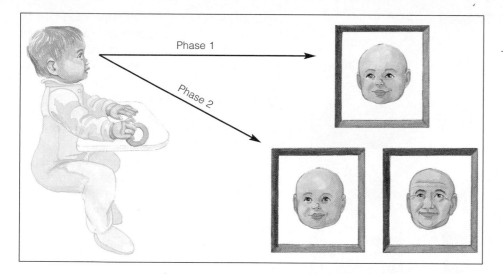

FIGURE 5.8

Example of how the habituation–dishabituation sequence can be used to study infant perception and memory. In Phase 1, infants are shown (habituated to) a photo of a baby. In Phase 2, infants are again shown the baby photo, but this time it appears alongside a photo of a bald-headed man. If infants dishabituate to (spend more time looking at) the photo of the man, then we know they remembered the baby and perceive the man's face as different from it. (Adapted from Fagan & Singer, 1979.)

reveal, operant conditioning with mobiles has become a powerful technique for studying infant memory. Once babies of different ages learn to kick, researchers can see how long and under what conditions they retain the response when exposed to mobile again.

Operant conditioning soon modifies parents' and babies' reactions to each other. As the infant gazes into the adult's eyes, the adult looks and smiles back, and then the infant looks and smiles again. The behavior of each partner reinforces the other, and both continue their pleasurable interaction. In Chapter 7, we will see that this contingent responsiveness plays a role in the development of infant–caregiver attachment.

Look carefully at the findings just described, and you will see that young babies are active learners; they use any means they can to explore and control their surroundings in an effort to meet their needs for nutrition, stimulation, and social contact (Rovee-Collier, 1996). In fact, when infants' environments are so disorganized that their behavior does not lead to predictable outcomes, serious difficulties ranging from intellectual delays to apathy and depression can result (Cicchetti & Aber, 1986; Seligman, 1975).

HABITUATION AND DISHABITUATION

Take a moment to walk through the rooms of the library, your home, or wherever you happen to be reading this book. What did you notice? Probably those things that are new and different, such as a recently purchased picture on the wall or a piece of furniture that has been moved. The human brain is set up to be attracted to novelty. **Habituation** refers to a gradual reduction in the strength of a response due to repetitive stimulation. Looking, heart rate, and respiration may all decline, indicating a loss of interest. Once this has occurred, a new stimulus—some kind of change in the environment—causes responsiveness to return to a high level. This recovery is called **dishabituation.**

Habituation and dishabituation enable us to focus on those aspects of the environment we know least about. As a result, learning is more efficient. By studying the stimuli that infants of different ages habituate and dishabituate to, researchers can tell much about their understanding of the world. For example, a baby who first habituates to a visual pattern (a photo of a baby) and then dishabituates to a new one (a photo of a bald man) clearly remembers the first stimulus and perceives the second one as new and different from it. This method of studying infant perception and cognition, illustrated in Figure 5.8, can be used with newborn babies, even those who are preterm. It has even been used to study the fetus's sensitivity to external stimuli—for example, by measuring changes in fetal heart rate when various repeated sounds are presented (Hepper, 1997).

Habituation is evident as early as the third trimester of pregnancy. As fetuses and babies get older, they habituate to stimuli more quickly, indicating that they process information

habituation
A gradual reduction in the strength of a response due to repetitive stimulation.

dishabituation
Increase in responsiveness after stimulation changes.

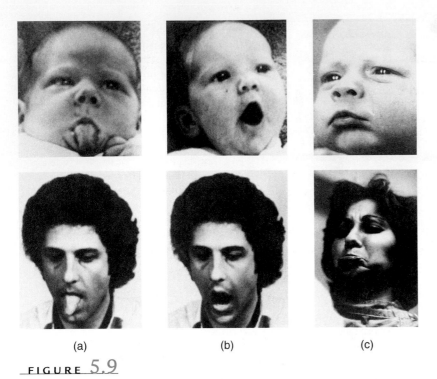

(a)   (b)   (c)

FIGURE 5.9

Photographs from two of the first studies of newborn imitation. Those on the left show 2- to 3-week-old infants imitating tongue protrusion (a), and mouth opening (b). The one on the right shows a 2-day-old infant imitating a sad (c) adult facial expression. (From A. N. Meltzoff & M. K. Moore, 1977, "Imitation of Facial and Manual Gestures by Human Neonates," *Science, 198,* p. 75; and T. M. Field et al., 1992, "Discrimination and Imitation of Facial Expressions by Neonates," *Science, 218,* p. 180. Copyright 1977 and 1982, respectively, by the AAAS. Reprinted by permission.)

more efficiently. Yet a fascinating exception to this trend exists. Two-month-olds actually take longer to habituate to novel visual forms than do newborns and older infants (Slater et al., 1996). Later, we will see that 2 months is also a time of dramatic gains in visual perception. Perhaps when young babies are first able to perceive certain information, they require more time to take it in (Johnson, 1996).

The habituation–dishabituation sequence provides researchers with a marvelous window into early mental development. We will return to it in this chapter, when we discuss perception, and in Chapter 6, when we consider attention, memory, and other aspects of infant cognition.

IMITATION

Newborn babies come into the world with a primitive ability to learn through **imitation**— by copying the behavior of another person. For example, Figure 5.9 shows infants from 2 days to several weeks old imitating a variety of adult facial expressions (Field et al., 1982; Meltzoff & Moore, 1977). The newborn's capacity to imitate extends to certain gestures, such as head movements, and has been demonstrated in many ethnic groups and cultures (Meltzoff & Kuhl, 1994).

But a few studies have failed to reproduce these findings (see, for example, Anisfeld et al., 2001). And imitation is more difficult to induce in babies 2 to 3 months old than just after birth. Therefore, some investigators regard the capacity as little more than an automatic response that declines with age, much like a reflex. Others claim that newborns imitate diverse facial expressions and head movements with apparent effort and determination, even after short delays—when the adult is no longer demonstrating the behavior (Butterworth, 1999). Furthermore, imitation does not decline, as reflexes do. Babies several months old often do not imitate an adult's behavior right away because they try to play social games they are used to in face-to-face interaction—smiling, cooing, and waving their arms. When an adult models a gesture repeatedly, older babies soon get down to business and imitate (Meltzoff & Moore, 1994).

According to Andrew Meltzoff and Keith Moore (1999), newborns imitate in much the same way we do—by actively trying to match body movements they "see" with ones they "feel" themselves make. Later in this chapter, we will encounter evidence that young babies are surprisingly good at coordinating information across sensory systems. Taken together, these findings support a view of newborn imitation as a flexible, voluntary capacity.

As we will see in Chapter 6, a baby's ability to imitate improves greatly over the first 2 years. But however limited it is at birth, imitation is a powerful means of learning. Using imitation, young infants begin to explore their social world, getting to know people by matching behavioral states with them. In the process, babies notice similarities between their own actions and those of others, and they start to find out about themselves. Furthermore, through imitation, adults can get young infants to express desirable behaviors, and once they do, adults can encourage these further. Finally, caregivers take great pleasure in a baby who imitates their facial gestures and actions. Newborn imitation seems to be one of those capacities that helps get the infant's relationship with parents off to a good start.

imitation
Learning by copying the behavior of another person. Also called modeling or observational learning.

review   Using examples, describe the difference between classical and operant conditioning. Why is each type of learning useful to infants?

apply   Nine-month-old Byron has a toy with large, colored push buttons on it. Each time he pushes a button, he hears a nursery tune. Which learning capacity is the manufacturer of this toy taking advantage of?

apply   Recall that infants with nonorganic failure to thrive are unlikely to smile at a friendly adult. Also, they keep track of nearby adults in an anxious, fearful way. Explain these reactions, citing the learning capacities discussed in the preceding sections.

connect   Return to the section on intervening with preterm infants on pages 147–149 of Chapter 4. Why might a preterm baby seek contact with a soft, "breathing" teddy bear, as reported in our discussion of operant conditioning on page 186?

Motor Development

Carolyn, Monica, and Vanessa each kept baby books, filling them with proud notations about when their children held up their heads, reached for objects, sat by themselves, and walked alone. Parents' enthusiasm for these achievements makes perfect sense. They are, indeed, milestones of development. With each new motor skill, babies master their bodies and the environment in a new way. For example, sitting alone grants infants an entirely different perspective on the world. Voluntary reaching permits babies to find out about objects by acting on them. And when infants can move on their own, their opportunities for exploration multiply.

Babies' motor achievements have a powerful effect on their social relationships. When Caitlin began to crawl at 7½ months, Carolyn and David began to restrict her movements by saying no, expressing mild anger and impatience, and picking her up and moving her—strategies that were unnecessary before. When Caitlin started walking three days after her first birthday, first "testing of wills" occurred (Biringen et al., 1995). Despite her mother's warnings, she sometimes pulled items from shelves that were "off limits." "Oh, Caitlin, I said not to do that!" Carolyn would remark as she took Caitlin by the hand and redirected her activities.

At the same time, expressions of affection and playful activities expanded as Caitlin sought her parents out for greetings, hugs, and a gleeful game of hide-and-seek (Campos, Kermoian, & Zumbahlen, 1992). Soon after, Caitlin turned the pages of a cardboard picture book and pointed while Carolyn named the objects. Caitlin's expressions of delight—laughing, smiling, and babbling—as she worked on new motor competencies triggered pleasurable reactions in others, which encouraged her efforts further (Mayes & Zigler, 1992). Motor skills, social competencies, cognition, and language developed together and supported one another.

THE SEQUENCE OF MOTOR DEVELOPMENT

Gross motor development refers to control over actions that help infants get around in the environment, such as crawling, standing, and walking. In contrast, *fine motor development* has to do with smaller movements, such as reaching and grasping. Table 5.1 on page 190 shows the average age at which infants and toddlers achieve a variety of gross and fine motor skills. Most (but not all) children follow this sequence.

Notice that the table also presents the age ranges during which the majority of babies accomplish each skill. These indicate that although the *sequence* of motor development is fairly uniform across children, large individual differences exist in *rate* of motor progress. Also,

TABLE 5.1

Gross and Fine Motor Development in the First Two Years

MOTOR SKILL	AVERAGE AGE ACHIEVED	AGE RANGE IN WHICH 90 PERCENT OF INFANTS ACHIEVE THE SKILL
When held upright, holds head erect and steady	6 weeks	3 weeks–4 months
When prone, lifts self by arms	2 months	3 weeks–4 months
Rolls from side to back	2 months	3 weeks–5 months
Grasps cube	3 months, 3 weeks	2–7 months
Rolls from back to side	4½ months	2–7 months
Sits alone	7 months	5–9 months
Crawls	7 months	5–11 months
Pulls to stand	8 months	5–12 months
Plays pat-a-cake	9 months, 3 weeks	7–15 months
Stands alone	11 months	9–16 months
Walks alone	11 months, 3 weeks	9–17 months
Builds tower of two cubes	11 months, 3 weeks	10–19 months
Scribbles vigorously	14 months	10–21 months
Walks up stairs with help	16 months	12–23 months
Jumps in place	23 months, 2 weeks	17–30 months
Walks on tiptoe	25 months	16–30 months

Sources: Bayley, 1969, 1993.

a baby who is a late reacher is not necessarily going to be a late crawler or walker. We would be concerned about a child's development only if many motor skills were seriously delayed.

Look at Table 5.1 once more, and you will see organization and direction in infants' motor achievements. The *cephalocaudal trend* is evident. Motor control of the head comes before control of the arms and trunk, which comes before control of the legs. You can also see the *proximodistal trend*: head, trunk, and arm control is advanced over coordination of the hands and fingers. These similarities between physical and motor development suggest a genetic contribution to motor progress.

But we must be careful not to think of motor skills as isolated, unrelated accomplishments that follow a fixed maturational timetable. Instead, each skill is a product of earlier motor attainments and a contributor to new ones. Furthermore, children acquire motor skills in highly individual ways. For example, most babies crawl before they pull to a stand and walk. Yet Grace, who spent most of her days lying in a hammock until her adoption, did not try to crawl because her biological mother rarely placed her on her tummy or on firm surfaces that enabled her to move on her own. As a result, she pulled to a stand and walked before she crawled!

Many influences—both internal and external—combine to support the vast transformations in motor competencies of the first 2 years. The *dynamic systems perspective*, a new theoretical approach introduced in Chapter 1 (see pages 29–30), helps us understand how motor development takes place.

MOTOR SKILLS AS DYNAMIC SYSTEMS

According to **dynamic systems theory of motor development,** mastery of motor skills involves acquiring increasingly complex *systems of action.* When motor skills work as a *system,* separate abilities blend together, each cooperating with others to produce more effective ways

dynamic systems theory of motor development
A theory that views new motor skills as reorganizations of previously mastered skills that lead to more effective ways of exploring and controlling the environment. Each new skill is a product of central nervous system development, movement possibilities of the body, the goal the child has in mind, and environmental supports for the skill.

of exploring and controlling the environment. For example, control of the head and upper chest combine into sitting with support. Kicking, rocking on all fours, and reaching combine to become crawling. Then crawling, standing, and stepping unite into walking (Thelen, 1989).

Each new skill is a joint product of the following factors: (1) central nervous system development; (2) movement possibilities of the body; (3) the goal the child has in mind; and (4) environmental supports for the skill. Change in any element makes the system less stable, and the child starts to explore and select new, more effective motor patterns.

The factors that induce change vary with age. In the early weeks of life, brain and body growth are especially important as infants achieve control over the head, shoulders, and upper torso. Later, the baby's goals (getting a toy or crossing the room) and environmental supports (parental encouragement, objects in the infants' everyday setting) play a greater role. The broader physical world also has a profound impact on motor skills. For example, had Caitlin, Grace, and Timmy been reared in the moon's reduced gravity, they would have preferred jumping to walking or running!

When a skill is first acquired, it is tentative and uncertain. Infants must practice and refine it so that it becomes smooth and accurate. For example, when Caitlin began to crawl, she often collapsed on her tummy and ended up moving backward instead of forward. Gradually, she figured out how to propel herself along by alternately pulling with her arms and pushing with her feet. As she experimented with muscle patterns and observed the consequences of her movements, she perfected the crawling motion (Adolph, Vereijkin, & Denny, 1998). Her efforts fostered the growth of new synaptic connections in the brain that govern motor activity.

Look carefully at dynamic systems theory, and you will see why motor development cannot be a genetically predetermined process. Since exploration and the desire to master new tasks motivate it, heredity can map it out only at a very general level. Instead of behaviors being *hardwired* into the nervous system, they are *softly assembled* (Hopkins & Butterworth, 1997; Thelen & Smith, 1998). This means that each skill is acquired by revising and combining earlier accomplishments into a more complex system that permits the child to reach a desired goal. Consequently, different paths to the same motor skill exist.

DYNAMIC MOTOR SYSTEMS IN ACTION

To study infants' mastery of motor milestones, researchers have conducted *microgenetic studies* (see Chapter 1, pages 45–46), following babies from their first attempts at a skill until it becomes smooth and effortless. Using this research strategy, Esther Thelen (1994) illustrated how infants acquire motor skills by modifying what the body can already do to fit a new task. She placed 3-month-olds under the special mobile attached to the baby's foot with a long cord, described earlier in this chapter. To produce the dazzling sight of the dancing mobile, infants quickly learned to kick with one foot or two feet in alternation.

Then Thelen changed the movement environment; she linked the babies' legs together with a soft piece of elastic attached to ankle cuffs (see Figure 5.10). Although this permitted single- or alternate-leg kicking, it made kicking both legs in unison much more effective for activating the mobile. When the elastic was in place, infants gradually discovered the new motion. They began with a few tentative simultaneous kicks and, seeing the effects, replaced earlier movements with this new form. When the elastic was removed, infants quickly gave up simultaneous kicking in favor of their previous behavior. They readily experimented, revising their motor behavior to fit changing conditions of the task.

CULTURAL VARIATIONS IN MOTOR DEVELOPMENT

Cross-cultural research demonstrates how early movement opportunities and a stimulating environment contribute to motor development. Several decades ago, Wayne Dennis (1960) observed infants in Iranian orphanages who were deprived of the tantalizing surroundings that motivate infants in most homes to acquire motor skills. The Iranian babies spent their days lying on their backs in cribs without toys to play with—conditions far worse than Grace experienced lying in a hammock in her Cambodian home. As a result, most did not move about on

FIGURE 5.10

A 3-month-old infant in the mobile experiment, with legs linked together by an elastic ankle cuff. Consistent with dynamic systems theory, the baby revised previously learned motor acts into a more effective motor system for activating the mobile. In response to the cuff, he replaced single- and alternate-leg kicking with simultaneous kicks. (Courtesy of Esther Thelen, Indiana University.)

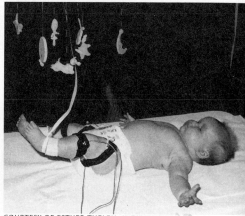

COURTESY OF ESTHER THELEN, INDIANA UNIV.

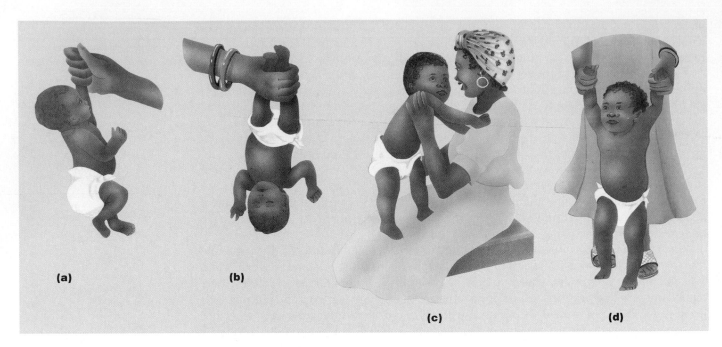

FIGURE 5.11

West Indians of Jamaica use a formal handling routine with their babies. Exercises practiced in the first few months include (a) stretching each arm while suspending the baby and (b) holding the infant upside-down by the ankles. Later in the first year, the baby is (c) "walked" up the mother's body and (d) encouraged to take steps on the floor while supported. (Adapted from B. Hopkins & T. Westra, 1988, "Maternal Handling and Motor Development: An Intracultural Study," *Genetic, Social and General Psychology Monographs, 14,* pp. 385, 388, 389. Reprinted by permission of the Helen Dwight Reid Educational Foundation. Published by Heldref Publications, 1319 Eighteenth St., N.W., Washington, DC 20036-1802.)

their own until after 2 years of age. When they finally did move, the constant experience of lying on their backs led them to scoot in a sitting position rather than crawl on their hands and knees. Since babies who scoot come up against objects such as furniture with their feet, not their hands, they are far less likely to pull themselves to a standing position in preparation for walking. Indeed, only 15 percent of the Iranian orphans walked alone by 3 to 4 years of age.

Cultural variations in infant-rearing practices also affect motor development. Take a quick survey of several parents you know, asking this question: Should sitting, crawling, and walking be deliberately encouraged? Answers vary widely from culture to culture. Japanese mothers, for example, believe such efforts are unnecessary. Among the Zinacanteco Indians of southern Mexico, rapid motor progress is actively discouraged. Babies who walk before they know enough to keep away from cooking fires and weaving looms are viewed as dangerous to themselves and disruptive to others (Greenfield, 1992).

In contrast, among the Kipsigis of Kenya and the West Indians of Jamaica, babies hold their heads up, sit alone, and walk considerably earlier than do North American infants. Kipsigi parents deliberately teach these motor skills. In the first few months, babies are seated in holes dug in the ground, and rolled blankets are used to keep them upright. Walking is promoted by frequently bouncing babies on their feet (Super, 1981). Unlike the Kipsigis, the West Indians of Jamaica do not train their infants in specific skills. As Figure 5.11 shows, they use a highly stimulating, formal handling routine, explaining that exercise helps infants grow strong, healthy, and physically attractive (Hopkins & Westra, 1988).

Putting together the evidence we have discussed so far, we must conclude that development of early motor skills is due to complex transactions between nature and nurture. As dynamic systems theory suggests, heredity establishes the broad outlines of change. But the precise sequence and rate of development result from an ongoing dialogue between the brain, the body, and the physical and social environment.

prereaching
The poorly coordinated, primitive reaching movements of newborn babies.

FINE MOTOR DEVELOPMENT: VOLUNTARY REACHING AND GRASPING

Of all motor skills, voluntary reaching may play the greatest role in infant cognitive development, since it opens up a whole new way of exploring the environment (Bushnell & Boudreau, 1993). By grasping things, turning them over, and seeing what happens when they are released, infants learn a great deal about the sights, sounds, and feel of objects.

The development of reaching and grasping, shown in Figure 5.12, provides an excellent example of how motor skills start out as gross, diffuse activity and move toward mastery of fine movements. Newborns make poorly coordinated swipes or swings, called **prereaching,** toward an object dangled in front of them. Because they cannot control their arms and hands, they rarely contact the object. Like the reflexes we discussed in Chapter 4, prereaching eventually drops out, around 7 weeks of age.

■ **DEVELOPMENT OF VOLUNTARY REACHING AND GRASPING.** At about 3 months, as infants develop the eye-gaze and head and shoulder postural control to support the skill, voluntary reaching appears and gradually improves in accuracy (Bertenthal & von Hofsten, 1998; Thelen & Spencer, 1998). By 5 to 6 months, infants can reach for and grasp an object that has been darkened during the reach, by switching off either the room lights or the illumination within the object. By 9 months, infants can reach for a darkened object just as quickly and accurately as an object that remains visible (Clifton et al., 1994; McCarty & Ashmead, 1999). This indicates that reaching does not require visual guidance of the arms and hands. Instead, it is largely controlled by *proprioception,* our sense of movement and location in space, arising from stimuli within the body. Early on, vision is freed from the basic act of reaching so it can focus on more complex adjustments, such as fine-tuning actions to fit the distance and shape of objects.

Improvements in reaching are largely a matter of gains in control of body posture and of arm and hand movements. Around 5 months, babies reduce their efforts when an object is moved beyond their reach (Robin, Berthier, & Clifton, 1996; Yonas & Hartman, 1993). By 7 months, their arms become more independent; they reach for objects with one arm rather than by extending both (Fagard & Pezé, 1997). And at 9 months, they can obtain a moving object that changes direction (Ashmead et al., 1993).

Individual differences in movement styles affect how the skill is perfected (Thelen, Corbetta, & Spencer, 1996). For example, Timmy's motions were large and forceful; he had to make them less vigorous to reach for a toy accurately. In contrast, Caitlin's gentle actions became faster and more energetic as she moved toward smoothly executed reaching (Thelen et al., 1993). Each infant builds the act of reaching uniquely by exploring the match between current movements and those demanded by the task (Thelen & Smith, 1998).

Of all motor skills, voluntary reaching is believed to play the greatest role in infant cognitive development. This 8-month-old can tip the basket with one hand while reaching in with the other. By exploring its contents, he adds to his knowledge of the sights, sounds, and feel of objects.

_FIGURE 5.12

Some milestones of voluntary reaching. The average age at which each skill is attained is given. (Ages from Bayley, 1969; Rochat, 1989.)

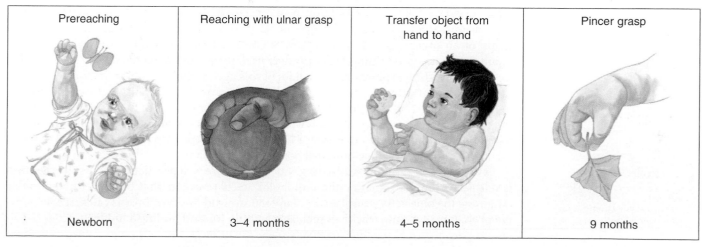

Prereaching	Reaching with ulnar grasp	Transfer object from hand to hand	Pincer grasp
Newborn	3–4 months	4–5 months	9 months

Caregiving Concerns

Keeping Infants and Toddlers Safe

STRATEGY	DESCRIPTION
Provide safe toys.	Match all toys to the child's age and abilities (see the Educational Concerns table in Chapter 6, page 223).
	Inspect all toys for small parts that can be swallowed, sharp edges that can cut, and materials that can shatter.
	Avoid cord-activated toys and toys intended to be attached to a crib or playpen; the infant's neck can become entangled in the cord or clothing can catch on a part of the toy, resulting in strangulation.
	Remove crib mobiles and crib gyms when the baby begins to push up on hands and knees; although researchers often use such toys to investigate infant capacities, the risk of becoming entangled is high.
	Do not let young children play with balloons, which can be inhaled if the child tries to blow them up.
Child-proof all rooms.	Keep lids of toilets closed and buckets of water used for cleaning away from infants and toddlers; a curious toddler who tries to play in the water can fall in and drown.
	Keep all medicines, cosmetics, cleaners, paints, glues, and other toxic substances out of reach, preferably in locked cabinets; make sure that medicine bottles have child-resistant safety caps.
	Put safety plugs in all unused electrical outlets.
	Unplug all appliances or remove dials when not in use so the child cannot turn them on. Keep cords for window blinds and curtains out of reach.
	Remove unstable furniture, such as tall floor lamps and freestanding bookshelves.
	When the infant starts to crawl, install safety gates at top and bottom of stairs.
Continuously monitor the infant or toddler in situations that pose any risk of injury.	Never leave a young child alone in the bath or on a changing table, even for a moment. At mealtimes, strap the infant or toddler into a high chair, and do not leave the child unattended.
Use a federally approved car seat.	When driving, always strap the young child into the car seat. Never permit an infant or toddler to ride on your lap; in an accident, your body could crush the child as you are thrown forward.
Report any unsafe toys and equipment.	If you discover any toys or equipment that seem unsafe, report them to the Consumer Product Safety Commission—(800) 638-2772. It keeps a record of complaints and initiates recalls of dangerous products.

Source: American Academy of Pediatrics, 1993.

Once infants can reach, they start to modify their grasp. When the grasp reflex of the newborn period weakens, it is replaced by the **ulnar grasp,** a clumsy motion in which the fingers close against the palm. Still, even 3-month-olds readily adjust their grasp to the size and shape of an object (Case-Smith, Bigsby, & Clutter, 1998). Around 4 to 5 months, when infants begin to master sitting, they no longer need their arms to maintain body balance. This frees both hands to explore objects. Babies of this age can hold an object in one hand while the other scans it with the tips of the fingers, and they frequently transfer objects from hand to hand (Rochat, 1992; Rochat & Goubet, 1995). By the latter part of the first year, infants use the thumb and index finger opposably in a well-coordinated **pincer grasp.** Then the ability to manipulate objects expands greatly. The 1-year-old can pick up raisins and blades of grass, turn knobs, and open and close small boxes.

Between 8 and 11 months, reaching and grasping are well practiced. As a result, attention is released from coordinating the motor skill itself to events that occur before and after obtaining the object. As we will see in Chapter 6, around this time infants can first solve simple problems involving reaching, such as searching for and finding a hidden toy.

ulnar grasp
The clumsy grasp of the young infant, in which the fingers close against the palm.

pincer grasp
The well-coordinated grasp emerging at the end of the first year, involving thumb and forefinger opposition.

■ **EARLY EXPERIENCE AND VOLUNTARY REACHING.** Like other motor milestones, early experience affects voluntary reaching. In a well-known study, Burton White and Richard Held (1966) found that institutionalized babies provided with a moderate amount of visual stimulation—at first, simple designs and later, a mobile hung over their crib—reached for objects 6 weeks earlier than did infants given nothing to look at. A third group of babies provided with massive stimulation—patterned crib bumpers and mobiles at an early age—also reached sooner than unstimulated babies. But this heavy dose of enrichment took its toll. These infants looked away and cried a great deal, and they were not as advanced in reaching as the moderately stimulated group. White and Held's findings remind us that more stimulation is not necessarily better. Trying to push infants beyond their current readiness to handle stimulation can undermine the development of important motor skills.

Of course, as motor skills permit infants and toddlers to move about and manipulate objects independently, caregivers must devote more energy to protecting them from harm. Refer to the Caregiving Concerns table on the previous page for a variety of suggestions for keeping infants and toddlers safe. In Chapter 8, we will consider the topic of unintentional injuries in greater detail.

ELIZABETH CREWS

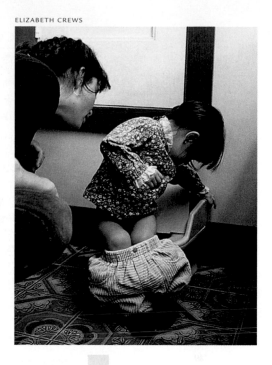

BOWEL AND BLADDER CONTROL

More than any other aspect of early muscular development, parents wonder about bowel and bladder control. Two or three generations ago, many mothers tried to toilet train infants. However, they did not succeed in teaching anything. They only caught the baby's reflexive release of urine or a bowel movement at a convenient moment.

Toilet training is best delayed until the end of the second or the beginning of the third year. Not until then can toddlers consistently identify the signals from a full bladder or rectum and wait until they get to the right place to permit these muscles to open—physiological developments essential for the child to cooperate with training (Brazelton et al., 1999). Research indicates that mothers who postpone training until age 2 have infants fully trained within 4 months. Starting earlier does not produce a more reliably trained preschooler; the whole process just takes longer (Brazelton, 1997). In addition, as we will see in Chapter 7, pressuring too much in this area, as well as in others, can negatively affect the toddler's emotional well-being.

Toddlers are not ready for toilet training until around age 2, when they can control bladder and rectal muscles consistently. The parents of this 2-year-old girl bought a small toilet on which she can sit comfortably, and they make toileting a pleasant experience. She is likely to be fully trained within a few months.

Ask **YOURSELF...**

review   *Cite evidence indicating that motor development is not hardwired into the brain but rather is a joint product of biological, psychological, and social factors.*

apply   *Rosanne read in a magazine that infant motor development could be accelerated through visual stimulation, so she hung mobiles and pictures above her newborn baby's crib and surrounded it with a brightly colored, patterned crib bumper. Is Rosanne doing the right thing? Why or why not?*

connect   *Cite several examples of how motor development influences infants' and toddlers' social experiences. How might social experiences, in turn, influence motor development?*

reflect   *Do you favor early training of infants in motor skills, such as crawling, walking, running, hopping, and stair climbing? Why or why not?*

Perceptual Development

In Chapter 4, you learned that the senses of touch, taste, smell, and hearing—but not vision—are remarkably well developed at birth. Now let's turn to a related question: How does perception change over the first year of life?

Our discussion will focus on hearing and vision because almost all research addresses these two aspects of perceptual development. Unfortunately, we know little about how touch, taste, and smell develop after birth. Also, in Chapter 4 we used the word *sensation* to talk about these capacities. Now we are using the word *perception*. The reason is that *sensation* suggests a fairly passive process—what the baby's receptors detect when they are exposed to stimulation. In contrast, *perception* is much more active. When we perceive, we organize and interpret what we see.

As we review the perceptual achievements of infancy, you will probably find it hard to tell where perception leaves off and thinking begins. Thus, the research we are about to discuss provides an excellent bridge to the topic of Chapter 6—cognitive development during the first 2 years.

HEARING

On Timmy's first birthday, Vanessa bought several tapes of nursery songs, and she turned one on each afternoon at naptime. Soon Timmy let her know his favorite tune. If she put on "Twinkle, Twinkle," he stood up in his crib and whimpered until she replaced it with "Jack and Jill." Timmy's behavior illustrates the greatest change in hearing over the first year of life: babies start to organize sounds into complex patterns. Between 4 and 7 months, they have a sense of musical phrasing. They prefer Mozart minuets with pauses between phrases to those with awkward breaks (Krumhansl & Jusczyk, 1990). And around 12 months, if two melodies differ only slightly, infants can tell that they are not the same (Morrongiello, 1986).

As we will see in the next chapter, throughout the first year babies are preparing to acquire language. Recall from Chapter 4 that newborns can distinguish between almost all sounds in human languages, and they prefer listening to their native tongue. As infants continue to listen to the talk of people around them, they learn to focus on meaningful sound variations. By 6 months of age, they start to "screen out" sounds not used in their own language (Kuhl et al., 1992; Polka & Werker, 1994).

In the second half of the first year, infants focus on the larger speech units crucial for figuring out meaning. They recognize familiar words in spoken passages (Jusczyk & Aslin, 1995; Jusczyk & Hohne, 1997). Older infants can also detect clauses and phrases in sentences. In one study, researchers recorded two versions of a mother telling a story. In the first, she spoke naturally, with pauses occurring between clauses: "Cinderella lived in a great big house [pause], but it was sort of dark [pause] because she had this mean stepmother." In the second version, the mother inserted pauses in unnatural places—in the middle of clauses: "Cinderella lived in a great big house, but it was [pause] sort of dark because she had [pause] this mean stepmother." Like adults, 7-month-olds clearly preferred speech with natural breaks (Hirsh-Pasek et al., 1987).

Around 7 to 9 months, infants extend this rhythmic sensitivity to individual words. They listen much longer to speech with stress patterns and sound sequences common in their own language (Jusczyk, Cutler, & Redanz, 1993; Morgan & Saffran, 1995). And they use these cues to divide the speech stream into word-like segments. Seven-month-olds can distinguish sound patterns that begin words from those that do not. For example, English learners often rely on the onset of a strong syllable to indicate a new word, as in "<u>an</u>imal" and "<u>pud</u>ding." By 10 months, infants can detect words that start with weak syllables, such as "sur<u>prise</u>," by listening for sound regularities before and after the words (Jusczyk, 1997).

Taken together, these findings reveal that between 7 and 9 months, infants have begun to analyze the internal structure of sentences and words (Werker & Tees, 1999). This information will be vital for linking speech units with their meanings in the second year.

VISION

If you had to choose between hearing and vision, which would you select? Most people pick vision, for good reason. More than any other sense, humans depend on vision for active exploration of the environment. Although at first the baby's visual world is fragmented, it undergoes extraordinary changes during the first 7 to 8 months of life.

Visual development is supported by rapid maturation of the eye and visual centers in the cerebral cortex. Recall from Chapter 4 that the newborn baby focuses and perceives color poorly. By 2 months, infants can discriminate colors across the entire spectrum, and by 3 months, they can focus on objects as well as adults can (Banks, 1980; Burr, Morrone, & Fiorentini, 1996). Visual acuity (fineness of discrimination) improves steadily throughout the first year. In Chapter 4, we noted that newborns see about as clearly at 20 feet as adults do at 600 feet. By 6 months, their acuity is about 20/100. At 11 months, it reaches a near-adult level (Courage & Adams, 1990). Over the first 6 months, the ability to track moving objects becomes more accurate (Hofsten & Rosander, 1998).

As infants see more clearly and explore their visual field more adeptly, they figure out the characteristics of objects and how they are arranged in space. We can best understand how they do so by examining the development of three aspects of vision: depth, pattern, and object perception.

■ **DEPTH PERCEPTION.** *Depth perception* is the ability to judge the distance of objects from one another and from ourselves. It is important for understanding the layout of the environment and for guiding motor activity. To reach for objects, babies must have some sense of depth. Later, when infants crawl, depth perception helps prevent them from bumping into furniture and falling down stairs. However, as we will see shortly, parents are unwise to trust the baby's judgment entirely in these situations!

Figure 5.13 shows the well-known *visual cliff*, designed by Eleanor Gibson and Richard Walk (1960) and used in the earliest studies of depth perception. It consists of a glass-covered table with a platform at the center, a "shallow" side with a checkerboard pattern just under the glass, and a "deep" side with a checkerboard several feet below the glass. The researchers found that crawling babies readily crossed the shallow side, but most reacted with fear to the deep side. They concluded that around the time that infants crawl, most distinguish deep from shallow surfaces and avoid drop-offs that look dangerous.

Gibson and Walk's research shows that crawling and avoidance of drop-offs are linked, but it does not tell us how they are related or when depth perception first appears. To better understand the development of depth perception, recent research has looked at babies' ability to detect specific depth cues, using methods that do not require that they crawl.

Emergence of Depth Perception. How do we know when an object is near rather than far away? Try these exercises to find out. Pick up a small object (such as your cup) and move it toward and away from your face. Did its image grow larger as it approached and smaller as it receded? When you next take a bike or car ride, notice that nearby objects move past your field of vision more quickly than those far away.

Motion provides a great deal of information about depth, and it is the first depth cue to which infants are sensitive. Babies 3 to 4 weeks of age blink their eyes defensively when an object moves toward their face as if it is going to hit (Nánez,

FIGURE 5.13

The visual cliff. By refusing to cross the deep side and showing a preference for the shallow surface, this infant demonstrates the ability to perceive depth.

BIRNBACH/MONKMEYER PRESS

1987; Nánez & Yonas, 1994). As they are carried about and people and things turn and move before their eyes, infants learn more about depth. For example, by the time they are 3 months old, motion has helped them figure out that objects are not flat but three dimensional (Arterberry, Craton, & Yonas, 1993).

Binocular (meaning two eyes) *depth cues* arise because our eyes have slightly different views of the visual field. The brain blends these two images but also registers the difference between them. Studies in which babies view images through special goggles, like those for 3-D movies, reveal that sensitivity to binocular cues emerges between 2 and 3 months and improves rapidly over the first half-year (Birch, 1993). Infants soon make use of binocular cues in their reaching, adjusting arm and hand movements to match the distance of objects from the eyes.

Last to develop are *pictorial depth cues*—the ones artists use to make a painting look three-dimensional. Examples are lines that create the illusion of perspective, changes in texture (nearby textures are more detailed than faraway ones), and overlapping objects (an object partially hidden by another object is perceived to be more distant). Research shows that 7-month-old babies are sensitive to a variety of pictorial cues, but 5-month-olds are not (Yonas et al., 1986).

Why does perception of depth cues emerge in the order just described? Researchers speculate that motor development is involved. For example, control of the head during the early weeks of life may help babies notice motion cues. Improved focusing ability at 3 months may permit detection of binocular cues. And around 5 to 6 months, the ability to turn, poke, and feel the surface of objects may promote perception of pictorial cues as infants pick up information about size, texture, and shape (Bushnell & Boudreau, 1993).

The close correspondence between depth perception and action reveals that these two aspects of development support one another (Bertenthal & Clifton, 1998). Indeed, as we will see next, research shows that one aspect of motor progress—the baby's ability to move about independently—plays a vital role in the refinement of depth perception.

Independent Movement and Depth Perception. Just before he reached the 6-month mark, Timmy started crawling. "He's like a fearless daredevil," exclaimed Vanessa. "If I put him down in the middle of the bed, he crawls right over the edge. Several times I stopped him just before he went overboard. The same thing's also happened by the stairs."

Will Timmy become more wary of the side of the bed and the staircase as he becomes a more experienced crawler? Research suggests that he will. In one study, infants with more crawling experience (regardless of when they started to crawl) were far more likely to refuse to cross the deep side of the visual cliff (Bertenthal, Campos, & Barrett, 1984). Avoidance of heights, the investigators concluded, is "made possible by independent locomotion" (Bertenthal & Campos, 1987, p. 563).

Independent movement contributes to other aspects of three-dimensional understanding. For example, crawling infants can better remember object locations and find hidden objects than can their noncrawling agemates. And the more crawling experience they have, the better they perform on these tasks (Bai & Bertenthal, 1992; Campos & Bertenthal, 1989).

Why does crawling make such a difference? Compare your experience of the environment when you are driven from one place to another as opposed to when you walk or drive yourself. When you move on your own, you are much more aware of landmarks, routes of travel, and what things look like from different points of view. The same is true for infants.

In fact, crawling is so important in structuring infants' experience of the world that it seems to promote a new level of brain organization. During the weeks in which babies master crawling, EEG brain-wave activity in the cerebral cortex becomes more organized.

FIGURE 5.14

The way two checkerboards differing in complexity look to infants in the first few weeks of life. Because of their poor vision, very young infants cannot resolve the fine detail in the more complex checkerboard. It appears blurred, like a gray field. The large, bold checkerboard appears to have more contrast, so babies prefer to look at it. (Adapted from M. S. Banks & P. Salapatek, 1983, "Infant Visual Perception," in M. M. Haith & J. J. Campos [Eds.], *Handbook of Child Psychology: Vol. 2. Infancy and Developmental Psychobiology* [4th ed.], New York: Wiley, p. 504. Copyright © 1983 by John Wiley & Sons. Reprinted by permission.)

Two checkerboards differing in complexity

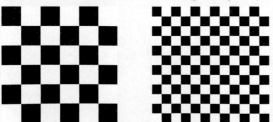

Appearance of checkerboards to very young infants

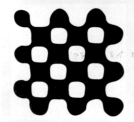

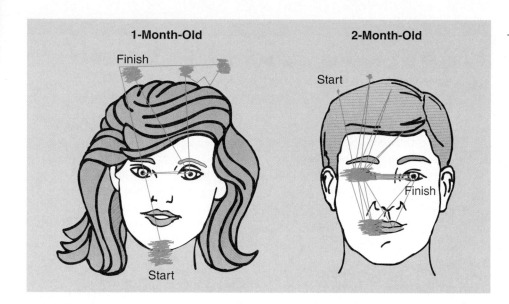

1-Month-Old

Finish

Start

2-Month-Old

Start

Finish

FIGURE 5.15

Visual scanning of the pattern of the human face by 1- and 2-month-old infants. One-month-olds limit their scanning to single features on the border of the stimulus, whereas 2-month-olds explore internal features. (From P. Salapatek, 1975, "Pattern Perception in Early Infancy," in L. B. Cohen & P. Salapatek [Eds.], *Infant Perception: From Sensation to Cognition,* New York: Academic Press, p. 201. Reprinted by permission.)

Crawling may lead to strengthening of certain neural connections, especially those involved in vision and understanding of space (Bell & Fox, 1996). As the Biology and Environment box on pages 200–201 reveals, the link between independent movement and spatial knowledge is evident in a population with very different perceptual experience: infants with severe visual impairments.

■ **PATTERN PERCEPTION.** Are young babies sensitive to the pattern, or form, of things they see, and do they prefer some patterns to others? Early research revealed that even newborns prefer to look at patterned as opposed to plain stimuli—for example, a drawing of the human face or one with scrambled facial features rather than a black-and-white oval (Fantz, 1961). As infants get older, they prefer more complex patterns. For example, 3-week-olds look longest at black-and-white checkerboards with a few large squares, whereas 8- and 14-week-olds prefer those with many squares (Brennan, Ames, & Moore, 1966). Infant preferences for many other patterned stimuli have been tested—curved versus straight lines, connected versus disconnected elements, and whether a pattern is organized around a central focus (as in a bull's eye), to name just a few.

Contrast Sensitivity. A general principle, called **contrast sensitivity,** explains these early pattern preferences (Banks & Ginsburg, 1985). *Contrast* refers to the difference in the amount of light between adjacent regions in a pattern. If babies *are sensitive to* (can detect) the contrast in two or more patterns, they prefer the one with more contrast.

To understand this idea, look at the two checkerboards in the top row of Figure 5.14 on the previous page. To us, the one with many small squares has more contrasting elements. Now look at the bottom row, which shows how these checkerboards appear to infants in the first few weeks of life. Because of their poor vision, very young babies cannot resolve the small features in more complex patterns, so they prefer to look at the large, bold checkerboard. By 2 months of age, when detection of fine-grained detail has improved considerably, infants become sensitive to the greater contrast in complex patterns and spend more time looking at them (Dodwell, Humphrey, & Muir, 1987).

Combining Pattern Elements. In the early weeks of life, infants respond to the separate parts of a pattern. For example, when shown drawings of human faces, 1-month-olds limit their visual exploration to the border of the stimulus and stare at single high-contrast features, such as the hairline or chin (see Figure 5.15). At about 2 months, when scanning ability and contrast sensitivity have improved, infants thoroughly explore a pattern's internal features, pausing briefly to look at each salient part (Bronson, 1991).

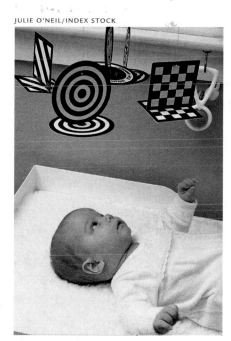

This 3-month-old looks at stimuli that match his level of visual development. His visual acuity has improved greatly since birth, so he can detect the contrast in complex patterns and spends more time looking at them.

contrast sensitivity
A general principle accounting for early pattern preferences, which states that if babies can detect a difference in contrast between two or more patterns, they will prefer the one with more contrast.

Biology & ENVIRONMENT

DEVELOPMENT OF INFANTS WITH SEVERE VISUAL IMPAIRMENTS

Research on infants who can see little or nothing at all dramatically illustrates the interdependence of vision, motor exploration, social interaction, and understanding of the world. In a longitudinal study, infants with a visual acuity of 20/800 or worse (they had only dim light perception or were blind) were followed through the preschool years. Compared with agemates who have less severe visual impairments, they showed serious delays in all aspects of development—motor, cognitive, language, and personal/social. Their motor and cognitive functioning suffered the most; with age, performance in both domains became increasingly distant from that of other children (Hatton et al., 1997).

What explains these profound developmental delays? Minimal or absent vision can alter the child's experiences in at least two crucial, interrelated ways.

IMPACT ON MOTOR EXPLORATION AND SPATIAL UNDERSTANDING

Infants with severe visual impairments attain gross and fine motor milestones many months later than do their sighted counterparts (Fraiberg, 1977; Tröster & Brambring, 1993). For example, on the average, blind infants do not reach for and manipulate objects until 12 months, crawl until 13 months, and walk until 19 months (compare these averages to the norms given in Figure 5.10 on page 191). Why is this so?

Infants with severe visual impairments must rely entirely on sound to identify the whereabouts of objects. But sound does not function as a precise clue to object location until much later than vision—around the middle of the first year (Litovsky & Ashmead, 1997). And because infants who cannot see may have difficulty engaging their caregivers, adults may not provide them with rich, early exposure to sounding objects. As a result, the baby comes to understand relatively late that there is a world of tantalizing objects to explore.

Until "reaching on sound" is achieved, infants with severe visual impairments are not motivated to move on their own (Fraiberg, 1977; Tröster & Brambring, 1993). Even after they do move, their coordination is poor due to many months of inactivity. Because of their own uncertainty and parents' protection and restriction to prevent injury, blind infants are typically tentative in their movements. These factors delay motor development further.

Motor and cognitive development are closely linked for infants with little or no vision, even more than for their sighted counterparts. These babies build an understanding of the location and arrangement of objects in space only after reaching and crawling (Bigelow, 1992). Inability to imitate the motor actions of others presents additional challenges as these children get older, contributing to declines in motor and cognitive progress relative to peers with better vision (Hatton et al., 1997).

IMPACT ON THE CAREGIVER– INFANT RELATIONSHIP

Infants who see very poorly have great difficulty evoking stimulating caregiver interaction. They cannot make eye contact, imitate, or pick up nonverbal social cues. Their emotional expressions are muted; for example, their smile is fleeting and unpredictable. Conse-

---

Once babies can detect all parts of a pattern, they integrate them into a unified whole. By 4 months, babies are so good at detecting pattern organization that they even perceive subjective boundaries that are not really present. For example, they perceive a square in the center of Figure 5.16a, just as you do (Ghim, 1990). Older infants carry this responsiveness to subjective form even further. For example, 9-month-olds show a special preference for an organized series of moving lights that resembles a human being walking, in that they look much longer at this display than at upside-down or scrambled versions (Bertenthal, 1993). By 12 months, infants detect objects represented by incomplete figures, even when as much as two-thirds is missing (see Figure 5.16b) (Rose, Jankowski, & Senior, 1997). By the end of the first year, a suggestive image is all that babies need to recognize a familiar form.

As these finding reveal, over time infants' knowledge of objects and actions increasingly governs pattern perception. We will see additional examples of this trend in the development of face perception.

quently, these infants may receive little adult attention, play, and other stimulation vital for all aspects of development (Tröster & Brambring, 1992).

When a visually impaired child does not learn how to participate in social interaction during infancy, communication is compromised in early childhood. In an observational study of blind children enrolled in preschools with sighted agemates, the blind children seldom initiated contact with peers and teachers. When they did interact, they had trouble interpreting the meaning of others' reactions and responding appropriately (Preisler, 1991, 1993).

INTERVENTIONS

Although many infants and preschoolers with severe visual impairments are substantially behind in development, considerable variation exists. Once language emerges and the child can rely on it for learning, some children with limited or no vision show impressive rebounds, eventually acquiring a unique capacity for abstract thinking and social and practical skills that permit them to lead productive, independent lives (Warren, 1994).

Parents and teachers can help infants with minimal vision overcome early developmental delays. Especially important is stimulating, responsive interaction. Until a close emotional bond with an adult is forged, visually impaired babies cannot establish vital links with their environments. Techniques that help infants become aware of their physical and social surroundings include heightened sensory input through combining sound and touch (holding, touching, or bringing the baby's hands to the adult's face while talking or singing), many repetitions, and consistently reinforcing the infant's efforts to make contact. Manipulative play with objects that make sounds is also vital. These experiences facilitate "reaching on sound," which motivates independent movement. Finally, rich, descriptive language stimulation—for example, saying "that large ball is soft and smooth, and it bounces very high" instead of "that ball"—can compensate for visual loss (Moore & McConachie, 1994). It grants young children a ready means of finding out about objects, events, and behaviors they cannot see.

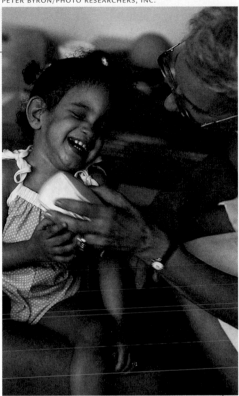

This 20-month-old, who is blind, reacts with glee as her father guides her exploration of a novel object through touch and sound. Adults who encourage and reinforce children's efforts to contact their physical and social surroundings prevent developmental delays typically associated with severely impaired vision.

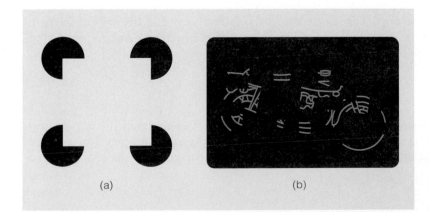

(a)   (b)

FIGURE 5.16

Subjective boundaries in visual patterns. (a) Do you perceive a square in the middle of the figure on the left? By 4 months of age, infants do, too. (b) What does the image on the right, missing two-thirds of its outline, look like to you? By 12 months, infants detect that it is a bicycle. After habituating to the incomplete bicycle image, they were shown an intact bicycle figure paired with a novel form. Twelve-month-olds dishabituated to (looked longest at) the novel figure, indicating that they recognized the bicycle pattern above on the basis of very little visual information. (Adapted from Ghim, 1990; Rose, Jankowski, & Senior, 1997.)

FIGURE 5.17

Early face perception. (a) Newborns prefer to look at the simple pattern resembling a face on the left over the upside-down version on the right. This preference for a crude, facelike stimulus disappears by age 6 weeks. Researchers believe it is innate, orients newborns toward people, and is supplanted by more complex perceptual learning as the cerebral cortex develops and visual capacities improve. (b) When the complex, stylized face on the left and the equally complex, scrambled version on the right are moved across newborns' field of vision, they follow the face longer—another finding that suggests a built-in capacity to orient toward people. But present the two stimuli in a static display, and infants show no preference for the face until 2 to 3 months of age. (From Johnson, 1999; Mondloch et al., 1999.)

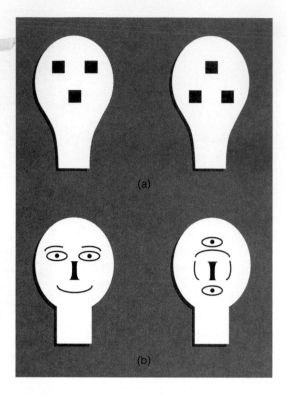

(a)

(b)

Perception of the Human Face. Do babies have an innate tendency to orient toward human faces? Some researchers think so, on the basis of evidence indicating that newborns prefer to look at a simple stimulus resembling a face over an upside down version (see Figure 5.17a) (Mondloch et al., 1999). In addition, newborns will track a facelike pattern moving across their visual field farther than they will track other stimuli (Easterbrook et al., 1999; Johnson, 1999). These behaviors may reflect a built-in, adaptive capacity to orient toward members of one's own species, just as many other newborn creatures do.

But most investigators agree that infants younger than 2 months do not prefer a static, stylized face over other equally complex patterns with scrambled facial features (see Figure 5.17b). As noted earlier, very young infants' visual acuity is poor, and they do not inspect the internal features of a stimulus.[2] At 2 to 3 months, when infants explore an entire stimulus and can combine its elements into an organized whole, they do prefer a stylized face to other stimulus arrangements (Dannemiller & Stephens, 1988).

Babies quickly apply their tendency to search for structure in a patterned stimulus. By 3 months of age, infants make fine distinctions between the features of different faces. For example, they can tell the difference between the photos of two strangers, even when the faces are moderately similar. Around this time, babies first recognize their mother's face in a photo, since they look longer at it than at the face of a stranger (Morton, 1993). Between 7 and 10 months, infants start to perceive emotional expressions as organized wholes. They treat positive faces (happy and surprised) as different from negative ones (sad and fearful), even when these expressions are demonstrated in slightly varying ways by different people (Ludemann, 1991). As we will see in Chapter 7, babies' developing sensitivity to the human face supports their earliest social relationships and helps regulate their exploration of the environment in adaptive ways.

The development of depth and pattern perception is summarized in Table 5.2. Note that several important changes take place around 2 months of age. Recall that 2 months also is a time when the frontal lobes of the cerebral cortex function more effectively. Brain development fosters babies' improved visual capacities, and babies' visual processing, in turn, promotes brain development.

OBJECT PERCEPTION

Research on pattern perception involves only two-dimensional stimuli, but our environment is made up of stable, three-dimensional objects. Do young infants perceive a world of independently existing objects—knowledge essential for distinguishing the self, other people, and things?

---

[2]Perhaps you are wondering how newborns can display the remarkable imitative capacities described earlier in this chapter if they do not scan the internal features of a face. The facial expressions in newborn imitation research were not static poses but live demonstrations. Their dynamic quality probably caused infants to notice them.

TABLE 5.2
Development of Visual Perception

	BIRTH–1 MONTH	2–4 MONTHS	5–12 MONTHS
Depth perception	Sensitivity to motion cues	Sensitivity to binocular cues	Sensitivity to pictorial cues; wariness of heights
Pattern perception	Preference for patterns with large elements Visual exploration limited to border of a stimulus and single features	Visual exploration of entire stimulus, including internal features Pattern elements combined into an organized whole	Detection of increasingly complex, meaningful patterns
Face perception	Preference for a simple, facelike pattern	Preference for a complex, stylized face over other, equally complex patterns and for mother's over stranger's face in a photo	More fine-grained discrimination of photos, including ability to perceive emotional expressions as organized wholes

■ **SIZE AND SHAPE CONSTANCY.** As we move around the environment, the images objects cast on our retina are constantly changing in size and shape. To perceive objects as stable and unchanging, we must translate these varying retinal images into a single representation.

Size constancy—perception of an object's size as the same, despite changes in the size of its retinal image—is evident in the first week of life. To test for it, researchers capitalized on the habituation–dishabituation response using the procedure described and illustrated in Figure 5.18. Perception of an object's shape as stable, despite changes in the shape projected on the retina, is called **shape constancy.** Habituation–dishabituation research reveals that it,

FIGURE 5.18

Testing newborns for size constancy. (a) First, infants were habituated to a small black-and-white cube at varying distances from the eye. In this way, the researchers hoped to desensitize the baby to changes in the cube's retinal image size and direct their attention to its actual size. (b) Next, the small cube and a new, large cube were presented together, but at different distances so they cast the same-size retinal image. All babies dishabituated to (looked much longer at) the novel large cube, indicating that they distinguish objects on the basis of actual size, not retinal image size. (Adapted from Slater, Mattock, & Brown, 1990.)

size constancy
Perception of an object's size as the same, despite changes in the size of its retinal image.

shape constancy
Perception of an object's shape as the same, despite changes in the shape projected on the retina.

FIGURE 5.19

Display used to test infants' ability to perceive object unity. (a) Infants are habituated to a rod moving back and forth behind a box against a textured background. Next, they are shown (b) a complete rod or (c) a broken rod with a gap corresponding to the location of the box. Each of these stimuli is moved back and forth against the textured background, in the same way as the habituation stimulus. Infants 2 months of age and older typically dishabituate (look longer at) the broken rod than the complete rod. This suggests that they perceive the rod behind the box in the first display as a single unit. (Adapted from Johnson, 1997.)

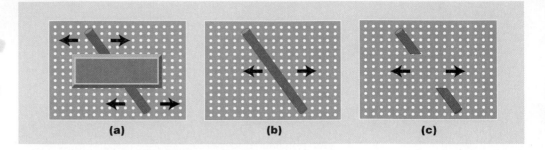

(a)   (b)   (c)

too, is present within the first week of life, long before babies can actively rotate objects with their hands and view them from different angles (Slater & Johnson, 1999).

In sum, both size and shape constancy seem to be innate capacities that assist babies in detecting a coherent world of objects. Yet they provide only a partial picture of young infants' object perception.

■ **PERCEPTION OF OBJECT UNITY.** When Vanessa dangled a colorful rattle in front of 4-month-old Timmy, he grabbed it eagerly. But when she placed the rattle on top of a book, Timmy no longer reached for it. Instead, he reached for the larger, supporting object. Timmy's behavior suggests that he did not perceive the boundary between two objects. Rather, he treated objects close together as a single unit.

Research reveals that at first, babies rely heavily on motion and spatial arrangement to identify objects (Kellman, 1996; Jusczyk et al., 1999; Spelke & Hermer, 1996). When two objects are touching and either move in unison or stand still, babies younger than 4 months of age cannot distinguish them. Infants, of course, are fascinated by moving objects; they almost always prefer a moving stimulus to an identical stationary one. As they track moving objects, they pick up additional information about their boundaries, such as shape, color, texture, and consistent distance from the eye of all the object's parts.

For example, as Figure 5.19 reveals, after 2 months of age, babies realize that a moving rod whose center is hidden behind a box is a complete rod rather than two rod pieces. Motion, a textured background, and a small box (so most of the rod is visible) are necessary for 2- to 4-month-olds to infer object unity; they cannot do so without all these cues to heighten the distinction between the objects in the display (Johnson & Aslin, 1996).

As infants become familiar with many types of objects, they rely more on shape, color, and texture and less on motion to identify objects as separate units (Johnson, 1997). Babies as young as 4½ months can distinguish two touching objects on the basis of their features in very simple, easy-to-process situations (Needham, 1998). In the second half of the first year, infants extend this capacity to more complex displays of objects.

INTERMODAL PERCEPTION

When we take in information from the environment, we often use **intermodal perception.** That is, we combine stimulation from more than one *modality,* or sensory system, at a time. For example, we know that the shape of an object is the same whether we see it or touch it, that lip movements are closely coordinated with the sound of a voice, and that dropping a rigid object on a hard surface will cause a sharp, banging sound. Recent evidence reveals that from the start, babies perceive the world in an intermodal fashion (Meltzoff, 1990; Spelke, 1987).

Recall that newborns turn in the general direction of a sound, and they reach for objects in a primitive way. These behaviors suggest that infants expect sight, sound, and touch to go

intermodal perception
Perception that combines stimulation from more than one sensory system at a time.

together. Experiencing the integration of sensory modalities in these ways prepares young babies for detecting the wealth of intermodal associations that pervade their everyday worlds (Slater et al., 1999).

Within a few months, infants make impressive intermodal matches. Three- and 4-month-olds can relate a child's or adult's moving lips to the corresponding sounds in speech. And 7-month-olds can link a happy or angry voice with the appropriate face of a speaking person (Bahrick, Netto, & Hernandez-Reif, 1998; Soken & Pick, 1992).

Of course, a great many intermodal associations, such as the way a train sounds or a teddy bear feels, must be based on direct exposure. Yet even newborn babies acquire these relationships remarkably quickly, often after just one contact with a new situation (Morrongiello, Fenwick, & Chance, 1998). In addition, when researchers try to teach intermodal matches by pairing sights and sounds that do not naturally go together, babies will not learn them (Bahrick, 1992). Intermodal perception is yet another capacity that helps infants build an orderly, predictable perceptual world.

UNDERSTANDING PERCEPTUAL DEVELOPMENT

Now that we have reviewed the development of infant perceptual capacities, how can we put together this diverse array of amazing achievements? Do any general principles account for perceptual development? Eleanor and James Gibson's **differentiation theory** provides widely accepted answers.

According to the Gibsons, infants actively search for **invariant features** of the environment—those that remain stable—in a constantly changing perceptual world. For example, in pattern perception, at first babies are confronted with a confusing mass of stimulation. But very soon, they search for features that stand out along the border of a stimulus and orient toward images that crudely represent a face. Soon they explore internal features, noticing stable relationships between those features. As a result, they detect patterns, such as squares and complex, stylized faces. The development of intermodal perception also reflects this principle. Babies seem to seek out invariant relationships, such as a similar tempo in an object's motion and sound, that unite information across modalities.

The Gibsons use the word *differentiation* (meaning analyze or break down) to describe their theory because over time, the baby makes finer and finer distinctions between stimuli. So one way of understanding perceptual development is to think of it as a built-in tendency to search for order and stability in the surrounding world, a capacity that becomes increasingly fine-tuned with age (Gibson, 1970; Gibson, 1979).

Acting on the environment plays a major role in perceptual differentiation. According to the Gibsons, perception is guided by the discovery of **affordances**—the action possibilities a situation offers an organism with certain motor capabilities (Gibson, 1988). As adults, we know when an object can be squeezed, bounced, or rolled and when a surface is appropriate for sitting or walking. Sensitivity to these affordances makes our actions future oriented and largely successful rather than reactive and blundering. Consequently, we spend far less time correcting ineffective actions than we otherwise would.

Infants discover affordances as they act on their world. To illustrate, let's consider how infants' changing capabilities for independent movement affect their perception. When babies start to crawl and again when they begin to walk, they gradually realize that a steeply sloping surface *affords the possibility* of falling (see Figure 5.20 on page 206). With added weeks of practicing each skill, they hesitate to crawl or walk down a risky incline. Experience in trying to keep their balance on various surfaces seems to make crawlers and walkers more aware of the consequences of their movements. Crawlers come to detect when surface slant places so much body weight on their arms that they will fall forward, walkers when an incline shifts body weight so their legs and feet can no longer hold them upright (Adolph, 1997; Adolph & Eppler, 1998, 1999). Experience with each skill leads infants to perceive surfaces in

differentiation theory
The view that perceptual development involves the detection of increasingly fine-grained, invariant features in the environment.

invariant features
In differentiation theory of perceptual development, features that remain stable in a constantly changing perceptual world.

affordances
The action possibilities a situation offers an organism with certain motor capabilities. Discovering affordances plays a major role in perceptual differentiation.

FIGURE 5.20

COURTESY OF KAREN ADOLPH, EMORY UNIVERSITY

Acting on the environment plays a major role in perceptual differentiation. Crawling and walking change the way babies perceive a steeply sloping surface. The newly crawling infant on the left plunges headlong down a steeply sloping surface. He has not yet learned that it affords the possibility of falling. The toddler on the right, who has been walking for more than a month, approaches the slope cautiously. Experience in trying to remain upright but frequently tumbling over has made him more aware of the consequences of his movements. He perceives the incline differently than he did at a younger age.

new ways that guide their current means of moving about the environment. As a result, they act more competently.

At this point, it is only fair to note that some researchers believe that babies do more than make sense of experience by searching for invariant features and discovering affordances. They also impose *meaning* on what they perceive, constructing categories of objects and events in the surrounding environment. We have already seen the glimmerings of this cognitive point of view in some of the evidence reviewed in this chapter. For example, older babies *interpret* a familiar face as a source of pleasure and affection and a pattern of blinking lights as a moving human being. We will save our discussion of infant cognition for the next chapter, acknowledging for now that the cognitive perspective also has merit in understanding the achievements of infancy. In fact, many researchers combine these two positions, regarding infant development as proceeding from a perceptual to a cognitive emphasis over the first year of life (Haith & Benson, 1998; Mandler, 1998).

Ask YOURSELF...

review   Cite evidence indicating that infants' expanding knowledge of objects and people influences their pattern perception.

apply   Not until age 2 months did Jana show keen interest in the bright wallpaper with detailed pictures on the wall of her room. What new visual abilities probably account for this change?

apply   After several weeks of crawling, Benjie learned to avoid going head-first down a steep incline. Now he has started to walk. Can his mother trust him not to try walking down the steep surface? Explain, using the concept of affordances.

connect   Motor development and perceptual development are closely linked. Provide as many examples as you can to support this statement.

Summary

BODY GROWTH

Describe major changes in body size, proportions, muscle–fat makeup, and skeletal growth over the first 2 years.

■ Height and weight gains are greater during the first 2 years than at any other time after birth. Physical growth of parts of the body follows **cephalocaudal** and **proximodistal trends.** Body fat is laid down quickly during the first 9 months, whereas muscle development is slow and gradual.

■ **Skeletal age,** a measure based on the number of **epiphyses** and the extent to which they are fused, is the best way to estimate the child's overall physical maturity. At birth, infants have six **fontanels,** which permit the skull bones to expand as the brain grows. The first tooth emerges around 4 to 6 months of age.

BRAIN DEVELOPMENT

Describe brain development during infancy and toddlerhood, at the level of individual brain cells and at the level of the cerebral cortex.

■ Early in development the brain grows faster than any other organ of the body. During infancy, **neurons** form **synapses,** or connections, at a rapid rate. During the peak period of synaptic growth in any brain area, many surrounding neurons die. Stimulation determines which neurons will survive and establish new synapses and which will lose their connective fibers through **synaptic pruning. Glial cells,** which are responsible for **myelinization,** multiply dramatically through the second year and contribute to large gains in brain weight.

■ Regions of the **cerebral cortex** develop in the same order in which various capacities emerge in the infant and child. Problems in early cortical functioning may lead to **sudden infant death syndrome,** a major cause of infant mortality. **Lateralization** refers to specialization of the hemispheres of the cortex. During the first few years, before many regions have taken on specialized roles, **brain plasticity** is high.

However, some lateralization exists at birth. Both heredity and early experience contribute to brain organization.

■ Gains in brain weight and skull size along with changes in neural activity indicate that brain growth spurts occur intermittently from infancy through adolescence. These may be sensitive periods in which appropriate stimulation is necessary for full development.

How does the organization of sleep and wakefulness change over the first 2 years?

■ Infants' changing arousal patterns are primarily affected by brain growth, but the social environment also plays a role. Short periods of sleep and wakefulness are put together and better coincide with a night and day schedule. Infants in Western nations sleep through the night much earlier than do babies throughout most of the world, who sleep with their parents.

FACTORS AFFECTING EARLY PHYSICAL GROWTH

Cite evidence indicating that heredity, nutrition, and parental affection and stimulation contribute to early physical growth.

■ Twin and adoption studies reveal that heredity contributes to body size and rate of physical maturation.

■ Breast milk is ideally suited to the growth needs of young babies and offers protection against disease. Breast-feeding prevents malnutrition and infant death in poverty-stricken areas of the world. Although breast-fed and bottle-fed babies do not differ in emotional adjustment, breast-fed babies are slightly advantaged in mental test performance.

■ Most chubby babies thin out during toddlerhood and early childhood. Infants and toddlers can eat nutritious foods freely, without risk of becoming overweight.

■ **Marasmus** and **kwashiorkor** are dietary diseases caused by malnutrition that affect

many children in developing countries. If allowed to continue, these diseases can cause body growth and brain development to be permanently stunted. **Nonorganic failure to thrive** illustrates the importance of parental affection and stimulation for normal physical growth.

LEARNING CAPACITIES

Describe infant learning capacities, the conditions under which they occur, and the unique value of each.

■ Classical conditioning enables infants to recognize which events usually occur together in the everyday world. In this form of learning, a neutral stimulus is paired with an **unconditioned stimulus (UCS)** that produces a reflexive, or **unconditioned response (UCR).** Once learning has occurred, the neutral stimulus, now called the **conditioned stimulus (CS),** elicits the response, which is called the **conditioned response (CR).** Young infants can be classically conditioned when the pairing of a UCS with a CS has a survival value, such as a feeding situation. However, classical conditioning of fear is difficult before 8 to 12 months.

■ **Operant conditioning** enables infants to explore and control their surroundings. In addition to food, interesting sights and sounds serve as effective **reinforcers,** increasing the occurrence of a response. **Punishment** involves removing a desirable stimulus or presenting an unpleasant one to decrease the occurrence of a response.

■ **Habituation** and **dishabituation** reveal that at birth, babies are attracted to novelty. Newborn infants also have a primitive ability to **imitate** the facial expressions and gestures of adults, a capacity that may promote social understanding and the early parent–infant relationship.

MOTOR DEVELOPMENT

Describe the general course of motor development during the first 2 years, along with factors that influence it.

Summary (continued)

- Like physical development, motor development follows the cephalocaudal and proximodistal trends. According to **dynamic systems theory of motor development,** new motor skills are a matter of combining existing skills into increasingly complex systems of action. Each new skill is a joint product of central nervous system development, movement possibilities of the body, the goal the child has in mind, and environmental supports for the skill.

- Movement opportunities and a stimulating environment profoundly affect motor development, as shown by research on infants raised in deprived institutions. Cultural values and child-rearing customs contribute to the emergence and refinement of early motor skills.

- During the first year, infants perfect their reaching and grasping. The poorly coordinated **prereaching** of the newborn period eventually drops out. As control of body posture and of arm and hand movements improves, voluntary reaching becomes more flexible and accurate, and the clumsy **ulnar grasp** is transformed into a refined **pincer grasp.**

- Young children are not physically and psychologically ready for toilet training until the end of the second or beginning of the third year of life.

PERCEPTUAL DEVELOPMENT

What changes in perception of speech sounds, depth, patterns, objects, and intermodal systems take place during infancy?

- Over the first year, infants organize sounds into more complex patterns. They also become more sensitive to the sounds and clause, phrase, and word units of their own language.

- Rapid development of the eye and visual centers in the brain supports the development of focusing, color discrimination, and visual acuity during the first half-year. The ability to track a moving object also improves.

- Research on depth perception reveals that responsiveness to motion develops first, followed by sensitivity to binocular and then pictorial cues. Experience in moving about independently promotes babies' three-dimensional understanding, including avoidance of edges and drop-offs (such as the deep side of the visual cliff) and memory for object locations.

- **Contrast sensitivity** accounts for babies' early pattern preferences. At first, infants look at the border of a stimulus and at single features. Around 2 months of age, they explore internal features of a pattern and start to detect pattern organization. Over time, they discriminate increasingly complex and meaningful patterns.

- Newborns prefer to look at and track simple, facelike stimuli, suggesting an innate tendency to orient toward human faces. At 2 to 3 months, with the capacity to combine pattern elements into organized wholes, they prefer a complex, stylized face to other stimulus arrangements. Gradually, they distinguish between faces and emotional expressions.

- At birth, **size** and **shape constancy** assist babies in building a coherent world of objects. At first, infants depend on motion and spatial arrangement to identify objects. After 4 months of age, they rely increasingly on other features, such as distinct shape, color, and texture.

- Infants have a remarkable, built-in capacity to engage in **intermodal perception.** They quickly combine information across sensory modalities, often after just one exposure to a new situation.

Explain differentiation theory of perceptual development.

- The Gibsons' **differentiation theory** is a widely accepted account of perceptual development. Over time, infants detect increasingly fine-grained, **invariant features** in a constantly changing perceptual world. Perception is guided by discovery of **affordances**—the action possibilities a situation offers the individual.

Important terms and concepts

affordances (p. 205)
brain plasticity (p. 175)
cephalocaudal trend (p. 171)
cerebral cortex (p. 175)
classical conditioning (p. 185)
conditioned response (CR) (p. 185)
conditioned stimulus (CS) (p. 185)
contrast sensitivity (p. 199)
differentiation theory (p. 205)
dishabituation (p. 187)
dynamic systems theory of motor
    development (p. 190)
epiphyses (p. 173)
extinction (p. 186)
fontanels (p. 173)

glial cells (p. 174)
habituation (p. 187)
imitation (p. 188)
intermodal perception (p. 204)
invariant features (p. 205)
kwashiorkor (p. 183)
lateralization (p. 175)
marasmus (p. 183)
myelinization (p. 174)
neurons (p. 173)
nonorganic failure to thrive (p. 184)
operant conditioning (p. 186)
pincer grasp (p. 194)
prereaching (p. 192)
proximodistal trend (p. 171)

punishment (p. 186)
reinforcer (p. 186)
shape constancy (p. 203)
size constancy (p. 203)
skeletal age (p. 173)
sudden infant death syndrome (SIDS)
    (p. 176)
synapses (p. 173)
synaptic pruning (p. 174)
ulnar grasp (p. 194)
unconditioned response (UCR)
    (p. 185)
unconditioned stimulus (UCS)
    (p. 185)

fyi . . . for further information and help

Consult the companion website for this book, where you will find additional weblinks and associated learning activities: www.abacon.com/berk

PHYSICAL GROWTH AND HEALTH

Healthy Mothers, Healthy Babies
www.hmhb.org

A coalition of national and state organizations concerned with maternal and child health. Serves as a network through which information on nutrition, injury prevention, and infant mortality is shared.

United Nations Children's Fund (UNICEF)
www.unicef.org

International organization dedicated to addressing the problems of children around the world. Develops and implements health and nutrition programs, campaigns to have children vaccinated against disease, and coordinates delivery of food and other aid to disaster-stricken areas.

World Health Organization (WHO)
www.who.int

International health agency of the United Nations that seeks to obtain the highest level of health care for all people. Promotes prevention and treatment of disease and strives to eliminate poverty. Places special emphasis on the health needs of developing countries.

Zero to Three
www.zerotothree.org

An organization that promotes the healthy development of infants and children from birth to 3 years of age. Provides information on many aspects of early development.

BREAST-FEEDING

La Leche League International
www.lalecheleague.org

International organization that provides information and support to breast-feeding mothers. Local chapters exist in many cities.

MALNUTRITION

Food Research and Action Center
www.frac.org

Provides assistance to community organizations trying to make federal food programs more responsive to the needs of millions of hungry Americans. Seeks to enhance public awareness of the problems of hunger and poverty in the United States.

SUDDEN INFANT DEATH SYNDROME (SIDS)

SIDS Network, Inc.
www.sids-network.org

Provides assistance to parents who have lost a child to SIDS. Works with families and health professionals in caring for infants at risk due to heart and respiratory problems.

National Sudden Infant Death Syndrome (SIDS) Resource Center
www.circsol.com/sids

Provides information on SIDS and related topics, including referral services.

"Happy Spring"

Soledad Urán

11 years, Argentina

Wide-eyed with amazement, a newly-walking toddler watches as his older sister plays with the family puppy. In Chapter 6, you will see that a stimulating environment combined with the guidance of more mature members of their culture ensures that young children's cognition will develop at its best.

Reprinted by permission from The International Museum of Children's Art, Oslo, Norway

Cognitive Development in Infancy and Toddlerhood

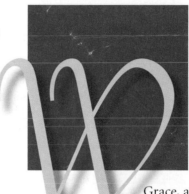

When Caitlin, Grace, and Timmy gathered at Ginette's child-care home, the playroom was alive with activity. The three spirited explorers, each nearly 18 months old, were bent on discovery. Grace dropped shapes through holes in a plastic box that Ginette held and adjusted so the harder ones would fall smoothly into place. Once a few shapes were inside, Grace grabbed and shook the box, squealing with delight as the lid fell open and the shapes scattered around her. The clatter attracted Timmy, who picked up a shape, carried it to the railing at the top of the basement steps, and dropped it overboard, then followed with a teddy bear, a ball, his shoe, and a spoon. In the meantime, Caitlin opened a drawer, unloaded a set of wooden bowls, stacked them in a pile, knocked it over, then banged two bowls together like cymbals. With each action, the children seemed to be asking, "How do things work? What makes interesting events happen? Which ones can I control?"

As the toddlers experimented, I could see the beginnings of language—a whole new way of influencing the world. Caitlin was the most vocal. "All gone baw!" she exclaimed as Timmy tossed the bright red ball down the basement steps. "Bye-bye," Grace chimed in, waving as the ball disappeared from sight. Later in the day, Grace revealed that she could use words and gestures to pretend. "Night-night," she said as she put her head down and closed her eyes, ever so pleased that in make-believe, she could decide for herself when and where to go to bed.

Over the first 2 years, the small, reflexive newborn baby becomes a self-assertive, purposeful being who solves simple problems and starts to master the most amazing human ability: language. Parents often wonder, "How does all this happen so quickly?" This question has also captivated researchers, yielding a wealth of findings along with vigorous debate over how to explain the astonishing pace of infant and toddler cognition.

In this chapter we take up three perspectives on early cognitive development: Piaget's *cognitive-developmental theory, information processing,* and Vygotsky's *sociocultural theory.* We will also consider the usefulness of tests that measure infants' and toddlers' intellectual progress. Our discussion concludes with the beginnings of language. We will see how toddlers' first words build on early cognitive achievements and how, very soon, new words and expressions increase the speed and flexibility of their thinking. Throughout development, cognition and language mutually support one another.

Piaget's Cognitive-Developmental Theory

Swiss theorist Jean Piaget inspired a vision of children as busy, motivated explorers whose thinking develops as they act directly on the environment. Influenced by his background in biology, he believed that the child's mind forms and modifies psychological structures to achieve a better adaptive fit with external reality. In the following sections we will first describe development as Piaget saw it. Then we will consider evidence indicating that the cognition of young infants is more advanced than Piaget imagined it to be.

KEY PIAGETIAN CONCEPTS

According to Piaget, between infancy and adolescence, children move through four stages of development. As the name **sensorimotor stage** implies, Piaget believed that infants and toddlers "think" with their eyes, ears, hands, and other sensorimotor equipment. They cannot yet carry out many activities inside their heads. But by the end of toddlerhood, children can solve practical, everyday problems and represent their experiences in speech, gesture, and play. To understand Piaget's view of how these vast changes take place, let's look at his ideas about development.

■ **WHAT CHANGES WITH DEVELOPMENT.** Piaget believed that *psychological structures*— the child's organized ways of making sense of experience—change with age. He referred to specific structures as **schemes.** At first, schemes are motor action patterns. For example, at age 6 months, Timmy dropped objects in a fairly rigid way, simply by letting go of a rattle or teething ring and watching with interest. By age 18 months, his "dropping scheme" had become much more deliberate and creative. He tossed all sorts of objects down the basement stairs, throwing some up in the air, bouncing others off walls, releasing some gently and others forcefully. Soon his schemes will move from an *action-based level* to a *mental level.* Instead of just acting on objects, he will show evidence of thinking before he acts. This change, as we will see later, marks the transition from sensorimotor to preoperational thought.

■ **HOW COGNITIVE CHANGE TAKES PLACE.** In Piaget's theory, two processes account for changes in schemes: *adaptation* and *organization.*

---

sensorimotor stage
Piaget's first stage, during which infants and toddlers "think" with their eyes, ears, hands, and other sensorimotor equipment. Spans the first 2 years of life.

scheme
In Piaget's theory, a specific structure, or organized way of making sense of experience, that changes with age.

adaptation
In Piaget's theory, the process of building schemes through direct interaction with the environment. Made up of two complementary processes: assimilation and accommodation.

Adaptation.   The next time you have a chance, notice how infants and toddlers tirelessly repeat actions that lead to interesting effects. **Adaptation** involves building schemes through direct interaction with the environment. It consists of two complementary activities: *assimilation* and *accommodation.* During **assimilation,** we use our current schemes to interpret the external world. For example, when Timmy dropped objects, he was assimilating them all into his sensorimotor dropping scheme. In **accommodation,** we create new schemes or adjust old ones after noticing that our current ways of thinking do not fit the environment completely. When Timmy dropped objects in different ways, he modified his dropping scheme to take account of the varied properties of objects.

According to Piaget, the balance between assimilation and accommodation varies over time. When children are not changing very much, they assimilate more than they accommodate. Piaget called this a state of cognitive *equilibrium,* implying a steady, comfortable condition. During times of rapid cognitive change, however, children are in a state of *disequilibrium,* or cognitive discomfort. They realize that new information does not match their current schemes, so they shift away from assimilation toward accommodation. Once they have modified their schemes, they move back toward assimilation, exercising their newly changed structures until they are ready to be modified again.

Each time this back-and-forth movement between equilibrium and disequilibrium occurs, more effective schemes are produced (Piaget, 1985). Because the times of greatest accommodation are the earliest ones, the sensorimotor stage is Piaget's most complex period of development.

© 2000 LAURA DWIGHT

According to Piaget's theory, at first schemes are motor action patterns. As this 1-year-old takes apart, bangs, and drops these containers, he discovers that his movements have predictable effects on objects and that objects influence one another in regular ways.

Organization.   Schemes change through a second process called **organization.** It takes place internally, apart from direct contact with the environment. Once children form new schemes, they rearrange them, linking them with other schemes to create a strongly interconnected cognitive system. For example, eventually Timmy will relate "dropping" to "throwing" and to his developing understanding of "nearness" and "farness." According to Piaget, schemes reach a true state of equilibrium when they become part of a broad network of structures that can be jointly applied to the surrounding world (Piaget, 1936/1952).

THE SENSORIMOTOR STAGE

The difference between the newborn baby and the 2-year-old child is so vast that the sensorimotor stage is divided into six substages. Piaget's observations of his own three children served as the basis for this sequence of development. Although this is a very small sample, Piaget watched carefully and also presented his son and two daughters with everyday problems (such as hidden objects) that helped reveal their understanding of the world. In the following sections we will first describe infant development as Piaget saw it. Then we will consider evidence that the cognitive competence of babies is more advanced than Piaget believed it to be.

■ **THE CIRCULAR REACTION.**   At the beginning of the sensorimotor stage, infants know so little about their world that they cannot purposefully explore it. The **circular reaction** provides them with a means of adapting their first schemes. It involves stumbling onto a new experience caused by their own motor activity. The reaction is "circular" because they try to repeat the event again and again. As a result, a sensorimotor response that first occurred by chance becomes strengthened into a new scheme. Consider Caitlin, who at age 2 months accidentally made a smacking sound after a feeding. The sound was new and intriguing, so Caitlin tried to repeat it until, after a few days, she became quite expert at smacking her lips.

During the first 2 years, the circular reaction changes in several ways. At first it centers around the infant's own body. Later it turns outward, toward manipulation of objects. Finally it becomes experimental and creative, aimed at producing novel effects in the environment.

assimilation
That part of adaptation in which the external world is interpreted in terms of current schemes.

accommodation
That part of adaptation in which new schemes are created and old ones adjusted to produce a better fit with the environment.

organization
In Piaget's theory, the internal rearrangement and linking together of schemes so that they form a strongly interconnected cognitive system.

circular reaction
In Piaget's theory, a means of building schemes in which infants try to repeat a chance event caused by their own motor activity.

TABLE 6.1

Summary of Piaget's Sensorimotor Stage

SENSORIMOTOR SUBSTAGE	TYPICAL ADAPTIVE BEHAVIORS
1. Reflexive schemes (birth to 1 month)	Newborn reflexes (see Chapter 4, page 153)
2. Primary circular reactions (1–4 months)	Simple motor habits centered around the infant's own body; limited anticipation of events
3. Secondary circular reactions (4–8 months)	Actions aimed at repeating interesting effects in the surrounding world; imitation of familiar behaviors
4. Coordination of secondary circular reactions (8–12 months)	Intentional, or goal-directed behavior; improved anticipation of events; imitation of behaviors slightly different from those the infant usually performs; ability to find a hidden object in the first location in which it is hidden (object permanence)
5. Tertiary circular reactions (12–18 months)	Exploration of the properties of objects by acting on them in novel ways; imitation of unfamiliar behaviors; ability to search in several locations for a hidden object (accurate AB search)
6. Mental representation (18 months–2 years)	Internal representation of objects and events, as indicated by sudden solutions to sensorimotor problems; ability to find an object that has been moved while out of sight; deferred imitation; and make-believe play

FIGURE 6.1

The newborn baby's schemes consist of reflexes, which will gradually be modified as they are applied to the surrounding environment.

intentional, or goal-directed, behavior A sequence of actions in which schemes are deliberately combined to solve a problem.

physical causality The causal action one object exerts on another through contact.

Piaget considered these revisions in the circular reaction so important that he named the sensorimotor substages after them. As you read about each substage, you may find it helpful to refer to the summary in Table 6.1.

■ **SUBSTAGE 1: REFLEXIVE SCHEMES (BIRTH TO 1 MONTH).** Piaget regarded newborn reflexes as the building blocks of sensorimotor intelligence. At first, babies suck, grasp, and look in much the same way, no matter what experiences they encounter (see Figure 6.1). Carolyn reported an amusing example of Caitlin's indiscriminate sucking at 2 weeks of age. She lay on the bed next to her father while he took a nap. Suddenly, he awoke with a start. Caitlin had latched on and begun to suck on his back!

■ **SUBSTAGE 2: PRIMARY CIRCULAR REACTIONS—THE FIRST LEARNED ADAPTATIONS (1 TO 4 MONTHS).** Infants start to gain voluntary control over their actions by repeating chance behaviors that lead to satisfying results. Consequently, they develop some simple motor habits, such as sucking their fists or thumbs and opening and closing their hands (see Figure 6.2). Babies at this substage also begin to vary their behavior in response to environmental demands. For example, they open their mouths differently for a nipple than for a spoon. Furthermore, infants begin to anticipate events. At age 3 months, when Timmy awoke from his nap, he cried out with hunger. But as soon as Vanessa entered the room and moved toward his crib, Timmy stopped crying. He knew that feeding time was near.

Piaget called the first circular reactions *primary,* and he regarded them as quite limited. Notice how, in the examples just given, infants' adaptations are oriented toward their own bodies and motivated by basic needs. According to Piaget, babies of this age are not yet very concerned with the effects of their actions on the external world.

FIGURE 6.2

At 2 months, Timmy sees his hand open and close and tries to repeat this action, in a primary circular reaction.

■ **SUBSTAGE 3: SECONDARY CIRCULAR REACTIONS—MAKING INTERESTING SIGHTS LAST (4 TO 8 MONTHS).** Between 4 and 8 months, infants sit up and become skilled at reaching for, grasping, and manipulating objects. These motor achievements play a major role in turning their attention outward toward the environment. Using the *secondary circular reaction,* they try to repeat interesting effects in the surrounding world that they cause by their own actions. For example, 4-month-old Caitlin accidentally knocked several toys Carolyn dangled in front of her, producing a swinging motion. Over the next 3 days, Caitlin tried to repeat this fascinating effect, at first by grasping and then by waving her arms and shaking herself. Finally, she succeeded in hitting a stuffed bear and gleefully repeated the motion (see Figure 6.3). She had built the hitting scheme.

FIGURE 6.3

At 4 months, Piaget's son Laurent accidentally hits a doll hung in front of him. He tries to recapture the interesting effect of the swinging doll. In doing so, he builds a new "hitting scheme" through the secondary circular reaction.

Improved control over their own behavior permits infants of this substage to imitate the behavior of others more effectively. However, they cannot adapt flexibly and quickly enough to imitate very novel behaviors (Kaye & Marcus, 1981). Therefore, although 4- to 8-month-olds enjoy watching an adult demonstrate a game of pat-a-cake or peekaboo, they are not yet able to participate.

■ **SUBSTAGE 4: COORDINATION OF SECONDARY CIRCULAR REACTIONS (8 TO 12 MONTHS).** Now infants start to organize schemes, combining secondary circular reactions into new, more complex action sequences. As a result, two landmark cognitive changes take place.

First, babies can engage in **intentional,** or **goal-directed, behavior.** By 8 months, infants have had enough practice with a variety of schemes that they combine them deliberately to solve sensorimotor problems. The clearest example is provided by Piaget's object-hiding tasks, in which he shows the baby an attractive toy and then hides it behind his hand or under a cover. Infants at this substage can find the object. In doing so, they coordinate two schemes—pushing aside the obstacle and grasping the toy. Piaget regarded these *means–end action sequences* as the first sign that babies appreciate **physical causality** (the causal action one object exerts on another through contact) and as the foundation for all later problem solving.

Second, when infants can retrieve hidden objects, they have begun to attain **object permanence,** the understanding that objects continue to exist when they are out of sight (see Figure 6.4). But awareness of object permanence is not yet complete. If an object is moved from one hiding place (A) to another (B), 8- to 12-month-olds will search for it only in the first hiding place (A). Because babies make this **A-not-B search error,** Piaget concluded that they do not have a clear image of the object as persisting when hidden from view.

FIGURE 6.4

Around 8 months, infants combine schemes deliberately in the solution of sensorimotor problems. They show an understanding of object permanence, since they can find an object in the first place in which it is hidden.

Substage 4 brings additional advances. First, infants anticipate events better, so they sometimes use their new capacity for intentional behavior to try to change those events. At 10 months, Timmy crawled after Vanessa when she put on her coat, whimpering to keep her from leaving. Second, babies can imitate behaviors slightly different from those they usually perform. After watching someone else, they try to stir with a spoon, push a toy car, or drop raisins in a cup. Once again, they draw on their capacity for intentional behavior, purposefully modifying schemes to fit an observed action (Piaget, 1945/1951).

■ **SUBSTAGE 5: TERTIARY CIRCULAR REACTIONS—DISCOVERING NEW MEANS THROUGH ACTIVE EXPERIMENTATION (12 TO 18 MONTHS).** At this substage, the circular reaction—now called *tertiary*—becomes experimental and creative. Toddlers repeat behaviors *with variation,* provoking new effects. Recall how Timmy dropped objects over the basement steps, trying this, then that, and then another action (see Figure 6.5 on page 216). Because they approach the world in this deliberately exploratory way, 12- to 18-month-olds are far better sensorimotor problem solvers than they were before. For example, Grace figured out how to fit a shape through a hole in a container by turning and twisting it until it fell through, and she discovered how to use a stick to get toys that were out of reach.

object permanence
The understanding that objects continue to exist when they are out of sight.

A-not-B search error
The error made by 8- to 12-month-olds after an object is moved from hiding place A to hiding place B. Infants in Piaget's Substage 4 search for it only in the first hiding place (A).

FIGURE 6.5

At 18 months, Timmy dropped a variety of objects down the basement stairs, throwing some up in the air, bouncing others off the wall, releasing some gently and others forcefully, in a deliberately experimental approach. Timmy displayed a tertiary circular reaction.

According to Piaget, this new capacity to experiment leads to a more advanced understanding of object permanence. Toddlers look in not just one but several locations to find a hidden toy; now they engage in an accurate AB search. Their more flexible action patterns also permit them to imitate many more behaviors, such as stacking blocks, scribbling on paper, and making funny faces.

■ **SUBSTAGE 6: MENTAL REPRESENTATION—INVENTING NEW MEANS THROUGH MENTAL COMBINATIONS (18 MONTHS TO 2 YEARS).** Substage 5 is the last truly *sensorimotor* stage, since Substage 6 brings with it the ability to create **mental representations** of reality—internal images of absent objects and past events. The Substage 6 toddler can solve problems symbolically instead of by trial-and-error. One sign of this new capacity is that children arrive at solutions to sensorimotor problems suddenly, suggesting that they experiment with actions inside their heads. For example, at 19 months, Grace received a new push toy. As she played with it for the first time, she rolled it over the carpet and ran into the sofa. She paused for a moment, as if to "think," and then immediately turned the toy in a new direction. Had she been in Substage 5, she would have pushed, pulled, and bumped it in a random fashion until it was free to move again.

With the capacity to represent, toddlers have a more advanced understanding of object permanence—that objects can move or be moved when out of sight. Try this object-hiding task with an 18- to 24-month-old as well as a younger child: Put a small toy inside a box and the box under a cover. Then, while the box is out of sight, dump the toy out, leave it under the cover, and show the toddler the empty box. The Substage 6 child finds the hidden toy easily. Younger toddlers are baffled by this situation.

Mental representation also brings with it the capacity for **deferred imitation**—the ability to remember and copy the behavior of models who are not immediately present. A famous and amusing example comes from Jacqueline, Piaget's daughter:

> Jacqueline had a visit from a little boy . . . who, in the course of the afternoon, got into a terrible temper. He screamed as he tried to get out of a playpen and pushed it backwards, stamping his feet. Jacqueline stood watching him in amazement. . . . The next day, she herself screamed in her playpen and tried to move it, stamping her foot lightly. (Piaget, 1936/1952, p. 63)

Finally, the sixth substage leads to a major change in play. Throughout the first year and a half, infants and toddlers engage in **functional play**—pleasurable motor activity with or without objects through which they practice sensorimotor schemes. At the end of the second year, children's growing capacity to represent experience permits them to engage in **make-believe play,** in which they act out everyday and imaginary activities. Like Grace's pretending to go to sleep at the beginning of this chapter, the make-believe of the toddler is very simple (see Figure 6.6). Make-believe expands greatly in early childhood, and it is so important for psychological development that we will return to it.

FIGURE 6.6

When Grace engaged in make-believe by pretending to go to sleep, she created a mental representation of reality. With the capacity for mental representation, the sensorimotor stage draws to a close.

RECENT RESEARCH ON SENSORIMOTOR DEVELOPMENT

Many studies show that infants display a wide array of understandings earlier than Piaget believed. For example, recall the operant conditioning research reviewed in Chapter 5, in which newborns sucked vigorously on a nipple to gain access to interesting sights and sounds. This behavior, which closely resembles Piaget's secondary circular reaction, shows that babies try to explore and control the external world long before 4 to 8 months. In fact, they do so as soon as they are born.

Piaget may have underestimated infant capacities because he did not have the sophisticated experimental techniques that are available today. As we consider recent research on sensorimotor development as well as information processing, we will see that operant conditioning and the habituation–dishabituation sequence have been used ingeniously to find out what the young baby knows.

Habituation Events

Short-carrot event

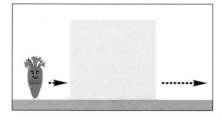

Tall-carrot event

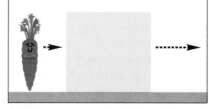

(a)

Test Events

Possible event

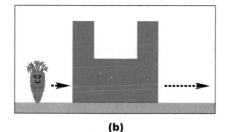

Impossible event

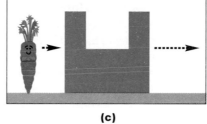

(b)   (c)

FIGURE 6.7

Testing infants for understanding of object permanence using the violation-of-expectation method. (a) First, infants were habituated to two events: a short carrot and a tall carrot moving behind a yellow screen, on alternative trials. Next the researchers presented two test events. The color of the screen was changed to help infants notice its window. (b) In the *possible event,* the carrot shorter than the window's lower edge moved behind the blue screen and reappeared on the other side. (c) In the *impossible event,* the carrot taller than the window's lower edge moved behind the screen, did not appear in the window, but then emerged intact on the other side. Infants as young as 3½ months dishabituated to (looked longer at) the impossible event, suggesting that they understood object permanence. (Adapted from R. Baillargeon & J. DeVos, 1991, "Object Permanence in Young Infants: Further Evidence," *Child Development, 62,* p. 1230. © The Society for Research in Child Development. Reprinted by permission.)

■ **REASONING ABOUT THE PHYSICAL WORLD.** Piaget concluded that not until 8 to 12 months of age do infants appreciate important regularities of their physical world—that objects continue to exist when out of sight and influence one another in predictable ways. Yet as findings reported in the following sections reveal, even very young babies are knowledgeable about object characteristics if procedures are used that do not require them to search actively for and obtain hidden objects.

To identify infants' grasp of object permanence and other aspects of physical reasoning, researchers often use a **violation-of-expectation method,** in which they habituate babies to a physical event and then determine whether they dishabituate to (look longer at) a possible event (a variation of the first event that follows physical laws) or an impossible event (a variation that violates physical laws). Dishabituation to the impossible event suggests surprise at a deviation from reality and, therefore, awareness of that aspect of physical reality.

Object Permanence. In a series of studies using the violation-of-expectation method, Renée Baillargeon and her collaborators found evidence for object permanence in the first few months of life. In one of Baillargeon's studies, described in Figure 6.7, 3½-month-olds indicated by their looking behavior that they understood that an object moved behind a screen continues to exist (Baillargeon & DeVos, 1991). Even 2½-month-olds display this understanding if the screens behind which the objects move are simplified (Aguiar & Baillargeon, 1999).

If 2- and 3-month-olds grasp the idea of object permanence, then what explains Piaget's finding that much older infants (who are quite capable of voluntary reaching) do not try to search for hidden objects? One explanation is that, just as Piaget's theory suggests, before 8 months infants cannot put together the separate schemes—pushing aside the obstacle and grasping the object—necessary to retrieve a hidden toy. In other words, what they *know* about object permanence is not yet *evident* in their searching behavior (Baillargeon et al., 1990). In support of this idea, when researchers simplify the search part of the task by reducing it to one action—permitting babies to reach directly for an object in the dark after hearing a sound signaling its location—even 6½-month-olds easily retrieve the object (Goubet & Clifton, 1998).

mental representation
An internal image of an absent object or a past event.

deferred imitation
The ability to remember and copy the behavior of models who are not immediately present.

functional play
A type of play involving pleasurable motor activity with or without objects. Enables infants and toddlers to practice sensorimotor schemes.

make-believe play
A type of play in which children pretend, acting out everyday and imaginary activities.

violation-of-expectation method
A method in which researchers habituate infants to a physical event and then determine whether they dishabituate to (look longer at) a possible event that conforms to physical laws or an impossible event that violates physical laws. Dishabituation to an impossible event suggests awareness of that aspect of physical reality.

Still, 8- to 12-month olds do not search for hidden objects under all conditions. They readily uncover an object after an experimenter places a cloth over it. Yet many do not search after the experimenter holds the object, moves it under a cloth, deposits the object, and shows the baby the empty palm (Moore & Meltzoff, 1999). This suggests that babies first understand object permanence in two ways: (1) an object still exists after being hidden if it stays on a consistent path of movement (as in the example in Figure 6.7), and (2) an object still exists after being hidden if it remains in the same location. Notice that an object covered by a cloth is in the same place when uncovered, but an object not in a palm when the hand reappears violates the baby's expectations! Indeed, many babies turn away from the empty palm, avoiding this confusing event.

In sum, although a beginning appreciation of object permanence is present early, a full understanding comes gradually. As we will see next, the A-not-B search error provides further evidence that at first, infants' object-permanence performance is limited to certain task conditions. Only later do infants succeed in obtaining hidden objects in increasingly complex and subtle situations.

Searching for Objects Hidden in More Than One Location.

For some years, researchers thought that babies made the A-not-B search error because they had trouble remembering an object's new location after it was hidden in more than one place. But recent findings reveal that poor memory cannot fully account for infants' unsuccessful performance. Between 5 and 12 months, babies increasingly *look* at the correct location while *reaching* incorrectly (Hofstadter & Reznick, 1996). And in violation-of-expectation procedures, in which an experimenter hides a toy at A, moves it to B, and then retrieves it either from B (possible event) or from A (impossible event), 8- to 12-month-olds look longer at the impossible event (Ahmed & Ruffman, 1998). This indicates that they remember where the object was last hidden (at B) and expect it to be there.

Perhaps babies search at A (where they first found the object) instead of B (its most recent location) because they have trouble inhibiting a previously rewarded response (Diamond, Cruttenden, & Neiderman, 1994). A more comprehensive explanation is that a complex, dynamic system of factors—memory for a previous reach, continuing to look at A, a hiding place at B that looks similar to the one at A, and a constant body posture—increase the chances that the baby will make the error. In a series of studies, disrupting any one of these factors increased 10-month-olds' searching at B (Smith et al., 1999).

Once again, before 12 months, infants have difficulty translating what they *know* about an object moving from one place to another into a successful search strategy under a broad range of task circumstances. The ability to integrate knowledge with action coincides with rapid development of the frontal lobes of the cerebral cortex at the end of the first year (Bell, 1998; Diamond, 1991). Also crucial are a wide variety of experiences perceiving, acting on, and remembering objects.

Other Aspects of Physical Reasoning.

The violation-of-expectation method suggests that young infants are aware of many object properties and the rules governing their behavior. For example, 3- to 4-month-olds realize that one solid object cannot move through another solid object. By 5 to 6 months, infants also appreciate that an object much larger than an opening cannot pass through that opening. Furthermore, in the first half-year, infants are sensitive to the effects of gravity. They look intently when a moving object stops in midair without support (Sitskoorn & Smitsman, 1995; Spelke et al., 1992).

In the next few months, infants apply these understandings to a wider range of circumstances. For example, with respect to gravity, 7-month-olds are aware that an object on a sloping surface will roll down, not up (Kim & Spelke, 1992). And as Figure 6.8 shows, between 6 and 7 months, infants realize that an object placed on top of another object will fall unless a large part of its bottom surface contacts the lower object (Baillargeon, 1994a).

A beginning grasp of physical causality also develops around the middle of the first year. Around 5 to 7 months, babies realize that when a moving ball collides with a stationary ball, it causes the stationary ball to be displaced immediately along the same path of movement. Infants of this age also figure out that a larger moving object can cause a stationary object to

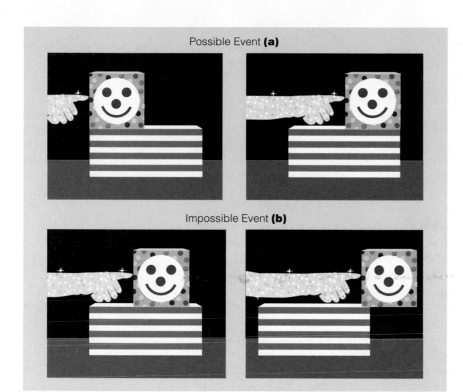

Possible Event **(a)**

Impossible Event **(b)**

FIGURE 6.8

Testing infants' understanding of object support using the violation-of-expectation method. First, infants were habituated to an event in which a hand pushed an attractive box partway across a long platform (not shown). Next, the researchers presented two test events in which the hand pushed the box across a shorter platform. (a) In the *possible event,* the hand pushed the box until its leading edge reached the end of the platform, so it remained fully supported. (b) In the *impossible event,* the hand pushed the box until only 15 percent of its bottom surface remained on the platform. Results indicated that 5½-month-olds looked equally at the two test events. In contrast, 6½-month-olds dishabituated to the impossible event, suggesting that they expect the object to fall unless a large portion of its bottom surface lies on the platform. (From R. Baillargeon, A. Needham, & J. DeVos, 1992, "The Development of Young Infants' Intuitions About Support," *Early Development and Parenting, 1,* p. 71. Copyright © 1992 John Wiley & Sons Limited. Reproduced with permission.)

travel farther (Cohen & Amsel, 1998; Kotovsky & Baillargeon, 1998). By 10 months, babies realize that if a moving ball hits a stationary ball off-center, the second ball will be deflected at an angle (Oakes & Cohen, 1995). Finally, between 10 and 15 months, toddlers appreciate three-step causal chains—that a toy vehicle can launch a second vehicle that, on impact with a toy doghouse, can cause a puppy's face to pop out (Cohen et al., 1999).

Clearly, infants appreciate the regularities of their physical world. Basic understandings— that objects continue to exist when hidden from view, cannot move through the space occupied by other solid objects, fall without support, and move along continuous paths—are present before 8 to 12 months, the age range of Piaget's Substage 4 (Haith & Benson, 1998). They are gradually refined during the second half-year.

■ **MENTAL REPRESENTATION.** In Piaget's theory, infants lead purely sensorimotor lives. They cannot represent experience until about 18 months of age. Yet new studies of deferred imitation and problem solving reveal that the transition to mental representation takes place earlier.

Deferred Imitation. Piaget studied imitation by noting when his three children demonstrated it in their everyday behavior. Under these conditions, a great deal must be known about the infant's daily life to be sure that deferred imitation has occurred.

Research reveals that deferred imitation, a form of representation, is present at 6 weeks of age! Infants who watched an unfamiliar adult's facial expression imitated the facial gesture when exposed to the same adult 24 hours later (Meltzoff & Moore, 1994). Perhaps young babies use this way of imitating to identify and communicate with people they have seen before.

As motor capacities improve, infants start to copy adults' actions on objects. In one study, 6- and 9-month-olds were shown an "activity" board with twelve novel objects secured to it—for example, a frog whose legs jump when a cord is pulled and an owl whose eyes flash when its belly is pushed. An experimenter modeled the actions of six objects. When tested 24 hours later, babies of both ages were far more likely to produce the actions they had seen than actions associated with objects that had not been demonstrated (Collie & Hayne, 1999). The babies retained and enacted not just one but, on average, three modeled behaviors.

[handwritten note: Deferred imitation—babies learn behavior from adults, then imitate that behavior.]

Deferred imitation greatly enriches young children's adaptations to their surrounding world. This toddler probably watched an adult watering flowers. Later, he imitates the behavior, having learned through observation what the sprinkling can is for.

By 14 to 15 months, toddlers use deferred imitation skillfully to enrich their range of schemes. They retain modeled behaviors for several months, copy the actions of peers as well as adults, and imitate across a change in context—for example, enact in the home a behavior learned at child care or on TV and generalize actions to similar objects varying in size and color (Barnat, Klein, & Meltzoff, 1996; Barr & Hayne, 1999; Hanna & Meltzoff, 1993).

Around 18 months, toddlers imitate not only an adult's behavior but the actions he or she *tries* to produce, even if these actions are not fully realized (Meltzoff, 1995). On one occasion, Ginette attempted to pour some raisins into a small bag but missed, spilling them onto the counter. A moment later, Grace climbed on a stool and began dropping the raisins into the bag, indicating that she had begun to infer others' intentions and perspectives. By age 2, children mimic entire social roles—such as mommy, daddy, or baby—during make-believe play.

Problem Solving. As Piaget indicated, infants develop intentional, means–end action sequences around 7 to 8 months, using them to solve simple problems, such as obtaining a toy resting on the far end of a cloth by pulling on the cloth (Willatts, 1999). Soon after, infants' representational skills permit more effective problem solving than Piaget's substages suggest. By 10 to 12 months, they can *solve problems by analogy*—take a strategy from one problem and apply it to other relevant problems. In one study, babies were given three similar problems, each requiring them to overcome a barrier, grasp a string, and pull it to get an attractive toy. The problems differed in all aspects of their specific features (see Figure 6.9). On the first problem, the parent demonstrated the solution and encouraged the infant to imitate. Babies obtained the toy more readily on each additional problem (Chen, Sanchez, & Campbell, 1997).

With age, children can better reason by analogy, applying relevant strategies across increasingly dissimilar situations (Goswami, 1996). But even in the first year, infants have some ability to move beyond trial-and-error experimentation, mentally represent a problem solution, and use it in new contexts.

FIGURE 6.9

Analogical problem solving by 10- to 12-month-olds. After the parent demonstrated the solution to problem (a), infants solved (b) and (c) with increasing efficiency, even though those problems differed in all aspects of their superficial features. (From Z. Chen, R. P. Sanchez, & T. Campbell, 1997, "From Beyond to Within Their Grasp: The Rudiments of Analogical Problem Solving in 10- to 13-month-olds," *Developmental Psychology, 33,* 790–801. Figure 1 (adapted), p. 792. Copyright © 1997 by the American Psychological Association. Adapted by permission of the publisher and author.)

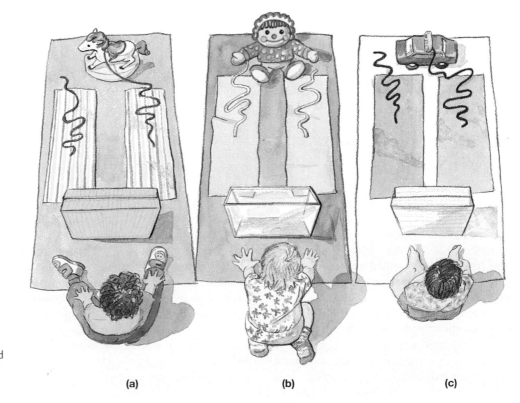

(a)   (b)   (c)

TABLE 6.2

Some Cognitive Attainments of Infancy and Toddlerhood

AGE	COGNITIVE ATTAINMENTS
Birth–1 month	Secondary circular reactions using limited motor skills, such as sucking a nipple to gain access to interesting sights and sounds
1–4 months	Awareness of many object properties and the rules governing their behavior, including object permanence, object solidity, and gravity; deferred imitation of an adult's facial expression after a short delay
4–8 months	Improved understanding of object permanence, object solidity, gravity, and object support; awareness of physical causality; deferred imitation of an adult's novel actions on objects after a short delay
8–12 months	Improved understanding of physical causality; ability to solve sensorimotor problems by analogy to a previous similar problem
12–18 months	Deferred imitation of an adult's novel actions on objects after a long delay (several months) and across a change in context
18 months–2 years	Deferred imitation of actions an adult tries to produce, even if these are not fully realized, indicating a beginning capacity to infer others' intentions and perspectives

Note: Which of the capacities listed in the table indicate that mental representation emerges earlier than predicted by Piaget's sensorimotor substages?

EVALUATION OF THE SENSORIMOTOR STAGE

Table 6.2 summarizes the remarkable cognitive attainments we have just considered. Compare this table with the description of Piaget's sensorimotor substages on page 214. You will see that infants anticipate events; display means–end problem solving; find hidden objects; flexibly vary their sensorimotor schemes; and engage in make-believe play within Piaget's time frame. Yet many other capacities—including secondary circular reactions, understanding of object properties (including permanence and physical causality), deferred imitation, and problem solving using mental representation (analogy)—emerge earlier than Piaget expected.

Notice, also, that the cognitive attainments of infancy and toddlerhood do not develop in the neat, stepwise fashion Piaget predicted. For example, deferred imitation and the beginnings of analogical problem solving are present long before toddlers can solve Piaget's most advanced object-hiding task. To obtain an object that has been moved while out of sight, infants must move beyond recall of a past event to a more complex form of representation; they must *imagine an event they have not seen* (Rast & Meltzoff, 1995). Yet Piaget assumed that all representational capacities develop at the same time, in Substage 6. These findings, and others like them, are among an accumulating body of evidence that questions Piaget's stages.

Disagreements between Piaget's observations and those of recent researchers raise controversial questions about how early development takes place. Consistent with Piaget's ideas, motor development facilitates the construction of some types of knowledge. For example, in Chapter 5 we noted that crawling babies are better than noncrawling peers at perceiving depth on the visual cliff and finding hidden objects. Yet we have also seen that infants comprehend a great deal before they are capable of the motor behaviors that Piaget assumed led to those understandings. How can we account for babies' amazing cognitive accomplishments? Let's explore three prominent ideas.

■ **A PERCEPTUAL VIEW.** Some researchers believe that infants build early schemes by looking and listening rather than just acting on the world. At the same time, they preserve Piaget's belief that the baby *constructs* new understandings.

Renée Baillargeon (1994b, 1995, 1998) argues that infants come to understand their physical world by first making all-or-none distinctions, to which they add as they are exposed to

ELIZABETH CREWS

Did this toddler figure out that one container can rest on top of another through rich, constructive interaction with objects, as Piaget assumed? Or did he begin life with innate knowledge that enables him to grasp the regularities of his physical world with very little hands-on exploration? The future is likely to bring compromises between these clashing viewpoints.

modular view of the mind
A nativist view that regards the mind as a collection of separate modules, or genetically prewired neural systems in the brain, each equipped with structures for making sense of a certain type of knowledge.

relevant information. At 3 months Caitlin realized that an object will fall when released in midair and stop falling when it contacts a surface, because she had seen adults drop toys in baskets and clothes in hampers many times. But not until the middle of the first year, when she could sit independently and put objects on surfaces herself, did she have a chance to observe that an object will fall unless much of its bottom surface is supported.

According to Lisa Oakes and Leslie Cohen, an appreciation of physical causality develops similarly (Cohen, 1998; Oakes & Cohen, 1995). As object perception improves (see Chapter 5) and infants have many opportunities to watch objects contacting one another, they detect increasingly fine-grained rules of physical causality.

■ **A NATIVIST VIEW.** Other researchers take a *nativist* (meaning inborn) view. They are convinced that infants' remarkable cognitive skills are based on innate knowledge. Development is a matter of these built-in, core understandings becoming more elaborate as infants come in contact with new information.

Elizabeth Spelke (1994) believes that infants know at birth that objects move on continuous paths, do not change shape or pass through one another as they move, and cannot act on one another until they come into contact. Later-emerging schemes directly extend these innate understandings, which channel infants' attention to relevant features of the environment. This gets their physical reasoning "off the ground" quickly (Spelke & Newport, 1998).

A growing number of researchers believe that innate knowledge also guides other aspects of development—for example, processing number, space, language, and social interaction. They assume that development is uneven because each type of knowledge has its own *module*, or genetically prewired neural system in the brain, and timetable of maturation. Consequently, this perspective has been called the **modular view of the mind.**

Think about this alternative to Piaget's theory. Since so much is laid down in advance, the child is much less active in constructing schemes than Piaget assumed. Critics complain that in emphasizing innate knowledge, the modular view sidesteps vital questions about development. As Caitlin, Grace, and Timmy explore their surroundings, they display many new skills. How these arise from built-in structures is not clear (Fischer & Bidell, 1998; Haith & Benson, 1998). Furthermore, the more predetermined we assume the child's mind to be, the less individual variability in thinking we would expect. Yet throughout this book, we will see many examples of wide individual differences in cognitive development.

Finally, according to the modular approach, we should be able to identify brain regions that govern specific types of knowledge at an early age. Yet research supports substantial brain plasticity in the early years and growth spurts across many areas of the cortex at once rather than in separate regions (see Chapter 5, pages 175–177). At present, neurological support for a separate brain/mind module is strongest for language. However, as we will see later in this chapter, non-nativist language theorists argue that this specialization is largely the *product* of development, not its starting point.

■ **A COMPROMISE POSITION.** How can we make sense of these clashing viewpoints? Clearly, babies must have some built-in mental equipment for making sense of experience, since they are not knowledge free. But much of this initial equipment may be little more than limited awareness. Although apparent in violation-of-expectation research, it must undergo considerable change before infants know how to use it purposefully (Bremner, 1998). In accord with this view, some theorists regard the baby's cognitive starting point as a set of biases, or learning procedures. Each grants the infant a means for constructing and flexibly adapting certain types of knowledge, some of which are acquired more easily than others (Elman et al., 1996; Haith & Benson, 1998; Karmiloff-Smith, 1992, 1996). Consequently, infant cognitive skills emerge gradually, depending on biological makeup and specific experiences encountered.

These ideas—that adultlike capacities are present during infancy in primitive form, that cognitive development occurs gradually and continuously rather than in abrupt stages, and that development is uneven because of the challenges of different types of tasks and children's varying exposure to those tasks—serve as the basis for a major competing approach to Piaget's theory: information processing, which we take up next.

Educational Concerns

Play Materials That Support Infant and Toddler Cognitive Development

FROM 2 MONTHS	FROM 6 MONTHS	FROM 1 YEAR
Crib mobile	Squeeze toys	Large dolls
Rattles and other handheld sound-making toys, such as a bell on a handle	Nesting cups	Toy dishes
	Clutch and texture balls	Toy telephone
Adult-operated music boxes, records, tapes, and CDs with gentle, regular rhythms, songs, and lullabies	Stuffed animals and soft-bodied dolls	Hammer-and-peg toy
	Filling and emptying toys	Pull and push toys
	Large and small blocks	Cars and trucks
	Pots, pans, and spoons from the kitchen	Rhythm instruments for shaking and banging, such as bells, cymbals, and drums
	Simple, floating objects for the bath	Simple puzzles
	Picture books	Sandbox, shovel, and pail
		Shallow wading pool and water toys

Note: Return to the Caregiving Concerns table in Chapter 5, page 194, to review safety concerns related to toys for infants and toddlers.
Source: Bronson, 1995.

But before we turn to this alternative view, let's conclude our discussion of the sensorimotor stage by recognizing Piaget's enormous contributions. Although not all his conclusions were correct, Piaget's work inspired a wealth of research on infant cognition, including studies that eventually challenged his ideas. In addition, Piaget's observations have been of great practical value. Teachers and caregivers continue to look to the sensorimotor stage for guidelines on how to create developmentally appropriate environments for infants and toddlers. Now that you are familiar with some milestones of infant and toddler development, consider playthings that would support the building of sensorimotor and representational schemes. Prepare your own list of infant and toddler toys, and justify it by making reference to the cognitive attainments of the first 2 years. Then compare your suggestions to the ones given in the Educational Concerns table above.

Ask YOURSELF...

review   Construct your own table providing an overview of infant and toddler cognitive development. Which entries in the table are consistent with Piaget's theory? Which ones develop earlier than Piaget anticipated?

apply   Seven-month-old Mimi banged her rattle on the tray of her highchair. Then she dropped the rattle, which fell out of sight on her lap. She did not try to retrieve it. Does Mimi know that the rattle still exists? Why doesn't she search for it? Use research findings to explain your answer.

connect   Recall from Chapter 5 (page 204) that around the middle of the first year, infants depend less on motion and more on features (shape, color, and texture) to perceive object unity. How might this change help infants understand physical causality, which also emerges around this time?

reflect   Which explanation of infants' cognitive competencies do you prefer, and why?

Information Processing

nformation-processing theorists agree with Piaget that children are active, inquiring beings, but they do not provide a single, unified theory of cognitive development. Instead, they focus on many aspects of thinking, from attention, memory, and categorization skills to complex problem solving.

Recall from Chapter 1 that the information-processing approach relies on computerlike flowcharts to describe the human cognitive system. The computer model of human thinking is attractive because it is explicit and precise. Information-processing researchers are not satisfied with general concepts, such as assimilation and accommodation, to describe how children think. Instead, they want to know exactly what individuals of different ages do when faced with a task or problem (Klahr & MacWhinney, 1998; Siegler, 1998).

STRUCTURE OF THE INFORMATION-PROCESSING SYSTEM

Most general models of the human information-processing system divide the mind into three basic parts: the *sensory register; working,* or *short-term, memory;* and *long-term memory* (see Figure 6.10). As information flows through each, we can operate on and transform it using **mental strategies,** increasing the efficiency of thinking and the chances that we will retain information for later use. These strategies also permit us to think flexibly, adapting information to changing circumstances. To understand this more clearly, let's take a brief look at each aspect of the mental system.

First, information enters the **sensory register.** Here, sights and sounds are represented directly and briefly. For example, look around you, and then close your eyes. An image of what you saw persists for a few seconds, but then it decays or disappears, unless you use mental strategies to preserve it. For example, you can *attend to* some information more carefully than others, increasing the chances that it will transfer to the next step of the information-processing system.

The second part of the mind is **working, or short-term, memory.** This is the conscious part of our mental system, where we actively "work" on a limited amount of information. For example, if you are studying this book effectively, you are taking notes, repeating information to yourself, or grouping pieces of information together—a strategy much like Piaget's notion of organization. Organization is an especially effective way to remember the many new concepts flowing into your working memory at the moment. If you permit information to remain disconnected, you can hold very little in working memory at once, since you must focus on each item separately. But organize it, and you will not just improve your memory. You will increase the chances that information will be transferred to the third, and largest, storage area.

Long-term memory is our permanent knowledge base. Its capacity is limitless. In fact, we store so much in long-term memory that we sometimes have problems with *retrieval,* or getting information back from the system. To aid retrieval, we apply strategies, just as we do in working memory. Information in your long-term memory is *categorized* according to a master plan based on contents, much like a library shelving system. As a result, you can retrieve it quite easily by following the same network of associations you used to store it in the first place.

Information-processing researchers believe that the basic structure of the human mental system is similar throughout life. However, the *capacity* of the system—the amount of information that can be processed at once and the speed with which it can be processed—increases, making possible more complex forms of thinking with age (Case, 1992, 1998; Miller & Vernon, 1997). Although gains in information-processing capacity are partly due to brain development, they are largely the result of improvements in strategies, such as attending to information and categorizing it effectively. The development of these strategies is already under way in the first 2 years of life.

mental strategies
In information processing, procedures that operate on and transform information, thereby increasing the efficiency and flexibility of thinking and the chances that information will be retained.

sensory register
In information processing, that part of the mental system in which sights and sounds are held briefly before they decay or are transferred to working, or short-term, memory.

working, or
short-term, memory
In information processing, the conscious part of the mental system, where we actively "work" on a limited amount of information to ensure that it will be retained.

long-term memory
In information processing, the part of the mental system that contains our permanent knowledge base.

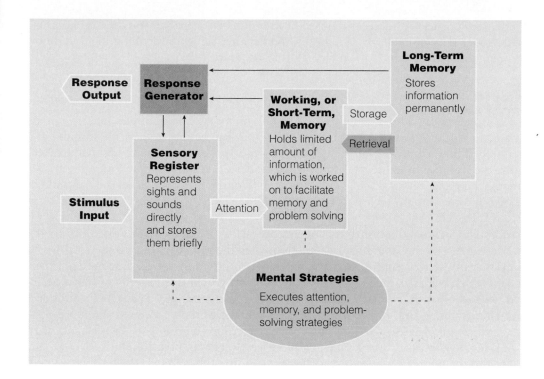

FIGURE 6.10

Structure of the human information-processing system. Information flows through three parts of the mental system: the sensory register; working, or short-term, memory; and long-term memory. In each, mental strategies can be used to manipulate information, increasing the efficiency of thinking and the chances that information will be retained. Strategies also permit us to think flexibly, adapting information to changing circumstances.

ATTENTION

Recall that between 1 and 2 months of age, infants shift from attending to a single high-contrast feature of their visual world to exploring objects and patterns more thoroughly. Besides attending to more aspects of the environment, infants gradually become more efficient at managing their attention, taking in information more quickly with age. Habituation–dishabituation research reveals that preterm and newborn babies require a long time to habituate and dishabituate to novel visual stimuli—about 3 or 4 minutes. But by 4 or 5 months, infants require as little as 5 to 10 seconds to take in a complex new visual stimulus and recognize that it differs from a previous one (Slater et al., 1996).

One reason that very young babies' habituation times are so long is that they have difficulty disengaging their attention from patterned stimuli, even when they try to do so (Frick, Colombo, & Saxon, 1999; Posner et al., 1997). Once, Carolyn held a doll dressed in red-and-white checked overalls in front of 2-month-old Caitlin, who stared intently until, unable to break her gaze, she burst into tears. Just as important as attending to a stimulus is the ability to shift attention from one stimulus to another. By 4 to 6 months, infants' attention becomes more flexible—a change believed to be due to development of structures in the cerebral cortex controlling eye movements (Hood, Atkinson, & Braddick, 1998).

During the first year, infants attend to novel and eye-catching events, orienting to them more quickly and tracking their movements more effectively (Richards & Holley, 1999). With the transition to toddlerhood, children become increasingly capable of intentional behavior (refer back to Piaget's Substage 4). Consequently, attraction to novelty declines (but does not disappear) and *sustained attention* improves, especially when children play with toys. When a toddler can plan a play activity even in a limited way, such as stacking blocks or putting them in a container, attention must be maintained to reach the goal. As plans and activities gradually become more complex, so does the duration of attention (Ruff & Lawson, 1990).

With age, infants and toddlers also become more interested in what others are attending to. And adults can foster infants' and toddlers sustained attention, introducing objects ("Look at this, Timmy!") and prompting the child to stay focused ("See, it makes a noise!")

(Findji, 1998). Later we will see that this joint attention between adult and child is important for language development. By 18 months, toddlers are skilled at dividing their attention between adult partners and toys in play (Ruff & Rothbart, 1996).

MEMORY

Habituation provides a window into infant memory. For example, infants can be exposed to a stimulus until they habituate. Then they can be shown the same stimulus at a later time. If they habituate more rapidly on the second occasion, this indicates that they recognize the stimulus from before. Using this method, studies show that by 3 months, infants remember a visual stimulus for 24 hours; by the end of the first year, for several days; and in the case of some stimuli (such as a photo of the human face), even weeks (Fagan, 1973; Martin, 1975; Pascalis et al., 1998).

Although habituation–dishabituation research tells us about infants' memory in the strange context of the laboratory, it underestimates their ability to remember real-world events they can actively control. Recall the operant conditioning research discussed in Chapter 5, in which babies learned to make a mobile move by kicking. In a series of studies, Carolyn Rovee-Collier found that 2- to 3-month-olds remember how to activate the mobile 1 week after training, and with a prompt (the experimenter briefly rotates the mobile for the baby), as long as 4 weeks. By 6 months of age, retention increases to 2 weeks and, with prompting, to 6 weeks (Rovee-Collier, 1999; Rovee-Collier & Bhatt, 1993).

Around the middle of the first year, operant conditioning tasks in which babies control stimulation by manipulating buttons, switches, or levers work well for studying memory. When infants and toddlers were shown how to press a lever to make a toy train move around a track, duration of memory continued to increase with age; 13 weeks after training, 18-month-olds still remembered how to press the lever (Hartshorn et al., 1998b). Speed of memory also improves. After infants had forgotten how the train worked, offering a prompt (briefly making the train move) led to more rapid recovery of lever pressing with age until, at 12 months, infants responded instantaneously (Hildreth & Rovee-Collier, 1999).

At first, memory is highly *context dependent*. If 2- to 6-month-olds are not tested in the same situation in which they were trained—with the same mobile and crib bumper and in the same room—they remember poorly (Boller, Grabelle, & Rovee-Collier, 1995; Hayne & Rovee-Collier, 1995). After 12 months, the importance of context declines. Toddlers remember how to make the toy train move, even when its features are altered and testing takes place in a different room (Hartshorne et al., 1998a; Hayne, Boniface, & Barr, 2000). As babies move on their own and experience frequent changes in context, their memory becomes increasingly *context free*. They can apply learned responses more flexibly, generalizing them to relevant new situations.

So far, we have discussed only **recognition,** the simplest form of memory because all that babies have to do is indicate (by looking, kicking, or pressing a lever) whether a new experience is identical or similar to a previous one. **Recall** is more challenging, since it involves remembering something in the absence of perceptual support. To recall, you must generate a mental image of the past experience. Can infants engage in recall? By the end of the first year, they can, since they find hidden objects and imitate the actions of others hours or days after they observed the behavior.

Between 1 and 2 years of age, children's recall for people, places, and objects is excellent. One-year-olds can imitate an experimenter's actions on a novel toy 1 month after a brief demonstration; 2-year-olds' retention persists for at least 3 months (Herbert & Hayne, 2000; Klein & Meltzoff, 1999). Older toddlers can even verbally express memories of events initially learned without the benefit of language (Bauer et al., 1998). For example, at age 25 months, Timmy said, "Bobby, go pool," recalling his water play with a friend as he passed the friend's house. Timmy had not seen Bobby for 7 months! Yet a puzzling finding is that older children and adults no longer recall their earliest experiences. See the Biology and Environment box on the following page for a discussion of *infantile amnesia*.

recognition
The simplest form of memory, which involves noticing whether a new experience is identical or similar to a previous one.

recall
The type of memory that involves remembering something in the absence of perceptual support.

autobiographical memory
Representations of special, one-time events that are long lasting because they are imbued with personal meaning.

Biology & ENVIRONMENT

INFANTILE AMNESIA

If toddlers remember many aspects of their everyday lives, then what explains infantile amnesia—the fact that practically none of us can retrieve events that happened to us before age 3? Forgetting cannot be due to the passage of time, since we can recall many events that happened long ago (Eacott, 1999). At present, there are several explanations of infantile amnesia.

One theory credits brain development. Growth of the frontal lobes of the cortex along with other structures may be necessary before experiences can be stored in ways that permit them to be retrieved many years later (Boyer & Diamond, 1992).

Yet the idea of vastly different approaches to remembering in younger and older individuals has been questioned, since even toddlers can describe memories verbally and retain them for extensive periods. A growing number of researchers believe that rather than a radical change in the way experience is represented, the cessation of infantile amnesia requires the emergence of a special form of recall—**autobiographical memory,** or representations of special, one-time events that are long lasting because they are imbued with personal meaning. For example, perhaps you recall the day a sibling was born, the first time you took an airplane, or a move to a new house.

For memories to become autobiographical, at least two developments are necessary. First, the child must have a well-developed image of the self. Yet in the first few years, the sense of self is not yet mature enough to serve as an anchor for one-time events (Howe & Courage, 1997). Second, autobiographical memory requires that children integrate personal experiences into a meaningful, time-organized life story. Recent evidence reveals that preschoolers learn to structure memories in narrative form by talking about them with adults, who expand on their recollections by explaining what happened when, where, and with whom (Nelson, 1993).

Between 2 and 5 years of age, children's interest in memory-related conversations increase greatly—a change that may underlie the age-related rise in autobiographical memories from this period. Interestingly, parents talk about the past in more detail with daughters (Bruce, Dolan, & Phillips-Grant, 2000; Reese, Haden, & Fivush, 1996). And collectivist cultural values lead Asian parents to discourage their children from talking about themselves (Han, Leichtman, & Wang, 1998). Perhaps because women's early experiences were integrated into more coherent narratives, they report an earlier age of first memory and more vivid early memories than do men. Similarly, first memories of Caucasian-American adults are, on the average, 6 months earlier than those of Asians (Mullen, 1994).

The cessation of infantile amnesia probably represents a change to which both biology and social experience contribute. One speculation is that vital changes in the frontal lobes of the cerebral cortex during toddlerhood pave the way for an *explicit memory* system—one in which children remember consciously rather than *implicitly,* without conscious awareness (Nelson, 1997). In Chapters 8 and 12, we will see that deliberate recall of information and events improves greatly during childhood. It undoubtedly supports the success of conversations about the past in structuring children's autobiographical memories.

When he gets older, this toddler won't recall the exciting party that took place on his second birthday. According to recent evidence, the offset of infantile amnesia after age 3 is due to the emergence of autobiographical memory. For this special form of recall to develop, young children must have a well-developed image of the self and the language skills to talk about personal experiences with adults, who assist them in constructing a meaningful, time-organized life story.

JEFF GREENBERG/INDEX STOCK

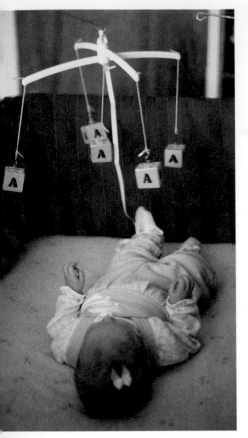

FIGURE 6.11

Investigating infant categorization using operant conditioning. Three-month-olds were taught to kick to move a mobile that was made of small blocks, all with the letter *A* on them. After a delay, kicking returned to a high level only if the babies were shown a mobile whose elements were labeled with the same form (the letter *A*). If the form was changed (from *A*s to *2*s), infants no longer kicked vigorously. While making the mobile move, the babies had grouped together its features. They associated the kicking response with the category *A* and, at later testing, distinguished it from the category *2*. (Courtesy of Carolyn Rovee-Collier/Rutgers University.)

CATEGORIZATION

As infants remember more information, they store it in a remarkably orderly fashion. Some creative variations of the task in which babies kicked to move a mobile have been used to find out about infant categorization. One such study is described in Figure 6.11. In fact, 3- to 5-month-olds categorize stimuli on the basis of shape, size, number (up to three elements), and other physical properties at such an early age that categorization is among the strongest evidence that infants structure their experience in adultlike ways (Mandler, 1998).

Habituation–dishabituation research also has been used to study infant categorization. Researchers show babies a series of pictures belonging to one category and then see whether they dishabituate to a picture that is not a member of the category. Findings reveal that 7- to 12-month-olds structure objects into an impressive array of meaningful categories—food items, furniture, birds, animals, vehicles, spatial location ("above" and "below"), and more (Mandler & McDonough, 1996, 1998; Oakes, Coppage, & Dingel, 1997; Quinn & Eimas, 1996; Younger, 1985, 1993). Besides organizing the physical world, infants of this age also categorize their emotional and social worlds. They sort people and their voices by gender and age (Bahrick, Netto, & Hernandez-Reif, 1998; Poulin-DuBois et al., 1994), have begun to distinguish emotional expressions, and can separate the natural movements of people from other motions (see Chapter 5, pages 200, 202).

The earliest categories are *perceptual*—based on similar overall appearance or prominent object part, such as legs for animals and wheels for vehicles (Rakison & Butterworth, 1998). By the end of the first year, categories are becoming *conceptual*—based on common function and behavior. Older infants can even make categorical distinctions when the perceptual contrast between two categories—animals and vehicles—is made as minimal as possible (for an illustration, see Figure 6.12).

In the second year, children become active categorizers. Around 12 months, toddlers touch objects that go together, without grouping them. Sixteen-month-olds can group objects into a single category. For example, when given four balls and four boxes, they put all the balls together but not the boxes. Around 18 months, toddlers can sort objects into two classes (Gopnik & Meltzoff, 1987).

Compared with the habituation–dishabituation sequence, sorting and other play behaviors better reveal the meanings that children attach to categories because they are applying those meanings in their everyday behavior. For example, after having watched an experimenter give a toy dog a drink from a cup, 14-month-olds shown a rabbit and a motorcycle usually offer the drink only to the rabbit (Mandler & McDonough, 1998). Their behavior reveals that they understand that certain actions are appropriate for some categories of items (animals) and not others (vehicles).

How does the perceptual-to-conceptual change in categorization take place? Although researchers disagree on whether this shift requires a new approach to analyzing experience, most acknowledge that exploration of objects and expanding knowledge of the world contribute to older infants' capacity to move beyond physical features and group objects by their functions and behaviors (Madole & Oakes, 1999; Mandler, 1999).

Finally, language builds on as well as facilitates categorization. Toddlers' advanced object-sorting behavior occurs at about the same time they show a "naming explosion," or vocabulary spurt (Gopnik & Meltzoff, 1992). At the same time, adult labeling of objects helps direct toddlers' attention to categories (Waxman, 1995). Korean children, who learn a language in which object names are often omitted from sentences, develop object-grouping skills later than do their English-speaking counterparts (Gopnik & Choi, 1990).

EVALUATION OF INFORMATION-PROCESSING FINDINGS

Information-processing research underscores the continuity of human thinking from infancy into adult life. In attending to the environment, remembering everyday events, and categorizing objects, Caitlin, Grace, and Timmy think in ways that are remarkably similar to our own, even though they are far from being the proficient mental processors we are. Findings on infant memory and categorization join with other research in challenging Piaget's view that early cognitive development takes place in discrete stages. If 2- to 3-month-olds can hold events in memory for as long as 1 to 4 weeks and categorize stimuli, then they clearly have some ability to mentally represent their experiences.

Information processing has contributed greatly to our view of infants and toddlers as sophisticated cognitive beings. Still, its greatest drawback stems from its central strength: By analyzing cognition into its components (such as perception, attention, memory, and categorization), information processing has had difficulty putting them back together into a broad, comprehensive theory.

During the past two decades, several attempts have been made to overcome this weakness. One approach has been to combine Piaget's theory with the information-processing approach, an effort we will take up in Chapter 12 (Case, 1985, 1998). A more recent trend has been the application of a dynamic systems view to early cognition. Researchers analyze each new attainment to see how it is the product of a complex system of prior accomplishments and the child's current goals (Smith & Katz, 1996; Thelen & Smith, 1998). These ideas have yet to be fully tested, but they may move the field closer to a more powerful view of how the mind of the infant and child develops.

The Social Context of Early Cognitive Development

Take a moment to review the short episode at the beginning of this chapter, in which Grace dropped shapes into a container. Notice that Grace does not discover how to use the toy on her own; she learns about it with Ginette's help. With adult support, Grace will gradually become better at matching shapes to openings and dropping them into the container. Then she will be able to perform the activity (and others like it) on her own.

Vygotsky's sociocultural theory has helped researchers realize that children live in rich social and cultural contexts that affect the way their cognitive world is structured (Rogoff, 1998; Wertsch & Tulviste, 1992). Vygotsky (1930–1935/1978) believed that complex mental activities, such as voluntary attention, deliberate memory, categorization, and problem solving, have their origins in social interaction. Through joint activities with more mature members of their society, children master activities and think in ways that have meaning in their culture.

A special Vygotskian concept, the **zone of proximal** (or potential) **development,** explains how this happens. It refers to a range of tasks that the child cannot yet handle alone but can accomplish with the help of more skilled partners. To understand this idea, think of a sensitive adult (such as Ginette) who introduces a child to a new activity. The adult picks a task that the child can master but that is challenging enough that the child cannot do it by herself. Or the adult capitalizes on an activity that the child has chosen. Such tasks are especially suited for spurring development. Then as the adult guides and supports, the child joins in the interaction and picks up mental strategies, and her competence increases. When this happens, the adult steps back, permitting the child to take more responsibility for the task.

As we will see in Chapters 9 and 12, Vygotsky's ideas have mostly been applied at older ages, when children are more skilled in language and social communication. But recently, Vygotsky's ideas have been extended to infancy and toddlerhood. Recall that babies are equipped with capabilities that ensure that caregivers will interact with them. Then adults adjust the environment and their communication in ways that promote learning adapted to their cultural circumstances.

A study by Barbara Rogoff and her collaborators (Rogoff, Malkin, & Gilbride, 1984) illustrates this process. The researchers watched how several adults played with Rogoff's son and

FIGURE 6.12

Categorical distinction made by 9- to 11-month-olds. After infants were given an opportunity to examine (by looking or touching) the objects in one category, they were shown a new object from each of the categories. They dishabituated to (spent more time looking at or touching) the object from the contrasting category, indicating that they distinguished the birds from the airplanes, despite their perceptual similarity. (Adapted from Mandler & McDonough, 1993.)

Children's thinking is promoted by their interactions w/others.

zone of proximal development
In Vygotsky's theory, a range of tasks that the child cannot yet handle alone but can accomplish with the help of more skilled partners.

© 2000 LAURA DWIGHT

This mother assists her toddler in making a musical top work through gestures and simple words. By presenting a task within the child's zone of proximal development and fine-tuning her support to the child's needs, the mother promotes her daughter's cognitive development.

daughter over the first 2 years while a jack-in-the-box toy was nearby. In the early months, adults tried to focus the baby's attention by working the toy, and as the bunny popped out, saying something like "My, what happened?" By the end of the first year (when the baby's cognitive and motor skills had improved), interaction centered on how to use the jack-in-the-box. When the infant reached for the toy, adults guided the baby's hand in turning the crank and putting the bunny back in the box. As the youngsters became toddlers, adults helped from a distance. They used gestures and verbal prompts, such as rotating a hand in a turning motion near the crank, while the child tried to make the toy work. Research indicates that this fine-tuned support is related to advances in play, language, and problem-solving skills during the second year (Bornstein et al., 1992b; Tamis-LeMonda & Bornstein, 1989).

Cultural variations in social experiences affect mental strategies as early as infancy and toddlerhood. Notice how, in the example just described, adults and children focused their attention on a single activity. This strategy, common in American middle-SES culture, is well suited to lessons in which children learn skills apart from the everyday situations in which those skills later will be used. In contrast, Guatemalan Mayan adults and toddlers often smoothly attend to several events at once. For example, one 12-month-old skillfully put objects in a jar while watching a passing truck and whistling on a toy whistle his mother had slipped into his mouth (Chavajay & Rogoff, 1999). Being able to process several competing events simultaneously may be vital in cultures in which children largely learn not through lessons but through keen observation of others at home, at work, and in public life.

Earlier in this chapter, we saw how infants and toddlers create new schemes by acting on the physical world (Piaget) and how certain skills become better developed as children represent their experiences more efficiently and meaningfully (information processing). Vygotsky adds a third dimension to our understanding by emphasizing that important aspects of cognitive development are socially mediated. The Cultural Influences box on the following page presents additional evidence for this idea. And we encounter even more in the next section, as we look at individual differences in mental development during the first 2 years.

Ask YOURSELF...

review   Cite evidence that categorization becomes less perceptual and more conceptual with age. What factors support this shift? How can adults facilitate the development of categorization?

apply   Caitlin played with toys in a far more intentional, goal-directed way as a toddler than as an infant. What impact is Caitlin's more advanced toy play likely to have on the development of attention? How is her cultural background likely to affect her attentional strategies?

connect   Review the research on page 220, indicating that by age 10 to 12 months, infants can solve problems by analogy. How might that capacity relate to a context-free memory, which develops about the same time?

reflect   Describe your earliest autobiographical memory. How old were you when the event occurred? Do your responses fit with research on infantile amnesia?

Cultural INFLUENCES

SOCIAL ORIGINS OF MAKE-BELIEVE PLAY

One of my husband Ken's activities with our two sons when they were young was to bake pineapple upside-down cake, a favorite treat. One Sunday afternoon when a cake was in the making, 21-month-old Peter stood on a chair at the kitchen sink, busily pouring water from one cup to another.

"He's in the way, Dad!" complained 4-year-old David, trying to pull Peter away from the sink.

"Maybe if we let him help, he'll give us some room," Ken suggested. As David stirred the batter, Ken poured some into a small bowl for Peter, moved his chair to the side of the sink, and handed him a spoon.

"Here's how you do it, Petey," instructed David, with an air of superiority. Peter watched as David stirred, then tried to copy his motion. When it was time to pour the batter, Ken helped Peter hold and tip the small bowl.

"Time to bake it," said Ken.

"Bake it, bake it," repeated Peter, as he watched Ken slip the pan into the oven.

Several hours later, we observed one of Peter's earliest instances of make-believe play. He got his pail from the sandbox and, after filling it with a handful of sand, carried it into the kitchen and put it down on the floor in front of the oven. "Bake it, bake it," Peter called to Ken. Together, father and son placed the pretend cake inside the oven.

Until recently, most researchers studied make-believe play apart from the social environment in which it occurs, while children played alone. Probably for this reason, Piaget and his followers concluded that toddlers discover make-believe as soon as they are capable of representational schemes. Vygotsky's theory has challenged this

view. He believed that society provides children with opportunities to represent culturally meaningful activities in play. Make-believe, like other complex mental activities, is initially learned under the guidance of experts (Berk, 1994). In the example just described, Peter's capacity to represent daily events was extended when Ken drew him into the baking task and helped him act it out in play.

Current evidence supports the idea that early make-believe is the combined result of children's readiness to engage in it and social experiences that promote it. In one observational study of middle-SES American toddlers, 75 to 80 percent of make-believe involved mother–child interaction (Haight & Miller, 1993). At 12 months, make-believe was fairly one-sided; almost all play episodes were initiated by mothers. By the end of the second year, mothers and children displayed mutual interest in getting make-believe started; half of pretend episodes were initiated by each.

When adults participate, toddlers' make-believe is more elaborate and advanced (O'Reilly & Bornstein, 1993). For example, play themes are more varied. And toddlers are more likely to combine schemes into complex sequences, as Peter did when he put the sand in the bucket ("making the batter"), carried it into the kitchen, and (with Ken's help) put it in the oven ("baking the cake"). The more parents pretend with their toddlers, the more

time their children devote to make-believe. And in certain collectivist societies, such as Argentina and Japan, mother–toddler other-directed pretending, as in feeding or putting a doll to sleep, is particularly rich in maternal expressions of affection and praise (Bornstein et al., 1999a).

In some cultures, adults do not spend much time playing with young children. Instead, older siblings take over this function. For example, in Indonesia and Mexico, where extended-family households and sibling caregiving are common, make-believe is more frequent and complex with older siblings than with mothers. As early as 3 to 4 years of age, children provide rich, challenging stimulation to their younger brothers and sisters. The fantasy play of these toddlers is just as well developed as that of their middle-SES American counterparts (Farver, 1993; Farver & Wimbarti, 1995).

As we will see in Chapter 9, make-believe is a major means through which children extend their cognitive skills and learn about important activities in their culture. Vygotsky's theory, and the findings that support it, tell us that providing a stimulating environment is not enough to promote early cognitive development. Toddlers must be invited and encouraged by more skilled members of their culture to participate actively in the social world around them.

KAREN HALVERSON/OMNI-PHOTO COMMUNICATIONS

In Mexico, where sibling caregiving is common, make-believe play is more frequent as well as complex with older siblings than with mothers. This 5-year-old provides rich, challenging stimulation to her younger sister within a pretend-play scene.

Individual Differences in Early Mental Development

Recall from Chapter 5 that because of Grace's deprived early environment, Kevin and Monica had a child psychologist give her one of many tests available for assessing mental development in infants and toddlers. Worried about Timmy's progress, Vanessa also arranged for him to be tested. At age 22 months, he had only a handful of words in his vocabulary, played in a less mature way than Caitlin and Grace, and seemed restless and overactive.

The testing approach differs from the cognitive theories we have just discussed, which try to explain the *process* of development—how children's thinking changes over time. In contrast, designers of mental tests focus on cognitive *products.* They seek to measure behaviors that reflect mental development and to arrive at scores that *predict* future performance, such as later intelligence, school achievement, and adult vocational success.

This concern with prediction arose nearly a century ago, when French psychologist Alfred Binet designed the first successful intelligence test, which predicted school achievement (see Chapter 1). It inspired the design of many new tests, including ones that measure intelligence at very early ages.

INFANT INTELLIGENCE TESTS

Accurately measuring the intelligence of infants is a challenge, since they cannot answer questions or follow directions. All we can do is present them with stimuli, coax them to respond, and observe their behavior. As a result, most infant tests consist of perceptual and motor responses along with some tasks that tap early language and problem solving. One commonly used infant test is the *Bayley Scales of Infant Development,* for children between 1 month and $3\frac{1}{2}$ years (Bayley, 1993). It is made up of two scales: (1) the Mental Scale, which includes such items as turning to a sound, looking for a fallen object, building a tower of cubes, and naming pictures; and (2) the Motor Scale, which assesses gross and fine motor skills, such as grasping, sitting, drinking from a cup, and jumping.

■ **COMPUTING INTELLIGENCE TEST SCORES.** Intelligence tests for infants, children, and adults are scored in much the same way. When a test is constructed, it is given to a large, representative sample of individuals. Performances of people at each age level form a *normal* or *bell-shaped curve,* in which most scores fall near the center (the mean or average) and progressively fewer fall out toward the extremes. On the basis of this distribution, the test designer computes norms, or standards against which future test takers can be compared. For example, if Timmy does better than 50 percent of his agemates, his score will be 100, an average test score. If he exceeds most children his age, his score will be much higher. If he does better than only a small percentage of 2-year-olds, his score will be much lower.

Scores computed in this way are called **intelligence quotients,** or **IQs,** a term you have undoubtedly heard before. Table 6.3 describes the meaning of a range of IQ scores. Notice how the IQ offers a way of finding out whether a child is ahead, behind, or on time (average) in mental development in relation to other children of the same age. The great majority of individuals (96 percent) have IQs that fall between 70 and 130; only a very few achieve higher or lower scores.

■ **PREDICTING LATER PERFORMANCE FROM INFANT TESTS.** Many people assume, incorrectly, that IQ measures native endowment, which does not change with age. Despite careful construction, many infant tests predict later intelligence poorly. Longitudinal research reveals that the majority of children show substantial IQ fluctuations between toddlerhood and adolescence—in most cases, 10 to 20 points and sometimes much more (McCall, 1993).

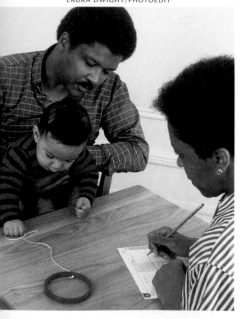

A trained examiner tests this baby with the Bayley Scales of Infant Development while his father holds him and looks on. The perceptual and motor items on most infant tests are different from the tasks given to older children, which emphasize verbal, conceptual, and problem-solving skills. Among normally developing children, infant tests predict later intelligence poorly.

Because infants and toddlers are especially likely to become distracted, fatigued, or bored during testing, their scores often do not reflect their true abilities. In addition, the perceptual and motor items on infant tests differ from the test questions given to older children, which emphasize verbal, conceptual, and problem-solving skills. Because of concerns that infant test scores do not tap the same dimensions of intelligence measured at older ages, they are conservatively labeled **developmental quotients, or DQs,** rather than IQs. Not until age 6 do IQ scores become stable, serving as reasonably good predictors of later performance (Hayslip, 1994).

Infant tests are somewhat better at making long-term predictions for extremely low-scoring babies. Today, they are used largely for *screening*—helping to identify for further observation and intervention babies whose very low scores mean that they are likely to have developmental problems in the future (Kopp, 1994).

Because infant tests do not predict later IQ for most children, researchers have turned to the information-processing approach to assess early mental progress. Their findings show that habituation and dishabituation to visual stimuli are the best available infant predictors of intelligence from early childhood into adolescence. Correlations between the speed of these responses and the IQs of 3- to 18-year-olds consistently range from the .30s to the .60s (McCall & Carriger, 1993; Sigman, Cohen, & Beckwith, 1997). The habituation–dishabituation sequence seems to be an especially effective early index of intelligence because it assesses quickness of thinking, a characteristic of bright individuals. It also taps basic cognitive processes—attention, memory, and response to novelty—that underlie intelligent behavior at all ages (Colombo, 1995; Rose & Feldman, 1997).

Piagetian object permanence tasks predict later IQ better than traditional infant tests, perhaps because they, too, reflect a basic intellectual process—problem solving (Wachs, 1975). The consistency of these findings prompted designers of the most recent edition of the Bayley test to include several items that tap higher-order cognitive skills, such as preference for novel stimuli, ability to find hidden objects, and categorization.

EARLY ENVIRONMENT AND MENTAL DEVELOPMENT

In Chapter 2, we indicated that intelligence is a complex blend of hereditary and environmental influences. Many studies have examined the relationship of environmental factors to infant and toddler mental test scores. As we consider this evidence, you will encounter findings that highlight the role of genetic factors as well.

■ **HOME ENVIRONMENT.** From what you have learned so far, what aspects of young children's home experiences would you expect to influence early mental development? The **Home Observation for Measurement of the Environment (HOME)** is a checklist for gathering information about the quality of children's home lives through observation and parental interview (Caldwell & Bradley, 1994). The Educational Concerns table on page 234 lists factors measured by HOME during the first 3 years. Each is positively related to toddlers' mental test performance. In addition, high HOME scores are associated with IQ gains between 1 and 3 years of age, whereas low HOME scores predict declines as large as 15 to 20 points (Bradley et al., 1989).

Regardless of the child's SES and ethnicity, an organized, stimulating physical setting and parental encouragement, involvement, and affection repeatedly predict language and IQ scores in toddlerhood and early childhood (Klebanov et al., 1998; Roberts, Burchinal, & Durham, 1999). The extent to which parents talk to infants and toddlers is particularly important. As the final section of this chapter will reveal, it contributes strongly to early language progress. Language progress, in turn, predicts intelligence and academic achievement in elementary school (Hart & Risley, 1995).

TABLE 6.3

Meaning of Various IQ Scores

SCORE	PERCENTILE RANK— CHILD DOES BETTER THAN ... PERCENT OF SAME-AGE CHILDREN	
70	2	
85	16	
100 (average IQ)	50	
115	84	
130	98	

intelligence quotient, or IQ
A score that reflects an individual's performance on an intelligence test compared with the performances of other individuals of the same age.

developmental quotient, or DQ
A score on an infant intelligence test, based primarily on perceptual and motor responses. Computed in the same manner as an IQ.

Home Observation for Measurement of the Environment (HOME)
A checklist for gathering information about the quality of children's home lives through observation and parental interview.

Educational Concerns

Home Observation for Measurement of the Environment (HOME): Infancy and Toddler Subscales

SUBSCALE	SAMPLE ITEM
Emotional and verbal responsiveness of the parent	Parent caresses or kisses child at least once during observer's visit.
Parental acceptance of the child	Parent does not interfere with child's actions or restrict child's movements more than three times during observer's visit.
Organization of the physical environment	Child's play environment appears safe and free of hazards.
Provision of appropriate play materials	Parent provides toys or interesting activities for child during observer's visit.
Parental involvement with the child	Parent tends to keep child within visual range and to look at child often during observer's visit.
Opportunities for variety in daily stimulation	Child eats at least one meal per day with mother and/or father, according to parental report.

Source: Elardo & Bradley, 1981.

Yet we must interpret these correlational findings with caution. In the research just mentioned, all the children were reared by their biological parents, with whom they share not just a common environment but also a common heredity. Parents who are genetically more intelligent might provide better experiences as well as give birth to genetically brighter children, who also evoke more stimulation from their parents. Note that this hypothesis refers to a *genetic–environmental correlation* (see Chapter 2, page 89).

Indeed, the HOME–mental development relationship is not as strong for adopted children as for biological children (Cherny, 1994). Yet heredity does not account for all of the association between home environment and mental tests scores. Family living conditions continue to predict children's IQ beyond the contribution of parental IQ (Luster & Dubow, 1992; Sameroff et al., 1993). In one study, infants and children growing up in less crowded homes had parents who were far more verbally responsive to them—a major contributor to language, intellectual, and academic progress (Evans, Maxwell, & Hart, 1999).

Can the research summarized so far help us understand Vanessa's concern about Timmy's development? Indeed, it can. Ben, the psychologist who tested Timmy, found that he scored slightly below average but well within normal range. Ben also talked with Vanessa about her child-rearing practices and watched her play with Timmy. A single parent, Vanessa worked long hours and had little energy for Timmy at the end of the day. Ben also noticed that Vanessa, anxious about how well Timmy was doing, tended to pressure him. She constantly tried to dampen his active behavior and bombarded him with directions, such as "Enough running. Sit down!" and "That's enough ball play. Stack these blocks."

Ben explained that when parents are intrusive in these ways, infants and toddlers are likely to be distractible, show less mature forms of play, and do poorly on mental tests (Bradley et al., 1989; Fiese, 1990). He coached Vanessa in how to interact sensitively with Timmy. At the same time, he assured her that Timmy's current performance need not forecast his future development, since warm, responsive parenting that builds on toddlers' current capacities is a much better indicator of how they will do later than is an early mental test score.

■INFANT AND TODDLER CHILD CARE. Home environments are not the only influential settings in which young children spend their days. Today, more than 60 percent of mothers with a child younger than age 2 are employed (U.S. Bureau of the Census, 2000). Child care for infants and toddlers is common, and its quality has a major impact on mental development. Research consistently shows that infants and young children exposed to poor-quality child care, regardless of whether they come from middle- or low-SES homes, score lower on measures of cognitive and social skills. In one American study, children who entered poor-quality child care during their first year and remained there during early childhood were rated as distractible, low in task involvement, and inconsiderate of others when they reached kindergarten (Howes, 1990).

In contrast, good child care can reduce the negative impact of a stressed, poverty-stricken home life, and it sustains the benefits of growing up in an economically advantaged family (Burchinal et al., 1996; Lamb, 1998). In Swedish longitudinal research, entering high-quality child care in infancy and toddlerhood was associated with cognitive, emotional, and social competence in middle childhood and adolescence (Andersson, 1989, 1992; Broberg et al., 1997).

Visit some child-care settings, and take notes on what you see. In contrast to conditions in Australia, New Zealand, and most European countries, where child care is nationally regulated and funded to ensure its quality, American child care is cause for deep concern. Standards are set by the states and vary greatly across the nation. In some places, caregivers need no special training in child development, and one adult cares for as many as 6 to 12 babies at once (Children's Defense Fund, 2000). In a study of several hundred randomly selected child-care centers in California, Colorado, Connecticut, and North Carolina, researchers judged that only 1 in 7 provided a level of care sufficient to promote healthy psychological development. As Figure 6.13 shows, the quality of infant/toddler programs was abysmal; the large majority were either mediocre or poor (Helburn, 1995). Research on child-care homes has yielded similar conclusions (Galinsky et al., 1994).

This child-care center meets rigorous, professionally established standards of quality. A generous caregiver–child ratio, a limited number of children in each room, an environment with appropriate equipment and toys, and training in child development enable caregivers to respond to infants' and toddlers' needs to be held, comforted, and stimulated.

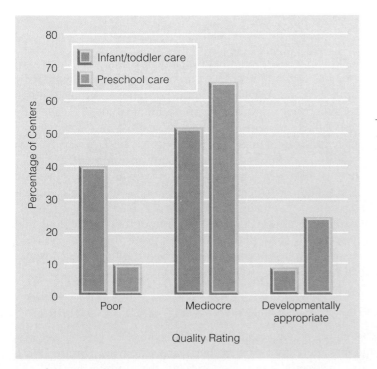

FIGURE 6.13

Quality ratings of child care for infants, toddlers, and preschoolers in the United States. Visits were made to 400 randomly selected child-care centers in California, Colorado, Connecticut, and North Carolina. Centers were classified as (1) *inadequate*—children's needs for health and safety are not met, and there is no warmth, support, and encouragement of learning; (2) *mediocre*—children's health and safety needs are met, and there is minimal to moderate warmth, support, and encouragement of learning; or (3) *developmentally appropriate*—children's health and safety needs are met, and warmth, support, and encouragement of learning are plentiful. (From Cost, Quality, and Outcomes Study Team, 1995, "Cost, Quality, and Child Outcomes in Child Care Centers: Key Findings and Recommendations," *Young Children, 50*(4), p. 41. © National Association for the Education of Young Children. Adapted by permission.)

Educational Concerns

Signs of Developmentally Appropriate Infant and Toddler Child Care

PROGRAM CHARACTERISTIC	SIGNS OF QUALITY
Physical setting	Indoor environment is clean, in good repair, well lighted, and well ventilated. Fenced outdoor play space is available. Setting does not appear overcrowded when children are present.
Toys and equipment	Play materials are appropriate for infants and toddlers and stored on low shelves within easy reach. Cribs, highchairs, infant seats, and child-sized tables and chairs are available. Outdoor equipment includes small riding toys, swings, slide, and sandbox.
Caregiver–child ratio	In child-care centers, caregiver–child ratio is no greater than 1 to 3 for infants and 1 to 6 for toddlers. Group size (number of children in one room) is no greater than 6 infants with 2 caregivers and 12 toddlers with 2 caregivers. In child-care homes, caregiver is responsible for no more than 6 children; within this group, no more than 2 are infants and toddlers. Staffing is consistent, so infants and toddlers can form relationships with particular caregivers.
Daily activities	Daily schedule includes times for active play, quiet play, naps, snacks, and meals. It is flexible rather than rigid, to meet the needs of individual children. Atmosphere is warm and supportive, and children are never left unsupervised.
Interactions between adults and children	Caregivers respond promptly to infants' and toddlers' distress; hold, talk to, sing, and read to them; and interact with them in a manner that respects the individual child's interests and tolerance for stimulation.
Caregiver qualifications	Caregiver has some training in child development, first aid, and safety.
Relationships with parents	Parents are welcome any time. Caregivers talk frequently with parents about children's behavior and development.
Licensing and accreditation	Child-care setting, whether a center or home, is licensed by the state. Accreditation by the National Academy of Early Childhood Programs or the National Association for Family Child Care is evidence of an especially high-quality program.

Sources: Bredekamp & Copple, 1997; National Association for the Education of Young Children, 1998.

The Educational Concerns table above lists signs of high-quality programs that can be used in choosing a child-care setting for an infant or toddler, based on standards for **developmentally appropriate practice** devised by the National Association for the Education of Young Children (Bredekamp & Copple, 1997). Caitlin, Grace, and Timmy are fortunate to be in a child-care home that meets these standards. Children from low-income and poverty-stricken families are especially likely to have inadequate child care (Pungello & Kurtz-Costes, 1999). These children receive a double dose of vulnerability—at home and in the child-care environment.

Child care in the United States is affected by a macrosystem of individualistic values and weak government regulation and funding. Furthermore, many parents think their children's child-care experiences are better than they actually are (Helburn, 1995). Inability to identify good care means that many parents do not demand it. Yet communities and nations that invest in child care have selected a highly cost-effective means of protecting children's well-being. Excellent child care can also serve as effective early intervention for children whose development is at risk, much like the programs we are about to consider.

developmentally appropriate practice
Standards devised by the National Association for the Education of Young Children that specify program characteristics that meet the developmental and individual needs of young children of varying ages, based on current research and the consensus of experts.

EARLY INTERVENTION FOR AT-RISK INFANTS AND TODDLERS

Many studies indicate that children living in poverty are likely to show gradual declines in intelligence test scores and to achieve poorly when they reach school age (Brody, 1992). These problems are largely due to stressful home environments that undermine children's ability to learn and increase the chances that they will remain poor throughout their lives. A variety of intervention programs have been developed to break this tragic cycle of poverty. Although most begin during the preschool years (we will discuss these in Chapter 9), a few start during infancy and continue through early childhood.

Some interventions are center based; children attend an organized child-care or preschool program where they receive educational, nutritional, and health services, and child-rearing and other social-service supports are provided to parents as well. Other interventions are home based. A skilled adult visits the home and works with parents, teaching them how to stimulate a very young child's development. In most intervention programs, participating youngsters score higher on mental tests by age 2 than do untreated controls. These gains persist as long as the program lasts and occasionally longer. The more intense the intervention (for example, full-day, year-round, high-quality child care plus support services for parents), the greater children's cognitive and academic performance when they reach school age (Campbell & Ramey, 1995; Ramey, Campbell, & Ramey, 1999).

The Carolina Abecedarian Project illustrates these positive outcomes. In the 1970s, more than one hundred 3-week- to 3-month-old infants from poverty-stricken families were randomly assigned to either a treatment or a control group. Treatment infants were enrolled in full-time, year-round child care, where they remained until they entered school. There they received stimulation aimed at promoting motor, cognitive, language, and social skills and, after age 3, prereading and math concepts. At all ages, special emphasis was placed on rich, responsive adult–child verbal communication. All children received nutrition and health services; the primary difference between treatment and controls was the child-care experience.

As Figure 6.14 shows, by 12 months of age, the IQs of the two groups diverged, and treatment children maintained their advantage into adolescence. In addition, at 12 and 15 years of age, treatment youths were achieving considerably better, especially in reading and math (Campbell & Ramey, 1991, 1994, 1995). While the children were in elementary school, the researchers conducted a second experiment to compare the impact of early and later intervention. From kindergarten through second grade, half the treatment and half the control group were provided a resource teacher, who introduced educational activities into the home

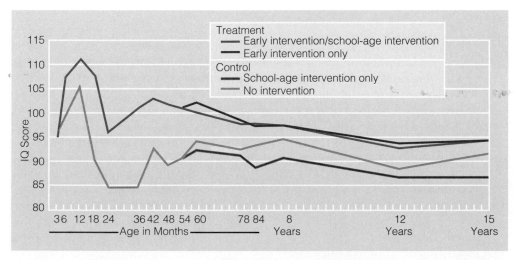

FIGURE 6.14

IQ scores of treatment and control children from 6 months to 15 years in the Carolina Abecedarian Project. School-based intervention had no impact on age-related changes in IQ; the effects of early intervention were powerful. (From F. A. Campbell & C. T. Ramey, 1995, "Cognitive and School Outcomes for High-Risk African-American Students at Middle Adolescence: Positive Effects of Early Intervention," *American Educational Research Journal, 32,* p. 757. Reprinted by permission of the American Educational Research Association.)

that addressed the child's specific learning needs. School-age intervention had no impact on IQ (refer again to Figure 6.14). And although it enhanced children's academic achievement, the effects were weaker than the impact of very early intervention (Campbell & Ramey, 1995).

Without some form of early intervention, many children born into economically disadvantaged families will not reach their potential. Recognition of this reality led the United States Congress to provide limited funding for intervention services directed at infants and toddlers who already have serious developmental problems or who are at risk for them because of poverty. At present, available programs are not nearly enough to meet the need (Children's Defense Fund, 2000). Nevertheless, those that exist are a promising beginning.

Ask YOURSELF...

review   *What probably accounts for the finding that speed of habituation and dishabituation to visual stimuli predicts later IQ better than does an infant mental test score?*

apply   *Fifteen-month-old Joey's developmental quotient (DQ) is 115. His mother wants to know exactly what this means and what she should do at home to support his mental development. How would you respond to her questions?*

connect   *Using what you learned about brain development in Chapter 5, explain why intensive intervention for poverty-stricken children beginning in the first 2 years has a greater impact on IQ than intervention at a later age?*

reflect   *Suppose you were seeking a child-care program for your baby. What would you want it to be like, and why?*

Language Development

As perception and cognition improve during infancy, they pave the way for an extraordinary human achievement—language. On the average, children say their first word at 12 months of age, with a range of about 8 to 18 months. Once words appear, language develops rapidly. Sometime between 1½ and 2 years, toddlers combine two words. Soon their utterances increase in length and complexity (Bloom, 1998). By age 6, children have a vocabulary of about 10,000 words, speak in elaborate sentences, and are skilled conversationalists.

Infants are communicative beings from the start, as this interaction between a 3-month-old and her grandfather indicates. How will she accomplish the awesome task of becoming a speaker of her native language? Theorists disagree sharply on answers to this question.

SOTOGRAPHS/LIAISON AGENCY

To appreciate what an awesome task this is, think about the many abilities involved in your own flexible use of language. When you speak, you must select words that match the underlying concepts you want to convey. Then you must combine them into phrases and sentences using a complex set of grammatical rules. Next, you must pronounce these utterances correctly, or you will not be understood. Finally, you must follow the rules of everyday conversation. For example, if you do not take turns, make comments that are relevant to what your partner just said, and use an appropriate tone of voice, then no matter how clear and correct your language, others may refuse to listen to you.

Infants and toddlers make remarkable progress in getting these skills under way. How do they do so? Several theories address how early language development takes place. Let's examine and evaluate each, based on what we know about the beginnings of language in the first 2 years.

THREE THEORIES OF LANGUAGE DEVELOPMENT

In the 1950s researchers did not take seriously the idea that very young children might be able to figure out important properties of the language they hear. As a result, the first two theories of how children acquire language were extreme views. One, *behaviorism*, regarded language development as entirely due to environmental influences. The second, *nativism*, assumed that children are prewired to master the intricate rules of their language.

■ **THE BEHAVIORIST PERSPECTIVE.** Well-known behaviorist B. F. Skinner (1957) proposed that language, just like any other behavior, is acquired through *operant conditioning*. As the baby makes sounds, parents reinforce those that are most like words with smiles, hugs, and speech in return. For example, at 12 months, my older son, David, often babbled something like this: "book-a-book-a-dook-a-dook-a-book-a-nook-a-book-aaa." One day while he babbled away, I held up his picture book and said, "Book!" Very soon David was saying "book-aaa" in the presence of books.

Some behaviorists rely on *imitation* to explain how children rapidly acquire complex utterances, such as whole phrases and sentences (Moerk, 1992; Whitehurst & Vasta, 1975). And imitation can combine with reinforcement to promote language, as when the parent coaxes, "Say 'I want a cookie,'" and delivers praise and a treat after the toddler responds, "Wanna cookie!"

Although reinforcement and imitation contribute to early language development, they are best viewed as supporting rather than fully explaining it. As Carolyn remarked one day, "It's amazing how creative Caitlin is with language. She combines words in ways she's never heard before, such as 'needle it' when she wants me to sew up her teddy bear and 'allgone outside' when she has to come in from the backyard." Carolyn's observations are accurate: Young children create many novel utterances that are not reinforced by or copied from others.

■ **THE NATIVIST PERSPECTIVE.** Linguist Noam Chomsky (1957) proposed a nativist theory that regards the young child's amazing language skill as etched into the structure of the human brain. Focusing on grammar, Chomsky reasoned that the rules of sentence organization are much too complex to be directly taught to or independently discovered by a young child. Instead, he argued, all children have a **language acquisition device (LAD),** a biologically based innate system that contains a set of rules common to all languages. It permits children, no matter which language they hear, to speak in a rule-oriented fashion as soon as they pick up enough words.

Are children biologically primed to acquire language? Recall from Chapter 4 that newborn babies are remarkably sensitive to speech sounds and prefer to listen to the human voice. In addition, children the world over reach major language milestones in a similar sequence—evidence that fits with a biologically based language program (Gleitman & Newport, 1996). Furthermore, efforts to teach language to nonhuman primates—using either specially devised artificial symbol systems or American Sign Language, a gestural language used by the deaf—have met with limited success (Miles, 1999). Apes master only a basic vocabulary, and they do not acquire complex grammatical forms—findings consistent with Chomsky's view that humans are uniquely prepared for language.

Evidence for specialized language areas in the brain and a sensitive period for language development have also been interpreted as supporting Chomsky's theory. Let's take a closer look at these findings.

language acquisition device (LAD)
In Chomsky's theory, a biologically based innate system for picking up language that permits children, no matter which language they hear, to speak in a rule-oriented fashion as soon as they have learned enough words.

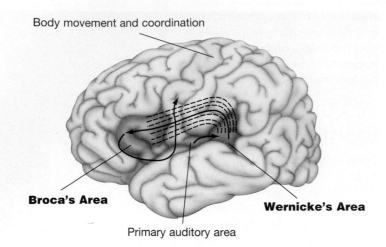

Body movement and coordination

Broca's Area

Wernicke's Area

Primary auditory area

FIGURE 6.15

Language-specific structures in the left hemisphere of the cerebral cortex. *Broca's area* controls language production by creating a detailed program for speaking, which it sends to the face area of the cortical region that controls body movement and coordination. *Wernicke's area* interprets language by receiving impulses from the primary auditory area, where sensations from the ears are sent. To produce a verbal response, Wernicke's area communicates with Broca's area through a bundle of nerve fibers, represented by dotted lines in the figure.

a sensitive period exists during which language must be acquired.

Broca's area
A language structure located in the frontal lobe of the left hemisphere of the cerebral cortex that controls language production.

Wernicke's area
A language structure located in the temporal lobe of the left hemisphere of the cerebral cortex that is responsible for interpreting language.

Language Areas in the Brain. Humans have evolved specialized regions in the brain that support language skills. Recall from Chapter 5 that for most people, language is housed in the left hemisphere of the cerebral cortex. Within it are two language-specific structures (see Figure 6.15). **Broca's area,** located in the frontal lobe, controls language production. **Wernicke's area,** located in the temporal lobe, is responsible for interpreting language.

Although Broca's and Wernicke's areas have been taken as support for an LAD, we must be cautious about this conclusion. In Chapter 5, we noted that at birth, the brain is not fully lateralized; instead, it is highly plastic. As children acquire language, the brain becomes more specialized. Furthermore, if the left hemisphere is injured in the early years, other regions take over its language functions (see page 175). So rather than the brain being innately programmed for language, language-learning experience seems to lead certain brain areas to become dedicated to language (Bates, 1999). Other research indicates that many parts of the brain participate in language activities in differing degrees, depending on the particular language skill and the individual's mastery of that skill (Kim et al., 1997; Neville & Bavelier, 1998).

A Sensitive Period for Language Development. Must language be acquired early in life, during an age span in which the brain is particularly responsive to language stimulation? Evidence for a sensitive period that coincides with brain lateralization would support the view that language development has unique biological properties.

To test this idea, researchers have tracked the recovery of severely abused children who experienced little human contact in childhood. The most thoroughly studied is Genie, a normally developing child who said her first words just before she was isolated in the back room of her parents' house at 1½ years of age. Until she was found at 13½, no one talked to her, and she was beaten when she made any noise. With several years of training by dedicated teachers, Genie's language developed, but not nearly to the same extent as that of normal children. Although she acquired a large vocabulary and good comprehension of conversation, her grammar and communication skills were limited (Curtiss, 1977, 1989). Genie's case, and others like it, fits with the notion of a sensitive period, although a precise age cutoff for a decline in language competence has not been established.

What about acquiring a second language? Is this task harder after a sensitive period has passed? In a study of Chinese and Korean adults who immigrated to the United States at varying ages, those who learned English between ages 3 and 7 scored as well as native speakers in grammar. As age of arrival increased, grammar scores declined. Similar trends exist for adults who became deaf in childhood or adolescence and learned American Sign Language at different ages (Mayberry, 1994; Newport, 1991). Furthermore, EEG and fMRI measures of neural activity indicate that second-language processing is less lateralized in older than younger learners (Dehaene et al., 1997). Although adolescents and adults can acquire a second language, children attain higher levels of mastery on a wide range of language skills (Harley & Wang, 1997).

■ **LIMITATIONS OF THE NATIVIST PERSPECTIVE.** Chomsky's theory has had a major impact on current views of language development. It is now widely accepted that humans have a unique, biological predisposition to acquire language. Yet as we have seen, the biological basis of Chomsky's LAD is far from clear. And his account of development has been challenged on other grounds.

First, researchers have had great difficulty identifying the single system of grammar that Chomsky believes underlies all languages. Even simple grammatical distinctions, such as the use of *the* versus *a,* are made in quite different ways around the world. For example, several African languages rely on tone patterns to express these articles. In Japanese and Chinese, they are inferred entirely from sentence context. Critics of Chomsky's theory doubt the existence of an LAD that can account for such varied approaches to conveying the same meaning (Maratsos, 1998; Tomasello, 1995).

Second, language is not acquired quite as quickly as nativist theory suggests. Although extraordinary strides are made during the early years, children master many sentence constructions gradually. As we will see in Chapter 12, complete mastery of some grammatical forms is not achieved until well into middle childhood (Tager-Flusberg, 1997). This suggests that more learning and discovery are involved than Chomsky assumed.

■ **THE INTERACTIONIST PERSPECTIVE.** In recent years, new ideas about language development have arisen, emphasizing *interactions* between inner capacities and environmental influences. Although several interactionist theories exist, all stress the social context of language learning. An active child, well endowed for acquiring language, observes and participates in social exchanges. From these experiences, children gradually build a communication system that relates the structure and content of language to their social meanings. According to this view, native capacity, a strong desire to interact with others, and a rich language and social environment combine to assist children in discovering the functions and regularities of language (Bohannon & Bonvillian, 2001).

Even among interactionists, debate continues over the precise nature of innate language abilities. Some theorists accept a modified view of Chomsky's position. They believe that children are primed to acquire language but form and refine hypotheses about its structure based on language experience (Slobin, 1985). Others believe that children make sense of their complex language environments by applying powerful cognitive strategies rather than ones specifically tuned to language (Bates, 1999; Tomasello & Brooks, 1999).

As we chart the course of early language growth, we will see a great deal of evidence for the interactionist position. But none of these theories has yet been fully tested. In reality, biology, cognition, and social experience may operate in different balances with respect to various aspects of language—pronunciation, vocabulary, grammar, and communication skills. Table 6.4 on page 242 provides an overview of early language milestones we will take up in the next few sections.

GETTING READY TO TALK

Before babies say their first word, they are preparing for language in many ways. They listen attentively to human speech, and they make speechlike sounds. As adults, we can hardly help but respond.

■ **COOING AND BABBLING.** Around 2 months, babies begin to make vowel-like noises, called **cooing** because of their pleasant "oo" quality. Gradually, consonants are added, and around 4 months **babbling** appears, in which infants repeat consonant–vowel combinations in long strings, such as "bababababa" or "nanananana."

The timing of early babbling seems to be due to maturation, since babies everywhere (even those who are deaf) start babbling at about the same age and produce a similar range of early sounds. But for babbling to develop further, infants must be able to hear human speech. Around 7 months, babbling starts to include the sounds of mature spoken languages. However, if a baby's hearing is impaired, these speechlike sounds are greatly delayed, and, in the case of deaf infants, are totally absent (Eilers & Oller, 1994; Oller, 2000). When deaf infants are exposed to sign language from birth, they babble with their hands in much the same way hearing infants do through speech (Petitto & Marentette, 1991).

cooing
Pleasant vowel-like noises made by infants, beginning around 2 months of age.

babbling
Repetition of consonant–vowel combinations in long strings, beginning around 4 months of age.

TABLE 6.4

Milestones of Language Development During the First Two Years

APPROXIMATE AGE	MILESTONE
2 months	Infants coo, making pleasant vowel sounds.
4 months on	Infants babble, adding consonants to their cooing sounds and repeating syllables. By 7 months, babbling of hearing infants starts to include many sounds of mature spoken languages.
	Infants and parents establish joint attention, and parents often verbally label what the baby is looking at.
	Interaction between parents and baby includes turn-taking games, such as pat-a-cake and peekaboo. By 12 months, babies participate actively.
8–12 months	Infants begin using preverbal gestures, such as showing and pointing, to influence the behavior of others. Word comprehension first appears.
12 months	Toddlers say their first recognizable word.
18–24 months	Vocabulary expands from about 50 to 200 words.
20–26 months	Toddlers combine two words.

When a baby coos or babbles and gazes at you, what are you likely to do? One day, as I stood in line at the post office behind a mother and her 7-month-old daughter, the baby babbled, and three adults—myself and two people standing beside me—started to talk to the infant. We cooed and babbled ourselves, imitating the baby, and also said such things as "My, you're a big girl, aren't you? Out to help Mommy mail letters today?" The baby smiled and babbled all the more.

As adults interact with infants and they listen to spoken language, babbling increases. By age 10 months, it contains the consonant–vowel and intonation patterns of the infant's language community, some of which are transferred to their first words (Boysson-Bardies & Vihman, 1991). Listen to an older baby babble, and notice that certain sounds appear in particular contexts—for example, when exploring objects, looking at books, and walking upright (Blake & Boysson-Bardies, 1992). Infants seem to be experimenting with the sound system and meaning of language before they speak in conventional ways.

■ **BECOMING A COMMUNICATOR.** Besides responding to cooing and babbling, adults interact with infants in many other situations. By age 4 months, infants start to gaze in the same direction adults are looking, a skill that becomes more accurate between 12 and 15 months of age (Tomasello, 1999). Adults also follow the baby's line of vision and, after establishing *joint attention,* comment on what the infant sees. In this way, they label the baby's environment. Researchers believe that joint attention contributes greatly to early language development. Infants and toddlers who often experience it talk earlier and show faster vocabulary development (Carpenter, Nagel, & Tomasello, 1998; Dunham, Dunham, & Curwin, 1993).

Around 4 to 6 months, interaction between parent and baby begins to include give-and-take, as in turn-taking games such as pat-a-cake and peekaboo. At first, the parent starts the game and the baby is an amused observer. Nevertheless, 4-month-olds are sensitive to the structure and timing of these interactions, smiling more to an organized than a disorganized peekaboo exchange (Rochat, Querido, & Striano, 1999). By 12 months, babies actively participate, exchanging roles with the parent. As they do so, they practice the turn-taking pattern of human conversation, a vital context for acquiring language and communication skills.

At the end of the first year, as infants become capable of intentional behavior, they use preverbal gestures to influence the behavior of others (Carpenter, Nagel, & Tomasello, 1998; Fenson et al., 1994). For example, Caitlin held up a toy to show it and pointed to the cupboard when she wanted a cookie. Carolyn responded to her gestures and also labeled them ("That's your bear!", "Oh, you want a cookie!"). In this way, toddlers learn that using language leads to desired

TONY FREEMAN/PHOTOEDIT

This 15-month-old delights in playing peekaboo with her mother. As she participates, she practices the turn-taking pattern of human conversation.

results. Soon they utter words with their reaching and pointing gestures, the gestures recede, and spoken language is under way (Iverson, Capirci, & Caselli, 1994; Namy & Waxman, 1998).

FIRST WORDS

Ask several parents to list their toddlers' first words. Notice how the words build on the sensorimotor foundations Piaget described and on categories children form during the first 2 years. Earliest words usually refer to important people ("Mama," "Dada"), objects that move ("ball," "car," "cat," "shoe"), familiar actions ("bye-bye," "up," "more"), or outcomes of familiar actions ("dirty," "hot," "wet"). In their first 50 words, toddlers rarely name things that just *sit there*, like "table" or "vase" (Nelson, 1973).

Some early words are linked to specific cognitive achievements. For example, toddlers begin to use disappearance words, like "all gone," at about the same time they master advanced object permanence problems. And success and failure expressions, such as "There!" and "Uh-oh!", appear when toddlers can solve sensorimotor problems suddenly, in Piaget's Substage 6. According to one pair of researchers, "Children seem to be motivated to acquire words that are relevant to the particular cognitive problems they are working on at the moment" (Gopnik & Meltzoff, 1986, p. 1057).

Besides cognition, emotion influences early word learning. At first, when acquiring a new word for an object, person, or event, 1½-year-olds say it neutrally; they need to listen carefully to learn, and strong emotion diverts their attention. As words become better learned, toddlers integrate talking and expressing feelings (Bloom, 1998). "Shoe!" said 22-month-old Grace as Monica tied her shoelaces before an outing. At the end of the second year, toddlers label their emotions with words like "happy," "mad," and "sad"—a development we will consider further in Chapter 7.

Toddlers often do not use new words just the way we do. Sometimes they apply them too narrowly, an error called **underextension.** For example, at 16 months, Caitlin used the word "bear" only to refer to the worn and tattered teddy bear she carried around much of the day. A more common error is **overextension**—applying a word to a wider collection of objects and events than is appropriate. For example, Grace used the word "car" for buses, trains, trucks, and fire engines.

Toddlers' overextensions reflect a remarkable sensitivity to categorical relations. They do not overextend randomly. Instead, they apply a new word to a group of similar experiences, such as "dog" to refer to furry, four-legged animals and "open" to mean opening a door, peeling fruit, and untying shoelaces. This suggests that children often overextend deliberately because they have difficulty recalling or have not acquired a suitable word (Bloom, 2000; Naigles & Gelman, 1995). In addition, when a word is hard to pronounce, toddlers are likely to substitute a related one they can say (Elsen, 1994). As vocabulary and pronunciation improve, overextensions gradually disappear.

underextension
An early vocabulary error in which a word is applied too narrowly, to a smaller number of objects and events than is appropriate.

overextension
An early vocabulary error in which a word is applied too broadly, to a wider collection of objects and events than is appropriate.

THE TWO-WORD UTTERANCE PHASE

Young toddlers add to their vocabularies slowly, at a rate of 1 to 3 words a month. Over time, the number of words learned accelerates. Between 18 and 24 months, a spurt in vocabulary often (but not always) takes place. Many children add 10 to 20 new words a week (Fenson et al., 1994; Reznick & Goldfield, 1992).

Why does vocabulary forge ahead in the second half of the second year? An improved ability to categorize experience and retrieve words from memory supports this "naming explosion" (Gershkoff-Stowe & Smith, 1997). Also, older toddlers can use language to represent a wider range of experiences as they talk not just about objects and events in the present, but also about nonpresent experiences (Morford & Goldin-Meadow, 1997). Furthermore, rapid word learning may depend on a growing capacity to grasp others' intentions, evident in toddlers' imitation around 18 months (see page 220). As a result, they can more easily figure out what others are talking about (Bloom, 2000).

As vocabulary size moves toward 200 words, toddlers combine two words, such as "Mommy shoe," "go car," "more cookie," and "my truck," in **telegraphic speech.** Like a telegram, they focus on high-content words and leave out smaller and less important ones, such as "can," "the," and "to." For children learning languages that emphasize word order (such as English and French), endings like "-s" and "-ed" are not yet present. In languages in which word order is flexible and small grammatical markers are stressed, children's first sentences include them from the start (de Villiers & de Villiers, 1999).

Even though the two-word utterance is very limited, toddlers the world over use it to express an impressive variety of meanings. In doing so, are they already applying a consistent grammar? Although toddlers rarely make gross grammatical errors (saying "chair my" instead of "my chair" or "eat Daddy" instead of "Daddy eat"), many early word combinations do not follow adult grammatical rules. At 20 months, Caitlin said "more hot" and "more read," expressions not acceptable in English.

Furthermore, two-word speech is largely made up of simple formulas, such as "eat + X" and "more + X" (with many different words inserted in the X position). These are usually copies of adult word pairings, as when Carolyn remarked to Caitlin, "Let's see if you can *eat the berries*" or "How about *more sandwich*?" (Tomasello & Brooks, 1999). When toddlers entering the two-word phase were taught several noun and verb nonsense words (for example, "meek" for a doll and "gop" for a snapping action), they easily combined the new nouns with words they knew well, as in "more meek." But they seldom formed word combinations with the new verbs (Tomasello et al., 1997). This suggests that they did not yet grasp subject–verb and verb–object relations, which are the foundation of grammar.

In sum, toddlers starting to combine words are absorbed in figuring out word meanings and using their limited vocabularies in whatever way possible to get their thoughts across (Maratsos, 1998). However, it does not take long for children to figure out grammatical rules. As we will see in Chapter 9, the beginnings of grammar are in place by age 2½.

COMPREHENSION VERSUS PRODUCTION

So far, we have focused on language **production**—the words and word combinations children use. What about **comprehension**—the language they understand? At all ages, comprehension develops ahead of production. For example, toddlers follow many simple directions, such as "Bring me your book" or "Don't touch the lamp," even though they cannot yet express all these words in their own speech. A 5-month lag exists between the time children comprehend 50 words (around 13 months) and the time they produce that many (around 18 months) (Menyuk, Liebergott, & Schultz, 1995).

Why is language comprehension ahead of production? Think back to the distinction made earlier in this chapter between two types of memory—recognition and recall. Comprehension requires only that children recognize the meaning of a word. Production is more difficult

telegraphic speech
Toddlers' two-word utterances that, like a telegram, leave out smaller and less important words.

production
In language development, the words and word combinations that children use.

comprehension
In language development, the words and word combinations that children understand.

because children must recall, or actively retrieve from their memories, the word as well as the concept for which it stands. Failure to say a word does not mean that toddlers do not understand it. If we rely only on what children say, we will underestimate their language progress.

INDIVIDUAL AND CULTURAL DIFFERENCES

Each child's progress in acquiring language results from a complex blend of biological and environmental influences. For example, earlier we saw that Timmy's spoken language was delayed, in part because of Vanessa's tense, directive communication with him. But Timmy is also a boy, and many studies show that girls are slightly ahead of boys in early vocabulary growth (Fenson et al., 1994). The most common biological explanation is girls' faster rate of physical maturation, believed to promote earlier development of the left cerebral hemisphere, where language is housed. But mothers also talk much more to toddler-age girls than boys (Leaper, Anderson, & Sanders, 1998).

Besides the child's sex, temperament and life circumstances make a difference. Toddlers who are very reserved and cautious often wait until they understand a great deal before trying to speak. When they finally do speak, their vocabularies grow rapidly (Nelson, 1973). In the week after her adoption, 16-month-old Grace spoke only a single Cambodian word, saying it when by herself. For the next 2 months, Grace listened to English conversation without speaking—a "silent period" typical of children beginning to acquire a second language (Saville-Troike, 1988). Around 18 months, words came quickly—first "Eli," then "doggie," "kitty," "Mama," "Dada," "book," "ball," "car," "cup," "clock," and "chicken," all within one week.

Young children have unique styles of early language learning. Caitlin and Grace (like most toddlers) used a **referential style;** their vocabularies consisted mainly of words that referred to objects. A smaller number of toddlers use an **expressive style.** Compared to referential children, they produce many more social formulas and pronouns, such as "stop it," "thank you," and "I want it," uttered as compressed phrases, much like single words (as in "Iwannit"). These styles reflect early ideas about the functions of language. Grace, for example, thought words were for naming things. In contrast, expressive-style children believe words are for talking about people's feelings and needs. The vocabularies of referential-style children grow faster, since all languages contain many more object labels than social phrases (Bates et al., 1994).

What accounts for a toddler's choice of a particular language style? Once again, both biological and environmental factors are involved. Grace was especially interested in exploring objects, and Monica and Kevin eagerly labeled them. She also freely imitated words she heard, and her parents responded by imitating back—a strategy that supports swift vocabulary growth because it helps children retain new labels in memory (Masur, 1995; Masur & Rodemaker, 1999). Expressive-style children tend to have highly sociable personalities, and their parents more often use verbal routines ("How are you?" "It's no trouble") designed to support social relationships (Goldfield, 1987).

The two language styles are also linked to culture. When speaking to infants and toddlers, American mothers label objects more frequently than do Japanese mothers. In contrast, Japanese mothers more often engage young children in social routines, perhaps because their culture stresses the importance of membership in the social group (Fernald & Morikawa, 1993). Similarly, African mothers of Mali, Mauritania, and Senegal respond verbally to their infant's glances and vocalizations to other people, not to the baby's exploration of objects (Jamin, 1994).

Sheer amount of parental speech is related to early word learning. The more words caregivers use, the more toddlers pick up. And words parents say very often tend to be acquired earliest (Huttenlocher et al., 1991). Whereas object words (nouns) are particularly common in the vocabularies of English-speaking toddlers, action words (verbs) are more numerous

DEVORE/ANTHRO-PHOTO

In Western societies, many mothers stress object labels to young language learners. In contrast, this African mother of Botswana responds verbally to her toddler's glances and vocalizations to other people, not to exploration of objects.

language learning = referential v. expressive

referential style
A style of early language learning in which toddlers use language mainly to label objects.

expressive style
A style of early language learning in which toddlers use language mainly to talk about the feelings and needs of themselves and other people. Initial vocabulary emphasizes social formulas and pronouns.

Educational Concerns
Supporting Early Language Learning

SUGGESTION	CONSEQUENCE
Respond to coos and babbles with speech sounds and words.	Encourages experimentation with sounds that can later be blended into first words. Provides experience with turn-taking pattern of human conversation.
Establish joint attention and comment on what child sees.	Predicts earlier onset of language and faster vocabulary development.
Play social games, such as pat-a-cake and peekaboo.	Provides experience with turn-taking pattern of human conversation.
Engage toddlers in joint make-believe play.	Promotes all aspects of conversational dialogue.
Engage toddlers in frequent conversations.	Predicts faster early language development and academic competence during the school years.
Read to toddlers often, engaging them in dialogues about picture books.	Provides exposure to many aspects of language, including vocabulary, grammar, communication skills, and information about written symbols and story structures.

among Korean and Mandarin Chinese toddlers. When caregivers' speech is examined in each culture, it reflects this difference (Choi & Gopnik, 1995; Tardif, Gelman, & Xu, 1999).

At what point should parents be concerned if their child does not talk or says very little? If a toddler's development is greatly delayed when compared to the norms given in Table 6.4, then parents should consult the child's doctor or a speech and language therapist. Late babbling may be a sign of slow and problematic language development that can be prevented with early intervention (Oller et al., 1999). Some toddlers who do not follow simple directions or who, after age 2, have difficulty putting their thoughts into words may suffer from a hearing impairment or a language disorder that requires immediate treatment (Ratner, 2001).

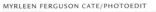

MYRLEEN FERGUSON CATE/PHOTOEDIT

This Chinese mother speaks to her baby daughter in short, clearly pronounced sentences with high-pitched, exaggerated intonation. Adults in many countries use this form of language, called child-directed speech, with infants and toddlers. It eases the task of early language learning.

SUPPORTING EARLY LANGUAGE DEVELOPMENT

There is little doubt that children are biologically prepared for acquiring language, since no other species can develop as flexible and creative a capacity for communication as we can. At the same time, a great deal of evidence fits with the interactionist view that a rich social environment builds on young children's natural readiness to speak their native tongue. The Educational Concerns table above summarizes ways that caregivers can consciously support early language learning. They also do so unconsciously—through a special style of speech.

Adults in many countries speak to young children in **child-directed speech (CDS),** a form of language made up of short sentences with high-pitched, exaggerated expression, clear pronunciation, and distinct pauses between speech segments (Fernald et al., 1989). CDS also contains many simplified words, such as "night-night," "bye-bye," and "tummy," that are easy for toddlers to pronounce. In addition, speakers of CDS often repeat phrases, ask questions, and give directions, perhaps as a way of checking to see if their message has been properly received. Deaf parents use a similar style of communication when signing to their babies (Masataka, 1996). Here is an example of Carolyn using CDS with 18-month-old Caitlin as she picked her up from child care:

Caitlin: "Go car."
Carolyn: "Yes, time to go in the car. Where's your jacket?"
Caitlin: (looks around, walks to the closet) "Dacket!" (pointing to her jacket)

© LAURA DWIGHT

Carolyn: "There's that jacket! (She helps Caitlin into the jacket.) On it goes! Let's zip up. (Zips up the jacket.) Now, say bye-bye to Grace and Timmy."

Caitlin: "Bye-bye, G-ace."

Carolyn: "What about Timmy? Bye to Timmy?"

Caitlin: "Bye-bye, Te-te."

Carolyn: "Where's your bear?"

Caitlin: (looks around)

Carolyn: (pointing) "See? Go get the bear. By the sofa." (Caitlin gets the bear.)

Parents do not seem to be deliberately trying to teach children to talk when they use CDS, since many of the same speech qualities appear when adults communicate with foreigners. CDS probably arises from adults' desire to keep young children's attention and ease their task of understanding, and it works effectively in these ways. From birth on, children prefer to listen to CDS over other kinds of adult talk (Cooper & Aslin, 1994). By 5 months, they are more emotionally responsive to it and can discriminate the tone quality of CDS with different meanings—for example, approving versus soothing utterances (Moore, Spence, & Katz, 1997; Werker, Pegg, & McLeod, 1994).

Parents constantly fine-tune CDS to fit with children's needs. Notice how Carolyn kept her utterance length just ahead of Caitlin's, creating a sensitive match between language stimulation and Caitlin's current capacities. In a study carried out in four cultures, American, Argentinean, French, and Japanese mothers tended to speak to 5-month-olds in emotion-laden ways, emphasizing greetings, repeated sounds, and affectionate names. At 13 months, when toddlers began to understand as well as respond, maternal speech became more information-laden—concerned with giving directions, asking questions, and describing what was happening at the moment (Bornstein et al., 1992a).

Many features of CDS support early language development. For example, parents who frequently repeat part of their own or the child's previous utterance and use simple questions have 2-year-olds who make faster language progress (Hoff-Ginsburg, 1986). As the Biology and Environment box on page 248 makes clear, when a child's disability makes it difficult for parents to engage in the sensitive communication of CDS, language and cognitive development are drastically delayed. This does not mean that we should deliberately load our speech to toddlers with repetitions, questions, and other characteristics of CDS! These qualities occur naturally as adults draw young children into dialogues, accepting their attempts to talk as meaningful and worthwhile.

Conversational give-and-take between parent and toddler is one of the best predictors of early language development and academic competence during the school years. It provides many examples of speech just ahead of the child's current level and a sympathetic environment in which children can try out new skills (Huttenlocher et al., 1991; Walker et al., 1994). Dialogues about picture books are particularly effective. They expose children to great breadth of language and literacy knowledge, from vocabulary, grammar, and communication skills to information about written symbols and story structures (Whitehurst & Lonigan, 1998). Low-income children benefit especially. Two- and 3-year-olds who experience daily reading at home or child care, compared with those who do not, are greatly advanced in language comprehension and production (Whitehurst et al., 1994).

Do social experiences that promote language development remind you of those that strengthen cognitive development in general? Notice how CDS and parent–child conversation create a *zone of proximal development* in which children's language expands. In contrast, impatience with and rejection of children's efforts to talk lead them to stop trying and result in immature language skills (Baumwell, Tamis-LeMonda, & Bornstein, 1997). In the next chapter we will see that sensitivity to children's needs and capacities supports their emotional and social development as well.

Dialogues about picture books are an especially effective way to stimulate young children's language development. As this father talks about the pictures with his 2-year-old daughter, he exposes her to great breadth of language and literacy knowledge.

child-directed speech (CDS)
A form of language adults use to speak to infants and toddlers that consists of short sentences with high-pitched, exaggerated expression, clear pronunciation, and distinct pauses between speech segments.

Biology & ENVIRONMENT

PARENT–CHILD INTERACTION AND COGNITIVE DEVELOPMENT OF DEAF CHILDREN

About 1 in every 1,000 American infants is born deaf (U.S. Department of Health and Human Services, 2000h). When a deaf child cannot participate fully in communication with parents and other caregivers, development is severely compromised. Yet the consequences of deafness for children's language and cognition vary with social context, as comparisons of deaf children of hearing parents with deaf children of deaf parents reveal.

Over 90 percent of deaf children have hearing parents. During toddlerhood and early childhood, these children often are delayed in language and complex make-believe play. In middle childhood, many achieve poorly in school and are deficient in social skills. Yet deaf children of deaf parents escape these difficulties! Their language (use of sign) and play maturity are on a par with hearing children's. After school entry, deaf children of deaf parents learn easily and get along well with adults and peers (Bornstein et al., 1999b; Spencer & Lederberg, 1997).

These differences can be traced to early parent–child communication. Beginning in infancy, hearing parents of deaf children are less positive, less effective at achieving joint attention and turn taking, and more directive and intrusive (Meadow-Orlans & Steinberg,

1993; Spencer & Meadow-Orlans, 1996). While helping their deaf preschoolers solve a challenging puzzle, hearing parents have trouble adjusting their verbal and nonverbal assistance to the child's needs (Jamieson, 1995). In contrast, the quality of interaction between deaf children of deaf parents is similar to that of hearing children of hearing parents.

Children with limited and less sensitive parental communication are behind their agemates in achieving verbal control over their behavior—in thinking before they act and in planning. Deaf children of hearing parents frequently display impulse-control problems (Arnold, 1999).

Hearing parents are not at fault for their deaf child's problems. Instead, they lack experience with visual communication, which enables deaf parents to respond readily to a deaf child's needs. Deaf parents know they must wait for the child to turn toward them before interacting (Spencer, Bodner-Johnson, & Gutfreund, 1992). Hearing parents tend to speak or gesture while the child's attention is directed elsewhere— a strategy that works with a hearing but not with a deaf partner. When the child is confused or unresponsive, hearing parents often feel overwhelmed and become more controlling (Jamieson, 1995). Furthermore, learning sign lan-

DAVID YOUNG-WOLFF/PHOTOEDIT

A teacher fluent in sign language interacts with this deaf toddler, born to hearing parents. Through early access to rich, natural language-learning experiences, he will be protected from serious developmental problems—delayed language, impulse-control difficulties, poor school achievement, and deficits in social skills.

guage is an immense task, and few hearing parents become fluent.

The impact of deafness on language and cognitive development can best be understood by considering its effects on parents and other significant people in the child's life. Deaf children need access to language models—deaf adults and peers—to experience a natural language-learning situation. And their hearing parents benefit from social support along with training in how to interact sensitively with a nonhearing partner.

Ask YOURSELF...

review Why is the interactionist perspective attractive to many investigators of language development? How does it differ from the behaviorist and nativist perspectives? Cite evidence that supports it.

apply Prepare a list of research-based recommendations for how to support language development during the first 2 years.

connect Cognition and language are interrelated. List examples of how cognition fosters language development. Next, list examples of how language fosters cognitive development.

Summary

PIAGET'S COGNITIVE-DEVELOPMENTAL THEORY

According to Piaget, how do schemes change over the course of development?

- In Piaget's theory, by acting directly on the environment, children move through four stages in which psychological structures, or **schemes,** achieve a better fit with external reality.

- Schemes change in two ways. The first is through **adaptation,** which is made up of two complementary activities—**assimilation** and **accommodation.** The second is through **organization,** the internal rearrangement of schemes into a strongly interconnected cognitive system.

Describe the major cognitive achievements of the sensorimotor stage.

- Piaget's **sensorimotor stage** is divided into six substages. In the first three substages, through the **circular reaction** the newborn baby's reflexes gradually transform into the more flexible action patterns of the older infant and finally into the representational schemes of the 2-year-old child. During Substage 4, infants develop **intentional,** or **goal-directed, behavior** and begin to understand **physical causality** and **object permanence.** Substage 5 brings a more exploratory approach to **functional play,** and infants no longer make the **A-not-B search error.** By Substage 6, toddlers can **mentally represent** reality, as shown by **deferred imitation** and **make-believe play.**

What does recent research say about the accuracy of Piaget's sensorimotor stage?

- Piaget underestimated many infant capacities. Secondary circular reactions and aspects of physical reasoning—including a grasp of object permanence, object solidity, gravity, and physical causality—are present in beginning form earlier than Piaget indicated, as revealed by the **violation-of-expectation method.** In addition, even young infants are capable of representation, as indicated by deferred imitation and problem solving by analogy.

Cognitive attainments do not develop in the neat, stepwise fashion predicted by Piaget's sensorimotor substages.

- Today, researchers believe that newborns have more built-in equipment for making sense of their world than Piaget assumed. Some speculate that infants build important schemes through perceptual learning. Others advocate a nativist, **modular view of the mind** that grants newborns substantial built-in knowledge. A compromise position suggests that babies begin life with a set of learning procedures for constructing certain types of knowledge; their progress depends on both biological makeup and specific experiences.

INFORMATION PROCESSING

Describe the information-processing view of cognitive development and the general structure of the information-processing system.

- Information-processing researchers regard development as gradual and continuous and study many aspects of thinking. They want to know exactly what individuals of different ages do when faced with a task or problem.

- Most general models of the information-processing system divide the mind into three parts: the **sensory register; working,** or **short-term, memory;** and **long-term memory.** As information flows through each, **mental strategies** operate on it to increase the efficiency of thinking as well as the chances that information will be retained.

What changes in attention, memory, and categorization take place over the first 2 years?

- With age, infants attend to more aspects of the environment, take information in more quickly, and flexibly shift their attention from one stimulus to another. In the second year, attention to novelty declines and sustained attention improves, especially during play with toys.

- As infants get older, they remember experiences longer and retrieve them more

quickly. After 12 months, memory persists despite changes in context. Young infants are capable of **recognition** memory; by the end of the first year, they can engage in **recall.** Between 1 and 2 years, recall for people, places, and objects is excellent. Both biology and social experience probably contribute to the emergence of **auto-biographical memory.**

- During the first year, infants group stimuli into increasingly complex categories, and categorization shifts from a perceptual to a conceptual basis. In the second year, toddlers become active categorizers, spontaneously sorting objects during their play.

Describe the contributions and limitations of the information-processing approach to our understanding of early cognitive development.

- Information-processing findings on memory and categorization challenge Piaget's view of infants as sensorimotor beings who cannot mentally represent experiences. However, information processing has not yet provided a broad, comprehensive theory of children's thinking.

THE SOCIAL CONTEXT OF EARLY COGNITIVE DEVELOPMENT

How does Vygotsky's concept of the zone of proximal development expand our understanding of early cognitive development?

- According to Vygotsky's sociocultural theory, complex mental activities originate in social interaction. Through the support and guidance of more skilled partners, infants master culturally meaningful tasks within the **zone of proximal development**—ones just ahead of their current capacities.

INDIVIDUAL DIFFERENCES IN EARLY MENTAL DEVELOPMENT

Describe the mental testing approach, the meaning of intelligence test scores, and the extent to which infant tests predict later performance.

Summary (continued)

- The mental testing approach measures intellectual development in an effort to predict future performance. **Intelligence quotients,** or **IQs,** are scores on mental tests that compare a child's performance to that of same-age children.

- Infant tests consist largely of perceptual and motor responses; they predict later intelligence poorly. As a result, scores on infant tests are called **developmental quotients,** or **DQs,** rather than IQs. Speed of habituation and dishabituation to visual stimuli and object permanence, which tap basic cognitive processes, are better predictors of future performance.

Discuss environmental influences on early mental development, including home, child care, and early intervention for at-risk infants and toddlers.

- Research with the **Home Observation for Measurement of the Environment (HOME)** reveals that a stimulating home environment and parental encouragement, involvement, affection, and verbal communication repeatedly predict higher mental test scores, no matter what the child's SES and ethnic background. Although the HOME–IQ relationship is partly due to heredity, family living conditions do affect mental development.

- The quality of infant and toddler child care has a major impact on cognitive and social skills. Standards for **developmentally appropriate practice** specify program characteristics that meet the developmental needs of young children. Intensive early intervention can prevent the gradual

declines in intelligence and the poor academic performance of poverty-stricken children.

LANGUAGE DEVELOPMENT

Describe three theories of language development, and indicate the emphasis each places on innate abilities and environmental influences.

- According to the behaviorist perspective, parents train children in language skills by relying on operant conditioning and imitation. Behaviorism has difficulty accounting for children's novel, rule-based utterances.

- Chomsky's nativist view regards children as naturally endowed with a **language acquisition device (LAD).** Consistent with this perspective, a complex language system is unique to humans, and language-specific structures—**Broca's** and **Wernicke's areas**—can be found in the left hemisphere of the cerebral cortex. Furthermore, research supports the existence of an early, sensitive period for language development. However, the role of language learning in brain lateralization, vast diversity among the world's languages, and children's gradual mastery of many constructions have raised questions about Chomsky's theory.

- New interactionist theories offer a compromise between these extreme views, stressing that innate abilities and a rich social environment combine to promote language development.

Describe major milestones of language development in the first 2 years, individual differ-

ences, and ways adults can support infants' and toddlers' emerging capacities.

- During the first year, much preparation for language takes place. Infants begin **cooing** at 2 months and **babbling** around 4 months. Adults encourage language progress by responding to infants' coos and babbles, playing turn-taking games with them, establishing joint attention and labeling what babies see, and acknowledging their preverbal gestures.

- Around 12 months, toddlers say their first word. Young children often make errors of **underextension** and **overextension.** Between 18 and 24 months, a spurt in vocabulary often occurs, and two-word utterances called **telegraphic speech** appear. At all ages, language **comprehension** develops ahead of **production.**

- Individual differences in early language development exist. Girls show faster progress than boys, and reserved, cautious toddlers may wait before trying to speak. Most toddlers use a **referential style** of language learning, in which early words consist largely of names for objects. A few use an **expressive style,** in which social formulas are common and vocabulary grows more slowly.

- Adults in many cultures speak to young children in **child-directed speech (CDS),** a simplified form of language that is well suited to their learning needs. CDS occurs naturally when caregivers engage toddlers in conversations that accept and encourage their early efforts to talk.

Important terms and concepts

A-not-B search error (p. 215)
accommodation (p. 213)
adaptation (p. 212)
assimilation (p. 213)
autobiographical memory (p. 226)
babbling (p. 241)
Broca's area (p. 240)
child-directed speech (CDS) (p. 247)
circular reaction (p. 213)
comprehension (p. 244)
cooing (p. 241)
deferred imitation (p. 217)
developmental quotient, or DQ
   (p. 233)
developmentally appropriate practice
   (p. 236)
expressive style (p. 245)

functional play (p. 217)
Home Observation for Measurement
   of the Environment (HOME)
   (p. 233)
intelligence quotient, or IQ (p. 233)
intentional, or goal-directed, behavior
   (p. 214)
language acquisition device (LAD)
   (p. 239)
long-term memory (p. 224)
make-believe play (p. 217)
mental representation (p. 217)
mental strategies (p. 224)
modular view of the mind (p. 222)
object permanence (p. 215)
organization (p. 213)
overextension (p. 243)

physical causality (p. 214)
production (p. 244)
recall (p. 226)
recognition (p. 226)
referential style (p. 245)
scheme (p. 212)
sensorimotor stage (p. 212)
sensory register (p. 224)
telegraphic speech (p. 244)
underextension (p. 243)
violation-of-expectation method
   (p. 217)
Wernicke's area (p. 240)
working, or short-term, memory
   (p. 224)
zone of proximal development
   (p. 229)

fyi . . . for further information and help

Consult the companion website for this book, where you will find additional weblinks and associated learning activities:
www.ablongman.com/berk

COGNITIVE DEVELOPMENT

Jean Piaget Society
www.piaget.org

An international organization of researchers and teachers interested in cognitive development. Includes an informative biography on Jean Piaget.

INFANT AND TODDLER DEVELOPMENT AND EDUCATION

Association for Childhood Education International (ACEI)
www.udel.edu/bateman/acei

An organization interested in promoting sound educational practice from infancy through early

adolescence. Student membership is available and includes a subscription to Childhood Education, *a bimonthly journal covering research, practice, and public policy issues.*

National Association for the Education of Young Children (NAEYC)
www.naeyc.org

An organization open to all individuals interested in acting on behalf of young children's needs, with primary focus on education. Membership includes a subscription to Young Children, *a bimonthly journal covering theory, research, and practice in infant and early childhood development and education. Student membership is available.*

National Association for Family Child Care
www.nafcc.org

Organization open to caregivers, parents, and other individuals involved or interested in high-quality, home-based child care.

EARLY INTERVENTION

High/Scope Educational Research Foundation
www.highscope.org

An organization devoted to improving development and education from infancy through the high school years. Has designed a parent–infant education program. Conducts longitudinal research to determine the effects of early intervention on development.

American Speech-Language-Hearing Association
www.asha.org

An association that provides information on early identification of speech and language delays and disorders, including signs that a child should be evaluated by a speech and language therapist.

"Happy Family"

Wang Yi

6 years, China

When families care for them with love and sensitivity, infants and toddlers develop a sense of trust that enables them to reach out and connect with their wider world. The importance of early family relationships for emotional and social development is a major theme of Chapter 7.

Emotional and Social Development in Infancy and Toddlerhood

ERIKSON'S THEORY OF INFANT AND TODDLER PERSONALITY
Basic Trust versus Mistrust · Autonomy versus Shame and Doubt

EMOTIONAL DEVELOPMENT
Development of Basic Emotions · Understanding and Responding to the Emotions of Others · Emergence of Self-Conscious Emotions · Beginnings of Emotional Self-Regulation

DEVELOPMENT OF TEMPERAMENT
The Structure of Temperament · Measuring Temperament · Stability of Temperament · Genetic Influences · Environmental Influences · Temperament and Child Rearing: The Goodness-of-Fit Model
■ *Biology & Environment: Biological Basis of Shyness and Sociability*

DEVELOPMENT OF ATTACHMENT
Bowlby's Ethological Theory · Measuring the Security of Attachment · Stability of Attachment · Cultural Variations · Factors that Affect Attachment Security · Multiple Attachments · From Attachment to Peer Sociability · Attachment and Later Development
■ *Social Issues/Health: Is Child Care in Infancy a Threat to Attachment Security?*
■ *Cultural Influences: Father–Infant Relationships Among the Aka*

SELF-DEVELOPMENT
Self-Awareness · Categorizing the Self · Emergence of Self-Control

 s Caitlin reached

8 months of age, her parents noticed some important changes. She had become more fearful. One evening when Carolyn and David left her with a babysitter, she wailed as soon as she saw them head for the door—an experience she had accepted easily a few weeks earlier. Caitlin and Timmy's caregiver Ginette also observed an increasing wariness of strangers in the two children and an active effort to remain close to her. When Ginette turned and headed for another room, both babies dropped their play to crawl after her. And a knock at the door from the mail carrier prompted Caitlin and Timmy to cling to Ginette's legs and reach out to be picked up.

At the same time, each baby seemed more willful. An object removed from the hand at 5 months produced little response, but at 8 months Timmy actively resisted when Vanessa took away a table knife he had managed to reach. He burst into angry screams and could not be consoled by the toys she offered in its place.

Monica and Kevin knew little about Grace's development during her first year. The orphanage director who placed 16-month-old Grace in Monica's arms reported that Grace had been deeply loved by her destitute, homeless mother. Repeated separations—first from her birth mother and then from the orphanage caregivers—followed by a long journey to an unfamiliar home, where strange people practicing foreign customs surrounded her, left Grace in shock. Monica and Kevin reported that at first, she was extremely sad. When they picked her up, her body went limp and she turned her head away. She did not smile for over a week.

But as Grace's new parents held her close, whispered softly, rocked her gently, and satisfied her nearly constant craving for food, Grace returned their affection. Two weeks after her arrival, her despondency gave way to a sunny, easygoing disposition. She burst into a wide grin, reached out at the sight of Monica and Kevin, and laughed at Eli's funny faces and other antics. Among her first words were the names of family members—"Eli," "Mama," and "Dada." As her second birthday approached, Grace pointed to photos of herself, exclaiming "Gwace!", and laid claim to treasured possessions. "Gwace's chicken!" she would announce at mealtimes, chewing the meat from the drumstick and then sucking out the marrow, a practice she brought with her from Cambodia.

Taken together, Caitlin's, Timmy's, and Grace's reactions reflect two related aspects of personality that develop during the first 2 years: *close ties to others and a sense of self*—an awareness of one's own separateness and uniqueness. Our discussion begins with Erikson's psychosocial theory, which provides an overview of personality development during infancy and toddlerhood. Then we chart the course of emotional development. As we do so, we will discover why fear and anger became more apparent in Caitlin's and Timmy's range of emotions by the end of the first year. Our attention then turns to individual differences in temperament and personality. We will examine biological and environmental contributions to these differences and their consequences for future development.

Next, we take up attachment to the caregiver, the child's first affectional tie that develops over the course of infancy. We will see how the feelings of security that grow out of this important bond support the child's exploration, sense of independence, and expanding social relationships.

Finally, we focus on early self-development. By the end of toddlerhood, Grace recognized herself in mirrors and photographs, labeled herself as a girl, and showed the beginnings of self-control. "Don't touch!" she instructed herself one day as she resisted the desire to pull a lamp cord out of its socket. Cognitive advances combine with social experiences to produce these changes during the second year.

Erikson's Theory of Infant and Toddler Personality

basic trust versus mistrust
In Erikson's theory, the psychological conflict of infancy, which is resolved positively if caregiving, especially during feeding, is sympathetic and loving.

autonomy versus shame and doubt
In Erikson's theory, the psychological conflict of toddlerhood, which is resolved positively if parents provide young children with suitable guidance and reasonable choices.

Our discussion of major theories in Chapter 1 revealed that psychoanalytic theory is no longer in the mainstream of child development research. But one of its lasting contributions is its ability to capture the essence of personality development during each phase of life. Recall that Sigmund Freud, founder of the psychoanalytic movement, believed that psychological health and maladjustment could be traced to the early years—in particular, to the quality of the child's relationships with parents. Although Freud's limited concern with the channeling of instincts and his neglect of important experiences beyond infancy and early childhood came to be heavily criticized, the basic outlines of his theory were accepted and elaborated in several subsequent theories of personality development. The leader of these neo-Freudian perspectives is Erik Erikson's *psychosocial theory*, also introduced in Chapter 1.

BASIC TRUST VERSUS MISTRUST

Freud called the first year the *oral stage* and regarded gratification of the infant's need for food and oral stimulation as vital. Erikson accepted Freud's emphasis on the importance of feeding, but he expanded and enriched Freud's view. A healthy outcome during infancy, Erikson believed, does not depend on the *amount* of food or oral stimulation offered but rather on the *quality* of the caregiver's behavior. A mother who supports her baby's development relieves discomfort promptly and sensitively. For example, she holds the infant gently during feedings, patiently waits until the baby has had enough milk, and weans when the infant shows less interest in the breast or bottle.

Erikson recognized that no parent can be perfectly in tune with the baby's needs. Many factors affect parental responsiveness—feelings of personal happiness, momentary life conditions (for example, additional small children in the family), and culturally valued child-rearing practices. But when the *balance of care* is sympathetic and loving, then the psychological conflict of the first year—**basic trust versus mistrust**—is resolved on the positive side. The trusting infant expects the world to be good and gratifying, so he feels confident about venturing out and exploring it. The mistrustful baby cannot count on the kindness and compassion of others, so she protects herself by withdrawing from people and things around her.

According to Erikson, basic trust grows out of the quality of the early caregiving relationship. A parent who relieves the baby's discomfort promptly and holds the baby tenderly, during feedings and at other times, promotes basic trust—the feeling that the world is good and gratifying.

AUTONOMY VERSUS SHAME AND DOUBT

In the second year, during Freud's *anal stage,* instinctual energies shift to the anal region of the body. Freud viewed toilet training, in which children must bring their impulses in line with social requirements, as crucial for personality development. (Return to Chapter 5, page 195, to review how adults can best support toddlers' attainment of bladder and bowel control.)

Erikson agreed that the parent's manner of toilet training is essential for psychological health. But he regarded it as only one of many important experiences for newly walking, talking toddlers. Their familiar refrains—"No!" and "Do it myself!"—reveal that they have entered a period of budding selfhood. Toddlers want to decide for themselves—not just in toileting, but in other situations as well. The great conflict of this stage, **autonomy versus shame and doubt,** is resolved favorably when parents provide young children with suitable guidance and reasonable choices. A self-confident, secure 2-year-old has been encouraged not just to use the toilet but also to eat with a spoon and to help pick up his toys. His parents do not criticize or attack him when he fails at these new skills. And they meet his assertions of independence with tolerance and understanding. For example, they grant him an extra 5 minutes to finish his play before leaving for the grocery store and wait patiently while he tries to zip his jacket.

According to Erikson, the parent who is over- or undercontrolling in toileting is likely to be so in other aspects of the toddler's life. The outcome is a child who feels forced and shamed and who doubts his ability to control his impulses and act competently on his own.

In sum, basic trust and autonomy grow out of warm, sensitive parenting and reasonable expectations for impulse control starting in the second year. If children emerge from the first few years without sufficient trust in caregivers and without a healthy sense of individuality, the seeds are sown for adjustment problems. Adults who have difficulty establishing intimate ties, who are overly dependent on a loved one, or who continually doubt their own ability to meet new challenges may not have fully mastered the tasks of trust and autonomy during infancy and toddlerhood.

This 2-year-old is intent on using a spoon to feed herself. Toddlers who are allowed to decide and do things for themselves in appropriate situations develop a sense of autonomy—the feeling that they can control their bodies and act competently on their own.

Emotional Development

In the previous chapter, I suggested that you observe babies' increasingly effective schemes for controlling the environment and ways that adults support cognitive and language development. Now focus on another aspect of infant and caregiver behavior: the exchange of emotions. While you observe, note the various emotions the infant displays, the cues you rely on to interpret the baby's emotional state, and how the caregiver responds. Researchers have conducted many such observations to find out how effectively infants and toddlers communicate their emotions and interpret those of others. They have discovered that emotions play a powerful role in organizing the developments that Erikson regarded as so important—relationships with caregivers, exploration of the environment, and discovery of the self (Izard, 1991; Lazarus, 1991; Saarni, Mumme, & Campos, 1998).

Think back to the *dynamic systems perspective,* introduced in Chapters 1 and 4. As you read about early emotional development in the sections that follow, notice how emotions interact with young children's dynamic systems of action. Emotions energize development. At the same time, they are an aspect of the system that develops, becoming more varied and complex as children reorganize their behavior to attain new goals.

Since infants cannot describe their feelings, determining exactly which emotions they are experiencing is a challenge. Although vocalizations and body movements provide some information, facial expressions offer the most reliable cues. Cross-cultural evidence reveals that people around the world associate photographs of different facial expressions with emotions in the same way (Ekman & Friesen, 1972). These findings, which suggest that emotional expressions are built-in social signals, inspired researchers to analyze infants' facial patterns carefully to determine the range of emotions they display at different ages. A commonly used method for doing so, the MAX System, is illustrated in Figure 7.1.

FIGURE 7.1

Which emotions are these babies displaying? The MAX (Maximally Discriminative Facial Movement) System is a widely used method for classifying infants' emotional expressions. Facial muscle movements are carefully rated to determine their correspondence with basic feeling states, since people around the world associate different facial gestures with emotions in the same way. For example, cheeks raised and corners of the mouth pulled back and up signal happiness (a). Eyebrows raised, eyes widened, and mouth opened with corners pulled straight back denote fear (b). (From Izard, 1979)

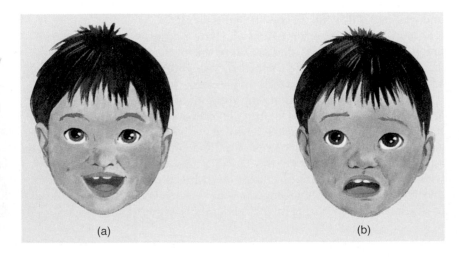

(a)   (b)

TABLE 7.1

Milestones of Emotional Development During the First Two Years

APPROXIMATE AGE	MILESTONE
Birth	Infants' emotions are relatively undifferentiated, consisting largely of two global arousal states: attraction to pleasant stimulation and withdrawal from unpleasant stimulation.
2–3 months	Infants engage in social smiling and respond in kind to adults' facial expressions.
3–4 months	Infants begin to laugh at very active stimuli. Expressions of sadness appear when parent–infant interaction is seriously disrupted.
6–8 months	Expressions of basic emotions are well organized and clearly related to social events. Infants start to become angry more often and in a wider range of situations. Fear, especially stranger anxiety, begins to rise. Attachment to the familiar caregiver is clearly evident, and separation anxiety appears. Infants use caregivers as a secure base for exploration.
8–12 months	Infants perceive facial expressions as organized patterns, and meaningful understanding of them improves. Social referencing appears. Infants laugh at subtle elements of surprise.
18–24 months	Self-conscious emotions of shame, embarrassment, guilt, and pride appear. A vocabulary for talking about feelings develops rapidly, and emotional self-regulation improves. Toddlers begin to appreciate that others' emotional reactions may differ from their own. First signs of empathy appear.

DEVELOPMENT OF BASIC EMOTIONS

Do infants come into the world with the ability to express **basic emotions**—those that can be directly inferred from facial expressions, such as happiness, interest, surprise, fear, anger, sadness, and disgust? Although signs of some emotions are present in early infancy, at first babies' emotional life is relatively undifferentiated, consisting of little more than two global arousal states: attraction to pleasant stimulation and withdrawal from unpleasant stimulation (Fox, 1991; Sroufe, 1979). Over time, emotions become clear, well-organized signals.

The dynamic systems perspective helps us understand how this happens. According to this view, children coordinate separate skills into more effective capacities as the central nervous system develops and the child's goals and experiences change. Videotaping the facial expressions of her daughter from 6 to 14 weeks, Linda Camras (1992) found that in the early weeks, the baby displayed a fleeting angry face as she was about to cry and a sad face as her crying waned. These expressions first appeared on the way to or away from full-blown distress and were not clearly related to the baby's experiences and desires. With age, she was better able to sustain an angry signal when she encountered a blocked goal and a sad signal when she could not overcome it.

Around 6 months, face, gaze, voice, and posture form distinct patterns that vary meaningfully with environmental events. For example, Caitlin typically responded to her parents' playful interaction with a joyful face, pleasant sounds, and a relaxed posture, as if to say, "This is fun!" In contrast, an unresponsive parent is likely to evoke a sad face, fussy sounds, and a tense body (sending the message, "I'm overwhelmed") or an angry face, crying, and "pick-me-up" gestures (stating, "Change this unpleasant event!"). In sum, by the middle of the first year, emotional expressions are well organized and specific—and therefore able to tell us a great deal about the infant's internal state (Weinberg & Tronick, 1994, 1996).

Four basic emotions—happiness, anger, sadness. and fear—have received the most research attention. Refer to Table 7.1 for an overview of changes during the first 2 years in these emotions as well as others we will take up in this chapter.

■ **HAPPINESS.** Happiness—first in terms of blissful smiles and later through exuberant laughter—contributes to many aspects of development. Infants smile and laugh when they conquer new skills, expressing their delight in motor and cognitive mastery. The smile also encourages caregivers to be affectionate and stimulating, so the baby smiles even more.

basic emotions
Emotions that can be directly inferred from facial expressions, such as happiness, interest, surprise, fear, anger, sadness, and disgust.

© BOB STERN/THE IMAGE WORKS

This 11-month-old smiles and laughs as he takes his first independent steps. His exuberance leads caregivers to return his joy and encourage his efforts. As a result, he masters new skills with enthusiasm.

Happiness binds parent and baby into a warm, supportive relationship that fosters the infant's developing competence.

During the early weeks, newborn babies smile when full, during sleep, and in response to gentle touches and sounds, such as stroking of the skin, rocking, and the mother's soft, high-pitched voice. By the end of the first month, infants start to smile at interesting sights, but these must be dynamic and eye-catching, such as a bright object jumping suddenly across the baby's field of vision. Between 6 and 10 weeks, the human face evokes a broad grin called the **social smile** (Sroufe & Waters, 1976). By 3 months, infants smile most often when interacting with people (Ellsworth, Muir, & Hains, 1993). These changes parallel the development of infant perceptual capacities—in particular, babies' sensitivity to visual patterns, including the human face (see Chapter 5).

Laughter, which appears around 3 to 4 months, reflects faster processing of information than does smiling. But like smiling, the first laughs occur in response to very active stimuli, such as the parent saying playfully, "I'm gonna get you!" and kissing the baby's tummy. As infants understand more about their world, they laugh at events that contain subtler elements of surprise. At 10 months, Timmy chuckled as Vanessa played a silent game of peekaboo. At 1 year, he laughed heartily as she crawled on all fours and then walked like a penguin (Sroufe & Wunsch, 1972).

Around the middle of the first year, infants smile and laugh more often when interacting with familiar people, a preference that supports and strengthens the parent–child bond. Toward the end of the first year, expressions of happiness differentiate further. Like adults, 10- to 12-month-olds have several smiles, which vary with context. They show a broad, "cheek-raised" smile to a parent's greeting; a reserved, muted smile to a friendly stranger; and a "mouth-open" smile during stimulating play (Dickson, Fogel, & Messinger, 1998). During the second year, the smile becomes a deliberate social signal. Toddlers break their play with an interesting toy to communicate their delight to an attentive adult (Jones & Raag, 1989).

■ **ANGER AND SADNESS.** Newborn babies respond with generalized distress to a variety of unpleasant experiences, including hunger, painful medical procedures, changes in body temperature, and too much or too little stimulation (see Chapter 4). From 4 to 6 months into the second year, angry expressions increase in frequency and intensity. Older infants react with anger in a wider range of situations—for example, when an interesting object or event is removed, their arms are restrained, the caregiver leaves for a brief time, or they are put down for a nap (Camras et al., 1992; Stenberg & Campos, 1990).

Why do angry reactions increase with age? Cognitive and motor development are involved. As infants become capable of intentional behavior (see Chapter 6), they want to control their own actions and the effects they produce (Alessandri, Sullivan, & Lewis, 1990). They are also better at identifying the person who caused pain or blocked their goal. The rise in anger is also adaptive. New motor capacities permit babies to use the energy mobilized by anger to defend themselves or overcome obstacles. At the same time, anger is a powerful social signal that motivates caregivers to ease a baby's distress.

Expressions of sadness also occur in response to pain, removal of an object, and brief separations, but they are usually less frequent than anger. Separation from a familiar caregiver can evoke extreme sadness, as Grace's despondency in the weeks after her adoption illustrates.

Sadness is especially common when parent–infant interaction is seriously disrupted. In several studies, researchers had parents assume either a still-faced, unreactive pose or a depressed emotional state. Their 3- to 7-month-old babies tried facial expressions, vocalizations, and body movements to get their mother or father to respond again. When these efforts failed, they turned away, frowned, and cried (Hernandez & Carter, 1996; Segal et al., 1995). The still-face reaction is identical in American, Canadian, and Chinese babies, suggesting that it is a built-in withdrawal response to caregivers' lack of communication (Kisilevsky et al., 1998). Return to Chapter 4, page 162, and note that infants of depressed

social smile
The smile evoked by the stimulus of the human face. First appears between 6 and 10 weeks.

parents respond this way. When allowed to persist, a sad, vacant outlook disrupts all aspects of early development.

SERGE ATTAL/TIMEPIX

■ **FEAR.** Like anger, fear rises during the second half of the first year. Older infants hesitate before playing with a new toy that they would have grasped immediately at an earlier age. And, as we saw in Chapter 5, newly crawling infants soon show fear of heights. But the most frequent expression of fear is to unfamiliar adults, a response called **stranger anxiety.**

Many infants and toddlers are quite wary of strangers, although the reaction does not always occur. It depends on several factors: temperament (some babies are generally more fearful), past experiences with strangers, and the situation in which baby and stranger meet (Thompson & Limber, 1991). When an unfamiliar adult picks up the infant in a new situation, stranger anxiety is likely. But if the adult sits still while the baby moves around and a parent is nearby, infants often show positive and curious behavior (Horner, 1980). The stranger's style of interaction—expressing warmth, holding out an attractive toy, playing a familiar game, and approaching slowly rather than abruptly—reduces the baby's fear.

Culture can modify stranger anxiety through infant-rearing practices. Maternal deaths are high among the Efe hunters and gatherers of Zaire, Africa. To ensure infant survival, a collective caregiving system exists in which beginning at birth, Efe babies are passed from one adult to another. Consequently, Efe infants show little stranger anxiety (Tronick, Morelli, & Ivey, 1992). In contrast, in Israeli kibbutzim (cooperative agricultural settlements), frequent terrorist attacks have led to widespread wariness of strangers. By the end of the first year, when (as we will see shortly) infants look to others for cues about how to respond emotionally, kibbutz babies display far more stranger anxiety than do their city-reared counterparts (Saarni, Mumme, & Campos, 1998).

The rise in fear after 6 months of age keeps newly crawling and walking babies' enthusiasm for exploration in check, generally keeping them close to the caregiver and careful about approaching unfamiliar people and objects. Eventually, stranger anxiety and other fears decline as cognitive development permits toddlers to discriminate more effectively between threatening and nonthreatening people and situations. This change is also adaptive, since adults other than caregivers will be soon be important in children's development.

Frequent terrorist attacks have led to widespread wariness of strangers among kibbutz residents—emotional reactions that are communicated to young children. These infants, who live on a kibbutz in the Golan Heights, enjoy a morning stroll. They are calm and comfortable with their caregiver, but should an unfamiliar person approach, they probably would show intense stranger anxiety.

UNDERSTANDING AND RESPONDING TO THE EMOTIONS OF OTHERS

Infants' emotional expressions are closely tied to their ability to interpret the emotional cues of others. Already we have seen that in the first few months, babies match the feeling tone of the caregiver in face-to-face communication. Early on, babies detect others' emotions through a fairly automatic process of *emotional contagion,* just as we tend to smile, laugh, or feel sad when we sense these emotions in others.

Between 7 and 10 months, infants perceive facial expressions as organized patterns, and they can match the emotion in a voice with the appropriate face of a speaking person (see Chapter 5). Responding to emotional expressions as organized wholes indicates that these signals have become meaningful to babies. As their skill at establishing joint attention improves (see Chapter 6), infants realize that an emotional expression not only has meaning but is a meaningful reaction to a specific object or event (Tomasello, 1999; Walker-Andrews, 1997).

Once these understandings are in place, infants engage in **social referencing,** in which they actively seek emotional information from a trusted person in an uncertain situation. Beginning at 8 to 10 months, when infants start to evaluate events with regard to their safety and security, social referencing occurs often. Many studies show that a caregiver's emotional expression (happy, angry, or fearful) influences whether a 1-year-old will be wary of strangers, play with

stranger anxiety
The infant's expression of fear in response to unfamiliar adults. Appears in many babies after 6 months of age.

social referencing
Relying on a trusted person's emotional reaction to decide how to respond in an uncertain situation.

an unfamiliar toy, or cross the deep side of the visual cliff (Repacholi, 1998; Rosen, Adamson, & Bakeman, 1992; Sorce et al., 1985).

Social referencing provides infants with a powerful means of learning about the world through indirect experience. By recognizing and responding to caregivers' emotional cues, babies can avoid harmful situations (such as a shock from an electric outlet or a fall down a steep staircase) without first experiencing their unpleasant consequences. And parents can capitalize on social referencing to teach their youngster, whose capacity to explore is rapidly expanding, how to react to a great many novel events.

Social referencing also permits toddlers to compare their own assessments of events with those of others. By the middle of the second year, they begin to appreciate that others' emotional reactions may differ from their own. In a recent study, an experimenter showed 14- and 18-month-olds broccoli and crackers. In one condition, she acted delighted with the taste of broccoli but disgusted with the taste of crackers. In the other condition, she showed the reverse preference. When asked to share the food, 14-month-olds offered only the type of food they themselves preferred—usually crackers. In contrast, 18-month-olds gave the experimenter whichever food they saw she liked, regardless of their own preferences (Repacholi & Gopnik, 1997).

In sum, toddlers no longer simply react to others' emotional messages. They use those signals to find out about others' intentions and preferences and to guide their own actions (Saarni, Mumme, & Campos, 1998).

EMERGENCE OF SELF-CONSCIOUS EMOTIONS

Besides basic emotions, humans are capable of a second, higher-order set of feelings, including shame, embarrassment, guilt, envy, and pride. These are called **self-conscious emotions** because each involves injury to or enhancement of our sense of self. For example, when we are ashamed or embarrassed, we feel negatively about our behavior or accomplishments, and we want to retreat so that others will no longer notice our failings. Guilt occurs when we know that we have harmed someone, and we wish to correct the wrongdoing and repair the relationship. In contrast, pride reflects delight in the self's achievements, and we are inclined to tell others what we have accomplished (Saarni, Mumme, & Campos, 1998).

Self-conscious emotions first appear in the middle of the second year, as the sense of self emerges. Shame and embarrassment can be seen as 18- to 24-month-olds lower their eyes, hang their heads, and hide their faces with their hands. Guiltlike reactions are also evident. After noticing Grace's unhappiness, 22-month-old Caitlin returned a toy she had grabbed and patted Grace in a soothing gesture. Pride, as well, emerges around this time (Barrett, 1998; Lewis et al., 1989). Besides self-awareness, self-conscious emotions require an additional ingredient: adult instruction in when to feel ashamed, guilty, or proud. Parents begin to provide this tutoring early, when they say, "My, look how far you can throw that ball!" or "Shame on you for grabbing that toy!"

As these comments indicate, self-conscious emotions play important roles in children's achievement-related and moral behaviors. The situations in which adults encourage these feelings vary from culture to culture. In most of the United States, children are taught to feel pride over personal achievement—throwing a ball the farthest, winning a game, and (later on) getting good grades. Among the Zuni Indians, shame and embarrassment occur in response to purely personal success, whereas generosity, helpfulness, and sharing evoke pride (Benedict, 1934b). In Japan, violating cultural standards of concern for others—a parent, a teacher, or an employer—causes intense shame (Lewis, 1992).

BEGINNINGS OF EMOTIONAL SELF-REGULATION

Besides expanding their range of emotional reactions, infants and toddlers begin to manage their emotional experiences. **Emotional self-regulation** refers to the strategies we use to

CELIA ROBERTS/EARTH IMAGES

Self-conscious emotions appear at the end of the first year. This Guatemalan 2-year-old undoubtedly feels a sense of pride as she helps care for her elderly grandmother—an activity highly valued in her culture.

adjust our emotional state to a comfortable level of intensity so we can accomplish our goals (Thompson, 1994). If you reminded yourself that an anxiety-provoking event would be over soon or decided not to see a scary horror movie, you were engaging in emotional self-regulation. A good start regulating emotion during the first 2 years contributes greatly to autonomy and mastery of cognitive and social skills, whereas early regulation difficulties predict adjustment problems (Crockenberg & Leerkes, 2000).

In the early months of life, infants have only a limited capacity to regulate their emotional states. Although they can turn away from unpleasant stimulation and mouth and suck when their feelings get too intense, they are easily overwhelmed by internal and external stimuli. As a result, they depend on the soothing interventions of caregivers—being lifted to the shoulder, rocked, and talked to softly—for help in adjusting their emotional reactions.

Rapid development of the cerebral cortex (see Chapter 5) gradually increases the baby's tolerance for stimulation. Between 2 and 4 months, caregivers start to build on this capacity by initiating face-to-face play and attention to objects. In these interactions, parents arouse pleasure in the baby while sensitively adjusting the pace of their own behavior so the infant does not become overwhelmed and distressed. As a result, the baby's tolerance for stimulation increases further (Field, 1994). By 4 months of age, the ability to shift attention helps infants control emotion. Babies who more readily turn away from unpleasant events are less prone to distress (Axia, Bonichini, & Benini, 1999; Johnson, Posner, & Rothbart, 1991). Around the end of the first year, crawling and walking enable infants to regulate emotion more effectively by approaching or retreating from various stimuli.

As caregivers help infants regulate their emotional states, they contribute to the child's style of emotional self-regulation. Parents who successfully read and respond contingently and sympathetically to the baby's emotional cues have infants who are less fussy, more easily soothed, and more interested in exploration. In contrast, parents who wait to intervene until the infant has become extremely agitated reinforce the baby's rapid rise to intense distress (Eisenberg, Cumberland, & Spinrad, 1998). This makes it harder for parents to soothe the baby in the future—and for the baby to learn to calm herself. When caregivers fail to regulate stressful experiences for infants who cannot yet regulate them for themselves, brain structures that buffer stress may fail to develop properly, resulting in an anxious, reactive temperament (Nelson & Bosquet, 2000).

As caregivers help infants regulate their emotions, they also provide lessons in socially approved ways of expressing feelings. Beginning in the first few months, mothers more often match their baby's positive than negative emotions. Boys get more of this training in controlling unhappiness than do girls, in part because infant boys have a harder time regulating negative emotion. As a result, the well-known sex difference—females as emotionally expressive and males as emotionally controlled—is promoted at a tender age (Malatesta et al., 1986; Weinberg et al., 1999). Furthermore, cultures that stress collectivism over individualism usually emphasize socially appropriate emotional behavior. Compared with Americans, Chinese and Japanese adults place more value on emotional restraint and discourage strong emotional expression in babies (Fogel, 1993). By the end of the first year, Chinese and, to a lesser extent, Japanese infants smile and cry less than do American babies (Camras et al., 1998).

In the second year, growth in representation and language leads to more effective ways of regulating emotions. A vocabulary for talking about feelings, such as "happy," "love," "surprised," "scary," "yucky," and "mad," develops rapidly after 18 months (Dunn, Bretherton, & Munn, 1987). Children of this age are not yet good at using language to comfort themselves (Grolnick, Bridges, & Connell, 1996). But by describing their emotions, toddlers can guide caregivers to help them feel better. For example, while listening to a story about monsters, Grace whimpered, "Mommy, scary." Monica put the book down and gave Grace a comforting hug.

Toddlers' use of words to label feelings shows that they already have a remarkable understanding of themselves and others as emotional beings. As we will see in later chapters, with the ability to think about feelings, emotional self-regulation improves greatly during early and middle childhood.

self-conscious emotions
Emotions that involve injury to or enhancement of the sense of self. Examples are shame, embarrassment, guilt, envy, and pride.

emotional self-regulation
Strategies for adjusting our emotional state to a comfortable level of intensity so we can accomplish our goals.

Ask YOURSELF...

review   *Why do many infants show stranger anxiety in the second half of the first year? What factors can increase or decrease wariness of strangers?*

apply   *At 14 months, Timmy danced joyfully to the tune "Old MacDonald" as several adults and children watched. At 20 months, he stopped dancing after a few steps, hiding his face behind his hands. What explains this change in Timmy's behavior?*

connect   *How do babies of depressed mothers fare in development of emotional self-regulation? (See Chapter 4, page 162.)*

reflect   *Do you believe that teaching infants and toddlers to control the expression of negative emotion is very important? Explain.*

Development of Temperament

Beginning in early infancy, Caitlin, Grace, and Timmy showed unique patterns of emotional reaction and behavior. Caitlin's sociability was unmistakable to everyone who met her. She smiled and laughed in response to adults and felt at ease in the company of other children, whom she readily approached during the second year. Meanwhile, Monica marveled at Grace's calm, relaxed disposition. At 19 months, she sat through a lengthy family celebration at a restaurant, contented in her high chair for almost 2 hours. In contrast, Timmy was constantly in motion. During his first few weeks, he wriggled about in his crib and squirmed vigorously on the changing table. When he became mobile, Vanessa found herself chasing him as he dropped one toy, moved on to the next, and climbed on chairs and tables.

When we describe one person as cheerful and "upbeat," another as active and energetic, and still others as calm, cautious, or prone to angry outbursts, we are referring to **temperament**—stable individual differences in quality and intensity of emotional reaction, activity level, attention, and emotional self-regulation (Rothbart & Bates, 1998). Researchers have become increasingly interested in temperamental differences among children, since the psychological traits that make up temperament are believed to form the cornerstone of the adult personality.

The New York Longitudinal Study, initiated in 1956 by Alexander Thomas and Stella Chess, is the longest and most comprehensive study of temperament to date. A total of 141 children were followed from early infancy well into adulthood. Results showed that temperament increases the chances that a child will experience psychological problems or, alternatively, be protected from the effects of a highly stressful home life. However, Thomas and Chess (1977) also found that temperament is not fixed and unchangeable. Parenting practices can modify children's emotional styles considerably.

These findings inspired a growing body of research on temperament, including its stability, its biological roots, and its interaction with child-rearing experiences. Let's begin to explore these issues by looking at the structure, or makeup, of temperament and how it is measured.

THE STRUCTURE OF TEMPERAMENT

Thomas and Chess's nine dimensions, listed in Table 7.2, served as the first influential model of temperament, inspiring all others that followed. When detailed descriptions of infants' and children's behavior obtained from parental interviews were rated on these dimensions, certain characteristics clustered together, yielding three types of children:

temperament
Stable individual differences in quality and intensity of emotional reaction, activity level, attention, and emotional self-regulation.

easy child
A child whose temperament is characterized by establishment of regular routines in infancy, general cheerfulness, and easy adaptation to new experiences.

difficult child
A child whose temperament is characterized by irregular daily routines, slow acceptance of new experiences, and negative and intense reactions.

slow-to-warm-up child
A child whose temperament is characterized by inactivity; mild, low-key reactions to environmental stimuli; negative mood; and slow adjustment when faced with new experiences.

TABLE 7.2

Two Models of Temperament

THOMAS AND CHESS		ROTHBART	
DIMENSION	**DESCRIPTION AND EXAMPLE**	**DIMENSION**	**DESCRIPTION**
Activity level	Proportion of active periods to inactive ones. Some babies are always in motion. Others move about very little.	Activity level	Level of gross motor activity
Rhythmicity	Regularity of body functions. Some infants fall asleep, wake up, get hungry, and have bowel movements on a regular schedule, whereas others are much less predictable.	Soothability	Reduction of fussing, crying, or distress in response to soothing techniques by the caregiver or baby
Distractibility	Degree to which stimulation from the environment alters behavior. Some hungry babies stop crying temporarily if offered a pacifier or a toy to play with. Others continue to cry until fed.	Attention span/persistence	Duration of orienting or interest
Approach/withdrawal	Response to a new object or person. Some babies accept new foods and smile and babble at strangers, whereas others pull back and cry on first exposure.	Fearful distress	Wariness and distress in response to intense or novel stimuli, including time taken to adjust to new situations
Adaptability	Ease with which the child adapts to changes in the environment. Although some infants withdraw when faced with new experiences, they quickly adapt, accepting the new food or person on the next occasion. Others continue to fuss and cry.	Irritable distress	Extent of fussing, crying, and showing distress when desires are frustrated
Attention span and persistence	Amount of time devoted to an activity. Some babies watch a mobile or play with a toy for a long time, whereas others lose interest after a few minutes.	Positive affect	Frequency of expression of happiness and pleasure
Intensity of reaction	Intensity or energy level of response. Some infants laugh and cry loudly, whereas others react only mildly.		
Threshold of responsiveness	Intensity of stimulation required to evoke a response. Some babies startle at the slightest change in sound or lighting. Others take little notice of these changes in stimulation.		
Quality of mood	Amount of friendly, joyful behavior as opposed to unpleasant, unfriendly behavior. Some babies smile and laugh frequently when playing and interacting with people. Others fuss and cry often.		

Sources: Left, Thomas & Chess, 1977; Right, Rothbart, 1981; Rothbart, Ahadi, & Evans, 2000.

- The **easy child** (40 percent of the sample). This child quickly establishes regular routines in infancy, is generally cheerful, and adapts easily to new experiences.

- The **difficult child** (10 percent of the sample). This child is irregular in daily routines, is slow to accept new experiences, and tends to react negatively and intensely.

- The **slow-to-warm-up child** (15 percent of the sample). This child is inactive, shows mild, low-key reactions to environmental stimuli, is negative in mood, and adjusts slowly to new experiences.

Note that 35 percent of the children did not fit any of these categories. Instead, they showed unique blends of temperamental characteristics.

Of the three temperamental types, the difficult pattern has sparked the most interest, since it places children at high risk for adjustment problems—both anxious withdrawal and aggressive behavior in middle childhood (Bates, Wachs, & Emde, 1994; Thomas, Chess, & Birch, 1968). Unlike difficult children, slow-to-warm-up children do not present many problems as infants and toddlers. However, they tend to show excessive fearfulness and slow, constricted behavior in the late preschool and school years, when they are expected to respond actively and quickly in classrooms and peer groups (Chess & Thomas, 1984; Schmitz et al., 1999).

A second model of temperament, developed by Mary Rothbart (1981), is also shown in Table 7.2. It combines overlapping dimensions of Thomas and Chess and other researchers. For example, "distractibility" and "attention span and persistence" are considered opposite ends of the same dimension and are simply called "attention span/persistence." It also includes a dimension not identified by Thomas and Chess—"irritable distress"—that taps emotional self-regulation. And it deletes what Rothbart considers overly broad dimensions, such as "rhythmicity," "intensity of reaction," "threshold of responsiveness" (Rothbart, Ahadi, & Evans, 2000). A child who is rhythmic in sleeping is not necessarily rhythmic in eating or bowel habits. And a child who smiles and laughs quickly and intensely is not necessarily quick and intense in fear or irritability.

Notice how Rothbart's six dimensions represent three underlying components of temperament: (1) emotion ("fearful distress," "irritable distress," "positive affect," and "soothability"), (2) attention ("attention span/persistence"), and (3) action ("activity level"). According to Rothbart, these components form an integrated system of capacities and limitations. Overall, the characteristics shown in Table 7.2 provide a fairly complete picture of the temperamental traits most often studied.

MEASURING TEMPERAMENT

Researchers measure temperament in diverse ways. Typically, they select from a variety of methods that assess children's behavior. But new techniques are focusing on physiological reactions in an effort to identify biological processes at the heart of temperamental styles.

■ **ASSESSMENTS OF BEHAVIOR.** Temperament is often assessed through interviews or questionnaires given to parents, although behavior ratings by pediatricians, teachers, and others familiar with the child, as well as direct observations by researchers, have also been used. Parental reports have been emphasized because of their convenience and parents' depth of knowledge about the child.

At the same time, information from parents has been criticized for being biased and subjective. For example, parents' prebirth expectations for their infant's temperament affect their reports after the infant arrives (Diener, Goldstein, & Mangelsdorf, 1995). And mothers who are anxious, depressed, and low in self-esteem tend to regard their babies as more difficult (Mebert, 1991; Vaughn et al., 1987). Nevertheless, parental ratings are moderately related to researchers' observations of children's behavior (Rothbart & Bates, 1998). And parent perceptions are useful for understanding the way parents view and respond to their child.

inhibited, or shy, child
A child whose temperament is characterized by negative reaction to and withdrawal from novel stimuli. Resembles slow-to-warm-up child.

uninhibited, or sociable, child
A child whose temperament is characterized by positive emotional reaction and approach to novel stimuli.

■ **ASSESSMENTS OF PHYSIOLOGICAL REACTIONS**. To explore the biological basis of temperament, researchers turn to psychophysiological measures. Most efforts have focused on **inhibited,** or **shy, children,** who react negatively to and withdraw from novel stimuli (much like Thomas and Chess's slow-to-warm-up children), and **uninhibited,** or **sociable, children,** who react positively to and approach novel stimuli. As the Biology and Environment box on pages 266–267 reveals, heart rate, hormone levels, and EEG waves in the frontal region of the cerebral cortex differentiate children with inhibited and uninhibited temperaments.

Investigators do not yet know how or when these diverse psychophysiological measures become interrelated—information that would shed light on the integrated role of various brain structures in shyness and sociability. And as we will see in the following sections, more research is needed to clarify how brain mechanisms combine with experience to support consistency and change in children's temperamental styles.

STABILITY OF TEMPERAMENT

It would be difficult to claim that something like temperament really exists if children's emotional styles were not stable over time. Indeed, many studies support the long-term stability of temperament. Infants and young children who score low or high on attention span, irritability, sociability, or shyness are likely to respond similarly when assessed again a few years later and, occasionally, even into the adult years (Caspi & Silva, 1995; Kochanska & Radke-Yarrow, 1992; Pedlow et al., 1993; Rothbart, Ahadi, & Evans, 2000; Ruff & Rothbart, 1996).

When the evidence as a whole is examined carefully, however, temperamental stability from one age period to the next is generally low to moderate. Although quite a few children remain the same, a good number have changed when assessed again. In fact, some characteristics, such as shyness and sociability, are stable over the long term only in children at the extremes—those who are very inhibited or very outgoing to begin with (Kerr et al., 1994; Sanson et al., 1996).

Why is temperament not more stable? A major reason is that temperament itself develops with age; early behaviors reorganize into new, more complex systems. To illustrate, let's look at irritability and activity level. Recall from Chapter 4 that the early months are a period of fussing and crying for most babies. As infants can better regulate their attention and emotions, many who initially seemed irritable become calm and content. In the case of activity level, the meaning of the behavior changes. At first, an active, wriggling infant tends to be highly aroused and uncomfortable, whereas an inactive baby is often alert and attentive. As infants move on their own, the reverse is so! An active crawler is usually alert and interested in exploration, whereas a very inactive baby might be fearful and withdrawn.

These inconsistencies help us understand why long-term prediction from early temperament is best achieved from the second year of life and after, when the child's system of emotion, attention, and action is better established (Caspi, 1998; Lemery et al., 1999). At the same time, the changes shown by many children suggest that experience can modify biologically based temperamental traits (although children rarely change from one extreme to another—that is, a shy toddler practically never becomes highly sociable). With these ideas in mind, let's turn to genetic and environmental contributions to temperament and personality.

GENETIC INFLUENCES

The word *temperament* implies a genetic foundation for individual differences in personality. To what extent are temperament and personality heritable? To answer this question, many kinship studies have compared individuals with various genetic relationships to one another. The most common approach is to compare identical with fraternal twins.

Findings reveal that identical twins are more similar than fraternal twins across a wide range of temperamental traits (activity level, shyness/sociability, irritability, attention span, and persistence) and personality measures (introversion/extroversion, anxiety, agreeableness, and impulsivity) (Caspi, 1998; DiLalla, Kagan, & Reznick, 1994; Emde et al., 1992; Goldsmith, Buss, & Lemery, 1997; Goldsmith et al., 1999). In Chapter 2, we indicated that heritability estimates derived from twin studies suggest a moderate role for genetic factors in temperament and personality: About half of individual differences can be traced to differences in genetic makeup.

Consistent ethnic and sex differences in early temperament exist, again implying a role for heredity. Compared to Caucasian infants, Asian babies tend to be less active, irritable, and vocal, more easily soothed when upset, and better at quieting themselves (Kagan et al., 1994; Lewis, Ramsay, & Kawakami, 1993). Grace's capacity to remain contentedly seated in her high chair through a long family dinner certainly fits with this evidence. And Timmy's high rate of activity is consistent with sex differences in emotional styles (Campbell & Eaton, 1999).

At birth, Chinese infants are calmer, more easily soothed when upset, and better at quieting themselves than are Caucasian infants. These differences are probably hereditary, but cultural variations in child rearing support them.

Biology & ENVIRONMENT

BIOLOGICAL BASIS OF SHYNESS AND SOCIABILITY

At age 4 months, Larry and Mitch visited the laboratory of Jerome Kagan, who observed their reactions to a variety of unfamiliar experiences. When exposed to new sights and sounds, such as a moving mobile decorated with colorful toys, Larry tensed his muscles, moved his arms and legs with agitation, and began to cry. Mitch's body remained relaxed and quiet, and he smiled and cooed pleasurably at the excitement around him.

Larry and Mitch returned to the laboratory as toddlers. This time, each experienced a variety of procedures designed to induce uncertainty. For example, electrodes were placed on their bodies and blood pressure cuffs on their arms to measure heart rate; highly stimulating toy robots, animals, and puppets moved before their eyes; and unfamiliar people entered and behaved in atypical ways or wore novel costumes. Larry whimpered and quickly withdrew, seeking his mother's protection. Mitch watched with interest, laughed at the strange sights, and approached the toys and strangers.

On a third visit, at age 4½ years, Larry barely talked or smiled during an interview with an unfamiliar adult. In contrast, Mitch asked questions and communicated his pleasure at each intriguing activity. In a playroom with two unfamiliar peers, Larry pulled back, keeping an anxious eye on the other children. Mitch made friends quickly.

In longitudinal research on several hundred Caucasian children, Kagan (1998) found that about 20 percent of 4-month-old babies were easily upset by novelty (like Larry), whereas 40 percent were comfortable, even delighted, with new experiences (like Mitch). About 30 percent of these extreme groups retained their temperamental styles as they grew older. Those resembling Larry tended to become fearful, inhibited toddlers and preschoolers; those resembling Mitch developed into outgoing, uninhibited youngsters (Kagan, Snidman, & Arcus, 1998).

PHYSIOLOGICAL CORRELATES OF SHYNESS AND SOCIABILITY

Kagan believes that individual differences in arousal of the *amygdala,* an inner brain structure that controls avoidance reactions, contribute to these contrasting temperamental styles. In shy, inhibited children, novel stimuli easily excite the amygdala and its con-nections to the cerebral cortex and sympathetic nervous system, which prepares the body to act in the face of threat. The same level of stimulation evokes minimal neural excitation in highly sociable, uninhibited children. In support of this theory, several physiological responses of shy infants and children resemble those of highly timid animals and are known to be mediated by the amygdala:

- **Heart Rate.** As early as the first few weeks of life, the heart rates of shy children are consistently higher than those of sociable youngsters, and they speed up further in response to unfamiliar events (Snidman et al., 1995).

- **Cortisol.** Saliva concentration of cortisol, a hormone that regulates blood pressure and is involved in resistance to stress, tends to be higher in shy than sociable children (Gunnar & Nelson, 1994; Kagan & Snidman, 1991).

- **Pupil dilation, blood pressure, and skin surface temperature.** Compared with sociable children, shy children show greater pupil dilation, rise in blood pressure, and cooling of the fingertips when faced with novelty and challenge (Kagan et al., 1999).

From an early age, boys tend to be more active and daring and girls more anxious and timid—a difference reflected in boys' higher injury rates throughout childhood and adolescence.

ENVIRONMENTAL INFLUENCES

Although genetic influences on temperament are clear, no study has shown that infants maintain their early emotional styles without environmental supports. Instead, heredity and environment combine to strengthen the stability of temperament, since a child's approach to the world affects the experiences to which she is exposed. To see how this works, let's take a second look at ethnic and sex differences in temperament.

When asked about their approach to child rearing, Japanese mothers respond that babies come into the world as independent beings who must learn to rely on their mothers through

Yet another physiological correlate of approach–withdrawal to people and objects is the pattern of EEG waves in the frontal region of the cerebral cortex. Recall from Chapter 5 that the left cortical hemisphere is specialized to respond with positive emotion, the right hemisphere with negative emotion. Shy infants and preschoolers show greater right than left frontal brain wave activity; their sociable counterparts show the opposite pattern (Calkins, Fox, & Marshall, 1996; Fox, Calkins, & Bell, 1994). Neural activity in the amygdala is transmitted to the frontal lobe and may influence these patterns.

LONG-TERM CONSEQUENCES

According to Kagan (1998), extremely shy or sociable children inherit a physiology that biases them toward a particular temperamental style. Among Caucasians, shy children are more likely to have certain physical traits—blue eyes and thin faces—known to be affected by heredity (Arcus & Kagan, 1995; Kagan et al., 1999). The genes controlling these characteristics may also influence the excitability of the amygdala.

Yet heritability research indicates that genes contribute only modestly to shyness and sociability. Experience also plays a part. When early inhibition persists, it can lead to adjustment difficulties, such as excessive cautiousness, social withdrawal, low self-esteem, and loneliness (Fordham & Stevenson-Hinde, 1999; Rubin, Stewart, & Coplan, 1995). At the same time, many inhibited infants and young children cope with novelty more effectively as they get older.

Child-rearing practices affect the chances that an emotionally reactive baby will become a fearful child. Warm, supportive parenting reduces cortisol production in inhibited babies, buffer-ing the child's fear, whereas cold, intrusive parenting heightens the cortisol response (Gunnar, 1998). In addition, when parents protect infants who dislike novelty from minor stresses, they make it harder for the child to overcome an urge to retreat from unfamiliar events. In contrast, parents who make appropriate demands for their baby to approach new experiences help the child learn to overcome fear (Rubin et al., 1997). In sum, for children to develop at their best, parenting must be tailored to their temperaments—a theme we will encounter again in this and later chapters.

A strong physiological response to uncertain situations prompts this 2-year-old's withdrawal when a friend of her parents bends down to chat with her. Her mother's patient but insistent encouragement can modify her physiological reactivity and help her overcome her urge to retreat from unfamiliar events.

close physical contact. North American mothers are likely to believe just the opposite—that they must wean the baby away from dependence into autonomy (Kojima, 1986). Consistent with these beliefs, Asian mothers interact gently, soothingly, and gesturally with their babies, whereas Caucasian mothers use a more active, stimulating, verbal approach—behaviors that enhance early temperamental differences between their infants (Fogel, Toda, & Kawai, 1988). Also, recall from our discussion of emotional self-regulation that Chinese and Japanese adults discourage babies from expressing strong emotion, an effort that contributes further to their infants' tranquility.

A similar process seems to contribute to sex differences in temperament. Within the first 24 hours after birth (before they could have had much experience with the baby), parents already perceive male and female newborns differently. Sons are rated as larger, better coordinated, more alert, and stronger. Daughters are viewed as softer, more awkward, weaker, and more delicate

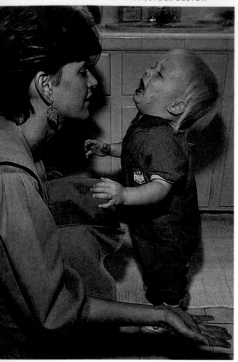

© NUBAR ALEXANIAN/STOCK BOSTON

This mother is perplexed because her 1-year-old is not responding to her efforts to help him calm down. Difficult children react negatively and intensely. When parents are patient and make firm but reasonable demands for mastering new experiences, difficultness often subsides.

goodness-of-fit model
Thomas and Chess's model, which states that an effective match, or "good fit," between child-rearing practices and a child's temperament leads to favorable development and psychological adjustment. A "poor fit" leads to adjustment problems.

(Stern & Karraker, 1989; Vogel et al., 1991). Gender-stereotyped beliefs carry over into the way parents treat their infants and toddlers. For example, parents more often encourage their young sons to be physically active and their daughters to seek help and physical closeness (Ruble & Martin, 1998). These practices promote temperamental differences between boys and girls.

In families with several children, an additional influence on temperament is at work. Parents often look for and emphasize each child's unique characteristics (Plomin, 1994b). This is reflected in the comments parents make after the birth of a second baby: "He's so much calmer," "She's a lot more active," or "He's more sociable." Research shows that when one child in a family is viewed as easy, another is likely to be perceived as difficult, even though the second child might not be very difficult when compared with children in general (Schachter & Stone, 1985). Each child, in turn, evokes responses from caregivers that are consistent with parental beliefs and the child's actual temperamental style.

Besides different experiences within the family, siblings have unique experiences with peers, teachers, and others in their community that can profoundly affect development (Caspi, 1998). These findings demonstrate that temperament and personality can be understood only in terms of complex interdependencies between genetic and environmental factors.

TEMPERAMENT AND CHILD REARING: THE GOODNESS-OF-FIT MODEL

We have already indicated that the temperaments of many children change with age. This suggests that environments do not always act in the same direction as a child's temperament. If a child's disposition interferes with learning or getting along with others, adults must gently but consistently counteract the child's maladaptive behavior.

Thomas and Chess (1977) proposed a **goodness-of-fit model** to explain how temperament and environmental pressures can together produce favorable outcomes. Goodness of fit involves creating child-rearing environments that recognize each child's temperament while encouraging more adaptive functioning.

Goodness of fit helps explain why children with difficult temperaments are at high risk for later behavior problems. These children, at least in many Western middle-SES families, frequently experience parenting that fits poorly with their dispositions. Without encouragement to try new experiences, their dislike of novelty can lead to overwhelming anxiety in the face of academic and social challenges. In addition, difficult infants are less likely to receive sensitive caregiving (van den Boom & Hoeksma, 1994). By the second year, their parents often resort to angry, punitive discipline. In response, the child reacts with defiance and disobedience. Then parents often behave inconsistently, rewarding the child's noncompliant behavior by giving in to it, although they initially resisted (Lee & Bates, 1985). The difficult child's temperament combined with harsh, inconsistent child rearing forms a poor fit that maintains and even increases the child's irritable, conflict-ridden style. In contrast, when parents are positive, involved, and engage in the sensitive, face-to-face play that helps infants regulate emotion, difficultness declines by age 2 (Feldman, Greenbaum, & Yirmiya, 1999).

However, effective caregiving also depends on life conditions and cultural values. During a famine in Africa, difficult infant temperament was associated with survival—probably because difficult babies demanded and received more maternal attention and food (deVries, 1984). In low-SES Puerto Rican families, difficult children are treated with sensitivity and patience; they are not at risk for adjustment problems (Gannon & Korn, 1983).

In Western nations, shy, withdrawn children are regarded as socially incompetent, yet Chinese adults evaluate such children positively—as advanced in social maturity and understanding (Chen, Rubin, & Li, 1995). In line with this view, in a study comparing Canadian and Chinese children, the Chinese children scored much higher in inhibition. Furthermore, when their children were shy, Canadian mothers reported more protection and punishment and less acceptance and encouragement of achievement. Chinese mothers of shy children indicated just the opposite—less punishment and rejection and more acceptance and encouragement (Chen et al., 1998).

In cultures where particular temperamental styles are linked to adjustment problems, an effective match between rearing conditions and child temperament is best accomplished early, before unfavorable temperament–environment relationships produce maladjustment that is hard to undo. Both difficult and shy children benefit from warm, accepting parenting that makes firm but reasonable demands for mastering new experiences. In the case of reserved, inactive toddlers, research shows that highly stimulating maternal behavior (frequent questioning, instructing, and pointing out objects) fosters exploration of the environment. Yet these same parental behaviors have a negative impact on very active toddlers, inhibiting their exploration (Gandour, 1989; Miceli et al., 1998). Recall from Chapter 6 that Vanessa often behaved in a harsh, directive way with Timmy. A "poor fit" between her parenting and Timmy's active temperament may have contributed to his tendency to move from one activity to the next with little involvement.

The goodness-of-fit model reminds us that babies come into the world with unique dispositions that adults have to accept. Parents can neither take full credit for their children's virtues nor be blamed for all their faults. But parents can turn an environment that exaggerates a child's problems into one that builds on the youngster's strengths, helping each child master the challenges of development.

In the following sections, we will see that goodness of fit is also at the heart of infant–caregiver attachment. This first intimate relationship grows out of interaction between parent and baby, to which the emotional styles of both partners contribute.

Ask YOURSELF...

review   *Why is the stability of temperament only low to moderate?*

apply   *At 18 months, highly active Jake climbed out of his high chair long before his meal was finished. Exasperated, his father made him sit at the table until he had eaten all his food. Soon Jake's behavior escalated into a full-blown tantrum. Using the concept of goodness of fit, suggest another way of handling Jake.*

connect   *Do findings on ethnic and sex differences in temperament illustrate genetic–environmental correlation, discussed on pages 89–91 of Chapter 2? Explain.*

reflect   *How would you describe your temperament as a young child? What type of parenting fits well with that temperament?*

Development of Attachment

Attachment is the strong, affectional tie we feel for special people in our lives that leads us to feel pleasure and joy when we interact with them and to be comforted by their nearness during times of stress. By the second half of the first year, infants have become attached to familiar people who have responded to their needs for physical care and stimulation. Watch babies of this age, and notice how parents are singled out for special attention. A whole range of responses are reserved just for them. For example, when the mother enters the room, the baby breaks into a broad, friendly smile. When she picks him up, he pats her face, explores her hair, and snuggles against her body. When he feels anxious or afraid, he crawls into her lap and clings closely.

Freud first suggested that the infant's emotional tie to the mother provides the foundation for all later relationships. We will see shortly that research on the consequences of attachment

attachment
The strong, affectional tie that humans feel toward special people in their lives.

is consistent with Freud's idea. But attachment has also been the subject of intense theoretical debate. Turn back to the description of Erikson's theory at the beginning of this chapter, and notice how the psychoanalytic perspective regards feeding as the central context in which caregivers and babies build this close emotional bond. Behaviorism, too, emphasizes the importance of feeding, but for different reasons. According to a well-known behaviorist drive reduction explanation, as the mother satisfies the baby's hunger (primary drive), infants learn to prefer her soft caresses, warm smiles, and tender words of comfort (secondary drive) because these events have been paired with tension relief.

Although feeding is an important context in which mothers and babies build a close relationship, attachment does not depend on hunger satisfaction. In the 1950s, a famous experiment showed that rhesus monkeys reared with terry-cloth and wire-mesh "surrogate mothers" clung to the soft terry-cloth substitute, even though the wire-mesh "mother" held the bottle and infants had to climb on it to be fed. (Harlow & Zimmerman, 1959). Observations of human infants also reveal that they become attached to family members who seldom if ever feed them, including fathers, siblings, and grandparents. And perhaps you have noticed that toddlers in Western cultures who sleep alone and experience frequent daytime separations from their parents sometimes develop strong emotional ties to cuddly objects, such as blankets or teddy bears (Passman, 1987). Yet such objects have never played a role in infant feeding!

Another problem with drive reduction and psychoanalytic accounts of attachment is that much is said about the caregiver's contribution to the attachment relationship. But little attention is given to the role of the infant's characteristics.

BOWLBY'S ETHOLOGICAL THEORY

Today, **ethological theory of attachment** is the most widely accepted view of the infant's emotional tie to the caregiver. According to ethology, many human behaviors have evolved over the history of our species because they promote survival. John Bowlby (1969), who first applied this idea to the infant–caregiver bond, was originally a psychoanalyst. In his theory, he retained the psychoanalytic idea that quality of attachment to the caregiver has profound implications for the child's feelings of security and capacity to form trusting relationships.

At the same time, Bowlby was inspired by Konrad Lorenz's studies of imprinting in baby geese (see Chapter 1). He believed that the human infant, like the young of other animal species, is endowed with a set of built-in behaviors that keep the parent nearby, increasing the chances that the infant will be protected from danger. Contact with the parent also ensures that the baby will be fed, but Bowlby was careful to point out that feeding is not the basis for attachment. Instead, the attachment bond has strong biological roots. It can best be understood in an evolutionary context in which survival of the species is of utmost importance.

According to Bowlby, the infant's relationship with the parent begins as a set of innate signals that call the adult to the baby's side. Over time, a true affectional bond forms, which is supported by new emotional, cognitive, and motor capacities as well as a history of warm, sensitive care. Attachment develops in four phases:

1. *The preattachment phase* (birth to 6 weeks). A variety of built-in signals—grasping, smiling, crying, and gazing into the adult's eyes—help bring newborn babies into close contact with other humans. Once an adult responds, infants encourage her to remain nearby, since they are comforted when picked up, stroked, and talked to softly. Babies of this age can recognize their own mother's smell and voice (see Chapter 4). However, they are not yet attached to her, since they do not mind being left with an unfamiliar adult.

2. *The "attachment in the making" phase* (6 weeks to 6–8 months). During this phase, infants start to respond differently to a familiar caregiver than to a stranger. For example, at 4 months, Timmy smiled, laughed, and babbled more freely when interacting with his mother and quieted more quickly when she picked him up. As infants engage in face-to-face interaction with the parent and experience relief from distress, they learn that their own actions affect the behavior of those around them. They begin to develop a sense of

© MARTIN ROGERS/STOCK BOSTON

Baby monkeys reared with "surrogate mothers" preferred to cling to a soft terry-cloth "mother" instead of a wire-mesh "mother" that held a bottle. These findings contradict the drive reduction explanation of attachment, which assumes that the parent–infant relationship is based on feeding.

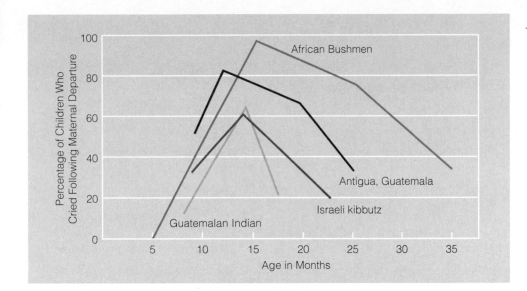

FIGURE 7.2

Development of separation anxiety.
In cultures around the world, separa-
tion anxiety emerges in the second
half of the first year, increasing until
about 15 months and then declining.
(Reprinted by permission of the pub-
lisher from *Infancy: Its Place in Human
Development* by Jerome Kagan,
Richard B. Kearsley, and Philip
Kelazo. Cambridge, Mass.: Harvard
University Press. Copyright © 1978
by the President and Fellows of
Harvard College.)

trust—the expectation that the caregiver will respond when signaled. But even though they recognize the parent, babies still do not protest when separated from her.

3. *The phase of "clear-cut" attachment* (6–8 months to 18 months–2 years). Now, attachment to the familiar caregiver is evident. Babies display **separation anxiety,** becoming upset when the adult they have come to rely on leaves. In many cultures, separation anxiety emerges around 6 months of age, increasing until about 15 months (see Figure 7.2). Its appearance suggests that infants have a clear understanding that the caregiver continues to exist when not in view. Consistent with this idea, babies who have not yet mastered Piagetian object permanence usually do not become anxious when separated from their mothers (Lester et al., 1974).

   Besides protesting the parent's departure, older infants and toddlers try hard to main-tain her presence. They approach, follow, and climb on her in preference to others. And they use her as a **secure base** from which to explore, venturing into the environment and then returning for emotional support.

4. *Formation of a reciprocal relationship* (18 months–2 years and on). By the end of the sec-ond year, rapid growth in representation and language permits toddlers to understand the parent's coming and going and to predict her return. As a result, separation protest declines. Now children negotiate with the caregiver, using requests and persuasion rather than crawling after and clinging to her. For example, at age 2, Caitlin asked Carolyn and David to read her a story before leaving her with a baby-sitter. The extra time with her parents, along with a better understanding of where they were going ("to have dinner with Uncle Sean") and when they would be back ("right after you go to sleep"), helped Caitlin withstand her parents' absence.

According to Bowlby (1980), out of their experiences during these four phases, children construct an enduring affectional tie to the caregiver that they can use as a secure base in the parent's absence. This inner representation becomes a vital part of personality. It serves as an **internal working model,** or set of expectations about the availability of attachment figures, their likelihood of providing support during times of stress, and the self's interaction with those figures. This image becomes the model, or guide, for all future close relationships— through childhood and adolescence and into adult life (Bretherton, 1992).

MEASURING THE SECURITY OF ATTACHMENT

Although virtually all family-reared babies become attached to a familiar caregiver by the second year, the quality of this relationship differs greatly from child to child. Some infants

ethological theory of attachment
A theory formulated by Bowlby, which views the infant's emotional tie to the caregiver as an evolved response that promotes survival.

separation anxiety
An infant's distressed reaction to the departure of the familiar caregiver.

secure base
The use of the familiar care-giver as a base from which the infant confidently explores the environment and to which he returns for emotional support.

internal working model
A set of expectations derived from early caregiving experi-ences concerning the availabil-ity of attachment figures, their likelihood of providing sup-port during times of stress, and the self's interaction with those figures. Becomes a model, or guide, for all future close relationships.

TABLE 7.3

Episodes in the Strange Situation

EPISODE	EVENTS	ATTACHMENT BEHAVIOR OBSERVED
1	Experimenter introduces parent and baby to playroom and then leaves.	
2	Parent is seated while baby plays with toys.	Parent as a secure base
3	Stranger enters, is seated, and talks to parent.	Reaction to unfamiliar adult
4	Parent leaves room. Stranger responds to baby and offers comfort if upset.	Separation anxiety
5	Parent returns, greets baby, and if necessary offers comfort. Stranger leaves room.	Reaction to reunion
6	Parent leaves room.	Separation anxiety
7	Stranger enters room and offers comfort.	Ability to be soothed by stranger
8	Parent returns, greets baby, if necessary offers comfort, and tries to reinterest baby in toys.	Reaction to reunion

Note: Episode 1 lasts about 30 seconds; the remaining episodes each last about 3 minutes. Separation episodes are cut short if the baby becomes very upset. Reunion episodes are extended if the baby needs more time to calm down and return to play.

Source: Ainsworth et al., 1978.

appear relaxed and secure in the presence of the caregiver; they know they can count on her for protection and support. Others seem anxious and uncertain.

A widely used technique for measuring the quality of attachment between 1 and 2 years of age is the **Strange Situation.** In designing it, Mary Ainsworth and her colleagues (1978) reasoned that if the development of attachment has gone well, infants and toddlers should use the parent as a secure base from which to explore an unfamiliar playroom. In addition, when the parent leaves for a brief period, the child should show separation anxiety, and an unfamiliar adult should be less comforting than the parent. As summarized in Table 7.3, the Strange Situation takes the baby through eight short episodes in which brief separations from and reunions with the parent occur.

Observing the responses of infants to these episodes, researchers have identified a secure attachment pattern and three patterns of insecurity; a few babies cannot be classified (Ainsworth et al., 1978; Main & Solomon, 1990; Barnett & Vondra, 1999). Which pattern do you think Grace displayed after adjusting to her adoptive family (see the description at the beginning of this chapter)?

Strange Situation
A procedure involving short separations from and reunions with the parent that assesses the quality of the attachment bond.

secure attachment
The quality of attachment characterizing infants who are distressed by parental separation and easily comforted by the parent when she returns.

avoidant attachment
The quality of insecure attachment characterizing infants who usually are not distressed by parental separation and who avoid the parent when she returns.

resistant attachment
The quality of insecure attachment characterizing infants who remain close to the parent before departure and display angry, resistive behavior when she returns.

- **Secure attachment.** These infants use the parent as a secure base. When separated, they may or may not cry, but if they do, it is due to the parent's absence, since they show a strong preference for her over the stranger. When the parent returns, they actively seek contact, and their crying is reduced immediately. About 65 percent of North American infants show this pattern.

- **Avoidant attachment.** These babies seem unresponsive to the parent when she is present. When she leaves, they usually are not distressed, and they react to the stranger in much the same way as the parent. During reunion, they avoid or are slow to greet the parent, and when picked up, they often fail to cling. About 20 percent of North American infants show this pattern.

- **Resistant attachment.** Before separation, these infants seek closeness to the parent and often fail to explore. When she returns, they display angry, resistive behavior, sometimes hitting and pushing. In addition, many continue to cry after being picked up and cannot be comforted easily. About 10 to 15 percent of North American infants show this pattern.

■ **Disorganized/disoriented attachment.** This pattern reflects the greatest insecurity. At reunion, these infants show a variety of confused, contradictory behaviors. For example, they might look away while being held by the parent or approach her with a flat, depressed gaze. Most of these babies communicate their disorientation with a dazed facial expression. A few cry out unexpectedly after having calmed down or display odd, frozen postures. About 5 to 10 percent of American infants show this pattern.

Infants' reactions in the Strange Situation closely resemble their use of the parent as a secure base and their response to separation at home (Blanchard & Main, 1979; Pederson & Moran, 1996). For this reason, the procedure is a powerful tool for assessing attachment security.

Recently, an alternative, more efficient method has become popular: the **Attachment Q-Sort** (Waters et al., 1995). It is suitable for children between 1 and 5 years of age. An observer—the parent or an expert informant—sorts a set of 90 descriptors of attachment-related behaviors (such as "Child greets mother with a big smile when she enters the room" and "If mother moves very far, child follows along") into nine categories, ranging from highly descriptive to not at all descriptive of the child. Then a score is computed that assigns children to securely or insecurely attached groups. Q-Sort responses of expert observers correspond well with Strange Situation attachment classifications (Pederson et al., 1998). And when mothers are carefully trained and supervised, their responses are reasonably consistent with those of expert observers (Seifer et al., 1996; Teti & McGourty, 1996).

STABILITY OF ATTACHMENT

Studies assessing the stability of attachment patterns between 1 and 2 years of age yield a wide range of findings. In some, the percentage of children whose reactions to parents remain the same is as low as 30 to 40 percent; in others, it is as high as 70 to 90 percent (Thompson, 1998).

A closer look at which infants stay the same and which ones change yields a more consistent picture. Quality of attachment is usually secure and stable for middle-SES babies experiencing favorable life conditions. And infants who move from insecurity to security typically have well-adjusted mothers with positive family and friendship ties. Perhaps many of these mothers became parents before they were psychologically ready but, with social support, grew into the role. In contrast, for low-SES families with many daily stresses, little social support, and parental psychological problems, attachment status generally moves away from security or changes from one insecure pattern to another (Owen et al., 1984; Vaughn et al., 1979; Vondra, Hommerding, & Shaw, 1999).

These findings indicate that securely attached babies more often maintain their attachment status than do insecure babies, whose relationship with the caregiver is, by definition, fragile and uncertain. The single exception to this trend is disorganized/disoriented attachment—an insecure pattern that is as stable as attachment security, with nearly 70 percent retaining this classification over the second year (Barnett, Ganiban, & Cicchetti, 1999). As we will see, many disorganized/disoriented infants experience extremely negative caregiving—a circumstance that may disrupt emotional self-regulation so severely that the baby's confused behavior persists.

Overall, many children show short-term instability in attachment quality. Yet three studies reported high long-term stability: More than 75 percent of children responded similarly to parental reunion in infancy and middle childhood (Howes, Hamilton, & Phillipsen, 1998; Main & Cassidy, 1988; Wartner et al., 1994). But these children were from middle-SES homes, and most probably had stable family lives. Even in the face of family stress and change, these parents may have been able to maintain a stable relationship with the child. When we take up factors that predict attachment security, we will consider evidence that supports this idea.

CULTURAL VARIATIONS

Cross-cultural evidence indicates that attachment patterns may have to be interpreted differently in other cultures. For example, as Figure 7.3 on page 274 reveals, German infants show

disorganized/disoriented attachment
The quality of insecure attachment characterizing infants who respond in a confused, contradictory fashion when reunited with the parent.

Attachment Q-Sort
An efficient method for assessing the quality of the attachment bond, in which a parent or an expert informant sorts a set of 90 descriptors of attachment-related behaviors on the basis of how well they describe the child. A score is then computed that assigns children to securely or insecurely attached groups.

FIGURE 7.3

A cross-cultural comparison of infants' reactions in the Strange Situation. A high percentage of German babies seem avoidantly attached, whereas a substantial number of Japanese infants appear resistantly attached. Note that these responses may not reflect true insecurity. Instead, they are probably due to cultural differences in child-rearing practices. (Adapted from van IJzendoorn & Kroonenberg, 1988.)

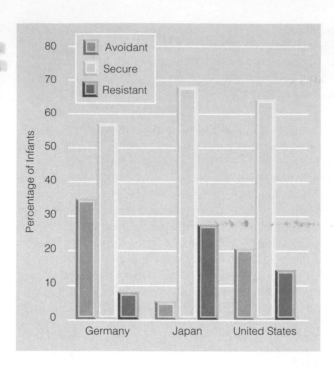

considerably more avoidant attachment than American babies do. But German parents encourage their infants to be nonclingy and independent, so the baby's behavior may be an intended outcome of cultural beliefs and practices (Grossmann et al., 1985). An unusually high number of Japanese infants display a resistant response, but the reaction may not represent true insecurity. Japanese mothers rarely leave their babies in the care of unfamiliar people, so the Strange Situation probably creates far greater stress for them than it does for infants who frequently experience maternal separations (Takahashi, 1990).

Despite these cultural variations and others, the secure pattern is still the most common attachment classification in all societies studied to date (van IJzendoorn & Kroonenberg, 1988; van IJzendoorn & Sagi, 1999). And when the Attachment Q-Sort is used to assess conceptions of the ideal child, mothers from diverse cultures—China, Germany, Israel, Japan, Norway, and the United States—prefer that their young children behave in a securely attached fashion (Posada et al., 1995).

FACTORS THAT AFFECT ATTACHMENT SECURITY

What factors might influence attachment security? Researchers have looked closely at four important influences: (1) opportunity to establish a close relationship; (2) quality of caregiving; (3) the baby's characteristics; and (4) family context, including parents' internal working models.

■ **OPPORTUNITY FOR ATTACHMENT.** The powerful effect of the baby's affectional tie to the familiar caregiver is most evident when it is absent. In a series of studies, René Spitz (1945, 1946) observed institutionalized infants who had been given up by their mothers between 3 and 12 months of age. The infants were placed on a large ward where they shared a nurse with at least seven other babies. In contrast to the happy, outgoing behavior they had shown before separation, they wept and withdrew from their surroundings, lost weight, and had difficulty sleeping. If a caregiver whom the baby could get to know did not replace the mother, the depression deepened rapidly.

These institutionalized babies had emotional difficulties because they were prevented from forming a bond with one or a few adults (Rutter, 1996). Another study supports this conclusion. Researchers followed the development of infants in an institution with a good caregiver–child ratio and a rich selection of books and toys. However, staff turnover was so rapid that the average child had 50 different caregivers by age 4½! Many of these children became "late adoptees" who were placed in homes after age 4. Most developed deep ties with their adoptive parents, indicating that a first attachment bond can develop as late as 4 to 6 years of age (Tizard & Rees, 1975).

But throughout childhood and adolescence, these youngsters displayed adjustment problems, including an excessive desire for adult attention, "overfriendliness" to unfamiliar adults and peers, and few friendships (Hodges & Tizard, 1989; Tizard & Hodges, 1978). Although fol-

low-ups into adulthood are necessary to be sure, these findings suggest that fully normal development depends on establishing close bonds with caregivers during the first few years of life.

■ QUALITY OF CAREGIVING. **Sensitive caregiving** distinguishes securely from insecurely
attached infants in diverse cultures. In a combined analysis of 66 studies involving more than
4,000 mother–infant pairs, the extent to which mothers responded promptly, consistently,
and appropriately to infant signals and held their babies tenderly and carefully was moderately related to attachment security (De Wolff & van IJzendoorn, 1997). In contrast, insecurely attached infants tend to have mothers who engage in less physical contact, handle
them awkwardly, behave in a "routine" manner, and are sometimes negative, resentful, and
rejecting (Ainsworth et al., 1978; Isabella, 1993; Pederson & Moran, 1996).

Do other caregiver behaviors support babies' feelings of trust? In several studies, a special
form of communication called **interactional synchrony** separated the experiences of secure
from insecure babies (Isabella & Belsky, 1991; Kochanska, 1998). It is best described as a sensitively tuned "emotional dance," in which caregiver–infant interaction appears to be mutually rewarding. The caregiver responds to infant signals in a well-timed,
appropriate fashion, and both partners match emotional states, especially the
positive ones. In one instance, Carolyn responded to Caitlin's excited shaking of a rattle with an enthusiastic "That-a-girl!" When Caitlin babbled and
looked at her mother, Carolyn smiled and spoke expressively in return.
When she fussed and cried, Carolyn soothed with gentle touches and soft
words.

Earlier we saw that sensitive face-to-face play, in which interactional synchrony occurs, helps infants regulate emotion. But more evidence is needed
to document the link between interactional synchrony and secure attachment. Observations reveal that only 30 percent of the time are mothers and
babies emotionally "in sync." The remaining 70 percent of the time, interactive errors occur (Tronick, 1989). Perhaps warm, sensitive caregivers become
especially skilled at repairing these errors and returning to a synchronous
state. Also, finely tuned, coordinated interaction does not characterize parent–infant interaction everywhere. Among the Gusii people of Kenya,
mothers rarely cuddle, hug, and interact playfully with their babies, although
they are very responsive to their infants' needs (LeVine et al., 1994). This suggests that secure
attachment depends on attentive caregiving, but its association with moment-by-moment
contingent interaction is probably limited to certain cultures.

Compared with securely attached infants, avoidant babies tend to receive overstimulating
and intrusive care. Their mothers might, for example, talk energetically to them while they
are looking away or falling asleep. By avoiding the mother, these infants appear to be escaping from overwhelming interaction. Resistant infants often experience inconsistent care.
Their mothers are minimally involved in caregiving and unresponsive to infant signals. Yet
when the baby begins to explore, these mothers interfere, shifting the infant's attention back
to themselves. As a result, the baby shows exaggerated dependence as well as anger and frustration at the mother's lack of involvement (Cassidy & Berlin, 1994; Isabella & Belsky, 1991).

When caregiving is highly inadequate, it is a powerful predictor of disruptions in attachment. Child abuse and neglect (topics we will consider in Chapter 10) are associated with all
three forms of attachment insecurity. Among maltreated infants, disorganized/disoriented
attachment is especially high (Barnett, Ganiban, & Cicchetti, 1999; Lyons-Ruth & Block,
1996). Depressed mothers and parents suffering from a traumatic event (such as loss of a
loved one) also tend to promote the uncertain behaviors of this pattern (Teti et al., 1995; van
IJzendoorn, 1995a). How do they do so? Research indicates that they often display frightening, contradictory, and other unpleasant behaviors, such as looking scared, mocking or teasing the baby, holding the baby stiffly at a distance, roughly pulling the baby by the arm, or
seeking reassurance from the upset child (Lyons-Ruth, Bronfman, & Parsons, 1999; Schuengel et al., 1999).

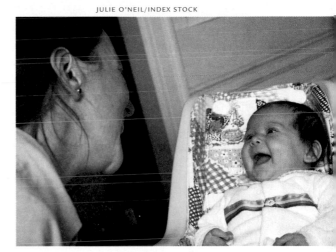

JULIE O'NEIL/INDEX STOCK

This mother and baby engage
in sensitively tuned communication called interactional synchrony, in which they match
emotional states, especially
the positive ones. Although
interactional synchrony may
support the development of
secure attachment, it does not
characterize parent–infant
interaction everywhere.

sensitive caregiving
Caregiving involving prompt,
consistent, and appropriate
responding to infant signals.

interactional synchrony
A sensitively tuned "emotional
dance," in which the caregiver
responds to infant signals in a
well-timed, appropriate fashion and both partners match
emotional states, especially
the positive ones.

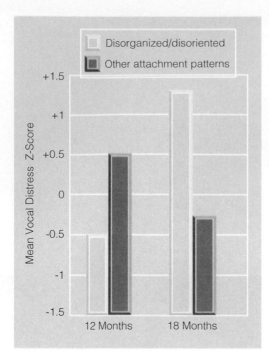

FIGURE 7.4

Mean vocal distress (ranging from brief frustration sounds to continuous crying and screaming) in the Strange Situation by disorganized/disoriented babies and babies with other attachment patterns. Babies were rated at two ages: 12 months and 18 months. At 12 months, the disorganized/disoriented infants appeared to suppress their distress, perhaps out of fear of their mother's response; they scored lower than did infants with other attachment patterns. By 18 months, the distress of disorganized/disoriented toddlers had risen sharply, whereas the distress of other toddlers had declined. A disorganized/disoriented attachment pattern appeared to promote an emotionally reactive temperament. (Adapted from Barnett, Ganiban, & Cicchetti, 1999.)

■ **INFANT CHARACTERISTICS.** Since attachment is the result of a *relationship* that builds between two partners, infant characteristics should affect how easily it is established. In chapters 3 and 4 we saw that prematurity, birth complications, and newborn illness make caregiving more taxing for parents. In poverty-stricken, stressed families, these difficulties are linked to attachment insecurity (Wille, 1991). But when parents have the time and patience to care for a baby with special needs and the infant is not very sick, at-risk newborns fare quite well in the development of attachment (Pederson & Moran, 1995).

Infants also vary considerably in temperament, but its role in attachment security has been intensely debated. Some researchers believe that infants who are irritable and fearful may simply react to brief separations with intense anxiety, regardless of the parent's sensitivity to the baby (Kagan, 1989, 1998). Consistent with this view, emotionally reactive, difficult babies are more likely to develop later insecure attachments (Seifer et al., 1996; Vaughn & Bost, 1999).

But other evidence argues for temperament as only a modest influence. Although quality of attachment to the mother and the father is often similar, quite a few infants establish distinct attachment relationships with each parent and with their professional caregivers (Goossens & van IJzendoorn, 1990; van IJzendoorn & De Wolff, 1997). If temperament were very powerful, we would expect attachment quality to be more constant across familiar adults than it is.

Furthermore, caregiving seems to be involved in the relationship between difficultness and attachment insecurity. In one study, distress-prone infants who became insecurely attached tended to have rigid, controlling mothers who probably had trouble comforting their reactive babies (Mangelsdorf et al., 1990). In another study, disorganized/disoriented 1-year-olds (many of whom were maltreated) increased sharply in emotional reactivity over the second year (see Figure 7.4). Attachment disorganization was not caused by difficult temperament but rather seemed to promote it (Barnett, Ganiban, & Cicchetti, 1999). Furthermore, an intervention that taught mothers how to respond sensitively to their irritable 6-month-olds led to gains in maternal responsiveness and in children's attachment security, exploration, cooperativeness, and sociability that were still present at 3½ years of age (van den Boom, 1995).

Other evidence confirms that caregiving can override the impact of infant characteristics on attachment security. When researchers combined data from 34 studies including more than 1,600 mother–infant pairs, they found that maternal problems—such as mental illness, teenage parenthood, and child abuse—were associated with increased attachment insecurity (see Figure 7.5). In contrast, infant problems—ranging from prematurity and developmental delays to serious physical disabilities and psychological problems—had little impact on attachment quality (van IJzendoorn et al., 1992).

A major reason that temperament and other infant characteristics do not show strong relationships with attachment security may be that their influence depends on goodness of fit. From this perspective, *many* child attributes can lead to secure attachment as long as the caregiver sensitively adjusts her behavior to fit the baby's needs (Seifer & Schiller, 1995). But when a parent's capacity to do so is strained—for example, by stressful life conditions or her own personality—then infants with illnesses, disabilities, and difficult temperaments are at greater risk for attachment problems.

■ **FAMILY CIRCUMSTANCES.** Timmy's parents divorced shortly after he was born, and his father moved to a distant city. Although Vanessa tried not to let his departure affect her caregiving, she became anxious and distracted. To make ends meet, she placed 1-month-old Timmy in Ginette's child-care home and began working 50- to 60-hour weeks. When Vanessa stayed late at the office, a baby-sitter picked Timmy up, gave him dinner, and put him to bed. Once or twice a week, Vanessa went to get Timmy. As he neared his first birthday, she couldn't help but notice that the other children reached out, crawled, or ran to their mothers and fathers to be picked up and hugged. Timmy, in contrast, ignored Vanessa. When she said, "It's time to go," he passively allowed himself to be taken.

Timmy's behavior reflects a repeated finding in the attachment literature: Job loss, a failing marriage, financial difficulties, and other stressors are linked to attachment insecurity. These problems can undermine attachment by interfering with the sensitivity of parental care. Or they may affect babies' sense of security directly, by exposing them to angry adult interactions or unfavorable child-care arrangements (Owen & Cox, 1997; Thompson, 1998). The availability of social supports, especially assistance in caregiving, reduces stress and fosters attachment security. Ginette's sensitivity with Timmy and the parenting advice that Ben, a psychologist, offered Vanessa were helpful. As Timmy turned 2, his relationship with his mother seemed warmer.

■ **PARENTS' INTERNAL WORKING MODELS.** Parents bring to the family context a long history of attachment experiences, out of which they construct internal working models that they apply to the bonds established with their babies. Carolyn remembered her mother as deeply affectionate and caring and viewed her as a positive influence in her own parenting. Monica recalled her mother as tense and preoccupied and expressed regret that they had not had a closer relationship. Do these images of parenthood affect the quality of Caitlin's and Grace's attachments to their mothers?

To answer this question, researchers have assessed adults' internal working models by having them recall and evaluate childhood attachment experiences. Parents who show objectivity and balance in discussing their childhoods, whether they were positive or negative, tend to have securely attached infants. In contrast, parents who dismiss the importance of early relationships or describe them in angry, confused ways usually have insecurely attached babies (Steele, Steele, & Fonagy, 1996; van IJzendoorn, 1995a). Caregiving behavior helps explain these associations. Mothers with secure representations are warmer and more sensitive with their babies. They are also more likely to be supportive and to encourage learning and mastery in their older children, who are more affectionate and comfortably interactive with them (Cohn et al., 1992; Pederson et al., 1998).

But we must not assume any direct transfer of parents' childhood experiences to their inner representations and quality of attachment to their own children. Internal working models are *reconstructed memories* affected by many factors, including relationship experiences over the life course, personality, and current life satisfaction. Indeed, according to longitudinal research, certain negative life events can weaken the link between attachment security in infancy and a secure internal working model in adulthood. And insecurely attached babies who become adults with insecure internal working models often have lives that, based on adulthood self-reports, are fraught with family crises (Waters et al., 2000; Weinfeld, Sroufe, & Egeland, 2000).

In sum, our early rearing experiences do not destine us to become sensitive or insensitive parents. Rather, the way we *view* our childhoods—our ability to come to terms with negative events, to integrate new information into our working models, and to look back on our own parents in an understanding, forgiving way—appears to be much more influential in how we rear our children than the actual history of care we received (van IJzendoorn, 1995b).

■ **ATTACHMENT IN CONTEXT.** Carolyn and Vanessa returned to work when their babies were 2 to 3 months old. Monica did the same a few weeks after Grace's adoption. When mothers divide their time between work and parenting and place their infants and toddlers in child care, is the quality of attachment affected? Turn to the Social Issues: Health box on page 278 for research that addresses this issue.

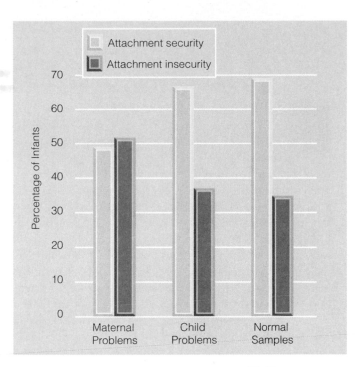

FIGURE 7.5

Comparison of the effects of maternal and child problem behaviors on the attachment bond. Maternal problems were associated with increased attachment insecurity. In contrast, child problems had little impact on the rate of attachment security and insecurity, which resembled that of normal samples. (Adapted from van IJzendoorn et al., 1992.)

Social

ISSUES: HEALTH

IS CHILD CARE IN INFANCY A THREAT TO ATTACHMENT SECURITY?

Research suggests that American infants placed in full-time child care before 12 months of age are more likely than home-reared babies to display insecure attachment—especially avoidance—in the Strange Situation (Belsky, 1989, 1992). Does this mean that babies who experience daily separations from their employed parents and early placement in child care are at risk for developmental problems? A close look at the evidence reveals that we should be cautious about concluding that child care is harmful to infants.

First, in studies reporting a child care–attachment association, the rate of insecurity among child-care infants is somewhat higher than among non-child-care infants (36 versus 29 percent), but it nevertheless resembles the overall rate of insecurity reported for children in industrialized countries (Lamb, Sternberg, & Prodromidis, 1992). In fact, most infants of employed mothers are securely attached! Furthermore, not all investigations report a difference in attachment quality between child-care and non-child-care infants (NICHD Early Child Care Research Network, 1997; Roggman et al., 1994).

Second, we have seen that family conditions affect attachment security. Many employed women find the pressures of handling two full-time jobs (work and motherhood) stressful. Some respond less sensitively to their babies because they are fatigued and harried, thereby risking the infant's security (Stifter, Coulehan, & Fish, 1993). Other employed mothers probably value and encourage their infant's independence. Or their babies are unfazed by brief separations in the Strange Situation because they are used to separating from their parents. In these cases, avoidance in the Strange Situation may represent healthy autonomy rather than insecurity (Lamb, 1998).

Third, poor-quality child care and many hours in child care may contribute to a higher rate of insecure attachment among infants of employed mothers. In the National Institute of Child Health and Development (NICHD) Study of Early Child Care—the largest longitudinal study to date, including 1,000 infants and their mothers in 10 areas of the country—child care alone did not contribute to attachment insecurity. But when babies were exposed to combined home and child-care risk factors—insensitive caregiving at home with insensitive caregiving in child care, long hours in child care, or more than one child-care arrangement—the rate of insecurity increased. Overall, mother–child interaction was more positive between 6 months and 3 years of age when children attended higher-quality child care and were in child care for fewer hours (NICHD Early Child Care Research Network, 1997, 1999).

Fourth, assessing attachment security while infants adapt to child care may yield an inaccurate picture. On entering child care, infants must adjust to new routines and daily separations from the parent. Under these conditions, signs of distress are expected. But after a few months, infants enrolled in high-quality programs become more comfortable. They smile, play actively, seek comfort from sensitive caregivers they have come to know well, and begin to interact with other children (Barnas & Cummings, 1994; Fein, Gariboldi, & Boni, 1993).

Finally, results of the NICHD study indicate that parenting has a far stronger impact on preschoolers' problem behavior than does early, extensive child care (NICHD Early Child Care Research Network, 1998). Indeed, having the opportunity to form a warm bond with a professional caregiver is helpful to infants whose relationship with one or both parents is insecure. When followed into the preschool and early school years, such children show higher self-esteem and socially skilled behavior than do their insecurely attached agemates who did not attend child care (Egeland & Hiester, 1995).

Taken together, research suggests that some infants may be at risk for attachment insecurity due to inadequate child care and the joint pressures of full-time employment and parenthood experienced by their mothers. However, using this as evidence to justify a reduction in infant child-care services is inappropriate. When family incomes are limited or mothers who want to work are forced to stay at home, children's emotional security is not promoted.

Instead, it makes sense to increase the availability of high-quality child care and to educate parents about the vital role of sensitive caregiving in early emotional development. Return to Chapter 6, page 236, to review signs of developmentally appropriate child care for infants and toddlers. For child care to foster attachment security, the professional caregiver's relationship with the baby is vital. When caregiver–child ratios are generous, group sizes are small, and caregivers are educated about child development and child rearing, caregivers' interactions are more positive (NICHD Early Child Care Research Network, 1996). Child care with these characteristics can become part of an ecological system that relieves rather than intensifies parental and child stress, thereby promoting healthy attachment and development.

After reading the box on child care and attachment, take a moment to consider each factor that influences the development of attachment. These include infant and parent characteristics, the parents' relationship with each other, outside-the-family stressors, the availability of social supports, parents' views of their attachment history, and child-care arrangements. Although attachment builds within the warmth and intimacy of caregiver–infant interaction, it can only be fully understood from an ecological systems perspective (Cowan, 1997). Return to Chapter 1, page 27, to review Bronfenbrenner's ecological systems theory. Notice how research confirms the importance of each level of the environment for attachment security.

MULTIPLE ATTACHMENTS

We have already indicated that babies develop attachments to a variety of familiar people— not just mothers, but fathers, siblings, grandparents, and professional caregivers. Although Bowlby (1969) made room for multiple attachments in his theory, he believed that infants are predisposed to direct their attachment behaviors to a single special person, especially when they are distressed. For example, when an anxious, unhappy 1-year-old is permitted to choose between the mother and the father as a source of comfort and security, the infant usually chooses the mother (Lamb, 1997). This preference typically declines over the second year of life. An expanding world of attachments enriches the emotional and social lives of many babies.

■ **FATHERS.** Like mothers', fathers' sensitive caregiving predicts secure attachment—an effect that becomes stronger the more time they spend with their babies (van IJzendoorn & De Wolff, 1997). Also, fathers of 1- to 5-year-olds enrolled in full-time child care report feeling just as much anxiety as do mothers about separating from their child and just as much concern about the impact of these daily separations on the child's welfare (Deater-Deckard et al., 1994).

As infancy progresses, mothers and fathers from a variety of cultures—Australia, India, Israel, Italy, Japan, and the United States—relate to babies in different ways. Mothers devote more time to physical care and expressing affection. Fathers spend more time in playful interaction (Lamb, 1987; Roopnarine et al., 1990). Mothers and fathers also play differently with babies. Mothers more often provide toys, talk to infants, and initiate conventional games, such as pat-a-cake and peekaboo. In contrast, fathers tend to engage in more exciting, highly physical bouncing and lifting games, especially with their infant sons (Yogman, 1981).

However, this picture of "mother as caregiver" and "father as playmate" has changed in some families due to the revised work status of women. Employed mothers tend to engage in more playful stimulation of their babies than do unemployed mothers, and their husbands are some- what more involved in caregiving (Cox et al., 1992). When fathers are the primary caregivers, they retain their arousing play style (Lamb & Oppenheim, 1989). Such highly involved fathers are less gender stereotyped in their beliefs; have sympathetic, friendly personalities; and regard parenthood as an especially enriching experience (Lamb, 1987; Levy-Shiff & Israelashvili, 1988).

Paternal involvement with babies takes place within a complex system of family attitudes and relationships. When mothers and fathers believe that men are capable of nurturing infants and they value being involved, fathers devote more time to caregiving (Beitel & Parke, 1998). A warm, gratifying marital bond supports both parents' sensitivity and involvement, but it is particularly important for fathers (Bruangart-Rieker, Courtney, & Garwood, 1999; Owen & Cox, 1997). See the Cultural Influences box on page 280 for cross-cultural evidence that supports this conclusion.

■ **SIBLINGS.** Despite a declining family size, 80 percent of North American children still grow up with at least one sibling. The arrival of a baby brother or sister is a difficult experi- ence for most preschoolers, who quickly realize that now they must share their parents' atten- tion and affection. They often become demanding and clingy for a time and engage in deliberate naughtiness. And their security of attachment typically declines, more so if they are over age 2 (old enough to feel threatened and displaced) and the mother is under stress due to marital or psychological problems (Teti et al., 1996).

Cultural INFLUENCES

FATHER–INFANT RELATIONSHIPS AMONG THE AKA

Among the Aka hunters and gatherers of Central Africa, fathers devote more time to infants than in any other known society. Observations reveal that Aka fathers are within arm's reach of their infants more than half the day. They pick up and cuddle their babies at least five times more often than do fathers in other African hunting-and-gathering societies in Africa and elsewhere in the world.

Why are Aka fathers so involved with their babies? Research shows that when husband and wife help each other with many tasks, fathers assist more with infant care. The relationship between Aka husband and wife is unusually cooperative and intimate. Throughout the day, they share hunt-ing, food preparation, and social and leisure activities. Babies are brought along on hunts, and mothers find it hard to carry them long distances. This explains, in part, why fathers spend so much time holding their infants. But when the Aka return to the campground, fathers continue to devote many hours to infant caregiving. The more Aka parents are together, the greater the father's interaction with his baby (Hewlett, 1992).

BARRY HEWLETT

This Aka father spends much time in close contact with his baby. In Aka society, husband and wife share many tasks of daily living and have an unusually cooperative and intimate relationship. Infants are usually within arm's reach of their fathers, who devote many hours to caregiving.

Although the arrival of a baby brother or sister is a difficult experience for most pre-schoolers, a rich emotional relationship quickly builds between siblings. This toddler is already actively involved in play with his 4-year-old brother, and both derive great pleasure from the interaction.

Yet resentment is only one feature of a rich emotional relationship that starts to build between siblings after a baby's birth. The older child can also be seen kissing, patting, and calling out "Mom, he needs you" when the baby cries—signs of affection and sympathetic concern. By the end of the baby's first year, siblings typically spend much time together, with the preschooler helping, sharing toys, imitating, and expressing friendliness in addition to anger and ambivalence (Dunn & Kendrick, 1982). Infants of this age are comforted by the presence of their preschool-age brother or sister during the mother's short absences (Stewart, 1983). And during the second year, toddlers often imitate and join in play with the older child (Dunn, 1989).

Nevertheless, individual differences in the quality of sibling relationships appear shortly after a baby's birth and persist into middle childhood (Dunn, 1992). Temperament plays an important role. For example, conflict increases when one sibling is emotionally intense or highly active (Brody, Stoneman, & McCoy, 1994; Dunn, 1994). Parenting also makes a difference. Secure infant–mother attachment and warmth toward both children are related to positive sibling interaction, whereas coldness is associated with sibling friction (MacKinnon-Lewis et al., 1997; Volling & Belsky, 1992).

Still, when a mother is more positive and playful with her new baby than her preschooler, she can spark rivalry and behavior problems in the older child along with less friendliness toward the baby (Moore, Cohn, & Campbell, 1997; Volling & Elins, 1998). This does not mean that parents should limit the attention they give to infants, but it does indicate the importance of setting aside special times to devote to the older child. In addition,

ERIKA STONE/PHOTO RESEARCHERS, INC.

Caregiving Concerns

Encouraging Affectional Ties Between Infants and Their Preschool Siblings

SUGGESTION	DESCRIPTION
Spend extra time with the older child.	To minimize the older child's feelings of being deprived of affection and attention, set aside time to spend with her. Fathers can be especially helpful in this regard, planning special outings with the preschooler and taking over care of the baby so the mother can be with the older child.
Handle sibling misbehavior with patience.	Respond patiently to the older sibling's misbehavior and demands for attention, recognizing that these reactions are temporary. Give the preschooler opportunities to feel proud of being more grown-up than the baby. For example, encourage the older child to assist with feeding, bathing, dressing, and offering toys, and show appreciation for these efforts.
Discuss the baby's wants and needs.	By helping the older sibling understand the baby's point of view, parents can promote friendly, considerate behavior. Say, for example, "He's so little that he just can't wait to be fed" or "He's trying to reach his rattle and can't."

Sources: Dunn & Kendrick, 1982; Howe & Ross, 1990.

mothers who often discuss the baby's feelings and intentions have preschoolers who are more likely to comment on the infant as a person with special wants and needs. And such children behave in an especially considerate and friendly manner when interacting with the baby (Howe & Ross, 1990).

The Caregiving Concerns table above suggests ways to promote positive relationships between babies and their preschool siblings. Research on brothers and sisters as attachment figures reminds us of the complex, multidimensional nature of the infant's social world. Siblings offer a rich social context in which children learn and practice a wide range of skills, including affectionate caring, conflict resolution, and control of hostile and envious feelings.

FROM ATTACHMENT TO PEER SOCIABILITY

In cultures where agemates have regular contact during the first year of life, peer sociability begins early. By age 6 months, Caitlin and Timmy occasionally looked, reached, smiled, and babbled when they saw one another. These isolated social acts increased until by the end of the first year, an occasional reciprocal exchange occurred in which the children grinned, gestured, or otherwise imitated a playmate's behavior (Vandell & Mueller, 1995; Vandell, Wilson, & Buchanan, 1980).

Between 1 and 2 years, coordinated interaction occurs more often, largely in the form of mutual imitation involving jumping, chasing, or banging a toy. These imitative, turn-taking games mark an advance in social awareness. They indicate that the toddler is not only interested in the playmate but aware of the playmate's interest in him or her. And such imitation creates joint understandings that aid verbal communication. Around age 2, toddlers begin to use words to talk about and influence a peer's behavior, as when Caitlin said to Grace, "Let's play chase," and after the game got going, "Hey, good running!" (Eckerman & Didow, 1996; Eckerman & Whitehead, 1999). Reciprocal play and positive emotion are especially frequent in toddlers' interactions with familiar agemates, suggesting that they are building true peer relationships (Ross et al., 1992).

Grace and Caitlin pause for a photo during outdoor play at Ginette's child-care home. As familiar playmates, they often engage in imitative games and exchange expressions of pleasure. As they approach their second birthdays, already they are building a warm, gratifying peer relationship.

CAROLYN MERRILL

As we will see when we take up self-development, toddlers' budding social understanding sometimes leads to clever efforts to annoy others. And struggles with peers, often over objects, occur as well. But peer sociability is present in the first 2 years, and it is fostered by the early caregiver–child bond. From interacting with sensitive adults, babies learn how to send and interpret emotional signals in their first peer associations. Consistent with this idea, infants with a warm parental relationship engage in more extended peer exchanges (Vandell & Wilson, 1987). And for toddlers in child care, a secure attachment to a stable professional caregiver predicts advanced peer and play behavior (Howes & Hamilton, 1993).

ATTACHMENT AND LATER DEVELOPMENT

According to psychoanalytic and ethological theories, the inner feelings of affection and security that result from a healthy attachment relationship support all aspects of psychological development. Consistent with this view, many researchers have addressed the link between infant–mother attachment and cognitive, emotional, and social development.

In the most comprehensive longitudinal study of this kind, Alan Sroufe and his collaborators reported that children who were securely attached as babies showed more elaborate make-believe play and greater enthusiasm, flexibility, and persistence in problem solving by 2 years of age. Preschool teachers rated these children at age 4 as socially competent, cooperative, popular, empathic, and high in self-esteem. In contrast, they viewed avoidantly attached agemates as isolated and disconnected and resistantly attached agemates as disruptive and difficult. Studied again at age 11 in summer camp, children who had been secure as infants had more favorable relationships with peers, closer friendships, and better social skills, as judged by camp counselors (Elicker, Englund, & Sroufe, 1992; Frankel & Bates, 1990; Matas, Arend, & Sroufe, 1978).

These findings have been taken by some researchers to mean that secure attachment in infancy causes improved cognitive, emotional, and social competence during later years. Yet more evidence is needed before we can be certain of this conclusion. Other short-term longitudinal studies yield a mixed picture. Secure infants do not always show more favorable development than do their insecure counterparts (Belsky & Cassidy, 1994). And one long-term study revealed that secure, avoidant, and resistant attachment at age 1 did not predict psychological adjustment at age 18 (Lewis, 1997). Disorganized/disoriented attachment, however, is an exception. It is consistently related to high hostility and aggression in early and middle childhood (Lyons-Ruth, 1996; Lyons-Ruth, Easterbrooks, & Cibelli, 1997).

Why, overall, is research on the consequences of attachment quality unclear? Michael Lamb and his colleagues (1985) suggest that *continuity of caregiving* determines whether attachment security is linked to later development. When parents respond sensitively not just in infancy but during later years, children are likely to develop favorably. In contrast, children of parents who react insensitively for a long time are at increased risk for maladjustment.

Several findings support this interpretation. Recall that many mothers of disorganized/disoriented infants have serious psychological difficulties and engage in highly maladaptive caregiving—problems that usually persist and are strongly linked to children's maladjustment (Lyons-Ruth, Bronfman, & Parsons, 1999). Furthermore, a close look at Sroufe's longitudinal study reveals that the few securely attached infants who did develop later behavior problems had mothers who became less positive and supportive in early childhood. Similarly, the handful of insecurely attached babies who became well-adjusted preschoolers had mothers who were sensitive and provided their young children with clear structure and guidance (Egeland et al., 1990; Thompson, 1999).

Do these trends remind you of our discussion of *resiliency* in Chapter 1? A child whose parental caregiving improves or who has compensating affectional ties outside the immediate family can bounce back from adversity. In sum, efforts to create warm, responsive environments are not important just in infancy and toddlerhood; they are vital at later ages, as we will see in subsequent chapters.

I-self
A sense of self as subject, or agent, who is separate from but attends to and acts on objects and other people.

review   Which attachment patterns tend to be stable over infancy and toddlerhood? Which ones often change, and why?

apply   What attachment pattern did Timmy display when Vanessa picked him up from child care, and what factors probably contributed to it? Will Timmy's insecurity necessarily compromise his development? Explain.

connect   Review research on emotional self-regulation on pages 260–261. How do the caregiving experiences of securely attached infants promote the development of emotional self-regulation?

reflect   How would you characterize your internal working model? What factors, in addition to your early relationship with your parents, might have influenced it?

Self-Development

nfancy is a rich, formative period for the development of physical and social understanding. In Chapter 6 you learned that infants develop an appreciation of the permanence of objects—an understanding that objects continue to exist when no longer in view. And in this chapter we have seen that over the first year, infants recognize and respond appropriately to others' emotions and distinguish familiar people from strangers. The fact that both objects and people achieve an independent, stable existence for the infant implies that knowledge of the self as a separate, permanent entity emerges around this time.

SELF-AWARENESS

After Caitlin's daily bath, Carolyn often held her in front of the bathroom mirror. As early as the first few months, Caitlin smiled and returned friendly behaviors to her image. At what age did she realize that the charming baby gazing and grinning back was really herself?

■ **EMERGENCE OF THE I-SELF AND THE ME-SELF.** To answer this question, researchers have exposed infants and toddlers to images of themselves in mirrors, on videotapes, and in photos. When shown two side-by-side video images of their kicking legs, one from their own perspective (camera behind the baby) and one from an observer's perspective (camera in front of the baby), 3-month-olds looked longer at the observer's view (see Figure 7.6a). In another video-image comparison, they looked longer at a reversal of their leg positions than at a normal view (see Figure 7.6b) (Rochat, 1998). Within the first few months, then, infants seem to have some sense of their own body as a distinct entity and have habituated to it, as indicated by their interest in novel views of the body.

Researchers agree that the earliest aspect of the self to emerge is the **I-self**—a sense of self as *subject*, or *agent*, who is separate from objects and other people but attends to and acts on them. How do infants develop this awareness? According to many theorists, the beginnings of the I-self lie in infants' recognition that their own actions cause objects and people to react in predictable ways (Harter, 1998). Parents who encourage babies to explore and who respond to their signals consistently and sensitively help them construct a sense of self as agent (Pipp, Easterbrooks, & Brown, 1993).

Baby's View   Observer's View
(a)

Left   Right   Right   Left
Normal View   Reversed View
(b)

FIGURE 7.6

Three-month-olds' emerging self-awareness, as indicated by reactions to video images.
(a) When shown two side-by-side views of their kicking legs, babies looked longer at the novel, observer's view than at their own view. (b) When shown a normal view of their leg positions alongside a reversed view, infants looked longer at the novel, reversed view. (Adapted from Rochat, 1998.)

This infant notices the correspondence between his own movements and the movements of the image in the mirror, a cue that helps him figure out that the grinning baby is really himself.

PAUL DAMIEN/STONE

Then, as infants act on the environment, they notice different effects that may help them sort out self from other people and objects. For example, batting a mobile and seeing it swing in a pattern different from the infant's own actions informs the baby about the relation between self and physical world. Smiling and vocalizing at a caregiver who smiles and vocalizes back helps specify the relation between self and social world. And watching the movements of one's own hands and feet provides still another kind of feedback— one under much more direct control than other people or objects (Lewis, 1994). The contrast between these experiences may help infants build an image of self as separate from external reality.

During the second year, toddlers start to construct a second aspect of self: the **me-self**, a reflective observer who treats the self as an object of knowledge and evaluation. Consequently, they become consciously aware of the self's features. In one study, 9- to 24-month-olds were placed in front of a mirror. Then, under the pretext of wiping the baby's face, each mother was asked to rub red dye on her child's nose. Younger infants touched the mirror as if the red mark had nothing to do with any aspect of themselves. But by 15 months, toddlers began to rub their strange-looking little red noses. They were keenly aware of their unique visual appearance (Lewis & Brooks-Gunn, 1979). By age 2, almost all children use their name or a personal pronoun ("I" or "me") to label their image or refer to themselves.

■ **SELF-AWARENESS AND EARLY EMOTIONAL AND SOCIAL DEVELOPMENT.** Self-awareness quickly becomes a central part of children's emotional and social lives. Recall that self-conscious emotions depend on toddlers' emerging sense of self. Self-awareness also leads to first efforts to appreciate another's perspective. For example, it is associated with the beginnings of self-conscious behavior—bashfulness and embarrassment. It also precedes the appearance of sustained, mutual peer imitation (recall that such imitation indicates that the toddler realizes a playmate is interested in him or her) (Asendorpf, Warkentin, & Baudonniere, 1996). And self-awareness is accompanied by the first signs of **empathy**—the capacity to understand another's emotional state and *feel with* that person, or respond emotionally in a similar way. For example, toddlers start to give to others what they themselves find comforting—a hug, a reassuring comment, or a favorite doll or blanket (Bischof-Köhler, 1991; Zahn-Waxler et al., 1992).

Along with an increase in empathic behavior comes a much clearer awareness of how to upset and frustrate other people. One 18-month-old heard her mother comment to another adult, "Anny (sibling) is really frightened of spiders. In fact, there's a particular toy spider that we've got that she just hates" (Dunn, 1989, p. 107). The innocent-looking toddler ran to get the spider from the toy box, returned, and pushed it in Anny's face!

me-self
A sense of self as a reflective observer that treats the self as an object of knowledge and evaluation.

empathy
The capacity to understand another's emotional state and *feel with* that person, or respond emotionally in a similar way.

CATEGORIZING THE SELF

Once children have a me-self, they use their representational and language capacities to create a mental image of themselves. One of the first signs of this change is that toddlers begin to compare themselves to other people. Between 18 and 30 months, children label themselves and others on the basis of age ("baby," "boy," or "man"), gender ("boy" versus "girl" and "lady" versus "man"), physical characteristics ("big," "strong"), and even goodness and badness ("I good girl." "Tommy mean!"). They also start to refer to the self's competencies ("Did it!" "I can't") (Stipek, Gralinski, & Kopp, 1990).

Toddlers' understanding of these social categories is quite limited. But as soon as they categorize themselves, they use this knowledge to organize their own behavior. For example, toddlers' ability to label their own gender is associated with a sharp rise in gender-stereotyped responses (Fagot & Leinbach, 1989). As early as 18 months, children select and play in a more involved way with toys that are stereotyped for their own gender—dolls and tea sets for girls, trucks and cars for boys. Then parents encourage these preferences further by responding more positively when toddlers display them (Fagot, Leinbach, & O'Boyle, 1992). As we will see in Chapter 10, gender-typed behavior increases dramatically over early childhood.

© LAURA DWIGHT

Encouraging this toddler to help wipe up spilled milk fosters compliance and the beginnings of self-control. He joins in the clean-up task with an eager, willing spirit, which suggests he is beginning to adopt the adult's directive as his own.

EMERGENCE OF SELF-CONTROL

Self-awareness also provides the foundation for **self-control,** the capacity to resist an impulse to engage in socially disapproved behavior. Self-control is essential for morality, another dimension of the self that will flourish during childhood and adolescence. To behave in a self-controlled fashion, children must think of themselves as separate, autonomous beings who can direct their own actions. And they must have the representational and memory capacities to recall a caregiver's directive (such as "Caitlin, don't touch that light socket!") and apply it to their own behavior. The ability to shift attention from a captivating stimulus and focus on a less attractive alternative, supported by development of the frontal lobes of the cerebral cortex, is also essential (Rothbart & Bates, 1998).

As these capacities improve, the first glimmerings of self-control emerge in the form of **compliance.** Between 12 and 18 months, children start to show clear awareness of caregivers' wishes and expectations and can voluntarily obey simple requests and commands (Kaler & Kopp, 1990). And, as every parent knows, they can also decide to do just the opposite! One way toddlers assert their sense of autonomy is by resisting adult directives. But among toddlers who experience warm, sensitive caregiving and reasonable expectations for mature behavior, opposition is far less common than eager, willing compliance (Kochanska, Aksan, & Koenig, 1995). Compliance quickly leads to toddlers' first morally relevant verbalizations—for example, correcting the self by saying "no, can't" before touching a light socket or jumping on the sofa (Kochanska, 1993).

Around 18 months, self-control appears and improves steadily with age. In one study, toddlers were given three tasks that required them to resist temptation. In the first, they were asked not to touch an interesting toy telephone that was within arm's reach. In the second, raisins were hidden under cups, and they were instructed to wait until the experimenter said it was all right to pick up a cup and eat a raisin. In the third, they were told not to open a gift until the experimenter had finished her work. On all three problems, the ability to wait increased between 18 and 30 months (Vaughn, Kopp, & Krakow, 1984).

Early, large individual differences in self-control remain modestly stable into middle childhood and adolescence (Shoda, Mischel, & Peake, 1990). Girls in general and children who are advanced in sustained attention and language development are more self-controlled (Cournoyer, Solomon, & Trudel, 1998; Rothbart, 1989). Already, some toddlers use verbal techniques, such as singing and talking to themselves, to keep from engaging in a prohibited act. In addition, mothers who are sensitive and supportive have toddlers who show greater

self-control
The capacity to resist an impulse to engage in socially disapproved behavior.

compliance
Voluntary obedience to adult requests and commands.

Caregiving Concerns

Helping Toddlers Develop Compliance and Self-Control

SUGGESTION	RATIONALE
Respond to the toddler warmly and sensitively.	Toddlers who experience warmth and sensitivity are far more compliant and cooperative than negative and resistant.
Provide advance notice when the toddler must stop an enjoyable activity.	Toddlers find it more difficult to stop a pleasant activity already under way than to wait before engaging in a desired action.
Offer many prompts and reminders.	Toddlers' ability to remember and comply with rules is limited; they need continuous adult oversight.
Respond to self-controlled behavior with verbal and physical approval.	Praise and hugs reinforce appropriate behavior, increasing its likelihood of occurring again.
Encourage sustained attention (see Chapter 6, pages 225–226).	Early sustained attention is related to self-control. Children who can shift attention from a captivating stimulus and focus on a less attractive alternative are better at controlling their impulses.
Support language development (see Chapter 6, pages 246–247).	Early language development is related to self-control. During the second year, children begin to use language to remind themselves about adult expectations.
Gradually increase rules in accord with the toddler's developing capacities.	As cognition and language improve, toddlers can follow more rules related to safety, respect for people and property, family routines, manners, and simple chores.

gains in self-control (Kochanska, Murray, & Harlan, 2000). Such parenting seems to encourage as well as model patient, nonimpulsive behavior.

As self-control improves, mothers increase the rules they require toddlers to follow, from safety and respect for property and people to family routines, manners, and simple chores (Gralinski & Kopp, 1993). Still, toddlers' control over their own actions is fragile. It depends on constant oversight and reminders by parents. To get Caitlin to stop playing and go on an errand, several prompts ("Remember, we're going to go in just a minute") and gentle insistence were usually necessary. The Caregiving Concerns table above summarizes ways to help toddlers develop compliance and self-control.

As the second year of life drew to a close, Carolyn, Monica, and Vanessa were delighted with their youngsters' newfound capacity for compliance and self-control. It signaled that the three toddlers were ready to learn the rules of social life. As we will see in Chapter 10, advances in cognition and language, along with parental warmth and reasonable demands for maturity, lead children to make tremendous strides in this area during early childhood.

Ask YOURSELF...

apply Nine-month-old Harry turned his cup upside down, spilling juice on the tray of his high chair. His mother directed, "Harry, put your cup back the right way!" Why can't Harry comply? When will he be able to do so?

connect What type of early parenting fosters the development of emotional self-regulation, attachment, and self-control? Why, in each instance, is it effective?

Summary

ERIKSON'S THEORY OF INFANT AND TODDLER PERSONALITY

What personality changes take place during Erikson's stages of basic trust versus mistrust and autonomy versus shame and doubt?

- According to Erikson, warm, responsive caregiving leads infants to resolve the psychological conflict of **basic trust versus mistrust** on the positive side. The trusting infant expects the world to be good and gratifying, so he feels confident about venturing out and exploring it.

- During toddlerhood, the conflict of **autonomy versus shame and doubt** is resolved favorably when parents provide appropriate guidance and reasonable choices. The outcome is a child who feels self-confident, secure, and able to control her impulses and act competently on her own. If children emerge from the first few years without sufficient trust and autonomy, the seeds are sown for adjustment problems.

EMOTIONAL DEVELOPMENT

Describe changes in happiness, anger, sadness, and fear over the first year, noting the adaptive function of each.

- During the first half-year, **basic emotions** become clear, well-organized signals. The **social smile** appears between 6 and 10 weeks, laughter around 3 to 4 months. Happiness strengthens the parent–child bond and reflects as well as supports physical and cognitive mastery.

- Anger and fear, especially in the form of **stranger anxiety,** increase in the second half of the first year as infants better evaluate objects and events. These reactions have special adaptive value as infants' motor capacities improve. Expressions of sadness appear in response to pain, removal of an object, brief separations, and disruptions of caregiver–infant interaction, but they are less frequent than anger.

Summarize changes that occur during the first 2 years in understanding others' emotions, expression of self-conscious emotions, and emotional self-regulation.

- The ability to understand the feelings of others expands over the first year. Between 7 and 10 months, babies perceive facial expressions as organized patterns. Soon after, **social referencing** appears; infants actively seek emotional information from caregivers in uncertain situations. By the middle of the second year, infants begin to appreciate that others' emotional reactions may differ from their own.

- During toddlerhood, self-awareness and adult instruction provide the foundation for **self-conscious emotions,** such as shame, embarrassment, guilt, envy, and pride. Caregivers help infants with **emotional self-regulation** by relieving distress, engaging in stimulating play, and discouraging negative emotion. During the second year, growth in representation and language leads to more effective ways of regulating emotion.

DEVELOPMENT OF TEMPERAMENT

What is temperament, and how is it measured?

- Infants differ greatly in **temperament, or** quality and intensity of emotional reaction, activity level, attention, and emotional self-regulation. On the basis of parental descriptions of children's behavior, three patterns of temperament—the **easy child,** the **difficult child,** and the **slow-to-warm-up child**—were identified in the New York Longitudinal Study. Difficult children, especially, are likely to display adjustment problems. Rothbart's dimensions of temperament represent three underlying components—emotion, attention, and action—that form an integrated system of capacities and limitations.

- Psychophysiological measures of temperament have supplemented parental reports, behavior ratings by adults familiar with the child, and direct observations. These assessments distinguish **inhibited, or shy, children** from **uninhibited, or sociable, children.** Shy and sociable youngsters may inherit a physiology that biases them toward a particular temperamental style.

Discuss the role of heredity and environment in the stability of temperament, including the goodness-of-fit model.

- Because temperament develops with age and can be modified by experience, stability from one age period to the next is generally low to moderate. Long-term prediction from early temperament is best achieved from the second year of life and after.

- Temperament has biological roots, but child rearing has much to do with whether a child's emotional style remains the same or changes over time. Ethnic and sex differences in temperament are due to the combined influence of heredity and child rearing.

- The **goodness-of-fit model** describes how temperament and environment work together to affect later development. Parenting practices that create a good fit with the child's temperament help difficult, shy, and highly active children achieve more adaptive functioning.

DEVELOPMENT OF ATTACHMENT

What are the unique features of ethological theory of attachment in comparison to drive reduction and psychoanalytic views?

- The development of **attachment,** infants' strong affectional tie to familiar caregivers, has been the subject of intense theoretical debate. Psychoanalytic and drive reduction (behaviorist) explanations emphasize the importance of feeding to attachment. The most widely accepted perspective is the **ethological theory of attachment.** It views babies as biologically prepared to contribute actively to ties established with their caregivers, which promote survival.

Summary (continued)

■ In early infancy, a set of built-in behaviors encourages the parent to remain close to the baby. Around 6 to 8 months, **separation anxiety** and use of the parent as a **secure base** indicate that a true attachment bond has formed. As representation and language develop, toddlers better understand the parent's coming and going, and separation anxiety declines. Out of early caregiving experiences, children construct an **internal working model** that serves as a guide for all future close relationships.

Cite the four attachment patterns assessed by the Strange Situation and the Attachment Q-Sort, and discuss factors that affect attachment security.

■ A widely used technique for measuring the quality of attachment between 1 and 2 years of age is the **Strange Situation.** A more efficient method is the **Attachment Q-Sort,** which is suitable for children between 1 and 5 years of age. Four attachment patterns have been identified: **secure, avoidant, resistant,** and **disorganized/ disoriented.**

■ Securely attached babies more often maintain their attachment status than do insecure babies. An exception is the disorganized/disoriented pattern, which is as stable as attachment security. Cultural conditions must be considered in interpreting reactions to the Strange Situation.

■ A variety of factors affect the development of attachment. Infants deprived of affectional ties with one or a few adults show lasting emotional and social problems. **Sensitive caregiving** is moderately related to secure attachment. **Interactional synchrony** also separates the experiences of secure from insecure babies, but its impor-

tance is probably limited to certain cultures. Overstimulating, intrusive care is linked to avoidant attachment, inconsistent care to resistant attachment. Many disorganized/disoriented babies experience extremely negative caregiving.

■ Even ill and temperamentally irritable infants are likely to become securely attached if parents adapt their caregiving to suit the baby's needs. Family conditions, including stress and instability, influence caregiving behavior and attachment security. Parents' internal working models also predict the quality of infants' attachment bonds. However, these reconstructed memories are influenced by many factors besides parents' childhood experiences. The development of attachment clearly takes place within a complex ecological system.

Discuss infants' attachments to fathers and siblings, and indicate how attachment paves the way for early peer sociability.

■ Infants develop strong affectional ties to fathers, whose sensitive caregiving predicts secure attachment. Fathers devote more time to stimulating, playful interaction than do mothers. Early in the first year, infants begin to build rich emotional relationships with siblings that mix rivalry and resentment with affection and sympathetic concern. Individual differences in the quality of sibling relationships are influenced by temperament and parenting practices.

■ Peer sociability begins in infancy with isolated social acts that are gradually replaced by reciprocal exchanges, largely in the form of mutual imitation, in the second year of life. Sensitive interaction between caregiver and child fosters the development of peer sociability.

Describe and interpret the relationship between secure attachment in infancy and cognitive, emotional, and social competence in childhood.

■ Evidence for the impact of early attachment pattern on cognitive, emotional, and social competence in later years is mixed. Continuity of parental care may be the crucial factor that determines whether attachment security is linked to later development.

SELF-DEVELOPMENT

Describe the development of self-awareness in infancy and toddlerhood, along with the emotional and social capacities it supports.

■ The earliest aspect of the self to emerge is the **I-self,** a sense of self as subject, or agent. Its beginnings lie in infants' recognition that their own actions cause objects and people to react in predictable ways. During the second year, toddlers start to construct the **me-self,** a reflective observer who treats the self as an object of knowledge and evaluation.

■ Self-awareness leads to toddlers' first efforts to appreciate another's perspective and to compare themselves to others. Social categories based on age, gender, physical characteristics, and goodness and badness are evident in toddlers' language. Self-awareness also provides the foundation for self-conscious emotions, leading to **empathy, compliance,** and **self-control.** Development of attention and language along with sensitive, supportive parenting promote gains in self-control from toddlerhood into early childhood.

Important terms and concepts

attachment (p. 269)
Attachment Q-Sort (p. 273)
autonomy versus shame and doubt (p. 254)
avoidant attachment (p. 272)
basic emotions (p. 257)
basic trust versus mistrust (p. 254)
compliance (p. 284)
difficult child (p. 262)
disorganized/disoriented attachment (p. 273)
easy child (p. 262)

emotional self-regulation (p. 261)
empathy (p. 284)
ethological theory of attachment (p. 271)
goodness-of-fit model (p. 268)
I-self (p. 282)
inhibited, or shy, child (p. 264)
interactional synchrony (p. 275)
internal working model (p. 271)
me-self (p. 284)
resistant attachment (p. 272)
secure attachment (p. 272)

secure base (p. 271)
self-conscious emotions (p. 261)
self-control (p. 284)
sensitive caregiving (p. 275)
separation anxiety (p. 271)
slow-to-warm-up child (p. 262)
social referencing (p. 259)
social smile (p. 258)
Strange Situation (p. 272)
stranger anxiety (p. 259)
temperament (p. 262)
uninhibited, or sociable, child (p. 264)

fyi . . . for further information and help

Consult the companion website for this book, where you will find additional weblinks and associated learning activities:
www.ablongman.com/berk

MENTAL HEALTH

American Academy of Child and Adolescent Psychiatry
www.aacap.org

An organization of medical professionals dedicated to treating and improving quality of life for infants, children, and adolescents with emotional or behavior disorders. Distributes Facts for Families, *an information sheet on childhood mental health, which can be accessed through its website. Also disseminates scholarly research through its journal.*

American Academy of Pediatrics
www.aap.org

An organization of more than 50,000 pediatricians dedicated to the physical and mental health of infants, children, and adolescents. Disseminates a wide variety of health-related information to professionals and parents through its publications, which include Pediatrics, *a scholarly journal;* Healthy Kids *magazine; and childcare books and brochures.*

Milestones of development in infancy and toddlerhood

AGE	PHYSICAL	COGNITIVE	LANGUAGE	EMOTIONAL/SOCIAL
Birth–6 months	■ Rapid height and weight gain. (170) ■ Reflexes decline. (154) ■ Sleep organized into a day–night schedule. (178) ■ Holds head up, rolls over, and reaches for objects. (190) ■ Can be classically and operantly conditioned. (185–187) ■ Habituates to unchanging stimuli; dishabituates to novel stimuli. (187) ■ Hearing well developed; by the end of this period, displays greater sensitivity to speech sounds of own language. (196) ■ Sensitive to motion and binocular depth cues. (197–198) ■ Perceives stimuli as organized patterns; recognizes and prefers pattern of human face. (199–202)	■ Engages in deferred imitation of adults' facial expressions. (219) ■ Repeats chance behaviors leading to pleasurable and interesting results. (214) ■ Aware of object permanence and other object properties in violation-of-expectation studies. (217) ■ Attention becomes more efficient and flexible. (225) ■ Recognition memory for people, places, and objects improves. (226) ■ Forms perceptual categories, based on objects' similar features. (228)	■ Engages in cooing and, by the end of this period, babbling. (241) ■ Establishes joint attention with caregiver, who labels objects and events. (242) 	■ Social smile and laughter emerge. (258) ■ Matches adults' emotional expressions during face-to-face interaction. (259) ■ Emotional expressions become better organized and clearly tied to social events. (259–260) ■ I-self emerges. (283) 
7–12 months	■ Sits alone, crawls, walks. (190) ■ Shows refined pincer grasp. (194) ■ Perceives larger speech units crucial to understanding meaning. (196) ■ Sensitive to pictorial depth cues. (197) ■ Organizes many stimuli into meaningful patterns. (199–200) ■ Relies on shape, color, and texture to distinguish objects from their surroundings. (204)	■ Combines sensorimotor schemes. (215) ■ Engages in intentional, or goal-directed, behavior. (215) ■ Finds objects hidden in one place. (215) ■ Understanding of object properties and physical causality expands. (217–219) ■ Engages in deferred imitation of adults' actions with objects. (219–220) ■ Recall memory for people, places, and objects improves. (226) ■ Solves simple problems by analogy. (220) ■ Groups stimuli into a wide range of meaningful categories. (228)	■ Babbling expands to include sounds of spoken languages and the child's language community. (241–242) ■ Uses preverbal gestures (showing, pointing) to communicate. (242) 	■ Anger and fear increase in frequency and intensity. (258–259) ■ Stranger anxiety and separation anxiety appear. (259, 271) ■ Uses caregiver as a secure base for exploration. (271) ■ Engages in social referencing. (259) ■ Shows "clear-cut" attachment to familiar caregivers. (271)

AGE	PHYSICAL	COGNITIVE	LANGUAGE	EMOTIONAL/SOCIAL
13–18 months	■ Height and weight gain rapid but not as great as in first year. (171) ■ Walking better coordinated. (190) ■ Manipulates small objects with improved coordination. (194) 	■ Experiments with objects in a trial-and-error fashion. (215) ■ Finds object hidden in more than one place. (216) ■ Sorts objects into categories. (228) ■ Imitates actions across a change in context—for example, from child care to home. (221) ■ Sustained attention improves. (225) ■ Memory becomes less dependent on context. (226)	■ Joint attention with caregiver becomes more accurate. (225–226) ■ Actively takes turns in games, such as pat-a-cake and peekaboo. (242) ■ Uses preverbal gestures to influence others' behavior. (242) ■ Says first word. (243) 	■ Joins in play with familiar adults, siblings, and peers. (280) ■ Me-self emerges; recognizes image of self in mirror and on videotape. (284) ■ Begins to realize others' emotional reactions may differ from one's own. (260) ■ Shows signs of empathy. (284) ■ Complies with simple directives. (285)
19–24 months	■ Jumps, runs, and climbs. (190) ■ Manipulates small objects with good coordination. (194) 	■ Solves sensorimotor problems through representation. (216) ■ Finds object moved while out of sight. (216) ■ Engages in deferred imitation of actions an adult tries to produce, even if not fully realized. (219–220) ■ Engages in make-believe play. (216) ■ Sorts objects into categories more effectively. (228) ■ Recall memory for people, places, and objects improves further. (226)	■ Vocabulary increases to 200 words. (244) ■ Combines two words. (244) 	■ Self-conscious emotions (shame, embarrassment, guilt, and pride) emerge. (260) ■ Acquires a vocabulary of emotional terms. (261) ■ Begins using language to assist with emotional self-regulation. (261) ■ Begins to tolerate caregiver's absences more easily. (271) ■ Starts to use words to influence a playmate's behavior. (281) ■ Uses own name or personal pronoun to label image of self. (285) ■ Categorizes the self and others on the basis of age, sex, physical characteristics, goodness and badness, and competencies. (285) ■ Shows gender-stereotyped toy choices. (285) ■ Self-control appears. (285)

Note: Numbers in parentheses indicate the page(s) on which each milestone is discussed.

8

"My Family"
Alyshia Hale
4 years, Australia

A transformed body and explosion of new motor skills contribute to an expanding sense of competence in early childhood, captured in this child's first painting of the human form. Chapter 8 highlights the close link between early childhood physical growth and other aspects of development.

Physical Development in Early Childhood

or more than a decade, my fourth-floor office window overlooked the preschool and kindergarten play yard of our university laboratory school. Sitting at my desk, I spent many fascinating moments watching young children at play. On mild fall and spring mornings, the doors of the preschool and kindergarten swung open, and sand table, woodworking bench, easels, and large blocks spilled out into a small, fenced courtyard. Around the side of the building was a grassy area with jungle gyms, swings, a small playhouse, and a flower garden planted by the children. Beyond it, I could see a circular path lined with tricycles and wagons. Each day the setting was alive with activity.

Even from my distant vantage point, the physical changes of early childhood were evident. Children's bodies were longer and leaner than they had been a year or two earlier. The awkward gait of toddlerhood had disappeared in favor of more refined movements that included climbing, jumping, galloping, and skipping. Throughout the morning, children scaled the jungle gym, searched for imaginary pirates behind trees and bushes, chased one another across the play yard, and pedaled tricycles vigorously over the pavement.

Just as impressive as these gross motor achievements were gains in fine motor skills. At the sand table, children built hills, valleys, caves, and roads and prepared trays of pretend cookies and cupcakes. Nearby, blocks of wood were hammered into small sculptures. And as children grew older, the paintings that hung out to dry took on greater form and detail as family members, houses, trees, birds, sky, monsters, and letterlike forms appeared in the colorful creations.

The years from 2 to 6 are often called "the play years," and aptly so, since play blossoms during this time and supports every aspect of development. We begin our consideration of early childhood by tracing the physical achievements of this period—growth in body size, improvements in motor coordination, and refinements in perception. Our discussion pays special attention to biological and environmental factors that support these changes as well as to their intimate connection with cognitive, emotional, and social development. The preschoolers I came to know well, first by watching from my office window and later by observing at close range in their classrooms, will provide us with many examples of developmental trends and individual differences.

Body Growth

Although Darryl visited the doctor only once a year during early childhood, his parents continued to measure his growth every 3 months in a corner of the kitchen, where they recorded his height on the wall. Each time, Darryl backed up with shoulders straight and head held high, eagerly awaiting the results. On his fifth birthday, the family took an overall look at how he'd grown. Compared to the earliest marks, those of the preschool years were closer together and more evenly spaced.

CHANGES IN BODY SIZE AND PROPORTIONS

Look at Figure 8.1, and you will see that the rapid increase in body size in infancy tapers off into a slower pattern of growth during early childhood. On average, children add 2 to 3 inches in height and about 5 pounds in weight each year. Boys continue to be slightly larger than girls.

At the same time, the "baby fat" that began to decline in toddlerhood drops off further. The child gradually becomes thinner, although girls retain somewhat more body fat, and boys are slightly more muscular. As the torso lengthens and widens, internal organs tuck neatly inside, and the spine straightens. By age 5, the top-heavy, bowlegged, potbellied toddler has become a more streamlined, flat-tummied, longer-legged child with body proportions similar to those of adults. Consequently, posture and balance improve—changes that support the gains in motor coordination that we will take up later.

Individual differences in body size are even more apparent during early childhood than in infancy and toddlerhood. Looking down at the play yard one day, I watched 5-year-old Darryl speed around the bike path. At 48 inches tall and 55 pounds, he towered over his kindergarten classmates and was, as his mother put it, "off the growth charts" at the doctor's office (the average North American 5-year-old boy is 43 inches tall and weighs 42 pounds). Priti, an Asian-Indian child, was unusually small due to hereditary factors linked to her cultural ancestry. Lynette and Hallie, two Caucasian children with impoverished home lives, were well below average for reasons we will discuss shortly.

The existence of cultural variations in body size reminds us that growth norms for one population (those in Figure 8.1 apply to North American children) are not good standards for many youngsters around the world. Consider the Efe of Zaire, an African people who

© BOB DAEMMRICH/STOCK BOSTON

Toddlers and 5-year-olds have very different body shapes. During early childhood, body fat declines, the torso enlarges to better accommodate the internal organs, and the spine straightens. Compared to her younger brother, this girl looks more streamlined. Her body proportions resemble those of an adult.

physical changes in kids are in accordance w/ development in other areas, esp. motor skills.

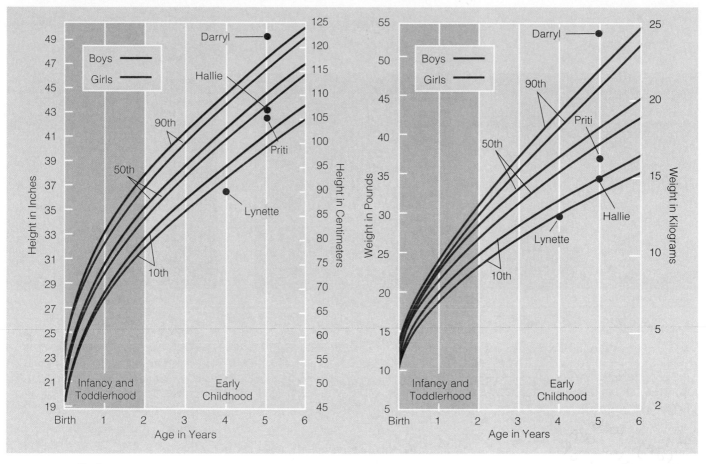

FIGURE 8.1

Gains in height and weight during early childhood among North American children. Compared to the first 2 years of life, growth is slower. Girls continue to be slightly shorter and lighter than boys. Wide individual differences in body size exist, as the percentiles on these charts reveal. Darryl, Priti, Lynette, and Hallie's heights and weights differ greatly.

normally grow to an adult height of less than 5 feet. Between 1 and 6 years, the growth of Efe children tapers off to a greater extent than that of American preschoolers. By age 5, the average Efe child is shorter than more than 97 percent of 5-year-olds in the United States. For genetic reasons, the hormones controlling body size have less effect on Efe youngsters than they do on other children (Bailey, 1990). We would be mistaken to take the Efe youngster's small stature as a sign of serious growth or health problems. However, this concern is warranted for an extremely slow-growing Caucasian child, such as Lynette, who falls below the tenth percentile for her age.

SKELETAL GROWTH

Skeletal changes under way in infancy continue throughout early childhood. Between ages 2 and 6, approximately 45 new *epiphyses,* or growth centers in which cartilage hardens into bone, emerge in various parts of the skeleton. Other epiphyses will appear in middle childhood. Figure 8.2 on page 296, which shows X-rays of a girl's hand at three ages, illustrates changes in the epiphyses over time. Such X-rays permit doctors to estimate children's *skeletal age,* the best available measure of progress toward physical maturity (see Chapter 5, page 172). During early and middle childhood, information about skeletal age is helpful in diagnosing growth disorders.

New epiphyses emerge in young children.

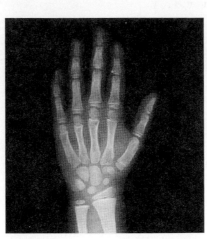
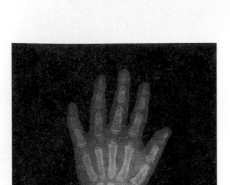
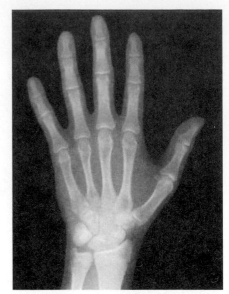

| 2½ years | 6½ years | 14½ years |

FIGURE 8.2

X-rays of a girl's hand, showing skeletal maturity at three ages. Notice how, at age 2½, wide gaps exist between the wrist bones and at the ends of the finger and arm bones. By age 6½, these have filled in considerably. At age 14½ (when this girl reached her adult size), the wrist and long bones are completely fused. (From J. M. Tanner, R. H. Whitehouse, N. Cameron, W. A. Marshall, M. J. R. Healy, & H. Goldstein, 1983, *Assessment of Skeletal Maturity and Prediction of Adult Height [TW2 Method],* 2nd ed., Academic Press [London, Ltd.], p. 86. Reprinted by permission.)

Secondary teeth growth is also an indicator of physical growth.

Parents and children are especially aware of another aspect of skeletal growth. By the end of the preschool years, children start to lose their primary, or "baby," teeth. The age at which they do so varies considerably and is heavily influenced by genetic factors. For example, girls, who are ahead of boys in physical development, lose their primary teeth sooner. Cultural ancestry also makes a difference. For example, North American children typically get their first secondary (permanent) tooth at 6½ years, children in Ghana at just over 5 years, and children in Hong Kong around the sixth birthday (Burns, 2000). Environmental influences, especially prolonged malnutrition, can delay the age at which children cut their permanent teeth.

Even though preschoolers will eventually lose their primary teeth, dental care is important, since decay in baby teeth is a strong predictor of decay in permanent teeth (al-Shalan, Erickson, & Hardie, 1997). Brushing consistently, avoiding sugary foods, drinking fluoridated water, and getting topical fluoride treatments and sealants (plastic coatings that protect tooth surfaces) prevent cavities. Unfortunately, childhood tooth decay remains high, especially among low-SES children. An estimated 60 percent of American poverty-stricken 3- to 5-year-olds have at least some tooth decay. Their cavaties advance at an especially rapid pace, affecting an average of 2.5 tooth sufaces each year. By the time American young people graduate from high school, five out of six have decayed teeth (Siegal, Farquhar, & Bouchard, 1997). Poor diet, lack of fluoridation in some communities, and inadequate health care are responsible.

ASYNCHRONIES IN PHYSICAL GROWTH

rapid slow rapid

general growth curve
A curve that represents overall changes in body size—rapid growth during infancy, slower gains in early and middle childhood, and rapid growth again during adolescence.

Body systems differ in their unique, carefully timed patterns of maturation. As Figure 8.3 shows, physical growth is *asynchronous*. Body size (as measured by height and weight) and a variety of internal organs follow the **general growth curve**. It involves rapid growth during infancy, slower gains in early and middle childhood, and rapid growth again during adolescence. Yet there are exceptions to this trend. The genitals develop slowly from birth to age

growth seems to accelerate during infancy + adolescence + wane in middle childhood.

4, change little throughout middle childhood, and then grow rapidly during adolescence. In contrast, the lymph tissue (small clusters of glands found throughout the body) grows at an astounding pace in infancy and childhood, but its growth declines in adolescence. The lymph system helps fight infection and assists in the absorption of nutrients, thereby supporting children's health and survival (Malina & Bouchard, 1991).

Figure 8.3 illustrates another growth trend with which you are familiar: During the first few years, the brain grows faster than any other part of the body. It develops especially rapidly during infancy and toddlerhood and continues to enlarge in early childhood, increasing from 70 percent of its adult weight at age 2 to 90 percent by age 6. Let's look at some highlights of brain development during early childhood.

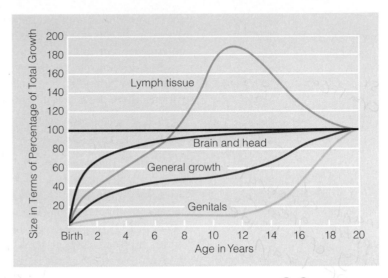

FIGURE 8.3

Growth of three different organ systems and tissues contrasted with the body's general growth. Growth is plotted in terms of percentage of change from birth to 20 years. Notice how growth of lymph tissue rises to nearly twice its adult level by the end of childhood. Then it declines. (Reprinted by permission of the publisher from J. M. Tanner, 1990, *Foetus into Man,* 2nd ed., Cambridge, MA: Harvard University Press, p. 16. Copyright © 1990 by J. M. Tanner. All rights reserved.)

Brain Development

Between ages 2 and 6, children gain in physical coordination, perception, attention, memory, language, logical thinking, and imagination. Virtually all theorists agree that brain development contributes to these changes. During early childhood, neural fibers in the brain continue to form *synapses* and *myelinate,* as they did during infancy and toddlerhood.

SYNAPTIC GROWTH AND PRUNING

Neuroimaging studies reveal that brain metabolism reaches a peak around 4 years of age, when it is well above what it will be in adulthood. Researchers speculate that by this time, many cortical regions have actually overproduced synapses, resulting in a very high energy need (Johnson, 1998). This overabundance of synaptic connections supports the *plasticity* of the young brain. Many synapses serve identical functions, helping to ensure that the child will acquire certain abilities even if some areas are damaged.

Next, *synaptic pruning* occurs: Neurons seldom stimulated lose their connective fibers, and the number of synapses is reduced (see Chapter 5, page 174). As the connective structures of stimulated neurons become more elaborate, they require additional space, and surrounding neurons die. As these changes occur, plasticity of the brain is reduced. By age 8 to 10, energy consumption of most cortical regions declines to near-adult levels (Chugani, 1994).

LATERALIZATION

In Chapter 5 we saw that the cerebral cortex is made up of two *hemispheres* with distinct functions. In several studies, EEG and fMRI measures of the neural activity of various cortical regions were taken at different ages. Results revealed especially rapid growth from 3 to 6 years in frontal-lobe areas devoted to planning and organizing behavior. Furthermore, for most children, the left hemisphere is especially active between 3 and 6 years and then levels off. In contrast, activity in the right hemisphere increases steadily throughout early and middle childhood, with a slight spurt between ages 8 and 10 (Thatcher, Walker, & Giudice, 1987; Thompson et al., 2000).

These findings fit nicely with what we know about several aspects of cognitive development. Language skills (typically housed in the left hemisphere) increase at an astonishing

Rate differences in brain specialization suggest Continuing lateralization.

dominant cerebral hemisphere - greater capacity of 1 side of brain.

LAURA DWIGHT

Twins typically lie in the uterus in opposite orientations during the prenatal period, which may explain why they are more often opposite-handed than are ordinary siblings. Although left-handedness is associated with developmental problems, the large majority of left-handed children are completely normal.

dominant cerebral hemisphere
The hemisphere of the brain responsible for skilled motor action. The left hemisphere is dominant in right-handed individuals. In left-handed individuals, the right hemisphere may be dominant, or motor and language skills may be shared between the hemispheres.

pace in early childhood, and they support children's increasing control over behavior. In contrast, spatial skills (such as finding one's way from place to place, drawing pictures, and recognizing geometric shapes) develop gradually over childhood and adolescence. Differences in rate of development of the two hemispheres suggest that they are continuing to *lateralize* (specialize in functions). Let's take a closer look at brain lateralization during early childhood by focusing on the development of handedness.

HANDEDNESS

One morning on a visit to the preschool, I watched 3-year-old Moira as she drew pictures, worked puzzles, joined in snack time, and played outside. Unlike most of her classmates, Moira does most things—drawing, eating, and zipping her jacket—with her left hand. But she also uses her right hand for a few activities, such as throwing a ball. Hand preference is evident in 10 percent of 1-year-olds and strengthens during early childhood. At age 5, 90 percent of children clearly prefer one hand over the other (Öztürk et al., 1999).

A strong hand preference reflects the greater capacity of one side of the brain—often referred to as the individual's **dominant cerebral hemisphere**—to carry out skilled motor action. Other abilities located on the dominant side may be superior as well. In support of this idea, for right-handed people, who make up 90 percent of the population, language is housed with hand control in the left hemisphere. For the remaining left-handed 10 percent, language is often shared between the hemispheres rather than located in only one. This indicates that the brains of left-handers tend to be less strongly lateralized than those of right-handers (Dean & Anderson, 1997). Consistent with this idea, many left-handed individuals (like Moira) are also *ambidextrous.* Although they prefer their left hand, they sometimes use their right hand skillfully as well (McManus et al., 1988).

Is handedness hereditary? Researchers disagree on this issue. Left-handed parents show only a weak tendency to have left-handed children. One genetic theory proposes that most children inherit a gene that *biases* them for right-handedness and left-hemispheric localization of language. However, that bias is not strong enough to overcome experiences that sway them toward a left-hand preference. Left-handed mothers are more likely to have left-handed children than are left-handed fathers. Therefore, male left-handers are believed to carry the right-hand bias gene more often than do female left-handers (Annett, 1994, 1999).

The genetic right-hand bias theory acknowledges that experience can profoundly affect handedness. In support of that view, twins—whether identical or fraternal—are more likely than ordinary siblings to display opposite-handedness. The hand preference of each twin is related to body position during the prenatal period; twins usually lie in opposite orientations (Derom et al., 1996). This suggests that prenatal events can affect lateralization. Most singleton fetuses orient toward the left, which may promote greater postural control by the right side of the body (Previc, 1991).

Another possibility is that practice heavily affects hand preference. Strength of handedness is strongest for complex skills requiring considerable training, such as eating with utensils, writing, and engaging in athletic skills. Also, wide cultural differences in the percentage of left-handers exist. For example, in Tanzania, Africa, children are physically restrained and punished for favoring the left hand. Less than 1 percent of the Tanzanian population is left-handed (Provins, 1997).

Perhaps you have heard that left-handedness is more frequent among severely retarded and mentally ill people than it is in the general population. Although this is true, recall that when two variables are correlated, this does not mean that one causes the other. Atypical brain lateralization is probably not responsible for the problems of these individuals. Instead, they may have suffered early damage to the left hemisphere, which caused their disabilities and also led to a shift in handedness. In support of this idea, left-handedness is associated

left-handedness is (not) related to developmental problems

with prenatal and birth difficulties that can result in brain damage, including prolonged labor, prematurity, Rh incompatibility, and breech delivery (Coren & Halpern, 1991; Powls et al., 1996).

Keep in mind, however, that only a small number of left-handers show developmental problems of any kind. The great majority, like Moira, are normal in every respect. In fact, unusual brain lateralization may have certain advantages. Left- and mixed-handed youngsters are more likely than their right-handed agemates to develop outstanding verbal and mathematical talents (Flannery & Liederman, 1995). More even distribution of these cognitive abilities across both hemispheres may be responsible.

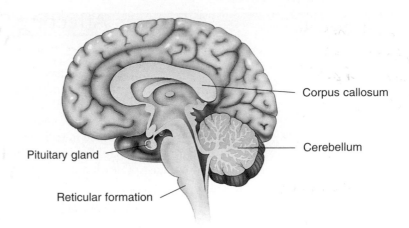

Corpus callosum

Cerebellum

Pituitary gland

Reticular formation

OTHER ADVANCES IN BRAIN DEVELOPMENT

Besides the cerebral cortex, several other areas of the brain make strides during early childhood. Figure 8.4 shows where each of these structures is located. As we look at these changes, you will see that they all involve establishing links between parts of the brain, increasing the coordinated functioning of the central nervous system.

At the rear and base of the brain is the **cerebellum**, a structure that aids in balance and control of body movement. Fibers linking the cerebellum to the cerebral cortex begin to myelinate after birth, but they do not complete this process until about age 4 (Tanner, 1990). This change undoubtedly contributes to dramatic gains in motor control, so that by the end of the preschool years, children can play hopscotch, pump a playground swing, and throw a ball with a well-organized set of movements.

The **reticular formation**, a structure in the brain stem that maintains alertness and consciousness, myelinates throughout early childhood, continuing its growth into adolescence. Neurons in the reticular formation send out fibers to other areas of the brain. Many go to the frontal lobes of the cerebral cortex, contributing to improvements in sustained, controlled attention (McGuinness & Pribram, 1980).

A final brain structure that undergoes major changes during early childhood is the **corpus callosum.** It is a large bundle of fibers that connects the two hemispheres so they can communicate directly. Myelinization of the corpus callosum does not begin until the end of the first year of life. By age 4 to 5, its development is fairly advanced, but it continues to enlarge throughout childhood and adolescence (Giedd et al., 1999; Witelson & Kigar, 1988). The corpus collosum supports gains in the integration of many aspects of thinking, including perception, attention, memory, language, and problem solving. The more complex the task, the more critical communication between the hemispheres becomes.

corpus callosum allows the hemispheres to communicate w/1 another.

FIGURE 8.4

Cross section of the human brain, showing the location of the cerebellum, the reticular formation, and the corpus callosum. These structures undergo considerable development during early childhood. Also shown is the pituitary gland, which secretes hormones that control body growth (see page 300).

cerebellum
A brain structure that aids in balance and control of body movement.

reticular formation
A brain structure that maintains alertness and consciousness.

corpus callosum
The large bundle of fibers that connects the two hemispheres of the brain.

 YOURSELF...

review Explain why brain growth in early childhood involves not only an increase in neural connections but loss of synapses and cell death.

apply Both Crystal and Shana are shorter and lighter than 97 percent of other North American 4-year-old girls. What are the possible causes of their very short stature?

connect What stance on the nature–nurture issue does evidence on development of handedness support? Document your answer with research findings.

[Handwritten margin notes:]

physical growth depends on:
① emotional health
② sleep
③ nutrition
④ freedom from disease

① growth hormone
② thyroid-stimulating hormone

Factors Affecting Physical Growth and Health

In earlier chapters we considered a wide variety of influences on physical growth during the prenatal period and infancy. As we discuss growth and health during early childhood, you will encounter some familiar themes. Although heredity remains important, environmental factors continue to play crucial roles. Emotional well-being, restful sleep, good nutrition, and relative freedom from disease are essential. Finally, like infant mortality, childhood mortality is largely preventable. Unintentional injuries are the leading cause of death during the preschool years.

HEREDITY AND HORMONES

The impact of heredity on physical growth is evident throughout childhood. Children's physical size and rate of growth (as measured by skeletal age) are related to their parents'. Genes influence growth by controlling the body's production of hormones, especially two that are released by the **pituitary gland,** located near the base of the brain (return to Figure 8.4).

The first is **growth hormone (GH),** which is necessary for physical development from birth on. GH affects the development of all body tissues except the central nervous system and the genitals. Children who lack it reach an average mature height of only 4 feet, 4 inches, although they are normal in physical proportions and healthy in all other respects. When treated with injections of GH starting at an early age, such children show catch-up growth and then grow at a normal rate. Consult the Biology and Environment box on the following page for a current controversy surrounding GH treatment—whether it should be used for short children who are not GH deficient.

The second pituitary hormone affecting children's growth is **thyroid-stimulating hormone (TSH).** It stimulates the thyroid gland (located in the neck) to release *thyroxine,* which is necessary for normal development of the nerve cells of the brain and for GH to have its full impact on body size. Infants born with a deficiency of thyroxine must receive it at once or they will be mentally retarded. At later ages, children with too little thyroxine grow at a below-average rate. However, the central nervous system is no longer affected, since the most rapid period of brain development is complete. With prompt treatment, such children catch up in body growth and eventually reach normal size (Tanner, 1990).

EMOTIONAL WELL-BEING

In childhood as in infancy, emotional well-being can have a profound effect on growth and health. Preschoolers with very stressful home lives (due to divorce, financial difficulties, or a change in their parents' employment status) suffer more respiratory and intestinal illnesses as well as unintentional injuries.

Extreme emotional deprivation can interfere with the production of GH and lead to **deprivation dwarfism,** a growth disorder observed between 2 and 15 years of age (Doeker et al., 1999). Lynette, the very small 4-year-old mentioned earlier in this chapter, was diagnosed with this condition. She had been placed in foster care after child welfare authorities discovered that she spent most of the day at home alone, unsupervised. She may also have been physically abused. To help her recover, authorities enrolled Lynette in our laboratory preschool. She showed the typical physical characteristics of deprivation dwarfism—very short stature (she was no taller than an average 2½-year-old), weight in proportion to her height, immature skeletal age, and decreased GH secretion.

Deprivation dwarfism usually can be distinguished from a biologically based GH deficiency and from normal shortness by the child's severe adjustment problems (Voss, Mulligan, & Betts, 1998). When such children are removed from their emotionally inadequate environments, their GH levels quickly return to normal, and they grow rapidly. But if treatment is delayed, the dwarfism can be permanent.

[Handwritten note at bottom:] there is a window where a child must be taken out of the bad home to resume normal growth.

pituitary gland
A gland located near the base of the brain that releases hormones affecting physical growth.

growth hormone (GH)
A pituitary hormone that affects the development of all body tissues except the central nervous system and the genitals.

thyroid-stimulating hormone (TSH)
A pituitary hormone that stimulates the thyroid gland to release thyroxine, which is necessary for normal brain development and body growth.

deprivation dwarfism
A growth disorder observed between 2 and 15 years of age. Characterized by very short stature, weight that is usually appropriate for height, immature skeletal age, and decreased GH secretion. Caused by emotional deprivation.

Biology & ENVIRONMENT

TREATING SHORT CHILDREN WITH GROWTH HORMONE

Through childhood and adolescence, Stephen was among the shortest 3 percent of his age group. He recalls being teased and tormented by insensitive peers and being called "shrimp," "pea," "midget," "squirt," and a dozen other insults. He looks back on these experiences calmly, perhaps because a late growth spurt led him to reach a final height of 5 feet 6 inches (Hall, 1996). But now, as he awaits the birth of his first child, he wonders, "Would treatment with GH have relieved the pain I experienced? Would it have added to or merely accelerated my growth? If my child is short, should I have him or her treated with a powerful drug to avoid the psychological pain induced by society's prejudices?"

Genetically engineered GH has been available since 1985, permitting successful treatment of short stature for children with GH deficiency. Since then, research has been conducted on unusually short, normal-GH children to see if they might benefit from hormone injections. Thousands of concerned parents have sought GH therapy for their children.

ARE SHORT, NORMAL-GH CHILDREN MALADJUSTED?

A major justification for treating short, non-GH-deficient children is to improve their psychological well-being. Frequently reported problems include social stigma due to deviant appearance, poor social skills, social isolation, low self-esteem, and poor academic achievement. But most studies include only GH-deficient children (Meyer-Bahlburg, 1990). Do these negative outcomes apply to short, normal-GH children as well?

Recent findings are mixed. In a British investigation comparing very short with average-stature children on self-esteem, social behavior, and academic achievement, differences between the two groups were minimal on some measures and nonexistent on others (Vance, 1994). An American study found very short 4- to 18-year-old boys, but not girls, to have an above-average incidence of parent-reported emotional and behavior problems. But when boys themselves—not their parents—were asked, they reported good self-esteem as well as athletic competence. They seemed to find their niche in certain sports in which height is not essential (Sandberg, Brook, & Campos, 1994).

In sum, research suggests that a biological height deficit by itself does not lead to poor psychological adjustment. Family attitudes and social experiences that sensitize children to their short stature appear to be very powerful.

DOES GH TREATMENT LEAD TO HEIGHT GAINS?

Many studies show that the final height of GH-deficient children is considerably greater than it would have been without treatment. In contrast, follow-ups of short, normal-GH children who began GH treatment in late childhood or early adolescence reveal faster initial growth—an outcome that may be emotionally beneficial for some youngsters. Final stature varies greatly. Some studies show only slight gains over previously predicted adult height (Guyda, 1999; Vance & Mauras, 1999). Others, in which treatment began 4 years or more prior to puberty and involved higher GH doses, show larger gains of 2 to 3 inches (Kelnar et al., 1999).

Both biological and social forces influence a doctor's decision to prescribe GH for a short but otherwise normal child. On the biological side, doctors are more likely to treat an extremely short child who is growing very slowly yet has a normal skeletal age—a combination of factors that increases the chances of becoming a very short adult. On the social side, family wishes clearly influence medical recommendations. When the child's parents strongly desire treatment, the child is more likely to get it (Cuttler et al., 1996).

Yet until more evidence is in, great caution should be exercised in prescribing GH for short, GH-normal children (Bercu, 1996). The estimated cost is staggering—$15,000 to $30,000 annually for a regimen that must continue until the child reaches near-adult height. Potential side effects include allergy, diabetic-like symptoms, fluid retention, and—for genetically susceptible individuals—curvature of the spine and leukemia. And wide individual differences in responsiveness exist, with some children profiting little or not at all from treatment.

Because "heightism" exists in society, treatment of short children may be warranted in some instances. But doctors and parents should recognize the unjust social values that lead them to consider intervening in a condition that results from biologically normal human diversity.

LAURA DWIGHT

Should the very short boy on the left in this class of kindergartners be given GH to speed his growth, increase his height, and protect him from social stigma? Research indicates that the cost of doing so is staggering and the outcome uncertain.

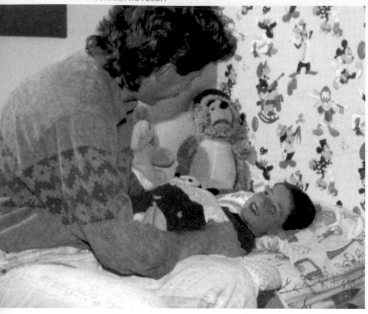

TONY FREEMAN/PHOTOEDIT

Parents of preschoolers often report that their children have sleep difficulties. Bedtime rituals, such as a story and a hug and kiss before turning out the light, help young children adjust to falling asleep in a room by themselves.

SLEEP HABITS AND PROBLEMS

Sleep contributes to body growth, since GH is released during the child's sleeping hours. A well-rested child is better able to play, learn, and contribute positively to family functioning. By disrupting parents' sleep, children who sleep poorly can cause significant family stress—a major reason that sleep difficulties are among the most common concerns parents raise with their preschooler's doctor (Mindell, Owens, & Carskadon, 1999).

On the average, total sleep declines in early childhood; 2- and 3-year-olds sleep 12 to 13 hours, 4- to 6-year-olds 10 to 11 hours. Younger preschoolers typically take a 1- to 2-hour nap in the early afternoon, although their daytime sleep needs vary widely. Some continue to take two naps, as they did in toddlerhood; others give up napping entirely. Unless a preschooler becomes irritable and overtired from lack of sleep, there is no need to force a nap. Between ages 3 and 5, most North American children give up naps, although a quiet play period or rest after lunch helps them rejuvenate for the rest of the day (Dahl, 1998). In some cultures, daytime naps persist through adulthood.

Western preschoolers often become rigid about bedtime rituals, such as using the toilet, listening to a story, getting a drink of water, taking a security object to bed, and hugging and kissing before turning off the light. These practices, which typically take as long as 30 minutes, help young children adjust to feelings of uneasiness at being left by themselves in a darkened room. Difficulty falling asleep—calling to the parent or asking for another drink of water—is generally due to lingering separation anxiety (Lansky, 1991). A night-light and a favorite blanket or stuffed animal tucked in with the child can ease these feelings. Intense bedtime struggles sometimes result from inconsistent discipline, which often accompanies family turmoil. Preschoolers with behavior problems tend to sleep considerably less than other children (Lavigne et al., 1999). In these cases, addressing family stress and conflict is the key to improving children's sleep.

[handwritten margin note: Sleep trouble is linked to lingering separation anxiety.]

[handwritten note across text: Separation anxiety + inconsistent discipline lead to disruptive sleeping patterns.]

NUTRITION

Early childhood often brings a dramatic change in the quantity and variety of foods that children will eat. Suddenly, appetite becomes unpredictable. Preschoolers may eat well at one meal and barely touch their food at the next. Many become picky eaters. One father I know wistfully recalled his son's eager sampling of the cuisine at a Chinese restaurant during toddlerhood. "He ate rice, chicken chow mein, egg rolls, and more. Now, at age 3, the only thing he'll try is the ice cream!"

This decline in the appetite is normal. It occurs because growth has slowed. And preschoolers' wariness of new foods may be adaptive. By sticking to familiar foods, young children are less likely to swallow dangerous substances when adults are not around to protect them (Birch & Fisher, 1995). Parents need not worry about variations in amount eaten from meal to meal. Over the course of a day, preschoolers' food intake is fairly constant. They compensate for a meal in which they ate little with a later one in which they eat more (Hursti, 1999).

Even though they eat less, preschoolers need a high-quality diet. They require the same foods that make up a healthy adult diet—only smaller amounts. Milk and milk products, meat or meat alternatives (such as eggs, dried peas or beans, and peanut butter), vegetables and fruits, and breads and cereals should be included. Fats and salt are needed but should be kept to a minimum because of their early link to heart disease in adulthood (Winkleby et al., 1999). Foods high in sugar should also be avoided. In addition to causing tooth decay, they lessen young children's appetite for healthy foods and increase their risk of overweight and obesity—a topic we will take up in Chapter 11.

[handwritten margin note: decline in appetite b/c not as much growth.]

[handwritten note at bottom: sugar is bad b/c of: 1) tooth decay 2) lessening appetite for healthy foods 3) ↑ risk of obesity.]

The social environment has a powerful impact on preschoolers' food preferences. Children tend to imitate the food choices and eating practices of people they admire—peers as well as adults. For example, in Mexico, children often see family members delighting in the taste of peppery foods. Consequently, Mexican preschoolers enthusiastically eat chili peppers, whereas American children reject them (Birch, Zimmerman, & Hind, 1980).

Repeated exposure to a new food (without any direct pressure to eat it) also increases children's acceptance. In one study, preschoolers were given one of three versions of a food they had never eaten before (sweet, salty, or plain tofu). After 8 to 15 exposures, they readily ate the food. But they preferred the version they had already tasted. For example, children in the "sweet" condition liked sweet tofu best, and those in the "plain" condition liked plain tofu best (Sullivan & Birch, 1990). These findings reveal that children's tastes are trained by foods they encounter repeatedly. Adding sugar or salt in hopes of increasing a young child's willingness to eat healthy foods simply strengthens the child's desire for a sugary or salty taste.

The emotional climate at mealtimes has a powerful impact on children's eating habits. Many parents worry about how well their preschoolers eat, so meals become unpleasant and stressful. Sometimes parents bribe their children, saying, "Finish your vegetables, and you can have an extra cookie." This practice causes children to like the healthy food less and the treat more (Birch, Johnson, & Fisher, 1995). Forbidding access to certain foods also increases children's preference for those foods. Although children's healthy eating depends on a healthy food environment, too much parental control over children's eating limits their opportunities to develop self-control (Birch, 1998). The Caregiving Concerns table below offers some suggestions for promoting healthy, varied eating in young children.

TOM MCCARTHY/PHOTOEDIT

Children's food tastes are trained by foods served often in their culture. Many Western children would refuse the spicy noodle dish these Japanese preschoolers are eating with enthusiasm.

Exposure, social environment, & parental control influence the diet of a child.

Caregiving Concerns

Encouraging Good Nutrition in Early Childhood

SUGGESTION	DESCRIPTION
Offer a varied, healthy diet.	Provide a well-balanced variety of nutritious foods that are colorful and attractively served. Avoid serving sweets and "junk" foods as a regular part of meals and snacks.
Offer predictable meals as well as several snacks each day.	Preschoolers' stomachs are small, and they may not be able to eat enough in three meals to satisfy energy requirements. They benefit from extra opportunities to eat.
Offer small portions, and permit the child to ask for seconds.	When too much food is put on the plate, preschoolers may be overwhelmed and not even try to eat.
Offer new foods early in a meal and over several meals, and respond with patience if the child rejects the food.	Introduce new foods before the child's appetite is satisfied. Let children see you eat and enjoy the new food. If the child rejects it, accept the refusal and serve it again at another meal. As foods become more familiar, they are more readily accepted.
Keep mealtimes pleasant, and include the child in mealtime conversations.	A pleasant, relaxed eating environment helps children develop positive attitudes about food. Refrain from constantly offering food and prompting eating, which fosters excessively fast eating and, possibly, overeating. Avoid confrontations over disliked foods and table manners, which may lead to refusal to eat.
Avoid using food as a reward and forbidding access to certain foods.	Saying "No dessert until you clean your plate" tells children that they must eat regardless of how hungry they are and that dessert is the best part of the meal. Restricting access to a food increases children's valuing of that food and their efforts to obtain it.

Sources: Birch, 1999; Drucker et al., 1999.

Important nutrients!
iron
calcium
vitamin A
vitamin C

Finally, as indicated in earlier chapters, many children in the United States and in developing countries lack diets that support healthy growth. Five-year-old Hallie was bused to our laboratory preschool from a poor neighborhood. His mother's welfare check barely covered her rent, let alone food. Hallie's diet was deficient in protein as well as essential vitamins and minerals—iron (to prevent anemia), calcium (to support development of bones and teeth), vitamin A (to help maintain eyes, skin, and a variety of internal organs), and vitamin C (to facilitate iron absorption and wound healing). These are the most common dietary deficiencies of the preschool years (Kennedy, 1998). Not surprisingly, Hallie was thin, pale, and tired. By age 7, American low-SES children are, on average, about 1 inch shorter than their economically advantaged counterparts (Yip, Scanlon, & Trowbridge, 1993).

INFECTIOUS DISEASE

Two weeks into the school year, I looked outside my window and noticed that Hallie was absent from the play yard. Several weeks passed; still I did not see him. When I asked Leslie, his preschool teacher, what had happened, she explained, "Hallie's been hospitalized with the measles. He's had a difficult time recovering—lost weight when there wasn't much to lose in the first place." In well-nourished children, ordinary childhood illnesses have no effect on physical growth. But when children are undernourished, disease interacts with malnutrition in a vicious spiral, and the consequences for physical growth can be severe.

BRUCE AYERS/STONE

Widespread, government-sponsored immunization of infants and young children is a cost-effective means of supporting healthy growth by dramatically reducing the incidence of childhood diseases. Although this boy finds a routine inoculation painful, it will offer him lifelong protection.

oral rehydration therapy (ORT)
A treatment for diarrhea in which sick children are given a glucose, salt, and water solution that quickly replaces fluids the body loses.

■ **INFECTIOUS DISEASE AND MALNUTRITION.** Hallie's reaction to the measles is commonplace among children in developing nations, where a large proportion of the population lives in poverty. In these countries, many children do not receive a program of immunizations. Illnesses such as measles and chicken pox, which typically do not appear until after age 3 in industrialized nations, occur much earlier. This is because poor diet depresses the body's immune system, making children far more susceptible to disease. Of the 10 million annual worldwide deaths in children under age 5, 99 percent are in developing countries and 70 percent are due to infectious diseases (World Health Organization, 2000).

Disease, in turn, is a major cause of malnutrition and, through it, affects physical growth. Illness reduces appetite, and it limits the body's ability to absorb foods. These outcomes are especially severe among children with intestinal infections. In developing countries, diarrhea is widespread and increases in early childhood due to unsafe water and contaminated foods, leading to several million childhood deaths each year (Shann & Steinhoff, 1999). Research in poverty-stricken Guatemalan villages showed that 7-year-olds who had been relatively free of diarrhea since birth were significantly heavier than their frequently ill peers (Martorell, 1980).

Most growth retardation and deaths due to diarrhea can be prevented with nearly cost-free **oral rehydration therapy (ORT),** in which sick children are given a glucose, salt, and water solution that quickly replaces fluids the body loses. Since 1990, public health workers have taught nearly half of families in the developing world how to administer ORT. As a result, the lives of more than 1 million children are being saved annually (Bellamy, 2000).

■ **IMMUNIZATION.** In industrialized nations, childhood diseases have declined dramatically during the past half-century, largely due to widespread immunization of infants and young children. Hallie got the measles because, unlike his classmates from more advantaged homes, he did not receive a full program of immunizations during his first 2 years of life.

About 20 percent of American infants and toddlers are not fully immunized. Of the 80 percent who receive a complete schedule of vaccinations in the first two years, some do not receive vital early childhood immunizations. Overall, 24 percent of American preschoolers lack essential immunizations, a rate that rises to 40 percent for poverty stricken children (U.S. Department of Health and Human Services, 2000a). In contrast, fewer than 10 percent of preschoolers

Cultural INFLUENCES

CHILD HEALTH CARE IN THE UNITED STATES AND OTHER WESTERN NATIONS

Historically, Americans have been strongly committed to the idea that parents should assume total responsibility for the care and rearing of children. This belief, in addition to powerful economic interests in the medical community, has prevented government-sponsored health services from being offered to all children.

American health insurance is an optional, employment-related fringe benefit. Many businesses that rely on low-wage and part-time help do not insure their employees. If they do, they often do not cover other family members, including children. Although a variety of public health programs are available in the United States, they reach only the most needy individuals. This leaves nearly 11.5 million children from poor, low-income, and moderate-income families (14 percent of the child population) uninsured and, therefore, without affordable medical care (Children's Defense Fund, 2000).

Because of the high cost of medical treatment, American uninsured, low-SES children see a doctor only half as often as insured, higher-SES children with similar illnesses (Newacheck, Hughes, & Stoddard, 1996). Consequently, an estimated 37 percent of children younger than age 5 who come from poverty-stricken families are in less than very good health. Partly because of weak health-care services, 13 percent of children living in poverty have activity limitations due to chronic illnesses—a rate nearly twice as high as

the national average (U.S. Department of Health and Human Services, 2000h). Furthermore, most employed parents have no solution to the problem of providing child care when their child becomes ill. Currently, only one-half of American employees receive paid sick leave of any kind (U.S. Bureau of the Census, 2000).

The inadequacies of American child health care stand in sharp contrast to services provided in other industrialized nations, where medical insurance is government sponsored and available to all citizens, regardless of income. Let's look at two examples.

In the Netherlands, every child receives free medical examinations from birth through adolescence. During the early years, health care also includes parental counseling in nutrition, disease prevention, and child development (de Winter, Balledux, & de Mare, 1997). The Netherlands achieves its extraordinarily high childhood immunization rate by giving parents of every newborn baby a written schedule that shows exactly when and where the child should be immunized. If the child is not brought in at the specified time, a public health nurse calls the family. In instances of repeated missed appointments, the nurse goes to the home to ensure that the child receives the recommended immunizations (Bradley & Bray, 1996).

In Norway, federal law requires that well baby and child clinics be established in all communities and that examinations by doctors take place

three times during the first year and at ages 2 and 4. Specialized nurses see children on additional occasions, monitoring their growth and development, providing immunizations, and counseling parents on physical and mental health. Although citizens pay a small fee for routine medical visits, hospital services are free of charge. Parents with a seriously ill child are given leave from work with full salary, a benefit financed by the government (Scarr et al., 1993).

In Australia, Canada, Europe, New Zealand, and other industrialized nations, child health care is regarded as a fundamental human right, no different from the right to education. Currently, many organizations, government officials, and concerned citizens committed to improving child health are working to guarantee every American child necessary medical care. In 1999, a new health initiative—the State Children's Health Insurance Program (CHIP) was launched. Under CHIP, the states receive $4 billion a year in federal matching funds for upgrading children's health insurance. State control over program implementation enables each state to adapt insurance coverage to meet its unique needs. But it also means that advocates for children's health must exert pressure for family-friendly policies. A state can, for example, require that families share in the cost of participation. For low-income parents making choices about how to stretch their limited budgets, even a small premium or co-payment could make CHIP unaffordable.

lack immunizations in Denmark and Norway and fewer than 7 percent in Canada, the Netherlands, and Sweden (Bellamy, 2000; Health Canada, 2000).

How have these countries managed to achieve higher rates of immunization than the United States? In earlier chapters we noted that many children in the United States do not have access to the medical care they need. The Cultural Influences box above examines child health care in the United States and other Western nations.

In 1994, all medically uninsured American children were guaranteed free immunizations, a program that has led to steady improvement in early childhood immunization rates. Inability to pay for vaccines, however, is only one cause of inadequate immunization in the United States. Misconceptions also contribute. American parents often report that they delay bringing their child in for a vaccination because they fear that the child might have an adverse reaction. And some believe, incorrectly, that the vaccines do not work or that vaccine-preventable diseases have been eradicated in the United States (U.S. Centers for Disease Control, 2000c). Public education programs directed at increasing parental knowledge about the safety and importance of timely immunizations are badly needed.

A final point regarding communicable disease in early childhood deserves mention. Research in Europe and the United States indicates that childhood illness rises with child-care attendance. On average, a child-care infant becomes sick 9 to 10 times a year, a child-care preschool child 6 to 7 times. Diseases that spread most rapidly are diarrhea and respiratory infections—the most frequent illnesses suffered by young children. The risk that a respiratory infection will result in otitis media, or middle ear infection, is almost double that of children remaining at home (Uhari, Mäntysaari, & Niemelä, 1996). To learn about its consequences for development and how to prevent it, consult the Social Issues: Health box on the following page. The Caregiving Concerns table below summarizes strategies for controlling the spread of infectious disease in child care.

CHILDHOOD INJURIES

Three-year-old Tory caught my eye as I visited the preschool classroom one day. More than any other child, he had trouble sitting still and paying attention at story time. Outside, he darted from one place to another, spending little time at a single activity. On a field trip to our campus museum, Tory ignored Leslie's directions and ran across the street without holding his partner's hand. Later in the year, I read in our local newspaper that Tory had narrowly escaped serious injury when he put his mother's car in gear while she was outside scraping its windows. The vehicle rolled through a guardrail and over the side of a 10-foot

*C*aregiving Concerns

Controlling the Spread of Infectious Disease in Child Care

STRATEGY	DESCRIPTION
Follow good personal hygiene.	Illness rates decline when adults and children routinely wash their hands—before touching food, after wiping noses, after toileting, and after touching clothing or objects contaminated with body secretions.
Clean the child-care environment regularly.	Regular cleaning reduces the spread of illness. Because infants and young children frequently put toys in their mouths, these objects should be rinsed frequently with a disinfectant solution.
Arrange the child-care environment to minimize infection.	Food preparation and toileting areas should be physically separated. Spacious, well-ventilated rooms and small group sizes limit the spread of illness.
Make sure that all children have a full program of infant and early childhood immunizations.	Over the first 2 years, immunizations should be given for diphtheria-tetanus-pertussis (DTP); polio; measles-mumps-rubella (MMR); hepatitis B; haemophilus B (meningitis); and chicken pox. Follow-up immunizations—DTP, MMR, and polio—should be given between 4 and 6 years.
Isolate children with communicable diseases that spread rapidly.	An isolation area should be provided for children who come down with a rapidly spreading infection or illness at child care. As long as good personal hygiene is followed, children with mild respiratory infections, such as the common cold, can continue to attend child care with little impact on the health of other youngsters.

Sources: Roberts et al., 2000; U.S. Centers for Disease Control, 2000b; Uhari & Möttönen, 1999.

concrete underpass. There it hung until rescue workers arrived. Tory's mother was charged with failing to use a restraint seat for children under age 5.

Unintentional injuries—auto collisions, pedestrian accidents, drownings, firearm wounds, burns, falls, poisoning, and swallowing of foreign objects—are the leading cause of childhood mortality in industrialized nations (Roberts & DiGuiseppi, 1999). These largely preventable events are highest in the United States, where they account for 40 to 50 percent of deaths in early and middle childhood and as many as 75 percent during adolescence. Approximately 22,000 youngsters die from these incidents each year. And for each death, thousands of other injured children survive but suffer pain, brain damage, or permanent physical disabilities. Overall, about one-fourth of American children experience at least one injury requiring medical treatment annually (Tremblay & Peterson, 1999).

Social ISSUES: HEALTH
OTITIS MEDIA AND DEVELOPMENT

During his first year in child care, 18-month-old Alex caught five colds, had the flu on two occasions, and experienced repeated *otitis media* (middle ear infection). Alex is not unusual. By age 3, over 70 percent of children have had respiratory illnesses that resulted in at least one bout of otitis media; 33 percent have had three or more bouts. Some episodes are painful, but as many as half are accompanied by few or no symptoms. Parents learn of them only on routine visits to the doctor. Although antibiotics eliminate the bacteria responsible for otitis media, they do not reduce fluid buildup in the middle ear, which causes mild to moderate hearing loss that can last for weeks or months.

The incidence of otitis media is greatest between 6 months and 3 years, when children are first acquiring language. Frequent infections predict delayed language progress and social isolation in early childhood and poorer academic performance after school entry (Rvachew, 1999; Teele et al., 1990; Vernon-Feagans, Manlove, & Volling, 1996).

How might otitis media disrupt language and academic progress? Difficulties in hearing speech sounds, particularly in noisy settings, may be responsible. Early and recurrent episodes of infection are consistently associated with impaired speech perception and production (Feagans & Proctor, 1994). Furthermore, children with many bouts are less attentive to the speech of others and less persistent at tasks (Feagans et al., 1987; Roberts, Burchinal, & Campbell, 1994). Their distractibility may be due to an inability to make out what people around them are saying. When children have trouble paying attention, they may reduce the quality of others' interactions with them. In one study, mothers of preschoolers with many illness episodes were less effective in teaching their child a task (Paradise et al., 1995).

Current evidence argues strongly in favor of early prevention of otitis media, especially since the illness is so widespread. Crowded living conditions and exposure to cigarette smoke and other pollutants are linked to the disease—factors that probably account for its high incidence among low-SES children. In addition, enrollment of millions of infants and young children in child care creates opportunities for close contact, greatly increasing otitis media episodes.

Early otitis media can be prevented in the following ways:

- *Preventive doses of xylitol, a sweetener derived from birch bark.* A Finnish study revealed that children in child-care centers given a daily dose of xylitol in gum or syrup form show a 30 to 40 percent drop in otitis media compared to controls receiving gum or syrup without the sweetener. Xylitol appears to have natural, bacteria-fighting ingredients (Uhari, Kontiokari, & Niemelä, 1998). However, dosage must be carefully monitored, since too much xylitol can cause abdominal pain and diarrhea.

- *Frequent screening of infants and preschoolers for otitis media, followed by prompt medical intervention.* Plastic tubes that drain the inner ear often are used to treat chronic otitis media, although their effectiveness remains controversial.

- *Infection-control procedures in child-care programs.* (See the Caregiving Concerns table on page 306)

- *Verbally stimulating adult–child interaction.* Developmental problems associated with otitis media are reduced or eliminated in high-quality child-care centers. When caregivers are verbally stimulating and keep noise to a minimum, children have more opportunities to hear and benefit from spoken language (Feagans, Kipp, & Blood, 1994; Roberts, Burchinal, & Campbell, 1994).

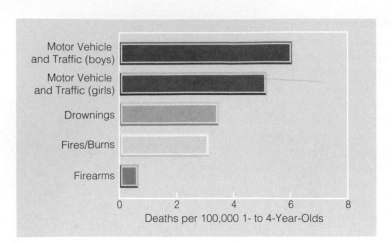

Deaths per 100,000 1- to 4-Year-Olds

FIGURE 8.5

Rate of injury mortality in the United States for children between 1 and 4 years of age by type of injury. Between 1 and 4 years of age, motor vehicle and traffic fatalities are greater for boys than girls. For other injuries depicted here, death rates for boys and girls are similar until age 5, when boys begin to outdistance girls in all categories. (From U.S. Department of Health and Human Services, 2000h.)

As Figure 8.5 shows, auto and traffic accidents, drownings, and burns are the most common injuries during the early childhood years. Motor vehicle collisions are by far the most frequent source of injury at all ages. They are the leading cause of death among children older than 1 year of age.

■ **FACTORS RELATED TO CHILDHOOD INJURIES.** We are used to thinking of childhood injuries as "accidental," a word that encourages us to believe that chance is responsible for them and that they cannot be prevented (Kronenfeld & Glik, 1995). But a close look at childhood injuries reveals that individual, family, community, and societal factors are related to them. As with other aspects of development, they take place within a complex *ecological system.* This suggests that meaningful causes underlie them, and we can, indeed, do something about them.

As Tory's case suggests, individual differences exist in the safety level of children's everyday behaviors. Because of their higher activity level and greater willingness to take risks during play, boys are more likely to be injured than girls (Laing & Logan, 1999). Temperamental characteristics—irritability, inattentiveness, and negative mood—are also related to childhood injuries. As we saw in Chapter 7, children with these traits present child-rearing challenges. They are likely to protest when placed in auto seat restraints, refuse to take a companion's hand when crossing the street, and disobey after repeated instruction and discipline (Matheny, 1991).

At the same time, poverty, low parental education, and more children in the home are strongly associated with injury (Bradbury et al., 1999). Parents who must cope with many daily stresses often have little time and energy to monitor the safety of their youngsters. And the homes and neighborhoods of such families pose further risks. Noise, crowding, and confusion characterize these run-down, inner-city neighborhoods with few safe places to play (Kronenfeld & Glik, 1995).

Broad societal conditions also affect childhood injury. Among Western industrialized nations, the United States ranks among the highest in childhood injury mortality. Although injury deaths have declined steadily in nearly all developed countries during the past 30 years, they have dropped only minimally in the United States (U.S. Department of Health and Human Services, 2000).

What accounts for this worrisome picture? Widespread poverty, a shortage of high-quality child care (to supervise children in their parents' absence), and a high rate of births to teenagers (who are neither psychologically nor financially ready to raise a child) are believed to play important roles. But children from economically advantaged families are also at greater risk for injury in the United States than in European nations (Williams & Kotch, 1990). This indicates that besides reducing poverty and teenage pregnancy and upgrading the status of child care, additional steps must be taken to ensure children's safety.

■ **PREVENTING CHILDHOOD INJURIES.** Childhood injuries have many causes, so a variety of approaches are needed to control them (Tremblay & Peterson, 1999). Laws prevent a great many injuries by requiring car safety seats, child-resistant caps on medicine bottles, flameproof clothing, and fenced-in backyard swimming pools (the site of 90 percent of early childhood drownings).

Communities can help by modifying their physical environments. For example, public transportation can reduce the time children spend in cars. Playgrounds, an especially common site of injury, can be covered with protective surfaces, such as rubber matting, sand, and wood chips (Dowd, 1999). Free, easily installed window guards can be given to families living in high-rise apartment buildings to prevent falls. And widespread media and information campaigns can inform parents and children about safety issues.

Nevertheless, many dangers cannot be eliminated from the environment. And even though they know better, many parents and children behave in ways that compromise safety. For example, about 15 percent of parents (like Tory's mother) fail to place their children in car safety seats, and many others do not use the seats correctly (Kronenfeld & Glik, 1995). Adults often leave caps off medicine bottles, neglect to replace batteries in home smoke detectors, and leave handguns within reach of children.

How can we change human behavior? A variety of programs based on *applied behavior analysis* (modeling and reinforcement) have improved child safety. In one, counselors helped parents identify dangers in the home—fire hazards, objects that young children might swallow, poisonous substances, firearms, and others. Then they demonstrated specific ways to eliminate the dangers (Tertinger, Greene, & Lutzker, 1984). Some interventions reward parents and children with prizes if the children arrive at child care or school restrained in car seats (Roberts, Alexander, & Knapp, 1990).

Efforts like these have been remarkably successful, yet their focus is fairly narrow—on decreasing specific environmental risks and risky behaviors (Peterson & Brown, 1994). Attention must also be paid to family conditions that can prevent childhood injury—relieving crowding and chaos in the home, providing social supports to ease parental stress, and teaching parents to establish safety rules and use effective discipline—a topic we take up in Chapter 10. Refer to the Caregiving Concerns table below for ways to reduce unintentional injuries in early childhood.

This child's parents insist that she ride properly restrained in an age-appropriate safety seat in the back of the car. In doing so, they greatly reduce her chances of injury and teach good safety practices.

  ## *C*aregiving Concerns

Reducing Unintentional Injuries in Early Childhood

SUGGESTION	DESCRIPTION
Provide age-appropriate supervision and safety instruction.	Despite increasing self-control, preschoolers need nearly constant supervision. Establish and enforce safety rules, explain the reasons behind them, and praise children for following them, thereby encouraging the child to remember, understand, and obey.
Know the child's temperament.	Children who are unusually active, distractible, negative, or curious have more than their share of injuries and need extra monitoring.
Eliminate the most serious dangers from the home.	Examine all spaces for safety. For example, in the kitchen, store dangerous products in high cabinets out of sight, and keep sharp implements in a latched drawer. Remove guns; if that is impossible, store them unloaded in a locked cabinet. Always accompany young preschoolers to the bathroom, and keep all medicines in containers with safety caps.
During automobile travel, always restrain the child properly in the back seat of the car.	Use an age-appropriate, properly installed car seat, and strap the child in correctly every time. Children should always ride in the back seat; passenger-side air bags in the front seat deploy so forcefully that they can cause injury or death to a child.
Select safe playground equipment and sites.	Make sure sand, wood chips, or rubberized matting has been placed under swings, see-saws, and jungle gyms. Check yards for dangerous plants. Always supervise outdoor play.
Be extra cautious around water.	Constantly observe children during water play; even shallow, inflatable pools can be sites of drownings. While swimming, young children's heads should not be immersed in water; they may swallow so much that they develop water intoxication, which can lead to convulsions and death.
Practice safety around animals.	Wait to get a pet until the child is mature enough to handle and care for it—usually around age 5 or 6. Never leave a young child alone with an animal; bites often occur during playful roughhousing. Model and teach humane pet treatment.

Source: Dowd, 1999; Tremblay & Peterson, 1999.

Motor Development

Visit a playground at a neighborhood park, preschool, or child-care center, and observe several 2- to 6-year-olds. You will see that an explosion of new motor skills occurs in early childhood, each of which builds on the simpler movement patterns of toddlerhood.

The same principle that governs motor development during the first 2 years of life continues to operate during the preschool years. Children integrate previously acquired skills into more complex *dynamic systems of action*. Then they revise each new skill as their bodies become larger and stronger, their central nervous systems develop, and their environments present new challenges.

GROSS MOTOR DEVELOPMENT

As children's bodies become more streamlined and less top-heavy, their center of gravity shifts downward, toward the trunk. As a result, balance improves greatly, paving the way for new motor skills involving large muscles of the body (Ulrich & Ulrich, 1985). By age 2, preschoolers' gaits become smooth and rhythmic—secure enough that soon they leave the ground, at first by running and later by jumping, hopping, galloping, and skipping.

As children become steadier on their feet, their arms and torsos are freed to experiment with new skills—throwing and catching balls, steering tricycles, and swinging on horizontal bars and rings. Then upper and lower body skills combine into more refined actions. Five- and 6-year-olds simultaneously steer and pedal a tricycle and flexibly move their whole body when hopping and jumping. By the end of the preschool years, all skills are performed with greater speed and endurance. Table 8.1 provides an overview of gross motor development in early childhood.

Changes in ball skills provide an excellent illustration of preschoolers' gross motor progress. Play a game of catch with a 2- or 3-year-old, and watch the child's body. Young preschoolers stand still facing the target, throwing with their arm thrust forward. Catching is equally awkward. Two-year-olds extend their arms and hands rigidly, using them as a single unit to trap the ball. By age 3, children flex their elbows enough to trap the ball against the chest. But if the ball arrives too quickly, they cannot adapt, and it may bounce off the body (Roberton, 1984).

TABLE 8.1

Changes in Gross Motor Skills During Early Childhood

AGE	WALKING AND RUNNING	JUMPING AND HOPPING	THROWING AND CATCHING	PEDALING AND STEERING
2–3 years	Walks more rhythmically; feet are not as widely spaced; opposite arm–leg swing appears. Hurried walk changes to true run.	Jumps down from step. Jumps several inches off floor with both feet, no arm action. Hops 1 to 3 times on same foot with stiff upper body and non-hopping leg held still.	Throws ball with fore-arm extension only; feet remain stationary. Awaits thrown ball with rigid arms outstretched.	Pushes riding toy with feet; little steering.
3–4 years	Walks up stairs, alternating feet. Walks down stairs, leading with one foot. Walks straight line.	Jumps off floor, with coordinated arm action. Broad jumps about 1 foot. Hops 4 to 6 times on same foot, flexing upper body and swinging non-hopping leg.	Throws ball with slight body rotation but little or no transfer of weight between feet. Flexes elbows in preparation for catching; traps ball against chest.	Pedals and steers tricycle.
4–5 years	Walks down stairs, alternating feet. Walks circular line. Walks awkwardly on balance beam. Runs more smoothly. Gallops and skips with one foot.	Jumps upward and for-ward more effectively; travels greater distance. Hops 7 to 9 times on same foot; displays improved speed of hopping.	Throws ball with in-creased body rotation and some transfer of weight forward. Catches ball with hands; if unsuccessful, may still trap ball against chest.	Rides tricycle rapidly, steers smoothly.
5–6 years	Walks securely on balance beam. Increases speed of run. Gallops more smoothly. Engages in true skipping.	Jumps off floor about 1 foot. Broad jumps 3 feet. Hops 50 feet on same foot in 10 seconds. Hops with rhythmic al-ternation (2 hops on one foot and 2 on the other).	Has mature throwing and catching pattern. Moves arm more and steps forward during throw. Awaits thrown ball with relaxed posture, adjusting body to path and size of ball.	Rides bicycle with training wheels.

Sources: Cratty, 1986; Getchell & Roberton, 1989; Newborg, Stock, & Wnek, 1984; Roberton, 1984.

Gradually, children call on the shoulders, torso, trunk, and legs to support throwing and catching. By age 4, the body rotates as the child throws, and at 5 years, preschoolers shift their weight forward, stepping as they release the ball. As a result, the ball travels faster and farther. When the ball is returned, older preschoolers predict its place of landing by moving forward, backward, or sideways. Then they catch it with their hands and fingers, "giving" with arms and body to absorb the force of the ball (see Figure 8.6 on page 312).

[handwritten margin note: catching becomes increasingly refined with age.]

5–6 Years

2 Years

3 Years

FIGURE 8.6

Changes in catching during early childhood. At age 2, children extend their arms rigidly, and the ball tends to bounce off the body. At age 3, they flex their elbows in preparation for catching, trapping the ball against the chest. By ages 5 and 6, children involve the entire body, catching with the hands and fingers.

FINE MOTOR DEVELOPMENT

Like gross motor development, fine motor skills take a giant leap forward during early childhood (refer to Table 8.2). Because control of the hands and fingers improves, young children put puzzles together, build structures out of small blocks, cut and paste, and string beads. To parents, fine motor progress is most apparent in two areas: (1) children's increasing ability to care for their own bodies, and (2) the drawings and paintings that fill the walls at home, child care, and preschool.

■ **SELF-HELP SKILLS.** Young children gradually become self-sufficient at dressing and feeding. Two-year-olds put on and take off simple items of clothing. By age 3, they do so well enough to take care of toileting needs by themselves. Between age 4 and 5, children can dress

TABLE 8.2

Changes in Fine Motor Skills During Early Childhood

AGE	DRESSING	FEEDING	DRAWING, WRITING, AND OTHER
2–3 years	Puts on and removes simple items of clothing. Zips and unzips large zippers.	Uses spoon effectively.	Opens door by turning knob. Strings large beads.
3–4 years	Fastens and unfastens large buttons.	Serves self food without assistance.	Uses scissors to cut paper. Copies vertical line and circle. Draws first representational forms.
4–5 years	Dresses and undresses without assistance.	Uses fork effectively.	Cuts with scissors, following line. Copies triangle, cross, and some letters.
5–6 years		Uses knife to cut soft food.	Ties single overhand knot; around age 6, ties shoes. Copies some numerals and simple words. Creates more complex drawings. Draws salient parts of figures and objects. Uses an adult pencil grip.

Sources: Bracken, 2000; Greer & Lockman, 1998; Toomela, 1999.

and undress without supervision. At mealtimes, young preschoolers use a spoon well, and they can serve themselves. By age 4, they are adept with a fork, and around 5 to 6 years they can use a knife to cut soft foods. Roomy clothing with large buttons and zippers and child-sized eating utensils help children master these skills.

Preschoolers get great satisfaction from managing their own bodies. They are proud of their independence, and their new skills also make life easier for adults. But parents need to be patient about these abilities. When tired and in a hurry, young children often revert to eating with their fingers. And the 3-year-old who dresses himself in the morning sometimes ends up with his shirt on inside out, his pants on backward, and his left snow boot on his right foot!

Perhaps the most complex self-help skill of early childhood is shoe tying, mastered around age 6. Success requires a longer attention span, memory for an intricate series of hand movements, and the dexterity to perform them. Shoe tying illustrates the close connection between cognitive and motor development. Drawing and writing offer additional examples.

ELIZABETH ZUCKERMAN/PHOTOEDIT

Putting on and fastening clothing is challenging but rewarding to preschoolers. Young children enjoy a new sense of independence when they can dress themselves.

[handwritten note: examples of cognitive and motor development: (1) shoe tying (2) drawing (3) writing]

■ **DRAWING AND WRITING.** When given crayon and paper, even young toddlers scribble in imitation of others. As the young child's ability to mentally represent the world expands, marks on the page take on definite meaning. A variety of factors combine with fine motor control in the development of children's artful representations. These include cognitive advances—the realization that pictures can serve as symbols and gains in planning skills and spatial understanding (a move from a focus on separate objects to a broader visual perspective)—and exposure to pictorial images (Case & Okamoto, 1996; Golomb, 1992).

From Scribbles to Pictures. Typically, drawing progresses through the following sequence:

1. *Scribbles.* Western children begin to draw during the second year. At first, action rather than the resulting scribble contains the intended representation. For example, one 18-month-old took her crayon and hopped it around the page, explaining as she made a series of dots, "Rabbit goes hop-hop" (Winner, 1986). By labeling the scribble, she revealed a beginning awareness of the symbolic function of pictures.

2. *First representational forms.* By age 3, children's scribbles start to become pictures. Often this happens after they make a gesture with the crayon, notice that they have drawn a recognizable shape, and then decide to label it. In one case, a 2-year-old made some random marks on a page and then, realizing the resemblance between his scribbles and noodles, named the creation "chicken pie and noodles" (Winner, 1986). Although few 3-year-olds spontaneously draw so others can tell what their picture represents, after an adult shows the child how pictures can be used to stand for objects in a game, more children draw recognizable forms (Callaghan, 1999).

FIGURE 8.7

Examples of young children's drawings. The universal tadpolelike shape that children use to draw their first picture of a person is shown on the left. The tadpole soon becomes an anchor for greater detail as arms, fingers, toes, and facial features sprout from the basic shape. By the end of the preschool years, children produce more complex, differentiated pictures like the one on the right, drawn by a 6-year-old child. (Tadpole drawings from H. Gardner, 1980, *Artful Scribbles: The Significance of Children's Drawings,* New York: Basic Books, p. 64. Reprinted by permission of Basic Books, a division of HarperCollins Publishers, Inc. Six-year-old's picture from E. Winner, August 1986, "Where Pelicans Kiss Seals," *Psychology Today, 20*[8], p. 35. Reprinted with permission from *Psychology Today* magazine. Copyright © 1986 Sussex Publishers, Inc.)

A major milestone in drawing occurs when children begin to use lines to represent the boundaries of objects. This permits them to draw their first picture of a person by age 3 or 4. Look at the tadpole image—a circular shape with lines attached—on the left in Figure 8.7. It is a universal one in which fine motor and cognitive limitations lead the preschooler to reduce the figure down to the simplest form that still looks like a human being. Four-year-olds begin to add features, such as eyes, nose, mouth, hair, fingers, and feet, as the tadpole drawings in the figure illustrate.

3. *More realistic drawings.* Young children do not demand that a drawing be realistic. But as cognitive and fine motor skills improve, they learn to desire greater realism. As a result, they create more complex drawings, like the one on the right in Figure 8.7, made by a 6-year-old child. These drawings contain more conventional figures, in which the head and body are differentiated and arms and legs appear. (Look closely at the human and animal figures in the 6-year-old's drawing.) Over time, children improve the proportions of the head, trunk, and extremities and add more details. Still, children of this age are not very particular about mirroring reality. Their drawings contain perceptual distortions, since they have just begun to represent depth (Braine et al., 1993).

Greater realism in drawing occurs gradually. For geometric objects, it follows the steps illustrated in Figure 8.8. (1) Three- to 7-year olds draw a single unit to

Drawing Category and Approximate Age Range		
Single Units (3 to 7 years)		
Object Parts (4 to 13 years)		
Integrated Whole (8 years and older)		

FIGURE 8.8

Development of children's drawings of geometric objects—a cube and a cylinder. As these examples show, drawings change from single units to representation of object parts. Then the parts are integrated into a realistic whole. (Adapted from Toomela, 1999.)

stand for an object. To represent a cube, they draw a square; to represent a cylinder, they draw a circle, an oval, or a rectangle. (2) During the late preschool and school years, children represent salient object parts. They draw several squares to stand for a cube's sides and two circles and some lines to represent a cylinder. However, the parts are not joined properly. (3) Older school-age children and adolescents integrate object parts into a realistic whole (Toomela, 1999).

Preschoolers' free depiction of reality makes their artwork look fanciful and inventive. Accomplished artists, who also try to represent people and objects freely, often must work hard to do deliberately what they did without effort as 5- and 6-year-olds.

LAURA BERK

Cultural Variations in Development of Drawing. In cultures with little interest in art, children produce simpler forms. In cultures that emphasize artistic expression, children's drawings reflect the conventions of their culture and are more sophisticated. For example, the women of Walbiri, an Aboriginal group in Australia, draw symbols in sand to illustrate stories for preschoolers. When their children go to preschool or school, they often mix these symbols with more realistic images (Wales, 1990).

The Jimi Valley is a remote region of Papua New Guinea with no indigenous pictorial art. Many children do not go to school and therefore have little opportunity to develop drawing skills. When a Western researcher asked nonschooled Jimi 10- to 15-year-olds to draw a human figure for the first time, most produced nonrepresentational scribbles and shapes or simple "stick" or "contour" images (see Figure 8.9). Compared with the Western tadpole image, Jimi figures emphasize the body, hands, and feet over the head and face—a different view of the human form (Martlew & Connolly, 1996).

That older Jimi children with no schooling often produce nonrepresentational forms suggests that this is a universal beginning in drawing. When they realize that lines on the page must evoke human features, they find solutions to figure drawing that vary somewhat from culture to culture but, overall, follow the sequence described earlier.

Early Printing. As young children experiment with lines and shapes, notice print in storybooks, and observe the writing of others, they try to print letters and, later, words. Often the first word printed is the child's name. Initially, it may be represented by a single letter. "How do you make a *D*?" my older son David asked at 3 years of age. When I printed a large uppercase *D* for him, he tried to copy. "*D* for David," he said as he wrote, quite satisfied with his

When young children experiment with crayons and paint, they not only develop fine motor skills but acquire the artistic traditions of their culture. This Australian Aboriginal 4-year-old creates a dot painting. To Westerners, it looks abstract. To the child, it expresses a "dreamtime" story about the life and land of his ancestors. If asked about the painting, he might respond, "Here are the boulders on the creek line, the hills with kangaroos and emus, and the campsites."

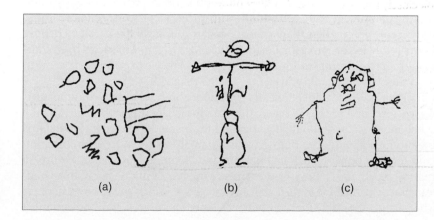

(a)   (b)   (c)

FIGURE 8.9

Drawings produced by nonschooled 10- to 15-year-old children of the Jimi Valley of Papua New Guinea when asked to draw a human figure for the first time. Many produced nonrepresentational scribbles and shapes (a), "stick" figures (b), or "contour" figures (c). Compared with the Western tadpole form, the Jimi "stick" and "contour" figures emphasize the hands and feet. Otherwise, the drawings of these older children, who had little opportunity to develop drawing skills, resemble those of young preschoolers. (Adapted from Martlew & Connolly, 1996.)

FIGURE 8.10

Variations in 3-year-olds' pencil grip. Through experimenting with different grips, preschoolers gradually discover an adult grip with one or two fingers on top of the pencil, which maximizes writing stability and efficiency. (Adapted from Greer & Lockman, 1998.)

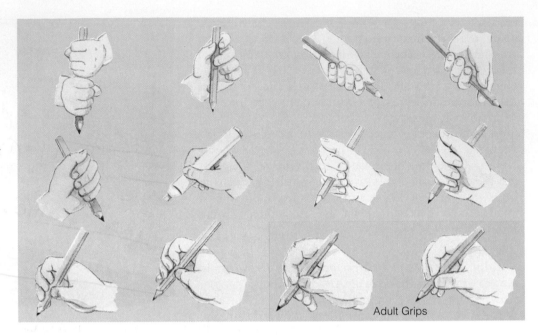

Adult Grips

backward, imperfect creation. A year later, David added several additional letters, and around age 5, he wrote his name clearly enough that others could read it.

Between 3 and 5 years, children acquire skill in gripping a pencil. As Figure 8.10 shows, 3-year-olds display diverse grip patterns and pencil angles against the surface. Depending on the direction and location of their marks on the page, they vary their grip. During this phase, preschoolers seem to be experimenting. As they try out different forms of pencil-holding, eventually they discover the pencil grip and angle that maximizes stability and writing efficiency. By age 5, most children use an adult grip pattern and a fairly constant pencil angle across a range of writing conditions (Greer & Lockman, 1998).

In addition to gains in fine motor control, advances in perception contribute to the ability to form letters and words. Like many children, David continued to reverse letters in his printing until well into second grade. When we take up early childhood perceptual development in the last section of this chapter, you will discover why these letter reversals are so common.

INDIVIDUAL DIFFERENCES IN MOTOR SKILLS

We have largely discussed motor milestones in terms of the average age at which children reach them in Western nations, but, of course, wide individual differences occur. Body build influences gross motor abilities. A child with a tall, muscular body tends to move more quickly and acquire certain skills earlier than a short, stocky youngster. Researchers believe that body build contributes to the superior performance of African-American over Caucasian-American children in running and jumping. African-American youngsters tend to have longer limbs, so they have better leverage (Lee, 1980; Wakat, 1978).

Sex differences in motor skills are evident in early childhood. Boys are slightly ahead of girls in skills that emphasize force and power. By age 5, they can jump slightly farther, run slightly faster, and throw a ball much farther (about 5 feet beyond the distance covered by girls). Girls have an edge in fine motor skills and in certain gross motor skills that require a combination of good balance and foot movement, such as hopping and skipping (Fischman, Moore, & Steele, 1992; Thomas & French, 1985). Boys' greater muscle mass and (in the case of throwing) slightly longer forearms may contribute to their skill advantages. And girls' greater overall physical maturity may be partly responsible for their better balance and precision of movement.

From an early age, boys and girls are usually encouraged into different physical activities. For example, fathers often play catch with their sons but seldom do so with their daughters. Baseballs and footballs are purchased for boys, jump ropes and hula hoops for girls. As children get older, differences in motor skills between boys and girls get larger, yet sex differences in physical capacity remain small until adolescence. These trends suggest that social pressures for boys to be active and physically skilled and for girls to play quietly at fine motor activities may exaggerate small, genetically based sex differences (Coakley, 1990; Greendorfer, Lewko, & Rosengren, 1996).

ENHANCING EARLY CHILDHOOD MOTOR DEVELOPMENT

Today, many parents provide preschoolers with early training in gymnastics, tumbling, and other lessons. These experiences offer excellent opportunities for physical exercise and social interaction. But aside from throwing (where direct instruction seems to make some difference), there is no evidence that preschoolers exposed to formal lessons are ahead in motor development. Instead, children seem to master the motor skills of early childhood naturally, as part of their everyday play.

Still, the physical environment in which informal play takes place can make a difference in mastery of complex motor skills. When children have play spaces and equipment appropriate for running, climbing, jumping, and throwing, along with encouragement to use them, they respond eagerly to these challenges. But if balls are too large and heavy to be properly grasped and thrown, or jungle gyms, ladders, and horizontal bars are suitable for only the largest and strongest youngsters, then children cannot easily develop new motor skills. Preschools, child-care centers, and city playgrounds must offer a variety of equipment to suit the needs of individual children.

This father encourages his daughter to derive feelings of pleasure and mastery from physical activity. Their regular bike rides promote endurance, coordination, and enjoyment of the out-of-doors. Boys get more parental encouragement to be physically active than do girls. Yet sex differences in physical capacity are small throughout childhood.

Similarly, fine motor development can be supported through daily routines, such as pouring juice and dressing, and play involving puzzles, construction sets, drawing, painting, sculpting, cutting, and pasting. Exposure to artwork of their own and other cultures enhances children's awareness of the creative possibilities of artistic media. Preschoolers should be encouraged to represent their own ideas and feelings rather than to color in predrawn forms.

Finally, the social climate created by adults can enhance or dampen preschoolers' motor development. When parents and teachers criticize a child's performance, push specific motor skills, or promote a competitive attitude, they risk undermining children's self-confidence and, in turn, their motor progress (Kutner, 1993). Adult involvement in young children's motor activities should focus on "fun" rather than winning or perfecting the "correct" technique.

When play spaces are properly designed and equipped for preschoolers, young children respond eagerly to motor challenges and develop new skills through informal play. This playground at a child-care center offers equipment suited to children of varying sizes; a safe, inviting tricycle path; and surfaces that protect young children from injury.

Perceptual Development

Think back to our discussion of infant perceptual development in Chapter 5. The most striking changes occurred in vision, the sense on which humans depend most for gathering information from the environment. For infants, the initial perceptual task involves figuring out how the space around them is organized. Once patterns and objects are located in space, infants start to sort them out. Recall that Eleanor and James Gibson's *differentiation theory* helps us understand this process. Over time, infants search for invariant features (those that remain stable in a changing perceptual world), making finer and finer distinctions between stimuli (to review this theory, return to page 205).

During early childhood, sensitivity to invariant features sharpens further, becoming more selective and efficient (Bornstein & Arterberry, 1999). Researchers have been especially interested in how detection of the fine-grained structure of visual patterns improves, since it helps us understand how children discriminate written symbols as they learn to read. Eleanor Gibson (1970) has applied differentiation theory to this process. Her research shows that preschoolers begin by recognizing letters as a set of items. By age 3 or 4, they can tell writing from nonwriting (scribbling and pictures), even though they cannot yet identify many letters of the alphabet. Then they discriminate particular letters. Those alike in shape are most difficult to tell apart. For example, because the invariant features of *C* and *G, E* and *F,* and *M* and *W* are subtle, many preschoolers confuse these letter pairs.

Letters that are mirror images of one another, such as *b* and *d* and *p* and *q,* are especially hard for young children to tell apart. This finding may remind you of a point made earlier in our discussion of writing. Until age 7 or 8, children print many letters backward. One reason is that until they learn to read, children do not find it especially useful to notice the difference between mirror-image forms. The ability to tune in to mirror images, as well as to scan a printed line from left to right, depends in part on experience with reading materials (Casey, 1986).

Of course, becoming a skilled reader is a long process, entailing much more than discriminating visual forms. Children must combine letters into words and sentences and use a variety of information-processing strategies to decipher their meaning, including sustained attention, memory, comprehension, and inference making. But perceptual skills do seem to be essential, since children with advanced visual abilities tend to read at higher levels (Fisher, Bornstein, & Gross, 1985). We will consider other aspects of early literacy development in the next chapter.

Ask YOURSELF...

review   Describe typical changes in children's drawings of people and objects during early childhood.

apply   Mabel and Chad want to do everything they can to support their 3-year-old daughter's athletic development. What advice would you give them?

connect   Does preschoolers' developing skill at gripping a pencil fit with dynamic systems theory of motor development? Explain, returning to Chapter 5, page 191, if you need to review.

Summary

BODY GROWTH

Describe changes in body size, proportions, and skeletal maturity during early childhood.

- Gains in body size taper off in early childhood. Body fat also declines, and children become longer and leaner. In various places in the skeleton, new epiphyses appear, where cartilage gradually hardens into bone. Individual differences in body size and rate of physical growth become very apparent during the preschool years.

- By the end of early childhood, children start to lose their primary teeth. Care of primary teeth is important, since diseased baby teeth can affect the health of permanent teeth. Childhood tooth decay remains high, especially among low-SES children.

What makes physical growth an asynchronous process?

- Different parts of the body grow at different rates. The **general growth curve** describes change in body size—rapid during infancy, slower during early and middle childhood, rapid again during adolescence. Exceptions to this trend include the genitals, the lymph tissue, and the brain.

BRAIN DEVELOPMENT

Describe brain development in early childhood.

- During the preschool years, neural fibers in the brain continue to form synapses and myelinate. By this time, many cortical regions have overproduced synapses, and synaptic pruning occurs. To make room for the connective structures of active neurons, many surrounding neurons die, and plasticity of the brain is reduced.

- The left cerebral hemisphere grows more rapidly than the right, supporting young children's rapidly expanding language skills.

- Hand preference strengthens during early childhood, indicating that lateralization increases during this time. Handedness indicates an individual's **dominant cerebral hemisphere.** According to one theory, most children inherit a gene that biases them for right-handedness, but experience can sway children toward a left-hand preference. Body position during the prenatal period and practice can affect handedness.

- Left-handers tend to be less strongly lateralized than right-handers. Although left-handedness is associated with developmental problems, the great majority of left-handed children are normal. Left- and mixed-handed youngsters are more likely to display outstanding verbal and mathematical talents.

- During early childhood, connections are established between brain structures. Fibers linking the **cerebellum** to the cerebral cortex myelinate, enhancing balance and motor control. The **reticular formation,** responsible for alertness and consciousness, and the **corpus callosum,** which connects the two cerebral hemispheres, also myelinate rapidly.

FACTORS AFFECTING PHYSICAL GROWTH AND HEALTH

Explain how heredity influences physical growth.

- Heredity influences physical growth by controlling the release of hormones from the **pituitary gland.** The most important pituitary hormones for childhood growth are **growth hormone (GH)** and **thyroid-stimulating hormone (TSH).**

Describe the effects of emotional well-being, restful sleep, nutrition, and infectious disease on physical growth and health in early childhood.

- Emotional well-being continues to influence body growth in early childhood. An emotionally inadequate home life can lead to **deprivation dwarfism.**

- Restful sleep in early childhood contributes to body growth and positive family functioning. Bedtime routines help Western children, who generally sleep alone, fall asleep. Almost all preschoolers awaken occasionally because of nightmares. Persistent sleep problems often are due to illness or family stress.

- Preschoolers' slower growth rate causes their appetite to decline, and often they become picky eaters. Young children's social environments have a powerful impact on food preferences. Modeling by others, repeated exposure to new foods, and a positive emotional climate at mealtimes can promote healthy, varied eating in young children.

- Malnutrition can combine with infectious disease to undermine healthy growth. In developing countries, diarrhea is widespread and claims millions of young lives. Teaching families how to administer **oral rehydration therapy (ORT)** can prevent most of these deaths.

- Immunization rates are lower in the United States than in other industrialized nations because many economically disadvantaged children do not have access to the medical care they need. In addition, parental misconceptions about safe immunization practices are not always corrected through public education.

- Childhood illness rises with child-care attendance. **Otitis media,** or middle ear infection, is especially common. Frequent bouts predict delayed language progress, social isolation, and poorer academic performance after school entry. High-quality child care and screening for otitis media can prevent these negative outcomes.

What factors increase the risk of unintentional injuries, and how can childhood injuries be prevented?

- Unintentional injuries are the leading cause of childhood mortality. Injury victims are more likely to be boys; to be temperamentally irritable, inattentive, and negative in mood; and to be growing up in stressed, poverty-stricken, crowded family environments.

Summary (continued)

■ A variety of approaches are needed to prevent childhood injuries. These include reducing poverty, teenage childbearing, and other sources of family stress; upgrading the quality of child care; passing laws that promote child safety; creating safer home, travel, and play environments; improving public education; and changing parent and child behaviors.

MOTOR DEVELOPMENT

Cite major milestones of gross and fine motor development in early childhood.

■ During early childhood, children continue to integrate previously acquired motor skills into more complex dynamic systems of action. Body growth causes the child's center of gravity to shift toward the trunk, and balance improves, paving the way for an explosion of gross motor skills.

■ Preschoolers' gaits become smooth and rhythmic, and they run, jump, hop, gallop, and skip. These abilities, as well as throwing and catching, become better coordi-

nated as movements of the entire body support each new skill.

■ Gains in control of the hands and fingers lead to dramatic changes in fine motor skills. Preschoolers gradually dress themselves and use a fork and knife at mealtime.

■ By age 3, children's scribbles become pictures. With age, their drawings increase in complexity and realism and are greatly influenced by the art of their society and by schooling. Young children try to print letters of the alphabet and, later, words, an ability that improves with gains in fine motor control and perception. Between 3 and 5 years, pencil grip becomes more adultlike as children discover the grip that maximizes stability and writing efficiency.

Describe individual differences in preschoolers' motor skills and ways to enhance motor development in early childhood.

■ Body build, ethnicity, and sex influence early childhood motor development. Differences in motor skills between boys and

girls are partly genetic, but environmental pressures exaggerate them.

■ Children master the motor skills of early childhood through informal play experiences. Richly equipped play environments that accommodate a wide range of physical abilities are important during the preschool years.

PERCEPTUAL DEVELOPMENT

Summarize perceptual development in early childhood, paying special attention to discrimination of written symbols.

■ The Gibsons' differentiation theory helps explain how children discriminate written symbols as they learn to read. Because preschoolers have little need to distinguish mirror-image forms in everyday life, left–right letter reversals are common in early childhood. Exposure to reading materials enhances children's ability to discriminate letters.

Important terms and concepts

cerebellum (p. 299)
corpus callosum (p. 299)
deprivation dwarfism (p. 300)
dominant cerebral hemisphere
    (p. 298)

general growth curve (p. 296)
growth hormone (GH) (p. 300)
oral rehydration therapy (ORT)
    (p. 304)

pituitary gland (p. 300)
reticular formation (p. 299)
thyroid-stimulating hormone (TSH)
    (p. 300)

. . . for further information and help

Consult the companion website for this book, where you will find additional weblinks and associated learning activities:
www.ablongman.com/berk

GROWTH DISORDERS

Human Growth Foundation
www.hgfound.org

Provides information on various growth disorders, including growth hormone (GH) deficiency.

INFECTIOUS DISEASES IN CHILDHOOD

American Academy of Pediatrics
www.aap.org

Provides public education on a variety of childhood health issues. Among the many pamphlets and publications available are written guidelines for effective control of infectious disease.

Child Care Information Exchange
www.ccie.com

A bimonthly publication written especially for child-care directors that addresses the practical issues of running a center. Articles discussing health and safety often are included.

U.S. Centers for Disease Control
www.cdc.gov

Surveys national disease trends and environmental health problems. Has organized an agency network to address problems of infectious disease in child care. Offers information to child-care staff on techniques that prevent the spread of infection.

CHILDHOOD INJURY CONTROL

U.S. Consumer Product Safety Commission
www.cpsc.gov

Establishes and enforces product safety standards. Operates a hotline providing information on safety issues and recall of dangerous consumer products.

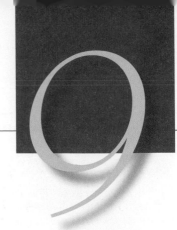

"Myself"
Bilgundi G. Mallinat
7 years, India

This image of an observant young painter portrays the most striking cognitive achievement of early childhood. As Chapter 9 reveals, mental representation takes a giant leap forward.

Cognitive Development in Early Childhood

One rainy morning, as I observed in our laboratory preschool, Leslie, the children's teacher, joined me at the back of the room to watch for a moment herself. "Preschoolers' minds are such a curious blend of logic, fantasy, and faulty reasoning," Leslie reflected. "Every day, I'm startled by the maturity and originality of many things they say and do. Yet other times, their thinking seems limited and inflexible."

Leslie's comments sum up the puzzling contradictions of early childhood cognition. Over the previous week, I had seen many examples in 3-year-old Sammy. That day, I found him at the puzzle table, moments after a loud clash of thunder outside. Sammy looked up, startled, then said to Leslie, "The man turned on the thunder!" Leslie patiently explained that people can't turn thunder on or off. But Sammy persisted. "Then a lady did it," he stated with certainty.

In other respects, Sammy's cognitive skills seemed surprisingly advanced. At snack time, he accurately counted, "One, two, three, four!" and then got four cartons of milk, giving one to each child at his table. Sammy's keen memory and ability to categorize were also evident. As he sat in the reading corner, he recited by heart *The Very Hungry Caterpillar* (Carle, 1969), a story he had heard many times. Sammy's favorite picture books were about animals, and he could name and categorize dozens of them.

Still, Sammy's cognitive skills seemed fragile. When more than four children joined his snack group, Sammy's counting broke down. And some of his notions about quantity seemed as fantastic as his understanding of thunder. Across the snack table, Priti dumped out her raisins, and they scattered in front of her. "How come you got lots, and I only got this little bit?" asked Sammy, failing to realize that he had just as many; they were simply all bunched up in a tiny red box. While Priti washed her hands after snack, Sammy put her remaining raisins in her cubby. When Priti returned and looked for her raisins, Sammy pronounced, "You know where they are!" He failed to grasp that Priti, who hadn't seen him move the raisins, believed they would be where she left them.

In this chapter, we explore the many facets of early childhood cognition, drawing from three theories with which you are already familiar. We begin with Piaget's preoperational stage, which, for the most part, emphasizes preschool children's deficits rather than strengths. Recent research along with two additional perspectives—Vygotsky's sociocultural theory and information processing—extends our understanding of preschoolers' cognitive competencies. Then we turn to a variety of factors that contribute to individual differences in mental development—the home environment, the quality of preschool and child care, and the many hours young children spend watching television. Our chapter concludes with language development, the most awesome achievement of early childhood.

Piaget's Theory: The Preoperational Stage

As children move from the sensorimotor to the **preoperational stage,** the most obvious change is an extraordinary increase in representational, or symbolic, mental activity. Recall that infants and toddlers have some ability to mentally represent the world. Between the ages of 2 and 7, this capacity blossoms.

ADVANCES IN MENTAL REPRESENTATION

As I looked around the preschool classroom, signs of developing representation were everywhere—in the children's drawings and paintings, in their re-creations of family life in the housekeeping area, and in their delight at story time. Especially impressive were strides in language skill. During free play, a hum of chattering voices rose from the classroom.

Piaget acknowledged that language is our most flexible means of mental representation. By detaching thought from action, it permits cognition to be far more efficient than it was during the sensorimotor stage. When we think in words, we overcome the limits of our momentary perceptions. We can deal with the past, present, and future all at once, combining images of the world in unique ways, as when we think about a hungry caterpillar eating bananas or monsters flying through the forest at night (Miller, 1993).

Despite the power of language, Piaget did not believe that it plays a major role in cognitive development or gives rise to representational thought. Instead, sensorimotor activity makes language possible, just as it leads to deferred imitation and make-believe play. Can you think of evidence that supports Piaget's view? Recall from Chapter 6 that the first words toddlers use have a strong sensorimotor basis. In addition, toddlers acquire an impressive range of cognitive categories long before they use words to label them (see page 228). Still, other theorists regard Piaget's account of the link between language and thought as incomplete, as we will see later in this chapter.

preoperational stage
Piaget's second stage, in which rapid growth in representation takes place but thought is not yet logical. Spans the years from 2 to 7.

[Handwritten note:] Piaget did not correlate language w/ cognitive development.

MAKE-BELIEVE PLAY

Make-believe play provides another excellent example of the development of representation during the preoperational stage. Piaget believed that through pretending, young children practice and strengthen newly acquired representational schemes. Drawing on Piaget's ideas, several investigators have traced changes in make-believe play during the preschool years.

■ **DEVELOPMENT OF MAKE-BELIEVE PLAY.** One day, Sammy's 18-month-old brother Dwayne came to visit the classroom. Dwayne wandered around, picked up the receiver of a toy telephone, said, "Hi, Mommy," and then dropped it. In the housekeeping area, he found a cup, pretended to drink, and toddled off again. In the meantime, Sammy joined a group of children in the block area for a space shuttle launch.

"That can be our control tower," he suggested to Vance and Lynette, pointing to a corner by a bookshelf. "Countdown!" Sammy announced, speaking into a small wooden block, his pretend walkie-talkie. "Five, six, two, four, one, blastoff!" Lynette made a doll push a pretend button, and the rocket was off!

A comparison of Dwayne's pretend with that of Sammy and his classmates illustrates three important advances in make-believe. Each reflects the preschool child's growing symbolic mastery:

ROSANNE OLSON/STONE

During the preschool years, make-believe play blossoms. This child directs pretend actions toward objects in a complex play scene.

1. *Over time, play increasingly detaches from the real-life conditions associated with it.* In early pretending, toddlers use only realistic objects—a toy telephone to talk into or a cup to drink from. Most of these earliest pretend acts imitate adults' actions and are not yet flexible. Dwayne, for example, pretended to drink from a cup, but he refused to pretend a cup was a hat (Tomasello, Striano, & Rochat, 1999). He had trouble using an object (cup) as a symbol for another object (hat) when the object (cup) already had an obvious use.

   Around age 2, children pretend with less realistic toys, such as a block for a telephone receiver. And sometime during the third year, they can imagine objects and events without support from the real world, as Sammy's imaginary control tower in a corner of the room illustrates (Corrigan, 1987; O'Reilly, 1995).

2. *The way the "child as self" participates in play changes with age.* When make-believe first appears, it is directed toward the self—for example, Dwayne pretends to feed only himself. A short time later, children direct pretend actions toward objects, as when the child feeds a doll. And early in the third year, they use objects as active agents, and the child becomes a detached participant who makes a doll feed itself or (in Lynette's case) push a button to launch a rocket. Make-believe gradually becomes less self-centered, as children realize that agents and recipients of pretend actions can be independent of themselves (McCune, 1993).

3. *Make-believe gradually includes more complex scheme combinations.* For example, Dwayne can pretend to drink from a cup, but he does not yet combine drinking with pouring. Later on, children combine pretend schemes with those of peers in **sociodramatic play,** the make-believe with others that is under way by age 2 1/2 and increases rapidly during the next few years (Haight & Miller, 1993). Already, Sammy and his classmates can create and coordinate several roles in an elaborate plot. By 4 years of age, children have a sophisticated understanding of role relationships and story lines (Göncü, 1993).

The appearance of complex sociodramatic play signals a major change in representation. Children do not just represent their world; they begin to display *awareness* that make-believe is a representational activity—an understanding that increases steadily from 4 to 8 years of age (Lillard, 1998, 2001). Listen closely to preschoolers as they jointly create an imaginary scene. You will hear them assign roles and negotiate make-believe plans: "*You pretend to be*

sociodramatic play
The make-believe play with others that is under way by age 2½.

[handwritten margin notes:]
A child has ↑ symbolism due to:
① ↑ detachment of play from real life
② use of self in play
③ combinations

the astronaut, *I'll act like* I'm operating the control tower!" "Wait, *I gotta set up* the spaceship." In communicating about pretend, children have started to reason about people's mental activities, a topic we will return to later in this chapter.

■ **ADVANTAGES OF MAKE-BELIEVE PLAY.** Today, Piaget's view of make-believe as mere practice of representational schemes is regarded as too limited. Research indicates that play not only reflects but contributes to children's cognitive and social skills. Sociodramatic play has been studied most thoroughly. In comparison to social nonpretend activities (such as drawing or putting puzzles together), during social pretend preschoolers' interactions last longer, show more involvement, draw larger numbers of children into the activity, and are more cooperative (Creasey, Jarvis, & Berk, 1998).

When we consider these findings, it is not surprising that preschoolers who spend more time at sociodramatic play are seen as more socially competent by their teachers (Connolly & Doyle, 1984). And many studies reveal that make-believe strengthens a wide variety of mental abilities, including sustained attention, memory, logical reasoning, language and literacy, imagination, creativity, and the ability to reflect on one's own thinking and take another's perspective (Bergen & Mauer, 2000; Dias & Harris, 1990; Kavanaugh & Engel, 1998; Newman, 1990; Ruff et al., 1990).

Some children spend much time in solitary make-believe, creating *imaginary companions*—special fantasized friends endowed with humanlike qualities. For example, one preschooler created Nutsy and Nutsy, a pair of boisterous birds living outside her bedroom window who often went along on family outings. Another child conjured up Maybe, a human of changing gender who could be summoned by shouting out the front door of the family house (Gleason, Sebanc, & Hartup, 2000; Taylor, 1999). In the past, imaginary companions were viewed as a sign of maladjustment, but recent research challenges this assumption. Between 25 and 45 percent of 3- to 7-year-olds have them, and those who do display more complex pretend play, are advanced in mental representation, and are often more (not less) sociable with peers (Taylor & Carlson, 1997; Taylor, Cartright, & Carlson, 1993).

The Educational Concerns table on the following page offers suggestions for enhancing make-believe at home and in preschool and child care. We will return to the topic of play in Chapter 10.

SYMBOL–REAL WORLD RELATIONS

Leslie set up a doll house, replete with tiny furnishings, in a corner of the classroom. Sammy often arranged the furniture to match his real-world living room, kitchen, and bedroom. Representations of reality, like Sammy's, are powerful cognitive tools. When we understand that a photograph, model, or map corresponds to circumstances in everyday life, we can use it to acquire information about objects and places we have not experienced.

When do children realize that a symbol stands for a specific state of affairs in the real world? In one study, $2\frac{1}{2}$- and 3-year-olds watched as an adult hid a small toy (little Snoopy) in a scale model of a room. Then they were asked to find a larger toy (big Snoopy) hidden in the room that the model represented. Not until age 3 could most children find big Snoopy (DeLoache, 1987). Younger children had trouble with **dual representation,** or viewing a symbolic object as both an object in its own right and a symbol. In the study just described, $2\frac{1}{2}$-year-olds did not realize that the model could be both *a toy room and a symbol of another room.*

Recall a similar limitation in early pretending—that $1\frac{1}{2}$- to 2-year-olds cannot use an object with an obvious use (cup) to stand for another object (hat). Likewise, 2-year-olds do not yet grasp that a drawing—an object in its own right—represents real-world objects. When an adult held up a drawing indicating which of two objects preschoolers should drop

Is this preschooler aware that the doll house is not just an interesting object in its own right, but can stand for a real house—that is, serve as a symbol of the real world? Not until age 3 do most young children grasp the *dual representation* of models.

DUAL representation - Snoopy experiment

Educational Concerns

Enhancing Make-Believe Play in Early Childhood

STRATEGY	DESCRIPTION
Provide sufficient space and play materials.	A generous amount of space and materials allows for many play options and reduces conflict.
Supervise and support children's play without controlling it.	Respond to, guide, and elaborate on preschoolers' play themes when they indicate a need for assistance. Excessive adult control destroys the creativity and joy of children's play.
Offer a wide variety of realistic materials and materials without clear functions.	Children use realistic materials, such as trucks, dolls, tea sets, dress-up clothes, and toy scenes (house, farm, garage, airport) to act out culturally relevant roles. Materials without clear functions, such as blocks, cardboard cylinders, paper bags, and sand, inspire fantastic role play, such as "pirate" and "creature from outer space."
Ensure that children have many rich, real-world experiences to inspire positive fantasy play.	Opportunities to participate in real-world activities with adults and to observe adult roles in the community provide children with rich social knowledge to integrate into make-believe. Restricting television viewing, especially programs with violent content, limits the degree to which violent themes and aggressive behavior become part of children's play. (See Chapter 10, pages 388–389.)
Help children solve social conflicts constructively.	Cooperation is essential for sociodramatic play. Guide children toward effective relations with agemates, using techniques that help them learn to resolve disagreements. (For example, ask, "What could you do if you want a turn?" If the child cannot think of possibilities, suggest some options and assist the child in implementing them.)

Sources: Berk, 2001; Frost, Shin, & Jacobs, 1998; Vandenberg, 1998.

down a chute, 3-year-olds used the drawing as a symbol to guide their behavior, but 2-year-olds did not (Callaghan, 1999).

How do children grasp the dual representation of models, drawings, and other symbols? Insight into one type of symbol–real world relation helps preschoolers understand others. For example, children understand photos as symbols very early, around age 2, since a photo's primary purpose is to stand for something; it is not an interesting object in its own right (DeLoache, 1991). And 3-year-olds who can use a model of a room to locate Big Snoopy readily transfer their understanding to a simple map (Marzolf & DeLoache, 1994).

Granting young children many opportunities to learn the functions of diverse symbols—picture books, photographs, drawings, make-believe, and maps—enhances their understanding that one object or event can stand for another (DeLoache & Smith, 1999). During childhood and adolescence, they come to understand a wide range of symbols that do not bear a strong physical similarity to what they represent (Liben, 1999). As a result, doors open to vast realms of knowledge.

LIMITATIONS OF PREOPERATIONAL THOUGHT

Aside from the development of representation, Piaget described preschool children in terms of what they cannot, rather than can, understand (Beilin, 1992). He compared them to older, more competent children in the concrete operational stage, as the term "*preoperational*" suggests. According to Piaget, young children are not capable of **operations**—mental representations of actions that obey logical rules. Instead, their thinking is rigid, limited to one aspect of a situation at a time, and strongly influenced by the way things appear at the moment.

■ **EGOCENTRIC AND ANIMISTIC THINKING.** For Piaget, the most serious deficiency of preoperational thinking, the one that underlies all others, is **egocentrism.** He believed that when children first mentally represent the world, they are unaware of any symbolic viewpoints

Piaget viewed children as limited beings. (handwritten margin note)

dual representation
Viewing a symbolic object as both an object in its own right and a symbol.

operations
Mental representations of actions that obey logical rules.

egocentrism
The inability to distinguish the symbolic viewpoints of others from one's own.

FIGURE 9.1

Piaget's three-mountains problem. A child is permitted to walk around a display of three mountains. Each is distinguished by its color and by its summit. One has a red cross, another a small house, and the third a snow-capped peak. Then the child stands on one side, and a doll is placed at various locations around the display. The child must choose a photograph that shows what the display looks like from the doll's perspective. Before age 6 or 7, most children select the photo that shows the mountains from their own point of view.

[handwritten: egocentrism is resp. 4 animistic thinking]

animistic thinking
The belief that inanimate objects have lifelike qualities, such as thoughts, wishes, feelings, and intentions.

conservation
The understanding that certain physical characteristics of objects remain the same, even when their outward appearance changes.

centration
The tendency to focus on one aspect of a situation and neglect other important features.

perception bound
Being easily distracted by the concrete, perceptual appearance of objects.

states rather than transformations
The tendency to treat the initial and final states in a problem as completely unrelated.

irreversibility
The inability to mentally go through a series of steps in a problem and then reverse direction, returning to the starting point.

hierarchical classification
The organization of objects into classes and subclasses on the basis of similarities and differences.

other than their own, and they believe that everyone else perceives, thinks, and feels the same way they do (Piaget, 1950).

Piaget's most convincing demonstration of egocentrism involves a task called the *three-mountains problem*, described in Figure 9.1. Egocentrism, he pointed out, shows up in other aspects of children's reasoning. Recall Sammy's firm insistence that someone must have turned on the thunder. Similarly, Piaget regarded egocentrism as responsible for preoperational children's **animistic thinking**—the belief that inanimate objects have lifelike qualities, such as thoughts, wishes, feelings, and intentions, just like themselves. The 3-year-old who charmingly explains that the sun is angry at the clouds and has chased them away is demonstrating this kind of reasoning. According to Piaget, because young children egocentrically assign human purposes to physical events, magical thinking is especially common during the preschool years.

Piaget argued that egocentrism leads to young children's rigid and illogical thinking. Thought proceeds so strongly from children's own point of view that they do not *accommodate,* or revise their faulty reasoning, in response to their physical and social worlds. But to appreciate this shortcoming fully, let's consider some additional tasks that Piaget gave children. *[handwritten: Thought comes from a kid's point of view so they do NOT accommodate.]*

■ **INABILITY TO CONSERVE.** Piaget's famous conservation tasks reveal a variety of deficiencies of preoperational thinking. **Conservation** refers to the idea that certain physical characteristics of objects remain the same, even when their outward appearance changes. At snack time, Sammy and Priti each had identical boxes of raisins, but after Priti spread hers out on the table, Sammy was convinced that she had more.

Another conservation task involves liquid. The child is shown two identical tall glasses of water and asked if they contain equal amounts. Once the child agrees, the water in one glass is poured into a short, wide container, changing the appearance of the water but not its amount. Then the child is asked whether the amount of water is the same or has changed. Preoperational children think the quantity has changed. They explain, "There is less now because the water is way down here" (that is, its level is so low) or "There is more because the water is all spread out." In Figure 9.2, you will find other conservation tasks that you can try with children.

Preoperational children's inability to conserve highlights several related aspects of their thinking. First, their understanding is *centered,* or characterized by **centration.** In other words, they focus on one aspect of a situation and neglect others. With conservation of liquid, the child centers on the height of the water in the two containers, failing to realize that all changes in height are compensated by changes in width. Second, their thinking is **perception bound.** They are easily distracted by the concrete, perceptual appearance of objects. It *looks like* the short, wide container has less water, so there *must be* less water. Third, children focus on **states rather than transformations.** In the conservation-of-liquid problem, they treat the initial and final *states* of the water as completely unrelated, ignoring the *dynamic transformation* (pouring of water) between them.

The most important illogical feature of preoperational thought is **irreversibility.** Children of this stage cannot mentally go through a series of steps in a problem and then reverse direction, returning to the starting point. *Reversibility* is part of every logical operation. After Priti spills her raisins, Sammy cannot reverse by thinking, "I know Priti doesn't have more raisins than I do. If we put them back in that little box, her raisins and mine would look just the same."

[handwritten: Kid's thinking is centered, perception bound, focus on states]

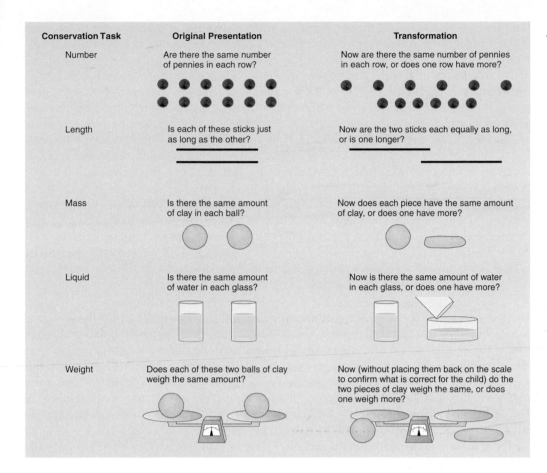

FIGURE 9.2

Some Piagetian conservation tasks. Children at the preoperational stage cannot yet conserve.

■ **LACK OF HIERARCHICAL CLASSIFICATION.** Lack of logical operations leads preschoolers to have difficulty with **hierarchical classification.** That is, they cannot organize objects into classes and subclasses on the basis of similarities and differences. Piaget's famous *class inclusion problem,* illustrated in Figure 9.3, demonstrates this limitation. Preoperational children center on the overriding feature of yellow and do not think reversibly by moving from the whole class (flowers) to the parts (yellow and blue) and back again.

RECENT RESEARCH ON PREOPERATIONAL THOUGHT

Over the past two decades, Piaget's account of a cognitively deficient preschooler has been challenged. If researchers give his tasks in just the way he originally designed them, preschoolers do indeed perform poorly. But many Piagetian problems contain unfamiliar elements or too many pieces of information for young children to handle at once. As a result, preschoolers' responses often do not reflect their true abilities. Piaget also missed many naturally occurring instances of preschoolers' effective reasoning. Let's look at some examples.

■ **EGOCENTRISM.** Are young children really so egocentric that they believe a person standing in a different location in a room sees the same thing they see? When researchers change the nature of Piaget's three-mountains problem to include

FIGURE 9.3

A Piagetian class inclusion problem. Children are shown 16 flowers, 4 of which are blue and 12 of which are yellow. Asked, "Are there more yellow flowers or more flowers?" the preoperational child responds, "More yellow flowers," failing to realize that both yellow and blue flowers are included in the category "flowers."

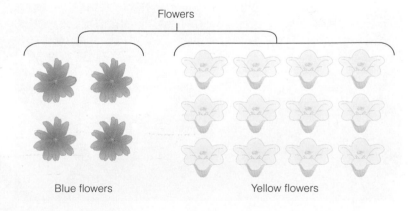

Flowers

Blue flowers

Yellow flowers

familiar objects and use methods other than picture selection (which is difficult even for 10-year-olds), 4-year-olds show clear awareness of others' vantage points (Borke, 1975; Newcombe & Huttenlocher, 1992).

Nonegocentric responses also appear in young children's conversations. For example, preschoolers adapt their speech to fit the needs of their listeners. Sammy uses shorter, simpler expressions when talking to his little brother Dwayne than when talking to agemates or adults (Gelman & Shatz, 1978). Also, in describing objects, children do not use such words as "big" and "little" in a rigid, egocentric fashion. Instead, they *adjust* their descriptions, taking account of context. By age 3, children judge a 2-inch shoe as small when seen by itself (because it is much smaller than most shoes) but as big for a very tiny, 5-inch doll (Ebeling & Gelman, 1994).

In previous chapters, we showed that even toddlers have some appreciation of others' perspectives. By 18 months, they have begun to infer others' intentions (see page 220) and appreciate that others' emotional reactions may differ from their own (see page 260). In sum, many findings challenge Piaget's description of young children as strongly egocentric, although (as we will see later) understanding of others' viewpoints develops gradually throughout childhood and adolescence.

stopping point

■ **ANIMISTIC AND MAGICAL THINKING.** Piaget also overestimated preschoolers' animistic beliefs because he asked children about objects with which they have little direct experience, such as the clouds, sun, and moon. Three-year-olds do make errors when questioned about certain vehicles, such as trains and airplanes. But these objects appear to be self-moving, a characteristic of almost all living things. And they also have some lifelike features—for example, headlights that look like eyes and animate-like movement patterns (Poulin-Dubois & Héroux, 1994; Richards & Siegler, 1986). Children's responses result from incomplete knowledge about objects, not from a rigid belief that inanimate objects are alive.

The same is true for other fantastic beliefs of the preschool years. Most 3- and 4-year-olds believe in the supernatural powers of fairies, goblins, and other enchanted creatures. But they deny that magic can alter their everyday experiences—for example, turn a picture into a real object or living being (Subbotsky, 1994). Instead, they think magic accounts for events that violate their expectations and that they cannot otherwise explain.

Between 4 and 8 years, as familiarity with physical events increases and scientific explanations are taught in school, magical beliefs decline. Children figure out who is really behind the activities of Santa Claus and the Tooth Fairy! They also realize that the antics of magicians are due to trickery, not special powers (Phelps & Woolley, 1994; Woolley et al., 1999). How quickly children give up certain fantastic ideas varies with religion and culture. For example, Jewish preschool and school-age children express greater disbelief in Santa Claus and the Tooth Fairy than do their Christian agemates. Having been taught at home about the unreality of Santa, they seem to generalize this attitude to other mythical figures (Woolley, 1997).

The importance of knowledge, experience, and culture can be seen in preschoolers' grasp of other natural concepts. Refer to the Social Issues: Education box on page 332–333 to find out about young children's developing understanding of death.

■ **ILLOGICAL THOUGHT.** Many studies have reexamined the illogical characteristics that Piaget saw in the preoperational stage. Results show that when preschoolers

Which of the children in this audience realize that a magician's powers depend on trickery? The younger children look surprised and bewildered. The older children think the magician's antics are funny. Between 4 and 8 years, as familiarity with physical events and principles increases, children's magical beliefs decline.

© J. SOHM/THE IMAGE WORKS

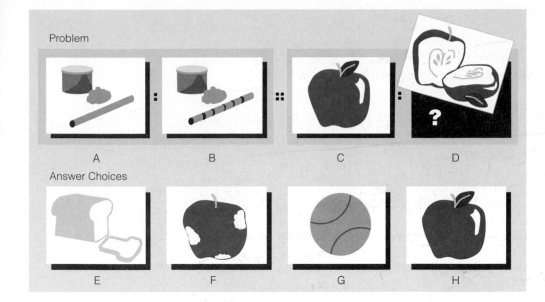

Problem

A B C D

Answer Choices

E F G H

FIGURE 9.4

Analogical problem about physical transformations. Preschoolers were told they would be playing a picture-matching game. Then the researchers showed each child the first three pictures of a four-picture sequence—in this example, playdough, cut up playdough, and apple—and asked the child to complete the sequence by choosing from five alternatives. Several wrong answers shared features with the right choice—for example, correct physical change but wrong object (E), correct object but wrong physical change (F). Children as young as 3 years of age could combine the correct physical change with the correct object and solve the problem. (Adapted from Goswami & Brown, 1989.)

most children are able 2 explain various phenomenons! They only have to be tailored to their mindset.

are given simplified tasks made relevant to their everyday lives, they do better than Piaget might have expected.

For example, when a conservation-of-number task is scaled down to include only three items instead of six or seven, 3-year-olds perform well (Gelman, 1972). And when preschoolers are asked carefully worded questions about what happens to familiar substances (such as sugar) after they are dissolved in water, they give very accurate explanations. Most 3- to 5-year-olds know that the substance is conserved—that it continues to exist, can be tasted, and makes the liquid heavier, even though it is invisible in the water (Au, Sidle, & Rollins, 1993; Rosen & Rozin, 1993).

Preschoolers' ability to reason about transformations is evident on other problems. For example, they can engage in impressive *reasoning by analogy* (taking an idea from one situation and applying it to another) about physical changes. As Figure 9.4 above shows, presented with the problem, *playdough is to cut-up playdough as apple is to ?*, even 3-year-olds choose the correct answer from a set of alternatives, several of which share physical features with the right choice. These findings indicate that preschoolers can overcome appearances and think logically about cause and effect in familiar contexts.

Furthermore, our discussion of physical causality in Chapter 6 revealed that the beginnings of causal reasoning are present in the first year of life (see page 215). By the preschool years, children say that the insides of animals differ from the insides of machines. Even though they have little detailed biological or mechanical knowledge, they know that animal insides are responsible for different cause–effect relations (such as willing oneself to move) than are possible for nonliving things (Keil & Lockhart, 1999).

Preschoolers also have a beginning sense of how illnesses can be transmitted. In a recent study, researchers told 3- to 12-year-olds and college students stories about people with either a physical ailment (having large blue spots appear on their skin) or a mental ailment (thinking that Big Bird was following them around and talking to them). Then others came in contact with the sick people. In one situation, the contact was physical (mistakenly drinking the sick person's soda); in the other, it was social (talking on the phone with the sick person). Even the youngest children said that a physical illness was more likely to be transmitted through physical contact and a mental illness through social contact (Keil et al., 1999).

Finally, 3- and 4-year-olds use causal expressions, such as *if–then* and *because*, with the same degree of accuracy as adults do (McCabe & Peterson, 1988). Illogical reasoning seems to occur only when they grapple with unfamiliar topics, too much information, or contradictory facts, which they have trouble reconciling (Ruffman, 1999).

Illogical reasoning occurs when:
① unfamiliar topics
② too much info
③ contradictory facts

Social

ISSUES: EDUCATION

YOUNG CHILDREN'S UNDERSTANDING OF DEATH

Five-year-old Miriam arrived at preschool the day after her dog Pepper died. Instead of running to play with the other children, she stayed close to Leslie, who noticed Miriam's discomfort. "What's wrong?" Leslie asked.

"Daddy said Pepper had a sick tummy. He fell asleep and died." For a moment, Miriam looked hopeful, "When I get home, Pepper might be up."

Leslie answered directly, "No, Pepper won't get up again. He's not asleep. He's dead, and that means he can't sleep, eat, run, or play anymore."

Miriam wandered off. Later, she returned to Leslie and confessed, "I chased Pepper too hard." Tears streamed from her eyes.

Leslie put her arm around Miriam. "Pepper didn't die because you chased him. He was very old and very sick," she explained.

Over the next few days, Miriam asked many more questions: "When I go to sleep, will I die?" "Can a tummy ache make you die?" "Does Pepper feel better now?" "Will Mommy and Daddy die?"

DEVELOPMENT OF THE DEATH CONCEPT

A realistic understanding of death is based on three ideas: (1) *Permanence:*
Once a living thing dies, it cannot be brought back to life. (2) *Universality:* All living things eventually die. (3) *Nonfunctionality:* All living functions, including thought, feeling, movement, and body processes, cease at death.

To understand death, children must acquire some very basic notions of biology—that animals and plants are living things with certain body parts that are essential for maintaining life. They must also break down their global category of *not alive* into *dead, inanimate, unreal,* and *nonexistent* (Carey, 1999). Until children grasp these ideas, they interpret death in terms of familiar experiences—as a change in behavior. Consequently, they may believe, as Miriam did, that they caused a relative's or pet's death, that having a stomachache can cause someone to die, and that death is like sleep. When researchers asked 4- to 6-year-olds whether dead people need food, air, water, and to go to the bathroom; whether they sleep and dream; and whether a cut on their body would heal, more than half of those who had not yet started to acquire biological understandings answered yes (Slaughter, Jaakkola, & Carey, 1999).

Most children master the three components of the death concept by age 7. *Permanence* is the first and most easily
understood idea. When Leslie explained that Pepper would not get up again, Miriam accepted this fact quickly, perhaps because she had seen it in other, less emotionally charged situations, such as the dead butterflies and beetles that she picked up and inspected while playing outside (Furman, 1990). Appreciation of *universality* comes slightly later. At first, children think that certain people do not die, especially those with whom they have close emotional ties or those who are like themselves—other children. Finally, *nonfunctionality* is the most difficult component of death for children to grasp, since many preschoolers view dead things as retaining living capacities (Lazar & Torney-Purta, 1991; Speece & Brent, 1992, 1996).

CULTURAL INFLUENCES

Although a mature appreciation of death is usually reached by middle childhood, ethnic variations suggest that religious teachings affect children's understanding. A comparison of four ethnic groups in Israel revealed that Druze and Moslem children's death concepts differed from those of Christian and Jewish children (Florian & Kravetz, 1985). The Druze emphasis on reincarnation and the greater religiosity of both the Druze and Moslem

■ **CATEGORIZATION.** Although preschoolers have difficulty with Piagetian class inclusion tasks, they organize their everyday knowledge into nested categories at an early age. By the second half of the first year, children have formed a variety of global categories, such as furniture, animals, vehicles, plants, and kitchen utensils (Mandler, 1998).

Notice that each of these categories includes objects that differ widely in perceptual features; the objects go together because of their common function and behavior. This challenges Piaget's assumption that preschoolers' thinking is always perception bound. Indeed, 2- to 5-year-olds readily draw inferences about nonobservable characteristics that category members share (Keil et al., 1999). For example, after being told that a bird has warm blood and a stegosaurus (dinosaur) has cold blood, preschoolers infer that a pterodactyl (labeled a dinosaur) has cold blood, even though it closely resembles a bird.

groups may have led more of their children to deny permanence and nonfunctionality. Similarly, children of Southern Baptist families, who believe in an afterlife, are less likely to endorse permanence than are children from Northern Unitarian families, who focus on the here and now—peace and justice in today's world (Candy-Gibbs, Sharp, & Petrun, 1985).

Experiences with death also influence understanding. Children growing up on Israeli kibbutzim (agricultural settlements) who have experienced terrorist attacks, family members' departure on army tours to high-tension areas, and parental anxiety about safety express a full grasp of the death concept by age 5 (Mahon, Goldberg, & Washington, 1999).

ENHANCING CHILDREN'S UNDERSTANDING

Parents often worry that discussing death candidly with children will fuel their fears, but this is not so. Instead, children with a good grasp of the facts of death have an easier time accepting it (Essa & Murray, 1994). Direct explanations, like Leslie's, that match the child's capacity to understand, work best.

When adults use clichés or make misleading statements, children may take these literally and react with confu-

sion. For example, after a parent said to her 5-year-old daughter, "Grandpa went on a long trip," the child wondered, "Why didn't he take me?" In another instance, a father whose wife had died of cancer said to his 9-year-old son that his mother "was sick," explaining nothing else about the illness. The father was surprised when, 10 months later, the boy caught the flu and became terribly afraid of dying (Wolfelt, 1997). Sometimes children ask very difficult questions, such as "Will I die? Will you die?" Parents can be truthful as well as comforting by taking advantage of children's sense of time. They can say something like "Not for many, many years. First I'm going to enjoy you as a grown-up and be a grandparent."

Discussions with children should also be culturally sensitive. Rather than presenting scientific evidence as counteracting religious beliefs, parents and teachers can assist children in blending the two sources of knowledge. As children get older, they often combine their appreciation of the death concept with spiritual and philosophical views, which offer solace

during times of bereavement (Cuddy-Casey & Orvaschel, 1997). Open, honest, and respectful communication about death contributes to children's cognitive development as well as their emotional well-being.

Examining this dead mouse will help these children understand the permanence of death. Appreciation of two additional components of the death concept—universality and nonfunctionality—will come later.

Over the early preschool years, children's global categories differentiate. They form many *basic-level categories*—ones at an intermediate level of generality, such as "chairs," "tables," "dressers," and "beds." Performance on object-sorting tasks indicates that by the third year, children easily move back and forth between basic-level categories and *general categories*, such as "furniture" (Blewitt, 1994). Soon after, they break down the basic-level categories into *subcategories*, such as "rocking chairs" and "desk chairs."

Preschoolers' rapidly growing vocabularies and expanding general knowledge support their impressive skill at categorizing. As they learn more about their world, they devise theories about underlying characteristics that category members share. For example, they realize that animals have an inborn potential for certain physical features and behaviors that determine their identity (Gelman & Wellman, 1991; Hirshfeld, 1995). In one study, researchers made up

Categories of Animals   **New Instances**

"Likes to fight"

"Likes to hide in trees"

FIGURE 9.5

Categories of imaginary animals shown to preschoolers. When given a theory about the coexistence of the animals' features—"likes to fight" and "likes to hide in trees"—4-year-olds easily classified new examples of animals with only one or two features. Without the theory, preschoolers could not remember the categories. Theories about underlying characteristics support the formation of many new categories in early childhood. (From R. M. Krascum & S. Andrews, 1998, "The Effects of Theories on Children's Acquisition of Family-Resemblance Categories," *Child Development*, 69, p. 336. © The Society for Research in Child Development, Inc. Reprinted by permission.)

two categories of animals: One had horns, armor, and a spiky tail; the other had wings, large ears, long toes, and a monkey-like tail (see Figure 9.5). Four-year-olds who were given a theory that explained the coexistence of the animals' features—animals in the first category "like to fight," those in the second category "like to hide in trees"—easily classified new examples of animals. Four-year-olds for whom animal features were merely pointed out or who were given a separate function for each feature could not remember the categories (Krascum & Andrews, 1998). In sum, young children's category systems are not yet very complex. But the capacity to classify hierarchically is present in early childhood.

■ **APPEARANCE VERSUS REALITY.** So far, we have seen that preschoolers show some remarkably advanced reasoning when presented with familiar situations and simplified problems. Yet in certain situations, young children are easily tricked by the outward appearance of things.

John Flavell and his colleagues presented children with objects that were disguised in various ways and asked what the items were "really and truly." Preschoolers had difficulty with problems involving sights and sounds, but not because (as Piaget suggested) they always confuse appearance and reality. Instead, the tasks required them to recall the real image of an object in the face of a second, contradictory representation. When asked whether a white piece of paper placed behind a blue filter is "really and truly blue" or whether a can that sounds like a baby crying when turned over is "really and truly a baby," preschoolers often respond "Yes!" Not until 6 to 7 years do children do well on these problems (Flavell, Green, & Flavell, 1987).

How do children master distinctions between appearance and reality? Make-believe play seems to contribute. Preschoolers can tell the difference between pretend play and real experiences long before they solve many appearance–reality tasks. And the more sociodramatic play they engage in, the better they distinguish the apparent and real identities of objects (Schwebel, Rosen, & Singer, 1999). The contrast between everyday and playful use of objects may help children figure out what is real and unreal in the surrounding world.

EVALUATION OF THE PREOPERATIONAL STAGE

Table 9.1 provides an overview of the cognitive attainments of early childhood we have just considered. Take a moment to compare them with Piaget's description of the preoperational child on pages 324–328. How can we make sense of the contradictions between Piaget's conclusions and the findings of recent research?

The evidence as a whole indicates that Piaget was partly wrong and partly right about young children's cognitive capacities. When given simplified tasks based on familiar experiences, preschoolers show the beginnings of logical operations long before the concrete operational stage. But their reasoning is not as well developed as that of school-age children, since they fail Piaget's three-mountains, conservation, and class inclusion tasks and have difficulty separating appearance from reality.

That preschoolers have some logical understanding suggests that they attain logical operations gradually. Over time, children rely on increasingly effective mental as opposed to perceptual approaches to solving problems. For example, research shows that children who cannot count cannot accurately compare two sets of items (Sophian, 1995). Once preschoolers can count, they apply this skill to conservation-of-number tasks with only a few items. As counting improves, they extend the strategy to problems with more items. By age 6, they have formed a mental understanding that a number remains the same after a transformation as long as nothing is added or taken away. Consequently, they no longer need to use counting to verify their answer (Klahr & MacWhinney, 1998; Siegler & Robinson, 1982). This sequence

TABLE 9.1

Some Cognitive Attainments of the Preschool Years

APPROXIMATE AGE	COGNITIVE ATTAINMENTS
2–4 years	Shows a dramatic increase in representational activity, as reflected in the development of language, make-believe play, and understanding of symbol–real world relations
	Takes the perspective of others in simplified, familiar situations and in everyday, face-to-face communication
	Distinguishes animate beings from inanimate objects; denies that magic can alter everyday experiences
	Notices transformations, reverses thinking, and explains events causally in familiar contexts
	Categorizes objects on the basis of common function and behavior (not just perceptual features) and devises theories about underlying characteristics that category members share
	Sorts familiar objects into hierarchically organized categories
4–7 years	Becomes increasingly aware that make-believe (and other thought processes) are representational activities
	Replaces magical beliefs about fairies, goblins, and events that violate expectations with plausible explanations
	Notices transformations, reverses thinking, and explains events causally in familiar contexts
	Shows improved ability to distinguish appearance from reality

indicates that children pass through several phases of understanding, although (as Piaget indicated) they do not fully grasp conservation until the early school years.

Evidence that preschool children can be trained to perform well on Piagetian problems also supports the idea that operational thought is not absent at one point in time and present at another. A variety of training methods are effective, including having children interact with more capable peers, explain an adult's correct reasoning, listen to an adult point out contradictions in the child's logic, or measure a transformed quantity (for example, determine how many ladles of liquid are in two differently shaped glasses) (Beilin, 1978; Roazzi & Bryant, 1997; Siegler, 1995).

That logical operations develop gradually poses a serious challenge to Piaget's stage concept, which assumes abrupt change toward logical reasoning around 6 or 7 years of age. Does a preoperational stage of development really exist? Some researchers no longer think so. They believe that children work out their understanding of each type of task separately. Their thought processes are regarded as basically the same at all ages—just present to a greater or lesser extent.

Piaget did not believe logical operations develop gradually.

Other experts think that the stage concept is still valid, but that it must be modified. For example, some *neo-Piagetian theorists* combine Piaget's stage approach with the information-processing emphasis on task-specific change (Case, 1992, 1998; Halford, 1993). They believe that Piaget's strict stage definition must be transformed into a less tightly knit concept, one in which a related set of competencies develops over an extended period, depending on brain development and specific experiences. These investigators point to findings indicating that as long as the complexity of tasks is carefully controlled, children approach them in similar, stage-consistent ways (Case & Okamoto, 1996; Marini & Case, 1994). For example, in drawing pictures, preschoolers depict objects separately, ignoring their spatial arrangement (return to the drawing on page 315 of Chapter 8 for an example). In understanding stories, they grasp only a single story line; they have difficulty with a main plot plus one or more subplots.

In sum, although Piaget's description of the preoperational child is no longer fully accepted, researchers are a long way from consensus on how to modify or replace it. Yet they continue to draw inspiration from his quest to understand how children acquire new cognitive capacities.

PIAGET AND EDUCATION

Piaget's theory has had a major impact on education, especially during early childhood. Three educational principles have served as the foundation for a variety of Piagetian-based preschool programs:

Handwritten margin notes:
① discovery learning
② sensitivity to kid's readiness to learn
③ individual diffs

1. *An emphasis on discovery learning.* In a Piagetian classroom, children are encouraged to discover for themselves through spontaneous interaction with the environment. Instead of presenting ready-made knowledge verbally, teachers provide a rich variety of materials and play areas designed to promote exploration and discovery—art, puzzles, table games, dress-up clothing, building blocks, books, measuring tools, musical instruments, and more.

2. *Sensitivity to children's readiness to learn.* A Piagetian classroom does not try to speed up development. Instead, Piaget believed that appropriate learning experiences build on children's current thinking. Teachers watch and listen to their pupils, introducing experiences that permit them to practice newly discovered schemes and that are likely to challenge their incorrect ways of viewing the world. But they do not impose new skills before children indicate that they are interested and ready, since this leads to superficial acceptance of adult formulas rather than true understanding.

3. *Acceptance of individual differences.* Piaget's theory assumes that all children go through the same sequence of development, but at different rates. Therefore, teachers must plan experiences for individuals and small groups rather than just for the total class (Ginsburg & Opper, 1988). In addition, teachers evaluate educational progress by comparing each child to his own previous development. They are less interested in how children measure up to normative standards, or the average performance of same-age peers.

Educational applications of Piaget's theory, like his stages, have met with criticism. Perhaps the greatest challenge has to do with his insistence that young children learn only through acting on the environment. In the next section we will see that they also use language-based routes to knowledge. Nevertheless, Piaget's influence on education has been powerful (Vergnaud, 1996). He gave teachers new ways to observe, understand, and enhance young children's development and offered strong theoretical justification for child-oriented approaches to classroom teaching and learning.

Ask YOURSELF...

review Select two of the following characteristics of the preoperational stage: egocentrism, perception-bound thought, illogical reasoning, lack of hierarchical classification. Cite findings that led Piaget to conclude that preschoolers are deficient in those ways. Then present evidence indicating that preschoolers are more capable thinkers than Piaget assumed.

apply At home, 4-year-old Will understands that his tricycle isn't alive and can't move by itself. Yet when Will went fishing with his family and his father asked, "Why do you think the river is flowing along?" Will responded, "Because it's alive and wants to." What explains this contradiction in Will's reasoning?

reflect Did you have an imaginary companion as a young child? If so, what was your companion like, and why did you create it? Were your parents aware of your companion? What was their attitude toward it?

Vygotsky's Sociocultural Theory

Piaget's de-emphasis on language as an important source of cognitive development brought on yet another challenge, this time from Vygotsky's sociocultural theory. We have seen that Vygotsky stressed the social context of cognitive development. In his theory, the child and the social environment collaborate to mold cognition in culturally adaptive ways.

According to Vygotsky, rapid growth in language broadens preschoolers' ability to participate in social dialogues while engaged in culturally important tasks. Soon children start to communicate with themselves in much the same way they converse with others. This greatly enhances the complexity of their thinking and their ability to control their own behavior. Let's see how this happens.

CHILDREN'S PRIVATE SPEECH

Watch preschoolers as they go about their daily activities, and you will see that they frequently talk out loud to themselves as they play and explore the environment. For example, as Sammy worked a puzzle one day, he said, "Where's the red piece? I need the red one. Now, a blue one. No, it doesn't fit. Try it here."

■ **PIAGET'S VIEW.** Piaget (1923/1926) called these utterances *egocentric speech,* a term expressing his belief that they reflect the preoperational child's inability to imagine the perspectives of others. For this reason, Piaget said, young children's talk is often "talk for self," in which they run off thoughts in whatever form they happen to occur, regardless of whether they are understandable to a listener.

Piaget believed that cognitive development and certain social experiences—namely, disagreements with peers—eventually bring an end to egocentric speech. Through arguments with agemates, children repeatedly see that others hold viewpoints different from their own. As a result, egocentric speech gradually declines and is replaced by social speech, in which children adapt what they say to their listeners.

■ **VYGOTSKY'S VIEW.** Vygotsky (1934/1987) voiced a powerful objection to Piaget's conclusion that young children's language is egocentric and nonsocial. He reasoned that children speak to themselves for self-guidance and self-direction. Because language helps children think about their own behavior and select courses of action, Vygotsky viewed it as the foundation for all complex mental activities. As children get older and tasks become easier, their self-directed speech declines and is internalized as silent, inner speech—the verbal dialogues we carry on with ourselves while thinking and acting in everyday situations.

Over the past three decades, researchers have carried out many studies to determine which of these two views—Piaget's or Vygotsky's—is correct. Almost all the findings have sided with Vygotsky (Berk, 2001). As a result, children's "speech to self" is now called **private speech** instead of egocentric speech. Research shows that children use more of it when tasks are difficult, after they make errors, or when they are confused about how to proceed (Berk, 1994). Also, just as Vygotsky predicted, private speech goes underground with age, changing into whispers and silent lip movements (Berk & Landau, 1993; Duncan & Pratt, 1997). Furthermore, children who use private speech during a challenging activity are more attentive and involved and show greater improvement in task performance than their less talkative agemates (Berk & Spuhl, 1995; Bivens & Berk, 1990; Winsler, Diaz, & Montero, 1997).

Finally, compared with their agemates, children with learning and behavior problems engage in private speech over a longer period of development (Berk & Landau, 1993; Winsler et al., 1999). They seem to call on private speech to help compensate for impairments in attention and cognitive processing that make many tasks more difficult for them.

SOCIAL ORIGINS OF EARLY CHILDHOOD COGNITION

Where does private speech come from? Vygotsky's answer to this question highlights the social origins of cognition—his main difference of opinion with Piaget. Recall from Chapter 6 that Vygotsky believed children's learning takes place within the *zone of proximal development*—a range of tasks too difficult for the child to do alone but possible to accomplish with the help of others. Consider the joint activity of Sammy and his mother, who assists him in putting together a difficult puzzle:

Sammy: "I can't get this one in." *[Tries to insert a piece in the wrong place]*

Mother: "Which piece might go down here?" *[Points to the bottom of the puzzle]*

KOPSTEIN/MONKMEYER PRESS

During the preschool years, children frequently talk to themselves as they play and explore the environment. Research supports Vygotsky's theory that children use private speech to guide their behavior when faced with challenging tasks. With age, private speech is transformed into silent, inner speech, or verbal thought.

[handwritten note] Vgotsky—children use speech to guide their behavior.

private speech
Self-directed speech that children use to plan and guide their own behavior.

Sammy: "His shoes." *[Looks for a piece resembling the clown's shoes but tries the wrong one]*

Mother: "Well, what piece looks like this shape?" *[Pointing again to the bottom of the puzzle]*

Sammy: "The brown one." *[Tries it, and it fits; then attempts another piece and looks at his mother]*

Mother: "Try turning it just a little." *[Gestures to show him]*

Sammy: "There!" *[Puts in several more pieces. His mother watches.]*

Sammy's mother keeps the puzzle within his zone of proximal development—at a manageable level of difficulty—by questioning, prompting, and suggesting strategies. Eventually, children take the language of these dialogues, make it part of their private speech, and use this speech to organize their independent efforts.

■ **EFFECTIVE SOCIAL INTERACTION.** To promote cognitive development, social interaction must have certain features. The first is **intersubjectivity,** the process whereby two participants who begin a task with different understandings arrive at a shared understanding (Newson & Newson, 1975). Intersubjectivity creates a common ground for communication, as each partner adjusts to the perspective of the other. Adults try to promote it when they translate their own insights in ways that are within the child's grasp. As the child stretches to understand the interpretation, she is drawn into a more mature approach to the situation (Rogoff, 1998).

The capacity for intersubjectivity is present early, in parent–infant mutual gaze, exchange of emotional signals, and imitation. Later, language facilitates it. As conversational skills improve, preschoolers become increasingly active in seeking others' help and in directing that assistance to ensure that it is beneficial (Whitington & Ward, 1999). Between ages 3 and 5, children increasingly strive for intersubjectivity in dialogues with peers, as when they affirm a playmate's message, add new ideas, and make contributions to ongoing play to sustain it. They can also be heard saying, "I think [this way]. What do you think?"—evidence of a willingness to share viewpoints, which assists preschoolers in resolving conflicts so play can continue (Berk, 2001). In these ways, children begin to create zones of proximal development for one another.

Another feature of social experience that fosters development is **scaffolding** (Bruner, 1983; Wood, 1989). It refers to a changing quality of social support over the course of a teaching session. Adults who offer an effective scaffold adjust the assistance they provide to fit the child's current level of performance. When the child has little notion of how to proceed, the adult uses direct instruction, breaking down the task into manageable units. As the child's competence increases, effective scaffolders—such as Sammy's mother—gradually and sensitively withdraw support, turning over responsibility to the child.

Scaffolding captures the form of teaching interaction that occurs as children work on school or school-like tasks, such as puzzles, model building, picture matching, and later, academic assignments. It may not apply to other contexts that are just as vital for cognitive development—for example, play or everyday activities, during which adults usually support children's efforts without deliberately instructing. To account for children's diverse opportunities to learn through involvement with others, Barbara Rogoff (1990, 1998) suggests the term **guided participation,** a broader concept than scaffolding. It calls attention to adult and child contributions to a cooperative dialogue without specifying the precise features of communication. Consequently, it allows for variations across situations and cultures.

■ **RESEARCH ON SOCIAL INTERACTION AND COGNITIVE DEVELOPMENT.** What evidence supports Vygotsky's ideas on the social origins of cognitive development? Think back to our discussion of caregiver–child interaction in previous chapters, and you will find a wealth of research indicating that when adults establish intersubjectivity with children by being stimulating, attentive, responsive, and supportive, they foster many competencies—attention, language, complex play, and understanding of others' perspectives. Furthermore,

---

intersubjectivity
The process whereby two participants who begin a task with different understandings arrive at a shared understanding.

scaffolding
A changing quality of social support over the course of a teaching session, in which the adult adjusts the assistance provided to fit the child's current level of performance. As competence increases, the adult gradually and sensitively withdraws support, turning over responsibility to the child.

guided participation
A concept that calls attention to adult and child contributions to a cooperative dialogue without specifying the precise features of communication, thereby allowing for variations across situations and cultures.

effective scaffolders have children who use more private speech and are more successful when asked to do a similar task by themselves (Berk & Spuhl, 1995; Conner, Knight, & Cross, 1997; Winsler, Diaz, & Montero, 1997).

Other research indicates that although young children benefit from working on tasks with same-age peers, their planning and problem solving show more improvement when their partner is either an "expert" peer (especially capable at the task) or an adult (Radziszewska & Rogoff, 1988). And peer disagreement (emphasized by Piaget) does not seem to be as important in fostering cognitive development as the extent to which children achieve intersubjectivity—by resolving differences of opinion and cooperating (Cannella, 1993; Tudge, 1992).

WILL FALLER

VYGOTSKY AND EDUCATION

Piagetian and Vygotskian classrooms clearly have features in common, such as opportunities for active participation and acceptance of individual differences. Yet a Vygotskian classroom goes beyond independent discovery. It promotes *assisted discovery.* Teachers guide children's learning with explanations, demonstrations, and verbal prompts, carefully tailoring their efforts to each child's zone of proximal development. Assisted discovery is helped along by *peer collaboration.* Children with varying abilities work in groups, teaching and helping one another.

Vygotsky (1935/1978) saw make-believe play as the ideal social context for fostering cognitive development in early childhood. As children create imaginary situations, they learn to follow internal ideas and social rules rather than respond to immediate impulses. For example, a child pretending to go to sleep follows the rules of bedtime behavior. Another child imagining himself to be a father and a doll to be a child conforms to the rules of parental behavior.

According to Vygotsky, make-believe play is a unique, broadly influential zone of proximal development in which children try a wide variety of challenging activities and acquire many new competencies (Smolucha & Smolucha, 1998). Turn back to page 326 to review findings that make-believe play enhances a diverse array of cognitive and social skills. Pretending is also rich in private speech—a finding that supports its role in helping children bring action under the control of thought (Krafft & Berk, 1998).

A Vygotskian classroom promotes assisted discovery. Teachers guide children's learning, carefully tailoring their efforts to each child's zone of proximal development. They also encourage peer collaboration, grouping together classmates of differing abilities and encouraging them to help one another.

[handwritten margin notes:]
Vgotsky classroom:
① indep. discovery
② assisted discovery
③ peer collaboration

EVALUATION OF VYGOTSKY'S THEORY

In granting social experience a fundamental role in cognitive development, Vygotsky's theory helps us understand the wide cultural variation in cognitive skills. It recognizes that children develop unique forms of thinking from engaging in activities that make up their culture's way of life. Nevertheless, some of Vygotsky's ideas have been challenged. Verbal communication may not be the only means, or the most important means, through which children learn in some cultures (Rogoff, 1998). For example, the child learning to sail a canoe in Micronesia or weave a garment on a loom in Mexico may gain more from direct observation and practice accompanied by nonverbal communication (a gaze, a change in posture, or a sensitive touch) than from verbal guidance. Turn to the Cultural Influences box on page 340 for research on Mayan preschoolers of Yucatan, Mexico, which supports this idea.

Finally, Vygotsky said little about how basic motor, perceptual, attention, memory, categorization, and problem-solving skills, discussed in Chapters 5 and 6, contribute to socially transmitted, complex mental activities. For example, his theory does not address how these elementary capacities spark changes in children's social experiences, from which more advanced cognition springs (Moll, 1994). Piaget paid far more attention than did Vygotsky to the development of basic cognitive processes. It is intriguing to speculate about the broader theory that might exist today had these two giants of developmental psychology had the chance to meet and weave together their extraordinary accomplishments.

[handwritten margin notes:]
child's uniqueness promotes development of activities in culture.
Yet is verbal communication the most important means of accomplishing this?

Vgotsky did not pay much attn. to basic cognitive processes like Piaget did.

Cultural INFLUENCES

YOUNG CHILDREN'S DAILY LIFE IN A YUCATEC MAYAN VILLAGE

Conducting ethnographic research in a remote Mayan village of the Yucatan, Mexico, Suzanne Gaskins (1999) found that child-rearing values, daily activities and, consequently, 2- to 5-year-olds' competencies differed sharply from those of Western preschoolers. Yucatec Mayan adults are subsistence farmers. Men spend their days tending corn-fields, aided by sons age 8 and older. Women oversee the household and yard, engaging in time-consuming meal preparation, clothes washing, and care of livestock and garden, assisted by daughters as well as sons not yet old enough to work in the fields.

In Yucatec Mayan culture, life is structured around adult work and religious and social events. Children join in these activities from the second year on. Adults make no effort to provide special experiences designed to satisfy children's interests or stimulate their development. When not participating with adults, children are expected to be independent. Even young children make many nonwork decisions for themselves—how much to sleep and eat, what to wear, when to bathe (as long as they do so every afternoon), and even when to start school.

As a result, Mayan preschoolers spend much time at self-care and are highly competent at it. In contrast, their make-believe play is limited; when it occurs, it involves brief imitations of adult work or more common scenes from adult life, organized and directed by older siblings. When not engaged in self-care or play, Mayan children watch others—for hours each day. By age 3, they can report the whereabouts and activities of all family members. At any moment, they may be called on to do a chore—fetch things from the house, run an errand, deliver a message, tend to livestock, or take care of toddler-age siblings. They are constantly "on call," to support adult work.

Mayan parents rarely converse with children or scaffold their learning. Rather, when children imitate adult tasks, parents conclude that they are ready for more responsibility. Then they assign chores, selecting ones the child can do with little help, so adult work is not disturbed. If a child cannot do a task, the adult takes over and the child observes, re-engaging when able to contribute. This give-and-take occurs smoothly, with parent and child focused on the primary goal of getting the job done.

Cultural priorities and daily activities lead Mayan preschoolers' skills and behavior to differ sharply from those of their Western agemates. Expected to be independent and helpful, Mayan children seldom display attention-getting behaviors or ask others for something interesting to do. From an early age, they can sit quietly for long periods with little fussing—through a lengthy religious service or dance, even a 3-hour truck ride into town. And when an adult interrupts their activity and directs them to do a chore, Mayan children respond eagerly to the command, which Western children frequently avoid or resent. By age 5, Mayan children spontaneously take responsibility for tasks beyond those assigned.

In Yucatec Mayan culture, adults rarely converse with children or scaffold their learning. Instead, children join in work and religious and social events from an early age, spending many hours observing the behavior of adults. These Mayan preschoolers watch intently as adults of their village celebrate the Yucatan Patron Festival, which honors the region's patron saint.

SUZANNE MURPHY LAURADO/D. DONNE BRYANT STOCK PHOTO

review Describe the characteristics of social interaction that support children's cognitive development. How does such interaction create a zone of proximal development?

apply Tanisha sees her 5-year-old son, Toby, talking out loud to himself while he plays. She wonders whether she should discourage this behavior. Use Vygotsky's theory to explain why Toby talks to himself. How would you advise Tanisha?

connect Are intersubjectivity and scaffolding involved in child-directed speech, discussed on pages 246–247 of Chapter 6? Explain.

Information Processing

Return for a moment to the model of information processing discussed on pages 224–225 of Chapter 6. Recall that information processing focuses on *mental strategies* that children use to operate on stimuli flowing into their mental systems, increasing the chances that they will retain the information and adapt it to the situation at hand. During early childhood, advances in representation and children's ability to guide their own behavior lead to more efficient and flexible ways of manipulating information and solving problems. In the following sections we look at preschoolers' attention, memory, problem solving, growing awareness of mental life, and literacy and mathematical skills.

ATTENTION

Recall from Chapter 6 that sustained attention improves in toddlerhood, a trend that continues over the preschool years, and fortunately so, since children will rely on this capacity greatly once they enter school. Nevertheless, parents and teachers are quick to notice that compared with school-age children, preschoolers spend relatively short times involved in tasks and are easily distracted.

During early childhood, attention also becomes more *planful*. **Planning** involves thinking out a sequence of acts ahead of time and allocating attention accordingly to reach a goal (Scholnick, 1995). As long as tasks are familiar and not too complex, preschoolers sometimes generate and follow a plan. For example, by age 4, they search for a lost object in a play yard systematically and exhaustively, looking only in locations between where they last saw the object and where they discovered it missing (Wellman, Somerville, & Haake, 1979).

Still, planful attention has a long way to go. When asked to compare detailed pictures, preschoolers fail to search thoroughly. And on complex tasks, they rarely decide what to do first and what to do next in an orderly fashion. Even when young children do plan, they often fail to implement important steps (Prevost, Bronson, & Casey, 1995; Scholnick, 1995).

MEMORY

Unlike infants and toddlers, preschoolers have the language skills to describe what they remember, and they can follow directions on simple memory tasks. As a result, memory development becomes easier to study in early childhood.

■ **RECOGNITION AND RECALL.** Try showing a young child a set of 10 pictures or toys. Then mix them up with some unfamiliar items and ask the child to point to the ones in the original set. You will find that preschoolers' *recognition* memory (ability to tell whether a stimulus is

planning
Thinking out a sequence of acts ahead of time and allocating attention accordingly to reach a goal.

Recognition is good, recall is bad

Preschoolers do not organize items into categories.

the same as or similar to one they have seen before) is remarkably good. It becomes even more accurate by the end of early childhood. In fact, 4- and 5-year-olds perform nearly perfectly.

Now give the child a more demanding task. While keeping the items out of view, ask the child to name the ones she saw. This requires *recall*—that the child generate a mental image of an absent stimulus. One of the most obvious features of young children's memories is that their recall is much poorer than their recognition. At age 2, they can recall no more than one or two items, at age 4 only about three or four (Perlmutter, 1984).

Of course, recognition is much easier than recall for adults as well, but in comparison to adults, children's recall is quite deficient. The reason is that young children are less effective at using **memory strategies,** deliberate mental activities that improve our chances of remembering. For example, when you want to retain information, you might *rehearse*, or repeat the items over and over again. Or you might *organize* it, intentionally grouping items that are alike so that you can easily retrieve them by thinking of their similar characteristics.

Preschoolers do show the beginnings of memory strategies. When circumstances permit, they arrange items in space to aid their memories. In one study, an adult seated at a table with a preschooler placed either an M&M or a wooden peg in each of 12 identical containers and handed them one by one to the child, who was asked to remember where the candy was hidden. By age 4, children devised the strategy of putting the candy containers in one place on the table and the peg containers in another, which almost always led to perfect recall (DeLoache & Todd, 1988). But preschoolers do not yet rehearse or organize items into *categories* (for example, all the vehicles together, all the animals together) when asked to recall a set of items. Even when trained to do so, their memory performance rarely improves, and they do not apply these strategies in new situations (Gathercole, Adams, & Hitch, 1994; Lange & Pierce, 1992).

Why do young children use memory strategies so rarely? One reason is that strategies tax young children's limited working memories (Bjorklund & Coyle, 1995). Preschoolers have difficulty holding on to the to-be-learned information and applying a strategy at the same time.

■ **MEMORY FOR EVERYDAY EXPERIENCES.** Think about the difference in your recall of listlike information and your memory for everyday experiences, or what researchers call **episodic memory.** In remembering lists, you recall isolated pieces of information and try to reproduce them exactly as you learned them. In remembering everyday experiences, you recall complex, meaningful events. Episodic memory involves selecting experiences, relating them to one another, and interpreting them on the basis of previous knowledge. Do children remember everyday experiences in these ways? The answer is clearly yes.

Memory for Familiar Events. Like adults, preschoolers remember familiar events—what you do when you get up in the morning, go to child care, or get ready for bed—in terms of **scripts,** general descriptions of what occurs and when it occurs in a particular situation. For very young children, scripts begin as a general structure of main acts. For example, when asked to tell what happens at a restaurant, a 3-year-old might say, "You go in, get the food, eat, and then pay." Although children's first scripts contain only a few acts, as long as events in a situation take place in logical order, they are almost always recalled in correct sequence (Bauer, 1997). With age, children's scripts become more elaborate, as in the following restaurant account given by a 5-year-old child: "You go in. You can sit in the booths or at a table. Then you tell the waitress what you want. You eat. If you want dessert, you can have some. Then you pay and go home" (Hudson, Fivush, & Kuebli, 1992).

Once formed, a script can be used to predict what will happen in the future. In this way, scripts help children organize and interpret repeated events. Children rely on them when listening to and telling stories. They recall more events from stories based on familiar event sequences than on unfamiliar ones (Hudson & Nelson, 1983). They also act out scripts in make-believe play as they pretend to put the baby to bed, go on a trip, or play school.

Memory for One-Time Events. In Chapter 6 we considered a second type of episodic memory—*autobiographical memory,* or representations of one-time events that are particu-

memory strategies
Deliberate mental activities that improve the likelihood of remembering.

episodic memory
Memory for everyday experiences.

scripts
General descriptions of what occurs and when it occurs in a particular situation. A basic means through which children organize and interpret repeated events.

larly meaningful in terms of the life story each of us creates. As 3- to 6-year-olds' cognitive and conversational skills improve, their descriptions of special events become better organized, detailed, and related to the larger context of their lives. As a result, children enter into the history of their family and community (Fivush, 1995; Haden, Haine, & Fivush, 1997).

Adults use two styles for eliciting children's autobiographical narratives. In the *elaborative style,* they ask many, varied questions; add information to children's statements; and volunteer their own recollections and evaluations of events. For example, after a field trip to the zoo, Leslie asked the children, "What was the first thing we did? Why weren't the parrots in their cages? I thought the roaring lion was scary. What did you think?" In contrast, adults who use the *repetitive style* provide little information and ask the same questions over and over. Preschoolers who experience the elaborative style produce more coherent and detailed personal stories when followed up 1 to 2 years later (McCabe & Peterson, 1991; Reese, Haden, & Fivush, 1993). In line with Vygotsky's ideas, early social experiences aid the development of memory skills.

WILL FALLER

Children's memory for everyday experiences improves greatly during early childhood. This girl cannot remember the details of what she did on a particular day when she washed her hands at preschool. Instead, she recalls the event in script form—in terms of what typically occurs when you get ready for lunch. Her account will become more elaborate with age. Scripts help us predict what will happen on similar occasions in the future.

PROBLEM SOLVING

How do preschoolers apply their cognitive competencies to discover new, useful problem-solving strategies that further cognitive development? To find out, let's look in on 5-year-old Darryl as he added marbles in pairs of small bags that Leslie set out on a table.

As Darryl dealt with each pair, his strategies varied. Sometimes he guessed, without applying any strategy. At other times, he counted from 1 on his fingers. For example, for bags containing 2 + 4 marbles, his fingers popped up one by one as he exclaimed, "1, 2, 3, 4, 5, 6!" On still other occasions, he started with the lower digit, 2, and "counted on" (2, 3, 4, 5, 6). Or he began with the higher digit, 4, and "counted on" (4, 5, 6)—a strategy called *min* because it minimizes the work. And sometimes, he took a quick look at the two sets of marbles and simply retrieved the answer from memory.

To study children's problem solving, Robert Siegler (1996) used the microgenetic research design (see Chapter 1, page 15), presenting children with a large number of problems over an extended time. He found that strategy use in basic addition tasks—and many other types of problems, including conservation, memory for lists of items, reading first words, spelling, and even tic-tac-toe—follows the overlapping waves pattern shown in Figure 9.6 on page 344. According to **overlapping-waves theory,** when given challenging problems, children generate a variety of strategies. While trying them out, they observe which work best, which work less well, and which are ineffective. Gradually, they select strategies that result in rapid, accurate solutions—in the case of basic addition, the *min* strategy. As children "home in" on more successful strategies, they learn more about the problems at hand. As a result, correct solutions become more strongly associated with problems, and children display the most efficient strategy—automatic retrieval of the answer.

How do children move from less to more efficient strategies? Often they discover a faster procedure by using a more time-consuming technique. For example, by repeatedly counting on fingers, Darryl began to recognize the number of fingers he held up. Soon after, he moved to the *min* strategy (Siegler & Jenkins, 1989). Also, certain problems dramatize the need for a better strategy. When Darryl opened a pair of bags with 10 marbles in one and 2 in the

overlapping-waves theory
A theory of problem solving, which states that when given challenging problems children generate a variety of strategies and gradually select those that result in rapid, accurate solutions, yielding an overlapping-waves pattern of development.

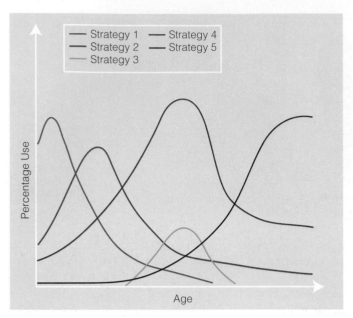

FIGURE 9.6

Overlapping-waves pattern of strategy use. When given challenging problems, children generate a variety of strategies, each represented by a wave. Several strategies may overlap at any given time. Use of each strategy, depicted by the height of the wave, is constantly changing. Gradually, the strategy that results in the most rapid, accurate solution wins out. (From *Emerging Minds: The Process of Change in Children's Thinking* by Robert S. Siegler, copyright © 1996 by Oxford University Press, Inc. Used by permission of Oxford University Press, Inc.)

children don't have a concept of social restraint

metacognition
Thinking about thought; awareness of mental activities.

other, he realized *min* would be best. Reasoning about concepts beneficial to the problems at hand is helpful (Canobi, Reeve, & Pattison, 1998). After Darrell understood that regardless of the order in which he combined 2 and 4, they yield the same result, he more often used *min*. Finally, when children are taught an effective strategy, they usually adopt it and abandon less successful techniques (Alibali, 1999).

Many factors—including practice, reasoning, tasks with new challenges, and adult assistance—contribute to improved problem solving. Children also profit greatly from experimenting with less mature strategies. By becoming familiar with them, children see their limitations and move toward more proficient approaches. Thus, overlapping-waves theory emphasizes that trying out many strategies is vital for developing new, more effective solution techniques. Even 2-year-olds solving simple problems, such as how to use a tool to obtain an out-of-reach toy, show the overlapping-waves pattern (Chen & Siegler, 2000). It characterizes problem solving across a wide range of ages.

THE YOUNG CHILD'S THEORY OF MIND

As their representation of the world and ability to remember and solve problems improve, children start to reflect on their own thought processes. They begin to construct a *theory of mind*, or set of ideas about mental activities. This understanding is also called **metacognition** (Flavell, 2000). The prefix "meta-," meaning beyond or higher, is applied to the term because the central meaning of metacognition is "thinking about thought."

As adults, we have a complex appreciation of our inner mental worlds. For example, you can tell the difference between believing, knowing, remembering, guessing, forgetting, and imagining, and you are aware of a great many factors that influence these cognitive activities. We rely on these understandings to interpret our own and others' behavior, as well as to improve our performance on various tasks. How early are preschoolers aware of their mental lives, and how complete and accurate is their knowledge?

■ **PRESCHOOLERS' UNDERSTANDING OF MENTAL LIFE.** Listen closely to the conversations of young children, and you will find evidence that awareness of mental activity emerges remarkably early. Such words as *think, remember,* and *pretend* are among the first verbs in children's vocabularies. After age 2½, children use them appropriately to refer to internal states (Wellman, 1990).

Despite a vocabulary of mentalistic terms, 2-year-olds have only a beginning grasp of the distinction between mental life and behavior. They think that people always behave in ways consistent with their desires; they do not understand that beliefs also affect people's actions (Bartsch & Wellman, 1995; Gopnik & Wellman, 1994).

Between ages 3 and 4, children figure out that both *beliefs* and *desires* determine behavior. In one instance, Sammy put a blanket over his head and, pretending to be a ghost, pushed Dwayne, who fell and began to cry. "I couldn't see him! The blanket was over my face," Sammy pleaded, trying to alter his mother's *belief* about his motive and, thereby, ward off any *desire* on her part to punish him. From early to middle childhood, efforts to alter others' beliefs increase, suggesting that children more firmly realize the power of belief to influence action.

A dramatic illustration of preschoolers' developing theory of mind comes from games that test whether they know that *false beliefs*—ones that do not represent reality accurately—can guide people's actions. To test for a grasp of false belief, researchers present situations like this one: Show a child two small closed boxes, one a familiar Band-Aid box and the other a plain, unmarked box. Then say, "Pick the box you think has the Band-Aids in it." Almost always, children pick the marked container. Next, ask the child to look inside both boxes;

when she does, contrary to her own belief, she finds that the marked one is empty and the unmarked one contains the Band-Aids. Finally, introduce the child to a hand puppet and explain, "Here's Pam. She has a cut, see? Where do you think she'll look for Band-Aids? Why would she look in there?" (Bartsch & Wellman, 1995). Only a handful of 3-year-olds but many 4-year-olds can explain why Pam would look in the marked box.

Many studies confirm that children's understanding of false belief strengthens over the preschool years, becoming more secure between ages 4 and 6. The better 3- to 6-year-olds perform on false-belief tasks, the more advanced they are in social skills, as rated by their teachers (Watson et al., 1999).

[handwritten note: better false-belief tasks, better social skills]

■ **HOW DOES A THEORY OF MIND DEVELOP?** How do such young children develop a theory of mind? Although great controversy surrounds this question, research suggests that language, cognitive abilities, make-believe play, and social experiences contribute.

[handwritten note: ① language ② cognitive abilities ③ make-believe play ④ social experiences]

Language. Understanding the mind requires the ability to reflect on thoughts, made possible by language. A grasp of false belief is related to language ability equivalent to that of an average 4-year-old or higher (Jenkins & Astington, 1996).

More specifically, use of complex sentences involving mental-state words, as in, "I *thought* the sock was in the drawer" is linked to false-belief understanding (de Villiers & de Villiers, 2000). Among the Quechua of the Peruvian highlands, adults refer to mental states such as "think" and "believe" indirectly, since their language lacks mental-state terms. Quechua children have difficulty with false-belief tasks for years after children in industrialized nations have mastered them (Vinden, 1996).

Cognitive Abilities. The ability of 3- and 4-year-olds to inhibit a previously rewarded response, think flexibly, and plan predicts performance on false-belief tasks one year later (Hughes, 1998). Like language, these skills are believed to enhance children's capacity to reflect on their experiences and mental states.

Make-Believe Play. As children act out various roles, they notice that the mind can change what objects and events mean. Often they create situations they know to be untrue in the real world and reason about their implications (Harris & Leevers, 2000). These experiences may trigger an awareness that belief influences behavior. In support of this idea, preschoolers who engage in extensive fantasy play are more advanced in their understanding of false belief and other aspects of the mind (Astington & Jenkins, 1995). And the better 3- and 4-year-olds are at reasoning about situations that contradict a real-world state of affairs, the more likely they are to pass false-belief tasks (Riggs & Peterson, 2000).

Social Interaction. Preschoolers with older siblings are advanced in performance on false-belief tasks. And those with several older siblings do better than those with only one (Ruffman et al., 1998). Having older siblings may allow for more interactions that highlight the influence of beliefs on behavior—through teasing, trickery, make-believe play, and discussing feelings.

Besides siblings, preschool friends may foster mental understanding. The more 3- and 4-year-olds engage in mental-state talk with friends, the better they perform on false-belief tasks more than a year later (Hughes & Dunn, 1998).

Interacting with more mature members of society also helps. In a study of Greek preschoolers with large networks of extended family and neighbors, daily contact with many adults and older children predicted mastery of false belief (Lewis et al., 1996). These encounters probably

Having older siblings fosters an understanding of false belief, probably because sibling interactions often highlight the influence of beliefs on behavior—through teasing, trickery, make-believe play, and discussing feelings.

TONY FREEMAN/PHOTOEDIT

provide young children with extra opportunities to talk about the reasons for peoples' behavior, speculate about what they might do in the future, and observe different points of view.

Many researchers believe that to profit from social experiences, preschoolers must be biologically prepared to develop a theory of mind. Consistent with this assumption, children with *infantile autism,* who are indifferent to other people, seem to be impaired in mental understanding. See the Biology and Environment box on the following page to find out more about "mindblindness" and infantile autism.

■ **LIMITATIONS OF THE YOUNG CHILD'S THEORY OF MIND.** Although surprisingly advanced, preschoolers' awareness of mental activities is far from complete. For example, without strong situational cues (a challenging task and a thoughtful expression), 3- and 4-year-olds deny that a person is thinking. They indicate that the minds of people waiting, looking at pictures, listening to stories, or reading books are "empty of thoughts and ideas." They do not realize that people are constantly talking to themselves and engaged in thought (Flavell, Green, & Flavell, 1993, 1995; Flavell et al., 1997).

Furthermore, preschoolers pay little attention to the *process* of thinking but, instead, focus on outcomes of thought. For example, 3-year-olds use the words "know" to refer to acting successfully (finding a hidden toy) and "forget" to refer to acting unsuccessfully (not finding the toy), even when another person is guessing the toy's location (Lyon & Flavell, 1994; Perner, 1991). And children younger than age 6 often claim they have always known information they just learned (Taylor, Esbenson, & Bennett, 1994). Finally, preschoolers believe that all events must be directly observed to be known. They do not understand that *mental inferences* can be a source of knowledge (Carpendale & Chandler, 1996).

How, then, should we describe the difference between the young child's theory of mind and that of the older child? Preschoolers know that people have an internal mental life. But they seem to believe that the mind is a passive container of information. Consequently, they greatly underestimate the amount of mental activity that goes on in people and are poor at inferring what people know or are thinking about. In contrast, older children view the mind as an active, constructive agent that selects and transforms information and affects how the world is perceived (Flavell, 1999; Wellman, 1990). We will consider this change further in Chapter 12 when we take up metacognition in middle childhood.

EARLY LITERACY AND MATHEMATICAL DEVELOPMENT

Researchers have begun to study how children's information-processing capacities affect the development of basic reading, writing, and mathematical skills that prepare them for school. The study of how preschoolers start to master these complex activities provides us with additional information on their cognitive strengths and limitations. In addition, we can use this knowledge to foster early literacy and mathematical development.

■ **EARLY CHILDHOOD LITERACY.** One week, Leslie's pupils brought empty food boxes to place on shelves in the classroom. Soon a make-believe grocery store opened. Children labeled items with prices, made shopping lists, and wrote checks at the cash register. A sign at the entrance announced the daily specials: "APLS BNS 5¢" ("apples bananas 5¢").

As their grocery store play reveals, preschoolers understand a great deal about written language long before they learn to read and write in conventional ways. This is not surprising when we consider that children in industrialized nations live in a world filled with written symbols. Each day, they observe and participate in activities involving storybooks, calendars, and lists. As part of these experiences, children try to figure out how written symbols convey meaning. Their active efforts to construct literacy knowledge through informal experiences are called **emergent literacy.**

Young preschoolers search for units of written language as they "read" memorized versions of stories and recognize familiar signs, such as "ON" and "OFF" on light switches and "PIZZA" at their favorite fast food counter. But their early ideas about written language differ from ours. For example, many preschoolers think that a single letter stands for a whole word or that each letter in a person's signature represents a separate name. Often they believe that letters (just like

emergent literacy
Young children's active efforts to construct literacy knowledge through informal experiences.

Biology & ENVIRONMENT

"MINDBLINDNESS" AND INFANTILE AUTISM

Sidney stood at the water table in Leslie's classroom, repeatedly filling a plastic cup and dumping out its contents. Dip-splash, dip-splash, dip-splash he went, until Leslie came over and redirected his actions. Without looking at Leslie's face, Sidney moved to a new repetitive pursuit: pouring water from one cup into another and back again. As other children entered the play space and conversed, Sidney hardly noticed. He rarely spoke, and when he did, he usually used words to get things he wanted, not to exchange ideas.

Sidney has *infantile autism,* the most severe behavior disorder of childhood. The term *autism* means "absorbed in the self," an apt description of Sidney. Like other children with the disorder, Sidney is impaired in the emotional and gestural (nonverbal) behaviors required for successful social interaction. In addition, his language is delayed and stereotyped; some autistic children do not speak at all. Sidney's interests, which focus on the physical world, are narrow and overly intense. For example, one day he sat for more than an hour making a toy ferris wheel go round and round.

Researchers agree that the disorder stems from abnormal brain functioning, usually due to genetic or prenatal environmental causes. However, psychophysiological research has not yet pinpointed a specific brain region (Tsai, 1999). Growing evidence suggests that one psychological factor involved is a severely deficient or absent theory of mind. Long after they reach the intellectual level of an average 4-year-old, autistic children have great difficulty with false-belief tasks. Most cannot attribute mental states to others or themselves. Such words as *believe, think, know, feel,* and *pretend* are rarely part of their vocabularies

(Happé, 1995; Yirmiya, Solomonica-Levi, & Shulman, 1996).

As early as the second year, autistic children show deficits in capacities that may contribute to awareness of others' mental states. For example, they less often establish joint attention, engage in social referencing, or imitate an adult's novel behaviors than do other children (Charman et al., 1997). Furthermore, they are relatively insensitive to a speaker's gaze as a cue to what he or she is talking about. Instead, autistic children often assume that another person's language refers to what they themselves are looking at—a possible reason they use many nonsensical expressions (Baron-Cohen, Baldwin, & Crowson, 1997). Finally, autistic children engage in much less make-believe play than do age- and mental-ability-matched comparison groups—both normal children and children with other developmental problems (Hughes, 1998).

Do these findings indicate that autism is due to a specific cognitive deficit that leaves the child "mindblind" and therefore unable to engage in human sociability? Some researchers think so (Baron-Cohen, 1993). But others point out that autistic individuals are not alone in poor performance on tasks assessing mental understanding; nonautistic, mentally retarded individuals also show it (Yirmiya et al., 1998). This suggests that some kind of general intellectual impairment may be involved.

Yet a third conjecture is that autism is due to a memory deficit, which makes it hard to stay focused on and retain the parts of complex tasks (Bennetto, Pennington, & Rogers, 1996). Perhaps this explains autistic children's preoccupation with simple, repetitive acts. It may also account for their difficulty with problems, such as

conservation, that require them to integrate several contexts at once (before, during, and after the transformation of a substance) (Yirmiya & Shulman, 1996). A memory deficit would also interfere with understanding the social world, since social interaction takes place quickly and requires integration of information from various sources.

At present, it is not clear which of these hypotheses is correct. Perhaps several biologically based deficits underlie the tragic social isolation of children like Sidney.

WILL HART

This autistic girl does not take note of a speaker's gaze to determine what that person is talking about. For this reason, the girl's teacher takes extra steps to capture her attention in a science lesson. Researchers disagree on whether autistic children's "mindblindness" is due to a specific social-cognitive deficit that leaves the child mindblind, to general intellectual impairment, or to a memory deficit.

FIGURE 9.7

A story (a) and a grocery list (b) written by a 4-year-old child. This child's writing has many features of real print. It also reveals an awareness of different kinds of written expression. (From L. M. McGee & D. J. Richgels, 2000, *Literacy's Beginnings* [3rd ed.], Boston: Allyn and Bacon, p. 69. Reprinted by permission.)

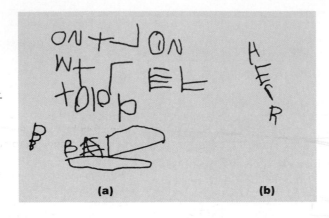

(a)   (b)

pictures) look like the meanings they represent. One child explained that the word deer begins with the letter O because it is shaped like a deer; then he demonstrated by drawing an O and adding antlers to it (Sulzby & Teale, 1991).

Gradually children revise these ideas as their perceptual and cognitive capacities improve, as they encounter writing in many contexts, and as adults help them with written communication. Soon preschoolers become aware of general characteristics of written language and create their own printlike symbols, as in the "story" and "grocery list" written by a 4-year-old in Figure 9.7. Eventually children figure out that letters are parts of words and are linked to sounds in systematic ways, as you can see in the invented spellings that are typical between ages 5 and 7. At first, children rely on sounds in the names of letters: "ADE LAFWTS KRMD NTU A LAVATR" ("eighty elephants crammed into a[n] elevator"). Over time, they grasp more subtle sound–letter correspondences. They also learn that some letters have more than one common sound and that context affects their use ("a" is pronounced differently in "cat" than "table") (Gentry, 1981; McGee & Richgels, 2000; Treiman et al., 1998).

Literacy development builds on a broad foundation of spoken language and knowledge about the world. The more informal literacy-related experiences young children have in their everyday lives, the better prepared they will be to tackle the complex tasks involved in reading and writing after they enter school. Adults can provide literacy-rich physical environments and encourage literacy-related play (Neuman, Copple, & Bredekamp, 2000). Storybook reading, in which adults engage preschoolers in discussion and interpretation of story content, is related to preschoolers' language and reading readiness scores, which predict later academic success. And adult-supported writing activities focusing on narrative (preparing a letter or a story) also foster literacy progress (Purcell-Gates, 1996; Whitehurst & Lonigan, 1998).

JIM PICKERELL

Preschoolers acquire a great deal of literacy knowledge informally as they participate in everyday activities involving written symbols. They try to figure out how print conveys meaningful information, just as they strive to make sense of other aspects of their world.

ordinality
A principle specifying order (more-than and less-than) relationships between quantities.

cardinality
A principle stating that the last number in a counting sequence indicates the quantity of items in the set.

Low-SES preschoolers generally have far less access to storybooks than do their higher-SES agemates (High et al., 1999). In a program that "flooded" child-care centers with high-quality children's books and provided training to caregivers on how to get 3- and 4-year-olds to interact with the books frequently and productively, children showed much greater gains in emergent reading and writing knowledge than did a control group not experiencing the intervention. These differences were still evident after the children entered kindergarten (Neuman, 1999). Regularly providing low-SES parents with children's books along with guidance in how to stimulate emergent literacy greatly enhances literacy activities in the home (High et al., 2000).

■ **YOUNG CHILDREN'S MATHEMATICAL REASONING.** Mathematical reasoning, like literacy, builds on informal knowledge. Young babies can discriminate the sizes of small sets (two versus three items), a sensitivity that provides the foundation for numerical under-

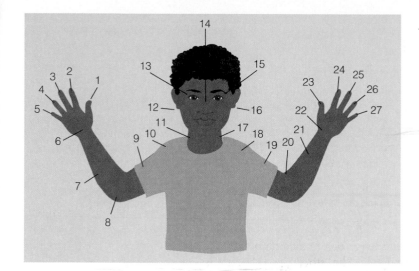

FIGURE 9.8

Sequence of body parts used for counting by the Oksapmin of Papua New Guinea. In the Oksapmin language, there are no terms for numbers aside from the body part names themselves (for example, "nose" represents "fourteen"). Children begin to use this system in the preschool years. Instead of counting on fingers, they can often be seen pointing to body parts. With age, they adapt the technique to handle more complex computation. (From G. B. Saxe, 1985, "Effects of Schooling on Arithmetical Understanding: Studies with Oksapmin Children in Papua New Guinea," *Journal of Educational Psychology, 77,* p. 505. Copyright © 1985 by the American Psychological Association. Reprinted by permission of the publisher and author.)

standings (Wynn, 1998). In the second year, children gain a grasp of **ordinality,** or order relationships between quantities, such as three is more than two. Soon they attach verbal labels (such as *lots, little, big,* and *small*) to amounts and sizes. And between ages 2 and 3, they begin to count. At first, counting is a memorized routine, as in "Onetwothreefourfivesix!" Or children repeat a few number words while vaguely pointing toward objects (Fuson, 1988).

Very soon, counting becomes more precise. Most 3- to 4-year-olds have established an accurate one-to-one correspondence between a short sequence of number words and the items they represent (Geary, 1995). Three-year-olds may not yet have memorized the correct number labels. For example, one child counted three items by saying, "1, 6, 10." But her general method was correct; she used only as many verbal tags as there were items to count. And pointing gestures show a one-to-one correspondence prior to number labels. This indicates that the child is about to master correct counting (Graham, 1999).

Sometime between ages 4 and 5, children grasp the vital principle of **cardinality.** They understand that the last number in a counting sequence indicates the quantity of items in the set (Bermejo, 1996). In the preschool scene described in the opening of this chapter, Sammy showed an appreciation of cardinality when he counted milk cartons. Mastery of cardinality increases the efficiency of children's counting. By age 4, children use counting to solve simple arithmetic problems. At first, their strategies are tied to the order of numbers presented; when given 2 + 4, they "count on" from 2 (Ginsburg, Klein, & Starkey, 1998). Soon they begin to experiment with various strategies. As a result, the *min* strategy, a more efficient approach (see page 343), appears.

The basic arithmetic knowledge just described emerges universally around the world, although ways of representing numbers vary. As Figure 9.8 shows, among the Oksapmin, an agricultural society of Papua New Guinea, counting is mapped onto 27 body parts, which serve as number terms. Using this system, Oksapmin children keep track of quantities, measure, and play number games. Instead of counting on fingers, they point to body parts as they expand their calculation skills (Saxe, 1985).

In homes and preschools where adults provide many occasions for counting and comparing quantities, children construct basic numerical concepts sooner (Geary, 1995). Then these concepts are solidly available as supports for the wide variety of mathematical skills children will be taught once they enter school.

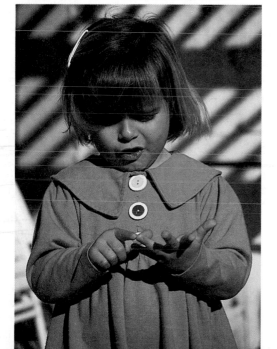

By counting on fingers, this child experiments with strategies for solving basic addition and subtraction problems. As she tries out various approaches and selects those that result in rapid, accurate solutions, gradually she will give up finger counting in favor of retrieving answers from memory.

Ask YOURSELF...

review
What factors influence children's problem-solving strategies, and why do they follow an overlapping-waves pattern of development?

apply
Lena notices that her 4-year-old son, Gregor, recognizes his name in print and counts to 20. She wonders why Gregor's preschool teacher permits him to spend so much time playing instead of teaching him academic skills. Gregor's teacher responds, "I am teaching him academics—through play." Explain why play is the best way for preschoolers to develop academically.

connect
Cite evidence on the development of memory, theory of mind, and literacy and mathematical understanding that is consistent with Vygotsky's sociocultural theory.

Individual Differences in Mental Development

In the preceding sections, we have seen many examples of wide individual differences in preschoolers' intellectual progress. Psychologists and educators typically measure how well preschoolers are developing cognitively by giving them intelligence tests. Scores are computed in the same way as they are for infants and toddlers (return to Chapter 6, page 232, to review). But instead of emphasizing perceptual and motor responses, tests for preschoolers sample a wide range of mental abilities.

Child development specialists are interested in young children's intelligence test scores because by age 5 to 6, they become good predictors of later intelligence and academic achievement (Hayslip, 1994). In addition, understanding the link between early childhood experiences and mental test performance gives us ways to intervene in support of children's cognitive growth.

EARLY CHILDHOOD INTELLIGENCE TESTS

Five-year-old Hallie sat in a small, strange testing room while Sarah, an adult he met only a short while ago, gave him an intelligence test. Some of the questions Sarah asked were *verbal*. For example, she held out a picture of a shovel and said, "Tell me what this shows?"—an item measuring vocabulary. Then she tested his memory by asking him to repeat sentences and lists of numbers back to her. She probed Hallie's quantitative knowledge and problem solving by seeing if he could count and solve simple addition and subtraction problems. Other tasks Sarah gave were *nonverbal* and largely assessed spatial reasoning. Hallie copied designs with special blocks, figured out the pattern in a series of shapes, and indicated what a piece of paper folded and cut would look like when unfolded (Thorndike, Hagen, & Sattler, 1986).

Before Sarah began the test, she took steps to ensure that Hallie's responses would accurately reflect his knowledge. Sarah was aware that Hallie came from an economically disadvantaged family. When low-SES and ethnic minority preschoolers are faced with an unfamiliar adult who bombards them with questions, they sometimes become anxious and afraid. Also, such children may not define the testing situation in achievement terms. Often they look for attention and approval from the examiner rather than focusing on the test questions themselves. As a result, they may settle for lower levels of performance than their abilities allow. Sarah spent time playing with Hallie before she began testing. In addition, she praised and encouraged him while the test was in progress. When testing conditions like these are used, low-SES preschoolers improve in performance (Bracken, 2000; Zigler & Finn-Stevenson, 1992).

Educational Concerns

Home Observation for Measurement of the Environment (HOME): Early Childhood Subscales

SUBSCALE	SAMPLE ITEM
Stimulation through toys, games, and reading material	Home includes toys to learn colors, sizes, and shapes.
Language stimulation	Parent teaches child about animals through books, games, and puzzles.
Organization of the physical environment	All visible rooms are reasonably clean and minimally cluttered.
Pride, affection, and warmth	Parent spontaneously praises child's qualities or behavior twice during observer's visit.
Stimulation of academic behavior	Child is encouraged to learn colors.
Modeling and encouragement of social maturity	Parent introduces interviewer to child.
Opportunities for variety in daily stimulation	Family member takes child on one outing at least every other week (picnic, shopping).
Avoidance of physical punishment	Parent neither slaps nor spanks child during observer's visit.

Source: Bradley & Caldwell, 1979.

Note that the questions Sarah asked Hallie tap knowledge and skills that not all children have had equal opportunity to learn. The issue of *cultural bias* in intelligence testing is a hotly debated topic that we will take up in Chapter 12. For now, keep in mind that intelligence tests do not sample the full range of human abilities, and performance is affected by cultural and situational factors (Sternberg, 1997). Nevertheless, test scores remain important because they predict school achievement, and this, in turn, is strongly related to vocational success in industrialized societies. Let's see how the environments in which children spend their days—home, preschool, and child care—affect mental test performance.

HOME ENVIRONMENT AND MENTAL DEVELOPMENT

A special version of the *Home Observation for Measurement of the Environment (HOME)*, covered in Chapter 6, assesses aspects of 3- to 6-year-olds' home lives that support intellectual growth (see the Educational Concerns table above). Physical surroundings and child-rearing practices play important roles. Preschoolers who develop well intellectually have homes rich in educational toys and books. Their parents are warm and affectionate, stimulate language and academic knowledge, and arrange outings to places where with interesting things to see and do. They also make reasonable demands for socially mature behavior—for example, that the child perform simple chores and behave courteously toward others. And when conflicts arise, these parents use reason to resolve them instead of physical force and punishment (Bradley & Caldwell, 1979, 1982).

As we saw in Chapter 2, these characteristics are less likely to be found in poverty-stricken families (Garrett, Ng'andu, & Ferron, 1994). When low-income parents manage, despite daily stresses, to obtain high HOME scores, their youngsters do substantially better on intelligence and achievement tests (Bradley & Caldwell, 1979, 1981). These findings, as well as others we will discuss in Chapter 12, suggest that the home plays a major role in the generally poorer intellectual performance of low-SES children in comparison to their higher-SES peers.

PRESCHOOL AND CHILD CARE

Children between ages 2 and 6 spend even more time away from their homes and parents than infants and toddlers do. Over the past 30 years, the number of young children enrolled

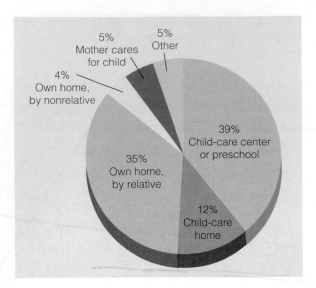

FIGURE 9.9

Who's minding America's preschoolers? The chart refers to settings in which 3- and 4-year-olds spend most time while their parents are at work. Over one-fourth of 3- and 4-year-olds experience more than one type of child care, a fact not reflected in the chart. (U.S. Bureau of the Census, 1997.)

[handwritten note: academic & child-centered preschools exist. Child-centered preschools are better.]

child-centered preschool
A preschool in which teachers provide a wide variety of activities from which children select, and most of the day is devoted to free play.

academic preschool
A preschool in which teachers structure the program, training children in academic skills through repetition and drill.

Project Head Start
The largest federally funded program in the United States, which provides low-income children with a year or two of preschool education, along with nutritional and medical services, and that encourages parent involvement in children's development.

in preschool or child care has steadily increased. Currently, 65 percent of preschool children have employed mothers (U.S. Bureau of the Census, 2000). Figure 9.9 shows where preschoolers spend their days while their parents are at work.

A *preschool* is a half-day program with planned educational experiences aimed at enhancing the development of 2- to 5-year-olds. In contrast, *child care* identifies a variety of arrangements for supervising children, ranging from care in someone else's or the child's own home to some type of center-based program. The line between preschool and child care is fuzzy. As Figure 9.9 indicates, parents often select a preschool as a child-care option. Many preschools (and public school kindergartens as well) have increased their hours to full days in response to the needs of employed parents (U.S. Department of Education, 2000). At the same time, good child care is not simply a matter of keeping children safe and adequately fed. It should provide the same high-quality educational experiences that an effective preschool does, the only difference being that children attend for an extended day.

■ **TYPES OF PRESCHOOL.** Preschool programs range along a continuum from child-centered to teacher-directed. In **child-centered preschools,** teachers provide activities from which children select, and most of the day is devoted to free play. In contrast, in **academic preschools,** teachers structure the program. Children are taught letters, numbers, colors, shapes, and other academic skills through repetition and drill.

Despite grave concern about the appropriateness of the academic approach, preschool teachers have felt increased pressure to stress formal academic training. Yet doing so in early childhood undermines motivation and emotional well-being. In a study of 3- to 6-year-olds, those in child-centered classrooms perceived their abilities to be higher than those in teacher-directed classrooms. In addition, they more often preferred challenging problems and expected to succeed on them, and they were less likely to seek adult approval or worry about school (Stipek et al., 1995). In yet another study, 4-year-olds in child-centered classrooms demonstrated greater mastery of motor, academic, language, and social skills at the end of the school year than did those in academic or philosophically unclear classrooms (Marcon, 1999a).

■ **EARLY INTERVENTION FOR AT-RISK PRESCHOOLERS.** In the 1960s, when the United States launched a "war on poverty," a wide variety of intervention programs for economically disadvantaged preschoolers were initiated. They were based on the assumption that learning problems are best treated early, before formal schooling begins.

Project Head Start, begun by the federal government in 1965, is the largest of these programs. A typical Head Start program provides children with a year or two of preschool, along with nutritional and medical services. Parent involvement is central to the Head Start philosophy. Parents serve on policy councils and contribute to program planning. They also work directly with children in classrooms, attend special programs on parenting and child development, and receive services directed at their own emotional, social, and vocational needs. Currently, more than 1,500 Head Start programs located around the country enroll about 826,000 children (Head Start Bureau, 2000).

Benefits of Preschool Intervention. Over two decades of research establishing the long-term benefits of preschool intervention has helped Head Start survive. The most important of these studies was coordinated by the Consortium for Longitudinal Studies, a group of investigators who combined data from seven university-based interventions. Results showed that children who attended the programs scored higher in IQ and academic achievement than did controls during the first 2 to 3 years of elementary school. After that time, differences in test scores declined (Lazar & Darlington, 1982).

Nevertheless, children who received intervention remained ahead on real-life measures of school adjustment into adolescence. They were less likely to be placed in special education classes or retained in grade, and a greater number graduated from high school. They also showed lasting benefits in attitude and motivation. Children who attended the programs were more likely to give achievement-related reasons (such as school or job accomplishments) for being proud of themselves. A separate report on one program—the High/Scope Perry Preschool Project—revealed benefits lasting into young adulthood. It was associated with a reduction in delinquency and teenage pregnancy, a greater likelihood of employment, and greater educational attainment, earnings, and marital stability at age 27 (Weikart, 1998).

These economically disadvantaged 4-year-olds benefit from the comprehensive early intervention services of Project Head Start. A rich, stimulating preschool experience is an essential part of the program. As parents like this classroom volunteer participate, they improve their own life circumstances as well as their children's development.

Does the impact of outstanding university-based programs on school adjustment generalize to Head Start programs in American communities? Outcomes are similar, although not as strong. Head Start preschoolers are more economically disadvantaged than are children in university-based programs, leading to more severe learning problems. And because Head Start is community based, quality of services is more variable across programs (Barnett, 1998).

Still, if preschool intervention yields long-term improvements in school adjustment, why do IQ and achievement gains fade so rapidly? One reason is that children graduating from Head Start and other interventions typically enter underfunded, inferior public schools (Currie & Thomas, 1997). The benefits of Head Start are easily undermined when children do not have continuing access to high-quality educational supports. In a program that began at age 4 and continued through third grade, children's achievement gains were still evident in junior high school (Reynolds & Temple, 1998). And recall from Chapter 6 that when intensive intervention persists from infancy through early childhood and children enter good-quality schools, IQ gains endure into adolescence (see page 237).

Despite Head Start children's declining test scores, their ability to meet school requirements is a remarkable intervention outcome. It may be due to program effects on parents, who create better rearing environments for their children. The more parents are involved in Head Start, the better their child-rearing practices and the more stimulating their home learning environments. These factors are positively related to preschoolers' year-end school-readiness scores, which tap academic, language, and social skills as well as independence and task persistence in the classroom (Marcon, 1999b; Parker et al., 1999).

The Future of Preschool Intervention. A typical component of early intervention focuses on teaching parenting skills and encouraging parents to act as supplementary intervenors for their children. By emphasizing developmental goals for *both* parents and children, program benefits might be extended (Smith, 1995). A parent helped to move out of poverty with education, vocational training, and other social services is likely to gain in psychological well-being, planning for the future, and beliefs and behaviors that foster children's motivation in school. When combined with child-centered intervention, these gains should translate into exceptionally strong benefits for children (Ramey & Ramey, 1998).

At present, this *two-generation approach* is too new to have yielded much research on long-term benefits (McLoyd, 1998). But one pioneering program, New Chance, is cause for optimism. In it, teenage mothers received services for themselves and their babies, including education, employment, family planning, life management, parent training, and child health care. A follow-up when children were 5 years old revealed that parent participants were less likely to be on welfare and had higher family earnings than did controls receiving less intensive intervention. In addition, program children experienced warmer and more stimulating

© ELLEN B. SENISI/THE IMAGE WORKS

This room has all the elements of a high-quality childcare program, including richly equipped activity areas, small group size, and children working individually or in small groups and granted many opportunities to select their own activities.

home environments, were more likely to have enrolled in Head Start, and had higher verbal IQs (Quint, Box, & Polit, 1997).

Although over one-fifth of American preschoolers are eligible for Head Start by virtue of their poverty level, at present the program serves only about one-third of these children. Yet Head Start and other interventions like it are highly cost effective. Program expenses are far less than the funds required to provide special education, treat delinquency, and support welfare dependency. Because of its demonstrated returns to society, a move is under way to expand and strengthen Head Start by starting intervention earlier, sustaining it longer, and intensifying services directed at parents and children (Zigler & Styfco, 1998).

■ **CHILD CARE.** We have seen that high-quality early intervention can enhance the development of economically disadvantaged children. However, as indicated in Chapter 6, much American child care lacks quality. Preschoolers exposed to poor-quality child care, whether they come from middle- or low-SES homes, score lower on measures of cognitive and social skills (Hausfather et al., 1997; Lamb, 1998).

What are the ingredients of high-quality child care? Large-scale studies of center- and home-based care reveal that the following factors are important: group size (number of children in a single space), caregiver–child ratio, caregiver's educational preparation, and caregiver's personal commitment to learning about and caring for children. When these characteristics are favorable, adults are more verbally stimulating and sensitive to children's needs. Children, in turn, do especially well on measures of cognitive, language, and social skills—effects that persist into the early school years for children of a wide range of family backgrounds (Burchinal et al., 2000; Helburn, 1995; Peiser-Feinberg, 1999). Other research shows that spacious, well-equipped environments and activities that meet the educational needs and interests of preschool children also contribute to positive outcomes (Scarr, 1998).

The Educational Concerns table on the following page summarizes characteristics of high-quality early childhood programs, based on standards for developmentally appropriate practice devised by the National Association for the Education of Young Children. Together, they offer a set of worthy goals as the United States strives to upgrade child-care and educational services for young children.

EDUCATIONAL TELEVISION

Besides home and preschool, young children spend much time in another learning environment: watching television. The average 2- to 6-year-old watches TV from 1½ to 3 hours a day—a very long time in the life of a young child (Comstock, 1993). However, large individual differences in TV viewing exist. In early and middle childhood, boys watch slightly more than girls. Low-SES, ethnic minority children are also more frequent viewers, perhaps because their families are less able to pay for out-of-home entertainment or their neighborhoods provide few alternative activities. And if parents watch a lot of TV, their children usually do so as well (Huston & Wright, 1998).

Each afternoon, Sammy looked forward to certain educational programs, including *Sesame Street*—his favorite. Find a time to watch an episode of *Sesame Street*. The program was originally designed for the same population served by Head Start—low-SES children who enter school academically behind their more economically advantaged peers. It uses lively visual and sound effects to stress basic literacy and number concepts, and engaging

Signs of Developmentally Appropriate Early Childhood Programs

PROGRAM CHARACTERISTIC	SIGNS OF QUALITY
Physical setting	Indoor environment is clean, in good repair, and well ventilated. Classroom space is divided into richly equipped activity areas, including make-believe play, blocks, science, math, games and puzzles, books, art, and music. Fenced outdoor play space is equipped with swings, climbing equipment, tricycles, and sandbox.
Group size	In preschools and child-care centers, group size is no greater than 18 to 20 children with 2 teachers.
Caregiver–child ratio	In child-care centers, teacher is responsible for no more than 8 to 10 children. In child-care homes, caregiver is responsible for no more than 6 children.
Daily activities	Most of the time, children work individually or in small groups. Children select many of their own activities and learn through experiences relevant to their own lives. Teachers facilitate children's involvement, accept individual differences, and adjust expectations to children's developing capacities.
Interactions between adults and children	Teachers move among groups and individuals, asking questions, offering suggestions, and adding more complex ideas. Teachers use positive guidance techniques, such as modeling and encouraging expected behavior and redirecting children to more acceptable activities.
Teacher qualifications	Teachers have college-level specialized preparation in early childhood development, early childhood education, or a related field.
Relationships with parents	Parents are encouraged to observe and participate. Teachers talk frequently with parents about children's behavior and development.
Licensing and accreditation	Program is licensed by the state. If a preschool or child-care center, accreditation by the National Academy of Early Childhood Programs is evidence of an especially high-quality program. If a child-care home, accreditation by the National Association for Family Child Care is evidence of high-quality experiences for children.

Sources: Bredekamp & Copple, 1997; National Association for the Education of Young Children, 1998.

puppet and human characters to teach general knowledge, emotional and social understanding, and social skills. More than 75 percent of American preschool children and 60 percent of kindergartners watch *Sesame Street* at least once a week, and it is broadcast in more than 40 countries (Zill, Davies, & Daly, 1994).

Sesame Street works well as an academic tutor. The more children watch, the higher they score on tests designed to measure the program's learning goals (Fisch, Truglio, & Cole, 1999). One study reported gains in academic achievement lasting into high school (Anderson et al., 1998). In recent years, *Sesame Street* has reduced its rapid-paced, adlike format in favor of leisurely episodes with a clear story line (Truglio, 2000). When types of programs are compared, ones with slow-paced action and easy-to-follow narratives, such as *Mr. Rogers' Neighborhood* and *Barney and Friends,* lead to more elaborate make-believe play. Those presenting quick, disconnected bits of information do not (Singer, 1999; Tower et al., 1979).

Does heavy TV viewing take children away from activities that promote cognitive development? Some evidence suggests that it does. The more preschool and school-age children watch TV—in particular, entertainment shows and cartoons—the less time they spend reading and interacting with others (Huston et al., 1999; Koolstra & van der Voort, 1996). Furthermore, children and adolescents who watch a great deal of TV achieve less well in school (Comstock & Scharrer, 1999).

But television can support cognitive and academic skills as long as viewing is not excessive and programs meet children's developmental needs. We will consider the impact of television on emotional and social development in the next chapter.

[Handwritten margin notes: too much TV leads to: (1) ↓ reading (2) ↓ interaction w/ others (3) low academic achievement]

Ask **YOURSELF...**

review   *Describe differences between child-centered and academic preschools. What findings indicate that parents who want to foster their preschooler's academic development should choose a child-centered preschool?*

apply   *Senator Smith heard that IQ and achievement gains resulting from Head Start do not last, so he plans to vote against funding for the program. Write a letter to Senator Smith explaining why he should support Head Start.*

reflect   *What TV programs did you watch as a child? How do you think they affected your play and learning?*

Language Development

anguage is intimately related to virtually all the cognitive changes discussed in this chapter. Through it, children express a wide variety of cognitive skills, and it extends many aspects of cognitive development. Between ages 2 and 6, children make awesome and momentous advances in language. Preschoolers' remarkable achievements, as well as their mistakes along the way, indicate that they master their native tongue in an active, rule-oriented fashion.

VOCABULARY DEVELOPMENT

At age 2, Sammy had a vocabulary of 200 words. By age 6, he will have acquired around 10,000 words. To accomplish this extraordinary feat, Sammy will learn an average of 5 new words each day (Anglin, 1993).

■ **RAPID GAINS IN VOCABULARY.** How do children build their vocabularies so quickly? Researchers have discovered that they can connect a new word with an underlying concept after only a brief encounter, a process called **fast mapping.** Even toddlers comprehend new labels remarkably quickly, but they need more repetitions of the word's use across several situations than do preschoolers, who better remember and categorize speech-based information (Akhtar & Montague, 1999; Gathercole et al., 1992; Woodward, Markman, & Fitzsimmons, 1994).

Once children fast-map a word, they often have to refine their first guess about its meaning. One day, Sammy heard Leslie announce to the children that they would soon take a field trip. He excitedly told his mother, "We're going on a field trip!" When she asked where the class would go, Sammy responded matter-of-factly, "To a field, of course."

Sammy's error suggests that young children fast-map some words more easily than others. They learn labels for objects especially rapidly because these refer to concrete items they already know much about, and caregivers' speech often emphasizes names for things (Bloom, 1998). Gradually, action words (*go, run, broke*), as well as modifiers referring to noticeable features of objects and people (*red, round, sad*), increase in frequency. If modifiers are related to one another in meaning, they take somewhat longer to learn. For example, 2-year-olds grasp the general distinction between *big* and *small*, but they do not understand more refined differences—between *tall* and *short, high* and *low*, and *long* and *short*—until age 3 to 5. Similarly, children acquire *now–then* before *yesterday–today–tomorrow* (Clark, 1983; Stevenson & Pollitt, 1987).

LAURA DWIGHT

To engage in effective verbal communication, these preschoolers must combine four components of language that have to do with sound, meaning, overall structure, and everyday use. How children accomplish this feat so rapidly raises some of the most puzzling questions about development.

■ **STRATEGIES FOR WORD LEARNING.** Preschoolers figure out the meanings of words by contrasting them with ones they already know and assigning the new label to a gap in their vocabulary (Clark, 1990). But exactly how they discover which concept each word picks out is not yet fully understood. Ellen Markman (1989, 1992) believes that in the early phases of vocabulary growth, children adopt a **principle of mutual exclusivity.** They assume that words refer to entirely separate (nonoverlapping) categories. The principle of mutual exclusivity works well as long as available referents are perceptually very distinct. For example, when 2-year-olds are told the names of two very different novel objects (a clip and a horn), they assign each label correctly, to the whole object and not a part of it (Waxman & Senghas, 1992).

But mutual exclusivity cannot account for what young children do when adults call a single object by more than one name. Children often draw on other aspects of language for help in these instances. According to one proposal, they figure out many word meanings by observing how words are used in *syntax*, or the structure of sentences—a hypothesis called **syntactic bootstrapping** (Gleitman, 1990). Consider an adult who says, "This is a *citron* one," while showing the child a yellow car. Two- and 3-year-olds interpret a new word used as an adjective as referring to a property of the object (Hall & Graham, 1999; Waxman & Markow, 1998).

Furthermore, drawing on their ability to infer others' intentions and perspectives, preschoolers often rely on social cues to identify word meanings (Baldwin & Tomasello, 1998). In one study, an adult performed an action on an object and then used a new label while looking back and forth between the child and the object, as if to invite the child to play. Two-year-olds capitalized on this social information to conclude that the label referred to the action, not the object (Tomasello & Akhtar, 1995).

Adults also provide direct information about the meaning of words. Consider an adult who says, "That soap is *made of lye.*" Relying on the phrase *made of,* preschoolers interpret lye to refer to the soap's material qualities rather than the dish on which the soap rests (Deák, 2000). When no social cues or direct information is available, children as young as 2 demonstrate remarkable flexibility in their word-learning strategies. They treat a new word applied to an already-labeled object as a second name for the object (Deák & Maratsos, 1998; Mervis, Golinkoff, & Bertrand, 1994).

Once preschoolers have a sufficient vocabulary, they use words creatively to fill in for ones they have not yet learned. As early as age 2, children coin new words in systematic ways. For example, Sammy said *plant-man* for gardener (created a compound word) and *crayoner* for a child using crayons (added the ending *-er*) (Clark, 1995). Preschoolers also extend language meanings through metaphor. For example, one 3-year-old used the expression "fire engine in my tummy" to describe a stomachache (Winner, 1988). The metaphors of young preschoolers involve concrete, sensory comparisons, such as "clouds are pillows" and "leaves are dancers." Once vocabulary and general knowledge expand, they also appreciate nonsensory comparisons, such as "Friends are like magnets" (Karadsheh, 1991). Metaphors permit young children to communicate in especially vivid and memorable ways.

As these findings illustrate, children's cognitive capacities join with diverse patterns of information in the environment to guide word learning. Their word-learning strategies change as information processing, communication skills, vocabulary size, and knowledge of categories improve (Bloom, 2000; Hollich, Hirsh-Pasek, & Golinkoff, 2000). And all along, children strive to acquire conventional word meanings (Clark, 1995). To participate fully in their language community, they must abandon invented words in favor of those used by others.

GRAMMATICAL DEVELOPMENT

Grammar refers to the way we combine words into meaningful phrases and sentences. Between ages 2 and 3, children adopt the word order of the adult speech to which they are exposed. English-speaking children use simple sentences that follow a subject–verb–object word order. Children learning other languages adopt the word orders of the adult speech to which they are exposed (Maratsos, 1998). This shows that they have a beginning grasp of the grammar of their language.

fast mapping
Connecting a new word with an underlying concept after only a brief encounter.

principle of mutual exclusivity
The assumption by children in the early stages of vocabulary growth that words mark entirely separate (nonoverlapping) categories.

syntactic bootstrapping
Figuring out word meanings by observing how words are used in the structure of sentences.

■ **FROM SIMPLE SENTENCES TO COMPLEX GRAMMAR.** As young children conform to word-order rules, they make small additions and changes in words that enable us to express meanings flexibly and efficiently. For example, they add *-s* for plural (*cats*), use prepositions (*in* and *on*), and form various tenses of the verb *to be* (*is, are, were, has been, will*). All English-speaking children master these grammatical markers in a regular sequence, starting with the ones that involve the simplest meanings and the fewest structural changes (Brown, 1973; de Villiers & de Villiers, 1973). For example, children master the plural form *-s* before they learn tenses of the verb *to be.*

By age 3½, children have acquired a great many grammatical rules, and they apply them so consistently that they overextend the rules to words that are exceptions, a type of error called **overregularization.** "My toy car *breaked,*" "I *runned* faster than you," and "We each got two *feets*" are expressions that start to appear between 2 and 3 years of age. Children over-regularize only occasionally, in about 5 to 8 percent of instances in which they use irregular words (such as *ran, broke,* and *feet*)—a rate that remains constant into middle childhood (Marcus, 1995; Marcus et al., 1992). Overregularization shows that children apply grammatical rules creatively, since they do not hear mature speakers use these forms.

Between 3 and 6 years, children master even more complex grammatical structures, although they make predictable errors along the way. In asking questions, preschoolers are reluctant to let go of the "subject–verb–object" sequence that is so basic to the English language. At first, they form questions by using rising intonation and failing to invert the subject and verb, as in "Mommy baking cookies?" and "What you doing, Daddy?" (Stromswold, 1995).

Other early errors also occur because young children tend to cling to a consistent word order. For example, some passive sentences give them trouble. When told, "The car was pushed by the truck," preschoolers often make a toy car push a truck. By age 5, they understand expressions like these. Nevertheless, 3- to 6-year-olds almost always use abbreviated passives ("It got broken") rather than full passives ("The glass was broken by Mary"). Although they can be trained to produce full passives, they still make errors (Brooks & Tomasello, 1999). Mastery of the passive form is not complete until the end of middle childhood (Horgan, 1978).

Nevertheless, preschoolers' grasp of grammar is impressive. By age 4 to 5, they form embedded sentences ("I think *he will come*"), tag questions ("Dad's going to be home soon, *isn't he?*"), and indirect objects ("He showed *his friend* the present"). As the preschool years draw to a close, children use most of the grammatical constructions of their language competently (Tager-Flusberg, 2000).

■ **STRATEGIES FOR ACQUIRING GRAMMAR.** Evidence that grammatical development proceeds gradually has raised questions about Chomsky's language acquisition device (LAD), which assumes that children have innate, built-in knowledge of grammatical rules (see Chapter 6, page 239). Some experts believe that grammar is largely a product of general cognitive development—children's tendency to search the environment for consistencies and patterns of all sorts (Maratsos, 1998). Yet among these theorists, there is intense debate about how children acquire the structure of their language.

According to one view, young children rely on *semantics,* or word meanings, to figure out grammatical rules—an approach called **semantic bootstrapping.** For example, children might begin by grouping words with "agent qualities" (things that cause actions) as *subjects* and words with "action qualities" as *verbs.* Then they merge these categories with observations of how words are used in sentences (Bates & MacWhinney, 1987). Others take the view that children acquire grammar through direct observations of the structure of their language. That is, they notice which words appear in the same positions in sentences and are combined in the same way with other words. Over time, they group them into the same grammatical category (Braine, 1994).

Still other theorists agree with the essence of Chomsky's theory. One idea accepts semantic bootstrapping but proposes that the grammatical categories into which children group word meanings are innately given—present at the outset (Bloom, 1999; Pinker, 1989). Critics, however, point out that toddlers' two-word utterances do not show a grasp of grammatical categories. Instead, they consist of simple formulas, which mostly copy adult word pairings (return

overregularization
Application of regular grammatical rules to words that are exceptions.

semantic bootstrapping
Figuring out grammatical rules by relying on word meanings.

to Chapter 6, page 244, to review) (Tomasello, 2000). According to another theory, although children do not start with innate knowledge, they have a special *language-making capacity*—a set of procedures for analyzing the language they hear, which supports the discovery of grammatical regularities. Research on children learning more than 40 different languages reveals common patterns, consistent with a basic set of strategies (Slobin, 1985, 1997).

In sum, intense controversy continues over whether there is a universal, built-in language-processing device or whether children in different parts of the world develop strategies for acquiring grammar that are influenced by their information-processing skills and features of the language they hear (de Villiers & de Villiers, 1999). We still have much to discover about how children master grammar.

BECOMING AN EFFECTIVE CONVERSATIONALIST

Besides acquiring vocabulary and grammar, children must use language successfully in social contexts. For a conversation to go well, participants must take turns, stay on the same topic, state their messages clearly, and conform to cultural rules for social interaction. This practical side of language is called **pragmatics,** and preschoolers make considerable headway in mastering it.

At the beginning of early childhood, children are already skilled conversationalists. In face-to-face interaction, they initiate verbal exchanges, respond appropriately to their partner's remarks, and take turns (Bloom et al., 1996; Pan & Snow, 1999). The number of turns over which children can sustain interaction and their ability to maintain a topic over time increases with age, but even 2-year-olds are capable of effective conversation (Snow et al., 1996). And when asked to clarify their statements, they readily do so. For example, when a 2½-year-old said, "How Joey go here?" and her mother indicated lack of understanding, the child corrected, "How Joey get here?" These surprisingly advanced abilities probably grow out of early interactive experiences (see Chapter 7).

Indeed, the presence of a sibling seems to be especially conducive to acquiring the pragmatics of language. Preschoolers closely monitor conversations between their siblings and parents. They often try to join in, and when they do, verbal exchanges last longer, with each participant taking more turns. To be successful at participating, children must understand the other speakers' topic and think of a way to add to it (Barton & Strosberg, 1997; Barton & Tomasello, 1991). And as they listen to conversations, young language learners are exposed to important skills, such as use of personal pronouns ("I" versus "you"), which are more common in the early vocabularies of later-born than first-born siblings (Pine, 1995).

By age 4, children already adjust their speech to fit the age, sex, and social status of their listeners. In one study, 4- to 7-year-olds were asked to act out different roles with hand puppets. Even the youngest children used more commands when playing socially dominant and male roles, such as teacher, doctor, and father In contrast, they spoke more politely and used more indirect requests when playing less dominant and feminine roles, such as pupil, patient, and mother (Anderson, 1992).

Preschoolers' conversational skills occasionally do break down. For example, have you tried talking on the telephone with a preschooler lately? Here is an excerpt of one 4-year-old's telephone conversation with his grandfather:

Grandfather: "How old will you be?"

John: "Dis many." (Holding up four fingers)

Grandfather: "Huh?"

John: "Dis many." (Again holding up four fingers) (Warren & Tate, 1992, pp. 259–260)

Preschoolers' conversations appear less mature in highly demanding situations in which they cannot see their listeners' reactions or rely on typical conversational aids, such as gestures

© B. DAEMMRICH THE IMAGE WORKS

The presence of an older sibling seems to foster preschoolers' grasp of the pragmatics of language. To join in conversation, young children must understand the other speakers' topic and think of a way to add to it.

children tailor speech to demographic of the listener.

pragmatics
The practical, social side of language that is concerned with how to engage in effective and appropriate communication with others.

In highly demanding situations, such as conversing on the phone, preschoolers often do not communicate clearly. They lack the supports available in face-to-face interaction, such as visual access to a partner's reaction and to objects that are topics of conversation.

do parents
correcting have a
(+) or (−) effect?

expansions
Adult responses that elaborate on a child's utterance, increasing its complexity.

recasts
Adult responses that restructure children's incorrect speech into a more appropriate form.

and objects to talk about. However, when asked to tell a listener how to solve a simple puzzle, 3- to 6-year-olds' directions are more specific over the phone than in person, indicating that they realize that more verbal description is necessary in the phone context (Cameron & Lee, 1997). Between ages 4 and 8, both conversing and giving directions over the phone improve greatly. (Telephone talk provides yet another example of how preschoolers' competencies depend on the demands of the situation.)

SUPPORTING LANGUAGE LEARNING IN EARLY CHILDHOOD

From what you have learned so far, what experiences do you think would foster preschoolers' language acquisition? Interaction with more skilled speakers, which is so important during toddlerhood, remains vital during early childhood. Conversational give-and-take with adults, either at home or in preschool, is consistently related to language progress (Hart & Risley, 1995; Helburn, 1995).

Sensitive, caring adults use special techniques that promote preschoolers' language skills. When children use words incorrectly or communicate unclearly, such adults give helpful, explicit feedback, such as "I can't tell which ball you want. Do you mean a large or small one or a red or green one?" At the same time, they do not overcorrect, especially when children make grammatical mistakes. Criticism discourages children from actively experimenting with language rules in ways that lead to new skills.

Instead, adults provide subtle, indirect feedback about grammar by using two strategies, often in combination: **expansions** and **recasts** (Bohannon & Stanowicz, 1988). For example, if a child says, "I gotted new red shoes," the parent might respond, "Yes, you got a pair of new red shoes," *expanding* the complexity of the child's statement as well as *recasting* its incorrect features into appropriate form. Nevertheless, some researchers question whether expansions and recasts are as important in children's mastery of grammar as is mere exposure to a rich language environment. Adults do not use these techniques often, and they are not provided to children in all cultures (Marcus, 1993; Valian, 1996). Furthermore, whereas some studies report that parents' reformulations have a corrective effect, others show no impact on children's use of grammar (Morgan, Bonama, & Travis, 1995; Saxton, 1997). Rather than eliminating errors, perhaps expansions and recasts serve the broader purpose of modeling grammatical alternatives and encouraging children to experiment with them.

Do the findings just described remind you once again of Vygotsky's theory? In language as in other aspects of intellectual growth, parents and teachers gently prompt young children to take the next developmental step forward. Children strive to master language because they want to attain social connectedness to other people. Adults, in turn, respond to children's natural desire to become competent speakers by listening attentively, elaborating on what they say, modeling correct usage, and stimulating them to talk further. In the next chapter we will see that this special combination of warmth and encouragement of mature behavior is at the heart of early childhood emotional and social development as well.

Ask YOURSELF...

review   *What can adults do to support language development in early childhood? Provide a list of recommendations, noting research that supports each.*

apply   *One day, Jason's mother explained to him that the family would take a vacation in Miami. The next morning, Jason emerged from his room with belongings spilling out of a suitcase and remarked, "I gotted my bag packed. When are we going to Your-ami?" What do Jason's errors reveal about his approach to mastering language?*

connect   *Explain how children's strategies for word learning support the interactionist perspective on language development, described on page 241 of Chapter 6.*

Summary

PIAGET'S THEORY: THE PREOPERATIONAL STAGE

Describe advances in mental representation and limitations of thinking during the pre-operational stage.

■ Rapid advances in mental representation, notably language and make-believe play, mark the beginning of the **preoperational stage.** With age, make-believe becomes increasingly complex, evolving into **socio-dramatic play.** Preschoolers' make-believe supports many aspects of cognitive and social development.

■ **Dual representation** improves rapidly over the third year of life. Children realize that photographs, drawings, models, and simple maps correspond to circumstances in the real world. Insight into one type of symbol–real world relation helps preschoolers understand others.

■ For the most part, Piaget described the young child in terms of deficits rather than strengths. He viewed them as not yet capa-ble of **operations** because they are **egocen-tric**—unable to imagine the perspectives of others. Egocentrism leads to the rigidity and illogical nature of young children's thought.

■ According to Piaget, preschoolers engage in **animistic thinking,** and their cogni-tions are **centered, perception-bound,** focused on **states rather than transforma-tions,** and **irreversible.** Because of these difficulties, they fail **conservation** and **hierarchical classification** tasks.

What does recent research imply about the accuracy of the preoperational stage?

■ When young children are given simplified problems relevant to their everyday lives, their performance appears more mature than Piaget assumed. Under these condi-tions, they recognize differing perspectives, notice and reason about transformations, think logically about cause–effect relations, and organize knowledge into hierarchical categories. However, not until age 6 to 7 are children good at making distinctions between appearance and reality.

■ Operational thinking develops gradually over the preschool years, a finding that challenges Piaget's concept of stage.

What educational principles can be derived from Piaget's theory?

■ A Piagetian classroom promotes discovery learning, sensitivity to children's readiness to learn, and acceptance of individual differences.

VYGOTSKY'S SOCIOCULTURAL THEORY

Describe Vygotsky's perspective on the origins and significance of children's private speech.

■ Whereas Piaget minimized the role of lan-guage in cognitive development, Vygotsky regarded it as the foundation for all com-plex mental activities. According to Vygotsky, **private speech,** or self-directed language, emerges out of social communi-cation as adults and more skilled peers help children master challenging tasks within the zone of proximal development. Eventually private speech is internalized as inner, verbal thought.

■ **Intersubjectivity** and **scaffolding** are fea-tures of social interaction that promote transfer of cognitive processes to children. The term **guided participation** recognizes situational and cultural variations in adult support of children's efforts.

Describe applications of Vygotsky's theory to education, and evaluate his major ideas.

■ A Vygotskian classroom emphasizes assisted discovery. Verbal guidance from teachers and peer collaboration are vitally important. According to Vygotsky, make-believe play is a unique, broadly influential zone of proxi-mal development in early childhood.

■ In granting social experience a central role in cognitive development, Vygotsky's theory helps us understand the wide cultural varia-tion in cognitive skills. However, verbal communication may not be the only means, or the most important means, through which children learn in some cultures. Vygotsky said little about how elementary

cognitive capacities, which develop in infancy, contribute to socially transmitted, complex mental activities.

INFORMATION PROCESSING

How do attention, memory, and problem solving change during early childhood?

■ Attention gradually becomes more sus-tained, and **planning** improves. Neverthe-less, compared with older children, preschoolers spend relatively short periods involved in tasks and are less systematic in planning.

■ Young children's recognition memory is remarkably good and becomes even more accurate by the end of early childhood. Compared with older children and adults, preschoolers' recall for listlike information is poor because they use **memory strate-gies** less effectively.

■ **Episodic memory,** or memory for everyday experiences, is well developed in early child-hood. Like adults, preschoolers remember familiar experiences in terms of **scripts,** which become more elaborate with age. As adults converse with children about the past, autobiographical memory becomes better organized, detailed, and related to the larger context of children's lives.

■ According to **overlapping-waves theory,** when solving problems children generate a variety of strategies. As they try out those strategies they gradually select ones that result in rapid, accurate solutions.

Describe the young child's theory of mind.

■ Preschoolers begin to construct a theory of mind, indicating that they are capable of **metacognition,** or thinking about thought. Between ages 3 and 4, they understand that both beliefs and desires can influence be-havior and that people can hold false beliefs.

■ Many factors seem to contribute to young children's understanding of mental life, including language and cognitive abilities; make-believe play and reasoning about imaginary situations; and social interaction with older siblings, friends, and adults.

Summary (continued)

- Preschoolers' awareness of mental activities is far from complete. They regard the mind as a passive container of information rather than an active, constructive agent.

Summarize children's literacy and mathematical knowledge during early childhood.

- Young children's **emergent literacy** reveals that they understand a great deal about written language before they read and write in conventional ways. Preschoolers gradually revise incorrect ideas about the meaning of written symbols as their perceptual and cognitive capacities improve, as they encounter writing in many contexts, and as adults help them make sense of written information.

- Mathematical reasoning also builds on a foundation of informal knowledge. Toddlers display a beginning grasp of **ordinality,** which serves as the basis for more complex understandings. As children experiment with counting strategies, they discover additional mathematical principles, including **cardinality.** Gradually, counting becomes more flexible and efficient, and children use it to solve simple arithmetic problems. When adults provide many occasions for counting and comparing quantities, children construct basic numerical concepts sooner.

INDIVIDUAL DIFFERENCES IN MENTAL DEVELOPMENT

Describe the content of early childhood intelligence tests and testing conditions that affect children's performance.

- Intelligence tests in early childhood include a wide variety of verbal and nonverbal items that assess vocabulary, memory, quantitative knowledge, problem solving, spatial reasoning, and other cognitive skills. When taking an intelligence test, low-income and ethnic minority children, especially, benefit from having time to get to know the examiner and receiving generous praise and encouragement.

Describe the impact of home, preschool and child care, and educational television on mental development in early childhood.

- Children growing up in warm, stimulating homes with parents who make reasonable demands for mature behavior score higher on mental tests. Home environment plays a major role in the poorer intellectual performance of low-SES children in comparison to their more economically advantaged peers.

- Preschool programs come in great variety. **Child-centered preschools** emphasize free play. In **academic preschools,** teachers train academic skills through repetition and drill. Formal academic instruction, however, is inconsistent with young children's developmental needs and undermines their emotional well-being.

- **Project Head Start** is the largest federally funded preschool program for low-income children in the United States. High-quality preschool intervention results in immediate IQ and achievement gains and long-term improvements in school adjustment for economically disadvantaged children. The more parents are involved in Head Start, the better children score on year-end school readiness scores. To strengthen the impact of intervention, new two-generation models are being tried.

- Poor-quality child care disrupts the development of children from all walks of life. When group size, caregiver–child ratio, caregiver educational preparation, and caregiver commitment to the child-care field are favorable, preschoolers are advantaged in cognitive and social development.

- Children pick up many cognitive skills from educational television programs like *Sesame Street.* Programs with slow-paced action and easy-to-follow story lines foster more elaborate make-believe play. Heavy TV viewers of entertainment shows and cartoons spend less time reading and interacting with others and achieve less well in school.

LANGUAGE DEVELOPMENT

Trace the development of vocabulary, grammar, and conversational skills in early childhood.

- Supported by **fast mapping,** children's vocabularies grow dramatically during early

childhood. Preschoolers figure out the meaning of new words by contrasting them with ones they already know. The **principle of mutual exclusivity** explains children's acquisition of some, but not all, early words.

- In addition, preschoolers engage in **syntactic bootstrapping,** observing how words are used in the structure of sentences to figure out word meanings. They also make use of adults' social cues and directly provided information. Once preschoolers have a sufficient vocabulary, they extend language meanings, coining new words and creating metaphors.

- Between ages 2 and 3, children adopt the word order of their language. As they master additional grammatical constructions, they occasionally **overregularize,** or apply the rules to words that are exceptions. By the end of the preschool years, children have acquired a wide variety of complex grammatical forms.

- Some experts believe that grammar is a product of general cognitive development. According to one view, children engage in **semantic bootstrapping,** relying on word meanings to figure out grammatical rules. Others agree with the essence of Chomsky's theory that children's brains are specially tuned for acquiring grammar.

- **Pragmatics** refers to the practical, social side of language. In face-to-face interaction with peers, young preschoolers are already skilled conversationalists. By age 4, they adapt their speech to their listeners in culturally accepted ways. Preschoolers' communicative skills appear less mature in highly demanding contexts, such as the telephone.

Cite factors that support language learning in early childhood.

- Conversational give-and-take with more skilled speakers fosters preschoolers' language skills. Adults often provide explicit feedback on the clarity of children's utterances. They give indirect feedback about grammar through **expansions** and **recasts.** However, the impact of these strategies on grammatical development has been challenged. For this aspect of language, exposure to a rich language environment may be sufficient.

Important terms and concepts

academic preschool (p. 354)
animistic thinking (p. 330)
cardinality (p. 350)
centration (p. 330)
child-centered preschool (p. 354)
conservation (p. 330)
dual representation (p. 329)
egocentrism (p. 329)
emergent literacy (p. 348)
episodic memory (p. 344)
expansions (p. 362)
fast mapping (p. 359)
guided participation (p. 340)

hierarchical classification (p. 330)
intersubjectivity (p. 340)
irreversibility (p. 330)
memory strategies (p. 344)
metacognition (p. 346)
operations (p. 329)
ordinality (p. 350)
overlapping-waves theory (p. 345)
overregularization (p. 360)
perception bound (p. 330)
planning (p. 343)
pragmatics (p. 361)

preoperational stage (p. 326)
principle of mutual exclusivity (p. 359)
private speech (p. 339)
Project Head Start (p. 354)
recasts (p. 362)
scaffolding (p. 340)
scripts (p. 344)
semantic bootstrapping (p. 360)
sociodramatic play (p. 327)
states rather than transformations
   (p. 330)
syntactic bootstrapping (p. 359)

 . . . **for further information and help**

Consult the companion website for this book, where you will find additional weblinks and associated learning activities:
www.ablongman.com/berk

EARLY CHILDHOOD DEVELOPMENT AND EDUCATION

Association for Childhood Education International (ACEI)
www.udel.edu/bateman/acei

An organization interested in promoting sound educational practice from infancy through early adolescence. Student membership is available and includes a subscription to Childhood Education, *a bimonthly journal covering research, practice, and public policy issues.*

National Association for the Education of Young Children (NAEYC)
www.naeyc.org

An organization open to all individuals interested in acting on behalf of young children's needs, with primary focus on educational services. Membership includes a subscription to Young Children, *a bimonthly journal covering theory, research, and practice in infant and early childhood development and education. Student membership is available.*

LITERACY

U.S. Department of Education
Helping Your Child Learn to Read
www.ed.gov/pubs/parents/Reading

A website with suggested strategies and activities for fostering literacy development from infancy through age 10.

The Children's Literature Web Guide
www.acs.ucalgary.ca/~dkbrown

A website that categorizes the growing number of books for children and young adults. Also provides information on authors and illustrators of children's books, and movies and television programs based on children's stories.

PRESCHOOL INTERVENTION

High/Scope Educational Research Foundation
www.highscope.org

An organization devoted to improving development and education from infancy through adolescence. Conducts longitudinal research to determine the effects of early intervention on development.

National Head Start Association
www.nhsa.org

An association of Head Start directors, parents, staff, and others interested in the Head Start program. Works to upgrade the quantity and quality of Head Start services.

CHILD CARE

National Association of Child Care Resource and Referral Agencies
www.naccrra.net

An organization that works for high-quality child care and provides information on available services to parents seeking child care for young children.

National Association of Family Child Care
www.nafcc.org

An organization open to caregivers, parents, and other individuals involved or interested in child-care homes. Serves as a national voice that promotes high-quality home child care.

National Network for Child Care
www.nncc.org

An organization that offers extensive information on child care and child development, communication with others concerned about child-care quality, and newsletters for center-based, home-based, and school-age child-care providers.

"I Listen to the Birds Singing under the Tree"

Cui Tao Ren

7 years, China

This scene of young children engaged in joint outdoor play depicts the expanding peer activities and first friendships of early childhood. Chapter 10 describes these emotional and social capacities.

Emotional and Social Development in Early Childhood

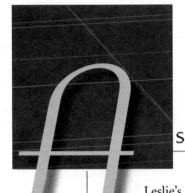

s the children in Leslie's classroom moved through the preschool years, their personalities took on clearer definition. By age 3, they voiced firm likes and dislikes as well as new ideas about themselves. "Stop bothering me," Sammy said to Mark, who tried to reach for Sammy's beanbag as Sammy aimed it toward the mouth of a large clown face. "See, I'm great at this game," Sammy announced with confidence, an attitude that kept him trying, even though most of his throws missed the target.

The children's conversations also revealed their first notions about morality. Often they combined statements about right and wrong they had heard from adults with forceful attempts to defend their own desires. "You're 'posed to take turns and share," stated Mark while he grabbed Sammy's beanbag.

"I was here first! Gimme it back," demanded Sammy, who pushed Mark while reaching for the beanbag. The two boys continued to struggle until Leslie intervened, provided an extra set of beanbags, and showed them how they could both play.

As Sammy and Mark's interaction reveals, preschoolers quickly become complex social beings. Although arguments and aggression take place among all young children, cooperative exchanges are far more frequent. Between the years of 2 and 6, first friendships form, in which children converse, act out complementary roles, and learn that their own desires for companionship and toys are best met when they consider the needs and interests of others.

The children's play highlighted their developing understanding of their social world. This was especially apparent in the attention they gave the dividing line between male and female. While Lynette and Karen cared for a sick baby doll in the housekeeping area, Sammy, Vance, and Mark transformed the block corner into a busy intersection. "Green light, go!" shouted police officer Sammy as Vance and Mark pushed large wooden cars and trucks across the floor. Already, the children preferred same-sex peers, and their play themes mirrored the gender stereotypes of their cultural community.

This chapter is devoted to the many facets of emotional and social development in early childhood. The theory of Erik Erikson provides an overview of personality change during the preschool years. Then we consider children's concepts of themselves, their insights into their social and moral worlds, their gender typing, and their increasing ability to manage their emotional and social behaviors. In the final sections of this chapter, we answer the question, What is effective child rearing? We also consider the complex conditions that support good parenting or lead it to break down. Today, child abuse and neglect are serious, widespread problems.

Erikson's Theory: Initiative versus Guilt

Erikson (1950) described early childhood as a period of "vigorous unfolding." Once children have a sense of autonomy and feel secure about separating from parents, they become more relaxed and less contrary than they were as toddlers. Their energies are freed for tackling the critical psychological conflict of the preschool years: **initiative versus guilt.** The word *initiative* means spirited, enterprising, and ambitious. It suggests that the young child has a new sense of purposefulness. Preschoolers are eager to tackle new tasks, join in activities with peers, and discover what they can do with the help of adults.

Erikson regarded play as a central means through which young children find out about themselves and their social world. Play permits preschoolers to try new skills with little risk of criticism and failure. It also creates a small social organization of children who must cooperate to achieve common goals. Around the world, children act out family scenes and highly visible occupations—police officer, doctor, and nurse in our society; rabbit hunter and potter among the Hopi Indians; and hut builder and spear maker among the Baka of West Africa (Roopnarine et al., 1998).

Recall that Erikson's theory builds on Freud's psychosexual stages (see Chapter 1, page 16, to review). In Freud's well-known Oedipus and Electra conflicts, to avoid punishment and maintain parental affection, preschoolers form a superego, or conscience, by *identifying* with the same-sex parent. That is, they take the parent's characteristics into their personality, and, as a result, adopt the moral and gender-role standards of their society. Each time the child disobeys standards of conscience, painful feelings of guilt occur.

For Erikson, the negative outcome of early childhood is an overly strict superego, one that causes children to feel too much guilt because they have been threatened, criticized, and punished excessively by adults. When this happens, preschoolers' exuberant play and bold efforts to master new tasks break down.

Although Freud's Oedipus and Electra conflicts are no longer accepted as satisfactory explanations of conscience development, Erikson's image of initiative

[handwritten note:] preschoolers form a superego by identifying w/same-sex parent.

As this Mexican Indian folk healer administers herbal remedies to a patient, the healer's grandchildren watch and play at the art of healing. By acting out highly visible occupations in their culture during play, children acquire insight into what they can do and develop a sense of initiative.

captures diverse changes in young children's emotional and social lives. The preschool years are, indeed, a time when children develop a confident self-image, more effective control over emotions, new social skills, the foundations of morality, and a clear sense of themselves as boy or girl. Now let's take a close look at each of these aspects of development.

Self-Development

Children emerge from toddlerhood with a firm awareness of their separateness from others. During the preschool years, new powers of representation through language enable them to reflect on themselves. Language permits children to talk about the *I-self*—their own subjective experience of being (Harter, 1998). In Chapter 9 we noted that preschoolers acquire a vocabulary for talking about their inner mental lives and refine their understanding of mental states. As the I-self becomes more firmly established, children focus more intently on the *me-self*—knowledge and evaluation of the self's characteristics. They start to develop a **self-concept,** the set of attributes, abilities, attitudes, and values that an individual believes defines who he or she is. Let's see what children's earliest self-descriptions are like.

© LAURA DWIGHT

A firmer sense of self permits young children to cooperate in solving simple problems. These 3-year-olds work together to sweep up spilled sand in their preschool classroom.

FOUNDATIONS OF SELF-CONCEPT

Ask a 3- to 5-year-old to tell you about him- or herself, and you are likely to hear something like this: "I'm Tommy. See, I got this new red T-shirt. I'm 4 years old. I can brush my teeth, and I can wash my hair all by myself. I have a new Tinkertoy set, and I made this big, big tower." As these statements indicate, preschoolers' self-concepts are very concrete. Usually they mention observable characteristics, such as their name, physical appearance, possessions, and everyday behaviors (Harter, 1996; Watson, 1990).

By age 3½, children also describe themselves in terms of typical emotions and attitudes, as in "I'm happy when I play with my friends" or "I don't like being with grown-ups" (Eder, 1989). This suggests a beginning understanding of their unique psychological characteristics. As further support for this budding grasp of personality, when someone is given a trait label, such as "shy" or "mean," 4-year-olds infer appropriate motives and feelings. For example, they know that a shy person doesn't like to be with unfamiliar people (Heyman & Gelman, 1999). But preschoolers do not refer directly to traits, by making such statements as "I'm helpful," "I'm shy," or "I'm usually truthful." This capacity must wait for greater cognitive maturity.

In fact, very young preschoolers' concepts of themselves are so bound up with specific possessions and actions that they spend much time asserting their rights to objects, as Sammy did in the beanbag incident at the beginning of this chapter. The stronger the child's self-definition, the more possessive he or she tends to be about objects (Levine, 1983). Rather than a sign of selfishness, early struggles over objects seem to be a sign of developing selfhood, an effort to clearly mark off boundaries between self and others.

A firmer sense of self also permits children to cooperate in resolving disputes over objects, in playing games, and in solving problems (Brownell & Carriger, 1990; Caplan et al., 1991). Accordingly, when trying to promote friendly peer interaction, parents and teachers can accept the young child's possessiveness as a sign of self-assertion ("Yes, that's your toy") and then encourage compromise ("but in a little while, can you give someone else a turn?"), rather than insisting on sharing.

initiative versus guilt
In Erikson's theory, the psychological conflict of early childhood, which is resolved positively through play experiences that foster a healthy sense of initiative and through development of a superego, or conscience, that is not overly strict and guilt ridden.

self-concept
The set of attributes, abilities, attitudes, and values that an individual believes defines who he or she is.

Cultural
INFLUENCES

CULTURAL VARIATIONS IN PERSONAL STORYTELLING: IMPLICATIONS FOR EARLY SELF-CONCEPT

Preschoolers of many cultural backgrounds participate in personal storytelling with their parents. Striking cultural differences exist in parents' selection and interpretation of events in these early narratives, affecting the way children come to view themselves.

In ethnographic research, Peggy Miller and her colleagues spent hundreds of hours over a 2-year period studying the storytelling practices of six middle-SES Irish-American families in Chicago and six middle-SES Chinese families in Taiwan. From extensive videotapes of adults' conversations with 2½-year-olds, the researchers identified personal stories and coded them for content, quality of their endings, and evaluation of the child (Miller, Fung, & Mintz, 1996; Miller et al., 1997).

Parents in both cultures discussed pleasurable holidays and family excursions about as often and in similar ways. Chinese parents, however, more often told lengthy stories about the child's misdeeds, such as using impolite language, writing on the wall, or playing in an overly rowdy way. These narratives were conveyed with warmth and caring, stressed the impact of misbehavior on others ("You made Mama lose face"), and often ended with direct teaching of proper behavior ("Saying dirty words is not good"). In the few instances in which Irish-American stories referred to transgressions, parents downplayed their seriousness, attributing them to the child's spunk and assertiveness.

Early narratives about the child seem to launch preschoolers' self-concepts on culturally distinct paths. Influenced by Confucian traditions of strict discipline and social obligations, Chinese parents integrated these values into their personal stories, affirming the importance of not disgracing the family and explicitly teaching proper behavior in the story's conclusion. Although Irish-American parents disciplined their children, they rarely dwelt on misdeeds in storytelling. Rather, they cast the child's shortcomings in a positive light, perhaps to encourage a positive sense of self. Hence, the Chinese child's self-image emphasizes obligations to others, whereas the American child's is more autonomous (Markus, Mullally, & Kitayama, 1997).

This Chinese child on an outing with her mother was about to eat a sweet treat she had been told to save until later. Her mother stops the bike and speaks gently to her. Chinese parents often tell preschoolers stories about the child's misdeeds, emphasizing their negative impact on others. The Chinese child's self-concept, in turn, emphasizes social obligations.

© OWEN FRANKLIN/STOCK BOSTON

In Chapters 6 and 9 we noted that adult–child conversations about the past contribute to development of an autobiographical memory. Parents often use these discussions to impart evaluative information about the child, as when they say, "You were a big boy when you did that!" Consequently, they serve as a rich source of early self-knowledge and, as the Cultural Influences box above reveals, as a major means through which the young child's self-concept is imbued with cultural values.

UNDERSTANDING INTENTIONS

As children learn more about themselves by reflecting on their own behavior, they distinguish actions that are intentional from those that are accidental. By age 2, preschoolers already say "gonna," "hafta," and "wanna" to announce actions they are about to perform. Soon they use this grasp of purposefulness to defend themselves. After being scolded for bumping into a playmate or spilling a glass of milk, they often exclaim, "It was an accident!" or "I didn't do it on purpose!"

By 2½ to 3 years, this understanding extends to others. Preschoolers sense when another person is acting intentionally. At first, they focus on the person's statements. If a person says he is going to do something and then does it, 3-year-olds judge the behavior as deliberate. (Astington, 1993).

Around age 4, children start to understand intention as a mental state that guides but can be distinguished from behavior. Consequently, they realize that a desired outcome can be reached intentionally or accidentally. In one study, preschoolers heard two stories. In one, a girl threw bread crumbs, and birds ate them. In the other, a girl accidentally dropped bread crumbs, and birds ate them. When asked which girl meant for the birds to eat the crumbs, 3-year-olds were equally likely to choose either girl. In contrast, 4- and 5-year-olds correctly chose the first girl (Astington, 1991).

By the end of the preschool years, children use a much wider range of information to judge intentionality. For example, 5-year-olds note whether a person is concentrating on what she is doing, whether her action leads to positive or negative outcomes (negative ones are usually not intended), and whether the person has the necessary knowledge to intend the behavior (Joseph & Tager-Flusberg, 1999; Smith, 1978).

How do preschoolers acquire these understandings? Conversations in which adults and peers clarify their intentions, using such terms as "tries to" and "means to," are important (Astington, 1999). Also, over time, preschoolers probably notice that their own thoughts and feelings are very different when they intend to do something than when they do not (Flavell & Miller, 1998).

EMERGENCE OF SELF-ESTEEM

Another aspect of self-concept emerges in early childhood: **self-esteem,** the judgments we make about our own worth and the feelings associated with those judgments. Self-esteem ranks among the most important aspects of self-development, since evaluations of our own competencies affect emotional experiences, future behavior, and long-term psychological adjustment. Take a moment to think about your own self-esteem. Besides a global appraisal of your worth as a person, you have a variety of separate self-judgments. For example, you may regard yourself as very good at schoolwork and getting along with others but only so-so at sports.

By age 4, preschoolers have several self-esteems, such as learning things well in school, trying hard at challenging tasks, making friends, and treating others kindly (Marsh, Craven, & Debus, 1998). However, their understanding is not as differentiated as that of older children. And when asked how well they can do something, they usually rate their own ability as extremely high and often underestimate task difficulty (Harter, 1990, 1998). Sammy's announcement that he was great at beanbag throwing despite his many misses is a typical self-evaluation during early childhood.

High self-esteem contributes greatly to preschoolers' initiative during a period in which they must master many new skills. Nevertheless, by age 4, some children give up easily when faced with a challenge, such as working a hard puzzle or building a tall block tower. They are discouraged after failure and conclude that they cannot do the task (Cain & Dweck, 1995; Smiley & Dweck, 1994). When these young nonpersisters are asked to act out with dolls an adult's reaction to failure, they often respond, "He's punished because he can't do the puzzle" or "Daddy's mad and is going to spank her" (Burhans & Dweck, 1995). They also are likely to report that their parents would berate them for making small mistakes (Heyman, Dweck, & Cain, 1992). The Caregiving Concerns table on page 370 suggests ways to avoid these self-defeating reactions and foster a healthy self-image in young children.

High self-esteem contributes greatly to preschoolers' enthusiasm for mastering many new skills. This boy's belief in his ability to master riding a bike is supported by his mother's patience and encouragement.

[handwritten margin note: preschoolers acquire understanding of intention via: ① convos w/ adults ② self-realization that their intentions are different from their behavior.]

self-esteem
The aspect of self-concept that involves judgments about one's own worth and the feelings associated with those judgments.

Caregiving Concerns

Fostering a Healthy Self-Image in Young Children

SUGGESTION	DESCRIPTION
Build a positive relationship.	Indicate that you want to be with the child by arranging times to be fully available. Listen without being judgmental, and express some of your own thoughts and feelings. Mutual sharing helps children feel valued.
Nurture success.	Adjust expectations appropriately, and provide assistance when asking the child to do something beyond his or her current limits. Accentuate the positive in the child's work or behavior. Promote self-motivation by emphasizing praise over concrete rewards. Instead of simply saying, "That's good," mention effort and specific accomplishments. Display the child's artwork and other products, pointing out increasing skill.
Foster the freedom to choose.	Choosing gives children a sense of responsibility and control over their own lives. Where children are not yet capable of deciding on their own, involve them in some aspect of the choice, such as when and in what order a task will be done.
Acknowledge the child's emotions.	Accept the child's strong feelings, and suggest constructive ways to handle them. When a child's negative emotion results from an affront to his or her self-esteem, offer sympathy and comfort along with a realistic appraisal of the situation so the child feels supported and secure.
Use a warm, rational approach to child rearing.	The strategies discussed on pages 380 and 397 (induction and authoritative child rearing) promote self-confidence and self-control.

Ask YOURSELF...

apply   Reread the description of Sammy and Mark's argument at the beginning of this chapter. On the basis of what you know about self-development, why was it a good idea for Leslie to resolve the dispute by providing an extra set of beanbags so that both boys could play at once?

connect   Around age 4, children understand intention as a mental state. How is this advance similar to children's mastery of false belief (see Chapter 9, page 344)? Are experiences that promote understanding of intention similar to those that foster a grasp of false belief? Explain.

emotional development is supported by:
① gains in mental rep.
② language
③ self-concept

Emotional Development

ains in mental representation, language, and self-concept support emotional development in early childhood. Between the ages of 2 and 6, children better understand their own and others' feelings, and they can better regulate the expression of emotion. Self-development also contributes to a rise in *self-conscious emotions*—shame, embarrassment, guilt, envy, and pride.

UNDERSTANDING EMOTION

Preschoolers' vocabulary for talking about emotion expands rapidly, and they use it skillfully to reflect on their own and others' behavior. Here are some excerpts from conversations in which 2-year-olds and 6-year-olds commented on emotionally charged experiences:

> *Two-year-old: (After father shouted at child, she became angry, shouting back)* "I'm mad at you, Daddy. I'm going away. Good-bye."

Two-year-old: (Commenting on another child who refused to nap and cried) "Mom, Annie cry. Annie sad."

Six-year-old: (In response to mother's comment, "It's hard to hear the baby crying") "Well, it's not as hard for me as it is for you." *(When mother asked why)* "Well, you like Johnny better than I do! I like him a little, and you like him a lot, so I think it's harder for you to hear him cry."

Six-year-old: (Trying to comfort a small boy in church whose mother had gone up to communion) "Aw, that's all right. She'll be right back. Don't be afraid. I'm here." (Bretherton et al., 1986, pp. 536, 540, 541)

■ **COGNITIVE DEVELOPMENT AND EMOTIONAL UNDERSTANDING.** As the examples just given show, early in the preschool years, children refer to causes, consequences, and behavioral signs of emotion, and over time their understanding becomes more accurate and complex (Stein & Levine, 1999). By age 4 to 5, children correctly judge the causes of many basic emotional reactions. When asked why a nearby playmate is happy, sad, or angry, they describe events similar to those identified by adults, such as "He's happy because he's swinging very high" or "He's sad because he misses his mother." However, they are likely to emphasize external factors over internal states as explanations—a balance that changes with age (Fabes et al., 1991; Levine, 1995).

Preschoolers are also good at predicting what a playmate expressing a certain emotion might do next. Four-year-olds know that an angry child might hit someone and that a happy child is more likely to share (Russell, 1990). And they realize that thinking and feeling are interconnected—that a person reminded of a previous sad experience is likely to feel sad (Lagattuta, Wellman, & Flavell, 1997). Furthermore, they come up with effective ways to relieve others' negative feelings, such as hugging to reduce sadness (Fabes et al., 1988). Overall, preschoolers have an impressive ability to interpret, predict, and change others' feelings.

At the same time, in situations with conflicting cues about how a person is feeling, preschoolers have difficulty making sense of what is going on. For example, when asked what might be happening in a picture showing a happy-faced child with a broken bicycle, 4- and 5-year-olds tended to rely only on the emotional expression ("He's happy because he likes to ride his bike"). Older children more often reconciled the two cues ("He's happy because his father promised to help fix his broken bike") (Gnepp, 1983). Also, preschoolers do not realize that people can experience more than one emotion at a time—that they can have "mixed feelings" (Wintre & Vallance, 1994). As in their approach to Piagetian tasks, young children focus on the most obvious aspect of a complex emotional situation to the neglect of other relevant information.

■ **SOCIAL EXPERIENCE AND EMOTIONAL UNDERSTANDING.** Although cognitive development leads to gains in emotional understanding, social experience also contributes. The more mothers label emotions and explain them in conversing with preschoolers, the more emotion words children use in these discussions. Maternal prompting of emotional thoughts, as in "What makes him afraid?" is a good predictor of 2-year-olds' emotion language. Explanations—"He's sad because his dog ran away"—are more important for older preschoolers (Cervantes & Callanan, 1998). Does this remind you of the concept of *scaffolding*—that to be effective, adult teaching must adjust to children's increasing competence?

Preschoolers growing up in families that frequently talk about feelings are better at judging the emotions of others when tested at later ages (Denham, Zoller, & Couchoud, 1994; Dunn, 1999b). Discussions in which family members disagree about their feelings are particularly helpful. These dialogues seem to help children step back from the experience of emotion and reflect on its causes and consequences.

As preschoolers learn more about emotion from conversing with adults, they transfer this knowledge to other contexts, engaging in more emotion talk with siblings and friends, especially during sociodramatic play (Brown, Donelan-McCall, & Dunn, 1996; Hughes & Dunn,

© CREWS/THE IMAGE WORKS

A group of 2-year-olds stop their play at child care to figure out why this baby is crying. During the preschool years, children's grasp of the causes, consequences, and behavioral signs of emotion expands rapidly.

Social experiences also contribute to gains in emotional understanding.

1998). Make-believe, in turn, contributes to emotional understanding, especially when children play with siblings (Youngblade & Dunn, 1995). The intense nature of the sibling relationship, combined with frequent acting out of feelings, makes pretending an excellent context for early learning about emotions.

Emotional knowledge helps children greatly in their efforts to get along with others. As early as 3 to 5 years of age, it is related to friendly, considerate behavior, willingness to make amends after harming another, and peer acceptance (Brown & Dunn, 1996; Dunn, Brown, & Maguire, 1995; Garner, Jones, & Miner, 1994).

EMOTIONAL SELF-REGULATION

Language also contributes to preschoolers' improved emotional *self-regulation,* or ability to control the expression of emotion. By age 3 to 4, children verbalize a variety of strategies for adjusting their emotional arousal to a more comfortable level. For example, they know that emotions can be blunted by restricting sensory input (covering your eyes or ears to block out a scary sight or sound), talking to yourself ("Mommy said she'll be back soon"), or changing your goals (deciding that you don't want to play anyway after being excluded from a game) (Thompson, 1990a).

Children's increasing awareness and use of these strategies means that emotional outbursts become less frequent over the preschool years. In fact, by age 3, children can even pose an emotion they do not feel and have begun to realize when others might be hiding their true feelings (Denham, 1998). These emotional "masks" are largely limited to the positive feelings of happiness and surprise. Children of all ages (and adults as well) find it more difficult to act sad, angry, or disgusted than pleased (Lewis, Sullivan, & Vasen, 1987). To promote good social relations, most cultures encourage their members to communicate positive feelings and inhibit unpleasant ones, and young children try hard to conform to this rule.

Temperament affects the development of emotional self-regulation. Children who experience negative emotion very intensely have greater difficulty inhibiting their feelings and shifting their focus of attention away from disturbing events. As early as the preschool years, they are more likely to respond with irritation to others' distress, get along poorly with peers, and have few or no friends (Eisenberg et al., 1997; Fabes et al., 1999; Walden, Lemerise, & Smith, 1999).

If emotionally reactive children are to avoid social difficulties, they must develop effective emotion-regulation strategies (Eisenberg, 1998b). Adult behavior powerfully affects their capacity to cope with stress. By watching parents handle their own feelings, children pick up strategies for regulating emotion. When parents have difficulty controlling anger and hostility, particularly when reacting to their preschooler's negative emotions, children have continuing problems with regulating emotion that seriously interfere with psychological adjustment (Eisenberg et al., 1999).

Adults' conversations with children also provide techniques for regulating feelings. Parents who prepare children for difficult experiences by describing what to expect and ways to handle anxiety offer coping strategies that children can apply. Preschoolers' vivid imaginations combined with their difficulty in separating appearance from reality make fears common in early childhood. The Caregiving Concerns table on the following page lists ways that parents can help young children manage them.

SELF-CONSCIOUS EMOTIONS

One morning in Leslie's classroom, a group of children crowded around for a bread-baking activity. Leslie asked them to wait patiently while she got a baking pan. In the meantime, Sammy reached to feel the dough, but the bowl tumbled over the side of the table. When Leslie returned, Sammy looked at her for a moment, covered his eyes with his hands, and said, "I did something bad." He was feeling ashamed and guilty.

As children's self-concepts become better developed, they become increasingly sensitive to praise and blame or (as in Sammy's case) the possibility of such feedback. As a result, they

Caregiving Concerns

Helping Children Manage Common Fears of Early Childhood

FEAR	SUGGESTION
Monsters, ghosts, and darkness	Reduce exposure to frightening stories in books and on TV until the child is better able to sort out appearance from reality. Make a thorough "search" of the child's room for monsters, showing him that none are there. Leave a night-light burning, sit by the child's bed until he falls asleep, and tuck in a favorite toy for protection.
Preschool or child care	If the child resists going to preschool but seems content once there, then the fear is probably separation. Under these circumstances, provide a sense of warmth and caring while gently encouraging independence. If the child fears being at preschool, try to find out what is frightening—the teacher, the children, or perhaps a crowded, noisy environment. Provide extra support by accompanying the child at the beginning and lessening the amount of time you are present.
Animals	Do not force the child to approach a dog, cat, or other animal that arouses fear. Let the child move at her own pace. Demonstrate how to hold and pet the animal, showing the child that when treated gently, the animal reacts in a friendly way. If the child is bigger than the animal, emphasize this: "You're so big. That kitty is probably afraid of *you*!"
Very intense fears	If a child's fear is very intense, persists for a long time, interferes with daily activities, and cannot be reduced in any of the ways just suggested, it has reached the level of a *phobia*. Sometimes phobias are linked to family problems, and special counseling is needed to reduce them. At other times, phobias diminish without treatment.

experience *self-conscious emotions* more often—feelings that involve injury to or enhancement of their sense of self (see Chapter 7). By age 3, self-conscious emotions are clearly linked to self-evaluation (Lewis, 1995a; Lewis, Alessandri, & Sullivan, 1992).

Nevertheless, since preschoolers are still developing standards of excellence and conduct, they depend on adults' messages to know when to feel self-conscious emotions (Stipek, 1995). Parents who repeatedly give feedback about the worth of the child and her performance ("That's a bad job! I thought you were a good girl") have children who experience self-conscious emotions intensely—more shame after failure and pride after success. In contrast, parents who focus on how to improve performance ("You did it this way; you should have done it that way") induce moderate, more adaptive levels of shame and pride (Lewis, 1998).

Beginning in early childhood, intense shame is associated with feelings of personal inadequacy ("I'm stupid," "I'm a terrible person") and is linked to maladjustment—withdrawal and depression as well as aggression. In contrast, guilt—as long as it occurs in appropriate circumstances and shame does not accompany it—is related to good adjustment, perhaps because guilt helps children resist expressing harmful impulses. And when children do transgress, guilt motivates them to repair the damage and behave more considerately in the future (Ferguson et al., 1999; Tangney, 1998).

EMPATHY AND SYMPATHY

Another emotional capacity—*empathy*—becomes more common in early childhood. It continues to serve as an important motivator of **prosocial, or altruistic, behavior**—actions that benefit another person without any expected reward for the self (Eisenberg & Fabes, 1998). Compared with toddlers, preschoolers rely more on words than gestures to console others, a change that indicates a more reflective level of empathy. When a 6-year-old noticed that his mother was distressed at not being able to find a motel after a long day's travel, he said, "You're pretty upset, aren't you, Mom? You're pretty sad. Well, I think, it's going to be all right. I think we'll find a nice place and it'll be all right" (Bretherton et al., 1986, p. 540). As children can better take the perspective of others, empathic responding increases.

prosocial, or altruistic, behavior
Actions that benefit another person without any expected reward for the self.

ROBERT VAN DER HILST/STONE

During a field trip to the seashore with her preschool classmates, this Australian 3-year-old bursts into tears, and her friend offers comfort. As young children's language skills expand and their ability to take the perspective of others improves, empathy increases and becomes an important motivator of pro-social, or altruistic, behavior.

sympathy
Feelings of concern or sorrow for another's plight.

Yet empathy, or feeling with another person and responding emotionally in a similar way, does not always yield acts of kindness and helpfulness. In some children, empathizing with an upset adult or peer escalates into personal distress. In trying to reduce these feelings, the child focuses on himself rather than the person in need. As a result, empathy does not give way to **sympathy**—feelings of concern or sorrow for another's plight.

Whether empathy prompts sympathetic, prosocial behavior or a personally distressed, self-focused response is related to both temperament and early experience. Children who are sociable, assertive, and good at regulating emotion are more likely to help, share, and comfort others in distress. In contrast, children who are poor emotion regulators less often display sympathetic concern and prosocial behavior (Eisenberg et al., 1992, 1996, 1998).

These differences are evident in children's facial and psychophysiological responses to situations that call for empathy. In a series of studies, researchers showed children videotapes of people in need, such as two children who had fallen from a playground climber and were lying on the ground crying. Children who reacted with facial or physiological markers of empathy—either a concerned expression or a decrease in heart rate, suggesting orienting and attention—usually behaved prosocially when offered a chance to help. Those who showed facial and physiological distress—frowning, lip biting, and a rise in heart rate—were less prosocial (Fabes et al., 1994; Miller et al., 1996).

Recall that parenting influences emotional self-regulation, and it affects empathy and sympathy as well. Parents who are warm and encouraging and show a sensitive, sympathetic concern for their preschoolers have children who are likely to react in a concerned way to the distress of others—relationships that persist into adolescence and young adulthood (Eisenberg & McNally, 1993; Koestner, Franz, & Weinberger, 1990). Besides modeling sympathy, teaching children the importance of kindness and intervening when they display inappropriate emotion predict high levels of sympathetic responding (Eisenberg et al., 1991; Zahn-Waxler & Radke-Yarrow, 1990).

In contrast, angry, punitive parenting disrupts the development of empathy at an early age. In one study, researchers observed physically abused preschoolers at a child-care center to see how they reacted to other children's distress. Compared with nonabused agemates, they rarely showed any signs of empathy. Instead, they responded with fear, anger, and physical attacks (Klimes-Dougan & Kistner, 1990). The children's reactions resembled the behavior of their parents, since both responded insensitively to the suffering of others.

Ask YOURSELF...

review   *What do preschoolers understand about emotion, and how do cognition and social experience contribute to their understanding?*

apply   *Four-year-old Tia had just gotten her face painted at a carnival. As she walked around with her mother, the heat of the afternoon caused her balloon to pop. When Tia started to cry, her mother said, "Oh, Tia, balloons aren't such a good idea when it's hot outside. We'll get another on a cooler day. If you cry, you'll mess up your beautiful face painting." What aspect of emotional development is Tia's mother trying to promote, and why is her intervention likely to help Tia?*

connect   *Explain why good emotional self-regulation is vital for empathy to result in sympathetic concern and prosocial behavior. How can parents promote emotional self-regulation, empathy, and sympathy at the same time?*

Peer Relations

As children become increasingly self-aware, more effective at communicating, and better at understanding the thoughts and feelings of others, their skill at interacting with peers improves rapidly. Peers provide young children with learning experiences they can get in no other way. Because peers interact on an equal footing, they must assume responsibility for keeping a conversation going and setting goals and cooperating in play. With peers, children form friendships—special relationships marked by attachment and common interests. Let's look at how peer interaction changes over the preschool years.

ADVANCES IN PEER SOCIABILITY

Mildred Parten (1932), one of the first to study peer sociability among 2- to 5-year-olds, noticed a dramatic rise with age in the ability to engage in joint, interactive play. She concluded that social development proceeds in a three-step sequence. It begins with **nonsocial activity**—unoccupied, onlooker behavior and solitary play. Then it shifts to a limited form of social participation called **parallel play,** in which a child plays near other children with similar materials but does not try to influence their behavior. At the highest level, preschoolers engage in two forms of true social interaction. One is **associative play,** in which children engage in separate activities, but they interact by exchanging toys and commenting on one another's behavior. The other is **cooperative play**—a more advanced type of interaction in which children orient toward a common goal, such as acting out a make-believe theme or working on the same product, such as a sand castle or painting.

■RECENT EVIDENCE ON PEER INTERACTION. Find a time to observe young children of varying ages, and note how long they spend in each of these types of play. You will probably discover that the play forms just described emerge in the order suggested by Parten, but they do not form a neat, developmental sequence in which later-appearing ones replace earlier ones (Howes & Matheson, 1992). Instead, all types coexist during the preschool years. Furthermore, although nonsocial activity declines with age, it is still the most frequent form of behavior among 3- to 4-year-olds. Even among kindergartners it continues to take up as much as a third of children's free-play time. Also, solitary and parallel play remain fairly stable from 3 to 6 years, accounting for as much of the young child's play as highly social, cooperative interaction.

We now understand that it is the *type,* rather than the amount, of solitary and parallel play that changes during early childhood. In studies of preschoolers' play in Taiwan and the United States, researchers rated the *cognitive maturity* of nonsocial, parallel, and cooperative play by applying the categories shown in Table 10.1 on page 376. Within each of Parten's play types, 5-year-olds engaged in more cognitively mature behavior than did 4-year-olds (Pan, 1994; Rubin, Watson, & Jambor, 1978).

Often parents wonder if a preschooler who spends large amounts of time playing alone is developing normally. Only *certain types* of nonsocial activity—aimless wandering, hovering near peers, and functional play involving immature, repetitive motor action—are cause for concern. Children who behave in these ways are usually temperamentally inhibited, anxious preschoolers who have not learned to regulate their high social fearfulness (Coplan et al., 1994; Rubin & Coplan, 1998). Often they depend too much on teachers, clinging and asking for help when they do not need it (Birch & Ladd, 1998).

But not all preschoolers with low rates of peer interaction are socially anxious. To the contrary, most like to play by themselves, and their solitary activities are positive and constructive. Teachers encourage such play when they set out art materials, books, puzzles, and building

GEORGE GOODWIN/MONKMEYER PRESS

These children are engaged in parallel play. Although they sit side by side and use similar materials, they do not try to influence one another's behavior. Parallel play remains frequent and stable over the preschool years, accounting for about one-fifth of children's play time.

nonsocial activity
Unoccupied, onlooker behavior and solitary play.

parallel play
A form of limited social participation in which the child plays near other children with similar materials but does not try to influence their behavior.

associative play
A form of true social participation, in which children are engaged in separate activities, but they interact by exchanging toys and commenting on one another's behavior.

cooperative play
A form of true social participation, in which children orient toward a common goal, such as acting out a make-believe theme or working on the same product.

TABLE 10.1

Developmental Sequence of Cognitive Play Categories

PLAY CATEGORY	DESCRIPTION	EXAMPLES
Functional play	Simple, repetitive motor movements with or without objects. Especially common during the first 2 years of life.	Running around a room, rolling a car back and forth, kneading clay with no intent to make something
Constructive play	Creating or constructing something. Especially common between 3 and 6 years.	Making a house out of toy blocks, drawing a picture, putting together a puzzle
Make-believe play	Acting out everyday and imaginary roles. Especially common between 2 and 6 years.	Playing house, school, or police officer; acting out storybook or television characters

Source: Rubin, Fein, & Vandenberg, 1983.

JEFF GREENBERG/PHOTOEDIT

These Chinese girls demonstrate an intricate hand-clapping game in which they must respond quickly and in unison. Preschoolers in the People's Republic of China frequently perform such games for classmates and parents. Their play reflects the value their culture places on group harmony.

toys. Preschoolers who spend much time at these activities are not maladjusted (Rubin et al., 1995). Instead, they are bright children who, when they do play with peers, display socially skilled behavior.

As noted in Chapter 9, *sociodramatic play* becomes especially common during the preschool years. It supports both cognitive and social development. In joint make-believe, preschoolers act out and respond to one another's pretend feelings. They also explore and gain control of fear-arousing experiences when they play doctor or pretend to search for monsters in a magical forest. As a result, they are better able to understand others' feelings and regulate their own. Finally, to create and manage complex plots, preschoolers must resolve their disputes through negotiation—experiences that contribute greatly to their ability to get along with others (Garvey, 1990; Howes, 1992).

■ **CULTURAL VARIATIONS.** Peer sociability in collectivist societies, which stress group harmony, differs from that in Western individualistic cultures. For example, children in India generally play in large groups that require high levels of cooperation. Much of their behavior during sociodramatic play and early games is imitative, occurs in unison, and involves close physical contact. In a game called Atiya Piatiya, children sit in a circle, join hands, and swing while they recite a jingle. In Bhatto Bhatto, they act out a script about a trip to the market, touching each other's elbows and hands as they pretend to cut and share a tasty vegetable (Roopnarine et al., 1994).

Cultural beliefs about the importance of play also affect early peer associations. Caregivers who view play as mere entertainment are less likely to provide props and encourage pretend than are those who value its cognitive and social benefits (Farver & Wimbarti, 1995). Korean-American parents, who emphasize task persistence as the means to academic success, have preschoolers who spend less time at joint make-believe and more time unoccupied and in parallel play than do their Caucasian-American counterparts. (Farver, Kim, & Lee, 1995).

Return to the description of Yucatec Mayan preschoolers' pretending on page 340 of Chapter 9. Mayan parents do not promote children's play, and when it interferes with important cultural activities, they discourage it. Yet even though they spend little time pretending, Mayan children are socially competent (Gaskins, 1999). Perhaps Western-style sociodramatic play, with its elaborate materials and wide-ranging themes, is particularly important for social development in societies where child and adult worlds are distinct. It may be less crucial when children participate in adult activities from an early age.

FIRST FRIENDSHIPS

As preschoolers interact, first friendships form that serve as important contexts for emotional and social development. Take a moment to jot down what the word *friendship* means to you. You probably thought of a mutual relationship involving companionship, sharing, understanding of thoughts and feelings, and caring for and comforting one another in times of need. In addition, mature friendships endure over time and survive occasional conflicts.

Preschoolers understand something about the uniqueness of friendship. They know that a friend is someone "who likes you" and with whom you spend a lot of time playing (Youniss, 1980). Yet their ideas about friendship are far from mature. We have already seen that young children typically describe themselves in concrete, activity-based terms. Their notion of friendship is much the same. Four- to 7-year-olds regard friendship as pleasurable play and sharing of toys. As yet, friendship does not have a long-term, enduring quality based on mutual trust (Selman, 1980). Indeed, Sammy declared, "Mark's my best friend" on days when the boys got along well. But he would state just the opposite—"Mark, you're not my friend!"—when a dispute was not quickly settled.

Nevertheless, interactions between young friends are unique. Preschoolers give twice as much reinforcement—greetings, praise, and compliance—to children they identify as friends, and they also receive more from them. Friends are also more emotionally expressive, talking, laughing, and looking at each other more than nonfriends (Hartup, 1999). Furthermore, early childhood friendships offer social support. When children begin kindergarten with friends from preschool in their class, they adjust to school more favorably (Ladd & Price, 1987). Perhaps the company of friends serves as a secure base from which to develop new relationships, enhancing children's feelings of comfort in the new classroom.

The extent to which kindergartners make new friends and are accepted by their classmates predicts cooperative participation in classroom activities and self-directed completion of learning tasks. These behaviors, in turn, are related to gains in achievement over the kindergarten year (Ladd, Birch, & Buhs, 1999; Ladd, Kochenderfer, & Coleman, 1997). As kindergartners forge new friendships, they seem to integrate themselves into the learning environment in ways that foster academic competence.

SOCIAL PROBLEM SOLVING

Children, even when they are best friends, sometimes come into conflict. Yet even preschoolers seem to handle most quarrels constructively, and only rarely do their disagreements result in hostile encounters. Although friends get into more conflicts than other peers do, they are more likely to work out their differences (Hartup & Laursen, 1991). Overall, conflicts are not very frequent when compared with children's friendly, cooperative interactions.

Nevertheless, peer conflicts are important. Watch children engage in disputes over play objects ("That's mine!" "I had it first!"), entry into and control over play activities ("I'm on your team, Jerry." "No, you're not!"), and disagreements over facts, ideas, and beliefs ("I'm taller than he is." "No, you aren't!"). You will see that they take these matters quite seriously. In Chapter 9 we noted that resolution of conflict, rather than conflict per se, promotes development. Social conflicts offer children invaluable learning opportunities for **social problem solving.** In their attempts to resolve conflicts effectively—in ways acceptable to others and beneficial to the self—children must bring together diverse social understandings.

■ **THE SOCIAL PROBLEM-SOLVING PROCESS.** Nicki Crick and Kenneth Dodge (1994) organize the steps of social problem solving into the circular model shown in Figure 10.1 on page 378. Notice how this flowchart takes an information-processing approach, clarifying exactly what a child must do to grapple with a social problem and arrive at a solution. Once this is known, then processing deficits can be identified, and intervention can be tailored to meet children's individual needs.

social problem solving
Resolving social conflicts in ways that are both acceptable to others and beneficial to the self. Involves noticing and accurately interpreting social cues, formulating goals that enhance relationships, generating and evaluating problem-solving strategies, and enacting a response.

[handwritten margin note: RESOLUTION of conflict promotes development]

FIGURE 10.1

An information-processing model of social problem solving. The model is circular, since children often engage in several information-processing activities at once—for example, interpreting information as they notice it and continuing to consider the meaning of another's behavior while they generate and evaluate problem-solving strategies. The model also takes into account the impact of mental state on social information processing—in particular, children's knowledge of social rules, their representations of past social experiences, and their expectations for future experiences. Peer evaluations and responses to enacted strategies are also important factors in social problem solving. (Adapted from N. R. Crick & K. A. Dodge, 1994, "A Review and Reformulation of Social Information-Processing Mechanisms in Children's Social Adjustment," *Psychological Bulletin, 115*, 74–101, Figure 2 (adapted), p. 76. Copyright © 1994 by the American Psychological Association. Adapted by permission.)

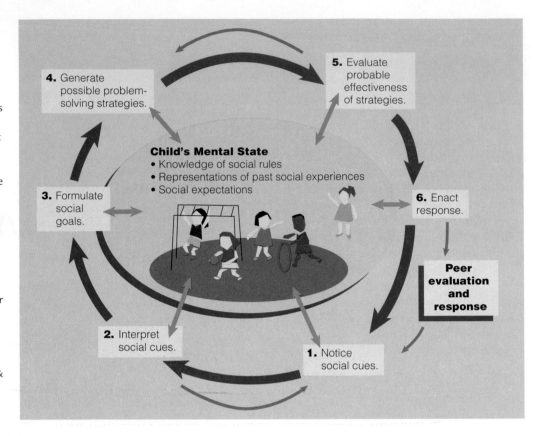

Social problem solving profoundly affects peer relations. Children who get along well with agemates interpret social cues accurately, formulate goals that enhance relationships (being helpful to peers), and have a repertoire of effective problem-solving strategies. For example, they make polite requests to play and ask for an explanation when they do not understand another child's behavior. In contrast, children with peer difficulties often hold biased social expectations. Consequently, they attend selectively to social cues (such as hostile acts) and misinterpret others' behavior (an unintentional jostle as hostile). Their social goals (satisfying an impulse, getting even with or avoiding a peer) often lead to strategies that damage relationships (Crick & Dodge, 1994; Rose & Asher, 1999). They might barge into a play group without asking, use threats and physical force, or fearfully hover around peers' activities.

From the preschool to the early school years, social problem solving improves. Although younger children more often use ineffective strategies, such as grabbing, hitting, or ordering another child to obey, older children are more likely to rely on friendly persuasion and compromise. Sometimes they suggest that a conflict be solved by creating new, mutual goals. In doing so, they recognize that solutions to current problems have an important bearing on the future of the relationship (Downey & Walker, 1989; Yeates, Schultz, & Selman, 1991). By kindergarten to second grade, the accuracy and effectiveness of each component of social problem solving is related to socially competent behavior, such as how effectively children join peer play activities (Dodge et al., 1986).

■ **TRAINING SOCIAL PROBLEM SOLVING.** Intervening with children who have weak social problem-solving skills can enhance development in several ways. Besides improving peer relations, effective social problem solving provides children with a sense of mastery in the face of stressful life events. It reduces the risk of adjustment difficulties in children from low-SES and troubled families (Goodman, Gravitt, & Kaslow, 1995).

In one widely applied social problem-solving training program, preschoolers and kindergartners discuss how to resolve social problems acted out with puppets in daily sessions over several months. In addition, teachers intervene as conflicts arise in the classroom, point out the consequences of children's behavior, and suggest alternative strategies. In several studies, trained children, in contrast to untrained controls, improved in their ability to think about social problems and in teacher-rated adjustment—gains still evident months after the program ended (Shure, 1997).

Practice in enacting responses may strengthen these positive outcomes. Often preschoolers know how to solve a social problem effectively, but they do not apply their knowledge (Rudolph & Heller, 1997). Also, for children who have enacted mal-adaptive responses repeatedly, rehearsal of alternatives may be necessary to overcome their habitual behaviors, change their social expectations, and spark more adaptive social information processing.

PARENTAL INFLUENCES ON EARLY PEER RELATIONS

Outside preschool, child care, and kindergarten, young children are limited in their ability to find playmates. They depend on parents to help them establish rewarding peer associations. Parents who frequently arrange informal peer play activities tend to have preschoolers with larger peer networks and more advanced social skills (Ladd, LeSieur, & Profilet, 1993). In providing opportunities for peer play, parents show children how to initiate their own peer contacts and encourage them to be good "hosts" who are concerned about their playmates' needs.

Parents also influence their children's peer interaction skills by offering advice, guidance, and effective examples of how to act toward others. Parents who phrase their directives positively and politely ("Please . . ." or "Why don't you try . . ." instead of "Don't" or "No, you can't") have preschoolers who are more successful in influencing peers (Kochanska, 1992). And children securely attached to warm, responsive parents, who help them regulate negative emotion and give skillful suggestions about how to solve peer problems, get along especially well with agemates (Gottman, Katz, & Hooven, 1996; Harrist et al., 1994).

Mothers provide most of this verbal advice and coaching, and it is particularly effective with daughters (Mize & Petit, 1997). In contrast, fathers more often influence preschoolers' peer relations through style of parent–child play. Highly involved, emotionally positive, cooperative play between fathers and sons predicts good social skills and favorable peer ties (Pettit et al., 1998). Perhaps such play is particularly effective in helping boys acquire skills for regulating emotion, solving social problems, and sustaining enjoyable play.

As early as the preschool years, some children have great difficulty getting along with age-mates. In Leslie's classroom, Robbie was one of them. Wherever he happened to be, such comments as "Robbie ruined our block tower," and "Robbie hit me for no reason" could be heard. You will learn more about how Robbie's family environment contributed to his problems as we take up moral development in the next section.

© CREWS/THE IMAGE WORKS

Parents influence children's peer interaction skills by offering advice, guidance, and examples of how to behave. This father teaches his 3-year-old son how to offer a present as a guest at a birthday party.

Ask **YOURSELF...**

review Among children who spend much time playing alone, what factors distinguish those who are likely to have adjustment difficulties from those who are well adjusted and socially skilled?

apply Three-year-old Bart lives in the country, with no other preschoolers nearby. His parents wonder whether it is worth driving Bart into town once a week to play with his 3-year-old cousin. What advice would you give Bart's parents, and why?

connect Illustrate the influence of temperament on social problem solving by explaining how an impulsive child and a shy, inhibited child might respond at each social problem-solving step in Figure 10.1 on page 378.

reflect Think back to your earliest friendship. How old were you? What did you and your friend like to do, and how would you describe the quality of your relationship?

Foundations of Morality

Children's morality develops (from external control) to inner standards

Preschoolers' first concepts of morality emerge in interactions with adults and peers. If you watch young children's behavior and listen in on their conversations, you will find many examples of their developing moral sense. By age 2, they often react with alarm to behaviors that are aggressive or that might otherwise harm someone. Soon they comment directly on their own and others' actions: "I naughty. I wrote on the wall" or (after having been hit by another child) "Connie not nice" (Kochanska, Casey, & Fukumoto, 1995).

Throughout the world, adults take note of this budding capacity to distinguish right from wrong and to accommodate the needs of others. Some cultures have special terms for it. The Utku Indians of Hudson Bay say the child develops *ihuma* (reason). The Fijians believe that *vakayalo* (sense) appears. In response, parents hold children more responsible for their behavior (Kagan, 1998). By the end of early childhood, children can state a great many moral rules, such as "You're not supposed to take things without asking" or "Tell the truth!" In addition, they argue over matters of justice, as when they say, "You sat there last time, so it's my turn" or "It's not fair. He got more!"

All theories of moral development recognize that conscience begins to take shape during the preschool years. And most agree on the general direction of moral growth. At first, the child's morality is *externally controlled* by adults. Gradually, it becomes regulated by *inner standards*. That is, truly moral individuals do not do the right thing for the sake of social conformity or when authority figures are around. Instead, they have developed a compassionate concern for others and principles of good conduct, which they follow in a wide variety of situations.

Although points of agreement exist among major theories, so do important differences. Psychoanalytic theory stresses the *emotional side* of conscience development—in particular, identification and guilt as motivators of good conduct. Social learning theory focuses on *moral behavior* and how it is learned through reinforcement and modeling. And the cognitive-developmental perspective emphasizes *thinking*—children's ability to reason about justice and fairness.

THE PSYCHOANALYTIC PERSPECTIVE

From our discussion of psychoanalytic theory earlier in this chapter, you already know something about this approach to moral development. To briefly review, in Freud's Oedipus and Electra conflicts, children desire to possess the parent of the other sex, but they give up this wish because they fear punishment and loss of parental love. Instead, they form a *superego*, or conscience, by *identifying* with the same-sex parent, whose moral standards they adopt. Children obey the superego to avoid *guilt*, a painful emotion that arises each time they are tempted to misbehave. According to Freud, moral development is largely complete by 5 to 6 years of age.

Today, most researchers disagree with Freud's account of conscience development. Notice how fear of punishment and loss of parental love are assumed to motivate young children to behave morally (Tellings, 1999). Yet children whose parents frequently use threats, commands, or physical force usually feel little guilt after harming others. In the case of love withdrawal—for example, when a parent refuses to speak to or actually states a dislike for the child—children often respond with high levels of self-blame after misbehaving. They might think to themselves, "I'm no good, and nobody loves me." Eventually, these children may protect themselves from overwhelming feelings of guilt by denying the emotion when they do something wrong. So they, too, develop a weak conscience (Kochanska, 1991; Zahn-Waxler et al., 1990b).

■ **THE POWER OF INDUCTIVE DISCIPLINE.** In contrast, a special type of discipline called **induction** supports conscience formation. It involves pointing out the effects of the child's misbehavior on others, noting especially others' distress and making clear that the child caused it. For example, the parent might say, "She feels so sad because you won't give back her doll" or "If you keep pushing him, he'll fall down and cry" (Hoffman, 2000). Induction works with children as early as 2 years of age. In one study, mothers who used inductive reasoning

induction
A type of discipline in which the effects of the child's misbehavior on others are communicated to the child.

had children who were more likely to make up for their misdeeds. They also showed more prosocial behavior, in that they spontaneously gave hugs, toys, and verbal sympathy to others in distress (Zahn-Waxler, Radke-Yarrow, & King, 1979).

The success of induction may lie in its power to cultivate children's active commitment to moral standards (Turiel, 1998). How does it do so? First, induction tells children how to behave so they can call on this information in future situations. Second, by pointing out the impact of the child's actions on others, parents encourage empathy and sympathetic concern, which motivates prosocial behavior (Krevans & Gibbs, 1996). Third, providing children with reasons for changing their behavior invites them to judge the appropriateness of parental expectations, which fosters adoption of standards because they make sense.

In contrast, discipline that relies too heavily on threats of punishment or love withdrawal produces such high levels of fear and anxiety that children cannot think clearly enough to figure out what they should do. These practices may stop unacceptable behavior temporarily, but they do not get children to internalize moral standards. At times, however, mild warnings and disapproval are necessary to get children to listen to the inductive message.

Although parent–child discipline is vitally important, children's characteristics can affect the success of parenting techniques. Turn to the Biology and Environment box on page 382 for recent findings on temperament and moral internalization.

NANCY SHEEHAN

This teacher uses inductive discipline to explain to a child the impact of her transgression on others. Induction supports conscience development by clarifying how the child should behave, encouraging empathy and sympathetic concern, and permitting the child to grasp reasons behind parental expectations.

■ **THE ROLE OF GUILT.** Although current research offers little support for Freudian ideas about conscience development, Freud was correct that guilt is an important motivator of moral action. Early in the preschool years, guilt reactions are evident, and internalization of the parent's moral voice has begun, as this typical preschooler's statement reveals, "Didn't you hear my mommy? We'd better not play with these toys" (Emde & Buchsbaum, 1990).

Inducing guilt in children by explaining that their behavior is causing pain or distress is a means of influencing them without using coercion. Guilt reactions are associated with stopping harmful actions, repairing damage caused by misdeeds, and engaging in future prosocial behavior—outcomes that maintain close interpersonal ties (Baumeister, 1998). At the same time, parents must help children deal with guilt feelings constructively—by doing one's best to make up for immoral behavior rather than minimizing or excusing it (Bybee, Merisca, & Velasco, 1998).

Finally, contrary to what Freud believed, guilt is not the only force that compels us to act morally. And moral development is not an abrupt event that is virtually complete by the end of early childhood. Instead, it is gradual process, beginning in the preschool years and extending into adulthood.

BEHAVIORISM AND SOCIAL LEARNING THEORY

According to the traditional behaviorist view, *operant conditioning* is an important way in which children pick up new responses. From this perspective, children start to behave in accord with adult moral standards because parents and teachers *reinforce* "good behavior" with approval, affection, and other rewards.

■ **THE IMPORTANCE OF MODELING.** Operant conditioning is not enough for children to acquire moral responses. Recall from Chapter 5 that for a behavior to be reinforced, it must first occur spontaneously. Yet many prosocial behaviors, such as sharing, helping, or comforting an unhappy playmate, do not occur often enough at first for reinforcement to explain their rapid development in early childhood. Instead, social learning theorists

Biology & ENVIRONMENT

TEMPERAMENT AND CONSCIENCE DEVELOPMENT IN YOUNG CHILDREN

When her mother reprimanded her sharply for pouring water on the floor as she played in her bath, 3-year-old Katherine burst into tears. An anxious, sensitive child, Katherine was so distressed that it took her mother 10 minutes to calm her down. Outside in the front yard the next day, Katherine's mother watched as her next-door neighbor patiently asked her 3-year-old son, who was about to pick the first tulips to blossom in the garden, not to touch the flowers. Alex, an active, adventurous child, paid no attention. As he pulled at another tulip, Alex's mother grabbed him, scolded him harshly, and carried him inside. Alex responded by kicking, hitting, and screaming, "Let me down! Let me down!"

What explains Katherine and Alex's very different reactions to firm parental discipline? Grazyna Kochanska (1995) points out that children's biologically based temperaments affect the parenting practices that best promote responsibility and concern for others. She found that for temperamentally inhibited 2- and 3-year-olds, gentle maternal discipline—reasoning, polite requests, suggestions, and distractions—predicted conscience development at age 5, measured in terms of not cheating in some games and completing stories about moral issues with prosocial themes (saying "I'm sorry," not taking someone else's toys, helping a child who is hurt). In contrast, for relatively fearless, impulsive children, mild disciplinary tactics showed no relationship to moral internalization. Instead, a secure attachment bond with the mother predicted a mature conscience (Kochanska, 1997).

According to Kochanska, inhibited children like Katherine, who are prone to anxiety, are easily overcome by intense discipline. Mild, patient tactics are sufficient to motivate them to internalize parental messages. But impulsive children, such as Alex, may not respond to gentle interventions with enough discomfort to promote internalization. Yet frequent use of power-assertive methods is not effective either, since these techniques spark anger and resentment, which interfere with the child's processing of parental messages.

Why does secure attachment predict conscience development in nonanxious children? Kochanska suggests that when children are so low in anxiety that typically effective disciplinary practices fail, a close bond with the caregiver provides an alternative foundation for conscience formation. It motivates children unlikely to experience negative emotion to internalize rules as a means of preserving a spirit of affection and cooperation with the parent.

To foster early moral development, parents must tailor their child-rearing strategies to their child's temperament. In Katherine's case, a soft-spoken correction would probably be effective. For Alex, taking extra steps to build a warm, caring relationship during times when he behaves well is likely to promote moral internalization. In addition, Alex's parents need to use firmer and more frequent discipline than Katherine's do. Without consistent parental controls, children who repeatedly resist parental directives become more unruly with age (Bates et al., 1998). At the same time, emphasizing power assertion is counterproductive for both children. Do these findings remind you of the notion of *goodness of fit,* discussed in Chapter 7? Return to page 268 to review this idea.

---

believe that children largely learn to act morally through *modeling*—by observing and imitating models who demonstrate appropriate behavior (Bandura, 1977; Grusec, 1988). Once children acquire a moral response, such as sharing or telling the truth, reinforcement in the form of praising the act ("That was a very nice thing to do") and the child's character ("You're a very kind and considerate boy") increases its frequency (Mills & Grusec, 1989).

Many studies show that models who behave helpfully or generously increase young children's prosocial responses. The model's characteristics affect children's willingness to imitate in the following ways:

- *Warmth and responsiveness.* Preschoolers are more likely to copy the prosocial actions of an adult who is warm and responsive rather than one who is cold and distant (Yarrow, Scott, & Waxler, 1973). Warmth seems to make children more attentive and receptive to the model, and it is an example of a prosocial response.

- *Competence and power.* Children admire and therefore tend to select competent, powerful models to imitate—the reason they are especially willing to copy the behavior of older peers and adults (Bandura, 1977).

- *Consistency between assertions and behavior.* When models say one thing and do another—for example, announce that "it's important to help others" but rarely engage in helpful acts—children generally choose the most lenient standard of behavior that adults demonstrate (Mischel & Liebert, 1966).

Models exert their most powerful effect during the preschool years. At the end of early childhood, children with a history of consistent exposure to caring adults tend to behave prosocially regardless of whether a model is present. By that time, they have internalized prosocial rules from repeated observations and encouragement by others (Mussen & Eisenberg-Berg, 1977).

■ **EFFECTS OF PUNISHMENT.** Most parents are aware of the limited usefulness of *punishment,* such as scolding, criticism, and spankings, and apply it sparingly. Using sharp reprimands or physical force to restrain or move a child from one place to another is justified when immediate obedience is necessary—for example, when a 3-year-old is about to run into the street. In fact, parents are most likely to use forceful techniques under these conditions. When they are interested in fostering long-term goals, such as acting kindly toward others, they tend to rely on warmth and reasoning (Kuczynski, 1984). Furthermore, parents often combine power assertion with reasoning when children commit very serious transgressions, such as lying or stealing (Grusec & Goodnow, 1994).

Indeed, much research shows that punishment promotes only momentary compliance, not lasting changes in children's behavior. For example, Robbie's parents punished often—spanking, shouting, and criticizing when he did something wrong. Robbie usually stopped misbehaving when his mother and father were around, but he displayed the behavior again as soon as they were out of sight and he thought he could get away with it. As a result, Robbie was especially unmanageable in settings away from home, such as preschool (Strassberg et al., 1994).

Harsh punishment also has undesirable side effects. First, when parents spank, they often do so in response to children's aggression (Holden, Coleman, & Schmidt, 1995). Yet the punishment itself models aggression! Second, children who are frequently punished soon learn to avoid the punishing adult. When Robbie's parents came into the room, Robbie braced himself for something unpleasant and kept his distance. Consequently, they had little opportunity to teach him desirable behaviors. Finally, as punishment "works" to stop children's misbehavior temporarily, it offers immediate relief to adults, and they are reinforced for using coercive discipline. For this reason, a punitive adult is likely to punish with greater frequency over time, a course of action that can spiral into serious abuse.

■ **ALTERNATIVES TO HARSH PUNISHMENT.** Alternatives to criticism, slaps, and spankings can reduce the side effects of punishment. A technique called **time out** involves removing children from the immediate setting—for example, by sending them to their rooms—until they are ready to act appropriately. Time out is useful when a child is out of control and other effective methods of discipline cannot be applied at the moment (Betz, 1994). It usually requires only a few minutes to change behavior, and it also offers a "cooling off" period for angry parents. Another approach is *withdrawal of privileges,* such as playing outside or going to the movies. Removing privileges often generates some resentment in children, but it allows parents to avoid harsh techniques that could easily intensify into violence.

When parents do decide to use punishment, they can increase its effectiveness in several ways:

- *Consistency.* Punishment that is unpredictable is related to especially high rates of disobedience in children. In a study in which researchers had mothers carry on a telephone conversation while their 2-year-olds played, reprimanding half of the children's inappropriate demands for attention ("Please don't interrupt") and giving in to the other half led to a dramatic increase in children's negative emotion and unruly behavior (see Figure 10.2 on page 384) (Acker & O'Leary, 1996). Allowing children to act inappropriately on some occasions but scolding them on others confuses them, and the unacceptable act persists.

- *A warm parent–child relationship.* Children of involved and caring parents find the interruption in parental affection that accompanies punishment to be especially

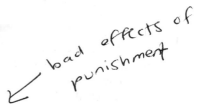

One alternative to harsh punishment is time out, in which children are removed from the immediate setting until they are ready to act appropriately. Time out is useful when a child is out of control and other methods of discipline cannot be applied at the moment. But the best way to motivate good conduct is to let children know ahead of time how to act and praise them when they behave well. Then time out will seldom be necessary.

time out
A form of mild punishment in which children are removed from the immediate setting until they are ready to act appropriately.

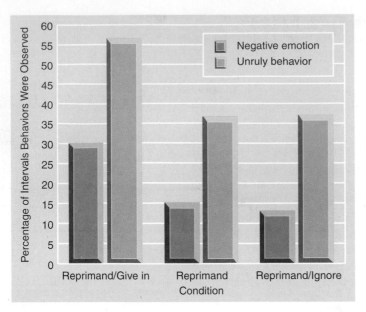

FIGURE 10.2

How does inconsistent punishment affect children's behavior? To find out, researchers conducted an experiment in which they had mothers talk on the telephone while their children played. Mothers in the "reprimand/give in" condition (who reprimanded half of their children's inappropriate demands and gave in to the other half) had children with far higher rates of negative emotion and unruly behavior than did mothers in the "reprimand" condition (who reprimanded every inappropriate demand) and mothers in the "reprimand/ignore" condition (who reprimanded half the inappropriate demands and ignored the other half). (Adapted from Acker & O'Leary, 1996.)

unpleasant. As a result, they want to regain the warmth and approval of parents as quickly as possible.

- *Explanations.* Explanations help children recall the misdeed and relate it to expectations for future behavior. Consequently, pairing reasons with mild punishment (such as time out) leads to a far greater reduction in misbehavior than using punishment alone (Larzelere et al., 1996).

■ **POSITIVE DISCIPLINE.** The most effective forms of discipline encourage good conduct. Instead of waiting for children to misbehave, parents build a positive, cooperative relationship with the child, serve as good examples, let children know ahead of time how to act, and praise them when they behave well (Zahn-Waxler & Robinson, 1995). When preschoolers have positive and cooperative relationships with parents, they show firmer conscience development—in the form of responsible behavior, fair play in games, and consideration for others' welfare. These outcomes continue into the early school years (Kochanska & Murray, 2000). Mutually responsive parent–child ties lead children to heed parental demands because children feel a sense of commitment to the relationship.

Parents who use positive discipline reduce opportunities for misbehavior. For example, on a long car trip, they bring back-seat activities that relieve children's restlessness and boredom. At the supermarket, where exciting temptations abound, they can engage preschoolers in conversation and encourage them to assist with shopping (Holden & West, 1989). When adults help children acquire acceptable behaviors that they can use to replace forbidden acts, the need for punishment is reduced.

THE COGNITIVE-DEVELOPMENTAL PERSPECTIVE

The psychoanalytic and behaviorist approaches to morality focus on how children acquire ready-made standards of good conduct from adults. In contrast, the cognitive-developmental perspective regards children as *active thinkers* about social rules. As early as the preschool years, children make moral judgments, deciding what is right or wrong on the basis of concepts they construct about justice and fairness (Gibbs, 1991).

Piaget's (1932/1965) work served as the original inspiration for the cognitive-developmental approach to morality. We will consider his theory of moral development in Chapter 16 because it has implications for adolescent moral understanding. Today, we know that Piaget underestimated young children's moral reasoning, just as he overlooked their ability to think about many aspects of their physical world (see Chapter 9).

■ **PRESCHOOLERS' MORAL UNDERSTANDING.** Young children have some well-developed ideas about morality. Three-year-olds know that a child who intentionally knocks a playmate off a swing is worse than one who does so accidentally (Yuill & Perner, 1988). Around age 4, children can tell the difference between truthfulness and lying (Bussey, 1992). By the end of early childhood, children evaluate lying on the basis of whether a person's intentions were prosocial or antisocial. Influenced by collectivist values of social harmony and humility, Chinese children are more likely than Canadian children to judge lying favorably when an intention involves modesty—for example, when a child who generously picks up garbage in the school yard says, "I didn't do it." In contrast, both Chinese and Canadian children rate lying about antisocial acts as "very naughty" (Lee et al., 1997).

Furthermore, preschoolers distinguish *moral imperatives,* which protect people's rights and welfare, from two other types of action: *social conventions,* or customs such as table manners and dress styles; and *matters of personal choice,* which do not violate rights and are up to the individual (Nucci, 1996; Smetana, 1995). Three-year-olds judge moral violations (stealing an apple) as more wrong than social-conventional violations (eating ice cream with fingers). And by 3½ years, children say moral (but not social conventional) violations would still be wrong if an adult did not see them and no rules existed to prohibit them (Smetana & Braeges, 1990). Concern with personal choice, conveyed through such statements as "I'm gonna wear *this* shirt," emerge as the sense of self strengthens in the early preschool years (Killen & Smetana, 1999; Nucci & Weber, 1995).

How do young children arrive at these distinctions? According to cognitive-developmental theorists, they do so by actively making sense of their experiences. They observe that after a moral offense, peers react emotionally, describe their own injury or loss, tell another child to stop, or retaliate. And an adult who intervenes is likely to call attention to the rights and feelings of the victim. In contrast, peers seldom react to violations of social convention. And in these situations, adults tend to demand obedience with no explanation or point to the importance of obeying rules and keeping order. Furthermore, preschoolers see that adults offer choices on personal matters and sometimes compromise on social conventions, but not on moral concerns.

With age, children start to appreciate the interdependence of moral, social-conventional, and personal matters. At times, violating a social convention (not saying "thank you") or exercising a personal choice (making statements that incite prejudice) can have moral implications because the behavior offends or otherwise hurts another. An early grasp of matters of personal choice serves as a springboard for moral concepts of individual rights and freedoms, which will strengthen in adolescence (Nucci, 1996).

■ **SOCIAL EXPERIENCE AND MORAL UNDERSTANDING.** Although cognition and language support preschoolers' moral understanding, social experiences are vital. Disputes over rights, possessions, and property usually occur when children interact with peers and siblings, providing important opportunities to work out first ideas about justice and fairness (Killen & Nucci, 1995).

The way parents handle rule violations and discuss moral issues also helps children reason about morality. Children who are advanced in moral thinking and prosocial behavior have parents who adapt their communications about fighting, honesty, and ownership to what their child can understand; respect the child's opinion; and gently stimulate the child to think further, without being hostile or critical (Janssens & Dekovic, 1997; Walker & Taylor, 1991a).

Preschoolers who are disliked by peers because of their aggressive approach to resolving conflict show difficulties with moral reasoning. They have trouble distinguishing moral rules from social conventions, and they violate both often (Sanderson & Siegal, 1988). Without special help, such children show long-term disruptions in moral development.

THE OTHER SIDE OF MORALITY: DEVELOPMENT OF AGGRESSION

Beginning in late infancy, all children display aggression from time to time, and as opportunities to interact with siblings and peers increase, aggressive outbursts occur more often. Although at times aggression serves prosocial ends (for example, stopping a victimizer from harming others), the large majority of human aggressive acts are clearly antisocial. By the early preschool years, two general types of aggression emerge. The most common is **instrumental aggression.** In this form, children want an object, privilege, or space, and in trying to get it, they push, shout at, or otherwise attack a person who is in the way. The other type, **hostile aggression,** is meant to hurt another person.

Hostile aggression comes in at least two varieties. The first is **overt aggression,** which harms others through physical injury or the threat of such injury—for example, hitting, kicking, or threatening to beat up a peer. The second is **relational aggression,** which damages another's peer relationships, as in social exclusion ("Go away, I'm not going to be your friend anymore!") or rumor spreading ("Don't play with Margie; she's a nerd").

For most preschoolers, instrumental aggression declines with age as they learn to compromise over possessions. In contrast, hostile, person-oriented outbursts rise slightly as children become better at detecting others' intentions (Shantz, 1987). Older preschoolers are

instrumental aggression
Aggression aimed at obtaining an object, privilege, or space with no deliberate intent to harm another person.

hostile aggression
Aggression intended to harm another person.

overt aggression
A form of hostile aggression that harms others through physical injury or the threat of such injury—for example, hitting, kicking, or threatening to beat up a peer.

relational aggression
A form of hostile aggression that does damage to another's peer relationships, as in social exclusion or rumor spreading.

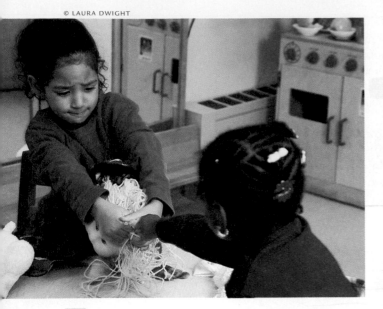

© LAURA DWIGHT

An occasional expression of aggression is normal in early childhood. This preschooler displays instrumental aggression as she grabs an attractive toy from a classmate. Instrumental aggression declines with age as children learn how to compromise and share.

better able to recognize malicious behavior and, as a result, more often respond with a hostile retaliation.

Although children of both sexes show this general pattern of development, on the average boys are more overtly aggressive than girls, a trend that appears in many cultures (Whiting & Edwards, 1988b). The sex difference is, in part, due to biology—in particular, to male sex hormones, or androgens. In humans, androgens contribute to boys' higher rate of physical activity, possibly increasing their opportunities for physically aggressive encounters (Collaer & Hines, 1995). At the same time, development of gender roles (a topic we will take up shortly) is also important. As soon as 2-year-olds become dimly aware of gender stereotypes—that males and females are expected to behave differently—overt aggression drops off in girls but is maintained in boys (Fagot & Leinbach, 1989).

But preschool and school-age girls are not less aggressive than boys! Instead, they are likely to express their hostility differently—through relational aggression (Crick, Casas, & Mosher, 1997; Crick & Grotpeter, 1995). When trying to harm a peer, children seem to do so in ways especially likely to thwart that child's social goals. Boys more often attack physically to block the dominance goals that are typical of boys. Girls resort to relational aggression because it interferes with the close, intimate bonds especially important to girls.

An occasional aggressive exchange between young children is normal. As we saw earlier, preschoolers sometimes assert their developing sense of self through these encounters, which become important learning experiences as adults intervene and teach alternative ways of satisfying desires. But some preschoolers—especially those who are impulsive and overactive—are at risk for high aggression. Whether they become so, however, depends on child-rearing conditions.

■ **THE FAMILY AS TRAINING GROUND FOR AGGRESSIVE BEHAVIOR.** "I can't control him, he's impossible," complained Nadine, Robbie's mother, to Leslie one day. When Leslie asked if Robbie might be troubled by something going on at home, she discovered that his parents fought constantly. Their conflict led to high levels of family stress and a "spillover" of hostility into child rearing. The same parenting practices that undermine moral internalization and self-control predict aggression. Love withdrawal, power assertion, physical punishment, and inconsistent discipline are linked to antisocial behavior from early childhood through adolescence, in children of both sexes (Coie & Dodge, 1998; Stormshak et al., 2000).

Observations in families like Robbie's reveal that anger and punitiveness quickly create a conflict-ridden family atmosphere and an "out of control" child. The pattern begins with forceful discipline, which occurs more often with stressful life experiences (such as economic hardship or an unhappy marriage), a parent's unstable personality, or a temperamentally difficult child (Coie & Dodge, 1998). Once the parent threatens, criticizes, and punishes, then the child whines, yells, and refuses until the parent "gives in." This sequence is likely to be repeated, since at the end of each exchange, both parent and child get relief from stopping the unpleasant behavior of the other. The next time the child misbehaves, the parent is even more coercive and the child more defiant, until one member of the pair "begs off" (Dodge, Pettit, & Bates, 1994; Patterson, 1995, 1997).

As these cycles become more frequent, they generate anxiety and irritability among other family members, who soon join in the hostile interactions. Compared with siblings in typical families, preschool siblings of critical, punitive parents are more verbally and physically aggressive toward one another. Destructive sibling conflict, in turn, contributes to a rise in poor impulse control and antisocial behavior by the early school years (Dunn & Munn, 1986; Garcia et al., 2000).

Because they are more active and impulsive and therefore harder to control, boys are more likely than girls to be targets of harsh, physical discipline and parental inconsistency. Children

[handwritten note in margin: Cycle of aggression b/w parent & child.]

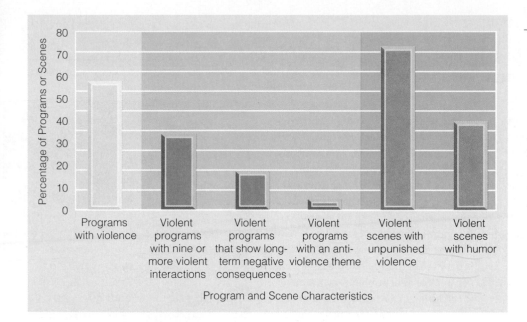

FIGURE 10.3

Violent characteristics of American television, based on a representative sample of more than 3,000 programs broadcast between 6 A.M. and 11 P.M. Violence occurs in the majority of programs. It often consists of repeated aggressive acts that go unpunished and that are embedded in humor. Only rarely do programs show long-term negative consequences of violence or present it in the context of an antiviolence theme. (Center for Communication and Social Policy, 1998.)

who are products of these family processes soon view the world from a violent perspective. Because they expect others to react with anger and physical force, they see hostile intent where it does not exist (Weiss et al., 1992). As a result, they make many unprovoked attacks. Soon they conclude that aggression "works" to produce rewards—getting others to comply and relieving teasing, taunting, and other unpleasant behaviors. And they come to value this control over others. These cognitions contribute to the aggressive cycle (Egan, Monson, & Perry, 1998).

Unfortunately, highly aggressive children have serious adjustment problems. Because of their hostility and poor self-control, they tend to be rejected by peers, to fail in school, and to form relationships with deviant peers, which lead them toward delinquency and adult criminality (see Chapter 16).

■ **TELEVISION AND AGGRESSION.** The National Television Violence Study, a recent large-scale survey of the amount, nature, and context of TV violence in the United States, concluded that violence pervades American TV (see Figure 10.3). Fifty-seven percent of programs between 6 A.M. and 11 P.M. contain violent scenes, often in the form of repeated aggressive acts against a victim that go unpunished. In fact, most violent portrayals do not show victims experiencing any serious physical harm, and few condemn violence or depict alternative ways of solving problems. Violent content is 9 percent above average in children's programming, and cartoons are the most violent (Center for Communication and Social Policy, 1998).

Young children are especially likely to be influenced by television. One reason is that before age 8, children fail to understand a great deal of what they see on TV. Because they have difficulty connecting separate scenes into a meaningful story line, they do not relate the actions of a TV character to motives or consequences (Collins et al., 1978). A villain who gets what he wants by punching, shooting, and killing may not be a "bad guy" to a preschooler, who fails to notice that the character was brought to justice in the end. Young children also find it hard to separate true-to-life from fantasized television content. Not until age 7 do children fully grasp the unreality of TV fiction—that characters do not retain their roles in real life and that their behavior is scripted (Wright et al., 1994). These misunderstandings increase young children's willingness to uncritically accept and imitate what they see on TV.

Reviewers of thousands of studies have concluded that television provides children with "an extensive how-to course in aggression" (Comstock & Scharrer, 1999; Slaby et al., 1995, p. 163). The case is strengthened by the fact that research using a wide variety of research designs, methods, and participants has yielded similar findings. In addition, the relationship of TV violence to hostile behavior remains the same after many factors—including family background and child characteristics—that might otherwise account for this association are controlled.

Social ISSUES : EDUCATION

REGULATING CHILDREN'S TELEVISION

Exposure to television is almost universal in the United States and other Western industrialized nations. Ninety-eight percent of American homes have at least one television set, and a TV is switched on in a typical household for a total of 7.1 hours a day. TV enters the lives of children at an early age, becoming a major teacher of undesirable attitudes and behavior. Yet television has as much potential for good as it does for ill. If the content of television were changed, it could promote prosocial attitudes and behavior and convey information about nonviolent aspects of the world, such as history, science, literature, fine arts, and other cultures (Graves, 1993).

Unfortunately, recent changes in the media world have increased children's exposure to harmful messages. Over 60 percent of American families are cable subscribers, and over 80 percent own VCRs—rates that are increasing (U.S. Bureau of the Census, 2000). Children with cable or VCR access can see films with far more graphic violence and sexual content than are shown on commercial TV. Although the greatest concern is violence, TV messages fostering gender and ethnic stereotyping and uncritical consumerism also damage children.

Many organizations concerned with the well-being of children and families have recommended government regulation of TV. But the First Amendment

right to free speech has made the federal government reluctant to place limits on television content. Consequently, professionals and committed public officials have sought ways to counteract the negative impact of television that are consistent with the First Amendment. Instead of regulatory control, the government now requires broadcasters to provide at least 3 hours per week of educational programming for children. In addition, broadcasters must rate television content and manufacturers must build the V-Chip (also called the Violence-Chip) into new TV sets so that viewers can program ratings codes into their TVs to block undesired violent and sexual material.

The V-Chip, however, is far from a complete solution. The rating system is largely based on frequency of offensive content, not harmfulness. Yet research indicates that the context of violent acts—their realism, intensity, motivation, and consequences—affects children's emotional reactions, evaluations, and imitation. Furthermore, the ratings may make shows more appealing to young audiences— an outcome supported for boys (Cantor & Harrison, 1996). Children may go to other homes to watch programs forbidden by their parents. And it will take years for the V-Chip to reach every TV.

Sometimes it takes a tragedy to mobilize action to protect children. In

PAUL DAMIEN/STONE

Using television to promote children's prosocial behavior and active engagement with their surroundings is a great challenge for American parents, given the antisocial content of many programs. Here a trip to the zoo brings to life an educational TV program on wildlife.

1992, a Canadian teenager, who believed that TV violence contributed to his sister's rape and murder, organized a petition to reduce violent TV programming. More than 1 million

Violent programming creates both short- and long-term difficulties in parent and peer relations. Longitudinal research reveals that highly aggressive children have a greater appetite for violent TV. As they watch more, they become increasingly likely to resort to hostile ways of solving problems, a spiraling pattern of learning that contributes to serious antisocial acts by adolescence and young adulthood (Huesmann & Miller, 1994). Television violence also "hardens" children to aggression, making them more willing to tolerate it in others. (Donnerstein, Slaby, & Eron, 1994).

The ease with which television can manipulate the beliefs and behavior of children has resulted in strong public pressures to improve its content. As the Social Issues: Education box above indicates, these efforts have not been very successful in the United States. At present,

ℰducational Concerns

Regulating Children's TV Viewing

STRATEGY	DESCRIPTION
Limit TV viewing.	Avoid using TV as a baby-sitter. Provide clear rules that limit what children can watch—for example, an hour a day and only certain programs—and stick to the rules. Do not place a TV in the child's bedroom, where TV viewing is difficult to monitor.
Refrain from using TV as a reinforcer.	Do not use television to reward or punish children, a practice that increases its attractiveness.
Encourage child-appropriate viewing.	Encourage children to watch programs that are child-appropriate, informative, and prosocial.
Explain televised information to children.	As much as possible, watch with children, helping them understand what they see. When adults express disapproval of on-screen behavior, raise questions about the realism of televised information, and encourage children to discuss it, they teach children to evaluate TV content rather than accept it uncritically.
Link televised content to everyday learning experiences.	Build on TV programs in constructive ways, encouraging children to move away from the set into active engagement with their surroundings. For example, a program on animals might spark a trip to the zoo, a visit to the library for books about animals, or new ways of observing and caring for the family pet.
Model good viewing practices.	Avoid excess television viewing, especially violent programs, yourself. Parental viewing patterns influence children's viewing patterns.
Use a warm, rational approach to child rearing.	Respond to children with warmth and reasonable demands for mature behavior. Children who experience these practices prefer programs with prosocial content and are less attracted to violent TV.

Source: Slaby et al., 1995.

people signed it (Dubow & Miller, 1996). The Canadian television industry responded with a voluntary code that bans gratuitous violence (unnecessary to the plot) and that requires the consequences of violence to be shown in all children's programs. Still, programs from the United States that violate the code slip through on Canadian cable TV.

Parents face an awesome task in monitoring and controlling children's TV viewing, given the extent of harmful messages on the screen. The Educational Concerns table above lists some strategies parents can use. In addition, the television industry must take a more responsible attitude toward limiting such content. Public education about the impact of television on children's development is vital, since consumer pressure is a powerful instrument of change.

it is up to parents to regulate their child's exposure—a heavy burden, given that children find TV so attractive.

■ **HELPING CHILDREN AND PARENTS CONTROL AGGRESSION.** Treatment for aggressive children must begin early, before their antisocial behavior becomes so well practiced that it is difficult to change. Breaking the cycle of hostilities between family members and replacing it with effective interaction styles is crucial. The coercive cycles of parents and aggressive children are so persistent that these children often get punished when they do behave appropriately (Strassberg, 1995).

Leslie suggested that Robbie's parents see a family therapist, who observed their inept practices, demonstrated alternatives, and had Nadine and her husband practice them. They learned not to give in to Robbie, to pair commands with reasons, to replace verbal insults and spankings with more effective punishments (such as time out and withdrawal of privileges), and to limit his access to TV with violent content (Patterson, 1982). The therapist also encouraged Robbie's parents to be warmer and more supportive and to give him attention and approval for prosocial acts.

At the same time, Leslie began teaching Robbie more successful ways of relating to peers. As opportunities arose, she encouraged Robbie to talk about a playmate's feelings and express his own. This helped Robbie take the perspective of others, empathize, and feel sympathetic concern (Denham, 1998). Soon he showed greater willingness to share and cooperate. Robbie also participated in social problem-solving training (return to page 377 to review). From observing and participating in family conflict, aggressive children acquire maladaptive social problem-solving tactics that must be replaced with more effective techniques (Goodman et al., 1999). Finally, Robbie's parents got help with their marital problems. This, in addition to their improved ability to manage Robbie's behavior, greatly reduced tension and conflict in the household.

Ask YOURSELF...

review   *Cite a major difference between the cognitive-developmental and the psychoanalytic and behaviorist perspectives on moral development. How do preschoolers distinguish between moral imperatives, social conventions, and matters of personal choice? Why are these distinctions important for moral development?*

apply   *Nanette told her 3-year-old son, Darren, not to go into the front yard without asking, since the house faces a very busy street. Darren disobeyed several times, and now Nanette thinks it's time to punish him. How would you recommend that Nanette discipline Darren, and why?*

reflect   *Did you display a strong, internalized conscience as a child? How do you think temperament, parenting practices, and TV viewing affected your childhood moral maturity?*

Gender Typing

The process of developing *gender roles,* or gender-linked preferences and behaviors valued by the larger society, is called gender typing. Early in the preschool years, **gender typing** is well under way. In Leslie's classroom, children tended to play and form friendships with peers of their own sex. Girls spent more time in the housekeeping, art, and reading corners, whereas boys more often gathered in blocks, woodworking, and active play spaces.

The same three theories that provide accounts of morality have been used to explain gender-role development. According to *psychoanalytic theory,* gender-stereotyped beliefs and behaviors develop in the same way as other social standards—through identification with the same-sex parent. But as in the area of morality, Freud's ideas have difficulty accounting for gender typing. Research shows that the same-sex parent is only one of many influences in gender-role development. The other-sex parent, peers, siblings, teachers, and the broader social environment are important as well.

Social learning theory, with its emphasis on modeling and reinforcement, and *cognitive-developmental theory,* with its focus on children as active thinkers about their social world, are major current approaches to understanding gender typing. We will see that neither has

gender typing
The process of developing gender roles, or gender-linked preferences and behaviors valued by the larger society.

[handwritten note:] Social learning theory + cognitive-developmental theory lead to gender typing.

proved adequate by itself. Consequently, a third perspective that combines elements of both, called *gender schema theory*, has gained favor. In the following sections, we consider the early development of gender typing, along with genetic and environmental contributions to it.

gender schema theory = social learning theory plus cognitive developmental theory

GENDER-STEREOTYPED BELIEFS AND BEHAVIORS

Recall from Chapter 7 that around age 2, children begin to label their own sex and that of other people. As soon as basic gender categories are established, children sort out what they mean in terms of activities and behaviors.

Preschoolers associate many toys, articles of clothing, tools, household items, games, occupations, behaviors, and even colors (pink and blue) with one sex or the other (Ruble & Martin, 1998). And their actions fall in line with their beliefs—not only in play preferences, but in personality traits. We have already seen that boys tend to be more active, assertive, and overtly aggressive. In contrast, girls tend to be more fearful, dependent, compliant, considerate, emotionally sensitive, and relationally aggressive (Brody & Hall, 1993; Eisenberg & Fabes, 1998; Feingold, 1994; Saarni, 1993).

Over the preschool years, children's gender-stereotyped beliefs become stronger—so much so that they operate like blanket rules rather than flexible guidelines (Biernat, 1991; Martin, 1989). Once, when Leslie showed the children a picture of a Scottish bagpiper wearing a kilt, they insisted, "Men don't wear skirts!" During free play, they often exclaimed that girls don't drive fire engines and can't be police officers and boys don't take care of babies and can't be the teacher.

These one-sided judgments are a joint product of gender stereotyping in the environment and preschoolers' cognitive limitations—in particular, their difficulty coordinating conflicting sources of information. Most preschoolers do not yet realize that characteristics associated with gender—activities, toys, occupations, hairstyle, and clothing—do not determine whether a person is male or female. (They have trouble understanding that males and females can be different in terms of their bodies yet similar in many other ways.)

While preschoolers are sexist due to gender stereotyping, it's also b/c they can't reconcile these stereotypes w/ other beliefs.

GENETIC INFLUENCES ON GENDER TYPING

The sex differences just described appear in many cultures around the world (Whiting & Edwards, 1988a). Certain of them—the preference for same-sex playmates as well as male activity level and overt aggression—are widespread among animal species as well (Beatty, 1992). So it is reasonable to ask whether gender typing might be influenced by genetic factors. We have already considered evidence that aggression is indirectly linked to sex hormones in human children. That is, androgens promote active play among boys, increasing the likelihood of hostile encounters.

Eleanor Maccoby (1990, 1998) argues that hormonal differences between males and females have important consequences for gender typing. Early on, hormones affect play styles, leading to rough, noisy movements among boys and calm, gentle actions among girls. Then, as children interact with peers, they choose same-sex partners whose interests and behaviors are compatible with their own. By age 2, girls already appear overwhelmed by boys' rambunctious behavior. When paired with a boy in a laboratory play session, the girl is likely to stand idly by while he explores the toys (Jacklin & Maccoby, 1978). Nonhuman primates react similarly. When a male juvenile initiates rough, physical play, male peers join in, whereas females withdraw (Beatty, 1992).

heredity + genetic factors provide a basis for gender typing.

Over the preschool years, girls increasingly seek out other girls and like to play in pairs because of a common preference for quieter activities involving cooperative roles. And boys come to prefer larger-group play with other boys, who respond positively to one another's desire to run, climb, play-fight, and build up and knock down. At age 4, children already spend three times as much time with same-sex as other-sex playmates. By age 6, this ratio climbs to 11 to 1 (Benenson, Apostoleris, & Parnass, 1997; Maccoby & Jacklin, 1987).

However, we must not overemphasize the contribution of heredity to gender typing. As we will see in the next section, a wide variety of environmental forces build on hereditary influences to promote children's awareness of and conformity to gender roles.

ENVIRONMENTAL INFLUENCES ON GENDER TYPING

A wealth of evidence reveals that family influences, encouragement by teachers and peers, and examples in the broader social environment combine to promote the vigorous gender typing of early childhood.

■ **THE FAMILY.** Beginning at birth, parents hold different perceptions and expectations of their sons and daughters (see Chapter 7). Many parents state that they want their children to play with "gender-appropriate" toys, and when asked about their child-rearing values, parents describe achievement, competition, and control of emotion as important for sons and warmth, "ladylike" behavior, and closely supervised activities as important for daughters (Brody, 1999; Turner & Gervai, 1995).

These beliefs carry over into parenting practices. Mothers and fathers are far more likely to purchase guns, cars, and footballs for sons and dolls, tea sets, and jump ropes for daughters—toys that promote very different play styles. In addition, parents actively reinforce many gender-stereotyped behaviors. For example, they react more positively when a young son plays with cars and trucks, demands attention, or tries to take toys from others—rewarding active and assertive behavior (Fagot & Hagan, 1991; Leaper et al., 1995). In contrast, they more often direct play activities and provide help to a daughter—encouraging dependency (Lytton & Romney, 1991).

Furthermore, parents converse differently with preschool boys and girls. Mothers more often *label emotions* when talking to girls, thereby teaching them to "tune in" to others' feelings. In contrast, they more often *explain emotions,* noting causes and consequences, to boys—an approach that emphasizes why it is important to control the expression of emotion (Cervantes & Callanan, 1998).

In most aspects of differential treatment of boys and girls, fathers discriminate more than mothers do. In Chapter 7 we saw that fathers tend to engage in more physically stimulating play with their infant sons than daughters, whereas mothers usually play in a quieter way with infants of both sexes. In childhood, fathers more than mothers encourage "gender-appropriate" behavior, and they place more pressure to achieve on sons than daughters (Gervai, Turner, & Hinde, 1995; Lytton & Romney, 1991).

These factors influence gender-role learning, since parents who hold nonstereotyped values and apply them in their daily lives have less gender-typed children (Turner & Gervai, 1995; Weisner & Wilson-Mitchell, 1990). Other family members also contribute to gender typing. For example, preschoolers with older, other-sex siblings have many more opportunities to imitate and participate in "cross-gender" play (Stoneman, Brody, & MacKinnon, 1986).

In any case, of the two sexes, boys are clearly the more gender typed. One reason is that parents—particularly fathers—are less tolerant of "cross-gender" behavior in their sons than daughters. They are more concerned if a boy acts like a "sissy" than if a girl acts like a "tomboy."

■ **TEACHERS.** Besides parents, teachers encourage children to conform to gender roles. Several times, Leslie caught herself responding in ways that furthered sex segregation and stereotyping in her classroom (Thorne, 1993). One day when the class was preparing to leave for a field trip, she called out, "Will the girls line up on one side and the boys on the other?" Then, as the class became noisy with excitement, she pleaded, "Boys, I wish you'd quiet down like the girls!"

As in their experiences at home, girls get more encouragement to participate in adult-structured activities at preschool. They can frequently be seen clustered around the teacher, following directions in an activity. In contrast, boys more often choose areas of the classroom where teachers are minimally involved or entirely absent (Carpenter, 1983; Powlishta, Serbin, & Moller, 1993). As a result, boys and girls engage in very different social behaviors. Compliance and bids for help occur more often in adult-structured contexts, whereas assertiveness, leadership, and creative use of materials appear more often in unstructured pursuits.

E. ZUCKERMAN/PHOTOEDIT

Gender-stereotyped game and toy choices are present by age 2 and strengthen with age. Already, these 3-year-olds play in highly gender-stereotyped ways.

[handwritten margin notes:] parents promote gender-typed behavior by reinforcing "gender appropriate" behavior.

[handwritten note at bottom:] different teaching styles used for different genders.

family
teachers
peers
TV
broader social env.

■ **PEERS.** Children's same-sex peer relationships are powerful environments for strengthening stereotyped beliefs and behavior. By age 3, same-sex peers positively reinforce one another for gender-typed play by praising, imitating, or joining in. Similarly, when preschoolers engage in "gender-inappropriate" activities—for example, when boys play with dolls or girls with cars and trucks—peers criticize them. Boys are especially intolerant of "cross-gender" play in their male companions (Carter & McCloskey, 1984; Fagot, 1984). A boy who frequently crosses gender lines is likely to be ignored by other boys even when he does engage in "masculine" activities!

Children also develop different styles of social influence in sex-segregated peer groups. To get their way with male peers, boys often rely on commands, threats, and physical force. In contrast, girls use polite requests and persuasion. These strategies succeed with other girls but not with boys, who pay little attention to girls' gentle tactics (Leaper, 1994; Leaper, Tenenbaum, & Shaffer, 1999). Consequently, girls may have an additional reason to prefer girls: they find boys to be unresponsive, unrewarding social partners.

Over time, children form beliefs about peers' play preferences, which contribute further to sex segregation. In one study 3- to 6-year-olds believed that peers would be more likely to approve of their behavior when they played with same-sex than other-sex agemates—a conviction that predicted children's actual association with same-sex peers at their child-care center (Martin et al., 1999). As boys and girls separate, they evaluate members of the other group more negatively—a bias that also characterizes adults. This "own-sex favoritism" is yet another factor that sustains the separate social worlds of boys and girls.

strengthening same-sex bonds cause girls to view boys even more negatively + vice-versa.

■ **TELEVISION.** Television is yet another powerful source of children's gender stereotypes. In prime-time TV programs, women appear less often than men, filling only one-third or less of major character roles (Comstock & Scharrer, 1999). Compared with two decades ago, today women are more often shown as involved in careers. But they continue to be portrayed as young, attractive, caring, emotional, victimized, and in romantic and family contexts. In contrast, men are depicted as dominant and powerful (Allan & Coltrane, 1996; Zillman, Bryant, & Huston, 1994).

Gender roles are especially stereotypic in entertainment programs for children and youths. For example, male cartoon characters are usually problem solvers, whereas females are sweet, childlike followers (Huston et al., 1992). Music television (MTV), designed for teenagers but also viewed by many children, includes males twice as often as females. When women appear, they tend to be dressed in revealing clothing and to be the object of sexual advances (Sommers-Flanagan, Sommers-Flanagan, & Davis, 1993).

cartoons + MTV are especially stereo-typical.

■ **THE BROADER SOCIAL ENVIRONMENT.** Although American society has changed to some degree, children's everyday social environments contain many examples of traditional gender-role behavior—in occupations, leisure activities, and achievements of men and women (Ruble & Martin, 1998). As we will see in the next section, young children do not just imitate the many gender-linked responses they observe. They also start to view themselves and their environment in gender-biased ways, a perspective that can seriously restrict their interests, experiences, and skills.

gender identity- our image as masculine or feminine.

GENDER IDENTITY

As adults, each of us has a **gender identity**—an image of oneself as relatively masculine or feminine in characteristics. By middle childhood, researchers can measure gender identity by asking children to rate themselves on personality traits, since at that time self-concepts begin to emphasize psychological attributes over concrete behaviors.

Individuals differ considerably in responses to these questionnaires. A child or adult with a "masculine" identity scores high on traditionally masculine items (such as "self-sufficient," "ambitious," and "forceful") and low on traditionally feminine ones (such as "affectionate," "soft-spoken," and "cheerful"). Someone with a "feminine" identity does just the reverse. Although the majority of individuals view themselves in gender-typed terms, a substantial minority (especially females) have a gender identity called **androgyny.** They score high on *both* masculine and feminine personality characteristics (Boldizar, 1991).

gender identity
An image of oneself as relatively masculine or feminine in characteristics.

androgyny
A type of gender identity in which the person scores high on both traditionally masculine and traditionally feminine personality characteristics.

Gender identity is a good predictor of psychological adjustment. Masculine and androgynous children and adults have a higher sense of self-esteem, whereas feminine individuals often think poorly of themselves, perhaps because many feminine traits are not highly valued in our society (Alpert-Gillis & Connell, 1989; Boldizar, 1991). In line with their flexible self-definitions, androgynous individuals are more adaptable in behavior—for example, able to show masculine independence or feminine sensitivity, depending on the situation (Taylor & Hall, 1982). Research on androgyny shows that children can acquire a mixture of positive qualities traditionally associated with each gender—an orientation that may best help them realize their potential.

■ **EMERGENCE OF GENDER IDENTITY.** How do children develop a gender identity? Both social learning and cognitive-developmental answers to this question exist. According to *social learning theory*, behavior comes before self-perceptions. Preschoolers first acquire gender-typed responses through modeling and reinforcement. Only later do they organize these behaviors into gender-linked ideas about themselves.

In contrast, *cognitive-developmental theory* regards the direction of development as the other way around. Over the preschool years, children first acquire a cognitive appreciation of the permanence of their sex. They develop **gender constancy,** the understanding that sex is biologically based and remains the same even if clothing, hairstyle, and play activities change. Then children use this idea to guide their behavior (Kohlberg, 1966).

Research indicates that gender constancy is not fully developed until the early school years, when children typically pass Piagetian conservation tasks (De Lisi & Gallagher, 1991). Shown a doll whose hairstyle and clothing are transformed before their eyes, a child younger than age 6 is likely to insist that the doll's sex has changed as well (McConaghy, 1979). And when asked such questions as "When you (a girl) grow up, could you ever be a daddy?" or "Could you be a boy if you wanted to?" young children freely answer yes (Slaby & Frey, 1975).

In many households in Western societies, young children do not see members of the other sex naked. They distinguish males and females using the only information they do have—the way each gender dresses and behaves and the stereotypes they have acquired through social experience. Preschoolers who are aware of genital differences usually answer gender constancy questions correctly (Bem, 1989). But when asked to justify their responses, they still do not refer to sex as an innate, unchanging quality of people, as 6- to 8-year-olds do (Szkrybalo & Ruble, 1999).

Is cognitive-developmental theory correct that gender constancy is responsible for children's gender-typed behavior? Perhaps you have already concluded that evidence for this assumption is weak. "Gender-appropriate" behavior appears so early in the preschool years that modeling and reinforcement must account for its initial appearance, as social learning theory suggests. At present, researchers disagree on just how gender constancy contributes to gender-role development (Bussey & Bandura, 1992; Lutz & Ruble, 1995). But they do know that once children begin to reflect on gender roles, they form basic gender categories that strengthen gender-typed self-images and behavior. Yet another theoretical perspective shows how this happens.

■ **GENDER SCHEMA THEORY.** **Gender schema theory** is an information-processing approach to gender typing that combines social learning and cognitive-developmental features. It emphasizes that environmental pressures and children's cognitions together shape gender-role development (Martin, 1993; Martin & Halverson, 1987).

At an early age, children respond to instruction from others, picking up gender-stereotyped preferences and behaviors. At the same time, they start to organize their experiences into *gender schemas,* or masculine and feminine categories, that they use to interpret their world. A young child who says, "Only boys can be doctors" or "Cooking is a girl's job" already has some well-formed gender schemas. As soon as preschoolers can label their own gender, they select gender schemas that are consistent with it, applying those categories to themselves. As a result, self-perceptions become gender typed and serve as additional schemas that children use to process information and guide their own behavior.

Let's look at the example in Figure 10.4 to see exactly how this network of gender schemas strengthens gender-typed preferences and behavior. Three-year-old Mandy has been taught that

---

gender constancy
The understanding that sex remains the same even if clothing, hairstyle, and play activities change.

gender schema theory
An information-processing approach to gender typing that combines social learning and cognitive-developmental features to explain how environmental pressures and children's cognitions together shape gender-role development.

[Handwritten margin note: gender constancy – realization that sex is biologically based]

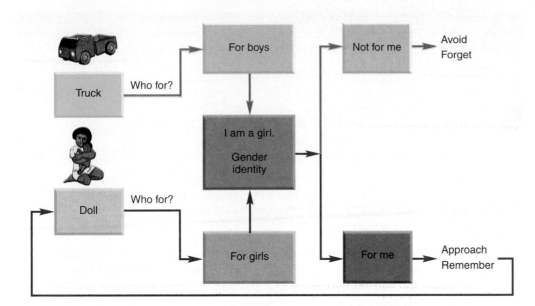

FIGURE 10.4

Effect of gender schemas on gender-stereotyped preferences and behavior. Mandy's network of gender schemas leads her to approach and explore "feminine" toys, such as dolls, and to avoid "masculine" ones, such as trucks. (From C. L. Martin & C. F. Halverson, 1981, "A Schematic Processing Model of Sex Typing and Stereotyping in Children," *Child Development, 52*, p. 1121. © The Society for Research in Child Development, Inc. Adapted by permission.)

"dolls are for girls" and "trucks are for boys." She also knows that she is a girl. Mandy uses this information to make decisions about how to behave. Because her schemas lead her to conclude that "dolls are for me," when given a doll she approaches it, explores it, and learns more about it. In contrast, on seeing a truck, she uses her gender schemas to conclude that "trucks are not for me" and responds by avoiding the "gender-inappropriate" toy (Martin & Halverson, 1981).

In research examining this pattern of reasoning, 4- and 5-year-olds were shown gender-neutral toys varying in attractiveness. An experimenter labeled some as boys' toys and others as girls' toys and left a third group unlabeled. Children engaged in gender-based reasoning, preferring toys labeled for their gender. Highly attractive toys, especially, lost their appeal when they were labeled as for the other gender (Martin, Eisenbud, & Rose, 1995).

Gender schemas are so powerful that when children see others behaving in "gender-inconsistent" ways, they often cannot remember the behavior or they distort their memory to make it "gender consistent" (Liben & Signorella, 1993). As a result, they increase their knowledge of "things for me" that fit with their gender schemas, but they learn much less about "cross-gender" activities and behaviors.

REDUCING GENDER STEREOTYPING IN YOUNG CHILDREN

How can we help young children avoid rigid gender schemas that restrict their behavior and learning opportunities? No easy recipe exists for accomplishing this difficult task. Even children who grow up in homes and schools that minimize stereotyping will eventually encounter it in the media and in what men and women typically do in their communities. Consequently, children need early experiences that counteract their readiness to absorb the extensive network of gender-linked associations that surrounds them.

Adults can begin by eliminating gender stereotyping from their own behavior and from the alternatives they provide for children. For example, mothers and fathers can take turns making dinner, bathing children, and driving the family car. They can provide sons and daughters with both trucks and dolls and pink and blue clothing. And teachers can make sure that all children spend some time each day in both adult-structured and unstructured activities. Also, efforts can be made to shield children from television and other media presentations that portray rigid gender differences.

Once children notice the vast array of gender stereotypes in their society, parents and teachers can point out exceptions. For example, they can arrange for children to see men and women pursuing nontraditional careers. And they can reason with children, explaining that interests and skills, not sex, should determine a person's occupation and activities. Research shows that such reasoning is very effective in reducing children's tendency to view the world in a gender-biased fashion (Bigler & Liben, 1990, 1992). And, as we will see in the next section, a rational approach to child rearing promotes healthy, adaptable functioning in many other areas as well.

Ask YOURSELF...

review   *Cite biological, social, and cognitive influences on sex segregation in children's peer associations.*

apply   *When 4-year-old Roger was in the hospital, he was cared for by a male nurse named Jared. After Roger recovered, he told his friends about Dr. Jared. Using gender schema theory, explain why Roger remembered Jared as a doctor, not a nurse.*

reflect   *Think back to storybooks you read and TV shows you watched as a child. Was their content gender stereotyped? Examine children's books at your local bookstore, and watch some children's TV shows. Do you think that portrayals of gender have changed? Cite examples.*

Child Rearing and Emotional and Social Development

In this and previous chapters, we have discussed many ways in which parents can foster children's development—by building a parent–child relationship based on affection and cooperation; by serving as models and reinforcers of mature behavior; by using reasoning, explanation, and inductive discipline; by firmly insisting on appropriate behavior yet avoiding harsh punishment; and by guiding and encouraging children's mastery of new skills. Now let's put these elements together into an overall view of effective parenting.

STYLES OF CHILD REARING

In a landmark series of studies, Diana Baumrind gathered information on child-rearing practices by watching parents interact with their preschoolers. Two broad dimensions of child rearing emerged. The first is *demandingness*. Some parents establish high standards for their children and insist that they meet those standards. Other parents demand very little and rarely try to influence their child's behavior. The second dimension is *responsiveness*. Some parents are accepting of and responsive to their children. They frequently engage in open discussion and verbal give-and-take. Others are rejecting and unresponsive.

As Figure 10.5 shows, the various combinations of demandingness and responsiveness yield four styles of child rearing. Baumrind's research focused on three of them: authoritative, authoritarian, and permissive. The fourth type, the uninvolved style, has been studied by other researchers.

■ AUTHORITATIVE CHILD REARING. The **authoritative style** is the most adaptive approach to child rearing. Authoritative parents make reasonable demands for maturity, and they enforce these demands by setting limits and insisting that the child obey. At the same time, they express warmth and affection, listen patiently to their child's point of view, and encourage participation in family decision making. Authoritative child rearing is a rational, democratic approach that recognizes and respects the rights of parents and children.

FIGURE 10.5

A two-dimensional classification of child-rearing styles. The various combinations of demandingness and responsiveness yield four styles of child rearing: authoritative, authoritarian, permissive, and uninvolved.

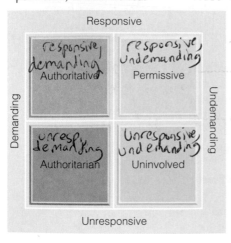

Responsive

responsive, demanding
Authoritative

responsive, undemanding
Permissive

Demanding

unresp, demanding
Authoritarian

Unresponsive, undemanding
Uninvolved

Undemanding

Unresponsive

Baumrind's findings revealed that children of these parents were developing especially well. They were lively and happy in mood, self-confident in their mastery of new tasks, and self-controlled in their ability to resist engaging in disruptive behavior (Baumrind, 1967). These children also seemed less gender typed. Girls scored particularly high in independence and desire to master new tasks and boys in friendly, cooperative behavior (Baumrind & Black, 1967).

■ **AUTHORITARIAN CHILD REARING.** Parents who use an **authoritarian style** are also demanding, but they place such a high value on conformity that they are unresponsive—even outright rejecting—when children do not obey. "Do it because I said so!" is the attitude of these parents. As a result, they engage in very little give-and-take with children, who are expected to accept their parent's word for what is right in an unquestioning manner. If they do not, authoritarian parents resort to force and punishment.

Baumrind found that preschoolers with authoritarian parents were anxious, withdrawn, and unhappy. When interacting with peers, they tended to react with hostility when frustrated (Baumrind, 1967). Boys, especially, showed high rates of anger and defiance. Girls were dependent and lacking in exploration, and they retreated from challenging tasks (Baumrind, 1971).

■ **PERMISSIVE CHILD REARING.** The **permissive style** of child rearing is nurturant and accepting, but it avoids making demands or imposing controls of any kind. Permissive parents allow children to make many of their own decisions at an age when they are not yet capable of doing so. They can eat meals and go to bed when they feel like it and watch as much television as they want. They do not have to learn good manners or do any household chores. Although some permissive parents truly believe this approach is best, many others lack confidence in their ability to influence their child's behavior and are disorganized and ineffective in running their households.

Baumrind found that children of permissive parents were very immature. They had difficulty controlling their impulses and were disobedient and rebellious when asked to do something that conflicted with their momentary desires. They were also overly demanding and dependent on adults, and they showed less persistence at tasks in preschool than did children of parents who exerted more control. The link between permissive parenting and dependent, nonachieving behavior was especially strong for boys (Baumrind, 1971).

■ **UNINVOLVED CHILD REARING.** The **uninvolved style** combines undemanding with indifferent, rejecting behavior. Uninvolved parents show little commitment to their role as caregivers beyond the minimal effort required to feed and clothe the child (Maccoby & Martin, 1983). At its extreme, uninvolved parenting is a form of child maltreatment called *neglect*. It is likely to characterize depressed parents with many stresses in their lives, such as marital conflict, little or no social support, and poverty. Especially when it begins early, it disrupts virtually all aspects of development, including attachment, cognition, play, and emotional and social skills (Cummings & Davies, 1994b). Even when parental disengagement is less extreme, children display many problems—low tolerance for frustration, poor emotional control, school achievement difficulties, and delinquency in adolescence (Kurdek & Fine, 1994; Lamborn et al., 1991).

WHAT MAKES AUTHORITATIVE CHILD REARING EFFECTIVE?

Since Baumrind's early work, a great many studies have confirmed her findings. Throughout childhood and adolescence, authoritative parenting is associated with task persistence, social maturity, high self-esteem, internalized moral standards, and superior academic achievement (Denham, Renwick, & Holt, 1991; Parke & Buriel, 1998; Steinberg, Darling, & Fletcher, 1995).

Why does this approach to parenting work so well? The following processes may be at work:

■ Control that appears fair and reasonable to the child, not abrupt and arbitrary, is far more likely to be complied with and internalized.

■ Nurturant parents who are secure in the standards they hold for their children provide models of caring concern as well as confident, self-controlled behavior.

authoritative style
A child-rearing style that is demanding and responsive. A rational, democratic approach in which parents' and children's rights are respected.

authoritarian style
A child-rearing style that is demanding but low in responsiveness to children's rights and needs. Conformity and obedience are valued over open communication with the child.

permissive style
A child-rearing style that is responsive but undemanding. An overly tolerant approach to child rearing.

uninvolved style
A child-rearing style that is both undemanding and unresponsive. Reflects minimal commitment to parenting.

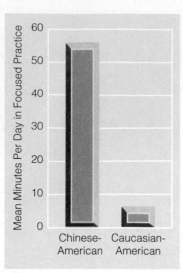

FIGURE 10.6

Daily time spent by Chinese-American and Caucasian-American preschoolers and kindergartners in focused practice on a task (usually math, music, or drawing), as reported by parents. Chinese-American young children exceeded their Caucasian-American agemates in focused practice by nearly tenfold. In addition, Chinese-American parents indicated that they were more likely to set aside daily periods for such practice and taught their children in more formal ways. (Adapted from Huntsinger, Jose, & Larson, 1998.)

- Authoritative parents make demands that fit children's ability to take responsibility for their own behavior. As a result, these parents let children know that they are competent individuals who can do things successfully for themselves, thereby fostering high self-esteem and cognitive and social maturity.

- Supportive aspects of the authoritative style, including parental warmth, involvement, and discussion, help protect children from the negative effects of family stress and poverty (Pettit, Bates, & Dodge, 1997).

CULTURAL VARIATIONS

Despite broad agreement on the advantages of authoritative child rearing, ethnic groups often have distinct child-rearing beliefs and practices. Some involve variations in warmth and demandingness that are adaptive when viewed in light of cultural values and family circumstances.

For example, compared with Caucasian Americans, Chinese adults describe their own parenting techniques and those they experienced as children as more demanding (Berndt et al., 1993). As Figure 10.6 shows, this greater emphasis on control continues to characterize Chinese parents who have immigrated to the United States, who are more directive in teaching and in scheduling their children's time beginning in early childhood (Huntsinger, Jose, & Larson, 1998). High control in Chinese families reflects the Confucian belief in strict discipline, respect for elders, and socially desirable behavior, taught by parents who are deeply concerned and involved in the lives of their children (Chao, 1994; Lin & Fu, 1990).

Chinese parents appear less warm than do Western parents because they believe that frequent praise may threaten their authority, cause children to be self-satisfied, and interfere with motivation to achieve (Chen, 2001). Nevertheless, *within* Chinese culture, variations in child-rearing styles predict children's adjustment in much the same way as in Western nations. Chinese preschoolers with authoritative parents tend to be communicative and cooperative; those with authoritarian parents tend to be unresponsive, resistant, and defiant, especially boys (Chen et al., 2000).

In Hispanic and Asian Pacific Island families, firm insistence on respect for parental authority, particularly that of the father, is paired with unusually high maternal warmth. As in Chinese families, this combination reflects parental commitment rather than authoritarianism. Parents say they use strict discipline to promote compliance and strong feelings of family loyalty (Fracasso & Busch-Rossnagel, 1992; Harrison et al., 1994).

Although wide variation exists among African Americans, black mothers (especially those who are younger, less educated, and single) often rely on an adult-centered approach in which they expect immediate obedience from children (Kelley, Power, & Wimbush, 1992; Kelley, Sanchez-Hucies, & Walker, 1993). Strict demands for compliance, however, make sense under certain conditions. When parents have few social supports and live in dangerous neighborhoods, forceful discipline may be necessary to protect children from becoming victims of crime or involved in antisocial activities. Other research suggests that African-American parents use strict discipline for broader reasons—to promote self-reliance, self-control, and a watchful attitude in risky surroundings (Brody & Flor, 1998).

Consistent with this view, low-SES, ethnic minority parents who use more controlling strategies tend to have more cognitively and socially competent young children (Brody, Stoneman, & Flor, 1996; O'Neil & Parke, 1997). And in several studies, physical discipline in early childhood predicted aggression and other conduct problems during the school years for Caucasian-American children only, not for African-American children (Deater-Deckard & Dodge, 1997; Deater-Deckard et al., 1996). This does not mean that slaps and spankings are effective strategies. But it does suggest that ethnic group differences in how children view parental behavior can modify its consequences. Most African-American parents who use strict, "no-nonsense" discipline seldom physically punish. And they typically combine strictness with warmth and reasoning, which predict favorable adjustment, regardless of ethnicity (Bluestone & Tamis-LeMonda, 1999; Pettit, Bates, & Dodge, 1998).

CHILD-REARING STYLES IN CONTEXT

The cultural variations we have just considered are a reminder that child-rearing styles can be fully understood only in their larger ecological context. As we have seen in earlier chapters, a great many factors contribute to parents' capacity to be appropriately warm, consistent, and demanding. These include personal characteristics of child and parent, socioeconomic well-being, access to extended family and community supports, cultural values and practices, and public policies that assist parents in their child-rearing roles (Parke & Buriel, 1998).

As we turn to the topic of child maltreatment, our discussion will underscore, once again, that effective child rearing is sustained not just by the desire of mothers and fathers to be good parents. Almost all want to be. Unfortunately, when vital supports for good parenting break down, children—as well as parents—can suffer terribly.

CHILD MALTREATMENT

Child abuse is as old as the history of humankind, but only recently has the problem been recognized and research been directed at understanding it. Perhaps public concern has increased because child maltreatment is especially common in large, industrialized nations. It occurs so often in the United States that a recent government committee called it "a national emergency." A total of 3.1 million cases were reported to juvenile authorities in 1998, an increase of 132 percent over the previous decade (U.S. Department of Health and Human Services, 2000). The true figure is surely much higher, since most cases go unreported.

Child maltreatment takes the following forms:

- *Physical abuse:* assaults on children, such as kicking, biting, shaking, punching, or stabbing, that produce pain, cuts, welts, bruises, burns, broken bones, and other injuries

- *Sexual abuse:* sexual comments, fondling, intercourse, and other forms of sexual exploitation

- *Physical neglect:* living conditions in which children do not receive enough food, clothing, medical attention, or supervision

- *Emotional neglect:* failure of caregivers to meet children's needs for affection and emotional support

- *Psychological abuse:* actions, such as ridicule, humiliation, scapegoating, or terrorizing, that damage children's cognitive, emotional, or social functioning

Although all experts recognize that these five types exist, they do not agree on how frequent and intense an adult's actions must be to be called maltreatment. The greatest problems arise in the case of subtle, ambiguous behaviors (Cicchetti & Toth, 1998a). All of us can agree that broken bones, cigarette burns, and bite marks are abusive, but the decision is harder to make in instances in which an adult touches or makes degrading comments to a child.

Some investigators regard psychological and sexual abuse as the most destructive forms, but psychological abuse may be the most common, since it accompanies most other types. More than 200,000 cases of child sexual abuse are reported each year (U.S. Department of Health and Human Services, 2000). Yet this statistic greatly underestimates the actual number, since affected children may feel frightened, confused, and guilty and usually are pressured into silence. Although children of all ages are targets, the largest number of sexual abuse victims are identified in middle childhood. We will pay special attention to this form of maltreatment in Chapter 13.

- **ORIGINS OF CHILD MALTREATMENT.** Early findings suggested that child maltreatment was rooted in adult psychological disturbance (Kempe et al., 1962). But it soon became clear that although child abuse was more common among disturbed parents, a single "abu-

CLEVE BRYANT/PHOTOEDIT

African-American mothers often use strict, no-nonsense discipline combined with warmth and reasoning—an approach well suited to promoting self-reliance, self-control, and a watchful attitude in dangerous neighborhoods.

TABLE 10.2

Factors Related to Child Maltreatment

FACTOR	DESCRIPTION
Parent characteristics	Psychological disturbance; alcohol and drug abuse; history of abuse as a child; belief in harsh, physical discipline; desire to satisfy unmet emotional needs through the child; unreasonable expectations for child behavior; young age (most under 30); low educational level
Child characteristics	Premature or very sick baby; difficult temperament; inattentiveness and overactivity; other developmental problems
Family characteristics	Low income; poverty; unemployment; homelessness; marital instability; social isolation; spouse or partner abuse; frequent moves; large families with closely spaced children; overcrowded living conditions; disorganized household; other signs of high life stress
Community	Unstable, run-down, and characterized by social isolation; few parks, child-care centers, preschool programs, recreation centers, and churches to serve as family supports
Culture	Approval of physical force and violence as ways to solve problems

Sources: Kotch et al., 1999; Wolfe, 1999.

sive personality type" does not exist. Sometimes even "normal" parents harm their children! Also, parents who were abused as children do not necessarily repeat the cycle with their own youngsters (Buchanan, 1996; Simons et al., 1991).

For help in understanding child maltreatment, researchers turned to *ecological systems theory* (see Chapters 1 and 2). They discovered that many interacting variables—at the family, community, and cultural levels—promote child abuse and neglect. Table 10.2 summarizes factors associated with child maltreatment. The more of these risks that are present, the greater the likelihood that abuse will occur. Let's examine each set of influences in turn.

The Family. Within the family, certain children—those whose characteristics make them more of a challenge to rear—are more likely to become targets of abuse. These include premature or very sick babies and children who are temperamentally difficult, inattentive and overactive, or who have other developmental problems (Kotch, Muller, & Blakely, 1999). But whether such children actually are maltreated depends on parents' characteristics.

Maltreating parents are less skillful than other parents in handling discipline confrontations and getting children to cooperate in working toward common goals. They also suffer from biased thinking about their child. For example, they often evaluate transgressions as worse than they are and attribute their child's misdeeds to a stubborn or bad disposition—perspectives that lead them to move quickly toward physical force (Milner, 1993; Rogosch et al., 1995).

Once abuse gets started, it quickly becomes part of a self-sustaining relationship. The small irritations to which abusive parents react—a fussy baby, a preschooler who knocks over a glass of milk, or a child who will not mind immediately—soon become bigger ones. Then the harshness of parental behavior increases. By the preschool years, abusive and neglectful parents seldom interact with their children. When they do, they rarely express pleasure and affection; the communication is almost always negative (Wolfe, 1999).

Most parents, however, have enough self-control not to respond to their children's misbehavior with abuse, and not all children with developmental problems are mistreated. Other factors must combine with these conditions to prompt an extreme parental response. Abusive parents respond to stressful situations with high emotional arousal. At the same time, such factors as low income and education (less than a high-school diploma), unemployment, young maternal age, alcohol and drug use, marital conflict, overcrowded living conditions, frequent moves, and extreme household disorganization are common in abusive homes (Gelles, 1998; Kotch et al., 1999). These personal and situational conditions increase the chances that parents will be too overwhelmed to meet basic child-rearing responsibilities or will vent their frustrations by lashing out at their children.

The Community. The majority of abusive parents are isolated from both formal and informal social supports in their communities. There are at least two causes of this social isolation. First, because of their own life histories, many of these parents have learned to mistrust and avoid others. They do not have the skills necessary for establishing and maintaining positive relationships with friends and relatives (Polansky et al., 1985). Second, abusive parents are more likely to live in unstable, run-down neighborhoods that provide few links between family and community, such as parks, child-care centers, preschool programs, recreation centers, and churches (Coulton, Korbin, & Su, 1999; Garbarino & Kostelny, 1993). For these reasons, they lack "lifelines" to others and have no one to turn to for help during stressful times.

The Larger Culture. One final set of factors—cultural values, laws, and customs—profoundly affects the chances that child maltreatment will occur when parents feel overburdened. Societies that view violence as an appropriate way to solve problems set the stage for child abuse. These conditions exist in the United States. Although all 50 states have laws designed to protect children from maltreatment, strong support still exists for the use of physical force with children. For example, during the past 30 years, the United States Supreme Court has twice upheld the right of school officials to use corporal punishment to discipline children. Crime rates are high in American cities, and television sets beam graphic displays of violence into family living rooms.

In view of the widespread acceptance of violent behavior in American culture, it is not surprising that over 90 percent of American parents report using slaps and spankings at one time or another to discipline their children (Staub, 1996). In countries where physical punishment is not accepted, such as Japan, Luxembourg, and Sweden, child abuse is rare (Zigler & Hall, 1989).

[handwritten margin note: U.S. seems to uphold physical force as a means of punishing children.]

■ **CONSEQUENCES OF CHILD MALTREATMENT.** The family circumstances of maltreated children impair the development of emotional self-regulation, self-concept, and social skills. Over time, these youngsters show serious learning and adjustment problems, including difficulties with peers, academic failure, severe depression, substance abuse, and delinquency (Cicchetti & Toth, 1998).

How do these damaging consequences occur? Think back to our earlier discussion of the effects of hostile cycles of parent–child interaction, which are especially severe for abused children. Indeed, a family characteristic strongly associated with child abuse is spouse abuse, in which physical and psychological brutality permeate parents' relationship (Margolin, 1998). Clearly, the home lives of abused children overflow with opportunities to learn to use aggression as a way of solving problems.

Furthermore, demeaning parental messages, in which children are ridiculed, humiliated, rejected, or terrorized, result in low self-esteem, high anxiety, self-blame, depression, and efforts to escape from extreme psychological pain—at times severe enough to prompt a suicide attempt in adolescence (Kaplan, Pelcovitz, & Labruna, 1999; Wolfe, 1999). At school, maltreated children are serious discipline problems. Their noncompliance, poor motivation, and cognitive immaturity interfere with academic achievement—an outcome that further undermines their chances for life success (Margolin & Gordis, 2000).

Finally, the trauma of repeated abuse can lead to psychophysiological changes, including abnormal EEG brain-wave activity and altered production of stress hormones (Ito et al., 1998; Nelson & Carver, 1998). These effects on brain functioning increase the chances that adjustment problems will endure.

■ **PREVENTING CHILD MALTREATMENT.** Since child maltreatment is embedded in families, communities, and society as a whole, efforts to prevent it must be directed at each of these levels. Many approaches have been suggested, including interventions that teach high-risk parents effective child-rearing and disciplinary strategies, high school child development courses that include direct experience with children, and broad social programs aimed at bettering economic conditions for low-SES families (Wolfe, 1999).

Children learn
by repetition.

You don't have to hit
to hurt.

San Francisco
Child Abuse Council
(415) 668-0494

Public service announcements help prevent child abuse by educating people about the problem and informing them of where to seek help. This poster reminds adults that degrading remarks can hit as hard as a fist.

In early parts of this book, we saw that providing social supports to families is very effective in easing parental stress. This approach sharply reduces child maltreatment as well (Azar & Wolfe, 1998). Research indicates that a trusting relationship with another person is the most important factor in preventing mothers with childhood histories of abuse from repeating the cycle with their own youngsters (Egeland, Jacobvitz, & Sroufe, 1988). Parents Anonymous, a national organization that has as its main goal helping child-abusing parents learn constructive parenting practices, does so largely through providing social supports to families. Its local chapters offer self-help group meetings, daily phone calls, and regular home visits to relieve social isolation and teach alternative child-rearing skills.

Besides these efforts, changes are needed in American culture. Many experts believe that child maltreatment cannot be eliminated as long as violence is widespread and corporal punishment is regarded as an acceptable child-rearing alternative. In addition, combating poverty and its diverse correlates—family stress and disorganization, inadequate food and medical care, teenage parenthood, low-birth-weight babies, and parental hopelessness—would reduce child maltreatment.

Although more cases reach the courts than in decades past, child maltreatment remains a crime that is difficult to prove. Most of the time, the only witnesses are the child victims or other loyal family members. Even in court cases in which the evidence is strong, judges hesitate to impose the ultimate safeguard against further harm: permanently removing the child from the family.

There are several reasons for this reluctant attitude. First, in American society, government intervention into family life is viewed as a last resort. Second, despite destructive family relationships, maltreated children and their parents usually are attached to one another. Most of the time, neither desires separation. Finally, the American legal system tends to regard children as parental property rather than as human beings in their own right, and this also has stood in the way of court-ordered protection.

Even with intensive treatment, some adults persist in their abusive acts. An estimated 1,500 American children die from maltreatment each year (U.S. Department of Health and Human Services, 2000). When parents are unlikely to change their behavior, the drastic step of separating parent from child and legally terminating parental rights is the only reasonable course of action.

Child maltreatment is a distressing and horrifying topic—a sad note on which to end our discussion of a period of childhood that is so full of excitement, awakening, and discovery. But there is reason to be optimistic. Great strides have been made over the past several decades in understanding and preventing child maltreatment.

Ask YOURSELF...

review   *Summarize findings on ethnic variations in child-rearing styles. Is the concept of authoritative parenting useful for understanding effective parenting across cultures? Explain.*

apply   *Chandra heard a news report that 10 severely neglected children, living in squalor in an inner-city tenement, were discovered by Chicago police. Chandra thought to herself, "What could possibly lead parents to mistreat their children so badly?" How would you answer Chandra's question?*

connect   *Which child-rearing style is most likely to be associated with use of inductive discipline, and why?*

reflect   *How would you classify your parents' child-rearing styles? What factors might have influenced their approach to child rearing?*

Summary

ERIKSON'S THEORY: INITIATIVE VERSUS GUILT

What personality changes take place during Erikson's stage of initiative versus guilt?

- Preschoolers develop a new sense of purposefulness as they grapple with the psychological conflict of **initiative versus guilt.** A healthy sense of initiative depends on exploring the social world through play, forming a conscience through identifying with the same-sex parent, and receiving supportive child rearing. Erikson's image of initiative captures the diverse emotional and social changes of early childhood.

SELF-DEVELOPMENT

Describe preschoolers' self-concepts, understanding of intentions, and self-esteem.

- Preschoolers' **self-concepts** largely consist of observable characteristics and typical emotions and attitudes. Their increasing self-awareness underlies struggles with other children over objects as well as first efforts to cooperate. By the end of early childhood, children understand intention as a mental state and use a wider range of information to distinguish intentional from unintentional acts.

- During early childhood, **self-esteem** has already begun to differentiate into several self-judgments. Preschoolers' high self-esteem contributes to their mastery-oriented approach to the environment. However, even a little adult disapproval can undermine a young child's self-esteem and enthusiasm for learning.

EMOTIONAL DEVELOPMENT

Cite changes in understanding and expressing emotion during early childhood, along with factors that influence those changes.

- Young children have an impressive understanding of the causes, consequences, and behavioral signs of emotion. By age 3 to 4, they are also aware of a variety of strategies that assist with emotional self-regulation. Temperament, adult modeling, and conversations about feelings influence the development of effective techniques for handling negative emotion.

- Preschoolers experience self-conscious emotions more often as their self-concepts become better developed and they become increasingly sensitive to the praise and criticism of others. Young children are likely to feel shame and guilt for any act that can be described as wrongdoing, even if it is accidental. Parents who repeatedly give feedback about the worth of the child and her performance have children who experience overly high, maladaptive levels of shame and pride.

- Empathy becomes more common over the preschool years. Temperament and parenting affect the extent to which empathy prompts **sympathy** and results in **prosocial,** or **altruistic, behavior.**

PEER RELATIONS

Describe peer sociability, friendship, and social problem solving in early childhood, and discuss parent and sibling influences on early peer relations.

- During early childhood, peer interaction increases. According to Parten, it moves from **nonsocial activity** to **parallel play** and then to **associative** and **cooperative play.** However, preschoolers do not follow this straightforward developmental sequence. Solitary play and parallel play remain common throughout early childhood. Sociodramatic play becomes especially frequent and supports many aspects of emotional and social development.

- Preschoolers view friendship in concrete, activity-based terms. Their interactions with friends are especially positive and cooperative and serve as effective sources of social support as they enter kindergarten and adjust to school.

- Conflicts with peers offer children invaluable learning opportunities for **social problem solving,** which profoundly affects peer relations. Social problem solving improves from the preschool to early school years. By kindergarten to second grade, each of its information-processing components is related to socially competent behavior. Training in social problem solving improves peer relations and psychological adjustment.

- Parents influence early peer relations by arranging informal peer play activities and offering advice, guidance, and examples of how to act toward others. Mothers provide most of this verbal coaching, whereas fathers more often influence preschoolers' peer relations through style of parent–child play. Children with stressful home lives often generalize their negative sibling interactions to peers.

FOUNDATIONS OF MORALITY

What are the central features of psychoanalytic, behaviorist and social learning, and cognitive-developmental approaches to moral development?

- The psychoanalytic and behaviorist approaches to morality focus on how children acquire ready-made standards held by adults. Freud was correct that guilt is an important motivator of moral action. However, discipline promoting fear of punishment and loss of parental love does not foster conscience development. **Induction** is far more effective in encouraging self-control and prosocial behavior.

- Behaviorism and social learning theory regard reinforcement and modeling as the basis for moral action. Effective adult models are warm and powerful, and they practice what they preach. Harsh punishment does not promote moral internalization and socially desirable behavior. Alternatives, such as **time out** and withdrawal of privileges, can help parents

Summary (continued)

avoid the undesirable side effects of punishment. When parents decide to use punishment, they can increase its effectiveness by being consistent; maintaining a warm, caring relationship with their child; and accompanying the punishment with explanations. The most effective forms of discipline encourage good conduct by building a positive, cooperative relationship with the child.

- The cognitive-developmental perspective views children as active thinkers about social rules. By age 4, preschoolers consider intentions in making moral judgments and can tell the difference between truthfulness and lying. They also distinguish moral imperatives from social conventions and matters of personal choice. Peer interaction provides children with important opportunities to work out their first ideas about justice and fairness. Parents who discuss moral issues with their children help them reason about morality.

Describe the development of aggression in early childhood, including family and television as influences.

- All children display aggression from time to time. During early childhood, **instrumental aggression** declines while **hostile aggression** increases. Two types of hostile aggression appear: **overt aggression,** which is more common in boys, and **relational aggression,** which is more common in girls.

- Ineffective discipline and a conflict-ridden family atmosphere promote and sustain aggression in children. Televised violence also promotes childhood aggression. Young children's limited understanding of TV content increases their willingness to uncritically accept and imitate what they see.

- Teaching parents effective child-rearing practices, providing children with social problem-solving training, intervening in hostile family relationships, and shielding children from violent TV help to reduce aggressive behavior.

GENDER TYPING

Discuss genetic and environmental influences on preschoolers' gender-stereotyped beliefs and behavior.

- **Gender typing** is well under way in early childhood. Preschoolers acquire a wide range of gender stereotypes and behaviors. Their gender-stereotyped beliefs operate like blanket rules rather than flexible guidelines.

- Genetic factors are believed to play a role in boys' higher activity level and overt aggression and children's preference for same-sex playmates. At the same time, parents, teachers, peers, television, and the broader social environment encourage many gender-typed responses.

Describe and evaluate major theories on the emergence of gender identity.

- Researchers measure **gender identity** by asking children and adults to rate themselves on gender-stereotyped personality traits. Although most people have traditional gender identities, some are **androgynous,** scoring high on both masculine and feminine characteristics.

- According to social learning theory, preschoolers first acquire gender-typed responses through modeling and reinforcement and then organize them into gender-linked ideas about themselves. Cognitive-developmental theory suggests that **gender constancy** must be mastered before children develop gender-typed behavior, but in contrast to cognitive-developmental predictions, gender-role behavior is acquired long before gender constancy.

- **Gender schema theory** is an information-processing approach to gender typing that combines social learning and cognitive-developmental features. As children acquire gender-stereotyped preferences and behaviors, they form masculine and feminine categories, or gender schemas, that they apply to themselves and use to interpret their world.

CHILD REARING AND EMOTIONAL AND SOCIAL DEVELOPMENT

Describe the impact of child-rearing styles on children's development, and explain why authoritative parenting is effective.

- Two broad dimensions, demandingness and responsiveness, yield four styles of child rearing. The **authoritative style,** which is demanding and responsive, promotes cognitive, emotional, and social competence. Parental explanations, caring concern, and reasonable demands for mature behavior account for its effectiveness.

- The **authoritarian style,** which is high in demandingness but low in responsiveness, is associated with anxious, withdrawn behavior and hostility when frustrated. The **permissive style** is responsive but undemanding; children who experience it are typically very immature and show poor self-control and achievement. The **uninvolved style** is low in demandingness and responsiveness. It disrupts virtually all aspects of development.

Discuss the multiple origins of child maltreatment, its consequences for development, and prevention strategies.

- Child maltreatment is related to factors within the family, community, and larger culture. Child and parent characteristics often feed on one another to produce abusive behavior. Unmanageable parental stress and social isolation greatly increase the chances that abuse and neglect will occur. When a society approves of force and violence as a means for solving problems, child abuse is promoted.

- Maltreated children are impaired in emotional self-regulation, self-concept, social skills, and learning in school. Over time they show a wide variety of serious adjustment problems. Successful prevention of child maltreatment requires efforts at the family, community, and societal levels.

Important terms and concepts

androgyny (p. 393)
associative play (p. 375)
authoritarian style (p. 397)
authoritative style (p. 397)
cooperative play (p. 375)
gender constancy (p. 394)
gender identity (p. 393)
gender schema theory (p. 394)
gender typing (p. 390)

hostile aggression (p. 385)
induction (p. 380)
initiative versus guilt (p. 366)
instrumental aggression (p. 385)
nonsocial activity (p. 375)
overt aggression (p. 385)
parallel play (p. 375)
permissive style (p. 397)

prosocial, or altruistic, behavior (p. 373)
relational aggression (p. 385)
self-concept (p. 367)
self-esteem (p. 368)
social problem solving (p. 377)
sympathy (p. 373)
time out (p. 383)
uninvolved style (p. 397)

fyi . . . for further information and help

Consult the companion website for this book, where you will find additional weblinks and associated learning activities:
www.ablongman.com/berk

CHILDREN'S TELEVISION

National Institute on Media and the Family
www.mediaandthefamily.org

An organization that provides research, education, and information on the impact of electronic media on children and families. Website features a rating system for evaluating various media, resources for parents and educators, and quizzes for evaluating family media habits.

Center for Communication and Social Policy
www.ccsp.ucsb.edu

An organization that conducts research and promotes discussion of policy issues related to communication. One of the Center's priorities is increasing public sensitity to the harmful effects of media violence. The National Television Violence Study is available on its website.

CHILD ABUSE AND NEGLECT

Child Help USA, Inc.
www.childhelpusa.org

An organization that promotes public awareness of child abuse through publications, media campaigns, and a speakers' bureau. Supports the National Child Abuse Hotline, 1-800-4-A-CHILD. Callers may request information about child abuse or speak with a crisis counselor.

Parents Anonymous
www.parentsanonymous.org

A support group dedicated to prevention and treatment of child abuse. Local groups provide support to child-abusing parents and training in nonviolent child-rearing techniques.

National Clearinghouse on Child Abuse and Neglect Information
www.calib.com/nccanch

An organization that provides information to states and communities wishing to develop programs and activities that identify, prevent, and treat child abuse and neglect.

Milestones of development in early childhood

AGE	PHYSICAL	COGNITIVE	LANGUAGE	EMOTIONAL/SOCIAL
2 years	■ Slower gains in height and weight than in toddlerhood. (294) ■ Balance improves; walking becomes better coordinated. (310) ■ Running, jumping, hopping, throwing, and catching develop. (310) ■ Puts on and removes some items of clothing. (312) ■ Uses spoon effectively. (312)	■ Make-believe becomes less dependent on realistic toys, less self-centered, and more complex. (325) ■ Can take the perspective of others in simple situations. (330) ■ Recognition memory is well developed. (341–342) ■ Aware of the difference between inner mental and outer physical events. (344–346) 	■ Vocabulary increases rapidly. (356) ■ Sentences follow word order of native language; adds grammatical markers. (358) ■ Displays effective conversational skills. (359)	■ Begins to develop a self-concept and self-esteem. (367) ■ Distinguishes own intentional from unintentional acts. (369) ■ Cooperation and instrumental aggression appear. (367, 385) ■ Understands causes, consequences, and behavioral signs of basic emotions. (371) ■ Empathy increases. (373–374) ■ Gender-stereotyped beliefs and behavior increase. (391)
3–4 years	■ May no longer need a daytime nap. (303) ■ Running, jumping, hopping, throwing, and catching become better coordinated. (310) ■ Galloping and one-foot skipping appear. (311) ■ Rides tricycle. (311) ■ Uses scissors. (312) ■ Draws first picture of a person. (314) ■ Can distinguish writing from nonwriting. (318)	■ Masters dual representation. (326) ■ Notices and reasons about transformations, reverses thinking, and understands causality in familiar situations. (328) ■ Classifies familiar objects hierarchically. (329) ■ Uses private speech to guide behavior in challenging tasks. (337) ■ Attention becomes more sustained and planful. (341) ■ Uses scripts to recall familiar experiences. (342) ■ Understands that both beliefs and desires determine behavior. (344) ■ Aware of some meaningful features of written language. (346, 348) ■ Counts small numbers of objects and grasps cardinality. (349)	■ Masters increasingly complex grammatical structures. (357–358) ■ Occasionally over-extends grammatical rules to exceptions. (358) ■ Understands many culturally accepted ways of adjusting speech to fit the age, sex, and social status of speakers and listeners. (359)	■ Begins to distinguish others' intentional from unintentional acts. (369) ■ Emotional self-regulation improves. (372) ■ Experiences self-conscious emotions more often. (372–373) ■ Nonsocial activity declines and interactive play increases. (375) ■ Instrumental aggression declines, and hostile aggression increases. (385) ■ Forms first friendships. (377) ■ Distinguishes moral from social-conventional and personal matters. (384–385) ■ Preference for same-sex playmates strengthens. (391)

AGE	PHYSICAL	COGNITIVE	LANGUAGE	EMOTIONAL/SOCIAL
5–6 years	■ Body is streamlined and longer-legged with proportions similar to those of adults. (274)	■ Ability to distinguish appearance from reality improves. (334)	■ Vocabulary reaches about 10,000 words. (356)	■ Bases understanding of people's intentions on a wider range of social cues. (369)
	■ First permanent tooth erupts. (296)	■ Attention continues to improve. (341)	■ Uses many complex grammatical structures. (358)	■ Ability to interpret, predict, and influence others' emotional reactions improves. (371)
	■ Gross motor skills increase in speed and endurance. (310)	■ Recall, scripted memory, and autobiographical memory improve. (341–343)		
	■ Skipping appears. (311)	■ Understanding of false belief improves. (344–345)		■ Relies more on language to express empathy. (373–374)
	■ Shows mature throwing and catching patterns. (311)			■ Becomes better at social problem solving. (377–379)
	■ Ties shoes, draws more complex pictures, uses an adultlike pencil grip, and writes name. (312–316)	■ Understands that letters and sounds are linked in systematic ways. (346, 348)		■ Has acquired many morally relevant rules and behaviors. (380)
	■ Can discriminate letters of the alphabet. (318)	■ Counts on and counts down, engaging in simple addition and subtraction. (349)		■ Gender-stereotyped beliefs and behavior continue to increase. (390–393)

Note: Numbers in parentheses indicate the page(s) on which each milestone is discussed.

"My World in the Year 2000"
Sherry Alef Georgy
12 years, Egypt

Middle childhood brings great advances in motor coordination, and children strive to acquire new athletic skills. This fantastic painting depicts these developments in motor mastery as eager children climb to the planets and stars. Chapter 11 takes up the diverse physical attainments of the school years.

Physical Development in Middle Childhood

I'm on my way,

Mom!" hollered 10-year-old Joey as he stuffed the last bite of toast into his mouth, slung his book bag over his shoulder, dashed out the door, jumped on his bike, and headed down the street for school. Joey's 8-year-old sister Lizzie followed, kissing her mother goodbye and pedaling furiously until she caught up with Joey. Rena, the children's mother and one of my colleagues at the university, watched from the front porch as her son and daughter disappeared in the distance.

"They're branching out," Rena remarked to me over lunch that day as she described the children's expanding activities and relationships. Homework, household chores, soccer teams, music lessons, scouting, friends at school and in the neighborhood, and Joey's new paper route were all part of the children's routine. "It seems as if the basics are all there; I don't have to monitor Joey and Lizzie so constantly anymore. Although being a parent is still very challenging, it's more a matter of refinements—helping them become independent, competent, and productive individuals."

Joey and Lizzie have entered the phase of development called middle childhood, which spans the years from 6 to 11. Around the world, children of this age are assigned new responsibilities as they begin the process of entering the adult world. Joey and Lizzie, like other youngsters in industrialized nations, spend long hours in school. Indeed, middle childhood is often called the "school years," since its onset is marked by the start of formal schooling. In village and tribal cultures, the school may be a field or a jungle rather than a classroom. But universally, mature members of society guide children of this age period toward tasks that increasingly resemble those they will perform as adults (Rogoff, 1996).

This chapter focuses on physical growth in middle childhood—changes less spectacular than in earlier years. By age 6, the brain has reached 95 percent of its adult size, and the body continues to grow slowly. In this way, nature grants school-age children the mental powers to master challenging tasks as well as added time to learn before reaching physical maturity.

We begin by reviewing typical growth trends as well as special health concerns of middle childhood. Then we turn to rapid gains in motor abilities, which support practical everyday activities, athletic skills, and participation in organized games. We will see that each of these achievements is affected by and contributes to cognitive, emotional, and social development. Our discussion will echo a familiar theme—that all domains are interrelated.

Body Growth

The rate of physical growth during the school years extends the pattern that characterized early childhood. Compared with the rapid height and weight gain of the first 2 years, growth is slow and regular.

CHANGES IN BODY SIZE AND PROPORTIONS

At age 6, the average North American child weighs about 45 pounds and is $3^{1}/_{2}$ feet tall. As Figure 11.1 shows, children continue to add about 2 to 3 inches in height and 5 pounds in weight each year. However, when researchers carefully track individuals, growth is not quite as steady as these norms suggest. A longitudinal study of Scottish children, who were followed between ages 3 and 10, revealed slight spurts in height. Girls tended to forge ahead at ages $4^{1}/_{2}$, $6^{1}/_{2}$, $8^{1}/_{2}$, and 10, boys slightly later, at $4^{1}/_{2}$, 7, 9, and $10^{1}/_{2}$. Between these spurts were lulls in which growth was slower (Butler, McKie, & Ratcliffe, 1990).

Look again at Figure 11.1, and you will see that girls are slightly shorter and lighter than boys at ages 6 to 8. By age 9, this trend reverses. Already, Rena noticed, Lizzie was starting to catch up with Joey in physical size. For many girls, the 10-year-old height spurt overlaps with the much more dramatic adolescent growth spurt, which takes place 2 years earlier in girls than boys.

During middle childhood, the lower portion of the body is growing fastest, so children appear longer-legged than they had in early childhood. They grow out of their jeans more quickly than their jackets and frequently need larger shoes.

Because the lower portion of the body is growing fastest at this age period, Joey and Lizzie appeared longer-legged than they had in early childhood. Rena discovered that they grew out of their jeans more quickly than their jackets and frequently needed larger shoes. As in early childhood, school-age girls have slightly more body fat and boys more muscle. After age 8, girls begin accumulating fat at a faster rate, and they will add even more during adolescence (Tanner, 1990).

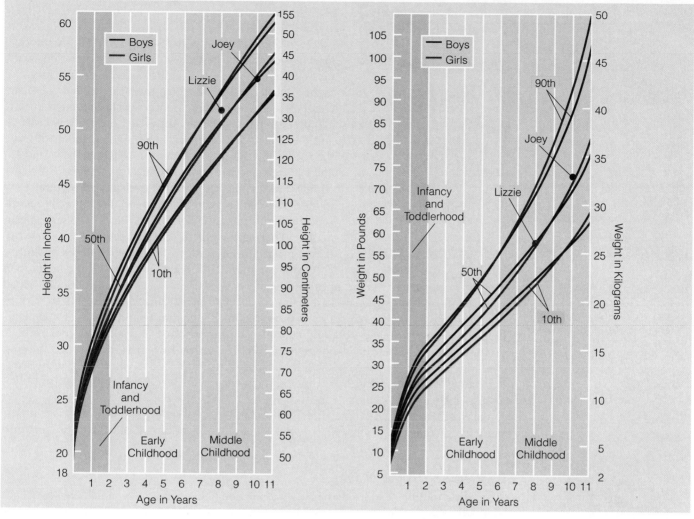

FIGURE 11.1

WORLDWIDE VARIATIONS IN BODY SIZE

A glance into any elementary school classroom reveals that individual differences in body growth remain great in middle childhood. Diversity in physical size is especially apparent when we travel to different nations. Measurements of 8-year-olds living in many parts of the world reveal a 9-inch gap between the smallest and the largest youngsters. The shortest children tend to be found in South America, Asia, the Pacific Islands, and parts of Africa and include such ethnic groups as Colombian, Burmese, Thai, Vietnamese, Ethiopian, and Bantu. The tallest children reside in Australia, northern and central Europe, and the United States and consist of Czech, Dutch, Latvian, Norwegian, Swiss, and black and white American children (Meredith, 1978). These findings remind us that growth norms based largely on Caucasian children, such as those in Figure 11.1, must be applied with caution, especially in countries with high immigration rates and many ethnic minority children.

What accounts for these vast differences in physical size? Both heredity and environment are involved. Body size sometimes results from evolutionary adaptations to a particular climate. For example, long, lean physiques are typical in hot, tropical regions and short, stocky ones in cold, Arctic areas. At the same time, children who grow tallest usually reside in developed countries, where food is plentiful and infectious diseases are largely controlled. In contrast, small children tend to live in less developed regions, where poverty, hunger, and disease are common (Tanner, 1990).

Gains in height and weight during middle childhood among North American children. The slow rate of growth established in early childhood extends into the school years. Girls are slightly shorter and lighter than boys until age 9, at which time this trend is reversed, as girls approach the adolescent growth spurt. Eight-year-old Lizzie is beginning to catch up with 10-year-old Joey in physical size. Wide individual differences in body size continue to exist, as the percentiles on these charts reveal.

Body size is sometimes the result of evolutionary adaptations to a particular climate. These boys of the Sudan, who live on the hot African plains, have long, lean physiques, which permit the body to cool easily.

SECULAR TRENDS IN PHYSICAL GROWTH

Over the past 150 years, **secular trends in physical growth**—changes in body size from one generation to the next—have taken place in industrialized nations. Joey and Lizzie are taller and heavier than their parents and grandparents were as children. These trends have been found in nearly all European nations, Japan, Australia, Canada, New Zealand, and the United States. For example, measurements of more than 24,000 Bogalusa, Louisiana, schoolchildren between 1973 and 1992 revealed an average height gain of nearly 1/3 inch per decade (Freedman et al., 2000). The secular gain appears early in life and becomes greater over childhood and early adolescence. Then, as mature body size is reached, the secular gain declines. The pattern suggests that the larger size of today's children is mostly due to a faster rate of physical development.

Why are so many children growing faster and larger than their ancestors? Once again, improved health and nutrition play major roles. Orphaned children from developing countries who are adopted by parents in industrialized nations often show more rapid physical growth and attain greater stature and weight than do children remaining in their land of origin. Secular trends are not as large for low-income children, who have poorer diets and are more likely to suffer from growth-stunting illnesses. And in regions of the world with widespread poverty, famine, and disease, either no secular change or a secular decrease in body size has occurred (Barnes-Josiah & Augustin, 1995; Proos, 1993).

Although secular gain in height has slowed in recent decades, gain in weight is continuing at a high rate. As we will see later, overweight and obesity have reached epic proportions.

SKELETAL GROWTH

During middle childhood, the bones of the body lengthen and broaden. However, ligaments are not yet firmly attached to bones. This, combined with increasing muscle strength, grants children unusual flexibility of movement. School-age youngsters often seem like "physical contortionists," turning cartwheels and doing splits and handstands. As their bodies become stronger, many children experience a greater desire for physical exercise. About 13 to 18 percent complain of evening "growing pains"—stiffness and aches in the legs—as muscles adapt to an enlarging skeleton (Walco, 1997).

One of the most striking aspects of skeletal growth in middle childhood is replacement of primary, or "baby," teeth with permanent teeth. Recall from Chapter 8 that children lose their first tooth at the end of early childhood. Between ages 6 and 12, all 20 primary teeth are replaced by permanent ones, with girls losing their teeth slightly earlier than boys. The first teeth to go are the central incisors (lower and then upper front teeth), giving many first and second graders a "toothless" smile. For a while, permanent teeth seem much too large. Gradually, facial bones grow, especially those of the jaw and chin, causing the child's face to lengthen and mouth to widen, accommodating the newly erupting teeth.

Care of the teeth is essential during the school years, since dental health affects the child's appearance, speech, and ability to chew properly. Children often neglect to brush thoroughly, and they usually cannot floss by themselves until about 9 years of age. Parents need to remind and help them with these tasks.

More than 50 percent of American school-age children have at least some tooth decay (U.S. Department of Health and Human Services, 2000e). As in the preschool years, low-SES children have especially high levels (see Chapter 8). Children without health insurance are three times more likely to have unmet dental needs. As decay progresses, they experience pain, embarrassment at damaged teeth, distraction from play and learning, and school absences due to dental-related illnesses.

secular trends in physical growth
Changes in body size from one generation to the next.

malocclusion
A condition in which the upper and lower teeth do not meet properly.

neurotransmitters
Chemicals that permit neurons to communicate across synapses.

© BETTY PRESS/WOODFIN CAMP & ASSOCIATES

One-third of school-age children suffer from **malocclusion,** a condition in which the upper and lower teeth do not meet properly. In about 14 percent of cases, serious difficulties in biting and chewing result. Malocclusion can be caused by thumb and finger sucking after permanent teeth erupt (Vogel, 1998). Children who were eager thumb suckers during infancy and early childhood may require gentle but persistent encouragement to give up the habit by school entry. A second cause of malocclusion is crowding of permanent teeth. In some children, this problem clears up as the jaw grows. Others need braces, a common sight by the end of elementary school.

BRAIN DEVELOPMENT

Brain development in middle childhood largely involves more efficient functioning of various structures. The *frontal lobes* of the cerebral cortex (responsible for thought and consciousness) show a slight increase in surface area between ages 5 and 7 due to continuing myelinization. Brain-imaging research reveals that the *corpus callosum* thickens, leading to improved communication between the two cortical hemispheres (see Chapter 8, page 299). As children acquire more abilities, synaptic connections between active neurons strengthen and neural fibers become more elaborate. *Synaptic pruning* (reduction of unused synapses) and death of surrounding neurons support this process. In addition, *lateralization* of the cerebral hemispheres, already well established in early childhood, increases over the school years.

Little information is available on how the brain changes in other ways during this age period. One idea is that development occurs largely at the level of **neurotransmitters,** chemicals that permit neurons to communicate across synapses (see Chapter 5, pages 173–174). Over time, neurons become increasingly selective, responding only to certain chemical messages. This change may contribute to the more efficient and flexible thinking and behavior of school-age children. Secretions of particular neurotransmitters are related to cognitive performance, social and emotional adjustment, and ability to withstand stress in children and adults. Children may suffer serious developmental problems, such as inattention and overactivity, emotional disturbance, and epilepsy (an illness involving brain seizures and loss of motor control) when neurotransmitters are not present in appropriate balances (Barr et al., 2000; Dammerman & Kriegstein, 2000).

Researchers also believe that brain functioning may change in middle childhood because of the influence of hormones. Around age 7 to 8, an increase in *androgens* (male sex hormones), secreted by the adrenal glands (located on top of the kidneys), occurs in children of both sexes. Androgens will rise further among boys at puberty, when the testes release them in large amounts. In many animal species, androgens affect brain organization and behavior, and they do so in humans as well (Hines & Green, 1991). Recall from Chapter 10 that androgens contribute to boys' higher activity level. They may also promote social dominance and play-fighting, topics we will take up at the end of this chapter (Maccoby, 1998).

Ask YOURSELF...

review   *What aspects of physical growth account for the long-legged appearance of many 8- to 12-year-olds?*

apply   *Joey complained to his mother that it wasn't fair that his younger sister Lizzie was almost as tall as he was. He worried that he wasn't growing fast enough. How should Rena respond to Joey's concern?*

connect   *Relate secular trends in physical growth to the concept of cohort effects, discussed on page 44 of Chapter 1.*

reflect   *In your family, how do members of your generation compare with members of your parents' generation in height and weight? How about your grandparents' generation? Do your observations illustrate secular trends?*

Common Health Problems

Children like Joey and Lizzie, who come from economically advantaged homes, appear to be at their healthiest during middle childhood, full of energy and play. The cumulative effects of good nutrition, combined with rapid development of the body's immune system, offer greater protection against disease. Infections occur less often now. At the same time, growth in lung size permits more air to be exchanged with each breath, so children are better able to exercise vigorously without tiring.

Nevertheless, a variety of health problems do occur. We will see that many of them are more prevalent among low-SES youngsters. Return to Chapter 8, page 305, to review the status of children's health care in the United States compared with other nations. Because economically disadvantaged American families often lack health insurance and cannot afford to pay for medical visits on their own, many children continue to be deprived of regular access to a doctor. And a growing number also lack such basic necessities as a comfortable home and regular meals. Not surprisingly, poverty continues to be a powerful predictor of poor health during middle childhood.

VISION AND HEARING

The most common vision problem in middle childhood is **myopia,** or nearsightedness. By the end of the school years, nearly 25 percent of children are affected, a rate that rises to 60 percent by early adulthood (Sperduto et al., 1996).

Kinship studies reveal that heredity contributes to myopia. Identical twins are more likely than fraternal twins to have the condition to a similar degree, and children with two myopic parents are more than six times as likely to become myopic as children with one or no myopic parents (Pacella et al., 1999; Teikari et al., 1992). Early biological trauma can also induce myopia. School-age children with low birth weights show an especially high rate, believed to result from immaturity of visual structures at birth, slower eye growth throughout childhood, and a greater incidence of eye disease (Robinson, 1999).

But myopia is also related to experience, as it has increased in recent generations, in developed and developing nations alike. Parents often warn their youngsters not to read in dim light or sit too close to the TV or computer screen, exclaiming, "You'll ruin your eyes!" Their concern is well founded. Myopia progresses much more rapidly during the school year, when children spend more time reading and doing other close work, than during the summer months (Goss & Rainey, 1998). Furthermore, myopia is one of the few health conditions that increase with family income and education. For example, a dramatic rise in myopia among Hong Kong Chinese children has occurred only in the past 50 years, during which the country changed from a largely illiterate to a highly educated society (Wu & Edwards, 1999). Fortunately, for those children who develop nearsightedness because they love reading, sewing, drawing, or model building, the condition can be corrected easily with glasses.

During middle childhood, the eustachian tube (the canal that runs from the inner ear to the throat) becomes longer, narrower, and more slanted, preventing fluid and bacteria from traveling so easily from the mouth to the ear. As a result, *otitis media* (middle ear infection) becomes less frequent (see Chapter 8). Still, some children have chronic ear infections that, if left untreated, can lead to permanent hearing defects. About 3 to 4 percent of the school-age population, and as many as 20 percent of low-SES youngsters, develop some hearing loss for this reason (Daly, Hunter, & Giebink, 1999). Regular screening tests for both vision and hearing are important so that defects can be corrected before they lead to serious learning difficulties.

MALNUTRITION

School-age children need a well-balanced, plentiful diet to provide energy for successful learning in school and increased physical activity. Many youngsters are so focused on play,

myopia
Nearsightedness; inability to see distant objects clearly.

friendships, and new activities that they spend little time at the table. Joey's hurried breakfast, described at the beginning of this chapter, is a common event during middle childhood. Also, the percentage of children eating dinner with their families drops sharply between 9 and 14 years, and family dinnertimes have waned in general over the past decade. Yet eating an evening meal with parents leads to higher consumption of fruits and vegetables and lower consumption of fried foods and soft drinks (Gillman et al., 2000). And the majority of children who experience regular family dinners report that their parents provide useful nutrition information during mealtime conversation (Gallup Organization, 1995).

Readily available, healthy between-meal snacks—cheese, fruit, raw vegetables, and peanut butter—can help meet school-age children's nutritional needs. As long as parents encourage healthy eating, mild nutritional deficits have no impact on development. But as we have seen in earlier chapters, many poverty-stricken children in developing countries and in the United States suffer from serious and prolonged malnutrition. By middle childhood, the effects are apparent in retarded physical growth, low intelligence test scores, poor motor coordination, inattention, and distractibility.

This negative impact of malnutrition on learning and behavior may be extended during the school years in at least two ways. First, compared with their adequately nourished agemates, growth-stunted school-age children respond with greater fear to stressful situations. Their blood levels of cortisol and their heart rates rise more sharply (Fernald & Grantham-McGregor, 1998). Perhaps the gnawing pain of hunger permanently alters their stress response. Second, animal evidence reveals that a deficient diet alters the production of neurotransmitters in the brain—an effect that can disrupt all aspects of psychological functioning (Levitsky & Strupp, 1995).

Unfortunately, when malnutrition persists for many years, permanent physical and mental damage results. As the Biology and Environment box on page 416 reveals, growth-stunted children whose diets eventually improve are more vulnerable to excessive weight gain. And even with dietary enrichment, catch-up growth in middle childhood is a poorer predictor of cognitive gains than is catch-up growth in infancy and early childhood (Grantham-McGregor, Walker, & Chang, 2000).

Prevention of malnutrition—through government-sponsored food programs beginning in the early years and continuing throughout childhood—is necessary. In studies carried out in Kenya and Egypt, total calorie and protein intakes of school-age children were positively related to mental test scores (Sigman et al., 1989; Wachs et al., 1995). In both nations, better-quality protein (from animal sources) was the strongest dietary predictor of cognitive development in middle childhood.

OBESITY

Mona, a very overweight child in Lizzie's class, often stood on the sidelines and watched during recess. When she did join the children's games, she was slow and clumsy. On a daily basis, Mona was the target of unkind comments: "Move it, Tubs!" "Tree trunks for legs!" "No fatsoes allowed!" Although Mona was a good student, other children continued to reject her inside the classroom. When it was time to choose partners for a special activity, Mona was one of the last to be selected. On most afternoons, she walked home from school by herself while the other children gathered in groups, talking, laughing, and chasing. Once home and in the kitchen, Mona sought comfort in high-calorie snacks, which promoted further weight gain.

Mona is one of over 25 percent of American children who suffer from **obesity,** a greater-than-20-percent increase over average body weight, based on the child's age, sex, and physical build. Large increases in overweight and obesity during the past several decades have been reported for Canada, Denmark, Finland, Great Britain, New Zealand, and, especially, the United States. From 1980 to 2000, the rate of obesity in the American population climbed from 15 to 27 percent (U.S. Department of Health and Human Services, 2000h). Smaller increases have occurred in other industrialized nations, including Australia, Germany, Israel, the Netherlands, and Sweden (Flegal, 1999). Obesity rates are also increasing rapidly in

obesity
A greater-than-20-percent increase over average body weight, based on the child's age, sex, and physical build.

Biology & ENVIRONMENT

GROWTH STUNTING DUE TO EARLY MALNUTRITION: RISK FACTOR FOR CHILDHOOD OBESITY

In research on overweight children in four developing nations, a disheartening link between early growth stunting due to malnutrition and childhood obesity has emerged. Nationwide surveys in Brazil, China, Russia, and South Africa yielded information on height for age (a measure of poor diet and stunting) and weight for height (a measure of obesity) for thousands of children (Popkin, Richards, & Montiero, 1996). The percentage of children who were stunted (very short for their age) ranged from 15 percent in Brazil to 22 percent in China and 30 percent in South Africa. In Russia, stunting is a new problem. It has emerged only in the past decade, after poverty rose while government-sponsored maternal and child nutrition programs deteriorated. About 9 percent of Russian children are growth stunted.

As Figure 11.2 shows, in each country except Brazil, rate of overweight was far greater among stunted than nonstunted children. Short, growth-retarded children were twice as likely as their peers to be fat in South Africa, three times as likely in China, and seven times as likely in Russia. Family income seemed to account for the lack of association between stunting and fatness in Brazil; many overweight Brazilian children come from financially better-off homes.

What explains excessive weight gain among growth-stunted children? Researchers believe that two physiological changes are involved:

- To protect itself, a malnourished body establishes a low basal metabolism rate, stretching its energy resources as far as possible—a change that may endure after nutrition improves.

- Early malnutrition may cause brain structures responsible for appetite control to be reset at a higher level. Consequently, stunted children are likely to overeat when food—especially high-fat products—becomes more widely available, which generally occurs as developing nations gain economically and modernize (Barker, 1994; Popkin, 1994).

The growth stunting–obesity link is evident among certain low-income, ethnic minorities in the United States, including Mexican-American and Hmong (Laotian) groups (Himes et al., 1992; Valdez et al., 1994). As economic conditions improve worldwide, children everywhere need a high-quality diet from the earliest ages. It may be vital for shielding them from an epidemic of obesity.

FIGURE 11.2

Relationship of growth stunting to overweight among 3- to 9-year-olds in four developing nations. Children identified as growth stunted were below the second percentile in height for their age, based on World Health Organization standards. Children identified as overweight were above the ninety-eighth percentile in weight for their height. Stunted children were twice as likely as their peers to be fat in South Africa, three times as likely in China, and seven times as likely in Russia. Family income seems to account for the lack of association between stunting and overweight in Brazil. (Adapted from Popkin, Richards, & Montiero, 1996.)

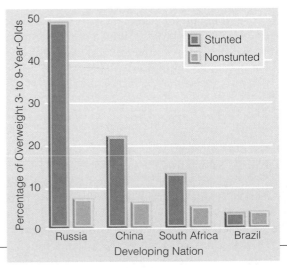

developing countries, as urbanization shifts the population toward sedentary lifestyles and diets high in meats and refined foods (Troiana & Flegal, 1998).

About 80 percent of youngsters like Mona become overweight adults. Besides serious emotional and social difficulties, obese children are at risk for lifelong health problems. High blood pressure and cholesterol levels along with respiratory abnormalities begin to appear in the

TABLE 11.1

Factors Associated with Childhood Obesity

FACTOR	DESCRIPTION
Heredity	Obese children are likely to have at least one obese parent, and concordance for obesity is greater in identical than fraternal twins.
Socioeconomic status	Obesity is more common in low-SES families.
Early growth pattern	Infants who gain weight rapidly during the first year are at slightly greater risk for obesity (see Chapter 5).
Family eating habits	When parents purchase high-calorie treats and junk food and use them to reward children and reduce anxiety, their youngsters are more likely to be obese.
Responsiveness to food cues	Obese children often decide when to eat on the basis of external cues, such as taste, smell, sight, and time of day, rather than hunger.
Physical activity	Obese children are less physically active than their normal-weight peers.
Television viewing	Children who spend many hours watching television are more likely to become obese.
Early malnutrition and growth stunting	Severe early malnutrition resulting in growth stunting increases the risk of later obesity.

early school years, symptoms that are powerful predictors of heart disease, adult-onset diabetes, gallbladder disease, certain forms of cancer, and early death (Strauss, 1999). As you can see from Table 11.1, childhood obesity is a complex physical disorder with multiple causes.

■ CAUSES OF OBESITY. Not all children are equally at risk for becoming overweight. Fat children tend to have fat parents, and concordance for obesity is greater in identical than fraternal twins. (Return to Chapter 2, page 86, to review the concept of concordance.) But similarity among family members is not strong enough for genetics to account for more than a tendency to gain weight (Bouchard, 1994).

One indication that environment is powerfully important is the consistent relation between low SES and obesity (Stunkard & Sørenson, 1993). Among the factors responsible are lack of knowledge about healthy diet; a tendency to buy high-fat, low-cost foods; and family stress, which prompts overeating in some individuals. Furthermore, 6 percent of American low-SES children are growth stunted due to early malnutrition and are therefore at increased risk for obesity. And 50 percent of infants born to diabetic mothers are obese by middle childhood (Dabelea, Knowler, & Pettitt, 2000). Researchers suspect that abnormally high blood sugar during pregnancy alters the appetite control system in the baby's brain.

Parental feeding practices contribute to childhood obesity as well. Fatter children are more likely to prefer and eat larger quantities of high-fat foods, perhaps because these foods are prominent in the diets offered by their parents, who also tend to be overweight (Fisher & Birch, 1995). Some parents anxiously overfeed their infants and young children, interpreting almost all their discomforts as a desire for food. Others are overly controlling, constantly monitoring what their children eat. In either case, they fail to help children learn to regulate their own food intake. Furthermore, parents of obese children often use food to reinforce other behaviors—a practice that leads children to attach great value to the treat (Birch & Fisher, 1995).

Because of these feeding experiences, obese children soon develop maladaptive eating habits (Johnson & Birch, 1994). They are more responsive to external stimuli associated with food— taste, sight, smell, and time of day—and less responsive to internal hunger cues than are normal-weight individuals (Ballard et al., 1980). They also eat faster and chew their food less thoroughly, a behavior pattern that appears as early as 18 months of age (Drabman et al., 1979).

Furthermore, fat children are less physically active than their normal-weight peers. This inactivity is both cause and consequence of their overweight condition. Recent evidence indicates that the rise in childhood obesity in the United States is, in part, due to television viewing. In a

FIGURE 11.3

Relationship between television viewing and development of childhood obesity. Researchers tracked 10- to 15-year-olds' television viewing over a 4-year-period. The more hours young people spent in front of the TV, the greater the likelihood that they became obese by the end of the study. (Adapted from Gortmaker et al., 1996.)

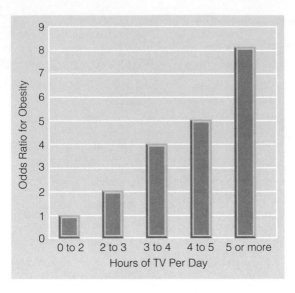

STEPHEN TRIMBLE

This Pima Indian medicine man of Arizona is very obese. By the time his children reach adolescence, they are likely to follow in his footsteps. Because of a high-fat diet, the Pima residing in the Southwestern United States have one of the highest rates of obesity in the world. In contrast, the Pima living in the remote Sierra Madre region of Mexico are average weight.

study that tracked children's TV viewing over a 4-year period, children who watched more than 5 hours per day were more than 8 times more likely to become obese than were children who watched 2 hours or less per day (see Figure 11.3) (Gortmaker et al., 1996). Television greatly reduces time devoted to physical exercise, and TV ads encourage children to eat fattening, unhealthy snacks. When researchers gave third and fourth graders 2 months of twice-weekly lessons in reducing TV viewing and videogame use, the children not only watched less but lost weight (Robinson, 1999).

Finally, the broader food environment affects the incidence of obesity. The Pima Indians of Arizona, who recently changed from a traditional diet of plant foods to an affluent, high-fat diet, have one of the highest rates of obesity in the world. Compared with descendants of their ancestors living in the remote Sierra Madre region of Mexico, the Arizona Pima have body weights 50 percent higher. Half the population has diabetes (8 times the national average), with many disabled by the disease in their twenties and thirties—blind, in wheelchairs, and on kidney dialysis (Gladwell, 1998; Ravussin et al., 1994). Although the Pima have a genetic susceptibility to overweight, it emerges only under Western dietary conditions.

■ **CONSEQUENCES OF OBESITY.** Unfortunately, physical attractiveness is a powerful predictor of social acceptance in our culture. Both children and adults rate obese youngsters as unlikable, stereotyping them as lazy, sloppy, dirty, ugly, stupid, and deceitful (Kilpatrick & Sanders, 1978). By middle childhood, obese children report feeling more depressed and display more behavior problems than their normal-weight agemates. A vicious cycle emerges in which unhappiness and overeating contribute to one another, and the child remains overweight (Braet & Mervielde, 1997).

The psychological consequences of obesity combine with continuing discrimination to result in reduced life chances. By early adulthood, overweight individuals have completed fewer years of schooling, have lower incomes, and are less likely to marry than are individuals with other chronic health problems. These outcomes are particularly strong for females (Gortmaker et al., 1993).

■ **TREATING OBESITY.** Childhood obesity is difficult to treat because it is a family disorder. In Mona's case, the school nurse suggested that Mona and her obese mother enter a weight loss program together. But Mona's mother, unhappily married for many years, had her own reasons for continuing to overeat. She rejected this idea, claiming that Mona would eventually decide to lose weight on her own.

Although many obese youngsters do try to slim down in adolescence, they often go on crash diets that deprive them of essential nutrients during a period of rapid growth. These efforts can make matters worse. Temporary starvation leads to physical stress, discomfort, and fatigue. Soon the child returns to old eating patterns, and weight rebounds to a higher level. Then, to protect itself, the body burns calories more slowly and becomes more resistant to future weight loss (Pinel, 2000).

When parents decide to seek treatment for an obese child, long-term changes in body weight do occur. The most effective interventions are family based and focus on changing behaviors. In one study, both parent and child revised eating patterns, exercised daily, and reinforced each other with praise and points for progress, which they exchanged for special activities and times together. Follow-ups after 5 and 10 years showed that children maintained their weight loss more effectively than did adults—a finding that underscores the importance of intervening at an early age. Furthermore, weight loss was greater when treatments focused on both dietary and lifestyle changes, including regular, vigorous exercise (Epstein, 1995).

Getting obese children to exercise, however, is challenging, since they find being sedentary so pleasurable. A successful technique is to reinforce them for spending less time inactive. In two studies, giving obese children tickets to the zoo or a baseball game (or similar rewards) for reducing sedentary time led to greater liking for physical activity and more weight loss than did reinforcing them directly for exercising or punishing them (by loss of privileges) for remaining inactive (Epstein, Saelens, & O'Brien, 1995; Epstein et al., 1997). Rewarding children for giving up sedentary pursuits seems to increase their sense of personal control over exercising—a factor linked to sustained physical activity.

Schools can help reduce obesity by ensuring regular physical activity and serving healthier meals. A comprehensive survey revealed that American schools typically serve high-fat lunches and snacks (Burghardt, Devaney, & Gordon, 1995). The makeup of school lunches can greatly affect body weight, since children consume one-third of their daily energy intake at school. In Singapore, school interventions consisting of nutrition education, low-fat food choices, and daily physical activity led child and adolescent obesity to decline from 14 to 11 percent over a 3-year period (Schmitz & Jeffery, 2000).

BEDWETTING

One Friday afternoon, Terry called Joey to see if he could sleep over, but Joey refused. "I can't," said Joey anxiously, without giving an explanation.

"Why not? We can take our sleeping bags out in the backyard. Come on, it'll be super!"

"My mom won't let me," Joey responded, unconvincingly. "I mean, well, I think we're busy, we're doing something tonight."

"Gosh, Joey, this is the third time you've said no. See if I'll ask you again!" snapped Terry as he hung up the phone.

Joey is one of 10 percent of American school-age children who suffer from **nocturnal enuresis,** or bedwetting during the night (Tobias, 2000). Enuresis evokes considerable distress in children and parents alike. In the overwhelming majority of cases, the problem has biological roots. Heredity is a major contributing factor. Parents with a history of bedwetting are far more likely to have a child with the problem, and concordance is greater among identical than fraternal twins (Christophersen & Edwards, 1992). Most often, it is caused by a failure of muscular responses that inhibit urination or by a hormonal imbalance that permits too much urine to accumulate during the night. Some children also have difficulty awakening to the sensation of a full bladder (Hjälmäs, 1998). Punishing a school-age child for wetting is only likely to make matters worse.

To treat enuresis, doctors often prescribe antidepressant drugs, which reduce the amount of urine produced. Although medication is a short-term solution for children attending camp or visiting a friend's house, once children stop taking it, they typically begin wetting again. Also, a small number of youngsters show side effects, such as anxiety, loss of sleep, and personality changes (Goin, 1998; Harari & Moulden, 2000). The most effective treatment is a urine alarm that wakes the child at the first sign of dampness and works according to conditioning principles. Success rates of about 60 to 70 percent occur after 4 to 6 months of treatment. Most children who relapse achieve dryness after trying the alarm a second time (Houts, Berman, & Abramson, 1994).

Treatment of enuresis in middle childhood has immediate positive psychological consequences. It leads to gains in parents' evaluation of their child's behavior and in children's self-esteem (Longstaffe, Moffatt, & Whalen, 2000). Although many children outgrow enuresis without any form of intervention, it generally takes years.

nocturnal enuresis
Repeated bedwetting during the night.

ILLNESSES

Children experience a somewhat higher rate of illness during the first 2 years of elementary school than they will later, due to exposure to sick children and the fact that their immune system is still developing. On average, illness causes children to miss about 11 days of school per year, but most absences can be traced to a few students with chronic health problems (Madan-Swain, Fredrick, & Wallander, 1999). Among children without diagnosed health difficulties, girls are more likely to miss school than are boys, with intestinal and respiratory infections, allergies, and muscle sprains being the most frequently reported reasons (Kornguth, 1990). When a child shows symptoms of illness, gender stereotypes may cause parents to perceive their daughters as more vulnerable than their sons.

About 19 percent of American children living at home have chronic diseases and conditions (including physical disabilities). By far the most common—accounting for nearly one-third of childhood chronic illness and the most frequent cause of school absence and childhood hospitalization—is **asthma** (Lemanek & Hood, 1999; Newacheck & Halfon, 2000). In this illness, the bronchial tubes (passages that connect the throat and lungs) are highly sensitive. In response to a variety of stimuli, such as cold weather, infection, exercise, allergies, and emotional stress, they fill with mucus and contract, leading to coughing, wheezing, and serious breathing difficulties.

The number of children with asthma has more than doubled in the past 30 years, and asthma-related deaths have also risen. Although heredity contributes to asthma, researchers believe that environmental factors are necessary to spark the illness. Boys, African-American children, and children who were born underweight, whose parents smoke, and who live in poverty are at greatest risk (Creer, 1998). Perhaps African-American and poverty-stricken youngsters experience a higher rate of asthma and more severe asthma attacks because of pollution in inner-city areas (which triggers allergic reactions), stressful home lives, and lack of access to good health care.

About 2 percent of American children have chronic illnesses that are more severe than asthma, such as sickle cell anemia, cystic fibrosis (see Table 2.3, pages 60–61 for a brief description of these conditions), diabetes, arthritis, cancer, and acquired immune deficiency syndrome (AIDS). Painful medical treatments, physical discomfort, and changes in appearance often disrupt the sick child's daily life, making it difficult to concentrate in school and causing withdrawal from peers. As the illness worsens, family stress increases. Mothers, who typically bear the burden of caring for a very ill child, report more health problems of their own (Drotar, 1997). For these reasons, chronically ill youngsters are at risk for academic, emotional, and social difficulties.

A strong link between parent psychological adjustment, good family functioning, and child well-being exists for chronically ill children, just as it does for physically healthy children (Barakat & Kazak, 1999). Interventions that foster positive family interactions and help parent and child cope with the disease improve children's adjustment. These include the following:

- Family and health education, in which parents and children learn about the illness and get training in how to manage it

- Home visits by health professionals, who offer counseling and social support to enhance parents' and children's strategies for handling the stress of chronic illness

- Disease-specific summer camps, which teach children self-help skills and grant parents time off from the demands of caring for an ill youngster

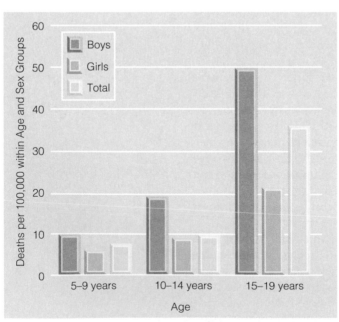

FIGURE 11.4

Rate of injury mortality in the United States from middle childhood to adolescence. Injury fatalities increase, and the gap between boys and girls expands. Motor vehicle (passenger and pedestrian) accidents are the leading cause, with bicycle injuries next in line. (From U.S. Department of Health and Human Services, 2000a.)

■ Parent and peer support groups

■ Individual and family therapy

UNINTENTIONAL INJURIES

As we conclude our discussion of threats to children's health during the school years, let's return for a moment to the topic of unintentional injuries (discussed in detail in Chapter 8). As Figure 11.4 on the previous page reveals, the frequency of injury fatalities increases from middle childhood into adolescence, with the rate for boys rising considerably above that for girls. In addition, poverty and rural or inner-city residence—factors associated with dangerous environments and reduced parental monitoring of children—are linked to high injury rates (Rivara & Aitken, 1998).

Motor vehicle accidents, involving children as passengers or pedestrians, continue to be the leading cause of injury during the school years, with bicycle accidents next in line (U.S. Department of Health and Human Services, 2000c). Pedestrian injuries most often result from midblock dart-outs; bicycle accidents, from disobeying traffic signals and rules. Young school-age children are not yet good at thinking before they act, especially when many stimuli impinge on them at once (Tuchfarber, Zins, & Jason, 1997). Whether on foot or bicycle, they need frequent reminders, supervision, and prohibitions against venturing into busy traffic on their own.

As children spend more time away from parents and range farther from home, safety education becomes especially important. School-based programs with lasting effects use extensive modeling, role playing, and rehearsal of safety practices; give children feedback about their performance along with praise and tangible rewards for acquiring safety skills; and provide occasional booster sessions (Zins et al., 1994). An important part of injury prevention is educating parents about children's age-related safety capacities, since parents often overestimate their child's safety knowledge and behavior (Rivara, 1995).

Insisting that children wear protective helmets while bicycling, roller blading, skateboarding, or using scooters is a vital safety intervention. These simple precautions lead to an 85 percent decline in the risk of head injury—a leading cause of permanent physical disability and death during the school years (Peterson & Oliver, 1995). When helmet use is combined with other prevention strategies, injury reduction can be dramatic. In the Harlem Hospital Injury Prevention Program, inner-city children received safety education in classrooms and in a simulated traffic environment. They also attended bicycle safety clinics, during which helmets were distributed. In addition, existing playgrounds were improved and new ones constructed to provide expanded off-street play areas. And more community-sponsored, supervised recreational activities were provided. As a result, motor vehicle and bicycle injuries among school-age children declined by 36 percent (Durkin et al., 1999).

Not all school-age children respond to efforts to increase their safety. By middle childhood, the greatest risk takers tend to be children whose parents do not act as safety-conscious models or who try to enforce rules by using punitive or inconsistent discipline (Tuchfarber, Zins, & Jason, 1997). These child-rearing techniques, as we saw in Chapter 10, spark defiance in children, reduce their willingness to comply, and may actually promote high-risk behavior.

Highly active boys remain particularly susceptible to injury in middle childhood. Although they have just as much safety knowledge as their peers, they are far less likely to implement it (Mori & Peterson, 1995). Compared with girls, boys judge risky play activities as less likely to result in injury, and they pay less attention to injury-risk cues in the situation, such as a peer who looks hesitant or fearful (Morrongiello & Rennie, 1998). The greatest challenge for injury control programs is reaching these "more difficult to reach" youngsters, altering high-risk factors in their families, and reducing the dangers to which they are exposed.

MICHAEL NEWMAN/PHOTOEDIT

Fast-paced scooters are popular among children but very dangerous, resulting in thousands of serious injuries annually. Small wheels add speed but often send children flying when they hit a bump. This boy should be wearing a helmet, as well as arm and knee protection.

asthma
An illness in which, in response to a variety of stimuli, highly sensitive bronchial tubes fill with mucus and contract, leading to episodes of coughing, wheezing, and serious breathing difficulties.

ISSUES: EDUCATION

CHILDREN'S UNDERSTANDING OF HEALTH AND ILLNESS

Lizzie lay on the living room sofa with a stuffy nose and sore throat, disappointed that she was missing her soccer team's final game and pizza party. "How'd I get this dumb cold anyhow?" she wondered aloud to Joey. "I probably got it by playing outside when it was freezing cold."

"No, no," Joey contradicted. "You can't get sick that way. Some creepy little viruses got into your bloodstream and attacked, just like an army."

"Gross. I didn't eat any viruses," answered Lizzie, puzzled.

"You don't eat them, silly, you breathe them in. Somebody probably sneezed them all over you at school. That's how you got sick!"

Lizzie and Joey are at different developmental levels in their understanding of health and illness—due to cognitive development and exposure to biological knowledge. Researchers have asked preschool through high school students questions designed to tap what they know about the causes of health and certain illnesses, such as colds, AIDS, and cancer.

During the preschool and early school years, children do not have much biological knowledge to bring to bear on their understanding of health and illness. For example, if you ask 4- to 8-year-olds to tell you what is inside their bodies, you will find that they know little about their internal organs and how they work. As a result, young children fall back on their rich knowledge of people's behavior to account for health and illness (Carey, 1995, 1999; Simons & Keil, 1995). Children of this age regard health as a matter of engaging in specific practices (eating the right foods, getting enough exercise, and wearing warm clothing on cold days) and illness as a matter of failing to follow these rules or of coming too close to a sick person (Bibace & Walsh, 1980).

Older school-age children acquire more knowledge about their bodies and are better able to make sense of it. By age 9 or 10, they name a wide variety of internal organs and view them as interconnected, working as a system. Around this time, children's concepts of health and illness shift to biological explanations (Carey, 1999).

Joey understands that illness can be caused by contagion—breathing in a harmful substance (a virus), which affects the operation of the body in some way. He also realizes that we eat not just because food tastes good or to stay alive (younger children's explanations) but to build new muscle and bone (Inagaki & Hatano, 1993).

By early adolescence, explanations become more elaborate and precise. Eleven- to 14-year-olds recognize health as a long-term condition that depends on the interaction of body, mind, and environment (Hergenrather & Rabinowitz, 1991). And the adolescent's notions of illness involve clearly stated ideas about interference in normal biological processes: "You get a cold when your sinuses fill with mucus. Sometimes your lungs do, too, and you get a cough. Colds come from viruses. They get into the bloodstream and make your platelet count go down" (Bibace & Walsh, 1980).

School-age children can grasp basic biological ideas, but whether or not they do so depends on information in their everyday environments. When

Health Education

Child development specialists are intensely interested in finding ways to help school-age youngsters understand their bodies, acquire mature conceptions of health and illness, and develop patterns of behavior that foster good health throughout life. Successful health intervention requires information on children's current health-related knowledge. What can they understand? What reasoning processes do they use? What factors influence what they know? The Social Issues: Education box above summarizes findings on children's concepts of health and illness during middle childhood.

The school-age period may be especially important for fostering healthy lifestyles because of the child's growing independence, increasing cognitive capacities, and rapidly developing self-concept, which includes a sense of physical well-being (Harter, 1998). During middle childhood, children can acquire a wide range of health information—about the structure and

supplied with relevant facts and new biological concepts, such as *gene*, *germ*, or *virus*, even 5- and 6-year-olds can use the concepts to organize those facts, and their understanding advances (Solomon & Johnson, 2000).

Without such knowledge, children readily generalize their knowledge of familiar diseases to less familiar ones. As a result, they often conclude that risk factors for colds (sharing a Coke or sneezing on someone) can cause AIDS. And lacking much understanding of cancer, they assume that it (like colds) is communicable through casual contact. These incorrect ideas can lead to unnecessary anxiety about getting a serious disease. In surveys of school-age children, about half incorrectly believed that everyone is at risk for AIDS. And more than half said they worry about getting AIDS and cancer (Chin et al., 1998; Holcomb, 1990).

Although misconceptions decline with age, culturally transmitted attitudes can lead to gaps between knowledge and behavior. When certain diseases take on powerful symbolic meanings—for example, cancer as a malignant, destructive evil and AIDS as a sign of moral decay—even adults with an accurate biological understanding irrationally expect bad things to happen from associating with affected people. These beliefs are quickly picked up by children, and they help explain the severe social rejection experienced by some youngsters with chronic diseases. As one school-age child admitted, "I'd be scared to even talk to them because they had AIDS, even though you can't get it that way" (Whalen et al., 1995, p. 434).

Education about the causes of various illnesses leads to an increasingly accurate appreciation of disease transmission and prevention throughout middle childhood and adolescence (Walsh & Bibace, 1991). To combat irrational fears and prejudices, teachers can offer reassurance that children usually do not get seriously ill. They can also encourage young people to examine their attitudes and feelings. Instruction that gives AIDS, cancer, and other debilitating and deadly illnesses "a human face"—by bringing chronically ill people into the class-

This child comforts her grandmother, who is dying of cancer. Helping school-age children understand that cancer is not communicable can prevent them from developing negative attitudes toward its victims.

room or talking about the experiences of people who died of an illness—may help children and adolescents respond rationally and compassionately (Pryor & Reeder, 1993).

functioning of their bodies, about good nutrition, and about the causes and consequences of physical injuries and diseases (Perry, Story, & Lytle, 1997; Stewart et al., 1995).

Yet most efforts to impart health concepts to school-age children have little effect on health habits. Several related reasons underlie this gap between knowledge and practice:

- Health is usually not an important goal for children, who feel good most of the time. They are far more concerned about schoolwork, friends, and play.

- Children do not yet have an adultlike time perspective, which relates past, present, and future. Engaging in preventive behaviors is difficult when so much time intervenes between what children do now and later health consequences.

- Much health information that children get is contradicted by other sources, such as television advertising (see Chapter 10) and the examples of adults and peers.

This does not mean that teaching school-age children health-related facts is unimportant. But information must be supplemented by other efforts. As we have seen in this and earlier

Educational Concerns

Strategies for Fostering Healthy Lifestyles in School-Age Children

STRATEGY	DESCRIPTION
Increase health-related knowledge and encourage healthy behaviors.	Provide health education through developmentally appropriate, enjoyable activities that go beyond transmitting information to include modeling, role playing, rehearsal, and reinforcement of good health practices.
Involve parents in supporting health education.	Communicate with parents about health education in school, encouraging them to carry over these efforts to the home. Encourage proper parental supervision by providing information about the development of children's health-related skills.
Provide healthy environments in schools.	Breakfast and lunch services in schools should follow widely accepted dietary guidelines. Opportunities for pupils to voice food preferences in the context of those guidelines enhance food acceptance and healthy eating.
Make voluntary screening for risk factors available as part of health education.	Offer periodic measures of height, weight, body mass, blood pressure, and adequacy of diet. Educate children about the meaning of each index, and encourage improvement.
Promote pleasurable physical activity.	Provide opportunities for regular, moderate to vigorous physical exercise through activities that de-emphasize competition and stress skill-building and personal and social enjoyment.
Teach children to be critical of media advertising.	Children are a targeted market for food manufacturers. More than half the ads on Saturday morning TV are for unhealthy foods. Besides teaching children to be skeptical of such ads, reduce advertising for nonnutritious foods in schools, where such messages are widespread.
Work for public policies that create safer and healthier community environments for children.	Form community action groups to improve child safety, school nutrition, and play environments, and initiate programs that foster healthy physical activity.

Sources: Perry, Story, & Lytle, 1997; Strauss, 2000; Tuchfarber, Zins, & Jason, 1997.

chapters, a powerful means of fostering children's health is to reduce hazards, such as pollution, inadequate medical and dental care, and nonnutritious foods (Perry, Story, & Lytle, 1997; Rivara & Aitken, 1998). At the same time, since environments will never be totally free of health risks, parents and teachers need to coach children in good health practices and model and reinforce these behaviors as much as possible. Refer to the Educational Concerns table above for ways to foster healthy lifestyles in school-age children.

Ask YOURSELF...

review　Select one of the following health problems of middle childhood: myopia, obesity, bedwetting, asthma, or unintentional injuries. Explain how both genetic and environmental factors contribute to it.

apply　Nine-year-old Talia is afraid to hug and kiss her grandmother, who has cancer. What explains Talia's mistaken belief that the same behaviors that cause colds to spread might lead her to catch cancer? What would you do to change her thinking?

connect　How does the link between early malnutrition and later obesity, described in the Biology and Environment box on page 416, illustrate the concept of epigenesis, described on page 91 of Chapter 2?

reflect　List unintentional injuries that you experienced as a child. Were you injury-prone? Why or why not?

Motor Development and Play

isit a city park on a pleasant weekend afternoon, and watch several preschool and school-age children at play. You will see that gains in body size and muscle strength support improved motor coordination during middle childhood. In addition, greater cognitive and social maturity permits older children to use their new motor skills in more complex ways. A major change in children's play takes place at this time.

GROSS MOTOR DEVELOPMENT

During middle childhood, running, jumping, hopping, and ball skills become more refined. At Joey and Lizzie's school one day, I watched during recess for third to sixth graders. Children burst into sprints as they raced across the playground, jumped quickly over rotating ropes, engaged in intricate patterns of hopscotch, kicked and dribbled soccer balls, swung bats at balls pitched by their classmates, and balanced adeptly as they walked toe-to-toe across narrow ledges. Table 11.2 summarizes gross motor achievements between 6 and 12 years of age. These diverse skills reflect gains in four basic motor capacities:

- *Flexibility.* Compared with preschoolers, school-age children are physically more pliable and elastic, a difference that can be seen as they swing a bat, kick a ball, jump over a hurdle, or execute tumbling routines.

TABLE 11.2

Changes in Gross Motor Skills During Middle Childhood

SKILL	DEVELOPMENTAL CHANGE
Running	Running speed increases from 12 feet per second at age 6 to over 18 feet per second at age 12.
Other gait variations	Skipping improves. Sideways stepping appears around age 6 and becomes more continuous and fluid with age.
Vertical jump	Height jumped increases from 4 inches at age 6 to 12 inches at age 12.
Standing broad jump	Distance jumped increases from 3 feet at age 6 to over 5 feet at age 12.
Precision jumping and hopping (on a mat divided into squares)	By age 7 children can accurately jump and hop from square to square, a performance that improves until age 9 and then levels off.
Throwing	Throwing speed, distance, and accuracy increase for both sexes, but much more for boys than girls. At age 6, a ball thrown by a boy travels 39 feet per second, one by a girl 29 feet per second. At age 12, a ball thrown by a boy travels 78 feet per second, one by a girl 56 feet per second.
Catching	Ability to catch small balls thrown over greater distances improves with age.
Kicking	Kicking speed and accuracy improve, with boys considerably ahead of girls. At age 6, a ball kicked by a boy travels 21 feet per second, one by a girl 13 feet per second. At age 12, a ball kicked by a boy travels 34 feet per second, one by a girl 26 feet per second.
Batting	Batting motions become more effective with age, increasing in speed and accuracy and involving the entire body.
Dribbling	Style of hand dribbling gradually changes, from awkward slapping of the ball to continuous, relaxed, even stroking.

Sources: Cratty, 1986; Malina & Bouchard, 1991; Roberton, 1984.

During middle childhood, gross motor skills become more refined. Gains in flexibility, balance, and agility permit these children to play a game of hopscotch with fancy footwork and to bend on one foot to retrieve an object.

■ *Balance.* School-age children can walk a narrower balance beam than they could during early childhood, and they can remain in a one-foot stand longer. Improved balance supports advances in many athletic skills, including running, hopping, skipping, throwing, kicking, and the rapid changes of direction required in many team sports.

■ *Agility.* Quicker and more accurate movements are evident in the fancy footwork of jump rope and hopscotch, as well as in the forward, backward, and sideways motions older children use as they dodge opponents in tag and soccer.

■ *Force.* Older youngsters can throw and kick a ball harder and propel themselves farther off the ground when running and jumping than they could at earlier ages (Cratty, 1986).

Although body growth contributes greatly to the improved motor performance, more efficient information processing also plays an important role. Younger children often have difficulty with skills that require immediate responding. When they dribble a ball, they often lose control, and when up at bat, they usually swing too late. Steady improvements in responding only to relevant information and in reaction time occur, with 11-year-olds reacting twice as quickly as do 5-year-olds (Band et al., 2000; Kail, 1993).

Reaction time combines several cognitive skills that are crucial for effective motor performance—time to recognize a stimulus, time to formulate an appropriate response, and time for the plan of action to reach the muscles. That speed of reaction is not yet well developed in younger children has practical implications for physical education (Seefeldt, 1996). Since 6- and 7-year-olds are seldom successful at batting a thrown ball, T-ball is more appropriate than baseball. And handball, four-square, and kickball should precede instruction in tennis, basketball, and football.

FINE MOTOR DEVELOPMENT

Fine motor development also improves steadily over the school years, a change that is apparent in the activities children of this age period enjoy. On rainy afternoons, Joey and Lizzie experimented with yo-yos, built model airplanes, wove pot holders on small looms, and worked puzzles with hundreds of tiny pieces. Middle childhood is also the time when many children take up musical instruments, which demand considerable fine motor control.

Gains in fine motor skill are especially evident in children's writing and drawing. By age 6, most children can print the alphabet, their first and last names, and the numbers from 1 to 10 with reasonable clarity. However, their writing tends to be quite large because they use the entire arm to make strokes rather than just the wrist and fingers. Children usually master uppercase letters first because horizontal and vertical motions are easier to control than the small curves of the lowercase alphabet. Legibility of writing gradually increases as children produce more accurate letters with uniform height and spacing. These improvements prepare children for mastering cursive writing by third grade.

Children's drawings show dramatic gains in organization, detail, and representation of depth during middle childhood. By the end of the preschool years, children can accurately copy many two-dimensional shapes, and they integrate these into their drawings. Some depth cues have also begun to appear, such as making distant objects smaller than near ones (Braine et al., 1993). Yet recall from Chapter 8 that before age 8, children have trouble accurately copying a three-dimensional form, such as a cube or cylinder (see pages 314–315). Around this time, the third dimension is clearly evident in children's drawings through overlapping objects, diagonal placement, and converging lines. Furthermore, as Figure 11.5 shows, school-age children not only depict objects in considerable detail but relate them to one another as part of an organized whole (Case, 1998; Case & Okamoto, 1996).

LAURA BERK

FIGURE 11.5

Increase in organization, detail, and depth cues in school-age children's drawings. Compare both drawings to the one by a 6-year-old on page 314. In the drawing on the left, an 8-year-old depicts her family. Notice how all parts are related, and the human figures are given much more detail. (The artist is your author, as a third grader. In the drawing, Laura can be found between her older sister and younger brother.) Integration of depth cues increases over the school years, as shown in the drawing on the right, by a 10-year-old artist from Singapore. Here, depth is indicated by overlapping objects, diagonal placement, and converging lines, as well as by making distant objects smaller than near ones.

REPRINTED BY PERMISSION FROM THE INTERNATIONAL MUSEUM OF CHILDREN'S ART, OSLO, NORWAY

INDIVIDUAL AND GROUP DIFFERENCES

As at younger ages, during middle childhood, children show marked individual differences in motor capacities that are influenced by both heredity and environment. Body build continues to affect gross motor performance, with taller, more muscular children excelling in many tasks. At the same time, parents who encourage physical exercise tend to have youngsters who enjoy it more and who are also more skilled.

Family income affects children's opportunities to develop a variety of physical abilities. Economically advantaged children are far more likely to have ballet, tennis, gymnastics, and music lessons than are children from low-income families. School and community provisions for nurturing athletic abilities—lessons, equipment, and regular practice—are crucial for low-SES children. When combined with parental encouragement, many low-SES children with access to these experiences become highly skilled.

Sex differences in motor skills that began to appear during the preschool years extend into middle childhood and, in some instances, become more pronounced. Girls remain ahead in the fine motor area, including handwriting and drawing. They also continue to have an edge in skipping, jumping, and hopping, which depend on balance and agility. But on all other skills listed in Table 11.2, boys outperform girls, and in the case of throwing and kicking, the difference is large (Cratty, 1986).

School-age boys' genetic advantage in muscle mass is not great enough to account for their superiority in so many gross motor skills. Instead, environment plays a much larger role. American girls' sports participation has increased dramatically since the 1970s, when the federal government implemented Title IX, a law mandating that schools provide equal opportunities for males and females in all educational programs, including athletics. Nevertheless, girls' sports involvement does not equal that of boys (Greendorfer, Lewko, & Rosengren, 1996). And despite improved media attention to women's athletics, most players in public sports events continue to be men. Although Lizzie played in the city soccer league, her parents believed that Joey was better at athletics and that it was more crucial that he do well at sports.

A study of more than 800 elementary school pupils found that parents hold higher expectations for boys' athletic performance, and children absorb these social messages at an early age. Kindergartners through third graders viewed sports in a gender-stereotyped fashion—as more important for boys. Boys also indicated that it was more important to their parents that they participate in athletics. These attitudes affected children's physical self-esteem as well as their behavior. Girls saw themselves as having less talent at sports, and by sixth grade they devoted less time to athletics than did their male classmates (Eccles & Harold, 1991; Eccles, Jacobs, & Harold, 1990). At the same time, girls and older school-age children regard boys' advantage in sports as unjust. They indicate, for example, that coaches should spend equal time with children of each sex and that female sports should command just as much public attention as male sports (Solomon & Bredemeier, 1999).

These findings indicate that extra measures must be taken to increase girls' participation, self-confidence, and sense of fair treatment in athletics. Educating parents about the minimal differences in school-age boys' and girls' physical capacities and sensitizing them to biases against girls' athletic ability may prove helpful. Parental enjoyment of physical activity is also important.

Compared with children of inactive parents, children of one active parent are 2 to $3\frac{1}{2}$ times more likely to be active; children with two active parents are 6 times more likely to be active (Moore et al., 1991). In addition, greater emphasis on skill training for girls and increased attention to their athletic achievements are likely to increase involvement. Middle childhood is a crucial time to take these steps, since during the school years children start to discover what they are good at and make some definite skill commitments.

CHILD-ORGANIZED GAMES

The physical activities of school-age children reflect an important advance in the quality of their play: games with rules become common. In cultures around the world, children engage in an enormous variety of informally organized games. Some are variants on popular sports, such as soccer, baseball, basketball, and football. Others are well-known childhood games, such as tag, jacks, and hopscotch. Children have also invented hundreds of less well-known games and passed them from one generation to the next (Kirchner, 2000). You may remember some from your own childhood, such as red rover, statues, blind man's buff, leapfrog, one-o-cat, kick the can, and prisoner's base.

Gains in perspective taking—in particular, children's ability to understand the roles of several players in a game—permit this transition to rule-oriented games. These play experiences contribute greatly to emotional and social development. Child-invented games usually rely on simple physical skills and a sizable element of luck. As a result, they rarely become contests of individual ability. Instead, they permit children to try out different styles of cooperating, competing, winning, and losing with little personal risk. Also, in their efforts to organize a game, children discover

These Indonesian children play a rousing game of jump rope in front of their rural home. Informal, child-organized games come in enormous variety. Through them, children try out different styles of cooperating, competing, winning, and losing and discover why rules are necessary and which ones work well.

Educational Concerns

Pros and Cons of Adult-Organized Sports in Middle Childhood

PROS	CONS	RECOMMENDATIONS FOR COACHES AND PARENTS
Adult-structured athletics prepares children for realistic competition—the kind they may face as adults.	Adult involvement leads games to become overly competitive, placing too much pressure on children.	Permit children to select from among appropriate activities the ones that suit them best. Do not push children into sports they do not enjoy.
Regularly scheduled games and practices ensure that children get plenty of exercise and fill free time that might otherwise be devoted to less constructive pursuits.	When adults control the game, children learn little about leadership, followership, and fair play.	For children younger than age 9, emphasize basic skills, such as kicking, throwing, and batting, and simplified games that grant all participants adequate playing time. Permit children to progress at their own pace and to play for the fun of it, whether or not they become expert athletes.
Children get instruction in physical skills necessary for future success in athletics.	When adults assign children to specific roles (such as catcher, first base), children lose the opportunity to experiment with rules and strategies.	Adjust practice time to children's attention spans and need for unstructured time with peers, with family, and for homework. Two practices a week, each no longer than 30 minutes for younger school-age children and 60 minutes for older school-age children, are sufficient. Emphasize effort, skill gains, and teamwork rather than winning. Avoid criticism for errors and defeat, which promotes anxiety and avoidance of athletics.
Parents and children share an activity that both enjoy.	Highly structured, competitive sports are less fun than child-organized games; they resemble "work" more than "play."	Avoid all-star games and championship ceremonies that recognize individuals. Instead, recognize all participants. Involve children in decisions about team rules. To strengthen desirable responses, reinforce compliance rather than punishing noncompliance.

Sources: Smith & Smoll, 1997; Strayer, Tofler, & Lapchick, 1998.

why rules are necessary and which ones work well. In fact, they often spend as much time working out the details of how a game should proceed as they do playing the game! As we will see in Chapter 13, these experiences help children form more mature concepts of fairness and justice.

ADULT-ORGANIZED YOUTH SPORTS

Because child-organized games support children's development, some researchers are concerned about their recent decline. Today, school-age youngsters spend less time gathering on sidewalks and playgrounds than they did in generations past. Parental concern about neighborhood safety and children's attraction to television and video games account for some of this change. But adult-organized sports, such as baseball, softball, basketball, and soccer leagues, also fill many hours that children used to devote to spontaneous play.

The past several decades have witnessed a tremendous expansion of youth sports programs. In the United States, most of the youth population participates at some time during childhood and adolescence in organized sports (Stryer, Tofler, & Lapchick, 1998). Some researchers worry that adult-structured athletics, which mirror professional sports, are robbing children of crucial learning experiences and endangering their development. The Educational Concerns table above summarizes the pros and cons of adult-organized youth athletic leagues.

So far, research indicates that for most children, these experiences do not result in long-term psychological damage. But the arguments of critics are valid in some cases. Children who join teams so early that the skills demanded are beyond their capabilities soon lose interest

Is this Little League coach careful to encourage rather than criticize? To what extent does he emphasize teamwork, fair play, courtesy, and skill development over winning? These factors determine whether or not adult-organized sports are pleasurable, constructive experiences for children.

(Bailey & Rasmussen, 1996). And coaches who criticize rather than encourage and who react angrily to defeat prompt intense anxiety in some children. They also serve as poor models of good sportsmanship, self-control, and compassion. By the end of the school years, competence at sports is linked to peer admiration, especially among boys. When coaches create a climate in which winning is paramount, weaker performers generally experience social ostracism (Stryer, Tofler, & Lapchick, 1998).

Earlier we saw that parents powerfully influence children's athletic attitudes and capabilities—an effect that is stronger than that of coaches. In a few cases, parents value sports so highly that they recognize their child only for his or her athletic achievements. Parental behaviors resulting from excessive investment in children's success include denouncing and punishing the child for making mistakes, insisting that the child keep playing after injury, holding the child back in school to ensure a physical advantage, and requesting medical interventions to improve the child's performance. High parental pressure sets the stage for emotional difficulties and early athletic dropout, not elite performance (Marsh & Daigneault, 1999; Tofler, Knapp, & Drell, 1998). Children of such parents may find athletics so stressful and damaging to their self-worth that eventually they avoid it entirely.

Finally, sports-related injuries in school-age children are an issue to consider. Although frequent, organized-sports injuries usually are not serious (Bijur et al., 1995). However, intense, frequent practice sessions can lead to painful "overuse" injuries. In extreme cases, physical stress fractures the soft cartilage in the epiphyses of the long bones, leading to premature closure and arrested growth (Lord & Kozar, 1996).

Refer again to the Educational Concerns table for ways to make adult-structured athletics positive experiences. When coaches are trained to emphasize effort, improvement, participation, and teamwork, young athletes enjoy sports more, like their coach and teammates more, and gain in self-esteem. These effects are particularly strong for children whose self-confidence is low to begin with—and who are most in need of a rewarding sports experience (Smith & Smoll, 1997).

SHADOWS OF OUR EVOLUTIONARY PAST

Besides a new level of structure and organization, some additional qualities of physical play become common in middle childhood. While watching children at your city park, notice how they occasionally wrestle, roll, hit, and run after one another while smiling and laughing. This friendly chasing and play-fighting is called **rough-and-tumble play.** Research indicates that it is a good-natured, sociable activity that is quite distinct from aggressive fighting. Children in many cultures engage in it with peers whom they like especially well, and they continue interacting after a rough-and-tumble episode rather than separating, as they do at the end of an aggressive encounter (Smith & Hunter, 1992).

Children's rough-and-tumble play is similar to the social behavior of young mammals of many species. It seems to originate in parents' physical play with babies, especially fathers with sons (see Chapter 7). Similarly, childhood rough-and-tumble is more common among boys, although girls also display it. Girls' rough-and-tumble largely consists of running, chas-

rough-and-tumble play
A form of peer interaction involving friendly chasing and play-fighting that, in our evolutionary past, may have been important for the development of fighting skill.

ing, and brief physical contact. Boys engage in more playful wrestling, restraining, and hitting (Boulton, 1996).

In our evolutionary past, rough-and-tumble play may have been important for the development of fighting skill. Consistent with this idea, by age 11 children choose rough-and-tumble partners who are similar in strength to themselves, permitting safer physical contact (Humphreys & Smith, 1987). Another possibility is that rough-and-tumble assists children in establishing a **dominance hierarchy**—a stable ordering of group members that predicts who will win when conflict arises. Observations of arguments, threats, and physical attacks between children reveal a consistent lineup of winners and losers that becomes increasingly stable during middle childhood and adolescence, especially among boys. Through rough-and-tumble play, children can assess their own and others' strength before challenging a peer's dominance (Pellegrini & Smith, 1998).

Like dominance relations among nonhuman animals, those among children serve the adaptive function of limiting aggression among group members. Once a dominance hierarchy is clearly established, hostility is rare. When it occurs, it is very restrained, often taking the form of playful verbal insults that can be accepted cheerfully by a partner (Fine, 1980). For example, Joey rarely challenges Sean, a child much larger than he, on the playground. But when he is unhappy about how things are going in a game, Joey is likely to tumble over humorously on the grass while saying something like "Hey, Sean, you've been up at bat so long you'll fall over dead if you swing at one more ball! Come on, give one of us a chance." This gradual replacement of direct hostility with friendly insults provides an effective means of influencing physically more powerful peers.

TONY FREEMAN/PHOTOEDIT

Rough-and-tumble play can be distinguished from aggression by its good-natured quality. In our evolutionary past, it may have been important for the development of fighting skill.

PHYSICAL EDUCATION

In the preceding sections, we have seen that physical activity supports many aspects of children's development—the health of their bodies, their sense of self-worth as physically active and capable beings, and the cognitive and social skills necessary for getting along well with others. Physical education classes that provide regularly scheduled opportunities for exercise and play help ensure that all children have access to these benefits.

Yet physical education is not taught often enough in American schools. Only 17 percent of American children and adolescents have a daily physical education class; the average school-age child gets only 20 minutes of physical education a week (U.S. Department of Health and Human Services, 2000g; Wurtele, 1996). This means that children get most of their exercise outside school. But on their own, American children often do not engage in enough vigorous physical activity. On average, 7- to 15-year-old boys spend 30 minutes per day in aerobic activity, 7- to 15-year-old girls only 8 to 10 minutes (Livingstone et al., 1992). The growing fitness movement among adults has not filtered down to children, many of whom ride to and from school in buses and cars, sit in classrooms most of the day, and watch TV for 3 to 4 hours after they arrive home.

These findings indicate that American schools must do a better job of providing physical education. Besides offering daily classes from kindergarten through high school, many experts believe that schools should change the content of physical education programs. Training in competitive sports is often a high priority, but it is unlikely to reach the least physically fit youngsters, who draw back when an activity demands a high level of skill and they are criticized by peers for striking out at bat or missing a basket (Portman, 1995).

Instead, programs should emphasize informal games that most children can perform well and individual exercise—walking, running, jumping, tumbling, and climbing. These pursuits are the ones most likely to last into later years. Furthermore, children of widely varying skill

dominance hierarchy
A stable ordering of group members that predicts who will win when conflict arises.

levels tend to sustain physical activity when teachers focus on each child's personal progress and contribution to team accomplishment (Whitehead & Corbin, 1997). Then physical education fosters a healthy sense of self while satisfying school-age children's need for relatedness.

Physical fitness builds on itself. Children who are in good physical condition have more energy, and they take great pleasure in their rapidly developing motor skills and ability to control their own bodies. As a result, they seek out these activities in the future, developing rewarding interests in physical exercise. Physically fit children become more active adults who reap many benefits (Dennison et al., 1998). These include greater physical strength; resistance to many illnesses, from colds and flu to cancer, diabetes, and heart disease; enhanced psychological well-being; and a longer life.

Ask YOURSELF...

review　Explain the adaptive value of rough-and-tumble play and dominance hierarchies among children.

apply　Alex thinks he isn't good at sports, and he doesn't like physical education. Suggest some strategies his teacher can use to improve his enjoyment and involvement in physical activity.

connect　On Saturdays, 8-year-old Gina gathers with friends at a city park to play kickball. Besides improved ball skills, what else is she learning?

reflect　Did you participate in adult-organized sports as a child? If so, what kind of climate for learning did coaches and parents create? How do you think your experience affected your development?

Summary

BODY GROWTH

Describe changes in body size, proportions, and skeletal maturity during middle childhood.

■ School-age children's growth is slow and regular. On the average, they add about 5 pounds in weight and 2 to 3 inches in height each year; slight spurts in height are followed by lulls. By age 9, girls overtake boys in physical size.

■ Evolutionary adaptations to a particular climate, food resources, and infectious disease result in large individual and ethnic variations in physical growth. **Secular trends in physical growth** have occurred in industrialized nations. Because of improved health and nutrition, many children are growing larger and reaching physical maturity earlier than did their ancestors.

■ During middle childhood, bones continue to lengthen and broaden, and all 20 primary teeth are replaced by permanent ones. Tooth decay affects over half of American school-age children and is especially high among low-SES children. About one-third of school-age children suffer from **malocclusion,** a condition in which the upper and lower teeth do not meet properly. Braces are common by the end of elementary school.

Describe brain development in middle childhood.

■ Only a small increase in brain size occurs during middle childhood. The frontal lobes gain in surface area, the corpus callosum thickens, synaptic connections strengthen and become more elaborate, and lateralization of the cerebral hemispheres increases. Brain development during the school years is believed to involve **neurotransmitter** and hormonal influences.

COMMON HEALTH PROBLEMS

Describe the overall status of children's health during middle childhood.

■ School-age children from economically advantaged homes are at their healthiest, due to the cumulative effects of good nutrition combined with rapid development of the body's immune system. At the same time, a variety of health problems do occur, many of which are more common among low-SES children.

■ The most common vision problem is **myopia,** or nearsightedness. It is influenced by heredity, early biological trauma, and time spent reading and doing other close work. Myopia is one of the few health conditions that increase with family education and income. Although ear infections decline during the school years, many low-SES children experience some hearing loss because of chronic, untreated otitis media.

Describe the causes and consequences of serious nutritional problems in middle childhood, granting special attention to obesity.

■ Poverty-stricken children in developing countries and in the United States continue to suffer from malnutrition during middle childhood. When malnutrition is allowed to persist for many years, its negative impact on physical growth, intelligence, and motor performance is permanent. Severely malnourished, growth-stunted children display a heightened stress response, altered production of neurotransmitters in the brain, and greater vulnerability to obesity after their diets improve.

■ Overweight and **obesity** are growing problems in both industrialized and developing nations. Although heredity contributes to obesity, parental feeding practices, maladaptive eating habits, lack of exercise, and Western high-fat diets also play important roles. Obese children are often socially rejected, report feeling more depressed, and display more behavior problems than their normal-weight peers.

■ Family-based interventions in which parents and children revise eating patterns, engage in regular daily exercise, and reinforce one another's progress are the most effective approaches to treating childhood obesity. Rewarding obese children for reducing sedentary time is an effective approach to getting them to like and engage in more physical activity. Schools can help by ensuring regular physical activity and serving healthier meals.

What factors contribute to nocturnal enuresis and asthma, and how can these health problems be reduced?

■ In the majority of cases, heredity is responsible for **nocturnal enuresis,** or bedwetting during the night, through a failure of muscular responses that inhibit urination or a hormonal imbalance that permits too much urine to accumulate. The most effective treatment is a urine alarm that works according to conditioning principles.

■ The most common cause of school absence and childhood hospitalization is **asthma.** It occurs more often among African-American and poverty-stricken children, perhaps because of pollution, stressful home lives, and lack of access to good health care. Children with severe chronic illnesses are at risk for academic, emotional, and social difficulties and benefit from a variety of interventions.

Describe changes in unintentional injuries during middle childhood and effective interventions.

■ The rate of unintentional injury increases from middle childhood into adolescence. Motor vehicle accidents (with children as passengers or pedestrians) and bicycle accidents are the leading causes. Highly active boys often do not implement their safety knowledge and remain particularly susceptible to injury.

■ Effective school-based safety education programs make use of modeling, role playing, and rehearsal of safety practices; reward children for good performance; and provide occasional booster sessions. In addition, parents must be educated about children's age-related safety capacities.

Summary (continued)

HEALTH EDUCATION

What can parents and teachers do to encourage good health practices in school-age children?

■ Besides providing health-related information, adults must reduce health hazards in children's environments, coach children in good health practices, and model and reinforce these behaviors.

MOTOR DEVELOPMENT AND PLAY

Cite major changes in gross and fine motor development during middle childhood.

■ Gradual increases in body size and muscle strength support refinements in many gross motor skills. Gains in flexibility, balance, agility, and force occur. In addition, improvements in responding only to relevant information and in reaction time contribute to athletic performance.

■ Fine motor development also improves. Children's writing becomes more legible, and their drawings show dramatic increases in organization, detail, and representation of depth.

Describe individual and group differences in motor performance during middle childhood.

■ Children show wide individual differences in motor capacities that are influenced by both heredity and environment. Body build, parental encouragement, and opportunities to take lessons support a variety of physical abilities. Gender stereotypes, which affect parental expectations for children's athletic performance, largely account for school-age boys' superiority on a wide range of gross motor skills.

What qualities of children's play are evident in middle childhood?

■ Organized games with rules become common during the school years. Children's informally organized games support many aspects of emotional and social development. Expansion of youth sports programs has led to concerns about adult-organized athletics. Although most players are not harmed, coaches and parents who emphasize competition and winning promote undue anxiety and avoidance of sports in some children. Promoting effort, improvement, participation, and teamwork makes organized sports enjoyable and beneficial for self-esteem.

■ Some features of children's physical activity reflect our evolutionary past. **Rough-and-tumble play** may at one time have been important for the development of fighting skill and may assist children in establishing a **dominance hierarchy.** Dominance hierarchies become increasingly stable in middle childhood, especially among boys, and serve the adaptive function of limiting aggression among group members.

Why is high-quality physical education important during the school years?

■ Physical education classes help ensure that all children have access to the benefits of regular exercise and play. Yet physical education does not take place often enough in American schools. Daily classes that emphasize informal games that most children can perform well translate into lifelong psychological and physical health benefits.

Important terms and concepts

asthma (p. 421)
dominance hierarchy (p. 431)
malocclusion (p. 412)
myopia (p. 414)

neurotransmitters (p. 412)
nocturnal enuresis (p. 419)
obesity (p. 415)

rough-and-tumble play (p. 430)
secular trends in physical growth (p. 412)

. . . for further information and help

Consult the companion website for this book, where you will find additional weblinks and associated learning activities: www.ablongman.com/berk

INJURY PREVENTION

National SAFE KIDS Campaign
www.safekids.org

Dedicated to the prevention of unintentional injury in children and youths. Develops posters, stickers, brochures, and pamphlets about injury prevention designed in easy-to-read formats for children. Also produces materials to help parents protect children and minimize risks. State and local SAFE KIDS coalitions exist in all 50 U.S. States, the District of Columbia, and Puerto Rico.

CHRONIC ILLNESS

Asthma and Allergy Foundation of America
www.aafa.org

Devoted to solving health problems posed by allergic diseases, including asthma. Supports research and medical training and provides information to health professionals and the public.

Candlelighters Childhood Cancer Foundation
www.candlelighters.org

Increases public awareness of childhood cancer and provides information, guidance, and emotional support to parents with affected children. Has a crisis hotline: 1-800-366-2223.

Cystic Fibrosis Foundation
www.cff.org

Supports research, education, and care centers to benefit children and young adults with cystic fibrosis.

ADULT-ORGANIZED SPORTS

Little League Baseball
www.littleleague.org

Organizes baseball and softball programs for children 6 to 18 years of age. Operates a special division for children with disabilities and sponsors an annual world series.

United States Youth Soccer Association
www.usysa.org

Supports soccer programs for children 6 to 18 years of age throughout the United States. Seeks to encourage widespread participation and offer equal opportunity regardless of ability or sex. Distributes supplies and support necessary to form teams.

"My World in the Year 2000"
Bolor-Erdene
10 years, Mongolia

The school-age child's expanding ability to comprehend and represent people, objects, and events in the world is readily evident in this imaginative depiction of Earth in space. An improved capacity to remember, reason, solve problems, and create makes middle childhood a period of rapidly developing cognition—the topic of Chapter 12.

Cognitive Development in Middle Childhood

"**F**inally!" Lizzie exclaimed the day she entered first grade. "Now I get to go to real school just like Joey!" Rena remembered how 6-year-old Lizzie had walked confidently into her classroom, pencils, crayons, and writing pad in hand, ready for a more disciplined approach to learning than she had experienced in early childhood. As a preschooler, Lizzie had loved playing school, giving assignments as the "teacher" and pretending to read and write as the "student." Now she was there in earnest, eager to master the tasks that had sparked her imagination as a 4- and 5-year-old.

Lizzie entered a whole new world of challenging mental activities. In a single morning, she and her classmates wrote in journals, met in reading groups, worked on addition and subtraction, and sorted leaves gathered on the playground for a special science project. As Lizzie and Joey moved through the elementary school grades, they tackled increasingly complex tasks and gradually became more accomplished at reading, writing, math skills, and general knowledge of the world.

Cognitive development had prepared Joey and Lizzie for this new phase. We begin by returning to Piaget's theory and the information-processing approach. Together, they provide an overview of cognitive change during the school years. Then we take an in-depth look at individual differences in mental development. We examine the genetic and environmental roots of IQ scores, which often influence important educational decisions. Our discussion continues with language, which blossoms further during middle childhood. Finally, we consider the importance of schools in children's learning and development.

Piaget's Theory: The Concrete Operational Stage

When Lizzie visited my child development class as a 4-year-old, Piaget's conservation problems easily confused her (see Chapter 9, page 329). For example, she insisted that the amount of water had changed after it had been poured from a tall, narrow container into a short, wide one. At age 8, when Lizzie returned, these tasks were easy. "Of course it's the same," she exclaimed. "The water's shorter but it's also wider. Pour it back," she instructed the college student who was interviewing her. "You'll see, it's the same amount!"

Lizzie has entered Piaget's **concrete operational stage,** which spans the years from 7 to 11. Thought is now more logical, flexible, and organized than it was during early childhood.

CONSERVATION

The ability to pass *conservation tasks* provides clear evidence of *operations*—mental actions that obey logical rules (see Chapter 9, page 328, for examples). Notice how Lizzie coordinates several aspects of the task rather than *centering* on only one, as a preschooler would do. She engages in **decentration,** recognizing that a change in one aspect of the water (its height) compensates for a change in another aspect (its width). Lizzie also demonstrates **reversibility,** the capacity to mentally go through a series of steps and then reverse direction, returning to the starting point. Recall from Chapter 9 that reversibility is part of every logical operation. It is solidly achieved in middle childhood.

CLASSIFICATION

An improved ability to categorize underlies children's interest in collecting objects during middle childhood. These older school-age children sort baseball cards into an elaborate structure of classes and subclasses.

Between ages 7 and 10, children pass Piaget's *class inclusion problem* (see page 329). This indicates that they are more aware of classification hierarchies and can focus on relations between a general and two specific categories at the same time—that is, three relations at once (Ni, 1998; Hodges & French, 1988). You can see this in children's play activities. Collections—stamps, coins, baseball cards, rocks, bottle caps, and more—become common in middle childhood. At age 10, Joey spent hours sorting and resorting his large box of baseball cards. At times he grouped them by league and team membership, at other times by playing position and batting average. He could separate the players into a variety of classes and subclasses and flexibly move back and forth between them.

SERIATION

The ability to order items along a quantitative dimension, such as length or weight, is called **seriation.** To test for it, Piaget asked children to arrange sticks of different lengths from shortest to longest. Older preschoolers can create the series, but they do so haphazardly. They put the sticks in a row but make many errors and take a long time to correct them. In contrast, 6- to 7-year-olds are guided by an orderly plan. They create the series efficiently by beginning with the smallest stick, then moving to the next largest, and so on, until the ordering is complete.

The concrete operational child's improved grasp of quantitative arrangements is also evident in a more challenging seriation problem—

© BOB DAEMMRICH/THE IMAGE WORKS

one that requires children to seriate mentally. This ability is called **transitive inference.** In a well-known transitive inference problem, Piaget showed children pairings of differently colored sticks. From observing that stick A is longer than stick B and stick B is longer than stick C, children must make the mental inference that A is longer than C. Notice how this task, like Piaget's class inclusion task, requires children to integrate three relations at once—in this instance, A–B, B–C, A–C. About half of 6-year-olds perform well on such problems— performance that improves considerably around age 8 (Andrews & Halford, 1998; Markovitz, Dumas, & Malfait, 1995).

SPATIAL REASONING

Piaget found that school-age children have a more accurate understanding of space than they did in early childhood. Let's take two examples—children's understanding of distance and their ability to give directions.

■ DISTANCE. Comprehension of distance improves in middle childhood, as a special conservation task reveals. To give this problem, make two small trees out of modeling clay and place them apart on a table at which the child is seated. Next, put a block or thick piece of cardboard between the trees. Then ask the child whether the trees are nearer together, farther apart, or still the same distance apart.

Preschoolers say the distance has become smaller. They do not understand that a filled-up space has the same value as an empty space (Piaget, Inhelder, & Szeminska, 1948/1960). By the early school years, children grasp this idea easily. Four-year-olds can conserve distance when questioned about objects that are very familiar to them or when a path is marked between two objects, which helps them represent the distance. However, their understanding is not as solid and complete as that of the school-age child (Fabricius & Wellman, 1993; Miller & Baillargeon, 1990).

■ DIRECTIONS. School-age children's more advanced understanding of space can also be seen in their ability to give directions. Stand facing a 5- or 6-year-old, and ask the child to name an object on your left and one on your right. Children of this age answer incorrectly; they apply their own frame of reference. Between 7 and 8 years, children start to perform *mental rotations,* in which they align the self's frame to match that of a person in a different orientation. As a result, they can identify left and right for positions they do not occupy (Roberts & Aman, 1993).

Around 8 to 10 years, children can give clear, well-organized directions for how to get from one place to another. Aided by their capacity for operational thinking, they use a "mental walk" strategy in which they imagine another person's movements along a route (Gauvain & Rogoff, 1989b). Six-year-olds give more organized directions after they walk the route themselves or are specially prompted. Otherwise, they focus on the end point without describing exactly how to get there (Plumert et al., 1994).

LIMITATIONS OF CONCRETE OPERATIONAL THOUGHT

Although school-age children are far more capable problem solvers than they were during the preschool years, concrete operational thinking suffers from one important limitation. Children think in an organized, logical fashion only when dealing with concrete information they can perceive directly. Their mental operations work poorly with abstract ideas—ones not apparent in the real world.

Children's solutions to transitive inference problems provide a good illustration. When shown pairs of sticks of unequal length, Lizzie easily figured out that if stick A is longer than stick B and stick B is longer than stick C, then stick A is longer than stick C. But she had great difficulty with a hypothetical version of this task, such as "Susan is taller than Sally and Sally is taller than Mary. Who is the tallest?" Not until age 11 or 12 can children solve this problem easily.

That logical thought is at first tied to immediate situations helps account for a special feature of concrete operational reasoning. Perhaps you have already noticed that school-age

abstract thinking is hard [handwritten margin note]

concrete operational stage
Piaget's third stage, during which thought is logical, flexible, and organized in its application to concrete information. Spans the years from 7 to 11.

decentration
The ability to focus on several aspects of a problem at once and relate them.

reversibility
The ability to mentally go through a series of steps in a problem and then reverse direction, returning to the starting point.

seriation
The ability to order items along a quantitative dimension, such as length or weight.

transitive inference
The ability to seriate—or order items along a quantitative dimension—mentally.

[handwritten notes at top: ① # ② liquid, mass, length ④ ③ w-t]

© NOBORU KOMINE/PHOTO RESEARCHERS, INC.

In tribal and village societies, conservation is often delayed. These Vietnamese sisters gather firewood for their family. Although they have many opportunities to handle quantities, compared with their agemates in Western nations they may seldom see two identical quantities arranged in different ways.

[handwritten note: school helps w/operational reasoning]

horizontal décalage
Development within a Piagetian stage. Gradual mastery of logical concepts during the concrete operational stage is an example.

children master Piaget's concrete operational tasks step by step, not all at once. For example, they usually grasp conservation problems in a certain order: first number, followed by length, liquid, and mass, followed by weight. Piaget used the term **horizontal décalage** (meaning development within a stage) to describe this gradual mastery of logical concepts.

The horizontal décalage is another indication of the concrete operational child's difficulty with abstractions. School-age children do not come up with the general principle of conservation and then apply it to all relevant situations. Rather, they seem to work out the logic of each problem separately.

RECENT RESEARCH ON CONCRETE OPERATIONAL THOUGHT

From researchers' attempts to verify Piaget's assumptions about concrete operations, two themes emerge. The first has to do with the impact of specific experiences on the attainment of the concrete operational stage. The second deals with how best to explain children's sequential mastery of logical problems during middle childhood. Some theorists believe that the horizontal décalage can best be understood within an information-processing framework.

■ **IMPACT OF CULTURE AND SCHOOLING.** According to Piaget, brain development combined with exposure to a rich and varied external world should lead children in every culture to reach the concrete operational stage. Yet recent evidence indicates that specific experiences have much to do with Piagetian task performance.

In tribal and village societies, conservation is often delayed. For example, among the Hausa of Nigeria, who live in small agricultural settlements and rarely send their children to school, even the most basic conservation tasks—number, length, and liquid—are not understood until age 11 or later (Fahrmeier, 1978). This suggests that taking part in relevant everyday activities helps children master conservation and other Piagetian concepts (Light & Perret-Clermont, 1989). Joey and Lizzie, for example, have learned to think of fairness in terms of equal distribution—a value emphasized in their culture. They have many opportunities to divide materials, such as crayons, Halloween treats, and lemonade, equally among their friends. Because they often see the same quantity arranged in different ways, they grasp conservation early.

The very experience of going to school seems to promote concrete operational reasoning. When children of the same age are tested, those who have been in school longer do better on transitive inference problems (Artman & Cahan, 1993). The opportunities schooling affords for seriating objects, learning about order relations, and remembering the parts of a complex problem are probably responsible.

Yet certain nonschool, informal experiences can also foster operational thought. In one study, Brazilian 6- to 9-year-old street vendors, who seldom attend school, were given two class inclusion problems: (1) the traditional Piagetian task, and (2) an informal version in which the researcher became a customer. After setting aside four units of mint and two units of strawberry chewing gum, the researcher asked, "For you to get more money, is it better to sell me the mint chewing gum or [all] the chewing gum? Why?" Street vendors did much better on the informal problem, which captured their interest and motivation. In contrast, Brazilian schoolchildren from economically advantaged homes were more successful on the Piagetian task than a version in which they were asked to role-play street vendors—an activity unfamiliar to them (Ceci & Roazzi, 1994).

On the basis of findings like these, some investigators have concluded that the forms of logic required by Piagetian tasks do not emerge spontaneously in children but are generated by practical activities in particular cultures. This approach to cognitive development is much like Vygotsky's sociocultural theory, discussed in earlier chapters.

■ **AN INFORMATION-PROCESSING VIEW OF THE HORIZONTAL DÉCALAGE.** If you think carefully about the horizontal décalage, you will see that it raises a familiar question about Piaget's theory: Is an abrupt, stagewise transition to logical thought the best way to describe cognitive development in middle childhood? In Chapter 9 we showed that the beginnings of logical thinking are evident during the preschool years on simplified and familiar tasks. The horizontal décalage suggests that logical understanding improves gradually over the school years.

Some *neo-Piagetian theorists* argue that the development of operational thinking can best be understood in terms of gains in information-processing capacity rather than a sudden shift to a new stage (Case, 1992; Halford, 1993). For example, Robbie Case (1996, 1998) proposes that with practice, cognitive schemes demand less attention and become more automatic. This frees up space in *working memory* (see page 224) so children can focus on combining old schemes and generating new ones. For instance, the child confronted with water poured from one container to another recognizes that the height of the liquid changes. As this understanding becomes routine, the child notices that the width of the water changes as well. Soon the child coordinates both of these observations, and conservation of liquid is achieved. Then, as this logical idea becomes well practiced, the child transfers it to more demanding situations, such as area and weight.

Once the schemes of a Piagetian stage are sufficiently automatic, enough working memory is available to integrate them into an improved representational form. As a result, children acquire *central conceptual structures,* networks of concepts and relations that permit them to think about a wide range of situations in more advanced ways. The central conceptual structures that emerge from practice and integration of concrete operational schemes are highly efficient, abstract principles, which we will discuss in the context of formal operational thought in Chapter 15.

central conceptual structures

Case has successfully applied his information-processing view of gains in operational thought to a wide variety of tasks, including solving arithmetic word problems, understanding stories, drawing pictures, sight-reading music, handling money, and interpreting social situations (Case, 1998; Case & Okamoto, 1996). In each, preschoolers' schemes focus on only one dimension. In understanding stories, for example, they grasp only a single story line. In drawing pictures, they depict objects separately, ignoring their spatial arrangement. By the early school years, central conceptual structures coordinate two dimensions. Children combine two story lines into a single plot, and they create drawings that show both the features of objects and the relationship of objects to one another. Around 9 to 11 years, central conceptual structures integrate multiple dimensions. Children tell coherent stories with a main plot and several subplots. And their drawings follow a set of rules for representing perspective and, therefore, include several points of reference, such as near, midway, and far.

Why do children show a horizontal décalage? First, different forms of the same logical insight, such as conversation of liquid and weight, vary in the processing demands they make of the child. As a result, each successive task requires more working-memory resources for mastery. Second, children's task-specific experiences vary widely. A child who often listens to and tells stories but rarely draws pictures would display more advanced central conceptual structures in storytelling than in drawing. When tasks make similar processing demands, such as Piaget's class inclusion and transitive inference problems (each of which requires children to consider three relations simultaneously), children with relevant experiences should master them at the same time. Indeed, research shows that they do (Halford, Wilson, & Phillips, 1998).

Children who do not show central conceptual structures expected for their age can usually be trained to attain them. And their improved understanding readily transfers to academic tasks in school (Griffin & Case, 1996). Consequently, Case's neo-Piagetian theory is helping children who are behind their classmates in academic performance catch up and learn more effectively.

Some neo-Piagetian theorists explain the development of operational thinking in information-processing terms. As these children pour water from one container to another, they coordinate their observations of changes in the liquid's height and width, and conservation of liquid is achieved. Once this logical idea becomes automatic, enough space is available in working memory to form a more general representation of conservation that can be applied to a wider range of situations.

© LAWRENCE MIGDALE/STOCK BOSTON

EVALUATION OF THE CONCRETE OPERATIONAL STAGE

Piaget was correct that school-age youngsters approach a great many problems in systematic and rational ways not possible during early childhood. But whether this difference occurs because of *continuous* improvement in logical skills or *discontinuous* restructuring of children's thinking (as Piaget's stage idea assumes) is an issue that prompts much disagreement. Many researchers think that both types of change may be involved (Carey, 1999; Case, 1996, 1998). From early to middle childhood, children apply logical schemes to a much wider range of tasks. Yet in the process, their thought seems to undergo qualitative change—toward a more comprehensive grasp of the underlying principles of logical thought.

Piaget himself seems to have recognized this possibility in the very concept of the horizontal décalage. So perhaps some blend of Piagetian and information-processing ideas holds greatest promise for understanding cognitive development in middle childhood. With this in mind, let's take a closer look at changes in information processing during the school years.

YOURSELF...

review Mastery of conservation problems provides one illustration of Piaget's horizontal décalage. Review the preceding sections. Then list additional examples showing that operational reasoning develops gradually during middle childhood.

apply Nine-year-old Adrienne spends many hours helping her father build furniture in his woodworking shop. Explain how this experience may have contributed to her advanced performance on Piagetian seriation problems.

connect Examine the children's drawings on pages 314 and 427—the first by a 6-year-old, the second by an 8-year-old, and the third by a 10-year-old. Explain how the drawings illustrate Case's information-processing view of the development of operational thought.

Information Processing

In contrast to Piaget's focus on cognitive change, the information-processing perspective examines separate aspects of thinking. Attention and memory, which underlie every act of cognition, are central concerns in middle childhood, just as they were during infancy and the preschool years. In addition, researchers are interested in finding out how children's growing knowledge of the world and awareness of their own mental activities affect these basic components of thinking. Finally, increased understanding of how children process information is being applied to their academic learning in school—in particular, to reading and mathematics.

Researchers believe that brain development contributes to two basic changes in information processing, which facilitate the diverse aspects of thinking we are about to consider:

■ *An increase in information-processing capacity.* When children, adolescents, and young adults in three countries—Canada, Korea, and the United States—were given a variety of cognitive tasks and asked to react as quickly as possible, a consistent pattern emerged: fairly rapid decline during middle childhood in time needed to process information, with this decline trailing off around age 12 (Kail & Park, 1992, 1994). Similarity across many tasks in several cultures suggests a biologically based, age-related gain in speed of thinking, possibly due to myelinization and synaptic pruning in the brain (Kail, 2000;

Miller & Vernon, 1997). More efficient thinking leads to greater working-memory capacity, since a faster thinker can hold onto and operate on more information at once.

- *Gains in cognitive inhibition.* The ability to resist interference from internal and external distracting stimuli, or **cognitive inhibition,** improves from infancy on. But considerable progress occurs during middle childhood. EEG recordings reveal that brain waves involved in evaluating stimuli and preparing a response become more pronounced from 5 to 12 years of age (Ridderinkhof & Molen, 1997). Gains in cognitive inhibition, believed to be due to further development of the frontal lobes of the cerebral cortex, permit children to keep their minds from straying to irrelevant thoughts (Bjorklund & Harnishfeger, 1995; Dempster & Corkill, 1999). By ensuring that working memory is not cluttered with irrelevant information, cognitive inhibition supports a wide range of information-processing skills.

Besides brain development, strategy use contributes to more effective information processing. As we will see, school-age children think far more strategically than do preschoolers. At the same time, neurological change supports gains in strategy use.

ATTENTION

During middle childhood, attention changes in three ways. It becomes more selective, adaptable, and planful.

- **SELECTIVITY AND ADAPTABILITY.** As Joey and Lizzie moved through the elementary school years, they became better at deliberately attending to just those aspects of a situation that were relevant to their task goals, ignoring other sources of information. One approach to studying this increasing selectivity of attention requires children to respond selectively to certain information in a stream of largely irrelevant information. For example, researchers might present a stream of numbers on a computer screen and ask children to press a button whenever a particular sequence of two digits ("1" then "9") appears. Findings with this task, and others, show that selective attention improves sharply between 6 and 9 years of age (Aslin & Smith, 1988; Lin, Hsiao, & Chen, 1999; Smith et al., 1998).

Older children are also more adaptable, flexibly adjusting their attention to the momentary requirements of situations. For example, in judging whether pairs of stimuli are the same or different, sixth graders quickly shift their basis of judgment (from size to shape to color) when asked to do so. Second graders have trouble with this type of task (Pick & Frankel, 1974). Older children also adapt their attention to changes in their own learning. When studying for a spelling test, 10-year-old Joey devoted most attention to the words he knew least well. Lizzie was much less likely do so (Masur, McIntyre, & Flavell, 1973).

How do children acquire attentional strategies that focus on relevant information and adapt to task requirements? Children's performance on many tasks reveals that strategy development follows a predictable, four-step sequence:

1. **Production deficiency.** Preschoolers rarely engage in attentional strategies. In other words, they fail to *produce* strategies when they could be helpful.

2. **Control deficiency.** Young elementary school children sometimes produce strategies, but not consistently. They fail to *control,* or execute, strategies effectively.

3. **Utilization deficiency.** Slightly later, children execute strategies consistently, but their performance does not improve.

4. **Effective strategy use.** By the mid-elementary school years, children use strategies consistently, and performance improves (Miller & Seier, 1994).

As we will see shortly, these phases also characterize the development of memory strategies. Why, when children first use a strategy, does it not work well? A likely reason is that applying a new strategy takes so much effort and attention that children do not have enough left over to perform other parts of the task well (Miller et al., 1991; Miller, Woody-Ramsey, & Aloise, 1991).

cognitive inhibition
The ability to resist interference from internal and external distracting stimuli, thereby ensuring that working memory is not cluttered with irrelevant information.

production deficiency
The failure to produce a mental strategy when it could be helpful.

control deficiency
The inability to execute a mental strategy consistently.

utilization deficiency
The inability to improve performance even with consistent use of a mental strategy.

effective strategy use
Consistent use of a mental strategy that leads to improvement in performance.

FIGURE 12.1

Play grocery store used to investigate children's planning. Five- to 9-year-olds were given "shopping lists," consisting of five cards with a picture of a food item on each. Along the walls and on the shelves of the doll-sized store were pictures of food items that could be picked up by moving a figurine called the "shopper" down the aisles. Researchers recorded children's scanning of the store before starting on a shopping trip and along the way. The length of the route used to gather the items served as the measure of planning effectiveness. (Adapted from Szepkouski, Gauvain, & Carberry, 1994.)

rehearsal
The memory strategy of repeating information.

organization
The memory strategy of grouping together related items.

■ **PLANNING.** School-age children's attentional strategies also become more planful. They scan detailed pictures and written materials for similarities and differences more thoroughly than do preschoolers (Vurpillot, 1968). And on complex tasks, school-age children decide what to do first and what to do next in an orderly fashion. In one study, 5- to 9-year-olds were given lists of items to obtain from a play grocery store. Older children more often took time to scan the store before starting on a shopping trip. They also paused more often along the way to look for each item before moving to get it (see Figure 12.1). Consequently, they followed shorter routes through the aisles (Gauvain & Rogoff, 1989a; Szepkouski, Gauvain, & Carberry, 1994).

The development of planning illustrates how attention becomes coordinated with other cognitive processes. To solve problems involving multiple steps, children must postpone action in favor of weighing alternatives, organizing task materials (such as items on a grocery list), and remembering the steps of their plan so they can attend to each one in sequence. Along the way, they must monitor how well the plan is working and revise it if necessary.

Children learn much about how to plan effectively by collaborating on tasks with more expert planners, who model and scaffold planning-related behaviors. With age, children take on more responsibility in these joint endeavors, such as organizing task materials and suggesting planning strategies. The demands of school tasks—and teachers' explanations for how to plan—also contribute to gains in planning. And parents can foster planning by encouraging it in everyday activities and routines, from completing homework assignments to rinsing and loading dishes into the dishwasher. In a longitudinal study involving observations of parent–child interaction at ages 4, 9, and 15, parent–child discussions involving planning predicted adolescents' initiations of planning interactions with other family members (Gauvain, 1999). Many opportunities to practice planning help children understand its components and increase the likelihood that they will use this knowledge to guide future activities.

The attentional strategies we have considered are crucial for success in school. Unfortunately, some children have great difficulty paying attention during the school years. See the Biology and Environment box on pages 446–447 for a discussion of the serious learning and behavior problems of children with attention-deficit hyperactivity disorder.

MEMORY STRATEGIES

As attention improves with age, so do *memory strategies,* deliberate mental activities we use to store and retain information. During the school years, these techniques for holding information in working memory and transferring it to our long-term knowledge base take a giant leap forward (Schneider & Pressley, 1997).

■ **REHEARSAL AND ORGANIZATION.** When Lizzie had a list of things to learn, such as a phone number, the capitals of the United States, or the names of geometric shapes, she immediately used **rehearsal,** repeating the information to herself over and over again. This memory strategy first appears in the early grade school years. Soon after, a second strategy becomes common: **organization** (Gathercole, 1998). Children group related items (for example, all capitals in the same part of the country), an approach that improves recall dramatically.

Memory strategies require time and effort to perfect. At first, *control deficiencies* are evident (Bjorklund & Coyle, 1995). For example, at age 8, Lizzie rehearsed in a piecemeal fashion. After being given the word "cat" in a list of items, she said, "Cat, cat, cat." In contrast, 10-year-old Joey combined previous words with each new item, saying, "Desk, man, yard, cat, cat" (Kunzinger, 1985). Not surprisingly, Joey retained much more information. Joey also organized more skillfully, grouping items into fewer categories. And he used organization in a wide range of memory tasks, whereas Lizzie used it only when relations between items were very obvious. Experience with materials that form clear categories helps children organize more effectively and begin to apply the strategy to less clearly related materials (Bjorklund et al., 1994).

Furthermore, both Joey and Lizzy often applied several memory strategies at once—rehearsing, organizing, and stating the category name of a group of items as they tried to learn them. With age, children use more strategies simultaneously, and the more they use, the better they remember (Coyle & Bjorklund, 1997).

Although younger school-age children's use of multiple strategies has little impact on performance (a *utilization deficiency*), their tendency to experiment is adaptive. By generating a variety of memory strategies, they discover which ones work best on different tasks and how to combine strategies effectively. For example, second to fourth graders know that organizing the items first, rehearsing category names second, and then rehearsing individual items is a good way to study lists (Hock, Park, & Bjorklund, 1998). By trying out memory strategies, children select better strategies and strategy combinations. Recall from *overlapping-waves theory*, discussed in Chapter 9, that children experiment with strategies when faced with many cognitive challenges, and memory is no exception.

■ **ELABORATION.** Children start to use a third memory strategy, **elaboration,** by the end of middle childhood. It involves creating a relationship, or shared meaning, between two or more pieces of information that are not members of the same category. For example, suppose "fish" and "pipe" are among a list of words you need to learn. If, in trying to remember them, you generate a mental image of a fish smoking a pipe, you are using elaboration. Once children discover this memory technique, they find it so effective that it tends to replace other strategies. The very reason elaboration is so successful explains why it is late to develop. To use elaboration, we must translate items into images and think of a relationship between them. Children's working memories must expand before they can carry out these activities at the same time (Schneider & Pressley, 1997). Elaboration becomes increasingly common during adolescence and young adulthood.

Because the strategies of organization and elaboration combine items into *meaningful chunks*, they permit children to hold on to much more information. As a result, the strategies further expand working memory. In addition, when children store a new item in long-term memory by linking it to information they already know, they can *retrieve* it easily by thinking of other items associated with it. As we will see in the next section, this is one reason that memory improves steadily during the school years.

THE KNOWLEDGE BASE AND MEMORY PERFORMANCE

During middle childhood, the long-term knowledge base grows larger and becomes organized into increasingly elaborate, hierarchically structured networks. This rapid growth of knowledge helps children use strategies and remember (Schneider, 1993). In other words, knowing more about a particular topic makes new information more meaningful and familiar so it is easier to store and retrieve.

To test this idea, researchers classified fourth graders as experts or novices in knowledge of soccer. Then they gave both groups lists of soccer and nonsoccer items to learn. Experts remembered far more items on the soccer list (but not on the nonsoccer list) than did nonexperts. And during recall, the experts' listing of items was better organized (as indicated by clustering of items into categories) (Schneider & Bjorklund, 1992). These findings suggest that very knowledgeable children apply an organizational strategy to information in their area of expertise with little or no effort—through rapid associations of new items with the large number they already know. Consequently, experts can devote more working-memory resources to using recalled information to reason and solve problems (Bjorklund & Douglas, 1997).

elaboration
The memory strategy of creating a relationship, or shared meaning, between two or more pieces of information that are not members of the same category.

Biology & ENVIRONMENT

CHILDREN WITH ATTENTION-DEFICIT HYPERACTIVITY DISORDER

While the other fifth graders worked quietly at their desks, Calvin squirmed in his seat, dropped his pencil, looked out the window, fiddled with his shoelaces, and talked out. "Hey Joey," he yelled over the top of several desks, "wanna play ball after school?"

Joey and the other children weren't eager to play with Calvin. Out on the playground, Calvin was a poor listener and failed to follow the rules of the game. When up at bat, he had difficulty taking turns. In the outfield, he tossed his mitt up in the air and looked elsewhere when the ball came his way. Calvin's desk at school and his room at home were a chaotic mess. He often lost pencils, books, and other materials necessary for completing assignments. And very often, he had difficulty remembering his assignments and when they were due.

SYMPTOMS OF ADHD

Calvin is one of 3 to 5 percent of school-age children with **attention-deficit hyperactivity disorder (ADHD)** (American Psychiatric Association, 1994). Boys are diagnosed three to nine times more often than girls. However, many girls with ADHD may be overlooked because their symptoms usually are not as flagrant (Gaub & Carlson, 1997).

Children with ADHD cannot stay focused on a task that requires mental effort for more than a few minutes. In addition, they often act impulsively, ignoring social rules and lashing out with hostility when frustrated. Many (but not all) are *hyperactive*. They charge through their days with excessive motor activity, exhausting parents and teachers and so irritating other children that they are quickly rejected by their classmates. To be diagnosed with ADHD, these symptoms must have appeared before age 7 as an early and persistent problem. They must also be pervasive—evident in at least two settings—and have led to academic and social difficulties. According to one view that has amassed substantial research support, a common theme unifies ADHD symptoms: an impairment in inhibition, which makes it hard to delay action in favor of thought (Barkley, 1997, 1999).

The intelligence of ADHD children is normal, and they show no signs of serious emotional disturbance. Instead, because they have trouble thinking before they act, they do poorly on laboratory tasks requiring sustained attention and find it hard to ignore irrelevant information. Their distractibility results in forgetfulness and difficulties with planning, reasoning, and problem solving in academic and social situations (Barkley, 1997; Denckla, 1996). Although some children catch up in development, most continue to have problems concentrating and finding friends in adolescence and adulthood (Claude & Firestone, 1995).

ORIGINS OF ADHD

Heredity plays a major role in ADHD, since the disorder runs in families, and identical twins share it more often than do fraternal twins. Also, an adopted child who is inattentive and hyperactive is likely to have a biological parent (but not an adoptive parent) with similar symptoms (Rhee et al., 1999; Sherman, Iacono, & McGue, 1997). Recent psychophysiological research, including EEG and fMRI studies, reveals that ADHD children have reduced electrical and blood-flow activity in the frontal lobes of the cerebral cortex and in other areas responsible for attention and inhibition of behavior (Novak,

attention-deficit hyperactivity disorder (ADHD)
A childhood disorder involving inattentiveness, impulsivity, and excessive motor activity. Often leads to academic failure and social problems.

Although knowledge clearly plays an important role in memory development, it may have to be quite broad and well structured before it can facilitate the use of strategies and recall. A brief series of lessons designed to increase knowledge in a particular area does not affect children's ability to remember new information in that domain (DeMarie-Dreblow, 1991).

Finally, knowledge is not the only important factor in children's strategic memory processing. Children who are expert in a particular area, whether it be chess, math, social studies, or spelling, are usually highly motivated. As a result, they not only acquire knowledge more quickly, but they *actively use what they know* to add more. In contrast, academically unsuccessful children often fail to use previously stored information to clarify new material. This, in turn, interferes with the development of a broad knowledge base (Schneider & Bjorklund, 1998). So by the end of the school years, knowledge acquisition and use of memory strategies are intimately related and support one another.

ELENA ROORAID/PHOTOEDIT

The boy on the right frequently engages in disruptive behavior, disturbing his classmates while they try to work. Children with ADHD have great difficulty staying on task and often act impulsively.

Solanto, & Abikoff, 1995; Rapport & Chung, 2000). Several genes that affect neurotransmitter and hormone levels have been implicated in the disorder (Biederman & Spencer, 2000; Faraone et al., 1999).

At the same time, ADHD is associated with a variety of environmental factors. These children are somewhat more likely to come from homes in which marriages are unhappy and family stress is high (Bernier & Siegel, 1994). But researchers agree that a stressful home life rarely causes ADHD. Instead, the behaviors of these children can contribute to family problems, which, in turn, are likely to intensify the child's preexisting difficulties. Furthermore, prenatal teratogens (particularly those involving long-term exposure, such as illegal drugs, alcohol, and cigarettes) are linked to inattention and hyperactivity (Milberger et al., 1997).

TREATING ADHD

Calvin's doctor eventually prescribed stimulant medication, the most common treatment for ADHD. As long as dosage is carefully regulated, these drugs reduce activity level and improve attention, academic per-

formance, and peer relations for 70 to 75 percent of children who take them (Greenhill, Halperin, & Abikof, 1999). Stimulant medication seems to increase brain-wave activity in the frontal lobes, thereby increasing the child's capacity to sustain attention and to inhibit off-task and self-stimulating behavior.

Although stimulant medication is relatively safe, its impact is only short term. Drugs cannot teach children ways of compensating for inattention and impulsivity. Combining medication with interventions that model and reinforce appropriate academic and social behavior seems to be the most effective approach to treatment (Pelham, Wheeler, & Chronis, 1998).

Teachers can also create conditions in classrooms that support these students' special learning needs. Short work periods followed by a chance to get up and move around help them concentrate.

Finally, family intervention is particularly important. Inattentive, overactive children strain the patience of parents, who are likely to react punitively and inconsistently in return—a child-rearing style that strengthens inappropriate behavior. Breaking this cycle is as important for ADHD children as it is for the defiant, aggressive youngsters we discussed in Chapter 10. In fact, at least 35 percent of the time, these two sets of behavior problems occur together (Lahey & Loeber, 1997).

CULTURE, SCHOOLING, AND MEMORY STRATEGIES

Think about the situations in which the strategies of rehearsal, organization, and elaboration are useful. People usually employ these techniques when they need to remember information for its own sake. On many other occasions, they participate in daily activities and remember as a natural by-product of the activity (Rogoff & Chavajay, 1995). For example, Joey can spout off a wealth of facts about baseball teams and players—information he picked up from watching the game, discussing it, and trading baseball cards with his friends. And without prior rehearsal, he can recount the story line of an exciting movie or novel—narrative material that is already meaningfully organized.

A repeated finding of cross-cultural research is that people who have no formal schooling do not use or benefit from instruction in memory strategies. Tasks that require children to recall isolated bits of information are common in classrooms, and they provide children with

As these Guatemalan Mayan boys practice the intricate art of mat weaving, they demonstrate keen memory for information embedded in meaningful contexts. Yet when given a list-memory task of the kind American children often perform in school, they do poorly.

more refined thinking

a great deal of motivation to use memory strategies. In fact, schooled children get so much practice with this type of learning that they do not refine other techniques that rely on spatial location and arrangement of objects, cues that are readily available in everyday life. Australian Aboriginal and Guatemalan Mayan children are considerably better at these memory skills (Kearins, 1981; Rogoff, 1986).

Looked at in this way, the development of memory strategies is not just a matter of a more competent information-processing system. It is also a product of task demands and cultural circumstances.

THE SCHOOL-AGE CHILD'S THEORY OF MIND

During middle childhood, children's *theory of mind,* or set of beliefs about mental activities, becomes much more elaborate and refined. You may recall from Chapter 9 that this awareness of cognitive processes is called *metacognition.* School-age children's improved ability to reflect on their own mental life advances their thinking and problem solving. They become increasingly conscious of cognitive capacities and effective strategies.

■ **KNOWLEDGE OF COGNITIVE CAPACITIES.** Unlike preschoolers, who view the mind as a passive container of information, older children regard it as an active, constructive agent, capable of selecting and transforming information (Kuhn, 2000). Consequently, they have a much better understanding of the process of thinking and the impact of psychological factors on performance.

Six- and 7-year-olds, for example, realize that mental inferences can be a source of knowledge and that doing well on a task depends on focusing attention—concentrating on it, wanting to do it, and not being tempted by anything else (Carpendale & Chandler, 1996; Miller & Bigi, 1979). And by age 10, children realize that if you "remember," "know," or "understand," you are more certain of your knowledge than if you "guessed," "estimated," or "compared." They also grasp the interrelatedness of memory and understanding—that remembering is crucial for understanding and that understanding strengthens memory (Schwanenflugel, Fabricius, & Noyes, 1996; Schwanenflugel, Henderson, & Fabricius, 1998).

What promotes this more reflective, process-oriented view of the mind? Perhaps children become aware of mental activities through quiet-time observation of their own thinking and through exposure to talk about the mind in active terms, as when they hear people say, "I was thinking a lot" or "My mind wandered" (Wellman & Hickling, 1994). Schooling may contribute as well. Instructing children to keep their minds on what they are doing and to remember mental steps calls attention to the workings of the mind. And as children engage in reading, writing, and math, they often use private speech, at first speaking aloud and later silently to themselves. As they "hear themselves think," they probably detect many aspects of mental life (Flavell, Green, & Flavell, 1995).

■ **KNOWLEDGE OF STRATEGIES.** Consistent with their more active view of the mind, school-age children are far more conscious of mental strategies than are preschoolers. For example, they know quite a bit about effective memory techniques. When shown video clips of two children using different recall strategies and asked which one is likely to produce better memory, kindergarten and young elementary school children recognize large gaps in strategy effectiveness—that rehearsing or organizing is better than looking or naming. Older children are aware of more subtle differences—that organizing is better than rehearsing (Justice, 1986; Schneider, 1986). By third grade, children realize that in studying material for later recall, it is helpful to devote most effort to items they know least well (Kreutzer, Leonard, & Flavell, 1975).

Once children become conscious of the many factors that influence mental activity, they combine them into an integrated understanding. By the end of middle childhood, children take account of *interactions* between variables—how age and motivation of the learner, effective use of strategies, and nature and difficulty of the task together affect cognitive performance (Wellman, 1990). In this way, metacognition truly becomes a comprehensive theory.

© 1999 LAURA DWIGHT

COGNITIVE SELF-REGULATION

Although metacognition expands, school-age children often have difficulty putting what they know about thinking into action. They are not yet good at **cognitive self-regulation,** the process of continuously monitoring progress toward a goal, checking outcomes, and redirecting unsuccessful efforts. For example, Lizzie is aware that she should group items in a memory task and that she should reread a complicated paragraph to make sure she understands it. But she does not always do these things when working on an assignment.

To study cognitive self-regulation, researchers sometimes look at the impact of children's awareness of memory strategies on how well they remember. By second grade, the more children know about memory strategies, the more they recall—a relationship that strengthens over the elementary school years (Pierce & Lange, 2000; Schneider & Pressley, 1997). Furthermore, children who can explain why a memory strategy works use it more effectively; they show better memory performance (Justice et al., 1997).

Why does cognitive self-regulation develop gradually? Monitoring learning outcomes is cognitively demanding, requiring constant evaluation of effort and progress. By adolescence, self-regulation is a strong predictor of academic success (Joyner & Kurtz-Costes, 1997). Students who do well in school know when their learning is going well and when it is not. If they run up against obstacles, such as poor study conditions, a confusing text passage, or an unclear class presentation, they take steps to organize the learning environment, review the material, or seek other sources of support. This active, purposeful approach contrasts sharply with the passive orientation of students who achieve poorly (Zimmerman & Risemberg, 1997).

Parents and teachers can foster self-regulation by pointing out the special demands of tasks, encouraging the use of strategies, and emphasizing the value of self-correction. As adults ask children questions and help them monitor their cognitive activity in circumstances where they are likely to encounter difficulties, children internalize these procedures. In addition, explaining why strategies are effective encourages children to use them in new situations (Pressley, 1995; Schunk & Zimmerman, 1994). When adults tell children not just what to do but why to do it, they provide a rationale for future action. Then children learn not just how to get a task done but what to do when faced with new problems.

Children who acquire effective self-regulatory skills succeed at challenging tasks. As a result, they develop confidence in their own ability—a belief that supports the use of self-regulation in the future (Zimmerman, Bonner, & Kovach, 1996). Unfortunately, some children receive messages from parents and teachers that seriously undermine their academic self-esteem and self-regulatory skills. We will consider these learned helpless youngsters, along with ways to help them, in Chapter 13.

APPLICATIONS OF INFORMATION PROCESSING TO ACADEMIC LEARNING

Joey entered first grade able to recognize only a handful of written words. By fifth grade, he was a proficient reader. Similarly, at age 6, Joey had an informally acquired knowledge of number concepts. By age 10, he could add, subtract, multiply, and divide with ease, and he had begun to master fractions and percentages.

Over the past decade, fundamental discoveries about the development of information processing have been applied to children's learning of reading and mathematics. Researchers have begun to identify the cognitive ingredients of skilled performance, trace their development, and distinguish good from poor learners by pinpointing differences in cognitive skills. They hope, as a result, to design teaching methods that will help all children master these essential skills.

School-age children have an improved ability to reflect on their own mental life. This child is aware that external aids to memory are often necessary to ensure that information will be retained.

good cognitive self-regulation correlates w/academic success.

cognitive self-regulation
The process of continuously monitoring progress toward a goal, checking outcomes, and redirecting unsuccessful efforts.

WILL HART

In this first-grade whole-language classroom, children acquire a sight vocabulary and learn to read through exposure to whole, meaningful text. Research indicates that kindergartners just starting to read benefit from an emphasis on whole language. In the early grades, combining the whole-language and basic-skills approaches seems most effective.

whole-language approach
An approach to beginning reading instruction that parallels children's natural language learning and uses reading materials that are whole and meaningful.

basic-skills approach
An approach to beginning reading instruction that emphasizes training in phonics—the basic rules for translating written symbols into sounds—and simplified reading materials.

■ **READING.** While reading, we use a large number of skills at once, taxing all aspects of our information-processing systems. We must perceive single letters and letter combinations, translate them into speech sounds, hold chunks of text in working memory while interpreting their meaning, and combine the meanings of various parts of a text passage into an understandable whole. In fact, reading is so demanding that most or all of these skills must be done automatically. If one or more are poorly developed, they will compete for space in our limited working memories, and reading performance will decline (Perfetti, 1988).

Researchers do not yet know how children manage to acquire and combine all these varied skills into fluent reading. Currently, psychologists and educators are engaged in a "great debate" about how to teach beginning reading. On one side are those who take a **whole-language approach** to reading instruction. They argue that reading should be taught in a way that parallels natural language learning. From the very beginning, children should be exposed to text in its complete form—stories, poems, letters, posters, and lists—so they can appreciate the communicative function of written language. According to these experts, as long as reading is kept whole and meaningful, children will be motivated to discover the specific skills they need as they gain experience with the printed word (Goodman, 1986; Watson, 1989). On the other side of the debate are those who advocate a **basic-skills approach.** According to this view, children should be given simplified text materials. At first, they should be coached on *phonics*—the basic rules for translating written symbols into sounds. Only later, after they have mastered these skills, should they get complex reading material (Rayner & Pollatsek, 1989; Samuels, 1985).

As yet, research does not show clear-cut superiority for either of these approaches. In fact, a third group of experts believes that children learn best when they receive a mixture of both (Freppon & Dahl, 1998; Stahl, McKenna, & Pagnucco, 1994). Kindergartners just starting to read benefit from an emphasis on whole language, with gradual introduction of phonics as reading skills improve (Jeynes & Littell, 2000; Sacks & Mergendoller, 1997). In the early grades, balancing the two methods seems most effective. In one study, 7-year-old poor readers showed greater reading gains when assigned to a "phonics/meaningful reading" intervention than to either a "phonics alone" or a "reading alone" teaching condition (Hatcher, Hulme, & Ellis, 1994).

Why might combining phonics with whole language work best? Learning the basics—relations between letters and sounds—enables children to *decode,* or decipher, words they have never seen before. As this process becomes more automatic, it releases children's attention to the higher-level activities involved in comprehending the text's meaning (Adams, Treiman, & Pressley, 1998). Research shows that *phonological awareness*—the ability to segment, blend, and manipulate the sound structure of words—predicts early reading success. Children who enter school low in phonological awareness make far better reading progress when given training in phonics. Soon they detect new letter–sound relations on their own as they read (Castle, 1999; Goswami, 2000). Children who receive phonics instruction also display more accurate spelling by third grade than children experiencing only whole language (Bruck et al., 1998).

Yet if practice in basic skills is overemphasized, children may lose sight of the goal of reading—understanding. Many teachers report cases of students who can read aloud fluently but who register little or no meaning. Such children have little metacognitive knowledge of effective reading strategies—for example, that they must read more carefully if they will be tested on a passage than if they are reading for pleasure. And they do not monitor their reading comprehension. Providing instruction aimed at increasing children's knowledge and use of reading strategies readily enhances reading performance of children from third grade on (Cross & Paris, 1988; Dickson et al., 1998).

Table 12.1 charts the general sequence of reading development. Notice how a major shift occurs around age 7 to 8, from "learning to read" to "reading to learn" (Ely, 1997). As decod-

TABLE 12.1

Sequence of Reading Development

GRADE/AGE	DEVELOPMENT	METHOD OF LEARNING
Preschool and Kindergarten 2–6 years	"Pretends" to read; recognizes some familiar signs ("ON," "OFF," "PIZZA"); "pretends" to write; prints own name and other words	Informal literacy experiences through literacy-rich physical environments, literacy-related play, and storybook reading (see Chapter 9, page 348)
Grades 1 and 2 6–7 years	Masters letter–sound correspondences; sounds out one-syllable words; reads simple stories; reads about 600 words	Direct teaching, through exposure to many types of texts and the basic rules of decoding written symbols into sounds
Grades 2 and 3 7–8 years	Reads simple stories more fluently; masters basic decoding rules; reads about 3,000 words	Same as above
Grades 4 to 9 9–14 years	Reads to learn new knowledge, usually without questioning the reading material	Reading and studying; participating in classroom discussion; completing written assignments
Grades 10 to 12 15–17 years	Reads more widely, tapping materials with diverse viewpoints	Reading more widely; writing papers
College 18 years and older	Reads with a self-defined purpose; decoding and comprehension skills reach a high level of efficiency	Reading even more widely; writing more sophisticated papers

Source: Chall, 1983.

ing and comprehension skills reach a high level of efficiency, older readers can become actively engaged with the text. They adjust the way they read to fit their current purpose—at times seeking new facts and ideas, at other times questioning, agreeing, or disagreeing with the writer's viewpoint.

■ MATHEMATICS. Mathematics teaching in elementary school builds on and greatly enriches children's informal knowledge of number concepts and counting. Written notation systems and formal computational techniques enhance children's ability to represent number and compute. Over the early elementary school years, children acquire basic math facts through a combination of frequent practice and reasoning about number concepts. (Return to Chapter 9, pages 345–346, for research supporting the importance of both extended practice and a grasp of concepts.) Eventually children retrieve answers automatically and apply this basic knowledge to more complex problems.

Arguments about how to teach mathematics resemble those in reading. Extensive practice is pitted against "number sense," or understanding. Yet once again, a blend of these two approaches is most beneficial. In learning basic math, poorly performing students move too quickly toward trying to retrieve answers automatically. Their responses are often wrong because the children have not experimented with strategies long enough to test which ones result in rapid, accurate solutions (Siegler, 1996). And when asked to explain math concepts, their performance is weak (Canobi, Reeve, & Pattison, 1998). This suggests that encouraging students to apply strategies and making sure they understand why certain ones work well are vital for solid mastery of basic math.

A similar picture emerges for more complex skills, such as carrying in addition, borrowing in subtraction, and operating with decimals and fractions. Children's mistakes indicate that they draw on their experience with easier problems and invent strategies, which do not always work. Or they try to use a procedure they have been taught but do not understand the basis for it. For example, look at the following subtraction errors:

$$\begin{array}{r} 427 \\ -138 \\ \hline 311 \end{array} \qquad \begin{array}{r} {}^{6}\!\!\not{7}00{}^{1}\!\!\not{2} \\ -5445 \\ \hline 1447 \end{array}$$

© FUJI FOTOS/THE IMAGE WORKS

Culture and language-based factors contribute to Asian children's skill at mathematics. The abacus supports these Japanese pupils' understanding of place value. Ones, tens, hundreds, and thousands are each represented by a different column of beads, and calculations are performed by moving the beads to different positions. As children become skilled at using the abacus, they learn to think in ways that facilitate solving complex arithmetic problems.

In the first problem, the child consistently subtracts a smaller from a larger digit, regardless of which is on top. In the second, columns with zeros are skipped in a borrowing operation, and whenever there is a zero on top, the bottom digit is written as the answer. Researchers believe that drill-oriented math instruction that provides children with little opportunity to experiment with problem solving, to grasp the reasons behind strategies, and to evaluate solution techniques and answers is at the heart of these difficulties (Carpenter et al., 1999; Fuson, 1990).

In Asian countries, students receive a variety of supports for acquiring mathematical knowledge, but these are not broadly available in the United States. For example, use of the metric system, which presents ones, tens, hundreds, and thousands values in all areas of measurement, helps Asian children grasp place value. The consistent structure of number words in Asian languages ("ten two" for 12, "ten three" for 13) also makes this idea clear (Ho & Fuson, 1998; Miller et al., 1995). Furthermore, Asian number words are shorter and more quickly pronounced. This eases verbal counting strategies, since more digits can be held in working memory. It also increases the speed with which children can retrieve math facts from long-term memory (Geary et al., 1996; Jensen & Whang, 1994). Finally, as we will see later in this chapter, in Asian classrooms, much more time is spent exploring underlying math concepts and much less on drill and repetition.

Ask YOURSELF...

review   *Cite evidence indicating that school-age children view the mind as an active, constructive agent.*

apply   *One day, the children in Lizzie and Joey's school saw a slide show about endangered species. They were told to remember as many animal names as they could. Fifth and sixth graders recalled considerably more than did second and third graders. What factors might account for this difference?*

apply   *Lizzie knows that if you have difficulty learning part of a task, you should devote most of your attention to that aspect. But she plays each of her piano pieces from beginning to end instead of picking out the hard parts for extra practice. What explains Lizzie's failure to apply what she knows?*

reflect   *Describe the relative emphasis on computational practice and understanding of concepts in your elementary-school math education. How do you think that balance affected your interest and performance in math?*

Individual Differences in Mental Development

During middle childhood, educators rely heavily on intelligence tests for assessing individual differences in mental development. Around age 6, IQ becomes more stable than it was at earlier ages, and it correlates well with academic achievement, from .40 to .70 (Brody, 1997). Because IQ predicts school performance, it often plays a major role in educational decisions. Do intelligence tests provide an accurate indication of the school-age child's ability to profit from academic instruction? Let's take a close look at this controversial issue.

IQ predicts academic success.

DEFINING AND MEASURING INTELLIGENCE

Take a moment to jot down a list of behaviors that you regard as typical of a highly intelligent school-age child. Did you come up with just one or two or a great many? Virtually all intelligence tests provide an overall score (the IQ), which represents *general intelligence* or reasoning ability, and an array of separate scores measuring specific mental abilities. Intelligence is a collection of many capacities, and not all are included on currently available tests.

Test designers use a complicated statistical technique called *factor analysis* to identify the various abilities that intelligence tests measure. This procedure determines which sets of items on the test correlate strongly with one another. Those that do are assumed to measure a similar ability and therefore are designated as a separate factor. To understand the types of intellectual factors measured in middle childhood, let's consider some representative intelligence tests and how they are administered.

■ **REPRESENTATIVE INTELLIGENCE TESTS.** The intelligence tests that Joey and Lizzie take every so often in school are *group-administered tests.* They permit large numbers of students to be tested at once and require very little training of teachers who give them. Group tests are useful for instructional planning and identifying children who require more extensive evaluation with *individually administered tests.* Unlike group tests, individually administered ones demand considerable training and experience to give well. The examiner not only considers the child's answers but carefully observes the child's behavior, noting such things as attentiveness to and interest in the tasks and wariness of the adult. These reactions provide insight into whether the test score is accurate or underestimates the child's abilities.

Two individual tests—the Stanford-Binet and the Wechsler—are most often used to identify highly intelligent children and diagnose those with learning problems. As we look at each, refer to Figure 12.2 on page 454, which shows some of the items that typically appear on intelligence tests for children.

The Stanford-Binet Intelligence Scale. The modern descendent of Alfred Binet's first successful intelligence test is the **Stanford-Binet Intelligence Scale,** for individuals between 2 years of age and adulthood. Its latest version measures both general intelligence and four intellectual factors: verbal reasoning, quantitative reasoning, abstract/visual reasoning, and short-term memory (Thorndike, Hagen, & Sattler, 1986). Within these factors are 15 subtests that permit a detailed analysis of each child's mental abilities. The verbal and quantitative factors emphasize culturally loaded, fact-oriented information, such as vocabulary and sentence comprehension. In contrast, the abstract/visual reasoning factor is believed to be less culturally biased because it demands little in the way of specific information. Instead, it tests children's ability to see complex relationships, as illustrated by the spatial visualization item shown in Figure 12.2.

The Wechsler Intelligence Scale for Children–III. The **Wechsler Intelligence Scale for Children–III (WISC–III)** is the third edition of a widely used test for 6- through 16-year-olds. A downward extension of it—the *Wechsler Preschool and Primary Scale of Intelligence–Revised*

Wechsler Intelligence Scale for Children–III (WISC–III)
An individually administered intelligence test that includes both a measure of general intelligence and a variety of verbal and performance scores.

Stanford-Binet Intelligence Scale
An individually administered intelligence test that is the modern descendent of Alfred Binet's first successful test for children. Measures general intelligence and four factors: verbal reasoning, quantitative reasoning, abstract/visual reasoning, and short-term memory.

This test measures verbal + performance.

Item	Typical Verbal Items
Vocabulary	Tell me what *carpet* means.
General Information	How many ounces make a pound? What day of the week comes right after Thursday?
Verbal Comprehension	Why are police officers needed?
Verbal Analogies	A rock is hard; a pillow is _____.
Logical Reasoning	Five girls are sitting side by side on a bench. Jane is in the middle and Betty sits next to her on the right. Alice is beside Betty, and Dale is beside Ellen, who sits next to Jane. Who are sitting on the ends?
Number Series	Which number comes next in the series? **4 8 6 12** ___

Typical Nonverbal Items

Picture Oddities	Which picture does not belong with the others?

Spatial Visualization	Which of the boxes on the right can be made from the pattern shown on the left?

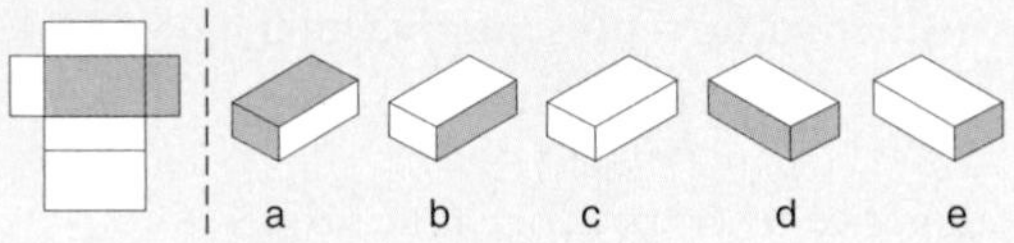

Typical Performance Items

Picture	Put the pictures in the right order so that what is happening makes sense.

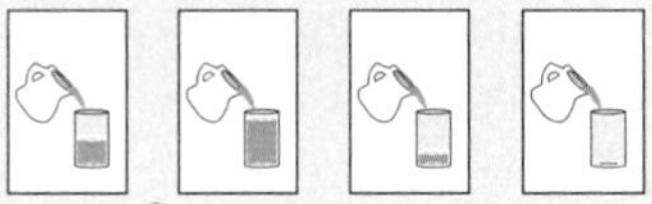

Puzzles	Put these pieces together so they make a wagon.

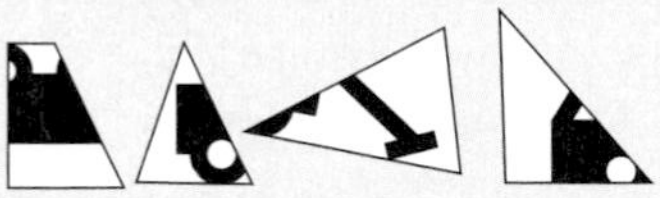

FIGURE 12.2

Test items like those on common intelligence tests for children. In contrast to verbal items, nonverbal items do not require reading or direct use of language. Performance items are also nonverbal, but they require the child to draw or construct something rather than merely give a correct answer. As a result, they appear only on individually administered intelligence tests. (Logical reasoning, picture oddities, and spatial visualization examples are adapted with permission of The Free Press, a Division of Simon & Schuster, Inc., from *Bias in Mental Testing* by Arthur R. Jensen. Copyright © 1980 by Arthur R. Jensen.)

(WPPSI–R)—is appropriate for children 3 through 8 (Wechsler, 1989, 1991). The Wechsler tests offered both a measure of general intelligence and a variety of factor scores long before the Stanford-Binet. As a result, over the past two decades, many psychologists and educators have come to prefer the WISC and WPPSI.

Both the WISC–III and the WPPSI–R measure two broad intellectual factors: verbal and performance. Each contains six subtests, yielding 12 separate scores in all. Performance items (see examples in Figure 12.2) require the child to arrange materials rather than talk to the examiner. Consequently, these tests provided one of the first means through which non-English-speaking children and children with speech and language disorders could demonstrate their intellectual strengths.

The Wechsler tests also were the first to be standardized on samples representing the total population of the United States, including ethnic minorities. Their broadly representative standardization samples have served as models for many other tests, including the recent version of the Stanford-Binet.

■ **RECENT DEVELOPMENTS IN DEFINING INTELLIGENCE.** Researchers have begun to combine the factor analytic approach to defining intelligence with the information-processing approach. They believe that factors on intelligence tests have limited use unless we can identify the cognitive processes responsible for them. Once we understand the underlying basis of IQ, we will know much more about why a particular child does well or poorly and what skills must be worked on to improve performance. These researchers conduct *componential analyses* of children's mental test scores. This means that they look for relationships between aspects (or components) of information processing and children's IQs.

Many studies reveal that speed of processing, measured in terms of reaction time on diverse cognitive tasks, is moderately related to IQ and to gains in mental test performance over time (Deary, 1995; Deary & Stough, 1996; Fry & Hale, 1996; Neubauer & Bucik, 1996). These findings suggest that individuals whose nervous systems function more efficiently, permitting them to take in and manipulate information quickly, have an edge in intellectual skills. In support of this interpretation, fast, strong EEG waves in response to stimulation also predict speedy processing and high mental test scores (Rijsdijk & Boomsma, 1997; Vernon, 1993).

But rapid responding is not the only processing correlate of mental test performance. Strategy use also makes a difference, and it explains some of the association between speed of thinking and IQ (Miller & Vernon, 1992). Children who apply strategies effectively acquire more knowledge. As a result, they develop fast, accurate thinking, which seems to carry over to performance on intelligence test items.

The componental approach has one major shortcoming: It regards intelligence as entirely due to causes within the child. Yet throughout this book, we have seen how cultural and situational factors profoundly affect children's cognitive skills. Recently, Robert Sternberg has expanded the componential approach into a comprehensive theory that regards intelligence as a product of inner and outer forces.

■ **STERNBERG'S TRIARCHIC THEORY.** As Figure 12.3 shows, Sternberg's (1985, 1997, 1999a) **triarchic theory of intelligence** is made up of three interacting subtheories. The first, the *componential subtheory,* spells out the information-processing skills that underlie intelligent behavior. You are already familiar with its main elements—strategy application, knowledge acquisition, metacognition, and self-regulation.

According to Sternberg, children's use of these components is not just a matter of internal capacity. It is also a function of the conditions under which intelligence is assessed. The *experiential subtheory* states that highly intelligent individuals, compared to less intelligent ones, process information more skillfully in novel situations. When given a relatively new task, the bright person learns rapidly, making strategies automatic so working memory is freed for more complex aspects of the situation.

Think, for a moment, about the implications of this idea for measuring children's intelligence. To accurately compare children in *brightness*—in ability to deal with novelty and learn efficiently—all children would have to be presented with equally unfamiliar test items. Otherwise, some children will appear more intelligent than others simply because of their past experiences, not because they are really more cognitively skilled. These children start with the unfair advantage of prior practice on the tasks.

This point brings us to the third part of Sternberg's model, the *contextual subtheory.* It proposes that intelligent people skillfully *adapt* their information-processing skills to fit their personal desires and the demands of their everyday worlds. When they cannot adapt to a situation, they try to *shape,* or change, it to meet their needs. If they cannot shape it, they *select* new contexts that are consistent with their goals. The contextual subtheory emphasizes that intelligent behavior is never culture free. Because of their backgrounds, some children come to value behaviors required for success on intelligence tests, and they easily adapt to the tasks and testing conditions. Others with different life histories misinterpret the testing context or reject it entirely because it does not suit their needs. Yet such children may display very sophisticated abilities in daily life—for example, telling stories, engaging in complex artistic activities, or interacting skillfully with other people (Sternberg, 1996b).

Sternberg's theory emphasizes the complexity of human mental skills and the limitations of current tests in assessing that complexity. Children often use different abilities in academic tasks than in nonacademic, everyday situations. Yet out-of-school, practical forms of intelligence are vital for life success, and they help explain why cultures vary widely in the behaviors they regard as intelligent (Sternberg et al., 1999). When ethnically diverse parents were asked for their idea of an intelligent first grader, Caucasian Americans valued cognitive traits over noncognitive ones. In contrast, ethnic minorities (Cambodian, Filipino, Vietnamese, and Mexican immigrants) saw noncognitive capacities—motivation, self-management, and social skills—as particularly important (Okagaki & Sternberg, 1993) As you can see, Sternberg's ideas are relevant to the controversy surrounding cultural bias in intelligence testing, which we will address shortly.

■ **GARDNER'S THEORY OF MULTIPLE INTELLIGENCES.** Howard Gardner's (1983, 1993, 1998b) **theory of multiple intelligences** provides yet another view of how information-processing skills underlie intelligent behavior. But unlike the componential approach, it does

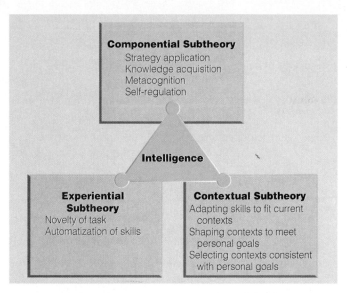

Componental Subtheory
Strategy application
Knowledge acquisition
Metacognition
Self-regulation

Intelligence

Experiential Subtheory
Novelty of task
Automatization of skills

Contextual Subtheory
Adapting skills to fit current contexts
Shaping contexts to meet personal goals
Selecting contexts consistent with personal goals

FIGURE 12.3

Sternberg's triarchic theory of intelligence.

triarchic theory of intelligence
Sternberg's theory, which states that information-processing skills, ability to learn efficiently in novel situations, and contextual (or cultural) factors interact to determine intelligent behavior.

theory of multiple intelligences
Gardner's theory, which proposes at least eight independent intelligences on the basis of distinct sets of processing operations that permit individuals to engage in a wide range of culturally valued activities.

TABLE 12.2

Gardner's Multiple Intelligences[a]

INTELLIGENCE	PROCESSING OPERATIONS	END-STATE PERFORMANCE POSSIBILITIES
Linguistic	Sensitivity to the sounds, rhythms, and meaning of words and the functions of language	Poet, journalist
Logico-mathematical	Sensitivity to, and capacity to detect, logical or numerical patterns; ability to handle long chains of logical reasoning	Mathematician
Musical	Ability to produce and appreciate pitch, rhythm (or melody), and aesthetic quality of the forms of musical expressiveness	Instrumentalist, composer
Spatial	Ability to perceive the visual-spatial world accurately, to perform transformations on those perceptions, and to re-create aspects of visual experience in the absence of relevant stimuli	Sculptor, navigator
Bodily-kinesthetic	Ability to use the body skillfully for expressive as well as goal-directed purposes; ability to handle objects skillfully	Dancer, athlete
Naturalist	Ability to recognize and classify all varieties of animals, minerals, and plants	Biologist
Interpersonal	Ability to detect and respond appropriately to the moods, temperaments, motivations, and intentions of others	Therapist, salesperson
Intrapersonal	Ability to discriminate complex inner feelings and to use them to guide one's own behavior; knowledge of one's own strengths, weaknesses, desires, and intelligences	Person with detailed, accurate self-knowledge

[a]Gardner (1998b) also has proposed a possible spiritual intelligence (gift for religion, mysticism, or the transcendent), existential intelligence (concern with "ultimate" issues, such as the significance of life and death), and moral intelligence (capacity to recognize and reason about moral issues). However, these potential intelligences are less well defined and more controversial than the eight intelligences listed above.
Sources: Gardner, 1983, 1993, 1998b.

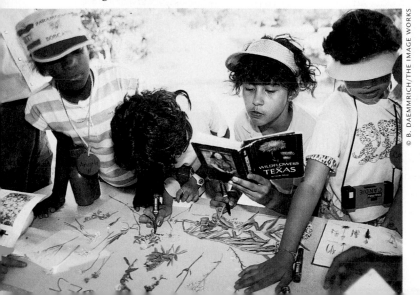

According to Gardner, children are capable of at least eight distinct intelligences. As these children classify wildflowers they collected during a walk through a forest and meadow, they enrich their naturalist intelligence.

not begin with existing mental tests and try to isolate the processing elements required to succeed on them. Instead, Gardner believes that intelligence should be defined in terms of distinct sets of processing operations that permit individuals to engage in a wide range of culturally valued activities. Therefore, Gardner dismisses the idea of general intelligence and proposes at least eight independent intelligences, which are described in Table 12.2.

Gardner argues that each intelligence has a unique biological basis, a distinct course of development, and different expert, or "end-state," performances. At the same time, he emphasizes that a lengthy process of education is required to transform any raw potential into a mature social role. This means that cultural values and learning opportunities have a great deal to do with the extent to which a child's intellectual strengths are realized and the ways in which they are expressed.

Gardner's theory has yet to be firmly grounded in research. For example, biological evidence for the independence of his abilities is weak. Similarly, some exceptionally gifted individuals have abilities that are broad rather than limited to a particular domain (Feldman, 1991). Finally, current mental tests do tap several of Gardner's intelligences (linguistic, logico-mathematical, and spatial), and evidence suggests that they have at least some common features.

Nevertheless, Gardner's theory highlights several intelligences not measured by IQ scores. For example, his interpersonal and intrapersonal intelligences include a set of capacities for understanding oneself and dealing with people that has become widely known as *emotional intelligence*. Emotional intelligence involves recognizing and regulating one's own emotions, detecting others' emotions, feeling empathy and sympathy, and working cooperatively with others. Recall from earlier chapters that these skills greatly enhance both cognitive and social competence. On the basis of that evidence, Daniel Goleman (1995, 1998) argues that valuing and cultivating emotional intelligence as much as we do IQ would make the world a far better place.

Finally Gardner's multiple intelligences have been helpful in efforts to understand and nurture children's special talents. We will take up this topic at the end of this chapter.

EXPLAINING INDIVIDUAL AND GROUP DIFFERENCES IN IQ

When we compare individuals in terms of academic achievement, years of education, and occupational status, it quickly becomes clear that certain sectors of the population are advantaged over others. In trying to explain these differences, researchers have examined the intelligence test performance of children varying in ethnicity and SES. Many studies show that American black children score, on average, 15 IQ points below American white children, although the difference has been shrinking (Hedges & Nowell, 1998; Loehlin, 2000). Hispanic children fall midway between black and white children (Ceci, Rosenblum, & Kumpf, 1998). SES differences in IQ also exist. In one large-scale study, low-SES children scored 9 points below children in the middle range of the SES distribution (Jensen & Figueroa, 1975).

These figures are, of course, averages. Considerable variation exists *within* each ethnic and SES group. Still, ethnic and SES differences in IQ are large enough and of serious enough consequence that they cannot be ignored.

In 1969, psychologist Arthur Jensen published a controversial article in the *Harvard Educational Review* entitled, "How Much Can We Boost IQ and Scholastic Achievement?" Jensen's answer to this question was "not much." He argued that heredity is largely responsible for individual, ethnic, and SES variations in intelligence, a position he continues to maintain (Jensen, 1985, 1998). Jensen's work received widespread public attention. It was followed by an outpouring of responses and research studies, leading to a heated nature–nurture debate on the origins of IQ. In the 1990s, the controversy was rekindled by Richard Herrnstein and Charles Murray's (1994) *The Bell Curve*. Like Jensen, these authors concluded that the contribution of heredity to individual and SES differences in IQ is substantial. And although they stated that the relative role of heredity and environment in the black–white IQ gap is unresolved, they implied a considerable role for heredity. Let's look closely at some important evidence.

■ **NATURE VERSUS NURTURE.** In Chapter 2 we introduced the *heritability estimate*. Recall that heritabilities are obtained from *kinship studies,* which compare family members. The most powerful evidence regarding heritability of IQ involves twin comparisons. Identical twins (who share all their genes) have more similar IQ scores than do fraternal twins (who are genetically no more alike than ordinary siblings). On the basis of this and other kinship evidence, current researchers estimate the heritability of IQ to be about .50 (Grigorenko, 2000). This means that about half the differences in IQ between children can be traced to their genetic makeup.

However, in Chapter 2 (pages 87–88) we noted that heritabilities risk overestimating genetic influences and underestimating environmental influences. Although research offers convincing evidence that genes contribute to IQ, disagreement persists over just how large the role of heredity really is (Sternberg & Grigorenko, 1997).

Furthermore, a widespread misconception exists that if a characteristic is heritable, then the environment can do little to affect it. A special type of kinship study, involving adopted children and their biological and adoptive relatives, shows that this assumption is incorrect. In one investigation of this kind, children of two extreme groups of biological mothers, those with IQs below 95 and those with IQs above 120, were chosen for special study. All the children were adopted at birth by parents who were well above average in income and education. During the school years, children of the low-IQ biological mothers scored above average in

LAWRENCE MIGDALE/STONE

IQ, indicating that test performance can be greatly improved by an advantaged home life. At the same time, they did not do as well as children of high-IQ biological mothers placed in similar adoptive families (Horn, 1983; Loehlin, Horn, & Willerman, 1997). Adoption research confirms the balanced position that both heredity and environment affect IQ scores.

Some intriguing adoption research also sheds light on the origins of the black–white IQ gap. African-American children placed in economically well-off white homes during the first year of life score high on intelligence tests. In two such studies, adopted black children attained mean IQs of 110 and 117 by middle childhood, well above average and 20 to 30 points higher than the typical scores of children growing up in low-income black communities (Moore, 1986; Scarr & Weinberg, 1983). However, a follow-up in one investigation revealed that adoptees' IQs declined in adolescence. Some researchers claim that adoptive rearing environments influence IQ only temporarily, in childhood. However, the IQ drop may have been due to use of different tests at the two ages and to the emotional challenge of establishing an ethnic identity that blends birth and rearing backgrounds (DeBerry, Scarr, & Weinberg, 1996; Waldman, Weinberg, & Scarr, 1994).

Adoption findings do not completely resolve questions about ethnic differences in IQ. Nevertheless, the IQ gains of black children "reared in the culture of the tests and schools" are consistent with a wealth of evidence indicating that poverty severely depresses the intelligence of large numbers of ethnic minority youngsters (Nisbett, 1998; Sternberg, 1996a). And in many other cases, unique cultural values and practices do not prepare these children for the kinds of tasks that are sampled by intelligence tests and valued in school.

■ **CULTURAL INFLUENCES.** Jermaine, a black child in Lizzie's third-grade class, participated actively in class discussion and wrote complex, imaginative stories. But he had not entered first grade feeling comfortable with classroom life. At the beginning, Jermaine responded, "I don't know," to the simplest of questions, including "What's your name?" Fortunately, Jermaine's teacher understood his uneasiness. Slowly and gently, she helped him build a bridge between the learning style fostered by his cultural background and the style necessary for academic success. A growing body of evidence reveals that IQ scores are affected by specific learning experiences, including exposure to certain language customs and knowledge.

Influenced by narrative practices in their homes, African-American children often tell topic-associating stories, which blend several similar experiences. This rich narrative style is at odds with the topic-focused formula valued in many classrooms. When teachers criticize African-American children's stories as "disorganized," they devalue the child's culture.

Language Customs. Ethnic minority subcultures often foster unique language skills that do not match the expectations of most classrooms and testing situations. Shirley Brice Heath (1982, 1989), an anthropologist who has spent many hours observing in low-income black homes in a southeastern American city, found that black adults asked children very different kinds of questions than are typical in white middle-SES families. From an early age, white parents ask knowledge-training questions, such as "What color is it?" and "What's this story about?" that resemble the questioning style of tests and classrooms. In contrast, the black parents asked only "real" questions—ones they themselves could not answer. Often these were analogy questions ("What's that like?") or story-starter questions ("Didja hear Miss Sally this morning?") that called for elaborate responses about personal experiences and no single right answer.

Heath and other researchers report that these experiences lead low-income black children to develop complex verbal skills at home, such as storytelling and exchanging quick-witted remarks. But their language differs from that of white middle-SES children in emphasizing emotional and social topics rather than facts about the world (Blake, 1994). Not surprisingly, black children may be confused by the "objective" questions they encounter in classrooms and withdraw into silence.

The impact of culture on language style is apparent in children's narratives. Most school-age children's narratives follow a *topic-focused formula;* they build to a high point, describe a critical event, and resolve it. African-American children, however, often tell *topic-associating stories,* which blend several similar experiences. One 9-year-old, for example, related having a tooth pulled, then described seeing her sister's tooth pulled, next told how she removed one

[handwritten note:] More openness to language in low-income black homes.

of her baby teeth, and concluded with her offer to take out her cousin's baby tooth: "So I told him, 'I'm a pullin' teeth expert . . . call me, and I'll be over'" (McCabe, 1997, p. 164). Yet many teachers criticize this approach as "disorganized'" (McCabe, 1998). And it is not assessed in verbal items on intelligence tests.

Other minority youngsters also develop distinct language customs. For example, children of Hispanic immigrants are taught to respect adult authority rather than express their own knowledge and opinions. Yet American teachers, who value self-assertive speaking, typically equate the silence of Hispanic children with having a negative attitude toward learning (Greenfield & Suzuki, 1998). As the child listens politely but does not answer out of deference to the adult, a culturally valued style of communicating quickly leads to unfair, negative evaluations in school and on mental tests.

Hispanic kids are taught to defer to their elders.

When faced with the strangeness of the testing situation, the minority child may look to the examiner for cues about how to respond. Some evidence suggests that African-American children—and perhaps other minority children as well—are more concerned with pleasing teachers than are white children (Ferguson, 1998). Yet on most intelligence tests, tasks can be presented in only one way, and those taking the test cannot get feedback. When an examiner refuses to reveal whether the child is on the right track, minority children may react with "disruptive apprehension"—giving any answer that comes to mind, rejecting the test situation as important to personal goals, and not revealing what they know.

Familiarity with Test Content. Many researchers argue that IQ scores are affected by specific information acquired as part of majority-culture upbringing. Unfortunately, attempts to change tests by eliminating fact-oriented verbal tasks and relying only on spatial reasoning and performance items (believed to be less culturally loaded) have not raised the scores of ethnic minority children very much (Reynolds & Kaiser, 1990).

Nevertheless, even these test items depend on learning opportunities. In one study, children's performance on a spatial reasoning task was related to the extent to which they had played a popular but expensive game that (like the test items) required them to arrange blocks to duplicate a design as quickly as possible (Dirks, 1982). Playing video games that require fast responding and mental rotation of visual images also fosters success on spatial test items (Subrahmanyam & Greenfield, 1996). Low-income minority children, who often grow up in more "people-oriented" than "object-oriented" homes, may lack opportunities to use games and objects that promote certain intellectual skills.

Furthermore, sheer amount of time a child spends in school is a strong predictor of IQ. When children of the same age who are in different grades are compared, those who have been in school longer score higher on intelligence tests. Similarly, dropping out of school leads to a decrease in IQ. The earlier young people leave school, the greater their loss of IQ points (Ceci 1991; Ceci & Williams, 1997). Although a more intelligent child may come to school with a greater ability to profit from instruction, increased exposure to the factual knowledge and ways of thinking valued in classrooms has a sizable impact on intelligence test performance.

REDUCING CULTURAL BIAS IN INTELLIGENCE TESTING

Although not all experts agree, many do acknowledge that IQ scores can underestimate the intelligence of culturally different children. A special concern exists about incorrectly labeling minority children as slow learners and assigning them to remedial classes, which are far less stimulating than regular school experiences. Because of this danger, test scores need to be combined with assessments of children's adaptive behavior—their ability to cope with the demands of their everyday environments. The child who does poorly on an IQ test yet plays a complex game on the playground, figures out how to rewire a broken TV, or cares for younger siblings responsibly is unlikely to be mentally deficient.

In addition, test designers are becoming more aware that minority children often are capable of the cognitive operations called for by test items. But because they are used to thinking in other ways in daily life, they may not access the required operation (Greenfield, 1997). **Dynamic testing,** an innovation consistent with Vygotsky's concept of the *zone of proximal*

dynamic testing
An approach to testing consistent with Vygotsky's concept of the zone of proximal development, in which individualized teaching is introduced into the testing situation to see what the child can attain with social support.

WILL HART/PHOTOEDIT

Dynamic testing introduces purposeful teaching into the situation to find out what the child can attain with social support. This teacher assists a second grader in writing the alphabet. Many ethnic minority children perform more competently after adult assistance. And the approach helps identify the teaching style to which the child is most responsive.

development (see Chapter 6, page 229), narrows this gap between actual and potential performance. Instead of emphasizing previously acquired knowledge, it introduces individualized teaching into the testing situation to see what the child can attain with social support (Grigorenko & Sternberg, 1998).

Several dynamic testing models exist, each of which uses a pretest–intervene–retest procedure with intelligence test items (Lidz, 1991, 1997). The best known is Reuben Feuerstein's (1979, 1980) *Learning Potential Assessment Device,* in which the adult tries to find the teaching style best suited to the child and communicates strategies that children can apply to new situations.

Evidence on the effectiveness of dynamic assessment reveals that the IQs of ethnic minority children underestimate their ability to perform intellectual tasks after adult assistance. Children's receptivity to teaching and their capacity to transfer what they have learned to novel problems add substantially to the prediction of future performance (Rand & Kaniel, 1987; Sternberg, 1999b; Tzuriel, 1989). As yet, dynamic assessment is not more effective in predicting academic achievement than are traditional tests. But better correspondence may emerge in classrooms where teaching interactions resemble the dynamic testing approach—namely, responsive assistance aimed at helping the child move beyond his or her current level of development.

Dynamic assessment is time consuming and requires extensive knowledge of minority children's cultural values and practices. Until we have the resources to implement these procedures broadly, should we suspend the use of intelligence testing in schools? Most experts regard this solution as unacceptable, since important educational decisions would be based only on subjective impressions—a policy that could increase discriminatory placement of minority children. Intelligence tests are useful as long as they are interpreted carefully by examiners who are sensitive to cultural influences on test performance. And despite their limitations, IQ scores continue to be valid measures of school learning potential for the majority of Western children.

Ask YOURSELF...

review   Using Sternberg's triarchic theory and Gardner's theory of multiple intelligences, explain the limitations of current mental tests in assessing the complexity of human intelligence.

apply   Desiree, an African-American child, was quiet and withdrawn while taking an intelligence test. Later she remarked to her mother, "I can't understand why that lady asked me all those questions, like what a ball and stove are for. She's a grownup. She must know what a ball and stove are for!" Using Sternberg's triarchic theory, explain Desiree's reaction to the testing situation. Why is Desiree's score likely to underestimate her intelligence?

connect   Referring to Chapter 2, pages 85–86, and evidence in this chapter, summarize the limitations of heritability estimates. Cite concepts discussed in Chapter 2 that support the position that heredity and environment cannot be divided into separate influences.

reflect   Do you think that intelligence tests are culturally biased? What evidence and observations influenced your conclusion?

Language Development

Vocabulary, grammar, and pragmatics continue to develop in middle childhood, although less obviously than at earlier ages. In addition, children's attitude toward language undergoes a fundamental shift. Whereas preschoolers view language largely as a means of communicating, school-age children treat it as an object of thought. They develop **metalinguistic awareness,** the ability to think about language as a system.

Besides promoting cognitive development, schooling contributes greatly to metalinguistic awareness. Talk about language is extremely common during literacy instruction but rare outside of classrooms (Gombert, 1992). In the following sections, we will see how an improved capacity to reflect on language supports a wide range of complex language skills.

VOCABULARY

Because the average 6-year-old's vocabulary is already quite large (about 10,000 words), parents and teachers usually do not notice rapid gains during the school years. Between the start of elementary school and its completion, vocabulary increases fourfold, eventually reaching about 40,000 words. On average, about 20 new words are learned each day—a rate of growth that exceeds that of early childhood. In addition to fast-mapping (discussed in Chapter 9), school-age children enlarge their vocabularies through analyzing the structure of complex words. From "happy," "wise," and "decide," they quickly derive the meanings of "happiness," "wisdom," and "decision" (Anglin, 1993). They also figure out many more word meanings from context, especially while reading (Nagy & Scott, 2000). Because written language contains a richer vocabulary than spoken language, reading contributes greatly to vocabulary growth in middle childhood.

As their knowledge base becomes better organized, school-age children think about and use words more precisely. Word definitions offer examples of this change. Five- and 6-year-olds give very concrete descriptions that refer to functions or appearance—for example, knife: "when you're cutting carrots"; bicycle: "it's got wheels, a chain, and handlebars." By the end of elementary school, synonyms and explanations of categorical relationships appear— for example, knife: "something you could cut with. A saw is like a knife. It could also be a weapon" (Wehren, DeLisi, & Arnold, 1981). This advance reflects the ability to deal with word meanings on an entirely verbal plane. Older children can add new words to their vocabulary simply by being given a definition, although examples of how to use the word in spoken or written communication enhance their understanding (Stahl, 1989).

School-age children's more reflective and analytical approach to language permits them to appreciate the multiple meanings of words. For example, they recognize that many words, such as "cool" or "neat," have psychological as well as physical meanings: "What a cool shirt!" or "That movie was really neat!" This grasp of double meanings permits 8- to 10-year-olds to comprehend subtle, mental metaphors, such as "sharp as a tack," "spilling the beans," and "left high and dry" (Nippold, Taylor, & Baker, 1996; Wellman & Hickling, 1994). It also leads to a change in children's humor. By the mid-elementary school years, riddles and puns are common:

"Hey, did you take a bath?" "No! Why, is one missing?"

"Why did the old man tiptoe past the medicine cabinet?" "Because he didn't want to wake up the sleeping pills."

Six-year-olds may laugh at these statements because they are nonsensical. But most cannot tell a good riddle or pun, nor do they understand why these jokes are funny (Ely & McCabe, 1994).

GRAMMAR

Although children have mastered most of the grammar of their language by the time they enter school, use of complex grammatical constructions improves. For example, children use the passive voice more frequently, and it expands from an abbreviated structure

metalinguistic awareness
The ability to think about language as a system.

("It got broken") into full statements ("The glass was broken by Mary") (Horgan, 1978). Older children also apply their grasp of the passive voice to a wider range of nouns and verbs. Preschoolers comprehend the passive best when the subject of the sentence is an animate being and the verb is an action word ("The boy is *kissed* by the girl"). During the school years, inanimate subjects, such as "drum" or "hat," and experiential verbs, such as "like" or "know," are included in passive constructions (Lempert, 1989; Pinker, Lebeaux, & Frost, 1987).

Another grammatical achievement of middle childhood is advanced understanding of infinitive phrases, such as the difference between "John is eager to please" and "John is easy to please" (Chomsky, 1969). Like gains in vocabulary, appreciation of these subtle grammatical distinctions is supported by metalinguistic awareness. During middle childhood, children can judge the grammatical correctness of a sentence even if its meaning is false or senseless, whereas preschoolers cannot (Bialystok, 1986).

PRAGMATICS

Improvements in *pragmatics,* the communicative side of language, take place in middle childhood. School-age children better adapt to the needs of listeners in challenging communicative situations, such as describing one object among a group of very similar objects. Whereas preschoolers tend to give ambiguous descriptions, such as "the red one," school-age children are much more precise. They might say, "the round red one with stripes on it" (Deutsch & Pechmann, 1982).

Gains in the ability to evaluate the clarity of others' messages occur as well. At first children realize when statements poorly describe objects. Later, they can tell when a message is inconsistent with something said earlier. To do so, children must recall a previous conversation and match it against currently spoken information—a capacity that improves gradually during middle childhood and adolescence (Sonnenschein, 1986).

School-age children's narratives about the past become longer and more complex, and they also refine their conversational strategies. For example, older children skillfully phrase things to get their way. When faced with an adult who refuses to hand over a desired object, 9-year-olds, but not 5-year-olds, state their second requests more politely (Axia & Baroni, 1985). School-age children are also more sensitive than preschoolers to distinctions between what people say and what they really mean. Lizzie, for example, knew that when her mother said, "The garbage is beginning to smell," she really meant, "Take that garbage out!" (Ackerman, 1978).

Opportunities to communicate for diverse purposes, in different situations, and with a variety of people help children refine their pragmatic skills (Ely, 2000). Because peers challenge unclear messages that adults may accept, peer interaction may contribute greatly to school-age children's conversational competence.

LEARNING TWO LANGUAGES AT A TIME

Like most American children, Joey and Lizzie speak only one language, their native tongue of English. Yet throughout the United States and the world, many children grow up *bilingual.* They learn two languages, and sometimes more than two, during childhood. An estimated 6 million American school-age children speak a language other than English at home, a figure expected to increase (U.S. Bureau of the Census, 2000).

■ **BILINGUAL DEVELOPMENT.** Children can become bilingual in two ways: (1) by acquiring both languages at the same time in early childhood, or (2) by learning a second language after mastering the first. Children of bilingual parents who learn both languages in early childhood show no special problems with language development. For a time, they mix the two languages. But this is not a sign of confusion, since bilingual parents do not maintain strict language separation either (Bhatia & Ritchie, 1999). Preschoolers acquire normal native ability in the language of their surrounding community and good-to-native ability in the second language, depending on their exposure to it. When school-age children acquire a second language after they already speak a first one, it generally takes them 3 to 5 years to become as competent in the second language as native-speaking agemates (Hakuta, 1999).

Recall from Chapter 6 that, as with first-language development, a sensitive period for second-language development exists. Mastery must begin sometime in childhood for full development to occur. Children who are fluent in two languages are advanced in cognitive development. They do better than others on tests of selective attention, analytical reasoning, concept formation, and cognitive flexibility (Bialystok, 1999; Hakuta, Ferdman, & Diaz, 1987). Also, their metalinguistic skills are particularly well developed. They are more aware that words are arbitrary symbols, more conscious of some aspects of language sounds, and better at noticing errors of grammar and meaning—capacities that enhance reading achievement (Bialystok, 1997; Bialystok & Herman, 1999; Campbell & Sais, 1995). *Bilingualism enhances Cognitive development*

ROBERT E. DAEMMRICH/STONE

These Pueblo children attend a bilingual education program in which they receive instruction in their native language and in English. In classrooms where both the first and second language are integrated into the curriculum, ethnic minority children are more involved in learning, participate more actively in class discussions, and acquire the second language more easily.

■ **BILINGUAL EDUCATION.** The advantages of bilingualism provide strong justification for bilingual education programs in schools. In Canada, where both English and French are official languages, *language immersion programs*—in which English-speaking children are taught entirely in French in kindergarten and first grade and English is introduced in second grade—succeed in developing fully bilingual children (Cummins, 1999).

Yet the question of how American ethnic minority children with limited English proficiency should be educated is hotly debated. On one side of the controversy are those who believe that time spent communicating in the child's native tongue detracts from English language achievement, which is crucial for success in the worlds of school and work. On the other side are educators committed to truly *bilingual* education—developing minority children's native language while fostering mastery of English. Providing instruction in the native tongue lets minority children know that their heritage is respected. In addition, it prevents *semilingualism,* or inadequate proficiency in both languages. When minority children gradually lose the first language as a result of being taught the second, they end up limited in both languages for a time, a circumstance that leads to serious academic difficulties (August & Garcia, 1988; Ovando & Collier, 1998). Semilingualism is one factor believed to contribute to the high rates of school failure and dropout among low-SES Hispanic youngsters, who make up nearly 50 percent of the American language-minority population.

loss of one language causes a loss (slightly) in both languages + thus academic difficulties

At present, public opinion sides with the first of these two viewpoints. Many states have passed laws declaring English to be their official language, creating conditions in which schools have no obligation to teach minority students in languages other than English. Yet in classrooms where both languages are integrated into the curriculum, minority children are more involved in learning, participate more actively in class discussions, and acquire the second language more easily. In contrast, when teachers speak only a language children can barely understand, minority children display frustration, boredom, withdrawal, and academic failure (Crawford, 1995, 1997).

American English-only supporters often point to the success of language immersion programs in Canada. Yet different educational strategies seem necessary for low-SES, minority children whose native language is not valued by the larger society (Mohanty & Perregaux, 1997). Bilingualism offers one of the best examples of how language, once learned, becomes an important tool of the mind and fosters cognitive development. From this perspective, the goals of schooling could reasonably be broadened to include helping all children become bilingual, thereby fostering the cognitive, linguistic, and cultural enrichment of the entire nation.

review Cite examples of language progress that benefit from school-age children's metalinguistic awareness.

apply Ten-year-old Shana arrived home from school after a long day, sank into the living room sofa, and commented, "I'm totally wiped out!" Megan, her 5-year-old sister, looked puzzled and asked, "What didya wipe out, Shana?" Explain Shana and Megan's different understanding of the meaning of this expression.

reflect Did you acquire a second language at home or study one in school? If so, when did you begin? Considering what you now know about bilingual development and education, what changes would you make in your second-language learning, and why?

Children's Learning in School

Throughout this chapter, we have touched on evidence indicating that schools are vital forces in children's cognitive development, affecting their modes of remembering, reasoning, problem solving, and acquiring language skills. How do schools exert such a powerful impact? Research looking at schools as complex social systems—their class size, educational philosophies, teacher–student interaction patterns, and larger cultural context in which they are embedded—provides important insights into this question. As you read about these topics, refer to the Educational Concerns table on the following page, which summarizes characteristics of high-quality education in elementary school.

CLASS SIZE

As each school year began, Rena telephoned the principal's office and asked, "How large will Joey and Lizzie's classes be?" Her concern is well founded. A large-scale field experiment revealed that class size influences children's learning.

More than 6,000 kindergartners in 76 Tennessee elementary schools were randomly assigned to three class types: small (13 to 17 students), regular (22 to 25 students), and regular with a full-time teacher's aide. These arrangements continued into third grade. Small-class students scored higher in reading and math achievement each year, an effect that was particularly strong for minority students. Placing teacher's aides in regular-size classes had no consistent impact. Finally, even after all students returned to regular-size classes in fourth and fifth grades, children who had experienced the small classes remained ahead in achievement (Mosteller, 1995).

Why is small class size beneficial? Teachers of fewer children spend less time disciplining and more time giving individual attention, and children's interactions with one another are more positive and cooperative. Also, when class size is small, teachers and students are more satisfied with school experiences. The achievement benefits of small classes are greatest in the early years of schooling, when children require more adult assistance (Blatchford & Mortimore, 1994). They might be even stronger if reductions in class size were accompanied by other changes, such as small-group and individualized teaching strategies.

EDUCATIONAL PHILOSOPHIES

Each teacher brings to the classroom an educational philosophy that plays a major role in children's learning experiences. Two philosophical approaches—traditional and open classrooms—have received the most research attention. They differ in what children are taught, the way they are believed to learn, and how their progress is evaluated.

*E*ducational Concerns

Signs of High-Quality Education in Elementary School

CLASSROOM CHARACTERISTICS	SIGNS OF QUALITY
Class Size	Optimum class size is no larger than 18 children.
Physical Setting	Space is divided into richly equipped activity centers—for reading, writing, playing math or language games, exploring science, working on construction projects, using computers, and engaging in other academic pursuits. Spaces are used flexibly for individual and small-group activities and whole-class gatherings.
Curriculum	The curriculum helps children both achieve academic standards and make sense of their learning in all subjects, including literacy, mathematics, social studies, art, music, health, and physical education. Subjects are integrated so children apply knowledge in one area to others. The curriculum is implemented through activities responsive to children's interests, ideas, and everyday lives, including their cultural backgrounds.
Daily Activities	Teachers provide challenging activities that include opportunities for small-group and independent work. Groupings vary in size and makeup of children, depending on the activity and children's learning needs. Teachers encourage cooperative learning and guide children in attaining it.
Interactions Between Teachers and Children	Teachers foster each child's progress, including children with academic difficulties and children capable of advanced performance. Teachers use intellectually engaging strategies, including posing problems, asking thought-provoking questions, discussing ideas, and adding complexity to tasks. They also demonstrate, explain, coach, and assist in other ways, depending on each child's learning needs.
Evaluations of Progress	Teachers regularly evaluate children's progress through written observations and work samples, which they use to enhance and individualize teaching. They help children reflect on their work and decide how to improve it. They also seek information and perspectives from parents on how well children are learning and include parents' views in evaluations.
Relationship with Parents	Teachers forge partnerships with parents. They hold periodic conferences and encourage parents to visit the classroom anytime, to observe and volunteer.

Source: Bredekamp & Copple, 1997.

■ **TRADITIONAL VERSUS OPEN CLASSROOMS.** In a **traditional classroom,** the teacher is the sole authority for knowledge, rules, and decision making and does most of the talking. Children are relatively passive, listening, responding when called on, and completing teacher-assigned tasks. Their progress is evaluated by how well they keep pace with a uniform set of standards for all students in their grade.

In contrast, in an **open classroom,** children are viewed as active agents in their own development. The teacher assumes a flexible authority role, sharing decision making with students, who learn at their own pace. Students are evaluated by considering their progress in relation to their own prior development. How well they compare to other same-age students is of lesser importance. A glance inside the door of an open classroom reveals richly equipped learning centers, small groups of students working on tasks they choose themselves, and a teacher who moves from one area to another, guiding and supporting in response to children's individual needs.

Over the past few decades, the pendulum in American education has swung back and forth between these two views. In the 1960s and early 1970s, open education gained in popularity, inspired by Piaget's vision of the child as an active, motivated learner. Then, as concern over the academic progress of American children and youths became widespread, a "back to basics" movement arose. Classrooms returned to traditional, teacher-directed instruction, a style still prevalent today.

traditional classroom
An elementary school classroom based on the educational philosophy that children are passive learners who acquire information presented by teachers. Children's progress is evaluated on the basis of how well they keep up with a uniform set of standards for all students in their grade.

open classroom
An elementary school classroom based on the educational philosophy that children are active agents in their own development and learn at different rates. Teachers share decision making with pupils. Children's progress is evaluated in relation to their own prior development.

Benefits of both kinds
of classrooms.

The combined results of many studies reveal that older school-age children in traditional classrooms have a slight edge in academic achievement. But open settings are associated with other benefits. Open-classroom students have more advanced critical thinking skills, and they value and respect individual differences in their classmates more. Students in open environments also like school better than those in traditional classrooms, and their attitude toward school becomes increasingly positive as they spend more time there (Walberg, 1986).

Recall from Chapter 9 that whole-class, teacher-directed instruction has filtered down to the preschools and kindergartens, and it is also common in the early school grades (see page 354). When kindergartners spend much time passively sitting and doing worksheets as opposed to being actively engaged in learning centers, they display more stress behaviors, such as wiggling and rocking, withdrawal, and talking out. Follow-ups reveal that traditional-classroom kindergartners show poorer study habits and achieve less well in grade school (Burts et al., 1992; Hart et al., 1998). These outcomes are strongest for low-SES children. Yet teachers tend to prefer a traditional approach for economically disadvantaged students—a disturbing trend in view of its negative impact on motivation and learning (Eccles et al., 1993b; Stipek & Byler, 1997).

The heavy emphasis in traditional kindergarten and primary classrooms on knowledge absorption and worksheet tasks has contributed to a growing trend among parents to delay their child's kindergarten entry for a year. Traditional teaching practices may also increase the incidence of grade retention. See the Social Issues: Education box on the following page for research on the consequences of "redshirting" and early retention.

■ **NEW VYGOTSKY-INSPIRED DIRECTIONS.** The philosophies of some teachers fall somewhere in between traditional and open. They want to foster high achievement as well as critical thinking, positive social relationships, and excitement about learning. New approaches to elementary education, grounded in Vygotsky's sociocultural theory, represent this point of view. Vygotsky's emphasis on the social origins of complex mental activities has inspired the following educational themes:

■ *Teachers and children as partners in learning.* A classroom rich in both teacher–child and child–child collaboration transfers culturally valued ways of thinking to children.

■ *Experience with many types of symbolic communication in meaningful activities.* As children master reading, writing, and quantitative reasoning, they become aware of their culture's communication systems, reflect on their own thinking, and bring it under voluntary control. (Can you identify research presented earlier in this chapter that supports this theme?)

■ *Teaching adapted to each child's zone of proximal development.* Assistance that responds to current understandings but that encourages children to take the next step forward helps ensure that each child will make the best progress possible.

Reciprocal teaching is a Vygotsky-inspired educational innovation in which a teacher and two to four pupils form a cooperative learning group and engage in dialogue about a text passage. Elementary and junior high school pupils who participate in reciprocal teaching show impressive gains in reading comprehension.

Let's look at two examples of a growing number of programs that have translated these ideas into action.

Reciprocal Teaching. Originally designed to improve reading comprehension in students achieving poorly, **reciprocal teaching** has been adapted to other subjects and is a useful model for all school-age children (Palincsar & Herrenkohl, 1999). A teacher and two to four students form a cooperative group and take turns leading dialogues on the content of a text passage. Within the dialogues, group members apply four cognitive strategies: questioning, summarizing, clarifying, and predicting.

The dialogue leader (at first a teacher, later a student) begins by *asking questions* about the content of the text passage. Students offer answers, raise additional questions, and, in case of disagreement, reread the original text. Next, the leader *summarizes* the passage, and

MARK POKEMPNER/IMPACT VISUALS

Social ISSUES: EDUCATION

WHEN ARE CHILDREN READY FOR SCHOOL? ACADEMIC REDSHIRTING AND EARLY RETENTION

While waiting to pick up their sons from preschool, Susan and Vicky struck up a conversation about kindergarten enrollment. "Freddy will be 5 in August," Susan announced. "He's a month older than the cutoff date."

"But he'll be one of the youngest in the class," Vicky countered. "Better check into what kids have to do in kindergarten these days. It's not just play, snack, and rest! Have you asked his teacher what she thinks?"

"Well," Susan admitted, "she did say Freddy was a bit young."

Although growing numbers of children are enrolling in preschool and child care, since the 1980s more parents have been delaying their child's kindergarten entry. On average, about 9 percent of American 5-year-olds are affected (Zill, West, & Lomax, 1997). Aware that boys lag behind girls in development, parents most often hold out sons whose birthdates are close to the kindergarten-entrance cutoff date. This trend has become common enough to acquire its own label—*academic redshirting*, adapted from the term used to refer to delaying a college student's participation in athletics for a year to make that student more competitive through additional growth and practice.

Is academic redshirting beneficial? Although teachers and principals often think so and recommend it, research has not revealed any advantages. Many studies indicate that younger children make just as much academic progress as do older children in the same grade (Cameron & Wilson, 1990; Graue & DiPerna, 2000; Jones & Mandeville, 1990). And younger first graders reap academic gains from on-time enrollment; they outperform same-age children a year behind them in school (Morrison, Griffith, & Alberts, 1997). Furthermore, redshirted children show no advantage in self-esteem, peer acceptance, or teacher ratings of behavior (Spitzer, Cupp, & Parke, 1995). Delaying kindergarten entry does not seem to prevent or solve emotional and social problems. To the contrary, children usually are aware that their school entry has been delayed, and some worry that they have failed (Graue, 1993).

A related dilemma concerns whether to retain a kindergartner not progressing well for a second kindergarten year. A wealth of research reveals no learning benefits and suggests negative consequences for motivation, self-esteem, and attitudes toward school as early as kindergarten (Carlton & Winsler, 1999). In one study, retained kindergartners scored lower than their classmates in academic achievement after entering the primary grades. In contrast, children recommended for retention but who nevertheless moved on to first grade did just as well as their normally promoted classmates (Dennebaum & Kulberg, 1994).

As an alternative to kindergarten retention, some school districts place poorly performing kindergarten children in a "transition" class—a waystation between kindergarten and first grade. Transition classes, however, are a form of homogeneous grouping. As with other "low-ability" groups, teachers may have lower expectations and teach transition children in a less stimulating fashion than they do other children (Dornbusch, Glasgow, & Lin, 1996).

Each of the options just considered is based on the view that readiness for school largely results from biological maturation. An alternative perspective, based on Vygotsky's sociocultural theory, is that children acquire the knowledge, skills, and attitudes for school success through the assistance of parents and teachers. The National Association for the Education of Young Children recommends that every child of legal age start kindergarten and be granted the classroom experiences summarized in the Educational Concerns table on page 465. Research shows that school readiness is not something to wait for; it can be cultivated.

---

children discuss the summary and *clarify* ideas that are unfamiliar to any group members. Finally the leader encourages students to *predict* upcoming content based on clues in the passage (Palincsar & Klenk, 1992).

Elementary and junior high school students exposed to reciprocal teaching show impressive gains in reading comprehension compared to controls taught in other ways (King & Johnson, 1999; Lederer, 2000; Rosenshine & Meister, 1994). Notice how reciprocal teaching creates a zone of proximal development in which children gradually assume more responsibility for comprehending complex text passages. Also, by collaborating with others, children forge group norms for good thinking and acquire skills vital for learning and success in everyday life.

reciprocal teaching
A method of teaching based on Vygotsky's theory in which a teacher and two to four pupils form a cooperative learning group. Dialogues occur that create a zone of proximal development in which reading comprehension improves.

The Kamehameha Elementary Education Program. The most well-known and extensive educational reform effort based on Vygotsky's theory is the **Kamehameha Elementary Education Program (KEEP).** To foster development, KEEP instruction is organized around activity settings specially designed to enhance teacher–child and child–child interaction. In each setting, small groups of students work on a project that ensures that their learning will be active and directed toward a meaningful goal. For example, they might read a story and discuss its meaning or draw a map of the playground to promote an understanding of geography.

All children enter a leading activity setting, called "Center One," at least once each morning for scaffolding of challenging literacy skills. Teachers carefully select text content to relate to children's experiences and engage them in discussion of what they have read, questioning, responding to, and building on children's ideas. The precise organization of each KEEP classroom is adjusted to fit the unique learning styles of its students, creating culturally responsive environments (Au, 1997; Tharp, 1993, 1994).

Thousands of low-SES minority children have attended KEEP classrooms in Hawaii, on a Navajo reservation in Arizona, and in Los Angeles. So far, research suggests that the approach is highly effective. In KEEP schools, minority students performed at their expected grade level in reading achievement, much better than children of the same background enrolled in traditional schools. Furthermore, KEEP students more often participated actively in class discussion, used elaborate language structures, and supported one another's learning than did non-KEEP controls (Tharp & Gallimore, 1988). As the KEEP model becomes more widely applied, perhaps it will be successful with all types of children because of its comprehensive goals and effort to meet the learning needs of a wide range of students.

TEACHER–STUDENT INTERACTION

Teachers vary in the way they interact with children—differences that affect academic achievement. Whereas Lizzie's teacher emphasized factual knowledge, Joey's teacher encouraged children to grapple with ideas and apply their knowledge to new situations. He asked, "Why is the main character in this story a hero?" and "Now that you are good at division, how many teams should we have at recess? How many children on each team?"

A disappointing finding is that American teachers emphasize rote, repetitive drill more than higher-level thinking, such as analyzing, synthesizing, and applying ideas and concepts (Campbell, Hombo, & Mazzeo, 2000). In a study of fifth-grade social studies and math lessons, students were far more attentive when teachers encouraged high-level thinking (Stodolsky, 1988). And in a longitudinal investigation of more than 5,000 seventh graders, those attending schools with a more stimulating and demanding academic climate showed better attendance and larger gains in math achievement during the following 2 years (Phillips, 1997).

Of course, teachers do not interact in the same way with all children. Some get more attention and praise than others. Well-behaved, high-achieving students typically experience positive interactions with teachers. In contrast, teachers may actively dislike children who achieve poorly and are also disruptive. These unruly students are often criticized and are rarely called on to contribute to class discussion. When they seek special help or permission, their requests are usually denied (Good & Brophy, 1994).

Unfortunately, once teachers' attitudes toward students are established, they are in danger of becoming more extreme than is warranted by children's behavior. A special concern is that an **educational self-fulfilling prophecy** can be set in motion: Children may adopt teachers' positive or negative views and start to live up to them. This effect is particularly strong when teachers emphasize competition and make public comparisons between children (Weinstein et al., 1987).

Teacher expectations have a greater impact on low achievers than high achievers (Madom, Jussim, & Eccles, 1997). High-achieving students have less room to improve when teachers think well of them, and they can fall back on their long history of success experiences when a teacher is critical. Low-achieving students' sensitivity to self-fulfilling prophecies can be

Kamehameha Elementary Education Program (KEEP)
The most well-known and extensive educational reform effort based on Vygotsky's theory. Instruction is organized around activity settings, designed to enhance teacher–child and child–child interaction and to be culturally responsive.

educational self-fulfilling prophecy
The idea that children may adopt teachers' positive or negative attitudes toward them and start to live up to these views.

beneficial when teachers believe in them. But unfortunately, biased teacher judgments are usually slanted in a negative direction, resulting in more unfavorable classroom experiences and achievement than would otherwise occur.

GROUPING PRACTICES

Children can be grouped for instruction in many ways. Often students are assigned to *homogenous groups,* or classes in which children of similar achievement levels are taught together. Ability groups can be a potent source of self-fulfilling prophecies, especially under conditions of grouping within the same class (Smith et al., 1998). Group labels quickly result in stereotyping. As a result, low-group students get more drill on basic facts and skills, less discussion, a slower learning pace, and less time on academic work. Gradually, such children show a drop in self-esteem and are viewed by themselves and others as "not smart." Not surprisingly, ability grouping widens the performance gap between high and low achievers and promotes segregated peer interaction (Dornbusch, Glasgow, & Lin, 1996; Fuligni, Eccles, & Barber, 1995).

Yet another approach to grouping has been to increase the *heterogeneity* of students. In *multigrade classrooms,* students of different grades are placed in the same classroom. When academic achievement differs between the multigrade and single-grade classrooms, it favors the multigrade arrangement. Self-esteem and attitudes toward school are also more positive, perhaps because multigrade classrooms often decrease competition and increase harmony (Lloyd, 1999). The opportunity that mixed-age grouping affords for peer tutoring may also contribute to its favorable outcomes. When older or more expert students teach younger or less expert students, both tutors and tutees benefit in achievement and self-esteem (Renninger, 1998).

Yet multigrade classrooms may not work well if principals create them for convenience (for example, to deal with uneven enrollments) rather than for philosophical reasons (Burns & Mason, 1998). Under these circumstances, they tend to place higher-ability and more independent pupils in the multigrade settings, producing an alternative form of homogeneous grouping!)

Furthermore, small, heterogeneous groups of students working together often yield poorer-quality interaction (less accurate explanations and answers) than do homogeneous groups of above-average students (Webb, Nemer, & Chizhik, 1998). For collaboration between heterogeneous peers to succeed, children need extensive training and guidance in **cooperative learning**—resolving differences of opinion, sharing responsibility, considering one another's ideas, and working toward common goals. When teachers explain, model, and have children role-play how to work together effectively, cooperative learning of heterogeneous peers promotes achievement across a wide range of school subjects (Gillies & Ashman, 1996, 1998).

COMPUTERS IN CLASSROOMS

Besides teachers and peers, another interactive aid to learning can be found in schools. In Joey and Lizzie's classrooms, several computers sat on desks in quiet corners. Virtually all American public schools have integrated computers into their instructional programs, and 95 percent can access the Internet (U.S. Bureau of the Census, 2000). These trends also are apparent in other industrialized nations.

Children prefer to use computers socially. Small groups often gather around the machine, and children more often collaborate when working with the computer than with other activities (Svensson, 2000). The common belief that computers channel children into solitary pursuits is unfounded. Research reveals that computers can have rich educational benefits.

■ **ADVANTAGES OF COMPUTERS.** Computers in classrooms are used in a variety of ways. In *computer-assisted instruction,* specially designed educational software permits children to practice basic skills and, in some instances, solve problems and acquire new knowledge. When

---

Handwritten margin notes:

Group labels can result in stereotypes.

yet ÷ of groups into high + low achievers weakens the self-esteem of low-achieving students.

grouping students from different grades increases the camraderie among students.

heterogenous grouping is more beneficial.

computers, counterintuitively, promote some form of social interaction among children.

cooperative learning
Collaboration on a task by a small group of students who resolve differences of opinion, share responsibility, consider one another's ideas, and work toward common goals.

Schools must take special steps to ensure that girls have generous access to computers. When classrooms emphasize cooperative learning and software is designed with the interests of girls in mind, they become enthusiastic users.

children use basic-skills programs regularly for several months, they gain in reading and math achievement. Benefits are greatest for younger students and those with learning difficulties (Fletcher-Flinn & Gravatt, 1995). However, too much emphasis on drill activities can undermine children's willingness to learn through active experimentation (Clements, Nastasi, & Swaminathan, 1993).

As soon as children begin to read and write, they can use the computer for *word processing*. It permits them to write freely and experiment with letters and words without having to struggle with handwriting at the same time. In addition, children can plan and revise the text's meaning and style as well as check their spelling. As a result, they worry less about making mistakes, and their written products tend to be longer and of higher quality (Clements, 1995). However, computers by themselves do not help children master the mechanics of writing (such as spelling and grammar). So it is best to use computers to build on and enhance, not replace, other classroom writing experiences.

Programming offers children the highest degree of control over the computer, since they must tell it what to do. Specially designed computer languages are available to introduce children to programming skills. As long as teachers encourage and support children's efforts, computer programming leads to improvements in concept formation, problem solving, and creativity (Clements, 1995; Clements & Nastasi, 1992). Also, since children must detect errors in their programs to get them to work, programming helps them reflect on their thought processes, leading to gains in metacognition and self-regulation (Clements, 1990).

Finally, widespread access to the Internet has permitted teachers to design e-mail and website-based learning activities, enabling children to access information and interact with people around the world (Windschitl, 1998). In one activity, groups of six to nine classrooms, from several countries, formed "learning circles." Each class planned a project and consulted with members of its circle to complete it. E-mail messages revealed a broadened understanding of other people and places (Reis, 1992). For example, students in Persian Gulf nations wrote candidly about their fears as one circle discussed world security and peace.

■ **CONCERNS ABOUT COMPUTERS.** Although computers provide children with many learning advantages, they also raise concerns. By the end of elementary school, boys spend much more time with computers than do girls, both in and out of school—a difference that may contribute to advantages for boys in problem solving and spatial abilities. Much software is unappealing to girls because it emphasizes themes of war, violence, and male-dominated sports (Collis et al., 1996; Griffiths, 1997). Yet girls' tendency to retreat from computers can be overcome. When teachers present computers in the context of cooperative rather than competitive learning activities and software is designed with the interests of girls in mind, they become enthusiastic users (Hawkins & Sheingold, 1986).

Video games account for most out-of-school, recreational computer use, especially by boys. Many parents are concerned that their children will become overly involved as well as more aggressive because of these fast-paced amusements with highly violent content. About 5 percent become "passionate," or excessive, players. Violent video games do seem to promote aggressive behavior, and they are full of ethnic and gender stereotypes (Dill & Dill, 1998; Griffiths, 1999; Phillips et al., 1995).

TEACHING CHILDREN WITH SPECIAL NEEDS

So far, we have seen that effective teachers flexibly adjust their teaching strategies to accommodate students with a wide range of abilities and characteristics. But such adjustments are increasingly difficult at the very low and high ends of the ability distribution. How do schools serve children with special learning needs?

■ **CHILDREN WITH LEARNING DIFFICULTIES.** The U.S. Individuals with Disabilities Education Act mandates that schools place children who require special supports for learning in the "least restrictive" environments that meet their educational needs. The law led to a rapid increase in **mainstreaming,** or placement of students with learning difficulties in regular classrooms for part of the school day, a practice designed to better prepare them for participation in society. Largely due to parental pressures, in some schools mainstreaming has been extended to **full inclusion**—placement in regular classrooms full time.

Some mainstreamed pupils are *mildly mentally retarded*—children whose IQs fall between 55 and 70 and who also show problems in adaptive behavior, or skills of everyday living (American Psychiatric Association, 1994). But the largest number have **learning disabilities.** Learning disabled students, who constitute 5 to 10 percent of school-age children, obtain average or above-average IQ scores but have great difficulty with one or more aspects of learning, usually reading. As a result, their achievement is considerably behind what would be expected on the basis of their IQ. Their problems cannot be traced to any obvious physical or emotional difficulty or to environmental disadvantage. Instead, faulty brain functioning is believed to be responsible. Some disorders run in families, suggesting a genetic influence (Ingalls & Goldstein, 1999). In many instances, however, the cause is unknown.

WILL HART

faulty brain functioning
heredity play role in
learning disabilities.

The pupil on the left, who has a learning disability, has been fully included in a regular classroom. Because his teacher encourages peer acceptance, individualizes instruction, minimizes comparisons with classmates, and promotes cooperative learning, this boy looks forward to school and is doing well.

social problems are
experienced by kids w/
learning disabilities.

■ **HOW EFFECTIVE ARE MAINSTREAMING AND FULL INCLUSION?** Does placement of students with disabilities in regular classes accomplish its two goals—providing more appropriate academic experiences and integrated participation in classroom life? At present, research findings are not positive on either of these points.

Although some mainstreamed and fully included students benefit academically, many do not. Achievement gains depend on both the severity of the disability and the support services available in the regular classroom (Klingner et al., 1998; Waldron & McLeskey, 1998). Furthermore, children with disabilities often are rejected by regular-classroom peers. Students who are mentally retarded are overwhelmed by the social skills of their classmates; they cannot interact adeptly in a conversation or game. And the processing deficits of some learning-disabled students lead to problems in social awareness and responsiveness (Greenham, 1999; Gresham & MacMillan, 1997).

Does this mean that special-needs children cannot be served in regular classrooms? This extreme conclusion is not warranted. Often these children do best when they receive instruction in a *resource room* for part of the day and in the regular classroom for the remainder—an arrangement the majority of school-age children with learning disabilities say they prefer (Vaughn & Klingner, 1998). In the resource room, a special education teacher works with students on an individual and small-group basis. Then, depending on their abilities, children are mainstreamed for varying subjects and amounts of time. This flexible approach makes it more likely that the unique academic needs of each child will be served (Hocutt, 1996).

Once children enter the regular classroom, special steps must be taken to promote peer acceptance. Cooperative learning and peer-tutoring experiences in which mainstreamed children and their classmates work together on the same task lead to friendly interaction and

① cooperative learning
② peer tutoring

full inclusion
Placement of pupils with learning difficulties in regular classrooms for the entire school day.

learning disabilities
Specific learning disorders that lead children to achieve poorly in school, despite an average or above-average IQ. Believed to be due to faulty brain functioning.

mainstreaming
Placement of pupils with learning difficulties in regular classrooms for part of the school day.

FIGURE 12.4

Responses of an 8-year-old who scored high on a figural measure of divergent thinking. This child was asked to make as many pictures as she could from the circles on the page. The titles she gave her drawings, from left to right, are as follows: "Dracula," "one-eyed monster," "pumpkin," "Hula-Hoop," "poster," "wheelchair," "earth," "moon," "planet," "movie camera," "sad face," "picture," "stoplight," "beach ball," "the letter O," "car," "glasses." Tests of divergent thinking tap only one of the complex cognitive contributions to creativity. (Reprinted by permission of Laura Berk.)

giftedness
Exceptional intellectual strengths. Includes high IQ, creativity, and talent.

creativity
The ability to produce work that is original yet appropriate—something that others have not thought of but that is useful in some way.

divergent thinking
The generation of multiple and unusual possibilities when faced with a task or problem. Associated with creativity.

convergent thinking
The generation of a single correct answer to a problem. The type of cognition emphasized on intelligence tests.

more favorable attitudes (Scruggs & Mastropieri, 1994; Siegel, 1996). Teachers also can prepare children for the arrival of a special-needs student. Under these conditions, mainstreaming may foster gains in emotional sensitivity and prosocial behavior among regular classmates.

■ **GIFTED CHILDREN.** In Joey and Lizzie's school, some children were **gifted.** They displayed exceptional intellectual strengths. Like mainstreamed students, their characteristics were diverse. In every grade were one or two students with IQ scores above 130, the standard definition of giftedness based on intelligence test performance (Gardner, 1998a). High-IQ children, as we have seen, are particularly quick at academic work. They have keen memories and an exceptional capacity to solve challenging academic problems rapidly and accurately.

Yet earlier in this chapter, we noted that intelligence tests do not sample the entire range of human mental skills. Recognition of this fact has led to an expanded conception of giftedness in schools.

Creativity and Talent. **Creativity** is the ability to produce work that is *original* yet *appropriate*—something that others have not thought of but that is useful in some way. High potential for creativity can result in a child being designated as gifted. Because most children are not mature enough to produce useful creative works, researchers have devised tests to tap their capacity for creative thought. These tests tap **divergent thinking**—the generation of multiple and unusual possibilities when faced with a task or problem. Divergent thinking contrasts sharply with **convergent thinking,** which involves arriving at a single correct answer and is emphasized on intelligence tests (Guilford, 1985).

Recognizing that highly creative children (like high-IQ children) are often better at some types of tasks than others, researchers have devised verbal, figural, and "real-world-problem" tests of divergent thinking (Runco, 1992; Torrance, 1988). A verbal measure might ask children to name as many uses for common objects (such as a newspaper) as they can. A figural measure might ask them to come up with as many drawings based on a circular motif as possible (see Figure 12.4). A "real-world" measure either gives children everyday problems or requires them to think of such problems and then suggest solutions. Responses to all these tests can be scored for the number of ideas generated and their originality.

Yet critics of these measures point out that at best, they are imperfect predictors of creative accomplishment in everyday life, since they tap only one of the complex cognitive contributions to creativity (Cramond, 1994). Also involved are the ability to define a new and important problem, to evaluate divergent ideas and choose the most promising, and to call on relevant knowledge to understand and solve the problem (Sternberg & Lubart, 1995).

Consider these additional ingredients, and you will see why people usually demonstrate expertise and creativity in only one or a few related areas. Even individuals designated as gifted by virtue of their high IQ often show uneven ability across academic subjects—for example, higher verbal than math scores, or vice versa (Achter, Lubinski, & Benbow, 1996). Partly for this reason, definitions of giftedness have been extended to include **talent.** Research consistently shows that outstanding performances in particular fields, such as creative writing, mathematics, science, music, visual arts, athletics, and leadership, have roots in specialized skills that first appear at an early age. Highly talented children are biologically prepared to master their domain of interest. And they display a passion—a burning drive—to do so (Gardner, 1998; Winner, 2000).

At the same time, talent must be nurtured in a favorable environment. Studies of the backgrounds of talented children and highly accomplished adults often reveal a family life focused on the child's needs—parents who are warm and sensitive, who provide a stimulating home life, and who are devoted to developing their child's extraordinary ability (Albert, 1994; Winner, 1996). These parents are not driving and overambitious but, instead, are reasonably demanding. They arrange for caring teachers while the child is young and for more rigorous master teachers as the talent develops (Bloom, 1985; Feldman, 1991).

Extreme giftedness often results in social isolation. The highly driven, nonconforming, and independent styles of many gifted children and adolescents lead them to spend more time alone, partly because of their rich inner lives and partly because solitude is necessary to develop their talents. Still, gifted children desire gratifying peer relationships, and some—more often girls than boys—try to hide their abilities to become better liked. Compared with their ordinary agemates, gifted youths, especially girls, report more emotional and social difficulties, including low self-esteem and depression (Gross, 1993; Winner, 2000).

Finally, whereas many talented youths become experts in their fields, few become highly creative. The skill involved in rapidly mastering an existing field is not the same as innovating, or changing that field. Gifted individuals who are restless with the status quo and daring about changing it are rare (Csikszentmihalyi, 1996; Gardner, 1993). The world, however, needs both experts and creators.

Educating the Gifted. Learning environments that permit gifted children to take risks and reflect on ideas are vital. When academically gifted and specially talented children are not sufficiently challenged, they sometimes lose their drive to excel. And when parents and teachers push them too hard, by adolescence they are likely to ask, "Who am I doing this for?" If the answer is not "myself," they may decide not to pursue their gift anymore (Winner, 1997, 2000, p. 166).

Although programs for the gifted exist in many schools, debate about their effectiveness usually focuses on factors irrelevant to giftedness—whether to offer enrichment in regular classrooms, to pull children out for special instruction (the most common practice), or to advance brighter students to a higher grade. Gifted children of all ages fare well academically and socially within each of these models (Moon & Feldhusen, 1994). Yet the extent to which programs foster talent and creativity depends on students' opportunities to acquire relevant skills.

Recently, Gardner's theory of multiple intelligences has inspired several model programs that provide enrichment to all students, so any child capable of high-level performance can manifest it. A wide variety of meaningful activities, each tapping a specific intelligence or set of intelligences, serve as contexts for assessing strengths and weaknesses and, on that basis, teaching new knowledge and original thinking. For example, linguistic intelligence might be fostered through storytelling or playwriting; spatial intelligence through drawing, sculpting, or taking apart and reassembling objects; and kinesthetic intelligence through dance or pantomime (Gardner, 1993).

AP/WIDE WORLD

People usually demonstrate expertise and creativity in only one or a few related areas, so definitions of giftedness have been extended to include talent. Highly talented children are biologically prepared to master their domain of interest and experience a favorable environment for doing so. Here Laurence Tai, age 11, conducts the New York Philharmonic Orchestra as it performs "Greenwich Overture," a piece that Laurence composed.

Social isolation often is associated w/ gifted children.

talent
Outstanding performance in a particular field.

INFLUENCES

EDUCATION IN JAPAN, TAIWAN, AND THE UNITED STATES

Why do Asian children perform so well academically? Research examining societal, school, and family conditions in Japan, Taiwan, and the United States provides some answers.

CULTURAL VALUING OF ACADEMIC ACHIEVEMENT

In Japan and Taiwan, natural resources are limited. Progress in science and technology is essential for economic well-being. Since a well-educated work force is necessary to meet this goal, children's mastery of academic skills is vital. Compared with Western countries, Japan, Taiwan, and other East Asian nations invest more in education, including paying higher salaries to teachers and granting them more prestige (Lewis, 1995; Rohlen, 1997). In the United States, attitudes toward academic achievement are far less unified. Many Americans believe that it is more important to encourage children to feel good about themselves and to explore various areas of knowledge than to perform well in school.

EMPHASIS ON EFFORT AND PARENT INVOLVEMENT IN EDUCATION

Japanese and Taiwanese parents and teachers believe that most children have the potential to master challenging academic tasks if they work hard enough. In contrast, American parents and teachers tend to regard native ability as key in academic success (Stevenson, 1992). These differences in attitude may contribute to the fact that American parents are less inclined to encourage activities at home that might enhance school performance. Japanese and Taiwanese parents promote their children's commitment to academics, and they devote many more hours to helping with homework than do American parents. As a result, Asian children spend far more free time studying, reading, and playing academic-related games than do children in the United States (Huntsinger, Jose, & Larson, 1998; Stevenson & Lee, 1990).

Furthermore, effort takes on different meaning in Asian collectivist societies than in Western individualistic societies. Japanese and Chinese youths strive to achieve in school because effort is a moral obligation—part of one's responsibility to family and community. In contrast, American young people regard working hard academically as matter of individual choice—of fulfilling personal goals (Bempechat & Drago-Severson, 1999). In high school, Asian students continue to devote more time to academic pursuits than do American students, who spend more time socializing with peers, pursuing sports and other leisure activities, and working at part-time jobs (Larson & Verma, 1999).

HIGH-QUALITY EDUCATION FOR ALL

Unlike American teachers, Japanese and Taiwanese teachers do not make early educational decisions on the basis of achievement. No separate ability groups or tracks exist in elementary school. Instead, all students receive the same high-quality instruction. Academic lessons are particularly well organized and presented in ways that capture children's attention. Topics in

---

Evidence is still needed on how effectively these programs nurture children's talents. But so far, they have succeeded in one way—by highlighting the strengths of some students who previously had been considered ordinary or even at risk for school failure. Consequently, they may be especially useful in identifying talented low-SES, minority children who are underrepresented in school programs for the gifted (Frazier, 1994).

HOW WELL EDUCATED ARE AMERICA'S CHILDREN?

Our discussion of schooling has largely focused on what teachers can do to support the education of children. Yet a great many factors, both within and outside schools, affect children's learning. Societal values, school resources, quality of teaching, and parental encouragement all play important roles. Nowhere are these multiple influences more apparent than when schooling is examined in cross-cultural perspective.

American children fare unevenly when their achievement is compared with that of children in other industrialized nations. In international studies of mathematics and science

mathematics are addressed in greater depth, and there is less repetition of material taught the previous year.

MORE TIME DEVOTED TO INSTRUCTION

In Japan and Taiwan, the school year is over 50 days longer than in the United States. When one American elementary school experimented by adding 30 days to its school year, extended-year students scored higher in reading, general knowledge, and (especially) math achievement than did students in similar-quality schools with a traditional calendar (Frazier & Morrison, 1998).

Furthermore, on a day-to-day basis, Japanese and Taiwanese teachers devote much more of the school day to academic pursuits, especially mathematics. However, Asian schools are not regimented places, as many Americans believe. An 8-hour school day permits extra recesses and a longer lunch period, with plenty of time for play, social interaction, field trips, and extracurricular activities. Frequent breaks may increase children's capacity to learn (Pellegrini & Smith, 1998; Stevenson, 1994).

Japanese children achieve considerably better than their American counterparts for a variety of reasons. A longer school day permits frequent alternation of academic instruction with pleasurable activity, an approach that fosters learning. During a break from academic subjects, these Japanese elementary-school children enjoy a class in the art of calligraphy.

COMMUNICATION BETWEEN TEACHERS AND PARENTS

Japanese and Taiwanese teachers get to know their students especially well. They teach the same children for 2 or 3 years and visit the home once or twice a year. Continuous communication between teachers and parents takes place with the aid of small notebooks that children carry back and forth every day with messages about assignments, academic performance, and behavior (Stevenson & Lee, 1990). No such formalized system of frequent teacher–parent communication exists in the United States.

Do Japanese and Taiwanese children pay a price for the pressure placed on them to succeed? By high school, academic work often displaces other experiences, since Asian adolescents must pass a highly competitive entrance exam to gain admission to college. Yet Asian parenting practices that encourage academic competence do not undermine children's adjustment. In fact, high-performing Asian students are socially competent (Crystal et al., 1994; Huntsinger, Jose, & Larson, 1998). Awareness of the ingredients of Asian success has prompted Americans to rethink current educational practices.

achievement, young people from Hong Kong, Japan, Korea, and Taiwan have consistently been among the top performers, whereas Americans have scored no better than at the mean and often below it (Lapointe, Askew, & Mead, 1992; Lapointe, Mead, & Askew, 1992). The most recent assessment revealed a sharp decline in performance with increasing grade. In math, fourth graders in the United States were comparable to those in many other countries; in science, they were near the top. By twelfth grade, American students' math and science knowledge was near the bottom of 21 participating nations—far below Australia, Canada, Iceland, and Sweden, to name just a few (U.S. Department of Education, 1998).

Why do American children fall behind in academic accomplishments? To find out, researchers have looked closely at learning environments in top-performing Asian nations. A common assumption is that Asian children are high achievers because they are "smarter," but this is not true. Except for the influence of language on early counting skills (see page 452), they do not start school with cognitive advantages over their American peers (Geary, 1996). Instead, as the Cultural Influences box above indicates, a variety of social forces combine to foster a much stronger commitment to learning in Asian families and schools.

The Japanese and Taiwanese examples underscore that families, schools, and the larger society must work together to upgrade education. The current educational reform movement in the United States is an encouraging sign. Throughout the country, academic standards and teacher certification requirements are being strengthened. In addition, many schools are working to increase parent involvement in children's education. Parents who create stimulating learning environments at home, monitor their child's academic progress, help with homework, and communicate often with teachers have children who consistently show superior academic progress (Connors & Epstein, 1996).

The returns of these efforts can be seen in recent national assessments of educational progress. The achievement of U.S. elementary and secondary school students has improved over the past decade in reading, math, and science (Campbell, Hombo, & Mazzeo, 2000). And elementary school students report reading more as part of school assignments and doing more homework than they did a decade ago.

Ask YOURSELF...

review — List teaching practices that foster children's academic achievement and those that undermine it. For each practice, provide a brief explanation.

apply — Ray is convinced that his 5-year-old son Tripper would do better in school if only Tripper's kindergarten would provide more teacher-directed lessons and worksheets and reduce the time devoted to learning-center activities. Is Ray correct? Explain.

apply — Sandy, a parent of a third grader, wonders whether she should support her school board's decision to teach first, second, and third graders together, in mixed-age classrooms. How would you advise Sandy, and why?

connect — Relate genetic–environmental correlation, *discussed in Chapter 2, pages 89–91,* to the development of gifted children. Which parenting and teaching practices can enhance that correlation, and which ones can undermine it?

Summary

PIAGET'S THEORY: THE CONCRETE OPERATIONAL STAGE

What are the major characteristics of concrete operational thought?

- During the **concrete operational stage**, thought is more logical, flexible, and organized than it was during the preschool years. Mastery of conservation tasks indicates that children can **decenter** and **reverse** their thinking. In addition, they are better at hierarchical classification and **seriation**, including **transitive inference**. School-age youngsters' spatial reasoning improves, as their understanding of distance and ability to give directions reveals.

- Concrete operational thought is limited in that children can reason logically only about concrete, tangible information; they have difficulty with abstractions. Piaget used the term **horizontal décalage** to describe the school-age child's gradual mastery of logical concepts, such as conservation.

Discuss recent research on concrete operational thought.

- Recent evidence indicates that specific cultural practices, especially those associated with schooling, affect children's mastery of Piagetian tasks. Some theorists believe that operational thinking can best be understood within an information-processing framework.

- Case's neo-Piagetian theory proposes that with brain development and practice, schemes demand less attention, freeing up space in working memory for combining old schemes and generating new ones. Eventually, children consolidate schemes into highly efficient, central conceptual structures and move up to a new Piagetian stage. Children show a horizontal décalage because tasks vary in their processing demands and children vary in their task-specific experiences.

INFORMATION PROCESSING

Cite two basic changes in information processing, and describe the development of attention and memory in middle childhood.

- Brain development contributes to gains in information-processing capacity and **cognitive inhibition** during the school years. These changes facilitate many aspects of information processing.

- During middle childhood, attention becomes more selective and adaptable. Attention (and memory) strategies develop in a four-step sequence: (1) **production deficiency** (failure to use the strategy); (2) **control deficiency** (failure to execute the strategy consistently); (3) **utilization deficiency** (consistent use of the strategy, but no improvement in performance); and (4) **effective strategy use.**

- School-age children also become better at planning. On tasks requiring systematic visual search or the coordination of many acts, they are more likely to decide ahead of time how to proceed and allocate their attention accordingly. Collaborating on tasks with more expert planners leads to gains in children's planning.

- Memory strategies improve during the school years. **Rehearsal** appears first, followed by **organization** and then **elaboration.** Development of the long-term knowledge base facilitates strategic memory processing. At the same time, children's motivation to use what they know contributes to memory development. Memory strategies are promoted by learning activities in school.

Describe the school-age child's theory of mind and capacity to engage in self-regulation.

- Metacognition expands over middle childhood as children gain a much better understanding of the process of thinking and factors that influence it. School-age children regard the mind as an active, constructive agent, and they combine their metacognitive knowledge into an integrated theory of mind.

- School-age children are not yet good at cognitive **self-regulation**—putting what they know about thinking into action. Providing children with instructions to monitor their cognitive activity improves self-regulatory skills and task performance.

Discuss current controversies in teaching reading and mathematics to elementary school children.

- Skilled reading draws on all aspects of the information-processing system. Experts disagree on whether a **whole-language approach** or a **basic-skills approach** should be used to teach beginning reading. A combination of both seems most effective.

- As with reading, instruction that combines practice in basic skills with conceptual understanding is best in mathematics. Students acquire basic math facts through a combination of frequent practice and reasoning about number concepts. Experimenting with problem solving and evaluating solution techniques is essential for mastering more complex skills.

INDIVIDUAL DIFFERENCES IN MENTAL DEVELOPMENT

Describe major approaches to defining intelligence.

- During the school years, IQ becomes more stable, and it correlates well with academic achievement. Most intelligence tests yield an overall score representing general intelligence as well as scores for separate intellectual factors. Current widely used intelligence tests for children are the **Stanford-Binet Intelligence Scale** and the **Wechsler Intelligence Scale for Children–III (WISC–III).**

- To search for the precise mental processes underlying mental ability factors, researchers have combined the factor analytic approach to defining intelligence with the information-processing approach. Findings reveal that speed of thinking and effective strategy use are related to IQ. Sternberg's **triarchic theory of intelligence** extends these efforts. It views intelligence as a complex interaction of information-processing skills, specific experiences, and contextual (or cultural) influences.

- According to Gardner's **theory of multiple intelligences,** mental abilities should be defined in terms of distinct sets of processing operations applied in culturally valued activities. He proposes at least eight independent intelligences, several of which are not measured by IQ scores. His theory has been helpful in efforts to understand and nurture children's special talents.

Describe evidence indicating that both heredity and environment contribute to intelligence.

Summary (continued)

- Heritability estimates and adoption research reveal that intelligence is a product of heredity and environment. Studies of African-American children adopted into economically well-off white homes indicate that the black–white IQ gap is substantially determined by environment.

- IQ scores are affected by specific learning experiences, including exposure to certain language customs and familiarity with the kind of knowledge sampled by the test. Sheer amount of time a child spends in school is a strong predictor of IQ. Because of cultural bias in intelligence testing, test scores can underestimate minority children's intelligence. By introducing individualized teaching into the testing situation, **dynamic testing** narrows the gap between a child's actual and potential performance.

LANGUAGE DEVELOPMENT

Describe changes in metalinguistic awareness, vocabulary, grammar, and pragmatics during middle childhood.

- During middle childhood, children develop **metalinguistic awareness,** which supports a wide range of complex language skills. Vocabulary continues to grow rapidly, and children have a more precise and flexible understanding of word meanings. Grasp of complex grammatical constructions also improves. School-age children can adapt to listeners' needs in challenging communicative situations, and they evaluate the clarity of others' messages. Narratives increase in length and complexity, and conversational strategies become more refined.

What are the advantages of bilingualism in childhood?

- Children who learn two languages in early childhood acquire normal native ability in the language of their surrounding community and good-to-native ability in the second language, depending on exposure. When school-age children acquire a second language after mastering the first, it takes 3 to 5 years to attain the competence of native-speaking agemates. Children who are fluent in two languages are advanced in cognitive development and metalinguistic awareness. These advantages provide strong justification for bilingual education programs in schools.

CHILDREN'S LEARNING IN SCHOOL

Describe the impact of class size and educational philosophies on children's motivation and academic achievement.

- As class size drops, academic achievement improves. Older students in **traditional classrooms** have a slight edge in academic achievement. Those in **open classrooms** tend to be critical thinkers who respect individual differences and have more positive attitudes toward school. Kindergartners in traditional classrooms display more stress behaviors, followed by poorer study habits and achievement in grade school.

- Vygotsky's sociocultural theory has inspired new experiments in elementary education, including **reciprocal teaching** and the **Kamehameha Elementary Education Program (KEEP).** In each, learning experiences are rich in teacher–child and child–child collaboration, children acquire literacy skills in meaningful activities, and teaching is adapted to each child's zone of proximal development. As a result, achievement improves.

Discuss the role of teacher–student interaction and grouping practices in academic achievement.

- Teaching that encourages high-level thinking and that creates a stimulating, demanding academic climate fosters children's interest, involvement, and academic achievement. **Educational self-fulfilling prophecies** are most likely to occur in classrooms that emphasize competition and public evaluation, and they have a greater impact on low achievers.

- Ability grouping is linked to poorer-quality instruction and a drop in self-esteem and achievement for children in low-ability groups. In contrast, multigrade classrooms promote self-esteem and positive school attitudes, perhaps because of greater classroom harmony and opportunity for peer tutoring. For collaboration between heterogeneous peers to lead to achievement gains, children need extensive training and guidance in **cooperative learning.**

Describe learning advantages of and concerns about computers.

- Computer-assisted instruction and word processing result in gains in academic performance. Programming promotes a variety of complex cognitive skills. However, boys spend much more time than girls with computers, perhaps leading to advantages for boys in problem solving and spatial abilities. Violent video games seem to contribute to aggressive behavior.

Under what conditions is placement of mildly mentally retarded and learning disabled children in regular classrooms successful?

- Students with mild mental retardation and **learning disabilities** are often placed in regular classrooms, usually through **mainstreaming** but also through **full inclusion.** The success of regular classroom placement depends on tailoring learning experiences to children's academic needs and promoting positive peer relations.

Describe the characteristics of gifted children and current efforts to meet their educational needs.

- **Giftedness** includes high IQ, **creativity,** and **talent.** Tests of creativity that tap **divergent** rather than **convergent** thinking focus on only one of the complex cognitive ingredients of creativity. People usually demonstrate creativity in one or a few related areas.

- Highly talented children seem biologically prepared to master their domain of interest, but they also have parents and teachers who nurture their extraordinary ability. Extreme giftedness often results in social isolation, and gifted youths—especially girls—report more emotional and social difficulties than do their ordinary agemates. Gifted children are best served by educational programs that build on their special strengths.

Why do American children fall behind children in Asian nations in academic achievement?

- In international studies of math and science achievement, students in Asian nations have consistently been among the top performers, whereas Americans have scored no better than at the mean and often below it. A strong cultural commitment to learning, which pervades homes and schools, seems to be responsible for the academic success of Asian students.

Important terms and concepts

attention-deficit hyperactivity
    disorder (ADHD) (p. 446)
basic-skills approach (p. 450)
cognitive inhibition (p. 443)
cognitive self-regulation (p. 449)
concrete operational stage (p. 439)
control deficiency (p. 443)
convergent thinking (p. 472)
cooperative learning (p. 469)
creativity (p. 472)
decentration (p. 439)
divergent thinking (p. 472)
dynamic testing (p. 459)
educational self-fulfilling prophecy
    (p. 468)

effective strategy use (p. 443)
elaboration (p. 445)
full inclusion (p. 471)
giftedness (p. 472)
horizontal décalage (p. 440)
Kamehameha Elementary Education
    Program (KEEP) (p. 468)
learning disabilities (p. 471)
mainstreaming (p. 471)
metalinguistic awareness (p. 461)
open classroom (p. 465)
organization (p. 444)
production deficiency (p. 443)
reciprocal teaching (p. 467)
rehearsal (p. 444)

reversibility (p. 439)
seriation (p. 439)
Stanford-Binet Intelligence Scale
    (p. 453)
talent (p. 473)
theory of multiple intelligences
    (p. 455)
traditional classroom (p. 465)
transitive inference (p. 439)
triarchic theory of intelligence
    (p. 455)
utilization deficiency (p. 443)
Wechsler Intelligence Scale for
    Children–III (WISC–III) (p. 453)
whole-language approach (p. 450)

 ... for further information and help

Consult the companion website for this book, where you will find additional weblinks and associated learning activities:
www.ablongman.com/berk

ATTENTION-DEFICIT HYPERACTIVITY DISORDER

Children and Adults with
Attention-Deficit Hyperactivity Disorder
www.chadd.org

Provides support and education to families of children and adults with attention-deficit hyper-activity disorder. Encourages schools and health care professionals to be responsive to their needs.

BILINGUAL EDUCATION

National Association for Bilingual Education
www.nabe.org

An organization of educators, public citizens, and students aimed at increasing public understand-ing of the importance of bilingual education.

LEARNING DISABILITIES

Learning Disabilities Association of America
www.ldanatl.org

An organization of interested professionals and parents of children with learning disabilities. Local groups provide parent support and educa-tion and sponsor recreational programs and summer camps for children.

GIFTEDNESS

The Association for the Gifted of the
Council for Exceptional Children
www.cec.sped.org

An organization of educators and parents aimed at stimulating interest in program development for gifted children. Publishes Journal for the Education of the Gifted.

National Association for Gifted Children
www.nagc.org

An association of scholars, educators, and librarians devoted to advancing education for gifted children. Distributes information and sponsors institutes. Publishes the journal Gifted Child Quarterly.

"My World in the Year 2000"

Emile Mavel

9 years, West Africa

Violence is part of the everyday existence of this artist, who has witnessed
devastation and death in a war-torn region of Africa. All children—and
especially those who face threatening living conditions—need the support
of parents, teachers, friends, and communities to maintain an image of a
moral world and a hopeful future. Chapter 13 takes up the widening social
understandings and experiences of school-age children.

Emotional and Social Development in Middle Childhood

One late afternoon, Rena heard Joey dash through the front door, run upstairs, and call up his best friend Terry. "Terry, gotta talk to you," pleaded Joey, out of breath from running home. "Everything was going great until that word I got—'porcupine,'" remarked Joey, referring to the fifth-grade spelling bee at school that day. "Just my luck! 'P-o-r-k,' that's how I spelled it! I can't believe it. Maybe I'm not so good at social studies," Joey confided, "but I *know* I'm better at spelling than that stuck-up Belinda Brown. And I'm better than most other kids, too. Gosh, I knocked myself out studying those spelling lists. Then *she* got all the easy words. Did'ya see how snooty she acted after she won? If I *had* to lose, why couldn't it be to a nice person?"

Joey's conversation reflects a whole new constellation of emotional and social capacities. First, Joey shows evidence of *industriousness*. By entering the spelling bee, he energetically pursued meaningful achievement in his culture—a major change of the middle childhood years. At the same time, Joey's social understanding has greatly expanded. He can size up strengths, weaknesses, and personality characteristics—a capacity

481

that was beyond him during the preschool years. Furthermore, friendship means something different to Joey than it did at younger ages. Terry is not just a convenient playmate; he is a best friend whom Joey counts on for understanding and emotional support.

We begin this chapter by returning to Erikson's theory for an overview of the personality changes of middle childhood. Then we take a close look at emotional and social development. We will see how, as children reason more effectively and spend more time in school and with peers, their views of themselves, of others, and of social relationships become more complex.

Although school-age children spend less time with parents than they did at earlier ages, the family remains powerfully influential. Joey and Lizzie, along with many children of their generation, are growing up in homes profoundly affected by social change. Rena, their mother, has been employed since her children were preschoolers. In addition, Joey and Lizzie's home life has been disrupted by family discord: Rena is divorced. Although family lifestyles are more diverse than ever before, Joey and Lizzie's experiences will help us appreciate that family functioning is far more important than family structure in ensuring children's well-being.

Finally, when stress is overwhelming and social support lacking, school-age children experience serious adjustment difficulties. Our chapter concludes with a discussion of some common emotional problems of middle childhood.

Erikson's Theory: Industry versus Inferiority

According to Erikson (1950), the personality changes of the school years build on Freud's *latency stage* (see Chapter 1, page 16). Although Freud's theory is no longer widely accepted, children whose experiences with caregivers have been positive do enter middle childhood with the calm confidence Freud intended by the term *latency.* And their energies are redirected from the make-believe of early childhood into realistic accomplishment.

Erikson believed that the combination of adult expectations and children's drive toward mastery sets the stage for the psychological conflict of middle childhood: **industry versus inferiority.** Industry means developing competence at useful skills and tasks. In cultures everywhere, improved physical and cognitive capacities mean that adults impose new demands. Children, in turn, are ready to meet these challenges and benefit from them:

■ Among the Baka hunters and gatherers of Cameroon, 5- to 7-year-olds fetch and carry water, bathe and mind younger siblings, and accompany adults on food-gathering missions. Behind the main camp stands a miniature village. In this "school" of the Baka society, children practice hut building, spear shaping, and fire making (Avis & Harris, 1991).

■ The Ngoni of Malawi, Central Africa, believe that when children shed their first teeth, they are ready for a different kind of life. Between ages 6 and 7, they stop their childish games and start skill training. Boys move out of the huts of family members into dormitories, where they enter a system of male domination and instruction. At that time, children are expected to show independence and are held personally accountable for irresponsible and disrespectful behavior (Read, 1968; Rogoff, 1996).

In industrialized nations, the transition to middle childhood is marked by the beginning of formal schooling. With it comes literacy training, which prepares children for the vast array of specialized careers in complex societies. In school, children become aware of their own and others' unique capacities, learn the value of division of labor, and develop a sense of moral commitment and responsibility. The danger at this stage is *inferiority,* reflected in the sad pessimism of some children who have little confidence in their ability to do things well. This sense of inadequacy can develop when family life has not prepared children for school life or when experiences with teachers and peers are so negative that they destroy children's feelings of competence and mastery.

Children become more adultlike in their concern for industry.

Improved physical and cognitive capacities of middle childhood mean that in cultures everywhere, adults impose new demands. These 9- and 13-year-old sisters of Mauritania, Africa, prepare a noon meal.

© LAUREN GOODSMITH/THE IMAGE WORKS

Erikson's sense of industry combines several developments of middle childhood: a positive but realistic self-concept, pride in accomplishment, moral responsibility, and cooperative participation with agemates. Let's look at how these aspects of self and social relationships change over the school years.

Self-Development

Several transformations in self-understanding take place in middle childhood. First, children can describe themselves in terms of psychological traits. Second, they start to compare their own characteristics to those of their peers. Finally, they speculate about the causes of their strengths and weaknesses. These ways of thinking about the self have a major impact on children's self-esteem.

SELF-CONCEPT

During the school years, children develop a much more refined *me-self*, or self-concept, organizing their observations of behaviors and internal states into general dispositions, with a major change taking place between ages 8 and 11. The following self-description from an 11-year-old reflects this change:

> My name is A. I'm a human being. I'm a girl. I'm a truthful person. I'm not pretty. I do so-so in my studies. I'm a very good cellist. I'm a very good pianist. I'm a little bit tall for my age. I like several boys. I like several girls. I'm old-fashioned. I play tennis. I am a very good swimmer. I try to be helpful. I'm always ready to be friends with anybody. Mostly I'm good, but I lose my temper. I'm not well liked by some girls and boys. I don't know if I'm liked by boys or not. (Montemayor & Eisen, 1977, pp. 317–318)

Notice that instead of specific behaviors, this child emphasizes competencies, as in "I'm a very good cellist" (Damon & Hart, 1988). Also, she clearly describes personality traits and mentions both positive and negative attributes—"truthful" but "not pretty," a "good cellist [and] pianist" but only "so-so in my studies." Older school-age children are far less likely than younger children to describe themselves in unrealistically positive, all-or-none ways (Harter, 1996).

Another change in self-concept takes place in middle childhood: Children make **social comparisons**—that is, they judge their appearance, abilities, and behavior in relation to those of others. In his comments about the spelling bee, Joey expressed some thoughts about how good he was compared with his peers—"better at spelling" but "not so good at social studies." Although 4- to 6-year-olds can compare their own performance to that of one peer and use that information as a basis for self-evaluation, older children can compare multiple individuals, including themselves (Butler, 1998; Ruble & Frey, 1991).

COGNITIVE, SOCIAL, AND CULTURAL INFLUENCES ON SELF-CONCEPT

What factors are responsible for these revisions in self-concept? Cognitive development certainly affects the changing *structure* of the self. School-age children, as we saw in Chapter 12, can better coordinate several aspects of a situation in reasoning about their physical world. They show an improved ability to relate separate observations in the social realm as well. Consequently, they combine typical experiences and behaviors into stable psychological dispositions, blend positive and negative characteristics into a consistent picture, and compare their own characteristics with those of many other peers (Harter, 1998, 1999). In middle childhood, children also gain a clearer understanding of traits as linked to specific desires (a "generous" person *wants* to share) and, therefore, as causes of behavior (Yuill & Pearson, 1998).

industry versus inferiority
In Erikson's theory, the psychological conflict of middle childhood, which is resolved positively when experiences lead children to develop a sense of competence at useful skills and tasks.

social comparisons
Judgments of appearance, abilities, and behavior, in relation to those of others.

concept of self-blends of what others think of us.

kids internalize an ideal self + compare it to their real self.

self-concept related to peers.

preschoolers have high self-esteem but that declines in middle childhood.

The changing *content* of self-concept is a product of both cognitive capacities and feedback from others. Early in this century, sociologist George Herbert Mead (1934) described the self as a blend of what important people in our lives think of us. He believed that a psychological self emerges when the child's *I-self* adopts a view of the *me-self* that resembles the attitudes of significant others. In other words, *perspective-taking* skills—in particular, an improved ability to imagine what other people are thinking—are crucial in the development of a self-concept based on personality traits. As we will see later in this chapter, perspective taking improves greatly over the school years. Children become better at "reading" messages they receive from others and incorporating these into their self-definitions. As school-age children internalize others' expectations, they form an *ideal self* that they use to evaluate their *real self*. A large discrepancy between the ideal and real selves can greatly affect self-esteem, leading to feelings of sadness, hopelessness, and depression.

During middle childhood, children look to more people for information about themselves as they enter a wider range of settings in school and community. This is reflected in children's frequent reference to social groups in their self-descriptions (Livesley & Bromley, 1973). "I'm a Boy Scout, a paper boy, and a Prairie City soccer player," Joey remarked when asked to describe himself. Gradually, as children move into adolescence, their sources of self-definition become more selective. Although parents remain influential, between ages 8 and 15, peers become more important. And over time, self-concept becomes increasingly vested in feedback from close friends (Oosterwegel & Openheimer, 1993).

Keep in mind, however, that the changes just described are based on interviews with North American and Western European children. Development of self-concept does not follow the same path in all societies. Recall from earlier chapters that Asian parents stress harmonious interdependence, whereas Western parents emphasize separateness and the importance of asserting the self. Consequently, in China and Japan, the self is defined in relation to the social group. In the United States, the self usually becomes the "property" of a self-contained individual (Markus & Kitayama, 1991). Turn back to Chapter 10, page 368, and notice this difference in mothers' personal storytelling with their young children.

A strong collectivist theme is also reflected in the values of many subcultures in Western nations. In one study, the self-descriptions of children in a Puerto Rican fishing village were compared with those of children in an American town. The Puerto Rican children more often described themselves as "polite," "nice," "respectful," and "obedient" and justified these social traits by noting the positive reactions they evoke from others. In contrast, the small-town children more often mentioned individualistic traits, such as interests, preferences, and skills (Damon & Hart, 1988).

SELF-ESTEEM

Self-esteem, the judgments children make about their own worth, is also reorganized in middle childhood. Recall from Chapter 10 that most preschoolers have extremely high self-esteem. As children enter school, they get much more feedback about their performance compared with that of their peers. Grades on papers and tests, report cards, and the comments of adults and other children are integrated into self-evaluations. As a result, self-esteem differentiates, and it also adjusts to a more realistic level (Stipek & Mac Iver, 1989).

■ **A HIERARCHICALLY STRUCTURED SELF-ESTEEM.** Susan Harter (1982, 1986) asked children to indicate the extent to which a variety of statements, such as "I am good at homework," "I'm usually the one chosen for games," and "Most kids like me," are true of themselves. Her findings, and those of other researchers, reveal that classrooms, playgrounds, and peer groups are key contexts in which children evaluate their own competence. By age 7 to 8, children have formed at least four separate self-esteems—academic competence, social competence, physical/athletic competence, and physical appearance—that become more refined with age. For example, academic self-worth divides into performance in each school subject, social self-worth into peer and parental relationships, and physical/athletic competence into skill at various sports (Marsh, 1990).

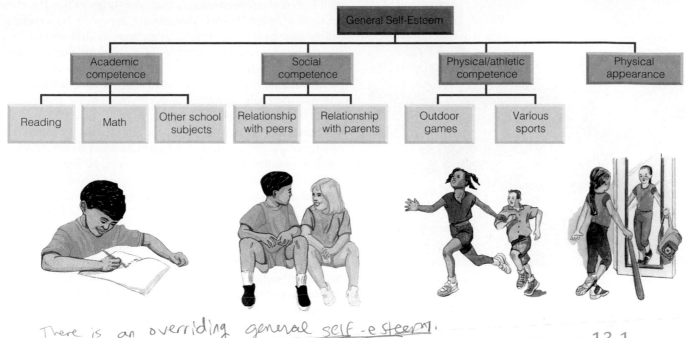

There is an overriding general self-esteem.

FIGURE 13.1

Hierarchical structure of self-esteem in the mid-elementary school years. From their experiences in different settings, children form at least four separate self-esteems: academic competence, social competence, physical/athletic competence, and physical appearance. These differentiate into additional self-evaluations and combine to form a general sense of self-esteem.

academic
social   *competences*
athletic
vanity

Furthermore, school-age children's newfound ability to view themselves in terms of stable dispositions permits them to combine their separate self-evaluations into a general psychological image of themselves—an overall sense of self-esteem (Harter, 1998, 1999). Consequently, by the mid-elementary school years, self-esteem takes on the hierarchical structure shown in Figure 13.1.

Separate self-evaluations, however, do not contribute equally to general self-esteem. Instead, as children attach greater importance to some aspects, those self-judgments are weighted more heavily in the total picture. For example, Joey commented, "Even though I'm not as good at social studies as I am at reading, math, and science, I still like myself. Social studies isn't very important to me." Although children and adolescents differ in the aspects of the self they deem most important, the way they perceive their physical appearance correlates more strongly with general self-worth than any other self-esteem factor (Harter, 1998; Hymel et al., 1999). The emphasis that society and the media place on appearance has major implications for young people's overall satisfaction with themselves.

■ **CHANGES IN LEVEL OF SELF-ESTEEM.** As children evaluate themselves in various areas, they lose the sunny optimism of early childhood. Self-esteem drops during the first few years of elementary school (Marsh, Craven, & Debus, 1998; Wigfield et al., 1997). This decline occurs as children adjust their self-judgments to fit the opinions of others and compare their own performance with that of agemates.

To protect their self-worth, children eventually balance social comparisons with personal achievement goals (Ruble & Flett, 1988). Perhaps for this reason, the drop in self-esteem in the early school years usually is not great enough to be harmful. Most (but not all) children appraise their characteristics and competencies realistically while maintaining an attitude of self-acceptance and self-respect. Then, from fourth to sixth grade, self-esteem rises for the majority of youngsters, who feel especially good about their peer relationships and athletic capabilities (Nottelmann, 1987; Zimmerman et al., 1997).

INFLUENCES ON SELF-ESTEEM

Beginning in middle childhood, strong relationships exist between self-esteem and everyday behavior. For example, academic self-esteem predicts children's school achievement as well as their willingness to try hard at challenging tasks (Marsh, Smith, & Barnes, 1985). Children

Children from collectivist cultures rarely call on social comparison to enhance their self-esteem. In a masquerade dance at their annual village carnival, these Caribbean children of St. Kitts display a strong sense of connection with their social group. Compared with children in individualistic societies, they are likely to be less concerned with whether another child is better at a skill than they are.

Attributions explain the causes of behavior.

attributions
Common, everyday explanations for the causes of behavior.

with high social self-esteem are consistently better liked by their peers (Harter, 1982). And as we saw in Chapter 11, boys come to believe they have more athletic talent than do girls, and they are also more advanced in a variety of physical skills. Furthermore, from age 5 on, children believe that self-esteem has important consequences. They say that people who like themselves would do better at a challenging task and cope more easily with a peer's rebuff (Daniels, 1998).

Because self-esteem is so powerfully related to individual differences in behavior, researchers have been intensely interested in identifying factors that cause it to be high for some children and low for others. If ways can be found to improve children's sense of self-worth, then many aspects of their development might be enhanced as well.

■ **CULTURE.** As with self-concept, cultural forces profoundly affect self-esteem. For example, the role of social comparison varies from culture to culture. Puerto Rican fishing-village children, mentioned earlier, almost never compare themselves to others by saying "I'm better at kickball than he is" or "How many math problems did you get right?" (Damon & Hart, 1988).

An especially strong emphasis on social comparison in school may underlie the finding that Japanese and Taiwanese children score lower in self-esteem than do American children, despite their higher academic achievement (Chiu, 1992–1993; Hawkins, 1994). In Asian classrooms, competition is tough and achievement pressure is high. At the same time, Asian children less often call on social comparisons to bolster their own self-esteem. Because their culture places a high value on modesty and social harmony, they tend to be reserved about judging themselves positively but generous in their praise of others (Falbo et al., 1997; Heine & Lehman, 1995).

■ **CHILD-REARING PRACTICES.** Children whose parents are warm and responsive and who provide firm but reasonable expectations for behavior—that is, who use an *authoritative* child-rearing style (see Chapter 10)—feel especially good about themselves (Deković & Meeus, 1997; Feiring & Taska, 1996). If you think carefully about this finding, you will see that it makes perfect sense. Warm, positive parenting lets children know that they are accepted as competent and worthwhile. And firm but appropriate expectations, backed with explanations, help children make sensible choices and evaluate their own behavior against reasonable standards.

In contrast, highly coercive parenting communicates a sense of inadequacy to children—that their behavior needs to be controlled by adults because they cannot manage it themselves. And indulgent parenting that promotes a "feel good" attitude no matter how children behave creates a false sense of self-esteem. Sooner or later, such children doubt their self-worth (Damon, 1995).

Although parental warmth and maturity demands are undoubtedly important ingredients of high self-esteem, we cannot tell the extent to which child-rearing styles are causes of or reactions to children's characteristics and behavior. Research on the precise content of adults' messages to children has been far more successful at isolating factors that affect children's sense of self-worth. Let's see how these messages mold children's evaluations of themselves in achievement contexts.

■ **ACHIEVEMENT-RELATED ATTRIBUTIONS.** **Attributions** are our common, everyday explanations for the causes of behavior—the answers we provide to the question, "Why did I (or another person) do that?" Look back at Joey's conversation about the spelling bee at the beginning of this chapter. Notice how he attributes his second-place performance to *luck* (Belinda got all the easy words) and his usual success at spelling to *ability* (he knows he's a better speller than Belinda). Joey also appreciates that *effort* makes a difference; he "knocked [himself] out studying those spelling lists."

Cognitive development permits school-age children to recognize and separate all these variables in explaining performance (Skinner, 1995). Yet children differ greatly in how they

[handwritten: a) learning goals]

account for their successes and failures. Those who are high in academic self-esteem develop **mastery-oriented attributions.** They believe that they succeed due to ability—a characteristic they can improve through trying hard and can count on when faced with new challenges. This *incremental view of ability*—that it can be altered—influences the way mastery-oriented children interpret negative events (Heyman & Dweck, 1998). When failure hits, they attribute it to factors that can be changed and controlled, such as insufficient effort or a very difficult task. So whether these children succeed or fail, they take an industrious, persistent, and enthusiastic approach to learning. *[handwritten: performance]*

Unfortunately, children who develop **learned helplessness** hold very discouraging explanations for their performance. They attribute their failures, not their successes, to ability. When they succeed, they are likely to conclude that external factors, such as luck, are responsible. Furthermore, unlike their mastery-oriented counterparts, they hold a *fixed view of ability*—that it cannot be changed (Cain & Dweck, 1995). They do not think that competence can be improved by trying hard. So when a task is difficult, these children experience an anxious loss of control—in Erikson's terms, a pervasive sense of inferiority. They quickly give up, saying "I can't do this," before they have really tried.

Children's attributions affect their goals. Mastery-oriented children focus on *learning goals*—increasing ability through effort and seeking information on how to do so. In contrast, learned-helpless children focus on *performance goals*—obtaining positive and avoiding negative evaluations of their fragile sense of ability. Over time, the ability of learned-helpless children no longer predicts how well they do. Many are very bright pupils who have concluded that they are incompetent (Wagner & Phillips, 1992). Because they fail to make the connection between effort and success, learned-helpless children do not develop the metacognitive and self-regulatory skills necessary for high achievement (see Chapter 12). Lack of effective learning strategies, reduced persistence, and a sense of being controlled by external forces sustain one another in a vicious cycle (Heyman & Dweck, 1992).

■ **INFLUENCES ON ACHIEVEMENT-RELATED ATTRIBUTIONS.** What accounts for the very different attributions of mastery-oriented and learned-helpless children? Adult communication plays a key role. Children with a learned-helpless style tend to have parents who set unusually high standards yet believe their child is not very capable and has to work much harder than others to succeed (Parsons, Adler, & Kaczala, 1982; Phillips, 1987). When these children fail, the adult might say, "You can't do that, can you? It's okay if you quit" (Hokoda & Fincham, 1995). And when the child succeeds, the adult might respond, "Gee, I'm surprised you got that A," or the adult might give feedback evaluating the child's traits, as in "You're so smart." When used often, trait statements promote a fixed view of ability, which encourages children to focus on performance, not learning, and respond helplessly to setbacks (Erdley et al., 1997).

A study following 1,600 third to eighth graders over a three-year period highlights the role of teacher communication in fostering a mastery-oriented approach (Skinner, Zimmer-Gembeck, & Connell, 1998). Students who viewed their teachers as warm and fair (for example, clarifying expectations, checking that the child understands) worked harder on assignments and participated more in class. Trying hard, in turn, predicted better academic performance, which sustained the child's belief in the role of effort. In contrast, children who experienced their teachers as unsupportive were more likely to regard their performance as externally controlled (by powerful teachers or luck). This predicted withdrawal from learning activities and declining achievement. These negative outcomes led children to doubt their ability and believe even more strongly in the power of external forces.

Some children are especially likely to have their performance undermined by adult feedback. Girls more often than boys blame their ability for poor performance. Girls also tend to receive messages from teachers and parents that their ability is at fault when they do not do well (Ruble & Martin, 1998). Low-SES, ethnic minority children also are at risk for learned helplessness. In several studies, African-American and Mexican-American children received less favorable teacher feedback than did other children (Aaron & Powell, 1982; Irvine, 1986; Losey, 1995). Furthermore, when ethnic minority children observe that adults in their own family are not rewarded by society for their achievement efforts, they may give up themselves.

MYRLEEN CATE/PHOTOEDIT

This second grader practices counting and writing numerals with effort, determination, and enthusiasm. Adult communication—the extent to which his parents and teachers implicate effort when he fails and express confidence in his ability to overcome obstacles and succeed—contributes to his mastery-oriented approach to learning.

[handwritten: learned helpless kids believe that their ability is fixed]

[handwritten: supportive teachers foster determination in kids.]

mastery-oriented attributions
Attributions that credit success to high ability and failure to insufficient effort. Leads to high self-esteem and a willingness to approach challenging tasks.

learned helplessness
Attributions that credit success to luck and failure to low ability. Leads to anxious loss of control in the face of challenging tasks.

Because their classrooms emphasize mastery and cooperation rather than ability and competition, Israeli children growing up on kibbutzim are shielded from learned helplessness. In this kibbutz school, children work collaboratively on art projects.

attribution retraining
An intervention that encourages learned-helpless children to believe that they can overcome failure by exerting more effort.

Many African-American children may come to believe that even if they do try in school, social prejudice will prevent them from succeeding (Ogbu, 1997).

Finally, cultural values for achievement affect the likelihood that children will develop learned helplessness. Compared with Americans, Chinese and Japanese parents and teachers believe that success in school depends much more on effort than ability—a message they transmit to children (Tuss, Zimmer, & Ho, 1995). And Israeli children growing up on *kibbutzim* (cooperative agricultural settlements) are shielded from learned helplessness by classrooms that emphasize mastery and interpersonal harmony rather than ability and competition (Butler & Ruzany, 1993).

■ **SUPPORTING CHILDREN'S SELF-ESTEEM.** Attribution research suggests that at times, well-intended messages from adults undermine children's competence. **Attribution retraining** is an intervention that encourages learned-helpless children to believe that they can overcome failure by exerting more effort. Most often, children are given tasks that are hard enough that they will experience some failure. Then they get repeated feedback that helps them revise their attributions, such as "You can do it if you try harder." Children also are taught to view their successes as due to ability and effort rather than chance factors, by giving them additional feedback after they succeed, such as "You're really good at this" or "You really tried hard on that one" (Schunk, 1983).

Another approach is to teach low-effort children to focus less on grades and more on mastery for its own sake. A large-scale study showed that classrooms emphasizing the intrinsic value of acquiring new knowledge led to impressive gains in failing pupils' academic self-esteem and motivation (Ames, 1992). Learned-helpless children also need instruction in metacognition and self-regulation to make up for development lost in this area and to ensure that renewed effort will pay off (Borkowski & Muthukrishna, 1995).

To work well, attribution retraining is best begun in middle childhood, before children's views of themselves become hard to change (Eccles, Wigfield, & Schiefele, 1998; Harter, 1999). An even better approach is to prevent low self-esteem before it happens. The Educational Concerns table on the following page lists ways to foster a mastery-oriented approach to learning and prevent learned helplessness in middle childhood.

Ask **YOURSELF...**

review How does level of self-esteem change in middle childhood, and what accounts for those changes?

apply Should parents try to promote children's self-esteem by telling them they're "smart" and "wonderful"? Is it harmful if children do not feel good about everything they do? Why or why not? How would you recommend that parents foster children's self-esteem?

connect What cognitive changes, described in Chapter 12, support the transition from a self-concept consisting of a collection of behaviors and internal states to a self-concept emphasizing competencies, personality traits, and social comparisons?

reflect Describe your attributions for academic successes and failures during childhood. What are those attributions like now? What experiences do you think contributed to your attributions?

ℰducational Concerns

Fostering a Mastery-Oriented Approach to Learning and Preventing Learned Helplessness

Provision of tasks	Select tasks that are meaningful, responsive to a diversity of pupil interests, and appropriately matched to current competence so the child is challenged but not overwhelmed.
Parent and teacher encouragement	Communicate warmth, confidence in the child's abilities, the value of achievement, and the importance of effort in success.
	Model high effort in overcoming failure.
	(For teachers) Communicate often with parents, suggesting ways to foster children's effort and progress.
	(For parents) Monitor schoolwork; provide scaffolded assistance that promotes knowledge of effective strategies and self-regulation.
Performance evaluations	Make evaluations private; avoid publicizing success or failure through wall posters, stars, privileges to "smart" children, and prizes for "best" performance.
	Stress individual progress and self-improvement.
School environment	Offer small classes, which permit teachers to provide individualized support for mastery.
	Provide for cooperative learning and peer tutoring, in which children assist each other; avoid ability grouping, which makes evaluations of children's progress public.
	Accommodate individual and cultural differences in styles of learning.
	Create an atmosphere that values academics and sends a clear message that all pupils can learn.

Sources: Ames, 1992; Eccles, Wigfield, & Schiefele, 1998.

Emotional Development

Greater self-awareness and social sensitivity support emotional development in middle childhood. Changes occur in children's experience of self-conscious emotions, understanding of emotional states, and emotional self-regulation.

SELF-CONSCIOUS EMOTIONS

As children integrate social standards into their self-definitions, a sense of personal responsibility clearly governs self-conscious emotions of pride and guilt. Unlike preschoolers, 6- to 11-year-olds experience these feelings in the absence of adult monitoring. A teacher or parent does not have to be present for a new accomplishment to spark a glowing sense of pride or for a transgression to arouse painful pangs of guilt (Harter, Wright, & Bresnick, 1987). Also, school-age children do not report guilt for any mishap, as they did at younger ages, but only for intentional wrongdoing, such as ignoring responsibilities, cheating, or lying (Ferguson, Stegge, & Damhuis, 1991). These changes reflect the older child's more mature sense of morality, a topic we will take up later in this chapter.

When school-age children feel pride or guilt, they view specific aspects of the self as leading to success or failure, as in "I tried hard on that difficult task, and it paid off" (pride) or "I made a mistake, and now I have to deal with it" (guilt). They tend to feel shame when they violated a standard but it was not under their control. For example, Lizzie felt ashamed when she dropped a spoonful of spaghetti at lunchtime and had a large spot on her shirt for the rest of the school day. But as children develop an overall sense of self-esteem, they may experience shame after a controllable breach of standards if the self-as-a-whole is blamed for it.

School-age children can experience shame that weakens their overall sense of self-esteem. While his classmates raise their hands eagerly, this boy has difficulty with the assignment and hangs his head in shame. He may be saying to himself, "I'm no good and stupid"—thoughts and feelings that are destructive to his development.

ZIGY KALZUNY/STONE

For example, the child who does poorly on a test and whose teacher or parent reprimands him ("Everyone else can do it! Why can't you?") may hang his head in shame while repeating to himself, "I'm stupid!" (Harter, 1999; Mascolo & Fischer, 1995).

Pride motivates children to take on further challenges. And guilt prompts them to make amends and strive for self-improvement. But profound feelings of shame (as noted in Chapter 10) are particularly destructive. They involve taking a single unworthy act to be the whole of self-worth, setting up maladaptive feelings of hopelessness and of passive retreat or intense anger at others who participated in the shame-evoking situation (Lindsay-Hartz, de Rivera, & Mascolo, 1995; Reimer, 1996).

EMOTIONAL UNDERSTANDING

School-age children's understanding of psychological dispositions means that they are likely to explain emotion by referring to internal states rather than physical events, as they did at younger ages (Strayer, 1993). They are also more aware of the diversity of emotional experiences. By age 8, children realize that they can experience more than one emotion at a time, each of which may be positive or negative and may differ in intensity (Harter & Buddin, 1987; Wintre & Vallance, 1994). For example, recalling the birthday present he received from his grandmother, Joey reflected, "I was very happy I got something but a little sad that I didn't get just what I wanted."

This appreciation that people can experience several feelings at once helps school-age children understand self-conscious emotions. When we feel proud, we combine two sources of happiness—joy over accomplishment and joy that a significant person recognized that accomplishment. When we feel ashamed, we are angry with ourselves for a personal inadequacy and sad at having disappointed another. Many 8- and 9-year-olds grasp self-conscious emotions in these ways. They say, for example, "I was proud of that A; I felt real happy, and my parents were happy for me, too," and "When I'm ashamed, I feel mad at myself for doing something bad, and I also feel sad for the other person" (Harter, 1999; Harter & Whitesell, 1989).

Similarly, school-age children appreciate that emotional reactions need not reflect a person's true feelings. Consequently, they become much better at masking their emotions. And whereas younger children hide feelings to avoid scolding and ridicule, older children do so because of social norms and concern for others (Jones, Abbey, & Cumberland, 1998). "I got all excited and told Grandma I liked that dumb plastic toy train she gave me when I don't" Joey said to Rena one day. "I wanted to be polite and make Grandma feel good."

Along with a more complex understanding of one's own feelings comes the ability to take more information into account in detecting the emotions of others. School-age children can reconcile contradictory facial and situational cues in figuring out another's emotions. Recall that preschoolers rely only on the facial expression (see Chapter 10, page 371). Furthermore, older children can use information about a person's past experiences to predict how he or she will feel in a new situation. They realize, for example, that a child rejected by her best friend will probably feel sad at later meeting the friend. Younger children rely only on the current situation, saying, "She'll be happy to see her friend" (Gnepp, 1989).

As with self-understanding, gains in emotional understanding are supported by cognitive development and social experiences, especially adults' sensitivity to children's feelings and willingness to discuss emotions. Together, these factors contribute to a rise in empathy as well (Ricard & Kamberk-Kilicci, 1995). The greater school-age children's perspective-taking skill and the more they recognize and accept their own feelings, the more likely they are to respond empathically. Empathy, in turn, continues to predict prosocial behavior in middle childhood (Roberts & Strayer, 1996).

As children move closer to adolescence, advances in perspective taking permit an empathic response not just to people's immediate distress but also to their general life condition (Hoffman, 2000). As Joey and Lizzie imagined how people who are chronically ill or hungry feel and evoked those emotions in themselves, their prosocial acts

At the end of middle childhood, empathy broadens as advances in perspective taking permit an empathic response to others' general life condition. As a result, prosocial acts expand. These 10-year-olds volunteer to box donated food items for a community food bank serving the needy.

© J. GREENBERG/THE IMAGE WORKS

expanded. They gave part of their allowance to charity and joined in fund-raising projects through school, church, and scouting organizations.

EMOTIONAL SELF-REGULATION

Rapid gains in emotional self-regulation occur in middle childhood. As children compare their accomplishments with their classmates' and care more about peer approval, they must learn to manage negative emotion that threatens their self-esteem.

By age 10, most children have an adaptive set of techniques for regulating emotion (Kliewer, Fearnow, & Miller, 1996). In situations where they have some control over an outcome (an anxiety-provoking test at the end of the week or a friend who is angry at them), they view problem solving and seeking social support as the best strategies. When outcomes are beyond their control (having received a bad grade or awaiting a painful injection at the doctor's office), they opt for distraction or redefining the situation in ways that help them accept current conditions ("Things could be worse. There'll be another test"). Compared with preschoolers, school-age children more often use these internal strategies to manage emotion, a change due to an improved ability to reflect on their thoughts and feelings (Brenner & Salovey, 1997).

Cognitive development and a wider range of social experiences permit children to flexibly adjust their emotion-regulation strategies to situations. When the development of emotional self-regulation has gone along well, school-age children acquire a sense of *emotional self-efficacy*—a feeling of being in control of their emotional experience (Saarni, 1999). This fosters a favorable self-image and an optimistic outlook, which assists them further in the face of emotional challenges.

Emotionally well-regulated children are generally upbeat in mood, more empathic and prosocial, and better liked by their peers. In contrast, poorly regulated children are overwhelmed by negative emotion, a response that interferes with prosocial behavior and peer acceptance. Girls with weak self-regulatory skills tend to freeze with anxiety, whereas boys more often lash out with hostility (Eisenberg, Fabes, & Losoya, 1997).

Recall from previous chapters that both temperament and parenting affect emotional self-regulation. In a striking illustration, researchers compared 6- to 9-year-olds in two subcultures in rural Nepal. In response to stories about emotionally charged situations (such as peer aggression or parental argument), Hindu children were far more likely to say they would feel angry and would try to mask their feelings. Buddhist children, in contrast, usually said they would feel just OK (see Figure 13.2). In line with this difference, Hindu mothers reported that they often teach their children how to behave emotionally. Buddhist mothers, in contrast, referred to the value their religion places on a calm, peaceful disposition and said that children learn emotional conduct on their own (Cole & Tamang, 1998). We will return to themes of temperament and parenting later when we take up peer acceptance and the ways children cope with stressful family circumstances.

Understanding Others: Perspective Taking

Already we have seen that middle childhood brings major advances in **perspective taking**—the capacity to imagine what other people are thinking and feeling. Now let's take a close look at these changes, which support self- and emotional understanding and a wide array of social skills. Robert Selman's five-stage sequence describes changes in perspective-taking skill, based on children's and adolescents' responses to social dilemmas in which characters have differing information and opinions about an event.

As Table 13.1 on page 492 indicates, at first, children have only a limited idea of what other people might be thinking and feeling. Over time, they become more aware that people can interpret the same event quite differently. Soon they can "step in another person's shoes" and reflect on how that person might regard their own thoughts, feelings, and behavior, as when

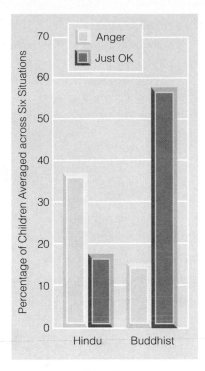

FIGURE 13.2

Hindu and Buddhist children's reports of feeling anger and just OK in response to emotionally charged situations. Hindu children reported that they would feel more anger. Buddhist children, whose religion values a calm, peaceful disposition, more often stated that they would feel just OK. (Adapted from Cole & Tamang, 1998.)

[handwritten note: temperament + parenting affect emotional self-regulation.]

perspective taking
The capacity to imagine what other people are thinking and feeling.

TABLE 13.1

Selman's Stages of Perspective Taking

STAGE	APPROXIMATE AGE RANGE	DESCRIPTION
Level 0: Undifferentiated perspective taking	3–6 years	Children recognize that self and other can have different thoughts and feelings, but they frequently confuse the two.
Level 1: Social-informational perspective taking	4–9 years	Children understand that different perspectives may result because people have access to different information.
Level 2: Self-reflective perspective taking	7–12 years	Children can "step in another person's shoes" and view their own thoughts, feelings, and behavior from the other person's perspective. They also recognize that others can do the same.
Level 3: Third-party perspective taking	10–15 years	Children can step outside a two-person situation and imagine how the self and other are viewed from the point of view of a third, impartial party.
Level 4: Societal perspective taking	14 years–adult	Individuals understand that third-party perspective taking can be influenced by one or more systems of larger societal values.

Sources: Selman, 1976; Selman & Byrne, 1974.

they make statements like this: "I *thought you would think* I was just kidding when I said that." Finally, they can evaluate two people's perspectives simultaneously, at first from the vantage point of a disinterested spectator and, finally, by making reference to societal values. The following explanation reflects this advanced level: "I know why Joey hid the stray kitten in the basement, even though his mom was against keeping it. He believes in not hurting animals. If you put the kitten outside or give it to the pound, it might die."

Although it improves with age, perspective-taking skill varies greatly among children of the same age. Cognitive maturity and experiences in which adults and peers explain their viewpoints, encouraging children to notice others' perspectives, contribute to these individual differences (Dixon & Moore, 1990). Children with poor social skills—in particular, the angry, aggressive styles we discussed in Chapter 10—have great difficulty imagining the thoughts and feelings of others. They often mistreat adults and peers without feeling the guilt and remorse prompted by awareness of another's viewpoint. Interventions that provide these children with coaching and practice in perspective taking help reduce antisocial behavior and increase empathy and prosocial responding (Chalmers & Townsend, 1990; Chandler, 1973).

Moral Development

Recall from Chapter 10 that preschoolers pick up a great many morally relevant behaviors through modeling and reinforcement. By middle childhood, they combine these experiences into rules for good conduct, such as "It's good to help others in trouble" or "It's wrong to take something that doesn't belong to you." Consequently, school-age children are not as dependent on adult oversight, modeling, and reinforcement as they were at younger ages. They can follow internalized standards.

These changes lead children to become considerably more independent and trustworthy. During middle childhood, they can take on many more responsibilities, including household chores, errands in the neighborhood, and care of younger siblings (Weisner, 1996). Of course, these advances take place only when children have had the consistent guidance and example of caring adults in their lives.

In Chapter 10 we also saw that children do not just copy their morality from those around them. As the cognitive-developmental approach emphasizes, from an early age they actively think about right and wrong. An expanding social world, the capacity to consider more variables when reasoning, and gains in perspective taking lead moral understanding to improve greatly in middle childhood.

distributive justice
Beliefs about how to divide material goods fairly.

LEARNING ABOUT JUSTICE THROUGH SHARING

In everyday life, children frequently experience situations that involve **distributive justice**—beliefs about how to divide material goods fairly. Heated discussions often take place over how much weekly allowance is to be given to siblings of different ages, who has to sit where in the family car on a long trip, and in what way an eight-slice pizza is to be shared by six hungry playmates. William Damon (1977, 1988) has traced children's changing concepts of distributive justice over early and middle childhood.

Preschoolers recognize the importance of sharing, but their reasons for doing so often seem contradictory and self-serving: "I shared because if I didn't, she wouldn't play with me" or "I let her have some, but most are for me because I'm older." As children enter middle childhood, they express more mature notions of distributive justice (see Table 13.2). At first, their ideas of fairness are based on equality. Children in the early school grades are intent on making sure that each person gets the same amount of a treasured resource, such as money, turns in a game, or a delicious treat. This strict-equality approach resembles young children's less flexible thinking in other areas.

A short time later, children view fairness in terms of *merit*. Extra rewards should be given to someone who has worked especially hard or otherwise performed in an exceptional way. Finally, around 8 years, children can reason on the basis of *benevolence*. They recognize that special consideration should be given to those at a disadvantage, like the needy or the disabled. Older children say that an extra amount might be given to a child who cannot produce as much or who does not get any allowance from his parents. They also adapt their basis of fairness to the situation—for example, relying more on merit when interacting with strangers and more on benevolence when interacting with friends (McGillicuddy-De Lisi, Watkins, & Vinchur, 1994).

According to Damon (1988), parental advice and encouragement support these developing standards of justice, but the give-and-take of peer interaction is especially important. Peer disagreements, along with efforts to resolve them, make children more sensitive to others' perspectives, and this supports their developing ideas of fairness (Kruger, 1993). Advanced distributive justice reasoning, in turn, is associated with more effective social problem solving and a greater willingness to help and share with others (Blotner & Bearison, 1984; McNamee & Peterson, 1986).

WILL FALLER

These five school-age children have figured out how to divide up two pizzas fairly among themselves. Already, they have a well-developed sense of distributive justice.

MORAL AND SOCIAL-CONVENTIONAL UNDERSTANDING

As their ideas about justice advance, children clarify and link moral rules and social conventions (Turiel, 1998). Over time, their understanding becomes more complex, taking

TABLE 13.2

Damon's Sequence of Distributive Justice Reasoning

BASIS OF REASONING	AGE	DESCRIPTION
Equality	5–6 years	Fairness involves strictly equal distribution of goods. Special considerations, such as merit and need, are not taken into account.
Merit	6–7 years	Fairness is based on deservingness. Children recognize that some people should get more because they have worked harder.
Benevolence	8 years	Fairness includes giving special consideration to those who are disadvantaged. More should be given to those who are in need.

Sources: Damon, 1977, 1988.

School-age children develop a sophisticated understanding of the links between moral rules and social conventions. They regard the social convention of respecting the flag as having moral implications. Not doing so, they say, harms others emotionally. At the same time, they acknowledge that flag burning is a form of freedom of expression that is warranted in an unfair country.

into account an increasing number of variables, including the purpose of the rule; people's intentions, knowledge, and beliefs; and the context of their behavior.

School-age children distinguish social conventions with a clear *purpose* (not running in school hallways because doing so might cause an accident) from ones with no obvious justification (crossing a "forbidden" line on the playground). They regard violations of purposeful social conventions as closer to violations of moral rules—that is, wrong even in the absence of authorities and stated rules to enforce them (Buchanan-Barrow & Barrett, 1998).

Furthermore, children age 6 and older realize that people's *intentions* and the *context* of their actions affect the moral implications of social-conventional transgressions—understandings that improve with age. In a Canadian study, 8- to 10-year-olds judged that because of a flag's symbolic value, burning it to express disapproval of a country or to start a cooking fire is worse than burning it accidentally. Older school-age children also stated that public flag-burning is worse than private flag-burning. When asked to explain, they referred to the emotional harm inflicted on others. At the same time, they recognized that burning a flag is a form of freedom of expression. Most acknowledged that in an unfair country, it would be acceptable (Helwig & Prencipe, 1999).

In middle childhood, children also realize that people whose *knowledge* differs may not be equally responsible for moral transgressions. Many 7-year-olds are tolerant of a teacher's decision to give more snack to girls than boys because she thinks (incorrectly) that girls need more food; they take into account the teacher's good intentions. But when a teacher gives girls more snack because she holds an *immoral belief* ("it's all right to be nicer to girls than boys"), almost all children judge her actions negatively (Wainryb & Ford, 1998). Children are more tolerant of people holding immoral beliefs than expressing them and more tolerant of people expressing such beliefs than acting on them—distinctions that sharpen in adolescence (Wainryb, Shaw, & Maianu, 1998). With age, young people refine their view of acceptable and unacceptable forms of dissent.

Children in Western and diverse non-Western cultures—such as Brazil, Korea, Indonesia, Nigeria, and Zambia—use the same criteria to distinguish moral and social-conventional concerns (Bersoff & Miller, 1993; Nucci, Camino, & Sapiro, 1996; Tisak, 1995). Increasingly over middle childhood, children say that even a child with no position of authority should be obeyed when giving fair and caring directives, such as to share candy, return lost money to its owner, and dispose of trash. This is true even for Korean children, whose culture places a high value on respect for and deference to authority. Korean 7- to 11-year-olds evaluate negatively a teacher or principal's order to engage in immoral acts, such as stealing or refusing to share—a response that strengthens with age (Kim, 1998; Kim & Turiel, 1996).

School-age children recognize an authority's right to set social conventions—for example, a principal's right to set rules and issue directives at school and a parent's right to do so at home (Laupa, 1995). But they know that more highly valued principles—ones independent of rule and authority—must govern when people's welfare is at stake.

MORAL EDUCATION

Debate over whether and how to teach morality in the public schools is vigorous and polemical. On one side are educators who call for *character education*—teaching students to follow a common set of moral virtues, such as honesty, kindness, fairness, and responsibility (De Roche & Williams, 1998). Critics claim that transmitting to school-age children a ready-made morality, such as "be honest and work hard," ignores their developing capacity to consider multiple variables in moral decision making (Kohn, 1997). As children get older, cognitive-developmental theorists point out, they benefit from increasing opportunities for *moral discussion*—evaluating beliefs and practices on moral grounds.

Darcia Narvaez and her colleagues (2001) recommend that moral education be broadened to promote four moral components, starting at a concrete level and moving toward more abstract understandings. Each component involves a different type of knowledge essential for moral functioning:

- *Interpreting the situation: moral sensitivity*—using cause–effect reasoning and perspective taking to predict how one's actions are likely to affect others, resulting in awareness that a situation involves a moral issue

- *Reasoning about right and wrong: moral judgment*—evaluating possible courses of action to determine which one is fair and just

- *Granting moral values a high priority: moral motivation*—elevating moral values above other personal values

- *Having the strength of one's convictions: moral character*—controlling impulses and steadfastly behaving in accord with moral values

At present, moral education programs for children are narrowly focused. Character education emphasizes *moral character*, whereas the cognitive-developmental approach stresses *moral judgment* (Bebeau, Rest, & Narvaez, 1999). Narvaez's four-component model offers a comprehensive basis for moral education. Children in highly successful programs should gain in each aspect of morality.

review How does emotional self-regulation improve in middle childhood? Do gains in emotional self-regulation have implications for children's self-esteem? Explain.

apply Joey's fourth-grade class participated in a bowl-a-thon to raise money for a charity serving children with cancer. Explain how activities like this one can foster emotional development, perspective taking, and moral understanding.

connect Describe how older children's capacity to take more information into account affects each of the following: self-concept, emotional understanding, perspective taking, and moral understanding.

Peer Relations

In middle childhood, the society of peers becomes an increasingly important context for development. Formal schooling exposes children to agemates who differ in many ways, including achievement, ethnicity, religion, interests, and personality. Peer contact, as we have seen, plays a major role in the school-age child's perspective taking and understanding of self and others. These developments, in turn, contribute to the quality of peer interaction, which becomes more prosocial over the school years. In line with this change, aggression declines, but the drop is greatest for physical attacks (Rubin, Bukowski, & Parker, 1998). As we will see, other types of aggression continue as school-age children form peer groups and distinguish "insiders" from "outsiders."

PEER GROUPS

Watch children in the schoolyard or neighborhood, and notice how groups of three to a dozen or more often gather. The organization of these collectives changes greatly with age. By the end of middle childhood, children display a strong desire for group belonging. Together, they generate unique values and standards for behavior. They also create a social structure of leaders and followers that ensures that group goals will be met. When these characteristics are present, a **peer group** is formed.

Peer groups organize on the basis of proximity (being in the same classroom) and similarity in gender, ethnicity, and popularity, and they are moderately stable. When tracked for 3 to 6 weeks, membership changes very little. When observed for a year or longer, substantial change can occur, depending on whether children are reshuffled into different classrooms and loyalties change within the group. When children remain together as a unit, 50 to 70 percent of groups consist mostly of the same children from year to year (Cairns, Xie, & Leung, 1998).

The practices of these informal groups lead to a "peer culture" that typically consists of a specialized vocabulary, dress code, and place to "hang out" during leisure hours. For example, Joey formed a club with three other boys. The children met at recess, after school, and on Saturdays in the treehouse in Joey's backyard and wore a "uniform" consisting of T-shirts, jeans, and tennis shoes. Calling themselves "the pack," the boys developed a secret handshake and chose Joey as their leader. Their activities included improving the clubhouse, trading baseball cards, playing basketball, making trips to the video arcade, and—just as important—keeping unwanted peers and adults out!

As children develop these exclusive associations, the codes of dress and behavior that grow out of them become more broadly influential. At school, children who deviate are often rebuffed by their peers. "Kissing up" to teachers, wearing the wrong kind of shirt or shoes, tattling on classmates, or carrying a strange-looking lunchbox are grounds for critical glances and comments. These special customs bind peers together, creating a sense of group identity. In addition, by participating in peer groups, children acquire many valuable social skills—cooperation, leadership, followership, and loyalty to collective goals. Through these experiences, children experiment with and learn about social organizations.

The beginning of peer group ties is also a time in which some of the "nicest children begin to behave in the most awful way" (Redl, 1966, p. 395). From third grade on, relational aggression—gossip, rumor spreading, and exclusion—rise among girls, who (because of gender-role expectations) express hostility in subtle, indirect ways (Crick & Grotpeter, 1995). Boys are more straightforward in their hostility toward the "outgroup." Overt aggression, in the form of verbal insults and pranks—toilet-papering a front yard or ringing a doorbell and running away—occurs among small groups of boys, who provide one another with temporary social support for these mildly antisocial behaviors.

Unfortunately, peer groups—at the instigation of their leaders—often direct their hostilities toward their own members, excluding no-longer "respected" children. These cast-outs are profoundly wounded, and many find new group ties hard to establish. Their previous behavior toward the outgroup, including expressed contempt for less popular children, reduces their chances of being included elsewhere. As one ejected fifth grader explained, "I think they didn't like me because when I was in the popular group we'd make fun of everyone. . . . I had been too mean to them in the past" (Adler & Adler, 1998, p. 70).

The school-age child's desire for group belonging can also be satisfied through formal group ties—Girl Scouts, Boy Scouts, 4-H, church groups, and other associations. Adult involvement holds in check the negative behaviors associated with children's informal peer groups. In addition, children gain in social and moral maturity as they negotiate and compromise while working on joint projects and as they help in their communities (Killen & Nucci, 1995; Vandell & Shumow, 1999).

© BOB DAEMMRICH/STOCK BOSTON

Peer groups first form in middle childhood. These fifth-grade girls have probably established a social structure of leaders and followers as they gather for play or just to talk. Their body language suggests that they feel a strong sense of group belonging.

peer group
Peers who form a social unit by generating shared values and standards of behavior and a social structure of leaders and followers.

FRIENDSHIPS

Whereas peer groups provide children with insight into larger social structures, close, one-to-one friendships contribute to the development of trust and sensitivity. During the school years, children's concepts of friendship become more complex and psychologically based. Consider the following 8-year-old's answers to questions about what makes a best friend:

Why is Shelly your best friend? Because she helps me when I'm sad, and she shares. . . . *What makes Shelly so special?* I've known her longer, I sit next to her and got to know her better. . . . *How come you like Shelly better than anyone else?* She's done the most for me. She never disagrees, she never eats in front of me, she never walks away when I'm crying, and she helps me on my homework. . . . *How do you get someone to like you?* . . . If you're nice to [your friends], they'll be nice to you. (Damon, 1988, pp. 80–81)

As these responses show, friendship is no longer just a matter of engaging in the same activities. Instead, it is a mutually agreed-on relationship in which children like each other's personal qualities and respond to one another's needs and desires. Since friendship involves both children wanting to be together, getting it started takes more effort than before. And once a friendship forms, *trust* becomes its defining feature. School-age children state that a good friendship is based on acts of kindness that signify that each person can be counted on to support the other. Consequently, events that break up a friendship are quite different than they were during the preschool years. Older children regard violations of trust, such as not helping when others need help, breaking promises, and gossiping behind the other's back, as serious breaches of friendship (Damon, 1977; Selman, 1980).

Because of these features, school-age children's friendships are more selective. Whereas preschoolers say they have lots of friends, by age 8 or 9, children have just a handful of people they call friends and, very often, only one best friend. Girls, especially, are exclusive in their friendships because they demand greater closeness than do boys. In addition, children tend to select friends like themselves in age, sex, race, ethnicity, and SES. Friends also resemble one another in personality (dependency, sociability, and prosocial and antisocial behavior), peer popularity, and academic achievement (Haselager et al., 1998; Kupersmidt, DeRosier, & Patterson, 1995). Note, however, that school and neighborhood characteristics affect friendship choices. For example, in integrated schools, as many as 50 percent of pupils report at least one close other-race friend (DuBois & Hirsch, 1990).

Friendships remain fairly stable over middle childhood; most last for several years. Through them, children learn the importance of emotional commitment. They come to realize that close relationships can survive disagreements if both parties are secure in their liking for one another and resolve conflicts in ways that meet both partners' needs (Laursen, Hartup, & Koplas, 1996; Rose & Asher, 1999). Yet the extent to which friendships support children's development depends on the company they keep.

Children who bring kindness and compassion to their friendships behave more prosocially toward others in general and also have more friends. In contrast, aggressive children's friendships usually magnify antisocial acts. Friendships of relationally aggressive girls are high in exchange of private feelings but full of jealousy, conflict, and betrayal (Grotpeter & Crick, 1996). Among boys, talk between aggressive friends contains frequent coercive statements and attacks, even during videotaping in a laboratory (Dishion, Andrews, & Crosby, 1995). These findings reveal that the social problems of aggressive children operate within their closest peer ties. As we will see next, these children also are at risk for rejection in the wider world of peers.

PEER ACCEPTANCE

Peer acceptance refers to likability—the extent to which a child is viewed by agemates as a worthy social partner. In Chapters 11 and 12, we saw that obese children and children with serious learning problems often have difficulty with peer acceptance. Yet there are other children whose appearance and intellectual abilities are quite normal; still, their classmates despise them.

During middle childhood, concepts of friendship become more psychologically based. Although these boys enjoy playing baseball, they want to spend time together because they like each other's personal qualities. Mutual trust is a defining feature of their friendship. Each child counts on the other to provide support and assistance.

Researchers usually assess peer acceptance with self-report measures called **sociometric techniques.** For example, children may be asked to nominate several peers in their class whom they especially like or dislike, to indicate for all possible pairs of classmates which one they prefer to play with, or to rate each peer on a scale from "like very much" to "like very little" (Cillessen & Bukowski, 2000).

Sociometric techniques yield four categories of peer acceptance: **popular children,** who get many positive votes; **rejected children,** who are actively disliked; **controversial children,** who get a large number of positive and negative votes; and **neglected children,** who are seldom chosen, either positively or negatively. About two-thirds of pupils in a typical elementary school classroom fit one of these categories. The remaining one-third are *average* in peer acceptance; they do not receive extreme scores (Coie, Dodge, & Coppotelli, 1982).

Peer acceptance is a powerful predictor of current as well as later psychological adjustment. Rejected children, especially, are unhappy, alienated, poorly achieving children with a low sense of self-esteem. Teachers and parents rate them as having a wide range of emotional and social problems. Peer rejection in middle childhood is also strongly associated with poor school performance, absenteeism, dropping out, antisocial behavior, and delinquency in adolescence and criminality in young adulthood (Bagwell, Newcomb, & Bukowski, 1998; Parker & Asher, 1987; Parker et al., 1995).

Although rejected status predicts and may contribute to later-life problems, preceding influences—children's characteristics, parenting practices, or some combination of the two—may explain the link between peer acceptance and psychological adjustment. In one study, 9-year-olds identified by their teachers as having peer-relationship problems were more likely to come from low-SES families and to have experienced parental changes (divorce, remarriage, death), insensitive caregiving, and punitive discipline. These children also showed high rates of childhood conduct problems—the strongest predictor of adolescent adjustment difficulties (Woodward & Fergusson, 1999).

Rejected children evoke a distinctive set of reactions from peers—and these experiences are believed to contribute to their unfavorable development. Let's turn to factors in the peer situation that increase the chances that a child will fall into a particular peer acceptance category.

■ **DETERMINANTS OF PEER ACCEPTANCE.** What causes one child to be liked and another to be rejected? A wealth of research reveals that social behavior plays a powerful role.

Popular Children. Although many popular children are kind and considerate, others are admired for their socially sophisticated yet belligerent behavior. Recently, researchers identified two subtypes of peer popularity:

■ **Popular-prosocial children.** Most popular children combine academic and social competence. They are good students and communicate with peers in sensitive, friendly, and cooperative ways. They are appropriately assertive; they rarely interfere with others' goals. When they do not understand another child's reaction, they ask for an explanation. If they disagree with a play partner in a game, they go beyond voicing their displeasure; they suggest what the other child could do instead. When they want to enter an ongoing play group, they adapt their behavior to the flow of the activity (Dodge, McClaskey, & Feldman, 1985; Newcomb, Bukowski, & Pattee, 1993).

■ **Popular-antisocial children.** This smaller subtype largely consists of "tough" boys who are athletically skilled but poor students. Popular-antisocial children are highly aggressive, often getting into fights, causing other trouble, and defying adult authority with nonchalance. Yet their peers view them as "cool," perhaps because of their athletic prowess and sophisticated social skills, through which they exploit others (Parkhurst & Hopmeyer, 1998; Rodkin et al., 2000).

Although popular-antisocial children are ethnically diverse, many are members of low-SES ethnic minorities. Recall from our discussion of achievement-related attributions that such children may conclude that they cannot succeed academically. Perhaps for this reason, their peer culture encourages troublemaking behavior. Consistent with this view, in classrooms with greater numbers of aggressive children, peers are more likely to rate such children

sociometric techniques
Self-report measures that ask peers to evaluate one another's likability.

popular children
Children who get many positive votes on sociometric measures of peer acceptance.

rejected children
Children who are actively disliked and get many negative votes on sociometric measures of peer acceptance.

controversial children
Children who get a large number of positive and negative votes on sociometric measures of peer acceptance.

neglected children
Children who are seldom chosen, either positively or negatively, on sociometric measures of peer acceptance.

popular-prosocial children
A subgroup of popular children who combine academic and social competence.

popular-antisocial children
A subgroup of popular children largely made up of "tough" boys who are athletically skilled, highly aggressive, defiant of adult authority, and poor students.

as "most liked" (Stormshak et al., 1999). So far, we do not know whether popular-antisocial children's likability protects them from future adjustment difficulties. But their antisocial activities require intervention, and positive classroom climates where they can succeed academically may be particularly helpful.

Rejected Children. Rejected children display a wide range of negative social behaviors. Consequently, they are likely to have few friends, and occasionally none at all. But like popular children, not all of these disliked children look the same. At least two subtypes exist.

- **Rejected-aggressive children,** the largest subgroup, show severe conduct problems—high rates of conflict, hostility, and hyperactive, inattentive, and impulsive behavior. These children are also deficient in social understanding and regulation of negative emotion. For example, they are more likely than others to be poor perspective takers, to misinterpret the innocent behaviors of peers as hostile, to blame others for their social difficulties, and to act on their angry feelings (Crick & Ladd, 1993; Deković & Gerris, 1994). Both boys' overt aggression and girls' relational aggression predict peer rejection (Crick, 1996).

- **Rejected-withdrawn children,** a smaller subgroup, are passive and socially awkward. These inhibited, timid children are also poor emotion regulators; overwhelmed by social anxiety, they withdraw in the face of social challenges (Hart et al., 2000; Rubin et al., 1995). As a result, they feel lonely, hold negative expectations for how peers will treat them, and are very concerned about being scorned and attacked (Boivin & Hymel, 1997; Ladd & Burgess, 1999). Because of their inept, submissive style of interaction, rejected-withdrawn children are at risk for abuse by bullies (see the Biology and Environment box on page 500).

Controversial Children. Consistent with the mixed peer opinion they engender, controversial children display a blend of positive and negative social behaviors. They are hostile and disruptive but also engage in high rates of positive, prosocial acts. Even though some peers dislike them, controversial children have qualities that protect them from social exclusion. They have as many friends as popular children do and are happy with their peer relationships (Newcomb, Bukowski, & Pattee, 1993; Parkhurst & Asher, 1992). The social status of controversial children often changes over time.

Neglected Children. Perhaps the most surprising finding on peer acceptance is that neglected children, once thought to be in need of treatment, are usually well adjusted. Although they engage in low rates of interaction and are considered shy by their classmates, they are not less socially skilled than average children. They do not report feeling lonely or unhappy about their social life, and when they want to, they can break away from their usual pattern of playing by themselves (Harrist et al., 1997; Ladd & Burgess, 1999). Perhaps for this reason, neglected status (like controversial status) is usually temporary.

Neglected children remind us that there are other paths to emotional well-being besides the outgoing, gregarious personality style so highly valued in our culture. In China, adults view cautious, inhibited children as advanced in social maturity! In accord with this standard, shyness and sensitivity are associated with peer acceptance and teacher-rated social competence and leadership among Chinese 8- to 10-year-olds (Chen, Rubin, & Li, 1995).

■ **HELPING REJECTED CHILDREN.** A variety of interventions exist to improve the peer relations and psychological adjustment of rejected children. Most involve coaching, modeling, and reinforcing positive social skills, such as how to begin interacting with a peer, cooperate in play, and respond to another child with friendly emotion and approval. Several of these programs have produced gains in social competence and peer acceptance still present from several weeks to a year later (Asher & Rose, 1997; Lochman et al., 1993; Mize & Ladd, 1990).

Some researchers believe that these interventions might be even more effective when combined with other treatments. Often, rejected children are poor students, and their low academic self-esteem magnifies their negative reactions to teachers and classmates (O'Neil et al., 1997). Intensive academic tutoring improves school achievement and social acceptance (Coie & Krehbiel, 1984).

rejected-aggressive children
A subgroup of rejected children who engage in high rates of conflict, hostility, and hyperactive, inattentive, and impulsive behavior.

rejected-withdrawn children
A subgroup of rejected children who are passive and socially awkward.

Biology & ENVIRONMENT

BULLIES AND THEIR VICTIMS

Follow the activities of aggressive children over a school day, and you will see that they reserve their hostilities for certain peers. A particularly destructive form of interaction is **peer victimization,** in which certain children become frequent targets of verbal and physical attacks or other forms of abuse. What sustains these repeated assault–retreat cycles between pairs of children?

Research indicates that the majority of victims reinforce bullies by giving into their demands, crying, assuming defensive postures, and failing to fight back. Victimized boys are passive when active behavior is expected; on the playground, they hang around chatting or wander on their own (Boulton, 1999). Biologically based traits—an inhibited temperament and a frail physical appearance—contribute to this reticent style. But victimized children also have histories of resistant attachment; overly intrusive, controlling parenting; and (among boys) maternal overprotectiveness. These parenting behaviors prompt anxiety, low self-esteem, and dependency, resulting in a fearful demeanor that radiates vulnerability (Ladd & Ladd, 1998; Olweus, 1993).

By elementary school, 10 percent of children are harassed by aggressive agemates, and peers expect these victims to give up desirable objects, show signs of distress, and fail to retaliate. In addition, children (especially those who are aggressive) feel less discomfort at the thought of causing pain and suffering to victims than nonvictims (Perry, Williard, & Perry, 1990). Although bullies and victims are more often boys, at times girls harass a vulnerable class-mate with relational hostility (Crick & Grotpeter, 1996). As early as kindergarten, victimization leads to a variety of adjustment difficulties, including sadness and depression, loneliness, difficulty controlling anger, and dislike and avoidance of school (Ladd, Kochendorfer, & Coleman, 1997).

Aggression and victimization are not polar opposites. A small number of extreme victims are also aggressive—picking arguments and fights or retaliating with relational aggression (Boulton & Smith, 1994; Crick & Bigbee, 1998). Perhaps these children foolishly provoke stronger agemates, who then prevail over them. Among rejected children, these bully/victims are the most despised, and they often experience extremely maladaptive parenting, including child abuse (Smith & Myron-Wilson, 1998). These home and peer influences place them at severe risk for maladjustment.

Interventions that change victimized children's negative opinions of themselves and that teach them to respond in nonreinforcing ways to their attackers are vital. Nevertheless, victimized children's behavior should not be taken to mean they are to blame for their abuse. Developing a school code against bullying, teaching child bystanders to inter-vene when it occurs, enlisting parents' assistance in changing both bullies' and victims' behavior, and moving aggressive children to another class or school can greatly reduce bully–victim problems, which account for a substantial portion of peer aggression in middle childhood (Olweus, 1995).

Another way to help victimized children is to assist them with the social skills needed to form and maintain a gratifying friendship. Anxious, withdrawn children who have a best friend seem better equipped to withstand peer attacks. They show fewer adjustment problems than do victims with no close friends (Hodges et al., 1999).

Children who are victimized by bullies have characteristics that make them easy targets. They are physically weak, rejected by their peers, and afraid to defend themselves. Both temperament and child-rearing experiences contribute to their cowering behavior, which reinforces their attackers' abusive acts.

MICHAEL NEWMAN/PHOTOEDIT

Other interventions focus on training in perspective taking and social problem solving. Still another approach is to increase rejected children's expectations for social success. Many rejected-withdrawn children develop a *learned-helpless* approach to peer acceptance. They conclude, after repeated rebuffs, that no matter how hard they try, they will never be liked.

In contrast, rejected-aggressive children tend to externalize their hostile actions with such claims as "They made me do it!" (Coie & Dodge, 1998; Toner & Munro, 1996). Both types of rejected children need help in attributing their peer difficulties to internal, changeable causes.

Finally, we have seen in previous chapters that children's socially incompetent behaviors often originate in a poor fit between the child's temperament and parenting practices. Therefore, interventions that focus on the child alone are unlikely to be sufficient. If the quality of parent–child interaction is not changed, rejected children may soon return to their old behavior patterns.

Gender Typing

Children's understanding of gender roles broadens in middle childhood, and their gender identities (views of themselves as relatively masculine or feminine) change as well. We will see that development differs for boys and girls, and it can vary considerably across cultures.

GENDER-STEREOTYPED BELIEFS

During the school years, children extend gender-stereotyped beliefs acquired in early childhood. As children think more about people as personalities, they label some traits as more typical of one sex than the other. For example, they regard "tough," "aggressive," "rational," and "dominant" as masculine and "gentle," "sympathetic," and "dependent" as feminine—stereotyping that increases steadily with age (Best et al., 1977; Serbin, Powlishta, & Gulko, 1993). Children derive these distinctions from observing gender differences as well as from adult treatment. Parents, for example, use more directive speech (telling the child what to do) with girls, are less likely to encourage girls to make their own decisions, and are less likely to express confidence in girls when praising them, through such statements as, "You must really enjoy your work!" (Leaper, Anderson, & Sanders, 1998; Pomerantz & Ruble, 1998).

Shortly after entering elementary school, children figure out which academic subjects and skill areas are "masculine" and which are "feminine." They regard reading, art, and music as more for girls, and mathematics, science, athletics, and mechanical skills as more for boys (Eccles, Jacobs, & Harold, 1990; Jacobs & Weisz, 1994). These stereotypes influence children's preferences for certain subjects and, in turn, how well they do at them. For example, boys feel more competent than girls at math and science, whereas girls feel more competent than boys at reading—even when children of equal skill level are compared (Andre et al., 1999; Eccles et al., 1993b). As we will see in Chapter 15, gender stereotypes of achievement become realities for many young people by adolescence.

Furthermore, girls seem to adopt a more general stereotype of males as smarter than females, which they apply to themselves. In a study of over 2,000 second to sixth graders from diverse cultures (Eastern and Western Europe, Japan, Russia, and the United States), girls consistently had higher school grades than boys. Yet they did not report stronger beliefs in their own ability, despite being aware of their performance standing. Compared with boys, girls discounted their talent (Stetsenko et al., 2000). Earlier in this chapter, we noted that when girls have difficulty with school tasks, teachers and parents are likely to tell them that they lack ability. Apparently, gender stereotyping of academic talent occurs in many parts of the world.

Although school-age children are aware of many stereotypes, they have an open-minded view of what males and females *can do*. As they develop the capacity to integrate conflicting social cues, children realize that a person's sex is not a certain predictor of his or her personality traits, activities, and behaviors. By the end of the school years, children regard gender typing as socially rather than biologically influenced (Bigler, 1995; Taylor, 1996). But acknowledging that people *can* cross gender lines does not mean that children always *approve* of doing so. One study showed that both children and adults are fairly tolerant of girls' violations of gender roles. But they judge boys' violations (such as "playing with dolls") harshly—as just as bad as violating a moral rule! (Levy, Taylor, & Gelman, 1995).

peer victimization
A destructive form of peer interaction in which certain children become frequent targets of verbal and physical attacks or other forms of abuse.

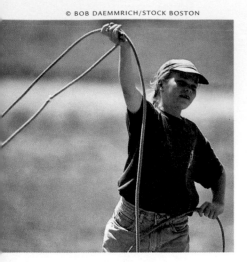

© BOB DAEMMRICH/STOCK BOSTON

During middle childhood, girls feel freer than boys to engage in "cross-gender" activities. This 10-year-old perfects her lasso technique.

GENDER IDENTITY AND BEHAVIOR

Boys' and girls' gender identities follow different paths in middle childhood. From third to sixth grade, boys strengthen their identification with the "masculine" role. In contrast, girls' identification with "feminine" attributes declines. Although girls still lean toward the "feminine" side, they begin to describe themselves as having some "other-gender" characteristics (Serbin, Powlishta, & Gulko, 1993). This difference also arises in the activities children choose in middle childhood. Whereas boys usually stick to "masculine" pursuits, girls experiment with a wider range of options. Besides cooking, sewing, and baby-sitting, they join organized sports teams, take up science projects, and build forts in the backyard.

In Chapter 10, we saw that parents are especially concerned about boys' gender-role conformity. Pressure from gender-segregated peer groups is similar. A tomboyish girl can make her way into boys' activities without losing status with her female peers, but a boy who hangs out with girls is likely to be ridiculed and rejected. Finally, perhaps school-age girls realize that society attaches greater prestige to "masculine" characteristics. As a result, they want to try some of the activities and behaviors associated with the more highly valued gender role.

CULTURAL INFLUENCES ON GENDER TYPING

Although the sex differences just described are typical, they do not apply to children everywhere. Girls are less likely to experiment with "masculine" activities in cultures and subcultures in which the gap between male and female roles is especially wide. And when social and economic conditions make it necessary for boys to take over "feminine" tasks, their personalities and behaviors are less stereotyped.

For example, in Nyansongo, a small agricultural settlement in Kenya, mothers work 4 to 5 hours a day in the gardens. They assign the care of young children, the tending of the cooking fire, and the washing of dishes to older siblings. Since children of both sexes perform these duties, girls are relieved of total responsibility for "feminine" tasks and have more time to interact with agemates. Their greater freedom and independence lead them to score higher than girls of other village and tribal cultures in dominance, assertiveness, and playful roughhousing. In contrast, boys' caregiving responsibilities mean that they often engage in help-giving and emotional support (Whiting & Edwards, 1988a, 1988b).

Do these findings suggest that boys in Western cultures should be assigned more "cross-gender" tasks? The consequences of doing so are not straightforward. Research shows that when fathers hold traditional gender-role beliefs and their sons engage in "feminine" housework, boys experience strain in the father–child relationship, feel stressed by their responsibilities, and judge themselves as less competent (McHale et al., 1990). So parental values may need to be consistent with task assignments for children to benefit.

Ask YOURSELF...

review   *Return to Chapter 10, page 393, and review the concept of* androgyny. *Which of the two sexes is more androgynous in middle childhood, and why?*

apply   *Apply your understanding of attributions to rejected children's social self-esteem. How are rejected children likely to explain their failure to gain peer acceptance? What impact on future efforts to get along with agemates will those attributions have?*

connect   *Cite similarities in school-age children's more mature self-concept and understanding of friendship.*

reflect   *Recall a popular child, a rejected child, a bully, and a victim from your own childhood. Describe the social behavior of each, and indicate whether it is consistent with research findings on peer acceptance.*

Family Influences

As children move into school, peer, and community contexts, the parent–child relationship changes. We will see that a gradual lessening of direct control supports development, as long as it is built on continuing parental warmth and involvement.

Our discussion will also reveal that families in industrialized nations have become more diverse. Today, there are fewer births per family unit, more lesbian and gay parents who are open about their sexual orientation, and more never-married parents. In addition, transitions in family life over the past several decades—a dramatic rise in marital breakup, remarried parents, and employed mothers—have reshaped the family system.

As you consider this array of family forms, think back to Bronfenbrenner's ecological systems theory. Notice how children's well-being continues to depend on the quality of family interaction, which is sustained by supportive ties to kin and community and favorable policies in the larger culture.

PARENT–CHILD RELATIONSHIPS

In middle childhood, the amount of time children spend with parents declines dramatically. The child's growing independence means that parents must deal with new issues. "I've struggled with how many chores to assign, how much allowance to give, and whether their friends are good influences," noted Rena. "And then there's the problem of how to keep track of them when they're out of the house or even when they're home and I'm not there to see what's going on."

Although parents face new concerns, child rearing actually becomes easier for those who established an authoritative style during the early years. Reasoning works more effectively with school-age children because of their greater capacity for logical thinking and respect for parents' expert knowledge (Braine et al., 1991). Of course, older children sometimes use their cognitive powers to bargain and negotiate. "Mom," Joey pleaded for the third time, "if you let Terry and me go to the mall tonight, I'll rake all the leaves in the yard, I promise."

Fortunately, parents can appeal to the child's better developed sense of self-esteem, humor, and morality to resolve these difficulties. "Joey, you have a test tomorrow," Rena responded. "You'll be unhappy at the results if you stay out late and don't study. Come on, no more wheeler-dealering!" Perhaps because parents and children have, over time, learned how to resolve conflicts, coercive discipline declines over the school years (Collins, Harris, & Susman, 1996).

As children demonstrate that they can manage daily activities and responsibilities, effective parents gradually shift control from adult to child. This does not mean that they let go entirely. Instead, they engage in **coregulation,** a form of supervision in which they exercise general oversight while permitting children to be in charge of moment-by-moment decision making. Coregulation grows out of a cooperative relationship between parent and child—one based on give-and-take and mutual respect. Parents must guide and monitor from a distance and effectively communicate expectations when they are with their children. And children must inform parents of their whereabouts, activities, and problems so parents can intervene when necessary (Maccoby, 1984). Coregulation supports and protects children while preparing them for adolescence, when they will make many important decisions themselves.

Although school-age children often press for greater independence, they also know how much they need their parents' support. In one study, fifth and sixth graders described parents as the most influential people in their lives. They often turned to them for affection, advice, enhancement of self-worth, and assistance with everyday problems (Furman & Buhrmester, 1992).

SIBLINGS

In addition to parents and friends, siblings are important sources of companionship, help with difficult tasks, and emotional support for school-age children. Yet sibling rivalry tends to increase in middle childhood. As children participate in a wider range of activities, parents

coregulation
A transitional form of supervision in which parents exercise general oversight while permitting children to be in charge of moment-by-moment decision making.

Although sibling rivalry tends to increase in middle childhood, siblings also provide one another with emotional support and help with difficult tasks.

often compare siblings' traits and accomplishments. The child who gets less attention, more disapproval, and fewer material resources is likely to resent a sibling who receives more favorable treatment (Brody, Stoneman, & McCoy, 1994; Dunn, 1996).

When siblings are close in age and the same sex, parental comparisons are more frequent, resulting in more quarreling and antagonism. This effect is particularly strong when fathers prefer one child. Perhaps because fathers usually spend less time with children, their favoritism is more noticeable and triggers greater anger (Brody, Stoneman, & McCoy, 1992; Brody et al., 1992).

Siblings often take steps to reduce this rivalry by differentiating themselves from one another (Huston, 1983). For example, two brothers I know deliberately selected different school subjects, athletic pursuits, and music lessons. If the older one did especially well at an activity, the younger one did not want to try it. Of course, parents can reduce these effects by making an effort not to compare children. But some feedback about their competencies is inevitable, and as siblings strive to win recognition for their own uniqueness, they shape important aspects of each other's development.

Birth order plays an important role in sibling experiences. For a time, oldest children have their parents' attention all to themselves. Even after brothers and sisters are born, they receive greater pressure for mature behavior from parents. For this reason, oldest children are slightly advantaged in IQ and school achievement (Zajonc & Mullally, 1997). Younger siblings, in contrast, tend to be more popular with agemates, perhaps as a result of becoming skilled at negotiating and compromising from interacting with more powerful brothers and sisters (Miller & Maruyama, 1976).

ONE-CHILD FAMILIES

Although sibling relationships bring many benefits, they are not essential for normal development. Contrary to popular belief, only children are not spoiled and selfish. Instead, they are just as well adjusted as other children and advantaged in some respects. Children growing up in one-child families score higher in self-esteem and achievement motivation. Consequently, they do better in school and attain higher levels of education (Falbo, 1992). A major reason may be that only children have somewhat closer relationships with parents, who exert more pressure for mastery and accomplishment (Falbo & Polit, 1986).

Favorable development also characterizes only children in China, where a one-child family policy has been strictly enforced for 2 decades to control overpopulation. Compared with agemates who have siblings, Chinese only children are advanced in performance on a variety of cognitive tasks and in academic achievement (Falbo & Poston, 1993; Jiao, Ji, & Jing, 1996). They also feel more emotionally secure, perhaps because government disapproval promotes tension in families with more than one child (Falbo & Poston, 1993; Yang et al., 1995). Although many Chinese adults remain convinced that the one-child family policy breeds self-centered "little emperors," Chinese only children do not differ from children with siblings in social skills and peer acceptance (Chen, Rubin, & Li, 1994).

Chinese only children report an earlier first autobiographical memory and give more self-focused descriptions of themselves than do their agemates with siblings (Wang, Leichtman, & White, 1998). The difference may be due to the attention Chinese parents and grandparents bestow on an only child—conversing often about past experiences and highlighting the child's thoughts, feelings, and other attributes.

GAY AND LESBIAN FAMILIES

Several million American gay men and lesbians are parents, most through heterosexual marriages that ended in divorce, some through adoption or reproductive technologies (Patterson & Chan, 1999). In the past, laws assuming that homosexuals could not be adequate parents led those who divorced a heterosexual partner to lose custody of their children.

Today, several states hold that sexual orientation is irrelevant to custody. In others, fierce prejudice against homosexual parents still prevails.

Families headed by a homosexual parent or a gay or lesbian couple are very similar to those of heterosexuals. Gay and lesbian parents are as effective at the parental role, and sometimes more so. Indeed, some research indicates that gay fathers are more consistent in setting limits and responding to their children's needs than are heterosexual fathers, perhaps because gay men's less traditional gender identity fosters involvement with children (Bigner & Jacobsen, 1989). In lesbian families, quality of mother–child interaction is at least as positive as in heterosexual families. And children of lesbian mothers regard their mother's partner as very much a parent (Brewaeys et al., 1997). Whether born to or adopted by their parents or conceived through donor insemination, children in homosexual families are as well adjusted as other children, and the large majority are heterosexual (Bailey et al., 1995; Chan, Raboy, & Patterson, 1998; Golombok & Tasker, 1996).

Overall, children of homosexuals can be distinguished from other children only by issues related to living in a nonsupportive society. The greatest concern of gay and lesbian parents is that their children will be stigmatized by their parents' sexual orientation (Hare, 1994).

TOM MCKITTERICK/IMPACT VISUALS

Homosexual parents are as committed to and as effective at child rearing as are heterosexual parents—and sometimes more so. Their children are well adjusted, and the large majority develop a heterosexual orientation.

NEVER-MARRIED SINGLE-PARENT FAMILIES

About 10 percent of American children have parents who have never married. Of these, 89 percent are mothers, 11 percent fathers (U.S. Bureau of the Census, 2000). More single women over age 30 in high-status occupations have become parents in recent years. However, they are still few in number, and little is known about how their children fare.

The largest group of never-married parents are African-American young women. Over 60 percent of births to black women in their twenties occur out of wedlock, compared with 18 percent to white women. African-American women postpone marriage more and childbirth less than do all other American ethnic groups (Glick, 1997). Job loss, persisting unemployment, and consequent inability of many black men to support a family have contributed to the postponement of marriage.

Never-married black mothers tap the extended family, especially their own mothers, for help in caring for children (Gasden, 1999). For most, marriage occurs several years after birth of the first child, not necessarily to the child's biological father. Nevertheless, these couples function much like other first-marriage parents. Their children often are unaware that the father is a stepfather, and parents do not report the child-rearing difficulties associated with remarriage that we will take up shortly (Ganong & Coleman, 1994).

Still, single mothers find it harder to overcome poverty. Many children in single-mother homes display problems associated with economic hardship. Also, when children of never-married mothers lack the warmth and involvement of a father, they achieve less well in school and engage in more antisocial behavior than do children in low-income, first-marriage families (Coley, 1998; Florsheim, Tolan, & Gorman-Smith, 1998). Strengthening social support, education, and employment opportunities for low-income parents would encourage marriage as well as help unmarried-mother families.

DIVORCE

Children's interactions with parents and siblings are affected by other aspects of family life. Joey and Lizzie's relationship, Rena told me, had been particularly negative only a few years before. Joey pushed, hit, taunted, and called Lizzie names. Although she tried to retaliate, she was little match for Joey's larger size. The arguments usually ended with Lizzie running in tears to her mother. Joey and Lizzie's fighting coincided with Rena and her husband's growing marital unhappiness. When Joey was 8 and Lizzie 5, their father, Drake, moved out.

The children were not alone in having to weather this traumatic event. Between 1960 and 1985, the divorce rate in the United States doubled and then stabilized. Currently, it is the

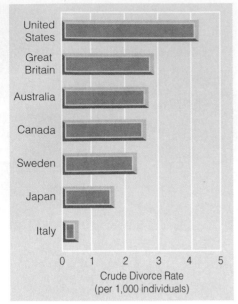

FIGURE 13.3

Divorce rate in seven industrialized nations. The divorce rate in the United States is the highest in the world. (From Australian Bureau of Statistics, 2000; Statistics Canada, 2000; U.S. Bureau of the Census, 2000; United Nations, 1999.)

highest in the world (see Figure 13.3). About half of American marriages end in divorce; three-fourths of these involve children. At any given time, about one-fourth of American children live in single-parent households. Although the large majority reside with their mothers, the percentage in father-headed households has increased steadily. Currently, it is about 15 percent (Hetherington & Stanley-Hagan, 1997).

The average child spends 5 years in a single-parent home, or almost a third of childhood. For many, divorce eventually leads to new family relationships. About two-thirds of divorced parents marry a second time. Half the children in this situation eventually experience a third major change—the end of their parent's second marriage (Hetherington & Henderson, 1997).

These figures reveal that divorce is not a single event in the lives of parents and children. Instead, it is a transition that leads to a variety of new living arrangements, accompanied by changes in housing, income, and family roles and responsibilities. Since the 1960s, many studies have reported that marital breakup is quite stressful for children (Hetherington, Bridges, & Insabella, 1998). But the research also reveals great individual differences in how children respond. The custodial parent's psychological health, the child's characteristics, and social supports within the family and surrounding community contribute to children's adjustment.

■ **IMMEDIATE CONSEQUENCES.** "Things were worst during the period in which Drake and I decided to separate," Rena reflected. "We fought over everything—from custody of the children to the living room furniture, and the kids really suffered. Once, sobbing, Lizzie told me she was 'sorry she made Daddy go away.' Joey kicked and threw things at home and didn't do his work at school. In the midst of everything, I could hardly deal with their problems. We had to sell the house; I couldn't afford it alone. And I needed a better-paying job."

Rena's description captures conditions in many newly divorced households. Family conflict often rises for a time as parents argue over child custody and personal belongings. Once one parent moves out, additional events threaten supportive interactions between parents and children. Mother-headed households typically experience a sharp drop in income. Three-fourths of divorced mothers in the United States get less than the full amount of child support from the absent father or none at all (Children's Defense Fund, 2000). They often have to move to new housing for economic reasons, reducing ties to neighbors and friends.

These life circumstances often lead to high maternal stress and a disorganized family situation called "minimal parenting" (Hetherington, 1989; Wallerstein & Kelly, 1980). "Meals and bedtimes were at all hours, the house didn't get cleaned, and I stopped taking Joey and Lizzie on weekend outings," said Rena. As children react with distress and anger to their less secure home lives, discipline may become harsh and inconsistent. Contact with noncustodial fathers decreases over time (Hetherington, Bridges, & Insabella, 1998; Lamb, 1999). When fathers see their children only occasionally, they are inclined to be permissive and indulgent. This often conflicts with the mother's style of parenting and makes her task of managing the child on a day-to-day basis even more difficult.

In view of these changes, it is not surprising that children experience painful emotional reactions. But the intensity of their feelings and the way these are expressed vary with the child's age, temperament, and sex.

Children's Age. Five-year-old Lizzie's fear that she had caused her father to leave home is not unusual. The cognitive immaturity of preschool and early school-age children makes it difficult for them to grasp the reasons behind their parents' separation. Younger children often blame themselves and take the marital breakup as a sign that both parents may abandon them. They may whine and cling, displaying intense separation anxiety. Preschoolers are especially likely to fantasize that their parents will get back together (Hetherington, 1989; Wallerstein, Corbin, & Lewis, 1988).

Older children are better able to understand the reasons behind their parents' divorce. They recognize that strong differences of opinion, incompatible personalities, and lack of caring for one another are responsible (Mazur, 1993). The ability to accurately assign blame may reduce some of the pain that children feel. Still, many school-age and adolescent young-sters react strongly to the end of their parents' marriage, particularly when family conflict is high. Escaping into undesirable peer activities—running away, truancy, early sexual activity, and delinquent behavior—and dropping out of school are common (Hetherington & Stan-ley-Hagan, 1999; Simons & Chao, 1996).

However, not all older children react this way. For some—especially the oldest child in the family—divorce can trigger more mature behavior. These youngsters may willingly take on extra burdens, such as household tasks, care and protection of younger siblings, and emo-tional support of a depressed, anxious mother. But if these demands are too great, older chil-dren may eventually become resentful and withdraw into some of the destructive behavior patterns just described (Hetherington, 1995, 1999b).

Children's Temperament and Sex. When temperamentally difficult children are exposed to stressful life events and inadequate parenting, their problems magnify (Lengua et al., 2000). In contrast, easy children are less often targets of parental anger and also are better at coping with adversity when it hits. After a moderately stressful divorce, some easy children (usually girls) actually emerge with enhanced coping skills (Hetherington, 1995).

These findings help us understand sex differences in children's response to divorce. Girls sometimes respond as Lizzie did, with internalizing reactions, such as crying, self-criticism, and withdrawal. More often, they show demanding, attention-getting behavior. But in mother-custody families, boys experience more serious adjustment problems. Recall from Chapter 10 that boys are more active and noncompliant—behaviors that increase with expo-sure to parental conflict and inconsistent discipline. Studies in Great Britain and the United States reveal that long before the marital breakup, many sons of divorcing couples were impulsive and defiant—behaviors that may have contributed to as well as been caused by their parents' problems (Cherlin et al., 1991; Shaw, Winslow, & Flanagan, 1999). As a result, these boys entered the period of turmoil surrounding divorce with a reduced capacity to cope with family stress.

Perhaps because their behavior is so unruly, boys of divorcing parents receive less emo-tional support from mothers, teachers, and peers. And as Joey's behavior toward Lizzie illus-trates, the coercive cycles of interaction between boys and their divorced mothers soon spread to sibling relations (MacKinnon, 1989). These outcomes compound boys' difficulties. School achievement declines for many children in the aftermath of divorce, but school prob-lems are greater for boys (Guidubaldi & Cleminshaw, 1985).

■ **LONG-TERM CONSEQUENCES.** Rena eventually found better-paying work and gained control over the daily operation of the household. Her own feelings of anger and rejection also declined. And after several meetings with a counselor, Rena and Drake realized the harmful impact of their quarreling on Joey and Lizzie. They resolved to keep the children out of future disagreements. Drake visited regularly and handled Joey's unruliness with firmness and consistency. Soon Joey's school performance improved, his behavior problems subsided, and both children seemed calmer and happier.

Most children show improved adjustment by 2 years after divorce. Yet a few continue to have serious difficulties into adulthood (Chase-Lansdale, Cherlin, & Kiernan, 1995). Boys and children with difficult temperaments are especially likely to drop out of school and dis-play antisocial behavior in adolescence. For both sexes, divorce is linked to problems with adolescent sexuality and with development of intimate ties. Young people who experienced parental divorce—especially more than once—display higher rates of early sexual activity, adolescent parenthood, and divorce in their adult lives (Booth, 1999; Cherlin, Kiernan, & Chase-Lansdale, 1995; Hetherington, 1997).

The overriding factor in positive adjustment following divorce is effective parenting—in particular, how well the custodial parent handles stress and shields the child from family con-flict, and the extent to which each parent engages in authoritative child rearing (Amato & Gilbreth, 1999; Whiteside & Becker, 2000). In a study of 8- to 15-year-olds whose parents had divorced in the previous 2 years, children reporting high maternal warmth and consistency

This divorced father welcomes his daughters for a visit. Keeping fathers involved in parenting and in assisting with financial support has great benefits for children's development. And when parents set aside their disagreements and support one another in their child-rearing roles, children of divorce have the best chance of growing up competent, stable, and happy.

divorce mediation
A series of meetings between divorcing adults and a trained professional, who tries to help them settle disputes. Aimed at avoiding legal battles that intensify family conflict.

joint custody
A child custody arrangement following divorce in which the court grants both parents equal say in important decisions about the child's upbringing.

of discipline were better able than other children to withstand divorce stressors and had the fewest adjustment problems (Wolchik et al., 2000).

Contact with fathers is also important. For girls, a good father–child relationship appears to protect against early sexual activity and unhappy romantic involvements. For boys, it seems to affect overall psychological well-being. In fact, several studies indicate that outcomes for sons are better when the father is the custodial parent (Camara & Resnick, 1988; Clarke-Stewart & Hayward, 1996). Fathers are more likely to praise a boy's good behavior and less likely to ignore his disruptiveness. The father's image of greater power and authority may also help him obtain more compliance from a son. Furthermore, boys in father-custody families may benefit from greater involvement of both parents, since noncustodial mothers participate more in their children's lives than do noncustodial fathers. One study showed that when both the mother and father engage in competent parenting, boys in single-parent families of divorce are at no greater risk for conduct problems than are boys in two-parent families (Simons et al., 1999).

Although divorce is painful for children, remaining in a high-conflict intact family is worse than making the transition to a low-conflict, single-parent household (Emery, 1999a; Hetherington, 1999a). When divorcing parents put aside their disagreements and support one another in their child-rearing roles, children have the best chance of growing up competent, stable, and happy. Caring extended-family members, teachers, siblings, and friends also reduce the likelihood that divorce will result in long-term disruption (DeGarmo & Forgatch, 1999; Grych & Fincham, 1997).

■ **DIVORCE MEDIATION, JOINT CUSTODY, AND CHILD SUPPORT.** Awareness that divorce is highly stressful for children and families has led to community-based services aimed at helping them through this difficult time. One is **divorce mediation.** It consists of a series of meetings between divorcing adults and a trained professional, who tries to help them settle disputes, such as property division and child custody. Its purpose is to avoid legal battles that intensify family conflict. Research reveals that mediation increases out-of-court settlements, compliance with these agreements, cooperation between parents in child rearing, and feelings of well-being reported by divorcing parents and their children (Emery, 1999; Walton, Oliver, & Griffin, 1999).

A relatively new child custody option tries to keep both parents involved with children. In **joint custody,** the court grants the mother and father equal say in important decisions about the child's upbringing. Joint custody results in a variety of living arrangements. In most instances, children reside with one parent and see the other on a fixed schedule, much like the typical sole-custody situation. But in other cases, parents share physical custody, and children must move between homes and sometimes schools and peer groups. These transitions introduce a new kind of instability that is especially hard on some children (Johnston, Kline, & Tschann, 1989). The success of joint custody requires a cooperative relationship between divorcing parents. If they continue to quarrel, it prolongs children's exposure to a hostile family atmosphere (Emery, 1999b).

Finally, many single-parent families depend on child support from the absent parent to relieve financial strain. In response to a recent federal law, all states have established procedures for withholding wages from parents who fail to make these court-ordered payments. Although child support is usually not enough to lift a single-parent family out of poverty, it can ease the burden substantially. An added benefit is that fathers are more likely to maintain contact with noncustodial children if they pay child support (Garfinkel & McLanahan, 1995). The Caregiving Concerns table on the following page summarizes ways to help children adjust to their parents' divorce.

BLENDED FAMILIES

"If you get married to Wendell and Daddy gets married to Carol," Lizzie wondered aloud to Rena, "then I'll have two sisters and one more brother. And let's see, how many grandmothers and grandfathers? Gosh, a lot!" exclaimed Lizzie. "But what will I call them all?" she asked, looking worried.

Caregiving Concerns
Helping Children Adjust to Their Parents' Divorce

SUGGESTION	EXPLANATION
Shield children from conflict.	Witnessing intense parental conflict is very damaging to children. If one parent insists on expressing hostility, children fare better if the other parent does not respond in kind.
Provide children with as much continuity, familiarity, and predictability as possible.	Children adjust better during the period surrounding divorce when their lives have some stability—for example, the same school, bedroom, baby-sitter, playmates, and daily schedule.
Explain the divorce and tell children what to expect.	Children are more likely to develop fears of abandonment if they are not prepared for their parents' separation. They should be told that their mother and father will not be living together anymore, which parent will be moving out, and when they will be able to see that parent. If possible, mother and father should explain the divorce together. Parents should provide a reason for the divorce that the child can understand and assure the child that he is not to blame.
Emphasize the permanence of the divorce.	Fantasies of parents getting back together can prevent children from accepting the reality of their current life. Children should be told that the divorce is final and they cannot change that fact.
Respond sympathetically to children's feelings.	Children need a supportive and understanding response to their feelings of sadness, fear, and anger. For children to adjust well, their painful emotions must be acknowledged, not denied or avoided.
Engage in authoritative parenting.	Provide children with affection and acceptance as well as reasonable demands for mature behavior and consistent, rational discipline. Parents who engage in authoritative parenting greatly reduce their children's risk of maladjustment following divorce.
Promote a continuing relationship with both parents.	When parents disentangle their lingering hostility toward the former spouse from the child's need for a continuing relationship with the other parent, children adjust well. Grandparents and other extended-family members can help by not taking sides.

Source: Teyber, 1992.

Life in a single-parent family is often temporary. Many parents find a new partner within a few years. Others cohabit, or share an intimate sexual relationship and residence with a partner outside of marriage. As Lizzie's comments indicate, entry into these **blended,** or **reconstituted, families** leads to a complex set of new relationships. For some children, this expanded family network is a positive turn of events that brings greater adult attention. But for most, it presents difficult adjustments. Stepparents often use different child-rearing practices than the child was used to, and having to switch to new rules and expectations can be stressful. In addition, children often regard steprelatives as "intruders." But how well children adapt is, once again, related to the overall quality of family functioning (Bray, 1999). This often depends on which parent forms a new relationship and on the child's age and sex. As we will see, older children and girls seem to have the hardest time.

■ **MOTHER–STEPFATHER FAMILIES.** The most frequent form of blended family is a mother–stepfather arrangement, since mothers generally retain custody of the child. Boys usually adjust quickly. They welcome a stepfather who is warm and responsive and who offers relief from the coercive cycles of interaction that tend to build with their divorced mothers. Mothers' friction with sons also declines due to greater economic security, another adult to share household tasks, and an end to loneliness (Stevenson & Black, 1995). In contrast, girls adapt less favorably when custodial mothers remarry. Stepfathers disrupt the close ties many girls established with their mother in the single-parent family, and girls often react to the new arrangement with sulky, resistant behavior (Hetherington, 1993).

blended, or **reconstituted, family**
A family structure resulting from cohabitation or remarriage that includes parent, child, and steprelatives.

Note, however, that age affects these findings. Older school-age children and adolescents of both sexes display more irresponsible, acting out, and antisocial behavior than do their agemates in nonstepfamilies. Parenting in stepfamilies—particularly families with stepsiblings—is highly challenging. Often parents are warmer and more involved with their biological children than with their stepchildren (Hetherington, Henderson, & Reiss, 1999). Older children are more likely to notice and challenge unfair treatment and other negative consequences of stepfamily living, sparking conflict-ridden family interaction.

■ **FATHER–STEPMOTHER FAMILIES.** Research reveals more confusion for children in father–stepmother families. Remarriage of noncustodial fathers often leads to reduced contact. They tend to withdraw from their "previous" families, more so if they have daughters than sons (Hetherington & Henderson, 1997). When fathers have custody, children typically react negatively to remarriage. One reason is that children living with fathers often start out with more problems. Perhaps the biological mother could no longer handle the unruly child (usually a boy), so the father and his new wife are faced with a youngster who has serious behavior problems. In other instances, the father is granted custody because of a very close relationship with the child, and his remarriage disrupts this bond (Buchanan, Maccoby, & Dornbusch, 1996).

Girls, especially, have a hard time getting along with their stepmothers. Sometimes (as just mentioned) this occurs because the girl's relationship with her father is threatened by the remarriage. In addition, girls often become entangled in loyalty conflicts between their two mother figures. But the longer girls live in father–stepmother households, the more positive their interaction with stepmothers becomes (Hetherington & Jodl, 1994). With time and patience they do adjust, and eventually girls benefit from the support of a second mother figure.

■ **SUPPORT FOR BLENDED FAMILIES.** In blended families, as in divorce, multiple pathways lead to diverse outcomes. Family life education and therapy can help parents and children adapt to the complexities of their new circumstances. Effective approaches encourage stepparents to move into their new roles gradually by first building a friendly relationship with the child. Only when a warm bond has formed between stepparents and stepchildren is more active parenting possible (Ganong & Coleman, 2000). In addition, therapy can offer couples help in forming a "parenting coalition" through which they cooperate and provide consistency in child rearing. By limiting loyalty conflicts, this allows children to benefit from stepparent relationships and increased diversity in their lives.

MATERNAL EMPLOYMENT AND DUAL-EARNER FAMILIES

Today, single and married American mothers are in the labor force in nearly equal proportions, and 78 percent of those with 6- to 13-year-olds are employed (U.S. Bureau of the Census, 2000). In Chapter 7, we saw that the impact of maternal employment on infant development depends on the quality of substitute care and the continuing parent–child relationship. This same conclusion applies during later years.

■ **CHILD CARE FOR SCHOOL-AGE CHILDREN.** High-quality child care is vital for parents' peace of mind and children's well-being, even during middle childhood. In recent years, much public concern has been voiced about the estimated 2.4 million 5- to 13-year-olds in the United States who regularly look after themselves during after-school hours.

Research on these **self-care children** reveals inconsistent findings. Some studies report that they suffer from low self-esteem, antisocial behavior, poor academic achievement, and fearfulness, whereas others show no such effects. Children's maturity and the way they spend their time seem to explain these contradictions. Among younger school-age children, those who spend more hours alone have more adjustment

In this after-school program in Los Angeles, children spend time productively and enjoyably while their parents are at work. A community volunteer assists children with learning and completing homework. Children who attend such programs display better school grades, work habits, and peer relations.

AMY ETRA/PHOTOEDIT

Caregiving Concerns
Helping Self-Care Children

SIGNS OF CHILDREN'S READINESS FOR SELF-CARE	HELPING CHILDREN MANAGE ON THEIR OWN
At least 9 or 10 years old[a]	Establish a telephone check-in procedure with the parent, a relative, or a friend.
Can follow important rules and directions	
Can recognize dangerous situations and respond appropriately	Leave emergency numbers, as well as the numbers of friends and neighbors, by the telephone.
Can make phone calls and take messages in an emergency	Teach safety skills, including a fire escape plan and basic first aid.
Can use household appliances safely	
Can respond to strangers properly (not opening the door, not saying she is alone)	Structure the child's after-school time by assigning regular responsibilities.
Can keep track of keys and can lock and unlock doors	Establish rules about having friends over, going out, watching television, and using appliances.
Can resolve sibling conflicts independently	Select a safe, well-traveled route home from school, and do not let the child wear a house key on a chain that advertises
Does not feel frightened or unhappy	his self-care status.

[a]Before age 9 or 10, children should not be left unsupervised because they do not yet have the cognitive and social skills to deal with emergencies.
Sources: Galambos & Maggs, 1991; Peterson, 1989.

difficulties (Vandell & Posner, 1999). As children become old enough to look after themselves, those who have a history of authoritative child rearing, are monitored from a distance by parental telephone calls, and have regular after-school chores appear responsible and well adjusted. In contrast, children left to their own devices are more likely to bend to peer pressures and engage in antisocial behavior (Steinberg, 1986).

The Caregiving Concerns table above lists signs of readiness for self-care, along with ways to help children manage on their own. Unfortunately, when children are not mature enough to handle the self-care arrangement, many employed parents have few alternatives. After-school programs for 6- to 13-year-olds are not yet widespread, and programs vary greatly in quality.

When high-quality "after-care" is available with a staff trained in child development; a generous adult–child ratio; positive adult–child communication; and stimulating, varied activities, children show better social skills and psychological adjustment (Pettit et al., 1997; Pierce, Hamm, & Vandell, 1999). And low-SES children of both sexes who otherwise would have few opportunities for enrichment activities (scouting, music lessons, and organized sports) display better work habits, school grades, and peer relations and fewer behavior problems. (Posner & Vandell, 1994, 1999).

■ **MATERNAL EMPLOYMENT AND CHILD DEVELOPMENT.** In addition to child-care quality, other factors—the mother's work satisfaction, the support she receives from her partner, and the child's sex—have a bearing on how maternal employment affects children's development. Mothers who enjoy their work and remain committed to parenting have children who show especially positive adjustment—a higher sense of self-esteem, more positive family and peer relations, less gender-stereotyped beliefs, and better grades in school. Girls, especially, profit from the image of female competence. Daughters of employed mothers perceive the woman's role as involving more freedom of choice and satisfaction and are more achievement and career oriented (Hoffman, 2000; Williams & Radin, 1993).

These benefits result from parenting practices. Employed mothers who value their parenting role are more likely to engage in authoritative child rearing and coregulation—granting

self-care children
Children who look after themselves during after-school hours.

their child greater independence with oversight. Also, children in dual-earner households devote more daily hours to doing homework under parental guidance and participate more in household chores. And maternal employment results in more time with fathers, who take on greater child-care responsibility (Gottfried et al., 1999; Hoffman & Youngblade, 1999). More paternal contact is related to higher intelligence and achievement, mature social behavior, and flexible gender-role attitudes (Gottfried, 1991; Radin, 1994).

However, when employment places heavy demands on the mother's schedule, children are at risk for ineffective parenting. Working long hours and spending little time with school-age children are associated with less favorable adjustment (Moorehouse, 1991). In contrast, part-time employment seems to have benefits for children of all ages, probably because it permits mothers to meet the needs of children with a wide range of characteristics (Lerner & Abrams, 1994; Williams & Radin, 1993).

■ **SUPPORT FOR EMPLOYED PARENTS AND THEIR FAMILIES.** As long as mothers have the necessary supports to engage in effective child rearing, maternal employment offers children many advantages. In dual-earner families, the husband's willingness to share responsibilities is crucial. If the father helps very little or not at all, the mother carries a double load, at home and at work, leading to fatigue, distress, and reduced time and energy for children.

Employed mothers and dual-earner parents need assistance from work settings and communities in their child-rearing roles. Part-time employment, flexible schedules, job-sharing, and paid leave when children are ill help parents juggle the demands of work and child rearing. Although these supports are available in other industrialized nations, at present only unpaid employment leave is mandated by U.S. federal law. Equal pay and employment opportunities for women are also important. Because these policies enhance financial status and morale, they improve the way mothers feel and behave when they arrive home at the end of the working day.

Ask YOURSELF...

review   List findings from our discussion of the family that highlight the influence of fathers on children's development.

apply   "How come you don't study hard and get good grades like your sister?" a mother exclaimed in exasperation after seeing her son's poor report card. What impact do remarks like this have on sibling interaction, and why?

apply   Steve and Marissa are in the midst of an acrimonious divorce. Their 9-year-old son Dennis has become hostile and defiant. How can Steve and Marissa help Dennis adjust?

connect   How does each level in Bronfenbrenner's ecological systems theory—microsystem, mesosystem, exosystem, and macrosystem—contribute to the effects of maternal employment on children's development?

Some Common Problems of Development

Throughout our discussion we have considered a variety of stressful experiences that place children at risk for future problems. In the following sections we touch on two more areas of concern: school-age children's fears and anxieties and the devastating consequences of child sexual abuse. Finally, we review factors that help school-age children cope effectively with stress.

FEARS AND ANXIETIES

Although fears of the dark, thunder and lightning, animals, and supernatural beings (often stimulated by movies and television) persist into middle childhood, older children's anxieties are also directed toward new concerns. As children begin to understand the realities of the wider world, the possibility of personal harm (being robbed, stabbed, or shot) and media events (war and disasters) often trouble them. Other common worries include academic failure, separation from parents, parents' health, physical injuries, the possibility of dying, and peer rejection (Muris et al., 2000; Silverman, La Greca, & Wasserstein, 1995).

Children's fears are shaped, in part, by their culture. For example, in China, where self-restraint and complying with social standards are highly valued, more children mention failure and adult criticism as salient fears than in Australia or the United States. Chinese children, however, are not more fearful overall. The number and intensity of fears they report resemble those of Western children (Ollendick et al., 1996).

Most children handle their fears constructively, by talking about them with parents, teachers, and friends and by relying on the more sophisticated emotional self-regulation strategies that develop in middle childhood. Consequently, fears decline steadily with age, especially for girls, who express more fears than do boys throughout childhood and adolescence (Gullone & King, 1997).

From 10 to 20 percent of school-age children develop an intense, unmanageable anxiety of some kind (Barrios & Dell, 1998). **School phobia** is an example. Typically, children with this disorder are middle-SES youngsters whose achievement is average or above. Still, they feel severe apprehension about attending school, often accompanied by physical complaints (dizziness, nausea, stomachaches, and vomiting) that disappear once the child is allowed to remain home. About one-third are 5- to 7-year-olds, most of whom do not fear school so much as separation from their mother. The difficulty often can be traced to a troubled parent–child relationship in which the mother encourages dependency. Family therapy and applied behavior analysis procedures that reinforce the child for going to school help these children (Elliott, 1999).

Most cases of school phobia appear later, around 11 to 13, during the transition from middle childhood to adolescence. These youngsters usually find a particular aspect of school experience frightening—an overcritical teacher, a school bully, the jeering remarks of insensitive peers, or too much parental pressure for school success. Treating this form of school phobia may require a change in school environment or parenting practices. Firm insistence that the child return to school along with training in how to cope with difficult situations is also helpful (Blagg & Yule, 1996).

Severe childhood anxieties may also arise from harsh living conditions. A great many children live in the midst of constant violence. In inner-city ghettos and in war-torn areas of the world, children learn to drop to the floor at the sound of gunfire, and they witness the wounding and killing of friends and relatives. As the Cultural Influences box on page 514 reveals, these youngsters often suffer from long-term emotional distress. Finally, as we saw in our discussion of child abuse in Chapter 10, too often, violence and other destructive acts become part of adult–child relationships. During middle childhood, child sexual abuse increases.

CHILD SEXUAL ABUSE

Until recently, child sexual abuse was viewed as a rare occurrence. When children came forward with it, adults usually did not take their claims seriously. In the 1970s, efforts by professionals along with media attention caused child sexual abuse to be recognized as a serious and widespread problem. Several hundred thousand cases are reported in the United States each year (see Chapter 10).

■ **CHARACTERISTICS OF ABUSERS AND VICTIMS.** Sexual abuse is committed against children of both sexes but more often against girls. Most cases are reported in middle

school phobia
Severe apprehension about attending school, often accompanied by physical complaints that disappear once the child is allowed to remain home.

Cultural INFLUENCES

THE IMPACT OF ETHNIC AND POLITICAL VIOLENCE ON CHILDREN

On May 27, 1992, Zlata Filipovic, a 10-year-old Bosnian girl, recorded in her diary the following reactions to the intensifying Serb attack on the city of Sarajevo:

SLAUGHTER! MASSACRE! HORROR! CRIME! BLOOD! SCREAMS! TEARS! DESPAIR! That's what Vaso Miskin Street looks like today. Two shells exploded in the street and one in the market. Mommy was nearby at the time. . . . Daddy and I were beside ourselves because she hadn't come home. I saw some of it on TV but I still can't believe what I actually saw. . . . I've got a lump in my throat and a knot in my tummy. HORRIBLE. They're taking the wounded to the hospital. It's a madhouse. We kept going to the window hoping to see Mommy, but she wasn't back. . . . Daddy and I were tearing our hair out. . . . I looked out the window one more time and . . . I SAW MOMMY RUNNING ACROSS THE BRIDGE. As she came into the house she started shaking and crying. Through her tears she told us how she had seen dismembered bodies. . . . Thank God, Mommy is with us. Thank God. (Filipovic, 1994, p. 55)

Violence stemming from ethnic and political tensions is being felt increasingly around the world. Today, virtually all armed conflicts are internal civil wars in which well-established ways of life are threatened or destroyed, and children are frequently victims (Mays et al., 1998).

Children's experiences under conditions of armed conflict are diverse. Some may participate in the fighting, either because they are forced or because they want to please adults. Others are kidnapped, terrorized, or tortured. Those who are bystanders often come under direct fire and may be killed or physically maimed for life. And as Zlata's diary entry illustrates, many children of war watch in horror as family members, friends, and neighbors flee, are wounded, or die (Ladd & Cairns, 1996).

When war and social crises are temporary, most children are comforted by caregivers' reassuring messages and do not show long-term emotional difficulties. But chronic danger requires children to make substantial adjustments, and their psychological functioning can be seriously impaired. Many children exposed to wartime trauma lose their sense of safety, become desensitized to violence, are haunted by terrifying memories, and build a pessimistic view of the future (Cairns, 1996).

These traumatized ethnic Albanian refugee children from Kosovo are victims of the Serbian program of "ethnic cleansing." Here they receive humanitarian aid at a refugee center. Some of the children have seen their homes burned and family members wounded or killed. Without special support from caring adults, they are likely to show lasting emotional problems.

The support and affection of parents, who help children redefine the world in moral and optimistic terms, is the best safeguard against lasting problems (Punamaeki, 1999). When children are separated from family members, communities can offer protection. In Israel, children who lost a parent in battle fared best when they lived in kibbutzim, where many adults knew the child well and felt responsible for her welfare (Lifschitz et al., 1977).

When wartime drains families and communities of resources, international organizations must step in and help children. Until we know how to prevent war, efforts to preserve children's physical, psychological, and educational well-being may be the best way to stop transmission of violence to the next generation in many parts of the world.

AP/WIDE WORLD PHOTOS

childhood, but sexual abuse also occurs at younger and older ages. Few children experience only a single episode. For some, the abuse begins early in life and continues for many years (Holmes & Slap, 1998; Trickett & Putnam, 1998).

Generally, the abuser is a male—a parent or someone the parent knows well. Often it is a father, stepfather, or live-in boyfriend; somewhat less often an uncle or older brother. In a few

TABLE 13.3

TABLE 13.3

Factors Related to Child Sexual Abuse

FACTOR	DESCRIPTION
Abuser	Usually a male and a member of the child's family. Finds children sexually arousing, has difficulty controlling impulses, rationalizes that the victim wants sex and will enjoy it, and has learned to believe that sexual abuse of others is appropriate. May have serious psychological disturbance, including alcohol or drug addiction, and may have experienced sexual abuse as a child.
Victim	More often female than male. Abusers tend to select children who seem like easy targets—ones who are physically weak, compliant in personality, emotionally needy, and socially isolated.
Family	Often associated with poverty and repeated marital breakup. However, abuse also occurs in relatively stable, middle-SES families.

instances, mothers are the offenders, more often with sons. If the abuser is a nonrelative, it is usually someone the child has come to know and trust (Kolvin & Trowell, 1996).

In the overwhelming majority of cases, the abuse is serious—vaginal or anal intercourse, oral–genital contact, fondling, and forced stimulation of the adult. Abusers make the child comply in a variety of distasteful ways, including deception, bribery, verbal intimidation, and physical force (Gomez-Schwartz, Horowitz, & Cardarelli, 1990).

You may be wondering how any adult—especially a parent or close relative—could possibly violate a child sexually. Many offenders deny their own responsibility. They blame the abuse on the willing participation of a seductive youngster. Yet children are not capable of making a deliberate, informed decision to enter into a sexual relationship! Even at older ages, they are not free to say yes or no.

Abusers tend to have characteristics that predispose them toward sexual exploitation. As Table 13.3 shows, they have great difficulty controlling their impulses and may suffer from psychological disorders, including alcohol and drug addiction. Often they pick children who are unlikely to defend themselves—those who are physically weak, emotionally deprived, and socially isolated (Faller, 1990).

Reported cases of child sexual abuse are strongly linked to poverty, marital instability, and resulting weakening of family ties. Children who live in homes with a history of constantly changing characters—repeated marriages, separations, and new partners—are especially vulnerable. But community surveys reveal that middle-SES children in stable homes are also victims; there, the perpetrators are simply more likely to escape detection (Gomez-Schwartz, Horowitz, & Cardarelli, 1990).

■ **CONSEQUENCES OF SEXUAL ABUSE.** The adjustment problems of sexually abused children often are severe. Depression, low self-esteem, mistrust of adults, and anger and hostility can persist for years after the abusive episodes. Younger children react with sleep difficulties, loss of appetite, and generalized fearfulness. Reactions of adolescents include severe depression, suicidal impulses, substance abuse, early sexual activity with more partners, running away, and delinquency. At all ages, persistent abuse accompanied by force and violence has a more severe impact (Feiring, Taska, & Lewis, 1999; Wolfe, 1998).

Sexually abused children frequently display sexual knowledge and behavior beyond their years. They have learned from their abusers that sexual overtures are acceptable ways to get attention and rewards. As they move toward young adulthood, abused girls often enter into unhealthy relationships. Many become promiscuous, believing that their bodies are for others to use. When they marry, they are likely to choose partners who abuse both them and their children. (Faller, 1990). As mothers, they often show poor parenting skills, abusing and neglecting their youngsters (Pianta, Egeland, & Erickson, 1989). In these ways, the harmful impact of sexual abuse is transmitted to the next generation.

LAPORTE COUNTY CHILD ABUSE PROTECTION COUNCIL

So there really was a monster in her bedroom.

For many kids, there's a real reason to be afraid of the dark.

Last year in Indiana, there were 6,912 substantiated cases of sexual abuse. The trauma can be devastating for the child and for the family. So listen closely to the children around you.

If you hear something you don't want to believe, perhaps you should. For helpful information on child abuse prevention, contact the LaPorte County Child Abuse Prevention Council, 7451 Johnson Road, Michigan City, IN 46360. (219) 874-0007

LaPorte County Child Abuse Prevention Council

This public service announcement reminds adults that child sexual abuse, until recently regarded as a product of children's vivid imaginations, is a devastating reality. Victims are in urgent need of protection and treatment.

This poster for *Keeping Ourselves Safe,* New Zealand's national, school-based child abuse prevention program described on page 516, illustrates the importance of teaching children to recognize abusive adult behaviors so they can take steps to protect themselves. Parents are informed about children's classroom learning experiences and encouraged to support and extend them at home.

■ **PREVENTION AND TREATMENT.** Treating child sexual abuse is difficult. The reactions of family members—anxiety about harm to the child, anger toward the abuser, and sometimes hostility toward the victim for telling—can increase children's distress. Sensitive work with parents is essential for helping the abused child. Since sexual abuse typically appears in the midst of other serious family problems, long-term therapy with children and families usually is necessary (Wolfe, 1998).

The best way to reduce the suffering of victims is to prevent sexual abuse from continuing. Today, courts are prosecuting abusers (especially nonrelatives) more vigorously and taking children's testimony more seriously (see the Social Issues: Health box on the following page).

Educational programs can teach children to recognize inappropriate sexual advances and show them where to go for help. Yet because of controversies over educating children about sexual abuse, few schools offer these interventions. New Zealand is the only country in the world with a national, school-based prevention program targeting sexual abuse. In *Keeping Ourselves Safe,* 5- to 13-year-olds learn that that abusers are rarely strangers but rather are close to their victims. Parent involvement ensures that home and school work together in teaching children self-protection skills. Evaluations reveal that virtually all New Zealand parents and children support the program and that it has helped many children avoid or report abuse (Briggs & Hawkins, 1996, 1999).

FOSTERING RESILIENCY IN MIDDLE CHILDHOOD

Throughout middle childhood—and other phases of development as well—children are confronted with challenging and sometimes threatening situations that require them to cope with psychological stress. In this trio of chapters, we have considered such topics as chronic illness, learning disabilities, achievement expectations, divorce, and sexual abuse. Each taxes children's coping resources, creating serious risks for development.

At the same time, many studies indicate only a modest relationship between stressful life experiences and psychological disturbance in childhood (Garmezy, 1993). Think back to our discussion in Chapter 4 of the long-term consequences of birth complications. We noted that some children manage to overcome the combined effects of birth trauma, poverty, and a deeply troubled family life. The same is true when we look at findings on school difficulties, family transitions, and child maltreatment.

Recall from Chapter 1 that three broad factors protect against maladjustment:

■ personal characteristics of children—an easy temperament, high self-esteem, and a mastery-oriented approach to new situations

■ a family environment that provides warmth, closeness, and organization in the child's life

■ a person outside the immediate family—a grandparent, teacher, or close friend—who develops a special relationship with the child, offering a support system and a positive coping model

Any one of these ingredients of resiliency can account for why one child fares well and another poorly when exposed to hardship. Yet most of the time, personal and environmental resources are interconnected (Smith & Prior, 1995; Sorenson, 1993). Throughout this book we have seen many examples of how unfavorable life experiences increase the chances that

Social ISSUES: HEALTH

CHILDREN'S EYEWITNESS TESTIMONY

Increasingly, children are being called on to testify in court cases involving child abuse and neglect, child custody, and other matters. Having to provide such information can be difficult and traumatic. Almost always, children must report on highly stressful events. In doing so, they may have to speak against a parent or other relative to whom they feel loyal. In some family disputes, they may fear punishment for telling the truth. In addition, child witnesses are faced with an unfamiliar situation—at the very least, an interview in the judge's chambers, and at most, an open courtroom with judge, jury, spectators, and the possibility of unsympathetic cross-examination. Not surprisingly, there is considerable debate about the accuracy of children's recall under these conditions.

AGE DIFFERENCES

Until recently, it was rare for children younger than age 5 to testify, whereas those age 6 and older often did so. Children between ages 10 and 14 have historically been assumed competent to testify. Yet as a result of societal reactions to rising rates of child abuse and difficulties in prosecuting perpetrators, legal requirements for child testimony have relaxed in Canada and the United States. Children as young as age 3 frequently serve as witnesses (Ceci & Bruck, 1998).

Compared with preschoolers, school-age children are better able to give detailed descriptions of past experiences and make accurate inferences about others' motives and intentions. Older children can better resist misleading questions of the sort asked by attorneys when they probe for more information or, in cross-examination, try to influence the content of the child's response (Ceci & Bruck, 1993; Goodman & Tobey, 1994). Nevertheless, when properly questioned, even 3-year-olds can recall recent events accurately—including highly stressful ones (Baker-Ward et al., 1993; Goodman et al., 1991).

SUGGESTIBILITY

Yet court testimony often involves repeated interviews. When adults lead children by suggesting incorrect facts ("He touched you there, didn't he?"), they increase the likelihood of incorrect reporting among preschool and school-age children alike. Events that children fabricate in response to leading questions can be quite fantastic. In one study, after a visit to a doctor's office, children said yes to questions about events that not only never occurred but that implied abuse—"Did the doctor lick your knee?" "Did the nurse sit on top of you?" (Ornstein et al., 1997). To ease the task of providing testimony, special interviewing methods have been devised for children. In many child sexual abuse cases, anatomically correct dolls are used to prompt children's recall. Although this method helps older children provide more detail about experienced events, it increases the suggestibility of preschoolers, who report physical and sexual contact that never happened (Ceci & Bruck, 1998; Goodman et al., 1999).

By the time children come to court, it is weeks, months, or even years after the occurrence of the target events. When a long delay is combined with suggestions about what happened and stereotyping of the accused ("He's in jail because he's been bad"), children can easily be misled into giving false information (Ceci, Leichtman, & Bruck, 1994; Leichtman & Ceci, 1995). And they may report features consistent with the recalled situation (for example, checking stomach in a physical exam) that were not really part of it (Ornstein et al., 1998).

INTERVENTIONS

Adults must prepare child witnesses so they understand the courtroom process and know what to expect. In some places, "court schools" exist in which children are taken through the setting and given an opportunity to role-play court activities. As part of this process, children can be encouraged to admit not knowing an answer rather than guessing or going along with what an adult expects of them. At the same time, legal professionals must lessen the risk of suggestibility—by limiting the number of times children are interviewed and by asking questions in nonleading ways.

If a child is likely to experience emotional trauma or later punishment (in a family dispute), then courtroom procedures can be adapted to protect them. For example, a child advocate can be present to offer emotional support, or children can testify behind a screen or over closed circuit TV so they do not have to face an abuser. When it is not wise for a child to participate directly, expert witnesses can provide testimony that reports on the child's psychological condition and includes important elements of the child's story. But for such testimony to be worthwhile, witnesses need to be impartial and trained in how to question to minimize false reporting (Bruck, Ceci, & Hembrooke, 1998).

parents and children will act in ways that expose them to further hardship. Children usually can handle one stressor in their lives, even if it is chronic. But when negative conditions pile up, such as marital discord, parental psychological disorder, abuse and neglect, poverty, crowded living conditions, and violent neighborhoods, the rate of maladjustment multiplies (Capaldi & Patterson, 1991; Sameroff et al., 1993).

Of great concern are children's violent acts. Despite substantial decline since the early 1990s, violence committed by American children and adolescents in schools and communities remains high, at times reaching the level of atrocities—maimings and murders of adults and peers. Because children spend extensive time in school, the quality of their relationships with teachers and classmates can strongly influence their social behavior (Henrich, Brown, & Aber, 1999).

Several highly effective school-based programs reduce violence and other antisocial acts by fostering social competence and supportive relationships. Among these is the *Resolving Conflict Creatively Program (RCCP)*. It provides children with up to 51 hour-long lessons in emotional and social understanding and skills. Topics covered include expressing feelings, regulating anger, resolving social conflicts, cooperating, appreciating diversity, identifying and standing up against prejudice, and recognizing one's role in creating a more peaceful world. Compared with children receiving few or no lessons, second to sixth graders experiencing an average of 23 lessons during the school year less often misinterpreted others' acts as hostile, less often behaved aggressively, more often engaged in prosocial behavior, and more often gained in academic achievement. Two years of intervention, as opposed to just one, strengthened these outcomes (Aber et al., 1998, 1999).

RCCP, and other programs like it, underscore that academic and social development are closely connected; warm, caring ties with adults and peers promote both domains. Throughout our discussion, we have seen how families, schools, communities, and society as a whole can enhance or undermine the school-age child's developing sense of competence. As the next three chapters reveal, young people whose childhood experiences helped them learn to overcome obstacles, strive for self-direction, and respond considerately and sympathetically to others meet the challenges of the next period—adolescence—quite well.

Ask YOURSELF...

review   *What can legal professionals do to increase the chances of accurate reporting when children must testify in court cases?*

apply   *Claire told her 6-year-old daughter to be very careful never to talk to or take candy from strangers. Why will Claire's directive* not *protect her daughter from sexual abuse?*

connect   *Explain how the three factors that protect against maladjustment, listed in the previous section, help account for variations in children's adjustment following divorce.*

Summary

ERIKSON'S THEORY: INDUSTRY VERSUS INFERIORITY

What personality changes take place during Erikson's stage of industry versus inferiority?

■ According to Erikson, children who successfully resolve the psychological conflict of **industry versus inferiority** develop the capacity to engage in productive work, learn the value of division of labor, and develop a sense of moral commitment and responsibility.

SELF-DEVELOPMENT

Describe school-age children's self-concept and self-esteem, and discuss factors that affect their achievement-related attributions.

■ During middle childhood, children's self-concepts include personality traits, positive and negative characteristics, and **social comparisons.** Self-esteem differentiates further, becomes hierarchically organized, and declines over the early school years as children adjust their self-judgments to feedback from the environment. Cultural forces affect self-esteem, as illustrated by variations in the role of social comparison. Authoritative child rearing is consistently related to high self-esteem.

■ Research on achievement-related **attributions** has identified adult messages that affect children's academic self-esteem. Children with **mastery-oriented attributions** credit their successes to high ability and their failures to insufficient effort. In contrast, those with **learned helplessness** attribute their successes to luck and their failures to low ability.

■ Children who receive negative feedback about their ability and messages evaluating their other traits are likely to develop learned helplessness. Supportive teachers and cultural valuing of effort increase the likelihood of a mastery-oriented approach.

■ **Attribution retraining** encourages learned-helpless children to revise their failure-related attributions, thereby improving self-esteem. Teaching children to focus less on grades and more on mastery for its own sake also leads to gains in failing students' academic self-esteem and motivation.

EMOTIONAL DEVELOPMENT

Cite changes in expression and understanding of emotion in middle childhood.

■ In middle childhood, a sense of personal responsibility clearly governs self-conscious emotions of pride and guilt. When children experience intense shame, their overall sense of self-worth can be profoundly shattered.

■ School-age children recognize that people can experience more than one emotion at a time. As a result, they have a better grasp of self-conscious emotions and ways to mask their feelings. They also attend to more cues—facial and situational cues and information about a person's past experiences—in interpreting others' feelings. Gains in perspective taking and emotional understanding lead empathy to increase in middle childhood.

■ By the end of middle childhood, most children have an adaptive set of techniques for regulating emotion. Emotionally well-regulated children are optimistic, prosocial, and well liked by peers.

UNDERSTANDING OTHERS: PERSPECTIVE TAKING

How does perspective taking change in middle childhood?

■ **Perspective taking** improves greatly over middle childhood, as Selman's five-stage sequence indicates. Cognitive maturity and experiences in which adults and peers encourage children to take note of another's viewpoint support school-age children's perspective-taking skill. Good perspective takers show more positive social skills.

MORAL DEVELOPMENT

Describe changes in moral understanding during middle childhood, and summarize current recommendations for moral education in schools.

■ By middle childhood, children follow internalized standards, so their need for adult oversight, modeling, and reinforcement declines. School-age children's concepts of **distributive justice** change from equality to merit to benevolence.

■ Children also clarify and create linkages between moral rules and social conventions. In judging the seriousness of transgressions, they take into account the purpose of the rule; people's intentions, knowledge, and beliefs; and the context of their behavior.

■ At present, moral education programs are narrowly focused. A comprehensive approach involves promoting four moral components: moral sensitivity, moral judgment, moral motivation, and moral character.

PEER RELATIONS

How do peer sociability and friendship change in middle childhood?

■ In middle childhood, peer interaction becomes more positive and prosocial, and physical aggression declines. By the end of the school years, children organize themselves into **peer groups.**

■ Friendships develop into mutual relationships based on trust. Children tend to select friends like themselves in age, sex, race, ethnicity, SES, personality, popularity, and academic achievement.

Describe major categories of peer acceptance and ways to help rejected children.

■ Sociometric techniques are used to distinguish four types of peer acceptance: (1) **popular children,** who are liked by many agemates; (2) **rejected children,** who are actively disliked; (3) **controversial children,** who are both liked and disliked; and (4) **neglected children,** who are seldom chosen, either positively or negatively.

■ Two subtypes of popular children exist: **popular-prosocial** children, who are academically and socially competent, and **popular-antisocial children,** who generally are athletically skilled, highly aggressive boys who are poor students. Rejected children

Summary (continued)

also divide into at least two subtypes: **rejected-aggressive children,** who show severe conduct problems, and **rejected-withdrawn children,** who are passive and socially awkward. Both subgroups often experience lasting adjustment difficulties.

■ Coaching in social skills, academic tutoring, and training in perspective taking and social problem solving have been used to help rejected youngsters. Teaching children to attribute peer difficulties to internal, changeable causes is also important. To produce lasting change, intervening in parent–child interaction is probably necessary.

GENDER TYPING

What changes in gender-stereotyped beliefs and gender-role identity take place during middle childhood?

■ School-age children extend their awareness of gender stereotypes to personality characteristics and academic subjects, and girls discount their academic talent. Although children develop a more open-minded view of what males and females can do, they often do not approve of males who violate gender-role expectations.

■ Boys strengthen their identification with the masculine role, whereas girls feel free to experiment with "opposite gender" activities. Cultural distinctions between male and female roles and tasks assigned to children influence their gender-typed behavior.

FAMILY INFLUENCES

How do parent–child communication and sibling relationships change in middle childhood?

■ Effective parents of school-age children engage in **coregulation,** exerting general oversight while permitting children to be in charge of moment-by-moment decision making. Coregulation depends on a cooperative relationship between parent and child.

■ During middle childhood, sibling rivalry tends to increase, as children participate in a wider range of activities and parents compare their traits and accomplishments. Siblings often try to reduce this rivalry by striving to be different from one another.

Older siblings are slightly advantaged in IQ and school achievement. Younger siblings tend to be more popular.

■ Only children are as well adjusted as are children with siblings. In addition, only children do better in school and attain higher levels of education, probably because of their closer relationships with parents, who exert more pressure for mastery and accomplishment.

How do children fare in gay and lesbian families and in single-parent, never-married families?

■ Gay and lesbian parents are as committed to and effective at child rearing as are heterosexuals, and sometimes more so. Their children are well adjusted and largely heterosexual.

■ The largest group of never-married parents are African-American young women, who postpone marriage more and childbirth less than do all other American ethnic groups. Many children of never-married mothers display problems associated with economic hardship. When they lack the warmth and involvement of a father, they achieve less well in school and engage in more antisocial behavior than do children in first-marriage families.

What factors influence children's adjustment to divorce and blended family arrangements?

■ Divorce is common in the lives of American children. Although painful emotional reactions usually accompany the period surrounding divorce, children with difficult temperaments and boys in mother-custody homes are more likely to show continuing school-performance difficulties and antisocial behavior. For children of both sexes, divorce is linked to problems with adolescent sexuality and with development of intimate ties.

■ The overriding factor in positive adjustment following divorce is effective parenting. Contact with fathers reduces the risk of lasting problems. Because **divorce mediation** helps parents resolve their disputes and cooperate in child rearing, it can help children through the difficult period surrounding divorce. If parents continue to quarrel, **joint custody** may create additional strains for children.

■ When divorced parents enter new relationships through cohabitation or remarriage, children must adapt to a **blended,** or **reconstituted, family.** How well they fare depends on which parent remarries and the age and sex of the child. Girls, older school-age children, adolescents, and children in father–stepmother families display the greatest adjustment problems.

How do maternal employment and life in dual-earner families affect children's development?

■ When mothers enjoy their work and remain committed to parenting, maternal employment is associated with favorable consequences for children, including a higher sense of self-esteem, more positive family and peer relations, less gender-stereotyped beliefs, and better grades in school. In dual-earner families, the father's willingness to share child rearing is linked to many positive outcomes for children. The availability of workplace supports, such as part-time employment and paid parental leave, assists parents in balancing the demands of work and child rearing.

■ **Self-care children** who are old enough to look after themselves, are monitored from a distance, and have a history of authoritative parenting appear responsible and well adjusted. In contrast, children left to their own devices are at risk for antisocial behavior. Children in high-quality after-school programs reap academic and social benefits.

SOME COMMON PROBLEMS OF DEVELOPMENT

Cite common fears and anxieties in middle childhood.

■ During middle childhood, children's fears are directed toward new concerns, including physical safety, media events, achievement, parents' health, the possibility of dying, and peer relations. Some children develop intense, unmanageable fears, such as **school phobia.** Severe anxiety can also result from harsh living conditions, such as constant violence.

Discuss factors related to child sexual abuse, its consequences for children's development, and prevention and treatment.

Summary (continued)

■ Child sexual abuse is generally committed by male family members, more often against girls than boys. Abusers have characteristics that predispose them toward sexual exploitation of children. Reported cases are strongly associated with poverty and marital instability. Adjustment problems of abused children often are severe. Common reactions are depression, low self-esteem, mistrust of adults, anger and hostility, and inappropriate sexual behavior.

■ Since sexual abuse is related to other serious family problems, long-term therapy with children and families is usually necessary. Educational programs that teach children to recognize inappropriate sexual advances and show them where to go for help reduce the risk of sexual abuse.

Cite factors that foster resiliency in middle childhood.

■ Overall, a modest relationship exists between stressful life experiences and psychological disturbance in childhood. Personal characteristics of children, a warm, well-organized home life, and social supports outside the family are related to resilience in the face of stress.

■ Because children spend extensive time in school, the quality of their relationships with teachers and classmates can strongly influence their social behavior. By fostering social competence and supportive relationships, school-based programs can reduce violence and other antisocial acts.

Important terms and concepts

attribution retraining (p. 488)
attributions (p. 486)
blended, or reconstituted, family (p. 509)
coregulation (p. 503)
controversial children (p. 498)
distributive justice (p. 492)
divorce mediation (p. 508)
industry versus inferiority (p. 483)

joint custody (p. 508)
learned helplessness (p. 487)
mastery-oriented attributions (p. 487)
neglected children (p. 498)
peer group (p. 496)
peer victimization (p. 501)
perspective taking (p. 491)
popular children (p. 498)
popular-antisocial children (p. 498)

popular-prosocial children (p. 498)
rejected-aggressive children (p. 499)
rejected children (p. 498)
rejected-withdrawn children (p. 499)
school phobia (p. 513)
self-care children (p. 511)
social comparisons (p. 483)
sociometric techniques (p. 498)

fyi . . . for further information and help

Consult the companion website for this book, where you will find additional weblinks and associated learning activities:
www.ablongman.com/berk

DIVORCE

Parents Without Partners
www.parentswithoutpartners.org

Organization of custodial and noncustodial single parents that provides support in the upbringing of children. Many local groups exist throughout the United States.

Center for Divorce Education
www.divorce-education.com

Organization of psychologists and lawyers committed to educating the public about the effects of divorce. Has developed a comprehensive education program for divorcing families.

BLENDED FAMILIES

Stepfamily Association of America
www.stepfam.org

Association of families interested in stepfamily relationships. Organizes support groups and offers education and children's services.

Stepfamily Foundation
www.stepfamily.org

Organization of remarried parents, interested professionals, and divorced individuals. Arranges group counseling sessions for stepfamilies and provides training for professionals.

CHILD SEXUAL ABUSE

Stop It Now!
www.stopitnow.com

Nonprofit organization that focuses on preventing child sexual abuse through working with families and children in how to confront abusers, encouraging abusers to seek help, and engaging in media campaigns to educate the public.

Milestones of development in middle childhood

AGE	PHYSICAL	COGNITIVE	LANGUAGE	EMOTIONAL/SOCIAL
6–8 years	■ Slow gains in height and weight continue until adolescent growth spurt. (410–412) ■ Gradual replacement of primary teeth by permanent teeth. (412) ■ Writing becomes smaller and more legible. Letter reversals decline. (426) ■ Drawings become more organized and detailed and include some depth cues. (426) ■ Organized games with rules and rough-and-tumble play become common. (428–430) ■ Dominance hierarchies become more stable, especially among boys. (431)	■ Thought becomes more logical, as shown by the ability to pass Piagetian conservation, class inclusion, and seriation problems. (438–439) ■ Understanding of spatial concepts improves, as illustrated by conservation of distance and ability to give clear, well-organized directions. (439) ■ Attention becomes more selective, adaptable, and planful. (443–444) ■ Uses memory strategies of rehearsal and organization. (444–445) ■ Regards the mind as an active, constructive agent, capable of transforming information. (448) ■ Awareness of memory strategies and the impact of psychological factors (attention, motivation) on task performance improve. (448) ■ By the end of this period, makes the transition from "learning to read" to "reading to learn." (450–451) ■ Uses informal knowledge of number concepts and counting to master more complex mathematical skills. (451–452)	■ Vocabulary increases rapidly throughout middle childhood. (461) ■ Word definitions are concrete, referring to functions and appearance. (461) ■ Metalinguistic awareness improves. (461)	■ Self-concept begins to include personality traits and social comparisons. (483) ■ Self-esteem differentiates, becomes hierarchically organized, and declines to a more realistic level. (484–485) ■ Self-conscious emotions of pride and guilt are governed by personal responsibility. (489) ■ Recognizes that individuals can experience more than one emotion at a time. (490) ■ Attends to more cues—facial, situational, and past experiences—in interpreting another's feelings. (491) ■ Understands that access to different information often causes people to have different perspectives. (491–492) ■ Becomes more responsible and independent. (492) ■ Distributive justice reasoning changes from equality to merit to benevolence. (493) ■ Peer interaction becomes more prosocial, and physical aggression declines. (497)

AGE	PHYSICAL	COGNITIVE	LANGUAGE	EMOTIONAL/SOCIAL
9–11 years	■ Adolescent growth spurt begins 2 years earlier for girls than for boys. (410) ■ Gross motor skills of running, jumping, throwing, catching, kicking, batting, and dribbling are executed more quickly and with better coordination. (425) ■ Reaction time improves, contributing to motor skill development. (426) ■ Representation of depth in drawings expands. (426–427) 	■ Logical thought remains tied to concrete situations until the end of middle childhood. (394–440) ■ Piagetian tasks continue to be mastered in a step-by-step fashion. (440) ■ Planning improves. (444) ■ Memory strategies of rehearsal and organization become more effective. (444) ■ Applies several memory strategies at once. (445) ■ Memory strategy of elaboration appears. (445) ■ Long-term knowledge base grows larger and becomes better organized. (445) ■ Cognitive self-regulation improves. (449)	■ Word definitions emphasize synonyms and categorical relations. (461) ■ Grasps double meanings of words, as reflected in comprehension of metaphors and humor. (461) ■ Understanding of complex grammatical constructions improves. (461–462) ■ Adapts messages to the needs of listeners in complex communicative situations. (462) ■ Narratives about the past become longer and more complex. (462) ■ Conversational strategies become more refined. (462) 	■ Self-esteem tends to rise. (485) ■ Distinguishes ability, effort, and luck in attributions for success and failure. (486) ■ Has an adaptive set of strategies for regulating emotion. (490) ■ Can "step into another's shoes" and view the self from that person's perspective. (491–492) ■ Later, can view the relationship between self and other from the perspective of a third, impartial party. (493) ■ Appreciates the linkage between moral rules and social conventions. (494) ■ Grasp of a unique domain of personal matters strengthens. ■ Peer groups emerge. (496) ■ Friendships are based on mutual trust. (497) ■ Becomes aware of more gender stereotypes, including personality traits and school subjects, but has a more flexible appreciation of what males and females can do. (501) ■ Sibling rivalry tends to increase. (503–504)

Note: Numbers in parentheses indicate the page(s) on which each milestone is discussed.

"My World in the Year 2000"

Martins Muzikants

11 years, Latvia

The dramatic physical and cognitive changes of adolescence lead teenagers to see themselves and their surroundings from new vantage points. As Chapter 14 indicates, puberty is both an exhilarating and an apprehensive phase. In all societies, young people are expected to give up childish ways in favor of greater responsibility.

Physical Development in Adolescence

n her eleventh birthday, Sabrina's friend Joyce gave her a surprise party, but Sabrina seemed somber during the celebration. Although Sabrina and Joyce had been close friends since third grade, their relationship was faltering. Sabrina was a head taller and some 20 pounds heavier than most of the girls in her sixth-grade class. Her breasts were well developed, her hips and thighs had broadened, and she had begun to menstruate. In contrast, Joyce still had the short, lean, flat-chested body of a school-age child.

Ducking into the bathroom while Joyce and the other girls set the table for cake and ice cream, Sabrina looked herself over in the mirror, straightened her blouse, smoothed her skirt, and whispered, "Gosh, I feel so big and heavy." At church youth group on Sunday evenings, Sabrina broke away from Joyce and spent time with the eighth-grade girls, around whom she didn't feel so large and awkward.

Once every 2 weeks, parents gathered at Sabrina and Joyce's school for discussions about child-rearing concerns.

Sabrina's Italian-American parents, Franca and Antonio, attended whenever they could. "How you know they are becoming teenagers is this," volunteered Antonio. "The bedroom door is closed, and they want to be alone. Also, they contradict and disagree. I tell Sabrina, 'You have to go to Aunt Gina's on Saturday for dinner with the family.' The next thing I know, she's arguing with me."

"All our four children were early developers," Franca added. "The three boys, too, were tall by age 12 or 13, but it was easier for them. They felt big and important. Sabrina is moody and doesn't want to be with her old friends. She was skinny as a little girl, but now she says she is too fat and wants to diet. She thinks about boys and doesn't concentrate on her studies. I try to be patient and listen to her," reflected Franca sympathetically.

Sabrina has entered adolescence, the transition between childhood and adulthood. In modern societies, the skills young people must master are so complex and the choices confronting them so diverse that adolescence lasts for nearly a decade. But around the world, the basic tasks of this phase are much the same. Sabrina must accept her full-grown body, acquire adult ways of thinking, attain emotional and economic independence, develop more mature ways of relating to peers of both sexes, and construct an identity—a secure sense of who she is, sexually, morally, politically, and vocationally.

The beginning of adolescence is marked by **puberty,** a flood of biological events leading to an adult-size body and sexual maturity. As Sabrina's reactions suggest, entry into adolescence can be trying, more so for some youngsters than for others. In this chapter we trace the events of puberty and take up a variety of health concerns—nutrition, sexual activity, and serious health problems affecting teenagers who encounter difficulties on the path to maturity. We conclude with a discussion of adolescent motor development, which highlights the large sex differences appearing at this time. But before we delve into these specifics, let's begin with an overview of changing views of adolescence over the past century.

Conceptions of Adolescence

hy is Sabrina self-conscious, argumentative, and in retreat from family activities? Historically, theorists explained the impact of puberty on psychological development by resorting to extremes—either a biological or environmental explanation. Today, researchers realize that biological, social, and cultural forces jointly determine adolescent psychological change.

THE BIOLOGICAL PERSPECTIVE

Ask several parents of young children what they expect their sons and daughters to be like as teenagers. You will probably get answers like these: "Rebellious and reckless," "Full of rages and tempers" (Buchanan & Holmbeck, 1998). This widespread view dates back to the ideas of eighteenth-century philosopher Jean-Jacques Rousseau. He believed that a natural outgrowth of the biological upheaval of puberty was heightened emotionality, conflict, and defiance of adults.

In the twentieth century, this storm-and-stress perspective was picked up by major theorists. The most influential was G. Stanley Hall, whose view of development was grounded in Darwin's theory of evolution (see Chapter 1, page 13). Hall (1904) described adolescence as a cascade of instinctual passions, a phase of growth so turbulent that it resembles the period in which human beings evolved from savages into civilized beings.

Sigmund Freud, as well, emphasized the emotional storminess of the teenage years. He called adolescence the *genital stage,* a period in which instinctual drives reawaken and shift to the genital region of the body, resulting in psychological conflict and volatile, unpredictable behavior. Gradually, as adolescents find intimate partners, inner forces achieve a new, more mature harmony, and the stage concludes with marriage, birth, and child rearing.

puberty
Biological changes at adolescence that lead to an adult-size body and sexual maturity.

In this way, young people fulfill their biological destiny: sexual reproduction and the survival of the species.

THE ENVIRONMENTAL PERSPECTIVE

Recent research suggests that the notion of adolescence as a biologically determined period of storm and stress is greatly exaggerated. A number of problems, such as eating disorders, depression, suicide, and law breaking, occur more often in adolescence than earlier. But the overall rate of serious psychological disturbance rises only slightly (by about 2 percent) from childhood to adolescence, when it is the same as in the adult population—about 20 percent (Costello & Angold, 1995). Although some teenagers encounter serious difficulties, emotional turbulence is not a routine feature of adolescence.

The first researcher to point out the wide variability in adolescent adjustment was anthropologist Margaret Mead (1928). She traveled to the Pacific islands of Samoa and returned with a startling conclusion: Because of the culture's relaxed social relationships and openness toward sexuality, adolescence "is perhaps the pleasantest time the Samoan girl (or boy) will ever know" (p. 308).

Mead offered an alternative view in which the social environment is entirely responsible for the range of teenage experiences, from erratic and agitated to calm and stress free. Yet this conclusion is just as extreme as the biological perspective it tried to replace! Later researchers found that Samoan adolescence was not as untroubled as Mead had assumed (Freeman, 1983). Still, Mead convinced researchers that greater attention must be paid to social and cultural influences for adolescent development to be understood.

A BALANCED POINT OF VIEW

Today we know that the experience of adolescence varies greatly and is a product of *both* biological and social forces. Biological changes are universal—found in all primates and all cultures. These internal stresses and the social expectations accompanying them—that the young person move away from childish ways of behaving, develop new interpersonal relationships, and take on greater responsibility—are likely to prompt moments of uncertainty, self-doubt, and disappointment in all teenagers.

At the same time, the length of adolescence and the number of hurdles a young person must overcome differ from one culture to the next. Although simpler societies have a shorter transition to adulthood, adolescence is not absent (Weisfield, 1997). A study of 186 tribal and village cultures revealed that almost all had an intervening phase, however brief, between childhood and full assumption of adult roles (Schlegel & Barry, 1991).

In industrialized nations, successful participation in economic life requires many years of education. Young people face extra years of dependence on parents and postponement of sexual gratification while they prepare for a productive work life. As a result, adolescence is greatly extended, and researchers commonly divide it into three phases:

1. *Early adolescence,* from 11 or 12 to 14 years of age, a period of rapid pubertal change

2. *Middle adolescence,* from 14 to 18 years, when pubertal changes are nearly complete

3. *Late adolescence,* from 18 to 21 years, when the young person achieves full adult appearance and faces more complete assumption of adult roles

These divisions correspond to the way industrialized societies commonly group adolescents—into middle or junior high school, high school, and college (Steinberg, 1999).

Throughout our discussion, we will see that the more the social environment supports young people in achieving adult responsibilities, the better they fare. For all the biological tensions and uncertainties about the future that teenagers feel, most are surprisingly good at negotiating the twists and turns of this period of life. With this idea in mind, let's look closely at puberty, the dawning of adolescent development.

Puberty: The Physical Transition to Adulthood

The changes of puberty are dramatic and momentous. Within a few years, the body of the school-age child is transformed into that of a full-grown adult. Genetically influenced hormonal processes regulate pubertal growth. Girls, who have been advanced in physical maturity since the prenatal period, reach puberty, on average, 2 years earlier than boys.

HORMONAL CHANGES

To young adolescents and their parents, signs of puberty seem to appear suddenly. But the complex hormonal changes that underlie them take place gradually and are under way by age 8 or 9 (see Figure 14.1). Recall from Chapter 8 that the *pituitary gland,* located at the base of the brain, releases *growth hormone (GH)* and stimulates other glands to produce hormones that act on body tissues, causing them to mature. Secretions of GH and *thyroxine* (a hormone released by the thyroid gland) increase, leading to tremendous gains in body size and attainment of skeletal maturity.

Sexual maturation is controlled by the sex hormones. Although *estrogens* are thought of as female hormones and *androgens* as male hormones, both types are present in each sex but in different amounts. The boy's testes release large quantities of the androgen *testosterone,* which leads to muscle growth, body and facial hair, and other male sex characteristics. Testosterone also contributes to gains in body size. The testes secrete small amounts of estrogen as well—the reason that 50 percent of boys experience temporary breast enlargement during the early phase of puberty (Larson, 1996).

Estrogens released by the girl's ovaries cause the breasts, uterus, and vagina to mature, the body to take on feminine proportions, and fat to accumulate. In addition, estrogens contribute

FIGURE 14.1

Hormonal influences on the body at puberty.

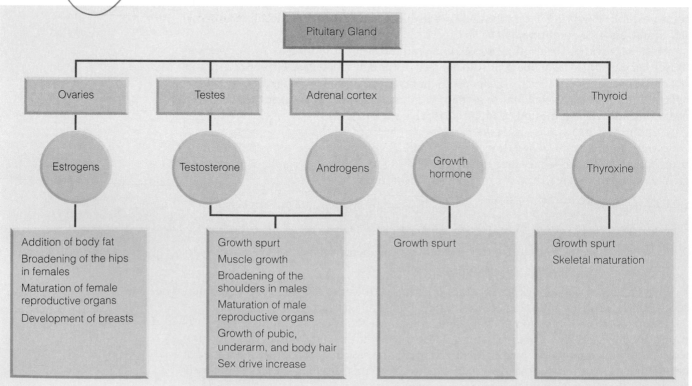

to regulation of the menstrual cycle. Girls' changing bodies are also affected by the release of androgens from the adrenal glands, located on top of each kidney. *Adrenal androgens* influence the girl's height spurt and stimulate growth of underarm and pubic hair. They have little impact on boys, whose physical characteristics are mainly influenced by androgen secretions from the testes.

As you can already tell, pubertal changes can be divided into two types: (1) overall body growth, including size, proportion, and muscle–fat makeup, and (2) maturation of sexual characteristics (Malina, 1990). Although we will discuss these changes separately, they are interrelated. We have already seen that the hormones responsible for sexual maturity also affect body growth; boys and girls differ in both aspects. In fact, puberty is the time of greatest sexual differentiation since prenatal life.

© BOB DAEMMRICH/STOCK BOSTON

CHANGES IN BODY SIZE, PROPORTIONS, AND MUSCLE–FAT MAKEUP

The first outward sign of puberty is the rapid gain in height and weight known as the **growth spurt.** On the average, it is under way for North American and European girls shortly after age 10, for boys around age 12½ (Malina, 1990). Because estrogens trigger and then restrain GH secretion more readily than do androgens, the girl is taller and heavier during early adolescence, but this advantage is short lived (Brook, 1999). At age 14 she is surpassed by the typical boy, whose adolescent growth spurt has started, whereas hers is almost finished. Growth in body size is complete for most girls by age 16 and for boys by age 17½, when the epiphyses at the ends of the long bones close completely (see Chapter 8, page 295).

Altogether, adolescents add almost 10 inches in height and about 40 pounds in weight during puberty. But even more striking is how fast these changes take place. When growing at their peak, boys add more than 4 inches and 26 pounds in a single year, girls about 3.5 inches and as much as 20 pounds. Figure 14.2 on page 530 provides an overview of general body growth from infancy through adolescence.

During puberty, the cephalocaudal trend of infancy and childhood reverses. At first, the hands, legs, and feet accelerate, and then the torso, which accounts for most of the adolescent height gain (Sheehy et al., 1999). This pattern of development helps us understand why early adolescents often appear awkward and out of proportion—long-legged and with giant feet and hands.

Large differences in boys' and girls' body proportions also appear, caused by the action of sex hormones on the skeleton. Boys' shoulders broaden relative to the hips, whereas girls' hips broaden relative to the shoulders and waist. Of course, boys also end up considerably larger than girls, and their legs are longer in relation to the rest of the body. The major reason is that boys have 2 extra years of preadolescent growth, when the legs are growing the fastest (Graber, Petersen, & Brooks-Gunn, 1996).

Compared with her later-developing girlfriends, Sabrina had accumulated much more fat, so she worried about her weight. Around age 8, girls start to add more fat than do boys on their arms, legs, and trunk, a trend that accelerates between ages 11 and 16. In contrast, the arm and leg fat of adolescent boys decreases (Siervogel et al., 2000). Although both sexes gain in muscle, this increase is much greater for boys, who develop larger skeletal muscles, hearts, and lung capacity. Also, the number of red blood cells, and therefore the ability to carry oxygen from the lungs to the muscles, increases in boys but not in girls. Altogether, boys gain far more muscle strength than do girls, a difference that contributes to boys' superior athletic performance during the teenage years (Ramos et al., 1998).

Sex differences in pubertal growth are obvious among these fifth graders. Although all are 10 to 11 years old, the girls are taller and more mature looking. The growth spurt takes place, on the average, 2 years earlier for girls than boys.

growth spurt
Rapid gain in height and weight during adolescence.

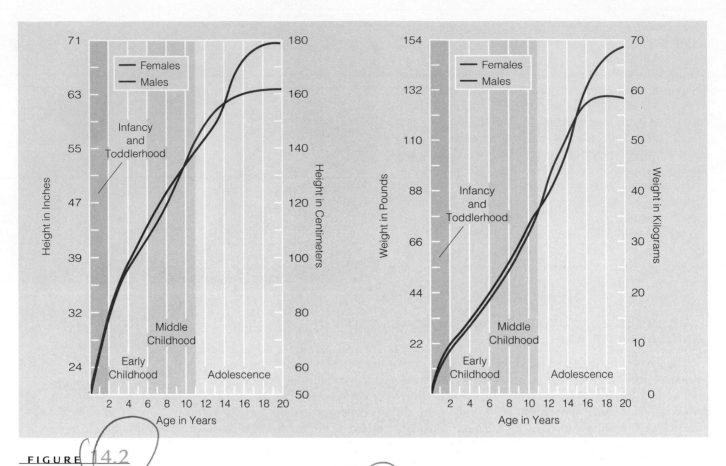

FIGURE 14.2

Average gains in height and weight from infancy through adolescence among North Americans. Note that the adolescent growth spurt takes place earlier for girls than boys. (From R. M. Malina, 1975, *Growth and Development: The First Twenty Years in Man,* Minneapolis: Burgess Publishing Company, p. 19. Adapted by permission.)

primary sexual characteristics
Physical features that involve the reproductive organs directly (ovaries, uterus, and vagina in females; penis, scrotum, and testes in males).

secondary sexual characteristics
Features visible on the outside of the body that serve as signs of sexual maturity but do not involve the reproductive organs (for example, breast development in females, appearance of underarm and pubic hair in both sexes).

menarche
First menstruation.

SEXUAL MATURATION

Accompanying the rapid increase in body size are changes in physical features related to sexual functioning. Some, called **primary sexual characteristics,** involve the reproductive organs directly (ovaries, uterus, and vagina in females; penis, scrotum, and testes in males). Others, called **secondary sexual characteristics,** are visible on the outside of the body and serve as additional signs of sexual maturity (for example, breast development in females, appearance of underarm and pubic hair in both sexes). As you can see in Table 14.1, these characteristics develop in a fairly standard sequence, although the age at which each begins and is completed varies greatly.

■ **SEXUAL MATURATION IN GIRLS.** **Menarche** (from the Greek word *arche,* meaning "beginning") is the scientific name for first menstruation. Because most people view it as the major sign that puberty has arrived in girls, you may be surprised to learn that it occurs late in the sequence of pubertal events. Female puberty usually begins with the budding of the breasts and the growth spurt. (For about 15 percent of girls, pubic hair is present before breast development.) Menarche typically happens around 12½ years for North American girls, 13 for Europeans. But the age range is wide, extending from 10½ to 15½ years. Following menarche, pubic hair and breast development are completed, and underarm hair appears. Most girls take 3 to 4 years to complete this sequence, although this, too, can vary greatly, from 1½ to 5 years (Tanner, 1990; Wheeler, 1991).

Table 14.1 shows that all girls experience menarche after the peak of the height spurt, a sequence that is adaptive. Nature delays menstruation until the girl's body is large enough for successful childbearing. As an extra measure of security, for 12 to 18 months following menarche, the menstrual cycle often takes place without an ovum being released from the ovaries. However, this temporary period of sterility does not apply to all girls, so it cannot be relied on for protection against pregnancy (Tanner, 1990).

TABLE 14.1

Average Age and Age Range of Major Pubertal Changes in North American Boys and Girls

GIRLS	AVERAGE	RANGE	BOYS	AVERAGE	RANGE
Breasts begin to "bud"	10	(8–13)	Testes begin to enlarge	11.5	(9.5–13.5)
Height spurt begins	10	(8–13)	Pubic hair appears	12	(10–15)
Pubic hair appears	10.5	(8–14)	Penis begins to enlarge	12	(10.5–14.5)
Peak of strength spurt	11.6	(9.5–14)	Height spurt begins	12.5	(10.5–16)
Peak of height spurt	11.7	(10–13.5)	Spermarche (first ejaculation) occurs	13	(12–16)
Menarche (first menstruation) occurs	12.8	(10.5–15.5)	Peak of height spurt	14	(12.5–15.5)
Adult stature reached	13	(10–16)	Facial hair begins to grow	14	(12.5–15.5)
Breast growth completed	14	(10–16)	Voice begins to deepen	14	(12.5–15.5)
Pubic hair growth completed	14.5	(14–15)	Penis and testes growth completed	14.5	(12.5–16)
			Peak of strength spurt	15.3	(13–17)
			Adult stature reached	15.5	(13.5–17.5)
			Pubic hair growth completed	15.5	(14–17)

Sources: Malina and Bouchard, 1991; Tanner, 1990.

■ **SEXUAL MATURATION IN BOYS.** The first sign of puberty in boys is the enlargement of the testes (glands that manufacture sperm), accompanied by changes in the texture and color of the scrotum. Pubic hair emerges a short time later, about the same time the penis begins to enlarge (Graber, Petersen, & Brooks-Gunn, 1996).

Refer again to Table 14.1, and you will see that the growth spurt occurs much later in the sequence of pubertal events for boys than for girls. Also, boys' height gain is more intense and longer lasting (Sheehy et al., 1999). When it reaches its peak (about age 14), enlargement of the testes and penis is nearly complete, and underarm hair appears soon after. Facial and body hair also emerge just after the peak in body growth and gradually increase for several years. Another landmark of male physical maturity is the deepening of the voice as the larynx enlarges and the vocal cords lengthen. (Girls' voices also deepen slightly.) Voice change usually takes place at the peak of the male growth spurt and often is not complete until puberty is over. When it first occurs, many boys have difficulty with voice control. Occasionally their newly acquired baritone breaks into a high-pitched sound.

While the penis is growing, the prostate gland and seminal vesicles (which together produce semen, the fluid in which sperm are bathed) enlarge. Then, around age 13, **spermarche,** or first ejaculation, occurs (Jorgensen & Keiding, 1991). For a while, the semen contains few living sperm. So, like girls, boys have an initial period of reduced fertility.

INDIVIDUAL AND GROUP DIFFERENCES IN PUBERTAL GROWTH

Heredity contributes substantially to the timing of puberty, since identical twins generally reach menarche within a month or two of each other, whereas fraternal twins differ by about 12 months (Kaprio et al., 1995; Tanner, 1990). Nutrition and exercise also make a difference. In females, a sharp rise in body weight and fat may trigger sexual maturation. Fat cells stimulate the production of sex hormones by the ovaries and adrenal glands—the likely reason that breast and pubic hair growth and menarche occur earlier for heavier and, especially, obese girls (Must & Strauss, 1999). In contrast, girls who begin rigorous athletic training at young ages or who eat very little (both of which reduce the percentage of body fat) often are delayed in sexual development (Rees, 1993).

spermarche
First ejaculation of seminal fluid.

Secular trends in physical growth have taken place in industrialized nations. The adolescent girl on the left is taller than her grandmother, mother, and aunt, and she probably reached menarche at an earlier age. Improved nutrition and health are responsible for gains in body size and faster physical maturation from one generation to the next.

Variations in pubertal growth also exist between regions of the world and SES groups. Heredity seems to play little role, since adolescents with very different genetic origins living under similarly advantaged conditions—for example, in Australia, Chile, Greece, Israel, Japan, and the United States—reach menarche at about the same average age (Morabia et al., 1998). Instead, physical health is largely responsible. In poverty-stricken regions where malnutrition and infectious disease are widespread, menarche is greatly delayed. In many parts of Africa, it does not occur until age 14 to 17. And within countries, girls from higher-income families consistently reach menarche 6 to 18 months earlier than do those living in economically disadvantaged homes.

Early family experiences also seem to contribute to the timing of puberty. One theory suggests that humans have evolved to be sensitive to the emotional quality of their childhood environments. When children's safety and security are at risk, it is adaptive for them to reproduce early. Consequently, strife-ridden families should promote earlier pubertal maturation. In support of this view, several studies indicate that girls exposed to early family conflict tend to reach menarche early, whereas those with highly affectionate family ties reach menarche relatively late (Ellis & Garber, 2000; Ellis et al., 1999; Moffitt et al., 1992).

Notice how, in the research we have considered, threats to physical health delay puberty, whereas threats to emotional health accelerate it. In a study carried out in Poland that distinguished physical stress (poverty) from emotional stress (father absence, parental illness, and parental alcohol abuse), opposite relationships with age at menarche were, indeed, found (Hulanicka, 1999).

THE SECULAR TREND

In Chapter 11 we saw that children in industrialized nations grow faster and larger than in generations past. Similarly, age of menarche has declined steadily from 1860 to 1970, by about 3 to 4 months per decade (see Figure 14.3). This *secular trend* in pubertal timing lends added support to the role of physical well-being in adolescent growth. Nutrition, health care, sanitation, and control of infectious disease have improved greatly during this time.

As noted in Chapter 11, the secular gain in height has slowed, but overweight and obesity rates have soared, contributing to the trend toward earlier menarche. In a large cross-sectional study, Louisiana girls were examined in 1978 and again in 1992. During that period, average age of menarche decreased sharply—by nearly a year in Caucasians (from 12.3 to 11.4 years) and by just over a half-year in African Americans (from 12.2 to 11.5). At the same time, obesity rates rose dramatically. And for both the 1978 and 1992 cohorts, obesity was a powerful predictor of early menarche (Wattigney et al., 1999).

A worrisome consequence for girls who reach sexual maturity by ages 10 and 11 is that they will feel pressure to act much older than they are. As we will see shortly, early maturing girls are at risk for unfavorable peer involvements, including sexual activity.

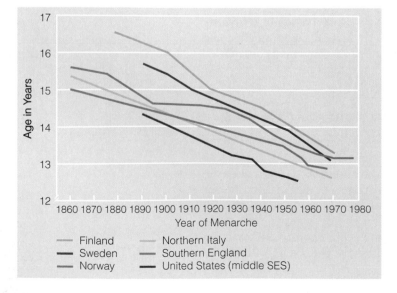

FIGURE 14.3

Secular trend in age of first menstruation (menarche) in industrialized nations. (Reprinted by permission of the publisher from J. M. Tanner, 1990, *Foetus into Man* [2nd ed., p. 160], Cambridge, MA: Harvard University Press. Copyright © 1990 by J. M. Tanner. All rights reserved.)

CHANGING STATES OF AROUSAL

Adolescence is a time of substantial change in sleep and wakefulness. On average, sleep declines from 10 hours in middle childhood to 7.5 to 8 hours in adolescence. Yet teenagers need almost as much sleep as they did during the school years—about 9.2 hours.

Adolescents go to bed much later than they did as children yet must get up early for school—before their sleep needs are satisfied. Biological changes may underlie this sleep "phase delay," as the tendency to stay up late strengthens with pubertal maturation (Carskadon, Viera, & Acebo, 1993). But afternoon and evening activities, part-time jobs, and social pressures also contribute. Although most teenagers say they enjoy staying up late, they also complain of daytime sleepiness (Wolfson & Carskadon, 1998). Sleep-deprived adolescents tend to achieve less well in school, more often suffer from depressed mood, and report irregular sleep schedules, which add to their daytime sleepiness and behavior problems (Link & Ancoli-Israel, 1995). Later school start times ease sleep loss but do not eliminate it (Kowalski & Allen, 1995).

review   *Many people believe that the rising sexual passions of puberty cause rebelliousness in adolescents. Where did this belief originate? Explain why it is incorrect.*

apply   *Sabrina, who reached menarche before age 11, was already much taller and heavier than her classmates. She worried that she was going to keep on growing larger and larger. How would you respond to Sabrina's concern?*

apply   *Sixteen-year-old Jonah, who used to go to bed early, stays up until 2 A.M., is often late for school, and dozes in his classes. Why might Jonah's sleep habits have changed, and what can his parents and his school do to help?*

The Psychological Impact of Pubertal Events

Think back to your late elementary school and junior high days. Were you early, late, or about on time in physical maturation with respect to your peers? How did your feelings about yourself and your relationships with others change? Research reveals that puberty affects the adolescent's self-image, mood, and interaction with parents and peers. Some of these outcomes are a response to dramatic physical change, regardless of when it occurs. Others have to do with the timing of pubertal maturation.

REACTIONS TO PUBERTAL CHANGES

How do girls and boys react to the massive physical changes of puberty? Most research aimed at answering this question has focused on girls' feelings about menarche.

■ **GIRLS' REACTIONS TO MENARCHE.** A generation or two ago, menarche often was traumatic. Today girls commonly react with "surprise," undoubtedly due to the sudden nature of the event. Otherwise, they typically report a mixture of positive and negative emotions—"excited and pleased" as well as "scared and upset" (Brooks-Gunn, 1988b). Yet wide individual differences exist that depend on prior knowledge and support from family members. Both are influenced by cultural attitudes toward puberty and sexuality.

For girls who have no advance information, menarche can be shocking and disturbing. In the 1950s, up to 50 percent were given no prior warning (Shainess, 1961). Today, no more

Cultural INFLUENCES

ADOLESCENT INITIATION CEREMONIES

An **adolescent initiation ceremony** is a ritualized announcement to the community that a young person is ready to make the transition from childhood into adolescence or full adulthood. These special rites of passage reach their fullest expression in small tribal and village societies. Besides celebration, they often include such features as separation from parents and members of the other sex; instruction in cultural customs and work roles; and fertility rituals that incorporate the young person into the sexual and childbearing world of adults. According to anthropologists, each of these ceremonial features is a cultural expression of the adaptive value of biological puberty.

SEPARATION

The beginning of an initiation ceremony usually is marked by separation from parents and members of the other sex, and sometimes by seclusion from the entire settlement. Among the !Kung hunters and gatherers of Botswana, Africa, a girl menstruating for the first time is carried to a special shelter by an old woman, who cares for her until the menstrual flow stops. At puberty, some Native American boys

must begin a lonely pilgrimage to seek their vision. The Tiwi, an Aboriginal group of northern Australia, greet male puberty by arranging to have a group of strange men take boys to a special campsite in the bush. Initiates are expected to shed their childish ways abruptly in favor of adultlike reverence and self-restraint (Spindler, 1970).

A same-sex nonparent usually oversees the initiation, since puberty is accompanied by a rise in conflict and psychological distancing between parent and child, which reduces parents' power to teach the adolescent (Eibl-Eibesfeldt, 1989). Gender segregation fosters the young person's assumption of adult gender roles, which are sharply divided in most tribal and village societies (Weisfield, 1986).

Boys are typically initiated in large peer groups, a custom that promotes social solidarity. When agemates undergo challenging and painful experiences together, they bond with one another, an outcome that enhances cooperation in hunting, defending the group, and other adult tasks (Schlegel & Barry, 1991). Girls, in contrast, are generally initiated singly. In adulthood, they will spend more time with their family and in small groups. Conse-

quently, large-group unity is deemed less important (Schlegel, 1995).

INSTRUCTION

During initiation rites, years of childhood teachings are supplemented with information on ceremonial matters, courtship, sexual techniques, duties to one's spouse and in-laws, and subsistence skills. Elders often convey tribal secrets and stress cultural values. Among the Mano of Liberia, older men take young boys off into the forest, where they teach them secret folklore along with farming and other skills they will need to earn a living. The boys return with a new name, signifying their adult identity, and an even stronger allegiance to their culture. !Kung women teach the newly menstruating girl not to shame her husband or touch his hunting gear and about birth and infant care (Fried & Fried, 1980).

ENTRY INTO ADULT SOCIETY

The training period culminates in a formal celebration, which usually grants young people permission to engage in sex and to marry. Most of the time, the appearance of initiates is changed so that all members of the community can identify them and treat

---

adolescent initiation ceremony
A ritual, or rite of passage, announcing to the community that a young person is making the transition into adolescence or full adulthood.

than 10 to 15 percent are uninformed (Brooks-Gunn, 1988b). This shift is probably due to modern parents' greater willingness to discuss sexual matters and more widespread health education classes. Almost all girls get some information from their mothers and at school. And girls whose fathers know about their daughters' pubertal changes adjust especially well. Perhaps a father's involvement reflects a family atmosphere that is highly understanding and accepting of physical and sexual matters (Brooks-Gunn & Ruble, 1980, 1983).

■ **BOYS' REACTIONS TO SPERMARCHE.** Like girls' reactions to menarche, boys' responses to spermarche reflect mixed feelings. Virtually all boys know about ejaculation ahead of time, but few get any information from parents. Usually they obtain it from reading material (Gaddis & Brooks-Gunn, 1985). Despite advance information, many boys say that their first ejaculation occurred earlier than they expected and that they were unprepared for it. As with girls, the better prepared boys feel, the more positively they react (Stein & Reiser, 1994).

This Ubi girl of Zaire, Africa, studied traditional dance and customs for a year before she was deemed ready for the adolescent initiation ceremony that will grant her adult status among her people.

them differently. Sometimes physical markers of increased status involve temporary body decorations, such as painting and jewelry. At other times, the changes are permanent, consisting of new types of clothing or scars engraved on some part of the body—usually the face, back, chest, or penis.

Many ceremonies include an ordeal, typically more severe for males than for females. A boy might need to kill game or endure cold and hunger, a girl might grind grain or remain secluded for several days. These rites stress responsibility, wisdom, and bravery. They also subject adolescents with a rebellious streak to the authority of their elders (Weisfield, 1997).

Male genital operations (usually circumcision) occur in about one-third of cultures with puberty rites and typically are followed by sexual activity. Female surgery (removal of part or all of the clitoris and sometimes the labia), to ensure the girl's continued virginity and therefore her value as a bride, takes place in 8 percent of initiation ceremonies (Weisfield, 1990).[1]

CULTURAL VARIATIONS

In the simplest societies, adolescent initiation ceremonies for girls are more common than those for boys. In small bands of hunters and gatherers, females are in short supply. The loss of any woman of childbearing age can threaten the survival of the group. In these cultures, female rites typically last for several weeks and are especially elaborate, designed to provide the girl with both social recognition and magical protection. As cultures move from simple foraging to farming communities, rituals for boys increase in frequency. Initiation rites in farming villages typically recognize young people of both sexes for their distinct reproductive and economic roles. In more complex cultures, adolescent initiation ceremonies recede in importance and disappear (Schlegel & Barry, 1980).

[1]*Female genital mutilation,* widespread in Africa, Indonesia, Malaysia, and the Middle East, as a means of guaranteeing chastity and therefore a good marriage partner, is usually performed on girls in infancy or early childhood, before they know enough to resist (Weisfield, 1997). Although illegal in many countries, the practice is difficult for governments to control. Today, there are millions of genitally mutilated girls and women in the developing world. International organizations are sending social scientists and health professionals into villages to work within each culture's belief system to bring an end to this violation of human rights (Bashir, 1997).

In addition, whereas almost all girls tell a friend that they are menstruating, far fewer boys tell anyone about spermarche (Brooks-Gunn et al., 1986; Downs & Fuller, 1991). Overall, boys seem to get much less social support for the physical changes of puberty than do girls. This suggests that boys might benefit, especially, from opportunities to ask questions and discuss feelings with a sympathetic parent or health professional.

■ **CULTURAL INFLUENCES.** The experience of puberty is affected by the larger culture in which boys and girls live. Many tribal and village societies celebrate puberty with a *rite of passage*—a community-wide event that marks an important change in privilege and responsibility. Consequently, all young people know that pubertal changes are honored and valued in their culture (see the Cultural Influences box above). In contrast, Western societies grant little formal recognition to movement from childhood to adolescence or from adolescence to adulthood. Certain religious ceremonies, such as confirmation and the Jewish bar or bat mitzvah, do resemble a rite of passage. But they usually do not lead to any meaningful change in social status.

Instead, Western adolescents are confronted with many ages at which they are granted partial adult status—for example, an age for starting employment, for driving, for leaving high school, for voting, and for drinking. In some contexts (on the highway and at work), they may be treated like adults. In others (at school and at home), they may still be regarded as children. The absence of a widely accepted marker of physical and social maturity makes the process of becoming an adult especially confusing.

PUBERTAL CHANGE, EMOTION, AND SOCIAL BEHAVIOR

In the preceding sections we considered adolescents' reactions to their sexually maturing bodies. Puberty can also affect the young person's emotional state and social behavior. A common belief is that pubertal change has something to do with adolescent moodiness and the desire for greater physical and psychological separation from parents.

■ **ADOLESCENT MOODINESS.** Recently, researchers have explored the role of sex hormones in adolescents' emotional reactions. Indeed, higher hormone levels are related to greater moodiness, in the form of anger and irritability for boys and anger and depression for girls (Buchanan, Eccles, & Becker, 1992; Nottelmann et al., 1990; Paikoff, Brooks-Gunn, & Warren, 1991). But these links are not strong, and we cannot really be sure that a rise in pubertal hormones causes adolescent moodiness.

What else might contribute to the common observation that adolescents are moody? In several studies, the mood fluctuations of children, adolescents, and adults were tracked over a week by having them carry electronic pagers. At random intervals, they were beeped and asked to write down what they were doing, whom they were with, and how they felt.

As expected, adolescents reported less favorable moods than did school-age children or adults (Csikszentmihalyi & Larson, 1984; Larson & Lampman-Petraitis, 1989). But young people whose moods were especially negative were experiencing a greater number of nega-

DAVID YOUNG-WOLFF/STONE

tive life events, such as difficulties in getting along with parents, disciplinary actions at school, and breaking up with a boyfriend or girlfriend. Number of negative events increased steadily from childhood to adolescence, and teenagers also seemed to react to them with greater emotion than did children (Larson & Ham, 1993).

Furthermore, compared with the moods of adults, adolescents' feelings were less stable. They often varied from cheerful to sad and back again. But teenagers also moved from one situation to another more often, and their mood swings were strongly related to these changes. High points of their days were times spent with friends and in self-chosen leisure and hobby activities. Low points tended to occur in adult-structured settings—class, job, school halls, school library, and religious services.

Not surprisingly, adolescents' emotional high points are Friday and Saturday evenings, especially at older ages (see Figure 14.4). As teenagers move from junior high to high school, frequency of going out with friends and romantic partners—to movies, sports events, and parties or just to cruise around town—increases dramatically, so much so that it becomes a "cultural script" for what is *supposed* to happen. This means that teenagers who fall short of the script—who spend weekend evenings at home—often experience profound loneliness (Larson & Richards, 1998).

Compared with children and adults, adolescents often seem moody. But young people whose moods are often negative experience more negative life events. This dispirited boy may have had an argument with his parents, received a detention at school, or broken up with his girlfriend. Events like these increase in adolescence.

Taken together, these findings suggest that situational factors combine with hormonal influences to affect teenagers' moodiness. Notice that this account is consistent with the balanced view of biological and social forces described earlier in this chapter.

■ **PARENT–CHILD RELATIONSHIPS.** Sabrina's father noticed that as his children entered adolescence, their bedroom doors started to close, they resisted spending time with the family, and they became more argumentative. Within a 2-day period, Sabrina and her mother squabbled over Sabrina's messy room ("Mom, it's *my* room. You don't have to live in it!") and her clothing purchases ("Sabrina, if you *buy* it, then *wear* it. Otherwise, you are wasting money!"). And Sabrina resisted the family's regular weekend visit to Aunt Gina's ("Why do I have to go *every* week?").

Many studies show that puberty is related to a rise in parent–child conflict. Although rate of conflict declines with age as parents and adolescents spend less time together, its emotional intensity rises into mid-adolescence. During this time, both parents and teenagers report feeling less close to one another. In late adolescence, heated arguments decline (Holmbeck, 1996; Laursen, Coy, & Collins, 1998). Frequency of conflict is surprisingly similar across American subcultures. It occurs about as often in families of European descent as it does in immigrant Chinese, Filipino, and Mexican families, whose traditions respect parental authority and downplay adolescent individuality (Fuligni, 1998).

Why should a youngster's more adultlike appearance trigger these disputes? The association may have some adaptive value. Among nonhuman primates, the young typically leave the family group around the time of puberty. The same is true in many nonindustrialized cultures (Caine, 1986; Schlegel & Barry, 1991). Departure of young people from the family discourages sexual relations between close blood relatives. But because children in industrialized societies remain economically dependent on parents long after they reach puberty, they cannot leave the family. Consequently, a modern substitute for physical departure seems to have emerged—psychological distancing (Steinberg, 1990).

In later chapters we will see that adolescents' new powers of reasoning may also contribute to a rise in family tensions. Also, the need for families to redefine relationships as children become physically mature and demand to be treated in adultlike ways can induce a temporary period of conflict. Parent–adolescent disagreements largely focus on mundane, day-to-day matters, such as driving, dating partners, and curfews. But beneath these disputes are serious concerns—parental efforts to protect their teenagers from substance use, auto accidents, and early sex. The greater the gap between parents' and adolescents' views of teenagers' readiness to take on developmental tasks, the greater the tendency for quarreling (Deković, Noom, & Meeus, 1997).

The conflict that does take place is generally mild. Only a small minority of families experience a serious break in parent–child relationships. In reality, parents and children display both conflict and affection throughout adolescence, and usually they agree on important values, such as honesty and the value of education (Arnett, 1999). This also makes sense from an evolutionary perspective. Although separation from parents is adaptive, both generations benefit from warm, protective family bonds that last for many years to come.

EARLY VERSUS LATE MATURATION

Recall that Sabrina's mother reported that all her children matured early, but her daughter had difficulty adjusting whereas her sons reacted with confidence. Maturational timing influences adolescent adjustment, in opposite directions for girls than for boys.

■ **EFFECTS OF MATURATIONAL TIMING.** Sabrina was self-conscious about her well-developed body, felt awkward and unsure of herself, and withdrew from her peers. In contrast, her brothers were confident and proud of their large, muscular physiques.

Findings of several studies match the experiences of Sabrina and her brothers. Both adults and peers viewed early maturing boys as relaxed, independent, self-confident, and physically

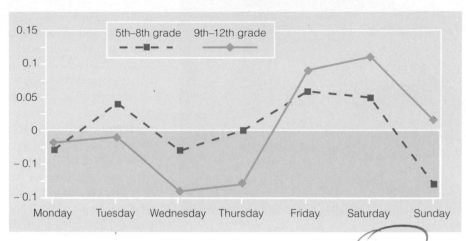

FIGURE 14.4

Younger and older adolescents' emotional experiences across the week. Adolescents' reports revealed that emotional high points are on Fridays and Saturdays, especially among ninth to twelfth graders. Mood drops on Sunday, before returning to school, and during the week, as students spend much time in adult-structured settings in school. (From R. Larson & M. Richards, 1998, "Waiting for the Weekend: Friday and Saturday Night as the Emotional Climax of the Week." In A. C. Crouter & R. Larson [Eds.], *Temporal Rhythms in Adolescence: Clocks, Calendars, and the Coordination of Daily Life.* San Francisco: Jossey-Bass, p. 41. Reprinted by permission.)

Each of these boys is 13 years old, yet they differ greatly in timing of pubertal maturation. The two early maturing boys are probably popular, self-confident, athletic stars with a positive body image. The three late maturing boys are likely to have a low sense of self-esteem and a negative body image.

body image
Conception of and attitude toward one's physical appearance.

attractive. Popular with agemates, they held many leadership positions in school and tended to be athletic stars. In contrast, late maturing boys were not well liked. Peers and adults viewed them as anxious, overly talkative, and attention seeking (Brooks-Gunn, 1988a; Clausen, 1975; Jones, 1965; Jones & Bayley, 1950).

Among girls, the impact of maturational timing was just the reverse. Early maturing girls were below average in popularity; appeared withdrawn, lacking in self-confidence, and psychologically stressed; and held few positions of leadership (Ge, Conger, & Elder, 1996; Graber et al., 1997; Jones & Mussen, 1958). In addition, they were more involved in deviant behavior (getting drunk, staying out late, participating in early sexual activity) and achieved less well in school (Caspi et al., 1993; Dick et al., 2000; Stattin & Magnusson, 1990). In contrast, their late maturing counterparts were well adjusted—regarded as physically attractive, lively, sociable, and leaders at school.

Two factors seem to account for these trends: (1) how closely the adolescent's body matches cultural ideals of physical attractiveness, and (2) how well young people "fit in" physically with their agemates.

■ **THE ROLE OF PHYSICAL ATTRACTIVENESS.** Flip through the pages of your favorite popular magazine. You will see evidence for our society's view of an attractive female as thin and long-legged and a good-looking male as tall, broad-shouldered, and muscular. The female image is a girlish shape that favors the late developer. The male image fits the early maturing boy.

As their bodies change, adolescents become preoccupied with their physical selves. Girls, especially, are likely to analyze their body's features (Wertheim, et al., 1997). In addition, teenagers get a great deal of feedback from others—both directly, through remarks about their appearance, and indirectly, through the tendency of children and adults to treat physically attractive people more positively. The conclusions young people draw about their appearance strongly affect their satisfaction with their bodies and, ultimately, their self-esteem and psychological well-being (Mendelson, White, & Mendelson, 1996; Usmiani & Daniluk, 1997).

In several studies, early maturing girls reported a less positive **body image**—conception of and attitude toward their physical appearance—than did their on-time and late maturing agemates. Among boys, the opposite occurred: early maturation was linked to a positive body image, whereas late maturation predicted dissatisfaction with the physical self (Alsaker, 1995). The difference in body image between early and late maturing boys was short lived; it disappeared as the late maturers reached puberty. Early maturing girls' less favorable body image not only persisted but became more extreme. In sum, society's "beauty is best" stereotype seems to affect adolescents' attitudes about their pubertal timing, particularly for girls.

■ **THE IMPORTANCE OF FITTING IN WITH PEERS.** Physical status in relation to peers also explains differences in adjustment between early and late maturers. From this perspective, early maturing girls and late maturing boys have difficulty because they fall at the extremes of physical development. Recall that Sabrina felt "out of place" when with her agemates. She was not just larger than the girls; she also towered over the boys. Late maturing boys are self-conscious about their childish appearance, and many harbor fears about whether they will grow larger. Not surprisingly, adolescents feel most comfortable with peers who match their own level of biological maturity (Brooks-Gunn et al., 1986; Stattin & Magnusson, 1990).

Because few agemates of the same physical status are available, early maturing adolescents of both sexes seek out older companions—at times with unfavorable consequences. Older peers often encourage them into activities they are not yet ready to handle emotionally, including sexual activity, drug and alcohol use, and minor delinquent acts. For example, the eighth graders Sabrina met at church introduced her to several high school boys, who were quite unconcerned that she was just a sixth grader! Sabrina welcomed their attentions, which gratified her desire to feel socially accepted and physically attractive. Perhaps because of involvements like these, the academic performance of early maturers tends to suffer (Caspi et al., 1993; Stattin & Magnusson, 1990).

Interestingly, school contexts can modify these maturational timing effects. In one study, early maturing sixth-grade girls felt better about themselves when they attended kindergarten through sixth grade (K–6) rather than kindergarten through eighth grade (K–8) schools, where they could mix with older adolescents. In the K–6 settings, they were relieved of pressures to adopt behaviors for which they were not ready (Blyth, Simmons, & Zakin, 1985). Similarly, a New Zealand study found that delinquency among early maturing girls was greatly reduced in all-girl schools, which limit opportunities to associate with norm-violating peers (most of whom are older boys) (Caspi et al., 1993).

■ **LONG-TERM CONSEQUENCES.** Do the effects of early and late maturation persist into adulthood? Long-term follow-ups show striking turnabouts. Many early maturing boys and late maturing girls, who had been so admired in adolescence, became rigid, inflexible, conforming, and somewhat discontented adults. In contrast, late maturing boys and early maturing girls, who were stress-ridden as teenagers, often developed into adults who were independent, flexible, cognitively competent, and satisfied with the direction of their lives (Livson & Peshkin, 1980; Macfarlane, 1971). What explains these remarkable reversals? Perhaps the confidence-inducing adolescence of early maturing boys and late maturing girls does not promote the coping skills needed to solve life's later problems. In contrast, the painful experiences associated with off-time pubertal growth may, in time, contribute to sharpened awareness, clarified goals, and greater stability.

Nevertheless, these long-term outcomes may not hold completely. In a Swedish study, achievement difficulties of early maturing girls persisted into young adulthood, in the form of lower educational attainment than their on-time and later maturing counterparts (Stattin & Magnusson, 1990). In countries with highly selective college entrance systems, perhaps it is harder for early maturers to recover from declines in school performance. Clearly, the effects of maturational timing involve a complex blend of biological, immediate social setting, and cultural factors.

Ask YOURSELF...

review List factors that contribute to pubertal timing. Then summarize the consequences of early versus late maturation for adolescent development.

apply After having been home on Friday and Saturday nights for three weekends in a row, 15-year-old Paul was particularly despondent. His parents attributed his gloomy mood to the storm and stress of adolescence. Provide another more likely explanation.

connect How might adolescent moodiness contribute to the psychological distancing between parents and children that accompanies puberty? (Hint: Think about bidirectional influences in parent–child relationships, discussed in previous chapters.)

reflect Think back to your own reactions to the physical changes of puberty. Are they consistent with research findings? Explain.

Health Issues

As young people move into adolescence, they begin to view physical health in a broader way—as more than just the absence of illness. To teenagers, being healthy means functioning physically, mentally, and socially at their best (Millstein & Litt, 1990). Consistent with this new view, the arrival of puberty is accompanied by new health concerns. As the body grows and takes on mature proportions, eating disturbances appear in many young people who worry about falling short of their idealized image of attractiveness and fitness. Sexual activity brings with it the risk of early pregnancy and sexually transmitted disease. Substance abuse and certain unintentional injuries also increase. (We will take up suicide—another serious adolescent health problem—in Chapter 16.)

As adolescents are granted greater autonomy, their personal decision making becomes important, in health as well as other areas (Bearison, 1998). Yet none of the health difficulties we are about to discuss can be traced to a single cause. Throughout development, biological, psychological, family, and cultural factors jointly contribute to health and well-being.

NUTRITIONAL NEEDS

When their sons reached puberty, Franca and Antonio reported a "vacuum cleaner effect" in the kitchen, as the boys routinely emptied the refrigerator. Rapid body growth leads to a dramatic rise in food intake. During the growth spurt, boys require about 2,700 calories a day and much more protein, girls about 2,200 calories and somewhat less protein than boys because of their smaller size and muscle mass. Calcium is especially important for skeletal growth. Extra iron is needed to support gains in muscle mass and blood volume in boys and to make up for the loss of blood in the menstrual flow of girls (Larson, 1996).

This increase in nutritional requirements comes at a time when the eating habits of many young people are the poorest. Of all age groups, adolescents are the most likely to skip breakfast (a practice linked to obesity), consume empty calories, and eat on the run (Siega-Riz, Popkin, & Carson, 1998). Fast-food restaurants, which are favorite teenage gathering places, have started to offer more healthful menu options. But adolescents need to know how to select these alternatives—baked foods and salads instead of fried foods, milk and fruit juice instead of soft drinks and high-calorie shakes. The eating habits of teenagers are particularly harmful if they extend a lifelong pattern of poor nutrition, less serious if they are just a temporary response to peer influences and a busy schedule.

The most common nutritional problem of adolescence is iron deficiency. A tired, listless, irritable adolescent may be suffering from anemia rather than unhappiness and should have a medical checkup. Most adolescents do not get enough calcium, and they are also deficient in riboflavin (vitamin B_2) and magnesium, both of which support metabolism. And contrary to what many parents believe, obese children rarely outgrow their weight problem when they become teenagers (Serdula et al., 1993).

Adolescents, especially girls who are concerned about their weight, tend to be attracted to the latest fad diets. Unfortunately, most are too limited in nutrients and calories to be healthful for fast-growing, active teenagers. Adolescence is also a time when many young people choose to become vegetarians. As they formulate a philosophy of life, some find the killing of animals distasteful. Others claim that meats are sources of impurities and toxins. A properly planned vegetarian diet can be healthy, but one not well chosen can be dangerous (Donatelle & Davis, 2000). When a youngster insists on trying a special diet, parents should, in turn, insist that they first consult with a doctor or dietitian.

SERIOUS EATING DISTURBANCES

Franca worried about Sabrina's desire to lose weight at such an early age, explained to her that she was really quite average in build for an adolescent girl, and reminded Sabrina that her Italian ancestors thought a plump female body was more beautiful than a thin one. Girls who reach puberty early, who are very dissatisfied with their body image, and who grow up in homes where concern with weight and thinness is high are at risk for eating problems. Severe dieting is the strongest predictor of the onset of an eating disorder in adolescence (Patton et al., 1999). The two most serious are anorexia nervosa and bulimia.

■ **ANOREXIA NERVOSA.** **Anorexia nervosa** is a tragic eating disturbance in which young people starve themselves because of a compulsive fear of getting fat. About 1 percent of teenage girls in the United States are affected, a rate that has increased sharply during the past 50 years, due to cultural admiration of female thinness. Occasionally, boys are diagnosed

anorexia nervosa
An eating disorder in which individuals (usually females) starve themselves because of a compulsive fear of getting fat and an extremely distorted body image

with the disorder; about half are homosexual or bisexual (Brown & Mehler, 2000). Asian-American, Caucasian-American, and Hispanic girls are at greater risk than are African-American girls, who are more satisfied with their size and shape (Abood & Chandler, 1997; Halpern et al., 1999; Rhea, 1999). Anorexia nervosa occurs equally often among economically advantaged and economically disadvantaged teenagers (Rogers et al., 1997).

Anorexics have an extremely distorted body image. Even after they have become severely underweight, they believe they are fat. Most lose weight by going on a self-imposed diet so strict that they struggle to avoid eating in response to hunger. To enhance weight loss, they exercise strenuously.

In their attempt to reach "perfect" slimness, anorexics lose between 25 and 50 percent of their body weight and are painfully thin. Because a normal menstrual cycle requires about 15 percent body fat, either menarche does not occur or menstrual periods stop. Malnutrition causes pale skin; brittle, discolored nails; fine, dark hairs all over the body; and extreme sensitivity to cold. If allowed to continue, anorexia nervosa can result in shrinking of the heart muscle and kidney failure. As many as 10 percent die of the disorder, as a result of either physical complications or suicide. Severe anorexics who survive may suffer from irreversible brain damage (Neumärker, 1997).

Forces within the individual, the family, and the larger culture give rise to anorexia nervosa. We have already seen that the societal image of "thin is beautiful" contributes to the poor body image of early maturing girls, who are at greatest risk for anorexia (Graber et al., 1994). But although almost all adolescent girls go on diets at one time or another, anorexics persist in weight loss to an extreme. Many have extremely high standards for their own behavior and performance. They also tend to be emotionally inhibited and to avoid intimate ties outside the family. Consequently, these girls are excellent students who are responsible and well behaved—ideal daughters in many respects.

Anorexia nervosa tends to run in families, suggesting a genetic influence (Strober et al., 2000). In addition, parent–child interactions reveal problems related to adolescent autonomy. Often mothers of these girls have high expectations for physical appearance (including body weight), achievement, and social acceptance and are overprotective and controlling; fathers tend to be emotionally distant. Instead of rebelling openly, the anorexic girl seems to do so covertly—by fiercely pursuing perfection in achievement, respectable behavior, and thinness (Sanders, Kapphahn, & Steiner, 1998). Nevertheless, whether maladaptive parent–child relationships precede the disorder, emerge as a response to it, or both is not yet clear.

Because anorexic girls typically deny that any problem exists, treating the disorder is difficult. Hospitalization often is necessary to prevent life-threatening malnutrition. Family therapy, aimed at changing parent–child interaction and expectations, is the most successful treatment (Becker et al., 1999). As a supplementary approach, applied behavior analysis—in which hospitalized anorexics are rewarded with praise, social contact, and opportunities for exercise when they eat and gain weight—is helpful (Robin, Gilroy, & Dennis, 1998). Still, only 50 percent of anorexics fully recover. For many others, eating problems continue in less extreme form. Ten percent show signs of a less severe disorder—bulimia—that is still physically and psychologically damaging (Fichter & Quadflieg, 1999).

■ **BULIMIA NERVOSA.** When Sabrina's 16-year-old brother Louis brought his girlfriend Cassie to the house, Sabrina admired her good figure. "What willpower! Cassie hardly touches food," Sabrina thought to herself. "But what in the world is wrong with Cassie's teeth?"

Willpower was not the secret of Cassie's slender shape. When it came to food, she actually had great difficulty controlling herself. Cassie suffered from **bulimia nervosa,** an eating disorder in which young people (again, mainly girls, but gay adolescent boys are also vulnerable) engage in strict dieting and excessive exercise accompanied by binge eating, often followed by deliberate vomiting and purging with laxatives. When by herself, Cassie had periods of feeling lonely, unhappy, and anxious. She responded with eating rampages, consuming thousands of

Cultural admiration of female thinness has contributed to a dramatic increase in anorexia nervosa. This girl died from the disorder. Her strict, self-imposed diet and obsession with strenuous physical exercise led her to become painfully thin. Even so, her body image was so distorted that she regarded herself as fat and continued her destructive behavior.

bulimia nervosa
An eating disorder in which individuals (mainly females) engage in strict dieting and excessive exercise accompanied by binge eating, often followed by deliberate vomiting and purging with laxatives.

calories in an hour or two. The vomiting that followed eroded the enamel on Cassie's teeth. In some cases, life-threatening damage to the throat and stomach occurs (Becker et al., 1999).

Bulimia is more common than anorexia nervosa. About 2 to 3 percent of teenage girls are affected; only 5 percent have previously been anorexic. Although bulimics share with anorexics a pathological fear of getting fat, they may have experienced their parents as disengaged and emotionally unavailable rather than overcontrolling (Fairburn et al., 1997). One conjecture is that bulimics turn to food to compensate for feelings of emptiness resulting from lack of parental involvement (Attie & Brooks-Gunn, 1996; Johnson & Connors, 1987).

Some bulimics, like anorexics, are perfectionists. Others lack self control not just in eating but in other areas of their lives, engaging in petty shoplifting and alcohol abuse (Garner & Garfinkel, 1997). Bulimics differ from anorexics in that they are aware of their abnormal eating habits, feel depressed and guilty about them, and usually are desperate to get help. As a result, bulimia is usually easier to treat through individual therapy focused on support groups, nutrition education, and revising eating habits and thoughts about food (Kaye et al., 2000).

SEXUAL ACTIVITY

Louis and Cassie hadn't planned to have intercourse after taking a ride in Louis's car one Friday night. It "just happened." But before and after, a lot of things passed through their minds. Cassie had been dating Louis for 3 months, and she began to wonder, "Will he think I'm normal if I don't have sex with him? If he wants to and I say no, will I lose him?" Both young people knew their parents wouldn't approve. In fact, when Franca and Antonio noticed how attached Louis was to Cassie, they talked to him about the importance of waiting and the dangers of pregnancy. But that Friday evening, Louis and Cassie's feelings for one another seemed overwhelming. As things went further and further, Louis thought, "If I don't make a move, will she think I'm a wimp?" And Cassie had heard from one of her girlfriends that you couldn't get pregnant the first time.

With the arrival of puberty, hormonal changes—in particular, the production of androgens in young people of both sexes—lead to an increase in sex drive (Halpern, Udry, & Suchindran, 1997; Udry, 1990). As Louis and Cassie's inner thoughts reveal, adolescents become very concerned about how to manage sexuality in social relationships. New cognitive capacities involving perspective taking and self-reflection affect their efforts to do so. Yet, like the eating behaviors we have just discussed, adolescent sexuality is heavily influenced by the young person's social context.

■ THE IMPACT OF CULTURE. Think, for a moment, about when you first learned "the facts of life" and how you found out about them. In your family, was sex discussed openly or treated with secrecy? Exposure to sex, education about it, and efforts to restrict the sexual curiosity of children and adolescents vary widely around the world. At one extreme are a number of Middle Eastern peoples, who are known to kill girls who lose their virginity before marriage. At the other extreme are several Asian and Pacific Island groups with very permissive sexual attitudes and practices. For example, among the Trobriand Islanders of Melanesia, older companions provide children with explicit instruction in sexual practices. Bachelor houses are maintained, where adolescents are expected to engage in sexual experimentation with a variety of partners (Benedict, 1934a; Ford & Beach, 1951).

Despite the publicity granted to the image of a sexually free adolescent, sexual attitudes in the United States are relatively restrictive. Typically, American parents give children little information about sex, discourage sex play, and rarely talk about sex in their presence. When young people become interested in sex, they seek information from friends, books, magazines, movies, and television. On prime-time TV shows, which adolescents watch the most, sex between partners with little commitment to each other occurs often and is spontaneous and passionate. Characters are rarely shown taking steps to avoid pregnancy and sexually transmitted disease (Ward, 1995).

The messages delivered by these two sets of sources are contradictory and confusing. On one hand, adults emphasize that sex at a young age and outside marriage is wrong. On the

TABLE 14.2

Teenage Sexual Activity Rates by Sex, Ethnic Group, and Grade

| SEX | ETHNIC GROUP | | | GRADE | | | | TOTAL |
	WHITE	BLACK	HISPANIC	9	10	11	12	
Male	45.4	75.7	62.9	44.5	51.1	51.4	63.9	52.2
Female	44.8	66.9	45.5	32.5	46.6	53.8	65.8	47.7
All	45.1	71.2	54.1	38.6	46.8	52.5	64.9	49.9

Note: Data reflect the percentage of high school students who report ever having had sexual intercourse.
Source: U.S. Department of Health and Human Services, 2000f.

other hand, adolescents encounter much in the broader social environment that extols the excitement and romanticism of sex. American teenagers are left bewildered, poorly informed about sexual facts, and with little sound advice on how to conduct their sex lives responsibly.

■ **ADOLESCENT SEXUAL ATTITUDES AND BEHAVIOR.** Although differences between subcultural groups exist, the sexual attitudes of American adolescents and adults have become more liberal over the past 40 years. Compared to a generation ago, more people believe that sexual intercourse before marriage is all right, as long as two people are emotionally committed to each other (Michael et al., 1994). Recently, a slight swing back in the direction of conservative sexual beliefs has occurred, largely due to the risk of sexually transmitted disease, especially AIDS (Glassman, 1996).

Trends in the sexual behavior of adolescents are quite consistent with their attitudes. The rate of premarital sex among young people rose over several decades but recently declined slightly. For example, among unmarried 15- to 19-year-olds, females claiming to have had sexual intercourse grew from 28 percent in 1971 to 55 percent in 1990 and then dropped to 48 percent in 1999 (U.S. Department of Health and Human Services, 2000f). Nevertheless, as Table 14.2 reveals, a substantial minority of boys and girls are sexually active quite early, by ninth grade. Males tend to have their first intercourse earlier than do females, and sexual activity is especially high among African-American adolescents—particularly boys.

Yet timing of first intercourse provides only a limited picture of adolescent sexual behavior. The majority of teenagers engage in relatively low levels of sexual activity. The typical sexually active 15- to 19-year-old—white, black, or Hispanic—has relations with only one partner at a time and spends much of the year with no partner. Only 16 percent of adolescents have had as many as four partners by their senior year of high school (Sonenstein, Pleck, & Ku, 1991; U.S. Department of Health and Human Services, 2000f). Overall, a runaway sexual revolution does not characterize American adolescents. In fact, the rate of teenage sexual activity in the United States is about the same as in Western European nations (Creatsas et al., 1995).

■ **CHARACTERISTICS OF SEXUALLY ACTIVE ADOLESCENTS.** Early and frequent teenage sexual activity is linked to a wide range of personal, family, peer, and educational variables. These include early physical maturation, parental divorce, single-parent and stepfamily homes, large family size, weak parental monitoring, disrupted parent–child communication, sexually active friends and older siblings, poor school performance, lower educational aspirations, and tendency to engage in norm-violating acts, including alcohol and drug use and delinquency (Cooper & Orcutt, 1997; Costa et al., 1995; Miller, Forehand, & Kotchick, 1999).

Since many of these factors are associated with growing up in a low-SES family, it is not surprising that early sexual activity is more common among young people from economically disadvantaged homes. Living in a hazardous neighborhood—one high in physical deterioration, crime, and violence—also increases the likelihood that teenagers will be sexually

Adolescence is an especially important time for the development of sexuality. American teenagers receive contradictory and confusing messages from the social environment about the appropriateness of sex. Although the rate of premarital sex has risen among adolescents, most engage in low levels of sexual activity and have only a single partner.

RICHARD HUTCHINGS/PHOTOEDIT

Biology & ENVIRONMENT

HOMOSEXUALITY: COMING OUT TO ONESELF AND OTHERS

Cultures vary as much in their acceptance of homosexuality as they do in their approval of premarital sex. In the United States, homosexuals are stigmatized, as shown by the degrading language often used to describe them. This makes forming a sexual identity a much greater challenge for gay and lesbian youths than for their heterosexual counterparts.

Wide variations in sexual identity formation exist, depending on personal, family, and community factors. Yet interviews with homosexual adolescents and adults reveal that many (but not all) move through a three-phase sequence in coming out to themselves and others.

FEELING DIFFERENT

Many gay men and some lesbians say that they felt different from other children when they were young (Diamond, 1998; Savin-Williams, 1998). Typically, this first sense of their biologically determined sexual orientation appears between ages 6 and 12 and results from play interests more like those of the other gender (Mondimore, 1996). Boys may find that they are less interested in sports, drawn to quieter activities, and more emotionally sensitive than other boys, girls that they are more athletic and active than other girls.

In Chapter 10 we saw that children who do not conform to traditional gender roles (especially boys) often are ridiculed—an early experience of many homosexuals. In addition, when children hear derogatory labels for homosexuality, they absorb a bias against their own sexual orientation at an early age.

CONFUSION

With the arrival of puberty, feeling different begins to include feeling sexually different. In research on ethnically diverse gay, lesbian, and bisexual youths, awareness of a same-sex attraction occurred, on average, between ages 11 and 12 for boys and 14 and 15 for girls, perhaps because adolescent social pressures toward heterosexuality are particularly intense for girls (Diamond, 1998; Herdt & Boxer, 1993). Realizing that same-sex attraction has personal relevance generally sparks confusion, largely because most young people had assumed they were heterosexual like everyone else.

A few adolescents resolve their discomfort by crystallizing a gay, lesbian, or bisexual identity quickly, with a flash of insight into their sense of being different. Most experience an inner struggle and deep sense of isolation—outcomes intensified by a lack of role models and social support. Some throw themselves into activities they have come to associate with heterosexuality. Boys may go out for athletic teams, girls may drop softball and basketball in favor of dance. And homosexual youths may try heterosexual dating. Others are so bewildered, uncomfortable, guilt ridden, and lonely that they escape into alcohol and drug abuse and suicidal thinking (Anhalt & Morris, 1998).

ACCEPTANCE

The majority of gay and lesbian teenagers reach a point of accepting their sexual identity. Then they face another crossroad: whether to tell oth-

---

active (Upchurch et al., 1999). In such neighborhoods, social ties are weak, and adults exert little oversight and control over adolescents' activities.

✂ ■ CONTRACEPTIVE USE. Although adolescent contraceptive use has increased in recent years, one-third to one-half of sexually active American teenagers are at risk for unplanned pregnancy because they do not use contraception at all or delay using it for months after they have become sexually active (Moore et al., 1998). Why do so many teenagers fail to take precautions? As we will see when we take up adolescent cognitive development in Chapter 15, teenagers can consider many possibilities when faced with a problem. But at first, they fail to apply this reasoning to everyday situations. When asked to explain why they did not use contraception, they often give answers like these: "I was waiting until I had a steady boyfriend." "I wasn't planning to have sex."

One reason for responses like these is that advances in perspective taking lead teenagers, for a time, to be extremely concerned about others' opinion of them. Recall how Cassie and Louis each worried about what the other would think if they decided not to have sex. Another reason for lack of planning before sex is that intense self-reflection leads many adolescents to believe that they are unique and invulnerable to danger. In the midst of everyday social pressures, they often seem to overlook the consequences of engaging in risky behaviors (Beyth-Marom & Fischhoff, 1997).

ers. The most difficult disclosure is to parents, but many fear rejection by peers as well (Cohen & Savin-Williams, 1996). Powerful stigma against their sexual orientation at home and school lead some to decide that no disclosure is possible. As a result, they self-define but otherwise "pass" as heterosexual. In one interview study of gay adolescents, 85 percent said they tried concealment for a time (Newman & Muzzonigro, 1993).

Many young people eventually acknowledge their sexual orientation publicly, usually by telling trusted friends first, then family members and acquaintances. When people react positively, coming out strengthens the adolescent's view of homosexuality as a valid, meaningful, and fulfilling identity. Contact with other gays and lesbians is important for reaching this phase, and changes in society permit many adolescents in urban areas to attain it earlier than they did a decade or two ago (Diamond, Savin-Williams, & Dubé, 1999). Gay and lesbian communities exist in large cities, along with specialized inter-

This gay couple enjoys an evening at a high school prom. As long as friends and family members react with acceptance, coming out strengthens the young person's view of homosexuality as a valid, meaningful, and fulfilling identity.

est groups, social clubs, religious groups, newspapers, and periodicals. Increasing numbers of favorable media images also are helpful. Small towns and rural areas remain difficult places to meet other homosexuals and to find a supportive environment. Teenagers in these locales have a special need for caring adults and peers who can help them find self and social acceptance.

Gay and lesbian youths who succeed in coming out to themselves and others integrate their sexual orientation into a broader sense of identity, a process we will address in Chapter 16. As a result, they no longer need to focus so heavily on their homosexual self, and energy is freed for other aspects of psychological growth. In sum, coming out has the potential to foster many aspects of adolescent development, including self-esteem, psychological well-being, and relationships with family, friends, and co-workers.

Although adolescent cognition may have something to do with teenagers' reluctance to use contraception, the social environment also contributes to it. Among girls, feeling depressed and "like a failure" are linked to unprotected intercourse; among boys, feeling "in control" is associated with it (Kowaleski-Jones & Mott, 1998). Teenagers who do not have the rewards of meaningful education and work are especially likely to engage in irresponsible sex, sometimes within relationships characterized by exploitation and victimization. Twelve percent of high school girls and 5 percent of boys say they were forced to have sexual intercourse (U.S. Department of Health and Human Services, 2000f).

In contrast, teenagers who report good relationships with parents and who talk openly with them about sex and contraception are more likely to use birth control (Miller et al., 1998; Whitaker & Miller, 2000). Unfortunately, many adolescents say they are too scared or embarrassed to ask parents questions. And too many leave sex education classes with incomplete or factually incorrect knowledge. Some do not know where to get birth control counseling and devices. When they do, they often worry that a doctor or family planning clinic might not keep their visits confidential (American Academy of Pediatrics, 1999).

■ SEXUAL ORIENTATION. Up to this point, our discussion has focused only on heterosexual behavior. About 3 to 6 percent of young people discover that they are lesbian or gay (see the Biology and Environment box above). An as-yet-unknown but significant number are bisexual (Michael et al., 1994; Patterson, 1995). Adolescence is an equally crucial time for the sexual development of these individuals, and societal attitudes, once again, loom large in how well they fare.

Recent evidence indicates that heredity makes an important contribution to homosexuality. Identical twins of both sexes are much more likely than fraternal twins to share a homosexual orientation; the same is true for biological as opposed to adoptive relatives (Bailey & Pillard, 1991; Bailey et al., 1993). Furthermore, male homosexuality tends to be more common on the maternal than paternal side of families. This suggests that it might be X-linked (see Chapter 2). Indeed, one gene-mapping study found that among 40 pairs of homosexual brothers, 33 (82 percent) had an identical segment of DNA on the X chromosome. One or several genes in that region might predispose males to become homosexual (Hamer et al., 1993).

How might heredity lead to homosexuality? According to some researchers, certain genes affect the level or impact of prenatal sex hormones, which modify brain structures in ways that induce homosexual feelings and behavior (Bailey et al., 1995; LeVay, 1993). Keep in mind, however, that both genetic and environmental factors can alter prenatal hormones. Girls exposed prenatally to very high levels of androgens or estrogens—because of either a genetic defect or drugs given to the mother to prevent miscarriage—are more likely to become homosexual or bisexual (Meyer-Bahlburg et al., 1995). Furthermore, homosexual men tend to be later in birth order and have a higher-than-average number of older brothers (Blanchard et al., 1995, 1996; Blanchard & Bogaert, 1996). One controversial speculation is that mothers with several male children sometimes produce antibodies to androgens, which reduce the prenatal impact of male sex hormones on the brains of later-born boys.

Family factors are also linked to homosexuality. Looking back at their childhoods, both male and female homosexuals tend to view their same-sex parent as cold, rejecting, or distant (Bell, Weinberg, & Hammersmith, 1981; McConaghy & Silove, 1992). This does not mean that parents cause their youngsters to become homosexual. Rather, for some children, an early biological bias away from traditional gender-role behavior may prompt negative reactions from same-sex parents and peers. A strong desire for affection from people of their own sex may join with biology to strengthen their homosexual orientation (Green, 1987).

Once again, however, homosexuality does not always develop in this way, since some homosexuals are very comfortable with their gender role and have warm relationships with their parents. Homosexuality probably results from a variety of biological and environmental combinations that are not well understood (Huwiler & Remafedi, 1998).

SEXUALLY TRANSMITTED DISEASE

Sexually active adolescents, both homosexual and heterosexual, are at risk for sexually transmitted disease (STD) (see Table 14.3). Adolescents have the highest incidence of STD of any age group. Despite a recent decline in STD in the United States, one out of six sexually active teenagers contracts one of these illnesses each year, a rate much higher than that of other industrialized nations (Panchaud et al., 2000). If left untreated, sterility and life-threatening complications can result. Teenagers in greatest danger of STD are the same ones who tend to engage in irresponsible sexual behavior—poverty-stricken young people who feel a sense of inferiority and hopelessness about their lives (Holmbeck, Waters, & Brookman, 1990).

By far the most serious STD is AIDS. One-fifth of cases in the United States occur between ages 20 and 29. Nearly all of these originate in adolescence, since AIDS symptoms typically take 8 to 10 years to develop in a person infected with HIV. Drug-abusing and homosexual adolescents account for most cases, but heterosexual spread of the disease has increased, especially among females. It is at least twice as easy for a male to infect a female with any STD, including AIDS, as it is for a female to infect a male (U.S. Centers for Disease Control, 2000a).

As the result of school courses and media campaigns, over 90 percent of high school students are aware of basic facts about AIDS. But some hold false beliefs that put them at risk—for example, that birth control pills provide some protection or that it is possible to tell whether people have AIDS by looking at them (DiClemente, 1993). Almost all parents favor

TABLE 14.3

Most Common Sexually Transmitted Diseases of Adolescence

DISEASE	INCIDENCE AMONG 15- TO 19-YEAR-OLDS (RATE PER 100,000)	CAUSE	SYMPTOMS AND CONSEQUENCES	TREATMENT
AIDS	20[a]	Virus	Fever, weight loss, severe fatigue, swollen glands, and diarrhea. As the immune system weakens, severe pneumonias and cancers, especially of the skin, appear. Death due to other diseases usually occurs.	No cure; experimental drugs prolong life
Chlamydia	1,132	Bacteria	Discharge from the penis in males; painful itching, burning vaginal discharge, and dull pelvic pain in females. Often no symptoms. If left untreated, can lead to inflammation of the pelvic region, infertility, and sterility.	Antibiotic drugs
Cytomegalovirus	Unknown[b]	Virus of the herpes family	No symptoms in most cases. Sometimes, a mild flu-like reaction. In a pregnant woman, can spread to the embryo or fetus and cause miscarriage or serious birth defects (see page 120).	None; usually disappears on its own
Genital warts	451	Virus	Warts that grow near the vaginal opening in females, on the penis or scrotum in males. Can cause severe itching. Related to cancer of the cervix.	Removal of warts
Gonorrhea	570	Bacteria	Discharge from the penis or vagina, painful urination. Sometimes no symptoms. If left untreated, can spread to other regions of the body, resulting in such complications as infertility, sterility, blood poisoning, arthritis, and inflammation of the heart.	Antibiotic drugs
Herpes simplex 2 (genital herpes)	267	Virus	Fluid-filled blisters on the genitals, high fever, severe headache, and muscle aches and tenderness. No symptoms in a few people. In a pregnant woman, can spread to the embryo or fetus and cause birth defects (see page 120).	No cure; can be controlled with drug treatment
Syphilis	6	Bacteria	Painless chancre (sore) at site of entry of germ and swollen glands, followed by rash, patchy hair loss, and sore throat within 1 week to 6 months. These symptoms disappear without treatment. Latent syphilis varies from no symptoms to damage to the brain, heart, and other organs after 5 to 20 years. In pregnant women, can spread to the embryo and fetus and cause birth defects (see page 120).	Antibiotic drugs

[a]This figure includes both adolescents and young adults. For most of these cases, the virus is contracted in adolescence, and symptoms appear in early adulthood.

[b]Cytomegalovirus is the most common STD. Because there are no symptoms in most cases, its precise rate of occurrence is unknown. Half the population or more may have had the virus sometime during their lives.

Source: U.S. Centers for Disease Control, 2000a.

AIDS education in the public schools, and most states now require it. The Educational Concerns table on page 548 lists strategies for preventing STD.

ADOLESCENT PREGNANCY AND PARENTHOOD

Cassie was lucky not to get pregnant after having sex with Louis, but some of her high school classmates weren't so fortunate. She'd heard about Veronica, who missed several periods, pretended nothing was wrong, and didn't go to a doctor until a month before she gave

Educational Concerns

Preventing Sexually Transmitted Disease

STRATEGY	DESCRIPTION
Know your partner well.	Take time to get to get to know your partner. Find out whether your partner has had sex with many people or has used injectable drugs.
Maintain mutual faithfulness.	For this strategy to work, neither partner can have an STD at the start of the relationship.
Do not use drugs.	Using a needle, syringe, or drug liquid previously used by others can spread STD. Alcohol, marijuana, or other illegal substances impair judgment, reducing your capacity to think clearly about the consequences of behavior.
Always use a latex condom and vaginal contraceptive when having sex with a nonmarital partner.	Latex condoms give good (but not perfect) protection against STD by reducing the passage of bacteria and viruses. Vaginal contraceptives containing nonoxynol-9 can kill several kinds of STD microbes. They increase protection when combined with condom use.
Do not have sex with a person you know has an STD.	Even if you are protected by a condom, you still risk contracting STD. In the case of the AIDS virus, you risk your life. If either partner has engaged in behavior that might have risked HIV infection, a blood test to detect infection must be administered and repeated at least 6 months after that behavior, since it takes time for the body to develop antibodies.
If you get an STD, inform all recent sexual partners.	Notifying people you may have exposed to STD permits them to get treatment before spreading the disease to others.

birth. Veronica lived at home until she became pregnant a second time. At that point, her parents told her they didn't have room for a second baby. So Veronica dropped out of school and moved in with her 17-year-old boyfriend, Todd, who worked in a fast-food restaurant. A few months later, Todd left Veronica because he couldn't stand being tied down with the babies. Veronica had to apply for public aid to support herself and the two infants.

More than 900,000 American teenage girls—20 percent of those who have had sexual intercourse—become pregnant annually, 30,000 younger than age 15. Despite a steady decline since 1991, the adolescent pregnancy rate in the United States is higher than that of most other industrialized countries (see Figure 14.5). The United States differs from these nations in three important ways: (1) effective sex education reaches fewer teenagers; (2) convenient, low-cost contraceptive services for adolescents are scarce; and (3) many more families live in poverty, which encourages young people to take risks without considering the future implications of their behavior.

About 40 percent of teenage pregnancies end in abortion, 14 percent in miscarriage (Alan Guttmacher Institute, 1998). Because the United States has one of the highest adolescent abortion rates of any developed country, the total number of teenage births is actually lower than it was 30 years ago (Ventura & Freedman, 2000). But teenage parenthood is a much greater problem today because modern adolescents are far less likely to marry before childbirth. In 1960 only 15 percent of teenage births were to unmarried females, whereas today 75 percent are (Coley & Chase-Lansdale, 1998).

Increased social acceptance of single motherhood, along with the belief of many teenage girls that a baby might fill a void in their lives, means that only a small number give up their infants for adoption. Each year,

FIGURE 14.5

Teenage pregnancy rate in eight industrialized nations. (Adapted from Singh & Darroch, 2000.)

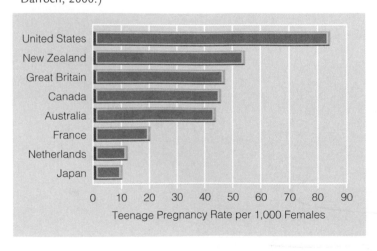

about 320,000 unmarried adolescent girls take on the responsibilities of parenthood before they are psychologically mature.

■ **CORRELATES AND CONSEQUENCES OF ADOLESCENT PARENTHOOD.** Becoming a parent is challenging and stressful for any person, but it is especially difficult for adolescents. Teenage parents have not yet established a clear sense of direction for their own lives.

As we have seen, adolescent sexual activity is linked to economic disadvantage. Teenage mothers are many times more likely to be poor than are agemates who postpone childbearing. Their life experiences often include low parental warmth and involvement; poor school performance; alcohol and drug use; antisocial behavior; adult models of unmarried parenthood, limited education, and unemployment; and residence in neighborhoods where other adolescents also display these risks (Fagot et al., 1998; Scaramella et al., 1998; Woodward & Fergusson, 1999). A high percentage of out-of-wedlock births are to members of low-income minorities, especially African-American, Native-American, and Hispanic teenagers (see Figure 14.6). Many of these young people seem to turn to early parenthood as a way to move into adulthood when educational and career avenues are unavailable (Luker, 1996).

Early childbearing imposes lasting hardships on two generations—adolescent and newborn baby. The lives of pregnant teenagers are troubled in many ways, and after the baby is born, their circumstances tend to worsen in at least three respects:

■ *Educational attainment.* Giving birth before age 18 reduces the likelihood of finishing high school. Only 50 percent of adolescent mothers graduate with either a diploma or general equivalency diploma (GED), compared with 96 percent of girls who wait to become parents (Hotz, McElroy, & Sanders, 1997).

■ *Marital patterns.* Teenage motherhood reduces the chances of marriage. When these mothers do marry, they are more likely to divorce than are their peers who delay childbearing (Moore et al., 1993). Consequently, teenage mothers spend more of their parenting years as single parents. Sometimes they have additional out-of-wedlock births in quick succession.

■ *Economic circumstances.* Because of low educational attainment, marital instability, and poverty, many teenage mothers are on welfare. If they are employed, their limited education restricts them to unsatisfying, low-paid jobs (Moore et al., 1993). Adolescent fathers work more hours than their nonparent agemates in the years following their child's birth. Perhaps for this reason, they obtain less education and are also economically disadvantaged (Brien & Willis, 1997).

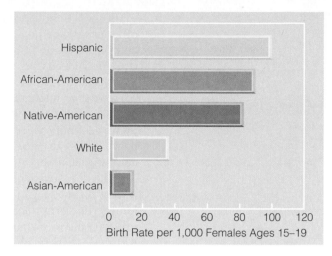

FIGURE 14.6

Births per 1,000 females ages 15 to 19 by ethnic group. Poverty, weak academic skills, and resulting narrowing of life options are key reasons birth rates are much higher among Hispanic, African-American, and Native-American teenagers than among whites and Asian Americans. (From U.S. Department of Health and Human Services, 2000f.)

Adolescent parenthood imposes lasting hardships on two generations. Early childbearing reduces the chances that teenage mothers will finish high school, marry, and enter a satisfying, well-paid vocation. Because of stressful life conditions, children of teenagers are at risk for poor parenting. These girls and their babies benefit from an intervention program that provides parenting classes and infant child care while the girls go to school. The program aims to increase both mothers' and babies' life chances.

Because many pregnant teenage girls have inadequate diets; smoke and use alcohol and other drugs; and do not receive early prenatal care, their babies often experience pregnancy and birth complications—especially low birth weight (Scholl, Heidiger, & Belsky, 1996). Children of teenagers also are at risk for poor parenting. Compared with adult mothers, adolescent mothers know less about child development, have unrealistically high expectations, perceive their infants as more difficult, and interact less effectively with them (Brooks-Gunn & Chase-Lansdale, 1995). Many of their children score low on intelligence tests, achieve poorly in school, and engage in disruptive social behavior. As the Social Issues: Health box on page 551 reveals, too often the cycle of adolescent parenthood is repeated in the next generation (Furstenberg, Hughes, & Brooks-Gunn, 1992; Moore, Morrison, & Green, 1997).

Still, how well adolescent parents and their children fare varies a great deal. If the adolescent finishes high school, avoids additional births, and finds a stable marriage partner, long-term disruptions in her own and her child's development are less severe. The small minority of young mothers who fail in all three of these ways face a life of continuing misfortune (Furstenberg, Brooks-Gunn, & Morgan, 1987).

■ **PREVENTION STRATEGIES.** Preventing teenage pregnancy means addressing the many factors underlying early sexual activity and lack of contraceptive use. Informing adolescents about sex and contraception is crucial. Too often, sex education courses are given too late (after sexual activity has begun), last only a few sessions, and are limited to a catalogue of facts about anatomy and reproduction. Sex education that goes beyond this minimum does not encourage early sex, as some opponents claim. It does improve awareness of sexual facts—knowledge that is necessary for responsible behavior (Katchadourian, 1990).

Knowledge, however, is not sufficient to influence teenagers' behavior. Sex education must help them build a bridge between what they know and what they do. Today, more effective sex education programs have emerged with the following key elements:

■ teaching skills for handling sexual situations through creative discussion and role-playing techniques, which permit teenagers to confront situations similar to those they will encounter in everyday life and acquire skills for resisting peer pressures for sexual activity;

■ promoting the value of abstinence to teenagers not yet sexually active; and

■ providing information about and ready access to contraceptives.

The combined results of many studies reveal that sex education with these components can delay the initiation of sexual activity, increase contraceptive use, and reduce pregnancy rates (Franklin et al., 1997; Frost & Forrest, 1995; Kirby, 1997).

The most controversial aspect of adolescent pregnancy prevention is increasing the availability of contraceptives. Many Americans argue that making birth control pills or condoms available to teenagers is equivalent to saying that early sex is okay. Yet in Western Europe, where clinics that distribute contraceptives are common, teenage sexual activity is no higher than in the United States, but pregnancy, childbirth, and abortion rates are much lower (Zabin & Hayward, 1993). Research confirms that knowledge and distribution of contraceptives is the most effective aspect of sex education for preventing adolescent pregnancy (Franklin & Corcoran, 2000).

Efforts to prevent adolescent pregnancy and parenthood must go beyond improving sex education and access to contraception to build social competence. In one study, researchers randomly assigned at-risk high school students to either a year-long community service class, called Teen Outreach, or to regular classroom experiences in health or social studies. In Teen Outreach, adolescents participated in at least 20 hours per week of volunteer work tailored to their interests. They returned to school for discussions that focused on enhancing their community service skills and ability to cope with everyday challenges. At the end of the school year, pregnancy, school failure, and school suspension were substantially lower in the group enrolled in Teen Outreach, which fostered social skills, connectedness to the community, and self-respect (Allen et al., 1997).

Social ISSUES:HEALTH

LIKE MOTHER, LIKE CHILD: INTERGENERATIONAL CONTINUITY IN ADOLESCENT PARENTHOOD

What are the long-term consequences of being the child of an adolescent parent? Does adolescent parenthood increase the chances of teenage childbearing in the next generation? To find out, Janet Hardy and her collaborators (1998) conducted a 30-year follow-up of more than 1,700 inner-city mothers (first generation) and their children (second generation). The first generation became parents between 1960 and 1964—about 28 percent as teenagers. As young people in the second generation grew up, they too became parents between the mid-1970s and early 1990s—25 percent as teenagers.

The researchers capitalized on extensive childhood data that had been gathered on the second generation, including IQ and achievement scores and information about family conditions. In addition, they interviewed both generations between 1992 and 1994, when the second generation reached 27 to 33 years of age, asking for recollec-

tions of the second generation's adolescent and early-adult life course.

First-generation mothers' age at first birth was strongly associated with the age at which second-generation young people became parents (see Figure 14.7). Yet becoming a second-generation teenage parent was not just a matter of having been born to an adolescent mother. Rather, adolescent parenthood was linked to a wide array of unfavorable rearing conditions, which predicted intergenerational continuity in teenage childbearing. For example, compared with second-generation daughters who postponed parenthood, daughters who became teenage mothers were more likely to grow up in a single-parent household, have four or more siblings (reducing parental attention and resources available to each), score lower in IQ and reading skill, repeat one or more grades, and (in adolescence) have a higher frequency of police arrests for delinquency. Similar trends were

found for second-generation sons who became teenage parents. And as these early child bearers moved into adulthood, they fared less well in education, physical and mental health, and financial security than did their age-mates who waited to become parents.

Finally, even when children born to teenage mothers did not repeat the pattern of early childbearing, their development was compromised. Although they fared better than their counterparts who became adolescent parents, they scored lower than other second-generation members in virtually all child and adult indicators of well-being. In sum, the likelihood of graduating from high school; achieving financial independence; enjoying good physical and mental health; and avoiding adolescent parenthood with all its costly future consequences is much greater for children born to older mothers than for those born to teenagers.

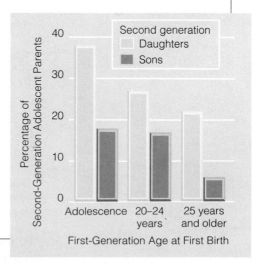

FIGURE 14.7

Intergenerational continuity in adolescent parenthood in a 30-year study of more than 1,700 inner-city parents and their children. The graph shows the percentage of second-generation daughters and sons who became adolescent parents for each of three groups of first-generation parents: those who had a first child as a teenager, between ages 20 and 24, or at age 25 or older. First-generation adolescent parents were more likely to have children who were adolescent parents, a tendency that was stronger for second-generation girls than for boys. Fewer boys in this study reported adolescent parenthood. They might not always have known about the birth of a child. And in some cases, they might have chosen not to disclose it. (Adapted from Hardy et al., 1998.)

Finally, teenagers who look forward to a promising future are far less likely to engage in early and irresponsible sex. Society can provide young people with good reasons to postpone early childbearing by expanding their educational, vocational, and employment opportunities. We will take up these issues in Chapter 15.

This teenager is a member of City Year Corps, an organization of young volunteers who represent a cross section of their communities and who serve as teachers' aides in public schools. Building competence through community service reduces teenage pregnancy and school failure among at-risk high school students.

■ **INTERVENING WITH ADOLESCENT PARENTS.** The most difficult and costly way to deal with adolescent parenthood is to wait until it has happened. Young single mothers need health care for themselves and their children, encouragement to stay in school, job training, instruction in parenting and life-management skills, and high-quality, affordable child care. School programs that provide these services reduce the incidence of low-birth-weight babies, increase mothers' educational success, and decrease their likelihood of rapid additional child-bearing (Seitz & Apfel, 1993, 1994; Seitz, Apfel, & Rosenbaum, 1991).

Adolescent mothers also benefit from family relationships that are sensitive to their developmental needs. In our discussion of the African-American extended family in Chapter 2, we noted that older teenage mothers display more effective parenting when they establish their own residence with the help of relatives—an arrangement that grants the adolescent a balance of autonomy and support. Similarly, teenage mothers of other ethnic backgrounds who live apart from their parents but receive high levels of assistance from them have warmer extended-family ties and children who develop more favorably (East & Felice, 1996). These findings raise questions about a U.S. welfare policy that requires teenage mothers to live at home to receive benefits (U.S. Department of Health and Human Services, 2000b).

Programs focusing on fathers are attempting to increase their emotional and financial commitment to the baby (Coley & Chase-Lansdale, 1998). Although almost half of young fathers visit their children during the first few years after birth, contact usually diminishes. By the time the child reaches school age, fewer than one-fourth are still involved with their fathers (Lerman, 1993). But new laws that encourage mothers to help establish paternity and that enforce child support payments may lead to a turnabout in paternal responsibility and interaction. Teenage mothers who receive financial and child-care assistance from the child's father are less distressed and interact more favorably with their infants (Caldwell & Antonucci, 1997). And the fewer stressful life events teenage mothers experience, the more likely fathers are to stay involved (Cutrona et al., 1998). Infants with lasting ties to their teenage fathers receive warmer, more stimulating caregiving and show better long-term adjustment (Furstenberg & Harris, 1993).

SUBSTANCE USE AND ABUSE

At age 14, Louis took some cigarettes out of his uncle's pack, waited until he was alone in the house, and smoked. At an unchaperoned party, he and Cassie drank several cans of beer, largely because everyone else was doing it. One summer at a beach gathering, someone pulled out some marijuana, and Louis and his friends lit up. Louis got little physical charge out of these experiences. He was a good student, well liked by peers, and close to his parents. He had no need for drugs as an escape valve from daily life. But he knew of others at his school for whom things were different—students who started with alcohol and cigarettes, increased their consumption, moved to harder substances, and eventually were hooked.

In the United States and many other industrialized nations, teenage alcohol and drug use is pervasive (Bauman & Phongsavan, 1999). By age 14, 56 percent of American young people have tried smoking; 70 percent, drinking; and 32 percent, at least one illegal drug (usually marijuana). At the end of high school, 22 percent smoke cigarettes regularly, 60 percent have engaged in heavy drinking at least once, and over 50 percent have experimented with illegal drugs. About 30 percent have tried at least one highly addictive and toxic substance, such as amphetamines, cocaine, phencyclidine (PCP), inhalants, or heroin (U.S. Department of Health and Human Services, 2000a).

These high figures represent a decade of decline in alcohol and drug use, followed by a steady increase during the past few years and then a slight drop (see Figure 14.8). Why do so many young people subject themselves to the health risks of these substances? Part of the reason is cultural. Adolescents live in a drug-dependent society. They see adults using caffeine to wake up in the morning, cigarettes to cope with daily hassles, a drink to calm down in the evening, and other remedies to relieve stress, headaches, depression, and physical illness. Reduced parent, school, and media focus on the hazards of drugs, followed by renewed public attention, may explain recent trends in adolescent drug taking.

For most young people, substance use simply reflects their intense curiosity about "adult-like" behaviors. Research reveals that the majority of teenagers dabble in alcohol as well as tobacco and marijuana. These minimal *experimenters* are not headed for a life of decadence and addiction. Instead, they are psychologically healthy, sociable, curious young people (Shedler & Block, 1990). In a society in which substance use is commonplace, some involvement with drugs is normal and to be expected.

Yet adolescent drug experimentation should not be taken lightly. Because most drugs impair perception and thought processes, a single heavy dose can lead to permanent injury or death. And a worrisome minority of high-risk teenagers move from substance *use* to *abuse*—taking drugs regularly, requiring increasing amounts to achieve the same effect, finding themselves unable to stop, and using enough to impair their ability to meet school, work, or other responsibilities (Luthar, Cushing, & McMahon, 1997). Three percent of high school seniors are daily drinkers, and 6 percent have taken illegal drugs on a daily basis over the past month (U.S. Department of Health and Human Services, 2000d).

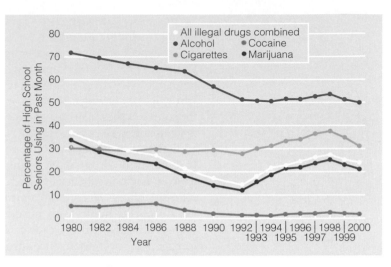

FIGURE 14.8

Percentages of high school seniors reporting use of alcohol, cigarettes, and illegal drugs in the past month, 1980–2000. Substance use continues to be widespread among adolescents. Although it declined from 1982 to 1992, a sharp increase over the 1990s—largely accounted for by marijuana and cigarette smoking—sounded a note of alarm. During the past few years, alcohol and drug use has again declined. (From U.S. Department of Health and Human Services, 2000d.)

Of all teenage drug habits, cigarette smoking has received the least attention because its short-term effects are minimal. Yet in the long run, it may be the deadliest substance, since it is an established cause of heart and lung disease and cancer. Cigarette use usually begins in early adolescence; 15 percent of American eighth graders say they smoked in the last month. Of high school students who smoke half a pack or more a day, 50 percent indicate that they tried to quit but could not (U.S. Department of Health and Human Services, 2000d).

These teenagers appear to be having fun, but their drinking and smoking are serious. Repeated substance use often leads to abuse and is associated with other serious adjustment problems of adolescence, including unprotected sexual activity, early pregnancy and parenthood, depression, antisocial behavior, and unintentional injury (especially auto accidents).

■ **CORRELATES AND CONSEQUENCES OF ADOLESCENT SUBSTANCE ABUSE.** In contrast to experimenters, drug abusers are seriously troubled young people who are inclined to express their unhappiness through antisocial acts. Longitudinal evidence reveals that their impulsive, disruptive, sensation-seeking style often is evident in early childhood (Weinberg et al., 1998). Although it probably has genetic roots, a wide range of environmental factors promote it. These include low-SES, family mental health problems, parental and older sibling drug abuse, lack of parental warmth and involvement, physical and sexual abuse, and poor school performance. By early adolescence, peer encouragement—friends who use drugs and provide access to illegal substances—is a strong predictor of substance abuse. Once an adolescent associates with drug-using peers, her own substance use approaches their level (Anda et al., 1999; Kilpatrick et al., 2000; Wills et al., 1996).

Teenage substance abuse often has lifelong consequences. When adolescents depend on alcohol and hard drugs to deal with daily stresses, they fail to learn responsible decision-making skills and alternative coping techniques—crucial lessons during this time of transition to adulthood. These young people show serious adjustment problems, including depression and antisocial behavior (Luthar & Cushing, 1997). They often enter into marriage, childbearing, and the work world prematurely and fail at them readily. Adolescent drug addiction is associated with high rates of divorce and job loss—painful outcomes that encourage further addictive behavior (Newcomb & Bentler, 1988).

© BOB DAEMMRICH/STOCK BOSTON

■ **PREVENTION AND TREATMENT.** School-based programs that promote effective parenting (including monitoring of teenagers' activities) and that teach adolescents skills for resisting peer pressure reduce drug experimentation to some degree (Steinberg, Fletcher, & Darling, 1994). But this approach is effective only if adults do not "pathologize" adolescents' tendency to try drugs from time to time. When teenagers are labeled "sick," "screwed up," or "druggies" for having taken a sip or puff of an illegal substance, they are likely to rebel against the source of these alarmist and insulting messages. Under these conditions, the frequency of drug use often rises. Scare tactics, such as showing graphic films of the dire consequences of addiction, also work poorly (Newcomb & Bentler, 1989; Shedler & Block, 1990).

Since some drug-taking seems to be inevitable, interventions that prevent adolescents from endangering themselves and others when they do experiment are essential. Many communities offer weekend on-call transportation services that any young person can contact for a safe ride home, with no questions asked. Providing appealing substitute activities, such as drug-free video arcades, dances, and sports activities, is also helpful. And educating teenagers about the dangers of drugs and alcohol is vital, since an increase in perceived risk closely paralleled the decline in substance use in the 1980s and early 1990s (O'Malley, Johnston, & Bachman, 1995).

Drug abuse, as we have seen, occurs for quite different reasons than does occasional use. Therefore, different preventive strategies are required. One approach is to work with parents early, reducing family adversity and improving parenting skills, before children are old enough to become involved with drugs. Addicted mothers may be especially responsive to such interventions, since many seek treatment out of concern for the well-being of their children (Luthar, Cushing, & McMahon, 1997). Programs that teach at-risk teenagers effective strategies for handling life stressors and that build competence through community service reduce alcohol and drug use, just as they reduce teenage pregnancy (Richards-Colocino, McKenzie, & Newton, 1996).

When an adolescent becomes a drug abuser, hospitalization is often a necessary and even life-saving first step. Once the young person is weaned from the drug, family and individual therapy to treat maladaptive parent–child relationships, low self-esteem, anxiety, and impulsivity are generally needed. Academic and vocational training to improve life success and satisfaction make a difference as well. Not much is known about the best way to treat adolescent drug abuse. Even comprehensive programs have alarmingly high relapse rates—from 35 to 85 percent (Gilvarry, 2000).

INJURIES

Adolescent risk taking, fueled by sensation seeking and a tendency to act without forethought, results in a rise in certain kinds of unintentional injuries. As we saw in Chapter 11, the total rate of unintentional injuries increases during adolescence (see page 421). Automobile accidents are largely responsible. They are the leading killer of American teenagers, accounting for 42 percent of deaths between ages 15 and 19. Many result from driving at high speeds, using alcohol, and not wearing seat belts (U.S. Department of Health and Human Services, 2000c). Parents must set firm limits on their teenager's car use, particularly with respect to drinking and seat belt use. These efforts are more likely to succeed in families with a history of good parent–child communication—a powerful preventive of adolescent injury (Millstein & Irwin, 1988).

Other injuries account for an additional 11 percent of adolescent deaths. The majority are caused by firearms. Although violence-related behaviors among high school students have declined in the past decade, 17 percent report having carried a weapon within the past month—5 percent, a gun (U.S. Department of Health and Human Services, 2000c). The rate of disability and death resulting from firearms—mostly homicidal but occasionally accidental—is especially high in inner-city ghettos (Weissberg & Greenberg, 1998). In response, many schools have installed metal detectors and security guards. Unfortunately, these environmental changes increase teenagers' fear of crime but have little impact on violence (Duncan, 1996). School-based violence prevention programs (see Chapter 13, page 518) help reduce assaults. Banning handgun sales is an especially powerful tactic. In countries where people cannot purchase handguns, firearm injuries almost never happen.

A third type of adolescent injury—less prevalent but still serious and largely avoidable—is sports related. Each year, about one-third of students involved in sports experience injuries requiring medical treatment (U.S. Department of Health and Human Services, 2000c). Most are muscle strains and bruises, but occasionally, severe injuries occur. These generally result from contact and collision with others in basketball, football, and soccer and from physical fights between players (Cheng et al., 2000).

Coaches are an important source of athletic injuries. In their drive to win, they sometimes make unreasonable demands of players and fail to enforce safety rules. Young adolescents are especially vulnerable. Many coaches match competitors on the basis of age and weight without considering physical maturity. Too often, this allows "[120 pounds] of mature muscle and mustache to compete against [120 pounds] of peach fuzz and baby fat" (Malina & Beunen, 1996; Malina & Stanitski, 1989, p. 35). The safest athletic activities during the period of rapid pubertal growth are limited-contact team sports, such as basketball, softball, and volleyball, and individual sports, such as track, swimming, and tennis.

Ask **YOURSELF...**

review   *What unfavorable life experiences do teenagers who engage in early and frequent sexual activity and who abuse drugs have in common? How do those experiences contrast with those of girls at risk for anorexia nervosa?*

apply   *Return to page 548 to review Veronica's life circumstances after becoming a teenage mother. Why are Veronica and her children likely to experience long-term hardships?*

connect   *Return to Chapter 1, page 10, and Chapter 13, page 516, to review factors that promote resiliency in the face of high life stress. Then list characteristics common to effective pregnancy and substance abuse prevention programs. Are these components well suited to fostering resiliency in at-risk adolescents? Explain.*

reflect   *Describe health education (including drug use prevention) programs that you experienced in secondary school. Did they assist you in resisting peer pressures to engage in sexual activity and alcohol and drug experimentation? Explain.*

Motor Development, Sports Participation, and Physical Activity

Puberty is accompanied by steady improvement in motor performance, but the pattern of change differs for boys and girls. Girls' gains are slow and gradual, leveling off by age 14. In contrast, boys show a dramatic spurt in strength, speed, and endurance that continues through the teenage years. The gender gap in physical skill widens over time. By mid-adolescence, very few girls perform as well as the average boy in running speed, broad jump, or throwing distance. And practically no boys score as low as the average girl (Malina & Bouchard, 1991).

Because girls and boys are no longer well matched physically, sex-segregated physical education usually begins in junior high school. At the same time, athletic options for both sexes expand. Many new sports are added to the curriculum—track and field, wrestling, tackle football, weight lifting, floor hockey, archery, tennis, and golf, to name just a few.

These high school relay racers compete at an interschool meet. After the U.S. government required schools receiving public funds to provide equal opportunities for males and females in athletics, girls' sports participation increased substantially. Still, throughout childhood and adolescence, girls get less encouragement and recognition for athletic achievement than do boys.

Since competence at sports is strongly related to peer admiration among adolescent boys, it becomes even more important in boys' self-esteem than it was earlier. Some adolescents—about twice as many boys as girls—become so obsessed with physical prowess that they turn to anabolic steroids to increase their skill artificially. In the United States, about 5 percent of adolescent boys and 2 percent of girls take these illegal drugs to boost muscle size and strength, ignoring their serious side effects (U.S. Department of Health and Human Services, 2000g; Yesalis et al., 1997). These include damage to the liver, circulatory system, and reproductive organs, as well as an increase in mood swings and aggressive behavior. Coaches and health professionals should inform teenagers of the dangers of steroids.

In 1972 the federal government required schools receiving public funds to provide equal opportunities for males and females in all educational programs, including athletics. As Figure 14.9 shows, high school girls' sports participation quadrupled during the following decade and has continued to increase, although it still falls far short of boys'. In Chapter 11 we saw that beginning at an early age, girls get less encouragement and recognition for athletic achievement, a pattern that persists into the teenage years.

The sex differences just described also characterize physical activity rates of American adolescents. Overall, 73 percent of high school boys but only 57 percent of girls report regular vigorous physical activity (at least 20 minutes 3 days a week). The number of boys engaging in regular strenuous exercise declines by 7 percent from ninth to twelfth grade. Among girls, the drop is more than twice as great—about 15 percent (U.S. Department of Health and Human Services, 2000g).

Besides improving motor performance, sports and exercise influence cognitive and social development. Interschool and intramural athletics provide important lessons in competition, assertiveness, problem solving, and teamwork. And regular physical activity is associated with enhanced functioning of the immune system, cardiovascular health, and improved psychological well-being (Newcombe & Boyle, 1995). Yet only 56 percent of American high school students are enrolled in physical education, and only 29 percent attend a class daily. Attendance drops off with each grade, especially for girls (U.S. Department of Health and Human Services, 2000g).

Required daily physical education, aimed at helping all teenagers find pleasure in sports and exercise, is a vital means of promoting adolescent—and lifelong—health. A positive sign is that enrollment in high school physical education is gradually increasing. And the sex difference in team sports participation is shrinking. Although we still have a long way to go, we are closer today than ever before to equality of opportunity for the sexes in sports as well as in other areas of human skill.

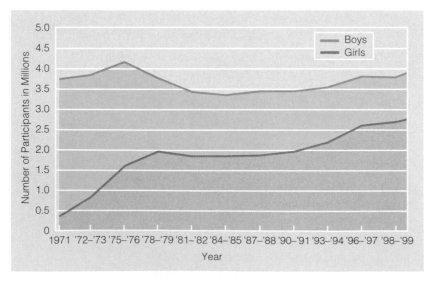

FIGURE 14.9

High school sports participation trends in the United States, 1971–1999. A legal mandate for equality of opportunity in school athletic participation led girls' involvement in sports to increase dramatically from the early 1970s to 1980. Since then, girls' participation has continued to rise gradually, although it still falls far short of boys'. (From National Federation of State High School Associations, 2000.)

Summary

CONCEPTIONS OF ADOLESCENCE

How have conceptions of adolescence changed over the twentieth century?

■ Early biologically oriented theories viewed **puberty** as an inevitable period of storm and stress. An alternative perspective regarded the social environment as entirely responsible for the wide variability in adolescent adjustment.

■ Current research shows that adolescence is neither biologically nor socially determined but a product of the two. In cultures where many years of education are required for successful participation in the work life of the community, adolescence is greatly extended.

PUBERTY: THE PHYSICAL TRANSITION TO ADULTHOOD

Describe pubertal changes in body size, proportions, and sexual maturity.

■ Hormonal changes starting in middle childhood initiate puberty, which arrives, on average, 2 years earlier for girls than for boys. The first outward sign of puberty is the rapid gain in height and weight known as the **growth spurt.** In early adolescence, the cephalocaudal trend of body growth reverses. Lengthening of the torso accounts for most height gain. As the body enlarges, girls' hips and boys' shoulders broaden. Girls add more fat, boys more muscle.

■ Sex hormones regulate changes in **primary** and **secondary sexual characteristics. Menarche** occurs relatively late in the girl's sequence of pubertal events, following the rapid increase in body size. After menarche, growth of the breasts and pubic and underarm hair are completed. Among boys, as the sex organs and body enlarge and pubic and underarm hair appear, **spermarche** takes place. This is followed by growth of facial and body hair and deepening of the voice.

What factors influence the timing of puberty?

■ Heredity, nutrition, and overall health contribute to the timing of puberty. Menarche is delayed in poverty-stricken regions of the world and among girls from economically disadvantaged homes. In contrast, girls exposed to early family conflict tend to reach menarche early. Because of improved nutrition, health care, and control of infectious disease, a secular trend toward an earlier age of menarche has occurred in industrialized nations.

How does the organization of sleep and wakefulness change in adolescence?

■ Adolescents tend to go to bed much later than they did as children, a pattern that strengthens with pubertal maturation. Sleep deprivation contributes to depressed mood and behavior problems.

THE PSYCHOLOGICAL IMPACT OF PUBERTAL EVENTS

What factors influence adolescents' reactions to the physical changes of puberty?

■ Girls generally react to menarche with surprise and mixed emotions, but whether their feelings lean in a positive or negative direction depends on advance information and support from family members. Boys usually know ahead of time about spermarche, but they receive less support for the physical changes of puberty than do girls.

■ Tribal and village societies often celebrate puberty with an **adolescent initiation ceremony.** The absence of a widely accepted marker for physical and social maturity in contemporary society makes the process of becoming an adult especially confusing.

■ Besides higher hormone levels, negative life events and adult-structured situations are associated with adolescents' negative moods. In contrast, teenagers feel upbeat when with friends and in self-chosen leisure activities, making weekend evenings emotional high points.

■ Puberty is accompanied by psychological distancing between parent and child. The reaction may be a modern substitute for physical departure from the family, which typically occurs at sexual maturity in primate species. Parent–adolescent conflict also reflects parents' efforts to protect teenagers from such risks as substance use, auto accidents, and early sex.

Describe the impact of maturational timing on adolescent adjustment, noting sex differences.

■ Timing of puberty influences adolescent psychological adjustment. Early maturing boys and late maturing girls, whose appearance closely matches cultural standards of physical attractiveness, have a more positive **body image,** feel more self-confident, and hold more positions of leadership. In contrast, early maturing girls and late maturing boys, who fit in least well physically with peers, experience emotional and social difficulties.

■ School contexts can modify maturational timing effects. Although long-term follow-ups show some striking turnabouts in adjustment, the consequences of early and late maturation may persist.

HEALTH ISSUES

Describe nutritional needs, and cite factors related to serious eating disturbances during adolescence.

■ As the body grows, nutritional requirements increase, at a time when the eating habits of young people are the poorest. Many adolescents suffer from iron, vitamin, and mineral deficiencies.

■ Girls who reach puberty early, who are very dissatisfied with their body images, and who grow up in homes where a concern with thinness is especially strong are at risk for eating disorders. **Anorexia nervosa** tends to run in families, suggesting a genetic influence, and to affect girls with perfectionist personalities, overprotective and controlling mothers, and emotionally

Summary (continued)

distant fathers. The impulsive eating and purging of **bulimia nervosa** is associated with disengaged parenting. Some bulimics, like anorexics, are perfectionists; others lack self-control not just in eating but in other areas of their lives.

Discuss social and cultural influences on adolescent sexual attitudes and behavior.

■ The hormonal changes of puberty lead to an increase in sex drive, but social factors affect how teenagers manage their sexuality. Compared with most other cultures, the United States is fairly restrictive in its attitude toward adolescent sex. Young people receive contradictory messages from the larger social environment. Sexual attitudes and behavior of adolescents have become more liberal, with a slight swing back in recent years, largely due to the risk of sexually transmitted disease.

■ Early and frequent sexual activity is linked to a variety of factors associated with economic disadvantage. One-third to one-half of sexually active American teenagers do not practice contraception regularly. Adolescent cognitive processes and a lack of social support for responsible sexual behavior underlie the failure of so many young people to protect themselves against pregnancy. Teenagers who talk openly with their parents about sex are more likely to use birth control.

Describe factors involved in the development of homosexuality.

■ About 3 to 6 percent of young people discover that they are lesbian or gay; an unknown number are bisexual. Although heredity makes an important contribution, homosexuality probably results from a variety of biological and environmental

combinations that are not yet well understood. Gay and lesbian teenagers face special challenges in establishing a positive sexual identity.

Discuss factors related to sexually transmitted disease and teenage pregnancy and parenthood.

■ Early sexual activity combined with inconsistent contraceptive use results in high rates of sexually transmitted disease (STD) among American teenagers. Many young adults with AIDS contracted HIV as adolescents. An important goal of sex education is prevention of STD.

■ Teenage pregnancy, abortion, and childbearing are more prevalent in the United States than in many industrialized nations. Adolescent parenthood is often associated with high school dropout, reduced chances of marriage, greater likelihood of divorce, and poverty—circumstances that risk the well-being of both adolescent and newborn child.

■ Improved sex education, access to contraceptives, and programs that build social competence help prevent early pregnancy. Adolescent mothers benefit from school programs that provide job training, instruction in parenting and life-management skills, and child care and extended-family support that is sensitive to their developmental needs. When teenage fathers stay involved, their children develop more favorably.

What personal and social factors are related to adolescent substance use and abuse?

■ Teenage alcohol and drug use is widespread in the United States and many other industrialized nations. For most young people, drug experimentation

reflects curiosity about these forbidden substances. Those who move from use to abuse have serious personal, family, school, and peer problems. Programs that work with parents early to reduce family adversity and improve parenting skills and that build teenagers' competence help prevent substance abuse.

Cite common unintentional injuries in adolescence.

■ Motor vehicle collisions are the leading cause of adolescent injury and death. The rate of disability and death caused by firearms is also high. A third, less prevalent type of injury is sports related.

MOTOR DEVELOPMENT, SPORTS PARTICIPATION, AND PHYSICAL ACTIVITY

Describe sex differences in motor development during adolescence.

■ Pubertal changes lead both sexes to improve in gross motor performance during adolescence; boys show much larger gains than girls. Although their involvement in high school sports has increased, girls continue to receive less encouragement and recognition for developing athletic skill than do boys.

■ More high school boys than girls report regular vigorous physical activity, but the number of physically active adolescents of both sexes declines from ninth to twelfth grade. Similarly, too few adolescents are enrolled in physical education classes. Required daily physical education that helps all teenagers find pleasure in sports and exercise is vital for promoting adolescent and lifelong health.

Important terms and concepts

adolescent initiation ceremony
  (p. 534)
anorexia nervosa (p. 540)
body image (p. 538)

bulimia nervosa (p. 541)
growth spurt (p. 529)
menarche (p. 530)
puberty (p. 526)

primary sexual characteristics (p. 530)
secondary sexual characteristics
  (p. 530)
spermarche (p. 531)

fyi . . . for further information and help

Consult the companion website for this book, where you will find additional weblinks and associated learning activities:
www.ablongman.com/berk

EATING DISORDERS

Anorexia Nervosa and Related Eating Disorders
www.anred.com

An association of anorexics and bulimics, their families and friends, and concerned professionals that provides information about the disorders.

SEXUAL BEHAVIOR

Alan Guttmacher Institute
www.agi-usa.org

Compiles statistics on sexual behavior and promotes public policy related to birth control. Publishes the journal Family Planning Perspectives, *which includes articles on adolescents.*

SEXUALLY TRANSMITTED DISEASE (STD)

American Social Health Association
www.ashastd.org

A national health agency that works to expand research, provide information to communities, and improve public health policy related to STD.

U.S. Centers for Disease Control
www.cdc.gov

A government agency devoted to promoting health and quality of life by preventing and controlling disease, injury, and disability. Compiles statistics on disease incidence and disseminates health information. Sponsors the National AIDS Hotline, 1-800-342-AIDS, and the National STD Hotline, 1-800-227-8922.

SUBSTANCE ABUSE

Cocaine Anonymous
www.ca.org

An organization devoted to helping adolescents and adults recover from addiction to cocaine and other mood-altering drugs.

(See page 131 for additional organizations related to substance abuse.)

"My World in the Year 2000"
Shellie Lee Korth
12 years, United States of America

During adolescence, cognition moves from the real to the possible. This drawing depicts one young person's vision of the many ways human thinking can contribute to humanity. Chapter 15 delves into the new, abstract reasoning powers of this transitional phase between childhood and adulthood.

Cognitive Development in Adolescence

ne mid-December

evening, a knock at the front door announced the arrival of Franca and Antonio's oldest son, Jules, home for vacation after the fall semester of his sophomore year at college. Moments later, the family gathered around the kitchen table. "How did it all go, Jules?" inquired Antonio while passing out pieces of apple pie.

"Well, math was only so-so. But physics and philosophy were awesome. The last few weeks, our physics prof introduced us to Einstein's theory of relativity. Boggles my mind, it's so incredibly counterintuitive."

"Counter-what?" asked 11-year-old Sabrina, trying hard to follow the conversation.

"Counterintuitive. Unlike what you'd normally expect," explained Jules. "Imagine this. You're on a train, going unbelievably fast, like 160,000 miles a second. The faster you go approaching the speed of light, the slower time passes and the denser and heavier things get relative to on the ground. The theory revolutionized the way we think about time, space, matter—the entire universe."

Sabrina wrinkled her forehead in a puzzled expression, unable to comprehend Jules's other-worldly reasoning. "Time slows down when I'm bored, like right now, not on a train when I'm going somewhere exciting. No speeding train ever made me denser and heavier, but this apple pie will if I eat any more of it," Sabrina announced with finality, getting up and leaving the table.

Sixteen-year-old Louis reacted differently. "Totally cool, Jules. So what'd you do in philosophy?"

"It was a course in philosophy of technology. One of the things we studied was the ethics of futuristic methods in human reproduction. For example, we argued the pros and cons of a world in which all embryos develop in artificial wombs."

"What do you mean?" asked Louis. "You order your kid at the lab?"

"That's right. I wrote my term paper on it. I had to evaluate it in terms of principles of justice and freedom. I can see some advantages but also lots of dangers. . . ."

As this conversation illustrates, adolescence brings with it vastly expanded powers of reasoning. At age 11, Sabrina's logic is still concrete, tied to the here-and-now. She finds it difficult to move beyond her own firsthand experiences into a world of possibilities. Over the next few years, her thinking will take on the abstract qualities of her older brother's thought. Jules juggles variables in complex combinations and thinks about situations that are not easily detected in the real world or that do not exist at all—cognitive capacities that open up whole new realms of learning. Adolescents can grasp complex scientific and mathematical principles, grapple with puzzling social and political issues, and detect the hidden meaning of a poem or story. Compared to school-age children's thinking, adolescent thought is more enlightened, imaginative, and rational.

The first part of this chapter traces these extraordinary changes, from both Piaget's and the information-processing points of view. Next, we take a close look at research findings that have attracted a great deal of public attention: sex differences in mental abilities. We also discuss important gains in language that reflect as well as contribute to the advanced thinking of the teenage years. The middle portion of this chapter is devoted to the primary setting in which adolescent thought takes shape: the school. We conclude with a consideration of vocational development during the teenage years.

Piaget's Theory: The Formal Operational Stage

According to Piaget, the capacity for abstract thinking begins around age 11. At the **formal operational stage,** the adolescent reasons much like a scientist searching for solutions in the laboratory. Concrete operational children can only "operate on reality," but formal operational adolescents can "operate on operations." In other words, concrete things and events are no longer required as objects of thought. Instead, adolescents can come up with new, more general logical rules through internal reflection (Brainerd, 1978; Inhelder & Piaget, 1955/1958). Table 15.1 summarizes two major features of formal operational reasoning.

HYPOTHETICO-DEDUCTIVE REASONING

At adolescence, young people first become capable of **hypothetico-deductive reasoning.** When faced with a problem, they start with a *general theory* of all possible factors that might affect the outcome and *deduce* from it specific *hypotheses* (or predictions) about what might happen. Then they test these hypotheses in an orderly fashion to see which ones work in the real world. Notice how this form of problem solving begins with possibility and proceeds to

TABLE 15.1

Major Characteristics of Formal Operational Thought

CHARACTERISTIC	DESCRIPTION	EXAMPLE
Hypothetico-deductive reasoning	When faced with a problem, formal operational adolescents think of all possible factors that could affect the outcome, even those not immediately suggested by concrete features of the situation. Then they try them out in a step-by-step fashion to find out which ones work in the real world.	In biology class, Louis had to determine which of two fertilizers was best for growing African violets. Louis thought, "The kind of fertilizer might not be the only factor that's important. Its concentration and how often the plant is fed might also make a difference." So Louis planned an experiment in which each fertilizer would be applied in several strengths and according to different feeding schedules. He made sure to design the experiment so that he could determine the separate effects of each factor, and their combined effects, on plant growth.
Propositional thought	Formal operational adolescents can evaluate the logic of statements by reflecting on the statements themselves. They do not need to consider them against real-world circumstances.	Louis was given the following propositional task and asked whether the conclusion was true, false, or uncertain: Major Premise: All animals are purple. Second Premise: A frobe is purple. Conclusion: A frobe is an animal. Louis concluded, correctly, that whether a frobe is an animal is uncertain. "A frobe might be an animal," he answered, "but it might also be a purple thing that is not an animal."

reality. In contrast, concrete operational children start with reality—with the most obvious predictions about a situation. When these are not confirmed, they cannot think of alternatives and fail to solve the problem.

Adolescents' performance on Piaget's famous *pendulum problem* illustrates this new hypothetico-deductive approach. Suppose we present several school-age children and adolescents with strings of different lengths, objects of different weights to attach to the strings, and a bar from which to hang the strings (see Figure 15.1). Then we ask each of them to figure out what influences the speed with which a pendulum swings through its arc.

Formal operational adolescents come up with four hypotheses: (1) the length of the string; (2) the weight of the object hung on it; (3) how high the object is raised before it is released; and (4) how forcefully the object is pushed. Then, by varying one factor at a time while holding all the others constant, they try out each possibility. Eventually they discover that only string length makes a difference.

In contrast, concrete operational children's experimentation is unsystematic. They cannot separate out the effects of each variable. For example, they may test for the effect of string length without holding weight constant by comparing a short, light pendulum with a long, heavy one. Also, school-age youngsters fail to notice variables that are not immediately suggested by the concrete materials of the task—the height and forcefulness with which the pendulum is released.

FIGURE 15.1

The pendulum problem. Adolescents who engage in hypothetico-deductive reasoning think of all possibilities. Then they vary one factor at a time while holding all others constant. Soon they discover that the weight of the object, the height from which it is released, and how forcefully it is pushed have no effect on the speed with which the pendulum swings through its arc. Only string length makes a difference.

PROPOSITIONAL THOUGHT

A second important characteristic of the formal operational stage is **propositional thought.** Adolescents can evaluate the logic of propositions (verbal statements) without referring to real-world circumstances. In contrast, concrete operational children can evaluate the logic of statements only by considering them against concrete evidence in the real world.

WILL HART

In Piaget's formal operational stage, adolescents engage in propositional thought. As these students discuss problems in a precalculus class, they show that they can reason with symbols that do not necessarily represent objects in the real world.

In a study of propositional reasoning, an experimenter showed children and adolescents a pile of poker chips and indicated that some statements would be made about them. Each participant was asked to tell whether each statement was true, false, or uncertain. In one condition, the experimenter hid a chip in her hand and then asked the young person to evaluate the following propositions:

"*Either* the chip in my hand is green *or* it is not green."

"The chip in my hand is green *and* it is not green."

In another condition, the experimenter held either a red or a green chip in full view and made the same statements.

School-age children focused on the concrete properties of the poker chips rather than on the logic of the statements. As a result, they replied that they were uncertain to both statements when the chip was hidden from view. When it was visible, they judged both statements to be true if the chip was green and false if it was red. In contrast, adolescents analyzed the logic of the statements as propositions. They understood that the "either–or" statement is always true and the "and" statement is always false, regardless of the poker chip's color (Osherson & Markman, 1975).

Although Piaget did not view language as playing a central role in cognitive development (see Chapter 9), he acknowledged that it is more important during adolescence. Abstract thought requires language-based systems of representation that do not stand for real things, such as those that exist in higher mathematics. Secondary school students use these systems in algebra and geometry. Formal operational thought also involves verbal reasoning about abstract concepts. Jules showed that he could think in this way when he pondered the relationships between time, space, and matter in physics and wondered about justice and freedom in philosophy.

RECENT RESEARCH ON FORMAL OPERATIONAL THOUGHT

Recent research on formal operational thought poses questions similar to those we discussed with respect to Piaget's earlier stages: Does abstract reasoning appear earlier than Piaget expected? And do all individuals reach formal operations during their teenage years?

■ **ARE YOUNG CHILDREN CAPABLE OF ABSTRACT THINKING?** School-age children show the glimmerings of hypothetico-deductive reasoning, but they are not as competent at it as adolescents and adults. For example, in simplified situations—ones involving no more than two possible causal variables—6-year-olds understand that hypotheses must be confirmed by appropriate evidence. They also realize that once supported, a hypothesis shapes predictions about what might happen in the future (Ruffman et al., 1993). But unlike adolescents, children cannot sort out evidence that bears on three or more variables at once. And as we will see when we take up information-processing research on scientific reasoning in a later section, children have difficulty explaining why a pattern of observations supports a hypothesis, even when they recognize the connection between the two.

School-age children's capacity for propositional thought is also limited. For example, they have great difficulty reasoning from premises that contradict reality or their own beliefs. Consider the following set of statements: "If dogs are bigger than elephants and elephants are bigger than mice, then dogs are bigger than mice." Children younger than 10 judge this reasoning to be false, since all relations specified do not occur in real life (Moshman & Franks, 1986). They fail to grasp the **logical necessity** of propositional reasoning—that the accuracy of conclusions drawn from premises rests on the rules of logic, not on real-world confirmation.

Furthermore, in reasoning with propositions, school-age children do not think carefully

logical necessity
A basic property of propositional thought, which specifies that the accuracy of conclusions drawn from premises rests on the rules of logic, not on real-world confirmation.

about the major premise and, therefore, violate the most basic rules of logic (Markovits, Schleifer, & Fortier, 1989). For example, when given the following problem, they almost always draw an incorrect conclusion:

Major Premise: If Susan hits a tambourine, then she will make a noise.

Second Premise: Suppose that Susan does not hit a tambourine.

Question: Did Susan make a noise?

Wrong Conclusion: No, Susan did not make a noise.

Notice that the major premise did *not* state that Susan can make noise *if, and only if,* she hits a tambourine. School-age children, however, represent the premise incompletely—as including only the elements mentioned in it—so they reason as follows: *tambourine hit →noise; tambourine not hit → no noise.* In contrast, adolescents generally detect that Susan could make noise in other ways (Klaczynski & Narasimham, 1998b). Also, adolescents are better than school-age children at searching their knowledge base for examples that contradict wrong conclusions, including ones that are not obvious. To induce children to come up with counterexamples, researchers have rephrased premises to refer to *categories of relevant items,* as follows: "*A tambourine is something that can be used* to make noise. Suppose that something is not a tambourine. Can it be used to make a noise?" Under these circumstances, 8-year-olds reason much more effectively (Markovits et al., 1998).

Around age 11, young people can analyze the logic of a series of propositions under increasingly varied circumstances. As Piaget's theory indicates, propositional thought improves steadily over the adolescent years (Markovits & Bouffard-Bouchard, 1992; Markovits & Vachon, 1989, 1990).

■ **DO ALL INDIVIDUALS REACH THE FORMAL OPERATIONAL STAGE?** Try giving the tambourine problem to some of your friends and see how well they do. You are likely to find that some well-educated adults have difficulty! About 40 to 60 percent of college students fail Piaget's formal operational problems (Keating, 1979).

Why is it that so many college students, and adults in general, are not fully formal operational? The reason is that people are most likely to think abstractly in situations in which they have had extensive experience. This is supported by evidence that taking college courses leads to improvements in formal operational reasoning related to course content (Lehman & Nisbett, 1990). The physics student grasps Piaget's pendulum problem with ease. The English enthusiast excels at analyzing the themes of a Shakespeare play, whereas the history buff skillfully evaluates the causes and consequences of the Vietnam War. Because of differences in training and interest, the person who does well at one task may not be especially good at the others. Consider these findings, and you will see that formal operations, like the concrete reasoning that preceded it, does not emerge in all contexts at once. Rather, it is specific to situation and task (Keating, 1990).

Furthermore, in many tribal and village societies, formal operational tasks are not mastered at all (Cole, 1990). For example, when asked to engage in propositional thought, people in nonliterate societies often refuse. Take this hypothetical proposition: "In the North, where there is snow, all bears are white. Novaya Zemlya is in the Far North, and it always has snow. What color are the bears there?" In response, a Central Asian peasant explains that he must see the event to discern its logical implications. The peasant insists on firsthand knowledge, whereas the interviewer states that truth can be based on ideas alone. Yet the peasant uses propositions to defend his point of view: "*If* a man . . . had seen a white bear and had told about it, *[then]* he could be believed, *but* I've never seen one and *hence* I can't say" (Luria

If asked, these nonliterate Mongolian nomads would probably refuse to engage in propositional thought, explaining that an event must be seen to discern its logical implications. Without opportunities to solve hypothetical problems, people are unlikely to engage in formal operational thought.

1976, pp. 108–109). Although he rarely displays it in everyday life, clearly the peasant is capable of formal operational thought!

Piaget acknowledged that if people in some societies lack the opportunity to solve hypothetical problems, they might not demonstrate formal operations. Still, these findings raise further questions about Piaget's stage sequence. Does the formal operational stage largely result from children and adolescents' independent efforts to make sense of their world? Or is it a culturally transmitted way of thinking that is particularly useful in literate societies and fostered by experiences encountered in school?

Finally, critics claim that Piaget's theory is unclear about how individuals make the transition from concrete to formal operational thought. They state that his explanation of cognitive change—in particular, the processes of *adaptation* and *organization* (see page 213)—is too vague and imprecise. This issue, especially, has prompted many investigators to turn toward an information-processing view.

An Information-Processing View of Adolescent Cognitive Development

Information-processing theorists agree with the broad outlines of Piaget's description of adolescent cognition (Case, 1992, 1998; Demetriou et al., 1993). However, they refer to a variety of specific mechanisms of cognitive change, each of which was discussed in previous chapters. Now let's draw them together:

- *Attention* becomes more thorough and better adapted to the demands of tasks (see page 443).

- *Strategies* become more effective, improving storage, representation, and retrieval of information (see pages 443–445).

- *Knowledge* increases, easing strategy use (see pages 445–446).

- *Metacognition* (awareness of thought) expands, leading to new insights into effective strategies for acquiring information and solving problems (see page 448).

- *Processing capacity* increases due to the joint effects of brain development and the factors just mentioned. Consequently, space in working memory is freed so more information can be held at once and combined into highly efficient, abstract representations (see page 441).

As we look at some influential findings from an information-processing perspective, we will see some of these mechanisms of change in action. And we will discover that researchers regard one of them—*metacognition*—as central to the development of abstract thought.

SCIENTIFIC REASONING: COORDINATING THEORY WITH EVIDENCE

During a free moment in physical education class, Sabrina wondered why more of her tennis serves and returns seemed to pass the net and drop in her opponent's court when she used a particular brand of balls. "Maybe it's something about their color or size? Hmm, possibly it's their surface texture, which might affect their bounce," she thought to herself as she carefully inspected several balls.

The heart of scientific reasoning is coordinating theories with evidence. A scientist can clearly describe the theory he or she favors, knows what evidence is needed to support it and what would refute it, and can explain how pitting evidence against available theories led to the acceptance of one theory as opposed to others. What evidence would Sabrina need to confirm her theory about the tennis balls?

Deanna Kuhn has conducted extensive research into the development of scientific reasoning, giving children and adolescents problems that resemble those used by Piaget in that they involve several variables that might affect an outcome. In one series of studies, third, sixth, and ninth graders; adults of mixed educational backgrounds; and professional scientists were provided with evidence, sometimes consistent and sometimes conflicting with theories. Then they were asked questions about the accuracy of each theory.

Good Serve

Bad Serve

FIGURE 15.2

Which features of these sports balls—size, color, surface texture, or presence or absence of ridges—influence the quality of a player's serve? This set of evidence suggests that color might be important, since light-colored balls are largely in the good-serve basket and dark-colored balls in the bad-serve basket. But the same is true for texture! The good-serve basket has mostly smooth balls; the bad-serve basket, rough balls. Since all light-colored balls are smooth and all dark-colored balls are rough, we cannot tell whether color or texture makes a difference. But we can conclude that size and presence or absence of ridges are not important, since these features are equally represented in the good-serve and bad-serve baskets. (Adapted from Kuhn, Amsel, & O'Loughlin, 1988.)

For example, participants were given a problem much like the one Sabrina posed. They were asked to theorize about which of four features of sports balls—size (large or small), color (light or dark), surface texture (rough or smooth), or presence or absence of ridges—influences the quality of a player's serve. Next, they were told about the theory of Mr. (or Ms.) S, who believes that size of the ball is important, and the theory of Mr. (or Ms.) C, who thinks that color makes a difference. Finally, the interviewer presented evidence by placing balls with certain characteristics in two baskets labeled "good serve" and "bad serve" (see Figure 15.2).

■ **AGE-RELATED CHANGE.** Kuhn and her collaborators (1988) found that the capacity to reason like a scientist improved with age. The youngest participants often ignored conflicting evidence or distorted it in ways consistent with their theory. When one third grader, who judged that size was causal (with large balls producing good serves and small balls, bad serves), was shown incomplete evidence (a single large, light-colored ball in the good-serve basket and no balls in the bad-serve basket), he insisted on the accuracy of Mr. S's theory (which was also his own). Asked to explain, he stated flatly, "Because this ball is big . . . the color doesn't really matter" (Kuhn, 1989, p. 677).

These findings, and others like them, reveal that instead of viewing evidence as separate from and bearing on a theory, children often blend the two into a single representation of "the way things are." The ability to distinguish theory from evidence and use logical rules to examine their relationship in complex, multivariable situations improves from adolescence into adulthood (Foltz, Overton, & Ricco, 1995; Kuhn et al., 1995; Schauble, 1996).

■ **HOW SCIENTIFIC REASONING DEVELOPS.** What factors support adolescents' skill at coordinating theory with evidence? Adolescents benefit from exposure to increasingly complex problems and instruction that highlights critical features of tasks and effective strategies. Consequently, scientific reasoning is strongly influenced by years of schooling, whether individuals grapple with traditional scientific tasks (like the sports ball problem or Piaget's pendulum task) or engage in informal reasoning—for example, justify a theory about what causes children to fail in school (Kuhn, 1993).

Many investigators believe that sophisticated *metacognitive understanding* is at the heart of advanced cognitive development (Kuhn, 1999; Moshman, 1999). When children receive continuous opportunities to pit theory against evidence, eventually they *reflect* on their current strategies, revise them, and become aware of the nature of logic. Then they apply their abstract appreciation of logical necessity to a wide variety of situations. Although children can distinguish a hypothesis from data and test it in simplified situations, the ability to *think*

© MARK RICHARDS/PHOTOEDIT

Compared with when they were in high school, these college students are more aware of a diversity of opinions on almost any topic. They have moved toward a type of postformal thought called relativistic reasoning, which accepts the existence of multiple truths.

about theories, *deliberately isolate* variables, and *actively seek* disconfirming evidence is rarely present before adolescence (Moshman, 1998b).

Although much better at scientific reasoning than children, adolescents and adults continue to show a self-serving bias in their thinking. They apply logic more effectively to ideas they doubt than to ones they favor (Klaczynski, 1997; Klaczynski & Narasimham, 1998a). Reasoning scientifically, however, requires the metacognitive capacity to evaluate one's objectivity—a disposition to be fairminded rather than self-serving (Moshman, 1999). As we will see in Chapter 16, this flexible, open-minded approach is not just a cognitive attainment but a personality trait—one that assists teenagers greatly in forming an identity and developing morally.

Research reveals that adolescents develop formal operational abilities in a similar, step-by-step fashion on different kinds of tasks. In a series of studies, 10- to 20-year olds were given sets of problems graded in difficulty. For example, one set consisted of quantitative-relational tasks like the pendulum problem on page 563. Another set contained verbal propositional tasks like the tambourine problem on page 565. And in still another set were causal-experimental tasks, such as the sports ball problem described in the previous section and the fertilizer problem in Table 15.1.

In each task domain, adolescents mastered component skills in sequential order by expanding their metacognitive awareness. For example, on causal-experimental tasks, they first became aware of the many variables—separately and in combination—that could influence an outcome. This enabled them to formulate and test hypotheses. Over time, adolescents combined separate skills into a smoothly functioning system. They constructed a general model that they could apply to many instances of a given type of problem. In the researchers' words, young people seem to form a "hypercognitive system," or supersystem, that understands, organizes, and influences other aspects of cognition (Demetriou, Efklides, & Platsidou, 1993; Demetriou et al., 1993, 1996).

Return to Chapter 12, page 441, and review Robbie Case's information-processing view of development during Piaget's concrete operational stage. Does Case's concept of *central conceptual structures* remind you of the metacognitive advances just described? Piaget also underscored the role of metacognition in formal operational thought when he spoke of "operating on operations" (see page 562). However, information-processing findings reveal that scientific reasoning does not result from an abrupt, stagewise change, as Piaget believed. Instead, it develops gradually out of many specific experiences that require children and adolescents to match theory against evidence and reflect on their thinking.

A RATIONAL APPROACH TO THINKING

How can we sum up the cognitive advances we have just considered? Ideally, adolescence opens the door to truly rational thought—a "critical spirit," in which the person seeks relevant evidence and alternative views and is willing to alter his or her beliefs in accord with them. Teenagers, as we have seen, make great strides toward becoming rational thinkers. Yet researchers who study **postformal thought** have shown that cognitive development is not complete at adolescence.

Piaget (1967) acknowledged the possibility that important advances in cognition follow the attainment of formal operations. He observed that many adolescents prefer a logical, internally consistent perspective on the world to one that is vague, contradictory, and constantly open to revision. Their theories often take on the status of right or wrong, good or bad. College-educated young people are much more aware of a diversity of opinions on

postformal thought
Cognitive development beyond Piaget's formal operational stage.

relativistic reasoning
A type of postformal thought that views all knowledge as embedded in a framework of thought and that accepts the existence of multiple truths.

almost any topic. They move toward **relativistic reasoning,** viewing all knowledge as embedded in a framework of thought (Perry, 1970, 1981). As a result, they give up the possibility of absolute truth in favor of multiple truths, each relative to its context. Then they seek good reasons for choosing a belief or course of action, recognizing that in certain instances, one option may be better justified than others.

Most adolescents can think relativistically about hypothetical situations related to their personal experiences. For example, they realize that a group of parents who favor a later driving age and a group of high school students who want the driving age to stay the same each has legitimate claims (Chandler, Boyes, & Ball, 1990). But exposure to the multiple viewpoints typical of a college education greatly enhances relativistic thinking, permitting it to be applied in a much wider range of situations (King & Kitchener, 1994).

In sum, over time abstract thinking becomes increasingly flexible—less constrained by the need to find one answer and more responsive to its context. As we turn now to adolescents' reasoning in everyday life, we will see additional examples of this change.

Consequences of Abstract Thought

The development of formal operations results in dramatic revisions in the way adolescents see themselves, others, and the world in general. Adjusting to thinking on a higher plane presents as many challenges as coming to terms with the physical changes of puberty. Just as adolescents are occasionally awkward in the use of their transformed bodies, they are initially faltering and clumsy in the use of abstract thought.

Parents and teachers must be careful not to mistake the many typical reactions of the teenage years—argumentativeness, self-concern, insensitive remarks, and indecisiveness—for anything other than inexperience with new reasoning powers. Although these behaviors often perplex and worry adults, they usually are beneficial in the long run. The Caregiving Concerns table below suggests ways to handle the everyday consequences of teenagers' newfound capacity for abstraction.

  Caregiving Concerns

Ways to Handle the Consequences of Teenagers' New Capacity for Abstraction

CONSEQUENCE	SUGGESTION
Argumentativeness	During disagreements, remain calm, rational, and focused on principles. Express your point of view and the reasons behind it. Although adolescents may continue to challenge, explanations permit them to consider the validity of your beliefs at a later time.
Sensitivity to public criticism	Refrain from finding fault with the adolescent in front of others. If the matter is important, wait until you can speak to the teenager alone.
Exaggerated sense of personal uniqueness	Acknowledge the adolescent's unique characteristics. At opportune times, point out how you felt similarly as a young teenager, encouraging a more balanced perspective.
Idealism and criticism	Respond patiently to the adolescent's grand expectations and critical remarks. Point out positive features of targets, helping adolescents see that all worlds and people are blends of virtues and imperfections.
Difficulty making everyday decisions	Refrain from deciding for the adolescent. Offer patient reminders and diplomatic suggestions until he or she can make choices more confidently.

ARGUMENTATIVENESS

As adolescents acquire formal operations, they are motivated to use them. The once pliable school-age child becomes a feisty, argumentative teenager who can marshal facts and ideas to build a case (Elkind, 1994). "A simple, straightforward explanation used to be good enough to get Louis to obey," complained Antonio. "Now, he wants a thousand reasons. And worse yet, he finds a way to contradict them all!" Antonio was reflecting on the previous evening, when he had taken a strong stand in forbidding Louis to go to a movie with Cassie. Here is what happened:

Antonio: "Louis, no going out tonight. It's a school night, and you have homework."

Louis: "Dad, I've done most of my homework. I can do the rest before class in the morning. Besides, I fell asleep this afternoon. There's no way I'll be able to go to bed early."

Antonio: "You fell asleep because you didn't get enough rest the night before. You've been out several evenings in a row. You need to stay home."

Louis: "You never made Jules stay in on school nights when he was my age. How come you don't treat me equally?"

Antonio: "I did just the same thing with Jules. Homework is one of your responsibilities. It comes before going out on school nights."

Louis: "If it's my responsibility, then I'll take care of it. It's my personal business, so don't worry about it."

Antonio: "But you're not taking care of it unless you stay home and do it."

Louis: "Dad, you're unfair! You treat Jules like an adult. You treat me like a child!"

Parents often comment that teenagers "argue for the sake of arguing." As long as parent–child disagreements remain focused on principles and do not deteriorate into meaningless battles, they can promote development. Through discussions of family rules and practices, adolescents become more aware of their parents' values and the reasons behind them. Gradually, they come to see the validity of parental beliefs and adopt many as their own (Alessandri & Wozniak, 1987).

Teenagers' capacity for effective argument opens the door to intellectually stimulating pastimes, such as debate teams and endless bull sessions with friends over ethical and political concerns. By proposing, justifying, criticizing, and defending a variety of solutions, adolescents often move to a higher level of understanding than they attain in individual reasoning—on challenging scientific tasks as well as social and moral problems (Moshman, 1998b, 1999).

SELF-CONSCIOUSNESS AND SELF-FOCUSING

Adolescents' ability to reflect on their own thoughts, combined with the physical and psychological changes they are undergoing, means that they start to think more about themselves. Piaget believed that the arrival of formal operations is accompanied by a new form of egocentrism: the inability to distinguish the abstract perspectives of self and others (Inhelder & Piaget, 1955/1958). As teenagers imagine what others must be thinking, two distorted images of the relation between self and other appear.

The first is called the **imaginary audience.** Young teenagers regard themselves as always on stage. They are convinced that they are the focus of everyone else's attention and concern (Elkind & Bowen, 1979). As a

These adolescents are acting for the camera. But the imaginary audience leads them to think that everyone is monitoring their performance at other times as well. Consequently, young teenagers are extremely self-conscious and go to great lengths to avoid embarrassment.

DAVID YOUNG-WOLFF/PHOTOEDIT

result, they become extremely self-conscious, often going to great lengths to avoid embarrassment. Sabrina, for example, woke up one Sunday morning with a large pimple on her chin. "I can't possibly go to church!" she cried. "*Everyone* will notice how ugly I look." The imaginary audience helps us understand the long hours adolescents spend in the bathroom inspecting every detail of their appearance as they envision the response of the rest of the world. It also accounts for their extreme sensitivity to public criticism. To teenagers, who believe that everyone is monitoring their performance, a critical remark from a parent or teacher can be mortifying.

A second cognitive distortion is the **personal fable.** Because teenagers are so sure that others are observing and thinking about them, they develop an inflated opinion of their own importance. They start to feel that they are special and unique. Many adolescents view themselves as reaching great heights of glory as well as sinking to unusual depths of despair—experiences that others could not possibly understand (Elkind, 1994). On one occasion, for example, Sabrina had a crush on a boy who failed to return her affections. As she lay on the sofa feeling depressed, Franca tried to assure her that there would be other boys. "Mom," Sabrina snapped. "You don't know what it's like to be in love!" The personal fable may also contribute to adolescent risk taking. Teenagers who have sex without using contraceptives or who weave in and out of traffic at 80 miles an hour seem, at least for the moment, to be convinced of their uniqueness and invulnerability.

The imaginary audience and personal fable are strongest during the transition from concrete to formal operations. They gradually decline as abstract thinking becomes better established (Enright, Lapsley, & Shukla, 1979; Lapsley et al., 1988). Yet these distorted visions of the self probably are not due to egocentrism, as Piaget suggested. Instead, they seem to be an outgrowth of advances in perspective taking, which cause young teenagers to be very concerned with what others think (Lapsley, 1985; Lapsley et al., 1986).

Take a moment to look back at Selman's stages of perspective taking on page 492 of Chapter 13. Recent evidence indicates that the *self-reflective* approach of late childhood and early adolescence contributes to the imaginary audience and personal fable (Vartanian & Powlishta, 1996). Adolescents also may have emotional reasons for clinging to the idea that others are preoccupied with their thoughts and feelings. Doing so helps them maintain a hold on important relationships as they struggle to separate from parents and establish an independent sense of self (Lapsley, 1993).

IDEALISM AND CRITICISM

Because abstract thinking permits adolescents to go beyond the real to the possible, it opens up the world of the ideal and of perfection. Teenagers can imagine alternative family, religious, political, and moral systems, and they want to explore them. Doing so is part of investigating new realms of experience, developing larger social commitments, and defining their own values and preferences.

The idealism of teenagers leads them to construct grand visions of a perfect world—with no injustice, discrimination, or tasteless behavior. They do not make room for the shortcomings of everyday life. Adults, with their longer life experience, have a more realistic outlook. The disparity between adults' and teenagers' world views is often called the "generation gap," and it creates tension between parent and child. Aware of the perfect

This teenage girl looks as if she has nothing in common with her parents. Her idealistic image of a perfect world, to which her family cannot measure up, leads to a " generation gap," creating tension between parent and adolescent child. Over time, she will forge a better balance between the ideal and the real.

imaginary audience
Adolescents' belief that they are the focus of everyone else's attention and concern.

personal fable
Adolescents' belief that they are special and unique. Leads them to conclude that others cannot possibly understand their thoughts and feelings. May promote a sense of invulnerability to danger.

family against which their real parents and siblings do not measure up, adolescents become fault-finding critics.

Yet overall, teenage idealism and criticism are advantageous. Once adolescents learn to see other people as having both strengths and weaknesses, they have a much greater capacity to work constructively for social change and to form positive and lasting relationships (Elkind, 1994). Parents can help teenagers forge a better balance between the ideal and the real by tolerating their criticism while reminding the young person that all people, including adolescents themselves, are blends of virtues and imperfections.

PLANNING AND DECISION MAKING

Adolescents, who think more analytically, handle cognitive tasks more effectively than they did at younger ages. Given a homework assignment, they are far better at *cognitive self-regulation*—planning what to do first and what to do next, monitoring progress toward a goal, and redirecting actions that prove unsuccessful. For this reason, study skills improve from middle childhood into adolescence.

In addition, adolescents are better at a form of self-regulation called **comprehension monitoring.** While reading or listening, they continually evaluate how well they understand. Compared with younger students, 12- and 13-year-olds more often notice when a passage does not make sense. Rather than just moving ahead, they slow down and look back to see if they missed some important information (Garner, 1990). Their greater sensitivity to text errors means that they are more likely to revise their written work (Beal, 1990).

But when it comes to planning and decision making in everyday life, teenagers (especially young ones) often feel overwhelmed by the possibilities before them. As a result, their efforts to choose among alternatives frequently break down, and they may resort to habit, act on impulse, or not make a decision at all (Elkind, 1994). On many mornings, for example, Sabrina tried on five or six outfits before leaving for school. Often she shouted from the bedroom, "Mom, what shall I wear?" Then, when Franca made a suggestion, Sabrina rejected it, opting for one of the two or three sweaters she had worn for weeks. Similarly, Louis procrastinated about registering for college entrance tests. When Franca mentioned that he was about to miss the deadline, Louis sat over the forms, unable to decide when or where he wanted to take the test.

Everyday planning and decision making are challenging for teenagers because they have so many opportunities. When they were younger, adults usually specified their options, reducing the number of decisions they had to make. As adolescents gather more experience, they make choices with greater confidence and certainty.

Ask YOURSELF...

review   Describe and cite examples of the role of metacognition in adolescent cognitive development.

apply   Louis suggested that Franca and Antonio vote for a certain candidate in the upcoming election, offering many good reasons. Franca and Antonio countered with reasons that Louis's favored candidate might not be best, but Louis insisted that his view was right. What aspects of adolescent cognition may have prevented Louis from seeing beyond his own perspective?

connect   What questions raised about Piaget's formal operational stage are similar to those raised about the concrete operational stage? (See Chapter 12, page 440.)

reflect   Can you recall displaying the imaginary audience, the personal fable, and idealistic thinking when you were a young teenager? Cite examples of each.

Sex Differences in Mental Abilities

Sex differences in intellectual performance have been studied since the beginning of this century, and they have sparked almost as much controversy as the ethnic and SES differences in IQ considered in Chapter 12. Although boys and girls do not differ in general intelligence, they do vary in specific mental abilities. Girls, as we saw in Chapter 6, are ahead in early language development. Throughout the school years, girls attain higher scores in reading and writing and account for a lower percentage of children referred for remedial reading instruction (Campbell, Hombo, & Mazzeo, 2000; Halpern, 2000). Girls' advantage on tests of general verbal ability is still present in adolescence. However, it is so slight that it is not really meaningful (Hyde & Linn, 1988).

Sex differences in mathematical ability are apparent by second grade among academically talented students. By adolescence an overall difference between boys and girls exists (Bielinski & Davison, 1998; Linn & Hyde, 1989). Again, however, the gender gap is largest among the academically talented. In some widely publicized research on more than 40,000 bright seventh and eighth graders who were invited to take the Scholastic Aptitude Test (SAT) long before they needed to do so for college admission, boys outscored girls on the mathematics subtest year after year. Twice as many boys as girls had scores above 500; 13 times as many scored over 700 (Benbow & Stanley, 1983; Lubinski & Benbow, 1994). However, sex differences only show up on some test items. Boys and girls do equally well in basic math knowledge, and girls do better in computational skills. The difference appears in abstract reasoning, primarily in solving complex word problems (Hyde, Fenema, & Lamon, 1990).

A subgroup of the academically talented students just mentioned—boys and girls whose SAT math scores were in the top 1 percent for 12- to 14-year-olds—were followed into adulthood. Both sexes demonstrated high achievement, earning bachelor's, master's, and doctoral degrees at rates far higher than those of the general population. But the occupations they chose were consistent with early sex differences in math ability. Men entered engineering, math, physical science, and computer science careers at higher rates than did women, who surpassed men in medicine and other health professions (Benbow et al., 2000).

Some researchers believe that the gender gap in mathematics—especially the tendency for many more boys to be extremely talented in math—is genetic. One common assumption is that sex differences in mathematical ability are rooted in boys' biologically based superior spatial reasoning. See the Biology and Environment box on pages 574–575 for a discussion of this issue.

Although heredity is involved, social pressures also contribute to girls' underrepresentation among the mathematically talented. The mathematics gender gap is related to student attitudes and self-esteem. Long before sex differences in math achievement are present, elementary school boys and girls view math as a "male domain" (see Chapter 13, page 501). In addition, girls regard math as less useful for their future lives, perceive themselves as having to work harder at it to do well, and more often blame their errors on lack of ability. These beliefs, in turn, lead girls to become less interested in math, to be less likely to consider math- or science-related careers, and to enroll in fewer math and science courses in high school and college (Byrnes & Takahira, 1993; Catsambis, 1994; Hyde et al., 1990). The result of this chain of events is that girls—even those who are highly talented academically—are less likely to develop abstract mathematical concepts and effective problem-solving strategies.

A positive sign is that sex differences in cognitive abilities of all kinds have declined steadily over the past several decades. Today, American boys are ahead of girls in mathematical reasoning and in science achievement by a much smaller margin than in the 1970s. Paralleling this change is an increase in girls' enrollment in advanced high school math and science courses. Today, boys and girls reach advanced levels of math and science study in equal proportions—a critical factor in reducing sex differences in knowledge and skill (Campbell, Hombo, & Mazzeo, 2000).

Still, extra steps must be taken to promote girls' interest in and confidence at math and science. When parents hold nonstereotyped gender-role values, daughters are less likely to

© BOB DAEMMRICH/STOCK BOSTON

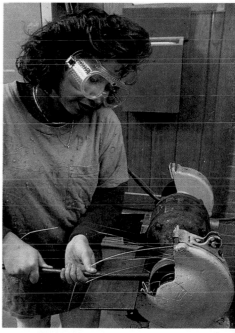

This girl is probably the only female enrolled in her high school metal shop class. Experience with manipulative activities, including model building and carpentry, contribute to sex differences in spatial abilities. Superior spatial skills and confidence at doing math, in turn, affect the ease with which young people solve complex math problems.

comprehension monitoring
Continually evaluating how well one understands a spoken or written message.

Biology & ENVIRONMENT

SEX DIFFERENCES IN SPATIAL ABILITIES

Spatial skills have become a key focus of researchers' efforts to explain sex differences in mathematics performance. Clear sex differences on some spatial reasoning tasks exist by age 4 (Levine et al., 1999). From middle childhood on, the gender gap favoring males is large for *mental rotation tasks,* in which individuals must rotate a three-dimensional figure rapidly and accurately inside their heads (see Figure 15.3). In addition, males do considerably better on *spatial perception tasks,* in which people must determine spatial relationships by considering the orientation of the surrounding environment. Sex differences on *spatial visualization tasks,* involving analysis of complex visual forms, are weak or nonexistent, perhaps because many strategies can be used to solve them. Both sexes may come up with effective procedures (Linn & Petersen, 1985; Voyer, Voyer, & Bryden, 1995).

Sex differences in spatial abilities persist throughout the lifespan (Kerns & Berenbaum, 1991). The pattern is consistent enough to suggest a biological explanation. One hypothesis is that heredity, perhaps through prenatal exposure to androgen hormones, enhances right hemispheric functioning, granting males a spatial advantage. (Recall that for most people, spatial skills are housed in the right hemisphere of the cerebral cortex.) Consistent with this idea, girls and women whose prenatal androgen levels were abnormally high show superior performance on spatial rotation tasks (Collaer & Hines, 1995). And people with severe prenatal deficits in either male or female hormones have difficulty with spatial reasoning (Hier & Crowley, 1982; Temple & Carney, 1995).

However, research on hormone variations within normal range is less clear. Two studies report a link between prenatal androgens and spatial abilities during the preschool years, but only for girls and in the opposite direction expected: The greater the hormone exposure, the lower the spatial score (Finegan, Niccols, & Sitarenios, 1992; Jacklin, Wilcox, & Maccoby, 1988). Prenatal hormones seem to affect spatial skills, but not in a straightforward fashion.

Other evidence suggests more rapid development of the right hemisphere of the cerebral cortex (where spatial abilities are housed) in boys than girls. In one study of human fetal brains, males' right cerebral hemispheres were larger (de Lacoste, Horvath, & Woodward, 1991). Also, auditory stimulation evokes greater electrical activity in the right hemisphere of infant boys (Grattan et al., 1992; Shucard, Shucard, & Thomas, 1984).

Although biology is involved in sex differences in spatial performance, experience also makes a difference. Children who engage in manipulative activities, such as block play, model building, and carpentry, do better on spatial tasks (Baenninger & Newcombe, 1995). Furthermore, playing video games that require rapid mental rotation of visual images enhances spatial scores of boys and girls alike (Okagaki & Frensch, 1996; Subrahmanyam & Greenfield, 1996). Boys spend far more time at all these pursuits than do girls. At the same time, research suggests a genetic–environmental correlation—that is, young people with a genetic

show declines in math and science achievement in adolescence (Updegraff, McHale, & Crouter, 1996). In schools, teachers must better demonstrate the relevance of math and science to everyday life. Girls, especially, respond positively to math and science instruction taught from an applied, hands-on perspective (Eccles, 1994). At the same time, teachers must ensure that girls participate fully in hands-on group activities and are not reduced to a passive role by boys' more assertive style of peer interaction (Jovanovic & King, 1998). And all students benefit from encouragement and constructive feedback rather than criticism when engaged in problem solving.

Finally, a common assumption is that girls show better math and science achievement in single-sex secondary schools, where they may encounter fewer gender-biased messages and more same-sex role models. Although past research supported this belief, recent evidence indicates that gender-segregated schools do not enhance boys' or girls' learning or self-esteem (Bryk, Lee, & Holland, 1993; LePore & Warren, 1997). Recently, both single-sex and coeducational schools have sharpened their focus on reducing gender discrimination. Consequently, the gender makeup of the student body seems to be far less relevant than it once was for girls' academic development.

spatial-skill advantage more often seek out spatial activities. When girls with one or more left-handed close relatives (suggesting a genetic, right-hemispheric bias) grow up with brothers and, therefore, in homes rich in spatial activities, they excel at mental rotation tasks (Casey, Nuttall, & Pezaris, 1999).

Do superior spatial skills contribute to the greater ease with which males solve complex math problems? Research indicates that they do (Casey et al., 1995). Yet in a recent study of high-ability college-bound adolescents, *both* mental rotation ability and self-

confidence at doing math predicted higher scores on the math subtest of the SAT (Casey, Nuttall, & Pezaris, 1997). Boys are advantaged not only in mental rotation but in math self-confidence. Even when their grades are

poorer than girls', boys judge themselves to be better at math (Eccles et al., 1993b). In sum, biology and environment jointly determine variations in spatial and math performance—within and between the sexes.

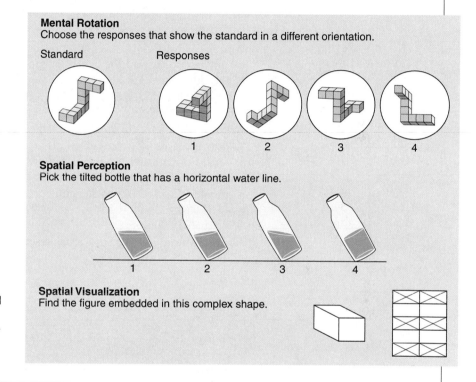

Mental Rotation
Choose the responses that show the standard in a different orientation.

Standard   Responses

                                          1   2   3   4

Spatial Perception
Pick the tilted bottle that has a horizontal water line.

                    1   2   3   4

Spatial Visualization
Find the figure embedded in this complex shape.

FIGURE 15.3

Types of spatial tasks. Large sex differences favoring males appear on mental rotation, and males do considerably better than females on spatial perception. In contrast, sex differences on spatial visualization are weak or nonexistent. (From M. C. Linn & A. C. Petersen, 1985, "Emergence and Characterization of Sex Differences in Spatial Ability: A Meta-Analysis," *Child Development, 56*, pp. 1482, 1483, 1485. © The Society for Research in Child Development, Inc. Reprinted by permission.)

Language Development

Although language development is largely complete by the end of childhood, subtle but important changes take place during adolescence. These gains are largely influenced by adolescents' improved capacity for reflective thought and abstraction, which enhances their *metalinguistic awareness,* or ability to think about language as a system.

VOCABULARY AND GRAMMAR

Adolescents add a wide variety of abstract words to their vocabularies. In the conversation at the beginning of this chapter, note Jules's use of *counterintuitive, incredible, revolutionized, philosophy, reproduction,* and *justice.* As a 9- or 10-year-old, he rarely used such words, and he had difficulty grasping their meaning. From high school to college, definitions of abstract words improve greatly in clarity and accuracy (Nippold et al., 1999). For example, in explaining the meaning of *burden,* Louis said, "It's like a heavy weight on your shoulders." Louis elaborated, "Yes, it's a heavy weight that must be carried, but the word can be used either literally or figuratively. Figuratively, a burden is an unpleasant responsibility or a long-term problem."

Abstract thinking also permits adolescents to master irony and sarcasm (Winner, 1988). "Don't have a major brain explosion," Louis commented to Sabrina when she complained about having to work on an essay for school. And when Franca fixed a dish for dinner that Louis disliked, he quipped, "Oh boy, my favorite!" Young children sometimes realize that a sarcastic remark is insincere if it is said in a very exaggerated, mocking tone of voice. But adolescents and adults need only notice the discrepancy between the statement and its context to grasp the intended meaning (Capelli, Nakagawa, & Madden, 1990).

Furthermore, adolescents can better grasp figurative language. Proverbs—especially those that express subtle attitudes—are among the most challenging. They can be used to comment ("Blood is thicker than water"), interpret ("His bark is worse than his bite"), advise ("Humility often gains more than pride"), warn ("Of idleness comes no goodness"), and encourage ("Every cloud has a silver lining"). And they make sense only in certain situations. "Too many cooks spoil the broth" is good advice when someone offers to help balance a checkbook but bad advice when that person offers to assist with cleaning up a classroom (Nippold, 2000). Understanding of proverbs improves greatly during adolescence and is positively related to academic achievement (Nippold et al., 1998). Furthermore, increased sensitivity to the nuances of language enables teenagers to appreciate adult literary works.

Adolescents also use more elaborate grammatical constructions. Their sentences are longer and consist of a greater number of subordinate clauses than do those of children. Persuasive speaking and writing, which draw on adolescents' advanced perspective-taking skill, illustrate this change. With age, this challenging form of communication contains many more connecting words, such as "although," "moreover," "on the other hand," and "consequently" (Crowhurst, 1990). Finally, teenagers can more effectively analyze and correct their grammar. Not surprisingly, diagramming sentences is a skill reserved for the junior high and high school years.

PRAGMATICS

One of the most obvious changes in adolescents' communication skill is an improved capacity to vary language style according to the situation (Obler, 2000). This change is partly the result of opportunities to enter many more situations. To succeed on the debate team, Louis had to speak in a rapid-fire, well-organized, persuasive manner. In theater class, he worked on reciting memorized lines as if they were natural. At work, his boss insisted that he respond to customers cheerfully and courteously. The ability to reflect on the features of language and engage in cognitive self-regulation also supports effective use of language styles. Teenagers are far more likely than school-age children to practice what they want to say in an expected situation, review what they did say, and figure out how they could say it better (Romaine, 1984).

Adolescents' mastery of language styles is particularly apparent in their slang. Teenagers use slang as a sign of group belonging and as a way of distinguishing themselves from adults. Doing so is part of separating from parents and seeking a temporary self-definition in the peer group. We will discuss these developments in Chapter 16.

Learning in School

In complex societies, adolescence coincides with entry into secondary school. Most young people move into either a middle or junior high school and then into a high school. With each change, academic achievement becomes more serious business, affecting college choices and job opportunities. In the following sections, we take up various aspects of secondary school life. We also consider the serious problem of high school dropouts and how well prepared American high school graduates are for life in a technologically advanced, rapidly changing world.

SCHOOL TRANSITIONS

When Sabrina started junior high, she left a small, intimate, self-contained sixth-grade classroom for a much larger school, where she was with a different teacher and group of students each period. "I don't know my way around the school yet, so I'm always lost, and there's a different notebook and folder for each class, so I never have the right one when I need it," Sabrina complained to her mother at the end of the first week. "Besides, there's too much homework. I get assignments in all my classes at once. I can't do all this!" she shouted, bursting into tears.

■ **IMPACT OF SCHOOL TRANSITIONS.** As Sabrina's reactions suggest, school transitions can create adjustment problems. With each school change—from elementary to middle or junior high and then to high school—adolescents' course grades decline. The drop is partly due to tighter academic standards. At the same time, the transition to junior high school often brings with it less personal attention, more whole-class instruction, and fewer opportunities to participate in classroom decision making (Eccles, Lord, & Buchanan, 1996).

In view of these changes, it is not surprising that students rate their junior-high learning experiences less favorably than their elementary school experiences (Wigfield & Eccles, 1994). They also report that their junior high teachers care less about them, are less friendly, grade less fairly, and stress competition more and mastery and improvement less. Consequently, many young people feel less academically competent and show a drop in motivation (Anderman & Midgley, 1997; Eccles et al., 1993c).

Inevitably, the transition to junior high and then to high school requires students to readjust their feelings of self-confidence and self-worth as academic expectations are revised and students enter a more complex social world. A comprehensive study revealed that the timing of school transition is important, especially for girls (Simmons & Blyth, 1987). More than 300 adolescents living in a large Midwestern city were followed from sixth to tenth grade. Some were enrolled in school districts with a 6–3–3 grade organization (a K–6 elementary school, a 3-year junior high, and a 3-year high school). These students made two school changes, one to junior high and one to high school. A comparison group attended schools with an 8–4 grade organization. They made only one school transition, from a K–8 elementary school to high school.

For the sample as a whole, gradepoint average dropped and feelings of anonymity increased after each transition. Participation in extracurricular activities declined more in

© JOHN MAHER/STOCK BOSTON

Moving from a small, self-contained elementary school classroom to a large, impersonal secondary school is stressful for adolescents. As this cafeteria line suggests, feelings of anonymity increase, and school grades and extracurricular participation also decline. The stress of school transition can be particularly harmful to adolescents with academic and emotional difficulties, increasing the risk of school failure and dropout.

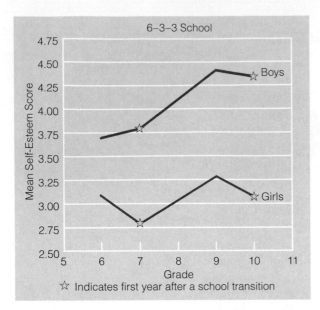

6–3–3 School

☆ Indicates first year after a school transition

FIGURE 15.4

Self-esteem from sixth to tenth grade in 6–3–3 schools. In this longitudinal study of more than 300 adolescents, boys' self-esteem remained stable after school transition. In contrast, girls' self-esteem dropped sharply in the year after each school change. (Adapted from Simmons & Blyth, 1987.)

the 6–3–3 than in the 8–4 arrangement, although the drop was greater for girls. Furthermore, in 8–4 schools, school transition led to gains in self-esteem. In contrast, in 6–3–3 schools, sex differences in self-esteem were striking. Whereas boys remained stable, girls showed a sharp drop with each school change (see Figure 15.4).

These findings show that any school transition is likely to temporarily depress adolescents' psychological well-being, but the earlier it occurs, the more dramatic and long lasting its impact. Girls in 6–3–3 schools fared poorest, the researchers argued, because movement to junior high tended to coincide with other life changes—namely, the onset of puberty and dating. Adolescents who must cope with added transitions, such as family disruption, parental unemployment, or a shift in residence around the time they change schools, are at greatest risk for academic and emotional difficulties (Flanagan & Eccles, 1993).

Emotionally distressed young people whose school performance drops sharply in junior high school often show a persisting pattern of poor self-esteem, academic motivation, and achievement. In another study, researchers compared "multiple-problem" youths (having both academic and mental health problems), youths having difficulties in just one area (either academic or mental health), and well-adjusted youths (doing well in both areas) across the transition to high school. Although all groups declined in grade point average, well-adjusted students continued to get high marks and multiple-problem youths low marks, with the remaining groups falling in between. And as Figure 15.5 shows, the multiple-problem youths showed a far greater rise in truancy and out-of-school problem behaviors (doing something dangerous for the thrill of it, damaging public property, or getting drunk) (Roeser, Eccles, & Freedman-Doan, 1999).

Adolescents with academic and emotional difficulties often turn to similarly alienated peers, whose values they describe as increasingly antisocial, for the support they lack in other spheres of life (Seidman et al., 1994). For some, the transition to high school initiates a downward spiral in school performance and involvement that eventually leads to failure and dropping out (Eccles et al., 1997b).

■ **HELPING ADOLESCENTS ADJUST TO SCHOOL TRANSITIONS.** Consider the findings just reviewed, and you will see that school transitions often lead to environmental changes that fit poorly with adolescents' developmental needs. They disrupt close relationships with teachers at a time when adolescents need adult support. They emphasize competition during a period of heightened self-focusing. They reduce decision making and choice as the desire for autonomy is increasing. And they interfere with peer networks at a time of increased concern with peer acceptance.

Enhanced support from parents, teachers, and peers eases the strain of school transition (Fenzel, 2000; Isakson & Jarvis, 1999). Since most students do better in an 8–4 school arrangement, school districts thinking about reorganization might give serious thought to this plan.[1] When early school transitions cannot be avoided, smaller social units can be formed within large schools, permitting closer relations with teachers and peers and greater extracurricular involvement (Seidman & French, 1997).

Other, less extensive changes also help. During the first year after a school transition, homerooms can be provided in which teachers offer academic and personal counseling and

---

[1]Recall from Chapter 14 (page 539) that girls who reach puberty early fare better in K–6 schools, where they are relieved of pressures from older adolescents to become involved in dating, sexual activity, and drug experimentation before they are ready. Although the 8–4 organization is best for the majority of adolescents, early maturing girls require special support under these conditions.

work closely with parents to promote favorable school adjustment. Students can also be assigned to classes with several familiar peers or a constant group of new peers—arrangements that promote emotional security and social support. In one investigation, high school freshmen experiencing these interventions showed much better academic performance and psychological adjustment at the end of the school year than did controls. A follow-up after 4 years revealed that only half as many students in the intervention group had dropped out of school (Felner & Adan, 1988).

Finally, successful transitions are most likely to occur in schools that foster adolescents' self-respect and capacity for autonomy and responsibility. Teenagers' perceptions of the sensitivity and flexibility of their school learning environments contribute substantially to their adjustment. When schools minimize competition and differential treatment by ability, students are less likely to feel angry and depressed, to be truant, and to show declines in academic values, self-esteem, and achievement during junior high school (Roeser & Eccles, 1998). School rules that strike young people as fair rather than punitive also foster satisfaction with school life (Eccles et al., 1993a).

ACADEMIC ACHIEVEMENT

Adolescent achievement results from a long history of cumulative effects. Early on, positive educational environments, both family and school, lead to personal traits that support achievement—intelligence, confidence in one's own abilities, the desire to succeed, and high educational aspirations (Masten & Coatsworth, 1998). In contrast, living in an environment that provides little encouragement or opportunity for success results in a decline in ability and the belief that trying hard is futile. Yet improving an unfavorable environment can help a poorly performing young person bounce back and open the door to a more satisfying adult life. The Educational Concerns table on page 580 summarizes environmental factors that enhance achievement during the teenage years.

■ **CHILD-REARING PRACTICES.** Authoritative parenting (which combines warmth with firm, reasonable demands for maturity) is linked to achievement in adolescence, just as it predicts mastery-oriented behavior during the childhood years. Research involving thousands of adolescents reveals that the authoritative style is related to higher grades for boys and girls varying widely in SES. In contrast, authoritarian and permissive styles often are associated with lower grades (Dornbusch et al., 1987; Steinberg, Darling, & Fletcher, 1995). Of all parenting approaches, a neglectful style (low in both warmth and maturity demands) predicts the poorest grades along with worsening school performance over time (Baumrind, 1991; Glasgow et al., 1997; Lamborn et al., 1991; Steinberg et al., 1994).

The child rearing–school performance relationships just described vary somewhat with ethnicity. Recall from Chapter 10 that some Asian and African-American parents are more demanding of their children than are Caucasian-American parents (see page 398). For Asian parents, high control represents deep parental concern and commitment, stemming from Confucian values. For African-American parents, dangerous inner-city neighborhoods may require greater strictness to foster children's competence. Consistent with these trends, parenting especially high in control is often linked to better grades among Asian and African-American teenagers (Avenevoli, Sessa, & Steinberg, 1999; Glasgow et al., 1997; Leung, Lau, & Lam, 1998).

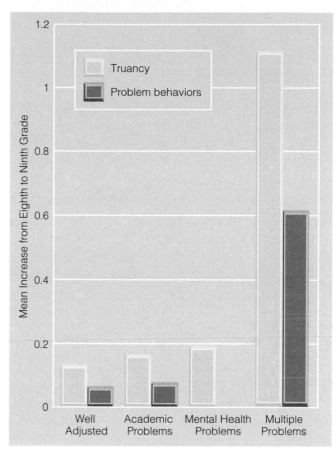

FIGURE 15.5

Increase in truancy and out-of-school problem behaviors across the transition to high school in four groups of students. Well-adjusted students, students with only academic problems, and students with only mental health problems showed little change. (Good students with mental health problems actually declined in problem behaviors, so no purple bar is shown for them.) In contrast, multiple-problem students— with both academic and mental health difficulties— increased sharply in truancy and problem behaviors after changing schools from eighth to ninth grade. (Adapted from Roeser, Eccles, & Freedman-Doan, 1999.)

$\mathcal{E}$ducational Concerns

Factors That Support High Achievement During Adolescence

FACTOR	DESCRIPTION
Child-rearing practices	Authoritative parenting (warmth with moderate to high demandingness, in accord with the young person's ethnic background)
	Joint parent–adolescent decision making
	Parent involvement in the adolescent's education
Peer influences	Peer valuing of and support for high achievement
School characteristics	Teachers who are warm and supportive, develop personal relationships with parents, and show them how to support their child's learning
	Learning activities that encourage high-level thinking
	Active student participation in learning activities and classroom decision making
Employment schedule (see page 592)	Job commitment limited to less than 15 hours per week
	High-quality vocational education for non-college-bound adolescents

Why does combining warmth with moderate to high demandingness promote intellectual persistence during adolescence? In Chapter 10, we noted that authoritative parents adjust their expectations to children's capacity to take responsibility for their own behavior. Parents who engage in joint decision making with adolescents, gradually permitting more autonomy with age, have youngsters who achieve especially well (Dornbusch et al., 1990). Open discussion accompanied by warmth and firmness makes adolescents feel competent and valued, encourages constructive thinking and self-regulation, and increases awareness of the importance of doing well in school. These factors, in turn, are related to mastery-oriented attributions, effort, achievement, and high educational expectations (Aunola, Stattin, & Nurmi, 2000; Trusty, 1999; Wentzel & Feldman, 1993).

■ **PARENT–SCHOOL INVOLVEMENT.** High-achieving young people typically have parents who keep tabs on their child's progress, communicate with teachers, and make sure their child is enrolled in challenging, well-taught classes. Although many parents reduce their school involvement as their children get older, it is just as important during junior and senior high school as it was earlier. Parents who are in frequent contact with the school send a message to their child about the value of education, promote wise educational decisions, and model constructive solutions to academic problems. Involved parents can also prevent school personnel from placing a bright student who is not working up to potential in unstimulating learning situations.

In a study of a nationally representative sample of more than 15,000 American students, parent involvement in eighth grade strongly predicted students' grade point average in tenth grade, beyond the influence of SES and previous academic achievement. This relationship held for each ethnic group included—black, white, Native American, and Asian (Keith et al., 1998). Schools can increase parent involvement in the following ways:

■ fostering personal relationships between parents and teachers;

■ showing parents how to support their child's education at home;

■ building bridges between minority home cultures and the culture of the school;

■ developing assignments that give parents a meaningful role to play, such as having students find out about their parents' experiences while growing up;

■ including parents in basic planning and governance to ensure that they are invested in school goals (Eccles & Harold, 1993).

Family and community characteristics affect the ease with which schools attain these goals. Low-SES parents living in high-risk neighborhoods are harder for schools to reach. These parents often are more preoccupied with protecting their youngsters from danger than developing their talents. Furthermore, they face many daily stresses that strain relationships with their teenagers and reduce time and energy available for school involvement—factors that are consistently linked to poor academic performance (Gutman & Eccles, 1999). Yet schools could relieve some of this stress by forging stronger home–school links. Parents of every SES level and in every type of neighborhood are highly involved in their adolescents' education (Eccles & Harold, 1996).

This father is involved in his adolescent daughter's school career. Besides keeping tabs on her progress, he is probably in regular contact with the school. He sends a message to his daughter about the importance of education and teaches her how to solve academic problems and make wise educational decisions.

■ **PEER INFLUENCES.** Peers also play an important role in achievement during adolescence, in a way that relates to both family and school. Adolescents whose parents value achievement generally choose friends who share those values (Berndt & Keefe, 1995; Kinderman, 1993). For example, when Sabrina began to make new friends in junior high, she often studied with her girlfriends and called them to check answers to homework assignments. Each girl wanted to do well in school and reinforced the same desire in the others.

Peer support for high achievement also depends on the overall climate of the peer culture, which—in the case of ethnic minority youths—is powerfully affected by the surrounding social order. Low-SES minority adolescents often react against working hard, convinced that getting good grades will have little payoff for their future and may threaten their peer relationships and ethnic identity (Ogbu, 1997). Yet not all economically disadvantaged minority students respond this way. As the Social Issues: Education box on pages 582–583 illustrates, when African-American students view achievement as part of a struggle against oppression, they are highly motivated, even in the face of peer pressures against doing well in school and powerful social obstacles to success.

■ **SCHOOL CHARACTERISTICS.** Adolescents need school environments that are responsive to their expanding powers of reasoning and emotional and social needs. Without appropriate learning experiences, the potential for abstract thought is unlikely to be realized.

Classroom Learning Experiences. As we discussed earlier, the transition to junior high school often brings impersonal schools and classrooms that offer few opportunities for active participation. In a study focusing on math classes, researchers found that students moving from an elementary school classroom perceived high in support (in terms of teacher friendliness, fairness, and student involvement) to a junior high classroom low in support showed a sharp decline in their liking for and personal sense of competence in the subject. When the direction of change was reversed—that is, when students moved from classrooms low in support to ones high in support—their evaluations of themselves and attitudes toward the subject improved (Midgley, Feldlaufer, & Eccles, 1989).

The perception of many adolescents that their classes lack warmth and supportiveness is the result of a large, departmentalized school organization that makes it difficult for teachers and students to get to know each other well. Adolescents, like children, need opportunities to form close relationships with teachers. As they begin to develop an identity beyond the family, they seek adult models other than their parents (Eccles & Harold, 1996).

Social

ISSUES:EDUCATION

DISPOSITIONS TOWARD COLLECTIVE STRUGGLE: HIGHLY ACHIEVING, OPTIMISTIC AFRICAN-AMERICAN HIGH SCHOOL STUDENTS

Adolescents' recognition of limited opportunities promotes a pessimistic outlook, which increases the likelihood of disengagement from school. Witness the remarks of Benita, a 16-year-old African-American low achiever:

> My friends on the street . . . They say, "What can an education get you?" . . . You can have fifty hundred years of high school and college, and the White man come up in there with the same thing you got; they going to pick the White man over the Black man. . . . We got a White president, a White everything—everybody, they just so down, and they ain't got no self-esteem. . . . *Why should we try?*" (O'Connor, 1997, p. 594)

In contrast, Sharon, a 16-year-old African-American high achiever, spoke this way:

> Some Black people still think the White people still got a hold on us. We still got to be less than the White people. Only thing we could do is be their secretaries, take care of their house, and things like that. . . . The White people

do have a hold on us, but the hold ain't full. You know, they own most everything, control most everything, and they got more money. But we can break that hold—we can fight it. *If we don't at least try to break that hold, we never going nowhere.*" (O'Connor, 1997, p. 594)

Benita and Sharon grew up in the same segregated inner-city neighborhood and go to the same high school. Both their families are poor and on public assistance. Nevertheless, they hold very different views of the potential for social change and of their own chances for success. Benita feels powerless and is cynical about the future. Well aware of racial oppression, Sharon believes in struggling against it. She is confident of her own and her people's ability to improve social and economic opportunities.

The girls' school behaviors are as different as their ways of thinking. Benita's grade point average is 0.2 on a 4-point scale. She attended school only twice in the past month, doesn't expect to graduate, and has little hope for a good life. Sharon's grade point

average is 3.3; she ranks first in her sophomore class of 335 students and is in the honors program.

Do the girls' differing beliefs in the power of collective struggle figure into their orientations toward school? To find out, Carla O'Connor (1997) conducted clinical interviews with 47 African-American high school sophomores in two predominantly black, inner-city Chicago high schools. All participants were from poverty-stricken homes. O'Connor asked such questions as, "What can prevent students from doing well in school? Which people have better opportunities to get ahead today than in the past? Which people have the worst chance of getting ahead, and why?"

Six young people, including Sharon, stood out from the rest of the sample in being both optimistic and high achieving. All had in common a disposition toward collective struggle. How did they develop this strong sense of agency? Parents and other family members had convinced them through discussion and example that injustice

Of course, an important reason for separate classes in each subject is that adolescents can be taught by experts, who are more likely to expect students to perform well and encourage high-level thinking—factors that promote school attendance and achievement (Phillips, 1997). But the classroom experiences of many junior and senior high school students do not work out this way. In a study of seventh- through tenth-grade English, social studies, and science teachers with reputations for excellence, students were not equally or consistently given assignments that stimulated abstract thought (Sanford, 1985).

Because of the uneven quality of instruction in American schools, a great many seniors graduate from high school poorly equipped with basic academic skills. Although the achievement gap separating African-American and Hispanic students from white students has declined since the 1970s, mastery of reading, mathematics, and science by low-SES ethnic minority students remains disappointing (Campbell, Hombo, & Mazzeo, 2000). Many attend underfunded schools with run-down buildings, outdated equipment, and textbook shortages. In some, crime and discipline have become so overwhelming that attention to these problems has taken the lead over

should not be tolerated and that together, blacks could overcome it.

Sharon, for example, related that when her aunt and uncle had applied for the same job, her uncle was hired, despite her aunt's better qualifications. Her aunt responded by filing a discrimination suit. Sharon also described how her father had refused to cower when white people tried, through vandalism and murder of the family's pet cat, to make the family move out of an integrated New Orleans housing complex. One by one, the other African-American families left. Explaining why her family did not move, Sharon said, "'Cause my daddy said we going to leave when we ready to leave. *Nobody going to shove us when we ain't ready to move.*"

Family members' messages about the importance of fighting for justice appeared to enhance students' hopefulness about the future and their willingness to work hard in school. The study included several high-achieving, pessimistic adolescents, who did not expect to realize their ambitions. None

voiced a commitment to struggle against racial oppression by significant adults in their lives. Consequently, when these young people became aware of obstacles to their ambitions, they could not imagine how to overcome them.

The six high-achieving, optimistic students had lofty goals, despite life in racially segregated schools and communities where high school dropout, adolescent parenthood, drug dealing, and gang violence were ever-present. Each aspired to a high-status career—in business administration, computer science, law, or medicine. As their images of collective struggle reveal,

these young people did not succeed academically at the expense of connecting with their African-American heritage. To the contrary, they achieved while maintaining a strong ethnic identity.

© TOM AND DEEANN MCCARTHY/THE STOCK MARKET

High-achieving, optimistic African-American adolescents attending predominantly black, inner-city Chicago high schools believed strongly in fighting for justice. Family members' messages about the power of collective struggle seemed to support these students' hopefulness and willingness to work hard in school.

learning and instruction. By junior high, large numbers of poverty-stricken minority students have been placed in low academic tracks, compounding their learning difficulties.

Tracking. Ability grouping, as we saw in Chapter 12, is detrimental during the elementary school years. Students in low groups generally get poor-quality instruction. Soon they view themselves as failures, and their peers label them this way as well. Students in the same ability groups typically stick together, forming separate subcultures. High-group students often feel superior, and low-group students respond with hostility and resentment. These influences severely undermine the motivation and academic progress of low-group students. At least into the early years of secondary school, mixed-ability classes are desirable. Research suggests that they do not stifle the more able students, and they have intellectual and social benefits for poorly performing youngsters (see Chapter 12, page 469).

By high school, some grouping is unavoidable because certain aspects of education must dovetail with the young person's future educational and career plans. In the United States, high school students are counseled into college preparatory, vocational, or general education tracks. Unfortunately, this sorting tends to perpetuate educational inequalities of earlier years.

Low-income minority students are assigned in large numbers to noncollege tracks. One study found that a good student from a low-SES family had only half as much chance of ending up in an academically oriented program as a student of equal ability from a middle-SES background (Vanfossen, Jones, & Spade, 1987). When high-ability students (as indicated by eighth-grade math score) end up in low tracks, they "sink" to the achievement level of their trackmates. Furthermore, teachers of noncollege-track classes are less likely to communicate with parents about what they can do to support their adolescent's learning. Parents, in turn, often are unaware of their child's noncollege-track placement (Dornbusch & Glasgow, 1997).

These unfavorable features of low tracks combine with less stimulating teaching and more disruptive classroom behavior. Not surprisingly, longitudinal research following the school performance of thousands of American students from eighth to twelfth grade revealed that assignment to an academic track accelerates academic growth, whereas assignment to vocational or general education tracks decelerates it (Hallinan & Kubitschek, 1999).

High school students are separated into academic and vocational tracks in virtually all industrialized nations. But in China, Japan, and most Western European nations, students take a national examination to determine their placement in high school. The outcome usually fixes future possibilities for the young person. In the United States, educational decisions are more fluid. Students who are not assigned to a college preparatory track or who do poorly in high school can still get a college education. But by the adolescent years, SES differences in quality of education and academic achievement have already sorted American students more drastically than is the case in other countries. In the end, many young people do not benefit from this more open system. Compared with other developed nations, the United States has a higher percentage of high school dropouts and adolescents with very limited academic skills.

DROPPING OUT

Across the aisle from Louis in math class sat Norman, who daydreamed, crumpled his notes into his pocket, and rarely did his homework. On test days, he twirled a rabbit's foot for good luck but left most of the questions blank. Louis had been in school with Norman since fourth grade, but the two boys had little to do with one another. To Louis, who was quick at schoolwork, Norman seemed to live in another world.

Once or twice each week, Norman cut class, and one spring day, he stopped coming altogether. Several months later, Louis ran into Norman at the supermarket, where Norman had a part-time job stocking shelves.

"Norm, where ya been? Haven't seen you at school lately," remarked Louis.

"Come on, Louis, you oughta know. There wasn't nothin' for me there. Got to the point where I just couldn't go back. I'd go to those classes, and the minute I got there I'd wanna get out. My mind just turned off, I felt so ashamed and stupid."

Norman is one of 12 percent of American young people who, by 18 years of age, leave high school without a diploma (U.S. Department of Education, 2000). The dropout rate is particularly high among low-SES ethnic minority youths, especially Hispanic teenagers (see Figure 15.6). The decision to leave school has dire consequences. Dropouts are far less likely to be employed than are high school graduates who do not go to college. And even when they are employed, they have a much greater chance of remaining in menial, low-paying jobs and of being out of work from time to time.

■ **FACTORS RELATED TO DROPPING OUT.** Table 15.2 lists the diverse factors related to leaving school early. The more that are present at once, the greater the risk that an adolescent will drop out. Although many dropouts

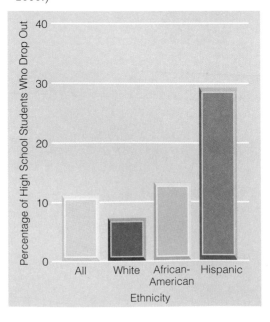

FIGURE **15.6**

Percentage of high school dropouts in the United States by ethnicity. Because African-American and Hispanic teenagers are more likely to come from low-income and poverty-stricken families, their dropout rates are above the national average. The rate for Hispanic young people is especially high. (From U.S. Department of Education, 2000.)

TABLE 15.2

Factors Related to Dropping Out of High School

STUDENT CHARACTERISTICS	FAMILY CHARACTERISTICS	SCHOOL CHARACTERISTICS
Poor school attendance	Parents who do not support or emphasize achievement	Unstimulating classes
Inattentiveness in class		Lack of opportunity to form personal relationships with teachers
School discipline problems, especially aggressive behavior	Parents who were high school dropouts	Curriculum irrelevant to student interests and needs
Inability to get along with teachers	Parents who are uninvolved in the adolescent's education	School authority structure that emphasizes the teacher and discourages student input
1 to 2 years behind in grade level	Parents who react with anger and punishment to the adolescent's low grades	
Low academic achievement		
A sharp drop in achievement after school transition		Large student body
Dislike of school	Single-parent household	Frequent school changes
Enrollment in a general education or vocational track	Low income	
Low educational aspirations		
Low self-esteem, especially academic self-esteem		
Friendships with peers who have left school		
Low involvement in extracurricular activities		
Drug use		
Law-breaking behavior		
Adolescent parenthood		

Sources: Kushman, Sieber, & Heariold-Kinney, 2000; Rumberger & Larson, 1998; Rumberger & Thomas, 2000.

achieve poorly and show high rates of misbehavior, a substantial number—like Norman—are young people with few behavior problems who experience academic difficulties and quietly disengage from school (Janosz et al., 2000). Norman had a long history of marginal to failing school grades, and he regarded his ability as extremely low. He gave up on tasks that presented the least challenge and counted on luck—his rabbit's foot—to get him by. As Norman got older, he attended class less regularly, failed to pay attention when he was there, and rarely did his homework. He didn't join any school clubs or participate in athletics. Because he was uninvolved in activities within and outside the classroom, few teachers and students got to know him well. The day Norman left, he felt alienated from all aspects of school life.

Compared with other students, even those with the same grade profile, dropouts are more likely to have parents who are less involved in their youngster's education. Many did not finish high school themselves and are unemployed, on welfare, or coping with the aftermath of divorce. When their youngsters bring home poor report cards, these parents are more likely to respond with punishment and anger—reactions that cause adolescents to rebel further against academic work (Garnier, Stein, & Jacobs, 1997; Melby & Conger, 1996). Sometimes suspension or expulsion for serious misbehavior prompts the teenager to leave altogether. And more often in ethnic minority families, a daughter has to care for adult relatives or children (her own or those of family members) and cannot handle school at the same time (Jordan, Lara, & McPartland, 1996).

Academically marginal students who drop out often have school experiences that undermine their chances for success—large classes that focus more on discipline than learning, that are unrelated to students' interests, and that provide little opportunity for student participation (Kasen, Cohen, & Brook, 1998; Rumberger & Thomas, 2000). Recent reports indicate that over 60 percent of students in some inner-city high schools do not graduate. Students in general education and vocational tracks, where teaching tends to be the least stimulating, are three times more likely to drop out as those in a college preparatory track (U.S. Department of Education, 2000). Some young people leave with a powerful critique of their school experiences, claiming that what happens in the classroom is irrelevant to their cultural background and everyday lives. As one African-American student who dropped out of school reflected,

> "I'm not smart, but I'm wise. I understand people and situations. Don't take much for me to know what's going on. I know what people be thinkin'. But I don't know what they be talkin' about in history class." (Fine, 1986, p. 402)

■ **PREVENTION STRATEGIES.** Many programs have been developed to help teenagers who are at risk for leaving school early. The strategies used are diverse, but several common themes are related to success:

■ *High-quality vocational training.* At-risk young people often benefit from special school programs that emphasize high-quality vocational training. For many marginal students, the real-life nature of vocational education is more comfortable and effective than purely academic work. But to work well, it must carefully integrate academic and job-related instruction so students can see the relevance to their future goals of what happens in the classroom (Ianni & Orr, 1996).

■ *Remedial instruction and counseling that offer personalized attention.* Most potential dropouts need intensive remedial instruction in small classes that permit warm, caring teacher–student relationships to form. To overcome the negative psychological effects of repeated school failure, good academic assistance must be combined with social support and special counseling (Kushman, Sieber, & Heariold-Kinney, 2000). One successful approach is to match at-risk students with retired adults, who serve as tutors, mentors, and role models in addressing academic needs and offering information and advice on vocational options (Lunenburg, 2000).

■ *Efforts to address the many factors in students' lives related to leaving school early.* Programs that strengthen parent involvement, offer flexible work–study arrangements, and provide on-site child care for teenage mothers can make staying in school easier for at-risk adolescents (Jordan, Lara, & McPartland, 1996).

■ *Participation in extracurricular activities.* Another way of helping marginal students is to draw them into the school community. Extracurricular participation is related to reduced rates of school dropout and antisocial behavior (Mahoney & Cairns, 1997; Mahoney & Stattin, 2000). The most powerful influence on extracurricular involvement is small school size. In smaller high schools (500 to 700 students or fewer), a

WILL HART/PHOTOEDIT

Because extracurricular participation draws marginal students into the school community, it reduces school dropout and antisocial behavior. These students enjoy rehearsing a school play.

greater proportion of the student body is needed to staff and operate activities. As a result, potential dropouts are far more likely to participate, gain recognition for their abilities, feel a sense of competence and efficacy, and remain until graduation. Note that "house" plans, which create smaller units within large schools, can have the same effect (Berk, 1992).

In a follow-up of poorly achieving eighth graders who lacked confidence in finishing high school, a combination of factors predicted recovery from low academic performance. Students reporting family supports, school responsiveness, and involvement in extracurricular activities were more likely to show academic resiliency, turning around their poor academic record by tenth grade (Catterall, 1998).

As we conclude our discussion of academic achievement, let's place the school dropout problem in historical perspective. Over the past half-century, the percentage of American adolescents completing high school has risen dramatically—from 39 percent in 1940 to 89 percent in 2000 (U.S. Department of Education, 2000). During that same period, college attendance also increased. Today, nearly 40 percent of 18- to 24-year-old high school graduates are working toward college degrees—one of the highest rates in the world. Finally, about one-third of all high school dropouts return on their own to finish their education within a few years, and some extend their schooling further (Children's Defense Fund, 2000). Although leaving school early is a very serious problem, as the end of adolescence approaches, many young people realize how essential education is for a rewarding job and career.

review   *List ways that parents can promote their adolescent's academic achievement, citing reasons that each is effective.*

apply   *Tanisha is finishing sixth grade. She could either continue in her current school through eighth grade or switch to a much larger junior high school in town. What would you suggest she do, and why?*

connect   *How are educational practices that prevent school dropout similar to those that improve learning for adolescents in general?*

reflect   *Describe your experiences in making the transition to middle school or junior high school and then to high school. What helped you adjust? What increased the stress of these transitions?*

Vocational Development

During late adolescence, young people face a major life decision: the choice of a suitable work role. As we will see in Chapter 16, selecting a vocation is central to identity development for contemporary adolescents. This is not surprising, since paid employment, economic independence, and career progress are hallmarks of adulthood in industrialized societies.

Being a productive worker calls for many of the same qualities needed to be an active citizen and nurturant family member—good judgment, responsibility, dedication, and cooperation. An adolescent well prepared for work can better fulfill other adult roles. How do young people make decisions about careers, and what influences their choices? What is the transition from school to work like, and what factors make it easy or difficult?

SELECTING A VOCATION

In societies with an abundance of career possibilities, occupational choice is a gradual process, beginning long before adolescence. Major theorists view the young person as moving through several phases of vocational development (Ginzberg, 1988; Super, 1980, 1984).

■ **PHASES OF VOCATIONAL DEVELOPMENT.** Sabrina, Louis, and Jules are each at different points in the development of occupational plans. All three began to toy with career possibilities during early and middle childhood. Louis is further along than Sabrina in selecting a vocational direction. Jules is close to crystallizing his career choice.

1. The **fantasy period** (early and middle childhood). As we saw in Chapter 10, young children gain insight into career options by fantasizing about them. When Sabrina announced at age 8 that she wanted to be an astronaut, a dancer, or a news reporter, her choices were determined by familiarity, glamour, and excitement. They did not include a realistic appraisal of her strengths, weaknesses, and special talents.

2. The **tentative period** (early and middle adolescence). Between ages 11 and 17, adolescents start to think about careers in more complex ways. During early adolescence, they evaluate vocational options in terms of their *interests*. For example, Sabrina wrote a paper on the pyramids of Egypt and was fascinated by what she learned. For a time, she wanted to be an archeologist. One summer, she visited a national park, learned to ride a horse, and thought it would be fun to be a forest ranger.

   By mid-adolescence, young people become more aware of personal and educational requirements for different vocations. Louis weighed possibilities not just against his interests but also against his *abilities* and *values*. "I like business and selling things," he said one day to Jules. "I won a prize for raising the most money for our class trip. Trouble is, I'm not a very exacting person. I'm good with people, though, and I'd like to do something to help others. So maybe counseling or social work would fit my needs."

3. The **realistic period** (late adolescence and young adulthood). By the end of adolescence, the economic and practical realities of adulthood are just around the corner, and young people narrow their options. At first, many do so through further *exploration*, gathering more information about a set of possibilities that blends with their personal characteristics. Then they enter a final phase of *crystallization*, in which they focus on a general vocational category. Within it, they experiment for a time before settling on a single occupation. As a college sophomore, Jules plans to enter a scientific field, but he is not sure whether he prefers chemistry, math, or physics. Within the next few months, he will choose a major. Then he will consider whether he wants to work for a company following graduation or study further to become a doctor or research scientist.

■ **FACTORS INFLUENCING VOCATIONAL CHOICE.** Most, but not all, adolescents follow this general pattern of vocational development. A few know from an early age just what they want to be and follow a direct path to a career goal. Some young people decide and change their minds, and still others remain undecided for an extended period. College students are granted added time to explore various options. In contrast, the life conditions of many low-SES youths restrict their range of choices. Furthermore, adolescents who vary in progress toward a career decision differ in how comfortable they are with their situation (Gordon, 1998).

Consider for a moment how an occupational choice is made, and you will see that it is not just a rational process in which young people match abilities, interests, and values against career options. Like other developmental milestones, it is the result of a dynamic interaction between person and environment. A great many influences feed into the decision.

fantasy period
The period of vocational development in which young children fantasize about career options through make-believe play. Spans early and middle childhood.

tentative period
The period of vocational development in which adolescents weigh vocational options against their interests, abilities, and values. Spans early and middle adolescence.

realistic period
The period of vocational development in which adolescents focus on a general career category and, slightly later, settle on a single occupation. Spans late adolescence and young adulthood.

Personality. People are attracted to occupations that complement their personalities. John Holland (1966, 1985) has identified six personality types that affect vocational choice:

- The *investigative person,* who enjoys working with ideas and is likely to select a scientific occupation (for example, anthropologist, physicist, or engineer).

- The *social person,* who likes interacting with people and gravitates toward human services (counseling, social work, or teaching).

- The *realistic person,* who prefers real-world problems and work with objects and tends to choose a mechanical occupation (construction, plumbing, or surveying).

- The *artistic person,* who is emotional and high in need for individual expression and looks toward an artistic field (writing, music, or the visual arts).

- The *conventional person,* who likes well-structured tasks and values material possessions and social status—traits well suited to certain business fields (accounting, banking, or quality control).

- The *enterprising person,* who is adventurous, persuasive, and a strong leader and is drawn to sales and supervisory positions and politics.

Research reveals a clear relationship between personality and vocational choice, but it is only moderate. Personality is not a stronger predictor because many people are blends of several personality types and can do well at more than one kind of occupation. Louis, for example, is both enterprising and social—dispositions that led him to consider both business and human services. Furthermore, as ecological systems theory reminds us, career decisions are the joint result of individual and contextual factors, including family background, educational opportunities, and societal conditions.

Family Influences. Adolescents' vocational aspirations correlate strongly with the jobs of their parents. Teenagers from higher-SES homes are more likely to select high-status, white-collar occupations, such as doctor, lawyer, scientist, and engineer. In contrast, those with lower-SES backgrounds tend to choose less prestigious, blue-collar careers—for example, plumber, construction worker, food service employee, and secretary. Parent–child similarity is partly a function of educational attainment. The single best predictor of occupational status is number of years of schooling completed (Featherman, 1980).

Family resemblance in occupational choice also comes about for other reasons. Higher-SES parents are more likely to give their children important information about the world of work and to have connections with people who can help the young person obtain a high-status position (Grotevant & Cooper, 1988). Parenting practices also shape work-related values. Recall from Chapter 2 (page 77) that higher-SES parents tend to promote independence and curiosity, which are required in many high-status careers. Lower-SES parents, in contrast, are more likely to emphasize conformity and obedience. Eventually, young people choose careers that are compatible with these values. The jobs that appeal to them are often like those of their parents (Mortimer & Borman, 1988).

Still, parents can also foster higher aspirations. Parental pressure to do well in school and encouragement toward high-status occupations predict vocational attainment beyond SES (Bell et al., 1996). And as we saw in Chapter 13, maternal employment is linked to higher career aspirations among girls, regardless of SES (Hoffman, 2000).

Teachers. Teachers play a powerful role in adolescents' career decisions. Jules regards his high school chemistry teacher as the most important influence on his choice of a scientific vocation. "Mr. Garvin showed me how to think about chemistry—and science in

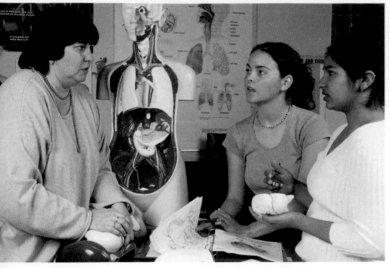

Teachers can powerfully affect adolescents' career decisions. This physiology teacher talks with two students about the wonders of the body systems, perhaps inspiring them to consider a career in the life sciences.

general. If I hadn't taken his class my junior year, I probably wouldn't have considered a career in science."

In one study, college freshmen were asked who had the greatest impact on their choice of a field of study. The people most often mentioned (by 39 percent of the sample) were high school teachers (Johnson, 1967, as cited in Rice, 1999). College-bound adolescents are likely to have closer relations with teachers than are other students. In contrast, students with academic and behavior problems generally have neither family nor teacher supports. Consequently, many feel discouraged about their career options, perceive barriers to attaining their goals, withdraw from making choices, and display larger discrepancies between their vocational aspirations and their expectations than their peers (Rojewski & Hill, 1998). These findings provide yet another reason for promoting positive teacher–student relations. The power of teachers as role models could serve as an important source of resiliency for these young people.

Gender Stereotypes. During the past three decades, high school boys' career preferences have remained strongly gender stereotyped, whereas girls have expressed increasing interest in occupations largely held by men (Gottfredson, 1996). Changes in gender-role attitudes along with the dramatic rise in employed mothers, who serve as career-oriented models for their daughters, are common explanations for girls' interest in nontraditional careers.

At the same time, women's progress in entering and excelling at male-dominated professions has been slow. As Table 15.3 shows, the percentage of women engineers, lawyers, and doctors increased between 1972 and 1999 in the United States, but it falls far short of equal representation. Women remain heavily concentrated in the less well-paid, traditionally feminine professions of literature, social work, education, and nursing (U.S. Bureau of the Census, 2000). In virtually all fields, their achievements lag behind those of men, who write more books, make more discoveries, hold more positions of leadership, and produce more works of art.

TABLE 15.3

Percentage of Females in Various Professions, 1972, 1983, 1999

PROFESSION	1972	1983	1999
Engineering	0.8	5.8	11.1
Law	3.8	15.8	28.5
Medicine	9.3	15.8	26.6
Business—executive and managerial	17.6	32.4	44.4[a]
Writing, art, entertainment	31.7	42.7	51.4
Social work	55.1	64.3	68.4
Elementary and secondary education	70.0	70.9	75.3
Higher education	28.0	36.3	42.3
Library, museum curatorship	81.6	84.4	80.8
Nursing	92.6	95.8	92.5

[a]This percentage includes executives and managers at all levels. Women make up only 10 percent of senior management at big firms, although that figure represents a three-fold increase in the past decade.

Source: U.S. Bureau of the Census, 2000.

Ability cannot account for these dramatic sex differences. As we have seen, the gender gap in cognitive performance of all kinds is small and is declining. Instead, gender-stereotyped messages from the social environment play a key role. Although girls' grades are higher than boys', girls reach secondary school less confident of their ability and more likely to under estimate their achievement (Bornholt, Goodnow, & Cooney, 1994). Between tenth and twelfth grade, the percentage of girls in gifted programs decreases. Girls make up about half the population in these programs in elementary school. By secondary school, they account for less than 30 percent, and their presence continues to drop during high school. Those who remain do not develop their talents to the same degree as do boys, either educationally or vocationally. When asked what discouraged them from continuing in gifted classes, parental and peer pressures and attitudes of teachers and counselors ranked high on girls' lists (Read, 1991; Winner, 1996).

During college, the career aspirations of academically talented females decline further. In one longitudinal study, high school valedictorians were followed over a 10-year period—through college and into the work world. By their sophomore year, young women showed a decline in estimates of their intelligence, whereas men did not. Women also shifted their expectations toward less demanding careers because of concerns about combining work with child rearing and unresolved questions about their ability. Even though female valedictorians outperformed their male counterparts in college courses, they achieved at lower levels after career entry (Arnold, 1994). Another study reported similar results. Educational aspirations of mathematically talented females declined considerably during college, as did the number majoring in the sciences (Benbow & Arjmand, 1990).

These findings reveal a pressing need for programs that sensitize parents, teachers, and school counselors to the special problems girls face in developing and maintaining high career aspirations. The aspirations of academically talented girls rise in response to parents' and teachers' confidence-building messages and career guidance that encourages girls to set goals that match their abilities. Models of accomplished women who have successfully dealt with family–career role conflict are also important (Pascarella et al., 1997; Schroeder, Blood, & Maluso, 1993; Zeldin & Pajares, 2000).

Access to Vocational Information. Adolescents could profit from greater access to career information. In a longitudinal study of a nationally representative sample of more than 1,200 American high school students followed for 5 years, youths of all SES levels and ethnicities were highly ambitious. Compared with previous generations, many more expected to graduate from college and enter professional jobs. But about half were unaware of the steps involved in reaching their goal (Schneider & Stevenson, 1999). They had only sketchy knowledge of their preferred vocation, of the educational requirements to enter it, and of the future demand for it.

These high-ambition/low-knowledge young people were at risk for becoming "drifting dreamers" who fail to make strategic choices about how to invest their efforts wisely. Especially if they entered a community college with plans to transfer to a 4-year institution, they frequently found that they did not have the high school prerequisites to take the courses they needed. And often they chose courses without checking to make sure that credit would transfer to a 4-year college. Consequently, some remained in school for an unnecessarily long time, whereas others did not complete their educational plans—for both academic and economic reasons.

Schools must do a better job of helping young people learn about the work that interests them and evaluate its fit with their personal attributes—by introducing students to people in those jobs, explaining entry requirements, encouraging participation in relevant extracurricular activities, and offering internships that provide firsthand experiences (Lent, Hackett, & Brown, 1999; Swanson & Fouad, 1999). As we will see next, the limited work knowledge and experience of American adolescents—especially those who terminate their education with a high school diploma—complicates the transition from school to work life.

MAKING THE TRANSITION FROM SCHOOL TO WORK

Franca and Antonio's middle son, 18-year-old Martin—who is a year younger than Jules and 2 years older than Louis—graduated from high school in a vocational track. Like 25 percent of young people with a high school diploma, he had no plans to go to college. He hoped to work in data processing after graduation, but 6 months later he was still a part-time sales clerk at the candy store where he had worked during high school. Although Martin had filled out many job applications, he got no interviews or offers.

Martin's inability to find a better job is typical for American non-college-bound high school graduates. As a college student, his older brother, Jules, will have a much easier time. Jules will emerge from school as a young adult, having profited from the advice of faculty in his major field of study, access to a wide variety of career services, and perhaps an internship in his chosen vocation.

Although high school graduates are more likely to find employment than those who drop out, they have fewer work opportunities than they did several decades ago. More than one-fifth of recent high school graduates who do not continue their education are unemployed (U.S. Department of Education, 2000). When they do find work, most are limited to low-paid, unskilled jobs. In addition, they lack access to vocational counseling and job placement resources as they make the transition from school to work (Bailey, 1993).

American employers regard the recent high school graduate as poorly prepared for a demanding, skilled occupation. Indeed, there is some truth to this conclusion. During high school, almost half of American adolescents are employed—a greater percentage than in any other developed country. But most of these are middle-SES students in pursuit of spending money rather than vocational exploration and training. Low-income teenagers who need to contribute to family income find it harder to get jobs (Children's Defense Fund, 2000).

Furthermore, the jobs adolescents hold are largely limited to low-level, repetitive tasks that provide little contact with adult supervisors. A heavy commitment to such jobs is actually harmful. High school students who work more than 15 hours per week have poorer school attendance, lower grades, and less time for extracurricular activities. They also report more drug and alcohol use and feel more distant from their parents. Although young people whose school performance is already compromised are more likely to work long hours, doing so makes a bad situation worse. And perhaps because of the menial nature of their jobs, employed teenagers tend to become cynical about work life. Many admit to having stolen from their employers (Barling, Rogers, & Kelloway, 1995; Steinberg & Dornbusch, 1991; Steinberg, Fegley & Dornbusch, 1993).

When work experiences are specially designed to meet educational and vocational goals and involve responsibility and challenge, outcomes are different. Participation in work–study programs is related to positive school and work attitudes, improved academic achievement, lower dropout rates, and continued work in the occupational area after high school graduation (Hamilton & Hamilton, 2000; Steinberg, 1984). Yet high-quality vocational preparation for American adolescents who do not go to college is scarce. Unlike some European nations, the United States has no widespread training system to prepare its youths for skilled business and industrial occupations and manual trades. For the same reason, many high school graduates in Canada and Great Britain also experience a "floundering period" (Grubb, 1999; Heinz, 1999a). The U.S. federal government does support some job-training programs, and funding for them has recently increased. But most are too short to make a difference in the lives of poorly skilled adolescents, who need intensive training and academic remediation before they are ready to enter the job market. And at present, these programs serve only a small minority of young people who need assistance (Children's Defense Fund, 2000).

Inspired by successful programs in Europe, youth apprenticeship strategies that coordinate on-the-job training with classroom instruction are being considered as an important dimension of educational reforms in the United States. The Cultural Influences box on the following page describes Germany's highly successful apprenticeship system. Bringing

Cultural INFLUENCES

WORK–STUDY APPRENTICESHIPS IN GERMANY

Rolf, an 18-year-old German vocational student, is an apprentice at Brandt, a large industrial firm known worldwide for its high-quality products. Like many German companies, Brandt has a well-developed apprenticeship program that includes a full-time professional training staff, a suite of classrooms, and a lab equipped with the latest learning aids. Apprentices move through more than 10 major company divisions that are carefully selected to meet their learning needs. Rolf has worked in purchasing, inventory, production, personnel, marketing, sales, and finance. Now in cost accounting, he assists Herr Stein, his supervisor, in designing a computerized inventory control system. Rolf draws a flowchart of the new system under the direction of Herr Stein, who explains that each part of the diagram will contain a set of procedures to be built into a computer program.

Rolf is involved in complex and challenging projects, guided by caring mentors who love their work and want to teach it to others. Two days a week, he attends the *Berufsschule,* a part-time vocational school. On the job, Rolf applies a wide range of academic skills, including reading, writing, problem solving, and logical thinking. His classroom learning is directly relevant to his daily life (Hamilton, 1990, 1994).

Germany has one of the most successful apprenticeship systems in the world for preparing young people to enter modern business and industry. Two-thirds of adolescents participate in it, making it the most common form of secondary education. German adolescents who do not go to the *Gymnasium* (college-preparatory high school) usually complete full-time schooling by age 15 or 16, but education remains compulsory until age 18. They fill the 2- to 3-year gap with part-time vocational schooling combined with apprenticeship. Students are trained for a wide range of crafts and blue- and white-collar occupations—more than 400, leading to more than 20,000 specialized careers. Each apprenticeship is jointly planned by educators and employers. Apprentices who complete training and pass a qualifying examination are certified as skilled workers and earn union-set wages for that occupation. Businesses provide financial support for the program because they know it guarantees a competent, dedicated work force (Heinz, 1999b).

The German apprenticeship system offers a smooth and rewarding path from school to career for young people who do not enter higher education. Many apprentices are hired by the firms that trained them. Most others find jobs in the same occupation. For those who change careers, the apprentice certificate is a powerful credential. Employers view successful apprentices as responsible and capable workers. They are willing to invest in further training to adapt the individual's skills to other occupations. As a result, German young people establish themselves in well-paid careers with security and advancement possibilities between the ages of 18 and 20 (Hamilton & Hamilton, 1999).

The success of the German system—and of similar systems in Austria, Denmark, Switzerland, and several East European countries—suggests that some kind of national apprenticeship program would improve the transition from school to work for young people in the United States. Nevertheless, implementing an American apprenticeship system poses major challenges. Perhaps the greatest is overcoming the reluctance of employers to assume part of the responsibility for vocational training. Whereas American companies are willing to provide training to college-educated workers, only about 10 percent of high school graduates receive company-sponsored training (Lewis et al., 1998).

Once the hurdle of employer-sponsored training is overcome, other barriers must be addressed. These include creating institutional structures that ensure cooperation between schools and businesses and preventing low-income youths from being concentrated in the lowest-skilled apprenticeship placements—an obstacle that Germany itself has not yet fully overcome (Hamilton & Hamilton, 2000; Heinz et al., 1998). Pilot apprenticeship projects are under way, in an effort to solve these problems and build bridges between learning and working in the United States.

© M. GRANITSAS/THE IMAGE WORKS

High-quality vocational training combined with apprenticeship enables German youths who do not go to college to enter well-paid careers. This electronics trainee works at a hydraulics system factory. His education involves integrating academic skills with on-the-job experience to ensure that he becomes competent at both.

together the worlds of schooling and work offers many benefits. These include helping non-college-bound adolescents establish productive lives right after graduation, motivating at-risk youths to stay in school, and contributing to the nation's economic growth (Hamilton, 1993; Safyer, Leahy, & Colan, 1995).

Although vocational development is a lifelong process, adolescence is a crucial period for defining occupational goals and launching a career. Young people well prepared for an economically and personally satisfying vocation are much more likely to become productive citizens, devoted family members, and contented adults. The support of families, schools, communities, and society as a whole can contribute greatly to a positive outcome.

Ask YOURSELF...

review   What steps can schools take to help ensure that adolescents' occupational choices match their interests, personality dispositions, and abilities?

apply   In high school, Valerie wanted to become an astronomer. By her second year in college, she continued to excel in physics classes, but she gave up her dream of becoming a research scientist. What factors might have led Valerie to change her mind?

connect   Review the discussion of achievement-related attributions on pages 486–487 of Chapter 13. Why are mastery-oriented attributions vital for optimum vocational development in adolescence? What steps can parents and teachers take to promote a mastery-oriented approach and, thereby, foster occupational choice and decision making at later ages?

reflect   Describe the career guidance you received from your family, school, and community. Which relationships and experiences were most influential? What assistance would you have liked that was not available?

Summary

PIAGET'S THEORY: THE FORMAL OPERATIONAL STAGE

What are the major characteristics of formal operational thought?

- During Piaget's **formal operational stage**, abstract thinking appears. Adolescents engage in **hypothetico-deductive reasoning.** When faced with a problem, they think of all possibilities, including ones that are not obvious, and test them against reality in an orderly fashion. **Propositional thought** also develops. Young people can evaluate the logic of verbal statements without considering them against real-world circumstances.

Discuss recent research on formal operational thought and its implications for the accuracy of Piaget's formal operational stage.

- Recent research reveals that school-age children display the beginnings of abstract reasoning, but they are not as cognitively competent as adolescents and adults. School-age children cannot sort out evidence that bears on three or more variables at once. Also, they do not grasp the **logical necessity** of propositional reasoning, they represent major premises incompletely, and they have difficulty thinking of examples that contradict wrong conclusions.

- Many college students and adults think abstractly only in situations in which they have had extensive experience, and formal operational tasks are not mastered in many village and tribal societies. These findings indicate that Piaget's highest stage is affected by specific learning opportunities.

AN INFORMATION-PROCESSING VIEW OF ADOLESCENT COGNITIVE DEVELOPMENT

How do information-processing researchers account for the development of abstract thought?

- Information-processing researchers believe that a variety of specific mechanisms of change foster abstract thought, including improved attention; more effective strategies; greater knowledge; gains in information-processing capacity; and, especially, advances in metacognition.

- Research on scientific reasoning reveals that the ability to coordinate theory with evidence improves from childhood to adolescence, as young people solve increasingly complex problems and reflect on their thinking, acquiring more sophisticated metacognitive understanding. Nevertheless, adolescents and adults continue to show a self-serving bias in their thinking; they apply logic more effectively to ideas they doubt than to ones they favor.

- Adolescents develop formal operational abilities in a similar, step-by-step fashion on different types of tasks, constructing general models they can apply to many instances of a given type of problem. Formal operational thought is not the result of an abrupt, stagewise change. Rather, it develops gradually.

- Researchers who study **postformal thought** have shown that cognitive development is not complete at adolescence. It becomes increasingly rational as young people move toward **relativistic reasoning**, or awareness of multiple truths.

CONSEQUENCES OF ABSTRACT THOUGHT

Describe typical reactions of adolescents that result from new abstract reasoning powers.

- Adolescents' new cognitive powers are reflected in many aspects of their daily behavior. Teenagers become more argumentative, idealistic, and critical. As they think more about themselves, two distorted images of the relation between self and other appear—the **imaginary audience** and the **personal fable.** Advances in perspective taking contribute to these visions of the self.

- Adolescents show gains in cognitive self-regulation and **comprehension monitoring** on academic tasks. However, they often have difficulty making decisions in everyday life.

SEX DIFFERENCES IN MENTAL ABILITIES

Describe sex differences in mental abilities at adolescence, along with factors that influence them.

- Although boys and girls do not differ in general intelligence, they do vary in specific mental abilities. During adolescence, the female advantage in general verbal ability is very slight. Boys do better in mathematical reasoning, especially in solving complex word problems. The gender gap in math is largest among the academically talented.

- Sex differences in mathematics stem, in part, from boys' biologically based advantage in spatial reasoning. At the same time, a variety of environmental factors, including girls' limited involvement in childhood play activities that foster spatial skills, gender stereotyping of math as a "male domain," and girls' doubts about their math ability, contribute to the gender gap.

LANGUAGE DEVELOPMENT

Describe changes in vocabulary, grammar, and pragmatics during adolescence.

- Adolescents add many abstract words to their vocabulary, and their definitions of these words increase in clarity and accuracy. The capacity to think flexibly about word meanings permits adolescents to better understand irony, sarcasm, and figurative language, such as proverbs.

- Adolescents use more elaborate grammatical constructions, a change evident in their persuasive speaking and writing. One of the most obvious advances in communication skill is the ability to make subtle adjustments in language style, depending

Summary (continued)

on the situation. The ability to reflect on the features of language and engage in cognitive self-regulation supports this change.

LEARNING IN SCHOOL

Discuss the impact of school transitions on adolescent adjustment.

- School transitions can be stressful. As school environments become larger and more impersonal, grades and feelings of competence decline. Girls experience more adjustment difficulties after the elementary to junior high transition, since other life changes (puberty and the beginning of dating) tend to occur at the same time. Emotionally distressed, poorly achieving young people whose school performance drops sharply in junior high school are at greatest risk for continuing academic difficulties and alienation from school.

Discuss family, peer, and school influences on academic achievement during adolescence.

- Authoritative parenting, joint parent–child decision making, and parent involvement in the adolescent's secondary school career promote high achievement. Teenagers with parents who encourage high achievement are likely to choose friends who do the same. The surrounding social order affects peer cultures of low-SES ethnic minority youths, who often react against working hard in school because they see little payoff for their future. Warm, supportive classroom learning environments with activities that emphasize high-level thinking enable adolescents to reach their cognitive potential.

- By high school, separate educational tracks that dovetail with adolescents' future plans are necessary. Unfortunately, high school

tracking in the United States usually extends the educational inequalities of earlier years. Low-SES students are at risk for unfair placement in noncollege tracks, reduced parental involvement in their education, less stimulating teaching, more disruptive classroom behavior, and resulting declines in school performance.

What factors are related to dropping out of school?

- Twelve percent of American young people leave high school without a diploma, many of them low-SES ethnic minority youths. Dropping out is the result of a cumulative process of disengagement from school. A variety of student characteristics and family and school influences combine to undermine the young person's chances for success. These include learning problems, dislike of school, antisocial behavior, lack of parental support for achievement, unstimulating teaching, and assignment to low tracks.

VOCATIONAL DEVELOPMENT

Trace the development of vocational choice.

- Vocational development moves through three phases: a **fantasy period,** in which children explore career options through play; a **tentative period,** in which teenagers weigh careers against their interests, abilities, and values; and a **realistic period,** in which older adolescents and young adults settle on a vocational category and, finally, a specific career.

What factors influence adolescents' vocational decisions?

- People are attracted to occupations that complement their personalities. However,

personality is only moderately related to vocational choice, since individual and contextual factors combine to influence adolescents' decisions.

- Adolescents' career aspirations correlate strongly with the jobs of their parents. The resemblance is due to educational opportunities, available information about the world of work, and teaching of work-related values. Teachers often have a powerful impact on adolescents' career decisions.

- Today, more girls express interest in male-dominated occupations. However, gender-stereotyped messages prevent many girls from reaching their career potential. Girls' career aspirations decline from high school into college.

What problems do American non-college-bound youths face in making the transition from school to work?

- Unlike some European nations, the United States has no widespread vocational training system to assist non-college-bound adolescents in preparing for challenging, well-paid careers in business, industry, and manual trades. The jobs available to teenagers are largely limited to low-level, repetitive tasks that provide little contact with adult supervisors. Too many hours in these work settings undermine school performance and work-related attitudes.

- In contrast, work–study programs designed to meet both educational and vocational goals foster a positive orientation toward academic achievement and work. Youth apprenticeships that coordinate on-the-job training with classroom instruction are being considered as part of American educational reforms.

Important terms and concepts

comprehension monitoring (p. 573)
fantasy period (p. 588)
formal operational stage (p. 562)
hypothetico-deductive reasoning
   (p. 562)

logical necessity (p. 564)
imaginary audience (p. 571)
personal fable (p. 571)
postformal thought (p. 568)

propositional thought (p. 562)
realistic period (p. 588)
relativistic reasoning (p. 568)
tentative period (p. 588)

 . . . for further information and help

Consult the companion website for this book, where you will find additional weblinks and associated learning activities:
www.ablongman.com/berk

ACADEMIC ACHIEVEMENT

National Assessment of Educational Progress
National Center for Education Statistics
United States Department of Education
nces.ed.gov/nationsreportcard

Conducts a nationally representative and continuing assessment of the achievement of American students in various subject areas. Distributes reports of recent findings.

Pursuing Excellence: The Third International Mathematics and Science Study
nces.ed.gov/timss

Presents findings of the largest, most comprehensive international comparison of mathematics and science achievement. A half-million students at five grade levels from 41 nations participated.

DROPOUT PREVENTION

National Dropout Prevention Center
www.dropoutprevention.org

Offers information on school dropout prevention and identifying high-risk youth. Provides consultation and referral services to school systems, agencies, and associations dealing with the dropout problem.

YOUTH EMPLOYMENT

National School-to-Work Learning and Information Center
www.stw.ed.gov

Provides information on the U.S. School-to-Work Opportunities Act, which offers seed money to the states for stimulating school-to-work partnerships between local businesses, schools, community organizations, and government. Each local program must combine relevant education with job training that meets industry standards.

"My World in the Year 2000"

Oguzcan Kaganoguzbeyolu

12 years, Turkey

As adolescents search for a set of values to have faith in, they bring a sense of idealism and hopefulness to society. This painting conveys a young person's belief in the power of theater, music, dance, and the visual arts to enrich human awareness and sensitivity.

Emotional and Social Development in Adolescence

ouis sat on the grassy hillside overlooking the high school, waiting for his best friend Darryl to arrive from his fourth-period class. The two boys often met at noontime and then crossed the street to have lunch together at a nearby hamburger stand.

Watching as hundreds of students poured onto the school grounds, Louis reflected on what he had learned in government class that day: "Suppose by chance I had been born in the People's Republic of China. I'd be sitting here, speaking a different language, being called by a different name, going home to different parents, and thinking about the world in different ways. I am who I am through some quirk of fate," Louis remarked to himself, looking around at the crowd of students picnicking on the grass.

Louis awoke from his thoughts with a start. Darryl stood in front of him. "Hey, dreamer! I've been shouting and waving from the bottom of the hill for 5 minutes."

"Sorry," Louis responded, jumping up and joining his friend.

As they walked off, Darryl asked, "How come you're so spaced out lately, Louis?"

"Oh, just wondering about stuff—like what I want, what I believe in. My older brother, Jules—I envy him. He seems to know just where he's going. Most of the time, I'm up in the air about it. You ever feel that way?"

"Yeah, a lot," admitted Darryl, looking at Louis seriously as they approached the hamburger stand. "I often think, What am I really like? Who will I become?"

Louis and Darryl's introspective remarks are signs of a major reorganization of the self at adolescence: the development of identity. Both young people are attempting to formulate who they are—their personal values and the directions they will pursue in life. Although important changes in self-concept occur throughout childhood, the restructuring of the self that happens in adolescence is profound. Rapid physical changes prompt teenagers to reconsider what they are like as people. And for the first time, adolescents can think hypothetically and, therefore, project themselves into the distant future. They start to realize the importance of their choice of values and goals for their later lives.

We begin this chapter with Erikson's account of identity development and the research it has stimulated on teenagers' thoughts and feelings about themselves. The quest for identity extends to many aspects of development. We will see how sense of cultural belonging, moral understanding, and masculine and feminine self-images are refined during adolescence. And as parent–child relationships are revised and young people become increasingly independent of the family, friendships and peer networks become crucial contexts for bridging the gap between childhood and adulthood. Our chapter concludes with a discussion of several serious adjustment problems of adolescence—depression, suicide, and delinquency.

Erikson's Theory: Identity versus Identity Confusion

Erikson (1950, 1968) was the first to recognize the formation of an **identity** as the major personality achievement of adolescence and as a crucial step toward becoming a productive, happy adult. Constructing an identity involves defining who you are, what you value, and the directions you choose to pursue in life. One expert described it as an explicit theory of oneself as a rational agent—one who acts on the basis of reason, takes responsibility for those actions, and can explain them (Moshman, 1999). This search for what is true and real about the self is the driving force behind many commitments—to a sexual orientation (see Chapter 14); a vocation (see Chapter 15); interpersonal relationships; community involvement; ethnic group membership; and moral, political, and religious ideals.

Erikson called the psychological conflict of adolescence **identity versus identity confusion.** He believed that successful outcomes of earlier stages pave the way toward its positive resolution. Young people who reach adolescence with a weak sense of *trust* have trouble finding ideals to have faith in. Those with little *autonomy* or *initiative* do not engage in the active exploration required to choose among alternatives. And those who lack a sense of *industry* fail to select a vocation that matches their interests and skills.

Although the seeds of identity formation are planted early, not until adolescence do young people become absorbed in this task. According to Erikson, in complex societies, teenagers experience an *identity crisis*—a temporary period of confusion and distress as they experiment with alternatives before settling on a set of values and goals. During this period, what adolescents once took for granted they question. "I've gone to church every Sunday morning since I was a little kid," Louis confided in Darryl. "Now I'm not so sure I can accept my parents' way of thinking about God." Teenagers who go through a process of inner soul-searching eventually arrive at a mature identity. They sift through characteristics that defined

identity
A well-organized conception of the self made up of values, beliefs, and goals to which the individual is solidly committed.

identity versus identity confusion
In Erikson's theory, the psychological conflict of adolescence, which is resolved positively when adolescents attain an identity after a period of exploration and inner soul-searching.

the self in childhood and combine them with new commitments. Then they mold these into a solid inner core that provides a sense of stability as they move through different roles in daily life. Once formed, identity continues to be refined in adulthood as people reevaluate earlier commitments and choices.

Current theorists agree with Erikson that questioning of values, plans, and priorities is necessary for a mature identity, but they no longer refer to this process as a "crisis" (Grotevant, 1998). For some young people, identity development is traumatic and disturbing, but for most it is not. *Exploration* better describes the typical adolescent's gradual, uneventful approach to identity formation. The many daily choices teenagers make—"whom to date; whether or not to break up, have intercourse, take drugs, go to college or work; which college; what major; whether to study or play; whether to become politically active"— gradually meld into an organized self-structure (Marcia, 1980, p. 161; Moshman, 1999).

The negative outcome of this stage is *identity confusion*. Some adolescents appear shallow and directionless, either because earlier conflicts have been resolved negatively or society restricts their choices to ones that do not match their abilities and desires. As a result, they are unprepared for the psychological challenges of adulthood. For example, individuals find it difficult to risk the self-sharing involved in Erikson's young adult stage—*intimacy*—if they do not have a firm sense of self (an identity) to which they can return.

Does research support Erikson's ideas about identity development? In the following sections we will see that adolescents go about the task of defining the self in ways that closely match Erikson's description.

© BOB DAEMMRICH/THE IMAGE WORKS

"Exploration" describes the typical adolescent's gradual, uneventful approach to identity formation. This teenager's eager experimentation with photography in his high school journalism class may help crystallize a vocational path or lead to an absorbing, long-term hobby.

Self-Development

During adolescence, cognitive changes transform the young person's vision of the self into a more complex, well-organized, and consistent picture. Changes in self-concept and self-esteem set the stage for development of a unified personal identity.

CHANGES IN SELF-CONCEPT

Recall from Chapter 13 that by the end of middle childhood, children describe themselves in terms of personality traits. In early adolescence, they unify separate traits, such as "smart" and "talented," into more abstract descriptors, such as "intelligent." But these generalizations about the self are not interconnected, and often they are contradictory. For example, 12- to 14-year-olds might mention such opposing traits as "intelligent" and "airhead" or "shy" and "outgoing." These disparities result from social pressures to display different selves in different relationships—with parents, classmates, close friends, and romantic partners. As adolescents' social world expands, contradictory self-descriptions increase, and teenagers frequently agonize over "which is the real me" (Harter, 1998; Harter & Monsour, 1992).

By middle to late adolescence, teenagers combine their traits into an organized system. And they begin to use qualifiers ("I have a *fairly* quick temper," "I'm not *thoroughly* honest"), which reveal their awareness that psychological qualities often change from one situation to the next. Older adolescents also add integrating principles, which make sense of formerly troublesome contradictions. For example, one young person remarked, "I'm very adaptable. When I'm around my friends, who think what I say is important, I'm very talkative; but around my family I'm quiet because they're never interested enough to really listen to me" (Damon, 1990, p. 88).

Compared with school-age children, teenagers place more emphasis on social virtues, such as being friendly, considerate, kind, and cooperative. Adolescents are very preoccupied with being liked and viewed positively by others, and their statements about themselves reflect this concern. In addition, personal and moral values appear as key themes in older adolescents' self-concepts. For example, here is how 16-year-old Ben described himself in terms of honesty to himself and others:

> I like being honest like with yourself and with everyone. . . . [A person] could be, in the eyes of everyone else the best person in the world, but if I knew they were lying or cheating, in my eyes they wouldn't be. . . . When I'm friendly, it's more to tell people that it's all right to be yourself. Not necessarily don't conform, but just whatever you are, you know, be happy with that. . . . So I'm not an overly bubbly person that goes around, "Hi, how are you?" . . . But if someone wants to talk to me, you know, sure. I wouldn't like, not talk to someone. (Damon & Hart, 1988, pp. 120–121)

Ben's well-integrated account of his personal traits and values is quite different from the fragmented, listlike self-descriptions of children. As adolescents revise their views of themselves to include enduring beliefs and plans, they move toward the kind of unity of self that Erikson described in his theory of identity development.

CHANGES IN SELF-ESTEEM

Self-esteem, the evaluative side of self-concept, continues to differentiate during the teenage years. To the self-evaluations of middle childhood—academic competence, social competence, physical/athletic competence, and physical appearance—are added several new dimensions: close friendship, romantic appeal, and job competence. These reflect important concerns of this new period (Harter, 1990, 1999).

Level of self-esteem changes as well. Except for temporary declines after school transitions for some adolescents (see Chapter 15, page 578), self-esteem is on the rise (Zimmerman et al., 1997). This increase is yet another reason that researchers question the assumption that adolescence is a time of emotional turmoil. To the contrary, for most young people, becoming an adolescent leads to feelings of pride and self-confidence (Powers, Hauser, & Kilner, 1989). This is true not just in the United States but elsewhere in the world. A study of self-esteem in 10 industrialized countries showed that the majority of teenagers had an optimistic outlook on life, a positive attitude toward school and work, and faith in their ability to cope with life's problems (Offer, 1988).

Still, young people vary greatly in their self-esteem profiles. Whereas some evaluate themselves similarly in all areas, others are more satisfied in one or two than in others. A profile of all highly favorable self-evaluations is not associated with better adjustment than is a profile that is generally positive. But teenagers who feel much better about their peer relations than their academic competence and family relations tend to have adjustment difficulties. And a profile of low self-regard in all areas is linked to anxiety, depression, and increasing antisocial behavior over time (DuBois et al., 1998, 1999).

INFLUENCES ON SELF-ESTEEM

In Chapters 14 and 15 we saw that adolescents who are off time in pubertal development, who are heavy drug users, and who fail in school feel poorly about themselves. Return to Figure 15.4 on page 578, and you will see that girls score lower than boys in overall sense of self-worth. When the results of many studies are considered, this difference is only slight (Kling et al., 1999). Nevertheless, of those young people whose self-esteem declines during adolescence, most are girls (Eccles et al., 1999; Zimmerman et al., 1997). Recall that teenage girls worry more about their physical appearance and feel more insecure about their abilities.

At the same time, the contexts in which young people find themselves can modify these group differences, since self-esteem continues to be profoundly affected by feedback from significant adults and peers. Parental warmth, approval, and appropriate expectations for maturity (authoritative parenting) predict high self-esteem in adolescence, just as they did in childhood. And encouragement from teachers is linked to a favorable self-image as well (Carlson, Uppal, & Prosser, 2000; Steinberg, Darling, & Fletcher, 1995).

In contrast, when support from adults or peers is *conditional* (withheld unless the young person meets very high standards), teenagers frequently engage in behaviors they consider "false"—not representative of their true self. Although most adolescents report acting "phony" from time to time, they usually do so to win temporary approval or to experiment with new roles. Those who display false-self behavior—"expressing things you don't really believe" or "putting on an act"—because others (and therefore they) devalue their true self suffer from low self-esteem, depression, and pessimism about the future (Harter et al., 1996).

The larger social environment also influences sense of self-worth. Caucasian-American adolescents' self-esteem is less positive than that of African Americans, who benefit from warm, extended families and a strong sense of ethnic pride (Gray-Little & Hafdahl, 2000). Also, white girls are far more likely to show declines in self-esteem in early adolescence than are black girls, who are more satisfied with their physical appearance and peer relations (Brown et al., 1999; Eccles et al., 1999). Furthermore, teenagers who attend schools or live in neighborhoods where their SES or ethnic group is well represented have fewer self-esteem problems because they have more opportunities for friendship, social support, and a sense of belonging (Gray-Little & Carels, 1997). Schools and communities that accept the young person's cultural heritage support a positive sense of self-worth. And as we will see shortly, they foster the development of a solid and secure personal identity as well.

PATHS TO IDENTITY

Adolescents' well-organized self-descriptions and expanded sense of self-esteem provide the cognitive foundation for forming an identity. Using a clinical interviewing procedure devised by James Marcia (1966, 1980), researchers group adolescents into four *identity statuses,* which show the progress they have made toward formulating a mature identity. Table 16.1 on page 604 summarizes these identity statuses: **identity achievement, moratorium, identity foreclosure,** and **identity diffusion.**

Identity development follows many paths. Some adolescents remain in one status, whereas others experience many status transitions. And the pattern often varies across identity domains. For example, in junior high school, Louis accepted his parents' religious beliefs (foreclosure) and gave only passing thought to a vocational direction (diffusion). In high school, he started to actively explore these identity issues. Like Louis, most adolescents change from "lower" statuses (foreclosure or diffusion) to "higher" statuses (moratorium or achievement) by late adolescence, but some move in the reverse direction (Kroger, 1995; Meeus, 1996)

Because college students have many opportunities to explore new career options and lifestyles, they make more progress toward formulating an identity than they did in high school (Meeus et al., 1999). Teenagers who go to work after high school graduation often settle on a self-definition earlier than do college-bound youths (Munro & Adams, 1977). However, those who find it difficult to realize their occupational goals because they lack training or vocational choices (see Chapter 15) are at risk for long-term identity foreclosure or diffusion (Archer, 1989b; Kroger, 1993).

At one time, researchers thought that adolescent girls postponed the task of establishing an identity and, instead, focused their energies on Erikson's next stage, intimacy development. Some girls do show more sophisticated reasoning in identity areas related to intimacy,

identity achievement
The identity status of individuals who have explored and committed themselves to self-chosen values and occupational goals.

moratorium
The identity status of individuals who are exploring alternatives in an effort to find values and goals to guide their life.

identity foreclosure
The identity status of individuals who have accepted ready-made values and goals that authority figures have chosen for them.

identity diffusion
The identity status of individuals who do not have firm commitments to values and goals and are not actively trying to reach them.

TABLE 16.1

The Four Identity Statuses

IDENTITY STATUS	DESCRIPTION	EXAMPLE
Identity achievement	Having already explored alternatives, identity-achieved individuals are committed to a clearly formulated set of self-chosen values and goals. They feel a sense of psychological well-being, of sameness through time, and of knowing where they are going.	When asked how willing she would be to change her career goal if something better came along, Darla responded, "Well, I might, but I doubt it. I've thought long and hard about law as a career. I'm pretty certain it's for me."
Moratorium	The word *moratorium* means "delay or holding pattern." These individuals have not yet made definite commitments. They are in the process of exploration—gathering information and trying out activities, with the desire to find values and goals to guide their life.	When asked if he had ever had doubts about his religious beliefs, Ramon said, "Yes, I guess I'm going through that right now. I just don't see how there can be a god and yet so much evil in the world."
Identity foreclosure	Identity-foreclosed individuals have committed themselves to values and goals without taking time to explore alternatives. Instead, they accept a ready-made identity that authority figures (usually parents but sometimes teachers, religious leaders, or romantic partners) have chosen for them.	When asked if she had ever reconsidered her political beliefs, Hillary answered, "No, not really, our family is pretty much in agreement on these things."
Identity diffusion	Identity-diffused individuals lack clear direction. They are not committed to values and goals, nor are they actively trying to reach them. They may have never explored alternatives, or they may have tried to do so but found the task too threatening and overwhelming.	When asked about his attitude toward nontraditional gender roles—a husband staying home to care for children while the wife works, for example—Joel responded, "Oh, I don't know. It doesn't make much difference to me. I can take it or leave it."

such as sexuality and family–career priorities. In this respect, they are actually ahead of boys in identity development. Otherwise, late adolescents of both sexes typically make progress on identity concerns before experiencing genuine intimacy in relationships (Archer & Waterman, 1994; Kroger, 2000; Meeus et al., 1999).

IDENTITY STATUS AND PSYCHOLOGICAL WELL-BEING

Identity achievement and moratorium are viewed as psychologically healthy routes to a mature self-definition, whereas foreclosure and diffusion are seen as maladaptive. Research supports this conclusion. Young people who are identity achieved or actively exploring have a higher sense of self-esteem, are more likely to engage in abstract and critical thinking, report greater similarity between their ideal self (what they hoped to become) and their real self, and are more advanced in moral reasoning (Josselson, 1994; Marcia et al., 1993). Although adolescents in moratorium are often highly anxious about the challenges that lie before them, they join with identity-achieved individuals in using an autonomous, information-gathering style when making decisions and solving problems (Berzonsky & Kuk, 2000; Kroger, 2000).

Adolescents who get stuck in either foreclosure or diffusion have adjustment difficulties. Foreclosed individuals tend to be dogmatic, inflexible, and intolerant. Some use their commitments in a defensive way, regarding any difference of opinion as a threat. Most are afraid of rejection by people on whom they depend for affection and self-esteem (Frank, Pirsch, & Wright, 1990; Kroger, 1995). A few foreclosed teenagers who are alienated from their families and society may join cults or other extremist groups, uncritically adopting a way of life that is different from their past.

Long-term diffused teenagers are the least mature in identity development. They typically entrust themselves to luck or fate, have an "I don't care" attitude, and tend to go along with whatever the "crowd" is doing at the moment. As a result, they often experience time-management and academic difficulties (Berzonsky & Kuk, 2000). And they are most likely to use and abuse drugs. At the heart of their apathy and impulsiveness is often a sense of hope-lessness about the future (Archer & Waterman, 1990). Both foreclosed and diffused young people often hold ethnic and religious prejudices. The foreclosed teenager tends to pick them up from authority figures, the diffused young person from peers (Streitmatter & Pate, 1989).

INFLUENCES ON IDENTITY DEVELOPMENT

Adolescent identity formation begins a lifelong process that reflects a dynamic blend of personality and context. Whenever the individual or the context changes, the possibility for reformulating identity exists (Grotevant, 1998). A wide variety of factors influence identity development.

■ **PERSONALITY.** Identity status, as we saw in the previous section, is linked to personal-ity characteristics. The attributes considered are both cause and consequence of identity development. Adolescents who assume that absolute truth is always attainable tend to be foreclosed, whereas those who lack confidence in the prospect of ever knowing anything with certainty are more often identity diffused. Adolescents who appreciate that they can use rational criteria to choose among alternatives are likely to be in a state of moratorium or identity achievement (Berzonsky & Kuk, 2000; Boyes & Chandler, 1992). This flexible, open-minded approach assists them greatly in defining educational, career, and other life goals.

■ **FAMILY.** Recall from Chapter 7 that toddlers with a healthy sense of self have mothers who provide both emotional support and freedom to explore. A similar link between parenting and identity exists at adolescence. When the family serves as a "secure base" from which teenagers can confidently move out into the wider world, identity development is enhanced. Adolescents who feel attached to their parents but who are also free to voice their own opinions tend to be identity achieved or in a state of moratorium (Grotevant & Cooper, 1998; Hauser, Powers, & Noam, 1991). Foreclosed teenagers usually have close bonds with parents, but they lack opportunities for healthy separation. And diffused young people report the lowest levels of warm, open communication at home (Papini, 1994).

■ **PEERS.** As adolescents interact with a diversity of peers, their exposure to ideas and values expands. Close friends assist young people in exploring options by providing emotional support, assistance, and role models of identity develop-ment (Josselson, 1992). As we will see later, within friendships, adolescents also learn much about themselves. In one study, late adolescents' attachment to friends predicted exploration of careers and progress in choosing one (Felsman & Blus-tein, 1999). In sum, friends—like parents—can serve as a "secure base" as adoles-cents grapple with possibilities.

■ **SCHOOL AND COMMUNITY.** Identity development also depends on schools and communities that offer rich and varied opportunities for exploration. Erikson (1968, p. 132) noted that it is "the inability to settle on an occupational identity which most disturbs young people." Schools can foster identity achievement in many ways—through classrooms that promote high-level thinking; extracurricular and com-munity activities that permit teenagers to take on responsible roles; teachers and counselors who encourage low-SES and ethnic minority students to go to college; and vocational training programs that immerse adolescents in the real world of adult work (Cooper, 1998; Hart, Atkins, & Ford, 1998).

Regional variations in opportunity can lead to differences in identity development. For example, between ages 13 and 17, exploration increases among Australian adolescents living in urban environments, whereas it decreases among youths in rural areas. Lack of educational

As these adolescents exchange opinions about a recent news event, they become more aware of a diversity of view-points. A flexible, open-minded approach to grappling with competing beliefs and values fosters identity development.

Cultural

INFLUENCES

IDENTITY DEVELOPMENT AMONG ETHNIC MINORITY ADOLESCENTS

Most Caucasian-American adolescents are aware of their cultural ancestry, but it is not a matter of intense concern for them. Since the values of their home lives are consistent with those of mainstream American culture, ethnicity does not prompt intense identity exploration (Phinney, 1993).

But for teenagers who are members of minority groups, **ethnic identity**—an enduring aspect of the self that includes a sense of ethnic-group membership and attitudes and feelings associated with that membership—is central to the quest for identity. Although ethnic identity increases with age, it presents complex challenges (Phinney, Ferguson, & Tate, 1997). As they develop cognitively and become more sensitive to feedback from the social environment, minority youths become painfully aware that they are targets of discrimination and inequality. One African-American journalist, looking back on his own adolescence, remarked, "If you were black, you didn't quite measure up . . . you didn't see any black people doing certain things, and you couldn't rationalize it. I mean, you don't think it out but you say, 'Well, it must mean that white people are better than we are. Smarter, brighter—whatever'" (Monroe, Goldman, & Smith, 1988, pp. 98–99).

Minority youths often feel caught between the standards of the larger society and the traditions of their culture of origin. In many immigrant families from collectivist cultures, adolescents' commitment to obeying their parents and fulfilling family obligations lessens the longer the family has been in the United States (Phinney, Ong, & Madden, 2000). Young people sometimes reject aspects of their ethnic background. In one study, Asian-American 15- to 17-year-olds were more likely than blacks and Hispanics to hold negative attitudes toward their subcultural group. Perhaps the absence of a social movement stressing ethnic pride of the kind available to black and Hispanic teenagers underlies this finding (Phinney, 1989).

Some immigrant parents are overly restrictive of their teenagers out of fear that assimilation into the larger society will undermine their cultural traditions, and their youngsters rebel. One Southeast-Asian refugee described his daughter's behavior: "She complains about going to the Lao temple on the weekend and instead joined a youth group in a neighborhood Christian Church. She refused to wear traditional dress on the Lao New Year. The girl is setting a very bad example for her younger sisters and brothers" (Nidorf, 1985, pp. 422–423).

Other minority teenagers react to years of shattered self-esteem, school failure, and barriers to success in the American mainstream by defining themselves in contrast to majority values. A Mexican-American teenager who had given up on school commented, "Mexicans don't have a chance to go on to college and make something of themselves." Another, responding to the question of what it takes to be a successful adult, pointed to his uncle, leader of a local gang, as an example (Matute-Bianche, 1986, pp. 250–251).

Because it is painful and confusing, minority high school students often dodge the task of forming an ethnic identity. Many are diffused or foreclosed on ethnic identity issues (Markstrom-Adams & Adams, 1995). How can society help them resolve identity conflicts constructively? A variety of efforts are relevant, including

- reducing poverty;
- promoting effective parenting, in which children and adolescents are encouraged to explore the meaning of ethnicity in their own lives;
- ensuring that schools respect minority youths' native language, unique learning styles, and right to a high-quality education; and
- fostering contact and respect between ethnic groups in integrated schools and neighborhoods (García Coll & Magnuson, 1997).

A secure ethnic identity is associated with higher self-esteem, optimism, and sense of mastery over the environment, and more positive attitudes toward one's own ethnic group (Carlson, Uppal, & Prosser, 2000; Phinney, Ferguson, & Tate, 1997; Smith et al., 1999). But forming a **bicultural identity**—by exploring and adopting values from both the adolescent's subculture and the dominant culture—offers added benefits. Biculturally identified adolescents tend to be achieved in other areas of identity as well. And their relations with members of other ethnic groups are especially favorable (Phinney & Kohatsu, 1997). In sum, ethnic-identity achievement enhances many aspects of emotional and social development.

These East Indian adolescents dress in traditional costumes for a folk dancing demonstration at a town festival. When minority youths encounter respect for their cultural heritage in schools and communities, they are more likely to retain ethnic values and customs as an important part of their identities.

RUDI VON BRIEL/PHOTOEDIT

Caregiving Concerns

Adult Practices That Support Healthy Identity Development

STRATEGY	RATIONALE
Warm, open communication	Provides both emotional support and freedom to explore values and goals.
Discussions at home and school that promote high-level thinking	Encourages rational and deliberate selection among competing beliefs and values.
Opportunities to participate in extracurricular activities and vocational training programs	Permits young people to explore the real world of adult work.
Opportunities to talk with adults and peers who have worked through identity questions	Offers models of identity achievement and advice on how to resolve identity concerns.
Opportunities to explore ethnic heritage and learn about other cultures in an atmosphere of respect	Fosters identity achievement in all areas and ethnic tolerance, which supports the identity explorations of others.

and vocational options in Australian rural regions is probably responsible (Nurmi, Poole, & Kalakoski, 1996). Regardless of where young people live, a chance to talk with adults and older peers who have worked through identity questions can be helpful.

■ **LARGER SOCIETY.** The larger cultural context and historical time period affect identity development. Among modern adolescents, exploration and commitment take place earlier in the identity domains of gender-role preference and vocational choice than in religious and political values. Yet a generation ago, when the Vietnam War divided Americans and disrupted the lives of thousands of young people, the political beliefs of American youths took shape sooner (Archer, 1989b). Societal forces are also responsible for the special problems that gay, lesbian, and bisexual youths (see Chapter 14) and ethnic minority adolescents face in forming a secure identity, as the Cultural Influences box on the previous page describes. The Caregiving Concerns table above summarizes ways that adults can support identity development in adolescence.

ethnic identity
An enduring aspect of the self that includes a sense of ethnic group membership and attitudes and feelings associated with that membership.

bicultural identity
The identity constructed by adolescents who explore and adopt values from both their subculture and the dominant culture.

Ask YOURSELF...

review   *Return to the opening of this chapter and review the conversation between Louis and Darryl. Which identity status best characterizes the two boys, and why? What personal and contextual factors may have contributed to their identity progress?*

apply   *At age 13, Jeremy described himself as both "cheerful" and "glum." At age 16, he said, "Sometimes I'm cheerful, at other times I'm glum, so I guess I'm kind of moody." What accounts for this change in Jeremy's self-concept?*

connect   *Jules is an identity-achieved young person, secure in his self-chosen values and future goals. What have you learned about Franca and Antonio's parenting style in previous chapters that helps explain Jules's adaptive approach to identity formation?*

reflect   *How would you characterize your identity status? Is it the same or different across identity domains of sexuality, vocation, religious beliefs, and political values? Describe the path of identity development you followed, along with factors that may have influenced it.*

Moral Development

Eleven-year-old Sabrina sat at the kitchen table reading the Sunday newspaper, her face wide-eyed with interest. "You gotta see this," she said to 16-year-old Louis, who was munching cereal across from her. Sabrina held up a page of large photos showing a 70-year-old woman standing in the center of her home. The floor and furniture were piled with stacks of newspapers, cardboard boxes, tin cans, glass containers, food, and clothing. The plaster on the walls was crumbling. And the accompanying article described crumbling plaster on the walls, frozen pipes, and sinks, a toilet, and a furnace that no longer worked. The headline read: "Loretta Perry: My Life Is None of Their Business."

"Look what they're trying to do to this poor lady," exclaimed Sabrina. "They wanna throw her out of her house and tear it down! Those city inspectors must not care about anyone. Here it says, 'Mrs. Perry has devoted much of her life to helping veterans and doing favors for people.' Why doesn't someone help her?"

"Sabrina, you missed the point," Louis responded. "Mrs. Perry is violating 30 building code standards. The law says you're supposed to keep your house clean and in good repair."

"But Louis, she's old and she needs help. She says her life will be over if they destroy her home."

"The building inspectors aren't being mean, Sabrina. Mrs. Perry is stubborn. She refuses to obey the law. By not taking care of her house, she's not just a threat to herself. She's a danger to her neighbors, too. Suppose her house caught fire. You can't live around other people and say your life is nobody's business."

"You don't just knock someone's home down," Sabrina replied angrily. "Where're her friends and neighbors in all this? Why aren't they over there fixing up that house? You're like those building inspectors, Louis. You've got no feeling!"

Louis and Sabrina's disagreement over Mrs. Perry's plight illustrates tremendous advances in moral understanding. Changes in cognition and social experience permit adolescents to better understand larger social structures—societal institutions and lawmaking systems—that govern moral responsibilities in complex cultures. As their grasp of social arrangements expands, adolescents construct new ideas about what ought to be done when the needs and desires of people conflict, and they move toward increasingly just and fair solutions to moral problems (Gibbs, 1995).

PIAGET'S THEORY OF MORAL DEVELOPMENT

The most influential approach to moral development is Lawrence Kohlberg's cognitive-developmental perspective, which was inspired by Piaget's early work on the moral judgment of the child. Piaget (1932/1965) saw children as moving through two broad stages of moral understanding.

The first stage is **heteronomous morality,** which extends from about 5 to 10 years of age. The word *heteronomous* means "under the authority of another." As the term suggests, children of this stage view rules as handed down by authorities (God, parents, and teachers), as having a permanent existence, as unchangeable, and as requiring strict obedience. Also, in judging an act's wrongness, they focus on objective consequences rather than intent to do harm. When asked to decide which child is naughtier—John, who accidentally breaks 15 cups while on his way to dinner, or Henry, who breaks 1 cup while stealing some jam—a 6- or 7-year-old chooses John.

According to Piaget, around age 10 children make the transition to the stage of **autonomous morality.** They realize that people can have different perspectives on moral matters and that intentions, not just outcomes, should serve as the basis for judging behavior. Piaget believed that improvements in perspective taking, which result from cognitive development and opportuni-

---

heteronomous morality
Piaget's first stage of moral development, in which children view moral rules as permanent features of the external world that are handed down by authorities, require strict obedience, and cannot be changed. Extends from about 5 to 10 years of age.

autonomous morality
Piaget's second stage of moral development, in which children view rules as flexible, socially agreed-on principles that can be revised when there is a need to do so. Begins around age 10.

ties to interact with peers, are responsible for this change. Autonomous individuals no longer view rules as fixed. Instead, they regard them as socially agreed-on principles that can be revised. In creating and changing rules, older children and adolescents use a standard of fairness called *reciprocity.* They express the same concern for the welfare of others as they do for themselves. Most of us are familiar with reciprocity in the form of the Golden Rule: "Do unto others as you would have others do unto you."

Think about Piaget's theory in light of what you learned about moral development in earlier chapters (return to pages 384–385 and 492–495 to review). You will see that school-age children do not view rules as fixed, show unquestioning respect for authorities, or ignore peoples' intentions in making moral judgments. Clearly, Piaget underestimated children's moral capacities. Nevertheless, his account of morality, like his cognitive theory, does describe the general direction of moral development. And in fairness, Piaget observed a mixture of heteronomous and autonomous reasoning in the responses of many children and recommended that the two moralities be viewed as overlapping phases rather than distinct stages.

Although children are less rigid moral thinkers than Piaget made them out to be, they are not as advanced as adolescents and adults. Piaget's groundbreaking work has been replaced by Kohlberg's more comprehensive theory, which regards moral development as extending beyond childhood into adolescence and adulthood in a six-stage sequence.

AARON HAUPT/PHOTO RESEARCHERS, INC.

This teenager's efforts to repair his friend's car may be motivated by his understanding of the Golden Rule: "Do unto others as you would have others do unto you." A sophisticated grasp of reciprocity—expressing the same concern for others as for oneself—contributes to advances in moral understanding in older children and adolescents.

KOHLBERG'S EXTENSION OF PIAGET'S THEORY

Kohlberg used a clinical interviewing procedure to study the development of moral understanding. He gave children, adolescents, and adults *moral dilemmas*—stories that present a genuine conflict between two moral values—and asked them what the main actor should do and why. The best known of these is the "Heinz dilemma," which presents a choice between the value of obeying the law (not stealing) and the value of human life (saving a dying person):

In Europe a woman was near death from cancer. There was one drug that the doctors thought might save her. A druggist in the same town had discovered it, but he was charging ten times what the drug cost him to make. The sick woman's husband, Heinz, went to everyone he knew to borrow the money, but he could only get together half of what it cost. The druggist refused to sell it cheaper or let Heinz pay later. So Heinz got desperate and broke into the man's store to steal the drug for his wife. Should Heinz have done that? Why? (paraphrased from Colby et al., 1983, p. 77)

Kohlberg emphasized that it is *the way an individual reasons* about the dilemma, not *the content of the response* (whether to steal or not to steal), that determines moral maturity. Individuals who believe that Heinz should take the drug and those who think that he should not can be found at each of Kohlberg's first four stages. At the highest two stages, people refer to broader principles, so moral reasoning and content come together. Individuals do not just agree on why certain actions are justified; they also agree on what people ought to do when faced with a moral dilemma. Given a choice between obeying the law and preserving individual rights, the most advanced moral thinkers support individual rights (in the Heinz dilemma, stealing the drug to save a life).

As we look at development in Kohlberg's scheme, we will see that moral reasoning and content are at first independent, but eventually they are integrated into a coherent ethical system (Kohlberg, Levine, & Hewer, 1983). Does this remind you of adolescents' effort to formulate a sound, well-organized set of personal values in identity development? According to some theorists, the development of identity and moral understanding are part of the same process (Blasi, 1994; Marcia, 1988).

TABLE 16.2

The Relation Between Kohlberg's Moral, Piaget's Cognitive, and Selman's Perspective-Taking Stages

KOHLBERG'S MORAL STAGE	DESCRIPTION	PIAGET'S COGNITIVE STAGE	SELMAN'S PERSPECTIVE-TAKING STAGE[a]
Punishment and obedience orientation	Fear of authority and avoidance of punishment are reasons for behaving morally.	Preoperational, early concrete operational	Social-informational
Instrumental purpose orientation	Satisfying personal needs determines moral choice.	Concrete operational	Self-reflective
"Good boy–good girl" orientation	Maintaining the affection and approval of friends and relatives motivates good behavior.	Early formal operational	Third-party
Social-order-maintaining orientation	A duty to uphold laws and rules for their own sake justifies moral conformity.	Formal operational	Societal
Social contract orientation	Fair procedures for changing laws to protect individual rights and the needs of the majority are emphasized.		
Universal ethical principle orientation	Abstract universal principles that are valid for all humanity guide moral decision making.		

[a]To review these stages, return to Chapter 13, page 492.

■ **KOHLBERG'S STAGES OF MORAL UNDERSTANDING.** Kohlberg organized his six stages into three general levels of moral development. He believed that moral understanding is promoted by the same factors that Piaget thought were important for cognitive development: (1) actively grappling with moral issues and noticing weaknesses in one's current thinking, and (2) advances in perspective taking, which permit individuals to resolve moral conflicts in more complex and effective ways. As Table 16.2 shows, Kohlberg's moral stages are related to Piaget's cognitive and Selman's perspective-taking stages. As we examine Kohlberg's developmental sequence and illustrate it with responses to the Heinz dilemma, look for changes in perspective taking that each stage assumes.

The Preconventional Level. At the **preconventional level,** morality is externally controlled. As in Piaget's heteronomous stage, children accept the rules of authority figures and judge actions by their consequences. Behaviors that result in punishment are viewed as bad, and those that lead to rewards are seen as good.

■ *Stage 1: The punishment and obedience orientation.* Children at this stage find it difficult to consider two points of view in a moral dilemma. As a result, they ignore people's intentions and, instead, focus on fear of authority and avoidance of punishment as reasons for behaving morally.

Prostealing: "If you let your wife die, you will get in trouble. You'll be blamed for not spending the money to help her and there'll be an investigation of you and the druggist for your wife's death." (Kohlberg, 1969, p. 381)

Antistealing: "You shouldn't steal the drug because you'll be caught and sent to jail if you do. If you do get away, [you'd be scared that] the police would catch up with you any minute." (Kohlberg, 1969, p. 381)

■ *Stage 2: The instrumental purpose orientation.* Children become aware that people can have different perspectives in a moral dilemma, but this understanding is, at first, very concrete. They view right action as flowing from self-interest. Reciprocity is understood as equal exchange of favors—"You do this for me, and I'll do that for you."

preconventional level
Kohlberg's first level of moral development, in which moral understanding is based on rewards, punishments, and the power of authority figures.

Prostealing: "The druggist can do what he wants and Heinz can do what he wants to do. . . . But if Heinz decides to risk jail to save his wife, it's his life he's risking; he can do what he wants with it. And the same goes for the druggist; it's up to him to decide what he wants to do." (Rest, 1979, p. 26)

Antistealing: "[Heinz] is running more risk than it's worth unless he's so crazy about her he can't live without her. Neither of them will enjoy life if she's an invalid." (Rest, 1979, p. 27)

The Conventional Level. At the **conventional level,** individuals continue to regard conformity to social rules as necessary, but not for reasons of self-interest. They believe that actively maintaining the current social system ensures positive human relationships and societal order.

■ ***Stage 3: The "good boy–good girl" orientation, or the morality of interpersonal cooperation.*** The desire to obey rules because they promote social harmony first appears in the context of close personal ties. Stage 3 individuals want to maintain the affection and approval of friends and relatives by being a "good person"—trustworthy, loyal, respectful, helpful, and nice. The capacity to view a two-person relationship from the vantage point of an impartial, outside observer supports this new approach to morality. At this stage, the individual understands reciprocity in terms of the Golden Rule.

Prostealing: "No one will think you're bad if you steal the drug, but your family will think you're an inhuman husband if you don't. If you let your wife die, you'll never be able to look anyone in the face again." (Kohlberg, 1969, p. 381)

Antistealing: "It isn't just the druggist who will think you're a criminal, everyone else will too. After you steal it, you'll feel bad thinking how you've brought dishonor on your family and yourself; you won't be able to face anyone again." (Kohlberg, 1969, p. 381)

■ ***Stage 4: The social-order-maintaining orientation.*** At this stage, the individual takes into account a larger perspective—that of societal laws. Moral choices no longer depend on close ties to others. Instead, rules must be enforced in the same evenhanded fashion for everyone, and each member of society has a personal duty to uphold them. The Stage 4 individual believes that laws must be obeyed under all circumstances because they are vital for ensuring societal order.

Prostealing: "He should steal it. Heinz has a duty to protect his wife's life; it's a vow he took in marriage. But it's wrong to steal, so he would have to take the drug with the idea of paying the druggist for it and accepting the penalty for breaking the law later."

Antistealing: "It's a natural thing for Heinz to want to save his wife, but it's still always wrong to steal. You have to follow the rules regardless of how you feel or regardless of the special circumstances. Even if his wife is dying, it's still his duty as a citizen to obey the law. No one else is allowed to steal, why should he be? If everyone starts breaking the law in a jam, there'd be no civilization, just crime and violence." (Rest, 1979, p. 30)

The Postconventional or Principled Level. Individuals at the **postconventional level** move beyond unquestioning support for the laws and rules of their own society. They define morality in terms of abstract principles and values that apply to all situations and societies.

■ ***Stage 5: The social contract orientation.*** At Stage 5, individuals regard laws and rules as flexible instruments for furthering human purposes. They can imagine alternatives to their social order, and they emphasize fair procedures for interpreting and changing the law. When laws are consistent with individual rights and the interests of the majority, each person follows them because of a *social contract orientation*—free and willing participation in the system because it brings about more good for people than if it did not exist.

conventional level
Kohlberg's second level of moral development, in which moral understanding is based on conforming to social rules to ensure positive human relationships and societal order.

postconventional level
Kohlberg's highest level of moral development, in which individuals define morality in terms of abstract principles and values that apply to all situations and societies.

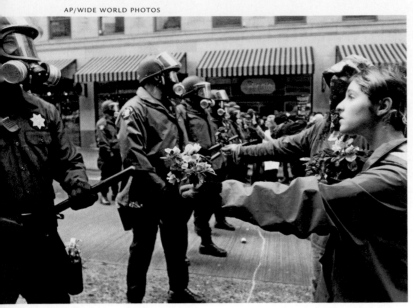

Young people make up a large sector of public demonstrations over moral issues. These students express a principled level of morality as they protest the meeting of the World Trade Organization in downtown Seattle in November, 1999. Despite the police crackdown, the Seattle demonstrators continued to object peacefully to a world market that benefits corporations at the expense of low-paid workers and farmers.

Prostealing: "Although there is a law against stealing, the law wasn't meant to violate a person's right to life. Taking the drug does violate the law, but Heinz is justified in stealing in this instance. If Heinz is prosecuted for stealing, the law needs to be reinterpreted to take into account situations in which it goes against people's natural right to keep on living."

Antistealing: No antistealing responses at this stage.

■ **Stage 6: *The universal ethical principle orientation.*** At this highest stage, right action is defined by self-chosen ethical principles of conscience that are valid for all humanity, regardless of law and social agreement. These values are abstract, not concrete moral rules like the Ten Commandments. Stage 6 individuals are guided by such principles as equal consideration of the claims of all human beings and respect for the worth and dignity of each person.

Prostealing: "If Heinz does not do everything he can to save his wife, then he is putting some value higher than the value of life. It doesn't make sense to put respect for property above respect for life itself. [People] could live together without private property at all. Respect for human life and personality is absolute, and accordingly [people] have a mutual duty to save one another from dying." (Rest, 1979, p. 37)

Antistealing: No antistealing responses at this stage.

■ **RESEARCH ON KOHLBERG'S STAGE SEQUENCE.** Longitudinal studies provide the most convincing evidence for Kohlberg's stage sequence. With few exceptions, individuals move through the stages in the order that Kohlberg expected (Colby et al., 1983; Walker, 1989; Walker & Taylor, 1991b). A striking finding is that moral development is very slow and gradual. Stages 1 and 2 decrease in early adolescence, whereas Stage 3 increases through mid-adolescence and then declines. Stage 4 rises over the teenage years until, by early adulthood, it is the typical response. Few people move beyond it to Stage 5. In fact, postconventional morality is so rare that there is no clear evidence that Kohlberg's Stage 6 actually follows Stage 5. The highest stage of moral development is still a matter of speculation.

■ **HYPOTHETICAL VERSUS REAL-LIFE MORAL DILEMMAS.** As you read the Heinz dilemma, you probably came up with your own solution to it. Now try to think of a moral dilemma you recently faced in everyday life. How did you solve it, and what factors influenced your choice? Did your reasoning fall at the same stage as your thinking about Heinz and his dying wife?

Kohlberg's theory has contributed greatly to our understanding of moral development. Yet in focusing on hypothetical dilemmas, it emphasizes rationally weighing alternatives to the neglect of other influences on moral judgment. When researchers had adolescents and adults recall and discuss a real-life moral dilemma, most often they focused on relationships—whether to continue helping a friend when she's taking advantage of you, whether to live with mother or father after their separation. Although participants endorsed reasoning to resolve these dilemmas, they also posed other strategies, such as talking through issues with others and relying on intuition that their decision was right. Especially striking was the expression of anguish in working through everyday dilemmas. People mentioned feeling drained, confused, and torn by temptation—a motivational and emotional side of moral judgment not tapped by hypothetical situations (Walker et al., 1995, 1999).

Although everyday moral reasoning corresponds to Kohlberg's scheme, it typically falls at a lower stage than do responses to hypothetical dilemmas (Carpendale, 2000). Real-life problems seem to elicit reasoning below a person's actual capacity because they bring out many practical considerations. The influence of situational factors on moral reasoning suggests that like Piaget's stages, Kohlberg's account of moral development is best viewed as a series of overlapping phases. Rather than developing in a neat, stepwise fashion, each individual draws on a range of moral responses that vary with context. With age, this range shifts upward, and more advanced moral thought gradually replaces less mature moral reasoning.

ARE THERE SEX DIFFERENCES IN MORAL REASONING?

As we have just seen, in real-life moral dilemmas, emotion often contributes to moral judgment. Return to Sabrina and Louis's moral discussion on page 608. Sabrina's argument focuses on caring and commitment to others. Louis's approach is more impersonal. He looks at the dilemma of Loretta Perry in terms of competing rights and justice.

Carol Gilligan (1982) is the most well-known figure among those who have argued that Kohlberg's theory does not adequately represent the morality of girls and women. She believes that feminine morality emphasizes an "ethic of care" that is devalued in Kohlberg's system. For example, Sabrina's reasoning falls at Stage 3 because it focuses on the importance of mutual trust and affection between people. Louis, who emphasizes the value of obeying the law to ensure societal order, is at Stage 4. According to Gilligan, a concern for others is a *different*, not less valid, basis for moral judgment than a focus on impersonal rights.

Many studies have tested Gilligan's claim that Kohlberg's approach underestimates the moral maturity of females, and most do not support it (Turiel, 1998). On hypothetical dilemmas as well as everyday moral problems, adolescent and adult females display reasoning at the same or higher stages as do their male counterparts. Also, themes of justice and caring appear in the responses of both sexes, and when girls do raise interpersonal concerns, they are not downscored in Kohlberg's system (Jadack et al., 1995; Kahn, 1992; Walker, 1995). These findings suggest that although Kohlberg emphasized justice rather than caring as the highest of moral ideals, his theory does include both sets of values.

Still, Gilligan makes a powerful claim that research on moral development has been limited by too much attention to rights and justice (a "masculine" ideal) and too little attention to care and responsiveness (a "feminine" ideal). Some evidence shows that although the morality of males and females taps both orientations, females do tend to stress care, or empathic perspective taking, whereas males stress justice or use justice and care equally (Galotti, Kozberg, & Farmer, 1991; Garmon et al., 1996; Wark & Krebs, 1996).

The difference in emphasis appears most often on real-life rather than hypothetical dilemmas. Consequently, it may be largely a function of women's greater involvement in daily activities involving care and concern for others. In one study, American and Canadian 17- to 26-year-old females showed more complex reasoning about care issues than did their male counterparts. But as Figure 16.1 shows, Norwegian males were just as advanced as Norwegian females in care-based understanding (Skoe, 1998). Perhaps Norwegian culture, which explicitly endorses gender equality at home, at school, and in the workplace, induces boys and men to think deeply about interpersonal obligations.

Taken together, these findings suggest that like her older brother Louis, Sabrina will one day reason at Kohlberg's Stage 4 or higher, but her justifications for moral action will continue to include concern for others. Although justice and caring are not gender-specific moralities, Gilligan's work has had the effect of broadening conceptions of the highly moral person.

INFLUENCES ON MORAL REASONING

Many factors predict maturity of moral reasoning. These include the young person's personality and a wide range of experiences—child-rearing practices, schooling, peer interaction, and aspects of culture. Growing evidence suggests these experiences present young people with cognitive challenges, which stimulate them to think about moral problems in more complex ways.

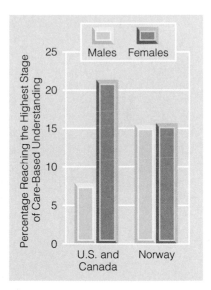

FIGURE 16.1

Complex reasoning about care issues among U.S. and Canadian versus Norwegian males and females. In this study of 17- to 26-year-olds, North American females scored much higher than males in complex care-based understanding. In contrast, Norwegian males and females displayed equally advanced care-based understanding. (Adapted from Skoe, 1998.)

■ **PERSONALITY.** A flexible, open-minded approach to new information and experiences is linked to gains in moral reasoning, just as it is to identity development (Hart et al., 1998; Matsuba & Walker, 1998). Because open-minded young people are more socially skilled, they have more opportunities for social participation (Block & Block, 1980). A richer social life enhances exposure to others' perspectives, and open-mindedness helps adolescents derive moral insights from that exposure. In contrast, adolescents who have difficulty adapting to new experiences are less likely to be interested in others' moral ideas and justifications.

■ **CHILD-REARING PRACTICES.** In Chapter 10 we saw that parents who are warm and consistent and who discuss moral concerns have children who are advanced in moral understanding. The same is true in adolescence. Teenagers who gain most in moral development have parents who tell stories with moral implications, encourage moral discussions, and create a supportive atmosphere by listening sensitively, asking clarifying questions, presenting higher-level reasoning, and using praise and humor (Pratt et al., 1999). In contrast, parents who lecture, use threats, or make sarcastic remarks have youngsters who change little or not at all (Walker & Taylor, 1991a). In sum, parents facilitate moral reasoning by using an authoritative approach that is verbal, rational, and affectionate and that promotes a cooperative style of family life.

■ **SCHOOLING.** Years of schooling completed is one of the most powerful predictors of moral development. Longitudinal research reveals that moral reasoning advances in late adolescence and young adulthood only as long as a person remains in school (Rest & Narvaez, 1991; Speicher, 1994). Perhaps higher education has a strong impact on moral development because it introduces young people to social issues that extend beyond personal relationships to entire political and cultural groups. Consistent with this idea, college students who report more academic perspective-taking opportunities (for example, classes that emphasize open discussion of opinions) and who indicate that they have become more aware of social diversity tend to be advanced in moral reasoning (Mason & Gibbs, 1993a, 1993b).

■ **PEER INTERACTION.** Many studies confirm Piaget's belief that peer experiences that confront adolescents with differing viewpoints promote moral understanding. For example, young people who report more close friendships, who more often participate in leisure activities and conversation with their friends, and who are viewed as leaders by their classmates score higher in moral reasoning (Schonert-Reichl, 1999).

But peer interaction must have certain features to be effective. Consider, once again, Sabrina and Louis's argument over the plight of Loretta Perry. Each teenager directly confronts and criticizes the other's statements, and emotionally intense expressions of disagreement occur. Peer discussions like this lead to much greater stage change than do those in which adolescents state their opinions in a disorganized, uninvolved way (Berkowitz & Gibbs, 1983; Haan, Aerts, & Cooper, 1985). Also, note that Sabrina and Louis do not revise their ways of thinking after just one discussion. Because moral development occurs gradually, it takes many peer interaction sessions over weeks or months to produce moral change.

■ **CULTURE.** Cross-cultural research reveals that individuals in technologically advanced, urban cultures move through Kohlberg's stages more quickly and advance to higher levels than do individuals in village societies. Members of these small, collectivist communities do not reach Stage 4 and above, whereas high school- and college-educated adolescents and adults in developed nations do (Snarey, 1995). (Keep in mind, however, that only a few adults in industrialized nations reach Stages 5 and 6.)

One explanation of these cultural differences focuses on the role of larger social structures in advanced moral understanding. In village societies, moral cooperation is based on direct relations between people. Yet Stages 4 to 6 reasoning depends on understanding the role of laws and government institutions in resolving moral conflict (Snarey, 1995). In support of this view, in cultures where young people participate in the institutions of their society at early ages, moral development is advanced. For example, on *kibbutzim,* small but technologically complex agricultural settlements in Israel, children receive training in the gover-

nance of their community in middle childhood. By third grade, they mention more concerns about societal laws and rules when
discussing moral conflicts than do Israeli city-
reared or American children (Fuchs et al.,
1986). During adolescence and young adulthood, a greater percentage of kibbutz than
American individuals reach Kohlberg's Stages
4 and 5 (Snarey, Reimer, & Kohlberg, 1985).

A second possible reason for cultural variation is that responses to dilemmas in some
cultures cannot be scored in Kohlberg's scheme.
Recall from Chapter 13 that self-concepts in
collectivist cultures (including village societies) are more other-directed than in Western
Europe and North America. This very difference seems to characterize moral reasoning as
well (Miller, 1994, 1997). In village societies,
moral statements that portray the individual as
vitally connected to the social group are common. For example, one New Guinea village
leader placed the blame for the Heinz dilemma on the entire social group, stating, "If I were
the judge, I would give him only light punishment because he asked everybody for help but
nobody helped him" (Tietjen & Walker, 1985, p. 990).

Similarly, members of Eastern collectivist nations grant obligations to others more weight
than do people in Western individualistic societies. In a study conducted in India, the most
morally mature individuals rarely appealed to personal ethical principles in discussing the
Heinz dilemma. Instead, they resisted choosing a course of action, explaining that a moral
solution should not be the burden of a single individual but of the entire society (Vasudev &
Hummel, 1987). These findings raise the question of whether Kohlberg's highest stages represent a culturally specific rather than universal way of thinking—one limited to Western
societies that emphasize individual rights and an appeal to an inner, private conscience.

Young people growing up on
Israeli kibbutzim receive training in the governance of their
community at an early age. As
a result, they understand the
role of societal laws in resolving moral conflict and are
advanced in moral reasoning.

MORAL REASONING AND BEHAVIOR

According to Kohlberg, moral thought and action should come together at the higher levels of moral understanding. Mature moral thinkers realize that behaving in line with their
beliefs is an important part of creating and maintaining a just social world (Gibbs, 1995). Consistent with this idea, advanced moral reasoning is related to positive social behavior. Higher-
stage adolescents more often act prosocially by helping, sharing, and defending victims of
injustice (Carlo et al., 1996; Fabes et al., 1999). They also less often engage in cheating, aggression, and other antisocial behaviors (Gregg, Gibbs, & Fuller, 1994; Taylor & Walker, 1997).

Yet even though a clear connection between moral thought and action exists, it is only
moderate. As we saw in earlier chapters, moral behavior is influenced by a great many factors
besides cognition, including the emotions of empathy, sympathy, and guilt; individual differences in temperament; and a long history of experiences that affect moral choice and decision making. Also, the degree to which morality is central to self-concept affects moral
behavior. In a study of low-SES African-American and Hispanic teenagers, those displaying
exceptional levels of community service emphasized moral traits and goals in their self-
descriptions. These highly prosocial young people, however, did not differ from their agemates in moral reasoning (Hart & Fegley, 1995). Researchers have yet to uncover just how
moral thought, emotion, and behavior influence one another. Still, as the Social Issues: Education box on pages 616–617 reveals, community involvement can help adolescents see the
connection between their personal interests and the public interest—an insight that may foster all aspects of morality at once.

Social ISSUES: EDUCATION

DEVELOPMENT OF CIVIC RESPONSIBILITY

During the summer, Louis and Cassie joined other high school students in a Habitat for Humanity project, building a home for the needy. Throughout the year, Sabrina volunteered on Saturday mornings at a nursing home, conversing with bedridden elders and assisting them with everyday tasks. In the months before a congressional election, all three young people attended special youth meetings with candidates, where they raised concerns. "What's your view on preserving our environment?" Louis asked. "How would you prevent the proposed tax cut from mostly benefiting the rich?" Sabrina chimed in. At school, Louis and Cassie, along with several other students, formed an organization devoted to promoting ethnic and racial tolerance.

Already, Louis, Cassie, and Sabrina have a strong sense of civic responsibility—a complex capacity that combines cognition, emotion, and behavior. Civic responsibility involves *knowledge* of political issues and the means through which citizens can resolve differing views fairly; *feelings* of attachment to the community, of wanting to make a difference in its welfare, and of trust in others' fairness and helpfulness; and *skills* for achieving civic goals, such as how to contact and question public officials and conduct meetings so that all participants have a voice (Flanagan & Faison, 2001). New research reveals that family, school, and community experiences contribute to adolescents' civic responsibility.

FAMILY INFLUENCES

Parents who bring up controversial issues and encourage their children to form opinions have teenagers who are more knowledgeable and interested in civic issues and better able to see them from more than one perspective (Santoloupo & Pratt, 1994). Also, adolescents who report that their families emphasize compassion for the less fortunate are more likely to hold socially responsible values themselves. When asked what causes such social ills as unemployment, poverty, and homelessness, these teenagers more often mention situational and societal factors (such as lack of education, government policies, or insufficient job opportunities) than individual factors (such as low intelligence or personal problems). Youths who endorse situational and societal causes, in turn, have more altruistic life goals. They say, for example, that they would be willing to have fewer luxuries themselves to help starving people or preserve the earth for future generations (Flanagan & Tucker, 1999).

Recall from Chapter 13 that as adolescence approaches, young people can empathize not only with people's immediate distress but with their general life condition (see page 490). Families that teach children to look beyond their own needs promote this advanced sense of empathy. Then young people draw on it to define altruistic goals.

SCHOOL AND COMMUNITY INFLUENCES

A democratic climate at school—one in which teachers hold the same high academic and moral standards for all students, express respect for students' ideas, and insist that students listen to and respect one another—fosters a sense of civic responsibility. Teenagers who say their teachers engage in these practices are more aware of political issues, better able to critically analyze them, and more committed to social causes—improving race relations, helping the

Gender Typing

As Sabrina entered adolescence, some aspects of her thinking and behavior became more gender typed. For example, she began to place more emphasis on excelling in the traditionally feminine subjects of language, art, and music than in math and science. And when with peers, Sabrina worried a great deal about how she should walk, talk, eat, dress, laugh, and compete, judged according to accepted social standards for maleness and femaleness.

Research suggests that early adolescence is period of **gender intensification**—increased gender stereotyping of attitudes and behavior (Basow & Rubin, 1999; Galambos, Almeida, & Petersen, 1990). Although it occurs in both sexes, gender intensification is stronger for girls.

gender intensification
Increased gender stereotyping of attitudes and behavior. Occurs in early adolescence.

During adolescence, young people develop a stronger sense of connection to their community. These teenagers test a polluted Texas tributary for signs of life. Teenagers' involvement in community service grows out of a sense of civic responsibility, which is supported by family, school, and community experiences.

downtrodden, and cleaning up their communities (Flanagan & Faison, 2001).

Participation in extracurricular activities at school and in youth organizations in the community is also associated with civic commitment that persists into adulthood (Verba, Schlozman, & Brady, 1995; Youniss, McLellan, & Yates, 1997). Researchers believe that two aspects of these involvements account for their lasting impact.

First, they introduce adolescents to the vision and skills required for mature civic engagement. Within clubs, teams, and other groups, young people see how their actions affect the wider school and community. They realize that collectively, they can achieve results greater than any one person can achieve alone. And to reach these goals, they learn to work together, balancing strong convictions with compromise.

Second, youth organizations promote identity development. While producing a weekly newspaper, participating in a dramatic production, or implementing a service project, young people explore political and moral ideals, selecting those they find meaningful. In one study, researchers tracked high school students' changing views during a year of volunteering at a soup kitchen. The students gradually gave up stereotypes of the "homeless," replacing them with images of people with complex life histories and problems. At the same time, they redefined themselves as more fortunate citizens with a responsibility to combat others' misfortunes. And they addressed the injustices of a political system that permits homelessness to increase (Youniss & Yates, 1997).

In an investigation of youth in seven countries—Australia, Bulgaria, the Czech Republic, Hungary, Russia, Sweden, and the United States—adolescents were more likely to regard civic responsibility as an important life goal when (1) their families empha-

sized compassion and social action, (2) their school engaged in democratic practices and they felt connected to its student body, and (3) they volunteered in their community. Each factor emerged as important in three or more countries (Flanagan et al., 1998).

Current evidence points to growing self-interest and materialism among American high school students (Rahn & Transue, 1998). Granting young people many opportunities to think in terms of *we* rather than *I* and to work with others toward a common good can combat this trend. The power of family, school, and community to promote civic responsibility may lie in discussions, educational practices, and activities that jointly foster moral thought, emotion, and behavior.

Recall from earlier chapters that girls are less gender typed than boys during childhood, a difference that extends into the teenage years. But early adolescent girls feel less free to experiment with "other gender" activities and behavior than they did in middle childhood (Huston & Alvarez, 1990).

What accounts for gender intensification? Biological, social, and cognitive factors are involved. Puberty magnifies sex differences in appearance, causing teenagers to spend more time thinking about themselves in gender-linked ways. Pubertal changes also prompt gender-typed pressures from others. Parents—especially those with traditional gender-role beliefs—may encourage "gender appropriate" activities and behavior to a greater extent than they did in middle childhood (Crouter, Manke, & McHale, 1995). And when adolescents start to date, they often become more gender typed as a way of increasing their attractiveness to other-sex peers (Maccoby, 1998). For example, in encounters with boys, girls

Early adolescence is a period of gender intensification. Puberty magnifies gender differences in appearance, causing teenagers to think about themselves in gender-linked ways. And when adolescents start to date, they often become more gender typed as a way of increasing their attractiveness to the other sex.

frequently use disclaimers, such as "I may be wrong" and "sort of"—a tentative speech style their male partners prefer (Carli, 1995). Finally, cognitive changes—in particular, greater concern with what others think—make young teenagers more responsive to gender-role expectations.

Gender intensification seems to decline by middle to late adolescence, but not all young people move beyond it to the same degree. The social environment is a primary force in promoting gender-role flexibility, just as it was at earlier ages. Teenagers who are encouraged to explore non-gender-typed options and to question the value of gender stereotypes for themselves and society are more likely to build an androgynous gender identity, selecting "masculine" and "feminine" traits that suit their personally chosen goals. Overall, androgynous adolescents tend to be psychologically healthier—more self-confident, more willing to speak their own mind, better liked by peers, and identity achieved (Dusek, 1987; Harter, 1998).

Ask YOURSELF...

review   In the discussion of Kohlberg's theory, why were examples of both prostealing and antistealing responses to the Heinz dilemma presented for Stages 1 through 4 but only prostealing responses for Stages 5 and 6?

apply   Tam grew up in a small village culture, Lydia in a large industrial city. At age 15, Tam reasons at Kohlberg's Stage 2, Lydia at Stage 4. What factors might account for the difference?

connect   Are environmental influences that foster identity development also likely to promote moral development, and vice versa?

reflect   Did you experience gender intensification in early adolescence? If so, how was it evident in your attitudes and behavior?

The Family

Franca and Antonio remember Louis's freshman year of high school as a difficult time. Because of a demanding project at work, Franca was away from home many evenings and weekends. Antonio took over in her absence, but when business declined at his hardware store, he, too, had less time for the family. That year, Louis and two friends used their computer know-how to crack the code of a long-distance telephone service. From the family basement, they made calls around the country. Louis's grades fell, and he often left the house without saying where he was going. Franca and Antonio began to feel uncomfortable about the long hours Louis spent in the basement and their lack of contact with him. Finally, when the telephone company traced the illegal calls to the family's phone number, Franca and Antonio knew they had cause for concern.

Development at adolescence involves striving for **autonomy** on a much higher plane than during the second year of life, when independence first became a major issue for the child. Teenagers seek to establish themselves as separate, self-governing individuals. This means relying more on oneself and less on parents for direction and guidance. It also involves carefully weighing one's own judgment and the suggestions of others to arrive at a well-reasoned course of action (Hill & Holmbeck, 1986; Steinberg & Silverberg, 1986). A major way that teenagers seek greater self-directedness is to shift away from family to peers and depart from earlier, more secure and stable patterns.

Nevertheless, parent–child relationships remain vital. And in line with ecological systems theory, effective family functioning during this period, like others, is greatly influenced by contextual factors, including the *chronosystem*, or changes in each family member's development (see Chapter 1, page 29), and family stresses and supports.

D. YOUNG-WOLFF/PHOTOEDIT

During her first summer away from her family as a foreign exchange student, this teenager will carry with her the memory of her mother's warm, supportive send-off. Adolescent autonomy is effectively achieved in the context of warm parenting that relaxes control in accord with the young person's readiness for new responsibilities.

PARENT–CHILD RELATIONSHIPS

Adolescents require freedom to experiment. Yet, as Franca and Antonio's episode with Louis reveals, they also need parental involvement and, at times, protection from danger. Think back to what we said earlier about parent–child relationships that foster academic achievement (Chapter 15), identity formation, and moral maturity. You will find a common thread. Effective parenting of adolescents strikes a *balance between connection and separation.*

Parental warmth and acceptance combined with firm (but not overly restrictive) monitoring of teenagers' activities is related to many aspects of competence—in adolescents of diverse SES and ethnic backgrounds and family structures (single-parent, two-parent, and stepparent) (Eccles et al., 1997a; Herman et al., 1997; Steinberg et al., 1994). Note that these features make up the authoritative style that was adaptive in childhood as well. The Caregiving Concerns table on page 620 summarizes practices emanating from authoritative parenting that foster adolescent cognitive and social development.

Maintaining an authoritative style with adolescents involves special challenges and adjustments. In Chapters 14 and 15, we showed that puberty brings increased parent–child conflict, for both biological and cognitive reasons. Teenagers' improved ability to reason about social relationships adds to family tensions. Perhaps you can recall a time during your own adolescence when you stopped viewing your parents as all-knowing and perfect and saw them as "just people." Once teenagers *de-idealize* their parents, they no longer bend as easily to parental authority as they did at earlier ages. The begin to regard many matters—such as cleaning their rooms and coming and going from the household—as their own personal business. Parents

autonomy
At adolescence, a sense of oneself as a separate, self-governing individual. Involves relying more on oneself and less on parents for direction and guidance and engaging in careful, well-reasoned decision making.

Caregiving Concerns

Parenting Practices That Foster Adolescent Competence

PARENTING PRACTICE	ADOLESCENT OUTCOMES
Warmth and acceptance	Promotes high self-esteem, identity exploration and achievement, prosocial behavior, more positive parent–adolescent communication.
Supervision and involvement	Promotes high self-esteem and reduced likelihood of engaging in antisocial behavior. Most effective when parents modify their supervision to fit adolescents' increasing competence.
Democratic decision making, verbal give-and-take	Promotes self-esteem and self-reliant, responsible behavior.
Firm control and consistent discipline	When accompanied by explanations and verbal give-and-take, promotes self-reliant, responsible behavior. (Firm control without explanations that lead adolescents to view parents' rules as legitimate can undermine self-reliance and responsibility.)
Information provision and skill modeling	Promotes competencies as diverse as academic achievement and effective negotiation and conflict resolution; protects against high-risk behaviors, such as sex without contraception and substance use.

Source: Holmbeck, Paikoff, & Brooks-Gunn, 1995.

continue to think of these as important social conventions—as shared concerns that permit family members to live together in harmony (Nucci, 1996; Smetana, 1995). Disagreements are harder to settle when parents and teenagers have such different perspectives.

In Chapter 2 we described the family as a *system* that must adapt to changes in its members. But when change occurs rapidly, the process of adjustment is harder. Adolescents may not be the only family members undergoing a major life transition. Many parents are in their forties and are reassessing their own lives. While teenagers face a boundless future and a wide array of choices, their parents must come to terms with the fact that their own possibilities are narrowing. In addition, parents of adolescents are often caught in a "middle-generation squeeze"—faced with competing demands of children, aging parents, and employment. As a result, they have a harder time caring for themselves.

The pressures of each generation oppose the other (Holmbeck, 1996). Parents often can't understand why the adolescent wants to skip family activities to be with peers. And teenagers fail to appreciate that parents want the family to be together as often as possible because an important stage in adult life—parenthood—will soon be over. In addition, parents and adolescents—especially early adolescents—differ sharply on the appropriate age for granting certain responsibilities and privileges, such as control over clothing, school courses, and going out with friends (Collins et al., 1997). Parents typically say that the young person is not yet ready for these signs of independence, whereas teenagers think they should have been granted long ago! Immigrant parents who place a high value on obedience to authority have great difficulty adapting to their teenagers' growing autonomy. Compared with nonimmigrant parents, they often react more strongly to adolescent disagreement. When they do, their teenagers report lower life satisfaction (Phinney & Ong, 2001).

As adolescents move closer to adulthood, the task for parents and children is not just one of separating. They must blend togetherness and independence so that parental control gradually relaxes without breaking the parent–child bond. When adolescents remain attached to parents and listen to their thoughts, feelings, and advice in a context of greater freedom, they display many positive outcomes—higher self-esteem, assertiveness, and dating competence; more advanced identity development; and greater ease of separation at the transition to college (Allen et al., 1994; Allen, Moore, & Kuperminc, 1996).

By middle to late adolescence, most parents and children achieve this more mature, mutual relationship. The mild conflict that occurs along the way facilitates adolescent identity and autonomy by helping family members learn to express and tolerate disagreement. Conflicts also inform parents of adolescents' changing needs and expectations, signaling them that adjustments in the parent–child relationship are necessary. The diminishing time teenagers spend with their families—for American youths, from 33 percent of waking hours in fifth grade to 14 percent in twelfth grade—actually has less to do with conflict than with expanding opportunities. By late adolescence, many teenagers drive, have part-time jobs, and are allowed to stay out (Larson et al., 1996). At the same time, positive parent–child interaction is on the rise.

FAMILY CIRCUMSTANCES

As Franca and Antonio's experience with Louis reminds us, difficulties at work as well as other life stresses can interfere with nurturant, involved child rearing and (in turn) with children's adjustment at any phase of development (Conger et al., 1994). However, we must keep in mind that maternal employment or a dual-earner family does not by itself reduce parental time spent with teenagers, nor is it harmful to adolescent development (Richards & Duckett, 1994). To the contrary, parents who are financially secure, invested in their work, and content with their marriages usually have fewer midlife difficulties and find it easier to grant teenagers appropriate autonomy (Seltzer & Ryff, 1994). When Franca and Antonio's work and financial stresses eased and they realized Louis's need for more support and guidance, his problems subsided.

Less than 10 percent of families with adolescents have seriously troubled relationships—chronic and escalating levels of conflict and repeated arguments over serious issues. Of these, most have difficulties that began in childhood—before the transition to adolescence. Young people who face multiple family stressors—arguing between parents, a depressed parent, an ill parent, and a hostile parent–child relationship—are at high risk for depression, antisocial behavior, and poor school performance (Forehand, Biggar, & Kotchick, 1998).

Table 16.3 summarizes family circumstances considered in earlier chapters that pose challenges for adolescents. Teenagers who develop well despite family difficulties continue to benefit from the personal and contextual factors that fostered resiliency in earlier years: an appealing, easygoing disposition; high self-esteem; a caring parent who combines warmth with high expectations; and (especially if parental supports are lacking) bonds to prosocial adults outside the family who care deeply about the adolescent's well-being (Masten & Coatsworth, 1998).

SIBLINGS

Like parent–child relationships, sibling interactions adapt to change at adolescence. As younger siblings mature and become more self-sufficient, they are no longer willing to accept as much direction from their older brothers and sisters. Consequently, teenage siblings relate to one another on a more equal footing than they did earlier. Furthermore, as teenagers become more involved in friendships and romantic relationships, they invest less time and energy in their siblings. And adolescents may not want to interact as much with siblings, who are part of

TABLE 16.3

Family Circumstances with Implications for Adolescent Adjustment

FAMILY CIRCUMSTANCE	TO REVIEW, TURN TO . . .
Type of Family	
Adoptive	Chapter 2, pages 70–72
	Chapter 12, pages 457–458
Never-married, single parent	Chapter 13, page 505
Divorced	Chapter 13, pages 505–508
Blended	Chapter 13, pages 508–510
Employed mother and dual-earner	Chapter 13, pages 510–512
Gay and lesbian	Chapter 13, pages 504–505
Family conditions	
Child maltreatment	Chapter 10, pages 399–402
	Chapter 13, pages 513–518
Economic hardship	Chapter 2, pages 77–78
Teenage childbearing	Chapter 14, pages 547–552

the family from which they are trying to establish autonomy (Furman & Buhrmester, 1992; Stocker & Dunn, 1994). As a result, sibling relationships often become less intense in adolescence, in both positive and negative feelings (Hetherington, Henderson, & Reiss, 1999).

Despite a drop in companionship, attachment between siblings, like closeness to parents, remains strong for most young people. Quality of sibling relationships is quite stable over time. Brothers and sisters who established a positive bond in early childhood are more likely to display affection and caring during the teenage years (Dunn, Slomkowski, & Beardsall, 1994). Older siblings with whom relations are positive are an important source of advice as young people face challenges in romantic relationships, schoolwork, and decisions about the future. In a study of Israeli Arab girls, a culturally prescribed role of older sister as caregiver helped teenage siblings adapt to social conditions radically different from their parents' traditional way of life. Older sisters assisted in academic and peer-relationship areas, where mothers were least helpful (Seginer, 1992).

Sibling interaction at adolescence continues to be affected by other relationships, both within and outside the family. Teenagers whose parents are warm and supportive seem to model their parents' behavior; they have more positive sibling ties (Bussell et al., 1999). And adolescents experiencing strains in peer relationships may turn to siblings. For example, when young people are having difficulty making friends, siblings can provide compensating emotional supports (East & Rook, 1992; Seginer, 1998). Adolescents without close bonds and enjoyable joint activities with either siblings or friends have more adjustment problems than do those with either positive sibling or positive friendship ties (Updegraff & Obeidallah, 1999).

Peer Relations

As adolescents spend less time with family members, peers become increasingly important. Contact between adolescents is common in all cultures, but it is especially high in industrialized societies, where young people spend most of each weekday with agemates in school. Teenagers also spend much out-of-class time together, especially in the United States. American teenagers average 18 nonschool hours a week with peers, compared to 12 hours for Japanese and 9 hours for Taiwanese adolescents (Fuligni & Stevenson, 1995). Less demanding academic standards, which lead American youths to spend far less time on schoolwork than Asian youths, account for this difference. Schoolwork fills close to one-half of waking hours among Korean adolescents, one-third among Japanese adolescents, but only one-quarter among American adolescents (Larson & Verma, 1999).

Is the large amount of time American teenagers spend together beneficial or harmful? We will see that adolescent peer relations can be both positive and negative. At their best, peers serve as crucial bridges between the family and adult social roles.

FRIENDSHIPS

When together, best friends Louis and Darryl relaxed, joked, watched TV, listened to tapes, or just talked about themselves, their classmates, and events in the wider world. During these times, the two boys felt they were understood and could fully be themselves. Adolescents report their most favorable moods when in the company of friends (Larson & Richards, 1991).

■ **CHARACTERISTICS OF ADOLESCENT FRIENDSHIPS.** The number of individuals young people call best friends declines from about four to six in early adolescence to one or two in adulthood (Hartup & Stevens, 1999). At the same time, the nature of the relationship changes. When asked to comment on the meaning of friendship, teenagers stress two characteristics. The first, and most important, is *intimacy*. Adolescents seek psychological closeness, trust, and mutual understanding from their friends—the reason that self-disclosure to friends increases steadily over the adolescent years (see Figure 16.2). Second, more than younger children, teenagers want their friends to be *loyal*—to stick up for them and not to leave them for somebody else (Buhrmester, 1996).

As frankness and faithfulness increase in friendships, teenagers get to know each other better as personalities. With age, best friends can describe one another's psychological traits with greater accuracy and completeness. Cooperation and mutual affirmation between friends rise as well—a change that may reflect greater effort and skill at preserving the relationship as well as increased sensitivity to a friend's needs and desires (Diaz & Berndt, 1982; Phillipsen, 1999). Teenagers are also less possessive of their friends than they were in childhood. They recognize that friends need a certain degree of autonomy, which they also desire for themselves (Rubin, Bukowski, & Parker, 1998).

With whom do adolescents share their innermost thoughts and feelings? Like school-age friends, adolescent friends are similar in sex, race, ethnicity, SES, personality, peer popularity, and school achievement. They are also alike in identity status, educational aspirations, political beliefs, and willingness to try drugs and engage in minor lawbreaking acts (Akers, Jones, & Coyl, 1998; Berndt & Keefe, 1995). Friendship similarity is partly due to the way the social world of adolescents is organized. Most teenagers live in neighborhoods that are segregated by income, ethnicity, and belief systems. And schools sort them through tracking. Teenagers may also choose companions like themselves to increase the supportiveness of friendship.

Nevertheless, most adolescents choose friends who differ in some ways from themselves. As they forge an identity, they grant themselves room to explore new attitudes and values within the security of a compatible relationship. African-American friends are less similar to each other in school achievement than are Caucasian-American friends. Many African-American adolescents seem to minimize academic performance in favor of identification with their ethnic group as a basis for friendship (Hamm, 2000; Tolson & Urberg, 1993).

Adolescent friendships are fairly stable and become more so with age (Degirmencioglu et al., 1998). Nevertheless, the transition to middle or junior high school brings a period of friendship change as adolescents encounter new peers and become interested in the other sex. For a time, young people are less focused on similarity and more concerned with superficial features—whether a potential friend is popular, physically attractive, or athletically skilled. Young teenagers of both sexes are attracted to aggressive boys as friends—a trend that contributes to a rise in antisocial behavior in early adolescence (Bukowski, Sippola, & Newcomb, 2000). Girls' tendency to strike up friendships with virile, aggressive boys who fit a stereotype of masculinity can lead to negative experiences in their first dating relationships. Over time, this widespread preference for friends who are prominent in the peer system subsides, and adolescents return to seeking friends whose traits, interests, and values resemble their own.

■ **SEX DIFFERENCES IN FRIENDSHIPS.** Ask several adolescent girls and boys to describe their close friendships. You are likely to find a consistent sex difference. Emotional closeness is more common in the friendships of girls than boys (Buhrmester & Prager, 1995). Whereas girls frequently get together to "just talk," boys more often gather for an activity—usually sports and competitive games that foster control, power, and excitement. When boys talk, their discussions often focus on recognition and mastery issues, such as the accomplishments of sports figures or their own attainments in sports and school (Buhrmester, 1998).

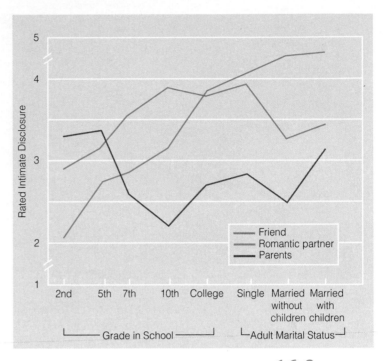

FIGURE 16.2

Age changes in reported self-disclosure to parents and peers, based on data from several studies. Self-disclosure to friends increases steadily during adolescence, reflecting intimacy as a major basis of friendship. Self-disclosure to romantic partners also rises. However, not until the college years does it surpass intimacy with friends. Self-disclosure to parents declines in early adolescence, a time of mild parent–child conflict. As family relationships readjust to the young person's increasing autonomy, self-disclosure to parents rises. (From D. Buhrmester, 1996, "Need Fulfillment, Interpersonal Competence, and the Developmental Contexts of Early Adolescent Friendship," in W. M. Bukowski, A. F. Newcomb, & W. W. Hartup, Eds., *The Company They Keep: Friendship during Childhood and Adolescence,* New York: Cambridge University Press, p. 168. Reprinted by permission of Cambridge University Press.)

CINDY CHARLES/PHOTOEDIT

During adolescence, intimacy and loyalty become defining features of friendship. Yet girls place a higher value on emotional closeness than do boys. Girls more often get together to "just talk," and they rate their friendships as higher in self-disclosure and emotional support.

Because of gender-role expectations, boys and girls seem to enter same-sex friendships with different social needs. Then their friendships nurture those needs further—girls toward communal concerns, boys toward achievement and status concerns. This does not mean that boys rarely form close friendship ties. They often do, but the quality of their friendships is more variable. The intimacy of boys' friendships is related to gender identity. Androgynous boys are just as likely as girls to form intimate same-sex ties, whereas boys who identify strongly with the traditional masculine role are less likely to do so (Jones & Dembo, 1989).

In early adolescence, young people who are either very popular or very unpopular are more likely to have other-sex friends. Boys have more other-sex friends than do girls, whose desire for closeness leads to a preference for same-sex friendships (Sippola, Bukowski, & Noll, 1997). Teenagers not accepted by their own sex sometimes look to the other sex for friendships. Among boys without same-sex friends, having an other-sex friend is associated with feelings of competence. Among girls who lack same-sex friends, other-sex friendships are linked to less positive well-being (Bukowski, Sippola, & Hoza, 1999). Perhaps these girls are especially likely to befriend boys with negative traits, such as aggression.

■ **BENEFITS OF ADOLESCENT FRIENDSHIPS.** As long as adolescent friendships are not based on attraction to antisocial behavior, they are related to many aspects of psychological health (Buhrmester, 1996). The reasons are several:

■ *Close friendships provide opportunities to explore the self and develop a deep understanding of another.* Through open, honest communication, adolescent friends become sensitive to each other's strengths and weaknesses, needs and desires. They get to know themselves and their friend especially well, a process that supports the development of self-concept, perspective taking, identity, and intimate ties beyond the family. Look again at Figure 16.2, and you will see that self-disclosure to friends precedes disclosure to romantic partners. The lengthy, often emotionally laden psychological discussions between adolescent friends appear to prepare the young person for love relationships (Savin-Williams & Berndt, 1990; Sullivan, 1953).

■ *Close friendships help young people deal with the stresses of adolescence.* Because friendship enhances sensitivity to and concern for another, it increases the likelihood of sympathy and prosocial behavior. Teenagers with supportive friendships report fewer daily hassles and more "uplifts" than do others (Kanner et al., 1987). As a result, anxiety and loneliness are reduced while self-esteem and sense of well-being are fostered.

■ *Close friendships can improve adolescents' attitudes toward school.* Close friendship ties promote good school adjustment in both middle- and low-SES students. When teenagers enjoy interacting with friends at school, perhaps they begin to view all aspects of school life more positively (Berndt & Keefe, 1995; Vandell & Hembree, 1994).

CLIQUES AND CROWDS

Friends do not just spend time in pairs. They also gather in *peer groups* (see Chapter 13), which become increasingly common during adolescence. The peer groups of the early teenage years are more tightly structured than those of middle childhood. They are organized around **cliques,** small groups of about five to seven members who are good friends and, therefore, resemble one another in family background, attitudes, and values.

clique
A small group of about five to seven members who are good friends and, therefore, resemble one another in family background, attitudes, and values.

In early adolescence, cliques are limited to same-sex members. Being in one predicts girls' academic and social competence, but not boys'. Clique membership is more important to girls, who often exchange expressions of emotional closeness and support (Henrich et al., 2000). By the mid-adolescent years, mixed-sex cliques become common. The cliques within a typical high school can be identified by their interests and social status, as the well-known "popular" and "unpopular" groups reveal (Cairns et al., 1995; Gillmore et al., 1997).

Often several cliques with similar values form a larger, more loosely organized group called a **crowd.** Unlike the more intimate clique, membership in a crowd is based on reputation and stereotype. Whereas the clique serves as the main context for direct interaction, the crowd grants the adolescent an identity within the larger social structure of the school. For example, Louis and Darryl hung out with the "studious" crowd—nonathletes who enjoy academics. Other prominent crowds include the "jocks," who are very involved in athletics; the "preppies," who have a boyfriend or girlfriend, are physically attractive, and wear brand-name clothes; the "headbangers," who use drugs, listen to heavy metal rock music, skip school, and get into fights; the "partyers," who value partying and popularity, care little about finishing high school, and are seen as troublemakers; and the "normals," average students who get along with students in most other crowds (Kinney, 1999; Stone & Brown, 1999).

What influences the assortment of teenagers into cliques and crowds? In addition to adolescent personality and interests, family factors seem to be important. In a study of 8,000 ninth to twelfth graders, adolescents who described their parents as authoritative tended to be members of "brain," "jock," and "preppie" groups that accepted both the adult and peer reward systems of the school. In contrast, boys with permissive parents valued interpersonal relationships and aligned themselves with the "partyer" crowd. And teenagers who viewed their parents as uninvolved more often affiliated with the "partyer" and "headbanger" crowds, suggesting lack of identification with adult reward systems (Durbin et al., 1993).

These findings indicate that many peer group values are extensions of ones acquired at home. But once adolescents join a clique or crowd, it can modify their beliefs and behaviors. For example, when adolescents associate with peers who have authoritative parents, their friends' competence "rubs off" on them in terms of better academic performance and lower levels of delinquency and substance abuse (Fletcher et al., 1995). However, the positive impact of having academically and socially skilled peers is greatest for teenagers whose own parents are authoritative. And the negative impact of having antisocial, drug-using friends is strongest for teenagers whose parents use less effective child-rearing styles (Mounts & Steinberg, 1995). In sum, family experiences affect the extent to which adolescents become like their peer associates over time.

In early adolescence, as interest in dating increases, boys' and girls' cliques come together. The merger takes place slowly. At junior high school dances and parties, clusters of boys and girls can be seen standing on opposite sides of the room, watching but seldom interacting. As mixed-sex cliques form and "hang out" together, they provide a supportive context for boys and girls to get to know each other. Cliques offer models for how to interact with the opposite sex and a chance to do so without having to be intimate. In addition, members can check with one another to find out if their attraction to someone is likely to be returned (Brown, 1999). Gradually, the larger group divides into couples, several of whom spend time together, going to parties and movies. By late adolescence, boys and girls feel comfortable enough about approaching each other directly that the mixed-sex clique is no longer needed and disappears (Connolly & Goldberg, 1999).

Crowds also decline in importance. As adolescents formulate their own personal values and goals, they no longer feel a strong need to broadcast, through dress, language, and preferred activities, who they are. And about half of young people switch crowds from tenth to twelfth grade, mostly in favorable directions. The "studious" and "normal" crowds grow and deviant crowds lose members as teenagers focus more on their future (Brown, Freeman, & Huang, 1992; Strouse, 1999). Strong, prosocial friendships and positive self-esteem are associated with these changes.

crowd
A large, loosely organized group consisting of several cliques. Membership is based on reputation and stereotype.

Both cliques and crowds serve vital functions. The clique provides a context for acquiring new social skills and for experimenting with values and roles. The crowd offers adolescents the security of a temporary identity as they separate from the family and construct a coherent sense of self (Stone & Brown, 1999).

DATING

Although sexual interest is affected by the hormonal changes of puberty (see Chapter 14), the beginning of dating is regulated by cultural expectations. Western societies tolerate and even encourage romantic involvements between teens, which typically begin in junior high school (Larson, Clore, & Wood, 1999). In one study, early, middle, and late adolescents were asked about their reasons for dating. Younger teenagers were more likely to say that they dated for recreation and to achieve status with agemates. In choosing a partner, they often focused on the person's external characteristics and approval by peers. By late adolescence, these factors were less important. As young people become ready for greater psychological intimacy in a dating relationship, they look for someone who shares their interests, who has clear goals for the future, and who is likely to make a good permanent partner (Roscoe, Diana, & Brooks, 1987).

Adolescent friendships, as mentioned earlier, prepare the young person for romantic bonds. Consequently, it is not surprising that the achievement of intimacy in dating relationships lags behind that in friendships. Perhaps because communication between boys and girls remains stereotyped and shallow through mid-adolescence, early dating does not foster social maturity. Instead, it is related to drug use and delinquency and poor academic achievement (Brown, Feiring, & Furman, 1999). And whereas early-adolescent boys involved in dating gain in status among their same-sex peers, girls often experience more conflicts due to competition and jealousy from other girls (Miller, 1990). Furthermore, romantic relationships often draw adolescents away from time with friends. Sticking with group activities, such as parties and dances, before becoming involved with a steady boyfriend or girlfriend is best for young teenagers.

Homosexual youths face special challenges in initiating and maintaining visible romances. Their first dating relationships seem to be short-lived and to involve little emotional commitment—but for different reasons than those of heterosexuals: They fear peer harassment and rejection. Recall from Chapter 14 that because of intense prejudice, homosexual adolescents often retreat into heterosexual dating. In addition, many have difficulty finding a same-sex partner because their homosexual peers have not yet come out. Often their first contacts with other sexual minority youths occur in support groups, where they are free to engage in dating publicly and can discuss concerns about coming out (Diamond, Savin-Williams, & Dubé, 1999). Homosexuals who have had several same-sex romances are usually "out" to peers. Yet a deep sense of isolation from the larger peer world frequently means that early dating partners place unreasonable demands on each other—for fulfilling all social needs (Savin-Williams, 1996).

As long as it does not begin too soon, dating provides adolescents with lessons in cooperation, etiquette, and dealing with people in a wide range of situations. As teenagers form a close emotional tie, sensitivity, empathy, capacity for intimacy, and identity development are enhanced (Connolly et al., 1999; Furman & Wehner, 1994). First romances usually serve as practice for later, more mature bonds. About half of heterosexual romances do not survive high school graduation and entry into college, and those that do become less satisfying over time (Shaver, Furman, & Buhrmester, 1985). Because young people are still forming their identities, those who like each other at one time often find that they have little in common later.

JEFF GREENBERG/INDEX STOCK

As long as dating does not begin too soon, it extends the benefits of adolescent friendships. Besides fun and enjoyment, dating promotes sensitivity, empathy, and identity development as teenagers relate to someone whose needs are different from their own.

PEER PRESSURE AND CONFORMITY

When Franca and Antonio discovered Louis's high school lawbreaking episode, they worried (as many parents do) about the negative side of adolescent peer networks. Conformity to peer pressure is greater during adolescence than in childhood or young adulthood—a finding that is not surprising when we consider how much time teenagers spend together. But contrary to popular belief, adolescence is not a period in which young people blindly do what their peers ask. Peer conformity is actually a complex process that varies with the adolescent's age and need for social approval and with the situation.

In one study of nearly 400 junior and senior high school students, adolescents felt greatest pressure to conform to the most obvious aspects of the peer culture—dressing and grooming like everyone else and participating in social activities, such as dating and going to parties and school dances. Peer pressure to engage in proadult behavior, such as getting good grades and cooperating with parents, was also strong. In contrast, although pressure toward misconduct rose in early adolescence, it was low. Many teenagers said that their friends actively discouraged antisocial acts. These findings reveal that peers and parents often act in concert, toward desirable ends! Finally, peer pressures correlated only modestly with teenagers' actual values and behaviors (Brown, Lohr, & McClenahan, 1986).

Perhaps because of greater concern with what their friends think of them, early adolescents are more likely than younger or older individuals to give in to peer pressure (Brown, Clasen, & Eicher, 1986). Yet when parents and peers disagree, even young teenagers do not consistently rebel against the family. Instead, parents and peers differ in their spheres of greatest influence. Parents have more impact on teenagers' basic life values and educational plans (Sebald, 1986). Peers are more influential in short-term, day-to-day matters, such as dress, music, and choice of friends. Adolescents' personal characteristics also make a difference. Young people who feel competent and worthwhile are less likely to fall in line behind peers.

Finally, authoritative parenting and resistance to unfavorable peer pressure are consistently related (Fletcher et al., 1995; Mason et al., 1996). Adolescents whose parents are supportive and exert appropriate oversight hold their parents in high regard, and this attitude of respect acts as an antidote to antisocial peer pressure (Sim, 2000). In contrast, adolescents who experience extremes of parental behavior—either too much or too little control and monitoring—tend to be highly peer oriented. They more often rely on friends for advice about their personal lives and future and are more willing to break their parents' rules, ignore their schoolwork, and hide their talents to be popular with agemates (Fuligni & Eccles, 1993).

Ask YOURSELF...

review   *What type of parenting fosters competence in adolescence? Explain why that style of parenting is effective, and cite its many positive outcomes.*

apply   *Phyllis likes her 14-year-old daughter Farrah's friends, but she wonders what Farrah gets out of hanging out at Jake's Pizza Parlor with them on Friday and Saturday evenings. Explain to Phyllis what Farrah is learning.*

connect   *How might gender intensification contribute to the shallow quality of early adolescent dating relationships?*

reflect   *To which crowd did you belong in junior high and high school? Did you change crowds? If so, why? How did family experiences influence your crowd membership?*

Problems of Development

Although most young people move through adolescence without serious difficulty, we have seen that some encounter major disruptions, such as premature parenthood, substance abuse, and school failure. Our discussion has also shown that no single factor can account for psychological and behavior problems. An ecological systems view reveals that biological and psychological change, families, schools, peers, communities, and society act together to produce a particular outcome. This theme is apparent in three additional problems of the teenage years: depression, suicide, and delinquency.

DEPRESSION

Depression—feeling sad, frustrated, and hopeless about life, accompanied by loss of pleasure in most activities and disturbances in sleep, appetite, concentration, and energy—is the most common psychological problem of adolescence. About 20 to 35 percent of American teenagers experience mild to moderate feelings of depression, bouncing back after a short time. Others display a more worrisome picture. About 15 to 20 percent have had one or more major depressive episodes (a rate comparable to that of adults). From 2 to 8 percent are chronically depressed—gloomy and self-critical for many months and sometimes years (Birmaher et al., 1996; Kessler et al., 1994).

Depression is not absent in the first decade of life; about 1 to 2 percent of children are seriously depressed, 70 to 75 percent of whom continue to display severe depression in adolescence (Kovacs et al., 1994). Yet as Figure 16.3 shows, depressive symptoms increase dramatically around the time of puberty. This change is understandable, if we stop and think about the many challenges adolescents face and their greater capacity for focusing on themselves. Depression occurs about twice as often in adolescent girls as in adolescent boys—a difference that peaks between ages 15 and 18 and persists throughout the lifespan in many industrialized nations (Hankin et al., 1998; Holsen, Kraft, & Vittersø, 2000).

Depression prevents young people from mastering important developmental tasks. Depressed teenagers' inability to imagine a worthwhile future for themselves seriously disrupts identity development (Chandler, 1994). Adolescent depression also is associated with persistent anxiety, poor school performance, drug abuse, lawbreaking, and auto accidents. Without treatment, depressed teenagers have a high likelihood of becoming depressed adults with persistent problems in employment, marriage, and child rearing (Harrington, Rutter, & Fombonne, 1996; Kovacs, 1996).

Unfortunately, depressive symptoms tend to be overlooked by parents and teachers; 70 to 80 percent of depressed teenagers do not receive any treatment. Because of the popular stereotype of adolescence as a period of storm and stress, many adults interpret depressive reactions as normal and just a passing phase. Depression is also hard to recognize in teenagers because they manifest it in a wide variety of ways. Some engage in excessive brooding, worries about their health, and restless, undirected behavior. Others act it out by running away or behaving rebelliously. The first of these patterns is more typical of girls, the second more characteristic of boys (Gjerde, 1995).

■ **FACTORS RELATED TO ADOLESCENT DEPRESSION.** Researchers believe that diverse combinations of biological and environmental factors lead to depression; the precise blend differs from one individual to the next (see Table 16.4). As we saw in Chapter 2, kinship studies reveal that heredity plays an important role. Genes can promote depression by affect-

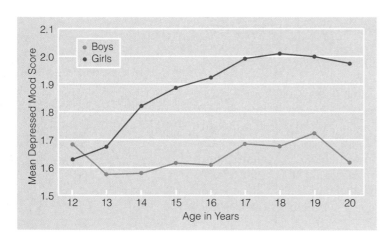

FIGURE 16.3

Change in depressive symptoms from age 12 to 20 in a cross-sectional study of more than 12,000 Norwegian adolescents. Girls showed a more rapid rise in depression around the time of puberty than did boys. Similar trends occur in other industrialized societies. (From L. Wichstrøm, 1999, "The Emergence of Gender Difference in Depressed Mood During Adolescence: The Role of Intensified Gender Socialization," *Developmental Psychology, 35,* pp. 232–245. Figure 2, p. 237. Copyright © 1999 by the American Psychological Association. Reprinted by permission of the publishers and author.)

TABLE 16.4

Factors Related to Adolescent Depression

FACTOR	DESCRIPTION
Heredity	The concordance rate for depression is higher among identical than fraternal twins. Depressed children and adolescents show a stronger resemblance to biological than adoptive relatives.
Stress	Depression is higher among teenagers who experience high levels of stress. It is also higher among adolescents who lack positive ties to parents or peers, who are dissatisfied with their school performance, and who are victims of child abuse.
Sex	In industrialized nations, the rate of depression is twice as high in girls as in boys.
Gender identity	Adolescents with a feminine gender identity are more likely to experience depression than those with a masculine or androgynous identity.
Thoughts about the self	Learned helplessness, the belief that trying hard will not improve negative life conditions, is related to depression. Identity development is often impaired, due to an inability to imagine a worthwhile future.

ing the balance of neurotransmitters in the brain, the development of brain regions involved in inhibiting negative emotion, or the body's hormonal response to stress (Cicchetti & Toth, 1998b).

But experience can also activate depression, promoting any of the biological changes just described. Parents of depressed children and adolescents have a high incidence of depression and other psychological disorders. Although a genetic risk may be passed from parent to child, in earlier chapters we saw that depressed or otherwise stressed parents often engage in maladaptive child rearing. As a result, their child's emotional self-regulation, attachment, and self-esteem may be impaired, with serious consequences for many cognitive and social skills (Garber, Braafladt, & Weiss, 1995; Garber et al., 1991).

Depressed youths usually display a learned-helpless attributional style (see Chapter 13), in which they view positive outcomes in school performance and peer relations as beyond their control. Consequently, numerous events can spark depression in a vulnerable young person—for example, failing at something important, parental divorce, the end of a close friendship or romantic partnership, or the challenges of school transition (see Chapter 14).

■ **SEX DIFFERENCES.** Why are adolescent girls more prone to depression? Biological changes associated with puberty cannot account for the gender gap, since it is limited to industrialized nations. In developing countries, rates of depression are similar for males and females and occasionally higher for males (Culbertson, 1997). Even in countries with a gender difference, its size varies considerably. For example, in a study of adolescent depression in the United States and China, the gender gap favoring females was smaller in China. Decades of efforts by the Chinese government to eliminate gender inequalities may have contributed to this finding (Greenberger et al., 2000).

Research suggests that stressful life events and gender-typed coping styles account for girls' higher rates of depression. The gender intensification girls experience in early adolescence often strengthens passivity and dependency—maladaptive approaches to the many challenges teenagers encounter in complex cultures (Nolen-Hoeksema & Girgus, 1994). Consistent with this explanation, girls more often say they feel overwhelmed when faced with problems—a response strongly linked to depression (Marcotte, Alain, & Gosselin, 1999). Furthermore, teenagers who identify with "feminine" traits are more depressed, regardless of their sex (Hart & Thompson, 1996). And girls with an androgynous or masculine gender identity show a much lower rate of depressive symptoms—one no different from that of masculine-identified boys (Wilson & Cairns, 1988).

As indicated in previous chapters, child abuse is related to severe depression, with sexual abuse having an especially powerful impact (Schraedley, Gotlib, & Hayward, 1999). Adolescent girls are more likely than boys to be sexually abused in family and dating relationships. As abuse

TONY FREEMAN/PHOTOEDIT

Depression in teenagers should not be dismissed as a temporary side effect of puberty. Because adolescent depression can lead to long-term emotional problems, it deserves to be taken seriously. Without treatment, depressed teenagers have a high likelihood of becoming depressed adults.

alters the young person's stress reactivity (see Chapter 10, page 401), victims may respond maladaptively to many stressors of daily life. In this way, feelings of helplessness can worsen.

Profound depression in adolescence predicts depression in adulthood and serious impairments in work, family life, and social life (Weissman et al., 1999). And depression often leads to suicidal thoughts, which all too often are translated into action.

▬ SUICIDE

Compared with his sister, who was an outstanding student, 17-year-old Brad just couldn't measure up. Brad's parents had been critical of his school performance for years. Now, with adulthood just around the corner, they berated him for being so undirected. "At your age, you oughta know where you're going!" Brad's father shouted one day. "Pick a college or get a trade. But for heaven's sake, stop sitting around."

Throughout high school, Brad had been a loner. Although he excelled in art class, his parents never showed much interest in his drawings, which were piled in a corner of his room. There, Brad spent hours by himself sketching. It bothered Brad's parents that he seemed unhappy and didn't have many friends. But at least he wasn't getting into much trouble like some other kids.

One day, Brad got up enough nerve to ask a girl out. His father, encouraged by Brad's interest in dating, gave him permission to use the family car. But when Brad arrived to pick the girl up, she wasn't home. Several hours later, Brad's parents got a call from the police. He had been picked up for speeding, "driving under the influence," and evading the police. The chase through city streets finally ended when Brad drove off the road into a ditch. Although he wasn't injured, the car was totaled. A terrible argument followed between Brad and his parents.

Over the next 2 days, Brad was somber and withdrawn. Then, after dinner one night, he seemed resolved to make things better. "I've taken care of things, I won't be any more trouble to you," he remarked to his parents. Handing several of his favorite drawings to his sister, he said, "Here, I want you to have these—for keeps, to think of me." Early the next morning, Brad's parents found him hanging from a rope in his room.

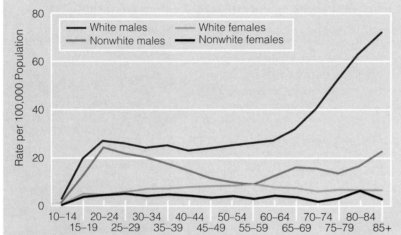

FIGURE 16.4

Suicide rates over the lifespan in the United States. Although teenagers do not commit suicide as often as adults and the aged, the suicide rate rises sharply from childhood to adolescence. Rates are greater for males than females and for white majority than nonwhite ethnic minority individuals. (From U.S. Bureau of the Census, 2000.)

■ **FACTORS RELATED TO ADOLESCENT SUICIDE.** The suicide rate increases over the lifespan. As Figure 16.4 shows, it is lowest in childhood and highest in old age, but it jumps sharply at adolescence. Currently, suicide is the third leading cause of death among young people, after motor vehicle collisions and homicides. It is a growing national problem, having tripled over the past 30 years, perhaps because modern teenagers face more stresses and have fewer supports than they did in past decades (McIntosh, 2000). The adolescent suicide rate varies widely among industrialized nations. Japan and most of Western Europe have low rates; Australia and Canada, like the United States, have intermediate rates; and Finland, New Zealand, and Estonia have high rates (Johnson, Krug, & Potter, 2000). Although many theories exist, international differences remain unexplained.

Striking sex differences in suicidal behavior exist. The number of boys who kill themselves exceeds the number of girls by 4 or 5 to 1. This may seem surprising, since girls show higher rates of depression and suicidal thoughts. Yet the findings are not inconsistent. In most industrialized nations, girls make more unsuccessful suicide attempts and use methods from which they can more likely be revived, such as a sleeping pill overdose. In contrast, boys tend to select more active techniques that lead to instant death, such as firearms or hanging. Once again, gender-role expectations may be responsible. Less tolerance exists for feelings of helplessness and failed efforts in males than females (Canetto & Sakinofsky, 1998).

Compared with the white majority, nonwhite ethnic minority teenagers (including African Americans, Hispanics, and Native Americans) have slightly lower suicide rates. Higher levels of support through extended families may be responsible. In contrast, when stress is overwhelming and social support is lacking, the suicide rate rises. Gay, lesbian, and bisexual youths are at high risk for suicide, making attempts at a rate three times higher than other adolescents. Those who have tried to kill themselves report more family conflict, inner turmoil about their sexuality, problems in romantic relationships, and peer victimization due to their sexual orientation (Hershberger, Pilkington, & D'Augelli, 1997).

Overall, suicide tends to occur in two types of young people. In the first group are adolescents much like Brad—highly intelligent but solitary, withdrawn, and unable to meet their own standards or those of important people in their lives. A second, larger group shows antisocial tendencies. These young people express their despondency through bullying, fighting, stealing, and increased risk taking and drug use (American Academy of Pediatrics, 2000; Fergusson, Woodward, & Horwood, 2000). Besides turning their anger and disappointment inward, they are hostile and destructive toward others. The fragile self-esteem of these teenagers quickly disintegrates in the face of stressful life events. Common circumstances just before a suicide include the breakup of an important peer relationship or the humiliation of having been caught engaging in irresponsible, antisocial acts.

Why is suicide rare in childhood but on the rise in adolescence? Teenagers' improved ability to plan ahead seems to be involved. Although some act impulsively, many depressed young people, such as Brad, take purposeful steps toward killing themselves (McKeown et al., 1998). Other cognitive changes contribute to the age-related increase in suicide. Belief in the personal fable leads many depressed young people to conclude that no one could possibly understand the intense pain they feel. As a result, their despair, hopelessness, and isolation deepen. Warning signs of suicide are listed in Table 16.5.

TABLE 16.5

Warning Signs of Suicide

Efforts to put personal affairs in order—smoothing over troubled relationships, giving away treasured possessions

Verbal cues—saying goodbye to family members and friends, making direct or indirect references to suicide ("I won't have to worry about these problems much longer"; "I wish I were dead"; "I wonder what dying is like")

Feelings of sadness, despondency, "not caring" anymore

Extreme fatigue, lack of energy, and boredom

No desire to socialize; withdrawal from friends

Easily frustrated

Emotional outbursts—spells of crying or laughing; bursts of energy

Inability to concentrate, distractible

Decline in grades, absence from school, discipline problems, running away

Neglect of personal appearance

Often gets drunk, uses marijuana daily

Sleep change—loss of sleep or excessive sleepiness

Appetite change—eating more or less than usual

Physical complaints—stomachaches, backaches, headaches

Sources: American Academy of Pediatrics, 2000; Capuzzi, 1989.

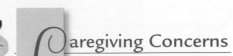

Caregiving Concerns

Ways to Respond to a Young Person Who Might Be Suicidal

STRATEGY	DESCRIPTION
Be psychologically and physically available.	Grant the young person your full attention; indicate when and where you can be located, and emphasize that you are always willing to talk.
Communicate a caring, capable attitude.	Such statements as "I'm concerned. I care about you" encourage the adolescent to discuss feelings of despair. Conveying a capable attitude helps redirect the young person's world of confusion toward psychological order.
Assess the immediacy of risk.	Gently inquire into the young person's motives with such questions as "Do you want to harm yourself? Do you want to die or kill yourself?" If the answer is yes, ask about the adolescent's plan. If it is specific (involves a method and a time), the risk of suicide is very high.
Empathize with the young person's feelings.	Empathy, through such statements as "I understand your confusion and pain," increases your persuasive power and defuses the adolescent's negative emotion.
Oppose the suicidal intent.	Communicate sensitively but firmly that suicide is not an acceptable solution and that you want to help the adolescent explore other options.
Offer a plan for help.	Offer to assist the young person in finding professional help and in telling others, such as parents and school officials, who need to know about the problem.
Obtain a commitment.	Ask the adolescent to agree to the plan. If he or she refuses, negotiate a promise to contact you or another supportive person if and when suicidal thoughts return.

Source: Kirk, 1993.

■ **PREVENTION AND TREATMENT.** Picking up on the signals that a troubled teenager sends is a crucial first step in suicide prevention. Parents and teachers must be trained in warning signs. Schools can help by providing sympathetic counselors, peer support groups, and information about telephone hot lines. Once a teenager takes steps toward suicide, staying with the young person, listening, and expressing sympathy and concern until professional help can be obtained is essential. The Caregiving Concerns table above suggests ways to respond to a young person who might be suicidal.

Intervention with depressed and suicidal adolescents takes many forms, from antidepressant medication to individual, family, and group therapy. Sometimes hospitalization is necessary to ensure the teenager's safety and swift entry into treatment. Until the adolescent improves, parents are usually advised to remove weapons, knives, razors, scissors, and drugs from the home. On a broader scale, gun control legislation that limits adolescents' access to the most frequent and deadly suicide method in the United States would greatly reduce both the number of suicides and the high teenage homicide rate.

After a suicide, family and peer survivors need support to assist them in coping with grief, anger, and guilt over not having been able to help the victim. Teenage suicides often take place in clusters. When one occurs, it increases the likelihood of others among depressed peers who knew the young person or heard about the death through the media (Grossman & Kruesi, 2000). In view of this trend, an especially watchful eye must be kept on vulnerable adolescents after a suicide happens. Restraint by journalists in reporting teenage suicides on television or in newspapers can also aid in prevention.

DELINQUENCY

Juvenile delinquents are children or adolescents who engage in illegal acts. Although youth crime in the United States has declined over the past decade, young people under the age of 21 continue to account for a large proportion of police arrests—about 30 percent (U.S.

Department of Justice, 2000). Yet when teenagers are asked directly, and confidentially, about lawbreaking, almost all admit that they are guilty of an offense of one sort or another (Farrington, 1987). Most of the time, they do not commit major crimes. Instead, they engage in petty stealing, disorderly conduct, and acts that are illegal only for minors, such as underage drinking, violating curfews, and running away from home.

Both police arrests and self-reports show that delinquency rises over the early teenage years, remains high during middle adolescence, and then diminishes into young adulthood. What is responsible for this trend? Recall that the desire for peer approval increases antisocial behavior among young teenagers. Over time, peers become less influential, moral reasoning improves, and young people enter social contexts (such as marriage, work, and career) that are less conducive to lawbreaking.

For most adolescents, a brush with the law does not forecast long-term antisocial behavior. But repeated arrests are cause for concern. Teenagers are responsible for 27 percent of violent crimes (homicide, rape, robbery, and assault) and 42 percent of property crimes (burglary and theft) (U.S. Department of Justice, 2000). A small percentage commit most of them, developing into recurrent offenders. Some enter a life of crime. As the Biology and Environment box on pages 634–635 reveals, childhood-onset conduct problems are far more likely to persist than are conduct problems that emerge during the teenage years.

■ **FACTORS RELATED TO DELINQUENCY.** Many personal and contextual factors are related to chronic delinquency. Depending on the estimate, about 3 to 8 times as many boys as girls commit major crimes. Although SES and ethnicity are strong predictors of arrests, they are only mildly related to teenagers' self-reports of antisocial acts. This is probably due to biases in the juvenile justice system—in particular, the tendency to arrest, charge, and punish low-SES, ethnic minority youths more often than their higher-SES white and Asian counterparts (Elliott, 1994).

Difficult temperament, low intelligence, poor school performance, peer rejection in childhood, and association with antisocial peers are linked to delinquency. How do these factors fit together? Think back to what you learned about the development of cognitive and social competence in earlier chapters. One of the most consistent findings about delinquent youths is that their families are low in warmth, high in conflict, and characterized by inconsistent discipline and low monitoring (Borduin & Schaefer, 1998). Because parental divorce and remarriage often lead to these conditions, adolescent boys who experience family transitions are especially prone to delinquency (Pagani et al., 1998, 1999). Youth crime peaks on weekdays between 2 and 8 o'clock, when many teenagers are unsupervised (U.S. Department of Justice, 2000).

Return for a moment to our discussion of the development of aggression on pages 386–387 of Chapter 10. It explains how ineffective parenting can promote and sustain hostile responding in all family members. Boys are more likely than girls to be targets of angry, inconsistent discipline because they are more active and impulsive and therefore harder to control. When children extreme in these characteristics are exposed to inept parenting, aggression rises during childhood, is transformed into criminality by adolescence, and persists into adulthood (refer again to the Biology and Environment box on pages 634–635).

Bonds with antisocial friends sustain delinquent behavior while providing relief from loneliness. Nevertheless, compared to youths with conventional friends, adolescents with deviant friends are more depressed—an outcome of their history of unfavorable family, school, and peer experiences and, perhaps, the conflict-ridden nature of their friendships (Brendgen, Vitaro, & Bukowski, 1998). Delinquent youths seem to stick with these friends to protect against social isolation and to bolster their fragile self-esteem. Indeed, many aggressive youths report overly high self-esteem. Despite their academic and social failings, they commonly believe they are competent and superior. When their arrogant, cocky behavior prompts others to challenge their inflated self-image, they react with anger and lash out (Baumeister, Smart, & Boden, 1996).

JIM SMITH/PHOTO RESEARCHERS, INC.

Most of the time, juvenile delinquency involves petty stealing, disorderly conduct, and acts that are illegal only for minors, such as underage drinking. Usually two or more peer commit these acts together. In early adolescence, the desire for peer approval increases antisocial behavior among young people.

Biology & ENVIRONMENT

TWO ROUTES TO ADOLESCENT DELINQUENCY

Persistent adolescent delinquency follows two paths of development, one with an onset of conduct problems in childhood, the second with an onset in adolescence. Longitudinal research reveals that the early-onset type is far more likely to lead to a life-course pattern of aggression and criminality. The late-onset type usually does not persist beyond the transition to young adulthood (Loeber & Stouthamer-Loeber, 1998).

Childhood-onset and adolescent-onset youths show comparable levels of serious offenses, involvement with deviant peers, substance abuse, unsafe sex, dangerous driving, and time spent in correctional facilities. Why does antisocial activity more often persist and escalate into lethal violence—including school and neighborhood knifings and shootings—in the first group than in the second? Longitudinal research extending from childhood into early adulthood sheds light on this question.

So far, investigators have focused only on boys because of their greater involvement in delinquent activity. Yet preliminary evidence suggests that girls who were aggressive in childhood are also at risk for adolescent and adult problems, including criminality and diverse psychiatric disorders (Wangby, Bergman, & Magnesson, 1999).

EARLY-ONSET TYPE

A difficult temperament distinguishes violence-prone boys; they are emotionally negative, restless, and willful as early as age 3. In addition, they show subtle deficits in cognitive functioning that seem to contribute to disruptions in the development of language, memory, and cognitive and emotional self-regulation (Loeber et al., 1999; Moffitt et al., 1996). Some have attention-deficit hyperactivity disorder (ADHD), which compounds their learning and self-control problems (see Chapter 12, page 446) (White et al., 1996).

Yet these biological risks are not sufficient to sustain antisocial behavior, since about half of early-onset boys do not display serious delinquency followed by adult criminality. Among those who follow the life-course path, inept parenting transforms their undercontrolled style into hostility and defiance. As they fail academically and are rejected by peers, they befriend other deviant youths, who provide the attitudes and motivations for violent behavior (see Figure 16.5). Compared with their adolescent-onset counterparts, early-onset teenagers feel distant from their families and leave school early (Moffitt et al., 1996). Their limited cognitive and social skills result in high rates of unemployment, contributing further to their antisocial involvements. Often these boys experience their first arrest before age 14—a strong predictor of becoming a chronic offender by age 18 (Patterson et al., 1998).

LATE-ONSET TYPE

A larger number of youths begin to display antisocial behavior around the time of puberty. Their conduct problems arise from the peer context of early adolescence, not from biological deficits and a history of unfavorable

---

Factors beyond the family and peer group also contribute to delinquency. Students enrolled in schools that fail to meet their developmental needs—those with large classes, poor-quality instruction, and rigid rules—show higher rates of lawbreaking, even after other influences are controlled (Hawkins & Lam, 1987). And in poverty-stricken neighborhoods with fragmented community ties and adult criminal subcultures, teenagers have few constructive alternatives to antisocial behavior (Pagani et al., 1999). Youth gangs often originate in these environments.

■ **PREVENTION AND TREATMENT.** Because delinquency often has roots in childhood and results from events in several contexts, prevention must start early and take place at multiple levels. Authoritative parenting, high-quality teaching in schools, and communities with healthy economic and social conditions would go a long way toward reducing adolescent criminality.

Treating serious offenders also requires an approach that recognizes the multiple determinants of delinquency. When interventions address only one aspect, they generally are ineffective. So far as possible, adolescents are best kept in their own homes and communities to

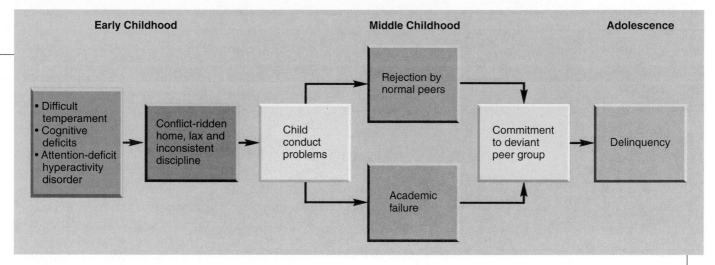

FIGURE 16.5

Developmental path to chronic delinquency for adolescents with childhood-onset antisocial behavior. Difficult temperament and deficits in cognitive functioning characterize many of these youths in early childhood; some have attention-deficit hyperactivity disorder. But these risks are not sufficient to sustain antisocial behavior. Instead, inept parenting transforms biologically based self-control difficulties into hostility and defiance. (Adapted from Patterson, DeBaryshe, & Ramsey, 1989.)

development (Moffitt, Lynam, & Silva, 1994). For some, quality of parenting may decline for a time, perhaps due to family stresses or the challenges of disciplining an unruly teenager. When age brings gratifying adult privileges, these young people draw on prosocial skills mastered before adolescence and give up their antisocial ways (Moffitt et al., 1996).

A few late-onset youths, however, continue to engage in antisocial acts.

The seriousness of their adolescent offenses seems to act as a "snare," trapping them in situations that rule out opportunities for responsible behavior. In one study, finding a steady, well-paying job and entering a happy marriage led to a large reduction in repeat offending. One former delinquent commented, "I worked steadily to support [my family] and take care of my responsibilities. I never had any time to get into trouble." In

contrast, the longer antisocial young people spent in prison, the more likely they were to sustain a life of crime (Sampson & Laub, 1993).

These findings suggest a need for a fresh look at policies aimed at stopping youth crime. Keeping adolescent and young adult offenders locked up for many years disrupts their vocational and marital lives during a crucial period of development, committing them to a future that is bleak.

increase the possibility that treatment changes will transfer to their daily lives. Many treatment models exist, including individual therapies, halfway houses, day treatment centers, special classrooms, work experience programs, and summer camps. However, delinquents who engage in serious, violent crimes usually must be removed from the community and placed in a correctional facility. Regardless of where treatment takes place, approaches that work best are lengthy and intensive and use problem-focused methods that teach cognitive and social skills needed to overcome family, peer, and school difficulties (Wasserman & Miller, 1998).

In one program, called EQUIP, *positive peer culture*—an adult-guided but youth-conducted small-group approach designed to create a climate in which prosocial acts replace antisocial behavior—served as the basis for treatment. By themselves, peer culture groups do not reduce antisocial behavior and, in one study, they increased it (Guerra, Attar, & Weissberg, 1997). But in EQUIP, the approach was supplemented with social skills training, anger management training, training to correct cognitive distortions (such as misperceiving others' intent as hostile and blaming the victim), and moral discussions to promote "catch-up" to age-appropriate moral reasoning (Gibbs, Potter, & Goldstein, 1995). Delinquents who participated in EQUIP displayed improved social skills and conduct within the institution relative to controls receiving no intervention. One year after their release, EQUIP youths were far less likely to have committed another crime (Leeman, Gibbs, & Fuller, 1993).

Yet even multidimensional treatments can fall short if adolescents remain embedded in hostile home lives, antisocial peer groups, and violent neighborhood settings. Intensive efforts to create nonaggressive environments—at the family, community, and cultural levels—are needed to support interventions for delinquent youths and to foster healthy development for all young people.

At the Threshold

Because some of the most complex and rapid changes of development take place during adolescence, teenagers are vulnerable to certain problems, but most do not show serious depression, suicidal tendencies, or persistent antisocial behavior. As we look back on the demands and expectations, the dangers and temptations of the adolescent period, the strength and vitality of young people are all the more remarkable.

We have seen that teenagers in industrialized nations confront challenges that are far more numerous and complex than those of adolescents in other cultures and at previous times during history. On a daily basis, young people must decide how vigorously to apply themselves in school, what kinds of friends to make, and whether to adopt risky behaviors, such as premarital sex and drug experimentation. These short-term choices can have a major impact on long-term options—length and type of formal education, vocational direction, and values and moral ideals. Yet as influential as the teenage years are, they occur within the context of an overall life course. Children enter adolescence having been shaped by heredity and a multitude of prior experiences. The paths adolescents choose and the contexts that affect their choices, in turn, influence many aspects of their future lives.

Society has good reason to treasure its youth as a rich national resource. Adolescents' ability to think seriously and deeply about possibilities, to commit themselves to idealistic causes, to be loyal to one another, and to experiment and take risks, while sometimes hazardous to themselves, energizes progress. Each new generation arrives at the threshold of adulthood with the capacity to benefit from the past while charting new, more fruitful directions. As individuals, as communities, and as a nation, we can do much to enhance adolescence as a final period of preparation for adulthood and a gateway to a better life for all. As we invest in the next generation, we invest in ourselves and the future of humankind. To our youth, we will entrust the task of taking care of us and our world.

Ask YOURExSELF...

review   Why are adolescent girls at greater risk for depression and adolescent boys at greater risk for suicide?

apply   Throughout his school years, Mac had difficulty learning, was disobedient, and picked fights with peers. At age 16 he was arrested for burglary. Zeke had been a well-behaved child in elementary school, but around age 13 he started spending time with the "wrong crowd." At age 16, he was arrested for property damage. Which boy is more likely to become a long-term offender, and why?

connect   Return to Chapter 14 and reread the sections on teenage pregnancy and substance abuse. What factors do these problems have in common with adolescent suicide and delinquency? How would you explain the finding that teenagers who experience one of these difficulties are likely to display others?

Summary

ERIKSON'S THEORY: IDENTITY VERSUS IDENTITY CONFUSION

According to Erikson, what is the major personality achievement of adolescence?

■ Erikson's theory emphasizes **identity** as the major personality achievement of adolescence. Young people who successfully resolve the psychological conflict of **identity versus identity confusion** construct a solid self-definition consisting of self-chosen values and goals.

SELF-DEVELOPMENT

Describe changes in self-concept and self-esteem during adolescence.

■ Adolescents' capacity for abstract thinking leads their self-descriptions to become more organized and consistent, and personal and moral values appear as key themes. New dimensions of self-esteem are also added.

■ For most adolescents, self-esteem rises, although it continues to be profoundly affected by feedback from others. Young people vary greatly in their profiles of self-esteem. Feeling much better about peer relations than other areas or feeling poorly about all areas is linked to adjustment difficulties. Parental warmth, approval, and appropriate expectations support self-esteem, as do schools and neighborhoods where the young person's SES or ethnic group is well represented.

Describe the four identity statuses, along with factors that promote identity development.

■ In complex societies, a period of exploration is necessary to form a personally meaningful identity. **Identity achievement** and **moratorium** are psychologically healthy identity statuses. Long-term **identity foreclosure** (commitment without exploration) and **identity diffusion** (absence of clear direction) are related to adjustment difficulties.

■ Adolescents who have a flexible, open-minded approach to grappling with competing beliefs and values and who feel attached to parents but free to voice their own opinions are likely to be advanced in identity development. Close friends support young people as they explore options. Schools and communities that provide young people of all backgrounds with rich and varied opportunities for exploration also foster identity achievement. Ethnic minority youths who construct a **bicultural identity** are advantaged in many aspects of emotional and social development.

MORAL DEVELOPMENT

Describe Piaget's theory of moral development, and evaluate its accuracy.

■ Piaget identified two broad stages of moral understanding: (1) **heteronomous morality,** in which moral rules are viewed as fixed dictates of authority figures; and (2) **autonomous morality,** in which rules are seen as flexible, socially agreed-on principles. Although Piaget's theory describes the general direction of moral development, it underestimates young children's moral capacities.

Describe Kohlberg's extension of Piaget's theory, and evaluate its accuracy.

■ According to Kohlberg, moral development is a gradual process that extends beyond childhood into adolescence and adulthood. By examining responses to moral dilemmas, Kohlberg found that moral reasoning advances through three levels, each of which contains two stages: (1) the **preconventional level,** in which morality is viewed as controlled by rewards, punishments, and the power of authority figures; (2) the **conventional level,** in which conformity to laws and rules is regarded as necessary to preserve positive human relationships and societal order; and (3) the **postconventional level,** in which individuals define morality in terms of abstract, universal principles of justice.

■ In focusing on hypothetical moral dilemmas, Kohlberg's theory emphasizes rational weighing of alternatives and overlooks other strategies that affect moral judgment. Because situational factors affect moral reasoning, Kohlberg's account of moral development is best viewed as a series of overlapping phases.

Evaluate claims that Kohlberg's theory does not adequately represent the morality of females.

■ Although Kohlberg's theory does not underestimate the moral maturity of females, it emphasizes justice rather than caring as a moral ideal. In resolving real-life moral dilemmas, females tend to stress care, whereas males stress justice or use justice and care equally.

Describe influences on moral reasoning and the relationship of moral reasoning to behavior.

■ A flexible, open-minded approach to new information and experiences is linked to gains in moral reasoning. Among experiences that contribute to moral maturity are warm, rational child-rearing practices, years of schooling, and peer discussion of moral issues. Young people in industrialized nations advance to higher levels of moral understanding than do those in village societies.

■ Kohlberg's theory does not fully capture moral understanding in collectivist cultures. This finding raises the question of whether his highest stages represent a culturally specific rather than universal way of thinking.

■ As individuals advance to higher stages, moral reasoning and behavior come closer together. Higher-stage reasoning is related to positive social behavior.

GENDER TYPING IN ADOLESCENCE

Why is early adolescence a period of gender intensification?

■ **Gender intensification** occurs in early adolescence for several reasons. Physical and cognitive changes prompt young teenagers to view themselves in gender-linked ways, and gender-typed pressures from parents and peers increase. Teenagers who eventually build an androgynous gender identity show better psychological adjustment.

THE FAMILY

Discuss changes in parent–child relationships during adolescence.

■ Effective parenting of adolescents strikes a balance between connection and separation.

Summary (continued)

Maintaining an authoritative style and adapting family interaction to meet adolescents' need for **autonomy** is especially challenging. As teenagers de-idealize their parents, they often question parental authority. Furthermore, many parents of adolescents are caught in a "middle-generation squeeze" and are undergoing major life transitions themselves.

■ Family circumstances continue to influence parent–child relationships during adolescence. Parents who are financially secure, invested in their work, and content with their marriages usually find it easier to grant teenagers support, guidance, and appropriate autonomy. When parents and adolescents have seriously troubled relationships, the difficulties usually began in childhood.

How do sibling relationships change during adolescence?

■ Sibling relationships become less intense as adolescents separate from the family and turn toward peers. Still, attachment to siblings remains strong for most young people. Teenagers whose parents are warm and supportive have more positive sibling ties. When young people have difficulty making friends, siblings can provide compensating emotional supports.

PEER RELATIONS

Describe adolescent friendships and their consequences for development.

■ Teenagers in industrialized nations spend many hours in the company of agemates. The nature of friendship changes, toward greater intimacy and loyalty. Adolescents resemble their friends in many ways. Although early adolescence is a period of friendship change, teenagers' friendships are fairly stable and become more so with age.

■ Girls' friendships place greater emphasis on intimate sharing, boys' on joint activities that foster control, power, and excitement. Among boys without same-sex friends, other-sex friendships are linked to feelings of competence. Among girls who lack same-sex friends, other-sex friendships are associated with less positive well-being.

■ As long as they are not based on attraction to antisocial behavior, adolescent friendships promote self-concept, perspective taking, identity, and the capacity for romantic involvements. They also help young people deal with the stresses of adolescence and can foster improved attitudes toward school.

Describe peer groups and dating relationships in adolescence.

■ Adolescent peer groups are organized around **cliques,** small groups of friends with common interests, dress styles, and behavior. Often several cliques form a larger, more loosely organized group called a **crowd** that grants the adolescent an identity within the larger social structure of the school. Parenting practices affect teenagers' choice of peer groups and the impact of group membership on their beliefs and behavior.

■ Mixed-sex cliques provide a supportive context for boys and girls to acquire social skills and get to know one another. Intimacy in dating relationships lags behind that in friendships. First romances serve as practice for later, more mature bonds. They generally dissolve or become less satisfying after graduation from high school. Because of intense prejudice, initiating and maintaining visible romances is especially challenging for homosexual youths.

Discuss conformity to peer pressure in adolescence.

■ Peer conformity is greater during adolescence than at younger or older ages. Young teenagers are more likely than older teenagers to give in to peer pressure for antisocial behavior. At the same time, few peer pressures are in conflict with important adult values. Peers have the greatest influence on short-term, day-to-day matters. Adults have more impact on long-term values and educational plans. Authoritative parenting is related to resistance to unfavorable peer pressure.

PROBLEMS OF DEVELOPMENT

What factors are related to adolescent depression and suicide?

■ Depression is the most common psychological problem of the teenage years. Adolescents who are severely depressed are likely to remain so as adults. Diverse combinations of biological and environmental factors lead to depression. Heredity contributes to depression, but maladaptive parenting and stressful life events of the teenage years may trigger it. Severe depression occurs twice as often in teenage girls as boys, a difference believed to be due to stressful life events and gender-typed coping styles.

■ Profound depression in adolescence predicts depression in adulthood, and it often leads to suicidal thoughts. The suicide rate increases dramatically at adolescence. Boys account for most suicides because their efforts usually succeed. Girls make more unsuccessful attempts. Whereas American nonwhite ethnic minority teenagers have slightly lower suicide rates, gay, lesbian, and bisexual youths are at high risk. Teenagers who try to commit suicide are sometimes solitary and withdrawn; more often, they are antisocial youths who react intensely to loss, failure, or humiliation.

Discuss factors related to delinquency.

■ Almost all teenagers become involved in some delinquent activity, but only a few are serious repeat offenders. Many more boys than girls commit major crimes.

■ Childhood-onset conduct problems are linked to difficult temperament, cognitive deficits, and inept parenting—a pattern likely to result in peer rejection, academic failure, association with antisocial peers, and persistent delinquency and criminality. Adolescent-onset antisocial behavior typically arises from peer pressures of the teenage years. It usually subsides by young adulthood.

■ Factors beyond the family and peer group contribute to delinquency. Schools that fail to meet adolescents' developmental needs and poverty-stricken neighborhoods with high crime rates and few constructive alternatives to antisocial activity promote adolescent lawbreaking.

Important terms and concepts

autonomous morality (p. 608)
autonomy (p. 619)
bicultural identity (p. 607)
clique (p. 624)
conventional level (p. 611)
crowd (p. 625)

ethnic identity (p. 607)
gender intensification (p. 616)
heteronomous morality (p. 608)
identity (p. 600)
identity achievement (p. 603)
identity diffusion (p. 603)

identity foreclosure (p. 603)
identity versus identity confusion
  (p. 600)
moratorium (p. 603)
postconventional level (p. 611)
preconventional level (p. 610)

fyi . . . for further information and help

Consult the companion website for this book, where you will find additional weblinks and associated learning activities:
www.ablongman.com/berk

SUICIDE

American Association of Suicidology
www.suicidology.org

Promotes research, public awareness, education, and training for professionals and volunteers on suicide and suicide prevention. Serves as a national clearinghouse for information on suicide.

American Foundation for Suicide Prevention
www.afsp.org

Supports research and education on suicide and suicide prevention. Includes a special section on youth suicide.

DELINQUENCY

Center for Youth as Resources
www.yar.org

A community-based program that provides small grants to young people to design and carry out service projects that contribute to community improvement. Adolescents in classrooms, neighborhood centers, youth organizations, and clubs tackle such social issues as health, housing, illiteracy, drug abuse, and crime.

National Crime Prevention Council
www.ncpc.org

An organization that aims to create safer, more caring communities by addressing the causes of crime and violence and reducing opportunities for crime to occur. A special focus is educating youth in crime prevention.

Milestones of development in adolescence

AGE	PHYSICAL	COGNITIVE	LANGUAGE	EMOTIONAL/SOCIAL
11–14 years	■ If a girl, reaches peak of growth spurt. (529) ■ If a girl, adds more body fat than muscle. (529) ■ If a girl, starts to menstruate. (530) ■ If a boy, begins growth spurt. (530) ■ If a boy, starts to ejaculate seminal fluid. (531) ■ Likely to become aware of sexual orientation. (544–546) ■ If a girl, motor performance gradually increases and then levels off. (555)	■ Becomes capable of formal operational reasoning. (562–563) ■ Becomes better at coordinating theory with evidence. (566–567) ■ Can argue more effectively. (570) ■ Becomes more self-conscious and self-focused. (570–571) ■ Becomes more idealistic and critical. (571) ■ Metacognition and cognitive self-regulation continue to improve. (567, 572) ■ Evaluates vocational options in terms of interests. (573)	■ Vocabulary continues to increase as abstract words are added. (575) ■ Grasps irony, sarcasm, and figurative language, such as proverbs. (576) ■ Understanding and use of complex grammatical constructions continue to improve. (576) ■ Can make subtle adjustments in speech style, depending on the situation. (576)	■ Moodiness and parent–child conflict increase. (536–537) ■ Is likely to show increased gender stereotyping of attitudes and behavior. (616–618) ■ As strives for autonomy, spends less time with parents and siblings. (621) ■ Spends more time with peers. (622) ■ Friendships are based on intimacy and loyalty. (622–623) ■ Peer groups become organized around cliques. (624) ■ Cliques with similar values form crowds. (625) ■ Conformity to peer pressure increases. (627)

AGE	PHYSICAL	COGNITIVE	LANGUAGE	EMOTIONAL/SOCIAL
Middle adolescence 14–18 years Late adolescence 18–21 years	■ If a girl, completes growth spurt. (529) ■ If a boy, reaches peak and then completes growth spurt. (529) ■ If a boy, voice deepens. (531) ■ If a boy, adds muscle while body fat declines. (529) ■ May have had sexual intercourse. (543) ■ If a boy, motor performance increases dramatically. (556) 	■ Is likely to show formal operational reasoning on familiar tasks. (565) ■ Displays relativistic reasoning in familiar situations. (569) ■ Masters the components of formal operational reasoning in sequential order on different types of tasks. (568) ■ Becomes less self-conscious and self-focused. (571) ■ Becomes better at everyday planning and decision making. (572) ■ Evaluates vocational options in terms of interests, abilities, and values. (588–594)	■ Can read and interpret adult literary works. (576) 	■ Combines features of the self into an organized self-concept. (601) ■ Self-esteem differentiates further. (602) ■ Self-esteem tends to rise. (602–603) ■ Is likely to be searching for an identity. (603) ■ Is likely to engage in societal perspective taking. (492, 610) ■ Is likely to have a conventional moral orientation. (611) ■ Gender stereotyping may decline. (618) ■ Has probably started dating. (626) ■ Conformity to peer pressure may decline. (627)
	■ If a boy, gains in motor performance continue. (555–556)	■ If goes to college, develops relativistic reasoning in a wide range of situations. (569) ■ Narrows vocational options and settles on a specific occupation. (592)		■ Is likely to be identity achieved. (603) ■ May develop a postconventional moral orientation. (611) ■ Cliques and crowds decline in importance. (624–625) ■ Is likely to move away from home.

Note: Numbers in parentheses indicate the page(s) on which each milestone is discussed.

Glossary

academic preschool
A preschool in which teachers structure the program, training children in academic skills through repetition and drill. Distinguished from *child-centered preschool*.

accommodation
That part of adaptation in which new schemes are created and old ones adjusted to produce a better fit with the environment. Distinguished from *assimilation*.

acquired immune deficiency syndrome (AIDS)
A relatively new viral infection that destroys the immune system and is spread through transfer of body fluids from one person to another. It can be transmitted prenatally.

adaptation
In Piaget's theory, the process of building schemes through direct interaction with the environment. Made up of two complementary processes: assimilation and accommodation.

adolescent initiation ceremony
A ritual, or rite of passage, announcing to the community that a young person is making the transition into adolescence or full adulthood.

affordances
The action possibilities a situation offers an organism with certain motor capabilities. Discovering affordances plays a major role in perceptual differentiation.

age of viability
The age at which the fetus can first survive if born early. Occurs sometime between 22 and 26 weeks.

allele
Each of two forms of a gene located at the same place on the autosomes.

amnion
The inner membrane that forms a protective covering around the prenatal organism.

amniotic fluid
The fluid that fills the amnion, helping to keep temperature constant and to provide a cushion against jolts caused by the mother's movement.

analgesic
A mild pain-relieving drug.

androgyny
A type of gender identity in which the person scores high on both traditionally masculine and traditionally feminine personality characteristics.

anesthetic
A strong painkilling drug that blocks sensation.

animistic thinking
The belief that inanimate objects have life-like qualities, such as thoughts, wishes, feelings, and intentions.

anorexia nervosa
An eating disorder in which individuals (usually females) starve themselves because of a compulsive fear of getting fat and an extremely distorted body image

A-not-B search error
The error made by 8- to 12-month-olds after an object is moved from hiding place A to hiding place B. Infants in Piaget's Substage 4 search for it only in the first hiding place (A).

anoxia
Inadequate oxygen supply.

Apgar Scale
A rating used to assess the newborn baby's physical condition immediately after birth.

applied behavior analysis
Procedures that combine reinforcement and modeling to eliminate undesirable behaviors and increase desirable responses.

assimilation
That part of adaptation in which the external world is interpreted in terms of current schemes. Distinguished from *accommodation*.

associative play
A form of true social participation, in which children are engaged in separate activities, but they interact by exchanging toys and commenting on one another's behavior. Distinguished from *nonsocial activity, parallel play*, and *cooperative play*.

asthma
An illness in which, in response to a variety of stimuli, highly sensitive bronchial tubes fill with mucus and contract, leading to episodes of coughing, wheezing, and serious breathing difficulties.

attachment
The strong, affectional tie that humans feel toward special people in their lives.

Attachment Q-Sort
An efficient method for assessing the quality of the attachment bond, in which a parent or an expert informant sorts a set of 90 descriptors of attachment-related behaviors on the basis of how well they describe the child. A score is then computed that assigns children to securely or insecurely attached groups.

attention-deficit hyperactivity disorder (ADHD)
A childhood disorder involving inattentiveness, impulsivity, and excessive motor activity. Often leads to academic failure and social problems.

attribution retraining
An intervention that encourages learned-helpless children to believe that they can overcome failure by exerting more effort.

attributions
Common, everyday explanations for the causes of behavior.

authoritarian style
A child-rearing style that is demanding but low in responsiveness to children's rights and needs. Conformity and obedience are valued over open communication with the child. Distinguished from *authoritative, permissive,* and *uninvolved styles.*

authoritative style
A child-rearing style that is demanding and responsive. A rational, democratic approach in which parents' and children's rights are respected. Distinguished from *authoritarian, permissive,* and *uninvolved styles.*

autobiographical memory
Representations of special, one-time events that are long lasting because they are imbued with personal meaning.

autonomous morality
Piaget's second stage of moral development, in which children view rules as flexible, socially agreed-on principles that can be revised when there is a need to do so. Begins around age 10.

autonomy
At adolescence, a sense of oneself as a separate self-governing individual. Involves relying more on oneself and less on parents for direction and guidance and engaging in careful, well-reasoned decision making.

autonomy versus shame and doubt
In Erikson's theory, the psychological conflict of toddlerhood, which is resolved positively if parents provide young children with suitable guidance and reasonable choices.

autosomes
The 22 matching chromosome pairs in each human cell.

avoidant attachment
The quality of insecure attachment characterizing infants who usually are not distressed by parental separation and who avoid the parent when she returns. Distinguished from *secure, resistant,* and *disorganized/disoriented attachment.*

babbling
Repetition of consonant– vowel combinations in long strings, beginning around 4 months of age.

basic emotions
Emotions that can be directly inferred from facial expressions, such as happiness, interest, surprise, fear, anger, sadness, and disgust.

basic-skills approach
An approach to beginning reading instruction that emphasizes training in phonics—the basic rules for translating written symbols into sounds—and simplified reading materials. Distinguished from *whole-language approach.*

basic trust versus mistrust
In Erikson's theory, the psychological conflict of infancy, which is resolved positively if caregiving, especially during feeding, is sympathetic and loving.

behavioral genetics
A field devoted to uncovering the contributions of nature and nurture to individual differences in human traits and abilities.

behaviorism
An approach that views directly observable events—stimuli and responses—as the appropriate focus of study and the development of behavior as taking place through classical and operant conditioning.

bicultural identity
The identity constructed by adolescents who explore and adopt values from both their subculture and the dominant culture.

blastocyst
The zygote 4 days after fertilization, when the tiny mass of cells forms a hollow, fluid-filled ball.

blended, or **reconstituted, family**
A family structure resulting from cohabitation or remarriage that includes parent, child, and steprelatives.

body image
Conception of and attitude toward one's physical appearance.

bonding
Parents' feelings of affection and concern for the newborn baby.

brain plasticity
The ability of other parts of the brain to take over functions of damaged regions. Disappears when hemispheres of the cerebral cortex lateralize.

breech position
A position of the baby in the uterus that would cause the buttocks or feet to be delivered first.

Broca's area
A language structure located in the frontal lobe of the left hemisphere of the cerebral cortex that controls language production.

bulimia nervosa
An eating disorder in which individuals (mainly females) engage in strict dieting and excessive exercise accompanied by binge eating, often followed by deliberate vomiting and purging with laxatives.

canalization
The tendency of heredity to restrict the development of some characteristics to just one or a few outcomes.

cardinality
A principle stating that the last number in a counting sequence indicates the quantity of items in the set.

carrier
A heterozygous individual who can pass a recessive trait to his or her children.

centration
The tendency to focus on one aspect of a situation and neglect other important features. Distinguished from *decentration.*

cephalocaudal trend
An organized pattern of physical growth and motor control that proceeds from head to tail.

cerebellum
A brain structure that aids in balance and control of body movement.

cerebral cortex
The largest, most complex structure of the human brain, and the one responsible for the highly developed intelligence of the human species. Surrounds the rest of the brain, much like a half-shelled walnut.

cerebral palsy
A general term for a variety of problems, all of which involve muscle coordination, that result from brain damage before, during, or just after birth.

cesarean delivery
A surgical delivery in which the doctor makes an incision in the mother's abdomen and lifts the baby out of the uterus.

child-centered preschool
A preschool in which teachers provide a wide variety of activities from which children select, and most of the day is devoted

to free play. Distinguished from *academic preschool.*

child development
A field of study devoted to understanding all aspects of human constancy and change from conception through adolescence.

child-directed speech (CDS)
A form of language adults use to speak to infants and toddlers that consists of short sentences with high-pitched, exaggerated expression, clear pronunciation, and distinct pauses between speech segments.

chorion
The outer membrane that forms a protective covering around the prenatal organism. It sends out tiny, fingerlike villi, from which the placenta begins to develop.

chromosomes
Rodlike structures in the cell nucleus that store and transmit genetic information.

chronosystem
In ecological systems theory, temporal changes in children's environments, which produce new conditions that affect development. These changes can be imposed externally or arise from within the child.

circular reaction
In Piaget's theory, a means of building schemes in which infants try to repeat a chance event caused by their own motor activity.

classical conditioning
A form of learning that involves associating a neutral stimulus with a stimulus that leads to a reflexive response.

clinical, or case study, method
A method in which the researcher attempts to understand the unique individual child by combining interview data, observations, test scores, and sometimes psychophysiological measures.

clinical interview
A method in which the researcher uses a flexible, conversational style to probe for the participant's point of view.

clique
A small group of about five to seven members who are good friends and, therefore, resemble one another in family background, attitudes, and values.

codominance
A pattern of inheritance in which both alleles in a heterozygous combination are expressed.

cognitive-developmental theory
An approach introduced by Piaget that views children as actively constructing knowledge as they manipulate and explore their world, and cognitive development as taking place in stages.

cognitive inhibition
The ability to resist interference from internal and external distracting stimuli, thereby ensuring that working memory is not cluttered with irrelevant information.

cognitive self-regulation
The process of continuously monitoring progress toward a goal, checking outcomes, and redirecting unsuccessful efforts.

cohort effects
The effects of cultural-historical change on the accuracy of findings: Children born in a particular time period are influenced by a particular set of cultural and historical conditions.

collectivist societies
Societies in which people define themselves as part of a group and stress group over individual goals. Distinguished from *individualistic societies.*

compliance
Voluntary obedience to adult requests and commands.

comprehension
In language development, the words and word combinations that children understand. Distinguished from *production.*

comprehension monitoring
Continually evaluating how well one understands a spoken or written message.

concordance rate
The percentage of instances in which both members of a twin pair show a trait when it is present in one pair member. Used to study the contribution of heredity to emotional and behavioral disorders that can be judged as either present or absent.

concrete operational stage
Piaget's third stage, during which thought is logical, flexible, and organized in its application to concrete information. Spans the years from 7 to 11.

conditioned response (CR)
In classical conditioning, an originally reflexive response that is produced by a conditioned stimulus (CS).

conditioned stimulus (CS)
In classical conditioning, a neutral stimulus that, through pairing with an unconditioned stimulus (UCS), leads to a new response (CR).

conservation
The understanding that certain physical characteristics of objects remain the same, even when their outward appearance changes.

contexts
Unique combinations of genetic and environmental circumstances that can result in markedly different paths of development.

continuous development
A view that regards development as a cumulative process that consists of gradually adding on more of the same types of skills that were there to begin with. Distinguished from *discontinuous development.*

contrast sensitivity
A general principle accounting for early pattern preferences, which states that if babies can detect a difference in contrast between two or more patterns, they will prefer the one with more contrast.

control deficiency
The inability to execute a mental strategy consistently. Distinguished from *production deficiency, utilization deficiency,* and *effective strategy use.*

controversial children
Children who get a large number of positive and negative votes on sociometric measures of peer acceptance. Distinguished from *popular, neglected,* and *rejected children.*

conventional level
Kohlberg's second level of moral development, in which moral understanding is based on conforming to social rules to ensure positive human relationships and societal order.

convergent thinking
The generation of a single correct answer to a problem. The type of cognition emphasized on intelligence tests. Distinguished from *divergent thinking.*

cooing
Pleasant vowel-like noises made by infants, beginning around 2 months of age.

cooperative learning
Collaboration on a task by a small group of students who resolve differences of opinion, share responsibility, consider one another's ideas, and work toward common goals.

cooperative play
A form of true social participation, in which children orient toward a common goal, such as acting out a make-believe theme or working on the same product. Distinguished from *nonsocial activity, parallel play,* and *associative play.*

coregulation
A transitional form of supervision in which parents exercise general oversight while permitting children to be in charge of moment-by-moment decision making.

correlation coefficient
A number, ranging from +1.00 to –1.00, that describes the strength and direction of the relationship between two variables.

correlational design
A research design in which the researcher gathers information without altering participants' experiences and examines relationships between variables. Does not permit inferences about cause and effect.

corpus callosum
The large bundle of fibers that connects the two hemispheres of the brain.

creativity
The ability to produce work that is original yet appropriate—something that others have not thought of but that is useful in some way.

crossing over
During meiosis, the exchange of genes between chromosomes next to each other.

cross-sectional design
A research design in which groups of people differing in age are studied at the same point in time. Distinguished from *longitudinal design.*

crowd
A large, loosely organized group consisting of several cliques. Membership is based on reputation and stereotype.

decentration
The ability to focus on several aspects of a problem at once and relate them. Distinguished from *centration.*

deferred imitation
The ability to remember and copy the behavior of models who are not immediately present.

deoxyribonucleic acid (DNA)
Long, double-stranded molecules that make up chromosomes.

dependent variable
The variable the researcher expects to be influenced by the independent variable in an experiment.

deprivation dwarfism
A growth disorder observed between 2 and 15 years of age. Characterized by very short stature, weight that is usually appropriate for height, immature skeletal age, and decreased GH secretion. Caused by emotional deprivation.

developmentally appropriate practice
Standards devised by the National Association for the Education of Young Children that specify program characteristics that meet the developmental and individual needs of young children of varying ages, based on current research and the consensus of experts.

developmental quotient, or DQ
A score on an infant intelligence test, based primarily on perceptual and motor responses. Computed in the same manner as an IQ.

differentiation theory
The view that perceptual development involves the detection of increasingly fine-grained, invariant features in the environment.

difficult child
A child whose temperament is characterized by irregular daily routines, slow acceptance of new experiences, and negative and intense reactions. Distinguished from *easy child* and *slow-to-warm-up child.*

dilation and effacement of the cervix
Widening and thinning of the cervix during the first stage of labor.

discontinuous development
A view in which new ways of understanding and responding to the world emerge at specific times. Distinguished from *continuous development.*

dishabituation
Increase in responsiveness after stimulation changes.

disorganized/disoriented attachment
The quality of insecure attachment characterizing infants who respond in a confused, contradictory fashion when reunited with the parent.

distributive justice
Beliefs about how to divide material goods fairly.

divergent thinking
The generation of multiple and unusual possibilities when faced with a task or problem. Associated with creativity. Distinguished from *convergent thinking.*

divorce mediation
A series of meetings between divorcing adults and a trained professional, who tries to help them settle disputes. Aimed at avoiding legal battles that intensify family conflict.

dominance hierarchy
A stable ordering of group members that predicts who will win when conflict arises.

dominant cerebral hemisphere
The hemisphere of the brain responsible for skilled motor action. The left hemisphere is dominant in right-handed individuals. In left-handed individuals, the right hemisphere may be dominant, or motor and language skills may be shared between the hemispheres.

dominant–recessive inheritance
A pattern of inheritance in which, under heterozygous conditions, the influence of only one allele is apparent.

dual representation
Viewing a symbolic object as both an object in its own right and a symbol.

dynamic systems perspective
A view that regards the child's mind, body, and physical and social worlds as a dynamic, integrated system. A change in any part of the system leads the child to reorganize his or her behavior so the various components of the system work together again but in a more complex and effective way.

dynamic systems theory of motor development
A theory that views new motor skills as reorganizations of previously mastered skills that lead to more effective ways of exploring and controlling the environment. Each new skill is a product of central nervous system development, movement possibilities of the body, the goal the child has in mind, and environmental supports for the skill.

dynamic testing
An approach to testing consistent with Vygotsky's concept of the zone of proximal development, in which individualized teaching is introduced into the testing situation to see what the child can attain with social support.

easy child
A child whose temperament is characterized by establishment of regular routines in infancy, general cheerfulness, and easy adaptation to new experiences. Distinguished from *difficult child* and *slow-to-warm-up child*.

ecological systems theory
Bronfenbrenner's approach, which views the child as developing within a complex system of relationships affected by multiple levels of the environment, from immediate settings of family and school to broad cultural values and programs.

educational self-fulfilling prophecy
The idea that children may adopt teachers' positive or negative attitudes toward them and start to live up to these views.

effective strategy use
Consistent use of a mental strategy that leads to improvement in performance. Distinguished from *production deficiency, control deficiency,* and *utilization deficiency.*

egocentrism
The inability to distinguish the symbolic viewpoints of others from one's own.

elaboration
The memory strategy of creating a relationship, or shared meaning, between two or more pieces of information that are not members of the same category.

embryo
The prenatal organism from 2 to 8 weeks after conception, during which time the foundations of all body structures and internal organs are laid down.

embryonic disk
A small cluster of cells on the inside of the blastocyst, from which the new organism will develop.

emergent literacy
Young children's active efforts to construct literacy knowledge through informal experiences.

emotional self-regulation
Strategies for adjusting our emotional state to a comfortable level of intensity so we can accomplish our goals.

empathy
The capacity to understand another's emotional state and *feel with* that person, or respond emotionally in a similar way.

epigenesis
Development of the individual resulting from ongoing, bidirectional exchanges between heredity and all levels of the environment.

epiphyses
Growth centers in the bones where new cartilage cells are produced and gradually harden.

episiotomy
A small incision made during childbirth to increase the size of the vaginal opening.

episodic memory
Memory for everyday experiences.

ethnic identity
An enduring aspect of the self that includes a sense of ethnic group membership and attitudes and feelings associated with that membership.

ethnography
A method in which the researcher attempts to understand the unique values and social processes of a culture or a distinct social group by living with its members and taking field notes for an extended period of time.

ethological theory of attachment
A theory formulated by Bowlby, which views the infant's emotional tie to the caregiver as an evolved response that promotes survival.

ethology
An approach concerned with the adaptive, or survival, value of behavior and its evolutionary history.

exosystem
In ecological systems theory, settings that do not contain children but that affect their experiences in immediate settings. Examples are parents' workplace and health and welfare services in the community, as well as parents' social networks.

expansions
Adult responses that elaborate on a child's utterance, increasing its complexity.

experimental design
A research design in which the investigator randomly assigns participants to treatment conditions. Permits inferences about cause and effect.

expressive style
A style of early language learning in which toddlers use language mainly to talk about the feelings and needs of themselves and other people. Initial vocabulary emphasizes social formulas and pronouns. Distinguished from *referential style.*

extended-family household
A household in which parent and child live with one or more adult relatives.

extinction
In classical conditioning, decline of the conditioned response (CR) as a result of presenting the conditioned stimulus (CS) enough times without the unconditioned stimulus (UCS).

fantasy period
The period of vocational development in which young children fantasize about career options through make-believe play. Spans early and middle childhood.

fast mapping
Connecting a new word with an underlying concept after only a brief encounter.

fetal alcohol effects (FAE)
The condition of children who display some but not all of the defects of fetal alcohol syndrome. Usually their mothers drank alcohol in smaller quantities during pregnancy.

fetal alcohol syndrome (FAS)
A set of defects that results when women consume large amounts of alcohol during most or all of pregnancy. Includes mental retardation, slow physical growth, and facial abnormalities.

fetal monitors
Electronic instruments that track the baby's heart rate during labor.

fetus
The prenatal organism from the beginning of the third month to the end of pregnancy, during which time completion of body structures and dramatic growth in size takes place.

fontanels
Six soft spots that separate the bones of the skull at birth.

forceps
Metal clamps placed around the baby's head, used to pull the infant from the birth canal.

formal operational stage
Piaget's final stage, in which adolescents develop the capacity for abstract, scientific thinking. Begins around 11 years of age.

fraternal, or **dizygotic, twins**
Twins resulting from the release and fertilization of two ova. They are genetically no more alike than ordinary siblings. Distinguished from *identical,* or *monozygotic, twins.*

full inclusion
Placement of pupils with learning difficulties in regular classrooms for the entire school day. Distinguished from *mainstreaming.*

functional play
A type of play involving pleasurable motor activity with or without objects. Enables infants and toddlers to practice sensorimotor schemes.

gametes
Human sperm and ova, which contain half as many chromosomes as a regular body cell.

gender constancy
The understanding that sex remains the same even if clothing, hairstyle, and play activities change.

gender identity
An image of oneself as relatively masculine or feminine in characteristics.

gender intensification
Increased gender stereotyping of attitudes and behavior. Occurs in early adolescence.

gender schema theory
An information-processing approach to gender typing that combines social learning and cognitive-developmental features to explain how environmental pressures and children's cognitions together shape gender-role development.

gender typing
The process of developing gender roles, or gender-linked preferences and behaviors valued by the larger society.

gene
A segment of a DNA molecule that contains hereditary instructions.

general growth curve
A curve that represents overall changes in body size—rapid growth during infancy, slower gains in early and middle childhood, and rapid growth again during adolescence.

genetic counseling
A communication process designed to help couples assess their chances of giving birth to a baby with a hereditary disorder and choose the best course of action in view of risks and family goals.

genetic–environmental correlation
The idea that heredity influences the environments to which individuals are exposed.

genetic imprinting
A pattern of inheritance in which alleles are imprinted, or chemically marked, in such a way that one pair member is activated, regardless of its makeup.

genotype
The genetic makeup of an individual.

giftedness
Exceptional intellectual strengths. Includes high IQ, creativity, and talent.

glial cells
Cells that are responsible for myelinization.

goodness-of-fit model
Thomas and Chess's model, which states that an effective match, or "good fit,"

between child-rearing practices and a child's temperament leads to favorable development and psychological adjustment. A "poor fit" leads to adjustment problems.

growth hormone (GH)
A pituitary hormone that affects the development of all body tissues except the central nervous system and the genitals.

growth spurt
Rapid gain in height and weight during adolescence.

guided participation
A concept that calls attention to adult and child contributions to a cooperative dialogue without specifying the precise features of communication, thereby allowing for variations across situations and cultures.

habituation
A gradual reduction in the strength of a response due to repetitive stimulation.

heritability estimate
A statistic that measures the extent to which individual differences in complex traits in a specific population are due to genetic factors.

heteronomous morality
Piaget's first stage of moral development, in which children view moral rules as permanent features of the external world that are handed down by authorities, require strict obedience, and cannot be changed. Extends from about 5 to 10 years of age.

heterozygous
Having two different alleles at the same place on a pair of chromosomes. Distinguished from *homozygous.*

hierarchical classification
The organization of objects into classes and subclasses on the basis of similarities and differences.

Home Observation for Measurement of the Environment (HOME)
A checklist for gathering information about the quality of children's home lives through observation and parental interview.

homozygous
Having two identical alleles at the same place on a pair of chromosomes. Distinguished from *heterozygous.*

horizontal décalage
Development within a Piagetian stage. Gradual mastery of logical concepts during the concrete operational stage is an example.

hostile aggression
Aggression intended to harm another person. Distinguished from *instrumental aggression*.

hypothetico-deductive reasoning
A formal operational problem-solving strategy, in which adolescents begin with a general theory of all possible factors that could affect an outcome and deduce from it specific hypotheses, which they test in an orderly fashion.

identical, or monozygotic, twins
Twins that result when a zygote, during the early stages of cell duplication, divides in two. They have the same genetic makeup. Distinguished from *fraternal*, or *dizygotic*, *twins*.

identity
A well-organized conception of the self made up of values, beliefs, and goals to which the individual is solidly committed.

identity achievement
The identity status of individuals who have explored and committed themselves to self-chosen values and occupational goals. Distinguished from *moratorium*, *identity foreclosure*, and *identity diffusion*.

identity diffusion
The identity status of individuals who do not have firm commitments to values and goals and are not actively trying to reach them. Distinguished from *identity achievement*, *moratorium*, and *identity foreclosure*.

identity foreclosure
The identity status of individuals who have accepted ready-made values and goals that authority figures have chosen for them. Distinguished from *identity achievement*, *moratorium*, and *identity diffusion*.

identity versus identity confusion
In Erikson's theory, the psychological conflict of adolescence, which is resolved positively when adolescents attain an identity after a period of exploration and inner soul-searching.

imaginary audience
Adolescents' belief that they are the focus of everyone else's attention and concern.

imitation
Learning by copying the behavior of another person. Also called modeling or observational learning. Also called *modeling* or *observational learning*.

implantation
Attachment of the blastocyst to the uterine lining 7 to 9 days after fertilization.

independent variable
The variable the researcher expects to cause changes in another variable in an experiment.

individualistic societies
Societies in which people think of themselves as separate entities and are largely concerned with their own personal needs.

induced labor
A labor started artificially by breaking the amnion and giving the mother a hormone that stimulates contractions.

induction
A type of discipline in which the effects of the child's misbehavior on others are communicated to the child.

industry versus inferiority
In Erikson's theory, the psychological conflict of middle childhood, which is resolved positively when experiences lead children to develop a sense of competence at useful skills and tasks.

infant mortality
The number of deaths in the first year of life per 1,000 live births.

information processing
An approach that views the human mind as a symbol-manipulating system through which information flows and regards cognitive development as a continuous process.

inhibited, or shy, child
A child whose temperament is characterized by negative reaction to and withdrawal from novel stimuli. Resembles slow-to-warm-up child. Distinguished from *uninhibited*, or *sociable, child*.

initiative versus guilt
In Erikson's theory, the psychological conflict of early childhood, which is resolved positively through play experiences that foster a healthy sense of initiative and through development of a superego, or conscience, that is not overly strict and guilt ridden.

instrumental aggression
Aggression aimed at obtaining an object, privilege, or space with no deliberate intent to harm another person. Distinguished from *hostile aggression.*

intelligence quotient, or IQ
A score that reflects an individual's performance on an intelligence test compared with the performances of other individuals of the same age.

intentional, or goal-directed, behavior
A sequence of actions in which schemes are deliberately combined to solve a problem.

interactional synchrony
A sensitively tuned "emotional dance," in which the caregiver responds to infant signals in a well-timed, appropriate fashion and both partners match emotional states, especially the positive ones.

intermodal perception
Perception that combines stimulation from more than one sensory system at a time.

internal working model
A set of expectations derived from early caregiving experiences concerning the availability of attachment figures, their likelihood of providing support during times of stress, and the self's interaction with those figures. Becomes a model, or guide, for all future close relationships.

intersubjectivity
The process whereby two participants who begin a task with different understandings arrive at a shared understanding.

invariant features
In differentiation theory of perceptual development, features that remain stable in a constantly changing perceptual world.

irreversibility
The inability to mentally go through a series of steps in a problem and then reverse direction, returning to the starting point. Distinguished from *reversibility*.

I-self
A sense of self as subject, or agent, who is separate from but attends to and acts on

objects and other people. Distinguished from *me-self*.

joint custody
A child custody arrangement following divorce in which the court grants both parents equal say in important decisions about the child's upbringing.

Kamehameha Elementary Education Program (KEEP)
The most well-known and extensive educational reform effort based on Vygotsky's theory. Instruction is organized around activity settings, designed to enhance teacher–child and child–child interaction and to be culturally responsive.

kinship studies
Studies comparing the characteristics of family members to determine the importance of heredity in complex human characteristics.

kwashiorkor
A disease usually appearing after weaning, between 1 and 3 years of age, that is caused by a diet low in protein. Symptoms include an enlarged belly, swollen feet, hair loss, skin rash, and irritable, listless behavior.

language acquisition device (LAD)
In Chomsky's theory, a biologically based innate system for picking up language that permits children, no matter which language they hear, to speak in a rule-oriented fashion as soon as they have learned enough words.

lanugo
A white, downy hair that covers the entire body of the fetus, helping the vernix stick to the skin.

lateralization
Specialization of functions of the two hemispheres of the cerebral cortex.

learned helplessness
Attributions that credit success to luck and failure to low ability. Leads to anxious loss of control in the face of challenging tasks. Distinguished from *mastery-oriented attributions*.

learning disabilities
Specific learning disorders that lead children to achieve poorly in school, despite an average or above-average IQ. Believed to be due to faulty brain functioning.

logical necessity
A basic property of propositional thought, which specifies that the accuracy of conclusions drawn from premises rests on the rules of logic, not on real-world confirmation.

longitudinal design
A research design in which participants are studied repeatedly at different ages. Distinguished from *cross-sectional design*.

longitudinal-sequential design
A research design with both longitudinal and cross-sectional components in which groups of participants born in different years are followed over time.

long-term memory
In information processing, the part of the mental system that contains our permanent knowledge base.

macrosystem
In ecological systems theory, cultural values, laws, customs, and resources that influence experiences and interactions at inner levels of the environment.

mainstreaming
Placement of pupils with learning difficulties in regular classrooms for part of the school day. Distinguished from *full inclusion*.

make-believe play
A type of play in which children pretend, acting out everyday and imaginary activities.

malocclusion
A condition in which the upper and lower teeth do not meet properly.

marasmus
A disease usually appearing in the first year of life that is caused by a diet low in all essential nutrients. Leads to a wasted condition of the body.

mastery-oriented attributions
Attributions that credit success to high ability and failure to insufficient effort. Leads to high self-esteem and a willingness to approach challenging tasks. Distinguished from *learned helplessness*.

maturation
A genetically determined, naturally unfolding course of growth.

meiosis
The process of cell division through which gametes are formed and in which the number of chromosomes in each cell is halved.

memory strategies
Deliberate mental activities that improve the likelihood of remembering.

menarche
First menstruation.

mental representation
An internal image of an absent object or a past event.

mental strategies
In information processing, procedures that operate on and transform information, thereby increasing the efficiency and flexibility of thinking and the chances that information will be retained.

me-self
A sense of self as a reflective observer that treats the self as an object of knowledge and evaluation. Distinguished from *I-self*.

mesosystem
In ecological systems theory, connections between children's immediate settings.

metacognition
Thinking about thought; awareness of mental activities.

metalinguistic awareness
The ability to think about language as a system.

microgenetic design
A research design in which researchers present children with a novel task and follow their mastery over a series of closely spaced sessions.

microsystem
In ecological systems theory, the activities and interaction patterns in the child's immediate surroundings.

mitosis
The process of cell duplication, in which each new cell receives an exact copy of the original chromosomes.

modifier genes
Genes that can enhance or dilute the effects of other genes.

modular view of the mind
A nativist view that regards the mind as a collection of separate modules, or geneti-

cally prewired neural systems in the brain, each equipped with structures for making sense of a certain type of knowledge.

moratorium
The identity status of individuals who are exploring alternatives in an effort to find values and goals to guide their life. Distinguished from *identity achievement, identity foreclosure,* and *identity diffusion.*

mutation
A sudden but permanent change in a segment of DNA.

myelinization
A process in which neural fibers are coated with an insulating fatty sheath (called myelin) that improves the efficiency of message transfer.

myopia
Nearsightedness; inability to see distant objects clearly.

natural, or **prepared, childbirth**
An approach designed to reduce pain and medical intervention and to make childbirth a rewarding experience for parents.

naturalistic observation
A method in which the researcher goes into the natural environment to observe the behavior of interest. Distinguished from *structured observation.*

nature–nurture controversy
Disagreement among theorists about whether genetic or environmental factors are more important determinants of development and behavior.

neglected children
Children who are seldom chosen, either positively or negatively, on sociometric measures of peer acceptance. Distinguished from *popular, rejected,* and *controversial children.*

Neonatal Behavioral Assessment Scale (NBAS)
A test developed to assess the behavior of the infant during the newborn period.

neonatal mortality
The number of deaths in the first month of life per 1,000 live births.

neural tube
The primitive spinal cord that develops from the ectoderm, the top of which swells to form the brain.

neurons
Nerve cells that store and transmit information.

neurotransmitters
Chemicals that permit neurons to communicate across synapses.

niche-picking
A type of genetic–environmental correlation in which individuals actively choose environments that complement their heredity.

noble savage
Rousseau's view of the child as naturally endowed with a sense of right and wrong and an innate plan for orderly, healthy growth.

nocturnal enuresis
Repeated bedwetting during the night.

nonorganic failure to thrive
A growth disorder usually present by 18 months of age that is caused by lack of affection and stimulation.

non-rapid-eye-movement (NREM) sleep
A "regular" sleep state in which the body is quiet and heart rate, breathing, and brainwave activity are slow and regular.

nonsocial activity
Unoccupied, onlooker behavior and solitary play. Distinguished from *parallel, associative,* and *cooperative play.*

normative approach
An approach in which age-related averages are computed to represent typical development.

obesity
A greater-than-20-percent increase over average body weight, based on the child's age, sex, and physical build.

object permanence
The understanding that objects continue to exist when they are out of sight.

open classroom
An elementary school classroom based on the educational philosophy that children are active agents in their own development and learn at different rates. Teachers share decision making with pupils. Children's progress is evaluated in relation to their own prior development.

operant conditioning
A form of learning in which a spontaneous behavior is followed by a stimulus that changes the probability that the behavior will occur again.

operations
Mental representations of actions that obey logical rules.

oral rehydration therapy (ORT)
A treatment for diarrhea in which sick children are given a glucose, salt, and water solution that quickly replaces fluids the body loses.

ordinality
A principle specifying order (more-than and less-than) relationships between quantities.

organization
In Piaget's theory, the internal rearrangement and linking together of schemes so that they form a strongly interconnected cognitive system.

organization
The memory strategy of grouping together related items.

overextension
An early vocabulary error in which a word is applied too broadly, to a wider collection of objects and events than is appropriate. Distinguished from *underextension.*

overlapping-waves theory
A theory of problem solving, which states that when given challenging problems children generate a variety of strategies and gradually select those that result in rapid, accurate solutions, yielding an overlapping-waves pattern of development.

overregularization
Application of regular grammatical rules to words that are exceptions.

overt aggression
A form of hostile aggression that harms others through physical injury or the threat of such injury—for example, hitting, kicking, or threatening to beat up a peer. Distinguished from *relational aggression.*

parallel play
A form of limited social participation in which the child plays near other children with similar materials but does not try to influence their behavior. Distinguished from *nonsocial , associative,* and *cooperative play.*

peer group
Peers who form a social unit by generating shared values and standards of behavior and a social structure of leaders and followers.

peer victimization
A destructive form of peer interaction in which certain children become frequent targets of verbal and physical attacks or other forms of abuse.

perception bound
Being easily distracted by the concrete, perceptual appearance of objects.

permissive style
A child-rearing style that is responsive but undemanding. An overly tolerant approach to child rearing. Distinguished from *authoritative* and *authoritarian styles.*

personal fable
Adolescents' belief that they are special and unique. Leads them to conclude that others cannot possibly understand their thoughts and feelings. May promote a sense of invulnerability to danger.

perspective taking
The capacity to imagine what other people are thinking and feeling.

phenotype
The individual's physical and behavioral characteristics, which are determined by both genetic and environmental factors.

physical causality
The causal action one object exerts on another through contact.

pincer grasp
The well-coordinated grasp emerging at the end of the first year, involving thumb and forefinger opposition.

pituitary gland
A gland located near the base of the brain that releases hormones affecting physical growth.

placenta
The organ that separates the mother's bloodstream from the embryo or fetal bloodstream but permits exchange of nutrients and waste products.

planning
Thinking out a sequence of acts ahead of time and allocating attention accordingly to reach a goal.

polygenic inheritance
A pattern of inheritance in which many genes determine a characteristic.

popular children
Children who get many positive votes on sociometric measures of peer acceptance. Distinguished from *rejected, controversial,* and *neglected children.*

popular-antisocial children
A subgroup of popular children largely made up of "tough" boys who are athletically skilled, highly aggressive, defiant of adult authority, and poor students. Distinguished from *popular-prosocial children.*

popular-prosocial children
A subgroup of popular children who combine academic and social competence. Distinguished from *popular-antisocial children.*

postconventional level
Kohlberg's highest level of moral development, in which individuals define morality in terms of abstract principles and values that apply to all situations and societies.

postformal thought
Cognitive development beyond Piaget's formal operational stage.

postpartum depression
Feelings of sadness and withdrawal that appear shortly after childbirth and that continue for weeks or months.

postterm
Infants who spend a longer-than-average time in the uterus—more than 42 weeks.

pragmatics
The practical, social side of language that is concerned with how to engage in effective and appropriate communication with others.

preconventional level
Kohlberg's first level of moral development, in which moral understanding is based on rewards, punishments, and the power of authority figures.

preformationism
Medieval view of the child as a miniature adult.

prenatal diagnostic methods
Medical procedures that permit detection of developmental problems before birth.

preoperational stage
Piaget's second stage, in which rapid growth in representation takes place but thought is not yet logical. Spans the years from 2 to 7.

prereaching
The poorly coordinated, primitive reaching movements of newborn babies.

preterm
Infants born several weeks or more before their due date. Although small in size, their weight may still be appropriate for the time they spent in the uterus.

primary sexual characteristics
Physical features that involve the reproductive organs directly (ovaries, uterus, and vagina in females; penis, scrotum, and testes in males). Distinguished from *secondary sexual characteristics.*

principle of mutual exclusivity
The assumption by children in the early stages of vocabulary growth that words mark entirely separate (nonoverlapping) categories.

private speech
Self-directed speech that children use to plan and guide their own behavior.

production
In language development, the words and word combinations that children use. Distinguished from *comprehension.*

production deficiency
The failure to produce a mental strategy when it could be helpful. Distinguished from *control deficiency, utilization deficiency,* and *effective strategy use.*

Project Head Start
The largest federally funded program in the United States, which provides low-income children with a year or two of preschool education, along with nutritional and medical services, and that encourages parent involvement in children's development.

propositional thought
A type of formal operational reasoning in which adolescents evaluate the logic of verbal statements without referring to real-world circumstances.

prosocial, or **altruistic, behavior**
Actions that benefit another person without any expected reward for the self.

proximodistal trend
An organized pattern of physical growth and motor control that proceeds from the center of the body outward.

psychoanalytic perspective
An approach to personality development introduced by Freud that assumes children move through a series of stages in which they confront conflicts between biological drives and social expectations. The way these conflicts are resolved determines psychological adjustment.

psychophysiological methods
Methods that measure the relationship between physiological processes and behavior. Among the most common are measures of autonomic nervous system activity (such as heart rate and respiration) and brain functioning (such as the EEG and fMRI).

psychosexual theory
Freud's theory, which emphasizes that how parents manage children's sexual and aggressive drives in the first few years of life is crucial for healthy personality development.

psychosocial theory
Erikson's theory, which emphasizes that at each Freudian stage, individuals not only develop a unique personality, but also acquire attitudes and skills that help them become active, contributing members of their society.

puberty
Biological changes at adolescence that lead to an adult-size body and sexual maturity.

public policies
Laws and government programs designed to improve current conditions.

punishment
In operant conditioning, a stimulus (removal of a desirable one or presentation of an unpleasant one) that decreases the occurrence of a response.

range of reaction
Each person's unique, genetically determined response to a range of environmental conditions.

rapid-eye-movement (REM) sleep
An "irregular" sleep state in which brain-wave activity is similar to that of the waking state; eyes dart beneath the lids; heart rate, blood pressure, and breathing are uneven; and slight body movements occur. Distinguished from *non-rapid-eye-movement (NREM) sleep*.

recall
The type of memory that involves remembering something in the absence of perceptual support.

recasts
Adult responses that restructure children's incorrect speech into a more appropriate form.

reciprocal teaching
A method of teaching based on Vygotsky's theory in which a teacher and two to four pupils form a cooperative learning group. Dialogues occur that create a zone of proximal development in which reading comprehension improves.

recognition
The simplest form of memory, which involves noticing whether a new experience is identical or similar to a previous one.

realistic period
The period of vocational development in which adolescents focus on a general career category and, slightly later, settle on a single occupation. Spans late adolescence and young adulthood.

referential style
A style of early language learning in which toddlers use language mainly to label objects.

reflex
An inborn, automatic response to a particular form of stimulation.

rehearsal
The memory strategy of repeating information.

reinforcer
In operant conditioning, a stimulus that increases the occurrence of a response.

rejected children
Children who are actively disliked and get many negative votes on sociometric measures of peer acceptance. Distinguished from *popular, controversial,* and *neglected children.*

rejected-aggressive children
A subgroup of rejected children who engage in high rates of conflict, hostility, and hyperactive, inattentive, and impulsive behavior. Distinguished from *rejected-withdrawn children.*

rejected-withdrawn children
A subgroup of rejected children who are passive and socially awkward. Distinguished from *rejected-aggressive children.*

relational aggression
A form of hostile aggression that does damage to another's peer relationships, as in social exclusion or rumor spreading. Distinguished from *overt aggression.*

relativistic reasoning
A type of postformal thought that views all knowledge as embedded in a framework of thought and that accepts the existence of multiple truths.

resistant attachment
The quality of insecure attachment characterizing infants who remain close to the parent before departure and display angry, resistive behavior when she returns. Distinguished from *secure, avoidant,* and *disorganized/disoriented attachment.*

respiratory distress syndrome
A disorder of preterm infants in which the lungs are so immature that the air sacs collapse, causing serious breathing difficulties. Also know as *hyaline membrane disease.*

reticular formation
A brain structure that maintains alertness and consciousness.

reversibility
The ability to mentally go through a series of steps in a problem and then reverse direction, returning to the starting point. Distinguished from *irreversibility.*

Rh factor
A protein that, when present in the fetus's blood but not in the mother's, can cause the mother to build up antibodies. If these return to the fetus's system, they destroy red blood cells, reducing the oxygen supply to organs and tissues.

rooming in
An arrangement in which the newborn baby stays in the mother's hospital room all or most of the time.

rough-and-tumble play
A form of peer interaction involving friendly chasing and play-fighting that, in

our evolutionary past, may have been important for the development of fighting skill.

rubella
Three-day German measles. Causes a wide variety of prenatal abnormalities, especially when it strikes during the embryonic period.

scaffolding
A changing quality of social support over the course of a teaching session, in which the adult adjusts the assistance provided to fit the child's current level of performance. As competence increases, the adult gradually and sensitively withdraws support, turning over responsibility to the child.

scheme
In Piaget's theory, a specific structure, or organized way of making sense of experience, that changes with age.

school phobia
Severe apprehension about attending school, often accompanied by physical complaints that disappear once the child is allowed to remain home.

scripts
General descriptions of what occurs and when it occurs in a particular situation. A basic means through which children organize and interpret repeated events.

secondary sexual characteristics
Features visible on the outside of the body that serve as signs of sexual maturity but do not involve the reproductive organs (for example, breast development in females, appearance of underarm and pubic hair in both sexes). Distinguished from *primary sexual characteristics*.

secular trends in physical growth
Changes in body size from one generation to the next.

secure attachment
The quality of attachment characterizing infants who are distressed by parental separation and easily comforted by the parent when she returns. Distinguished from *avoidant, resistant,* and *disorganized/ disoriented attachment.*

secure base
The use of the familiar caregiver as a base from which the infant confidently explores the environment and to which he returns for emotional support.

self-care children
Children who look after themselves during after-school hours.

self-concept
The set of attributes, abilities, attitudes, and values that an individual believes defines who he or she is.

self-conscious emotions
Emotions that involve injury to or enhancement of the sense of self. Examples are shame, embarrassment, guilt, envy, and pride.

self-control
The capacity to resist an impulse to engage in socially disapproved behavior.

self-esteem
The aspect of self-concept that involves judgments about one's own worth and the feelings associated with those judgments.

semantic bootstrapping
Figuring out grammatical rules by relying on word meanings.

sensitive caregiving
Caregiving involving prompt, consistent, and appropriate responding to infant signals.

sensitive period
A time that is optimal for certain capacities to emerge and in which the individual is especially responsive to environmental influences.

sensorimotor stage
Piaget's first stage, during which infants and toddlers "think" with their eyes, ears, hands, and other sensorimotor equipment. Spans the first 2 years of life.

sensory register
In information processing, that part of the mental system in which sights and sounds are held briefly before they decay or are transferred to working, or short-term, memory.

separation anxiety
An infant's distressed reaction to the departure of the familiar caregiver.

seriation
The ability to order items along a quantitative dimension, such as length or weight.

sex chromosomes
The twenty-third pair of chromosomes, which determines the sex of the child—in females, called XX; in males, called XY.

shape constancy
Perception of an object's shape as the same, despite changes in the shape projected on the retina.

size constancy
Perception of an object's size as the same, despite changes in the size of its retinal image.

skeletal age
An estimate of physical maturity based on development of the bones of the body.

slow-to-warm-up child
A child whose temperament is characterized by inactivity; mild, low-key reactions to environmental stimuli; negative mood; and slow adjustment when faced with new experiences. Distinguished from *easy child* and *difficult child.*

small for date
Infants whose birth weight is below normal when length of pregnancy is taken into account.

social comparisons
Judgments of appearance, abilities, and behavior, in relation to those of others.

social learning theory
An approach that emphasizes the role of modeling, or observational learning, in the development of behavior. Its most recent revision stresses the importance of thinking in social learning and is called *social-cognitive theory.*

social problem solving
Resolving social conflicts in ways that are both acceptable to others and beneficial to the self. Involves noticing and accurately interpreting social cues, formulating goals that enhance relationships, generating and evaluating problem-solving strategies, and enacting a response.

social referencing
Relying on a trusted person's emotional reaction to decide how to respond in an uncertain situation.

social smile
The smile evoked by the stimulus of the human face. First appears between 6 and 10 weeks.

sociocultural theory
Vygotsky's theory, in which children acquire the ways of thinking and behaving that make up a community's culture through cooperative dialogues with more knowledgeable members of society.

sociodramatic play
The make-believe play with others that is under way by age 2½.

socioeconomic status (SES)
A measure of a family's social position and economic well-being that combines three interrelated, but not completely overlapping, variables: (1) years of education and (2) the prestige of and skill required by one's job, both of which measure social status; and (3) income, which measures economic status.

sociometric techniques
Self-report measures that ask peers to evaluate one another's likability.

spermarche
First ejaculation of seminal fluid.

stage
A qualitative change in thinking, feeling, and behaving that characterizes a specific period of development.

Stanford-Binet Intelligence Scale
An individually administered intelligence test that is the modern descendent of Alfred Binet's first successful test for children. Measures general intelligence and four factors: verbal reasoning, quantitative reasoning, abstract/visual reasoning, and short-term memory.

states of arousal
Different degrees of sleep and wakefulness.

states rather than transformations
The tendency to treat the initial and final states in a problem as completely unrelated.

stranger anxiety
The infant's expression of fear in response to unfamiliar adults. Appears in many babies after 6 months of age.

Strange Situation
A procedure involving short separations from and reunions with the parent that assesses the quality of the attachment bond.

structured interview
A method in which each participant is asked the same questions in the same way.

structured observation
A method in which the investigator sets up a situation that evokes the behavior of interest and observes it in a laboratory. Distinguished from *naturalistic observation*.

subculture
A group of people with beliefs and customs that differ from those of the larger culture.

sudden infant death syndrome (SIDS)
The unexpected death, usually during the night, of an infant younger than 1 year of age that remains unexplained after thorough investigation.

sympathy
Feelings of concern or sorrow for another's plight.

synapses
The gaps between neurons, across which chemical messages are sent.

synaptic pruning
Loss of connective fibers by seldom-stimulated neurons, thereby returning them to an uncommitted state so they can support the development of future skills.

syntactic bootstrapping
Figuring out word meanings by observing how words are used in the structure of sentences.

tabula rasa
Locke's view of the child as a blank slate whose character is shaped by experience.

talent
Outstanding performance in a particular field.

telegraphic speech
Toddlers' two-word utterances that, like a telegram, leave out smaller and less important words.

temperament
Stable individual differences in quality and intensity of emotional reaction, activity level, attention, and emotional self-regulation.

tentative period
The period of vocational development in which adolescents weigh vocational options against their interests, abilities, and values. Spans early and middle adolescence.

teratogen
Any environmental agent that causes damage during the prenatal period.

thalidomide
A sedative widely available in Europe, Canada, and South America in the early 1960s. When taken by mothers between the fourth and sixth weeks after conception, it produced gross deformities of the embryo's arms and legs.

theory
An orderly, integrated set of statements that describes, explains, and predicts behavior.

theory of multiple intelligences
Gardner's theory, which proposes at least eight independent intelligences on the basis of distinct sets of processing operations that permit individuals to engage in a wide range of culturally valued activities.

thyroid-stimulating hormone (TSH)
A pituitary hormone that stimulates the thyroid gland to release thyroxine, which is necessary for normal brain development and body growth.

time out
A form of mild punishment in which children are removed from the immediate setting until they are ready to act appropriately.

toxemia
An illness of the last half of pregnancy, in which the mother's blood pressure increases sharply and her face, hands, and feet swell. If untreated, it can cause convulsions in the mother and death of the fetus. Also called *eclampsia*.

toxoplasmosis
A parasitic disease caused by eating raw or undercooked meat or coming in contact with the feces of infected cats. During the first trimester, it leads to eye and brain damage.

traditional classroom
An elementary school classroom based on the educational philosophy that children are passive learners who acquire information presented by teachers. Children's progress is evaluated on the basis of how well they keep up with a uniform set of standards for all students in their grade. Distinguished from *open classroom*.

transition
Climax of the first stage of labor, in which the frequency and strength of contractions are at their peak and the cervix opens completely.

transitive inference
The ability to seriate—or order items along a quantitative dimension—mentally.

triarchic theory of intelligence
Sternberg's theory, which states that information-processing skills, ability to learn efficiently in novel situations, and contextual (or cultural) factors interact to determine intelligent behavior.

trimesters
Three equal time periods in prenatal development, each of which lasts 3 months.

trophoblast
The thin outer ring of cells of the blastocyst, which will become the structures that provide protective covering and nourishment to the new organism.

ulnar grasp
The clumsy grasp of the young infant, in which the fingers close against the palm.

umbilical cord
The long cord connecting the prenatal organism to the placenta; it delivers nutrients and removes waste products.

unconditioned response (UCR)
In classical conditioning, a reflexive response that is produced by an unconditioned stimulus (UCS).

unconditioned stimulus (UCS)
In classical conditioning, a stimulus that leads to a reflexive response.

underextension
An early vocabulary error in which a word is applied too narrowly, to a smaller number of objects and events than is appropriate. Distinguished from *over extension.*

uninhibited, or sociable, child
A child whose temperament is characterized by positive emotional reaction and approach to novel stimuli. Distinguished from *inhibited,* or *shy, child.*

uninvolved style
A child-rearing style that is both undemanding and unresponsive. Reflects minimal commitment to parenting. Distinguished from *authoritative, authoritarian,* and *permissive style.*

utilization deficiency
The inability to improve performance even with consistent use of a mental strategy. Distinguished from *production deficiency, control deficiency,* and *effective strategy use.*

vacuum extractor
A plastic cup attached to a suction tube, used to help deliver the baby.

vernix
A white, cheeselike substance that covers the fetus and prevents the skin from chapping due to constant exposure to amniotic fluid.

violation-of-expectation method
A method in which researchers habituate infants to a physical event and then determine whether they dishabituate to (look longer at) a possible event that conforms to physical laws or an impossible event that violates physical laws. Dishabituation to an impossible event suggests awareness of that aspect of physical reality.

visual acuity
Fineness of visual discrimination.

Wechsler Intelligence Scale for Children–III (WISC–III)
An individually administered intelligence test that includes both a measure of general intelligence and a variety of verbal and performance scores.

Wernicke's area
A language structure located in the temporal lobe of the left hemisphere of the cerebral cortex that is responsible for interpreting language.

whole-language approach
An approach to beginning reading instruction that parallels children's natural language learning and uses reading materials that are whole and meaningful. Distinguished from *basic-skills approach.*

working, or short-term, memory
In information processing, the conscious part of the mental system, where we actively "work" on a limited amount of information to ensure that it will be retained.

X-linked inheritance
A pattern of inheritance in which a recessive gene is carried on the X chromosome. Males are more likely to be affected.

zone of proximal development
In Vygotsky's theory, a range of tasks that the child cannot yet handle alone but can accomplish with the help of more skilled partners.

zygote
The newly fertilized cell formed by the union of sperm and ovum at conception.

References

Aaron, R., & Powell, G. (1982). Feedback practices as a function of teacher and pupil race during reading groups instruction. *Journal of Negro Education, 51*, 50–59.

Abbott, S. (1992). Holding on and pushing away: Comparative perspectives on an eastern Kentucky child-rearing practice. *Ethos, 20*, 33–65.

Aber, J. L., Brown, J. L., Jones, S. M., & Mathew, K. E. (1999, April). *Impact of the Resolving Conflict Creatively Program on aggression-related cognitions and behaviors over two years.* Paper presented at the biennial meeting of the Society for Research in Child Development, Albuquerque, NM.

Aber, J. L., Jones, S. M., Brown, J. L., Chaudry, N., & Samples, F. (1998). Resolving conflict creatively: Evaluating the developmental effects of a school-based violence prevention program in neighborhood and classroom context. *Development and Psychopathology, 10*, 187–213.

Abood, D. A., & Chandler, S. B. (1997). Race and the role of weight, weight change, and body dissatisfaction in eating disorders. *American Journal of Health Behavior, 21*, 21–25.

Abramovitch, R., Freedman, J. L., Henry, K., & Van Brunschot, M. (1995). Children's capacity to consent to participation in psychological research: Some empirical findings. *Child Development, 62*, 1100–1109.

Achenbach, T. M., Phares, V., Howell, C. T., Rauh, V. A., & Nurcombe, B. (1990). Seven-year outcome of the Vermont program for low-birthweight infants. *Child Development, 61*, 1672–1681.

Achter, J. A., Luginski, D., & Benbow, C. P. (1996). Multipotentiality among the intellectually gifted: "It was never there and already it's vanishing." *Journal of Counseling Psychology, 43*, 65–76.

Acker, M. M., & O'Leary, S. G. (1996). Inconsistency of mothers' feedback and toddlers' misbehavior and negative affect. *Journal of Abnormal Child Psychology, 24*, 703–714.

Ackerman, B. P. (1978). Children's understanding of speech acts in unconventional frames. *Child Development, 49*, 311–318.

Adams, M. J., Treiman, R., & Pressley, M. (1998). Reading, writing, and literacy. In D. Kuhn & R. S. Siegler (Eds.), *Handbook of child psychology: Vol. 2. Cognition, perception, and language* (5th ed., pp. 275–355). New York: Wiley.

Adams, R. J., & Courage, M. L. (1998). Human newborn color vision: Measurement with chromatic stimuli varying in excitation purity. *Journal of Experimental Child Psychology, 68*, 22–34.

Adler, P. A., & Adler, P. (1998). *Peer power.* New Brunswick, NJ: Rutgers University Press.

Adolph, K. E. (1997). Learning in the development of infant locomotion. *Monographs of the Society for Research in Child Development, 62* (3, Serial No. 251).

Adolph, K. E. A., Vereijken, B., & Denny, M. A. (1998). Learning to crawl. *Child Development, 69*, 1299–1312.

Adolph, K. E., & Eppler, M. A. (1998). Development of visually guided locomotion. *Ecological Psychology, 10*, 303–321.

Adolph, K. E., & Eppler, M. A. (1999). Obstacles to understanding: An ecological approach to infant problem solving. In E. Winograd, R. Fivush, & W. Hirst (Eds.), *Ecological approaches to cognition* (pp. 31–58). Mahwah, NJ: Erlbaum.

Aguiar, A., & Baillargeon, R. (1999). 2.5-month-old infants' reasoning about when objects should and should not be occluded. *Cognitive Psychology, 39*, 116–157.

Ahaja, K. K., Emerson, G., Seaton, A., Mamiso, J., & Simons, E. G. (1997). Widow's attempt to use her dead husband's sperm. *British Medical Journal, 314*, 143.

Ahlsten, G., Cnattingius, S., & Lindmark, G. (1993). Cessation of smoking during pregnancy improves fetal growth and reduces infant morbidity in the neonatal period: A population-based prospective study. *Acta Paediatrica, 82*, 177–181.

Ahmed, A., & Ruffman, T. (1998). Why do infants make A not B errors in a search task, yet show memory for the location of hidden objects in a nonsearch task? *Developmental Psychology, 34*, 441–453.

Ainsworth, M. D. S., Blehar, M. C., Waters, E., & Wall, S. (1978). *Patterns of attachment.* Hillsdale, NJ: Erlbaum.

Akers, J. F., Jones, R. M., & Coyl, D. D. (1998). Adolescent friendship pairs: Similarities in identity status development, behaviors, attitudes, and intentions. *Journal of Adolescent Research, 13*, 178–201.

Akhtar, N., & Montague, L. (1999). Early lexical acquisition: The role of cross-situational learning. *First Language, 19*, 347–358.

Alan Guttmacher Institute. (1998). *Facts in brief—Teen sex and pregnancy.* New York: Author.

Albert, R. S. (1994). The achievement of eminence: A longitudinal study of exceptionally gifted boys and their families. In R. F. Sobotnik & K. D. Arnold (Eds.), *Beyond Terman: Contemporary studies of giftedness and talent* (pp. 282–315). Norwood, NJ: Ablex.

Alessandri, S. M., Bendersky, M., & Lewis, M. (1998). Cognitive functioning in 8- to 18-month-old drug-exposed infants. *Developmental Psychology, 34*, 565–573.

Alessandri, S. M., Sullivan, M. W., & Lewis, M. (1990). Violation of expectancy and frustration in early infancy. *Developmental Psychology, 26*, 738–744.

Alessandri, S. M., & Wozniak, R. H. (1987). The child's awareness of parental beliefs concerning the child: A developmental study. *Child Development, 58*, 316–323.

Alexander, J. M., Lucas, M. J., Ramin, S. M., McIntire, D. D., & Leveno, K. J. (1998). The course of labor with and without epidural analgesia. *American Journal of Obstetrics and Gynecology, 178*, 516–520.

Alfieri, T., Ruble, D. N., & Higgins, E. T. (1996). Gender stereotypes during adolescence: Developmental changes and the transition to junior high school. *Developmental Psychology, 32*, 1129–1137.

Alibali, M. W. (1999). How children change their minds: Strategy change can be gradual or abrupt. *Developmental Psychology, 35*, 127–145.

Allan, K., & Coltrane, S. (1996). Gender displaying television commercials: A comparative study of television commercials in the 1950s and 1980s. *Sex Roles, 35*, 185–203.

Allen, J. P., Hauser, S. T., Bell, K. L., & O'Connor, T. G. (1994). Longitudinal assessment of autonomy and relatedness in adolescent–family interactions as predictors of adolescent ego development and self-esteem. *Child Development, 65*, 179–194.

Allen, J. P., Moore, C. M., & Kuperminc, G. P. (1996). Developmental approaches to understanding adolescent deviance. In S. S. Luthar, J. A. Burack, D. Cicchetti, & J. R. Weisz (Eds.), *Developmental psychopathology: Perspectives on adjustment, risk, and disorder* (pp. 548–567). New York: Cambridge University Press.

Allen, J. P., Philliber, S., Herrling, S., & Kuperminc, G. P. (1997). Preventing teen pregnancy and academic failure: Experimental evaluation of a developmentally based approach. *Child Development, 64*, 729–742.

Alpert-Gillis, L. J., & Connell, J. P. (1989). Gender and sex-role influences on children's self-esteem. *Journal of Personality, 57*, 97–114.

Alsaker, F. D. (1995). Timing of puberty and reactions to pubertal changes. In M. Rutter (Ed.), *Psychosocial disturbances in young people: Challenges for prevention* (pp. 37–82). New York: Cambridge University Press.

Al-Shalan, T. A., Erickson, P. R., & Hardie, N. A. (1997). Primary incisor decay before age 4 as a risk factor for future dental caries. *Pediatric Dentistry, 19*, 273–276.

Amato, P. R., & Gilbreth, J. (1999). Nonresident fathers and children's well-being: A meta-analysis. *Journal of Marriage and the Family, 61*, 557–573.

American Academy of Pediatrics. (1993). *Caring for your baby and young child: Birth to age 5.* New York: Bantam.

American Academy of Pediatrics. (1999). Contraception and adolescents. *Pediatrics, 104,* 1161–1166.

American Academy of Pediatrics. (2000). Changing concepts of sudden infant death syndrome: Implications for infant sleeping environment and sleep position. *Pediatrics, 105,* 650–656.

American Academy of Pediatrics. (2000). Suicide and suicide attempts in adolescents. *Pediatrics, 105,* 871–874.

American Psychiatric Association. (1994). *Diagnostic and statistical manual of mental disorders* (4th ed.). Washington, DC: Author.

American Psychological Association. (1992). Ethical principles of psychologists and code of conduct. *American Psychologist, 44,* 1597–1611.

Ames, C. (1992). Classrooms: Goals, structures, and student motivation. *Journal of Educational Psychology, 84,* 261–271.

Ananth, C. V., Berkowitz, G., Savitz, D. A., & Lapinski, R. H. (1999). Placental abruption and adverse perinatal outcomes. *Journal of the American Medical Association, 282,* 1646–1651.

Anda, R. F., Croft, J. B., Felitti, V. J., Nordenberg, D., Giles, W. H., Williamson, D. F., & Giovino, G. A. (1999). Adverse childhood experiences and smoking during adolescence and adulthood. *Journal of the American Medical Association, 282,* 1652–1658.

Anderman, E. M., & Midgley, C. (1997). Changes in achievement goal orientations, perceived academic competence, and grades across the transition to middle-level schools. *Contemporary Educational Psychology, 22,* 269–298.

Anderson, D. M., Huston, A. C., Wright, J. C., & Collins, P. A. (1998). "Sesame Street" and educational television for children. In R. G. Noll & M. E. Price (Eds.), *A communications cornucopia: Markle Foundation essays on information policy* (pp. 279–296). Washington, DC: Brookings Institute.

Anderson, E. (1992). *Speaking with style: The sociolinguistic skills of children.* London: Routledge.

Anderson, J. W., Johnstone, B. M., & Remley, D. T. (1999). Breast-feeding and cognitive development: A meta-analysis. *American Journal of Clinical Nutrition, 70,* 525–535.

Andersson, B.-E. (1989). Effects of public day care—A longitudinal study. *Child Development, 60,* 857–866.

Andersson, B.-E. (1992). Effects of day care on cognitive and socio-emotional competence of thirteen-year-old Swedish schoolchildren. *Child Development, 63,* 20–36.

Andre, T., Whigham, M., Hendrickson, A., & Chambers, S. (1999). Competence beliefs, positive affect, and gender stereotypes of elementary students and their parents about science versus other school subjects. *Journal of Research in Science Teaching, 36,* 719–747.

Andrews, G., & Halford, G. S. (1998). Children's ability to make transitive inferences: The importance of premise integration and structural complexity. *Cognitive Development, 13,* 479–513.

Andrews, L. B., & Elster, N. (2000). Regulating reproductive technologies. *Journal of Legal Medicine, 21,* 35–65.

Anglin, J. M. (1993). Vocabulary development: A morphological analysis. *Monographs of the Society for Research in Child Development, 58* (10, Serial No. 238).

Anhalt, K., & Morris, T. L. (1998). Developmental and adjustment issues of gay, lesbian, and bisexual adolescents: A review of the empirical literature. *Clinical Child & Family Psychology Review, 1,* 215–230.

Anisfeld, M., Turkewitz, G., Rose, S. A., Rosenberg, F. R., Shelber, F. J., Couturier-Fagan, D. A., Ger, J. S., & Sommer I. (2001). No compelling evidence that newborns imitate oral gestures. *Infancy, 2,* 111–122.

Annett, M. (1994). Handedness as a continuous variable with dextral shift: Sex, generation, and family handedness in subgroups of left- and right-handers. *Behavioral Genetics, 24,* 51–63.

Annett, M. (1999). Left-handedness as a function of sex, maternal versus paternal inheritance, and report bias. *Behavior Genetics, 29,* 103–114.

Anslow, P. (1998). Birth asphyxia. *European Journal of Radiology, 26,* 148–153.

Apgar, V. (1953). A proposal for a new method of evaluation in the newborn infant. *Current Research in Anesthesia and Analgesia, 32,* 260–267.

Archer, S. L. (1989b). The status of identity: Reflections on the need for intervention. *Journal of Adolescence, 12,* 345–359.

Archer, S. L., & Waterman, A. S. (1990). Varieties of identity diffusions and foreclosures: An exploration of subcategories of the identity statuses. *Journal of Adolescent Research, 5,* 96–111.

Archer, S. L., & Waterman, A. S. (1994). Adolescent identity devel-opment: Contextual perspectives. In C. B. Fisher & R. M. Lerner (Eds.), *Applied developmental psychology* (pp. 76–100). New York: McGraw-Hill.

Arcus, D., & Kagan, J. (1995). Temperament and craniofacial variation in the first two years. *Child Development, 66,* 1529–1540.

Ariès, P. (1962). *Centuries of childhood.* New York: Random House.

Arnett, J. J. (1999). Adolescent storm and stress, reconsidered. *American Psychologist, 54,* 317–326.

Arnold, K. (1994). The Illinois Valedictorian Project: Early adult careers of academically talented male and female high school students. In R. F. Subotnik & K. D. Arnold (Eds.), *Beyond Terman: Contemporary longitudinal studies of giftedness and talent* (pp. 24–51). Norwood, NJ: Ablex.

Arnold, P. (1999). Emotional disorders in deaf children. In V. L. Schwean & D. H. Saklofske (Eds.), *Handbook of psychosocial characteristics of exceptional children* (pp. 493–522). New York: Kluwer.

Aronson, M., Hagberg, B., & Gillberg, C. (1997). Attention deficits and autistic spectrum problems in children exposed to alcohol during gestation: A follow-up study. *Developmental Medicine & Child Neurology, 39,* 583–587.

Arterberry, M. E., Craton, L. G., & Yonas, A. (1993). Infants' sensitivity to motion-carried information for depth and object properties. In C. E. Granrud (Ed.), *Visual perception and cognition in infancy* (pp. 215–234). Hillsdale, NJ: Erlbaum.

Artman, L., & Cahan, S. (1993). Schooling and the development of transitive inference. *Developmental Psychology, 29,* 753–759.

Asendorpf, J. B., Warkentin, V., & Baudonniere, P. (1996). Self-awareness and other-awareness II: Mirror self-recognition, social contingency awareness, and synchronic imitation. *Developmental Psychology, 32,* 313–321.

Asher, S. R., & Rose, A. J. (1997). Promoting children's social-emotional adjustment with peers. In P. Salovey & D. J. Sluyter (Eds.), *Emotional development and emotional intelligence* (pp. 193–195). New York: Basic Books.

Ashley-Koch, A. E., Robinson, H., Glicksman, A. E., Nolin, S. L., Schwartz, C. E., & Brown, W. T. (1998). Examination of factors associated with instability of the FMR1 CGG repeat. *American Journal of Human Genetics, 63,* 776–785.

Ashley-Koch, A., Yang, Q., & Olney, R. S. (2000). Sickle hemoglobin (HbS) allele and sickle cell dis-ease: A HuGE review. *American Journal of Epidemiology, 151,* 839–845.

Ashmead, D. H., McCarty, M. E., Lucas, L. S., & Belvedere, M. A. (1993). Visual guidance in infants' reaching toward suddenly displaced targets. *Child Development, 64,* 1111–1127.

Aslin, R. N., Jusczyk, P. W., & Pisoni, D. B. (1998). Speech and auditory processing during infancy: Constraints on and precursors to language. In D. Kuhn & R. S. Siegler (Eds.), *Handbook of child psychology: Vol. 2. Cognition, perception, and language* (5th ed., pp. 147–198). New York: Wiley.

Aslin, R. N., & Smith, L. B. (1988). Perceptual development. *Annual Review of Psychology, 39,* 435–473.

Astington, J. W. (1991). Intention in the child's theory of mind. In C. Moore & D. Frye (Eds.), *Children's theories of mind* (pp. 157–172). Hillsdale, NJ: Erlbaum.

Astington, J. W. (1993). *The child's discovery of the mind.* Cambridge, MA: Harvard University Press.

Astington, J. W. (1999). The language of intention: Three ways of doing it. In P. D. Zelazo & J. W. Astington (Eds.), *Developing theories of intention* (pp. 295–315). Mahwah, NJ: Erlbaum.

Astington, J. W., & Jenkins, J. M. (1995). Theory of mind development and social understanding. *Cognition & Emotion, 9,* 151–165.

Astley, S. J., Clarren, S. K., Little, R. E., Sampson, P. D., & Daling, J. R. (1992). Analysis of facial shape in children gestationally exposed to marijuana, alcohol, and/or cocaine. *Pediatrics, 89,* 67–77.

Atkinson, R. C., & Shiffrin, R. M. (1968). Human memory: A proposed system and its control processes. In K. W. Spence & J. T. Spence (Eds.), *Advances in the psychology of learning and motivation* (Vol. 2, pp. 90–195). New York: Academic Press.

Attie, I., & Brooks-Gunn, J. (1996). The development of eating regulation across the life span. In D. Cicchetti & D. J. Cohen (Eds.), *Developmental psychology: Vol. 2. Risk, disorder, and adaptation* (pp. 332–368). New York: Wiley.

Au, K. H. (1997). A sociocultural model of reading instruction: The Kamehameha Elementary Education Program. In S. A. Stahl & D. A. Hayes (Eds.), *Instructional models in reading* (pp. 181–202). Mahwah, NJ: Erlbaum.

Au, T. K., Sidle, A. L., & Rollins, K. B. (1993). Developing an intuitive understanding of conservation and contamination: Invisible particles as a plausible mechanism.

Developmental Psychology, 29, 286–299.

August, D., & Garcia, E. E. (1988). *Language minority education in the United States.* Springfield, IL: Thomas.

Aunola, K., Stattin, H., & Nurmi, J.-E. (2000). Parenting styles and adolescents' achievement strategies. *Journal of Adolescence, 23,* 205–222.

Australian Bureau of Statistics. (2000). *Divorce rates.* [On-line] www.abus.gov.au.

Avenevoli, S., Sessa, F. M., & Steinberg, L. (1999). Family structure, parenting practices, and adolescent adjustment: An ecological examination. In E. M. Hetherington (Ed.), *Coping with divorce, single parenting, and remarriage: A risk and resiliency perspective* (pp. 65–90). Mahwah, NJ: Erlbaum.

Avis, J., & Harris, P. L. (1991). Belief–desire reasoning among Baka children: Evidence for a universal conception of mind. *Child Development, 62,* 460–467.

Axia, G., & Baroni, R. (1985). Linguistic politeness at different age levels. *Child Development, 56,* 918–927.

Axia, G., Bonichini, S., & Benini, F. (1999). Attention and reaction to distress in infancy: A longitudinal study. *Developmental Psychology, 35,* 500–504.

Azar, S. T., & Wolfe, D. A. (1998). Child physical abuse and neglect. In E. J. Mash & R. A. Barkley (Eds.), *Treatment of childhood disorders* (2nd ed., pp. 501–544). New York: Guilford.

Bacharach, V. R., & Baumeister, A. A. (1998). Direct and indirect effects of maternal intelligence, maternal age, income, and home environment on intelligence of preterm, low-birth-weigh children. *Journal of Applied Developmental Psychology, 19,* 361–375.

Bader, A. P. (1995). Engrossment revisited: Fathers are still falling in love with their newborn babies. In J. L. Shapiro, M. J. Diamond, & M. Greenberg (Eds.), *Becoming a father* (pp 224–233). New York: Springer.

Baenninger, M., & Newcombe, N. (1995). Environmental input to the development of sex-related differences in spatial and mathematical ability. *Learning and Individual Differences, 7,* 363–379.

Bagwell, C. L., Newcomb, A. F., & Bukowski, W. M. (1998). Preadolescent friendship and peer rejection as predictors of adult adjustment. *Child Development, 69,* 140–153.

Bahrick, L. E. (1992). Infants' perception of substance and temporal synchrony in multimodal

events. *Infant Behavior and Development, 6,* 429–451.

Bahrick, L. E., Netto, D., & Hernandez-Reif, M. (1998). Intermodal perception of adult and child faces and voices by infants. *Child Development, 69,* 1263–1275.

Bai, D. L., & Bertenthal, B. I. (1992). Locomotor status and the development of spatial search skills. *Child Development, 63,* 215–226.

Bailey, D. A., & Rasmussen, R. L. (1996). Sport and the child: Physiological and skeletal issues. In F. L. Smoll & R. E. Smith (Eds.), *Children and youth in sport: A biopsychological perspective* (pp. 187–199). Dubuque, IA: Brown & Benchmark.

Bailey, J. M., Bobrow, D., Wolfe, M., & Mikach, S. (1995). Sexual orientation of adult sons of gay fathers. *Developmental Psychology, 31,* 124–129.

Bailey, J. M., & Pillard, R. C. (1991). A genetic study of male sexual orientation. *Archives of General Psychology, 43,* 808–812.

Bailey, J. M., Pillard, R. C., Neale, M. C., & Agyei, Y. (1993). Heritable factors influence sexual orientation in women. *Archives of General Psychiatry, 50,* 217–223.

Bailey, R. C. (1990). Growth of African pygmies in early childhood. *New England Journal of Medicine, 323,* 1146.

Bailey, T. (1993). Can youth apprenticeship thrive in the United States? *Educational Researcher, 22* (3), 4–10.

Baillargeon, R. (1994a). How do infants learn about the physical world? *Current Directions in Psychological Science, 3,* 133–140.

Baillargeon, R. (1994b). Physical reasoning in infancy. In M. S. Gazzaniga (Ed.), *The cognitive neurosciences* (pp. 181–204). Cambridge, MA: MIT Press.

Baillargeon, R. (1995). A model of physical reasoning in infancy. In C. Rovee-Collier & L. P. Lipsitt (Eds.), *Advances in infancy research* (Vol. 9, pp. 305–371). Norwood, NJ: Ablex.

Baillargeon, R. (1998). Infants' understanding of the physical world. In M. Sabourin, F. I. M. Craik, & M. Robert (Eds.), *Advances in psychological science: Vol. 1. Cognitive and biological aspects* (pp. 503–529). London: Psychology Press.

Baillargeon, R., & DeVos, J. (1991). Object permanence in young infants: Further evidence. *Child Development, 62,* 1227–1246.

Baillargeon, R., Graber, M., DeVos, J., & Black, J. (1990). Why do young infants fail to search for hidden objects? *Cognition, 36,* 255–284.

Baillargeon, R., Needham, A., & DeVos, J. (1992). The development of young infants' intuitions about support. *Early Development and Parenting, 1,* 68–78.

Baker-Ward, L., Gordon, B. N., Ornstein, P. A., Larus, D. M., & Clubb, P. A. (1993). Young children's long-term retention of a pediatric examination. *Child Development, 64,* 1519–1533.

Baldwin, D. A., & Tomasello, M. (1998). Word learning: A window on early pragmatic understanding. In E. V. Clark (Ed.), *Proceedings of the Twenty-Ninth Annual Child Language Research Forum* (pp. 3–23). Stanford, CA: Center for the Study of Language and Information.

Ballard, B. D., Gipson, M. T., Guttenberg, W., & Ramsey, K. (1980). Palatability of food as a factor influencing obese and normal-weight children's eating habits. *Behavior Research and Therapy, 18,* 598–600.

Band, G. P. H., van der Molen, M. W., Overtoom, C. C. E., & Verbaten, M. N. (2000). The ability to activate and inhibit speeded responses: Separate developmental trends. *Journal of Experimental Child Psychology, 75,* 263–290.

Bandura, A. (1977). *Social learning theory.* Englewood Cliffs, NJ: Prentice-Hall.

Bandura, A. (1986). *Social foundations of thought and action: A social cognitive theory.* Englewood Cliffs, NJ: Prentice-Hall.

Bandura, A. (1989). Social cognitive theory. In R. Vasta (Ed.), *Annals of child development* (Vol. 6, pp. 1–60). Greenwich, CT: JAI Press.

Bandura, A. (1992). Perceived self-efficacy in cognitive development and functioning. *Educational Psychologist, 28,* 117–118.

Bandura, A. (1997). *Self-efficacy: The exercise of control.* New York: Freeman.

Banish, M. T., & Heller, W. (1998). Evolving perspectives on lateralization of function. *Current Directions in Psychological Science, 7,* 1–2.

Banks, M. S. (1980). The development of visual accommodation during early infancy. *Child Development, 51,* 157–173.

Banks, M. S., & Bennett, P. J. (1988). Optical and photoreceptor immaturities limit the spatial and chromatic vision of human neonates. *Journal of the Optical Society of America, 5,* 2059–2079.

Banks, M. S., & Ginsburg, A. P. (1985). Early visual preferences: A review and new theoretical treatment. In H. W. Reese (Ed.), *Advances in child development and*

behavior (Vol. 19, pp. 207–246). New York: Academic Press.

Banks, M. S., & Salapatek, P. (1983). Infant visual perception. In M. M. Haith & J. J. Campos (Eds.), *Handbook of child psychology: Vol. 2. Infancy and developmental psychobiology* 4th ed., (pp. 435–571). New York: Wiley.

Barakat, L. P., & Kazak, A. E. (1999). Family issues. In R. T. Brown (Ed.), *Cognitive aspects of chronic illness in children* (pp. 333–354). New York: Guilford.

Barker, D. J. P. (1994). *Mothers, babies, and disease in later life.* London: British Medical Journal Publishing.

Barker, D. J. P. (1999). Fetal origins of cardiovascular disease. *Annals of Medicine, 31*(Suppl. 1), 3–6.

Barker, R. G. (1955). *Midwest and its children.* Stanford, CA: Stanford University Press.

Barkley, R. A. (1997). Behavioral inhibition, sustained attention, and executive functions: Constructing a unifying theory of ADHD. *Psychological Bulletin, 121,* 65–94.

Barkley, R. A. (1999). Theories of attention-deficit/hyperactivity disorder. In H. C. Quay & A. E. Hogan (Eds.), *Handbook of disruptive behavior disorders* (pp. 295–313). New York: Kluwer.

Barling, J., Rogers, K., & Kelloway, K. (1995). Some effects of teenagers' part-time employment: The quantity and quality of work make the differences. *Journal of Organizational Behavior, 16,* 143–154.

Barnas, M. V., & Cummings, E. M. (1994). Caregiver stability and toddlers' attachment-related behavior toward caregivers in day care. *Infant Behavior and Development, 17,* 141–147.

Barnat, S. B., Klein, P. J., & Meltzoff, A. N. (1996). Deferred imitation across changes in context and object: Memory and generalization in 14-month-old infants. *Infant Behavior and Development, 19,* 241–251.

Barnes-Josiah, D., & Augustin, A. (1995). Secular trend in the age at menarche in Haiti. *American Journal of Human Biology, 7,* 357–362.

Barnett, D., Ganiban, J., & Cicchetti, D. (1999). Maltreatment, negative expressivity, and the development of Type D attachments from 12 to 24 months of age. In J. I. Vondra & D. Barnett (Eds.), *Atypical attachment in infancy and early childhood among children at developmental risk. Monographs of the Society for Research in Child Development, 64*(3, Serial No. 258), pp. 97–118.

Barnett, D., & Vondra, J. I. (1999). Atypical patterns of early attachment: Theory, research, and current directions. In J. I. Vondra & D. Barnett (Eds.), Atypical attachment in infancy and early childhood among children at developmental risk. *Monographs of the Society for Research in Child Development, 64*(3, Serial No. 258), pp.1–24.

Barnett, W. S. (1998). Long-term cognitive and academic effects of early childhood education on children in poverty. *Preventive Medicine, 27,* 204–207.

Baron-Cohen, S. (1993). From attention–goal psychology to belief–desire psychology: The development of a theory of mind and its dysfunction. In S. Baron-Cohen, H. Tager-Flusberg, & D. Cohen (Eds.), *Understanding other minds: Perspectives from autism* (pp. 59–82). Oxford, England: Oxford University Press.

Baron-Cohen, S., Baldwin, D. A., & Crowson, M. (1997). Do children with autism use the speaker's direction of gaze strategy to crack the code of language? *Child Development, 68,* 48–57.

Barr, C. L., Wigg, K. G., Bloom, S., Schachar, R., Tannock, R., & Roberts, W. (2000). Further evidence from haplotype analysis for linkage of the dopamine D4 receptor gene and attention-deficit hyperactivity disorder. *American Journal of Medical Genetics, 96,* 262–267.

Barr, H. M., Streissguth, A. P., Darby, B. L., & Sampson, P. D. (1990). Prenatal exposure to alcohol, caffeine, tobacco, and aspirin: Effects on fine and gross motor performance in 4-year-old children. *Developmental Psychology, 26,* 339–348.

Barr, R., & Hayne, H. (1999). Developmental changes in imitation from television during infancy. *Child Development, 70,* 1067–1081.

Barratt, M. S., Roach, M. A., & Leavitt, L. A. (1996). The impact of low-risk prematurity on maternal behaviour and toddler outcomes. *International Journal of Behavioral Development, 19,* 581–602.

Barrett, K. C. (1998). The origins of guilt in early childhood. In J. Bybee (Ed.), *Guilt and children* (pp. 75–90). San Diego: Academic Press.

Barrios, B. A., & Dell, S. L. (1998). Fears and anxieties. In E. J. Mash & R. A. Barkley (Eds.), *Treatment of childhood disorders* (2nd ed., pp. 249–337). New York: Guilford.

Barton, M. E., & Strosberg, R. (1997). Conversational patterns of two-year-old twins in mother–twin–twin triads. *Journal of Child Language, 24,* 257–269.

Barton, M. E., & Tomasello, M. (1991). Joint attention and con-

versation in mother– infant– sibling triads. *Child Development, 62,* 517–529.

Bartsch, K., & Wellman, H. (1995). *Children talk about the mind.* New York: Oxford University Press.

Bashir, L. M. (1997). Female genital mutilation—balancing intolerance of the practice with tolerance of culture. *Journal of Women's Health, 6,* 11–14.

Basow, S. A., & Rubin, L. R. (1999). Gender influences on adolescent development. In N. G. Johnson & M. C. Roberts (Eds.), *Beyond appearance: A new look at adolescent girls* (pp. 25–52). Washington, DC: American Psychological Association.

Bates, E. (1999). Plasticity, localization, and language development. In S. H. Broman & J. M. Fletcher (Eds.), *The changing nervous system: Neurobehavioral consequences of early brain disorders* (pp. 214–247). New York: Oxford University Press.

Bates, E., Elman, J., Johnson, M. C., Karmiloff-Smith, A., Parisi, D., & Plunkett, K. (1998). Innateness and emergentism. In W. Bechtel & G. Graham (Eds.), *A companion to cognitive science* (pp. 590–601). New York: Oxford University Press.

Bates, E., & MacWhinney, B. (1987). Competition, variation, and language learning. In B. MacWhinney (Ed.), *Mechanisms of language acquisition* (pp. 157–193). Hillsdale, NJ: Erlbaum.

Bates, E., Marchman, V., Thal, D., Fenson, L., Dale, P., Reznick, J. S., Reilly, J., & Hartung, J. (1994). Developmental and stylistic variation in the composition of early vocabulary. *Journal of Child Language, 21,* 85–123.

Bates, J. E., Pettit, G. S., Dodge, K. A., & Ridge, B. (1998). Interaction of temperamental resistance to control and restrictive parenting in the development of externalizing behavior. *Developmental Psychology, 34,* 982–995.

Bates, J. E., Wachs, T. D., & Emde, R. N. (1994). Toward practical uses for biological concepts. In J. E. Bates & T. D. Wachs (Eds.), *Temperament: Individual differences at the interface of biology and behavior* (pp. 275–306). Washington, DC: American Psychological Association.

Bauer, P. J. (1997). Development of memory in early childhood. In N. Cowan (Ed.), *The development of memory in childhood* (pp. 83–111). Hove, UK: Psychology Press.

Bauer, P. J., Kroupina, M. G., Schwade, J. A., Dropik, P., & Wewerka, S. S. (1998). If memory

serves, will language? Later verbal accessibility of early memories. *Development and Psychopathology, 10,* 655–679.

Bauman, A., & Phongsavan, P. (1999). Epidemiology of substance use in adolescence: Trends and policy implications. *Drug and Alcohol Dependence, 55,* 187–207.

Baumeister, R. F. (1998). Inducing guilt. In J. Bybee (Ed.), *Guilt and children* (pp. 185–213). San Diego: Academic Press.

Baumeister, R. F., Smart, L., & Boden, J. M. (1996). Relation of threatened egotism to violence and aggression: The dark side of high self-esteem. *Psychological Review, 103,* 5–33.

Baumrind, D. (1967). Child are practices anteceding three patterns of preschool behavior. *Genetic Psychology Monographs, 75,* 43–88.

Baumrind, D. (1971). Current patterns of parental authority. *Developmental Psychology Monograph, 4* (No. 1, Pt. 2).

Baumrind, D. (1991). The influence of parenting style on adolescent competence and substance use. *Journal of Early Adolescence, 11,* 56–95.

Baumrind, D., & Black, A. E. (1967). Socialization practices associated with dimension of competence in preschool boys and girls. *Child Development, 38,* 291–327.

Baumwell, L., Tamis-LeMonda, C. S., & Bornstein, M. H. (1997). Maternal verbal sensitivity and child language comprehension. *Infant Behavior and Development, 20,* 247–258.

Bayley, N. (1969). *Bayley Scales of Infant Development.* New York: Psychological Corporation.

Bayley, N. (1993). *Bayley Scales of Infant Development* (2nd ed.). New York: Psychological Corporation.

Beal, C. R. (1990). The development of text evaluation and revision skills. *Child Development, 61,* 247–258.

Bearison, D. J. (1998). Pediatric psychology and children's medical problems. In I. G. Sigel & K. A. Renninger (Eds.), *Handbook of child psychology: Vol. 4. Child psychology in practice* (5th ed., pp. 635–711). New York: Wiley.

Beatty, W. W. (1992). Gonadal hormones and sex differences in nonreproductive behaviors. In A. A. Gerall, H. Moltz, & I. L. Ward (Eds.), *Handbook of behavioral neurobiology: Vol. 11. Sexual differentiation* (pp. 85–128). New York: Plenum.

Beauchamp, G. K., Cowart, B. J., Mennella, J. A., & Marsh, R. R. (1994). Infant salt taste: Developmental, methodological, and contextual factors. *Developmental Psychobiology, 27,* 353–365.

Bebeau, M. J., Rest, J. R., & Narvaez, D. (1999). Beyond the promise: A perspective on research in moral education. *Educational Researcher, 28*(4), 18–26.

Beck, M. (1994, January 17). How far should we push mother nature? *Newsweek,* pp. 54–57.

Becker, A. E., Grinspoon, S. K., Klibanski, A., & Herzog, D. B. (1999). Eating disorders. *New England Journal of Medicine, 14,* 1093–1098.

Beckmann, C. A., Buford, T. A., & Witt, J. B. (2000). Perceived barriers to prenatal care services. *American Journal of Maternal and Child Nursing, 25,* 43–46.

Beckwith, L., & Sigman, M. D. (1995). Preventive interventions in infancy. *Child and Adolescent Psychiatric Clinics of North America, 4,* 683–700.

Behrman, R. E., Kliegman, R. M., & Arvin, A. M. (1996). *Nelson textbook of pediatrics* (15th ed.). Philadelphia: Saunders.

Behrman, R. E., Kliegman, R. M., & Jenson, H. B. (2000). *Nelson textbook of pediatrics* (16th ed.). Philadelphia: Saunders.

Beilin, H. (1978). Inducing conservation through training. In G. Steiner (Ed.), *Psychology of the twentieth century* (Vol. 7, pp. 260–289). Munich: Kindler.

Beilin, H. (1992). Piaget's enduring contribution to developmental psychology. *Developmental Psychology, 28,* 191–204.

Beitel, A. H., & Parke, R. D. (1998). Paternal involvement in infancy: The role of maternal and paternal attitudes. *Journal of Family Psychology, 12,* 268–288.

Bell, A., Weinberg, M., & Hammersmith, S. (1981). *Sexual preference: Its development in men and women.* Bloomington, IN: Indiana University Press.

Bell, K. L., Allen, J. P., Hauser, S. T., & O'Connor, T. G. (1996). Family factors and young adult transitions: Educational attainment and occupational prestige. In J. A. Graber, J. Brooks-Gunn, & A. C. Petersen (Eds.), *Transitions through adolescence: Interpersonal domains and context* (pp. 345–366). Mahwah, NJ: Erlbaum.

Bell, M. A. (1998). Frontal lobe function during infancy: Implications for the development of cognition and attention. In J. E. Richards (Ed.), *Cognitive neuroscience of attention: A developmental perspective* (pp. 327–362). Mahwah, NJ: Erlbaum.

Bell, M. A., & Fox, N. A. (1994). Brain development over the first year of life: Relations between EEG frequency and coherence and cognitive and affective behaviors. In G. Dawson & K. W. Fischer (Eds.), *Human behavior and the developing brain* (pp. 314–345). New York: Guilford.

Bell, M. A., & Fox, N. A. (1996). Crawling experience is related to changes in cortical organization during infancy: Evidence from EEG coherence. *Developmental Psychobiology, 29,* 551–561.

Bell, M. A., & Fox, N. A. (1998). Crawling experience is related to changes in cortical organization during infancy: Evidence from EEG coherence. *Developmental Psychology.*

Bell, R. J., Palma, S. M., & Lumley, J. M. (1995). The effect of vigorous exercise during pregnancy on birth-weight. *Australian and New Zealand Journal of Obstetrics and Gynaecology, 35,* 46–51.

Bellamy, C. (1998). *The state of the world's children 1998.* New York: Oxford University Press (in cooperation with UNICEF).

Bellamy, C. (2000). *The state of the world's children 2000.* New York: Oxford University Press (in cooperation with UNICEF).

Bellinger, D., Leviton, A., Waternaux, C., Needleman, H., & Rabinowitz, M. (1987). Longitudinal analysis of prenatal and postnatal lead exposure and early cognitive development. *New England Journal of Medicine, 316,* 1037–1043.

Belsky, J. (1989). Infant–parent attachment and day care: In defense of the Strange Situation. In J. Lande, S. Scarr, & N. Gunzenhauser (Eds.), *Caring for children: Challenge to America* (pp. 23–48). Hillsdale, NJ: Erlbaum.

Belsky, J. (1992). Consequences of child care for children's development: A deconstructionist view. In A. Booth (Ed.), *Child care in the 1990s: Trends and consequences* (pp. 83–85). Hillsdale, NJ: Erlbaum.

Belsky, J., & Cassidy, J. (1994). Attachment: Theory and evidence. In M. Rutter & D. Hay (Eds.), *Development through life* (pp. 373–402). Oxford, England: Blackwell.

Belsky, J., & Kelly, J. (1994). *The transition to parenthood.* New York: Delacorte Press.

Beltramini, A. U., & Hertzig, M. E. (1983). Sleep and bedtime behavior in preschool-aged children. *Pediatrics, 71,* 153–158.

Bem, S. L. (1989). Genital knowledge and gender constancy in preschool children. *Child Development, 60,* 649–662.

Bempechat, J., & Drago-Severson, E. (1999). Cross-national differences in academic achievement: Beyond etic conceptions of children's

understandings. *Review of Educational Research, 69,* 287–314.

Benbow, C. P., & Arjmand, O. (1990). Predictors of high academic achievement in mathematics and science by mathematically talented students: A longitudinal study. *Journal of Educational Psychology, 82,* 430–441.

Benbow, C. P., Lubinski, D., Shea, D. L., & Eftekhara-Sanjani, H. (2000). Sex differences in mathematical reasoning ability at age 13: Their status 20 years later. *Psychological Science, 11,* 474–480.

Benbow, C. P., & Stanley, J. C. (1983). Sex differences in mathematical reasoning: More facts. *Science, 222,* 1029–1031.

Bench, R. J., Collyer, Y., Mentz, L., & Wilson, I. (1976). Studies in infant behavioural audiometry: I. Neonates. *Audiology, 15,* 85–105.

Bender, S. L., Word, C. O., DiClemente, R. J., Crittenden, M. R., Persaud, N. A., & Ponton, L. (1995). The Developmental Implications of prenatal and/or postnatal crackk cocaine exposure in preschool children: A preliminary report. *Developmental and Behavioral Pediatrics, 16,* 418–424.

Benedict, R. (1934a). Anthropology and the abnormal. *Journal of Genetic Psychology, 10,* 59–82.

Benedict, R. (1934b). *Patterns of culture.* Boston: Houghton Mifflin.

Benediktsson, R., Calder, A. A., Edwards, C. R., & Seckl, J. R. (1997). Placental 11 beta-hydroxysteroid dehydrogenase: A key regulator of fetal glucocorticoid exposure. *Clinical Endocrinology, 46,* 161–166.

Benenson, J. F., Apostoleris, N. H., & Parnass, J. (1997). Age and sex differences in dyadic and group interaction. *Developmental Psychology, 33,* 538–543.

Bennetto, L., Pennington, B. F., & Rogers, S. J. (1996). Intact and impaired memory functions in autism. *Child Development, 67,* 1816–1835.

Bercu, B. B. (1996). Use of growth hormone for non-growth hormone deficient children [letter]. *Journal of the American Medical Association, 276,* 1878.

Bergen, D., & Mauer, D. (2000). Symbolic play, phonological awareness, and literacy skills at three age levels. In K. A. Roskos & J. F. Christie (Eds.), *Play and literacy in early childhood: Research from multiple perspectives* (pp. 45–62). Mahwah, NJ: Erlbaum.

Berk, L. E. (1985). Relationship of caregiver education to child-oriented attitudes, job satisfaction, and behaviors toward children. *Child Care Quarterly, 14,* 103–129.

Berk, L. E. (1992). The extracurriculum. In P. W. Jackson (Ed.), *Handbook of research on curriculum* (pp. 1002–1043). New York: Macmillan.

Berk, L. E. (1994, November). Why children talk to themselves. *Scientific American, 271*(5), 78–83.

Berk, L. E. (2001). *Dialogues with children: Creating learning environments at home and school.* New York: Oxford University Press.

Berk, L. E., & Landau, S. (1993). Private speech of learning disabled and normally achieving children in classroom academic and laboratory contexts. *Child Development, 64,* 556–571.

Berk, L. E., & Spuhl, S. T. (1995). Maternal interaction, private speech, and task performance in preschool children. *Early Childhood Research Quarterly, 10,* 145–169.

Berkowitz, M. W., & Gibbs, J. C. (1983). Measuring the developmental features of moral discussion. *Merrill-Palmer Quarterly, 29,* 399–410.

Berkus, M. D., Langer, O., Samueloff, A., Xanakis, E. M., & Field, N. T. (1999). Electronic fetal monitoring: What's reassuring? *Acta Obstetrica et Gynecologica Scandinavica, 78,* 15–21.

Berlin, L. J., Brooks-Gunn, J., McCarton, C., & McCormick, M. C. (1998). The effectiveness of early intervention: Examining risk factors and pathways to enhanced development. *Preventive Medicine, 27,* 238–245.

Berman, P. W. (1980). Are women more responsive than men to the young? A review of developmental and situational variables. *Psychological Bulletin, 88,* 668–695.

Bermejo, V. (1996). Cardinality development and counting. *Developmental Psychology, 32,* 263-268.

Berndt, T. J., Cheung, P. C., Lau, S., Hau, K-T., & Lew, W. J. F. (1993). Perceptions of parenting in mainland China, Taiwan, and Hong Kong: Sex differences and societal differences. *Developmental Psychology, 29,* 156–164.

Berndt, T. J., & Keefe, K. (1995). Friends' influence on adolescents' adjustment to school. *Child Development, 66,* 1312–1329.

Bernier, J. C., & Siegel, D. H. (1994). Attention-deficit hyperactivity disorder: A family ecological systems perspective. *Families in Society, 75,* 142–150.

Bersoff, D. M., & Miller, J. G. (1993). Culture, context, and the development of moral accountability judgments. *Developmental Psychology, 29,* 664–676.

Bertenthal, B. I. (1993). Infants' perception of biomechanical motions:

Intrinsic image and knowledge-based constraints. In C. Granrud (Ed.), *Visual percpetion and cognition in infancy* (pp. 175–214). Hillsdale, NJ: Erlbaum.

Bertenthal, B. I., & Campos, J. J. (1987). New directions in the study of early experience. *Child Development, 58,* 560–567.

Bertenthal, B. I., Campos, J. J., & Barrett, K. (1984). Self-produced locomotion: An organizer of emotional, cognitive, and social development in infancy. In R. Emde & R. Harmon (Eds.), *Continuities and discontinuities in development* (pp. 174–210). New York: Plenum.

Bertenthal, B. I., & Clifton, R. K. (1998). Perception and action. In D. Kuhn & R. S. Siegler (Eds.), *Handbook of child psychology: Vol. 2. Cognition, perception, and language* (pp. 51–102). New York: Wiley.

Bertenthal, B., & von Hofsten, C. (1998). Eye, head and trunk control: The foundation for manual development. *Neuroscience and Biobehavioral Reviews, 22,* 515–520.

Berzonsky, M. D., & Kuk, L. S. (2000). Identity status, identity processing style, and the transition to university. *Journal of Adolescent Research, 15,* 81–98.

Best, D. L., Williams, J. E., Cloud, J. M., Davis, S. W., Robertson, L. S., Edwards, J. R., Giles, H., & Fowles, J. (1977). Development of sex-trait stereotypes among young children in the United States, England, and Ireland. *Child Development, 48,* 1375–1384.

Betz, C. (1994, March). Beyond time-out: Tips from a teacher. *Young Children, 49*(3), 10–14.

Beyth-Marom, R., & Fischhoff, B. (1997). Adolescents' decisions about risks: A cognitive perspective. In J. Schulenberg, J. L. Maggs, & K. Hurrelmann (Eds.), *Health risks and developmental transitions during adolescence* (pp. 110–135). New York: Cambridge University Press.

Bhatia, T. K., & Ritchie, W. C. (1999). The bilingual child: Some issues and perspectives. In W. C. Ritchie & T. K. Bhatia (Eds.), *Handbook of child language acquisition* (pp. 569–643). San Diego: Academic Press.

Bialystok, E. (1986). Factors in the growth of linguistic awareness. *Child Development, 57,* 498–510.

Bialystok, E. (1997). Effects of bilingualism and biliteracy on children's emerging concepts of print. *Developmental Psychology, 33,* 429–440.

Bialystok, E. (1999). Cognitive complexity and attentional control in the bilingual mind. *Child Development, 70*, 636–644.

Bialystok, E., & Herman, J. (1999). Does bilingualism matter for early literacy? *Bilingualism, 2*, 35–44.

Bianco, A., Stone, J., Lynch, L., Lapinski, R., Berkowitz, G., & Berkowitz, R. L. (1996). Pregnancy outcome at age 40 and older. *Obstetrics and Gynecology, 87*, 917–922.

Bibace, R., & Walsh, M. E. (1980). Development of children's concepts of illness. *Pediatrics, 66*, 912–917.

Bidell, T. R., & Fischer, K. W. (1992). Cognitive development in educational contexts: Implications for skill learning. In A. Demetriou, M. Shayer, & A. Efklides (Eds.), *Neo-Piagetian theories of cognitive development* (pp. 11–31). London: Routledge & Kegan Paul.

Biederman, J., & Spencer, T. J. (2000). Genetics of childhood disorders: XIX, ADHD, part 3: Is ADHD a noradrenergic disorder? *Journal of the American Academy of Child & Adolescent Psychiatry, 39*, 1330–1333

Bielinski, J., & Davison, M. L. (1998). Gender differences by item difficulty interactions in multiple-choice mathematics items. *American Educational Research Journal, 35*, 455–476.

Bigelow, A. (1992). Locomotion and search behavior in blind infants. *Infant Behavior and Development, 15*, 179–189.

Bigler, R. S. (1995). The role of classification skill in moderating environmental influences on children's gender stereotyping: A study of the functional use of gender in the classroom. *Child Development, 66*, 1072–1087.

Bigler, R. S., & Liben, L. S. (1990). The role of attitudes and interventions in gender-schematic processing. *Child Development, 61*, 1440–1452.

Bigler, R. S., & Liben, L. S. (1992). Cognitive mechanisms in children's gender stereotyping: Theoretical and educational implications of a cognitive-based intervention. *Child Development, 63*, 1351–1363.

Bigner, J. J., & Jacobsen, R. B. (1989). Parenting behaviors of homosexual and heterosexual fathers. *Journal of Homosexuality, 18*, 173–186.

Bijeljac-Babic, R., Bertoncini, J., & Mehler, J. (1993). How do 4-day-old infants categorize multisyllable utterances? *Developmental Psychology, 29*, 711–721.

Bijur, P. E., Trumble, A., Harel, Y., Overpeck, M. D., Jones, D., & Schneidt, P. C. (1995). Sports and recreation injuries in U.S. children and adolescents. *Archives of Pediatric and Adolescent Medicine, 149*, 1009–1016.

Birch, E. E. (1993). Stereopsis in infants and its developmental relation to visual acuity. In K. Simons (Ed.), *Early visual development: Normal and abnormal* (pp. 224–236). New York: Oxford University Press.

Birch, L. L. (1998). Psychological influences on the childhood diet. *Journal of Nutrition, 128*, 407S–410S.

Birch, L. L. (1999). Development of food preferences. *Annual Review of Nutrition, 19*, 41–62.

Birch, L. L., & Fisher, J. A. (1995). Appetite and eating behavior in children. *Pediatric Clinics of North America, 42*, 931–953.

Birch, L. L., Zimmerman, S., & Hind, H. (1980). The influence of social-affective context on preschool children's food preferences. *Child Development, 51*, 856–861.

Birch, S. H., & Ladd, G. W. (1998). Children's interpersonal behaviors and the teacher–child relationship. *Developmental Psychology, 34*, 934–946.

Bird, C. E. (1999). Gender, household labor, and psychological distress: The impact of the amount and division of housework. *Journal of Health and Social Behavior, 40*, 32–45.

Biringen, Z., Emde, R. N., Campos, J. J., & Appelbaum, M. I. (1995). Affective reorganization in the infant, the mother, and the dyad: The role of upright locomotion and its timing. *Child Development, 66*, 499–514.

Biringen, Z., Emde, R. N., Campos, J. J., & Appelbaum, M. I. (1995). Affective reorganization in the infant, the mother, and the dyad: The role of upright locomotion and its timing. *Child Development, 66*, 499–514.

Birmaher, B., Ryan, N., Williamson, D., Brent, D., & Kaufman, J. (1996). Childhood and adolescent depression: A review of the past 10 years. Part II. *Journal of the American Academy of Child and Adolescent Psychiatry, 35*, 1575–1583.

Bischof-Köhler, D. (1991). The development of empathy in infants. In M. E. Lamb & H. Keller (Eds.), *Infant development: Perspectives from German-speaking countries* (pp. 1–33). Hillsdale, NJ: Erlbaum.

Bivens, J. A., & Berk, L. E. (1990). A longitudinal study of the development of elementary school children's private speech. *Merrill-Palmer Quarterly, 36*, 443–463.

Bjorklund, D. F. (1997). In search of a metatheory for cognitive development (or, Piaget is dead and I don't feel so good myself). *Child Development, 68*, 144–148.

Bjorklund, D. F., & Coyle, T. R. (1995). Utilization deficiencies in

the development of memory strategies. In F. E. Weinert & W. Schneider (Eds.), *Research on memory development: State of the art and future directions* (pp. 161–180). Hillsdale, NJ: Erlbaum.

Bjorklund, D. F., & Douglas, R. N. (1997). The development of memory strategies. In N. Cowan (Ed.), *The development of memory in childhood* (pp. 83–111). Hove, UK: Psychology Press.

Bjorklund, D. F., & Harnishfeger, K. K. (1995). The evolution of inhibition mechanisms and their role in human cognition and behavior. In M. L. Howe & R. Pasnak (Eds.), *Emerging themes in cognitive development: Vol. 1. Foundations* (pp. 141–173). New York: Springer-Verlag.

Bjorklund, D. F., Schneider, W., Cassel, W. S., & Ashley, E. (1994). Training and extension of a memory strategy: Evidence for utilization deficiencies in high- and low-IQ children. *Child Development, 65*, 951–965.

Black, M. M., Hutcheson, J. J., Dubowitz, H., & Berenson-Howard, J. (1994). Parenting style and developmental status among children with nonorganic failure to thrive. *Journal of Pediatric Psychology, 19*, 689–707.

Blagg, N., & Yule, W. (1996). School phobia. In T. H. Ollendick, N. J. King, & W. Yule (Eds.), *International handbook of phobic and anxiety disorders in children and adolescents* (pp. 169–186). New York: Plenum.

Blake, I. K. (1994). Language development and socialization in young African-American children. In P. M. Greenfield & R. R. Cocking (Eds.), *Cross-cultural roots of minority child development* (pp. 167–195). Hillsdale, NJ: Erlbaum.

Blake, J., & Boysson-Bardies, B. de (1992). Patterns in babbling: A cross-linguistic study. *Journal of Child Language, 19*, 51–74.

Blanchard, M., & Main, M. (1979). Avoidance of the attachment figure and social-emotional adjustment in day-care infants. *Developmental Psychology, 15*, 445–446.

Blanchard, R., & Bogaert, A. F. (1996). Homosexuality in men and number of older brothers. *American Journal of Psychiatry, 153*, 27–31.

Blanchard, R., Zucker, K. J., Bradley, S. J., & Hume, C. S. (1995). Birth order and sibling sex ratio in homosexual male adolescents and probably prehomosexual feminine boys. *Developmental Psychology, 31*, 22–30.

Blanchard, R., Zucker, K. J., Cohen-Kettenis, P. T., Gooren, L. J. G., &

Bailey, J. M. (1996). Birth order and sibling sex ratio in two samples of Dutch gender-dysphoric homosexual males. *Archives of Sexual Behavior, 25*, 495–512.

Blasi, A. (1994). Moral identity: Its role in moral functioning. In B. Puka (Ed.), *Fundamental research in moral development: A compendium* (Vol. 2, pp. 123–167). New York: Garland.

Blass, E. M. (1999). Savoring sucrose and suckling milk: Easing pain, saving calories, and learning about mother. In M. Lewis & D. Ramsay (Eds.), *Soothing and stress* (pp. 79–107). Mahwah, NJ: Erlbaum.

Blass, E. M., Ganchrow, J. R., & Steiner, J. E. (1984). Classical conditioning in newborn humans 2–48 hours of age. *Infant Behavior and Development, 7*, 223–235.

Blatchford, P., & Mortimore, P. (1994). The issue of class size for young children in schools: What can we learn from research? *Oxford Review of Education, 20*, 411–428.

Blewitt, P. (1994). Understanding categorical hierarchies: The earliest levels of skills. *Child Development, 65*, 1279–1298.

Block, J., & Block, J. H. (1980). *The California Child Q-Set.* Palo Alto, CA: Consulting Psychologists Press.

Bloom, B. S. (Ed.). (1985). *Developing talent in young people.* New York: Ballantine Books.

Bloom, L. (1998). Language acquisition in its developmental context. In D. Kuhn & R. S. Siegler (Eds.), *Handbook of child psychology: Vol. 2. Cognition, perception, and language* (5th ed., pp. 309–370). New York: Wiley.

Bloom, L. (2000). The intentionality model of language development: How to learn a word, any word. In R. Golinkoff, K. Hirsh-Pasek, N. Akhtar, L. Bloom, G. Hollich, L. Smith, M. Tomasello, & A. Woodward (Eds.), *Becoming a word learner: A debate on lexical acquisition.* New York: Oxford University Press.

Bloom, L., Margulis, C., Tinker, E., & Fujita, N. (1996). Early conversations and word learning: Contributions from child and adult. *Child Development, 67*, 3154–3175.

Bloom, P. (1999). The role of semantics in solving the bootstrapping problem. In R. Jackendoff & P. Bloom (Eds.), *Language, logic, and concepts* (pp. 285–309). Cambridge, MA: MIT Press.

Bloom, P. (2000). *How children learn the meanings of words.* Cambridge, MA: MIT Press.

Blotner, R., & Bearison, D. J. (1984). Developmental consistencies in socio-moral knowledge: Justice reasoning and altruistic behavior. *Merrill-Palmer Quarterly, 30,* 349–367.

Bluestone, C., & Tamis-LeMonda, C. S. (1999). Correlates of parenting styles in predominantly working- and middle-class African American mothers. *Journal of Marriage and the Family, 61,* 881–893.

Blum, N. J., & Carey, W. B. (1996). Sleep problems among infants and young children. *Pediatrics in Review, 17,* 87–93.

Blumberg, M. S., & Lucas, D. E. (1996). A developmental and component analysis of active sleep. *Developmental Psychobiology, 29,* 1–22.

Blyth, D. A., Simmons, R. G., & Zakin, D. F. (1985). Satisfaction with body image for early adolescent females: The impact of pubertal timing within different school environments. *Journal of Youth and Adolescence, 14,* 207–225.

Bobak, I. M., Jensen, M. D., & Zalar, M. K. (1989). *Maternity and gynecologic care.* St. Louis: Mosby.

Bock, G. R., & Goode, J. A. (Eds.). (1996). *Genetics of criminal and antisocial behavior.* Ciba Foundation Symposium 194. Chichester, England: Wiley.

Bodmer, W., & McKie, R. (1997). *The book of man: The human genome project and the quest to discover our genetic heritage.* New York: Oxford University Press.

Bohannon, J. N., III, & Bonvillian, J. D. (2001). Theoretical approaches to language acquisition. In J. B. Gleason (Ed.), *The development of language* (5th ed., pp. 254–314). Boston: Allyn and Bacon.

Bohannon, J. N., III, & Stanowicz, L. (1988). The issue of negative evidence: Adult responses to children's language errors. *Developmental Psychology, 24,* 684–689.

Bohman, M. (1996). Predispositions to criminality: Swedish adoption studies in retrospect. In G. R. Bock & J. A. Goode (Eds.), *Genetics of criminal and antisocial behavior.* Ciba Foundation Symposium 194 (pp. 99–114). Chichester, England: Wiley.

Bohman, M., & Sigvardsson, S. (1990). Outcome in adoption: Lessons from longitudinal studies. In D. M. Brodzinsky & M. D. Schechter (Eds.), *The psychology of adoption* (pp. 93–106). New York: Oxford University Press.

Boivin, M., & Hymel, S. (1997). Peer experiences and social self-perceptions: A sequential model. *Developmental Psychology, 33,* 135–145.

Boldizar, J. P. (1991). Assessing sex typing and androgyny in children: The children's sex role inventory. *Developmental Psychology, 27,* 505–515.

Boller, K., Grabelle, M., & Rovee-Collier, C. (1995). Effects of postevent information on infants' memory for a central target. *Journal of Experimental Child Psychology, 59,* 372–396.

Booth, A. (1999). Causes and consequences of divorce: Reflections on recent research. In R. A. Thompson & P. R. Amato (Eds.), *The postdivorce family: Children, parenting, and society* (pp. 29–48). Thousand Oaks, CA: Sage.

Borduin, C. M., & Schaefer, C. M. (1998). Violent offending in adolescence: Epidemiology, correlates, outcomes, and treatment. In T. P. Gullotta, G. R. Adams, & R. Montemayor (Eds.), *Delinquent violent youth: Theory and interventions* (pp. 144–174). Thousand Oaks, CA: Sage.

Borke, H. (1975). Piaget's mountains revisited: Changes in the egocentric landscape. *Developmental Psychology, 11,* 240–243.

Borkowski, J. G., & Muthukrishna, N. (1995). Learning environments and skill generalization: How contexts facilitate regulatory processes and efficacy beliefs. In F. Weinert & W. Schneider (Eds.), *Memory performances and competence: Issues in growth and development* (pp. 283-300). Mahwah, NJ: Erlbaum.

Bornholt, L. J., Goodnow, J. J., & Cooney, G. H. (1994). Influences of gender stereotypes on adolescents' perceptions of their own achievement. *American Educational Research Journal, 31,* 675–692.

Bornstein, M. H. (1989). Sensitive periods in development: Structural characteristics and causal interpretations. *Psychological Bulletin, 105,* 179–197.

Bornstein, M. H., & Arterberry, M. E. (1999). Perceptual development. In M. H. Bornstein & M. E. Lamb (Eds.), *Developmental psychology: An advanced textbook* (pp. 231–274). Mahwah, NJ: Erlbaum.

Bornstein, M. H., Haynes, O. M., Pascual, L., Painter, K. M., & Galperin, C. (1999a). Play in two societies: Pervasiveness of process, specificity of structure. *Child Development, 70,* 317–331.

Bornstein, M. H., Selmi, A. M., Haynes, O. M., Painter, K. M., & Marx, E. S. (1999b). Representational abilities and the hearing status of child/mother dyads. *Child Development, 70,* 833–852.

Bornstein, M. H., Tal, J., Rahn, C., Galperín, C. Z., Pêcheux, M., Lamour, M., Toda, S., Azuma, H., Ogino, M., & Tamis-LeMonda, C. S. (1992a). Functional analysis of the contents of maternal speech to infants of 5 and 13 months in four cultures: Argentina, France, Japan, and the United States. *Developmental Psychology, 28,* 593–603.

Bornstein, M. H., Vibbert, M., Tal, J., & O'Donnell, K. (1992b). Toddler language and play in the second year: Stability, covariation, and influences of parenting. *First Language, 12,* 323–338.

Borstelmann, L. J. (1983). Children before psychology: Ideas about children from antiquity to the late 1800s. In W. Kessen (Ed.), *Handbook of child psychology: Vol. 1. History, theory, and methods* (pp. 1–40). New York: Wiley.

Bortolus, R., Parazzini, F., Chatenoud, L., Benzi, G., Bianchi, M. M., & Marini, A. (1999). The epidemiology of multiple births. *Human Reproduction Update, 5,* 179–187.

Bouchard, C. (1994). *The genetics of obesity.* Boca Raton, FL: CRC Press.

Bouchard, T. J., Jr., Lykken, D. T., McGue, M., Segal, N. L., & Tellegen, A. (1990). Sources of human psychological differences: The Minnesota Study of Twins Reared Apart. *Science, 250,* 223–228.

Boukydis, C. F. Z., & Burgess, R. L. (1982). Adult physiological response to infant cries: Effects of temperament of infant, parental status and gender. *Child Development, 53,* 1291–1298.

Boukydis, C. F. Z., & Lester, B. M. (1998). Infant crying, risk status and social support in families of preterm and term infants. *Early Development and Parenting, 7,* 31–39.

Boulton, M. J. (1996). A comparison of 8- and 11-year-old girls' and boys' participation in specific types of rough-and-tumble play and aggressive fighting: Implications for functional hypotheses. *Aggressive Behavior, 22,* 271–287.

Boulton, M. J. (1999). Concurrent and longitudinal relations between children's playground behavior and social preference, victimization, and bullying. *Child Development, 70,* 944–954.

Boulton, M. J., & Smith, P. K. (1994). Bully/victim problems in middle-school children: Stability, self-perceived competence, peer perceptions and peer acceptance. *British Journal of Developmental Psychology, 12,* 315–329.

Bowlby, J. (1969). *Attachment and loss: Vol. 1. Attachment.* New York: Basic Books.

Bowlby, J. (1980). *Attachment and loss: Vol. 3. Loss.* New York: Basic Books.

Boyer, K., & Diamond, A. (1992). Development of memory for temporal order in infants and young children. In A. Diamond (Ed.), *Development and neural bases of higher cognitive function* (pp. 267– 317). New York: New York Academy of Sciences.

Boyes, M. C., & Chandler, M. (1992). Cognitive development, epistemic doubt, and identity formation in adolescence. *Journal of Youth and Adolescence, 21,* 277–304.

Boysson-Bardies, B. de, & Vihman, M. M. (1991). Adaptation to language: Evidence from babbling and first words in four languages. *Language, 67,* 297–319.

Brackbill, Y., McManus, K., & Woodward, L. (1985). *Medication in maternity: Infant exposure and maternal information.* Ann Arbor: University of Michigan Press.

Bracken, B. A. (2000). Clinical observation of preschool assessment behavior. In B. A. Bracken (Ed.), *The psychoeducational assessment of preschool children* (3rd ed., pp. 45–56). Boston, MA: Allyn and Bacon.

Bracken, B. A. (2000). *The psychoeducational assessment of preschool children.* Boston: Allyn and Bacon.

Bradbury, K., Janicke, D. M., Riley, A. W., & Finney, J. W. (1999). Predictors of unintentional injuries to school-age children seen in pediatric primary care. *Journal of Pediatric Psychology, 24,* 423–433.

Bradley, P. J., & Bray, K. H. (1996). The Netherlands' Maternal-Child Health Program: Implications for the United States. *Journal of Obstetric, Gynecologic, and Neonatal Nursing, 25,* 471–475.

Bradley, R. H., & Caldwell, B. M. (1979). Home Observation for Measurement of the Environment: A revision of the preschool scale. *American Journal of Mental Deficiency, 84,* 235–244.

Bradley, R. H., & Caldwell, B. M. (1981). The HOME Inventory: A validation of the preschool scale for black children. *Child Development, 52,* 708–710.

Bradley, R. H., & Caldwell, B. M. (1982). The consistency of the home environment and its relation to child development. *International Journal of Behavioral Development, 5,* 445–465.

Bradley, R. H., Caldwell, B. M., Rock, S. L., Ramey, C. T., Barnard, D. E., Gray, C., Hammond, M. A., Mitchell, S., Gottfried, A., Siegel, L., & Johnson, D. L. (1989). Home environment and cognitive development in the first 3 years of life: A collaborative study involving six sites and three ethnic groups in North America. *Developmental Psychology, 25,* 217–235.

Bradley, R. H., Whiteside, L., Mundfrom, D. J., Casey, P. H., Kelleher, K. J., & Pope, S. K. (1994). Contribution of early intervention and early caregiving experiences to resilience in low-birthweight, premature children living in poverty. *Journal of Clinical Child Psychology, 23*, 425–434.

Braet, D., Mervielde, I., & Vandereycken, W. (1997). Psychological aspects of childhood obesity: A controlled study in a clinical and nonclinical sample. *Journal of Pediatric Psychology, 22*, 59–71.

Braine, L. G., Pomerantz, E., Lorber, D., & Krantz, D. H. (1991). Conflicts with authority: Children's feelings, actions, and justifications. *Developmental Psychology, 27*, 829–840.

Braine, L. G., Schauble, L., Kugelmass, S., & Winter, A. (1993). Representation of depth by children: Spatial strategies and lateral biases. *Developmental Psychology, 29*, 466–479.

Braine, M. D. S. (1994). Is nativism sufficient? *Journal of Child Language, 21*, 1–23.

Braungart, J. M., Plomin, R., DeFries, J. C., & Fulker, D. W. (1992). Genetic influence on tester-rated infant temperament as assessed by Bayley's Infant Behavior Record: Nonadoptive and adoptive siblings and twins. *Developmental Psychology, 28*, 40–47.

Braungart-Rieker, J., Courtney, S., & Garwood, M. M. (1999). Mother- and father–infant attachment: Families in context. *Journal of Family Psychology, 13*, 535–553.

Bray, J. H. (1999). From marriage to remarriage and beyond: Findings from the Developmental Issues in Stepfamilies Research Project. In E. M. Hetherington (Ed.), *Coping with divorce, single parenting, and remarriage: A risk and resiliency perspective* (pp. 295–319). Mahwah, NJ: Erlbaum.

Brazelton, T. B. (1997). *Toilet training your child*. New York: Consumer Visions.

Brazelton, T. B., Christopherson, E. R., Frauman, A. C., Gorski, P. A., Poole, J. M., Stadtler, A. C., & Wright, C. L. (1999). Instruction, timeliness, and medical influences affect toilet training. *Pediatrics, 103*, 1353–1358.

Brazelton, T. B., Koslowski, B., & Tronick, E. (1976). Neonatal behavior among urban Zambians and Americans. *Journal of the American Academy of Child Psychiatry, 15*, 97–107.

Brazelton, T. B., & Nugent, J. K. (1995). *Neonatal Behavioral Assessment Scale*. London: Mac Keith Press.

Brazelton, T. B., Nugent, J. K., & Lester, B. M. (1987). Neonatal Behavioral Assessment Scale. In J. D. Osofsky (Ed.), *Handbook of infant development* (2nd ed., pp. 780–817). New York: Wiley.

Bredekamp, S., & Copple, C. (Eds.). (1997). *Developmentally appropriate practice in early childhood programs* (rev. ed.). Washington, DC: National Association for the Education of Young Children.

Bremner, J. G. (1998). From perception to action: The early development of knowledge. In F. Simion & G. Butterworth (Eds.), *Development of sensory, motor, and cognitive capacities in early infancy* (pp. 239–255). East Sussex, UK: Psychology Press.

Brendgen, M., Vitaro, F., & Bukowski, W. M. (1998). Deviant friends and early adolescents' emotional and behavioral adjustment. *Journal of Research on Adolescence, 10*, 173–189.

Brennan, W. M., Ames, E. W., & Moore, R. W. (1966). Age differences in infants' attention to patterns of different complexities. *Science, 151*, 354–356.

Brenner, E., & Salovey, P. (1997). Emotional regulation during childhood: Developmental, interpersonal, and individual considerations. In P. Salovey & D. Sluyter (Eds.), *Emotional literacy and emotional development* (pp. 168–192). New York: Basic Books.

Brent, R. L. (1999). Utilization of developmental basic science principles in the evaluation of reproductive risks from pre- and postconception environmental radiation exposures. *Teratology, 59*, 182–204.

Bretherton, I. (1992). The origins of attachment theory: John Bowlby and Mary Ainsworth. *Developmental Psychology, 28*, 759–775.

Brewaeys, A., Ponjaert, I., Van Hall, E. V., & Golombok, S. (1997). Donor insemination: Child development and family functioning in lesbian mother families. *Human Reproduction, 12*, 1349–1359.

Brien, M. J., & Willis, R. J. (1997). Costs and consequences for the fathers. In R. A. Maynard (Ed.), *Kids having kids* (pp. 95–144). Washington, DC: Urban Institute.

Briggs, F., & Hawkins, R. (1996). *Keeping ourselves safe: Who benefits?* Wellington, NZ: New Zealand Council for Educational Research.

Briggs, F., & Hawkins, R. (1999). The importance of parent involvement in child protection curricula. In L. E. Berk (Ed.), *Landscapes of development* (pp. 321–335). Belmont, CA: Wadsworth.

Brindley, B. A., & Sokol, R. J. (1988). Induction and augmentation of labor: Basis and methods for current practice. *Obstetrics and Gynecology Survey, 43*, 730–743.

Broberg, A. G., Wessels, H., Lamb, M. E., & Hwang, C. P. (1997). Effects of day care on the development of cognitive abilities in 8-year-olds: A longitudinal study. *Developmental Psychology, 33*, 62–69.

Brody, G. H., & Flor, D. L. (1998). Maternal resources, parenting practices, and child competence in rural, single-parent African American families. *Child Development, 69*, 803–816.

Brody, G. H., Stoneman, Z., & Flor, D. (1996). Family wages, family processes, and youth competence in rural married African American families. In E. M. Hetherington & E. A. Blechman (Eds.), *Stress, coping, and resiliency in children and families. Family research consortium: Advances in family research* (pp. 173–188). Mahwah, NJ: Erlbaum.

Brody, G. H., Stoneman, Z., & McCoy, J. K. (1992). Associations of maternal and paternal direct and differential behavior with sibling relationships: Contemporaneous and longitudinal analyses. *Child Development, 63*, 82–92.

Brody, G. H., Stoneman, Z., & McCoy, J. K. (1994). Forecasting sibling relationships in early adolescence from child temperament and family processes in middle childhood. *Child Development, 65*, 771–784.

Brody, G. H., Stoneman, Z., McCoy, J. K., & Forehand, R. (1992). Contemporaneous and longitudinal associations of sibling conflict with family relationship assessments and family discussions about sibling problems. *Child Development, 63*, 391–400.

Brody, L. (1999). *Gender, emotion, and the family*. Cambridge, MA: Harvard University Press.

Brody, L. R., & Hall, J. A. (1993). Gender and emotion. In M. Lewis & J. M. Haviland (Eds.), *Handbook of emotions* (pp. 447–460). New York: Guilford.

Brody, N. (1992). *Intelligence* (2nd ed.). San Diego: Academic Press.

Brody, N. (1997). *Intelligence* (2nd ed.). San Diego: Academic Press.

Brody, N. (1997). Intelligence, schooling, and society. *American Psychologist, 52*, 1046–1050.

Bronfenbrenner, U. (1979). *The ecology of human development: Experiments by nature and design*. Cambridge, MA: Harvard University Press.

Bronfenbrenner, U. (1989). Ecological systems theory. In R. Vasta (Ed.), *Annals of child development* (Vol. 6, pp. 187–251). Greenwich, CT: JAI Press.

Bronfenbrenner, U. (1993). The ecology of cognitive development: Research models and fugitive findings. In R. H. Wozniak & K. W. Fischer (Eds.), *Development in context* (pp. 3–44). Hillsdale, NJ: Erlbaum.

Bronfenbrenner, U. (1995). The bioecological model from a life course perspective: Reflections of a participant observer. In P. Moen, G. H. Elder, Jr., & K. Lüscher (Eds.), *Examining lives in context* (pp. 599–618). Washington, DC: American Psychological Association.

Bronfenbrenner, U. (1998). The ecology of developmental processes. In R. M. Lerner (Ed.), *Handbook of child psychology: Vol 1. Theoretical models of human development* (5th ed., pp. 993–1028). New York: Wiley.

Bronfenbrenner, U., & Ceci, S. J. (1994). Nature–nurture reconceptualized in developmental perspective: A bioecological model. *Psychological Review, 101*, 568–586.

Bronfenbrenner, U., & Morris, P. A. (1998). The ecology of developmental processes. In R. M. Lerner (Ed.), *Handbook of child psychology: Vol. 1. Theoretical models of human development* (5th ed., pp. 535–584). New York: Wiley.

Bronson, G. W. (1991). Infant differences in rate of visual encoding. *Child Development, 62*, 44–54.

Bronson, M. B. (1995). *The right stuff for children birth to 8*. Washington, DC: National Association for the Education of Young Children.

Brook, C. G. D. (1999). Mechanism of puberty. *Hormone Research, 51*(suppl. 3), 52–54.

Brooks, P. J., & Tomasello, M. (1999). Young children learn to produce passives with nonce [nonsense] words. *Developmental Psychology, 35*, 29–44.

Brooks-Gunn, J. (1988a). Antecedents and consequences of variations in girls' maturational timing. *Journal of Adolescent Health Care, 9*, 365–373.

Brooks-Gunn, J. (1988b). The impact of puberty and sexual activity upon the health and education of adolescent girls and boys. *Peabody Journal of Education, 64*, 88–113.

Brooks-Gunn, J., & Chase-Lansdale, P. L. (1995). Adolescent parenthood. In M. H. Bornstein (Ed.), *Handbook of parenting: Vol. 3. Status and social conditions of parenting* (pp. 113–149). Mahwah, NJ: Erlbaum.

Brooks-Gunn, J., McCarton, C. M., Casey, P. H., McCormick, M. C., Bauer, C. R., Bernbaum, J. C., Tyson, J., Swanson, M., Bennett, F. C., Scott, D. T., Tonascia, J., & Meinert, C. L. (1994). Early intervention in low-birth-weight premature infants. *Journal of the*

American Medical Association, 272, 1257–1262.

Brooks-Gunn, J., & Ruble, D. N. (1980). Menarche: The interaction of physiology, cultural, and social factors. In A. J. Dan, E. A. Graham, & C. P. Beecher (Eds.), *The menstrual cycle: A synthesis of interdisciplinary research* (pp. 141–159). New York: Springer-Verlag.

Brooks-Gunn, J., & Ruble, D. N. (1983). The experience of menarche from a developmental perspective. In J. Brooks-Gunn & A. C. Peterson (Eds.), *Girls at puberty* (pp. 155–177). New York: Plenum.

Brooks-Gunn, J., Warren, M. P., Samelson, M., & Fox, R. (1986). Physical similarity of and disclosure of menarcheal status to friends: Effects of grade and pubertal status. *Journal of Early Adolescence, 6,* 3–14.

Brown, A. L. (1997). Transforming schools into communities of thinking and learning about serious matters. *American Psychologist, 52,* 399–413.

Brown, B., Clasen, D., & Eicher, S. (1986). Perceptions of peer pressure, peer conformity dispositions, and self-reported behavior among adolescents. *Developmental Psychology, 22,* 521–530.

Brown, B. B. (1999). "You're going out with who?": Peer group influences on adolescent romantic relationships. In W. Furman, B. B. Brown, & C. Feiring (Eds.), *The development of romantic relationships in adolescence* (pp. 291–329). New York: Cambridge University Press.

Brown, B. B., Feiring, C., & Furman, W. (1999). Missing the love boat: Why researchers have shied away from adolescent romance. In W. Furman, B. B. Brown, & C. Feiring (Eds.), *The development of romantic relationships in adolescence* (pp. 1–16). New York: Cambridge University Press.

Brown, B. B., Freeman, H., & Huang, B. (1992). *"Crowd hopping": Incidence, correlates, and consequences of change in crowd affiliation during adolescence.* Paper presented at the biennial meeting of the Society for Research on Adolescence, Washington, DC.

Brown, B. B., Lohr, M. J., & McClenahan, E. L. (1986). Early adolescents' perceptions of peer pressure. *Journal of Early Adolescence, 6,* 139–154.

Brown, J. M., & Mehler, P. S. (2000). Medical complications occurring in adolescents with anorexia nervosa. *Western Journal of Medicine, 172,* 189–193.

Brown, J. R., Donelan-McCall, N., & Dunn, J. (1996). Why talk about mental states? The significance of children's conversations with friends, siblings, and mothers. *Child Development, 67,* 836–849.

Brown, J. R., & Dunn, J. (1996). Continuities in emotion understanding from 3 to 6 years. *Child Development, 67,* 789–802.

Brown, K. M., McMahon, R. P., Biro, F. M., Crawford, P., Schreiber, G. B., & Similo, S. L. (1999). Changes in self-esteem in black and white girls between the ages of 9 and 14 years: The NHLBI Growth and Health Study. *Journal of Adolescent Health, 23,* 7–19.

Brown, R. W. (1973). *A first language: The early stages.* Cambridge, MA: Harvard University Press.

Bruce, D., Dolan, A., & Phillips-Grant, K. (2000). On the transition from childhood amnesia to recall of personal memories. *Psychological Science, 11,* 360–364.

Bruck, M., Ceci, S. J., & Hembrooke, H. (1998). Reliability and credibility of young children's reports. *American Psychologist, 53,* 136–151.

Bruck, M., Treiman, R., Caravolas, M., Genesee, F., & Cassar, M. (1998). Spelling skills of children in whole language and phonics classrooms. *Applied Psycholinguistics, 19,* 669–684.

Bruer, J. T. (1999). *The myth of the first three years.* New York: Free Press.

Bruerd, B., & Jones, C. (1996). Preventing baby bottle tooth decay: Eight-year results. *Public Health Reports, 111,* 63–65.

Bruner, J. S. (1983). *Child's talk: Learning to use language.* Oxford: Oxford University Press.

Bryant, B. K. (1985). The neighborhood walk: Sources of support in middle childhood. *Monographs of the Society for Research in Child Development, 50* (3, Serial No. 210).

Bryk, A. S., Lee, V. E., & Holland, P. B. (1993). *Catholic schools and the common good.* Cambridge, MA: Harvard University Press.

Buchanan, A. (1996). *Cycles of child maltreatment.* Chichester, UK: Wiley.

Buchanan, C. M., Eccles, J. S., & Becker, J. B. (1992). Are adolescents the victims of raging hormones? Evidence for activational effects of hormones on moods and behaviors at adolescence. *Psychological Bulletin, 111,* 62–107.

Buchanan, C. M., & Holmbeck, G. N. (1998). Measuring beliefs about adolescent personality and behavior. *Journal of Youth and Adolescence, 27,* 609–629.

Buchanan, C. M., Maccoby, E. E., & Dornbusch, S. M. (1996). *Adolescents after divorce.* Cambridge, MA: Harvard University Press.

Buchanan-Barrow, E., & Barrett, M. (1998). Children's rule discrimination within the context of the school. *British Journal of Developmental Psychology, 16,* 539–551.

Buekens, P., Kotelchuck, M., Blondel, B., Kristensen, F. B., Chen, J-H., & Masuy-Stroobant, G. (1993). A comparison of prenatal care use in the United States and Europe. *American Journal of Public Health, 83,* 31–36.

Buhrmester, D. (1996). Need fulfillment, interpersonal competence, and the developmental contexts of early adolescent friendship. In W. M. Bukowski, A. F. Newcomb, & W. W. Hartup (Eds.), *The company they keep: Friendship during childhood and adolescence* (pp. 158–185). New York: Cambridge University Press.

Buhrmester, D. (1998). Need fulfillment, interpersonal competence, and the developmental contexts of early adolescent friendship. In W. M. Bukowski & A. F. Newcomb (Eds.), *The company they keep: Friendship in childhood and adolescence* (pp. 158–185). New York: Cambridge University Press.

Buhrmester, D., & Furman, W. (1990). Perceptions of sibling relationships during middle childhood and adolescence. *Child Development, 61,* 1387–1398.

Buhrmester, D., & Prager, K. (1995). Patterns and functions of self-disclosure during childhood and adolescence. In K. J. Rotenberg (Ed.), *Disclosure processes in children and adolescents* (pp. 10–56). New York: Cambridge University Press.

Bukowski, W. M., Sippola, L. K., & Hoza, B. (1999). Same and other: Interdependency between participation in same- and other-sex friendships. *Journal of Youth and Adolescence, 28,* 439–459.

Bukowski, W. M., Sippola, L. K., & Newcomb, A. F. (2000). Variations in patterns of attraction of same- and other-sex peers during early adolescence. *Developmental Psychology, 36,* 147–154.

Bulatao, R. A. (1998). *The value of family planning programs in developing countries.* New York: Rand Corporation.

Burchinal, M. R., Peisner-Feinberg, E., Bryant, D. M., & Clifford, R. (2000). Children's social and cognitive development and child-care quality: Testing for differential associations related to poverty, gender, or ethnicity. *Applied Developmental Science, 4,* 149–165.

Burchinal, M. R., Roberts, J. E., Nabors, L. A., & Bryant, D. M. (1996). Quality of center child care and infant cognitive and language development. *Child Development, 67,* 606–620.

Burghardt, J. A., Devaney, B. L., & Gordon, A. R. (1995). The School Nutrition and Dietary Assessment Study: Summary and discussion. *American Journal of Clinical Nutrition, 61,* 252S–257S.

Burhans, K. K., & Dweck, C. S. (1995). Helplessness in early childhood: The role of contingent worth. *Child Development, 66,* 1719–1738.

Burns, C. E. (2000). *Pediatric primary care: A handbook for nurse practitioners.* Philadelphia: Saunders.

Burns, R. B., & Mason, D. A. (1998). Class formation and composition in elementary schools. *American Educational Research Journal, 35,* 739–772.

Burr, D. C., Morrone, C., & Fiorentini, A. (1996). Spatial and temporal properties of infant colour vision. In F. Vital-Durand, J. Atkinson, & O. J. Braddick (Eds.), *Infant vision* (pp. 63–77). Oxford, England: Oxford University Press.

Burts, D. C., Hart, C. H., Charlesworth, R., Fleege, P. O., Mosley, J., & Thomasson, R. H. (1992). Observed activities and stress behaviors of children in developmentally appropriate and inappropriate kindergarten classrooms. *Early Childhood Research Quarterly, 7,* 297–318.

Bushnell, E. W., & Boudreau, J. P. (1993). Motor development and the mind: The potential role of motor abilities as a determinant of aspects of perceptual development. *Child Development, 64,* 1005–1021.

Bussell, D. A., Neiderhiser, J. M., Pike, A., Plomin, R., Simmens, S., Howe, G. W., Hetherington, E. M., Carroll, E., & Reiss, D. (1999). Adolescents' relationships to siblings and mothers: A multivariate genetic analysis. *Developmental Psychology, 35,* 1248–1259.

Bussey, K. (1992). Lying and truthfulness: Children's definitions, standards, and evaluative reactions. *Child Development, 63,* 129–137.

Bussey, K., & Bandura, A. (1992). Self-regulatory mechanisms governing gender development. *Child Development, 63,* 1236–1250.

Butler, D., & Smaglik, P. (2000). Draft data leave geneticists with a mountain still to climb. *Nature, 405,* 984–985.

Butler, G. E., McKie, M., & Ratcliffe, S. G. (1990). The cyclical nature of prepubertal growth. *Annals of Human Biology, 17,* 177–198.

Butler, R. (1998). Age trends in the use of social and temporal comparison for self-evaluation: Examination of a novel developmental hypothesis. *Child Development, 69,* 1054–1073.

Butler, R., & Ruzany, N. (1993). Age and socialization effects on the development of social comparison motives and normative ability assessment in kibbutz and urban children. *Child Development, 64,* 532–543.

Butterworth, G. (1999). Neonatal imitation: Existence, mechanisms and motives. In J. Nadel & G. Butterworth (Eds.), *Imitation in infancy* (pp. 63–88). Cambridge, UK: Cambridge University Press.

Bybee, J., Merisca, R., & Velasco, R. (1998). The development of reactions to guilt-producing events. In J. Bybee (Ed.), *Guilt and children* (pp. 185–213). San Diego: Academic Press.

Byrnes, J. P., & Takahira, S. (1993). Explaining gender differences on SAT-math items. *Developmental Psychology, 29,* 805–810.

Cadoret, R. J., Cain, C. A., & Crowe, R. R. (1983). Evidence for gene–environment interaction in the development of adolescent antisocial behavior. *Behavior Genetics, 13,* 301–310.

Cain, K. M., & Dweck, C. S. (1995). The relation between motivational patterns and achievement cognitions through the elementary school years. *Merrill-Palmer Quarterly, 41,* 25–52.

Caine, N. (1986). Behavior during puberty and adolescence. In G. Mitchell & J. Erwin (Eds.), *Comparative primate biology: Vol. 2A. Behavior, conservation, and ecology* (pp. 327–361). New York: Liss.

Cairns, E. (1996). *Children and political violence.* Cambridge: Blackwell.

Cairns, R. B. (1998). The making of developmental psychology. In R. M. Lerner (Ed.), *Handbook of child psychology: Vol. 1. Theoretical models of human development* (5th ed., pp. 25–105). New York: Wiley.

Cairns, R. B., Leung, M., Buchanan, L., & Cairns, B. D. (1995). Friendships and social networks in childhood and adolescence: Fluidity, reliability, and interrelations. *Child Development, 66,* 1330–1345.

Cairns, R., Xie, H., & Leung, M.-C. (1998). The popularity of friendship and the neglect of social networks: Toward a new balance. In W. M. Bukowski & A. H. Cillessen (Eds.), *Sociometry then and now: Building on six decades of measuring children's experiences with the peer group* (pp. 25–53). San Francisco: Jossey-Bass.

Caldwell, B. M., & Bradley, R. H. (1994). Environmental issues in developmental follow-up research. In S. L. Friedman & H. C. Haywood (Eds.), *Developmental follow-up* (pp. 235–256). San Diego: Academic Press.

Caldwell, C. H., & Antonucci, T. C. (1997). Childbearing during adolescence: Mental health risks and opportunities. In J. Schulenberg, J. L. Maggs, & K. Hurrelmann (Eds.), *Health risks and developmental transitions during adolescence* (pp. 220–245). New York: Cambridge University Press.

Caldwell, J. (1999). Paths to lower fertility. *British Medical Journal, 319,* 985–987.

Calkins, S. D., Fox, N. A., & Marshall, T. R. (1996). Behavioral and physiological antecedents of inhibited and uninhibited behavior. *Child Development, 67,* 523–540.

Callaghan, T. C. (1999). Early understanding and production of graphic symbols. *Child Development, 70,* 1314–1324.

Camara, K. A., & Resnick, G. (1988). Interparental conflict and cooperation: Factors moderating children's post-divorce adjustment. In E. M. Hetherington & J. D. Arasteh (Eds.), *Impact of divorce, single parenting, and stepparenting on children* (pp. 169–195). Hillsdale, NJ: Erlbaum.

Cameron, C. A., & Lee, K. (1997). The development of children's telephone communication. *Journal of Applied Developmental Psychology, 18,* 55–70.

Cameron, M. B., & Wilson, B. J. (1990). The effects of chronological age, gender, and delay of entry on academic achievement and retention: Implications for academic redshirting. *Psychology in the Schools, 27,* 260–263.

Campbell, D. W., & Eaton, W. O. (1999). Sex differences in the activity level of infants. *Infant and Child Development, 8,* 1–17.

Campbell, F. A., & Ramey, C. T. (1991). *The Carolina Abecedarian Project.* Paper presented at the biennial meeting of the Society for Research in Child Development, Seattle, WA.

Campbell, F. A., & Ramey, C. T. (1994). Effects of early intervention on intellectual and academic achievement: A follow-up study of children from low-income families. *Child Development, 65,* 684–698.

Campbell, F. A., & Ramey, C. T. (1995). Cognitive and school outcomes for high-risk African-American students at middle adolescence: Positive effects of early intervention. *American Educational Research Journal, 32,* 743–772.

Campbell, J. R., Hombo, C. M., & Mazzeo, J. (2000). *NAEP 1999: Trends in academic progress.* Washington, DC: U.S. Department of Education.

Campbell, R., & Sais, E. (1995). Accelerated metalinguistic (phonological) awareness in bilingual children. *British Journal of Developmental Psychology, 13,* 61–68.

Campbell, S. B., Cohen, J. F., & Meyers, T. (1995). Depression in first-time mothers: Mother–infant interaction and depression chronicity. *Developmental Psychology, 31,* 349–357.

Campos, J. J., & Bertenthal, B. I. (1989). Locomotion and psychological development. In F. Morrison, K. Lord, & D. Keating (Eds.), *Applied developmental psychology* (Vol. 3, pp. 229–258). New York: Academic Press.

Campos, J. J., Kermoian, R., & Zumbahlen, M. R. (1992). Socioemotional transformation in the family system following infant crawling onset. In N. Eisenberg & R. A. Fabes (Eds.), *New directions for child development* (No. 55, pp. 25–40). San Francisco: Jossey-Bass.

Campos, R. G. (1989). Soothing pain-elicited distress in infants with swaddling and pacifiers. *Child Development, 60,* 781–792.

Camras, L. A. (1992). Expressive development and basic emotions. *Cognition and Emotion, 6,* 267–283.

Camras, L. A., Oster, H., Campos, J., Campos, R., Ujie, T., Miyake, K., Wang, L., & Meng, Z. (1998). Production of emotional and facial expressions in European American, Japanese, and Chinese infants. *Developmental Psychology, 34,* 616–628.

Camras, L. A., Oster, H., Campos, J. J., Miyake, K., & Bradshaw, D. (1992). Japanese and American infants' responses to arm restraint. *Developmental Psychology, 28,* 578–583.

Canadian Institute for Health Information. (2000). *Health care in Canada 2000.* Ottawa: Canadian Institute for Health Information.

Candy-Gibbs, S., Sharp, K., & Petrun, C. (1985). The effects of age, object, and cultural/religious background on children's concepts of death. *Omega, 15,* 329–345.

Canetto, S. S., & Sakinofsky, I. (1998). The gender paradox in suicide. *Suicide and Life-Threatening Behavior, 28,* 1–23.

Cannella, G. S. (1993). Learning through social interaction: Shared cognitive experience, negotiation strategies, and joint concept construction for young children. *Early Childhood Research Quarterly, 8,* 427–444.

Canobi, K. H., Reeve, R. A., & Pattison, P. E. (1998). The role of conceptual understanding in children's addition problem solving. *Developmental Psychology, 34,* 882–891.

Capaldi, D. M., & Patterson, G. R. (1991). Relation of parental transitions to boys' adjustment problems: I. A linear hypothesis. II. Mothers at risk for transitions and unskilled parenting. *Developmental Psychology, 27,* 489–504.

Capelli, C. A., Nakagawa, N., & Madden, C. M. (1990). How children understand sarcasm: The role of context and intonation. *Child Development, 61,* 1824–1841.

Capuzzi, D. (1989). *Adolescent suicide prevention.* Ann Arbor, MI: ERIC Counseling and Personnel Services Clearinghouse.

Carey, S. (1995). On the origins of causal understanding. In D. Sperber, D. Premack, & A. J. Premack (Eds.), *Causal cognition* (pp. 268–308). Oxford, UK: Clarendon Press.

Carey, S. (1999). Sources of conceptual change. In E. K. Scholnick, K. Nelson, S. A. Gelman, & P. H. Miller (Eds.), *Conceptual development: Piaget's legacy* (pp. 293–326). Mahwah, NJ: Erlbaum.

Carle, E. (1969). *The very hungry caterpillar.* New York: Philomel.

Carli, L. L. (1995). No: Biology does not create gender differences in personality. In M. R. Walsh (Ed.), *Women, men, and gender.* New Haven, CT: Yale University Press.

Carlo, G., Koller, S. H., Eisenberg, N., Da Silva, M., & Frohlich, C. (1996). A cross-national study on the relations among prosocial moral reasoning, gender role orientations, and prosocial behaviors. *Developmental Psychology, 32,* 231–240.

Carlson, C., Uppal, S., & Prosser, E. (2000). Ethnic differences in processes contributing to the self-esteem of early adolescent girls. *Journal of Early Adolescence, 20,* 44–67.

Carlson, K. J., Eisenstat, S. A., & Ziporyn, T. (1996). *The Harvard guide to women's health.* Cambridge, MA: Harvard University Press.

Carlton, M. P., & Winsler, A. (1999). School readiness: The need for a paradigm shift. *School Psychology Review, 28,* 338–352.

Carmichael, S. L., & Shaw, G. M. (2000). Maternal life stress and congenital anomalies. *Epidemiology, 11,* 30–35.

Carpendale, J. I. M. (2000). Kohlberg and Piaget on stages and moral reasoning. *Developmental Review, 20,* 181–205.

Carpendale, J. I., & Chandler, M. J. (1996). On the distinction between false belief understanding and subscribing to an interpretive theory of mind. *Child Development, 67,* 1686–1706.

Carpenter, C. J. (1983). Activity structure and play: Implications for socialization. In M. Liss (Eds.), *Social and cognitive skills: Sex roles and children's play* (pp. 117–145). New York: Academic Press.

Carpenter, M., Nagel, K., & Tomasello, M. (1998). Social cognition, joint attention, and communicative competence. *Monographs of the Society for Research in Child Development, 63*(4, Serial No. 255).

Carpenter, T. P., Fennema, E., Fuson, K., Hiebert, J., Human, P., & Murray, H. (1999). Learning basic number concepts and skills as problem solving. In E. Fennema & T. A. Romberg (Eds.), *Mathematics classrooms that promote understanding: Studies in mathematical thinking and learning series* (pp. 45–61). Mahwah, NJ: Erlbaum.

Carskadon, M. A., Viera, C., & Acebo, C. (1993). Association between puberty and delayed phase preference. *Sleep, 16,* 258–262.

Carter, D. B., & McCloskey, L. A. (1984). Peers and the maintenance of sex-typed behavior: The development of children's conceptions of cross-gender behavior in their peers. *Social Cognition, 2,* 294–314.

Casaer, P. (1993). Old and new facts about perinatal brain development. *Journal of Child Psychology and Psychiatry, 34,* 101–109.

Case, R. (1985). *Intellectual development: A systematic reinterpretation.* New York: Academic Press.

Case, R. (1992). *The mind's staircase: Exploring the conceptual underpinnings of children's thought and knowledge.* Hillsdale, NJ: Erlbaum.

Case, R. (1996). Introduction: Reconceptualizing the nature of children's conceptual structures and their development in middle childhood. In R. Case & Y. Okamoto (Eds.), The role of central conceptual structures in the development of children's thought. *Monographs of the Society for Research in Child Development, 246* (61, Serial No. 246), pp. 1–26.

Case, R. (1998). The development of conceptual structures. In D. Kuhn & R. S. Siegler (Eds.), *Handbook of child psychology: Vol. 2. Cognition, perception, and language* (pp. 745–800). New York: Wiley.

Case, R., & Okamoto, Y. (Eds.). (1996). The role of central conceptual structures in the development of children's thought. *Monographs of the Society for Research in Child Development, 61*(1–2, Serial No. 246).

Case-Smith, J., Bigsby, R., & Clutter, J. (1998). Perceptual-motor coupling in the development of grasp.

American Journal of Occupational Therapy, 52, 102–110.

Casey, M. B. (1986). Individual differences in selective attention among prereaders: A key to mirror-image confusions. *Developmental Psychology, 22,* 824–831.

Casey, M. B., Nuttall, R. L., & Pezaris, E. (1997). Mediators of gender differences in mathematics college entrance test scores: A comparison of spatial skills with internalized beliefs and anxieties. *Developmental Psychology, 33,* 669–680.

Casey, M. B., Nuttall, R. L., & Pezaris, E. (1999). Evidence in support of a model that predicts how biological and environmental factors interact to influence spatial skills. *Developmental Psychology, 35,* 1237–1247.

Casey, M. B., Nuttall, R., Pezaris, E., & Benbow, C. P. (1995). The influence of spatial ability on gender differences in mathematics college entrance test scores across diverse samples. *Developmental Psychology, 31,* 697–705.

Caspi, A. (1998). Personality development across the life course. In N. Eisenberg (Ed.), *Handbook of child psychology: Vol. 3. Social, emotional, and personality development* (5th ed., pp. 311–388). New York: Wiley.

Caspi, A., & Silva, P. A. (1995). Temperamental qualities at age three predict personality traits in young adulthood: Longitudinal evidence from a birth cohort. *Child Development, 66,* 486–498.

Caspi, A., Elder, G. H., Jr., & Bem, D. J. (1987). Moving against the world: Life-course patterns of explosive children. *Developmental Psychology, 23,* 308–313.

Caspi, A., Elder, G. H., Jr., & Bem, D. J. (1988). Moving away from the world: Life-course patterns of shy children. *Developmental Psychology, 24,* 824–831.

Caspi, A., Lynam, D., Moffitt, T. E., & Silva, P. A. (1993). Unraveling girls' delinquency: Biological, dispositional, and contextual contributions to adolescent misbehavior. *Developmental Psychology, 29,* 19–30.

Cassidy, J., & Berlin, L. J. (1994). The insecure/ambivalent pattern of attachment: Theory and research. *Child Development, 65,* 971–991.

Castle, J. M. (1999). Learning and teaching phonological awareness. In G. B. Thompson & T. Nicholson (Eds.), *Learning to read: Beyond phonics and whole language* (pp. 55–73). New York: Teachers College Press.

Catsambis, S. (1994). The path to math: Gender and racial-ethnic differences in mathematics partici-

pation from middle school to high school. *Sociology of Education, 67,* 199–215.

Catterall, J. (1998). Risk and resilience in student transitions to high school. *American Journal of Education, 106,* 302–333.

Ceci, S. J. (1991). How much does schooling influence general intelligence and its cognitive components? A reassessment of the evidence. *Developmental Psychology, 27,* 703–722.

Ceci, S. J., & Bruck, M. (1993). Suggestibility of the child witness: A historical review and synthesis. *Psychological Bulletin, 113,* 403–439.

Ceci, S. J., & Bruck, M. (1998). Children's testimony: Applied and basic issues. In I. Sigel & K. A. Renninger (Eds.), *Handbook of child psychology: Vol. 4. Child psychology in practice* (5th ed., pp. 713–774). New York: Wiley.

Ceci, S. J., Leichtman, M. D., & Bruck, M. (1994). The suggestibility of children's eyewitness reports: Methodological issues. In F. Weinert & W. Schneider (Eds.), *Memory development: State of the art and future directions.* Hillsdale, NJ: Erlbaum.

Ceci, S. J., & Roazzi, A. (1994). The effects of context on cognition: Postcards from Brazil. In R. J. Sternberg (Ed.), *Mind in context* (pp. 74–101). New York: Cambridge University Press.

Ceci, S. J., Rosenblum, T. B., & Kumpf, M. The shrinking gap between high- and low-scoring groups: Current trends and possible causes. In U. Neisser (Ed.), *The rising curve: Long-term gains in IQ and related measures* (pp. 287–302). Washington, DC: American Psychological Association.

Ceci, S. J., & Williams, W. M. (1997). Schooling, intelligence, and income. *American Psychologist, 52,* 1051–1058.

Center for Communication and Social Policy. (Ed.). (1998). *National Television Violence Study* (Vol. 2). Newbury Park, CA: Sage.

Central Intelligence Agency. (1999). *The world fact book.* Washington, DC: U.S. Government Printing Office.

Cernoch, J. M., & Porter, R. H. (1985). Recognition of maternal axillary odors by infants. *Child Development, 56,* 1593–1598.

Cervantes, C. A., & Callanan, M. A. (1998). Labels and explanations in mother–child emotion talk: Age and gender differentiation. *Developmental Psychology, 34,* 88–98.

Chall, J. S. (1983). *Stages of reading development.* New York: McGraw-Hill.

Chalmers, J. B., & Townsend, M. A. R. (1990). The effects of training in social perspective taking on socially maladjusted girls. *Child Development, 61,* 178–190.

Chamberlain, G., & Steer, P. (1999). Obstetric emergencies. *British Medical Journal, 318,* 1342–1345.

Chan, R. W., Raboy, B., & Patterson, C. J. (1998). Psychosocial adjustment among children conceived via donor insemination by lesbian and heterosexual mothers. *Child Development, 69,* 443–457.

Chandler, M. (1994). Adolescent suicide and the loss of personal continuity. In D. Cicchetti & S. L. Toth (Eds.), *Rochester Symposium on Developmental Psychopathology: Vol. 5. Disorders and dysfunctions of the self* (pp. 371–390). Rochester, NY: University of Rochester Press.

Chandler, M., Boyes, M., & Ball, L. (1990). Relativism and stations of epistemic doubt. *Journal of Experimental Child Psychology, 50,* 370–395.

Chandler, M. J. (1973). Egocentrism and antisocial behavior: The assessment and training of social perspective-taking skills. *Developmental Psychology, 9,* 326–332.

Chandra, R. K. (1991). Interactions between early nutrition and the immune system. In *Ciba Foundation Symposium No. 156* (pp. 77–92). Chichester, England: Wiley.

Chao, R. K. (1994). Beyond parental control and authoritarian parenting style: Understanding Chinese parenting through the cultural notion of training. *Child Development, 65,* 1111–1119.

Charman, T., Swettenham, J., Baron-Cohen, S., Cox, A., Baird, G., & Drew, A. (1997). Infants with autism: An investigation of empathy, pretend play, joint attention, and imitation. *Developmental Psychology, 33,* 781–789.

Chase-Lansdale, P. L., Brooks-Gunn, J., & Zamsky, E. S. (1994). Young African-American multigenerational families in poverty: Quality of mothering and grandmothering. *Child Development, 65,* 373–393.

Chase-Lansdale, P. L., Cherlin, A. J., & Kiernan, K. E. (1995). The long-term effects of parental divorce on the mental health of young children. *Child Development, 66,* 1614–1634.

Chase-Lansdale, P. L., & Vinovskis, M. A. (1995). *Escape from poverty: What makes a difference for children?* New York: Cambridge University Press.

Chasnoff, I. J., Anson, A., Hatcher, R., Stenson, H., Iaukea, K., &

Randolph, L. A. (1998). Prenatal exposure to cocaine and other drugs: Outcome at four to six years. In J. A. Harvey & B. E. Kosofsky (Eds.), *Annals of the New York Academy of Sciences* (Vol. 846, pp. 314–328). New York: New York Academy of Sciences.

Chatkupt, S., Mintz, M., Epstein, L. G., Bhansali, D., & Koenigsberger, M. R. (1989). Neuroimaging studies in children with human immunodeficiency virus type 1 infection. *Annals of Neurology, 26,* 453.

Chavajay, P., & Rogoff, B. (1999). Cultural variation in management of attention by children and their caregivers. *Developmental Psychology, 35,* 1079–1090.

Chen, X. (2001). Growing up in a collectivistic culture. Socialization and socio-emotional development in Chinese children. In A. L. Comunian & U. P. Gielen (Eds.), *Human development in cross-cultural perspective.* Padua, Italy: Cedam.

Chen, X., Hastings, P. D., Rubin, K. H., Chen, H., Cen, G., & Stewart, S. L. (1998). Child-rearing attitudes and behavioral inhibition in Chinese and Canadian toddlers: A cross-cultural study. *Developmental Psychology, 34,* 677–686.

Chen, X., Liu, M., Li, B., Cen, G., Chen, H., & Wang, L. (2000). Maternal authoritative and authoritarian attitudes and mother–child interactions and relationships in urban China. *International Journal of Behavioral Development, 24,* 119–126.

Chen, X., Rubin, K. H., & Li, Z. (1995). Social functioning and adjustment in Chinese children: A longitudinal study. *Developmental Psychology, 31,* 531–539.

Chen, Y.-C., Yu, M.-L., Rogan, W., Gladen, B., & Hsu, C.-C. (1994). A 6-year follow-up of behavior and activity disorders in the Taiwan Yu-cheng children. *American Journal of Public Health, 84,* 415–421.

Chen, Y.-J., & Hsu, C.-C. (1994). Effects of prenatal exposure to PCBs on the neurological function of children: A neuropsychological and neurophysiological study. *Developmental Medicine and Child Neurology, 36,* 312–320.

Chen, Z., Sanchez, R. P., & Campbell, T. (1997). From beyond to within their grasp: The rudiments of analogical problem solving in 10- to 13-month-olds. *Developmental Psychology, 33,* 790–801.

Chen, Z., & Siegler, R. S. (2000). Across the great divide: Bridging the gap between understanding of toddlers' and older children's thinking. *Monographs of the Society for Research in Child Development, 65*(2, Serial No. 261).

Cheng, T. L., Fields, C. B., Brenner, R. A., Wright, J. L., Lomax, T., Scheidt, P. C., & the District of Columbia Child/Adolescent Injury Research Network. (2000). Sports injuries: An important cause of morbidity in urban youth. *Pediatrics, 105,* e32.

Cherlin, A. J., Furstenberg, F. F., Jr., Chase-Lansdale, P. L., Kiernan, K. E., Robins, P. K., Morrison, D. R., & Teitler, J. O. (1991). Longitudinal studies of effects of divorce on children in Great Britain and the United States. *Science, 252,* 1386-1389.

Cherlin, A. J., Kiernan, K. E., & Chase-Lansdale, P. L. (1995). Parental divorce in childhood and demographic outcomes in young adulthood. *Demography, 32,* 299–318.

Cherny, S. S. (1994). Home environmental influences on general cognitive ability. In J. C. DeFries, R. Plomin, & D. W. Fulker (Eds.), *Nature and nurture during middle childhood* (pp. 262–280). Cambridge, MA: Blackwell.

Chess, S., & Thomas, A. (1984). *Origins and evolution of behavior disorders.* New York: Brunner/Mazel.

Chez, B. F. (1997). Electronic fetal monitoring then and now. *Journal of Perinatal and Neonatal Nursing, 10,* 1–4.

Children's Defense Fund. (2000). *The state of America's children: Yearbook 2000.* Washington, DC: Author.

Childs, C. P., & Greenfield, P. M. (1982). Informal modes of learning and teaching: The case of Zinacanteco weaving. In N. Warren (Ed.), *Advances in cross-cultural psychology* (Vol. 2, pp. 269–316). London: Academic Press.

Chin, D. G., Schonfeld, D. J., O'Hare, L. L., Mayne, S. T., Salovey, P., Showalter, D. R., & Cicchetti, D. V. (1998). Elementary school-age children's developmental understanding of the causes of cancer. *Developmental and Behavioral Pediatrics, 19,* 397–403.

Chiu, L-H. (1992-1993). Self-esteem in American and Chinese (Taiwanese) children. *Current Psychology: Research and Reviews, 11,* 309–313.

Choi, S., & Gopnik, A. (1995). Early acquisition of verbs in Korean: A cross-linguistic study. *Journal of Child Language, 22,* 497–529.

Chomsky, C. (1969). *The acquisition of syntax in children from five to ten.* Cambridge, MA: MIT Press.

Chomsky, N. (1957). *Syntactic structures.* The Hague: Mouton.

Christophersen, E. R., & Edwards, K. J. (1992). Treatment of elimination disorders: State of the art 1991. *Applied and Preventive Psychology, 1,* 15–22.

Chugani, H. T. (1994). Development of regional brain glucose metabolism in relation to behavior and plasticity. In G. Dawson & K. W. Fischer (Eds.), *Human behavior and the developing brain* (pp. 153–175). New York: Guilford.

Cicchetti, D., & Aber, J. L. (1986). Early precursors of later depression: An organizational perspective. In L. P. Lipsitt & C. Rovee-Collier (Eds.), *Advances in infancy research* (Vol. 4, pp. 87–137). Norwood, NJ: Ablex.

Cicchetti, D., & Garmezy, N. (1993). Prospects and promises in the study of resilience. *Development and Psychopathology, 5,* 497–502.

Cicchetti, D., & Toth, S. L. (1998a). Perspectives on research and practice in developmental psychology. In I. E. Sigel & K. A. Renninger (Eds.), *Handbook of child psychology: Vol. 4. Child psychology in practice* (5th ed., pp. 479–582). New York: Wiley.

Cicchetti, D., & Toth, S. L. (1998b). The development of depression in children and adolescents. *American Psychologist, 53,* 221–241.

Cillessen, A. H. N., & Bukowski, W. M. (2000). *Recent advances in the measurement of acceptance and rejection in the peer system.* San Francisco: Jossey-Bass.

Clark, E. V. (1983). Meanings and concepts. In J. H. Flavell & E. M. Markman (Eds.), *Handbook of child psychology: Vol. 3. Cognitive development* (pp. 787–840). New York: Wiley.

Clark, E. V. (1990). On the pragmatics of contrast. *Journal of Child Language, 17,* 417–431.

Clark, E. V. (1995). The lexicon and syntax. In J. L. Miller & P. D. Eimas (Eds.), *Speech, language, and communication* (pp. 303–337). San Diego: Academic Press.

Clark, R., Hyde, J. S., Essex, M. J. & Klein, M. H. (1997). Length of maternity leave and quality of mother-infant interaction. *Child Development, 68,* 364–383.

Clarke-Stewart, K. A. (1998). Historical shifts and underlying themes in ideas about rearing young children in the United States: Where have we been? Where are we going? *Early Development and Parenting, 7,* 101–117.

Clarke-Stewart, K. A., & Hayward, C. (1996). Advantages of father custody and contact for the psychological well-being of school-age children. *Journal of Applied Developmental Psychology, 17,* 239–270.

Claude, E., & Firestone, P. (1995). The development of ADHD boys: A 12-year follow-up. *Canadian Journal of Behavioural Science, 27,* 226–249.

Clausen, J. A. (1975). The social meaning of differential physical and sexual maturation. In S. E. Dragastin & G. H. Elder (Eds.), *Adolescence in the life cycle: Psychological change and the social context* (pp. 25–47). New York: Halsted.

Clements, D. H. (1990). Metacomponential development in a Logo programming environment. *Journal of Educational Psychology, 82,* 141–149.

Clements, D. H. (1995). Teaching creativity with computers. *Educational Psychology Review, 7,* 141–161.

Clements, D. H., & Nastasi, B. K. (1992). Computers and early childhood education. In M. Gettinger, S. N. Elliott, & T. R. Kratochwill (Eds.), *Advances in school psychology: Preschool and early childhood treatment directions* (pp. 187– 246). Hillsdale, NJ: Erlbaum.

Clements, D. H., Nastasi, B. K., & Swaminathan, S. (1993). Young children and computers: Crossroads and directions from research. *Young Children, 48*(2), 56–64.

Clifton, R. K., Rochat, P., Robin, D. J., & Berthier, N. E. (1994). Multimodal perception in the control of infant reaching. *Journal of Experimental Psychology: Human Perception and Performance, 20,* 876–886.

Cnattingius, S., Forman, M. R., Berendes, H. W., & Isotalo, L. (1992). Delayed childbearing and risk of adverse perinatal outcome: A population-based study. *Journal of the American Medical Association, 268,* 886–890.

Coakley, J. (1990). *Sport and society: Issues and controversies* (4th ed.). St. Louis: Mosby.

Cohen, F. L. (1993). Epidemiology of HIV infection and AIDS in children. In F. L. Cohen & J. D. Durham (Eds.), *Women, children, and HIV/ AIDS* (pp. 137–155). New York: Springer.

Cohen, K. M., & Savin-Williams, R. C. (1996). Developmental perspectives on coming out to self and others. *The lives of lesbians, gays, and bisexuals: Children to adults* (pp. 113–151). Ft. Worth, TX: Harcourt Brace.

Cohen, L. B. (1998). An information-processing approach to infant perception and cognition. In F. Simion & G. Butterworth (Eds.), *Development of sensory, motor, and cognitive capacities in early infancy* (pp. 270–300). East Sussex, UK: Psychology Press.

Cohen, L. B., & Amsel, G. (1998). The precursors to infants' perception of the causality of a simple event. *Infant Behavior and Development, 21,* 713–732.

Cohen, L. B., Rundell, L. J., Spellman, N. S., & Cashon, C. H. (1999). Infants' perception of causal chains. *Psychological Science, 10,* 412–418.

Cohen, S., & Williamson, G. M. (1991). Stress and infectious disease in humans. *Psychological Bulletin, 109,* 5–24.

Cohn, D. A., Cowan, P. A., Cowan, C. P., & Pearson, J. (1992). Mothers' and fathers' working models of childhood attachment relationships, parenting styles, and child behavior. *Development and Psychopathology, 4,* 417–432.

Coie, J. D., & Dodge, K. A. (1998). Aggression and antisocial behavior. In N. Eisenberg (Ed.), *Handbook of child psychology: Vol. 3. Social, emotional, and personality development* (5th ed., pp. 779–862). New York: Wiley.

Coie, J. D., Dodge, K. A., & Coppotelli, H. (1982). Dimensions and types of social status: A cross-age perspective. *Developmental Psychology, 18,* 557–570.

Coie, J. D., & Krehbiel, G. (1984). Effects of academic tutoring on the social status of low-achieving, socially rejected children. *Child Development, 55,* 1465–1478.

Colby, A., Kohlberg, L., Gibbs, J., & Lieberman, M. (1983). A longitudinal study of moral judgment. *Monographs of the Society for Research in Child Development, 48*(1–2, Serial No. 200).

Cole, M. (1990). Cognitive development and formal schooling: The evidence from cross-cultural research. In L. C. Moll (Ed.), *Vygotsky and education* (pp. 89–110). New York: Cambridge University Press.

Cole, P. M., & Tamang, B. L. (1998). Nepali children's ideas about emotional displays in hypothetical challenges. *Developmental Psychology, 34,* 640–648.

Coley, R. L. (1998). Children's socialization experiences and functioning in single-mother households: The importance of fathers and other men. *Child Development, 69,* 219–230.

Coley, R. L., & Chase-Lansdale, P. L. (1998). Adolescent pregnancy and parenthood: Recent evidence and future directions. *American Psychologist, 53,* 152–166.

Collaer, M. L., & Hines, M. (1995). Human behavioral sex differences: A role for gonadal hormones during early development? *Psychological Bulletin, 118,* 55–107.

Collie, R., & Hayne, H. (1999). Deferred imitation by 6- and 9-month-old infants: More evidence for declarative memory. *Developmental Psychobiology, 35,* 83–90.

Collins, W. A. (1997). Relationships and development during adolescence: Interpersonal adaptation to individual change. *Personal Relationships, 4,* 1–14.

Collins, W. A., Harris, M. L., & Susman, A. (1996). Parenting during middle childhood. In M. H. Bornstein (Ed.), *Handbook of parenting: Vol. 1. Children and parenting* (pp. 65–90). Mahwah, NJ: Erlbaum.

Collins, W. A., Laursen, B., Mortensen, N., Luebker, C., & Ferreira, M. (1997). Conflict processes and transitions in parent and peer relationships: Implications for autonomy and regulation. *Journal of Adolescent Research, 12,* 178–198.

Collins, W. A., Maccoby, E. E., Steinberg, L., Hetherington, E. M., & Bornstein, M. H. (2000). Contemporary research on parenting: The case for nature and nurture. *American Psychologist, 52,* 218–232

Collins, W. A., Wellman, H., Keniston, A. H., & Westby, S. D. (1978). Age-related aspects of comprehension and inference from a televised dramatic narrative. *Child Development, 49,* 389–399.

Collis, B. A., Knezek, G. A., Lai, K-W., Miyashita, K. T., Pelgrum, W. J., Plomp, T., & Sakamoto, T. (1996). *Children and computers in school.* Mahwah, NJ: Erlbaum.

Colman, L. L., & Colman, A. D. (1991). *Pregnancy: The psychological experience.* Noonday Press.

Colombo, J. (1993). *Infant cognition: Predicting later intellectual functioning.* Newbury Park, CA: Sage.

Colombo, J. (1995). On the neural mechanisms underlying developmental and individual differences in visual fixation in infancy. *Developmental Review, 15,* 97–135.

Coltrane, S. (1990). Birth timing and the division of labor in dual-earner families. *Journal of Family Issues, 11,* 157–181.

Comstock, G., & Scharrer, E. (1999). *Television: What's on, who's watching, and what it means.* San Diego: Academic Press.

Comstock, G. A. (1993). The medium and society: The role of television in American life. In G. L. Berry & J. K. Asamen (Eds.), *Children and television* (pp. 117–131). Newbury Park, CA: Sage.

Conel, J. L. (1959). *The postnatal development of the human cerebral cortex.* Cambridge, MA: Harvard University Press.

Conger, R., Patterson, G. R., & Ge, X. (1995). It takes two to replicate: A mediational model for the impact of parents' stress on adolescent adjustment. *Child Development, 66,* 80–97.

Conger, R. D., Ge, X., Elder, G. H., Jr., Lorenz, F. O., & Simons, R. L. (1994). Economic stress, coercive family process, and developmental problems of adolescents. *Child Development, 65,* 541–561.

Conner, D. B., Knight, D. K., & Cross, D. R. (1997). Mothers' and fathers' scaffolding of their 2-year-olds during problem-solving and literacy interactions. *British Journal of Developmental Psychology, 15,* 323–338.

Connolly, J., Craig, W., Goldberg, A., & Pepler, D. (1999). Conceptions of cross-sex friendships and romantic relationships in early adolescence. *Journal of Youth and Adolescence, 28,* 481–494.

Connolly, J., & Goldberg, A. (1999). Romantic relationships in adolescence: The role of friends and peers in their emergence and development. In W. Furman, B. B. Brown, & C. Feiring (Eds.), *The development of romantic relationships in adolescence* (pp. 266–290). New York: Cambridge University Press.

Connolly, J. A., & Doyle, A. B. (1984). Relations of social fantasy play to social competence in preschoolers. *Developmental Psychology, 20,* 797–806.

Connors, L. J., & Epstein, J. L. (1996). Parent and school partnerships. In M. H. Bornstein (Ed.), *Handbook of parenting: Vol. 4. Applied and practical parenting* (pp. 437–458). Mahwah, NJ: Erlbaum.

Cooke, R. A. (1982). The ethics and regulation of research involving children. In B. B. Wolman (Ed.), *Handbook of developmental psychology* (pp. 149–172). Englewood Cliffs, NJ: Prentice-Hall.

Cooper, C. R. (1998). *The weaving of maturity: Cultural perspectives on adolescent development.* New York: Oxford University Press.

Cooper, M. L., & Orcutt, H. K. (1997). Drinking and sexual experience on first dates among adolescents. *Journal of Abnormal Psychology, 106,* 191–202.

Cooper, P., & Murray, L. (1997). Prediction, detection, and treatment of postnatal depression. *Archives of Diseases of Children, 77,* 97–99.

Cooper, P. J., & Murray, L. (1998). Postnatal depression. *British Medical Journal, 316,* 1884–1886.

Cooper, R. P., & Aslin, R. N. (1994). Developmental differences in infant attention to the spectral properties of infant-directed speech. *Child Development, 65,* 1663–1677.

Coplan, R. J., Rubin, K. H., Fox, N. A., Calkins, S. D., & Stewart, S. L. (1994). Being alone, playing alone, and acting alone: Distinguishing among reticence and passive and active solitude in young children. *Child Development, 65,* 129–137.

Corah, N. L., Anthony, E. J., Painter, P., Stern, J. A., & Thurston, D. L. (1965). Effects of perinatal anoxia after seven years. *Psychological Monographs 79* (3, Whole No. 596).

Coren, S., & Halpern, D. F. (1991). Left-handedness: A marker for decreased survival fitness. *Psychological Bulletin, 109,* 90–106.

Cornelius, M. D., Day, N. L., Richardson, G. A., & Taylor, P. M. (1999). Epidemiology of substance abuse during pregnancy. In P. J. Ott & R. E. Tarter (Eds.), *Sourcebook on substance abuse: Etiology, epidemiology, assessment, and treatment* (pp. 1–13). Boston, MA: Allyn and Bacon.

Corrigan, R. (1987). A developmental sequence of actor–object pretend play in young children. *Merrill-Palmer Quarterly, 33,* 87–106.

Cosden, M., Peerson, S., & Elliott, K. (1997). Effects of prenatal drug exposure on birth outcomes and early child development. *Journal of Drug Issues, 27,* 525–539.

Cost, Quality, and Outcomes Study Team. (1995). Cost, quality, and child outcomes in child care centers: Key findings and recommendations. *Young Children, 50*(4), 40–44.

Costa, F. M., Jessor, R., Donovan, J. E., & Fortenberry, J. D. (1995). Early initiation of sexual intercourse: The influence of psychosocial unconventionality. *Journal of Research on Adolescence, 5,* 93–121.

Costello, E. J., & Angold, A. (1995). Developmental epidemiology. In D. Cicchetti & D. Cohen (Eds.), *Developmental psychopathology: Vol. 1. Theory and method* (pp. 23–56). New York: Wiley.

Coulton, C. J., Korbin, J. E., & Su, M. (1999). Neighborhoods and child maltreatment: A multi-level study. *Child Abuse and Neglect, 23,* 1019–1040.

Couper, R. T., & Couper, J. J. (2000). Prader-Willi syndrome. *Lancet, 356,* 673–675.

Courage, M. L., & Adams, R. J. (1990). Visual acuity assessment from birth to three years using the acuity card procedures: Cross-sectional and longitudinal samples. *Optometry and Vision Science, 67,* 713–718.

Cournoyer, M., Solomon, C. R., & Trudel, M. (1998). I speak then I expect: Language and self-control in the young child at home. *Canadian Journal of Behavioural Science, 30,* 69–81.

Cowan, C. P., & Cowan, P. A. (1995). Interventions to ease the transition to parenthood: Why they are needed and what they can do. *Family Relations, 44,* 412–423.

Cowan, C. P., & Cowan, P. A. (1997). Working with couples during stressful transitions. In S. Dreman (Ed.), *The family on the threshold of the 21st century* (pp. 17–47). Mahwah, NJ: Erlbaum.

Cowan, C. P., & Cowan, P. A. (2000). *When partners become parents.* Mahwah, NJ: Erlbaum.

Cowan, P. A. (1997). Beyond meta-analysis: A plea for a family systems view of attachment. *Child Development, 68,* 601–603.

Cowan, P. A., Cowan, C. P., Schulz, M., & Heming, G. (1994). Prebirth to preschool family factors predicting children's adaptation to kindergarten. In R. D. Parke & S. Kellam (Eds.) *Exploring family relationships with other social contexts: Advances in family research* (Vol. 4, pp. 75–114). Hillsdale, NJ: Erlbaum.

Cowan, P. A., Powell, D., & Cowan, C. P. (1998). Parenting interventions: A family systems perspective. In I. E. Sigel & K. A. Renninger (Eds.), *Handbook of child psychology: Vol. 4. Child psychology in practice* (5th ed., pp. 3–72). New York: Wiley.

Cox, K., & Schwartz, J. D. (1990). *The well-informed patient's guide to caesarean births.* New York: Dell.

Cox, M. J., Owen, M. T., Henderson, V. K., & Margand, N. A. (1992). Prediction of infant–father and infant–mother attachment. *Developmental Psychology, 28,* 474–483.

Coyle, T. R., & Bjorklund, D. F. (1997). Age differences in, and consequences of, multiple- and variable-strategy use on a multitrial sort-recall task. *Developmental Psychology, 33,* 372–380.

Cramond, B. (1994). The Torrance Tests of Creative Thinking: From design through establishment of predictive validity. In R. F. Subotnik & K. D. Arnold (Eds.), *Beyond Terman: Contemporary longitudinal studies of giftedness and talent* (pp. 229–254). Norwood, NJ: Ablex.

Cratty, B. J. (1986). *Perceptual and motor development in infants and children* (3rd ed.). Englewood Cliffs, NJ: Prentice-Hall.

Crawford, J. (1995). *Bilingual education: History, politics, theory, and practice.* Los Angeles: Bilingual Education Services.

Crawford, J. (1997). *Best evidence: Research foundations of the bilingual education act.* Washington, DC: National Clearinghouse for Bilingual Education.

Creasey, G. L., Jarvis, P. A., & Berk, L. E. (1998). Play and social competence. In O. N. Saracho & B. Spodek (Eds.), *Multiple perspectives on play in early childhood education* (pp. 116–143). Albany: State University of New York Press.

Creatsas, G. K., Vekemans, M., Horejsi, J., Uzel, R., Lauritzen, C., & Osler, M. (1995). Adolescent sexuality in Europe: A multicentric study. *Adolescent and Pediatric Gynecology, 8,* 59–63.

Creer, T. L. (1998). Childhood asthma. In T. H. Ollendick & M. Hersen (Eds.), *Handbook of child psychopathology* (3rd ed., pp. 395–415). New York: Plenum.

Crick, N. R. (1996). The role of overt aggression, relational aggression, and prosocial behavior in the prediction of children's future social adjustment. *Child Development, 67,* 2317–2327.

Crick, N. R., & Bigbee, M. A. (1998). Relational and overt forms of peer victimization: A multiinformant approach. *Journal of Consulting and Clinical Psychology, 66,* 337–347.

Crick, N. R., Casas, J. F., & Mosher, M. (1997). Relational and overt aggression in preschool. *Developmental Psychology, 33,* 579–588.

Crick, N. R., & Dodge, K. A. (1994). A review and reformulation of social information-processing mechanisms in children's social adjustment. *Psychological Bulletin, 115,* 74–101.

Crick, N. R., & Grotpeter, J. K. (1995). Relational aggression, gender, and social-psychological adjustment. *Child Development, 66,* 710–722.

Crick, N. R., & Grotpeter, J. K. (1996). Children's treatment by peers: Victims of relational and overt aggression. *Development and Psychopathology, 8,* 367–380.

Crick, N. R., & Ladd, G. W. (1993). Children's perceptions of their peer experiences: Attributions, loneliness, social anxiety, and social avoidance. *Developmental Psychology, 29,* 244–254.

Crockenberg, S., & Leerkes, E. (2000). Infant social and emotional development in family context. In C. H. Zeanah, Jr., *Handbook of infant mental health* (2nd ed., pp. 60–90). New York: Guilford.

Crook, C. K., & Lipsitt, L. P. (1976). Neonatal nutritive sucking: Effects of taste stimulation upon sucking rhythm and heart rate. *Child Development, 47,* 518–522.

Cross, D. R., & Paris, S. G. (1988). Developmental and instructional analyses of children's metacognition and reading comprehension. *Journal of Educational Psychology, 80,* 131–142.

Crouter, A. C., Manke, B. A., & McHale, S. M. (1995). The family context of gender intensification in early adolescence. *Child Development, 66,* 317–329.

Crowhurst, M. (1990). Teaching and learning the writing of persuasive/argumentative discourse. *Canadian Journal of Education, 15,* 348–359.

Crystal, D. S., Chen, C., Fuligni, A. J., Stevenson, H. W., Hsu, C.-C., Ko, H.-J., Kitamura, S., & Kimura, S. (1994). Psychological maladjustment and academic achievement: A cross-cultural study of Japanese, Chinese, and American high school students. *Child Development, 65,* 738–753.

Csikszentmihalyi, M. (1996). *Creativity: Flow and the psychology of discovery and invention.* New York: HarperCollins.

Csikszentmihalyi, M., & Larson, R. (1984). *Being adolescent. Conflict and growth in the teenage years.* New York: Basic Books.

Cuddy-Casey, M., & Orvaschel, H. (1997). Children's understanding of death in relation to child suicidality and homicidality. *Clinical Psychology Review, 17,* 33–45.

Culbertson, F. M. (1997). Depression and gender: An international review. *American Psychologist, 52,* 25–51.

Culnane, M., Fowler, M. G., Lee, S. S., McSherry, G., Brady, M., & O'Donnell, K. (1999). Lack of long-term effects of in utero exposure to zidovudine among uninfected children born to HIV-infected women. *Journal of the American Medical Association, 281,* 151–157.

Cummings, E. M., & Cicchetti, D. (1990). Towards a transactional model of relations between attachment and depression. In M. Greenberg, D. Cicchetti, & E. M. Cummings (Eds.), *Attachment in the preschool years: Theory, research, and intervention* (pp. 339–372). Chicago: University of Chicago Press.

Cummings, E. M., & Davies, P. T. (1994). Maternal depression and child development. *Journal of Child Psychology and Psychiatry, 35,* 73–112.

Cummings, E. M., & Zahn-Waxler, C. (1992). Emotions and the socialization of aggression: Adults' angry behavior and children's arousal and aggression. In A. Fraczek & H. Zumkley (Eds.), *Socialization and aggression* (pp. 61–84). New York: Springer-Verlag.

Cummins, J. (1999). Alternative paradigms in bilingual education research: Does theory have a place? *Educational Researcher, 28*(7), 26–32.

Currie, J., & Thomas, D. (1997). Can Head Start lead to long term gains in cognition after all? *SRCD Newsletter, 40*(2), 3–5.

Curtin, S. C. (1999). Recent changes in birth attendant, place of birth, and the use of obstetric interventions, United States, 1989–1997. *Journal of Nurse-Midwifery, 44,* 349–354.

Curtin, S. C., & Park, M. M. (1999). Trends in the attendant, place, and timing of births and in the use of obstetric interventions: United States, 1989–1997. *National Vital Statistics Report, 47*(27), 1–12.

Curtiss, S. (1977). *Genie: A psycholinguistic study of a modern day "wild child."* New York: Academic Press.

Curtiss, S. (1989). The independence and task-specificity of language. In M. H. Bornstein & J. S. Bruner (Eds.), *Interaction in human development* (pp. 105–137). Hillsdale, NJ: Erlbaum.

Cutrona, C. E., Hessling, R. M., Bacon, P. L., & Russell, D. W. (1998). Predictors and correlates of continuing involvement with the baby's father among adolescent mothers. *Journal of Family Psychology, 12,* 369–387.

Cuttler, L., Silvers, J. B., Singh, J., Marrero, U., Finkelstein, B., Tannin, G., & Neuhauser, D. (1996). Short stature and growth hormone therapy. *Journal of the American Medical Association, 276,* 531–537.

Dabelea, D., Knowler, W. C., & Pettitt, D. J. (2000). Effect of diabetes in pregnancy on offspring: Follow-up research in the Pima Indians. *Journal of Maternal and Fetal Medicine, 9,* 83–88.

D'Agostino, J. A., & Clifford, P. (1998). Neurodevelopmental consequences associated with the premature neonate. *AACN Clinical Issues, 9,* 11–24.

Dahl, R. E. (1998). The development and disorders of sleep. Advances in Pediatrics, 45, 73–90.

Dahl, R. E., Scher, M. S., Williamson, D. E., Robles, N., & Day, N. (1995). A longitudinal study of prenatal marijuana use: Effects on sleep and arousal at age 3 years. *Archives of Pediatric and Adolescent Medicine, 149,* 145–150.

Daly, K. A., Hunter, L. L., & Giebink, G. S. (1999). Chronic otitis media with effusion. *Pediatrics Review, 20,* 85–93.

Dammerman, R. S., & Kriegstein, A. R. (2000). Transient actions of neurotransmitters during neocortical development. *Epilepsia, 41,* 1080–1081.

Damon, W. (1977). *The social world of the child.* San Francisco: Jossey-Bass.

Damon, W. (1988). *The moral child.* New York: Free Press.

Damon, W. (1990). Self-concept, adolescent. In R. M. Lerner, A. C. Petersen, & J. Brooks-Gunn (Eds.), *The encyclopedia of adolescence* (Vol. 2, pp. 87–91). New York: Garland.

Damon, W. (1995). *Greater expectations: Overcoming the culture of indulgence in America's homes and schools.* New York: Free Press.

Damon, W., & Hart, D. (1988). *Self-understanding in childhood and adolescence.* New York: Cambridge University Press.

Daniels, D. H. (1998). Age differences in concepts of self-esteem. *Merrill-Palmer Quarterly, 44,* 234–259.

Daniels, K., & Lewis, G. M. (1996). Openness of information in the use of donor gametes: Developments in New Zealand. *Journal of Reproductive and Infant Psychology, 14,* 57–68.

Dannemiller, J. L., & Stephens, B. R. (1988). A critical test of infant pattern preference models. *Child Development, 59,* 210–216.

Darling, N., & Steinberg, L. (1997). Community influences on adolescent achievement and deviance. In J. Brooks-Gunn, G. Duncan, & L. Aber (Eds.), *Neighborhood poverty: Context and consequences for children: Conceptual, ethological, and policy approaches to studying neighborhoods* (Vol. 2, pp. 120–131). New York: Russell Sage Foundation.

Darnton-Hill, I., & Coyne, E. T. (1998). Feast and famine: Socioeconomic disparities in global nutrition and health. *Public Health and Nutrition, 1,* 23–31.

Darwin, C. (1877). Biographical sketch of an infant. *Mind, 2,* 285–294.

Darwin, C. (1936). *On the origin of species by means of natural selection.* New York: Modern Library. (Original work published 1859)

Datta-Bhutada, S., Johnson, H. L., & Rosen, T. S. (1998). Intrauterine cocaine and crack exposure: Neonatal outcome. *Journal of Perinatology, 18,* 183–188.

Dattel, B. J. (1997). Antiretroviral therapy during pregnancy. Beyond AZT (ZDV). *Obstetrics and Gynecology Clinics of North America, 24,* 645–657.

DaVanzo, J., & Adamson, D. M. (2000). *Family planning in developing countries: An unfinished success story.* New York: Rand Corporation.

Davidson, R. J. (1994). Asymmetric brain function, affective style, and psychopathology: The role of early experience and plasticity. *Development and Psychopathology, 6,* 741–758.

Davis, D. L., Gottlieb, M. B., & Stampnitzky, J. R. (1998). Reduced ratio of male to female births in several industrial countries. *Journal of the American Medical Association, 279,* 1018–1023.

Deák, G. O. (2000). Hunting the fox of word learning: Why "constraints" fail to capture it. *Developmental Review, 20,* 29–80.

Deák, G. O., & Maratsos, M. (1998). On having complex representations of things: Preschoolers use multiple words for objects and people. *Developmental Psychology, 34,* 224–240.

Dean, R. S., & Anderson, J. L. (1997). Lateralization of cerebral function. In A. M. Horton, Jr., D. Wedding, & J. Webster (Eds.), *The neuropsychology handbook: Vol. 1. Foundations and assessment* (2nd ed., pp. 139–168). New York: Springer.

Deary, I. J. (1995). Auditory inspection time and intelligence: What is the direction of causation? *Developmental Psychology, 31,* 237–250.

Deary, I. J., & Stough, C. (1996). Intelligence and inspection time: Achievements, prospects, and problems. *American Psychologist, 51,* 599–608.

Deater-Deckard, K., & Dodge, K. A. (1997). Externalizing behavior problems and discipline revisited: Nonlinear effects and variation by culture, context, and gender. *Psychological Inquiry, 8,* 161–175.

Deater-Deckard, K., & Dodge, K. A., Bates, J.E., & Petit, G.S. (1996). Physical discipline among African American and European American mothers: Links to children's externalizing behaviors. *Developmental Psychology, 32,* 1065-1072.

Deater-Deckard, K., Scarr, S., McCartney, K., & Eisenberg, M. (1994). Paternal separation anxiety: Relationships with parenting stress, child-rearing attitudes, and maternal anxieties. *Psychological Science, 5,* 341–346.

DeBerry, K. M., Scarr, S., & Weinberg, R. (1996). Family racial socialization and ecological competence: Longitudinal assessments of African-American transracial adoptees. *Child Development, 67,* 2375–2399.

DeBerry, K. M., Scarr, S., & Weinberg, R. (1996). Family racial socialization and ecological competence: Longitudinal assessments of African-American transracial adoptees. *Child Development, 67,* 2375–2399.

DeCasper, A. J., & Spence, M. J. (1986). Prenatal maternal speech influences newborns' perception of speech sounds. *Infant Behavior and Development, 9,* 133–150.

DeGarmo, D. S., & Forgatch, M. S. (1999). Contexts as predictors of changing maternal parenting practices in diverse family structures: A social interactional perspective of risk and resilience. In E. M. Hetherington (Ed.), *Coping with divorce, single parenting, and remarriage: A risk and resiliency perspective* (pp. 227–252). Mahwah, NJ: Erlbaum.

Degirmencioglu, S. M., Urberg, K. A., Tolson, J. M., & Richard, P. (1998). Adolescent friendship networks: Continuity and change over the school year. *Merrill-Palmer Quarterly, 44,* 313–337.

Dehaene, S., Dupoux, E., Mehler, J., Cohen, L., Perani, D., van de Moortele, P.-F., Leherici, S., & Le Bihan, D. (1997). Anatomical variability in the cortical representation of first and second languages. *Neuroreport, 17,* 3809–3815.

Dejin-Karlsson, E., Hanson, B. S., Estergren, P.-O., Sjoeberg, N.-O., & Marsal, K. (1998). Does passive smoking in early pregnancy increase the risk of small-for-gestational-age infants? *American Journal of Public Health, 88,* 1523–1527.

Deković, M., & Gerris, J. R. M. (1994). Developmental analysis of social cognitive and behavioral differences between popular and rejected children. *Journal of Applied Developmental Psychology, 15,* 367–386.

Deković, M., & Meeus, W. (1997). Peer relations in adolescence: Effects of parenting and adolescents' self-concept. *Journal of Adolescence, 20,* 163–176.

Dekovic, M., Noom, M. J., & Meeus, W. (1997). Expectations regarding development during adolescence: Parent and adolescent perceptions. *Journal of Youth and Adolescence, 26,* 253–271.

de Lacoste, M., Horvath, D. S., & Woodward, D. J. (1991). Possible sex differences in the developing human fetal brain. *Journal of Clinical & Experimental Neuropsychology, 13,* 831–846.

Delgado-Gaitan, C. (1994). Socializing young children in Mexican-American families: An intergenerational perspective. In P. M. Greenfield & R. R. Cocking (Eds.), *Cross-cultural roots of minority child development* (pp. 55–86). Hillsdale, NJ: Erlbaum.

De Lisi, R., & Gallagher, A. M. (1991). Understanding gender stability and constancy in Argentinean children. *Merrill-Palmer Quarterly, 37,* 483–502.

DeLoache, J. S. (1987). Rapid change in symbolic functioning of very young children. *Science, 238,* 1556–1557.

DeLoache, J. S. (1991). Symbolic functioning in very young children: Understanding of pictures and models. *Child Development, 62,* 736–752.

DeLoache, J. S., & Smith, C. M. (1999). Early symbolic representation. In I. E. Sigel (Ed.), *Development of mental representation* (pp. 61–86). Mahwah, NJ: Erlbaum.

DeLoache, J. S., & Todd, C. M. (1988). Young children's use of spatial categorization as a mnemonic strategy. *Journal of Experimental Child Psychology, 46,* 1–20.

DeMarie-Dreblow, D. (1991). Relation between knowledge and memory: A reminder that correlation does not imply causality. *Child Development, 62,* 484–498.

Demetriou, A., Efklides, A., & Platsidou, M. (1993). The architecture and dynamics of developing mind. *Monographs of the Society for Research in Child Development, 58*(No. 5–6, Serial No. 234).

Demetriou, A., Efklides, A., Papadaki, M., Papantoniou, G., & Economou, A. (1993). Structure and development of causal–experimental thought: From early adolescence to youth. *Developmental Psychology, 29,* 480–497.

Demetriou, A., Pachaury, A., Metallidou, Y., & Kazi, S. (1996). Universals and specificities in the structure and development of quantitative-relational thought: A cross-cultural study in Greece and India. *International Journal of Behavioral Development, 19,* 255–290.

Demo, D. H., & Acock, A. C. (1996). Family structure, family process, and adolescent well-being. *Journal of Research on Adolescence, 6,* 457–488.

Dempster, F. N., & Corkill, A. J. (1999). Interference and inhibition in cognition and behavior: Unifying themes for educational psychology. *Educational Psychology Review, 11,* 1–88.

Denckla, M. B. (1996). Biological correlates of learning and attention: What is relevant to learning disability and attention-deficit hyperactivity disorder? *Developmental and Behavioral Pediatrics, 17,* 114–119.

Denham, S. (1998). *Emotional development in young children.* New York: Guilford.

Denham, S., Zoller, D., & Couchoud, E. (1994). Socialization of preschoolers' emotion understanding. *Developmental Psychology, 30,* 928–936.

Denham, S. A., Renwick, S. M., & Holt, R. W. (1991). Working and playing together: Prediction of preschool social-emotional competence from mother–child interaction. *Child Development, 62,* 242–249.

Dennebaum, J. M., & Kulberg, J. M. (1994). Kindergarten retention and transitional classrooms: Their relationship to achievement. *Psychology in the Schools, 31,* 5–12.

Dennis, W. (1960). Causes of retardation among institutionalized children: Iran. *Journal of Genetic Psychology, 96,* 47–59.

Dennison, B. A., Straus, J. H., Mellits, D., & Charney, E. (1998). Childhood physical fitness tests: Predictor of adult physical activity levels? *Pediatrics, 82,* 342–330.

Dennison, E., Fall, C., Cooper, C., & Barker, D. (1997). Prenatal factors influencing long-term outcome. *Hormone Research, 48*(Suppl. 1), 25–29.

De Roche, E. F., & Williams, M. M. (1998). *Educating hearts and minds: A comprehensive character education framework.* Thousand Oaks, CA: Corwin Press.

Derom, C., Thiery, E., Vlietinck, R., Loos, R., & Derom, R. (1996). Handedness in twins according to zygosity and chorion type: A preliminary report. *Behavior Genetics, 26,* 407–408.

Deutsch, F. M., Ruble, D. N., Fleming, A., Brooks-Gunn, J., & Stangor, C. (1988). Information-seeking and maternal self-definition during the transition to motherhood. *Journal of Personality and Social Psychology, 55,* 420–431.

Deutsch, W., & Pechmann, T. (1982). Social interaction and the development of definite descriptions. *Cognition, 11,* 159–184.

de Villiers, J. G., & de Villiers, P. A. (1973). A cross-sectional study of the acquisition of grammatical morphemes in child speech. *Journal of Psycholinguistic Research, 2,* 267–278.

de Villiers, J.G., & de Villiers, P. A. (1999). Language development. In M. H. Bornstein & M. E. Lamb (Eds.), *Developmental psychology: An advanced textbook* (4th ed., pp. 313–373). Mahwah, NJ: Erlbaum.

de Villiers, J. G., & de Villiers, P. A. (2000). Linguistic determinism and the understanding of false beliefs. In P. Mitchell & K. J. Riggs (Eds.), *Children's reasoning and the mind* (pp. 87–99). Hove, UK: Psychology Press.

deVries, M. W. (1984). Temperament and infant mortality among the Masai of East Africa. *American Journal of Psychiatry, 141,* 1189–1194.

de Waal, F. B. M. (1999). The end of nature versus nurture. *Scientific American, 281*(6), 94–99.

de Winter, M., Balledux, M., & de Mare, J. (1997). A critical evaluation of Dutch preventive child health care. *Child: Care, Health and Development, 23,* 437–446.

de Wolff, M. S., & van IJzendoorn, M. H. (1997). Sensitivity and attachment: A meta-analysis on parental atnecedents of infant attachment. *Child Development, 68,* 571–591.

Dewsbury, D. A. (1992). Comparative psychology and ethology: A reassessment. *American Psychologist, 47,* 208–215.

Diamond, A. (1991). Neuropsychological insights into the meaning of object concept development. In S. Carey & R. Gelman (Eds.), *The epigenesis of mind: Essays on biology and knowledge* (pp. 67–110). Hillsdale, NJ: Erlbaum.

Diamond, A., Cruttenden, L., & Neiderman, D. (1994). AB with multiple wells: 1. Why are multiple wells sometimes easier than two wells? 2. Memory or memory + inhibition. *Developmental Psychology, 30,* 192–205.

Diamond, A., Prevor, M. B., Callender, G., & Druin, D. P. (1997). Prefrontal cortex cognitive deficits in children treated early and continuously for PKU. *Monographs of the Society for Research in Child Development, 62* (4, Serial No. 252).

Diamond, L. M. (1998). Development of sexual orientation among adolescent and young adult women. *Developmental Psychology, 34,* 1085–1095.

Diamond, L. M., Savin-Williams, R. C., & Dubé, E. M. (1999). Sex, dating, passionate friendships, and romance: Intimate peer relations among lesbian, gay, and bisexual adolescents. In W. Furman & B. B. Brown (Eds.), *The development of romantic relationships in adolescence* (pp. 175–210). New York: Cambridge University Press.

Diamond, M., & Hopson, J. (1999). *Magic trees of the mind.* New York: Plume.

Dias, M. G., & Harris, P. L. (1990). The influence of imagination on reasoning by young children. *British Journal of Developmental Psychology, 8,* 305–318.

Diaz, R. M., & Berndt, T. J. (1982). Children's knowledge of a best friend: Fact or fancy? *Developmental Psychology, 18,* 787–794.

Dick, D. M., Rose, R. J., Viken, R. J., & Kaprio, J. (2000). Pubertal timing and substance use: Associations between and within families across late adolescence. *Developmental Psychology, 36,* 180–189.

Dick-Read, G. (1959). *Childbirth without fear.* New York: Harper & Brothers.

Dickson, K. L., Fogel, A., & Messinger, D. (1998). The development of emotion from a social process view. In M. F. Mascolo (Ed.), *What develops in emotional development?* (pp. 253–271). New York: Plenum.

Dickson, S. V., Collins, V. L., Simmons, D. C., & Dameenui, E. J. (1998). Metacognitive strategies: Research bases. In D. C. Simmons & E. J. Kameenui (Eds.), *What reading research tells us about children with diverse learning needs: Bases and basics* (pp. 295–360). Mahwah, NJ: Erlbaum.

DiClemente, R. J. (1993). Preventing HIV/AIDS among adolescents. *Journal of the American Medical Association, 270,* 760–762.

Diener, M. L., Goldstein, L. H., & Mangelsdorf, S. C. (1995). The role of prenatal expectations in parents' reports of infant temperament. *Merrill-Palmer Quarterly, 41,* 172–190.

DiLalla, L. F., Kagan, J., & Reznick, J. S. (1994). Genetic etiology of behavioral inhibition among 2-year-old children. *Infant Behavior and Development, 17,* 405–412.

Dill, K. E., & Dill, J. C. (1998). Video game violence: A review of the empirical literature. *Aggression and Violent Behavior, 3,* 407–428.

DiMatteo, M. R., & Kahn, K. L. (1997). Psychosocial aspects of childbirth. In S. J. Gallant, G. P. Keita, & R. Royak-Schaler (Eds.), *Health care for women: Psychological, social, and behavioral influences* (pp. 175–186). Washington, DC: American Psychological Association.

DiPietro, J. A., Hodgson, D. M., Costigan, K. A., & Hilton, S. C. (1996a). Fetal neurobehavioral development. *Child Development, 67,* 2553–2567.

DiPietro, J. A., Hodgson, D. M., Costigan, K. A., & Johnson, T. R. B. (1996b). Fetal antecedents of infant temperament. *Child Development, 67,* 2568–2583.

Dirks, J. (1982). The effect of a commercial game on children's Block Design scores on the WISC–R test. *Intelligence, 6,* 109–123.

Dishion, T. J., Andrews, D. W., & Crosby, L. (1995). Antisocial boys and their friends in early adolescence: Relationship characteristics, quality, and interactional processes. *Child Development, 66,* 139–151.

Dixon, J. A., & Moore, C. F. (1990). The development of perspective taking: Understanding differences in information and weighting. *Child Development, 61,* 1502–1513.

Dixon, R. A., & Lerner, R. M. (1999). History and systems in developmental psychology. In M. H. Bornstein & M. E. Lamb (Eds.), *Developmental psychology: An advanced textbook* (4th ed., pp. 3–46). Mahwah, NJ: Erlbaum.

Dodge, K. A., McClaskey, C. L., & Feldman, E. (1985). A situational approach to the assessment of social competence in children. *Journal of Consulting and Clinical Psychology, 53,* 344–353.

Dodge, K. A., Pettit, G. S., & Bates, J. E. (1994). Socialization mediators of the relation between socioeconomic status and child conduct problems. *Child Development, 65,* 649–665.

Dodge, K. A., Pettit, G. S., McClaskey, C. L., & Brown, M. M. (1986). Social competence in children. *Monographs of the Society for Research in Child Development, 51*(2, Serial No. 213).

Dodwell, P. C., Humphrey, G. K., & Muir, D. W. (1987). Shape and pattern perception. In P. Salapatek & L. Cohen (Eds.), *Handbook of infant perception* (Vol. 2, pp. 1–77). Orlando, FL: Academic Press.

Doeker, B., Simic-Schleicher, A., Hauffa, B. P., & Andler, W. (1999). Psychosozialer Kleinwuchs maskiert als Wachstumshormonmangel. [Psychosocially stunted growth masked as growth hormone deficiency]. *Klinische Padiatrie, 211,* 394–398.

Donatelle, R. J., & Davis, L. G. (2000). *Health: The basics* (3rd ed.). Boston: Allyn and Bacon.

Dondi, M., Simion, F., & Caltran, G. (1999). Can newborns discriminate between their own cry and the cry of another newborn infant? *Developmental Psychology, 35,* 418–426.

Donnerstein, E., Slaby, R. G., & Eron, L. D. (1994). The mass media and youth aggression. In L. D. Eron, J. H. Gentry, & P. Schlegel (Eds.), *Reason to hope: A psychosocial perspective on violence and youth* (pp. 219–250). Washington, DC: American Psychological Association.

Dontas, C., Maratsos, O., Fafoutis, M., & Karangelis, A. (1985). Early social development in institutionally reared Greek infants: Attachment and peer interaction. In I. Bretherton & E. Waters (Eds.), Growing points of attachment theory and research. *Monographs of the Society for Research in Child Development, 50* (1–2, Serial No. 209).

Dornbusch, S. M., & Glasgow, K. L. (1997). The structural context of family–school relations. In A. Booth & J. F. Dunn (Eds.), *Family–school links: How do they affect educational outcomes?* (pp. 35–55). Mahwah, NJ: Erlbaum.

Dornbusch, S. M., Ritter, P. L., Liederman, P. H., Roberts, D. F., & Fraleigh, M. J. (1987). The relation of parenting style to adolescent school performance. *Child Development, 58,* 1244–1257.

Dornbusch, S. M., Glasgow, K. L., & Lin, I.-C. (1996). The social structure of schooling. *Annual Review of Psychology, 47,* 401–429.

Dornbusch, S. M., Ritter, P. L., Mont-Reynaud, R., & Chen, Z. (1990). Family decision making and academic performance in a diverse high school population. *Journal of Adolescent Research, 5,* 143–160.

Dorris, M. (1989). *The broken cord.* New York: Harper & Row.

Dowd, M. D. (1999). Childhood injury prevention at home and play. *Current Opinion in Pediatrics, 11,* 578–582.

Downey, G., & Walker, E. (1989). Social cognition and adjustment in children at risk for psychopathology. *Developmental Psychology, 25,* 835–845.

Downs, A. C., & Fuller, M. J. (1991). Recollections of spermarche: An exploratory investigation. *Current Psychology: Research and Reviews, 10,* 93–102.

Drabman, R. S., Cordua, G. D., Hammer, D., Jarvie, G. J., & Horton, W. (1979). Developmental trends in eating rates of normal and overweight preschool children. *Child Development, 50,* 211–216.

Drew, L. M., Richard, M. H., & Smith, P. K. (1998). Grandparenting and its relationship to parenting. *Clinical Child Psychology and Psychiatry, 3,* 465–480.

Drotar, D. (1997). Relating parent and family functioning to the psychological adjustment of children with chronic health conditions: What have we learned? What do we need to know? *Journal of Pediatric Psychology, 22,* 149–165.

Drotar, D., Pallotta, J., & Eckerle, D. (1994). A prospective study of family environments of children hospitalized for nonorganic failure-to-thrive. *Developmental and Behavioral Pediatrics, 15,* 78–85.

Drucker, R. R., Hammer, L. D., Agras, W. S., & Bryson, S. (1999). Can mothers influence their child's eating behavior? *Developmental and Behavioral Pediatrics, 20,* 88–92.

DuBois, D. L., Bull, C. A., Sherman, M. D., & Roberts, M. (1998). Self-esteem and adjustment in early adolescence: A social-contextual perspective. *Journal of Youth and Adolescence, 27,* 557–583.

DuBois, D. L., Felner, R. D., Brand, S., & George, G. R. (1999). Profiles of self-esteem in early adolescence: Identification and investigation of adaptive correlates. *American Journal of Community Psychology, 27,* 899–932.

DuBois, D. L., & Hirsch, B. J. (1990). School and neighborhood friendship patterns of black and whites in early adolescence. *Child Development, 61,* 524–536.

Dubow, E. F., & Miller, L. S. (1996). Television violence viewing and aggressive behavior. In T. M. MacBeth (Eds.), *Tuning into young viewers* (pp. 117–147). Thousand Oaks, CA: Sage.

Duncan, D. F. (1996). Growing up under the gun: Children and adolescents coping with violent neighborhoods. *Journal of Primary Prevention, 16,* 343–356.

Duncan, G. J., Brooks-Gunn, J., & Klebanov, P. K. (1994). Economic deprivation and early childhood development. *Child Development, 65,* 296–318.

Duncan, R. M., & Pratt, M. W. (1997). Microgenetic change in the quantity and quality of preschoolers' private speech. *International Journal of Behavioral Development, 20,* 367–383.

Dunham, P. J., Dunham, F., & Curwin, A. (1993). Joint-attentional states and lexical acquisition at 18 months. *Developmental Psychology, 29,* 827–831.

Duniz, M., Scheer, P. J., Trojovsky, A., Kaschnitz, W., Kvas, E., & Macari, S. (1996). *European Child & Adolescent Psychiatry, 5,* 93–100.

Dunn, J. (1989). Siblings and the development of social understanding in early childhood. In P. G. Zukow (Ed.), *Sibling interaction across cultures* (pp. 106–116). New York: Springer-Verlag.

Dunn, J. (1992). Sisters and brothers: Current issues in developmental research. In F. Boer & J. Dunn (Eds.), *Children's sibling relationships* (pp. 1–17). Hillsdale, NJ: Erlbaum.

Dunn, J. (1994). Temperament, siblings, and the development of relationships. In W. B. Carey & S. C. McDevitt (Eds.), *Prevention and early intervention* (pp. 50–58). New York: Brunner/Mazel.

Dunn, J. (1996). Sibling relationships and perceived self-competence: Patterns of stability between childhood and early adolescence. In A. J. Sameroff & M. M. Haith (Eds.), *The five to seven year shift* (pp. 253–270). Chicago: University of Chicago Press.

Dunn, J. (1999a). Making sense of the social world: Mindreading, emotion, and relationships. In P. D. Zelazo & J. W. Astington (Eds.), *Developing theories of intention* (pp. 229–242). Mahwah, NJ: Erlbaum.

Dunn, J. (1999b). Siblings, emotion and the development of understanding. In S. Braten (Ed.), *Intersubjective communication and emotion in early ontogeny* (pp. 158–168). Cambridge, UK: Cambridge University Press.

Dunn, J., Bretherton, I., & Munn, P. (1987). Conversations about feeling states between mothers and their young children. *Developmental Psychology, 23,* 132–139.

Dunn, J., Brown, J. R., & Maguire, M. (1995). The development of children's moral sensibility: Individual differences and emotion understanding. *Developmental Psychology, 31,* 649–659.

Dunn, J., & Kendrick, C. (1982). *Siblings: Love, envy and understanding.* Cambridge, MA: Harvard University Press.

Dunn, J., & Munn, P. (1986). Sibling quarrels and maternal intervention: Individual differences in understanding aggression. *Journal of the American Academy of Child Psychology and Psychiatry, 27,* 583–595.

Dunn, J., Slomkowski, C., & Beardsall, L. (1994). Sibling relationships from the preschool period through middle childhood and early adolescence. *Developmental Psychology, 30,* 315–324.

Durbin, D. L., Darling, N., Steinberg, L., & Brown, B. B. (1993). Parenting style and peer group membership among European-American adolescents. *Journal of Research on Adolescence, 3,* 87–100.

Durkin, M. S., Laraque, D., Lubman, I., & Barlow, B. (1999). Epidemiology and prevention of traffic injuries to urban children and adolescents. *Pediatrics, 103,* e74.

Dusek, J. B. (1987). Sex roles and adjustment. In D. B. Carter (Ed.), *Current conceptions of sex roles and sex typing* (pp. 211–222). New York: Praeger.

Dwyer, T., Ponsonby, A. L., & Couper, D. (1999). Tobacco smoke exposure at one month of age and subsequent risk of SIDS: A prospective study. *American Journal of Epidemiology, 149,* 593–602.

Dybing, E., & Sanner, T. (1999). Passive smoking, sudden infant death syndrome (SIDS), and childhood infections. *Human Experimental Toxicology, 18,* 202–205.

Dyer, C. (1999). Pathophysiology of phenylketonuria. *Mental Retardation & Developmental Disabilities Research Reviews, 5,* 104–112.

Dye-White, E. (1986). Environmental hazards in the work setting: Their effect on women of childbearing age. *American Association of Occupational Health and Nursing Journal, 34,* 76–78.

Eacott, M. J. (1999). Memory for the events of early childhood. *Current Directions in Psychological Science, 8,* 46–48.

East, P. L., & Felice, M. E. (1996). *Adolescent pregnancy and parenting: Findings from a racially diverse sample.* Mahwah, NJ: Erlbaum.

East, P. L., & Rook, K. S. (1992). Compensatory patterns of support among children's peer relationships: A test using school friends, nonschool friends, and siblings. *Developmental Psychology, 28,* 168–172.

Easterbrook, M. A., Kisilevsky, B. S., Muir, D. W., & LaPlante, D. P. (1999). Newborns discriminate schematic faces from scrambled faces. *Canadian Journal of Experimental Psychology, 53,* 231–241.

Ebeling, K. S., & Gelman, S. A. (1994). Children's use of context in interpreting "big" and "little." *Child Development, 65,* 1178–1192.

Eberhart-Phillips, J. E., Frederick, P. D., & Baron, R. C. (1993). Measles in pregnancy: A descriptive study of 58 cases. *Obstetrics and Gynecology, 82,* 797–801.

Ebrahim, S. H., Floyd, R. L., Merritt, R. K., Decoufle, P., & Holtzman, D. (2000). Trends in pregnancy-related smoking rates in the United States, 1987–1996. *Journal of the American Medical Association, 283,* 361–366.

Eccles, J., Barber, B., Jozefowicz, D., Malenchuk, O., & Vida, M. (1999). Self-evaluations of competence, task values, and self-esteem. In N. G. Johnson & M. C. Roberts (Eds.), *Beyond appearance: A new look at adolescent girls* (pp. 53–83). Washington, DC: American Psychological Association.

Eccles, J. S. (1994). Understanding women's educational and occupational choices: Applying the Eccles et al. model of achievement-related choices. *Psychology of Women Quarterly, 18,* 585–609.

Eccles, J. S., Early, D., Frasier, K., Belansky, E., & McCarthy, K. (1997a). The relation of connection, regulation, and support for autonomy to adolescents' functioning. *Journal of Adolescent Research, 12,* 263–286.

Eccles, J. S., & Harold, R. D. (1991). Gender differences in sport involvement: Applying the Eccles' expectancy-value model. *Journal of Applied Sport Psychology, 3,* 7–35.

Eccles, J. S., & Harold, R. D. (1993). Parent–school involvement during the early adolescent years. *Teachers College Record, 94,* 568–587.

Eccles, J. S., & Harold, R. D. (1996). Family involvement in children's and adolescents' schooling. In A. Booth & J. F. Dunn (Eds.),

Family–school links: How do they affect educational outcomes? (pp. 3–34). Mahwah, NJ: Erlbaum.

Eccles, J. S., Jacobs, J., & Harold, R. D. (1990). Gender-role stereotypes, expectancy effects, and parents' role in the socialization of gender differences in self-perceptions and skill acquisition. *Journal of Social Issues, 46,* 183–201.

Eccles, J. S., Lord, S., & Buchanan, C. M. (1996). School transitions in early adolescence: What are we doing to our young people? In J. A. Graber, J. Brooks-Gunn, & A. C. Petersen (Eds.), *Transitions through adolescence* (pp. 251–284). Mahwah, NJ: Erlbaum.

Eccles, J. S., Lord, S., Roeser, R. W., Barber, B., & Josefowicz-Hernandez, D. (1997b). The association of school transitions in early adolescence with developmental trajectories through high school. In J. Schulenberg, J. Maggs, & K. Hurrelmann (Eds.), *Health risks and developmental transitions during adolescence* (pp. 283–320). New York: Cambridge University Press.

Eccles, J. S., Midgley, C., Wigfield, A., Buchanan, C. M., Reuman, D., Flanagan, C., & Mac Iver, D. (1993a). Development during adolescence: The impact of stage–environment fit on young adolescents' experiences in schools and in families. *American Psychologist, 48,* 90–101.

Eccles, J. S., Wigfield, A., Harold, R., & Blumenfeld, P. B. (1993b). Age and gender differences in children's self- and task perceptions during elementary school. *Child Development, 64,* 830–847.

Eccles, J. S., Wigfield, A., Midgley, C., Reuman, D., Mac Iver, D., & Feldlaufer, H. (1993c). Negative effects of traditional middle schools on students' motivation. *Elementary School Journal, 93,* 553–574.

Eccles, J. S., Wigfield, A., & Schiefele, U. (1998). Motivation to succeed. In N. Eisenberg (Ed.), *Handbook of child psychology: Vol. 3. Social, emotional, and personality development* (5th ed., pp. 1017–1095). New York: Wiley.

Eckerman, C. O., & Didow, S. M. (1996). Nonverbal imitation and toddlers' mastery of verbal means of achieving coordinated action. *Developmental Psychology, 32,* 141–152.

Eckerman, C. O., & Whitehead, H. (1999). How toddler peers generate coordinated action: A cross-cultural exploration. *Early Education & Development, 10,* 241–266.

Eder, R. A. (1989). The emergent personologist: The structure and content of 3½-, 5½-, and 7½-year-olds' concepts of themselves and other persons. *Child Development, 60,* 1218–1228.

Egan, S. K., Monson, T. C., & Perry, D. G. (1998). Social-cognitive influences on change in aggression over time. *Developmental Psychology, 34,* 996–1006.

Egeland, B., & Hiester, M. (1995). The long-term consequences of infant daycare and mother–infant attachment. *Child Development, 66,* 474–485.

Egeland, B., Jacobvitz, D., & Sroufe, L. A. (1988). Breaking the cycle of abuse. *Child Development, 59,* 1080–1088.

Egeland, B., Kalkoske, M., Gottesman, N., & Erickson, M. F. (1990). Preschool behavior problems: Stability and factors accounting for change. *Journal of Child Psychology and Psychiatry, 31,* 891–909.

Eiben, B., Hammans, W., Hansen, S., Trawicki, W., Osthelder, B., Stelzer, A., Jaspers, K.-D., & Goebel, R. (1997). On the complication risk of early amniocentesis versus standard amniocentesis. *Fetal Diagnosis and Therapy, 12,* 140–144.

Eibl-Eibesfeldt, I. (1989). *Human ethology.* Hawthorne, NY: Aldine.

Eiden, R. D., & Reifman, A. (1996). Effects of Brazelton demonstrations on later parenting: A meta-analysis. *Journal of Pediatric Psychology, 21,* 857–868.

Eilers, R., & Oller, D. K. (1994). Infant vocalizations and the early diagnosis of severe hearing impairment. *Journal of Pediatrics, 124,* 199–203.

Eisenberg, L. (1999). Experience, brain, and behavior: The importance of a head start. *Pediatrics, 103,* 1031–1035.

Eisenberg, N. (1998a). Introduction. In N. Eisenberg (Ed.), *Handbook of child psychology: Vol. 3. Social, emotional, and personality development* (pp. 1–24). New York: Wiley.

Eisenberg, N. (1998b). The socialization of socioemotional competence. In D. Pushkar, W. M. Bukowski, A. E. Schwartzman, E. M. Stack, & D. R. White (Eds.), *Improving competence across the lifespan* (pp. 59–78). New York: Plenum.

Eisenberg, N., Cumberland, A., & Spinrad, T. L. (1998). Parental socialization of emotion. *Psychological Inquiry, 9,* 241–273.

Eisenberg, N., & Fabes, R. A. (1998). Prosocial development. In N. Eisenberg (Ed.), *Handbook of child psychology: Vol. 3. Social, emotional, and personality development* (5th ed., pp. 701–778). New York: Wiley.

Eisenberg, N., Fabes, R. A., Bernzweig, J., Karbon, M., Poulin, R., & Hanish, L. (1993). The relations of emotionality and regulation to preschoolers' social skills and sociometric status. *Child Development, 64,* 1418–1438.

Eisenberg, N., Fabes, R. A., Carlo, G., & Karbon, M. (1992). Emotional responsivity to others: Behavioral correlates and socialization antecedents. In N. Eisenberg & R. A. Fabes (Eds.), *New directions in child development* (No. 55, pp. 57–73). San Francisco: Jossey-Bass.

Eisenberg, N., Fabes, R. A., & Losoya, S. (1997). Emotional responding: Regulation, social correlates, and socialization. In P. Salovey & D. J. Sluyter (Eds.), *Emotional development and emotional intelligence* (pp. 129–162). New York: Basic Books.

Eisenberg, N., Fabes, R., Murphy, B., Karbon, M., Smith, M., & Maszk, P. (1996). The relations of children's dispositional empathy-related responding to their emotionality, regulation, and social functioning. *Developmental Psychology, 32,* 195–209.

Eisenberg, N., Fabes, R. A., Schaller, M., Carlo, G., et al. (1991). The relations of parental characteristics and practices to children's vicarious emotional responding. *Child Development, 27,* 1393–1408.

Eisenberg, N., Fabes, R. A., Shepard, S. A., Guthrie, I., Murphy, B. C., & Reiser, M. (1999). Parental reactions to children's negative emotions: Longitudinal relations to quality of children's social functioning. *Child Development, 70,* 513–534.

Eisenberg, N., Fabes, R. A., Shepard, S. A., Murphy, B. C., Jones, S., & Guthrie, I. K. (1998). Contemporaneous and longitudinal prediction of children's sympathy from dispositional regulation and emotionality. *Developmental Psychology, 34,* 910–924.

Eisenberg, N., & McNally, S. (1993). Socialization and mothers' and adolescents' empathy-related characteristics. *Journal of Research on Adolescence, 3,* 171–191.

Ekman, P., & Friesen, W. (1972). Constants across culture in the face and emotion. *Journal of Personality and Social Psychology, 17,* 124–129.

Elardo, R., & Bradley, R. H. (1981). The Home Observation for Measurement of the Environment (HOME) Scale: A review of research. *Developmental Review, 1,* 113–145.

Elicker, J., Englund, M., & Sroufe, L. A. (1992). Predicting peer competence and peer relationships in childhood from early parent–child relationships. In R. D. Parke & G. W. Ladd (Eds.), *Family–peer relationships: Modes of linkage* (pp. 77–106). Hillsdale, NJ: Erlbaum.

Elkind, D. (1994). *A sympathetic understanding of the child: Birth to sixteen* (3rd ed.). Boston: Allyn and Bacon.

Elkind, D., & Bowen, R. (1979). Imaginary audience behavior in children and adolescents. *Developmental Psychology, 15,* 33–44.

Elliott, D. S. (1994). Serious violent offenders: Onset, developmental course, and termination. *Criminology, 32,* 1–21.

Elliott, D. S., Wilson, W. J., Huizinga, D., Sampson, R. J., Elliott, A., & Rankin, B. (1996). The effects of neighborhood disadvantage on adolescent development. *Journal of Research in Crime and Delinquency, 33,* 389–426.

Elliot, J. G. (1999). School refusal: Issues of conceptualization, assessment, and treatment. *Journal of Child Psychology & Psychiatry & Allied Disciplines, 40,* 1001–1012.

Ellis, B. J., & Garber, J. (2000). Psychosocial antecedents of variation in girls' pubertal timing: Maternal depression, stepfather presence, and marital and family stress. *Child Development, 71,* 485–501.

Ellis, B. J., McFadyen-Ketchum, S., Dodge, K. A., Pettit, G. S., & Bates, J. E. (1999). Quality of early family relationships and individual differences in the timing of pubertal maturation in girls: A longitudinal test of an evolutionary model. *Journal of Personality and Social Psychology, 77,* 933–952.

Ellsworth, C. P., Muir, D. W., & Hains, S. M. J. (1993). Social competence and person–object differentiation: An analysis of the still-face effect. *Developmental Psychology, 29,* 63–73.

Elman, J. L., Bates, E. A., Johnson, M. H., Karmiloff-Smith, A., Parisi, D., & Plunkett, K. (1996). *Rethinking innateness: A connectionist perspective on development.* Cambridge, MA: MIT Press.

Elsen, H. (1994). Phonological constraints and overextensions. *First Language, 14,* 305–315.

El-Sheikh, M., Cummings, E. M., & Reiter, S. (1996). Preschoolers' responses to ongoing interadult conflict: The role of prior exposure to resolved versus unresolved arguments. *Journal of Abnormal Child Psychology, 24,* 665–679.

Ely, R. (1997). Language and literacy in the school years. In J. Berko Gleason (Ed.), *The development of language* (4th ed., pp. 398–439). Boston: Allyn and Bacon.

Ely, R. (2000). Language and literacy in the school years. In J. B. Gleason (Ed.), *The development of language* (pp. 409–454). Boston: Allyn and Bacon.

Ely, R., & McCabe, A. (1994). The language play of kindergarten children. *First Language, 14,* 19–35.

Emanuel, R. L., Robinson, B. G., Seely, E. W., Graves, S. W., Kohane, I., Saltzman, D., Barbieri, R., & Majzoub, J. A. (1994). Corticotrophin releasing hormone levels in human plasma and amniotic fluid during gestation. *Clinical Endocrinology, 40,* 257–262.

Emde, R. N. (1992). Individual meaning and increasing complexity: Contributions of Sigmund Freud and René Spitz to developmental psychology. *Developmental Psychology, 28,* 347–359.

Emde, R. N., & Buchsbaum, H. K. (1990). "Didn't you hear my mommy?" Autonomy with connectedness in moral self-emergence. In D. Cicchetti & M. Beeghly (Eds.), *Development of the self through transition* (pp. 35–60). Chicago: University of Chicago Press.

Emde, R. N., Plomin, R., Robinson, J., Corley, R., DeFries, J., Fulker, D. W., Reznick, J. S., Campos, J., Kagan, J., & Zahn-Waxler, C. (1992). Temperament, emotion, and cognition at fourteen months: The MacArthur Longitudinal Twin Study. *Child Development, 63,* 1437–1455.

Emery, R. E. (1999a). *Marriage, divorce, and children's adjustment* (2nd ed.). Thousand Oaks, CA: Sage.

Emery, R. E. (1999b). Postdivorce family life for children: An overview of research and some implications for policy. In R. A. Thompson & P. R. Amato (Eds.), *The postdivorce family: Children, parenting, and society* (pp. 3–27). Thousand Oaks, CA: Sage.

Emery, R. E., & Laumann-Billings, L. (1998). An overview of the nature, causes, and consequences of abusive family relationships: Toward differentiating maltreatment and violence. *American Psychologist, 53,* 121–135.

Emory, E. K., Schlackman, L. J., & Fiano, K. (1996). Drug–hormone interactions on neurobehavioral responses in human neonates. *Infant Behavior and Development, 19,* 213–220.

Engel, N. (1989). An American experience of pregnancy and childbirth in Japan. *Birth, 16,* 81–86.

Enright, R. D., Lapsley, D. K., & Shukla, D. (1979). Adolescent egocentrism in early and late adolescence. *Adolescence, 14,* 687–695.

Epstein, L. H. (1995). Do children lose and maintain weight easier than adults: A comparison of child and parent weight changes from six months to ten years. *Obesity Research, 3,* 411–417.

Epstein, L. H., Saelens, B. E., Myers, M. D., & Vito, D. (1997). Effects of decreasing sedentary behaviors on activity choice in obese children. *Health Psychology, 16,* 107–113.

Epstein, L. H., Saelens, B. E., & O'Brien, J. G. (1995). Effects of reinforcing increases in active versus decreases in sedentary behavior for obese children. *International Journal of Behavioral Medicine, 2,* 41–50.

Erdley, C. A., Cain, K. M., Loomis, C. C., Dumas-Hines, F., & Dweck, C. S. (1997). Relations among children's social goals, implicit personality theories, and responses to social failure. *Developmental Psychology, 33,* 263–272.

Erel, O., & Burman, B. (1995). Interrelatedness of marital relations and parent–child relations: A meta-analytic review. *Psychological Bulletin, 118,* 108–132.

Erikson, E. H. (1950). *Childhood and society.* New York: Norton.

Erikson, E. H. (1968). *Identity, youth, and crisis.* New York: Norton.

Eskenazi, B. (1993). Caffeine during pregnancy: Grounds for concern? *Journal of the American Medical Association, 270,* 2973–2974.

Eskenazi, B., Stapleton, A. L., Kharrazi, M., & Chee, W. Y. (1999). Associations between maternal decaffeinated and caffeinated coffee consumption and fetal growth and gestational duration. *Epidemiology, 10,* 242–249.

Espy, K. A., Kaufmann, P. M., & Glisky, M. L. (1999). Neuropsychological function in toddlers exposed to cocaine in utero: A preliminary study. *Developmental Neurospsychology, 15,* 447–460.

Essa, E. L., & Murray, C. I. (1994, May). Young children's understanding and experience with death. *Young Children, 49* (4), 74–81.

Evans, G. W., Maxwell, L. E., & Hart, B. (1999). Parental language and verbal responsiveness to children in crowded homes. *Developmental Psychology, 35,* 1020–1023.

Everman, D. B., & Cassidy, S. B. (2000). Genetics of childhood disorders: XII. Genomic imprinting: Breaking the rules. *Journal of the American Academy of Child and Adolescent Psychiatry, 38,* 386–389.

Fabes, R. A., Carlo, G., Kupanoff, K., & Laible, D. (1999). Early adolescence and prosocial/moral behavior I: The role of individual processes. *Journal of Early Adolescence, 19,* 5–16.

Fabes, R. A., Eisenberg, N., Jones, S., Smith, M., Guthrie, I., Poulin, R., Shepard, S., & Friedman, J. (1999). Regulation, emotionality, and preschoolers' socially competent peer interactions. *Child Development, 70,* 432–444.

Fabes, R. A., Eisenberg, N., Karbon, M., & Troyer, D., et al. (1994). The relations of children's emotion regulation to their vicarious emotional responses and comforting behaviors. *Child Development, 65,* 1678–1693.

Fabes, R. A., Eisenberg, N., McCormick, S. E., & Wilson, M. S. (1988). Preschoolers' attributions of the situational determinants of others' naturally occurring emotions. *Developmental Psychology, 24,* 376–385.

Fabes, R. A., Eisenberg, N., Nyman, M., & Michealieu, Q. (1991). Young children's appraisals of others' spontaneous emotional reactions. *Developmental Psychology, 27,* 858–866.

Fabricius, W. V., & Wellman, H. M. (1993). Two roads diverged: Young children's ability to judge distance. *Child Development, 64,* 399–414.

Facchinetti, F., Battaglia, C., Benatti, R., Borella, P., & Genazzani, A. R. (1992). Oral magnesium supplementation improves fetal circulation. *Magnesium Research, 3,* 179–181.

Fagan, J. F., III. (1973). Infants' delayed recognition memory and forgetting. *Journal of Experimental Child Psychology, 16,* 424–450.

Fagan, J. F., III, & Singer, L. T. (1979). The role of simple feature differences in infants' recognition of faces. *Infant Behavior and Development, 2,* 39–45.

Fagard, J., & Pezé, A. (1997). Age changes in interlimb coupling and the development of bimanual coordination. *Journal of Motor Behavior, 29,* 199–208.

Fagot, B. I. (1978). The influence of sex of child on parental reactions to toddler children. *Child Development, 49,* 459–465.

Fagot, B. I. (1984). The child's expectations of differences in adult male and female interactions. *Sex Roles, 11,* 593–600.

Fagot, B. I., & Hagan, R. I. (1991). Observations of parent reactions to sex-stereotyped behaviors: Age and sex effects. *Child Development, 62,* 617–628.

Fagot, B. I., & Leinbach, M. D. (1989). The young child's gender schema: Environmental input, internal organization. *Child Development, 60,* 663–672.

Fagot, B. I., Leinbach, M. D., & O'Boyle, C. (1992). Gender labeling, gender stereotyping, and parenting behaviors. *Developmental Psychology, 28,* 225–230.

Fagot, B. I., Pears, K. C., Apaldi, D. M., Crosby, L., & Lee, C. S. (1998). Becoming an adolescent father: Precursors and parenting. *Developmental Psychology, 34,* 1209–1219.

Fahrmeier, E. D. (1978). The development of concrete operations among the Hausa. *Journal of Cross-Cultural Psychology, 9,* 23–44.

Fairburn, C. G., Doll, H. A., Welch, S. L., Hay, P. J., Davies, B. A., & O'Conner, M. E. (1997). Risk factors for binge eating disorder: A community-based case control study. *Archives of General Psychiatry, 54,* 509–517.

Falbo, T. (1992). Social norms and the one-child family: Clinical and policy implications. In F. Boer & J. Dunn (Eds.), *Children's sibling relationships* (pp. 71–82). Hillsdale, NJ: Erlbaum.

Falbo, T., & Polit, D. (1986). A quantitative review of the only child literature: Research evidence and theory development. *Psychological Bulletin, 100,* 176–189.

Falbo, T., & Poston, D. L., Jr. (1993). The academic, personality, and physical outcomes of only children in China. *Child Development, 64,* 18–35.

Falbo, T., Poston, D. L., Jr., Triscari, R. S., & Zhang, X. (1997). Self-enhancing illusions among Chinese schoolchildren. *Journal of Cross-Cultural Psychology, 28,* 172–191.

Fall, C. H., Stein, C. E., Kumaran, K., Cox, V., Osmond, C., Barker, D. J., & Hales, C. N. (1998). Size at birth, maternal weight, and type 2 diabetes in South India. *Diabetic Medicine, 15,* 220–227.

Faller, K. C. (1990). *Understanding child sexual maltreatment.* Newbury Park, CA: Sage.

Fantz, R. L. (1961, May). The origin of form perception. *Scientific American, 204*(5), 66–72.

Faraone, S. V., Biederman, J., Weiffenbach, B., Keith, T., Chu, M. P., Weaver, A. (1999). Dopamine D-sub-4 gene 7-repeat allele and attention deficit hyperactivity disorder. *American Journal of Psychiatry, 156,* 768–770.

Farrington, D. P. (1987). Epidemiology. In H. C. Quay (Ed.), *Handbook of juvenile delinquency* (pp. 33–61). New York: Wiley.

Farver, J. M. (1993). Cultural differences in scaffolding pretend play: A comparison of American and Mexican mother–child and sibling–child pairs. In K. MacDonald (Ed.), *Parent–child play* (pp. 349–366). Albany, NY: SUNY Press.

Farver, J. M., & Branstetter, W. H. (1994). Preschoolers' prosocial responses to their peers' distress. *Developmental Psychology, 30,* 334–341.

Farver, J. M., Kim, Y. K., & Lee, Y. (1995). Cultural differences in Korean- and Anglo-American preschoolers' social interaction and play behaviors. *Child Development, 66,* 1099–1099.

Farver, J. M., & Wimbarti, S. (1995). Indonesian children's play with their mothers and older siblings. *Child Development, 66,* 1493–1503.

Fasouliostis, S. J., & Schenker, J. G. (2000). Ethics and assisted reproduction. *European Journal of Obstetrics, Gynecology, and Reproductive Biology, 90,* 171–180.

Fattibene, P., Mazzei, F., Nuccetelli, C., & Risica, S. (1999). Prenatal exposure to ionizing radiation: Sources, effects, and regulatory aspects. *Acta Paediatrica, 88,* 693–702.

Feagans, L., Sanyal, M., Henderson, F., et al. (1987). Relationship of middle ear disease in early childhood to later narrative and attention skills. *Journal of Pediatric Psychology, 12,* 581–594.

Feagans, L. V., Kipp, E., & Blood, I. (1994). The effects of otitis media on the attention skills of day-care-attending toddlers. *Developmental Psychology, 30,* 701–708.

Feagans, L. V., & Proctor, A. (1994). The effects of mild illness in infancy on later development: The sample case of the effects of otitis media (middle ear effusion). In C. B. Fisher & R. M. Lerner (Eds.), *Applied developmental psychology* (pp. 139–173). New York: McGraw-Hill.

Featherman, D. (1980). Schooling and occupational careers: Constancy and change in worldly success. In O. Brim, Jr., & J. Kagan (Eds.), *Constancy and change in human development* (pp. 675–738). Cambridge, MA: Harvard University Press.

Fein, G. G., Gariboldi, A., & Boni, R. (1993). The adjustment of infants and toddlers to group care: The first six months. *Early Childhood Research Quarterly, 8,* 1–14.

Feingold, A. (1994). Gender differences in personality: A meta-analysis. *Psychological Bulletin, 116,* 429–456.

Feiring, C., & Taska, L. S. (1996). Family self-concept: Ideas on its meaning. In B. Bracken (Ed.), *Handbook of self-concept* (pp. 317–373). New York: Wiley.

Feiring, C., Taska, L., & Lewis, M. (1999). Age and gender differences in children's and adolescents' adaptation to sexual abuse. *Child Abuse and Neglect, 23,* 115–128.

Feldman, D. H. (1991). *Nature's gambit.* New York: Teacher's College Press.

Feldman, D. H., & Goldsmith, L. T. (1991). *Nature's gambit.* New York: Teachers College Press.

Feldman, R., Greenbaum, C. W., & Yirmiya, N. (1999). Mother–infant affect synchrony as an antecedent of the emergence of self-control. *Developmental Psychology, 35,* 223–231.

Feldman, R., Weller, A., Leckman, J. F., Kuint, J., & Eidelman, A. I. (1999). The nature of the mother's tie to her infant: Maternal bonding under conditions of proximity, separation, and potential loss. *Journal of Child Psychology and Psychiatry, 40,* 929–939.

Felner, R. D., & Adan, A. M. (1988). The School Transitional Environment Project: An ecological intervention and evaluation. In R. H. Price, E. L. Cowan, R. P. Lorion, & J. Ramos-McKay (Eds.), *14 ounces of prevention: A casebook for practitioners* (pp. 111–122). Washington, DC: American Psychological Association.

Felsman, D. E., & Blustein, D. L. (1999). The role of peer relatedness in late adolescent career development. *Journal of Vocational Behavior, 54,* 279–295.

Fenson, L., Dale, P. S., Reznick, J. S., Bates, E., Thal, D. J., & Pethick, S. J. (1994). Variability in early communicative development. *Monographs of the Society for Research in Child Development, 59* (5, Serial No. 242).

Fenzel, L. M. (2000). Prospective study of changes in global self-worth and strain during the transition to middle school. *Journal of Early Adolescence, 20,* 93–116.

Ferguson, R. F. (1998). Teachers' perceptions and expectations and the black–white test score gap. In C. Jencks & M. Phillips (Eds.), *The black–white test score gap* (pp. 273–317). Washington, DC: Brookings Institution.

Ferguson, T. J., Stegge, H., & Damhuis, I. (1991). Children's understanding of guilt and shame. *Child Development, 62,* 827–839.

Ferguson, T. J., Stegge, H., Miller, E. R., & Olsen, M. E. (1999). Guilt, shame, and symptoms in children. *Developmental Psychology, 35,* 347–357.

Fergusson, D. M., & Woodward, L. J. (1999). Breast-feeding and later psychosocial adjustment. *Paediatric & Perinatal Epidemiology, 13,* 144–157.

Fergusson, D. M., Woodward, L. J., & Horwood, L. J. (2000). Risk factors and life processes associated with the onset of suicidal behaviour during adolescence and early adulthood. *Psychological Medicine, 30,* 23–39.

Fernald, A., & Morikawa, H. (1993). Common themes and cultural variations in Japanese and American mothers' speech to infants. *Child Development, 64,* 637–656.

Fernald, A., Taeschner, T., Dunn, J., Papousek, M., Boyssen-Bardies, B., & Fukui, I. (1989). A cross-language study of prosodic modifications in mothers' and fathers' speech to preverbal infants. *Journal of Child Language, 16,* 477–502.

Fernald, L. C., & Grantham-McGregor, S. M. (1998). Stress response in school-age children who have been growth retarded since early childhood. *American Journal of Clinical Nutrition, 68,* 691–698.

Fernandes, O., Sabharwal, M., Smiley, T., Pastuszak, A., Koren, G., & Einarson, T. (1998). Moderate to heavy caffeine consumption during pregnancy and relationship to spontaneous abortion and abnormal fetal growth: A meta-analysis. *Reproductive Toxicology, 12,* 435–444.

Feuerstein, R. (1979). *Dynamic assessment of retarded performers: The learning potential assessment device: Theory, instruments, and techniques.* Baltimore: University Park Press.

Feuerstein, R. (1980). *Instrumental enrichment.* Baltimore: University Park Press.

Ficca, G., Fagioli, I., Giganti, F., & Salzarulo, P. (1999). Spontaneous awakenings from sleep in the first year of life. *Early Human Development, 55,* 219–228.

Fichter, M. M., & Quadflieg, N. (1999). Six-year course and outcome of anorexia nervosa. *International Journal of Eating Disorders, 26,* 359–385.

Field, T. (1994). The effects of mother's physical and emotional unavailability on emotion regulation. In N. A. Fox (Ed.), The development of emotion regulation: Biological and behavioral considerations. *Monographs of the Society for Research in Child Development, 59*(2–3, Serial No. 240).

Field, T. (1998). Maternal depression effects on infants and early interventions. *Preventive Medicine, 27,* 200–203.

Field, T. M., Schanberg, S. M., Scafidi, F., Bauer, C. R., Vega-Lahr, N., Garcia, R., Nystrom, J., & Kuhn, C. M. (1986). Effects of tactile/kinesthetic stimulation on preterm neonates. *Pediatrics, 77,* 654–658.

Field, T. M., Woodson, R., Greenberg, R., & Cohen, D. (1982). Discrimination and imitation of facial expressions by neonates. *Science, 218,* 179–181.

Fiese, B. (1990). Playful relationships: A contextual analysis of mother–toddler interaction and symbolic play. *Child Development, 61,* 1648–1656.

Filipovic, Z. (1994). *Zlata's diary: A child's life in Sarajevo.* New York: Penguin.

Findji, F. (1998). Infant attention scaffolding at home. *European Journal of Psychology of Education, 13,* 323–333.

Fine, G. A. (1980). The natural history of preadolescent male friendship groups. In H. C. Foot, A. J. Chapman, & J. R. Smith (Eds.), *Friendship and social relations in children* (pp. 293–320). Chichester, England: Wiley.

Fine, M. (1986). Why urban adolescents drop into and out of public high school. *Teacher's College Record, 87,* 393–409.

Finegan, J. K., Niccols, G. A., & Sitarenios, G. (1992). Relations between prenatal testosterone levels and cognitive abilities at 4 years. *Developmental Psychology, 28,* 1075–1089.

Fisch, S. M., Truglio, R. T., & Cole, C. F. (1999). The impact of Sesame Street on preschool children: A review and synthesis of 30 years' research. *Media Psychology, 1,* 165–190.

Fischer, K. W., & Bidell, T. R. (1998). Dynamic development of psychological structures in action and thought. In R. M. Lerner (Ed.), *Handbook of child psychology: Vol. 1. Theoretical models of human development* (5th ed., pp. 467–562). New York: Wiley.

Fischer, K. W., & Rose, S. P. (1995, Fall). Concurrent cycles in the dynamic development of brain and behavior. *SRCD Newsletter,* pp. 3–4, 15–16.

Fischman, M. G., Moore, J. B., & Steele, K. H. (1992). Children's one-hand catching as a function of age, gender, and ball location. *Research Quarterly for Exercise and Sport, 63,* 349–355.

Fisher, C. B. (1993, Winter). Integrating science and ethics in research with high-risk children and youth. *Social Policy Report of the Society for Research in Child Development, 4*(4).

Fisher, C. B., Bornstein, M. H., & Gross, G. G. (1985). Left–right coding skills related to beginning reading. *Journal of Developmental and Behavioral Pediatrics, 6,* 279–283.

Fisher, J. A., & Birch, L. L. (1995). 3–5 year-old children's fat preferences and fat consumption are related to parental adiposity. *Journal of the American Dietetic Association, 95,* 759–764.

Fivush, R. (1995). Language, narrative, and autobiography. *Consciousness and Cognition, 4,* 100–103.

Flake, A., Roncarolo, M., Puck, J. M., Almeidaporada, G., Evins, M. I., Johnson, M. P., Abella, E. M., Harrison, D. D., & Zanjani, E. D. (1996). Treatment of X-linked severe combined immunodeficiency by in utero transplantation of paternal bone marrow. *New England Journal of Medicine, 335,* 1806–1810.

Flanagan, C. A., Bowes, J. M., Jonsson, B., Caspo, B., & Sheblanova, E. (1998). Ties that bind: Correlates of adolescents' civic commitments in seven countries. *Journal of Social Issues, 54,* 457–475.

Flanagan, C. A., & Eccles, J. S. (1993). Changes in parents' work status and adolescents' adjustment at school. *Child Development, 64,* 247–257.

Flanagan, C. A., & Faison, N. (2001). Youth civic development: Implications of research for social policy and programs. *Social Policy Report of the Society for Research in Child Development, 15*(1).

Flanagan, C. A., & Tucker, C. J. (1999). Adolescents' explanations for political issues: Concordance with their views of self and society. *Developmental Psychology, 35,* 1198–1209.

Flannery, K. A., & Liederman, J. (1995). Is there really a syndrome involving the co-occurrence of neurodevelopmental disorder, talent, non-right handedness and immune disorder among children? *Cortex, 31,* 503–515.

Flavell, J. H. (1999). Cognitive development: Children's knowledge about the mind. *Annual Review of Psychology, 50,* 21–45.

Flavell, J. H. (2000). Development of children's knowledge about the mental world. *International Journal of Behavioral Development, 24,* 15–23.

Flavell, J. H., Green, F. L., & Flavell, E. R. (1987). Development of knowledge about the appearance–reality distinction. *Monographs of the Society for Research in Child Development, 51* (1, Serial No. 212).

Flavell, J. H., Green, F. L., & Flavell, E. R. (1993). Children's understanding of the stream of consciousness. *Child Development, 64,* 387–398.

Flavell, J. H., Green, F. L., & Flavell, E. R. (1995). Young children's knowledge about thinking. *Monographs of the Society for Research in Child Development, 60* (1, Serial No. 243).

Flavell, J. H., Green, F. L., Flavell, E. R., & Grossman, J. B. (1997). The development of children's knowledge about inner speech. *Child Development, 68,* 39–47.

Flavell, J. H., & Miller, P. H. (1998). Social cognition. In D. Kuhn & R. S. Siegler (Eds.), *Handbook of child psychology: Vol. 2. Cognition, perception, and language* (4th ed., pp. 851–898). New York: Wiley.

Flegal, K. M. (1999). The obesity epidemic in children and adults: Current evidence and research issues. *Medicine & Science in Sports & Exercise, 31,* S509–S514.

Fletcher, A. C., Darling, N. E., Steinberg, L., & Dornbusch, S. M. (1995). The company they keep: Relation of adolescents' adjustment and behavior to their friends' perceptions of authoritative parenting in the social network. *Developmental Psychology, 31,* 300–310.

Fletcher, J. M., Landry, S. H., Bohan, T. P., Davidson, K. C., Brookshire, B. L., Lachar, D., Dramer, L. A., & Francis, D. J. (1997). Effects of intraventricular hemorrhage and hydrocephalus on the long-term neurobehavioral development of preterm very-low-birthweight infants. *Developmental Medicine & Child Neurology, 39,* 596–606.

Fletcher-Flinn, C. M., & Gravatt, B. (1995). The efficacy of computer-assisted instruction (CAI): A meta-analysis. *Journal of Educational Computing Research, 12,* 219–242.

Floccia, C., Christophe, A., & Bertoncini, J. (1997). High-amplitude sucking and newborns: The quest for underlying mechanisms. *Journal of Experimental Child Psychology, 64,* 175–198.

Florian, V., & Kravetz, S. (1985). Children's concepts of death: A cross-cultural comparison among Muslims, Druze, Christians, and Jews in Israel. *Journal of Cross-Cultural Psychology, 16,* 174–179.

Florsheim, P., Tolan, P., & Gorman-Smith, D. (1998). Family relationships, parenting practices, the availability of male family members, and the behavior of inner-city boys in single-mother and two-parent families. *Child Development, 69,* 1437–1447.

Flynn, J. R. (1996). What environmental factors affect intelligence: The relevance of IQ gains over time. In D. K. Detterman (Ed.), *The environment: Current topics in human intelligence* (Vol. 5, pp. 17–29). Norwood, NJ: Ablex.

Flynn, J. R. (1999). Searching for justice: The discovery of IQ gains over time. *American Psychologist, 54,* 5–20.

Fogel, A. (1993). *Developing through relationships: Origins of communication, self and culture.* New York: Harvester Wheatsheaf.

Foltz, C., Overton, W. F., & Ricco, R. B. (1995). Proof construction: Adolescent development from inductive to deductive problem-solving strategies. *Journal of Experimental Child Psychology, 59,* 179–195.

Fonagy, P., Steele, H., & Steele, M. (1991). Maternal representations of attachment during pregnancy predict the organization of infant–mother attachment at one year of age. *Child Development, 62,* 891–905.

Ford, C., & Beach, F. (1951). *Patterns of sexual behavior.* New York: Harper & Row.

Ford, W. C., North, K., Taylor, H., Farrow, A., Hull, M. G., & Golding, J. (2000). Increasing paternal age is associated with delayed conception in a large population of fertile couples: Evidence for declining fecundity in older men. The ALSPAC Study Team (Avon Longitudinal Study of Pregnancy and Childhood). *Human Reproduction, 15,* 1703–1708.

Fordham, K., & Stevenson-Hinde, J. (1999). Shyness, friendship quality, and adjustment during middle childhood. *Journal of Child Psychology and Psychiatry, 40,* 757–768.

Forehand, R., Biggar, H., & Kotchick, B. A. (1998). Cumulative risk across family stressors: Short- and long-term effects for adolescents. *Journal of Abnormal Child Psychology, 26,* 119–128.

Forsén, T., Eriksson, J., Tuomilehto, J., Reunanen, A., Osmond, C., & Barker, D. (2000). The fetal and childhood growth of persons who develop type 2 diabetes. *Annals of Internal Medicine, 133,* 176–182.

Fortier, I., Marcoux, S., & Beaulac-Baillargeon, L. (1993). Relation of caffeine intake during pregnancy to intrauterine growth retardation and preterm birth. *American Journal of Epidemiology, 137,* 931–940.

Fox, N. A. (1991). If it's not left, it's right: Electroencephalograph asymmetry and the development of emotion. *American Psychologist, 46,* 863–872.

Fox, N. A., Calkins, S. D., & Bell, M. A. (1994). Neural plasticity and development in the first two years of life: Evidence from cognitive and socioemotional domains of research. *Development and Psychopathology, 6,* 677–696.

Fox, N. A., & Card, J. A. (1998). Psychophysiological measures in the study of attachment. In J. Cassidy & P. Shaver (Eds.), *Handbook of attachment: Theory, research, and clinical applications* (pp. 226–245). New York: Guilford.

Fox, N. A., & Davidson, R. J. (1986). Taste-elicited changes in facial signs of emotion and the asymmetry of brain electrical activity in newborn infants. *Neuropsychologia, 24,* 417–422.

Fracasso, M. P., & Busch-Rossnagel, N. A. (1992). Parents and children of Hispanic origin. In M. E. Procidano & C. B. Fisher (Eds.), *Contemporary families* (pp. 83–98). New York: Teachers College Press.

Fraiberg, S. (1977). *Insights from the blind: Comparative studies of blind and sighted infants.* New York: Basic Books

Franco, P., Chabanski, S., Szliwowski, H., Dramaiz, M., & Kahn, A. (2000). Influence of maternal smoking on autonomic nervous system in healthy infants. *Pediatric Reasearch, 47,* 215–220.

Frank, S. J., Pirsch, L. A., & Wright, V. C. (1990). Late adolescents' perceptions of their relationships with their parents: Relationships among deidealization, autonomy, relatedness, and insecurity and implications for adolescent adjustment and ego identity status. *Journal of Youth and Adolescence, 19,* 571–588.

Frankel, K. A., & Bates, J. E. (1990). Mother–toddler problem solving: Antecedents in attachment, home behavior, and temperament. *Child Development, 61,* 810–819.

Franklin, C., & Corcoran, J. (2000). Preventing adolescent pregnancy: A review of programs and practices. *Social Work, 45,* 40–52.

Franklin, C., Grant, D., Corcoran, J., O'Dell-Miller, P., & Bultman, L. (1997). Effectiveness of prevention programs for adolescent pregnancy: A meta-analysis. *Journal of Marriage and the Family, 59,* 551–567.

Frazier, J. A., & Morrison, F. J. (1998). The influence of extended-year schooling on growth of achievement and perceived competence in early elementary school. *Child Development, 69,* 495–517.

Frazier, M. M. (1994). Issues, problems and programs in nurturing the disadvantaged and culturally different talented. In K. A. Heller, F. J. Jonks, & H. A. Passow (Eds.), *International handbook of research and development of giftedness and talent* (pp. 685–692). Oxford, England: Pergamon Press.

Freedman, D. S., Khan, L. K., Serdula, M. K., Srinivasan, S. R., & Berenson, G. S. (2000). Secular trends in height among children during 2 decades: The Bogalusa Heart Study. *Archives of Pediatric and Adolescent Medicine, 154,* 155–161.

Freeman, D. (1983). *Margaret Mead and Samoa: The making and unmaking of an anthropological myth.* Cambridge, MA: Harvard University Press.

Freppon, P. A., & Dahl, K. L. (1998). Balanced instruction: Insights and considerations. *Reading Research Quarterly, 33*, 240–251.

Freud, S. (1973). *An outline of psychoanalysis.* London: Hogarth. (Original work published 1938)

Freud, S. (1974). *The ego and the id.* London: Hogarth. (Original work published 1923)

Frick, J. E., Colombo, J., & Saxon, T. F. (1999). Individual and developmental differences in disengagement of fixation in early infancy. *Child Development, 70*, 537–548.

Fried, M. N., & Fried, M. H. (1980). *Transitions: Four rituals in eight cultures.* New York: Norton.

Fried, P. A., & Makin, J. E. (1987). Neonatal behavioral correlates of prenatal exposure to marijuana, cigarettes, and alcohol in a low risk population. *Neurobehavioral Toxicology and Teratology, 9*, 1–7.

Fried, P. A., Watkinson, B., & Gray, R. (1998). Differential effects on cognitive functioning in 9- to 12-year-olds prenatally exposed to cigarettes and marihuana. *Neurotoxicology and Teratology, 20*, 293–306.

Fried, P. A., Watkinson, B., & Gray, R. (1999). Growth from birth to early adolescence in offspring prenatally exposed to cigarettes and marijuana. *Neurotoxicology and Teratology, 21*, 513–525.

Friedman, J. M. (1996). *The effects of drugs on the fetus and nursing infant: A handbook for health care professionals.* Baltimore: Johns Hopkins University Press.

Frodi, A. (1985). When empathy fails: Aversive infant crying and child abuse. In B. M. Lester & C. F. Z. Boukydis (Eds.), *Infant crying: Theoretical and research perspectives* (pp. 263–277). New York: Plenum.

Frost, J. J., & Forrest, J. D. (1995). Understanding the impact of effective teenage pregnancy prevention programs. *Family Planning Perspectives, 27*, 188–195.

Frost, J. L., Shin, D., & Jacobs, P. J. (1998). Physical environments and children's play. In O. N. Saracho & B. Spodek (Eds.), *Multiple perspectives on play in early childhood education* (pp. 255–294). Albany: State University of New York Press.

Fry, A. F., & Hale, S. (1996). Processing speed, working memory, and fluid intelligence: Evidence for a developmental cascade. *Psychological Science, 7*, 237–241.

Fuchs, I., Eisenberg, N., Hertz-Lazarowitz, R., & Sharabany, R. (1986). Kibbutz, Israeli city, and American children's moral reasoning about prosocial moral conflicts. *Merrill-Palmer Quarterly, 32*, 37–50.

Fuligni, A. J. (1997). The academic achievement of adolescents from immigrant families: The roles of family background, attitudes, and behavior. *Child Development, 68*, 261–273.

Fuligni, A. J. (1998a). Authority, autonomy, and parent–adolescent conflict and cohesion: A study of adolescents from Mexican, Chinese, Filipino, and European backgrounds. *Developmental Psychology, 34*, 782–792.

Fuligni, A. J. (1998b). The adjustment of children from immigrant families. *Current Directions in Psychological Science, 7*, 99–103.

Fuligni, A. J., Burton, L., Marshall, S., Perez-Febles, A., Yarrington, J., Kirsh, L. B., & Merriwether-DeVries, C. (1999). Attitudes toward family obligations among American adolescents with Asian, Latin American, and European backgrounds. *Child Development, 70*, 1030–1044.

Fuligni, A. J., & Eccles, J. S. (1993). Perceived parent–child relationships and early adolescents' orientation toward peers. *Developmental Psychology, 29*, 622–632.

Fuligni, A. J., Eccles, J. S., & Barber, B. L. (1995). The long-term effects of seventh-grade ability grouping in mathematics. *Journal of Early Adolescence, 15*, 58–89.

Fuligni, A. J., & Stevenson, H. W. (1995). Time use and mathematics achievement among American, Chinese, and Japanese high school students. *Child Development, 66*, 830–842.

Furman, E. (1990, November). Plant a potato—learn about life (and death). *Young Children, 46*(1), 15–20.

Furman, W., & Buhrmester, D. (1992). Age and sex differences in perceptions of networks of personal relationships. *Child Development, 63*, 103–115.

Furman, W., & Wehner, E. A. (1994). Romantic views: Toward a theory of adolescent romantic relationships. In R. Montemayor, G. R. Adams, & T. P. Gullotta (Eds.), *Advances in adolescent development: Vol. 3. Relationships in adolescence* (pp. 168–195). Beverly Hills, CA: Sage.

Furstenberg, F. F., Jr., Brooks-Gunn, J., & Morgan, S. P. (1987). *Adolescent mothers and their children in later life.* Cambridge, England: Cambridge University Press.

Furstenberg, F. F., Jr., & Harris, K. M. (1993). When and why fathers matter: Impact of father involvement on children of adolescent mothers. In R. I. Lerman & T. J. Ooms (Eds.), *Young unwed fathers* (pp. 117–138). Philadelphia: Temple University Press.

Furstenberg, F. F., Jr., Hughes, M. E., & Brooks-Gunn, J. (1992). The next generation: Children of teenage mothers grow up. In M. K. Rosenheim & M. F. Testa (Eds.), *Early parenthood* (pp. 113–135). New Brunswick, NJ: Rutgers University Press.

Fuson, K. C. (1988). *Children's counting and concepts of number.* New York: Springer-Verlag.

Fuson, K. C. (1990). Issues in place-value and multidigit addition and subtraction learning and teaching. *Journal for Research in Mathematics Education, 21*, 273–280.

Gaddis, A., & Brooks-Gunn, J. (1985). The male experience of pubertal change. *Journal of Youth and Adolescence, 14*, 61–69.

Gaillard, W. D., Hertz-Pannier, L., Mott, S. H., Barnett, A. S., LeBihan, D., & Theodore, W. H. (2000). Functional anatomy of cognitive development: fMRI of verbal fluency in children and adults. *Neurology, 54*, 180–185.

Galambos, N. L., Almeida, D. M., & Petersen, A. C. (1990). Masculinity, femininity, and sex role attitudes in early adolescence: Exploring gender intensification. *Child Development, 61*, 1905–1914.

Galambos, S. J., & Maggs, J. L. (1991). Children in self-care: Figures, facts and fiction. In J. V. Lerner & N. L. Galambos (Eds.), *Employed mothers and their children* (pp. 131–157). New York: Garland.

Gale, G., & VandenBerg, K. A. (1998). Kangaroo care. *Neonatal Network, 17*(5), 69–71.

Galinsky, E., Howes, C., Kontos, S., & Shinn, M. (1994). *The study of children in family child care and relative care: Highlights of findings.* New York: Families and Work Institute.

Galler, J. R., Ramsey, C. F., Morley, D. S., Archer, E., & Salt, P. (1990). The long-term effects of early kwashiorkor compared with marasmus. IV. Performance on the National High School Entrance Examination. *Pediatric Research, 28*, 235–239.

Galler, J. R., Ramsey, F., & Solimano, G. (1985a). A follow-up study of the effects of early malnutrition on subsequent development: I. Physical growth and sexual maturation during adolescence. *Pediatric Research, 19*, 518–523.

Galler, J. R., Ramsey, F., & Solimano, G. (1985b). A follow-up study of the effects of early malnutrition on subsequent development: II. Fine motor skills in adolescence. *Pediatric Research, 19*, 524–527.

Galler, J. R., Ramsey, F., Solimano, G., Kucharski, L. T., & Harrison, R. (1984). The influence of early malnutrition on subsequent behavioral development: IV. Soft neurological signs. *Pediatric Research, 18*, 826–832.

Gallup Organization. (1995). *Food, physical activity, and fun: What kids think.* Chicago, IL: The International Food Information Council and The Presidents' Council on Physical Fitness and Sports.

Galotti, K. M., Kozberg, S. F., & Farmer, M. C. (1991). Gender and developmental differences in adolescents' conceptions of moral reasoning. *Journal of Youth and Adolescence, 20*, 13–30.

Gandour, M. J. (1989). Activity level as a dimension of temperament in toddlers: Its relevance for the organismic specificity hypothesis. *Child Development, 60*, 1092–1098.

Gannon, S., & Korn, S. J. (1983). Temperament, cultural variation, and behavior disorder in preschool children. *Child Psychiatry and Human Development, 13*, 203–212.

Ganong, L. H., & Coleman, M. (1994). *Remarried family relationships.* Thousand Oaks, CA: Sage.

Ganong, L. H., & Coleman, M. (2000). Remarried families. In C. Hendrick & S. S. Hendrick (Eds.), *Close relationships* (pp. 155–168). Thousand Oaks, CA: Sage.

Garbarino, J., & Kostelny, K. (1993). Neighborhood and community influences on parenting. In T. Luster & L. Okagaki (1993), *Parenting: An ecological perspective* (pp. 203–226). Hillsdale, NJ: Erlbaum.

Garber, J., Braafladt, N., & Weiss, B. (1995). Affect regulation in depressed and nondepressed children and young adolescents. *Developmental and Psychopathology, 7*, 93–115.

Garber, J., Quiggle, N., Panak, W., & Dodge, K. (1991). Aggression and depression in children: Comorbidity, specificity, and social cognitive processing. In D. Cicchetti & S. L. Toth (Eds.), *Rochester Symposium on Developmental Psychopathology: Vol. 2. Internalizing and externalizing expressions of dysfunction* (pp. 225–264). Hillsdale, NJ: Erlbaum.

Garcia, M. M., Shaw, D. S., Winslow, E. B., & Yaggi, K. E. (2000). Destructive sibling conflict and the development of conduct problems in young boys. *Developmental Psychology, 36*, 44–53.

García Coll, C., & Magnuson, K. (1997). The psychological experience of immigration: A developmental perspective. In A. Booth, A. C. Crouter, & N. Landale (Eds.), *Immigration and the family* (pp. 91–131). Mahwah, NJ: Erlbaum.

Gardner, H. (1980). *Artful scribbles: The significance of children's drawings.* New York: Basic Books.

Gardner, H. (1983). *Frames of mind: The theory of multiple intelligences.* New York: Basic Books.

Gardner, H. (1993). *Multiple intelligences: The theory in practice.* New York: Basic Books.

Gardner, H. (1998a). Extraordinary cognitive achievements (ECA): A symbol systems approach. In R. M. Lerner (Ed.), *Handbook of child psychology: Vol. 1. Theoretical models of human development* (5th ed., pp. 415–466). New York: Wiley.

Gardner, H. (1998b). *Intelligence reframed: Multiple intelligences for the 21st century.* New York: Basic Books.

Garfinkel, I., & McLanahan, S. (1995). The effects of child support reform on child well-being. In P. L. Chase-Lansdale & J. Brooks-Gunn (Eds.), *Escape from poverty: What makes a difference for children?* (pp. 211–238). New York: Cambridge University Press.

Garmezy, N. (1993). Children in poverty: Resilience despite risk. *Psychiatry, 56,* 127–136.

Garmon, L. C., Basinger, K. S., Gregg, V. R., & Gibbs, J. C. (1996). Gender differences in stage and expression of moral judgment. *Merrill-Palmer Quarterly, 42,* 418–437.

Garner, D. M., & Garfinkel, P. E. (Eds.). (1997). *Handbook of treatment for eating disorders* (2nd ed.). New York: Guilford.

Garner, P. W., Jones, D. C., & Miner, J. L. (1994). Social competence among low-income preschoolers: Emotion socialization practices and social cognitive correlates. *Child Development, 65,* 622–637.

Garner, R. (1990). Children's use of strategies in reading. In D. F. Bjorklund (Ed.), *Children's strategies: Contemporary views of cognitive development* (pp. 245–268). Hillsdale, NJ: Erlbaum.

Garnier, H. E., Stein, J. A., & Jacobs, J. K. (1997). The process of dropping out of high school: A 19-year perspective. *American Educational Research Journal, 34,* 395–419.

Garrett, P., Ng'andu, N., & Ferron, J. (1994). Poverty experiences of young children and the quality of their home environments. *Child Development, 65,* 331–345.

Garvey, C. (1990). *Play.* Cambridge, MA: Harvard University Press.

Gasden, V. (1999). Black families in intergenerational and cultural perspective. In M. E. Lamb (Ed.), *Parenting and child development in "nontraditional" families* (pp. 221–246). Mahwah, NJ: Erlbaum.

Gaskins, S. (1999). Children's daily lives in a Mayan village: A case study of culturally constructed roles and activities. In R. Göncü (Ed.), *Children's engagement in the world: Sociocultural perspectives* (pp. 25–61). Cambridge, U.K.: Cambridge University Press.

Gathercole, S. E. (1998). The development of memory. *Journal of Child Psychology and Psychiatry, 39,* 3–27.

Gathercole, S. E., Adams, A-M., & Hitch, G. (1994). Do young children rehearse? An individual-differences analysis. *Memory & Cognition, 22,* 201–207.

Gathercole, S. E., Willis, C. S., Emslie, H., & Baddeley, A. D. (1992). Phonological memory and vocabulary development during the early school years: A longitudinal study. *Developmental Psychology, 28,* 887–898.

Gaub, M., & Carlson, C. L. (1997). Gender differences in ADHD: A meta-analysis and critical review. *Journal of the American Academy of Child and Adolescent Psychiatry, 36,* 1036–1045.

Gauvain, M. (1999). Everyday opportunities for the development of planning skills: Sociocultural and family influences. In A. Göncü (Ed.), *Children's engagement in the world* (pp. 173–201). New York: Cambridge University Press.

Gauvain, M., & Rogoff, B. (1989a). Collaborative problem solving and children's planning skills. *Developmental Psychology, 25,* 139–151.

Gauvain, M., & Rogoff, B. (1989b). Ways of speaking about space: The development of children's skill in communicating spatial knowledge. *Cognitive Development, 4,* 295–307.

Gazmararian, J. A., Parker, R. M., & Baker, D. W. (1999). Reading skills and family planning knowledge and practices in a low-income managed-care population. *Obstetrics & Gynecology, 93,* 239–244.

Ge, X., Conger, R. D., & Elder, G. H., Jr. (1996). Coming of age too early: Pubertal influences on girls' vulnerability to psychological distress. *Child Development, 67,* 3386–3400.

Geary, D. C. (1994). *Children's mathematical development.* Washington, DC: American Psychological Association.

Geary, D. C. (1995). *Children's mathematical development: Research and practical applications.* Washington, DC: American Psychological Association.

Geary, D. C. (1996). International differences in mathematics achievement: The nature, causes, and consequences. *Current Directions in Psychological Science, 5,* 133–137.

Geary, D. C., Bow-Thomas, C. C., Liu, F., & Siegler, R. S. (1996). Development of arithmetical competencies in Chinese and American children: Influence of age, language, and schooling. *Child Development, 67,* 2022–2044.

Gelles, R. J. (1998). The youngest victims: Violence toward children. In R. Bergen & R. Kennedy (Eds.), *Issues in intimate violence* (pp. 5–24). Thousand Oaks, CA: Sage.

Gelman, R. (1972). Logical capacity of very young children: Number invariance rules. *Child Development, 43,* 75–90.

Gelman, R., & Shatz, M. (1978). Appropriate speech adjustments: The operation of conversational constraints on talk to two-year-olds. In M. Lewis & L. A. Rosenblum (Eds.), *Interaction, conversation, and the development of language* (pp. 27–61). New York: Wiley.

Gelman, S. A., & Wellman, H. M. (1991). Insides and essences: Early understandings of the nonobvious. *Cognition, 38,* 213–244.

Genome International Sequencing Consortium. (2001). Initial sequencing and analysis of the human genome. *Nature, 409,* 860–921.

Gentry, J. R. (1981, January). Learning to spell developmentally. *The Reading Teacher, 35*(2), 378–381.

Georgiewa, P., Rzanny, R., Hopf, J. M., Knab, R., Glauche, V., Kaiser, W. A., & Blanz, B. (1999). fMRI during word processing in dyslexic and normal reading children. *Neuroreport, 10,* 3459–3465.

Gershkoff-Stowe, L., & Smith, L. B. (1997). A curvilinear trend in naming errors as a function of early vocabulary growth. *Cognitive Psychology 34,* 37–71.

Gervai, J., Turner, P. J., & Hinde, R. A. (1995). Gender-related behaviour, attitudes, and personality in parents of young children in England and Hungary. *International Journal of Behavioral Development, 18,* 105–126.

Gesell, A. (1933). Maturation and patterning of behavior. In C. Murchison (Ed.), *A handbook of child psychology.* Worcester, MA: Clark University Press.

Getchell, N., & Roberton, M. A. (1989). Whole body stiffness as a function of developmental level in children's hopping. *Developmental Psychology, 25,* 920–928.

Ghim, H.R. (1990). Evidence for perceptual organization in infants: Perception of subjective contours by young infants. *Infant Behavior and Development, 13,* 221–248.

Gibbs, J. C. (1991). Toward an integration of Kohlberg's and Hoffman's theories of morality. In W. M. Kurtines & J. L. Gewirtz (Eds.), *Handbook of moral behavior and development* (Vol. 1, pp. 183–222). Hillsdale, NJ: Erlbaum.

Gibbs, J. C. (1995). The cognitive developmental perspective. In W. M. Kurtines & J. L. Gewirtz (Eds.), *Moral development: An introduction* (pp. 27–48). Boston: Allyn and Bacon.

Gibbs, J. C., Potter, G. B., & Goldstein, A. P. (1995). *The EQUIP program: Teaching youth to think and act responsibly through a peer-helping approach.* Champaign, IL: Research Press.

Gibson, E. J. (1970). The development of perception as an adaptive process. *American Scientist, 58,* 98–107.

Gibson, E. J. (1988). Exploratory behavior in the development of perceiving, acting, and the acquiring of knowledge. *Annual Review of Psychology, 39,* 1–41.

Gibson, E. J., & Walk, R. D. (1960). The "visual cliff." *Scientific American, 202,* 64–71.

Gibson, J. J. (1979). *The ecological approach to visual perception.* Boston: Houghton Mifflin.

Giedd, J. N., Blumenthal, J., Jeffries, N. O., Rajapakse, J. C., Vaituzis, C., & Liu, H. (1999). Development of the human corpus callosum during childhood and adolescence: A longitudinal MRI study. *Progress in Neuro-Psychopharmacology and Biological Psychiatry, 23,* 571–588.

Gillies, R. M., & Ashman, A. F. (1996). Teaching collaborative skills to primary school children in classroom-based workgroups. *Learning and Instruction, 6,* 187–200.

Gillies, R. M., & Ashman, A. F. (1998). Behavior and interactions of children in cooperative groups in lower and middle elementary grades. *Journal of Educational Psychology, 90,* 746–757.

Gilligan, C. F. (1982). *In a different voice.* Cambridge, MA: Harvard University Press.

Gillman, M. W., Rifas-Shiman, S. L., Frazier, A. L., Rockett, H. R. H., Camargo, C. A., Jr., Field, A. E., Berkey, C. S., & Colditz, G. A. (2000). Family dinner and diet quality among older children and adolescents. *Archives of Family Medicine, 9,* 235–240.

Gillmore, M. R., Hawkins, J. D., Day, L. E., & Catalano, R. F. (1997). Friendship and deviance: New evidence on an old controversy. *Journal of Early Adolescence, 16,* 80–95.

Gilvarry, E. (2000). Substance abuse in young people. *Journal of Child Psychology and Psychiatry, 41,* 55–80.

Ginsburg, H. P., Klein, A., & Starkey, P. (1998). The development of children's mathematical thinking: Connecting research with practice. In I. E. Sigel & K. A. Renninger (Eds.), *Handbook of child psychology: Vol. 4. Child Psychology in Practice* (5th ed., pp. 401–476). New York: Wiley.

Ginsburg, H. P., & Opper, S. (1988). *Piaget's theory of intellectual development* (3rd ed.). Englewood Cliffs, NJ: Prentice-Hall.

Ginzberg, E. (1988). Toward a theory of occupational choice. *Career Development Quarterly, 36*, 358–363.

Giusti, R. M., Iwamoto, K., & Hatch, E. E. (1995). Diethylstilbestrol revisited: A review of the long-term health effects. *Annals of Internal Medicine, 122*, 778–788.

Gjerde, P. F. (1995). Alternative pathways to chronic depressive symptoms in young adults: Gender differences in developmental trajectories. *Child Development, 66*, 1277–1300.

Gladwell, M. (1998, February 2). The Pima paradox. *The New Yorker,* pp. 44–57.

Glasgow, K. L., Dornbusch, S. M., Troyer, L., Steinberg, L., & Ritter, P. L. (1997). Parenting styles, adolescents' attributions, and educational outcomes in nine heterogeneous high schools. *Child Development, 68*, 507–523.

Glassman, B. S. (Ed.). (1996). *The new view almanac.* Woodbridge, CT: Blackbirch Press.

Gleason, T. R., Sebanc, A. M., & Hartup, W. W. (2000). Imaginary companions of preschool children. *Developmental Psychology, 36*, 419–428.

Gleitman, L. R., & Newport, E. (1996). The invention of language by children. Cambridge, MA: MIT Press.

Glick, P. C. (1997). Demographic pictures of African American families. In H. P. McAdoo (Ed.), *Black families* (3rd ed., pp. 118–138). Thousand Oaks, CA: Sage.

Glidden, L. M., & Pursley, J. T. (1989). Longitudinal comparisons of families who have adopted children with mental retardation. *American Journal on Mental Retardation, 94*, 272–277.

Glosten, B. (1998). Controversies in obstetric anesthesia. *Anesthesia and Analgesia, 428*(Suppl. 32-8), 32–38.

Gnepp, J. (1983). Children's social sensitivity: Inferring emotions from conflicting cues. *Developmental Psychology, 19*, 805–814.

Gnepp, J. (1989). Children's use of personal information to understand other people's feelings. In C. Saarni & P. Harris (Eds.), *Children's understanding of emotion*

(pp. 151–180). Cambridge, England: Cambridge University Press.

Goin, R. P. (1998). Nocturnal enuresis in children. *Child: Care, Health and Development, 24*, 277–288.

Goldfield, B. A. (1987). Contributions of child and caregiver to referential and expressive language. *Applied Psycholinguistics, 8*, 267–280.

Goldsmith, H. H., Buss, K. A., & Lemery, K. S. (1997). Toddler and childhood temperament: Expanded content, stronger genetic evidence, new evidence for the importance of the environment. *Developmental Psychology, 33*, 891–905.

Goldsmith, H. H., Lemery, K. S., Buss, K. A., & Campos, J. J. (1999). Genetic analyses of focal aspects of infant temperament. *Developmental Psychology, 35*, 972–985.

Goleman, D. (1995). *Emotional intelligence.* New York: Bantam.

Goleman, D. (1998). *Working with emotional intelligence.* New York: Bantam.

Golomb, C. (1992). *The child's creation of a pictorial world.* Berkeley: University of California Press.

Golombok, S., & Tasker, F. (1996). Do parents influence the sexual orientation of their children? Findings from a longitudinal study of lesbian families. *Developmental Psychology, 32*, 3–11.

Golombok, S., Cook, R., Bish, A., & Murray, C. (1995). Families created by the new reproductive technologies: Quality of parenting and social and emotional development of the children. *Child Development, 66*, 285–298.

Golub, M. S. (1996). Labor analgesia and infant brain development. Pharmacology, *Biochemistry, and Behavior, 55*, 619–628.

Gombert, J. E. (1992). *Metalinguistic development.* Chicago: University of Chicago Press.

Gomez-Schwartz, B., Horowitz, J. M., & Cardarelli, A. P. (1990). *Child sexual abuse: Initial effects.* Newbury Park, CA: Sage.

Göncü, A. (1993). Development of intersubjectivity in the dyadic play of preschoolers. *Early Childhood Research Quarterly, 8*, 99–116.

Gonzales, N. A., Cauce, A. M., Friedman, R. J., & Mason, C. A. (1996). Family, peer, and neighborhood influences on academic achievement among African-American adolescents: One-year prospective effects. *American Journal of Community Psychology, 24*, 365–387.

Good, T. L., & Brophy, J. E. (1994). *Looking in classrooms* (6th ed.). New York: HarperCollins.

Goodfellow, P. N., & Lovell, B. R. (1993). SRY and sex determination in mammals. *Annual Review of Genetics, 27*, 71–92.

Goodlet, C. R., & Johnson, T. B. (1999). Temporal windows of vulnerability within the third trimester equivalent: Why "knowing when" matters. In J. H. Hannigan, L. P. Spear, N. P. Spear, & C. R. Goodlet (Eds.), *Alcohol and alcoholism: Effects on brain and development* (pp. 59–91). Mahwah, NJ: Erlbaum.

Goodman, G. S., Hirschman, J. E., Hepps, D., & Rudy, L. (1991). Children's memory for stressful events. *Merrill-Palmer Quarterly, 37*, 109–158.

Goodman, G. S., Quas, J. A., Bulkley, J., & Shapiro, C. (1999). Innovations for child witnesses: A national survey. *Psychology, Public Policy, & Law, 5*, 255, 281.

Goodman, G. S., & Tobey, A. E. (1994). Memory development within the context of child sexual abuse investigations. In C. B. Fisher & R. M. Lerner (Eds.), *Applied developmental psychology* (pp. 46–75). New York: McGraw-Hill.

Goodman, K. S. (1986). *What's whole in whole language?* Portsmouth, NH: Heinemann.

Goodman, S. H., Barfoot, B., Frye, A. A., & Belli, A. M. (1999). Dimensions of marital conflict and children's social problem-solving skills. *Journal of Family Psychology, 13*, 33–45.

Goodman, S. H., Gravitt, G. W., Jr., & Kaslow, N. J. (1995). Social problem solving: A moderator of the relation between negative life stress and depression symptoms in children. *Journal of Abnormal Child Psychology, 23*, 473–485.

Goossens, F. A., & van IJzendoorn, M. H. (1990). Quality of infants' attachments to professional caregivers: Relation to infant–parent attachment and day-care characteristics. *Child Development, 61*, 832–837.

Gopnik, A., & Choi, S. (1990). Do linguistic differences lead to cognitive differences? A cross-linguistic study of semantic and cognitive development. *First Language, 11*, 199–215.

Gopnik, A., & Meltzoff, A. N. (1986). Relations between semantic and cognitive development in the one-word stage: The specificity hypothesis. *Child Development, 57*, 1040–1053.

Gopnik, A., & Meltzoff, A. N. (1992). Categorization and naming: Basic-level sorting in eighteen-month-olds and its relation to language. *Child Development, 63*, 1091–1103.

Gopnik, A., & Wellman, H. M. (1994). The 'theory' theory. In L. A. Hirschfeld & S. A. Gelman (Eds.), *Mapping the mind: Domain*

specificity in cognition and culture (pp. 257–293). Cambridge, U.K.: Cambridge University Press.

Gordon, V. N. (1998). Career decidedness types: A literature review. *Career Development Quarterly, 46*, 386–403.

Gortmaker, S. L., Must, A., Perrin, J. M., Sobol, A. M., & Dietz, W. H., Jr. (1993). Social and economic consequences of overweight in adolescence and young adulthood. *New England Journal of Medicine, 329*, 1008–1012.

Gortmaker, S. L., Must, A., Sobol, A. M., Peterson, K., Colditz, G. A., & Dietz, W. H. (1996). Television viewing as a cause of increasing obesity among children in the United States, 1986–1990. *Archives of Pediatric and Adolescent Medicine, 150*, 356–362.

Goss, D. A., & Rainey, B. B. (1998). Relation of childhood myopia progression rates to time of year. *Journal of the American Optometric Association, 69*, 262–266.

Goswami, U. (1996). Analogical reasoning and cognitive development. In H. Reese (Ed.), *Advances in child development and behavior* (Vol. 26, pp. 91–138). New York: Academic Press.

Goswami, U. (2000). Phonological and lexical processes. In M. L. Kamil & P. B. Mosenthal (Eds.), *Handbook of reading research* (Vol. 3, pp. 251–284). Mahwah, NJ: Erlbaum.

Goswami, U., & Brown, A. (1989). Melting chocolate and melting snowmen: Analogical reasoning and causal relations. *Cognition, 35*, 69–95.

Gott, V. L. (1998). Antoine Marfan and his syndrome: One hundred years later. *Maryland Medical Journal, 47*, 247–252.

Gottesman, I. I. (1963). Genetic aspects of intelligent behavior. In N. Ellis (Ed.), *Handbook of mental deficiency* (pp. 253– 296). New York: McGraw-Hill.

Gottesman, I. I. (1991). *Schizophrenia genetics: The origins of madness.* New York: Freeman.

Gottesman, I. I., Carey, G., & Hanson, D. R. (1983). Pearls and perils in epigenetic psychopathology. In S. B. Guze, E. J., Earls, & J. E. Barrett (Eds.), *Childhood psychopathology and development* (pp. 287–300). New York: Raven Press.

Gottfredson, L. S. (1996). Gottfredson's theory of circumscription and compromise. In D. Brown & L. Brooks (Eds.), *Career choice and development* (3rd ed.). San Francisco: Jossey-Bass.

Gottfried, A. E. (1991). Maternal employment in the family setting: Developmental and environmental issues. In J. V. Lerner & N. L. Galambos (Eds.), *Employed mothers and their children* (pp. 63–84). New York: Garland.

Gottfried, A. E., Gottfried, A. W., Bathurst, K., & Killian, C. (1999). Maternal and dual-earner employment. In M. E. Lamb (Ed.), *Parenting and child development in "nontraditional" families* (pp. 15–37). Mahwah, NJ: Erlbaum.

Gottlieb, G. (1992). *Individual development and evolution: The genesis of novel behavior.* New York: Oxford University Press.

Gottlieb, G. (1996). Developmental psychobiological theory. In R. B. Cairns, G. H. Elder, Jr., & E. J. Costello (Eds.), *Developmental science: Cambridge studies in social and emotional development* (pp. 63–77). New York: Cambridge University Press.

Gottlieb, G. (1998). Normally occurring environmental and behavioral influences on gene activity: From central dogma to probabilistic epigenesis. *Psychological Review, 105,* 792–802.

Gottlieb, G. (2000). Environmental and behavioral influences on gene activity. *Current Directions in Psychological Science, 9,* 93–97.

Gottman, J. M., Katz, L. F., & Hooven, C. (1996). *Meta-emotion: How families communicate emotionally.* Mahwah, NJ: Erlbaum.

Goubet, N., & Clifton, R. K. (1998). Object and event representation in 6½-month-old infants. *Developmental Psychology, 34,* 63–76.

Gould, J. L., & Keeton, W. T. (1996). *Biological science* (6th ed.). New York: Norton.

Graber, J. A., Brooks-Gunn, J., Paikoff, R. L., & Warren, M. P. (1994). Prediction of eating problems: An 8-year study of adolescent girls. *Developmental Psychology, 30,* 823–834.

Graber, J. A., Lewinsohn, P. M., Seeley, J. R., & Brooks-Gunn, J. (1997). Is psychopathology associated with the timing of pubertal development? *Journal of the American Academy of Child & Adolescent Psychiatry, 36,* 1768–1776.

Graber, J. A., Petersen, A. C., & Brooks-Gunn, J. (1996). Pubertal processes: Methods, measures, and models. In J. A. Graber, J. Brooks-Gunn, & A. C. Petersen (Eds.), *Transitions through adolescence* (pp. 23–53). Mahwah, NJ: Erlbaum.

Graham, S., Doubleday, C., & Guarino, P. A. (1984). The development of relations between perceived controllability and the emotions of pity, anger, and guilt. *Child Development, 55,* 561–565.

Graham, T. A. (1999). The role of gesture in children's learning to count. *Journal of Experimental Child Psychology, 74,* 333–355.

Gralinski, J. H., & Kopp, C. B. (1993). Everyday rules for behavior: Mothers' requests to young children. *Developmental Psychology, 29,* 573–584.

Granot, M., Spitzer, A., Aroian, K. J., Ravid, C., Tamir, B., & Noam, R. (1996). Pregnancy and delivery practices and beliefs of Ethiopian immigrant women in Israel. *Western Journal of Nursing Research, 18,* 299–313.

Grantham-McGregor, S., Powell, C., Walker, S., Chang, S., & Fletcher, P. (1994). The long-term follow-up of severely malnourished children who participated in an intervention program. *Child Development, 65,* 428–439.

Grantham-McGregor, S. M., Walker, S. P., & Chang, S. (2000). Nutritional deficiencies and later behavioral development. *Proceedings of the Nutrition Society, 59,* 47–54.

Grattan, M. P., De Vos, E., Levy, J., & McClintock, M. K. (1992). Asymmetric action in the human newborn: Sex differences in patterns of organization. *Child Development, 63,* 273–289.

Graue, M. E. (1993). Expectations and ideas coming to school. *Early Childhood Research Quarterly, 8,* 53–75.

Graue, M. E., & DiPerna, J. (2000). Redshirting and early retention: Who gets the "gift of time" and what are its outcomes? *American Educational Research Journal, 37,* 509–534.

Graves, S. B. (1993). Television, the portrayal of African Americans, and the development of children's attitudes. In G. L. Erry & J. K. Asamen (Eds.), *Children and television* (pp. 179–190). Newbury Park, CA: Sage.

Gray-Little, B., & Carels, R. (1997). The effects of racial and socioeconomic consonance on self-esteem and achievement in elementary, junior high, and high school students. *Journal of Research on Adolescence, 7,* 109–131.

Gray-Little, B., & Hafdahl, A. R. (2000). Factors influencing racial comparisons of self-esteem: A quantitative review. *Psychological Bulletin, 126,* 26–54.

Green, R. (1987). *The "sissy boy" syndrome and the development of homosexuality.* New Haven, CT: Yale University Press.

Greenberger, E., Chen, C., Tally, S. R., & Dong, Q. (2000). Family, peer, and individual correlates of depressive symptomatology among U.S. and Chinese adolescents.

Journal of Counseling and Clinical Psychology, 68, 209–219.

Greenberger, E., O'Neil, R., & Nagel, S. K. (1994). Linking workplace and homeplace: Relations between the nature of adults' work and their parenting behaviors. *Developmental Psychology, 30,* 990–1002.

Greendorfer, S. L., Lewko, J. H., & Rosengren, K. S. (1996). Family and gender-based socialization of children and adolescents. In F. L. Smoll & R. E. Smith (Eds.), *Children and youth in sport: A biopsychological perspective* (pp. 89–111). Dubuque, IA: Brown & Benchmark.

Greenfield, P. M. (1992, June). *Notes and references for developmental psychology.* Conference on Making Basic Texts in Psychology More Culture-Inclusive and Culture-Sensitive, Western Washington University, Bellingham, WA.

Greenfield, P. M. (1994). Independence and interdependence as developmental scripts: Implications for theory, research, and practice. In P. M. Greenfield & R. R. Cocking (Eds.), *Cross-cultural roots of minority child development* (pp. 1–37). Hillsdale, NJ: Erlbaum.

Greenfield, P. M. (1997). You can't take it with you: Why ability assessments don't cross cultures. *American Psychologist, 52,* 1115–1124.

Greenfield, P. M., & Suzuki, L. (1998). Culture and human development: Implications for parenting education, pediatrics, and mental health. In I. E. Sigel & K. A. Renninger (Eds.), *Handbook of child psychology: Vol. 4. Child psychology in practice* (5th ed., pp. 1059–1109). New York: Wiley.

Greenham, S. L. (1999). Learning disabilities and psychosocial adjustment: A critical review. *Child Neuropsychology, 5,* 171–196.

Greenhill, L. L., Halperin, J. M., & Abikof, H. (1997). Stimulant Medications. *Journal of the American Academy of Child & Adolescent Psychiatry, 38,* 503–512.

Greenough, W. T., & Black, J. E. (1992). Induction of brain structure by experience: Substrates for cognitive development. In M. R. Gunnar & C. A. Nelson (Eds.), *Minnesota Symposia on Child Psychology* (Vol. 25, pp. 155–200). Hillsdale, NJ: Erlbaum.

Greenough, W. T., Wallace, C. S., Alcantara, A. A., Anderson, B. J., Hawrylak, N., Sirevaag, A. M., Weiler, I. J., & Withers, G. S. (1993). Development of the brain: Experience affects the structure of neurons, glia, and blood vessels. In N. J. Anastasiow & S. Harel (Eds.), *At-risk infants: Interventions, fami-*

lies, and research (pp. 173–185). Baltimore: Paul H. Brookes.

Greer, T., & Lockman, J. J. (1998). Using writing instruments: Invariances in young children and adults. *Child Development, 69,* 888–902.

Gregg, V., Gibbs, J. C., & Fuller, D. (1994). Patterns of developmental delay in moral judgment by male and female delinquents. *Merrill-Palmer Quarterly, 40,* 538–553.

Gresham, F. M., & MacMillan, D. L. (1997). Social competence and affective characteristics of students with mild disabilities. *Review of Educational Research, 67,* 377-415.

Griffin, S., & Case, R. (1996). Evaluating the breadth and depth of training effects when central conceptual structures are taught. *Monographs of the Society for Research in Child Development, 246* (61, Serial No. 246), pp. 83–102.

Griffiths, M. (1997). Computer game playing in early adolescence. *Youth & Society, 29,* 223–237.

Griffiths, M. (1999). Violent video games and aggression: A review of the literature. *Aggression and Violent Behavior, 4,* 203–212.

Grigorenko, E. L. (2000). Psychology and educational practice: Snapshots of one relationship. *Educational & Child Psychology, 17,* 32–50.

Grigorenko, E. L., & Sternberg, R. J. (1998). *Dynamic testing. Psychological Bulletin, 124,* 75–111.

Grody, W. W. (1999). Cystic fibrosis: Molecular diagnosis, population screening, and public policy. *Archives of Pathology and Laboratory Medicine, 123,* 1041–1046.

Groff, J. Y., Mullen, P. D., Mongoven, M., & Burau, K. (1997). Prenatal weight gain patterns and infant birthweight associated with maternal smoking. *Birth, 24,* 234–239.

Grolnick, W. S., Bridges, L. J., & Connell, J. P. (1996). Emotion regulation in two-year-olds: Strategies and emotional expression in four contexts. *Child Development, 67,* 928–941.

Grolnick, W. S., & Slowiaczek, M. L. (1994). Parents' involvement in children's schooling: A multidimensional conceptualization and motivational model. *Child Development, 65,* 237–252.

Groome, L. J., Swiber, M. J., Atterbury, J. L., Bentz, L. S., & Holland, S. B. (1997). Similarities and differences in behavioral state organization during sleep periods in the perinatal infant before and after birth. *Child Development, 68,* 1–11.

Gross, M. (1993). *Exceptionally gifted children.* London: Routledge.

Gross, S. J., Geller, J., & Tomarelli, R. M. (1981). Composition of breast milk from mothers of preterm infants. *Pediatrics, 68,* 480–493.

Grossman, J. A., & Kruesi, M. J. P. (2000). Innovative approaches to youth suicide prevention: An update of issues and research findings. In R. W. Maris, S. S. Canetto, J. L. McIntosh, & M. M. Silverman (Eds.), *Review of Suicidology, 2000* (pp. 170–201). New York: Guilford.

Grossmann, K., Grossmann, K. E., Spangler, G., Suess, G., & Unzner, L. (1985). Maternal sensitivity and newborns' orientation responses as related to quality of attachment in Northern Germany. In I. Bretherton & E. Waters (Eds.), Growing points of attachment theory and research. *Monographs of the Society for Research in Child Development, 50* (1–2, Serial No. 209).

Grotevant, H. D. (1998). Adolescent development in family contexts. In N. Eisenberg (Ed.), *Handbook of child psychology: Vol. 3. Social, emotional, and personality development* (5th ed., pp. 1097–1149). New York: Wiley.

Grotevant, H. D., & Cooper, C. R. (1988). The role of family experience in career exploration during adolescence. In P. Baltes, D. Featherman, & R. Lerner (Eds.), *Life-span development and behavior* (Vol. 8, pp. 231–258). Hillsdale, NJ: Erlbaum.

Grotevant, H. D., & Cooper, C. R. (1998). Individuality and connectedness in adolescent development: Review and prospects for research on identity, relationships, and context. In E. Skoe & A. von der Lippe (Eds.), *Personality development in adolescence.* London: Routledge & Kegan Paul.

Grotevant, H. D., & Kohler, J. K. (1999). Adoptive families. In M. E. Lamb (Ed.), *Parenting and child development in nontraditional families* (pp. 161–190). Mahwah, NJ: Erlbaum.

Grotpeter, J. K., & Crick, N. R. (1996). Relational aggression, overt aggression, and friendship. *Child Development, 67,* 2328–2338.

Grubb, W. N. (1999). The subbaccalaureate labor market in the United States: Challenges for the school-to-work transition. In W. R. Heinz (Ed.), *From education to work: Cross-national perspectives* (pp. 171–193). New York: Cambridge University Press.

Grusec, J. E. (1988). *Social development: History, theory, and research.* New York: Springer-Verlag.

Grusec, J. E., & Goodnow, J. J. (1994). Impact of parental discipline methods on the child's internalization of values: A reconceptualization of current points of view. *Developmental Psychology, 30,* 4–19.

Grych, J. H., & Fincham, F. D. (1997). Children's adaptation to divorce: From description to explanation. In S. A. Wolchik & I. N. Sandler (Eds.), *Handbook of children's coping: Linking theory to intervention* (pp. 159– 193). New York: Plenum.

Guerra, N. G., Attar, B., & Weissberg, R. P. (1997). Prevention of aggression and violence among inner-city youths. In D. M. Stoff, J. Breiling, & J. D. Maser (Eds.), *Handbook of antisocial behavior* (pp. 375–383). New York: Wiley.

Guerri, C. (1998). Neuroanatomical and neurophysiological mechanisms involved in central nervous system dysfunctions induced by prenatal alcohol exposure. *Alcoholism: Clinical & Experimental Research, 22,* 304–312.

Guidubaldi, J., & Cleminshaw, H. K. (1985). Divorce, family health and child adjustment. *Family Relations, 34,* 35–41.

Guilford, J. P. (1985). The structure-of-intellect model. In B. B. Wolman (Ed.), *Handbook of intelligence* (pp. 225–266). New York: Wiley.

Gullone, E., & King, N. J. (1997). Three-year follow-up of normal fear in children and adolescents aged 7 to 18 years. *British Journal of Developmental Psychology, 15,* 97–111.

Gunn, A. J. (2000). Cerebral hypothermia for prevention of brain injury following perinatal asphyxia. *Current Opinion in Pediatrics, 12,* 111–115.

Gunnar, M. R. (1998). Quality of early care and buffering of neuroendocrine stress reactions: Potential effects on the developing human brain. *Preventive Medicine, 27,* 208–211.

Gunnar, M. R., & Nelson, C. A. (1994). Event-related potentials in year-old infants: Relations with emotionality and cortisol. *Child Development, 65,* 80–94.

Guo, G., & VanWey, L. K. (1999). Sibship size and intellectual development: Is the relationship causal? *American Sociological Review, 64,* 169–187.

Gustafson, G. E., Green, J. A., & Cleland, J. W. (1994). Robustness of individual identity in the cries of human infants. *Developmental Psychobiology, 27,* 1–9.

Gustafson, G. E., & Harris, K. L. (1990). Women's responses to young infants' cries. *Developmental Psychology, 26,* 144–152.

Gutman, L. M., & Eccles, J. S. (1999). Financial strain, parenting behaviors, and adolescents' achievement: Testing model equivalence between African-American and European-American single- and two-parent families. *Child Development, 70,* 1464–1476.

Guyda, H. J. (1999). Four decades of growth hormone therapy for short children: What have we achieved? *Journal of Clinical Endocrinology & Metabolism, 84,* 4307–4316.

Guyer, B., Hoyert, D. L., Martin, J. A., Ventura, S. J., MacDorman, M. F., & Strobino, D. M. (1999). Annual summary of vital statistics—1998. *Pediatrics, 104,* 1229–1246.

Haan, N., Aerts, E., & Cooper, B. (1985). *On moral grounds: The search for practical morality.* New York: New York University Press.

Hack, M., Wright, L. L., Shankaran, S., & Tyson, J. E. (1995). Very low birth weight outcomes of the National Institute of Child Health and Human Development Neonatal Network, November 1989 to October 1990. *American Journal of Obstetrics and Gynecology, 172,* 457–464.

Hack, M. B., Taylor, H. G., Klein, N., Eiben, R., Schatschneider, C., & Mercuri-Minich, N. (1994). School-age outcomes in children with birth weights under 750 g. *New England Journal of Medicine, 331,* 753–759.

Haddad, F. F., Yeatman, T. J., Shivers, S. C., & Reintgen, D. S. (1999). The Human Genome Project: A dream becoming a reality. *Surgery, 125,* 575–580.

Haden, C. A., Haine, R. A., & Fivush, R. (1997). Developing narrative structure in parent–child reminiscing across the preschool years. *Developmental Psychology, 33,* 295–307.

Hagekull, B., Bohlin, G., & Rydell, A. (1997). Maternal sensitivity, infant temperament, and the development of early feeding problems. *Infant Mental Health Journal, 18,* 92–106.

Haggerty, L. A. (1999). Continuous electronic fetal monitoring: Contradictions between practice and research. *Journal of Obstetric, Gynecologic, and Neonatal Nursing, 28,* 409–416.

Haight, W. L., & Miller, P. J. (1993). *Pretending at home: Early development in a sociocultural context.* Albany: State University of New York Press.

Haith, M. M., & Benson, J. B. (1998). Infant cognition. In D. Kuhn & R. S. Siegler (Eds.), *Handbook of child psychology: Vol. 2 Cognition, perception, and language* (pp. 199–254). New York: Wiley.

Hakuta, K. (1999). The debate on bilingual education. *Developmental and Behavioral Pediatrics, 20,* 36–37.

Hakuta, K., Ferdman, B. M., & Diaz, R. M. (1987). Bilingualism and cognitive development: Three perspectives. In S. Rosenberg (Ed.), *Advances in applied psycholinguistics: Vol. 2. Reading, writing, and language learning* (pp. 284–319). New York: Cambridge University Press.

Halford, G. S. (1993). *Children's understanding: The development of mental models.* Hillsdale, NJ: Erlbaum.

Halford, G. S., Wilson, W. H., Phillips, S. (1998). Processing capacity defined by relational complexity: Implications for comparative, developmental, and cognitive psychology. *Behavioral and Brain Sciences, 21,* 803–864.

Hall, D. G., & Graham, S. A. (1999). Lexical form class information guides word-to-object mapping in preschoolers. *Child Development, 70,* 78–91.

Hall, G. S. (1904). *Adolescence.* New York: Appleton-Century-Crofts.

Hall, S. S. (1996, January/ February). Short like me. *Health,* pp. 98–106.

Halliday, J. L., Watson, L. F., Lumley, J., Danks, D. M., & Sheffield, L. S. (1995). New estimates of Down syndrome risks at chorionic villus sampling, amniocentesis, and live birth in women of advanced maternal age from a uniquely defined population. *Prenatal Diagnosis, 15,* 455–465.

Hallinan, M. T., & Kubitschek, W. N. (1999). Curriculum differentiation and high school achievement. *Social Psychology of Education, 3,* 41–62.

Halpern, C. T., Udry, J. R., Campbell, B., & Schindran, C. (1999). Effects of body fat on weight concerns, dating, and sexual activity: A longitudinal analysis of black and white adolescent girls. *Developmental Psychology, 35,* 721–736.

Halpern, C. T., Udry, J. R., & Suchindran, C. (1997). Testosterone predicts initiation of coitus in adolescent females. *Psychosomatic Medicine, 59,* 161–171.

Halpern, D. F. (1997). Sex differences in intelligence. *American Psychologist, 52,* 1091–1102.

Halpern, D. F. (2000). *Sex differences in cognitive abilities* (3rd ed.). Mahwah, NJ: Erlbaum.

Halpern, L. F., MacLean, W. E., & Baumeister, A. A. (1995). Infant sleep–wake characteristics: Relation to neurological status and the prediction of developmental outcome. *Developmental Review, 15,* 255–291.

Hamelin, K., & Ramachandran, C. (1993, June). Kangaroo care. *Canadian Nurse, 89*(6), 15–17.

Hamer, D. H., Hu, S., Magnuson, V. L., Hu, N., & Pattatucci, A. M. L. (1993). A linkage between DNA markers on the X chromosome and male sexual orientation. *Science, 261,* 321–327.

Hamilton, S. F. (1990). *Apprenticeship for adulthood: Preparing youth for the future.* New York: Free Press.

Hamilton, S. F. (1993). Prospects for an American-style youth apprenticeship system. *Educational Researcher, 22*(3), 11–16.

Hamilton, S. F. (1994). Social roles for youths: Interventions in unemployment. In A. C. Petersen & J. T. Mortimer (Eds.), *Youth employment and society* (pp. 248–269). New York: Cambridge University Press.

Hamilton, S. F., & Hamilton, M. A. (1999). Creating new pathways to adulthood by adapting German apprenticeship in the United States. In W. R. Heinz (Ed.), *From education to work: Cross-national perspectives* (pp. 194–213). New York: Cambridge University Press.

Hamilton, S. F., & Hamilton, M. A. (2000). Research, intervention, and social change: Improving adolescents' career opportunities. In L. J. Crockett & R. K. Silbereisen (Eds.), *Negotiating adolescence in times of social change* (pp. 267–283). New York: Cambridge University Press.

Hamm, J. V. (2000). Do birds of a feather flock together? The variable bases for African American, Asian American, and European American adolescents' selection of similar friends. *Developmental Psychology, 36,* 209–219.

Hammersley, M. (1992). *What's wrong with ethnography?* New York: Routledge.

Han, J. J., Leichtman, M. D., & Wang, Q. (1998). Autobiographical memory in Korean, Chinese, and American children. *Developmental Psychology, 34,* 701–713.

Handler, A. S., Mason, E. D., Rosenberg, D. L., & Davis, F. G. (1994). The relationship between exposure during pregnancy to cigarette smoking and cocaine use and placenta previa. *American Journal of Obstetrics and Gynecology, 170,* 884–889.

Hankin, B. L., Abramson, L. Y., Moffitt, T. E., Silva, P., & McGee, R. (1998). Development of depression from preadolescence to young adulthood: Emerging gender differences in a 10-year longitudinal study. *Journal of Abnormal Psychology, 107,* 128–140.

Hanna, E., & Meltzoff, A. N. (1993). Peer imitation by toddlers in laboratory, home, and day-care contexts: Implications for social learning and memory. *Developmental Psychology, 29,* 701–710.

Happé, F. G. E. (1995). The role of age and verbal ability in the theory of mind task performance of subjects with autism. *Child Development, 66,* 843–855.

Harari, M. D., & Moulden, A. (2000). Nocturnal enuresis: What is happening? *Journal of Paediatrics and Child Health, 36,* 78–81.

Hardy, J. B., Astone, N. M., Brooks-Gunn, J., Shapiro, S., & Miller, T. L. (1998). Like mother, like child: Intergenerational patterns of age at first birth and associations with childhood and adolescent characteristics and adult outcomes in the second generation. *Developmental Psychology, 34,* 1220–1232.

Hare, J. (1994). Concerns and issues faced by families headed by a lesbian couple. *Families in Society, 43,* 27–35.

Harley, B., & Wang, W. (1997). The critical period hypothesis: Where are we now? In A. M. B. de Groot & J. F. Kroll (Eds.), *Tutorials in bilingualism* (pp. 19–51). Mahwah, NJ: Erlbaum.

Harlow, H. F., & Zimmerman, R. (1959). Affectional responses in the infant monkey. *Science, 130,* 421–432.

Harold, G. T., & Conger, R. D. (1997). Marital conflict and adolescent distress: The role of adolescent awareness. *Child Development, 68,* 333–350.

Harrington, R., Rutter, M., & Fombonne, E. (1996). Developmental pathways in depression: Multiple meanings, antecedents, and endpoints. *Development and Psychopathology, 8,* 601–616.

Harris, G. (1997). Development of taste perception and appetite regulation. In G. Bremner, A. Slater, & G. Butterworth (Eds.), *Infant development: Recent advances* (pp. 9–30). East Sussex, UK: Erlbaum.

Harris, I. B. (1996). *Children in jeopardy.* New Haven, CT: Yale University Press.

Harris, J. R. (1998). *The nurture assumption: Why children turn out the way they do.* New York: Free Press.

Harris, K. M. (2000). The health status and risk behavior of adolescents in immigrant families. In D. J. Hernandez (Ed.), *Children of immigrants: Health, adjustment, and public assistance.* Washington, DC: National Academy Press.

Harris, P. L., & Leevers, H. J. (2000). Reasoning from false premises. In P. Mitchell & K. J. Riggs (Eds.), *Children's reasoning and the mind* (pp. 67–99). Hove, UK: Psychology Press.

Harris, S., Kasari, C., & Sigman, M. (1996). Joint attention and language gains in children with Down syndrome. *American Journal of Mental Retardation, 100,* 608–618.

Harrison, A. O., Wilson, M. N., Pine, C. J., Chan, S. Q., & Buriel, R. (1994). Family ecologies of ethnic minority children. In G. Handel & G. G. Whitchurch (Eds.), *The psychosocial interior of the family* (pp. 187–210). New York: Aldine De Gruyter.

Harrison, M. R. (1993). Fetal surgery. *Western Journal of Medicine, 159,* 341–349.

Harrist, A. W., Pettit, G. S., Dodge, K. A., & Bates, J. E. (1994). Dyadic synchrony in mother–child interaction—relation with children's subsequent kindergarten adjustment. *Family Relations, 43,* 417–424.

Harrist, A. W., Zaia, A. F., Bates, J. E., Dodge, K. A., & Pettit, G. S. (1997). Subtypes of social withdrawal in early childhood: Sociometric status and social-cognitive differences across four years. *Child Development, 68,* 278–294.

Hart, B., & Risley, T. R. (1995). *Meaningful differences in the everyday experience of young American children.* Baltimore: Paul H. Brookes.

Hart, B. I., & Thompson, J. M. (1996). Gender role characteristics and depressive symptomatology among adolescents. *Journal of Early Adolescence, 16,* 407–426.

Hart, C. H., Burts, D. C., Durland, M. A., Charlesworth, R., DeWolf, M., & Fleege, P. O. (1998). Stress behaviors and activity type participation of preschoolers in more and less developmentally appropriate classrooms: SES and sex differences. *Journal of Research in Childhood Education, 13.*

Hart, C. H., Yang, C., Nelson, L. J., Robinson, C. C., Olsen, J. A., & Nelson, D. A. (2000). *International Journal of Behavioral Development, 24,* 73–81.

Hart, D., Atkins, R., & Ford, D. (1998). Urban America as a context for the development of moral identity in adolescence. *Journal of Social Issues, 54,* 513–530.

Hart, D., & Fegley, S. (1995). Prosocial behavior and caring in adolescence: Relations to self-understanding and social judgment. *Child Development, 66,* 1346–1359.

Hart, D., Keller, M., Edelstein, W., & Hofmann, V. (1998). Childhood personality influences on social-cognitive development: A longitudinal study. *Journal of Personality and Social Psychology, 74,* 1278–1289.

Harter, S. (1982). The perceived competence scale for children. *Child Development, 53,* 87–97.

Harter, S. (1986). Processes underlying the construction, maintenance, and enhancement of self-concept in children. In S. Suhls & A. Greenwald (Eds.), *Psychological perspectives of the self* (Vol. 3, pp. 136–182). Hillsdale, NJ: Erlbaum.

Harter, S. (1990). Issues in the assessment of the self-concept of children and adolescents. In A. LaGreca (Ed.), *Through the eyes of a child* (pp. 292–325). Boston: Allyn and Bacon.

Harter, S. (1996). Developmental changes in self-understanding across the 5 to 7 shift. In A. J. Sameroff & M. M. Haith (Eds.), *The five to seven year shift* (pp. 207–236). Chicago: University of Chicago Press.

Harter, S. (1998). The development of self-representations. In N. Eisenberg (Ed.), *Handbook of child psychology: Vol. 3. Social, emotional, and personality development* (5th ed., pp. 553–618). New York: Wiley.

Harter, S. (1999). *The construction of self: A developmental perspective.* New York: Guilford.

Harter, S., & Buddin, B. J. (1987). Children's understanding of the simultaneity of two emotions: A five-stage developmental acquisition sequence. *Developmental Psychology, 23,* 388–399.

Harter, S., Marold, D. B., Whitesell, N. R., & Cobbs, G. (1996). A model of the effects of parent and peer support on adolescent false self-behavior. *Child Development, 67,* 360–374.

Harter, S., & Monsour, A. (1992). Developmental analysis of conflict caused by opposing attributes in the adolescent self-portrait. *Developmental Psychology, 28,* 251–260.

Harter, S., & Whitesell, N. (1989). Developmental changes in children's understanding of simple, multiple, and blended emotion concepts. In C. Saarni & P. Harris (Eds.), *Children's understanding of emotion* (pp. 81–116). Cambridge, England: Cambridge University Press.

Harter, S., Wright, K., & Bresnick, S. (1987). A developmental sequence of the emergence of self affects. Paper presented at the biennial meeting of the Society for Research in Child Development, Baltimore.

Hartshorn, K., Rovee-Collier, C., Gerhardstein, P., Bhatt, R. S., Klein, P. J., Aaron, F., Wondoloski, T. L., & Wurtzel, N. (1998a). Developmental changes in the specificity of memory over the first year of life. *Developmental Psychobiology, 33,* 61–78.

Hartshorn, K., Rovee-Collier, C., Gerhardstein, P., Bhatt, R. S., Wondoloski, T. L., Klein, P., Gilch, J., Wurtzel, N., & Campos-de-Carvalho, M. (1998b). The ontogeny of long-term memory over the first year-and-a-half of life. *Developmental Psychobiology, 32,* 69–89.

Hartup, W. W. (1999). Peer experience and its developmental significance. In M. Bennett (Ed.), *Developmental psychology: Achievements and prospects* (pp. 106–125). Philadelphia, PA: Psychology Press.

Hartup, W. W., & Laursen, B. (1991). Relationships as developmental contexts. In R. Cohen & A. W. Siegel (Eds.), *Context and development* (pp. 253–279). Hillsdale, NJ: Erlbaum.

Hartup, W. W., & Stevens, N. (1999). Friendships and adaptation across the life span. *Current Directions in Psychological Science, 8,* 76–79.

Haselager, G. J. T., Hartup, W. W., van Lieshout, C. F. M., & Riksen-Walraven, J. M. A. (1998). Similarities between friends and non-friends in middle childhood. *Child Development, 69,* 1198–1208.

Hashimoto, K., Noguchi, M., & Nakatsuji, N. (1992). Mouse offspring derived from fetal ovaries or reaggregates which were cultured and transplanted into adult females. *Development: Growth & Differentiation, 34,* 233–238.

Hatch, M. C., Shu, X-O., McLean, D. E., Levin, B., Begg, M., Reuss, L., & Susser, M. (1993). Maternal exercise during pregnancy, physical fitness, and fetal growth. *American Journal of Epidemiology, 137,* 1105–1114.

Hatcher, P. J., Hulme, C., & Ellis, A. W. (1994). Ameliorating early reading failure by integrating the teaching of reading and phonological skills: The phonological linkage hypothesis. *Child Development, 65,* 41–57.

Hatton, D. D., Bailey, D. B., Jr., Burchinal, M. R., & Ferrell, K. A. (1997). Developmental growth curves of preschool children with vision impairments. *Child Development, 68,* 788–806.

Hauser, S. T., Powers, S. I., & Noam, G. G. (1991). *Adolescents and their families: Paths of ego development.* New York: Free Press.

Hausfather, A., Toharia, A., LaRoche, C., & Engelsmann, F. (1997). Effects of age of entry, day-care quality, and family characteristics on preschool behavior. *Journal of Child Psychology and Psychiatry, 38,* 441–448.

Hauth, J. C., Goldenberg, R. L., Parker, C. R., Cutter, G. R., & Cliver, S. P. (1995). Low-dose aspirin—lack of association with an increase in abruptio placentae or perinatal mortality. *Obstetrics and Gynecology, 85,* 1055–1058.

Hawke, S., & Knox, D. (1978). The one-child family: A new life-style. *The Family Coordinator, 27,* 215–219.

Hawkins, A. J., Christiansen, S. L., Sargent, K. P., & Hills, E. J. (1993). Rethinking fathers' involvement in child care: A developmental perspective. *Journal of Family Issues, 14,* 531–549.

Hawkins, D. J., & Lam, T. (1987). Teacher practices, social development, and delinquency. In J. D. Burchard & S. N. Burchard (Eds.), *Prevention of delinquent behavior* (pp. 241– 274). Newbury Park, CA: Sage.

Hawkins, J., & Sheingold, K. (1986). The beginnings of a story: Computers and the organization of learning in classrooms. In J. A. Culbertson & L. L. Cunningham (Eds.), *Microcomputers and education* (85th Yearbook of the National Society for the Study of Education, pp. 40–58). Chicago: University of Chicago Press.

Hawkins, J. N. (1994). Issues of motivation in Asian education. In H. F. O'Neil, Jr., & M. Drillings (Eds.), *Motivation: Theory and research* (pp. 101–115). Hillsdale, NJ: Erlbaum.

Hayne, H., Boniface, J., & Barr, R. (2000). The development of declarative memory in human infants: Age-related changes in deferred imitation. *Behavioral Neuroscience, 114,* 77–83.

Hayne, H., Rovee-Collier, C., & Perris, E. E. (1987). Categorization and memory retrieval by three-month-olds. *Child Development, 58,* 750–767.

Haynes, S. N. (1991). Clinical applications of psychophysiological assessment: An introduction and overview. *Psychological Assessment, 3,* 307–308.

Hayslip, B., Jr. (1994). Stability of intelligence. In R. J. Sternberg (Ed.), *Encyclopedia of human intelligence* (Vol. 2, pp. 1019–1026). New York: Macmillan.

Head Start Bureau. (2000). *2000 Head Start Fact Sheet.* [On-line] Available: *www2.acf.dhhs.gov/ programs/hsb/research/00_hsfs.htm*

Health Canada. (2000). *Paediatrics and child health: Canadian Report on Immunization, 1997.* [On-line] Available: *www.hc-sc.gc.ca*

Heath, S. B. (1982). Questioning at home and at school: A comparative study. In G. Spindler (Ed.), *Doing the ethnography of schooling: Educational anthropology in action* (pp. 102–127). New York: Holt.

Heath, S. B. (1989). Oral and literate traditions among black Americans living in poverty. *American Psychologist, 44,* 367–373.

Heath, S. B. (1990). The children of Trackton's children: Spoken and written language in social change. In J. Stigler, G. Herdt, & R. A. Shweder (Eds.), *Cultural psychology: Essays on comparative human development* (pp. 496–519). New York: Cambridge University Press.

Hedges, L. V., & Nowell, A. (1998). Black–white test score convergence since 1995. In C. Jencks & M. Phillips (Eds.), *The black–white test score gap* (pp.149–181). Washington, DC: Brookings Institution.

Heffner, R. W., & Kelley, M. L. (1994). Nonorganic failure to thrive: Developmental outcomes and psychosocial assessment and intervention issues. *Research in Developmental Disabilities, 15,* 247–268.

Heine, S. J., & Lehman, D. R. (1995). Cultural variation in unrealistic optimism: Does the West feel more invulnerable than the East? *Journal of Personality and Social Psychology, 68,* 595–607.

Heinz, W. R. (1999a). Introduction: Transitions to employment in a cross-national perspective. In W. R. Heinz (Ed.), *From education to work: Cross-national perspectives* (pp. 1–21). New York: Cambridge University Press.

Heinz, W. R. (1999b). Job-entry patterns in a life-course perspective. In W. R. Heinz (Ed.), *From education to work: Cross-national perspectives* (pp. 214–231). New York: Cambridge University Press.

Heinz, W. R., Kelle, U., Witzel, A., & Zinn, J. (1998). Vocational training and career development in Germany: Results from a longitudinal study. *International Journal of Behavioral Development, 22,* 77–101.

Helburn, S. W. (Ed.). (1995). *Cost, quality and child outcomes in child care centers.* Denver: University of Colorado.

Helwig, C. C., & Prencipe, A. (1999). Children's judgments of flags and flag-burning. *Child Development, 70,* 132–143.

Henrich, C. C., Brown, J. L., & Aber, J. L. (1999). Evaluating the effectiveness of school-based violence prevention: Developmental approaches. *Social Policy Report of the Society for Research in Child Development, 8*(3).

Henrich, C. C., Kuperminc, G. P., Sack, A., Blatt, S. J., & Leadbeater, B. J. (2000). Characteristics and homogeneity of early adolescent friendship groups: A comparison of male and female clique and nonclique members. *Applied Developmental Science, 4,* 15–26.

Hepper, P. G. (1997). Fetal habituation: Another Pandora's box? *Developmental Medicine and Child Neurology, 39,* 274–278.

Herbert, J., & Hayne, H. (2000). The ontogeny of long-term retention during the second year of life. *Developmental Science, 3,* 50–56.

Herdt, G., & Boxer, A. M. (1993). *Children of horizons: How gay and lesbian teens are leading a new way out of the closet.* Boston: Beacon Press.

Hergenrather, J. R., & Rabinowitz, M. (1991). Age-related differences in the organization of children's knowledge of illness. *Developmental Psychology, 27,* 952–959.

Herman, M. R., Dornbusch, S. M., Herron, M. C., & Herting, J. R. (1997). The influence of family regulation, connection, and psychological autonomy on six measures of adolescent functioning. *Journal of Adolescent Research, 12,* 34–67.

Hernandez, D. J. (1994, Spring). Children's changing access to resources: A historical perspective. *Social Policy Report of the Society for Research in Child Development, 8*(1).

Hernandez, F. D., & Carter, A. S. (1996). Infant response to mothers and fathers in the still-face paradigm. *Infant Behavior and Development, 19,* 502.

Herrnstein, R. J., & Murray, C. (1994). *The bell curve.* New York: Free Press.

Hershberger, S. L., Pilkington, N. W., & D'Augelli, A. R. (1997). Predictors of suicide attempts among gay, lesbian, and bisexual youth. *Journal of Adolescent Research, 12,* 477–497.

Hetherington, E. M. (1989). Coping with family transitions: Winners, losers and survivors. *Child Development, 60,* 1–14.

Hetherington, E. M. (1993). An overview of the Virginia Longitudinal Study of Divorce and Remarriage: A focus on early adolescence. *Journal of Family Psychology, 7,* 39–56.

Hetherington, E. M. (1997). Teenaged childbearing and divorce. In S. Luthar, J. A. Burack, D. Cicchetti, & J. Weisz (Eds.), *Developmental psychopathology: Perspectives on adjustment, risk, and disorders* (pp. 350-373). Cambridge: Cambridge University Press.

Hetherington, E. M. (1999a). Should we stay together for the sake of the children? In E. M. Hetherington (Ed.), *Coping with divorce, single-parenting, and remarriage: A risk and resiliency perspective* (pp. 93–116). Hillsdale, NJ: Erlbaum.

Hetherington, E. M. (1999b). Social capital and the development of youth from nondivorced, divorced, and remarried families. In A. Collins (Ed.), *Minnesota Symposia on Child Psychology* (Vol. 29). Hillsdale, NJ: Erlbaum.

Hetherington, E. M., Bridges, M., & Insabella, G. M. (1998). What matters? What does not? Five perspectives on the association between marital transitions and children's adjustment. *American Psychologist, 53,* 167–184.

Hetherington, E. M., & Henderson, S. H. (1997). Fathers in stepfamilies. In M. E. Lamb (Ed.), *The role of the father in child development* (pp. 212–226). New York: Wiley.

Hetherington, E. M., Henderson, S. H., & Reiss, D. (1999). Adolescent siblings in stepfamilies: Family functioning and adolescent adjustment. *Monographs of the Society for Research in Child Development, 64*(4, Serial No. 259).

Hetherington, E. M., & Jodl, K. M. (1994). Stepfamilies as settings for child development. In A. Booth & J. Dunn (Eds.) *Stepfamilies: Who benefits? Who does not?* (pp. 55–79). Hillsdale, NJ: Erlbaum.

Hetherington, E. M., & Stanley-Hagan, M. (1999). The adjustment of children with divorced parents: A risk and resiliency perspective. *Journal of Child Psychology and Psychiatry, 40,* 129–140.

Hetherington, E. M., & Stanley-Hagan, M. M. (1997). The effects of divorce on fathers and their children. In M. E. Lamb (Ed.), *The role of the father in child development* (pp. 191–211). New York: Wiley.

Hetherington, P. (1995, March). *The changing American family and the well-being of children.* Master lecture presented at the biennial meeting of the Society for Research in Child Development, Indianapolis.

Hetherington, S. E. (1990). A controlled study of the effect of prepared childbirth classes on obstetric outcomes. *Birth, 17,* 86–90.

Hewlett, B. S. (1992). Husband–wife reciprocity and the father–infant relationship among Aka pygmies. In B. S. Hewlett (Ed.), *Father–child relations: Cultural and biosocial contexts* (pp. 153–176). New York: Aldine De Gruyter.

Heyman, G. D., & Dweck, C. S. (1992). Achievement goals and intrinsic motivation: Their relation and their role in adaptive motivation. *Motivation and Emotion, 16,* 231–247.

Heyman, G. D., & Dweck, C. S. (1998). Children's thinking about traits: Implications for judgments of the self and others. *Child Development, 69,* 391–403.

Heyman, G. D., Dweck, C. S., & Cain, K. M. (1992). Young children's vulnerability to self-blame and helplessness: Relationship to beliefs about goodness. *Child Development, 63,* 401–415.

Heyman, G. D., & Gelman, S. A. (1999). The use of trait labels in making psychological inferences. *Child Development, 70,* 604–619.

Hickey, T. L., & Peduzzi, J. D. (1987). Structure and development of the visual system. In P. Salapatek & L. Cohen (Eds.), *Handbook of infant perception: Vol. 1. From sensation to perception* (pp. 1–42). New York: Academic Press.

Hier, D. B., & Crowley, W. F. (1982). Spatial ability in androgen-deficient men. *New England Journal of Medicine, 302,* 1202–1205.

High, P., Hopmann, M., LaGasse, L., Sege, R., Moran, J., Guiterrez, C., & Becker, S. (1999). Child centered literacy orientation: A form of social capital? *Pediatrics, 103,* e55.

High, P. C., LaGasse, L., Becker, S., Ahlgren, I., & Gardner, A. (2000). Literacy promotion in primary care pediatrics: Can we make a difference? *Pediatrics, 105,* 927–934.

Hildreth, K., & Rovee-Collier, C. (1999). Decreases in the response latency to priming over the first year of life. *Developmental Psychobiology, 35,* 276–289.

Hill, J. P., & Holmbeck, G. N. (1986). Attachment and autonomy during adolescence. In G. Whitehurst (Ed.), *Annals of child development* (Vol. 3, pp. 145–189). Greenwich, CT: JAI Press.

Himes, J. H., Story, M., Czaplinski, K., & Dahlberg-Luby, E. (1992). Indications of early obesity in low-income Hmong children. *American Journal of Diseases of Children, 146,* 67–69.

Hinde, R. A. (1989). Ethological and relationships approaches. In R. Vasta (Ed.), *Annals of child development* (Vol. 6, pp. 251–285). Greenwich, CT: JAI Press.

Hines, M., & Green, R. (1991). Human hormonal and neural correlates of sex-typed behaviors. *Review of Psychiatry, 10,* 536–555.

Hines, S., & Bennett, F. (1996). Effectiveness of early intervention for children with Down syndrome. *Mental Retardation & Develop-mental Disabilities Research Reviews, 2,* 96–101.

Hirschfeld, L. A. (1995). Do children have a theory of race? *Cognition, 54,* 209–252.

Hirsh-Pasek, K., Kemler Nelson, D. G., Jusczyk, P. W., Cassidy, K. W., Druss, B., & Kennedy, L. (1987). Clauses are perceptual units for young infants. *Cognition, 26,* 269–286.

Hjälmäs, K. (1998). Nocturnal enuresis: Basic facts and new horizons. *European Urology, 33*(suppl. 3), 53–57.

Ho, C. S., & Fuson, K. C. (1998). Children's knowledge of teen quantities as tens and ones: Comparisons of Chinese, British, and American kindergartners. *Journal of Educational Psychology, 90,* 536–544.

Hochschild, A. R. (1997). *The time bind: When work becomes home and home becomes work.* New York: Metropolitan Books.

Hock, H. S., Park, C. L., & Bjorklund, D. F. (1998). Temporal organization in children's strategy formation. *Journal of Experimental Child Psychology, 70,* 187–206.

Hocutt, A. M. (1996). Effectiveness of special education: Is placement the critical factor? *Future of Children, 6,* 77–102.

Hodapp, R. M. (1996). Down syndrome: Developmental, psychiatric, and management issues. *Child and Adolescent Psychiatric Clinics of North America, 5,* 881–894.

Hodges, E. V. E., Boivin, M., Vitaro, F., & Bukowski, W. M. (1999). The power of friendship: Protection against an escalating cycle of peer victimization. *Developmental Psychology, 35,* 94–101.

Hodges, J., & Tizard, B. (1989). Social and family relationships of ex-institutional adolescents. *Journal of Child Psychology and Psychiatry, 30,* 77–97.

Hodges, R. M., & French, L. A. (1988). The effect of class and collection labels on cardinality, class-inclusion, and number conservation tasks. *Child Development, 59,* 1387–1396.

Hoff-Ginsberg, E. (1986). Function and structure in maternal speech: Their relation to the child's development of syntax. *Developmental Psychology, 22,* 155–163.

Hoff-Ginsberg, E., & Tardiff, T. (1995). Socioeconomic status and parenting. In M. Bornstein (Ed.), *Handbook of parenting* (Vol. 2, pp. 161–188). Hillsdale, NJ: Erlbaum.

Hoffman, L. W. (1994). Commentary on Plomin, R. (1994). A proof and disproof questioned. *Social Development, 3,* 60–63.

Hoffman, L. W. (2000). Maternal employment: Effects of social context. In R. D. Taylor & M. C. Wang (Eds.), *Resilience across contexts: Family, work, culture, and community* (pp. 147–176). Mahwah, NJ: Erlbaum.

Hoffman, L. W., & Youngblade, L. M. (1999). *Mothers at work: Effects on children's well-being.* New York: Cambridge University Press.

Hoffman, M. L. (2000). *Empathy and moral development.* New York: Cambridge University Press.

Hoffman, S., & Hatch, M. C. (1996). Stress, social support and pregnancy outcome: A reassessment based on research. *Paediatric and Perinatal Epidemiology, 10,* 380–405.

Hofstadter, M., & Reznick, J. S. (1996). Response modality affects human infant delayed-response performance. *Child Development, 67,* 646–658.

Hokoda, A., & Fincham, F. D. (1995). Origins of children's helpless and mastery achievement patterns in the family. *Journal of Educational Psychology, 87,* 375–385.

Holcomb, T. F. (1990). Fourth graders' attitudes toward AIDS issues: A concern for the elementary school counselor. *Elementary School Guidance & Counseling, 25,* 83–90.

Holden, G. W., Coleman, S. M., & Schmidt, K. L. (1995). Why 3-year-old children get spanked: Determinants as reported by college-educated mothers. *Merrill-Palmer Quarterly, 41,* 431–452.

Holden, G. W., & West, M. J. (1989). Proximate regulation by mothers: A demonstration of how differing styles affect young children's behavior. *Child Development, 60,* 64–69.

Holland, J. L. (1966). *The psychology of vocational choice.* Waltham, MA: Blaisdell.

Holland, J. L. (1985). *Making vocational choices: A theory of vocational personalities and work environments.* Englewood Cliffs, NJ: Prentice-Hall.

Hollich, G. J., Hirsh-Pasek, K., & Golinkoff, R. M. (2000). Breaking the language barrier: An emergentist coalition model for the origins of word learning. *Monographs of the Society for Research in Child Development, 65*(3, Serial No. 262).

Holmbeck, G. N. (1996). A model of family relational transformations during the transition to adolescence: Parent–adolescent conflict and adaptation. In J. A. Graber, J. Brooks-Gunn, & A. C. Petersen

(Eds.), *Transitions through adolescence* (pp. 167–199). Mahwah, NJ: Erlbaum.

Holmbeck, G. N., Paikoff, R. L., & Brooks-Gunn, J. (1995). Parenting adolescents. In M. H. Bornstein (Ed.), *Handbook of parenting: Vol. 1. Children and parenting* (pp. 91–118). Mahwah, NJ: Erlbaum.

Holmbeck, G. N., Waters, K. A., & Brookman, R. R. (1990). Psychosocial correlates of sexually transmitted diseases and sexual activity in black adolescent females. *Journal of Adolescent Research, 5,* 431–448.

Holmes, W. C., & Slap, G. B. (1998). Sexual abuse of boys: Definition, prevalence, correlates, sequelae, and management. *Journal of the American Medical Association, 280,* 1855–1862.

Holsen, I., Kraft, P., & Vittersø, J. (2000). Stability in depressed mood in adolescence: Results from a 6-year longitudinal study. *Journal of Youth and Adolescence, 29,* 61–78.

Hood, B. M., Atkinson, J., & Braddick, O. J. (1998). Selection-for-action and the development of orienting and visual attention. In J. E. Richards (Ed.), *Cognitive neuroscience of attention: A developmental perspective* (pp. 219–251). Mahwah, NJ: Erlbaum.

Hopkins, B., & Butterworth, G. (1997). Dyamical systems approaches to the development of action. In G. Bremner, A. Slater, & G. Butterworth (Eds.), *Infant development: Recent advances* (pp. 75–100). East Sussex: Psychology Press.

Hopkins, B., & Westra, T. (1988). Maternal handling and motor development: An intracultural study. *Genetic, Social and General Psychology Monographs, 14,* 377–420.

Horgan, D. (1978). The development of the full passive. *Journal of Child Language, 5,* 65–80.

Horn, J. M. (1983). The Texas Adoption Project: Adopted children and their intellectual resemblance to biological and adoptive parents. *Child Development, 54,* 268–275.

Horne, R. S., Sly, D. J., Cranage, S. M., Chau, B., & Adamson, T. M. (2000). Effects of prematurity on arousal from sleep in the newborn infant. *Pediatric Research, 47,* 468–474.

Horner, T. M. (1980). Two methods of studying stranger reactivity in infants: A review. *Journal of Child Psychology and Psychiatry, 21,* 203–219.

Horowitz, F. D. (1987). *Exploring developmental theories: Toward a structural/behavioral model of child development.* Hillsdale, NJ: Erlbaum.

Horowitz, F. D. (1992). John B. Watson's legacy: Learning and environment. *Developmental Psychology, 28,* 360–367.

Hotz, V. J., McElroy, S. W., & Sanders, S. G. (1997). The costs and consequences of teenage childbearing for mothers. In R. A. Maynard (Ed.), *Kids having kids* (pp. 55–94). Washington, DC: Urban Institute.

Houts, A. C. (1991). Nocturnal enuresis as a biobehavioral problem. *Behavior Therapy, 22,* 133–151.

Houts, A. C., Berman, J. S., & Abramson, H. (1994). Effectiveness of psychological and pharmacological treatments for noctural enuresis. *Journal of Consulting and Clinical Psychology, 62,* 737–745.

Howard, V. F., Williams, B. F., & Port, P. (1999). Biological and genetic factors in human development. In V. L. Schwean & D. H. Saklofske (Eds.), *Handbook of psychosocial characteristics of exceptional children* (pp. 69–94). New York: Academic Press.

Howe, M. L., & Courage, M. L. (1997). The emergence and early development of autobiographical memory. *Psychological Review, 104,* 499–523.

Howe, N., & Ross, H. S. (1990). Socialization, perspective-taking, and the sibling relationship. *Developmental Psychology, 26,* 160–165.

Howes, C. (1988). Relations between early child care and schooling. *Developmental Psychology, 24,* 53–57.

Howes, C. (1992). *The collaborative construction of pretend.* Albany: State University of New York Press.

Howes, C., & Hamilton, C. E. (1993). The changing experience of child care: Changes in teachers and in teacher–child relationships and children's social competence with peers. *Early Childhood Research Quarterly, 8,* 15–32.

Howes, C., Hamilton, C. E., Phillipsen, L. C. (1998). Stability and continuity of child–caregiver and child–peer relationships. *Child Development, 69,* 418–426.

Howes, C., & Matheson, C. C. (1992). Sequences in the development of competent play with peers: Social and social pretend play. *Developmental Psychology, 28,* 961–974.

Hudson, J. A., Fivush, R., & Kuebli, J. (1992). Scripts and episodes: The development of event memory. *Applied Cognitive Psychology, 6,* 483–505.

Huesmann, L. R., & Miller, L. S. (1994). Long-term effects of repeated exposure to media violence in childhood. In L. R. Huesmann (Ed.), *Aggressive behavior: Current perspectives* (pp. 153–186). New York: Plenum.

Hughes, C. (1998). Finding your marbles: Does preschoolers' strategic behavior predict later understanding of mind? *Developmental Psychology, 34,* 1326–1339.

Hughes, C., & Dunn, J. (1998). Understanding mind and emotion: Longitudinal associations with mental-state talk between young friends. *Developmental Psychology, 34,* 1026–1037.

Hulanicka, B. (1999). Acceleration of menarcheal age of girls from dysfunctional families. *Journal of Reproductive and Infant Psychology, 17,* 119–132.

Human Genome Program. (2000). *Count of mapped genes by chromosome.* Washington, DC: U.S. Department of Energy, Office of Biological and Environmental Research.

Humphrey, L. T. (1998). Growth patterns in the modern human skeleton. *American Journal of Physical Anthropology, 105,* 57–72.

Humphrey, T. (1978). Function of the nervous system during prenatal life. In U. Stave (Ed.), *Perinatal physiology* (pp. 651–683). New York: Plenum.

Humphreys, A. P., & Smith, P. K. (1987). Rough and tumble, friendship, and dominance in schoolchildren: Evidence for continuity and change with age. *Child Development, 58,* 201–212.

Hunt, E., Streissguth, A. P., Kerr, B., & Olson, H. C. (1995). Mothers' alcohol consumption during pregnancy: Effects on spatial-visual reasoning in 14-year-old children. *Psychological Science, 6,* 339–342.

Huntsinger, C. S., Jose, P. E., & Larson, S. L. (1998). Do parent practices to encourage academic competence influence the social adjustment of young European and Chinese American children? *Developmental Psychology, 34,* 747–756.

Hursti, U. K. (1999). Factors influencing children's food choice. *Annals of Medicine, 31,* 26–32.

Huston, A. C. (1983). Sex-typing. In E. M. Hetherington (Ed.), *Handbook of child psychology: Vol. 4. Socialization, personality, and social development* (4th ed., pp. 387–467). New York: Wiley.

Huston, A. C., & Alvarez, M. M. (1990). The socialization context of gender role development in early adolescence. In R. Montemayor, G. R. Adams, & T. P. Gullotta (Eds.), *From childhood to adolescence: A transitional period?* (pp. 156–179). Newbury Park, CA: Sage.

Huston, A. C., Donnerstein, E., Fairchild, H., Feshbach, N. D., Katz, P. A., Murray, J. P., Rubinstein, E. A., Wilcox, B. L., & Zuckerman, D. (1992). *Big world, small screen: The role of television in American society.* Lincoln: University of Nebraska Press.

Huston, A. C., & Wright, J. C. (1998). Mass media and children's development. In I. E. Sigel & K. A. Renninger (Eds.), *Handbook of child psychology: Vol. 4. Child psychology in practice* (5th ed., pp. 999–1058). New York: Wiley.

Huston, A. C., Wright, J. C., Marquis, J., & Green, S. B. (1999). How young children spend their time: Television and other activities. *Developmental Psychology, 35,* 912–925.

Huston, T. L., & Vangelisti, A. L. (1995). How parenthood affects marriage. In M. A. Fitzpatrick & A. L. Vangelisti (Eds.), *Explaining family interactions* (pp. 147–176). Thousand Oaks, CA: Sage.

Huttenlocher, J., Haight, W., Bryk, A., Seltzer, M., & Lyons, T. (1991). Early vocabulary growth: Relation to language input and gender. *Developmental Psychology, 27,* 236–248.

Huttenlocher, P. R. (1994). Synaptogenesis in the human cerebral cortex. In G. Dawson & K. W. Fischer (Eds.), *Human behavior and the developing brain* (pp. 137–152). New York: Guilford.

Huttenlocher, P. R., & Dabholkar, A. S. (1997). Regional differences in synaptogenesis in human cerebral cortex. *Journal of Comparative Neurology, 387,* 167–178.

Huwiler, S. M. S., & Remafedi, G. (1998). Adolescent homosexuality. In L. A. Barness (Ed.), *Advances in pediatrics* (pp. 107–144). St. Louis: Mosby.

Hyde, J. S. (1995). Women and maternity leave: Empirical data and public policy. *Psychology of Women Quarterly, 19,* 299–313.

Hyde, J. S., Fenema, E., & Lamon, S. J. (1990). Gender differences in mathematics performance: A meta-analysis. *Psychological Bulletin, 107,* 139–155.

Hyde, J. S., Fenema, E., Ryan, M., Frost, L. A., & Hopp, C. (1990). Gender differences in mathematics attitudes and affect: A meta-analysis. *Psychology of Women Quarterly, 14,* 299–324.

Hyde, J. S., Klein, M. H., Essex, M. J., & Clark, R. (1995). Maternity leave and women's mental health. *Psychology of Women Quarterly, 19,* 257–285.

Hyde, J. S., & Linn, M. C. (1988). Gender differences in verbal ability: A meta-analysis. *Psychological Bulletin, 104,* 53–69.

Hymel, S., LeMare, L., Ditner, E., & Woody, E. Z. (1999). Assessing self-concept in children: Variations across self-concept domains. *Merrill-Palmer Quarterly, 45,* 602–623.

Ianni, F. A. J., & Orr, M. T. (1996). Dropping out. In J. A. Graber, J. Brooks-Gunn, & A. C. Petersen (Eds.), *Transitions through adolescence: Interpersonal domains and context* (pp. 285–322). Mahwah, NJ: Erlbaum.

Inagaki, K., & Hatano, G. (1993). Children's understanding of mind–body distinction. *Child Development, 64,* 1534–1549.

Ingalls, S., & Goldstein, S. (1999). Learning disabilities. In S. Goldstein & C. R. Reynolds (Eds.), *Handbook of neurodevelopmental and genetic disorders in children* (pp. 101–153). New York: Guilford.

Inhelder, B., & Piaget, J. (1958). *The growth of logical thinking from childhood to adolescence: An essay on the construction of formal operational structures.* New York: Basic Books. (Original work published 1955)

Irvine, J. J. (1986). Teacher-student interactions: Effects of student race, sex, and grade level. *Journal of Educational Psychology, 78,* 14–21.

Isabella, R. (1993). Origins of attachment: Maternal interactive behavior across the first year. *Child Development, 64,* 605–621.

Isabella, R., & Belsky, J. (1991). Interactional synchrony and the origins of infant–mother attachment: A replication study. *Child Development, 62,* 373–384.

Isakson, K., & Jarvis, P. (1999). The adjustment of adolescents during the transition into high school: A short-term longitudinal study. *Journal of Youth and Adolescence, 28,* 1–26.

Ismail, M. A., Nagib, N., Ismail, T., & Cibils, L. A. (1999). Comparison of vaginal and cesarean section delivery for fetuses in breech presentation. *Journal of Perinatal Medicine, 27,* 339–351.

Ito, Y., Teicher, M. H., Glod, C. A., & Ackerman, E. (1998). Preliminary evidence for aberrant cortical development in abused children: A quantitative EEG study. *Journal of Neuropsychiatry and Clinical Neuroscience, 10,* 298–307.

Iverson, J. M., Capirci, O., & Caselli, M. C. (1994). From communication to language in two modalities. *Cognitive Development, 9,* 23–43.

Izard, C. E. (1979). *The maximally discriminative facial movement scoring system.* Unpublished manuscript, University of Delware.

Izard, C. E. (1991). *The psychology of emotions.* New York: Plenum.

Izard, C. E., Haynes, O. M., Chisholm, G., & Baak, K. (1991).

Emotional determinants of infant–mother attachment. *Child Development, 62,* 906–917.

Jacklin, C. N., & Maccoby, E. E. (1978). Issues of gender differentiation in normal development. In M. D. Levine, W. B. Carey, A. C. Crocker, & R. T. Gross (Eds.), *Developmental-behavioral pediatrics* (pp. 174–184). Philadelphia: Saunders.

Jacklin, C. N., Wilcox, K. T., & Maccoby, E. E. (1988). Neonatal sex-steroid hormones and cognitive abilities at six years. *Developmental Psychology, 21,* 567–574.

Jacobs, J. E., & Weisz, V. (1994). Gender stereotypes: Implications for gifted education. *Roeper Review, 16,* 152–155.

Jacobson, J. L., Jacobson, S. W., Fein, G., Schwartz, P. M., & Dowler, J. (1984). Prenatal exposure to an environmental toxin: A test of the multiple effects model. *Developmental Psychology, 20,* 523–532.

Jacobson, J. L., Jacobson, S. W., Padgett, R. J., Brumitt, G. A., & Billings, R. L. (1992). Effects of prenatal PCB exposure on cognitive processing efficiency and sustained attention. *Developmental Psychology, 28,* 297–306.

Jacobson, S. W. (1998). Specificity of neurobehavioral outcomes associated with prenatal alcohol exposure. *Alcoholism: Clinical & Experimental Research, 22,* 313–320.

Jacobson, S. W., Jacobson, J. L., Sokol, R. J., Martier, S. S., & Ager, J. W. (1993). Prenatal alcohol exposure and infant information processing ability. *Child Development, 64,* 1706–1721.

Jadack, R. A., Hyde, J. S., Moore, C. F., & Keller, M. L. (1995). Moral reasoning about sexually transmitted diseases. *Child Development, 66,* 167–177.

James, D. (1998). Recent advances in fetal medicine. *British Medical Journal, 316,* 1580–1583.

Jameson, S. (1993). Zinc status in pregnancy: The effect of zinc therapy on perinatal mortality, prematurity, and placental ablation. *Annals of the New York Academy of Sciences, 678,* 178–192.

Jamieson, J. R. (1995). Interactions between mothers and children who are deaf. *Journal of Early Intervention, 19,* 108–117.

Jamin, J. R. (1994). Language and socialization of the child in African families living in France. In P. M. Greenfield & R. R. Cocking (Eds.), *Cross-cultural roots of minority child development* (pp. 147–166). Hillsdale, NJ: Erlbaum.

Janosz, M., Le Blanc, M., Boulerice, B., & Tremblay, R. E. (2000).

Predicting different types of school dropouts: A typological approach with two longitudinal samples. *Journal of Educational Psychology, 92,* 171–190.

Janssens, J. M. A. M., & Dekovic, M. (1997). Child rearing, prosocial moral reasoning, and prosocial behavior. *International Journal of Behavioral Development, 20,* 509–527.

Jenkins, J. M., & Astington, J. W. (1996). Cognitive factors and family structure associated with theory of mind development in young children. *Developmental Psychology, 32,* 70–78.

Jensen, A. R. (1969). How much can we boost IQ and scholastic achievement? *Harvard Educational Review, 39,* 1–123.

Jensen, A. R. (1985). The nature of the black–white difference on various psychometric tests: Spearman's hypothesis. *Behavioral and Brain Sciences, 8,* 193–219.

Jensen, A. R. (1998). *The g factor: The science of mental ability.* New York: Praeger.

Jensen, A. R., & Figueroa, R. A. (1975). Forward and backward digit-span interaction with race and IQ: Predictions from Jensen's theory. *Journal of Educational Psychology, 67,* 882–893.

Jensen, A. R., & Whang, P. A. (1994). Speed of accessing arithmetic facts in long-term memory: A comparison of Chinese-American and Anglo-American children. *Contemporary Educational Psychology, 19,* 1–12.

Jessor, R. (1996). Ethnographic methods in contemporary perspective. In R. Jessor, A. Colby, & R. A. Shweder (Eds.), *Ethnography and human development* (pp. 3–14). Chicago: University of Chicago Press.

Jeynes, W. H., & Littell, S. W. (2000). A meta-analysis of studies examining the effect of whole language instruction on the literacy of low-SES students. *Elementary School Journal, 101,* 21–33.

Jiao, S., Ji, G., & Jing, Q. (1996). Cognitive development of Chinese urban only children and children with siblings. *Child Development, 67,* 387–395.

Johanson, R. B., Rice, C., Coyle, M., Arthur, J., Anyanwu, L., Ibrahim, J., Warwick, A., Redman, C. W. E., & O'Brien, P. M. S. (1993). A randomised prospective study comparing the new vacuum extractor policy with forceps delivery. *British Journal of Obstetrics and Gynaecology, 100,* 524–530.

Johnson, C., & Connors, M. E. (1987). *The etiology and treatment of bulimia nervosa: A biopsycho-*

social perspective. New York: Basic Books.

Johnson, G. R., Krug, E. G., & Potter, L. B. (2000). Suicide among adolescents and young adults: A cross-national comparison of 34 countries. *Suicide and Life-threatening Behavior, 30,* 74–82.

Johnson, M. (1991). Infant and toddler sleep: A telephone survey of parents in one community. *Developmental and Behavioral Pediatrics, 12,* 108–114.

Johnson, M. H. (1998). The neural basis of cognitive development. In D. Kuhn & R. S. Siegler (Eds.), *Handbook of child psychology: Vol. 2. Cognition, perception, and language* (5th ed., pp. 1–49). New York: Wiley.

Johnson, M. H. (1999). Ontogenetic constraints on neural and behavioral plasticity: Evidence from imprinting and face processing. *Canadian Journal of Experimental Psychology, 55,* 77–90.

Johnson, M. H., Posner, M. I., & Rothbart, M. K. (1991). Components of visual orienting in early infancy: Contingency learning, anticipatory looking, and disengaging. *Journal of Cognitive Neuroscience, 3,* 335–344.

Johnson, S. L., & Birch, L. L. (1994). Parents' and children's adiposity and eating style. *Pediatrics, 94,* 653–661.

Johnson, S. P. (1996). Habituation patterns and object perception in young infants. *Journal of Reproductive and Infant Psychology, 14,* 207–218.

Johnson, S. P. (1997). Young infants' perception of object unity: Implications for development of attentional and cognitive skills. *Current Directions in Psychological Science, 6,* 5–11.

Johnson, S. P., & Aslin, R. N. (1996). Perception of object unity in young infants: The roles of motion, depth, and orientation. *Cognitive Development, 11,* 161–180.

Johnston, J. R., Kline, M., & Tschann, J. M. (1989). Ongoing post-divorce conflict. *American Journal of Orthopsychiatry, 57,* 587–600.

Jones, D. C., Abbey, B. B., & Cumberland, A. (1998). The development of display rule knowledge: Linkages with family expressiveness and social competence. *Child Development, 69,* 1209–1222.

Jones, G. P., & Dembo, M. H. (1989). Age and sex role differences in intimate friendships during childhood and adolescence. *Merrill-Palmer Quarterly, 35,* 445–462.

Jones, M. C. (1965). Psychological correlates of somatic development. *Child Development, 36,* 899–911.

Jones, M. C., & Bayley, N. (1950). Physical maturing among boys as related to behavior. *Journal of Educational Psychology, 41,* 129–148.

Jones, M. C., & Mussen, P. H. (1958). Self-conceptions, motivations, and interpersonal attitudes of early- and late-maturing girls. *Child Development, 29,* 491–501.

Jones, M. M., & Mandeville, G. K. (1990). The effect of age at school entry on reading achievement scores among South Carolina students. *Remedial and Special Education, 11,* 56–62.

Jones, N. A., Field, T., Fox, N. A., Lundy, B., & Davalos, M. (1997). EEG activation in 1-month-old infants of depressed mothers. *Development and Psychopathology, 9,* 491–505.

Jones, S. S., & Raag, T. (1989). Smile production in older infants: The importance of a social recipient for the facial signal. *Child Development, 60,* 811–818.

Jordan, B. (1993). *Birth in four cultures.* Prospect Heights, IL: Waveland.

Jordan, W. J., Lara, J., & McPartland, J. M. (1996). Exploring the causes of early dropout among race-ethnic and gender groups. *Youth & Society, 28,* 62–94.

Jorgensen, K. M. (1999). Pain assessment and management in the newborn infant. *Journal of Peri-Anesthesia Nursing, 14,* 349–356.

Jorgensen, M., & Keiding, N. (1991). Estimation of spermarche from longitudinal spermaturia data. *Biometrics, 47,* 177–193.

Joseph, R. (2000). Fetal brain behavior and cognitive development. *Developmental Review, 20,* 81–98.

Joseph, R. M. (1998). Intention and knowledge in preschoolers' conception of pretend. *Child Development, 69,* 966–980.

Joseph, R. M., & Tager-Flusberg, H. (1999). Preschool children's understanding of the desire and knowledge constraints on intended action. *British Journal of Developmental Psychology, 17,* 221–243.

Josselson, R. (1992). *The space between us.* San Francisco: Jossey-Bass.

Josselson, R. (1994). The theory of identity development and the question of intervention. In S. L. Archer (Ed.), *Interventions for adolescent identity development* (pp. 12–25). Thousand Oaks, CA: Sage.

Jovanovic, J., & King, S. S. (1998). Boys and girls in the performance-based science classroom: Who's doing the performing? *American Educational Research Journal, 35,* 477–496.

Joyner, M. H., & Kurtz-Costes, B. (1997). Metamemory develop-ment. In W. Schneider & F. E. Weinert (Eds.), *Memory performance and competencies: Issues in growth and development* (pp. 275–300). Hillsdale, NJ: Erlbaum.

Jusczyk, P. W. (1995). Language acquisition: Speech sounds and phonological development. In J. L. Miller & P. D. Eimas (Eds.), *Handbook of perception and cognition: Vol. 11. Speech, language, and communication* (pp. 263–301). Orlando, FL: Academic Press.

Jusczyk, P. W. (1997). Finding and remembering words: Some beginnings by English-learning infants. *Current Directions in Psychological Science, 6,* 170–174.

Jusczyk, P. W., & Aslin, R. N. (1995). Infants' detection of the sound patterns of words in fluent speech. *Cognitive Psychology, 29,* 1–23.

Jusczyk, P. W., Cutler, A., & Redanz, N. J. (1993). Infants' preference for the predominant stress patterns of English words. *Child Development, 64,* 675–687.

Jusczyk, P. W., & Hohne, E. A. (1997). Infants' memory for spoken words. *Science, 277,* 1984–1986.

Jusczyk, P. W., Johnson, S. P., Spelke, E. S., & Kennedy, L. J. (1999). Synchronous change and perception of object unity: Evidence from adults and infants. *Cognition, 71,* 257–288.

Justice, E. M. (1986). Developmental changes in judgments of relative strategy effectiveness. *British Journal of Developmental Psychology, 4,* 75–81.

Justice, E. M., Baker-Ward, L., Gupta, S., & Jannings, L. R. (1997). Means to the goal of remembering: Developmental changes in awareness of strategy use–performance relations. *Journal of Experimental Child Psychology, 65,* 293–314.

Kagan, J. (1989). *Unstable ideas: Temperament, cognition, and self.* Cambridge, MA: Harvard University Press.

Kagan, J. (1992). Behavior, biology, and the meanings of temperamental constructs. *Pediatrics, 90,* 510–513.

Kagan, J. (1998). Biology and the child. In N. Eisenberg (Ed.), *Handbook of child psychology: Vol. 3. Social, emotional, and personality development* (5th ed., pp. 177–236). New York: Wiley.

Kagan, J., Arcus, D., Snidman, N., Feng, W. Y., Hendler, J., & Greene, S. (1994). Reactivity in infants: A cross-national comparison. *Developmental Psychology, 30,* 342–345.

Kagan, J., Kearsley, R. B., & Zelazo, P. R. (1978). *Infancy: Its place in human development.* Cambridge, MA; Harvard University Press.

Kagan, J., & Snidman, N. (1991). Temperamental factors in human development. *American Psychologist, 46,* 856–862.

Kagan, J., Snidman, N., & Arcus, D. (1998). Childhood derivatives of high and low reactivity in infancy. *Child Development, 69,* 1483–1493.

Kagan, J., Snidman, N., Zentner, M., & Peterson, E. (1999). Infant temperament and anxious symptoms in school-age children. *Development and Psychopathology, 11,* 209–224.

Kahn, P. H., Jr. (1992). Children's obligatory and discretionary moral judgments. *Child Development, 63,* 416–430.

Kail, R. (1993). Processing time decreases globally at an exponential rate during childhood and adolescence. *Journal of Experimental Child Psychology, 57,* 281–291.

Kail, R. (2000). Speed of information processing: Developmental change and links to intelligence. *Journal of School Psychology, 38,* 51–61.

Kail, R., & Park, Y. (1992). Global developmental change in processing time. *Merrill-Palmer Quarterly, 38,* 525–541.

Kail, R., & Park, Y. (1994). Processing time, articulation time, and memory span. *Journal of Experimental Child Psychology, 57,* 281–291.

Kaitz, M., Good, A., Rokem, A. M., & Eidelman, A. I. (1987). Mothers' recognition of their newborns by olfactory cues. *Developmental Psychobiology, 20,* 587–591.

Kaitz, M., Good, A., Rokem, A. M., & Eidelman, A. I. (1988). Mothers' and fathers' recognition of their newborns' photographs during the postpartum period. *Journal of Developmental and Behavioral Pediatrics, 9,* 223–226.

Kaitz, M., Meirov, H., Landman, I., & Eidelman, A. I. (1993a). Infant recognition by tactile cues. *Infant Behavior and Development, 16,* 333–341.

Kaitz, M., Shiri, S., Danziger, S., Hershko, Z., & Eidelman, A. I. (1993b). Fathers can also recognize their newborns by touch. *Infant Behavior and Development, 17,* 205–207.

Kalb, C. (1997, May 5). How old is too old? *Newsweek,* p. 64.

Kaler, S. R., & Kopp, C. B. (1990). Compliance and comprehension in very young toddlers. *Child Development, 61,* 1997–2003.

Kamerman, S. B. (1993). International perspectives on child care policies and programs. *Pediatrics, 91,* 248–252.

Kamerman, S. B. (2000). From maternity to parental leave policies: Women's health, employment, and child and family well-being. *Journal of the American Medical Women's Association, 55,* 96–99.

Kandall, S. R., Gaines, J., Habel, L., Davidson, G., & Jessop, D. (1993). Relationship of maternal substance abuse to subsequent sudden infant death syndrome in offspring. *Journal of Pediatrics, 123,* 120–126.

Kanner, A. D., Feldman, S. S., Weinberger, D. A., & Ford, M. E. (1987). Uplifts, hassles, and adaptational outcomes in early adolescents. *Journal of Early Adolescence, 7,* 371–394.

Kao, G. (2000). Psychological well-being and educational achievement among immigrant youth. In D. J. Hernandez (Ed.), *Children of immigrants: Health, adjustment, and public assistance.* Washington, DC: National Academy Press.

Kao, G., & Tienda, M. (1995). Optimism and achievement: The educational performance of immigrant youth. *Social Science Quarterly, 76,* 1–19.

Kaplan, S. J., Pelcovitz, D., & Labruna, V. (1999). Child and adolescent abuse and neglect research: A review of the past 10 years. Part I: Physical and emotional abuse and neglect. *Journal of the American Academy of Child and Adolescent Psychiatry, 38,* 1214–1222.

Kaprio, J., Rimpela, A., Winter, T., Viken, R. J., Pimpela, M., & Rose, R. J. (1995). Common genetic influence on BMI and age at menarche. *Human Biology, 67,* 739–753.

Karadsheh, R. (1991). *This room is a junkyard!: Children's comprehension of metaphorical language.* Paper presented at the biennial meeting of the Society for Research in Child Development, Seattle, WA.

Karmiloff-Smith, A. (1992). *Beyond modularity: A developmental perspective on cognitive science.* Cambridge, MA: MIT Press.

Karmiloff-Smith, A. (1996, Fall). The connectionist infant: Would Piaget turn in his grave? *Newsletter of the Society for Research in Child Development,* pp. 1–2, 10.

Kasen, S., Cohen, P., & Brook, J. S. (1998). Adolescent school experiences and dropout, adolescent pregnancy, and young adult deviant behavior. *Journal of Adolescent Research, 13,* 49–72.

Katchadourian, H. (1990). Sexuality. In S. S. Feldman & G. R. Elliott (Eds.), *At the threshold: The developing adolescent* (pp. 330–351). Cambridge, MA: Harvard University Press.

Kavanaugh, R. D., & Engel, S. (1998). The development of pretense and narrative in early childhood. In O. N. Saracho & B. Spodek (Eds.), *Multiple perspectives on play in early childhood education* (pp. 80–99). Albany: State University of New York Press.

Kaye, K., & Marcus, J. (1981). Infant imitation: The sensory-motor agenda. *Developmental Psychology, 17*, 258–265.

Kaye, K., & Wells, A. J. (1980). Mothers' jiggling and the burst–pause pattern in neonatal feeding. *Infant Behavior and Development, 3*, 29–46.

Kaye, W. H., Klump, K. L., Frank, G. K. W., & Strober, M. (2000). Anorexia and bulimia nervosa. *Annual Review of Medicine, 51*, 299–313.

Kearins, J. M. (1981). Visual spatial memory in Australian aboriginal children of desert regions. *Cognitive Psychology, 13*, 434–460.

Keating, D. (1979). Adolescent thinking. In J. Adelson (Ed.), *Handbook of adolescent psychology* (pp. 211–246). New York: Wiley.

Keating, D. (1990). Adolescent thinking. In S. S. Feldman & G. R. Elliott (Eds.), *At the threshold* (pp. 54–89). Cambridge, MA: Harvard University Press.

Keil, F. C., Levin, D., Gutheil, G., & Richman, B. (1999). Mechanism and explanation in the development of biological thought: The case of disease. In D. Medin & S. Atran (Eds.), *Folkbiology* (pp. 285–318). Cambridge, U.K.: Cambridge University Press.

Keil, F. C., & Lockhart, K. L. (1999). Explanatory understanding in conceptual development. In E. K. Scholnick, K. Nelson, S. A. Gelman, & P. H. Miller (Eds.), *Conceptual development: Piaget's legacy* (pp. 103–130). Mahwah, NJ: Erlbaum.

Keith, T. Z., Keith, P. B., Quirk, K. J., Sperduto, J., Santillo, S., & Killings, S. (1998). Longitudinal effects of parent involvement on high school grades: Similarities and differences across gender and ethnic groups. *Journal of School Psychology, 36*, 335–363.

Kelley, M. L., Power, T. G., & Wimbush, D. D. (1992). Determinants of disciplinary practices in low-income black mothers. *Child Development, 63*, 573–582.

Kelley, M. L., Sanchez-Hucies, J., & Walker, R. (1993). Correlates of disciplinary practices in working-to middle-class African-American mothers. *Merrill-Palmer Quarterly, 39*, 252–264.

Kellman, P. J. (1996). The origins of object perception. In R. Gelman & T. K. Au (Eds.), *Perceptual and cognitive development* (pp. 3–48). San Diego: Academic Press.

Kelly, F. W., Terry, R., & Naglieri, R. (1999). A review of alternative

birthing positions. *Journal of the American Osteopathic Association, 99*, 470–474.

Kelnar, C. J. H., Albertsson-Wikland, K., Hintz, R. L., Ranke, M. B., & Rosenfeld, R. G. (1999). Should we treat children with idiopathic short stature? *Hormone Research, 52*, 150–157.

Kempe, C. H., Silverman, B. F., Steele, P. W., Droegemueller, P. W., & Silver, H. K. (1962). The battered-child syndrome. *Journal of the American Medical Association, 181*, 17–24.

Kennedy, C. M. (1998). Childhood nutrition. *Annual Review of Nursing Research, 16*, 3–38.

Kennell, J. H., Klaus, M., McGrath, S., Robertson, S., & Hinkley, C. (1991). Continuous emotional support during labor in a U.S. hospital. *Journal of the American Medical Association, 265*, 2197–2201.

Kerns, K. A., & Berenbaum, S. A. (1991). Sex differences in spatial ability in children. *Behavior Genetics, 21*, 383–396.

Kerr, M., Lambert, W. W., Stattin, H., & Klackenberg-Larsson, I. (1994). Stability of inhibition in a Swedish longitudinal sample. *Child Development, 65*, 138–146.

Kessen, W. (1967). Sucking and looking: Two organized congenital patterns of behavior in the human newborn. In H. W. Stevenson, E. H. Hess & H. L. Rheingold (Eds.), *Early behavior: Comparative and developmental approaches* (pp. 147–179). New York: Wiley.

Kessler, R., McGonagle, K., Zhao, S., Nelson, C., Hughes, M., Eshleman, S., Wittchen, H., & Kendler, K. (1994). Lifetime and 12-month prevalence of DSM-III-R psychiatric disorders in the United States: Results from the national comorbidity survey. *Archives of General Psychiatry, 51*, 8–19.

Killen, M., & Nucci, L. P. (1995). Morality, autonomy, and social conflict. In M. Killen & D. Hart (Eds.), *Morality in everyday life: Developmental perspectives* (pp. 52–86). Cambridge, UK: Cambridge University Press.

Killen, M., & Smetana, J. G. (1999). Social interactions in preschool classrooms and the development of young children's conceptions of the personal. *Child Development, 70*, 486–501.

Kilpatrick, D. G., Acierno, R., Saunders, B., Resnick, H. S., Best, C. L., & Schnurr, P. P. (2000). Risk factors for adolescent substance abuse and dependence: Data from a national sample. *Journal of Consulting and Clinical Psychology, 68*, 19–30.

Kilpatrick, S. W., & Sanders, D. M. (1978). Body image stereotypes: A developmental comparison. *Journal of Genetic Psychology, 132*, 87–95.

Kim, J. M. (1998). Korean children's concepts of adult and peer authority and moral reasoning. *Developmental Psychology, 34*, 947–955.

Kim, J. M., & Turiel, E. (1996). Korean children's concepts of adult and peer authority. *Social Development, 5*, 310–329.

Kim, K., & Spelke, E. S. (1992). Infants' sensitivity to effects of gravity on visible object motion. *Journal of Experimental Psychology: Human Perception and Performance, 18*, 385–393.

Kim, K. H. S., Relkin, N. R., Lee, K. M., & Hirsch, J. (1997). Distinct cortical areas associated with native and second languages. *Nature, 388*, 171–174.

Kinderman, T. A. (1993). Natural peer groups as contexts for individual development: The case of children's motivation in school. *Developmental Psychology, 29*, 970–977.

King, C. M., & Johnson, L. M. P. (1999). Constructing meaning via reciprocal teaching. *Reading Research and Instruction, 38*, 169–186.

King, P. M., & Kitchener, K. S. (1994). *Developing reflective judgment: Understanding and promoting intellectual growth and critical thinking in adolescents and adults.* San Francisco: Jossey-Bass.

Kinney, D. (1999). From "head-bangers" to "hippies": Delineating adolescents' active attempts to form an alternative peer culture. In J. A. McLellan & M. J. V. Pugh (Eds.), *The role of peer groups in adolescent social identity: Exploring the importance of stability and change* (pp. 21–35). San Francisco: Jossey-Bass.

Kirby, D. (1997). *No easy answers: Research findings on programs to reduce teen pregnancy.* Washington, DC: National Campaign to Prevent Teen Pregnancy.

Kirchner, G. (2000). *Children's games from around the world.* Boston: Allyn and Bacon.

Kirk, W. G. (1993). *Adolescent suicide.* Champaign, IL: Research Press.

Kisilevsky, B. S., Hains, S. M. J., Lee, K., Muir, D. W., Xu, F., Fu, G., Zhao, Z. Y., & Yang, R. L. (1998). The still-face effect in Chinese and Canadian 3- to 6-month-old infants. *Developmental Psychology, 34*, 629–639.

Kisilevsky, B. S., & Low, J. A. (1998). Human fetal behavior: 100 years of study. *Developmental Review, 18*, 1–29.

Klaczynski, P. A. (1997). Bias in adolescents' everyday reasoning and its relationships with intellectual ability, personal theories, and self-serving motivation. *Developmental Psychology, 33*, 273–283.

Klaczynski, P. A., & Narasimham, G. (1998a). Development of scientific reasoning biases: Cognitive versus ego-protective explanations. *Developmental Psychology, 34*, 175–187.

Klaczynski, P. A., & Narasimham, G. (1998b). Representations as mediators of adolescent deductive reasoning. *Developmental Psychology, 34*, 865–881.

Klahr, D., & MacWhinney, B. (1998). Information processing. In D. Kuhn & R. S. Siegler (Eds.), *Handbook of child psychology: Vol. 2. Cognition, perception, and language* (5th ed., pp. 631–678). New York: Wiley.

Klaus, M. H., & Kennell, J. H. (1982). *Parent–infant bonding.* St. Louis: Mosby.

Klebanov, P. K., Brooks-Gunn, J., McCarton, C., & McCormick, M. C. (1998). The contribution of neighborhood and family income to developmental test scores over the first three years of life. *Child Development, 69*, 1420–1436.

Kleeman, W. J., Schlaud, M., Fieguth, A., Hiller, A. S., Rothamel, T., & Troger, H. D. (1999). Body and head position, covering of the head by bedding and risk of sudden infant death (SID). *International Journal of Legal Medicine, 112*, 22–26.

Klein, P. J., & Meltzoff, A. N. (1999). Long-term memory, forgetting, and deferred imitation in 12-month-old infants. *Developmental Science, 2*, 102–113.

Kliewer, W., Fearnow, M. D., & Miller, P. A. (1996). Coping socialization in middle childhood: Tests of maternal and paternal influences. *Child Development, 67*, 2339–2357.

Klimes-Dougan, B., & Kistner, J. (1990). Physically abused preschoolers' responses to peers' distress. *Developmental Psychology, 26*, 599–602.

Kling, K. C., Hyde, J. S., Showers, C. J., & Buswell, B. N. (1999). Gender differences in self-esteem: A meta-analysis. *Psychological Bulletin, 125*, 470–500.

Klingner, J. K., Vaughn, S., Hughes, M. T., Schumm, J. S., & Elbaum, B. (1998). Outcomes for students with and without learning disabilities in inclusive classrooms. *Learning Disabilities Research and Practice, 13*, 153–161.

Klitzing, K. von, Simoni, H., Amsler, F., & Buergin, D. (1999). The role of the father in early family interactions. *Infant Mental Health Journal, 20,* 222–237.

Knobloch, H., & Pasamanick, B. (Eds.). (1974). *Gesell and Amatruda's Developmental Diagnosis.* Hagerstown, MD: Harper & Row.

Knoers, N., van den Ouweland, A., Dreesen, J. Verdijk, M., Monnens, L. S., & van Oost, B. A. (1993). Nephrongenic diabetes inspidus: Identification of the genetic defect. *Pediatric Nephrology, 7,* 685–688.

Kochanska, G. (1991). Socialization and temperament in the development of guilt and conscience. *Child Development, 62,* 1379–1392.

Kochanska, G. (1992). Children's interpersonal influence with mothers and peers. *Developmental Psychology, 28,* 491–499.

Kochanska, G. (1993). Toward a synthesis of parental socialization and child temperament in early development of conscience. *Child Development, 64,* 325–347.

Kochanska, G. (1995). Children's temperament, mothers' discipline, and security of attachment: Multiple pathways to emerging internalization. *Child Development, 66,* 597–615.

Kochanska, G. (1997). Multiple pathways to conscience for children with different temperaments: From toddlerhood to age 5. *Developmental Psychology, 33,* 228–240.

Kochanska, G. (1998). Mother–child relationship, child fearfulness, and emerging attachment: A short-term longitudinal study. *Developmental Psychology, 34,* 480–490.

Kochanska, G., Aksan, N., & Koenig, A. L. (1959). A longitudinal study of the roots of preschoolers' conscience: Committed compliance and emerging internalization. *Child Development, 66,* 643–656.

Kochanska, G., Casey, R. J., & Fukumoto, A. (1995). Toddlers' sensitivity to standard violations. *Child Development, 66,* 643–656.

Kochanska, G., & Murray, K. T. (2000). Mother–child mutually responsive orientation and conscience development: From toddler to early school age. *Child Development, 71,* 417–431.

Kochanska, G., Murray, K. T., & Harlan, E. T. (2000). Effortful control in early childhood: Continuity and change, antecedents, and implications for social development. *Developmental Psychology, 36,* 220–232.

Kochanska, G., & Radke-Yarrow, M. (1992). Inhibition in toddlerhood and the dynamics of the child's interaction with an unfamiliar peer at age five. *Child Development, 63,* 325–335.

Koestner, R., Franz, C., & Weinberger, J. (1990). The family origins of empathic concern: A 26-year longitudinal study. *Journal of Personality and Social Psychology, 58,* 709–717.

Kohlberg, L. (1966). A cognitive-developmental analysis of children's sex-role concepts and attitudes. In E. E. Maccoby (Ed.), *The development of sex differences* (pp. 82–173). Stanford, CA: Stanford University Press.

Kohlberg, L. (1969). Stage and sequence: The cognitive-developmental approach to socialization. In D. A. Goslin (Ed.), *Handbook of socialization theory and research* (pp. 347–480). Chicago: Rand McNally.

Kohlberg, L., Levine, C., & Hewer, A. (1983). *Moral stages: A current formulation and a response to critics.* Basel, Switzerland: Karger.

Kohlendorfer, U., Kiechl, S., & Sperl, W. (1998). Sudden infant death syndrome: Risk factor profiles for distinct subgroups. *American Journal of Epidemiology, 147,* 960–968.

Kohn, A. (1997). How not to teach values: A critical look at character education. *Phi Delta Kappan, 78*(6), 429–439.

Kojima, H. (1986). Childrearing concepts as a belief–value system of the society and the individual. In H. Stevenson, H. Azuma, & K. Hakuta (Eds.), *Child development and education in Japan* (pp. 39–54). New York: Freeman.

Kolominsky, Y., Igumnov, S., & Drozdovitch, V. (1999). The psychological development of children from Belarus exposed in the prenatal period to radiation from the Chernobyl atomic power plant. *Journal of Child Psychology and Psychiatry, 40,* 299–305.

Kolvin, I., & Trowell, J. (1996). Child sexual abuse. In I. Rosen (Ed.), *Sexual deviation* (3rd ed., pp. 337–360). Oxford, England: Oxford University Press.

Koo, M. R., Dekker, G. A., & van Geijn, H. P. (1998). Perinatal outcome of singleton term breech deliveries. *European Journal of Obstetrics, Gynecology, and Reproductive Biology, 78,* 19–24.

Koolstra, C. M., & van der Voort, T. H. (1996). Longitudinal effects of television on children's leisure-time reading. *Human Communication Research, 23,* 4–35.

Kopp, C. B. (1994). Infant assessment. In C. B. Fisher & R. M. Lerner (Eds.), *Applied developmental psychology* (pp. 265–293). New York: McGraw-Hill.

Korner, A. F. (1996). Reliable individual differences in preterm infants' excitation management. *Child Development, 67,* 1793–1805.

Kornguth, M. L. (1990). School illnesses: Who's absent and why? *Pediatric Nursing, 16,* 95–99.

Korte, D. (1997). *The VBAC companion: The expectant mother's guide to vaginal birth after cesarean.* Cambridge, MA: Harvard Common Press.

Kotch, J. B., Browne, D. C., Dufort, V., & Winsor, J. (1999). Predicting child maltreatment in the first four years of life from characteristics assessed in the neonatal period. *Child Abuse and Neglect, 23,* 305–319.

Kotch, J. B., Muller, G. O., & Blakely, C. H. (1999). Understanding the origins and incidence of spousal violence in North America. In T. P. Gullotta & S. J. McElhaney (Eds.), *Violence in homes and communities* (pp. 1–38). Thousand Oaks, CA: Sage.

Kotovsky, L., & Baillargeon, R. (1998). The development of calibration-based reasoning about collision events in young infants. *Cognition, 57,* 311–351.

Kovacs, M. (1996). Presentation and course of major depressive disorder during childhood and later years of the lifespan. *Journal of the American Academy of Child and Adolescent Psychiatry, 35,* 705–715.

Kovacs, M., Akiskal, H., Gatsonis, C., & Parrone, P. (1994). Childhood-onset dysthymic disorder: Clinical features and prospective naturalistic outcome. *Archives of General Psychiatry, 51,* 365–374.

Kowaleski-Jones, L., & Mott, F. L. (1998). Sex, contraception and childbearing among high-risk youth: Do different factors influence males and females? *Family Planning Perspectives, 30,* 163–169.

Kowalski, N., & Allen, R. (1995). School sleep lag is less but persists with a very late starting high school. *Sleep Research, 24,* 124.

Kraemer, H. C., Yesavage, J. A., Taylor, J. L., & Kupfer, D. (2000). How can we learn about developmental processes from cross-sectional studies, or can we? *American Journal of Psychiatry, 157,* 163–171.

Krafft, K., & Berk, L. E. (1998). Private speech in two preschools: Significance of open-ended activities and make-believe play for verbal self-regulation. *Early Childhood Research Quarterly, 13,* 637–658.

Krascum, R. M., & Andrews, S. (1998). The effects of theories on children's acquisition of family-resemblance categories. *Child Development, 69,* 333–346.

Kreutzer, M. A., Leonard, C., & Flavell, J. H. (1975). An interview study of children's knowledge about memory. *Monographs of the Society for Research in Child Development, 40* (1, Serial No. 159).

Krevans, J., & Gibbs, J. C. (1996). Parents' use of inductive discipline: Relations to children's empathy and prosocial behavior. *Child Development, 67,* 3263–3277.

Kroger, J. (1993). Identity and context: How the identity statuses choose their match. In R. Josselson & A. Lieblich (Eds.), *The narrative study of lives* (Vol. 1, pp. 130–162). Newbury Park, CA: Sage.

Kroger, J. (1995). The differentiation of "firm" and "developmental" foreclosure identity statuses: A longitudinal study. *Journal of Adolescent Research, 10,* 317–337.

Kroger, J. (2000). *Identity development: Adolescence through adulthood.* Thousand Oaks, CA: Sage.

Kronenfeld, J. J., & Glik, D. C. (1995). Unintentional injury: A major health problem for young children and youth. *Journal of Family and Economic Issues, 16,* 365–393.

Kruger, A. C. (1993). Peer collaboration: Conflict, cooperation, or both? *Social Development, 2,* 165–182.

Krumhansl, C. L., & Jusczyk, P. W. (1990). Infants' perception of phrase structure in music. *Psychological Science, 1,* 70–73.

Kuczynski, L. (1984). Socialization goals and mother–child interaction: Strategies for long-term and short-term compliance. *Developmental Psychology, 20,* 1061–1073.

Kuhl, P. K., Williams, K. A., Lacerda, F., Stevens, K. N., & Lindblom, B. (1992). Linguistic experience alters phonetic perception in infants by 6 months of age. *Science, 255,* 606–608.

Kuhn, D. (1989). Children and adults as intuitive scientists. *Psychological Review, 96,* 674–689.

Kuhn, D. (1993). Connecting scientific and informal reasoning. *Merrill-Palmer Quarterly, 39,* 74–103.

Kuhn, D. (1995). Microgenetic study of change: What has it told us? *Psychological Science, 6,* 133–139.

Kuhn, D. (1999). Metacognitive development. *Current Directions in Psychological Science, 9,* 178–181.

Kuhn, D. (2000). Theory of mind, metacognition, and reasoning: A life-span perspective. In P. Mitchell & K. J. Riggs (Eds.), *Children's reasoning and the mind* (pp. 301–326). Hove, UK: Psychology Press.

Kuhn, D., Garcia-Mila, M., Zohar, A., & Andersen, C. (1995). Strategies of knowledge acquisition. *Monographs of the Society for Research in Child Development, 60* (245, Serial No. 4).

Kuhn, L., & Stein, Z. (1997). Infant survival, HIV infection, and feeding alternatives in less-developed countries. *American Journal of Public Health, 87*, 926–931.

Kulakov, V. I., Sokus, T. N., Volobuev, A. I., Tzibulskaya, I. S., Malisheva, V. A., & Zikin, J. M. (1993). Female reproductive function in areas affected by radiation after the Chernobyl power station accident. *Environmental Health Perspective, 101*(suppl. 2), 117–123.

Kunzinger, E. L., III. (1985). A short-term longitudinal study of memorial development during early grade school. *Developmental Psychology, 21*, 642–646.

Kupersmidt, J. B., DeRosier, M. E., & Patterson, C. P. (1995). Similarity as the basis for children's friendships: The roles of sociometric status, aggressive and withdrawn behavior, academic achievement, and demographic characteristics. *Journal of Social and Personal Relationships, 12*, 439–452.

Kurdek, L. A., & Fine, M. A. (1994). Family acceptance and family control as predictors of adjustment in young adolescents: Linear, curvilinear, or interactive effects? *Child Development, 65*, 1137–1146.

Kushman, J. W., Sieber, C., & Heariold-Kinney, P. (2000). This isn't the place for me: School dropout. In D. Capuzzi & D. R. Gross (Eds.), *Youth risk: A prevention resource for counselors, teachers, and parents* (3rd ed., pp. 471–507). Alexandria, VA: American Counseling Association.

Kutner, L. (1993, June). Getting physical. *Parents*, Vol. 68, N. 6, pp. 96–98.

Ladd, G. W., Birch, S. H., & Buhs, E. S. (1999). Children's social and scholastic lives in kindergarten: Related spheres of influence? *Child Development, 70*, 1373–1400.

Ladd, G. W., & Burgess, K. B. (1999). Charting the relationship trajectories of aggressive, withdrawn, and aggressive/withdrawn children during early grade school. *Child Development, 70*, 910–929.

Ladd, G. W., & Cairns, E. (1996). Children: Ethnic and political violence. *Child Development, 67*, 14–18.

Ladd, G. W., Kochenderfer, B. J., & Coleman, C. C. (1997). Classroom peer acceptance, friendship, and victimization: Distinct relational systems that contribute uniquely to children's school adjustment? *Child Development, 68*, 1181–1197.

Ladd, G. W., & Ladd, B. K. (1998). Parenting behaviors and parent–child relationships: Correlates of peer victimization in kindergarten? *Developmental Psychology, 34*, 1450–1458.

Ladd, G. W., LeSieur, K., & Profilet, S. M. (1993). Direct parental influences on young children's peer relations. In S. Duck (Ed.), *Learning about relationships* (Vol. 2, pp. 152–183). London: Sage.

Ladd, G. W., & Price, J. M. (1987). Predicting children's social and school adjustment following the transition from preschool to kindergarten. *Child Development, 58*, 1168–1189.

LaGasse, L. L., Seifer, R., & Lester, B. M. (1999). Interpreting research on prenatal substance exposure in the context of multiple confounding factors. *Clinics in Perinatology, 26*, 39–54.

Lagattuta, K. H., Wellman, H. M., & Flavell, J. H. (1997). Preschoolers' understanding of the link between thinking and feeling: Cognitive cuing and emotional change. *Child Development, 68*, 1081–1104.

Lagercrantz, H., & Slotkin, T. A. (1986). The "stress" of being born. *Scientific American, 254*, 100–107.

Lahey, B. B., & Loeber, R. (1997). Attention-deficit/hyperactivity disorder, oppositional defiant disorder, conduct disorder, and adult antisocial behavior: A life span perspective. In D. M. Stoff, J. Breiling, & J. D. Maser (Eds.), *Handbook of antisocial behavior* (pp. 51–59). New York: Wiley.

Laing, G. J., & Logan, S. (1999). Patterns of unintentional injury in childhood and their relation to socio-economic factors. *Public Health, 113*, 291–294.

Lamaze, F. (1958). *Painless childbirth.* London: Burke.

Lamb, M. (1994). Infant care practices and the application of knowledge. In C. B. Fisher & R. M. Lerner (Eds.), *Applied developmental psychology* (pp. 23–45). New York: McGraw-Hill.

Lamb, M. E. (1987). *The father's role: Cross-cultural perspectives.* Hillsdale, NJ: Erlbaum.

Lamb, M. E. (1997). The development of father–infant relationships. In M. E. Lamb (Ed.), *The role of the father in child development* (3rd ed., pp. 104–120). New York: Wiley.

Lamb, M. E. (1998). Nonparental child care: Context, quality, correlates, and consequences. In I. E. Sigel & K. A. Renninger (Eds.), *Handbook of child psychology: Vol. 4. Child psychology in practice* (5th ed., pp. 73–133). New York: Wiley.

Lamb, M. E. (1999). Noncustodial fathers and their impact on the children of divorce. In R. A. Thompson & P. R. Amato (Eds.), *The postdivorce family: Children, parenting, and society* (pp. 105–125). Thousand Oaks, CA: Sage.

Lamb, M. E., & Oppenheim, D. (1989). Fatherhood and father–child relationships: Five years of research. In S. H. Cath, A. Gurwitt, & L. Gunsberg (Eds.), *Fathers and their families* (pp. 11–26). Hillsdale, NJ: Erlbaum.

Lamb, M. E., Sternberg, K. J., & Prodromidis, M. (1992). Nonmaternal care and the security of infant–mother attachment: A reanalysis of the data. *Infant Behavior and Development, 15*, 71–83.

Lamb, M. E., Thompson, R. A., Gardner, W., Charnov, E. L., & Connell, J. P. (1985). Infant-mother attachment: The origins and developmental significance of individual differences in the Strange Situation: Its study and biological interpretation. *Behavioral and Brain Sciences, 7*, 127–147.

Lamborn, S. D., Mounts, N. S., Steinberg, L., & Dornbusch, S. M. (1991). Patterns of competence and adjustment among adolescents from authoritative, authoritarian, indulgent, and neglectful families. *Child Development, 62*, 1049–1065.

Lampl, M. (1993). Evidence of saltatory growth in infancy. *American Journal of Human Biology, 5*, 641–652.

Lampl, M., Veldhuis, J. D., & Johnson, M. L. (1992). Saltation and stasis: A model of human growth. *Science, 258*, 801–803.

Landry, S. H., & Whitney, J. A. (1996). The impact of prenatal cocaine exposure: Studies of the developing infant. *Seminars in Perinatology, 20*, 99–106.

Lange, G., & Pierce, S. H. (1992). Memory-strategy learning and maintenance in preschool children. *Developmental Psychology, 28*, 453–462.

Lansky, V. (1991). *Getting your child to sleep . . . and back to sleep: Tips for parents of infants, toddlers, and preschoolers.* New York: Book Peddlers.

Lapointe, A. E., Askew, J. M., & Mead, N. A. (1992). *Learning mathematics.* Princeton, NJ: Educational Testing Service.

Lapointe, A. E., Mead, N. A., & Askew, J. M. (1992). *Learning science.* Princeton, NJ: Educational Testing Service.

Lapsley, D. K. (1985). Elkind on egocentrism. *Developmental Review, 5*, 227–236.

Lapsley, D. K. (1993). Toward an integrated theory of adolescent ego development: The "new look" at adolescent egocentrism. *American Journal of Orthopsychiatry, 63*, 562–571.

Lapsley, D. K., Jackson, S., Rice, K., & Shadid, G. (1988). Self-monitoring and the "new look" at the imaginary audience and personal fable: An ego-developmental analysis. *Journal of Adolescent Research, 3*, 17–31.

Lapsley, D. K., Milstead, M., Quintana, S., Flannery, D., & Buss, R. (1986). Adolescent egocentrism and formal operations: Tests of a theoretical assumption. *Developmental Psychology, 22*, 800–807.

Larson, D. E. (1996). *Mayo Clinic family health book.* New York: Morrow.

Larson, R., & Ham, M. (1993). Stress and "storm and stress" in early adolescence: The relationship of negative events with dysphoric affect. *Developmental Psychology, 29*, 130–140.

Larson, R., & Lampman-Petraitis, C. (1989). Daily emotional states as reported by children and adolescents. *Child Development, 60*, 1250–1260.

Larson, R., & Richards, M. (1998). Waiting for the weekend: Friday and Saturday night as the emotional climax of the week. In A. C. Crouter & R. Larson (Eds.), *Temporal rhythms in adolescence: Clocks, calendars, and the coordination of daily life* (pp. 37–51). San Francisco: Jossey-Bass.

Larson, R. W., Clore, G. L., & Wood, G. A. (1999). The emotions of romantic relationships: Do they wreak havoc on adolescents? In W. Furman, B. B. Brown, & C. Feiring (Eds.), *The development of romantic relationships in adolescence* (pp. 19–49). New York: Cambridge University Press.

Larson, R. W., & Richards, M. H. (1991). Daily companionship in late childhood and early adolescence: Changing developmental contexts. *Child Development, 62*, 284–300.

Larson, R. W., Richards, M. H., Moneta, G., Holmbeck, G., & Duckett, E. (1996). Changes in adolescents' daily interactions with their families from ages 10 to 18: Disengagement and transformation. *Developmental Psychology, 32*, 744-754.

Larson, R. W., & Verma, S. (1999). How children and adolescents spend time across the world: Work, play, and developmental opportunities. *Psychological Bulletin, 25*, 701–736.

Larzelere, R. E., Schneider, W. N., Larson, D. B., & Pike, P. L. (1996). The effects of discipline responses in delaying toddler misbehavior recurrences. *Child and Family Behavior Therapy, 18*, 35–7.

Latz, S., Wolf, A. W., & Lozoff, B. (1999). Sleep practices and problems in young children in Japan and the United States. *Archives of Pediatric and Adolescent Medicine, 153,* 339–346.

Laupa, M. (1995). Children's reasoning about authority in home and school contexts. *Social Development, 4,* 1–16.

Laursen, B., Coy, K., & Collins, W. A. (1998). Reconsidering changes in parent–child conflict across adolescence: A meta-analysis. *Child Development, 69,* 817–832.

Laursen, B., Hartup, W. W., & Koplas, A. L. (1996). Toward understanding peer conflict. *Merrill-Palmer Quarterly, 42,* 76–102.

Lavigne, J. V., Arend, R., Rosenbaum, D., Smith, A., Weissbluth, M., Binns, H. J., & Christoffel, K. K. (1999). Sleep and behavior problems among preschoolers. *Developmental and Behavioral Pediatrics, 20,* 164–169.

Law, C. M., Gordon, G. S., Shiell, A. W., Barker, D. J., & Hales, C. N. (1995). Thinness at birth and glucose tolerance in seven-year-old children. *Diabetic Medicine, 12,* 330–336.

Lazar, A., & Torney-Purta, J. (1991). The development of the subconcepts of death in young children: A short-term longitudinal study. *Child Development, 62,* 1321–1333.

Lazar, I., & Darlington, R. (1982). Lasting effects of early education: a report from the Consortium for Longitudinal Studies. *Monographs of the Society for Research in Child Development, 47*(2–3, Serial No. 195).

Lazarus, R. (1991). *Emotion and adaptation.* New York: Oxford University Press.

Leach, C. E. A., Blair, P. S., Fleming, P. J., Smith, I. J., Platt, M. W., & Berry, P. J. (1999). Epidemiology of SIDS and explained sudden infant deaths. *Pediatrics, 104,* e43.

Leaper, C. (1994). Exploring the correlates and consequences of gender segregation: Social relationships in childhood, adolescence, and adulthood. In C. Leaper (Ed.), *New directions for child development* (No. 65, pp. 67–86). San Francisco: Jossey-Bass.

Leaper, C., Anderson, K. J., & Sanders, P. (1998). Moderators of gender effects on parents' talk to their children: A meta-analysis. *Developmental Psychology, 34,* 3–27.

Leaper, C., Leve, L., Strasser, T., & Schwartz, R. (1995). Mother–child communication sequences: Play activity, child gender, and marital status effects. *Merrill-Palmer Quarterly, 41,* 307–327.

Leaper, C., Tenenbaum, H. R., & Shaffer, T. G. (1999). Communication patterns of African-American girls and boys from low-income, urban

backgrounds. *Child Development, 70,* 1489–1503.

Lederer, J. M. (2000). Reciprocal teaching of social studies in inclusive elementary classrooms. *Journal of Learning Disabilities, 33,* 91–106.

Lee, A. M. (1980). Child-rearing practices and motor performance of black and white children. *Research Quarterly for Exercise and Sport, 51,* 494–500.

Lee, C. L., & Bates, J. E. (1985). Mother–child interaction at age two years and perceived difficult temperament. *Child Development, 56,* 1314–1325.

Lee, K., Cameron, C., Xu, F., Fu, G., & Board, J. (1997). Chinese and Canadian children's evaluations of lying and truth telling: Similarities and differences in the context of pro- and antisocial behaviors. *Child Development, 68,* 924–934.

Lee, S. H., Ewert, D. P., Frederick, P. D., & Mascola, L. (1992). Resurgence of congenital rubella syndrome in the 1990s. *Journal of the American Medical Association, 267,* 2616–2620.

Leeman, L. W., Gibbs, J. C., & Fuller, D. (1993). Evaluation of a multicomponent group treatment program for juvenile delinquents. *Aggressive Behavior, 19,* 281–292.

Lehman, D. R., & Nisbett, R. E. (1990). A longitudinal study of the effects of undergraduate training on reasoning. *Developmental Psychology, 26,* 952–960.

Leichtman, M. D., & Ceci, S. J. (1995). The effect of stereotypes and suggestions on preschoolers' reports. *Developmental Psychology, 31.*

Lemanek, K. L., & Hood, C. (1999). Asthma. In R. T. Brown (Ed.), *Cognitive aspects of chronic illness in children* (pp. 78–104). New York: Guilford.

Lemery, K. S., Goldsmith, H. H., Klinnert, M. D., & Mrazek, D. A. (1999). Developmental models of infant and childhood temperament. *Developmental Psychology, 35,* 189–204.

Lempert, H. (1989). Animacy constraints on preschoolers' acquisition of syntax. *Child Development, 60,* 237–245.

Lengua, L. J., Wolchik, S., Sandler, I. N., & West, S. G. (2000). The additive and interactive effects of parenting and temperament in predicting problems of children of divorce. *Journal of Clinical Psychology, 29,* 232–244.

Lent, R. W., Hackett, G., & Brown, S. D. (1999). A social cognitive view of school-to-work transition. *Career Development Quarterly, 47,* 297–311.

Leonard, M. F., Rhymes, J. P., & Solnit, A. J. (1986). Failure to

thrive in infants: A family problem. *American Journal of Diseases of Children, 111,* 600–612.

LePore, P. C., & Warren, J. R. (1997). A comparison of single-sex and coeducational Catholic secondary schooling: Evidence from the National Educational Longitudinal Study of 1988. *American Educational Research Journal, 34,* 485–511.

Lerman, R. I. (1993). A national profile of young unwed fathers. In R. I. Lerman & T. J. Ooms (Eds.), *Young unwed fathers* (pp. 27–51). Philadelphia: Temple University Press.

Lerner, J. V., & Abrams, A. (1994). Developmental correlates of maternal employment influences on children. In C. B. Fisher & R. M. Lerner (Eds.), *Applied developmental psychology* (pp. 174–206). New York: McGraw-Hill.

Lester, B. M. (1985). Introduction: There's more to crying than meets the ear. In B. M. Lester & C. F. Z. Boukydis (Eds.), *Infant crying* (pp. 1–27). New York: Plenum.

Lester, B. M., Boukydis, C. F. Z., & Zachariah, C. F. (1992). No language but a cry. In H. Papousek (Ed.), *Nonverbal vocal communication: Comparative and developmental approaches* (pp.145–173). New York: Cambridge University Press.

Lester, B. M., & Dreher, M. (1989). Effects of marijuana use during pregnancy on newborn cry. *Child Development, 60,* 765–771.

Lester, B. M., Kotelchuck, M., Spelke, E., Sellers, M. J., & Klein, R. E. (1974). Separation protest in Guatemalan infants: Cross-cultural and cognitive findings. *Developmental Psychology, 10,* 79–85.

Leung, K., Lau, S., & Lam, W.-L. (1998). Parenting styles and academic achievement: A cross-cultural study. *Merrill-Palmer Quarterly, 44,* 157–172.

LeVay, S. (1993). *The sexual brain.* Cambridge, MA: MIT Press.

Levesque, R. J. R. (1996). International children's rights: Can they make a difference in American family policy? *American Psychologist, 51,* 1251–1256.

Levine, L. E. (1983). Mine: Self-definition in 2-year-old boys. *Developmental Psychology, 19,* 544–549.

Levine, L. J. (1995). Young children's understanding of the causes of anger and sadness. *Child Development, 66,* 697–709.

LeVine, R. A., Dixon, S., LeVine, S., Richman, A., Leiderman, P. H., Keefer, C. H., & Brazelton, T. B. (1994). *Child care and culture:*

Lessons from Africa. New York: Cambridge University Press.

Levine, S. C., Huttenlocher, J., Taylor, A., & Langrock, A. (1999). Early sex differences in spatial skill. *Developmental Psychology, 35,* 940–949.

Levitsky, D. A., & Strupp, B. J. (1995). Malnutrition and the brain: Changing concepts, changing concerns. *Journal of Nutrition, 125,* 2245S–2254S.

Levy, G. D., Taylor, M. G., & Gelman, S. A. (1995). Traditional and evaluative aspects of flexibility in gender roles, social conventions, moral rules, and physical laws. *Child Development, 66,* 515–531.

Levy-Shiff, R. (1994). Individual and contextual correlates of marital change across the transition to parenthood. *Developmental Psychology, 30,* 591–601.

Levy-Shiff, R., & Israelashvili, R. (1988). Antecedents of fathering: Some further exploration. *Developmental Psychology, 24,* 434–440.

Lewis, C. C. (1995). *Educating hearts and minds.* New York: Cambridge University Press.

Lewis, C., Freeman, N. H., Kyriadidou, C., Maridakikassotaki, K., & Berridge, D. M. (1996). Social influences on false belief access—specific sibling influences or general apprenticeship? *Child Development, 67,* 2930–2947.

Lewis, D. P., Van Dyke, D. C., Stumbo, P. J., & Berg, M. J. (1998). Drug and environmental factors associated with adverse pregnancy outcomes. Part III: Folic acid: Pharmacology, therapeutic recommendations, and economics. *Annals of Pharmacotherapy, 32,* 1087–1095.

Lewis, M. (1992). *Shame: The exposed self.* New York: Free Press.

Lewis, M. (1994). Myself and me. In S. T. Parker, R. W. Mitchell, & M. L. Boccia (Eds.), *Self-awareness in animals and humans: Developmental perspectives* (pp. 20–34). New York: Cambridge University Press.

Lewis, M. (1995a). Embarrassment: The emotion of self-exposure and evaluation. In J. P. Tangney & K. W. Fischer (Eds.), *Self-conscious emotions* (pp. 198–218). New York: Guilford Press.

Lewis, M. (1997). *Altering fate: Why the past does not predict the future.* New York: Guilford.

Lewis, M. (1998). Emotional competence and development. In D. Pushkar, W. M. Bukowski, A. E. Schwartzman, E. M. Stack, & D. R. White (Eds.), *Improving competence across the lifespan* (pp. 27–36). New York: Plenum.

Lewis, M., Alessandri, S. M., & Sullivan, M. W. (1992). Differences in shame and pride as a function of children's gender and task difficulty. *Child Development, 63,* 630–638.

Lewis, M., & Brooks-Gunn, J. (1979). *Social cognition and the acquisition of self.* New York: Plenum.

Lewis, M., Ramsay, D. S., & Kawakami, K. (1993). Differences between Japanese infants and Caucasian American infants in behavioral and cortisol response to inoculation. *Child Development, 64,* 1722–1731.

Lewis, M., Sullivan, M. W., Stanger, C., & Weiss, M. (1989). Self development and self-conscious emotions. *Child Development, 60,* 146–156.

Lewis, M., Sullivan, M. W., & Vasen, A. (1987). Making faces: Age and emotion differences in the posing of emotional expressions. *Developmental Psychology, 23,* 690–697.

Lewis, M. D. (1995b). Cognition-emotion feedback and the self-organization of developmental paths. *Human Development, 38,* 71–102.

Lewis, T., Stone, J., III, Shipley, W., & Madzar, S. (1998). The transition from school to work: An examination of the literature. *Youth & Society, 29,* 259–292.

Liaw, F., & Brooks-Gunn, J. (1993). Patterns of low-birthweight children's cognitive development. *Developmental Psychology, 29,* 1024–1035.

Liben, L. S. (1999). Developing an understanding of external spatial representations. In I. E. Sigel (Ed.), *Development of mental representation* (pp. 297–321). Mahwah, NJ: Erlbaum.

Liben, L. S., & Signorella, M. L. (1993). Gender-schematic processing in children: The role of initial interpretations of stimuli. *Developmental Psychology, 29,* 141–149.

Lidz, C. S. (1991). *Practitioner's guide to dynamic assessment.* New York: Guilford.

Lidz, C. S. (1997). Dynamic Assessment: Psychoeducational assessment with cultural sensitivity. *Journal of Social Distress and the Homeless, 6,* 95–111.

Lifschitz, M., Berman, D., Galili, A., & Gilad, D. (1977). Bereaved children: The effects of mother's perception and social system organization on their short range adjustment. *Journal of Child Psychiatry, 16,* 272–284.

Light, P., & Perret-Clermont, A.-N. (1989). Social context effects in learning and testing. In A. Gellatly, D. Rogers, & J. Sloboda (Eds.), *Cognition and social worlds* (pp. 99–112). Oxford, England: Clarendon Press.

Lillard, A. S. (1998). Playing with a theory of mind. In O. N. Saracho & B. Spodek (Eds.), *Multiple perspectives on play in early childhood education* (pp. 11–33). Albany: State University of New York Press.

Lillard, A. S. (2001). Pretending, understanding pretense, and understanding minds. In S. Reifel (Ed.), *Play and culture studies* (Vol. 3). Norwood, NJ: Ablex.

Lin, C. C., Hsiao, C. K., & Chen, W. J. (1999). Development of sustained attention assessed using the continuous performance test among children 6–15 years. *Journal of Abnormal Child Psychology, 27,* 403–412.

Lindgren, M. L., Byers, R. H., Jr., Thomas, P., Davis, S. F., Caldwell, B. R., & Rogers, M. (1999). Trends in perinatal transmission of HIV/AIDS in the United States. *Journal of the American Medical Association, 282,* 531–538.

Lindsay-Hartz, J., de Rivera, J., & Mascolo, M. F. (1995). Differentiating guilt and shame and their effects on motivation. In J. P. Tangney & K. W. Fischer (Eds.), *Self-conscious emotions* (pp. 274–300). New York: Guilford.

Link, S. C., & Ancoli-Isreal, S. (1995). Sleep and the teenager. *Sleep Research, 24a,* 184.

Linn, M. C., & Hyde, J. S. (1989). Gender, mathematics, and science. *Educational Researcher, 18,* 17–27.

Linn, M. C., & Petersen, A. C. (1985). Emergence and characterization of sex differences in spatial ability: A meta-analysis. *Child Development, 56,* 1479–1498.

Lissens, W., & Sermon, K. (1997). Preimplantation genetic diagnosis—current status and new developments. *Human Reproduction, 12,* 1756–1761.

Litovsky, R. Y., & Ashmead, D. H. (1997). Development of binaural and spatial hearing in infants and children. In R. H. Gilkey & T. R. Anderson (Eds.), *Binaural and spatial hearing in real and virtual environments* (pp. 571–592). Mahwah, NJ: Erlbaum.

Livesley, W. J., & Bromley, D. B. (1973). *Person perception in childhood and adolescence.* London: Wiley.

Livingstone, B. E., Coward, W. A., Prentice, A. M., Davies, P., Strain, J. J., & McKenna, G. (1992). Daily energy expenditure in free-living children: Comparison of heart-rate monitoring with the double labeled water method. *American Journal of Clinical Nutrition, 56,* 343–352.

Livson, N., & Peskin, H. (1980). Perspectives on adolescence from

longitudinal research. In J. Adelson (Ed.), *Handbook of adolescent psychology* (pp. 47–98). New York: Wiley.

Lloyd, L. (1999). Multi-age classes and high ability students. *Review of Educational Research, 69,* 187–212.

Lochman, J. E., Coie, J. D., Underwood, M. K., & Terry, R. (1993). Effectiveness of a social relations intervention program for aggressive and nonaggressive, rejected children. *Journal of Consulting and Clinical Psychology, 61,* 1053–1058.

Locke, J. (1892). Some thoughts concerning education. In R. H. Quick (Ed.), *Locke on education* (pp. 1–236). Cambridge, England: Cambridge University Press. (Original work published 1690)

Lockhart, R. S., & Craik, F. I. M. (1990). Levels of processing: A retrospective commentary on a framework for memory research. *Canadian Journal of Psychology, 44,* 87–112.

Loeber, R., & Stouthamer-Loeber, M. (1998). Development of juvenile aggression and violence: Some common misconceptions and controversies. *American Psychologist, 53,* 242–259.

Loeber, R. L., Farrington, D. P., Stouthamer-Loeber, M., Moffitt, T. E., & Caspi, A. (1999). The development of male offending: Key findings from the first decade of the Pittsburgh Youth Study. *Studies on Crime & Crime Prevention, 8,* 245–263.

Loehlin, J. C. (1992). *Genes and environment in personality development.* Newbury Park, CA: Sage.

Loehlin, J. C. (2000). Group differences in intelligence. In R. J. Sternberg (Ed.), *Handbook of intelligence* (pp. 176–193). New York: Cambridge University Press.

Loehlin, J. C., Horn, J. M., & Willerman, L. (1997). Heredity, environment, and IQ in the Texas Adoption Project. In R. J. Sternberg & E. L. Grigorenko (Eds.), *Intelligence, heredity, and environment* (pp. 105–125). New York: Cambridge University Press.

Loehlin, J. C., Willerman, L., & Horn, J. M. (1988). Human behavior genetics. *Annual Review of Psychology, 38,* 101–133.

Loganovskaja, T. K., & Loganovsky, K. N. (1999). EEG, cognitive and psychopathological abnormalities in children irradiated in utero. *International Journal of Psychophysiology, 34,* 213–224.

Longstaffe, S., Moffatt, M. E., & Whalen, J. C. (2000). Behavioral and self-concept changes after six months of enuresis treatment: A randomized, controlled trial. *Pediatrics, 105,* 935–940.

Lord, R. H., & Kozar, B. (1996). Overuse injuries in young athletes. In F. L. Smoll & R. E. Smith (Eds.), *Children and youth in sport: A biopsychological perspective* (pp. 281–294). Dubuque, IA: Brown & Benchmark.

Lorenz, K. Z. (1943). Die angeborenen Formen möglicher Erfahrung. *Zeitschrift für Tierpsychologie, 5,* 235–409.

Lorenz, K. Z. (1952). *King Solomon's ring.* New York: Crowell.

Losey, K. M. (1995). Mexican-American students and classroom interaction: An overview and critique. *Review of Educational Research, 65,* 283–318.

Louis, J., Cannard, C., Bastuji, H., & Challamel, M.-J. (1997). Sleep ontogenesis revisited: A longitudinal 24-hour home polygraphic study on 15 normal infants during the first two years of life. *Sleep, 20,* 323–333.

Lozoff, B., Askew, G. L., & Wolf, A. W. (1996). Cosleeping and early childhood sleep problems: Effects of ethnicity and socioeconomic status. *Developmental and Behavioral Pediatrics, 17,* 9–15.

Lozoff, B., Klein, N. K., Nelson, E. C., McClish, D. K., Manuel, M., & Chacon, M. E. (1998). Behavior of infants with iron-deficiency anemia. *Child Development, 69,* 24–36.

Lozoff, B., Wolf, A., Latz, S., & Paludetto, R. (1995, March). *Cosleeping in Japan, Italy, and the U.S.: Autonomy versus interpersonal relatedness.* Paper presented at the biennial meeting of the Society for Research in Child Development, Indianapolis.

Lubinski, D., & Benbow, C. P. (1994). The study of mathematically precocious youth: The first three decades of a planned 50-year study of intellectual talent. In R. F. Subotnik & K. D. Arnold (Eds.), *Beyond Terman: Contemporary longitudinal studies of giftedness and talent* (pp. 255–281). Norwood, NJ: Ablex.

Ludemann, P. M. (1991). Generalized discrimination of positive facial expressions by seven- and ten-month-old infants. *Child Development, 62,* 55–67.

Luker, K. (1996). *Dubious conceptions: The politics of teenage pregnancy.* Cambridge, MA: Harvard University Press.

Lunenburg, F. C. (2000). America's hope: Making schools work for all children. *Journal of Instructional Psychology, 27,* 39–46.

Luria, A. R. (1976). *Cognitive development: Its cultural and social foundations.* Cambridge, MA: Harvard University Press.

Luster, T., & Dubow, E. (1992). Home environment and maternal intelligence as predictors of verbal intelligence: A comparison of preschool and school-age children. *Merrill-Palmer Quarterly, 38,* 151–175.

Luthar, S. S., & Cushing, G. (1997). Substance use and personal adjustment among disadvantaged teenagers: A six-month prospective study. *Journal of Youth and Adolescence, 26,* 353–372.

Luthar, S. S., Cushing, T. J., & McMahon, T. J. (1997). Interdisciplinary interface: Developmental principles brought to substance abuse research. In S. S. Luthar, J. A. Burack, D. Cicchetti, & Weisz, J. R. (1997). *Developmental psychopathology* (pp. 437–456). Cambridge: Cambridge University Press.

Lutz, D. J., & Sternberg, R. J. (1999). Cognitive development. In M. H. Bornstein & M. E. Lamb (Eds.), *Developmental psychology: An advanced textbook* (4th ed., pp. 275–311). Mahwah, NJ: Erlbaum.

Lutz, S. E., & Ruble, D. N. (1995). Children and gender prejudice: Context, motivation, and the development of gender conception. In R. Vasta (Ed.), *Annals of child development* (Vol. 10, pp. 131–166). Greenwich, CT: JAI Press.

Lyon, T. D., & Flavell, J. H. (1994). Young children's understanding of "remember" and "forget." *Child Development, 65,* 1357–1371.

Lyons-Ruth, K. (1996). Attachment relationships among children with aggressive behavior problems: The role of disorganized early attachment patterns. *Journal of Consulting and Clinical Psychology, 64,* 64–73.

Lyons-Ruth, K., & Block, D. (1996). The disturbed caregiving system: Relations among childhood trauma, maternal caregiving, and infant affect and attachment. *Infant Mental Health Journal, 17,* 257–275.

Lyons-Ruth, K., Bronfman, E., & Parsons, E. (1999). Maternal frightened, frightening, or atypical behavior and disorganized infant attachment patterns. *Monographs of the Society for Research in Child Development, 64*(3, Serial No. 258), pp. 67–96.

Lyons-Ruth, K., Easterbrooks, A., & Cibelli, C. (1997). Infant attachment strategies, infant mental lag, and maternal depressive symptoms: Predictors of internalizing and externalizing problems at age 7. *Developmental Psychology, 33,* 681–692.

Lytton, H., & Romney, D. M. (1991). Parents' sex-related differential socialization of boys and girls: A

meta-analysis. *Psychological Bulletin, 109,* 267–296.

Maccoby, E. E. (1984). Middle childhood in the context of the family. In W. A. Collins (Ed.), *Development during middle childhood* (pp. 184–239). Washington, DC: National Academy Press.

Maccoby, E. E. (1990). Gender and relationships. *American Psychologist, 45,* 513–520.

Maccoby, E. E. (1998). *The two sexes: Growing up apart, coming together.* Cambridge, MA: Belknap/Harvard University Press.

Maccoby, E. E., & Jacklin, C. N. (1987). Gender segregation in childhood. In E. H. Reese (Ed.), *Advances in child development and behavior* (Vol. 20, pp. 239–287). New York: Academic Press.

Maccoby, E. E., & Martin, J. A. (1983). Socialization in the context of the family: Parent–child interaction. In E. M. Hetherington (Ed.), *Handbook of child psychology: Vol. 4. Socialization, personality, and social development* (4th ed., pp. 1–101). New York: Wiley.

MacDorman, M. F., & Atkinson, J. O. (1999). Infant mortality statistics from the 1997 period linked birth/infant death data set. *National Vital Statistics Report, 47*(23), 1–23.

Macfarlane, J. W. (1971). From infancy to adulthood. In M. C. Jones, N. Bayley, J. W. Macfarlane, & M. P. Honzik (Eds.), *The course of human development* (pp. 406–410). Waltham, MA: Xerox College Publishing.

Mackey, M. C. (1995). Women's evaluation of their childbirth performance. *Maternal–Child Nursing Journal, 23,* 57–72.

MacKinnon, C. E. (1989). An observational investigation of sibling interactions in married and divorced families. *Developmental Psychology, 25,* 36–44.

MacKinnon-Lewis, C., Starnes, R., Volling, B., & Johnson, S. (1997). Perceptions of parenting as predictors of boys' sibling and peer relations. *Developmental Psychology, 33,* 1024–1031.

Macknin, M. L., Piedmonte, M., Jacobs, J., & Skibinski, C. (2000). Symptoms associated with infant teething: A prospective study. *Pediatrics, 105,* 747–752.

Madan-Swain, A., Fredrick, L. D., & Wallander, J. L. (1999). Returning to school after a serious illness or injury. In R. T. Brown (Ed.), *Cognitive aspects of chronic illness in children* (pp. 312–332). New York: Guilford.

Madole, K. L., & Oakes, L. M. (1999). Making sense of infant categorization: Stable processes and chang-

ing representations. *Developmental Review, 19,* 263–296.

Madom, S., Jussim, L., & Eccles, J. (1997). In search of the powerful self-fulfilling prophecy. *Journal of Personality and Social Psychology, 72,* 791–809.

Mahon, M. M., Goldberg, E. Z., & Washington, S. K. (1999). Concept of death in a sample of Israeli kibbutz children. *Death Studies, 23,* 43–59.

Mahoney, J. L., & Cairns, R. B. (1997). Do extracurricular activities protect against early school dropout? *Developmental Psychology, 33,* 241–253.

Mahoney, J. L., & Stattin, H. (2000). Leisure activities and antisocial behavior: The role of structure and social context. *Journal of Adolescence, 23,* 113–127.

Main, M., & Cassidy, J. (1988). Categories of response to reunion with the parent at age 6: Predictable from infant attachment classifications and stable over a 1-month period. *Developmental Psychology, 24,* 415–426.

Main, M., & Solomon, J. (1990). Procedures for identifying infants as disorganized/disoriented during the Ainsworth Strange Situation. In M. Greenberg, D. Cicchetti, & M. Cummings (Eds.), *Attachment in the preschool years: Theory, research, and intervention* (pp. 121–160). Chicago: University of Chicago Press.

Makin, J. E., Fried, P. A., & Watkinson, B. (1991). A comparison of active and passive smoking during pregnancy: Long-term effects. *Neurotoxicology and Teratology, 13,* 5–12.

Malatesta, C. Z., Grigoryev, P., Lamb, C., Albin, M., & Culver, C. (1986). Emotion socialization and expressive development in preterm and full-term infants. *Child Development, 57,* 316–330.

Malina, R. M. (1990). Physical growth and performance during the transitional years (9–16). In R. Montemayor, G. R. Adams, & T. P. Gullotta (Eds.), *From childhood to adolescence: A transitional period?* (pp. 41–62). Newbury Park, CA: Sage.

Malina, R. M., & Beunen, G. (1996). Matching of opponents in youth sports. In O. Bar-Or (Ed.), *The child and adolescent athlete* (pp. 202–213). Oxford: Blackwell.

Malina, R. M., & Bouchard, C. (1991). *Growth, maturation, and physical activity.* Champaign, IL: Human Kinetics.

Malina, R. M., & Stanitski, C.L. (1989). Common injuries in preadolescent and adolescent athletes. *Sports Medicine, I,* 32–41.

Malloy, M. H., & Hoffman, H. J. (1995). Prematurity, sudden infant death syndrome, and age of death. *Pediatrics, 96,* 464–471.

Maloney, M., & Kranz, R. (1991). *Straight talk about eating disorders.* New York: Facts on File.

Maloni, J. A., Cheng, C. Y., Liebl, C. P., & Maier, J. S. (1996). Transforming prenatal care: Reflections on the past and present with implications for the future. *Journal of Obstetrics, Gynecology, and Neonatal Nursing, 25,* 17–23.

Mandler, J. M. (1998). Representation. In D. Kuhn & R. S. Siegler (Eds.), *Handbook of child psychology: Vol. 1. Theoretical models of human development* (5th ed., pp. 255–308). New York: Wiley.

Mandler, J. M. (1999). Seeing is not the same as thinking: Commentary on "Making Sense of Infant Categorization." *Developmental Review, 19,* 297–306.

Mandler, J. M., & McDonough, L. (1993). Concept formation in infancy. *Cognitive Development, 8,* 291–318.

Mandler, J. M., & McDonough, L. (1996). Drinking and driving don't mix: Inductive generalization in infancy. *Cognition, 59,* 307–335.

Mandler, J. M., & McDonough, L. (1998). On developing a knowledge base in infancy. *Developmental Psychology, 34,* 1274–1288.

Mange, E. J., & Mange, A. P. (1998). *Basic human genetics* (2nd ed.). Sunderland, MA: Sinauer Associates.

Mangelsdorf, S., Gunnar, M., Kestenbaum, R., Lang, S., & Andreas, D. (1990). Infant proneness-to-distress temperament, maternal personality, and mother–infant attachment: Associations and goodness of fit. *Child Development, 61,* 820–831.

Maratsos, M. (1998). The acquisition of grammar. In D. Kuhn & R. S. Siegler (Eds.), *Handbook of child psychology: Vol. 1. Theoretical models of human development* (5th ed., pp. 255–308). New York: Wiley.

March of Dimes. (2000). *International comparisons of infant mortality rates.* White Plains, NY: March of Dimes Birth Defects Foundation.

Marcia, J. E. (1966). Development and validation of ego identity status. *Journal of Personality and Social Psychology, 3,* 551–558.

Marcia, J. E. (1980). Identity in adolescence. In J. Adelson (Ed.), *Handbook of adolescent psychology* (pp. 159–187). New York: Wiley.

Marcia, J. E. (1988). Common processes underlying ego identity, cognitive/moral development, and individuation. In D. K. Lapsley &

F. P. Clark (Eds.), *Self, ego, and identity* (pp. 211–225). New York: Springer-Verlag.

Marcia, J. E., Waterman, A. S., Matteson, D., Archer, S. L., & Orlofsky, J. L. (1993). *Ego identity: A handbook for psychosocial research.* New York: Springer-Verlag.

Marcon, R. A. (1999a). Differential impact of preschool models on development and early learning of inner-city children: A three-cohort study. *Developmental Psychology, 35,* 358–375.

Marcon, R. A. (1999b). Positive relationships between parent–school involvement and public school inner-city preschoolers' development and academic performance. *School Psychology Review, 28,* 395–412.

Marcotte, D., Alain, M., & Gosselin, M.-J. (1999). Gender differences in adolescent depression: Gender-typed characteristics or problem-solving skills deficits? *Sex Roles, 41,* 31–48.

Marcus, G. F. (1993). Negative evidence in language acquisition. *Cognition, 46,* 53–85.

Marcus, G. F. (1995). Children's over-regularization of English plurals: A quantitative analysis. *Journal of Child Language, 22,* 447–459.

Marcus, G. F., Pinker, S., Ullman, M., Hollander, M., Rosen, T. J., & Xu, F. (1992). Overregularization in language acquisition. *Monographs of the Society for Research in Child Development, 57*(4, Serial No. 228).

Margolin, G. (1998). Effects of domestic violence on children. In P. K. Trickett & C. J. Schellenbach (Eds.), *Violence against children in the family and community* (pp. 57–102). Washington, DC: American Psychological Association.

Margolin, G., & Gordis, E. B. (2000). The effects of family and community violence on children. *Annual Review of Psychology, 51,* 445–479.

Marini, Z., & Case, R. (1994). The development of abstract reasoning about the physical and social world. *Child Development, 65,* 147–159.

Markman, E. M. (1989). *Categorization and naming in children.* Cambridge, MA: MIT Press.

Markman, E. M. (1992). Constraints on word learning: Speculations about their nature, origins, and domain specificity. In M. R. Gunnar & M. P. Maratsos (Eds.), *Minnesota Symposia on Child Psychology* (Vol. 25, pp. 59–101). Hillsdale, NJ: Erlbaum.

Markovits, H., & Bouffard-Bouchard, T. (1992). The belief-bias effect in reasoning: The development and activation of competence. *British Journal of Developmental Psychology, 10,* 269–284.

Markovits, H., Dumas, C., & Malfait, N. (1995). Understanding transitivity of a spatial relationship: A developmental analysis. *Journal of Experimental Child Psychology, 59,* 124–141.

Markovits, H., Fleury, M. L., Quinn, S., & Venet, M. (1998). The development of conditional reasoning and the structure of semantic memory. *Child Development, 69,* 742–755.

Markovits, H., Schleifer, M., & Fortier, L. (1989). Development of elementary deductive reasoning in young children. *Developmental Psychology, 25,* 787–793.

Markovits, H., & Vachon, R. (1989). Reasoning with contrary-to-fact propositions. *Journal of Experimental Child Psychology, 47,* 398–412.

Markovits, H., & Vachon, R. (1990). Conditional reasoning, representation, and level of abstraction. *Developmental Psychology, 26,* 942–951.

Markstrom-Adams, C., & Adams, G. R. (1995). Gender, ethnic group, and grade differences in psychosocial functioning during middle adolescence? *Journal of Youth and Adolescence, 24,* 397–414.

Markus, H. R., & Kitayama, S. (1991). Culture and the self: Implications for cognition, emotion, and motivation. *Psychological Review, 98,* 224–253.

Markus, H. R., Mullally, P. R., & Kitayama, S. (1997). Selfways: Diversity in modes of cultural participation. In U. Neisser & D. Jopling (Eds.), *The conceptual self in context* (pp. 13–61). New York: Cambridge University Press.

Marlier, L., & Schaal, B. (1997). La perception de la familiarité olfactive chez le nouveau-né: Influence différentielle du mode d'alimentation? [The perception of olfactory familiarity in the neonate: Differential influence of the mode of feeding?] *Enfance, 1,* 47–61.

Marlier, L., Schaal, B., & Soussignan, R. (1998). Neonatal responsiveness to the odor of amniotic and lacteal fluids: A test of perinatal chemosensory continuity. *Child Development, 69,* 611–623.

Marsh, H. W. (1990). The structure of academic self-concept: The Marsh/Shavelson model. *Journal of Educational Psychology, 82,* 623–636.

Marsh, H. W., Craven, R., & Debus, R. (1998). Structure, stability, and development of young children's self-concepts: A multicohort–multioccasion study. *Child Development, 69,* 1030–1053.

Marsh, H. W., Smith, I. D., & Barnes, J. (1985). Multidimensional self-concepts: Relations with sex and academic achievement. *Journal of Educational Psychology, 77,* 581–596.

Marsh, J. S., & Daigneault, J. P. (1999). The young athlete. *Current Opinion in Pediatrics, 11,* 84–88.

Marshall-Baker, A., Lickliter, R., & Cooper, R. P. (1998). Prolonged exposure to a visual pattern may promote behavioral organization in preterm infants. *Journal of Perinatal and Neonatal Nursing, 12,* 50–62.

Martin, C. L. (1989). Children's use of gender-related information in making social judgments. *Developmental Psychology, 25,* 80–88.

Martin, C. L. (1993). New directions for investigating children's gender knowledge. *Developmental Review, 13,* 184–204.

Martin, C. L., Eisenbud, L., & Rose, H. (1995). Children's gender-based reasoning about toys. *Child Development, 66,* 1453–1471.

Martin, C. L., Fabes, R. A., Evans, S. M., & Wyman, H. (1999). Social cognition on the playground: Children's beliefs about playing with girls versus boys and their relations to sex segregated play. *Journal of Social and Personal Relationships, 16,* 751–771.

Martin, C. L., & Halverson, C. F. (1981). A schematic processing model of sex typing and stereotyping in children. *Child Development, 52,* 1119–1134.

Martin, C. L., & Halverson, C. F. (1987). The role of cognition in sex role acquisition. In D. B. Carter (Ed.), *Current conceptions of sex roles and sex typing: Theory and research* (pp. 123–137). New York: Praeger.

Martin, J. A. (1981). A longitudinal study of the consequences of early mother–infant interaction: A microanalytic approach. *Monographs of the Society for Research in Child Development, 46*(3, Serial No. 190).

Martin, J. C., Barr, H. M., Martin, D. C., & Streissguth, A. P. (1996). Neonatal exposure to cocaine. *Neurotoxicology and Teratology, 18,* 617–625.

Martin, R. M. (1975). Effects of familiar and complex stimuli on infant attention. *Developmental Psychology, 11,* 178–185.

Martlew, M., & Connolly, K. J. (1996). Human figure drawings by schooled and unschooled children in Papua New Guinea. *Child Development, 67,* 2743–2762.

Martorell, R. (1980). Interrelationships between diet, infectious disease, and nutritional status. In L. S. Greene & F. E. Johnston (Eds.), *Social and biological predictors of nutritional status, physical growth, and neurological development* (pp. 81–106). New York: Academic Press.

Martyn, C. N., Barker, D. J. P., & Osmond, C. (1996). Mothers' pelvic size, fetal growth, and death from stroke and coronary heart disease in men in the UK. *Lancet, 348,* 1264–1268.

Marzolf, D. P., & DeLoache, J. S. (1994). Transfer in young children's understanding of spatial representations. *Child Development, 65,* 1–15.

Masataka, N. (1996). Perception of motherese in a signed language by 6-month-old deaf infants. *Developmental Psychology, 32,* 874–879.

Mascolo, M. F., & Fischer, K. W. (1995). Developmental transformations in appraisals for pride, shame, and guilt. In J. P. Tangney & K. W. Fischer (Eds.), *Self-conscious emotions* (pp. 114-139). New York: Guilford.

Mason, C. A., Cauce, A. M., Conzales, N., & Hiraga, Y. (1996). Neither too sweet nor too sour: Problem peers, maternal control, and problem behavior in African American adolescents. *Child Development, 67,* 2115–2130.

Mason, M. G., & Gibbs, J. C. (1993a). Role-taking opportunities and the transition to advanced moral judgment. *Moral Education Forum, 18,* 1–12.

Mason, M. G., & Gibbs, J. C. (1993b). Social perspective taking and moral judgment among college students. *Journal of Adolescent Research, 8,* 109–123.

Masten, A. S., & Coatsworth, J. D. (1998). The development of competence in favorable and unfavorable environments: Lessons from research on successful children. *American Psychologist, 53,* 205–220.

Masten, A. S., Hubbard, J. J., Gest, S. D., Tellegen, A., Garmezy, N., & Ramirez, M. (1999). Adaptation in the context of adversity: Pathways to resilience and maladaptation from childhood to late adolescence. *Development and Psychopathology, 11,* 143–169.

Mastropieri, D., & Turkewitz, G. (1999). Prenatal experience and neonatal responsiveness to vocal expressions of emotion. *Developmental Psychobiology, 35,* 204–214.

Masur, E. F. (1995). Infants' early verbal imitation and their later lexical development. *Merrill-Palmer Quarterly, 41,* 286–306.

Masur, E. F., McIntyre, C. W., & Flavell, J. H. (1973). Developmental changes in apportionment of study time among items in a multi-trial free recall task. *Journal of Experimental Child Psychology, 15,* 237–246.

Masur, E. F., & Rodemaker, J. E. (1999). Mothers' and infants' spontaneous vocal, verbal, and action imitation during the second year. *Merrill-Palmer Quarterly, 45,* 392–412.

Matas, L., Arend, R., & Sroufe, L. A. (1978). Continuity of adaptation in the second year: The relationship between quality of attachment and later competence. *Child Development, 49,* 547–556.

Matheny, A. P., Jr. (1991). Children's unintentional injuries and gender: Differentiation and psychosocial aspects. *Children's Environment Quarterly, 8,* 51–61.

Mathews, F., Yudkin, P., & Neil, A. (1999). Influence of maternal nutrition on outcome of pregnancy: Prospective cohort study. *British Medical Journal, 319,* 339–343.

Matsuba, M. K., & Walker, L. J. (1998). Moral reasoning in the context of ego functioning. *Merrill-Palmer Quarterly, 44,* 464–483.

Mattson, S. N., Riley, E. P., Delis, D. C., & Jones, K. L. (1998). Neuropsychological comparison of alcohol-exposed children with or without physical features of fetal alcohol syndrome. *Neuropsychology, 12,* 146–153.

Matute-Bianchi, M. E. (1986). Ethnic identities and patterns of school success and failure among Mexican-descent and Japanese-American students in a California high school: An ethnographic analysis. *American Journal of Education, 95,* 233–255.

Mayberry, R. I. (1994). The importance of childhood to language acquisition: Evidence from American Sign Language. In J. C. Goodman & H. C. Nusbaum (Eds.), *The development of speech perception: The transition from speech sounds to spoken words* (pp. 57–90). Cambridge, MA: MIT Press.

Mayes, L. C. (1999). Reconsidering the concept of vulnerability in children using the model of prenatal cocaine exposure. In T. B. Cohen & E. M. Hossein (Eds.), *The vulnerable child* (Vol. 3, pp. 35–54). Madison, CT: International Universities Press.

Mayes, L. C., & Bornstein, M. H. (1997). Attention regulation in infants born at risk: Prematurity and prenatal cocaine exposure. In J. A. Burack & J. T. Enns (Eds.), *Attention, development, and psychopathology* (pp. 97–122). New York: Guilford.

Mayes, L. C., Bornstein, M. H., Chawarska, K., & Haynes, O. M. (1996). Impaired regulation of arousal in 3-month-old infants exposed prenatally to cocaine and other drugs. *Development & Psychopathology, 8,* 29–42.

Mayes, L. C., & Zigler, E. (1992). An observational study of the affective concomitants of mastery in infants. *Journal of Child Psychology and Psychiatry, 33,* 659–667.

Mays, V. M., Bullock, M., Rosenzweig, M. R., & Wessells, M. (1998). Ethnic conflict: Global challenges and psychological conflict. *American Psychologist, 53,* 737–742.

Mazur, E. (1993). Developmental differences in children's understanding of marriage, divorce, and remarriage. *Journal of Applied Developmental Psychology, 14,* 191–212.

Mazzocco, M. M. (2000). Advances in research on the fragile X syndrome. *Mental Retardation and Developmental Disabilities Research Reviews, 6,* 96–106.

McAdoo, H. P. (1993). Ethnic families: Strengths that are found in diversity. In H. P. McAdoo (Ed.), *Family ethnicity* (pp. 3–14). Newbury Park, CA: Sage.

McCabe, A. (1997). Developmental and cross-cultural aspects of children's narration. In M. Bamberg (Ed.), *Narrative development: Six approaches* (pp. 137–174). Mahwah, NJ; Erlbaum.

McCabe, A. E. (1998). *Chameleon readers: Teaching children to appreciate all kinds of good stories.* New York: McGraw-Hill.

McCabe, A. E., & Peterson, C. (1988). A comparison of adults' versus children's spontaneous use of *because* and *so. Journal of Genetic Psychology, 149,* 257–268.

McCabe, A. E., & Peterson, C. (1991). Getting the story: A longitudinal study of parental styles in eliciting narratives and developing narrative skill. In A. McCabe & C. Peterson (Eds.), *Developing narrative structure* (pp. 217–253). Hillsdale, NJ: Erlbaum.

McCall, R. B. (1993). Developmental functions for general mental performance. In D. K. Detterman (Ed.), *Current topics in human intelligence* (Vol. 3, pp. 3–29). Norwood, NJ: Ablex.

McCall, R. B., & Carriger, M. S. (1993). A meta-analysis of infant habituation and recognition memory performance as predictors of later IQ. *Child Development, 64,* 57–79.

McCarton, C. (1998). Behavioral outcomes in low birth weight infants. *Pediatrics, 102,* 1293–1297.

McCarton, C. M., Brooks-Gunn, J., Wallace, I. F., Bauer, C. R., Bennett, F. C., Bernbaum, J. C., Broyles, R. S., Casey, P. H., McCormick, M. C., Scott, D. T., Tyson, J., Tonascia, J., & Meinert, C. L. (1997). Results at age 8 years of early intervention for low-birth-weight premature infants: The infant health and development program. *Journal of the American Medical Association, 277,* 126–132.

McCarty, M. E., & Ashmead, D. H. (1999). Visual control of reaching and grasping in infants. *Developmental Psychology, 35,* 620–631.

McClain, K., Cobb, P., & Bowers, J. (1998). A contextual investigation of three-digit addition and subtraction. In National Council of Teachers of Mathematics (Ed.), *Yearbook of the National Council of Teachers of Mathematics* (pp. 141–150). Reston, VA: Author.

McConaghy, M. J. (1979). Gender permanence and the genital basis of gender: Stages in the development of constancy of gender identity. *Child Development, 50,* 1223–1226.

McConaghy, N., & Silove, D. (1992). Do sex-linked behaviors in children influence relationships with their parents? *Archives of Sexual Behavior, 21,* 469–479.

McCune, L. (1993). The development of play as the development of consciousness. In M. H. Bornstein & A. O'Reilly (Eds.), *New directions for child development* (No. 59, pp. 67–79). San Francisco: Jossey-Bass.

McGee, G. (1997). Legislating gestation. *Human Reproduction, 12,* 407–408.

McGee, L. M., & Richgels, D. J. (2000). *Literacy's beginnings* (3rd ed.). Boston: Allyn and Bacon.

McGillicuddy-De Lisi, A. V., Watkins, C., & Vinchur, A. J. (1994). The effect of relationship on children's distributive justice reasoning. *Child Development, 65,* 1694–1700.

McGuffin, P., & Sargeant, M. P. (1991). Major affective disorder. In P. McGuffin & R. Murray (Eds.), *The new genetics of mental illness* (pp. 165–181). London: Butterworth-Heinemann.

McGuinness, D., & Pribram, K. H. (1980). The neuropsychology of attention: Emotional and motivational controls. In M. C. Wittcock (Ed.), *The brain and psychology* (pp. 95–139). New York: Academic Press.

McHale, S. M., Bartko, W. T., Crouter, A. C., & Perry-Jenkins, M. (1990). Children's housework and psychosocial functioning: The mediating effects of parents' sex-role behaviors and attitudes. *Child Development, 61,* 1413–1426.

McIntosh, J. L. (2000). Epidemiology of adolescent suicide in the United States. In R. W. Maris, S. S. Canetto, J. L. McIntosh, & M. M. Silverman (Eds.), *Review of Suicidology, 2000* (pp. 3–33). New York: Guilford.

McKeown, R. E., Garrison, C. Z., Cuffe, S. P., Waller, J. L., Jackson, K. L., & Addy, C. L. (1998). Incidence and predictors of suicidal behaviors in a longitudinal sample of young adolescents. Journal of the American *Academy of Child and Adolescent Psychiatry, 37,* 612–619.

McKusick, V. A. (1998). *Mendelian inheritance in man: A catalog of human genes and genetic disorders.* Baltimore: Johns Hopkins University Press.

McLean, M., Bisits, A., Davies, J., Woods, R., Lowry, P., & Smith R. (1995). A placental clock controlling the length of human pregnancy. *Nature Medicine, 1,* 460–463.

McLeod, J. D., & Shanahan, M. J. (1996). Trajectories of poverty and children's mental health. *Journal of Health and Social Behavior, 37,* 207–220.

McLoyd, V. C. (1998). Children in poverty: Development, public policy, and practice. In W. Damon (Ed.), *Handbook of child psychology: Vol. 4. Child psychology in practice* (pp. 135–208). New York: Wiley.

McLoyd, V. C., Jayaratne, T. E., Ceballo, R., & Borquez, J. (1994). Unemployment and work interruption among African American single mothers: Effects on parenting and adolescent socioemotional functioning. *Child Development, 65,* 562–589.

McManus, I. C., Sik, G., Cole, D. R., Mellon, A. F., Wong, J., & Kloss, J. (1988). The development of handedness in children. *British Journal of Developmental Psychology, 6,* 257–273.

McNamee, S., & Peterson, J. (1986). Young children's distributive justice reasoning, behavior, and role taking: Their consistency and relationship. *Journal of Genetic Psychology, 146,* 399–404.

MCR Vitamin Study Research Group. (1991). Prevention of neural tube defects: Results of the Medical Research Council Vitamin Study. *Lancet, 338,* 131–137.

Mead, G. H. (1934). *Mind, self, and society.* Chicago: University of Chicago Press.

Mead, M. (1928). *Coming of age in Samoa.* Ann Arbor, MI: Morrow.

Mead, M., & Newton, N. (1967). Cultural patterning of perinatal behavior. In S. Richardson & A. Guttmacher (Eds.), *Childbearing: Its social and psychological aspects* (pp. 142–244). Baltimore: Williams & Wilkins.

Meadow-Orlans, K. P., & Steinberg, A. G. (1993). Effects of infant hearing loss and maternal support on mother–infant interactions at 18 months. *Journal of Applied Developmental Psychology, 14*, 407–426.

Mebert, C. J. (1991). Dimensions of subjectivity in parents' ratings of infant temperament. *Child Development, 62*, 352–361.

Meeus, W. (1996). Studies on identity development in adolescence: An overview of research and some new data. *Journal of Youth and Adolescence, 25*, 569–598.

Meeus, W., Iedema, J., Helsen, M., & Vollebergh, W. (1999). Patterns of adolescent identity development: Review of literature and longitudinal analysis. *Developmental Review, 19*, 419–461.

Mehlmadrona, L., & Madrona, M. M. (1997). Physician- and midwife-attended home births—effects of breech, twin, and post-dates outcome data on mortality rates. *Journal of Nurse-Midwifery, 42*, 91–98.

Meisels, S. J., Dichtelmiller, M., & Liaw, F. R. (1993). A multidimensional analysis of early childhood intervention programs. In C. H. Zeanah (Ed.), *Handbook of infant mental health* (pp. 361–385). New York: Guilford.

Melby, J. N., & Conger, R. D. (1996). Parental behaviors and adolescent academic performance: A longitudinal analysis. *Journal of Research on Adolescence, 6*, 113–137.

Meltzoff, A. N. (1990). Towards a developmental cognitive science. *Annals of the New York Academy of Sciences, 608*, 1–37.

Meltzoff, A. N. (1995). Understanding the intentions of others: Re-enactment of intended acts by 18-month-old children. *Developmental Psychology, 31*, 838–850.

Meltzoff, A. N., & Kuhl, P. K. (1994). Faces and speech: Intermodal processing of biologically relevant signals in infants and adults. In D. J. Lewkowicz & R. Lickliter (Eds.), *The development of intersensory perception: Comparative perspectives* (pp. 335–369). Hillsdale, NJ: Erlbaum.

Meltzoff, A. N., & Moore, M. K. (1977). Imitation of facial and manual gestures by human neonates. *Science, 198*, 75–78.

Meltzoff, A. N., & Moore, M. K. (1994). Imitation, memory, and the representation of persons. *Infant Behavior and Development, 17*, 83–99.

Meltzoff, A. N., & Moore, M. K. (1999). Persons and representation: Why infant imitation is important for theories of human development. In J. Nadel & G. Butterworth (Eds.), *Imitation in infancy* (pp. 9–35). Cambridge, U.K.: Cambridge University Press.

Mendelson, B. K., White, D. R., & Mendelson, M. J. (1996). Self-esteem and body esteem: Effects of gender, age, and weight. *Journal of Applied Developmental Psychology, 17*, 321–346.

Mennella, J. A., & Beauchamp, G. K. (1998). Early flavor experiences: Research update. *Nutrition Reviews, 56*, 205–211.

Menyuk, P., Liebergott, J. W., & Schultz, M. C. (1995). *Early language development in full-term and premature infants.* Hillsdale, NJ: Erlbaum.

Meredith, N. V. (1978). *Human body growth in the first ten years of life.* Columbia, SC: State Printing.

Mervis, C. B., Golinkoff, R. M., & Bertrand, J. (1994). Two-year-olds readily learn multiple labels for the same basic-level category. *Child Development, 65*, 1163–1177.

Meyer-Bahlburg, H. F. L. (1990). Short stature: Psychological issues. In F. Lifshitz (Ed.), *Pediatric endocrinology: A clinical guide* (2nd ed., pp. 173–196). New York: Marcel Dekker.

Meyer-Bahlburg, H. F. L., Ehrhardt, A. A., Rosen, L. R., Gruen, R. S., Veridiano, N. P., Vann, F. H., & Neuwalder, H. F. (1995). Prenatal estrogens and the development of homosexual orientation. *Developmental Psychology, 31*, 12–21.

Meyers, C., Adam, R., Dungan, J., & Prenger, V. (1997). Aneuploidy in twin gestations: When is maternal age advanced? *Obstetrics & Gynecology, 89*, 248–251.

Miceli, P. J., Whitman, T. L., Borkowski, J. G., Braungart-Riekder, J., & Mitchell, D. W. (1998). Individual differences in infant information processing: The role of temperamental and maternal factors. *Infant Behavior and Development, 21*, 119–136.

Michael, R. T., Gagnon, J. H., Laumann, E. O., & Kolata, G. (1994). *Sex in America.* Boston: Little, Brown.

Michaels, G. Y. (1988). Motivational factors in the decision and timing of pregnancy. In G. Y. Michaels & W. A. Goldberg (Eds.), *The transition to parenthood: Current theory and research* (pp. 23–61). New York: Cambridge University Press.

Michels, K. B., Trichopoulos, D., Robins, J. M., Rosner, B. A., Manson, J. E., Hunter, D. J., Colditz, G. A., Hankinson, S. E., Speizer, F. E., & Willett, W. C. (1996). Birthweight as a risk factor for breast cancer. *Lancet, 348*, 1542–1546.

Midgley, C., Feldlaufer, H., & Eccles, J. S. (1989). Student/teacher relations and attitudes toward mathematics before and after the transition to junior high school. *Child Development, 60*, 981–992.

Milberger, S., Biederman, J., Faraone, S. V., Guite, J., & Tsuang, M. T. (1997). Pregnancy, delivery and infancy complications and attention-deficit hyperactivity disorder: Issues of gene–environment interaction. *Biological Psychiatry, 41*, 65–75.

Milberger, S., Biederman, J., Faraone, S. V., & Jones, J. (1998). Further evidence of an association between maternal smoking during pregnancy and attention-deficit hyperactivity disorder: Findings from a high-risk sample of siblings. *Journal of Clinical Child Psychology, 27*, 352–358.

Miles, H. L. (1999). Symbolic communication with and by great apes. In S. T. Parker, R. W. Mitchell, & H. L. Miles (Eds.), *The mentalities of gorillas and orangutans* (pp. 197–210). Cambridge, U.K.: Cambridge University Press.

Milgram, N. A., & Palti, G. (1993). Psychosocial characteristics of resilient children. *Journal of Research in Personality, 27*, 207–221.

Miller, J. G. (1994). Cultural diversity in the morality of caring: Individually oriented versus duty-based interpersonal moral codes. *Cross-cultural Research: The Journal of Comparative Social Science, 28*, 3–39.

Miller, J. G. (1997). Culture and self: uncovering the cultural grounding of psychological theory. In J. G. Snodgrass & R. L. Thompson (Eds.), *Annals of the New York Academy of Sciences* (Vol. 18, pp. 217–231). New York: New York Academy of Sciences.

Miller, K. E. (1990). Adolescents' same-sex and opposite-sex peer relations: Sex differences in popularity, perceived social competence and social cognitive skills. *Journal of Adolescent Research, 5*, 222–241.

Miller, K. F., & Baillargeon, R. (1990). Length and distance: Do preschoolers think that occlusion brings things together? *Developmental Psychology, 26*, 103–114.

Miller, K. F., Smith, C. M., Zhu, J., & Zhang, H. (1995). Preschool origins of cross-national differences in mathematical competence: The role of number-naming systems. *Psychological Science, 6*, 56–60.

Miller, K. S., Forehand, R., & Kotchick, B. A. (1999). Adolescent sexual behavior in two ethnic minority samples: The role of family variables. *Journal of Marriage and the Family, 61*, 85–98.

Miller, K. S., Levin, M. L., Whitaker, D. J., & Xu, X. (1998). Patterns of condom use among adolescents: The impact of mother–adolescent communication. *American Journal of Public Health, 88*, 1542–1544.

Miller, L. T., & Vernon, P. A. (1992). The general factor in short-term memory, intelligence, and reaction time. *Intelligence, 16*, 5–29.

Miller, L. T., & Vernon, P. A. (1997). Developmental changes in speed of information processing in young children. *Developmental Psychology, 33*, 549–554.

Miller, N., & Maruyama, G. (1976). Ordinal position and peer popularity. *Journal of Personality and Social Psychology, 33*, 123–131.

Miller, P. A., Eisenberg, N., Fabes, R. A., & Shell, R. (1996). Relations of moral reasoning and vicarious emotion to young children's prosocial behavior toward peers and adults. *Developmental Psychology, 32*, 210–219.

Miller, P. H. (1993). *Theories of developmental psychology* (3rd ed.). New York: Freeman.

Miller, P. H., & Bigi, L. (1979). The development of children's understanding of attention. *Merrill-Palmer Quarterly, 25*, 235–250.

Miller, P. H., & Seier, W. L. (1994). Strategy utilization deficiencies in children: When, where, and why. In H. W. Reese (Ed.), *Advances in child development and behavior* (Vol. 25, pp. 107–156). New York: Academic Press.

Miller, P. H., Seier, W. L., Probert, J. S., & Aloise, P. A. (1991). Age differences in the capacity demands of a strategy among spontaneously strategic children. *Journal of Experimental Child Psychology, 52*, 149–165.

Miller, P. H., Woody-Ramsey, J., & Aloise, P. A. (1991). The role of strategy effortfulness in strategy effectiveness. *Developmental Psychology, 27*, 738–745.

Miller, P. J., Fung, H., & Mintz, J. (1996). Self-construction through narrative practices: A Chinese and American comparison of early socialization. *Ethos, 24*, 1–44.

Miller, P. J., Wiley, A. R., Fung, H., & Liang, C.-H. (1997). Personal storytelling as a medium of socialization in Chinese and American families. *Child Development, 68*, 557–568.

Miller, S. A. (1998). *Developmental research methods* (2nd ed.). Englewood Cliffs, NJ: Prentice-Hall.

Mills, D. L., Coffey-Corina, S. A., & Neville, H. J. (1993). Language acquisition and cerebral specialization in 20-month-old infants. *Journal of Cognitive Neuroscience, 5*, 317–334.

Mills, D. L., Coffey-Corina, S. A., & Neville, H. J. (1994). Variability in cerebral organization during primary language acquisition. In G. Dawson & K. W. Fischer (Eds.), *Human behavior and the developing brain* (pp. 427–455). New York: Guilford.

Mills, R., Coffey-Corina, S., & Neville, H. J. (1997). Language comprehension and cerebral specialization from 13 to 20 months. *Developmental Neuropsychology, 13,* 397–445.

Mills, R., & Grusec, J. E. (1989). Cognitive, affective, and behavioral consequences of praising altruism. *Merrill-Palmer Quarterly, 35,* 299–326.

Millstein, S. G., & Irwin, C. E. (1988). Accident-related behaviors in adolescents: A biosocial view. *Alcohol, Drugs, and Driving, 4,* 21–29.

Millstein, S. G., & Litt, I. F. (1990). Adolescent health. In S. S. Feldman & G. R. Elliott (Eds.), *At the threshold: The developing adolescent* (pp. 431–456). Cambridge, MA: Harvard University Press.

Milner, J. S. (1993). Social information processing and physical child abuse. *Clinical Psychology Review, 13,* 275–294.

Minde, K. (2000). Prematurity and serious medical conditions in infancy: Implications for development, behavior, and intervention. In C. H. Zeanah, Jr. (Ed.), *Handbook of infant mental health* (pp. 176–194). New York: Guilford.

Mindell, J. A., Owens, J. A., & Carskadon, M. A. (1999). Developmental features of sleep. *Child and Adolescent Psychiatric Clinics of North America, 8,* 695–725.

Mischel, W., & Liebert, R. M. (1966). Effects of discrepancies between observed and imposed reward criteria on their acquisition and transmission. *Journal of Personality and Social Psychology, 3,* 45–53.

Mize, J., & Ladd, G. W. (1990). A cognitive–social learning approach to social skill training with low-status preschool children. *Developmental Psychology, 26,* 388–397.

Mize, J., & Pettit, G. S. (1997). Mothers' social coaching, mother–child relationship style, and children's peer competence: Is the medium the message? *Child Development, 68,* 312–332.

Moerk, E. L. (1992). *A first language taught and learned.* Baltimore: Paul H. Brookes.

Moffitt, T. E., Caspi, A., Belsky, J., & Silva, P. A. (1992). Childhood experience and onset of menarche: A test of a sociobiological model. *Child Development, 63,* 47–58.

Moffitt, T. E., Caspi, A., Dickson, N., Silva, P., & Stanton, W. (1996).

Childhood-onset versus adolescent-onset antisocial conduct problems in males: Natural history from ages 3 to 18 years. *Development and Psychopathology, 8,* 399–424.

Moffitt, T. E., Lynam, D. R., & Silva, P. A. (1994). Neuropsychological tests predicting persistent male delinquency. *Criminology, 32,* 277–300.

Mogford-Bevan, K. (1999). Twins and their language development. In A. C. Sandbank (Ed.), *Twin and triplet psychology.* New York: Routledge.

Mohanty, A. K., & Perregaux, C. (1997). Language acquisition and bilingualism. In J. W. Berry, P. R. Dasen, & T. S. Saraswathi (Eds.), *Handbook of cross-cultural psychology: Vol. 2. Basic processes and human development* (2nd ed., pp. 217–254). Boston: Allyn and Bacon.

Moll, I. (1994). Reclaiming the natural line in Vygotsky's theory of cognitive development. *Human Development, 37,* 333–342.

Mondimore, F. M. (1996). *A natural history of homosexuality.* Baltimore: Johns Hopkins University Press.

Mondloch, C. J., Lewis, T., Budreau, D. R., Maurer, D., Dannemillier, J. L., Stephens, B. R., & Kleiner-Gathercoal, K. A. (1999). Face perception during early infancy. *Psychological Science, 10,* 419–422.

Money, J. (1993). Specific neurocognitional impairments associated with Turner (45,X) and Klinefelter (47,XXY) syndromes: A review. *Social Biology, 40,* 147–151.

Monk, C., Fifer, W. P., Myers, M. M., Sloan, R. P., Trien, L., & Hurtado, A. (2000). Maternal stress responses and anxiety during pregnancy: Effects on fetal heart rate. *Developmental Psychobiology, 36,* 67–77.

Monroe, S., Goldman, P., & Smith, V. E. (1988). *Brothers: Black and poor—a true story of courage and survival.* New York: Morrow.

Montemayor, R., & Eisen, M. (1977). The development of self-conceptions from childhood to adolescence. *Developmental Psychology, 13,* 314–319.

Moon, C., Cooper, R. P., & Fifer, W. P. (1993). Two-day-old infants prefer their native language. *Infant Behavior and Development, 16,* 495–500.

Moon, S. M., & Feldhusen, J. F. (1994). The Program for Academic and Creative Enrichment (PACE): A follow-up study ten years later. In R. F. Subotnik & K. D. Arnold (Eds.), *Beyond Terman: Contemporary longitudinal*

studies of giftedness and talent (pp. 375–400). Norwood, NJ: Ablex.

Moore, D. S., Spence, M. J., & Katz, G. S. (1997). Six-month-olds' categorization of natural infant-directed utterances. *Developmental Psychology, 33,* 980–989.

Moore, E. G. J. (1986). Family socialization and the IQ test performance of traditionally and transracially adopted black children. *Developmental Psychology, 22,* 317–326.

Moore, G. A., Cohn, J. F., & Campbell, S. B. (1997). Mothers' affective behavior with infant siblings: Stability and change. *Developmental Psychology, 33,* 856–860.

Moore, K. A., Miller, B. C., Sugland, B. W., Morrison, D. R., Glei, D. A., & Blumenthal, C. (1998). *Beginning too soon: Adolescent sexual behavior, pregnancy and parenthood.* Washington, DC: U.S. Government Printing Office.

Moore, K. A., Morrison, D. R., & Green, A. D. (1997). Effects on the children born to adolescent mothers. In R. A. Maynard (Ed.), *Kids having kids* (pp. 145–180). Washington, DC: Urban Institute.

Moore, K. A., Myers, D. E., Morrison, D. R., Nord, C. W., Brown, B., & Edmonston, B. (1993). Age at first childbirth and later poverty. *Journal of Research on Adolescence, 3,* 393–422.

Moore, K. L., & Persaud, T. V. N. (1998). *Before we are born* (5th ed.). Philadelphia: Saunders.

Moore, K. L., Persaud, T. V. N., & Shiota, K. (1994). *Color atlas of clinical embryology.* Philadelphia: Saunders.

Moore, L. L., Lombardi, D. A., White, M. J., Campbell, J. L., Oliveria, S. A., Ellison, R. C. (1991). Influence of parents' physical activity levels on activity levels of young children. *Journal of Pediatrics, 118,* 215–219.

Moore, M. K., & Meltzoff, A. N. (1999). New findings on object permanence: A developmental difference between two types of occlusion. *British Journal of Developmental Psychology, 17,* 563–584.

Moore, V., & McConachie, H. (1994). Communication between blind and severely visually impaired children and their parents. *British Journal of Developmental Psychology, 12,* 491–502.

Moorehouse, M. J. (1991). Linking maternal employment patterns to mother–child activities and children's school competence. *Developmental Psychology, 27,* 295–303.

Morabia, A., Costanza, M. C., & the World Health Organization Collaborative Study of Neoplasia and Steroid Contraceptives. (1998).

International variability in ages at menarche, first live birth, and menopause. *American Journal of Epidemiology, 148,* 1195–1205.

Moran, G. F., & Vinovskis, M. A. (1986). The great care of godly parents: Early childhood in Puritan New England. *Monographs of the Society for Research in Child Development, 50*(4–5, Serial No. 211).

Morelli, G., Rogoff, B., Oppenheim, D., & Goldsmith, D. (1992). Cultural variation in infants' sleeping arrangements: Questions of independence. *Developmental Psychology, 28,* 604–613.

Morford, J. P., & Goldin-Meadow, S. (1997). From here and now to there and then: The development of displaced reference in homesign and English. *Child Development, 68,* 420–435.

Morgan, J. L., Bonama, K. M., & Travis, L. L. (1995). Negative evidence on negative evidence. *Developmental Psychology, 31,* 180–197.

Morgan, J. L., & Saffran, J. R. (1995). Emerging integration of sequential and suprasegmental information in preverbal speech segmentation. *Child Development, 66,* 911–936.

Morgane, P. J., Austin-LaFrance, R., Bronzino, J., Tonkiss, J., Diaz-Cintra, S., Cintra, L., Kemper, T., & Galler, J. R. (1993). Prenatal malnutrition and development of the brain. *Neuroscience and Biobehavioral Reviews, 17,* 91–128.

Mori, L., & Peterson, L. (1995). Knowledge of safety of high and low active–impulsive boys: Implications for child injury prevention. *Journal of Clinical Child Psychology, 24,* 370–376.

Morrison, F. E., Griffith, E. M., & Alberts, D. M. (1997). Nature–nurture in the classroom: Entrance age, school readiness, and learning in children. *Developmental Psychology, 33,* 254–262.

Morrongiello, B. A. (1986). Infants' perception of multiple-group auditory patterns. *Infant Behavior and Development, 9,* 307–319.

Morrongiello, B. A., Fenwick, K. D., & Chance, G. (1998). Crossmodal learning in newborn infants: Inferences about properties of auditory-visual events. *Infant Behavior and Development, 21,* 543–554.

Morrongiello, B. A. & Rennie, H. (1998). Why do boys engage in more risk taking than girls? The role of attributions, beliefs, and risk appraisals. *Journal of Pediatric Psychology, 23,* 33–43.

Mortimer, J. T., & Borman, K. M. (Eds.). (1988). *Work experience and psychological development throughout the lifespan.* Boulder, CO: Westview Press.

Morton, J. (1993). Mechanisms in infant face processing. In B. de Boysson-Bardies, S. de Schonen, P. Jusczyk, P. McNeilage, & J. Morton (Eds.), *Developmental neurocognition: Speech and face processing in the first year of life* (pp. 93–102). London: Kluwer.

Moshman, D. (1998a). *Adolescent psychological development: Rationality, morality, and identity.* Mahwah, NJ: Erlbaum.

Moshman, D. (1998b). Cognitive development beyond childhood. In D. Kuhn & R. S. Siegler (Eds.), *Handbook of child psychology: Vol. 2. Cognition, perception, and language* (5th ed., pp. 947– 978). New York: Wiley.

Moshman, D. (1999). *Adolescent psychological development: Rationality, morality, and identity.* Mahwah, NJ: Erlbaum.

Moshman, D., & Franks, B. A. (1986). Development of the concept of inferential validity. *Child Development, 57,* 153–165.

Moss, M., Colombo, J., Mitchell, D. W., & Horowitz, F. D. (1988). Neonatal behavioral organization and visual processing at three months. *Child Development, 59,* 1211–1220.

Mosteller, F. (1995). The Tennessee Study of Class Size in the Early School Grades. *Future of Children, 5*(2), 113–127.

Mounts, N. S., & Steinberg, L. (1995). An ecological analysis of peer influence on adolescent grade point average and drug use. *Developmental Psychology, 31,* 915–922.

Mullen, M. K. (1994). Earliest recollections of childhood: A demographic analysis. *Cognition, 52,* 55–79.

Muller, F., Rebiff, M., Taillandier, A., Qury, J. F., & Mornet, E. (2000). Parental origin of the extra chromosome in prenatally diagnosed fetal trisomy. *Human Genetics, 106,* 340–344.

Munro, G., & Adams, G. R. (1977). Ego identity formation in college students and working youth. *Developmental Psychology, 13,* 523–524.

Muris, P., Merckelbach, H., Gadet, B., & Moulaert, V. (2000). Fears, worries, and scary dreams in 4- to 12-year-old children: their content, developmental pattern, and origins. *Journal of Clinical Child Psychology, 29,* 43–52.

Murray, A. D. (1985). Aversiveness is in the mind of the beholder. In B. M. Lester & C. F. Z. Boukydis (Eds.), *Infant crying* (pp. 217–239). New York: Plenum.

Murray, L., & Cooper, P. J. (1997). Postpartum depression and child development. *Psychological Medicine, 27,* 253–260.

Murray, L., Sinclair, D., Cooper, P., Ducournau, P., & Turner, P. (1999). The socioemotional development of 5-year-old children of postnatally depressed mothers. *Journal of Child Psychology and Psychiatry, 40,* 1259–1271.

Mussen, P., & Eisenberg-Berg, N. (1977). *Roots of caring, sharing, and helping.* San Francisco: Freeman.

Must, A., & Strauss, R. S. (1999). Risks and consequences of childhood and adolescent obesity. *International Journal of Obesity, 23,* S2–S11.

Nachtigall, R. D. (1993). Secrecy: An unresolved issue in the practice of donor insemination. *American Journal of Obstetrics and Gynecology, 168,* 1846–1851.

Nachtigall, R. D., Becker, G., Quiroga, S. S., & Tschann, J. M. (1998). The disclosure decision: Concerns and issues of parents of children conceived through donor insemination. *American Journal of Obstetrics and Gynecology, 178,* 1165–1170.

Nachtigall, R. D., Pitcher, L., Tschann, J. M., Becker, G., & Quiroga, S. S. (1997). Stigma, disclosure, and family functioning among parents of children conceived through donor insemination. *Fertility and Sterility, 68,* 83–89.

Nagy, W. E., & Scott, J. A. (2000). Vocabulary processes. In M. L. Kamil & P. B. Mosenthal (Eds.), *Handbook of reading research* (Vol. 3, pp. 269–284). Mahwah, NJ: Erlbaum.

Naigles, L. G., & Gelman, S. A. (1995). Overextensions in comprehension and production revisited: Preferential-looking in a study of dog, cat, and cow. *Journal of Child Language, 22,* 19–46.

Nakamura, S., Wind, M., & Danello, M. A. (1999). Review of hazards associated with children in adult beds. *Archives of Pediatric and Adolescent Medicine, 153,* 1019–1023.

Namy, L. L., & Waxman, S. R. (1998). Words and gestures: Infants' interpretations of different forms of symbolic reference. *Child Development, 69,* 295–308.

Nanez, J. (1987). Perception of impending collision in 3- to 6-week-old infants. *Infant Behavior and Development, 11,* 447–463.

Nánez, J., Sr., & Yonas, A. (1994). Effects of luminance and texture motion on infant defensive reactions to optical collision. *Infant Behavior and Development, 17,* 165–174.

Narvaez, D., Mitchell, C., Bock, T., Endicott, L., & Gardner, J. (2001). *Guidelines for developing curricula for middle school students that meet graduation standards while teaching character.* In press.

National Association for the Education of Young Children. (1998). *Accreditation criteria and procedures of the National Academy of Early Childhood Programs* (2nd ed.). Washington, DC: Author.

National Center for Children in Poverty. (2000). *Child poverty in the United States.* New York: Author.

National Center for Health Statistics, U.S. Department of Health and Human Services. (2000). *Vital Statistics of the United States, 1996.* Washington, DC: U.S. Government Printing Office.

National Coalition for the Homeless. (1999a). *Homeless families with children.* Washington, DC: Author.

National Coalition for the Homeless. (1999b). *Why are people homeless?* Washington, DC: Author.

National Federation of State High School Associations. (2000). *High school athletic participation survey.* Kansas City, MO: Author.

National Institute for Child Health and Development, Early Child Care Research Network. (1996). Characteristics of infant care: Factors contributing to positive caregiving. *Early Childhood Research Quarterly, 11,* 269–306.

National Institute for Child Health and Development, Early Child Care Research Network. (1997). The effects of infant child care on infant–mother attachment security: Results of the NICHD Study of Early Child Care. *Child Development, 68,* 860–879.

National Institute for Child Health and Development, Early Child Care Research Network. (1998). Early child care and self-control, compliance, and problem behavior at twenty-four and thirty-six months. *Child Development, 69,* 1145–1170.

National Institute for Child Health and Human Development, Early Child Care Research Network. (1999). Child care and mother–child interaction in the first 3 years of life. *Developmental Psychology, 35,* 1399–1413.

National Law Center on Homelessness and Poverty. (1997). *"Back to school" is not for everybody.* Washington, DC: Author.

Navarrete, C., Martinez, I., & Salamanca, F. (1994). Paternal line of transmission in chorea of Huntington with very early onset. *Genetic Counseling, 5,* 175–178.

Needham, A. (1998). Infants' use of featural information in the segregation of stationary objects. *Infant Behavior and Development, 21,* 1–24.

Nelson, C. (1997). The neurobiological basis of early memory development. In N. Cowan (Ed.), *The development of memory in childhood. Studies in developmental psychology* (pp. 41–82). Hove, UK: Erlbaum.

Nelson, C. A., & Bosquet, M. (2000). Neurobiology of fetal and infant development: Implications for infant mental health. In C. H. Zeanah, Jr. (Ed.), *Handbook of infant mental health* (2nd ed., pp. 37–59). New York: Guilford.

Nelson, C. A., & Carver, L. J. (1998). The effects of stress and trauma on brain and memory: A view from developmental cognitive neuroscience. *Development and Psychopathology, 10,* 793–809.

Nelson, E. A. S., Schiefenhoevel, W., & Haimerl, F. (2000). Child care practices in nonindustrialized societies. *Pediatrics, 105,* e75.

Nelson, K. (1973). Structure and strategy in learning to talk. *Monographs of the Society for Research in Child Development, 38*(1–2, Serial No. 149).

Nelson, K. (1993). The psychological and social origins of autobiographical memory. *Psychological Science, 1,* 1–8.

Netley, C. T. (1986). Summary overview of behavioural development in individuals with neonatally identified X and Y aneuploidy. *Birth Defects, 22,* 293–306.

Neubauer, A. C., & Bucik, V. (1996). The mental speed–IQ relationship: Unitary or modular? *Intelligence, 22,* 23–48.

Neuman, S. B. (1999). Books make a difference: A study of access to literacy. *Reading Research Quarterly, 34,* 286–311.

Neuman, S. B., Copple, C., & Bredekamp, S. (2000). *Learning to read and write: Developmentally appropriate practices for young children.* Washington, DC: National Association for the Education of Young Children.

Neumärker, K. (1997). Mortality and sudden death in anorexia nervosa. *International Journal of Eating Disorders, 21,* 205–212.

Neville, H. J., & Bavelier, D. (1998). Neural organization and plasticity of language. *Current Opinion in Neurobiology, 8,* 254–258.

Newacheck, P. W., & Halfon, N. (2000). Prevalence, impact, and trends in childhood disability due to asthma. *Archives of Pediatric and Adolescent Medicine, 154,* 287–293.

Newacheck, P. W., Hughes, D. C., & Stoddard, J. J. (1996). Children's access to primary care: Differences by race, income, and insurance status. *Pediatrics, 97,* 26–32.

Newborg, J., Stock, J. R., & Wnek, L. (1984). *Battelle Developmental Inventory.* Allen, TX: LINC Associates.

Newcomb, A. F., Bukowski, W. M., & Pattee, L. (1993). Children's peer relations: A meta-analytic review of popular, rejected, neglected, controversial, and average sociometric status. *Psychological Bulletin, 113,* 99–128.

Newcomb, M. D., & Bentler, P. M. (1988). Consequences of adolescent substance use on young adult health status and utilization of health services: A structural equation model over four years. *Social Science and Medicine, 24,* 71–82.

Newcomb, M. D., & Bentler, P. M. (1989). Substance use and abuse among children and teenagers. *American Psychologist, 44,* 242–248.

Newcombe, N., & Huttenlocher, J. (1992). Children's early ability to solve perspective-taking problems. *Developmental Psychology, 28,* 635–643.

Newcombe, P. A., & Boyle, G. J. (1995). High school students' sports personalities: Variations across participation level, gender, type of sport, and success. *International Journal of Sports Psychology, 26,* 277–294.

Newman, B. S., Muzzonigro, P. G. (1993). The effects of traditional family values on the coming out process of gay male adolescents. *Adolescence, 28,* 213–226.

Newman, L. S. (1990). Intentional versus unintentional memory in young children: Remembering versus playing. *Journal of Experimental Child Psychology, 50,* 243–258.

Newnham, J. P., Evans, S. F., Michael, C. A., Stanley, F. J., & Landau, L. I. (1993). Effects of frequent ultrasound during pregnancy: A randomized controlled trial. *Lancet, 342,* 887–890.

Newport, E. L. (1991). Contrasting conceptions of the critical period for language. In S. Carey & R. Gelman (Eds.), *The epigenesis of mind: Essays on biology and cognition* (pp. 111–130). Hillsdale, NJ: Erlbaum.

Newson, J., & Newson, E. (1975). Intersubjectivity and the transmission of culture: On the social origins of symbolic functioning. *Bulletin of the British Psychological Society, 28,* 437–446.

Ni, Y. (1998). Cognitive structure, content knowledge, and classificatory reasoning. *Journal of Genetic Psychology, 159,* 280–296.

Nidorf, J. F. (1985). Mental health and refugee youths: A model for diagnostic training. In T. C. Owen (Ed.), *Southeast Asian mental health: Treatment, prevention, services, training, and research* (pp. 391–427). Washington, DC: National Institute of Mental Health.

Nilsson, L., & Hamberger, L. (1990). *A child is born.* New York: Delacorte.

Nippold, M. A. (2000). Language development during the adolescent years: Aspects of pragmatics, syntax, and semantics. *Topics in Language Disorders, 20,* 15–28.

Nippold, M. A., Hegel, S. L., Sohlberg, M. M., & Schwarz, I. E. (1999). Defining abstract entities: Development in preadolescents, adolescents, and young adults. *Journal of Speech, Language, and Hearing Research, 42,* 473–481.

Nippold, M. A., Hegel, S. L., Uhden, L. D., & Bustamante, S. (1998). Development of proverb comprehension in adolescents: Implications for instruction. *Journal of Children's Communication Development, 19,* 49–55.

Nippold, M. A., Taylor, C. L., & Baker, J. M. (1996). Idiom understanding in Australian youth: A cross-cultural comparison. *Journal of Speech and Hearing Research, 39,* 442–447.

Nisbett, R. E. (1998). Race, genetics, and IQ. In C. Jencks & M. Phillips (Eds.), *The black–white test score gap* (pp. 86–102). Washington, DC: Brookings Institution.

Nolen-Hoeksema, S., & Girgus, J. S. (1994). The emergence of gender differences in depression in adolescence. *Psychological Bulletin, 115,* 424–443.

Nottelmann, E. D. (1987). Competence and self-esteem during transition from childhood to adolescence. *Developmental Psychology, 23,* 441–450.

Nottelmann, E. D., Inoff-Germain, G., Susman, E. J., & Chrousos, G. P. (1990). Hormones and behavior at puberty. In J. Bancroft & J. M. Reinisch (Eds.), *Adolescence and puberty* (pp. 88–123). New York: Oxford University Press.

Nourse, C. B., & Butler, K. M. (1998). Perinatal transmission of HIV and diagnosis of HIV infection in infants: A review. *Irish Journal of Medical Science, 167,* 28–32.

Novak, G. P., Solanto, M., & Abikoff, H. (1995). Spatial orienting and focused attention in attention deficit hyperactivity disorder. *Journal of Psychophysiology, 32,* 546–559.

Nucci, L. P. (1996). Morality and the personal sphere of action. In E. Reed, E. Turiel, & T. Brown (Eds.), *Values and knowledge* (pp. 41–60). Hillsdale, NJ: Erlbaum.

Nucci, L. P., Camino, C., & Sapiro, C. M. (1996). Social class effects on Northeastern Brazilian children's conceptions of areas of personal choice and social regulation. *Child Development, 67,* 1223–1242.

Nucci, L. P., & Weber, E. (1995). Social interactions in the home and the development of young children's conceptions of the personal. *Child Development, 66,* 1438–1452.

Nuckolls, K., Cassel, J., & Kaplan, B. (1972). Psychosocial assets, life crisis, and the prognosis of pregnancy. *American Journal of Epidemiology, 95,* 431–441.

Nurmi, J., Poole, M. E., & Kalakoski, V. (1996). Age differences in adolescent identity exploration and commitment in urban and rural environments. *Journal of Adolescence, 19,* 443–452.

O'Connor, C. (1997). Dispositions toward (collective) struggle and educational resilience in the inner city: A case analysis of six African-American high school students. *American Educational Research Journal, 34,* 593–629.

O'Malley, P. M., Johnston, L. D., & Bachman, J. G. (1995). Adolescent substance use: Epidemiology and implications for public policy. *Pediatric Clinics of North America, 42,* 241–260.

O'Neil, R., & Parke, R. D. (1997, March). *Objective and subjective features of children's neighborhoods: Relations to parental regulatory strategies and children's social competence.* Paper presented at the biennial meeting of the Society for Research in Child Development, Washington, DC.

O'Neill, R., Welsh, M., Parke, R. D., Wang, S., & Strand, C. (1997). A longitudinal assessment of the academic correlates of early peer acceptance and rejection. *Journal of Clinical Psychology, 26,* 290–303.

O'Reilly, A. W. (1995). Using representations: Comprehension and production of actions with imagined objects. *Child Development, 66,* 999–1010.

O'Reilly, A. W., & Bornstein, M. H. (1993). Caregiver–child interaction in play. In M. H. Bornstein & A. W. O'Reilly (Eds.), *New directions for child development* (No. 59, pp. 55–66). San Francisco: Jossey-Bass.

Oakes, L. M., & Cohen, L. B. (1995). Infant causal perception. In C. Rovee-Collier & L. P. Lipsitt (Eds.), *Advances in infancy research* (Vol. 9, pp. 1–54). Norwood, NJ: Ablex.

Oakes, L. M., Coppage, D. J., & Dingel, A. (1997). By land or by sea: The role of perceptual similarity in infants' categorization of animals. *Developmental Psychology, 33,* 396–407.

Oberg, C. N., Bryant, N., & Bach, M. L. (1995). A portrait of America's children: The impact of poverty and a call to action. *Journal of Social Distress and the Homeless, 4,* 43–57.

Obler, L. K. (2000). Development and loss: Changes in the adult years. In J. B. Gleason (Ed.), *The development of language* (pp. 455–488). Boston: Allyn and Bacon.

Offer, D. (1988). *The teenage world: Adolescents' self-image in ten countries.* New York: Plenum.

Ogbu, J. U. (1997). Understanding the school performance of urban blacks: Some essential background knowledge. In H. J. Walberg, O. Reyes, & R. P. Weissberg (Eds.), *Children and youth: Interdisciplinary perspectives* (pp. 190–222). Thousand Oaks, CA: Sage.

Okagaki, L., & Frensch, P. A. (1996). Effects of video game playing on measures of spatial performance: Gender effects in late adolescence. In P. M. Greenfield & R. R. Cocking (Eds.), *Interacting with video* (pp. 115–140). Norwood, NJ: Ablex.

Okagaki, L., & Sternberg, R. J. (1993). Parental beliefs and children's school performance. *Child Development, 64,* 36–56.

Ollendick, T. H., Yang, B., King, N. J., Dong, Q., & Akande, A. (1996). Fears in American, Australian, Chinese, and Nigerian children and adolescents: A cross-cultural study. *Journal of Child Psychology and Psychiatry, 37,* 213–220.

Oller, D. K. (2000). *The emergence of the speech capacity.* Mahwah, NJ: Erlbaum.

Oller, D. K., Eilers, R. E., Neal, A. R., & Schwartz, H. K. (1999). Precursors to speech in infancy: The prediction of speech and language disorders. *Journal of Communication Disorders, 32,* 223–245.

Olsen, O. (1997). Meta-analysis of the safety of home birth. *Birth—Issues in Perinatal Care, 24,* 4–13.

Olson, H. C., Feldman, J. J., Streissguth, A. P., Sampson, P. D., & Bookstein, F. L. (1998). Neuropsychological deficits in adolescents with fetal alcohol syndrome: Clinical findings. *Alcoholism: Clinical and Experimental Research, 22,* 1998–2012.

Olweus, D. (1995). Bullying or peer abuse at school: Facts and intervention. *Current Directions in Psychological Science, 4,* 196–200.

Ondrusek, N., Abramovitch, R. P., & Koren, P. (1998). Empirical examination of the ability of children to consent to clinical research. *Journal of Medical Ethics, 24,* 158–165.

Oosterwegel, A., & Openheimer, L. (1993). *The self-system: Developmental changes between and within self-concepts.* Hillsdale, NJ: Erlbaum.

Ornstein, P. A., Merritt, K. A., Baker-Ward, L., Furtado, E., Gordon, B. N., & Principe, G. (1998). Children's knowledge, expectation, and long-term retention. *Applied Cognitive Psychology, 12,* 387–405.

Ornstein, P. A., Shapiro, L. R., Clubb, P. A., & Follmer, A. (1997). The influence of prior knowledge on children's memory for salient medical experiences. In N. Stein, P. A. Ornstein, C. J. Brainerd, & B. Tversky (Eds.), *Memory for everyday and emotional events* (pp. 83–112). Hillsdale, NJ: Erlbaum.

Osherson, D. N., & Markman, E. M. (1975). Language and the ability to evaluate contradictions and tautologies. *Cognition, 2,* 213–226.

Ovando, C. J., & Collier, V. P. (1998). *Bilingual and ESL classrooms: Teaching in multicultural contexts.* Boston: McGraw-Hill.

Overgaard, C., & Knudsen, A. (1999). Pain-relieving effect of sucrose in newborns during heel prick. *Biology of the Neonate, 75,* 279–284.

Owen, M. T., & Cox, M. J. (1997). Marital conflict and the development of infant–parent attachment relationships. *Journal of Family Psychology, 11,* 152–164.

Owen, M. T., Easterbrooks, M. A., Chase-Lansdale, L., & Goldberg, W. A. (1984). The relation between maternal employment status and the stability of attachment to mother and father. *Child Development, 55,* 1894–1901

Öztürk, C., Durmazlar, N., Ural, B., Karaagaoglu, E., Yalaz, K., & Anlar, B. (1999). Hand and eye preference in normal preschool children. *Clinical Pediatrics, 38,* 677–680.

Pacella, R., Mclellan, M., Grice, K., Del Bono, E. A., Wiggs, J. L. & Gwiazda, J. E. (1999). Role of genetic factors in the etiology of juvenile-onset myopia based on a longitudinal study of refractive error. *Optometry and Vision Science, 76,* 381–386.

Pagani, L., Boulerice, B., Vitaro, F., & Tremblay, E. (1999). Effects of poverty on academic failure and delinquency in boys: A change and process model approach. *Journal of Child Psychology and Psychiatry, 40,* 1209–1219.

Pagani, L., Tremblay, R. E., Vitaro, F., Kerr, M., & McDuff, P. (1998). The impact of family transition on the development of delinquency in adolescent boys: A 9-year longitudinal study. *Journal of Child Psychology and Psychiatry, 39,* 489–499.

Paikoff, R. L., Brooks-Gunn, J., & Warren, M. P. (1991). Effects of girls' hormonal status on depressive and aggressive symptoms over the course of one year. *Journal of Youth and Adolescence, 20,* 191–215.

Palincsar, A. S., & Herrenkohl, L. R. (1999). Designing collaborative contexts: Lessons from three research programs. In A. M. O'Donnell & A. King (Eds.), *Cognitive perspectives on peer learning. The Rutgers Invitational Symposium on Education Series* (pp. 151–177). Mahwah, NJ: Erlbaum.

Palincsar, A. S., & Klenk, L. (1992). Fostering literacy learning in supportive contexts. *Journal of Learning Disabilities, 25,* 211–225.

Palmlund, I. (1996). Exposure to a xenoestrogen before birth: The diethylstilbestrol experience. *Journal of Psychosomatic Obstetrics and Gynaecology, 17,* 71–84.

Palta, M., Sadek-Badawi, M., Evans, M., Weinstein, M. R., & McGuinness, G. (2000). Functional assessment of a multicenter very low-birth-weight cohort at age 5 years. *Archives of Pediatric and Adolescent Medicine, 154,* 23–30.

Pan, B. A., & Snow, C. E. (1999). The development of conversation and discourse skills. In M. Barrett (Ed.), *The development of language* (pp. 229–249). Hove, UK: Psychology Press.

Pan, H. W. (1994). Children's play in Taiwan. In J. L. Roopnarine, J. E. Johnson, & F. H. Hooper (Eds.), *Children's play in diverse cultures* (pp. 31–50). Albany, NY: SUNY Press.

Panchaud, C., Singh, S., Feivelson, D., & Darroch, J. E. (2000). Sexually transmitted diseases among adolescents in developed countries. *Family Planning Perspectives, 32,* 24–32.

Panigrahy, A., Filano, J. J., Sleeper, L. A., Mandell, F., Krous, H. F., & Rava, L. A. (1997). Decreased kainate binding in the arcuate nucleus of the sudden infant death syndrome. *Journal of Neuropathology and Experimental Neurology, 56,* 1253–1261.

Papini, D. R. (1994). Family interventions. In S. L. Archer (Ed.), *Interventions for adolescent identity development* (pp. 47–61). Thousand Oaks, CA: Sage.

Papousek, M., & Papousek, H. (1996). Infantile persistent crying, state regulation, and interaction with parents: A systems view. In M. H. Bornstein & J. L. Genevro (Eds.), *Child development and behavioral pediatrics* (pp. 11–33). Mahwah, NJ: Erlbaum.

Paradise, J. L., Haggard, M. P., Lous, J., Roberts, J. E., & Schilder, A. G. M. (1995). Developmental implications of early-life otitis media. *International Journal of Pediatric Otorhinolaryngology, 32,* S37.

Parer, J. T. (1998). Effects of fetal asphyxia on brain cell structure and function: Limits of tolerance. *Comparative Biochemistry and Physiology, 119A,* 711–716.

Parke, R. D., & Buriel, R. (1998). Socialization in the family: Ethnic and ecological perspectives. In N. Eisenberg (Ed.), *Handbook of child psychology: Vol. 3. Social, emotional, and personality development* (5th ed., pp. 463–552). New York: Wiley.

Parke, R. D., & Tinsley, B. R. (1981). The father's role in infancy: Determinants of involvement in caregiving and play. In M. E. Lamb (Ed.), *The role of the father in child development* (pp. 429–458). New York: Wiley.

Parker, F. L., Boak, A. Y., Griffin, K. W., Ripple, C., & Peay, L. (1999). Parent–child relationship, home learning environment, and school readiness. *School Psychology Review, 28,* 413–425.

Parker, J. G., & Asher, S. R. (1987). Peer relations and later personal adjustment: Are low-accepted children at risk? *Psychological Bulletin, 102,* 357–389.

Parker, J. G., Rubin, K. H., Price, J., & DeRosier, M. E. (1995). Peer relationships, child development, and adjustment: A developmental psychopathology perspective. In D. Cicchetti & D. Cohen (Eds.), *Developmental psychopathology: Vol. 2. Risk, disorder, and adaptation* (pp. 96–161). New York: Wiley.

Parkhurst, J. T., & Asher, S. R. (1992). Peer relations and later personal adjustment: Are low-accepted children at risk? *Psychological Bulletin, 102,* 357–389.

Parkhurst, J. T., & Hopmeyer, A. (1998). Sociometric popularity and peer-perceived popularity: Two distinct dimensions of peer status. *Journal of Early Adolescence, 18,* 125–144.

Parks, W. (1996). Human immunodeficiency virus. In R. D. Behrman, R. M. Kliegman, & A. M. Arvin (Eds.), *Nelson textbook of pediatrics* (15th ed., pp. 916–919). Philadelphia: Saunders.

Parsons, J. E., Adler, T. F., & Kaczala, C. M. (1982). Socialization of achievement attitudes and beliefs: Parental influences. *Child Development, 53,* 310–321.

Parten, M. (1932). Social participation among preschool children. *Journal of Abnormal and Social Psychology, 27,* 243–269.

Pascalis, O., de Haan, M., & Nelson, C. A. (1998). Long-term recognition memory for faces assessed by visual paired comparison in 3- and 6-month-old infants. *Journal of Experimental Psychology: Learning, Memory, and Cognition, 24,* 249–260.

Pascarella, E. T., Whitt, E. J., Edison, M. I., Nora, A., Hagedorn, L. S., Yeager, P. M., & Terenzini, P. T. (1997). Women's perceptions of a "chilly climate" and their cognitive outcomes during the first year of college. *Journal of College Student Development, 38,* 109–124.

Passman, R. H. (1987). Attachment to inanimate objects: Are children who have security blankets insecure? *Journal of Consulting and Clinical Psychology, 55,* 825–830.

Patterson, C. J., & Chan, R. W. (1999). Families headed by lesbian and gay parents. In M. E. Lamb (Ed.), *Parenting and child development in "nontraditional" families* (pp. 191–219). Mahwah, NJ: Erlbaum.

Patterson, G. R. (1982). *Coercive family processes.* Eugene, OR: Castilia Press.

Patterson, G. R. (1995). Coercion—A basis for early age of onset for arrest. In J. McCord (Ed.), *Coercion and punishment in long-term perspective* (pp. 81–105). New York: Cambridge University Press.

Patterson, G. R. (1997). Performance models for parenting: A social interactional perspective. In J. E. Grusec & L. Kuczynski (Eds.), *Parenting and children's internalization of values* (pp. 193–226). New York: Wiley.

Patterson, G. R., DeBaryshe, B. D., & Ramsey, E. (1989). A developmental perspective on antisocial behavior. *American Psychologist, 44,* 329–335.

Patterson, G. R., Forgatch, M. S., Yoerger, K. L., & Stoolmiller, M. (1998). Variables that initiate and maintain an early-onset trajectory for juvenile offending. *Development and Psychopathology, 10,* 531–547.

Patterson, G. R., Reid, J. B., & Dishion, T. J. (1992). *Antisocial boys.* Eugene, OR: Castalia.

Patton, G. C., Selzer, R., Coffey, C., Carlin, J. B., & Wolfe, R. (1999). Onset of adolescent eating disorders: Population based cohort study over 3 years. *British Medical Journal, 318,* 765–768.

Pearce, D., Cantisani, G., & Laihonen, A. (1999). Changes in fertility and family sizes in Europe. *Population Trends, 95,* 33–40.

Pearson, J. L., Hunter, A. G. Ensminger, M. E., & Kellam, S. G. (1990). Black grandmothers in multigenerational households: Diversity in family structure and parenting involvement in the Woodlawn community. *Child Development, 61*, 434–442.

Peckham, C. S., & Logan, S. (1993). Screening for toxoplasmosis during pregnancy. *Archives of Disease in Childhood, 68*, 3–5.

Pederson, D. R., Gleason, K. E., Moran, G., & Bento, S. (1998). Maternal attachment representations, maternal sensitivity, and the infant–mother attachment relationship. *Developmental Psychology, 34*, 925–933.

Pederson, D. R., & Moran, G. (1995). A categorical description of infant–mother relationships in the home and its relation to Q-sort measures of infant–mother interaction. In E. Waters, B. E. Vaughn, G. Posada, & K. Kondo-Ikemura K. (Eds.), Caregiving, cultural, and cognitive perspectives on secure-base behavior and working models: New growing points of attachment theory and research. *Monographs of the Society for Research in Child Development, 60* (2–3, Serial No. 244).

Pederson, D. R., & Moran, G. (1996). Expressions of the attachment relationship outside of the Strange Situation. *Child Development, 67*, 915–927.

Pedlow, R., Sanson, A., Prior, M., & Oberklaid, F. (1993). Stability of maternally reported temperament from infancy to 8 years. *Developmental Psychology, 29*, 998–1007.

Peiser-Feinberg, E. S. (1999). *The children of the Cost, Quality, and Outcomes Study go to school.* Chapel Hill, NC: University of North Carolina.

Pelham, W. E., Jr., Wheeler, T., & Chronis, A. (1998). Empirically supported psychosocial treatments for attention deficit hyperactivity disorder. *Clinical Child Psychology, 27*, 190–205.

Pellegrini, A. D., & Smith, P. K. (1998). Physical activity play: The nature and function of a neglected aspect of play. *Child Development, 69*, 577–598.

Pennington, B. F., Bender, B., Puck, M., Salbenblatt, J., & Robinson, A. (1982). Learning disabilities in children with sex chromosome abnormalities. *Child Development, 53*, 1182–1192.

Perfetti, C. A. (1988). Verbal efficiency in reading ability. In M. Daneman, G. E. MacKinnon, & T. G. Waller (Eds.), *Reading research: Advances in theory and practice* (Vol. 6, pp. 109–143). San Diego, CA: Academic Press.

Perlmutter, M. (1984). Continuities and discontinuities in early human

memory: Paradigms, processes, and performances. In R. V. Kail, Jr., & N. R. Spear (Eds.), *Comparative perspectives on the development of memory* (pp. 253–287). Hillsdale, NJ: Erlbaum.

Perner, J. (1991). *Understanding the representational mind.* Cambridge, MA: Bradford/ MIT Press.

Perry, C. L., Story, M., & Lytle, L. A. (1997). Promoting healthy dietary behaviors. In R. P. Weissberg, T. P. Gullotta, R. L. Hampton, B. A. Ryan, & G. R. Adams (Eds.), *Enhancing children's wellness* (pp. 214–249). Thousand Oaks, CA: Sage.

Perry, D. G., Williard, J. C., & Perry, L. C. (1990). Peers' perceptions of the consequences that victimized children provide aggressors. *Child Development, 61*, 1310–1325.

Perry, W. G., Jr. (1970). *Forms of intellectual and ethical development in the college years.* New York: Holt, Rinehart & Winston.

Perry, W. G., Jr. (1981). Cognitive and ethical growth. In A. Chickering (Ed.), *The modern American college* (pp. 76–116). San Francisco: Jossey-Bass.

Peshkin, A. (1978). *Growing up American: Schooling and the survival of the community.* Chicago: University of Chicago Press.

Peshkin, A. (1994). *Growing up American: Schooling and the survival of community.* Prospect Heights, IL: Waveland Press.

Peshkin, A. (1997). *Places of memory: Whiteman's schools and Native American communities.* Mahwah, NJ: Erlbaum.

Peters, B. R., Atkins, M. S., & McKay, M. M. (1999). Adopted children's behavior problems: A review of five explanatory models. *Clinical Psychology Review, 19*, 297–328.

Peterson, L. (1989). Latchkey children's preparation for self-care: Overestimated, underrehearsed, and unsafe. *Journal of Clinical Child Psychology, 18*, 36–43.

Peterson, L., & Brown, D. (1994). Integrating child injury and abuse–neglect research: Common histories, etiologies, and solutions. *Psychological Bulletin, 116*, 293–315.

Peterson, L., & Oliver, K. K. (1995). Prevention of injuries and disease. In M. C. Roberts (Ed.), *Handbook of pediatric psychology* (2nd ed., pp. 185–199). New York: Guilford.

Petitto, L. A., & Marentette, P. F. (1991). Babbling in the manual mode: Evidence for the ontogeny of language. *Science, 251*, 1493–1496.

Pettit, G. S., Bates, J. E., & Dodge, K. A. (1998). Supportive parenting, ecological context, and chil-

dren's adjustment: A seven-year longitudinal study. *Child Development, 68*, 908–923.

Pettit, G. S., Brown, E. G., Mize, J., & Lindsey, E. (1998). Mothers' and fathers' socializing behaviors in three contexts: Links with children's peer competence. *Merrill-Palmer Quarterly, 44*, 173–193.

Pettit, G. S., Laird, R. D., Bates, J. E., & Dodge, K. A. (1997). Patterns of after-school care in middle childhood: Risk factors and developmental outcomes. *Merrill-Palmer Quarterly, 43*, 15–38.

Phelps, K. E., & Woolley, J. D. (1994). The form and function of young children's magical beliefs. *Developmental Psychology, 30*, 385–394.

Phillips, C. A., Rolls, S., Rouse, A., & Griffiths, M. D. (1995). Home video game playing in schoolchildren—A study of incidence and patterns of play. *Journal of Adolescence, 18*, 687–691.

Phillips, D. A. (1987). Socialization of perceived academic competence among highly competent children. *Child Development, 58*, 1308–1320.

Phillips, M. (1997). What makes schools effective? A comparison of the relationships of communitarian climate and academic climate to mathematics achievement and attendance during middle school. *American Educational Research Journal, 34*, 633–662.

Phillips, M. (1997). What makes schools effective? A comparison of the relationships of communitarian climate and academic climate to mathematics achievement and attendance during middle school. *American Educational Research Journal, 34*, 633–662.

Phillipsen, L. C. (1999). Associations between age, gender, and group acceptance and three components of friendship quality. *Journal of Early Adolescence, 19*, 438–464.

Phinney, J., & Ong, A. (2001). *Family obligations and life satisfaction among adolescents from immigrant and non-immigrant families: Direct and moderated effects.* Unpublished manuscript, California State University, Los Angeles.

Phinney, J. S. (1989). Stages of ethnic identity development in minority group adolescents. *Journal of Early Adolescence, 9*, 34–49.

Phinney, J. S. (1993). A three stage model of ethnic identity development in adolescents. In M. E. Bernal & G. P. Knight (Eds.), *Ethnic identity: Formation and transmission among Hispanic and other minorities* (pp. 61–80). Albany, NY: State University of New York Press.

Phinney, J. S., Ferguson, D. L., & Tate, J. D. (1997). Intergroup attitudes

among ethnic minority adolescents: A causal model. *Child Development, 68*, 955–969.

Phinney, J. S., & Kohatsu, E. L. (1997). Ethnic and racial identity development and mental health. In J. Schulenberg, J. L. Maggs, & K. Hurrelmann (Eds.), *Health risks and developmental transitions during adolescence* (pp. 420–443). Cambridge, UK: Cambridge University Press.

Phinney, J. S., Ong, A., & Madden, T. (2000). Cultural values and intergenerational value discrepancies in immigrant and non-immigrant families. *Child Development, 71*, 528–539.

Piaget, J. (1926). *The language and thought of the child.* New York: Harcourt, Brace & World. (Original work published 1923)

Piaget, J. (1930). *The child's conception of the world.* New York: Harcourt, Brace, & World. (Original work published 1926)

Piaget, J. (1950). *The psychology of intelligence.* New York: International Universities Press.

Piaget, J. (1951). *Play, dreams, and imitation in childhood.* New York: Norton. (Original work published 1945)

Piaget, J. (1952). *The origins of intelligence in children.* New York: International Universities Press. (Original work published 1936)

Piaget, J. (1965). *The moral judgment of the child.* New York: Free Press. (Original work published 1932)

Piaget, J. (1967). *Six psychological studies.* New York: Vintage.

Piaget, J. (1971). *Biology and knowledge.* Chicago: University of Chicago Press.

Piaget, J. (1985). *The equilibration of cognitive structures: The central problem of intellectual development.* Chicago: University of Chicago Press.

Piaget, J., Inhelder, B., & Szeminska, A. (1960). *The child's conception of geometry.* New York: Basic Books. (Original work published 1948)

Pianta, R., Egeland, B., & Erickson, M. F. (1989). The antecedents of maltreatment: Results of the Mother–Child Interaction Research Project. In D. Cicchetti & V. Carlson (Eds.), *Child maltreatment* (pp. 203–253). New York: Cambridge University Press.

Pick, A. D., & Frankel, G. W. (1974). A developmental study of strategies of visual selectivity. *Child Development, 45*, 1162–1165.

Pickering, L. K., Granoff, D. M., Erickson, J. R., Mason, M. L., & Cordle, C. T. (1998). Modulation of the immune system by human milk and infant formula containing nucleotides. *Pediatrics, 101*, 242–249.

Pierce, K. M., Hamm, J. V., & Vandell, D. L. (1999). Experiences in after-school programs and children's adjustment in first-grade classrooms. *Child Development, 70,* 756–767.

Pierce, S. H., & Lange, G. (2000). Relationships among metamemory, motivation and memory performance in young school-age children. *British Journal of Developmental Psychology, 18,* 121–135.

Pierce, W. D., & Epling, W. F. (1995). *Behavior analysis and learning.* Englewood Cliffs, NJ: Prentice-Hall.

Pietz, J., Dunckelmann, R., Rupp, A., Rating, D., Meinck, H. M., Schmidt, H., & Bremer, H. J. (1998). Neurological outcome in adult patients with early-treated phenylketonuria. *European Journal of Pediatrics, 157,* 824–830.

Pine, J. M. (1995). Variation in vocabulary development as a function of birth order. *Child Development, 66,* 272–281.

Pinel, J. P. J. (2000). *Biopsychology* (4th ed.). Boston: Allyn and Bacon.

Pinker, S. (1989). *Learnability and cognition.* Cambridge, MA: MIT Press.

Pinker, S., Lebeaux, D. S., & Frost, L. A. (1987). Productivity and constraints in the acquisition of the passive. *Cognition, 26,* 195–267.

Pipes, P. L. (1996). *Nutrition in infancy and childhood* (6th ed.). St. Louis: Mosby.

Pipp, S., Easterbrooks, M. A., & Brown, S. R. (1993). Attachment status and complexity of infants' self- and other-knowledge when tested with mother and father. *Social Development, 2,* 1–14.

Pivarnik, J. M. (1998). Potential effects of maternal physical activity on birth weight: Brief review. *Medicine & Science in Sports & Exercise, 30,* 407–414.

Plessinger, M. A., & Woods, J. R., Jr. (1998). Cocaine in pregnancy: Recent data on maternal and fetal risks. *Substance Abuse in Pregnancy, 25,* 99–118.

Plomin, R. (1994a). *Genetics and experience: The interplay between nature and nurture.* Thousand Oaks, CA: Sage.

Plomin, R. (1994b). Nature, nurture, and social development. *Social Development, 3,* 37–53.

Plumert, J. M., Pick, H. L., Jr., Marks, R. A., Kintsch, A. S., & Wegesin, D. (1994). Locating objects and communicating about locations: Organizational differences in children's searching and direction-giving. *Developmental Psychology, 30,* 443–453.

Poindron, P., & Le Neindre, P. (1980). Endocrine and sensory regulation of maternal behavior in the ewe. In J. S. Rosenblatt, R. A. Hinde, C. Beer, & M. Busnel (Eds.), *Advances in the study of behavior* (pp. 76–119). New York: Academic Press.

Polansky, N. A., Gaudin, J. M., Ammons, P. W., & Davis, K. B. (1985). The psychological ecology of the neglectful mother. *Child Abuse & Neglect, 9,* 265–275.

Polka, L., & Werker, J. F. (1994). Developmental changes in perception of non-native vowel contrasts. *Journal of Experimental Psychology: Human Perception and Performance, 20,* 421–435.

Pollitt, E. (1996). A reconceptualization of the effects of undernutrition on children's biological, psychosocial, and behavioral development. *Social Policy Report of the Society for Research in Child Development, 10*(5).

Pollitt, E., Gorman, K. S., Engle, P. L., Martorell, R., & Rivera, J. (1993). Early supplementary feeding and cognition. *Monographs of the Society for Research in Child Development, 58*(7, Serial No. 235).

Pomerantz, E. M., & Ruble, D. N. (1998a). The multidimensional nature of control: Implications for the development of sex differences in self-evaluation. In J. Heckhausen & C. S. Dweck (Eds.), *Motivation and self-regulation across the lifespan* (pp. 159–184). New York: Cambridge University Press.

Pomerantz, E. M., & Ruble, D. N. (1998b). The role of maternal control in the development of sex differences in child self-evaluative factions. *Child Development, 69,* 458–478.

Popkin, B. M. (1994). The nutrition transition in low-income countries: An emerging crisis. *Nutrition Review, 52,* 285–298.

Popkin, B. M., Richards, M. K., & Montiero, C. A. (1996). Stunting is associated with overweight in children of four nations that are undergoing the nutrition transition. *Journal of Nurition, 126,* 3009–3016.

Porges, S. W. (1991). Autonomic regulation and attention. In B. A. Campbell, H. Hayne, & R. Richardson (Eds.), *Attention and information processing in infants and adults* (pp. 201–223). Hillsdale, NJ: Erlbaum.

Porter, R. H., Makin, J. W., Davis, L. B., & Christensen, K. M. (1992). An assessment of the salient olfactory environment of formula-fed infants. *Physiology & Behavior, 50,* 907–911.

Porter, R. H., & Winberg, J. (1999). Unique salience of maternal breast odors for newborn infants. *Neuroscience and Biobehavioral Reviews, 23,* 439–449.

Portman, P. A. (1995). Who is having fun in physical education classes? Experiences of sixth-grade students in elementary and middle schools. *Journal of Teaching in Physical Education, 14,* 445–453.

Posada, G., Gao, Y., Wu, F., Posada, R., Tascon, M., Schöelmerich, A., Sagi, A., Kondo-Ikemura, K., Haaland, W., & Synnevaag, B. (1995). The secure-base phenomenon across cultures: Children's behavior, mothers' preferences, and experts' concepts. In E. Waters, B. E. Vaughn, G. Posada, & K. Kondo-Ikemura K. (Eds.), *Caregiving, cultural, and cognitive perspectives on secure-base behavior and working models: New growing points of attachment theory and research. Monographs of the Society for Research in Child Development, 60* (2–3, Serial No. 244).

Posner, J. K., & Vandell, D. L. (1994). Low-income children's after-school care: Are there beneficial effects of after-school programs? *Child Development, 64,* 440–456.

Posner, J. K., & Vandell, D. L. (1999). After-school activities and the development of low-income urban children: A longitudinal study. *Developmental Psychology, 35,* 868–879.

Posner, M. I., Rothbart, M. K., Gerardi, G., & Thomas-Thrapp, L. (1997). Functions of orienting in early infancy. In P. Lange, M. Balaban, & R. F. Simmons (Eds.), *The study of attention: Cognitive perspectives from psychophysiology, reflexology, and neuroscience* (pp. 327–345). Hillsdale, NJ: Erlbaum.

Potischman, N., & Troisi, R. (1999). In-utero and early life exposures in relation to risk of breast cancer. *Cancer Causes and Control, 10,* 561–573.

Poulin-Dubois, D., & Héroux, G. (1994). Movement and children's attributions of life properties. *International Journal of Behavioral Development, 17,* 329–347.

Poulin-Dubois, D., Serbin, L. A., Kenyon, B., & Derbyshire, A. (1994). Infants' intermodal knowledge about gender. *Developmental Psychology, 30,* 436–442.

Powell, B., & Steelman, L. C. (1993). The educational benefits of being spaced out: Sibship density and educational progress. *American Sociological Review, 58,* 367–381.

Powers, S. I., Hauser, S. T., & Kilner, L. A. (1989). Adolescent mental health. *American Psychologist, 44,* 200–208.

Powers, W. F., & Wampler, N. S. (1996). Further defining risks confronting twins. *American Journal of Obstetrics and Gynecology, 175,* 1522–1528.

Powlishta, K. K., Serbin, L. A., & Moller, L. C. (1993). The stability of individual differences in gender typing: Implications for understanding gender segregation. *Sex Roles, 29,* 723–737.

Powls, A., Botting, N., Cooke, R. W. I., & Marlow, N. (1996). Handedness in very-low-birthweight (VLBW) children at 12 years of age: Relation to perinatal and outcome variables. *Developmental Medicine and Child Neurology, 38,* 594–602.

Pratt, M. W., Arnold, M. L., Pratt, A. T., & Diessner, R. (1999). Predicting adolescent moral reasoning from family climate: A longitudinal study. *Journal of Early Adolescence, 19,* 148–175.

Prechtl, H. F. R. (1958). Problems of behavioral studies in the newborn infant. In D. S. Lehrmann, R. A. Hinde, & E. Shaw (Eds.), *Advances in the study of behavior* (Vol. 1, pp. 75–98). New York: Academic Press.

Prechtl, H. F. R., & Beintema, D. (1965). *The neurological examination of the full-term newborn infant.* London: Heinemann Medical.

Preisler, G. M. (1991). Early patterns of interaction between blind infants and their sighted mothers. *Child: Care, Health and Development, 17,* 65–90.

Preisler, G. M. (1993). A descriptive study of blind children in nurseries with sighted children. *Child: Care, Health and Development, 19,* 295–315.

Pressley, M. (1995). More about the development of self-regulation: Complex, long-term, and thoroughly social. *Educational Psychologist, 30,* 207–212.

Previc, F. H. (1991). A general theory concerning the prenatal origins of cerebral lateralization. *Psychological Review, 98,* 299–334.

Prevost, R. A., Bronson, M. B., & Casey, M. B. (1995). Planning processes in preschool children. *Journal of Applied Developmental Psychology, 16,* 505–527.

Preyer, W. (1888). *The mind of the child* (2 vols.). New York: Appleton. (Original work published 1882)

Proos, L. A. (1993). Anthropometry in adolescence—secular trends, adoption, ethnic and environmental differences. *Hormone Research, 39,* 18–24.

Provins, K. A. (1997). Handedness and speech: A critical reappraisal of the role of genetic and environmental factors in the cerebral lateralization of function. *Psychological Review, 104,* 554–571.

Pryor, J. B., & Reeder, G. D. (1993). Collective and individual representations of HIV/AIDS stigma. In J. B. Pryor & G. D. Reeder (Eds.), *The social psychology of HIV infection* (pp. 263–286). Hillsdale, NJ: Erlbaum.

Prysak, M., Lorenz, R. P., & Kisly, A. (1995). Pregnancy outcome in nulliparous women 35 years and older. *Obstetrics and Gynecology, 85,* 65–70.

Punamaeki, R.-L. (1999). Concept formation of war and peace: A meeting point between child development and a politically violent society. In A. Raviv & L. Oppenheimer (Eds.), *How children understand war and peace* (pp. 127–144). San Francisco, CA: Jossey-Bass.

Pungello, E. P., & Kurtz-Costes, B. (1999). Why and how working women choose child care: A review with a focus on infancy. *Developmental Review, 19,* 31–96.

Purcell-Gates, V. (1996). Stories, coupons, and the TV guide: Relationships between home literacy experiences and emergent literacy knowledge. *Reading Research Quarterly, 31,* 406–428.

Pyeritz, R. E. (1998). Sex: What we make of it. *Journal of the American Medical Association, 279,* 269.

Qazi, Q. H., Sheikh, T. M., Fikrig, S., & Menikoff, H. (1988). Lack of evidence for craniofacial dysmorphism in perinatal human immunodeficiency virus infection. *Journal of Pediatrics, 11,* 7–11.

Quinn, P. C., & Eimas, P. D. (1996). Perceptual organization and categorization in young infants. In C. Rovee-Collier & P. P. Lipsitt (Eds.), *Advances in infancy research* (Vol. 10, pp. 1–36). Norwood, NJ: Ablex.

Quint, J. C., Box, J. M., & Polit, D. F. (1997). *New Chance: Final report on a comprehensive program for disadvantaged young mothers and their children.* New York: Manpower Demonstration Research Corporation.

Quintero, R. A., Puder, K. S., & Cotton, D. B. (1993). Embryoscopy and fetoscopy. *Obstetrics and Gynecology Clinics of North America, 20,* 563–581.

Quyen, G. T., Bird, H. R., Davies, M., Hoven, C., Cohen, P., Jensen, P. S., & Goodman, S. (1998). Adverse life events and resilience. *Journal of the American Academy of Child and Adolescent Psychiatry, 37,* 1191–1200.

Raag, T., & Rackliff, C. L. (1998). Preschoolers' awareness of social expectations of gender: Relationships to toy choices. *Sex Roles, 38,* 685–700.

Radin, N. (1994). Primary caregiving fathers in intact families. In A. E. Gottfried & A. W. Gottfried (Eds.), *Redefining families: Implications for children's development* (pp. 11–54). New York: Plenum.

Radziszewska, B., & Rogoff, B. (1988). Influence of adult and peer collaboration on the development of children's planning skills. *Developmental Psychology, 24,* 840–848.

Rahn, W. M., & Transue, J. E. (1998). Social trust and value change: The decline of social capital in American youth, 1976–1995. *Political Psychology, 19,* 545–565.

Raisler, J. (1999). Breast-feeding and infant illness: A dose-response relationship? *American Journal of Public Health, 89,* 25–30.

Rakison, D. H., & Butterworth, G. E. (1998). Infants' use of object parts in early categorization. *Developmental Psychology, 34,* 49–62.

Ramey, C. T., Campbell, F. A., & Ramey, S. L. (1999). Early intervention: Successful pathways to improving intellectual development. *Developmental Neuropsychology, 16,* 385–392.

Ramey, C. T., & Ramey, S. L. (1998). Early intervention and early experience. *American Psychologist, 53,* 109–120.

Ramos, E., Frontera, W. R., Llopart, A., & Feliciano, D. (1998). Muscle strength and hormonal levels in adolescents: Gender related differences. *International Journal of Sports Medicine, 19,* 526–531.

Rand, Y., & Kaniel, S. (1987). Group administration of the LPAD. In C. S. Lidz (Ed.), *Dynamic assessment: An interactional approach to evaluating learning potential* (pp. 196–214). New York: Guilford.

Ranly, D. M. (1998). Early orofacial development. *Journal of Clinical Pediatric Dentistry, 22,* 267–275.

Rapport, M. D., & Chung, K.-M. (2000). Attention deficit hyperactivity disorder. In M. Hersen & R. T. Ammerman (Eds.), *Advanced abnormal child psychology* (2nd ed., pp. 413–440). Mahwah, NJ: Erlbaum.

Rast, M., & Meltzoff, A. N. (1995). Memory and representation in young children with Down syndrome: Exploring deferred imitation and object permanence. *Development and Psychopathology, 7,* 393–407.

Ratcliffe, S. G., Pan, H., & McKie, M. (1992). Growth during puberty in the XYY boy. *Annals of Human Biology, 19,* 579–587.

Ratner, N. B. (2001). Atypical language development. In J. B. Gleason (Ed.), *The development of language* (4th ed., pp. 347–408). Boston: Allyn and Bacon.

Ravussin, E., Valencia, M. E., Esparza, J., Bennett, P. H., & Schulz, L. O. (1994). Effects of a traditional lifestyle on obesity in Pima Indians. *Diabetes Care, 17,* 1067–1074.

Rayner, K., & Pollatsek, A. (1989). *The psychology of reading.* Englewood Cliffs, NJ: Prentice-Hall.

Raz, S., Shah, F., & Sander, C. J. (1996). Differential effects of perinatal hypoxic risk on early developmental outcome: A twin study. *Neuropsychology, 10,* 429–436.

Read, C. R. (1991). Achievement and career choices: Comparisons of males and females. *Roeper Review, 13,* 188–193.

Read, M. (1968). *Children of their fathers: Growing up among the Ngoni of Malawi.* New York: Holt, Rinehart & Winston.

Redl, F. (1966). *When we deal with children.* New York: Free Press.

Rees, M. (1993). Menarche: When and why? *Lancet, 342,* 1375–1376.

Reese, E., Haden, C. A., & Fivush, R. (1993). Mother–child conversations about the past: Relationships of style and memory over time. *Cognitive Development, 8,* 403–430.

Reese, E., Haden, C. A., & Fivush, R. (1996). Mothers, fathers, daughters and sons: Gender differences in autobiographical reminiscing. *Research on Language and Social Interaction, 29*(1), 27–56.

Reifsnider, E., & Gill, S. L. (2000). Nutrition for the childbearing years. *Journal of Obstetrics, Gynecology, and Neonatal Nursing, 29,* 43–55.

Reilly, K. (2000). Nutrition, exercise, work, and sex in pregnancy. *Primary Care: Clinics in Office Practice, 27,* 105–115.

Reimer, M. (1996). "Sinking into the ground": The development and consequences of shame in adolescence. *Developmental Review, 16,* 321–363.

Reis, M. (1992). Making connections from urban schools. *Education and Urban Society, 24,* 477–488.

Reiser, J., Yonas, A., & Wikner, K. (1976). Radial localization of odors by human neonates. *Child Development, 47,* 856–859.

Reisman, J. E. (1987). Touch, motion, and proprioception. In P. Salapatek & L. Cohen (Eds.), *Handbook of infant perception: Vol. 1. From sensation to perception* (pp. 265–303). Orlando, FL: Academic Press.

Renninger, K. A. (1998). Developmental psychology and instruction: Issues from and for practice. In I. Sigel & K. A. Renninger (Eds.), *Handbook of child psychology: Vol. 4. Child psychology and practice* (pp. 211–274). New York: Wiley.

Repacholi, B. M. (1998). Infants' use of attentional cues to identify the referent of another person's emotional expression. *Developmental Psychology, 34,* 1017–1025.

Repacholi, B. M., & Gopnik, A. (1997). Early reasoning about desires: Evidence from 14- and 18-month-olds. *Developmental Psychology, 33,* 12–21.

Repke, J. T. (1992). Drug supplementation in pregnancy. *Current Opinion in Obstetrics and Gynecology, 4,* 802–806.

Resnick, M. B., Gueorguieva, R. V., Carter, R. L., Ariet, M., Sun, Y., Roth, J., Bucciarelli, R. L., Curran, J. S., & Mahan, C. S. (1999). The impact of low birth weight, perinatal conditions, and sociodemographic factors on educational outcome in kindergarten. *Pediatrics, 104,* e74.

Rest, J. R. (1979). *Development in judging moral issues.* Minneapolis: University of Minnesota Press.

Rest, J. R., & Narvaez, D. (1991). The college experience and moral development. In W. M. Kurtines & J. L. Gewirtz (Eds.), *Handbook of moral behavior and development* (Vol. 2, pp. 229–245). Hillsdale, NJ: Erlbaum.

Reynolds, A. J., & Temple, J. A. (1998). Extended early childhood intervention and school achievement: Age thirteen findings from the Chicago Longitudinal Study. *Child Development, 69,* 231–246.

Reynolds, C. R., & Kaiser, S. M. (1990). Test bias in psychological assessment. In T. B. Gutkin & C. R. Reynolds (Eds.), *The handbook of school psychology* (pp. 487–525). New York: Wiley.

Reznick, J. S., & Goldfield, B. A. (1992). Rapid change in lexical development in comprehension and production. *Developmental Psychology, 28,* 406–413.

Rhea, D. J. (1999). Eating disorder behaviors of ethnically diverse urban female adolescent athletes and non-athletes. *Journal of Adolescence, 22,* 379–388.

Rhee, S. H., Waldman, I. D., Hay, D. A., & Levy, F. (1999). Sex differences in genetic and environmental influences on DSM-III-R attention deficit/hyperactivity disorder. *Journal of Abnormal Psychology, 108,* 24–41.

Ricard, M., & Kamberk-Kilicci, M. (1995). Children's empathic responses to emotional complexity. *International Journal of Behavioral Development, 18,* 211–225.

Rice, F. P. (1999). *The adolescent: Development, relationships, and culture* (8th ed.). Boston: Allyn and Bacon.

Rice, M. L., Huston, A. C., Truglio, R., & Wright, J. (1990). Words from "Sesame Street": Learning vocabulary while viewing. *Developmental Psychology, 26,* 421–428.

Richards, D. D., & Siegler, R. S. (1986). Children's understandings of the attributes of life. *Journal of Experimental Child Psychology, 42,* 1–22.

Richards, J. E., & Holley, F. B. (1999). Infant attention and the development of smooth pursuit tracking. *Developmental Psychology, 35,* 856–867.

Richards, M. H., & Duckett, E. (1994). The relationship of maternal employment to early adolescent daily experience with and without parents. *Child Development, 65,* 225–236.

Richards-Colocino, N., McKenzie, P., & Newton, R. R. (1996). Project Success: Comprehensive intervention services for middle school high-risk youth. *Journal of Adolescent Research, 11,* 130–163.

Richardson, G. A., Hamel, S. C., Goldschmidt, L., & Day, N. L. (1996). The effects of prenatal cocaine use on neonatal neurobehavioral status. *Neurotoxicology and Teratology, 18,* 519–528.

Rich-Edwards, J. W., Colditz, G. A., Stampfer, M. J., Willett, W. C., Gillman, M. W., Hennekens, C. H., Speizer, F. E., & Manson, J. E. (1999). Birthweight and the risk for type 2 diabetes mellitus in adult women. *Annals of Internal Medicine, 130,* 278–284.

Rich-Edwards, J. W., Stampfer, M. J., Manson, J. E., Rosner, B., Hankinson, S. E., Colditz, G. A., Willett, W. C., & Hennekens, C. H. (1997). Birth weight and risk of cardiovascular disease in a cohort of women followed up since 1976. *British Medical Journal, 315,* 396–400.

Rickel, A. U., & Becker, E. (1997). *Keeping children from harm's way.* Washington, DC: American Psychological Association.

Ridderinkhof, K. R., & Molen, M. W. van der (1997). Mental resources, processing speed, and inhibitory control: A developmental perspective. *Biological Psychology, 45,* 241–261.

Riggs, K. J., & Peterson, D. M. (2000). Counterfactual thinking in preschool children: Mental state and causal inferences. In P. Mitchell & K. J. Riggs (Eds.), *Children's reasoning and the mind* (pp. 87–99). Hove, UK: Psychology Press.

Rijsdijk, F. V., & Boomsma, D. I. (1997). Genetic mediation of the correlation between peripheral nerve conduction velocity and IQ. *Behavior Genetics, 27,* 87–98.

Rivara, F. P. (1995). Developmental and behavioral issues in childhood injury prevention. *Developmental and Behavioral Pediatrics, 16,* 362–370.

Rivara, F. P., & Aitken, M. (1998). Prevention of injuries to children and adolescents. In L. A. Barness (Ed.), *Advances in pediatrics* (Vol. 45, pp. 37–72). St. Louis: Mosby.

Rivkin, M. J. (2000). Developmental neuroimagining of children using magnetic resonance techniques. *Mental Retardation & Developmental Disabilities Research, 6,* 68–80.

Roazzi, A., & Bryant, P. (1997). Explicitness and conservation: Social class differences. *International Journal of Behavioral Development, 21,* 51–70.

Roberton, M. A. (1984). Changing motor patterns during childhood. In J. R. Thomas (Ed.), *Motor development during childhood and adolescence* (pp. 48–90). Minneapolis, MN: Burgess.

Roberts, I., & DiGuiseppi, C. (1999). Injury prevention. *Archives of Disease in Childhood, 81,* 200–201.

Roberts, J. E., Burchinal, M. R., & Campbell, F. (1994). Otitis media in early childhood and patterns of intellectual development and later academic performance. *Journal of Pediatric Psychology, 19,* 347–367.

Roberts, J. E., Burchinal, M., & Durham, M. (1999). Parents' report of vocabulary and grammatical development of African American preschoolers: Child and environment associations. *Child Development, 70,* 92–106.

Roberts, L., Jorm, L., Patel, M., Smith, W., Douglas, R. M., & McGilchrist, C. (2000). Effect of infection control measures on the frequency of diarrheal episodes in child care: A randomized, controlled trial. *Pediatrics, 105,* 743–746.

Roberts, M. C., Alexander, K., & Knapp, L. G. (1990). Motivating children to use safety belts: A program combining rewards and "flash for life." *Journal of Community Psychology, 18,* 110–119.

Roberts, M. C., Fanurik, D., & Wilson, D. R. (1988). A community program to reward children's use of seat belts. *American Journal of Community Psychology, 16,* 395–407.

Roberts, R. J., Jr., & Aman, C. J. (1993). Developmental differences in giving directions: Spatial frames of reference and mental rotation. *Child Development, 64,* 1258–1270.

Roberts, W., & Strayer, J. (1996). Empathy, emotional expressiveness, and prosocial behavior. *Child Development, 67,* 449–470.

Robertson, N. J., & Edwards, A. D. (1998). Recent advances in developing neuroprotective strategies for perinatal asphyxia. *Current Opinion in Pediatrics, 10,* 575–580.

Robin, A. L., Gilroy, M., & Dennis, A. B. (1998). Treatment of eating disorders in children and adolescents. *Clinical Psychology Review, 18,* 421–446.

Robin, D. J., Berthier, N. E., & Clifton, R. K. (1996). Infants' predictive reaching for moving objects in the dark. *Developmental Psychology, 32,* 824–835.

Robinson, B. E. (1999). Factors associated with the prevalence of myopia in 6-year-olds. *Optometry and Vision Science, 76,* 266–271.

Robinson, T. N. (1999). Reducing children's television viewing to prevent obesity. *Journal of the American Medical Association, 282,* 1561–1567.

Rochat, P. (1989). Object manipulation and exploration in 2- to 5-month-old infants. *Developmental Psychology, 25,* 871–884.

Rochat, P. (1992). Self-sitting and reaching in 5- to 8-month-old infants: The impact of posture and its development on early eye–hand coordination. *Journal of Motor Behavior, 24,* 210–220.

Rochat, P. (1998). Self-perception and action in infancy. *Experimental Brain Research, 123,* 102–109.

Rochat, P., & Goubet, N. (1995). Development of sitting and reaching in 5- to 6-month-old infants. *Infant Behavior and Development, 18,* 53–68.

Rochat, P., Querido, J. G., & Striano, T. (1999). Emerging sensitivity to the timing and structure of protoconversation. *Developmental Psychology, 35,* 950–957.

Roche, A. F. (1981). The adipocyte-number hypothesis. *Child Development, 52,* 31–43.

Rodgers, J. L., Cleveland, H. H., van den Oord, E., & Rowe, D. C. (2000). Resolving the debate over birth order, family size, and intelligence. *American Psychologist, 55,* 599–612.

Rodkin, P. C., Farmer, T. W., Pearl, R., & Van Acker, R. (2000). Heterogeneity of popular boys: Antisocial and prosocial configurations. *Developmental Psychology, 36,* 14–24.

Roe, B., Whittington, L. A., Fein, S. B., & Teisl, M. F. (1999). Is there competition between breastfeeding and maternal employment? *Demography, 36,* 157–171.

Roebuck, T. M., Mattson, S. N., & Riley, E. P. (1999). Prenatal exposure to alcohol: Effects on brain structure and neuropsychological functioning. In J. H. Hannigan & L. P. Spear (Eds.), *Alcohol and alcoholism: Effects on brain and development* (pp. 1–16). Mahwah, NJ: Erlbaum.

Roeser, R. W., & Eccles, J. S. (1998). Adolescents' perceptions of middle school: Relation to longitudinal changes in academic and psychological adjustment. *Journal of Research on Adolescence, 8,* 123–158.

Roeser, R. W., Eccles, J. S., & Freedman-Doan, C. (1999). Academic functioning and mental health in adolescence: Patterns, progressions, and routes from childhood. *Journal of Adolescent Research, 14,* 135–174.

Roffwarg, H. P., Muzio, J. N., & Dement, W. C. (1966). Ontogenetic development of the human sleep–dream cycle. *Science, 152,* 604–619.

Rogers, C., & Shiff, M. (1996). Early versus late prenatal care in New Mexico: Barriers and motivators. *Birth, 23,* 26–30.

Rogers, L., Resnick, M. D., Mitchell, J. E., & Blum, R. W. (1997). The relationship between socioeconomic status and eating disordered behaviors in a community sample of adolescent girls. *International Journal of Eating Disorders, 22,* 15–23.

Roggman, L. A., Langlois, J. H., Hubbs-Tait, L., & Rieser-Danner, L. A. (1994). Infant day-care, attachment, and the "file drawer problem." *Child Development, 65,* 1429–1443.

Rogoff, B. (1986). The development of strategic use of context in spatial memory. In M. Perlmutter (Ed.), *Perspectives on intellectual development* (pp. 107–123). Hillsdale, NJ: Erlbaum.

Rogoff, B. (1990). *Apprenticeship in thinking.* New York: Oxford University Press.

Rogoff, B. (1996). Developmental transitions in children's participation in sociocultural activities. In A. J. Sameroff & M. M. Haith (Eds.), *The five to seven year shift: The age of reason and responsibility,* (pp. 273–294). Chicago: University of Chicago Press.

Rogoff, B. (1998). Cognition as a collaborative process. In D. Kuhn & R. S. Siegler (Eds.), *Handbook of child psychology: Vol. 2. Cognition, perception, and language* (5th ed., pp. 679–744). New York: Wiley.

Rogoff, B., & Chavajay, P. (1995). What's become of research on the cultural basis of cognitive development? *American Psychologist, 50,* 859–877.

Rogoff, B., Malkin, C., & Gilbride, K. (1984). Interaction with babies as guidance in development. In B. Rogoff & J. V. Wertsch (Eds.), *New directions for child development* (No. 23, pp. 31–44). San Francisco: Jossey-Bass.

Rogosch, F., Cicchetti, D., Shields, A., & Toth, S. L. (1995). Parenting dysfunction in child maltreatment. In M. H. Bornstein (Ed.), *Handbook of parenting* (Vol. 4, pp. 127–159). Hillsdale, NJ: Erlbaum.

Rohlen, T. P. (1997). Differences that make a difference: Explaining Japan's success. In W. K. Cummings & P. G. Altbach (Eds.), *The challenge of Eastern Asian education: Implications for America* (pp. 223–248). Albany, NY: SUNY Press.

Rohner, R. P., & Rohner, E. C. (1981). Parental acceptance– rejection and parental control: Cross-cultural codes. *Ethnology, 20,* 245–260.

Rojewski, J. W., & Hill, R. B. (1998). Influence of gender and academic risk behavior on career decision making and occupational choice in early adolescence. *Journal of Education for Students Placed at Risk, 3,* 265–287.

Romaine, S. (1984). *The language of children and adolescents: The acquisition of communicative competence.* Oxford, England: Blackwell.

Romans, S. M., Roeltgen, D. P., Kushner, H., & Ross, J. L. (1997). Executive function in girls with Turner's syndrome. *Developmental Neuropsychology, 13,* 23–40.

Rönnqvist, L., & Hopkins, B. (1998). Head position preference in the human newborn: A new look. *Child Development, 69,* 13–23.

Roopnarine, J. L., Hossain, Z., Gill, P., & Brophy, H. (1994). Play in the East Indian context. In J. L. Roopnarine, J. E. Johnson, & F. H. Hooper (Eds.), *Children's play in diverse cultures* (pp. 9–30). Albany, NY: SUNY Press.

Roopnarine, J. L., Lasker, J., Sacks, M., & Stores, M. (1998). The cultural contexts of children's play. In O. N. Saracho & B. Spodek (Eds.), *Multiple perspectives on play in early childhood education* (pp. 194–219). Albany: State University of New York Press.

Roopnarine, J. L., Talukder, E., Jain, D., Joshi, P., & Srivastav, P. (1990). Characteristics of holding, patterns of play, and social behaviors between parents and infants in New Delhi, India. *Developmental Psychology, 26,* 667–673.

Roscoe, B., Diana, M. S., & Brooks, R. H. (1987). Early, middle, and late adolescents' views on dating and factors influencing partner selection. *Adolescence, 22,* 59–68.

Rose, A. J., & Asher, S. R. (1999). Children's goals and strategies in response to conflicts within a friendship. *Developmental Psychology, 35,* 69–79.

Rose, L. (2000). Fathers of full-term infants. In N. Tracey (Ed.), *Parents of premature infants: Their emotional world* (pp. 105–116). London, UK: Whurr.

Rose, S. A., & Feldman, J. F. (1997). Memory and speed: Their role in the relation of infant information processing to later IQ. *Child Development, 68,* 610–620.

Rose, S. A., Jankowski, J. J., & Senior, G. J. (1997). Infants' recognition of contour-deleted figures. *Journal of Experimental Psychology: Human Perception and Performance, 23,* 1206–1216.

Rosen, A. B., & Rozin, P. (1993). Now you see it, now you don't: The preschool child's conception of invisible particles in the context of dissolving. *Developmental Psychology, 29,* 300–311.

Rosen, M. G., & Dickinson, J. C. (1992). Management of post-term pregnancy. *New England Journal of Medicine, 326,* 1628–1629.

Rosen, W. D., Adamson, L. B., & Bakeman, R. (1992). An experimental investigation of infant social referencing: Mothers' messages and gender differences. *Developmental Psychology, 28,* 1172–1178.

Rosenberg, D. R., Sweeney, J. A., Gillen, J. S., Kim J., Varanelli, M. J., O'Hearn, K. M., & Erb, P. A. (1997). Magnetic resonance imaging of children without sedation preparation with simulation. *Journal of the American Academy of Child and Adolescent Psychiatry, 36,* 853–859.

Rosenblatt, J. S., & Lehrman, D. (1963). Maternal behavior of the laboratory rat. In H. R. Rheingold (Ed.). *Maternal behavior in mammals* (pp. 8–57). New York: Wiley.

Rosenshine, B., & Meister, C. (1994). Reciprocal teaching: A review of nineteen experimental studies. *Review of Educational Research, 64,* 479–530.

Rosenstein, D., & Oster, H. (1990). Differential facial expressions in response to four basic tastes in infants. *Child Development, 59,* 1555–1568.

Rosenthal, J. A. (1992). *Special-needs adoption: A study of intact families.* New York: Praeger.

Ross, H. S., Conant, C., Cheyne, J. A., & Alevizos, E. (1992). Relationships and alliances in the social interactions of kibbutz toddlers. *Social Development, 1,* 1–17.

Rothbart, M. K. (1981). Measurement of temperament in infancy. *Child Development, 52,* 569–578.

Rothbart, M. K. (1989). Temperament and development. In G. A. Kohnstamm, J. A. Bates, & M. K. Rothbart (Eds.), *Temperament in childhood* (pp. 59–73). New York: Wiley.

Rothbart, M. K., Ahadi, S. A., & Evans, D. E. (2000). Temperament and personality: Origins and outcome. *Journal of Personality and Social Psychology, 78,* 122–135.

Rothbart, M. K., & Bates, J. E. (1998). Temperament. In N. Eisenberg (Ed.), *Handbook of child psychology: Vol. 3. Social, emotional, and personality development* (5th ed., pp. 105–176). New York: Wiley.

Rousseau, J. J. (1955). *Emile.* New York: Dutton. (Original work published 1762)

Rovee-Collier, C. (1999). The development of infant memory. *Current Directions in Psychological Science, 8,* 80–85.

Rovee-Collier, C. (1996). Shifting the focus from what to do why. *Infant Behavior and Development, 19,* 385–400.

Rovee-Collier, C. K. (1987). Learning and memory. In J. D. Osofsky (Ed.), *Handbook of infant development* (2nd ed., pp. 98–148). New York: Wiley.

Rovee-Collier, C. K., & Bhatt, R. S. (1993). Evidence of long-term memory in infancy. *Annals of Child Development, 9,* 1–45.

Rovet, J., Netley, C., Keenan, M., Bailey, J., & Stewart, D. (1996). The psychoeducational profile of boys with Klinefelter syndrome. *Journal of Learning Disabilities, 29,* 180–196.

Rowe, D. (1994). *The limits of family influence: Genes, experience, and behavior.* New York: Guilford.

Royal College of Obstetricians and Gynecologists. (l997, October). *Report of the panel to review fetal pain.* London: Author.

Rubin, K., Bukowski, W., & Parker, J. G. (1998). Peer interactions, relationships, and groups. In N. Eisenberg (Ed.), *Handbook of child psychology: Vol. 3. Social, emotional, and personality development* (5th ed., pp. 619–700). New York: Wiley.

Rubin, K. H., & Coplan, R. J. (1998). Social and nonsocial play in childhood: An individual differences perspective. In O. N. Saracho & B. Spodek (Eds.), *Multiple perspectives on play in early childhood education* (pp. 144–170). Albany, NY: State University of New York Press.

Rubin, K. H., Coplan, R. J., Fox, N. A., & Calkins, S. D. (1995). Emotionality, emotion regulation, and preschoolers' social adaptation. *Development and Psychopathology, 7,* 49–62.

Rubin, K. H., Fein, G. G., & Vandenberg, B. (1983). Play. In E. M. Hetherington (Ed.), *Handbook of child psychology: Vol. 4. Socialization, personality, and social development* (4th ed., pp. 693–744). New York: Wiley.

Rubin, K. H., Hastings, P. D., Stewart, S. L., Henderson, H. A., & Chen, X. (1997). The consistency and concomitants of inhibition: Some of the children, all of the time. *Child Development, 68,* 467–483.

Rubin, K. H., Stewart, S. L., & Coplan, R. J. (1995). Social withdrawal in childhood: Conceptual and empirical perspectives. In T. H. Ollendick & R. J. Prinz (Eds.), *Advances in clinical child psychology* (Vol. 17, pp. 157–196). New York: Plenum.

Rubin, K. H., Watson, K. S., & Jambor, T. W. (1978). Free-play behaviors in preschool and kindergarten children. *Child Development, 49,* 539–536.

Ruble, D. N., & Flett, G. L. (1988). Conflicting goals in self-evaluative information seeking: Developmental and ability level analyses. *Child Development, 59,* 97–106.

Ruble, D. N., & Frey, K. S. (1991). Changing patterns of comparative behavior as skills are acquired: A functional model of self-evaluation. In J. Suls & T. A. Wills (Eds.), *Social comparison: Contemporary theory and research* (pp. 70–112). Hillsdale, NJ: Erlbaum.

Ruble, D. N., & Martin, C. L. (1998). Gender development. In N. Eisenberg (Ed.), *Handbook of child psychology: Vol. 3. Social, emotional, and personality development* (pp. 933–1016). New York: Wiley.

Rudolph, D. K., & Heller, T. L. (1997). Interpersonal problem solving, externalizing behavior, and social competence in preschoolers: A knowledge-performance discrepancy? *Journal of Applied Developmental Psychology, 18,* 107–117.

Ruff, H. A., & Lawson, K. R. (1990). Development of sustained, focused attention in young children during free play. *Developmental Psychology, 26,* 85–93.

Ruff, H. A., Lawson, K. R., Parinello, R., & Weissberg, R. (1990). Long-term stability of individual differences in sustained attention in the early years. *Child Development, 61,* 60–75.

Ruff, H. A., & Rothbart, M. K. (1996). *Attention in early development.* New York: Oxford University Press.

Ruffman, T. (1999). Children's understanding of logical inconsistency. *Child Development, 70,* 872–886.

Ruffman, T., Perner, J., Naito, M., Parkin, L., & Clements, W. A. (1998). Older (but not younger) siblings facilitate false belief understanding. *Developmental Psychology, 34,* 161–174.

Ruffman, T., Perner, J., Olson, D. R., & Doherty, M. (1993). Reflecting on scientific thinking: Children's understanding of the hypothesis–evidence relation. *Child Development, 64,* 1617–1636.

Rumbaut, R. G. (1997). Ties that bind: Immigration and immigrant families in the United States. In A. Booth, A. C. Crouter, & N. Landale (Eds.), *Immigration and the family: Research and policy on U.S. immigrants* (pp. 3–46). Mahwah, NJ: Erlbaum.

Rumberger, R. W., & Larson, K. A. (1998). Student mobility and the increased risk of high school dropout. *American Journal of Education, 107,* 1–35.

Rumberger, R. W., & Thomas, S. L. (2000). The distribution of dropout and turnover rates among urban and suburban high schools. *Sociology of Education, 73,* 39–67.

Runco, M. A. (1992). Children's divergent thinking and creative ideation. *Developmental Review, 12,* 233–264.

Russell, J. A. (1990). The preschooler's understanding of the causes and consequences of emotion. *Child Development, 61,* 1872–1881.

Rutter, M. (1987). Psychosocial resilience and protective mechanisms. *American Journal of Orthopsychiatry, 57,* 316–331.

Rutter, M. (1996). Maternal deprivation. In M. H. Bornstein (Ed.), *Handbook of parenting: Vol. 4. Applied and practical parenting* (pp. 3–31). Mahwah, NJ: Erlbaum.

Rutter, M., et al. (1998). Developmental catch-up, and deficit, following adoption after severe global early privation. *Journal of Child Psychology and Psychiatry, 39,* 465–476.

Rvachew, S., Slawinski, E., Williams, M., & Green, C. L. (1999). The impact of early onset otitis media on babbling and early language development. *Journal of the Acoustical Society of America, 105,* 467–475.

Ryynänen, M., Kirkinen, P., Mannermaa, A., & Saarikoski, S. (1995). Carrier diagnosis of the fragile X syndrome—a challenge in antenatal clinics. *American Journal of Obstetrics and Gynecology, 172,* 1236–1239.

Saarni, C. (1993). Socialization of emotion. In M. Lewis & J. M. Haviland (Eds.), *Handbook of emotions* (pp. 435–446). New York: Guilford.

Saarni, C. (1999). *The development of emotional competence.* New York: Guilford.

Saarni, C., Mumme, D. L., & Campos, J. J. (1998). Emotional development: Action, communication, and understanding. In N. Eisenberg (Ed.), *Handbook of child psychology: Vol. 3. Social, emotional,*

and personality development (5th ed., pp. 237–309). New York: Wiley.

Sacks, C. H., & Mergendoller, J. R. (1997). The relationship between teachers' theoretical orientation toward reading and student outcomes in kindergarten children with different initial reading abilities. *American Educational Research Journal, 34,* 721–739.

Sadeh, A. (1997). Sleep and melatonin in infants: A preliminary study. *Sleep, 20,* 185–191.

Sadler, T. W. (1995). *Langman's medical embryology* (7th ed.). Baltimore: Williams & Wilkins.

Safyer, A. W., Leahy, B. H., & Colan, N. B. (1995). The impact of work on adolescent development. *Families in Society, 76,* 38–45.

Sahni, R., Schulze, K. F., Stefanski, M., Myers, M. M., & Fifer, W. P. (1995). Methodological issues in coding sleep states in immature infants. *Developmental Psychobiology, 28,* 85–101.

Salapatek, P. (1975). Pattern perception in early infancy. In L. B. Cohen & P. Salapatek (Eds.), *Infant perception: From sensation to cognition* (pp. 133–248). New York: Academic Press.

Sameroff, A. J., Seifer, R., Baldwin, A., & Baldwin, C. (1993). Stability of intelligence from preschool to adolescence: The influence of social and family risk factors. *Child Development, 64,* 80–97.

Sampson, R. J. (2000). A neighborhood-level perspective on social change and the social control of adolescent delinquency. In L. J. Crockett & R. K. Silbereisen (Eds.), *Negotiating adolescence in times of social change* (pp. 178–188). New York: Cambridge University Press.

Sampson, R. J., & Laub, J. H. (1993). *Crime in the making: Pathways and turning points through life.* Cambridge, MA: Harvard University Press.

Samson, L. F. (1988). Perinatal viral infections and neonates. *Journal of Perinatal Neonatal Nursing, 1,* 56–65.

Samuels, M., & Samuels, N. (1996). *The new well pregnancy book.* New York: Fireside.

Samuels, S. J. (1985). Toward a theory of automatic information processing in reading: Updated. In H. Singer & R. B. Ruddell (Eds.), *Theoretical models and processes of reading* (3rd ed., pp. 719–721). Newark, DE: International Reading Association.

Sandberg, D. E., Brook, A. E., & Campos, S. P. (1994). Short stature: A psychosocial burden requiring growth hormone therapy? *Pediatrics, 94,* 832–840.

Sanders, M. J., Kapphahn, C. J., & Steiner, H. (1998). Eating disorders. In R. T. Ammerman & J. V. Campo (Eds.), *Handbook of pediatric psychology and psychiatry* (Vol. 1, pp. 287–312). Boston: Allyn and Bacon.

Sanderson, J. A., & Siegal, M. (1988). Conceptions of moral and social rules in rejected and nonrejected preschoolers. *Journal of Clinical Child Psychology, 17,* 66–72.

Sanford, J. P. (1985). *Comprehension-level tasks in secondary classrooms.* Austin: Research and Development Center for Teacher Education, University of Texas at Austin.

Sansavini, A., Bertoncini, J., & Giovanelli, G. (1997). Newborns discriminate the rhythm of multisyllabic stressed words. *Developmental Psychology, 33,* 3–11.

Sanson, A. V., Pedlow, R., Cann, W., Prior, M., & Oberklaid, F. (1996). Shyness ratings: Stability and correlates in early childhood. *International Journal of Behavioural Development, 19,* 705–724.

Santoloupo, S., & Pratt, M. (1994). Age, gender, and parenting style variations in mother–adolescent dialogues and adolescent reasoning about political issues. *Journal of Adolescent Research, 9,* 241–261.

Savage, A. R., Petersen, M. B., Pettay, D., Taft, L., Allran, K., Freeman, S. B., Karadima, G., Avramopoulos, D., Torfs, C., Mikkelsen, M., & Hassold, T. J. (1998). Elucidating the mechanisms of paternal non-disjunction of chromosome 21 in humans. *Human Molecular Genetics, 7,* 1221–1227.

Saville-Troike, M. (1988). Private speech: Evidence for second language learning strategies during the 'silent' period. *Journal of Child Language, 15,* 567–590.

Savin-Williams, R. C. (1996). Dating and romantic relationships among gay, lesbian, and bisexual youths. In R. C. Savin-Williams & K. M. Cohen (Eds.), *The lives of lesbians, gays, and bisexuals* (pp. 166–180). Fort Worth, TX: Harcourt Brace.

Savin-Williams, R. C. (1998). *. . . And then I became gay: Young men's stories.* New York: Routledge.

Savin-Williams, R. C., & Berndt, T. J. (1990). Friendship and peer relations. In S. S. Feldman & G. R. Elliott (Eds.), *At the threshold: The developing adolescent* (pp. 277–307). Cambridge, MA: Harvard University Press.

Saxe, G. B. (1985). Effects of schooling on arithmetical understandings: Studies with Oksapmin children in Papua New Guinea. *Journal of Educational Psychology, 77,* 503–513.

Saxe, G. B. (1988, August–September). Candy selling and math learning.

Educational Researcher, 17(6), 14–21.

Saxton, M. (1997). The contrast theory of negative input. *Journal of Child Language, 24,* 139–161.

Scaramella, L. V., Conger, R. D., Simons, R. L., & Whitbeck, L. B. (1998). Predicting risk for pregnancy by late adolescence: A social contextual perspective. *Developmental Psychology, 34,* 1233–1245.

Scarr, S. (1985). Constructing psychology: Making facts and fables for our times. *American Psychologist, 40,* 499–512.

Scarr, S. (1996). Individuality and community: The contrasting role of the state in family life in the United States and Sweden. *Scandinavian Journal of Psychology, 37,* 93–102.

Scarr, S. (1997). Behavior-genetic and socialization theories of intelligence: Truce and reconciliation. In R. J. Sternberg & E. L. Grigorenko (Eds.), *Intelligence, heredity, and environment* (pp. 3–41). New York: Cambridge University Press.

Scarr, S. (1998). American child care today. *American Psychologist, 53,* 95–108.

Scarr, S., & McCartney, K. (1983). How people make their own environments: A theory of genotype → environment effects. *Child Development, 54,* 424–435.

Scarr, S., Phillips, D., McCartney, K., & Abbott-Shim, M. (1993). Quality of child care as an aspect of family and child care policy in the United States. *Pediatrics, 91,* 182–188.

Scarr, S., & Weinberg, R. A. (1983). The Minnesota adoption studies: Genetic differences and malleability. *Child Development, 54,* 260–267.

Schachter, F. F., & Stone, R. K. (1985). Difficult sibling– easy sibling: Temperament and the within-family environment. *Child Development, 56,* 1335–1344.

Schaffer, J., & Kral, R. (1998). Adoptive families. In C. S. Chilman, E. W. Nunnally, & F. M. Cox (Eds.), *Variant family forms* (pp. 165–184). Newbury Park, PA: Sage.

Schauble, L. (1996). The development of scientific reasoning in knowledge-rich contexts. *Developmental Psychology, 32,* 102–119.

Scher, A., Tirosh, E., Jaffe, M., Rubin, L., Sadeh, A., & Lavie, P. (1995). Sleep patterns of infants and young children in Israel. *International Journal of Behavioral lDevelopment, 18,* 701–711.

Schiavi, R. C., Theilgaard, A., Owen, D., & White, D. (1984). Sex chromosome anomalies, hormones, and aggressivity. *Archives of General Psychiatry, 41,* 93–99.

Schlaud, M., Eberhard, C., Trumann, B., Kleemann, W. J., Poets, C. F., Tietze, K. W., & Schwartz, F. W. (1999). Prevalence and determinants of prone sleeping position in infants: Results for two cross-sectional studies on risk factors for SIDS in Germany. *American Journal of Epidemiology, 150,* 51–57.

Schlegel, A. (1995). A cross-cultural approach to adolescence. *Ethos, 23,* 5–32.

Schlegel, A., & Barry, H., III. (1980). The evolutionary significance of adolescent initiation ceremonies. *American Ethnologist, 7,* 696–715.

Schlegel, A., & Barry, H., III. (1991). *Adolescence: An anthropological inquiry.* New York: Free Press.

Schmitz, M. K. H., & Jeffery, R. W. (2000). Public health interventions for the prevention and treatment of obesity. *Medical Clinics of North America, 84,* 491–512.

Schmitz, S., Fulker, D. W., Plomin, R., Zahn-Waxler, C., Emde, R. N., & DeFries, J. C. (1999). Temperament and problem behaviour during early childhood. *International Journal of Behavioral Development, 23,* 333–355.

Schneider, B., & Stevenson, D. (1999). *The ambitious generation: America's teenagers, motivated but directionless.* New Haven, CT: Yale University Press.

Schneider, W. (1986). The role of conceptual knowledge and metamemory in the development of organizational processes in memory. *Journal of Experimental Child Psychology, 42,* 218–236.

Schneider, W., & Bjorklund, D. F. (1992). Expertise, aptitude, and strategic remembering. *Child Development, 63,* 461–473.

Schneider, W., & Bjorklund, D. F. (1998). Memory. In D. Kuhn & R. S. Siegler (Eds.), *Handbook of child psychology: Vol. 2. Cognition, perception, and language* (5th ed., pp. 467–521). New York: Wiley.

Schneider, W., & Pressley, M. (1989). *Memory development between 2 and 20.* New York: Springer-Verlag.

Schneirla, T. C., Rosenblatt, J. S., & Tobach, E. (1963). Maternal behavior in the cat. In H. R. Rheingold (Ed.), *Maternal behavior in mammals* (pp. 122–168). New York: Wiley.

Scholl, T. O., Heidiger, M. L., & Belsky, D. (1996). Prenatal care and maternal health during adolescent pregnancy: A review and meta-analysis. *Journal of Adolescent Health, 15,* 444–456.

Scholnick, E. K. (1995, Fall). Knowing and constructing plans. *SRCD Newsletter,* pp. 1–2, 17.

Schonert-Reichl, K. A. (1999). Relations of peer acceptance, friendship adjustment, and social behavior to moral reasoning during early adolescence. *Journal of Early Adolescence, 19,* 249–279.

Schothorst, P. F., & van Engeland, H. (1996). Long-term behavioral sequelae of prematurity. *Journal of the American Academy of Child and Adolescent Psychiatry, 35,* 175–183.

Schraedley, P. K., Gotlib, I. H., & Hayward, C. (1999). Gender differences in correlates of depressive symptoms in adolescents. *Journal of Adolescent Health, 25,* 98–108.

Schroeder, K. A., Blood, L. L., & Maluso, D. (1993). Gender differences and similarities between male and female undergraduate students regarding expectations for career and family roles. *College Student Journal, 27,* 237–249.

Schuengel, G., Bakermans-Kranenburg, M. J., & van IJzendoorn, M. H. (1999). Attachment and loss: Frightening maternal behavior linking unresolved loss and disorganized infant attachment. *Journal of Consulting and Clinical Psychology, 67,* 54–63.

Schull, W. J., & Otake, M. (1999). Cognitive function and prenatal exposure to ionizing radiation. *Teratology, 59,* 222–226.

Schulman, J. D., & Black, S. H. (1997). Screening for Huntington disease and certain other dominantly inherited disorders: A case for preimplantation genetic testing. *Journal of Medical Screening, 4,* 58–59.

Schunk, D. H. (1983). Ability versus effort attributional feedback: Differential effects on self-efficacy and achievement. *Journal of Educational Psychology, 75,* 848–856.

Schunk, D. H., & Zimmerman, B. J. (Eds.). (1994). *Self-regulation of learning and performance.* Englewood Cliffs, NJ: Erlbaum.

Schwanenflugel, P. J., Fabricius, W. V., & Noyes, C. R. (1996). Developing organization of mental verbs: Evidence for the development of a constructivist theory of mind in middle childhood. *Cognitive Development, 11,* 265–294.

Schwanenflugel, P. J., Henderson, R. L., & Fabricius, W. V. (1998). Developing organization of mental verbs and theory of mind in middle childhood: Evidence from extensions. *Developmental Psychology, 34,* 512–524.

Schwebel, D. C., Rosen, C. S., & Singer, J. L. (1999). Preschoolers' pretend play and theory of mind: The role of jointly constructed pretense. *British Journal of Developmental Psychology, 17,* 333–348.

Scott, K. D., Berkowitz, G., & Klaus, M. (1999). A comparison of intermittent and continuous support during labor: A meta-analysis. *American Journal of Obstetrics and Gynecology, 180,* 1054–1059.

Scruggs, T. E., & Mastropieri, M. A. (1994). Successful mainstreaming in elementary science classes: A qualitative study of three reputational cases. *American Educational Research Journal, 31,* 785–811.

Sebald, H. (1986). Adolescents' shifting orientation toward parents and peers: A curvilinear trend over recent decades. *Journal of Marriage and the Family, 48,* 5–13.

Seefeldt, V. (1996). The concept of readiness applied to the acquisition of motor skills. In F. L. Smoll & R. E. Smith (Eds.), *Children and youth in sport: A biopsychological perspective* (pp. 49–56). Dubuque, IA: Brown & Benchmark.

Segal, L. B., Oster, H., Cohen, M., Caspi, B., Myers, M., & Brown, D. (1995). Smiling and fussing in seven-month-old preterm and full-term black infants in the still-face situation. *Child Development, 66,* 1829–1843.

Seginer, R. (1992). Sibling relationships in early adolescence: A study of Israeli Arab sisters. *Journal of Early Adolescence, 12,* 96–110.

Seginer, R. (1998). Adolescents' perceptions of relationships with older siblings in the context of other close relationships. *Journal of Research on Adolescence, 8,* 287–308.

Seidman, E., Allen, L., Aber, J. L., Mitchell, C., & Feinman, J. (1994). The impact of school transitions in early adolescence on the self-system and perceived social context of poor urban youth. *Child Development, 65,* 507–522.

Seidman, E., & French, S. E. (1997). Normative school transitions among urban adolescents: When, where, and how to intervene. In H. J. Walberg, O. Reyes, & R. P. Weissberg (Eds.), *Children and youth: Interdisciplinary perspectives* (pp. 166–189). Thousand Oaks, CA: Sage.

Seifer, R., & Schiller, M. (1995). The role of parenting sensitivity, infant temperament, and dyadic interaction in attachment theory and assessment. In E. Waters, B. E. Vaughn, G. Posada, & K. Kondo-Ikemura K. (Eds.), *Caregiving, cultural, and cognitive perspectives on secure-base behavior and working models: New growing points of attachment theory and research. Monographs of the Society for Research in Child Development, 60* (2–3, Serial No. 244).

Seifer, R., Schiller, M., Sameroff, A. J., Resnick, S., & Riordan, K. (1996). Attachment, maternal sensitivity, and infant temperament during the first year of life. *Developmental Psychology, 32,* 12–25.

Seitz, V., & Apfel, N. H. (1993). Adolescent mothers and repeated childbearing: Effects of a school-based intervention program. *American Journal of Orthopsychiatry, 63,* 572–581.

Seitz, V., & Apfel, N. H. (1994). Effects of a school for pregnant students on the incidence of low-birthweight deliveries. *Child Development, 65,* 666–676.

Seitz, V., Apfel, N. H., & Rosenbaum, L. K. (1991). Effects of an intervention program for pregnant adolescents: Educational outcomes at two years postpartum. *American Journal of Community Psychology, 6,* 911–930.

Seligman, M. E. P. (1975). *Helplessness: On depression, development, and death.* San Francisco: Freeman.

Selikowitz, M. (1997). *Down syndrome: The facts* (2nd ed.). Oxford: Oxford University Press.

Selman, R. L. (1976). Social-cognitive understanding: A guide to educational and clinical practice. In T. Lickona (Ed.), *Moral development and behavior: Theory, research, and social issues* (pp. 299–316). New York: Holt, Rinehart, & Winston.

Selman, R. L. (1980). *The growth of interpersonal understanding.* New York: Academic Press.

Selman, R. L., & Byrne, D. F. (1974). A structural-developmental analysis of levels of role taking in middle childhood. *Child Development, 45,* 803–806.

Seltzer, M. M., & Ryff, C. D. (1994). Parenting across the life span: The normative and nonnormative cases. In D. L. Featherman, R. M. Lerner, & M. Perlmutter (Eds.), *Life-span development and behavior* (pp. 1–40). Hillsdale, NJ: Erlbaum.

Serbin, L. A., Powlishta, K. K., & Gulko, J. (1993). The development of sex typing in middle childhood. *Monographs of the Society for Research in Child Development, 58*(2, Serial No. 232).

Serdula, M. K., Ivery, D., Coates, R. J., Freedman, D. S., Williamson, D. F., & Byers, T. (1993). Do obese children become obese adults? A review of the literature. *Preventive Medicine, 22,* 167–177.

Sever, J. L. (1983). Maternal infections. In C. C. Brown (Ed.), *Childhood learning disabilities and prenatal risk* (pp. 31–38). New York: Johnson & Johnson.

Seyb, S. T., Berka, R. J., Socol, M. L., & Dooley, S. L. (1999). Risk of cesarean delivery with elective induction of labor at term in nulliparous women. *Obstetrics and Gynecology, 94,* 600–607.

Shahar, S. (1990). *Childhood in the Middle Ages.* London: Routledge & Kegan Paul.

Shainess, N. (1961). A re-evaluation of some aspects of femininity through a study of menstruation: A preliminary report. *Comparative Psychiatry, 2,* 20–26.

Shann, F., & Steinhoff, M. C. (1999). Vaccines for children in rich and poor countries. *Paediatrics, 354,* 7–11.

Shantz, C. U. (1987). Conflicts between children. *Child Development, 58,* 283–305.

Shaver, P., Furman, W., & Buhrmester, D. (1985). Transition to college: Network changes, social skills, and loneliness. In S. Duck & D. Perlman (Eds.), *Understanding personal relationships: An interdisciplinary approach* (pp. 193–219). London: Sage.

Shaw, D. S., Winslow, E. B., & Flanagan, C. (1999). A prospective study of the effects of marital status and family relations on young children's adjustment among African-American and European-American families. *Child Development, 70,* 742–755.

Shea, K. M., Wilcox, A. J., & Little, R. E. (1998). Postterm delivery: A challenge for epidemiologic research. *Epidemiology, 9,* 199–204.

Shedler, J., & Block, J. (1990). Adolescent drug use and psychological health: A longitudinal inquiry. *American Psychologist, 45,* 612–630.

Sheehy, A., Gasser, T., Molinari, L., & Largo, R. H. (1999). An analysis of variance of the pubertal and midgrowth spurts for length and width. *Annals of Human Biology, 26,* 309–331.

Sherman, D. K., Iacono, W. G., & McGue, M. K. (1997). Attention-deficit hyperactivity disorder dimensions: A twin study of inattention and impulsivity-hyperactivity. *Journal of the American Academy of Child and Adolescent Psychiatry, 36,* 745–753.

Shields, P. J., & Rovee-Collier, C. K. (1992). Long-term memory for context-specific category information at six months. *Child Development, 63,* 245–259.

Shiloh, S. (1996). Genetic counseling: A developing area of interest for psychologists. *Professional Psychology: Research and Practice, 27,* 475–486.

Shime, J. (1988). Influence of prolonged pregnancy on infant development. *Journal of Reproductive Medicine, 33,* 277–284.

Shinn, M. W. (1900). *The biography of a baby.* Boston: Houghton Mifflin.

Shoda, Y., Mischel, W., & Peake, P. K. (1990). Predicting adolescent cognitive and self-regulatory competencies from preschool delay of gratification: Identifying diagnostic conditions. *Developmental Psychology, 26,* 978–986.

Shucard, J. L., Shucard, D. W., & Thomas, D. G. (1984). Auditory evoked potentials of probes of hemispheric differences in cognitive processing. *Science, 197,* 1295–1298.

Shure, M. B. (1997). Interpersonal cognitive problem solving: Primary prevention of early high-risk behaviors in the preschool and primary years. In G. W. Albee & T. P. Gullotta (Eds.), *Primary prevention works* (pp. 167–188). Thousand Oaks, CA: Sage.

Shweder, R. A. (1996). True ethnography: The lore, the law, and the lure. In R. Jessor, A. Colby, & R. A. Shweder (Eds.), *Ethnography and human development* (pp. 15–52). Chicago: University of Chicago Press.

Shweder, R. A., Goodnow, J., Hatano, G., LeVine, R. A., Markus, H., & Miller, P. (1998). The cultural psychology of development: One mind, many mentalities. In R. M. Lerner (Ed.), *Handbook of child psychology: Vol. 1. Theoretical models of human development* (5th ed., pp. 865–937). New York: Wiley.

Siegal, M. D., Farquhar, C. L., & Bouchard, J. M. (1997). Dental sealants. Who needs them? *Public Health Reports, 112,* 98–106.

Siega-Riz, A. M., Popkin, B. M., & Carson, T. (1998). Trends in breakfast consumption for children in the United States from 1965–1991. *American Journal of Clinical Nutrition, 67,* 748S–756S.

Siegel, B. (1996, Spring). Is the emperor wearing clothes? Social policy and the empirical support for full inclusion of children with disabilities in the preschool and early elementary school grades. *Social Policy Report of the Society for Research in Child Development, 10* (2–3), 2–17.

Siegler, R. S. (1992). The other Alfred Binet. *Developmental Psychology, 28,* 179–190.

Siegler, R. S. (1995). How does change occur? A microgenetic study of number conservation. *Cognitive Psychology, 28,* 225–273.

Siegler, R. S. (1996). *Emerging minds: The process of change in children's thinking.* New York: Oxford University Press.

Siegler, R. S. (1998). *Children's thinking* (3rd ed.). Upper Saddle River, NJ: Prentice-Hall.

Siegler, R. S., & Crowley, K. (1991). The microgenetic method:

A direct means for studying cognitive development. *American Psychologist, 46,* 606–620.

Siegler, R. S., & Crowley, K. (1992). Microgenetic methods revisited. *American Psychologist, 47,* 1241–1243.

Siegler, R. S., & Jenkins, E. A. (1989). *How children discover new strategies.* Hillsdale, NJ: Erlbaum.

Siegler, R. S., & Robinson, M. (1982). The development of numerical understandings. In H. W. Reese & L. P. Lipsitt (Eds.), *Advances in child development and behavior* (Vol. 16, pp. 241–312). New York: Academic Press.

Siervogel, R., M., Maynard, L. M., Wisemandle, W. A., Roche, A. F., Guo, S. S., Chumlea, W. C., & Towne, B. (2000). Annual changes in total body fat and fat-free mass in children from 8 to 18 years in relation to changes in body mass index: The Fels Longitudinal Study. *Annals of the New York Academy of Sciences, 904,* 420–423.

Sigman, M. (1995). Nutrition and child development: More food for thought. *Current Directions in Psychological Science, 4,* 52–55.

Sigman, M., Cohen, S. E., & Beckwith, L. (1997). Why does infant attention predict adolescent intelligence? *Infant Behavior and Development, 20,* 133–140.

Sigman, M., Neumann, C., Jansen, A. A. J., & Bwibo, N. (1989). Cognitive abilities of Kenyan children in relation to nutrition, family characteristics, and education. *Child Development, 60,* 1462–1474.

Sigman, M., & Whaley, S. E. (1998). The role of nutrition in the development of intelligence. In U. Neisser (Ed.), *The rising curve* (pp. 155–182). Washington, DC: American Psychological Association.

Silverman, W. K., La Greca, A. M., & Wasserstein, S. (1995). What do children worry about? Worries and their relation to anxiety. *Child Development, 66,* 671–686.

Sim, T. N. (2000). Adolescent psychosocial competence: The importance and role of regard for parents. *Journal of Research on Adolescence, 10,* 49–64.

Simmons, R. G., & Blyth, D. A. (1987). *Moving into adolescence.* New York: Aldine de Gruyter.

Simon, R., Altstein, H., & Melli, M. S. (1994). *The case for transracial adoption.* Washington, DC: American University Press.

Simons, D. J., & Keil, F. C. (1995). An abstract to concrete shift in the development of biological thought: The insider story. *Cognition, 56,* 129–163.

Simons, R. L., & Chao, W. (1996). Conduct problems. In R. L. Simons & Associates (Eds.), *Understanding differences between divorced and intact families* (pp. 125–143). Thousand Oaks, CA: Sage.

Simons, R. L., Lin, K.-H., Gordon, L. C., Conger, R. D., & Lorenz, F. O. (1999). Explaining the higher incidence of adjustment problems among children of divorce compared with those in two-parent families. *Journal of Marriage and the Family, 61,* 1020–1033.

Simons, R. L., Whitbeck, L. B., Conger, R. D., & Chyi-In, W. (1991). Intergenerational transmission of harsh parenting. *Developmental Psychology, 27,* 159–171.

Singer, D. G. (1999). Imaginative play and television: Factors in a child's development. In J. A. Singer & P. Salovey (Eds.), *At play in the fields of consciousness: Essays in honor of Jerome L. Singer* (pp. 303–326). Mahwah, NJ: Erlbaum.

Singh, S., & Darroch, J. E. (2000). Adolescent pregnancy and childbearing: Levels and trends in developed countries. *Family Planning Perspectives, 32,* 14–23.

Sippola, L., Bukowski, W. M., & Noll, R. B. (1997). Age differences in children's and early adolescents' liking for same-sex and other-sex peers. *Merrill-Palmer Quarterly, 43,* 547–561.

Sitskoorn, M. M., & Smitsman, A. W. (1995). Infants' perception of dynamic relations between objects: Passing through or support? *Developmental Psychology, 31,* 437–447.

Sivard, R. L. (1996). *World military and social expenditures* (16th ed.). Leesburg, VA: WMSE.

Skinner, B. F. (1957). *Verbal behavior.* New York: Appleton-Century-Crofts.

Skinner, E. A. (1995). *Perceived control, motivation, and coping.* Thousand Oaks, CA: Sage.

Skinner, E. A., Zimmer-Gembeck, M. J., & Connell, J. P. (1998). Individual differences and the development of perceived control. *Monographs of the Society for Research in Child Development, 63*(2–3, Serial No. 254).

Skoe, E. S. A. (1998). The ethic of care: Issues in moral development. In E. E. A. Skoe & A. L. von der Lippe (Eds.), *Personality development in adolescence* (pp. 143–171). London: Routledge.

Slaby, R. G., & Frey, K. S. (1975). Development of gender constancy and selective attention to same-sex models. *Child Development, 46,* 849–856.

Slaby, R. G., Roedell, W. C., Arezzo, D., & Hendrix, K. (1995). *Early violence prevention.* Washington, DC: National Association for the Education of Young Children.

Slater, A., Brown, E., Mattock, A., & Bornstein, M. H. (1996). Continuity and change in habituation in the first 4 months from birth. *Journal of Reproductive and Infant Psychology, 14,* 187–194.

Slater, A., & Johnson, S. P. (1999). Visual sensory and perceptual abilities of the newborn: Beyond the blooming, buzzing confusion. In A. Slater & S. P. Johnson (Eds.), *The development of sensory, motor and cognitive capacities in early infancy* (pp. 121–141). Hove, UK: Sussex Press.

Slater, A., Quinn, P. C., Brown, E., & Hayes, R. (1999) Intermodal perception at birth: Intersensory redundancy guides newborn infants' learning of arbitrary auditory–visual pairings. *Developmental Science, 2,* 333–338.

Slater, A. M., Mattock, A., & Brown, E. (1990). Size constancy at birth: Newborn infants' responses to retinal and real size. *Journal of Experimental Child Psychology, 49,* 314–322.

Slaughter, V., Jaakkola, R., & Carey, S. (1999). Constructing a coherent theory: Children's biological understanding of life and death. In M. Siegel & C. C. Petersen (Eds.), *Children's understanding of biology and health* (pp. 71–96). Cambridge, U.K.: Cambridge University Press.

Slobin, D. I. (1985). Crosslinguistic evidence for language-making capacity. In D. I. Slobin (Ed.), *The crosslinguistic study of language acquisition: Vol. 2. Theoretical issues* (pp. 1157– 1256). Hillsdale, NJ: Erlbaum.

Slobin, D. I. (1997). On the origin of grammaticalizable notions: Beyond the individual mind. In D. I. Slobin (Ed.), *The crosslinguistic study of language acquisition: Vol. 5.* Hillsdale, NJ: Erlbaum.

Smetana, J. G. (1995). Morality in context: Abstractions, ambiguities, and applications. In R. Vasta (Ed.), *Annals of child development* (Vol. 10, 83–130). London: Jessica Kingsley.

Smetana, J. G., & Braeges, J. L. (1990). The development of toddlers' moral and conventional judgments. *Merrill-Palmer Quarterly, 36,* 329–346.

Smiley, P. A., & Dweck, C. S. (1994). Individual differences in achievement goals among young children. *Child Development, 65,* 1723–1743.

Smith, A. E., Jussim, L., Eccles, J., VanNoy, M., Madon, S., & Palumbo, P. (1998). Self-fulfilling prophecies, perceptual biases, and accuracy at the individual and group levels. *Journal of Experimental Social Psychology, 34,* 530–561.

Smith, B. A., & Blass, E. M. (1996). Taste-mediated calming in premature, preterm, and full-term human infants. *Developmental Psychology, 32,* 1084–1089.

Smith, E. P., Walker, K., Fields, L., Brookins, C. C., & Seay, R. C. (1999). Ethnic identity and its relationship to self-esteem, perceived efficacy, and prosocial attitudes in early adolescence. *Journal of Adolescence, 22,* 867–880.

Smith, J., & Prior, M. (1995). Temperament and stress resilience in school-age children: A within-families study. *Journal of the American Academy of Child and Adolescent Psychiatry, 34,* 168–179.

Smith, L. B., & Katz, D. B. (1996). Activity-dependent processes in perceptual and cognitive development. In R. Gelman & T. K. Au (Eds.), *Perceptual and cognitive development* (pp. 414–445). San Diego: Academic Press.

Smith, L. B., Quittner, A. L., Osberger, M. J., & Miyamoto, R. (1998). Audition and visual attention: The developmental trajectory in deaf and hearing populations. *Developmental Psychology, 34,* 840–850.

Smith, L. B., Thelen, E., Titzer, R., & McLin, D. (1999). Knowing in the context of acting: The task dynamics of the A-not-B error. *Psychological Review, 106,* 235–260.

Smith, M. C. (1978). Cognizing the behavior stream: The recognition of intentional action. *Child Development, 49,* 736–743.

Smith, P. K., & Hunter, T. (1992). Children's perceptions of play-fighting, playchasing, and real fighting: A cross-national study. *Social Development, 1,* 211–229.

Smith, P. K., & Myron-Wilson, R. (1998). Parenting and school bullying. *Clinical Child Psychology and Psychiatry, 3,* 405–417.

Smith, R. (1999). The timing of birth. *Scientific American, 280*(3), 68–75.

Smith, R. E., & Smoll, F. L. (1997). Coaching the coaches: Youth sports as a scientific and applied behavior setting. *Current Directions in Psychological Science, 6,* 16–21.

Smith, S. (Ed.). (1995). Two-generation programs for famlies in poverty: A new intervention strategy. *Advances in applied developmental psychology* (Vol. 9). Norwood, NJ: Ablex.

Smolucha, L., & Smolucha, F. (1998). The social origins of mind: Post-Piagetian perspectives on pretend play. In O. N. Saracho & B. Spodek (Eds.), *Multiple perspectives on play in early childhood education* (pp. 34–58). Albany: State University of New York Press.

Snarey, J. (1995). In a communitarian voice: The sociological expansion of Kohlbergian theory, research, and practice. In W. M. Kurtines & J. L. Gewirtz (Eds.), *Moral development: An introduction* (pp. 109–134). Boston: Allyn and Bacon.

Snarey, J. R., Reimer, J., & Kohlberg, L. (1985). The development of social–moral reasoning among kibbutz adolescents: A longitudinal cross-cultural study. *Developmental Psychology, 21,* 3–17.

Snidman, N., Kagan, J., Riordan, L., & Shannon, D. C. (1995). Cardiac function and behavioral reactivity. *Psychophysiology, 32,* 199–207.

Snow, C. E., Pan, B. A., Imbens-Bailey, A., & Herman, J. (1996). Learning how to say what one means: A longitudinal study of children's speech act use. *Social Development, 5,* 56–84.

Society for Research in Child Development. (1993). Ethical standards for research with children. In *Directory of Members* (pp. 337–339). Ann Arbor, MI: Author.

Soken, H. H., & Pick, A. D. (1992). Intermodal perception of happy and angry expressive behaviors by seven-month-old infants. *Child Development, 63,* 787–795.

Solomon, G. B., & Bredemeier, B. J. L. (1999). Children's moral conceptions of gender stratification in sport. *International Journal of Sport Psychology, 30,* 350–368.

Solomon, G. E. A., & Johnson, S. C. (2000). Conceptual change in the classroom: Teaching young children to understand biological inheritance. *British Journal of Developmental Psychology, 18,* 81–96.

Sommers-Flanagan, R., Sommers-Flanagan, J., & Davis, B. (1993). What's happening on music television? A gender-role content analysis. *Sex Roles, 28,* 745–753.

Sonenstein, F. L., Pleck, J. H., & Ku, L. C. (1991). Levels of sexual activity among adolescent males in the United States. *Family Planning Perspectives, 23,* 162–167.

Sonnenschein, S. (1986). Development of referential communication skills: How familiarity with a listener affects a speaker's production of redundant messages. *Developmental Psychology, 22,* 549–552.

Sophian, C. (1995). Representation and reasoning in early numerical development: Counting, conservation, and comparisons between sets. *Child Development, 66,* 559–577.

Sorce, J., Emde, R., Campos, J., & Klinnert, M. (1985). Maternal emotional signaling: Its effect on the visual cliff behavior of 1-year-olds. *Developmental Psychology, 21,* 195–200.

Sorenson, E. S. (1993). *Children's stress and coping.* New York: Guilford.

Sosa, R., Kennell, J., Klaus, M., Robertson, S., & Urrutia, J. (1980). The effect of a supportive companion on perinatal problems, length of labor, and mother–infant interaction. *New England Journal of Medicine, 303,* 597–600.

Spätling, L., & Spätling, G. (1988). Magnesium supplementation in pregnancy: A double-blind study. *British Journal of Obstetrics and Gynecology, 95,* 120–125.

Speece, M. W., & Brent, S. B. (1992). The acquisition of a mature understanding of three components of the concept of death. *Death Studies, 16,* 211–229.

Speece, M. W., & Brent, S. B. (1996). The development of children's understanding of death. In C. A. Corr & D. M. Corr (Eds.), *Handbook of childhood death and bereavement* (pp. 29–50). New York: Springer.

Speicher, B. (1994). Family patterns of moral judgment during adolescence and early adulthood. *Developmental Psychology, 30,* 624–632.

Spelke, E. (1999). Save Mozart for later: Neurobiology offers no evidence that infancy is a privileged time for learning. *Nature, 401,* 643–644.

Spelke, E. S. (1987). The development of intermodal perception. In P. Salapatek & L. Cohen (Eds.), *Handbook of infant perception: Vol. 2. From perception to cognition* (pp. 233–273). Orlando, FL: Academic Press.

Spelke, E. S. (1994). Initial knowledge: Six suggestions. *Cognition, 50,* 431–445.

Spelke, E. S., Breinlinger, K., Macomber, J., & Jacobson, K. (1992). Origins of knowledge. *Psychological Review, 99,* 605–632.

Spelke, E. S., & Hermer, L. (1996). Early cognitive development: Objects and space. In R. Gelman & T. K. Au (Eds.), *Perceptual and cognitive development* (pp. 71–114). San Diego: Academic Press.

Spelke, E. S., & Newport, E. L. (1998). Nativism, empiricism, and the development of knowledge. In R. M. Lerner (Ed.), *Handbook of child psychology: Vol. 1. Theoretical models of human development* (5th ed., pp. 199–254). New York: Wiley.

Spence, M. J., & DeCasper, A. J. (1987). Prenatal experience with low-frequency maternal voice sounds influences neonatal perception of maternal voice samples. *Infant Behavior and Development, 10,* 133–142.

Spencer, P. E., Bodner-Johnson, B. A., & Gutfreund, M. K. (1992). Interacting with infants with a hearing loss: What can we learn from mothers who are deaf? *Journal of Early Intervention, 16,* 64–78.

Spencer, P. E., & Lederberg, A. (1997). Different modes, different models: Communication and language of young deaf children and their mothers. In L. B. Adamson & M. Romski (Eds.), *Communication and language acquisition: Discoveries from atypical development* (pp. 203–230). Baltimore: Paul H. Brookes.

Spencer, P. E., & Meadow-Orlans, K. P. (1996). Play, language, and maternal responsiveness: A longitudinal study of deaf and hearing infants. *Child Development, 67,* 3176–3191.

Sperduto, R. D., Hiller, R., Podgor, M. J., Freidlin, V., Milton, R. C., Wolf, P. A., Myers, R. H., Dagostine, R. B., Roseman, M. J., Stockman, M. E., & Wilson, P. W. (1996). Familial aggregation and prevalence of myopia in the Framingham Offspring Eye Study. *Archives of Ophthalmology, 114,* 326–333.

Spindler, G. D. (1970). The education of adolescents: An anthropological perspective. In D. Ellis (Ed.), *Adolescents: Readings in behavior and development* (pp. 152–161). Hinsdale, IL: Dryden.

Spitz, R. A. (1945). Hospitalism: An inquiry into the genesis of psychiatric conditions in early childhood. *Psychoanalytic Study of the Child, 1,* 113–117.

Spitz, R. A. (1946). Anaclitic depression. *Psychoanalytic Study of the Child, 2,* 313–342.

Spitzer, S., Cupp, R., & Parke, R. D. (1995). School entrance age, social acceptance, and self-perceptions in kindergarten and first grade. *Early Childhood Research Quarterly, 10,* 433–450.

Spock, B., & Parker, S. J. (1998). *Dr. Spock's baby and child care.* (7th ed.). New York: Pocket.

Sroufe, L. A. (1979). Socioemotional development. In J. D. Osofsky (Ed.), *Handbook of infant development* (pp. 462–516). New York: Wiley.

Sroufe, L. A., Egeland, B., & Kreutzer, T. (1990). The fate of early experience following developmental change: Longitudinal approaches to individual adaptation. *Child Development, 61,* 1363–1373.

Sroufe, L. A., & Waters, E. (1976). The ontogenesis of smiling and laughter: A perspective on the organization of development in infancy. *Psychological Review, 83,* 173–189.

Sroufe, L. A., & Wunsch, J. P. (1972). The development of laughter in the first year of life. *Child Development, 43,* 1324–1344.

Stahl, S. (1989). Task variations and prior knowledge in learning word meanings from context. In S. McCormick & J. Zutell (Eds.), *Cognitive and social perspectives for literacy research and instruction. Thirty-eighth yearbook of the National Reading Conference* (pp. 197–204). Chicago: National Reading Conference.

Stahl, S. A., McKenna, M. C., & Pagnucco, J. R. (1994). The effects of whole-language instruction: An update and a reappraisal. *Educational Psychologist, 29,* 175–185.

Standley, J. M. (1998). The effect of music and multimodal stimulation on responses of premature infants in neonatal intensive care. *Pediatric Nursing, 24,* 532–538.

Stark, L. J., Allen, K. D., Hurst, M., Nash, D. A., Rigney, B., & Stokes, T. F. (1989). Distraction: Its utilization and efficacy with children undergoing dental treatment. *Journal of Applied Behavior Analysis, 22,* 297–307.

Statistics Canada. (2000). *Divorces.* [On-line] www.statcan.ca.

Stattin, H., & Magnusson, D. (1990). *Pubertal maturation in female development.* Hillsdale, NJ: Erlbaum.

Staub, E. (1996). Cultural–societal roots of violence. *American Psychologist, 51,* 117–132.

Steele, C. D., Wapner, R. J., Smith, J. B., Haynes, M. K., & Jackson, L. G. (1996). Prenatal diagnosis using fetal cells isolated from maternal blood: A review. *Clinical Obstetrics and Gynecology, 39,* 801–813.

Steele, H., Steele, M., & Fonagy, P. (1996). Associations among attachment classifications of mothers, fathers, and their infants. *Child Development, 67,* 541–555.

Steihm, E. R., Lambert, J. S., Mofenson, L. M., Whitehouse, J., Nugent, R., & Move, J., Jr. (1999). Efficacy of zidovudine and human immunodeficiency virus (HIV) hyperimmune immunoglobulin for reducing perinatal HIV transmission from HIV-infected women with advanced disease: Results of Pediatric AIDS Clinical Trials Group protocol 185. *Journal of Infectious Disease, 179,* 567–575.

Stein, J. H., & Reiser, L. W. (1994). A study of white middle-class adolescent boys' responses to "semenarche" (the first ejaculation). *Journal of Youth and Adolescence, 23,* 373–384.

Stein, N., & Levine, L. J. (1999). The early emergence of emotional understanding and appraisal: Implications for theories of development. In T. Dalgleish & M. J. Power (Eds.), *Handbook of cognition and emotion* (pp. 383–408). Chichester, UK: Wiley.

Stein, Z., Susser, M., Saenger, G., & Marolla, F. (1975). *Famine and human development: The Dutch hunger winter of 1944–1945.* New York: Oxford.

Steinberg, L. (1984). The varieties and effects of work during adolescence. In M. Lamb, A. Brown, & B. Rogoff (Eds.), *Advances in developmental psychology* (pp. 1–37). Hillsdale, NJ: Erlbaum.

Steinberg, L. (1986). Latchkey children and susceptibility to peer pressure: An ecological analysis. *Developmental Psychology, 22,* 433–439.

Steinberg, L. (1990). Interdependence in the family: Autonomy, conflict, and harmony in the parent–adolescent relationship. In S. S. Feldman & G. R. Elliott (Eds.), *At the threshold: The developing adolescent* (pp. 255–276). Cambridge, MA: Harvard University Press.

Steinberg, L. (1999). *Adolescence* (5th ed.). New York: McGraw-Hill.

Steinberg, L., Darling, N. E., & Fletcher, A. C. (1995). Authoritative parenting and adolescent development: An ecological journey. In P. Moen, G. H. Elder, & K. Luscher (Eds.), *Examining lives in context* (pp. 423–466). Washington, DC: American Psychological Association.

Steinberg, L., & Dornbusch, S. M. (1991). Negative correlates of part-time employment during adolescence: Replication and elaboration. *Developmental Psychology, 27,* 304–313.

Steinberg, L., Lamborn, S. D., Darling, N., Mounts, N. S., & Dornbusch, S. M. (1994). Over-time changes in adjustment and competence among adolescents from authoritative, authoritarian, indulgent, and neglectful families. *Child Development, 65,* 754–770.

Steinberg, L., & Silverberg, S. B. (1986). The vicissitudes of autonomy in early adolescence. *Child Development, 57,* 841–851.

Steinberg, L. D., Fegley, S., & Dornbusch, S. (1993). Negative impact of part-time work on adolescent adjustment: Evidence from a longitudinal study. *Developmental Psychology, 29,* 171–180.

Steinberg, L. D., Fletcher, A., & Darling, N. (1994). Parental monitoring and peer influences on adolescent substance use. *Pediatrics, 93,* 1060–1064.

Steinberg, S., & Bellavance, F. (1999). Characteristics and treatment of women with antenatal and postpartum depression. *International Journal of Psychiatry in Medicine, 29,* 209–233.

Steiner, J. E. (1979). Human facial expression in response to taste and smell stimulation. In H. W. Reese & L. P. Lipsitt (Eds.), *Advances in child development and behavior* (Vol. 13, pp. 257–295). New York: Academic Press.

Stenberg, C., & Campos, J. (1990). The development of anger expressions in infancy. In N. Stein, B. Leventhal, & T. Trabasso (Eds.), *Psychological and biological approaches to emotion* (pp. 247–282). Hillsdale, NJ: Erlbaum.

Stern, M., & Karraker, K. H. (1989). Sex stereotyping of infants: A review of gender labeling studies. *Sex Roles, 20,* 501–522.

Sternberg, R. J. (1985). *Beyond IQ: A triarchic theory of human intelligence.* New York: Cambridge University Press.

Sternberg, R. J. (1996a). Myths, countermyths, and truths about intelligence. *Educational Researcher, 25,* 11–16.

Sternberg, R. J. (1996b). *Successful intelligence: How practical and creative intelligence determine success in life.* New York: Simon & Schuster.

Sternberg, R. J. (1997). *Successful intelligence.* New York: Plume.

Sternberg, R. J. (1999a). A triarchic approach to understanding and assessment of intelligence in multicultural populations. *Journal of School Psychology, 37,* 145–159.

Sternberg, R. J. (1999b). The theory of successful intelligence. *Review of General Psychology, 3,* 292–316.

Sternberg, R. J., & Grigorenko, E. L. (Eds.). (1997). *Intelligence, heredity, and environment.* New York: Cambridge University Press.

Sternberg, R. J., Grigorenko, E. L., Ferrari, M., & Clinkenbeard, P. (1999). A triarchic analysis of an aptitude–treatment interaction. *European Journal of Psychological Assessment, 15,* 1–11.

Sternberg, R. J., & Lubart, T. I. (1995). *Defying the crowd*. New York: Basic Books.

Stetsenko, A., Little, T. D., Gordeeva, T., Grasshof, M., & Oettingen, G. (2000). Gender effects in children's beliefs about school performance. *Child Development, 21*, 517–527.

Stevenson, H. W. (1992, December). Learning from Asian schools. *Scientific American, 267*(6), 32–38.

Stevenson, H. W. (1994). Extracurricular programs in East Asian schools. *Teachers College Record, 95*, 389–407.

Stevenson, H. W., & Lee, S-Y. (1990). Contexts of achievement: A study of American, Chinese, and Japanese children. *Monographs of the Society for Research in Child Development, 55* (1–2, Serial No. 221).

Stevenson, M. R., & Black, K. N. (1995). *How divorce affects offspring: A research approach*. Dubuque, IA: Brown & Benchmark.

Stevenson, R., & Pollitt, C. (1987). The acquisition of temporal terms. *Journal of Child Language, 14*, 533–545.

Stewart, K. J., Lipis, P. H., Seemans, C. M., McFarland, L. D., Weinhofer, J. J., & Brown, C. S. (1995). Heart-healthy knowledge, food patterns, fatness, and cardiac risk factors in children receiving nutrition edition. *Journal of Health Education, 26*, 381–387.

Stewart, P., Reihman, J., Lonky, E., Darvill, T., & Pagano, J. (2000). Prenatal PCB exposure and neonatal behavioral assessment scale (NBAS) performance. *Neurotoxicology and Teratology, 22*, 21–29.

Stewart, R. B. (1983). Sibling attachment relationships: Child–infant interactions in the Strange Situation. *Developmental Psychology, 19*, 192–199.

Stifter, C. A., Coulehan, C. M., & Fish, M. (1993). Linking employment to attachment: The mediating effects of maternal separation anxiety and interactive behavior. *Child Development, 64*, 1451–1460.

Stiles, J. (1998). The effects of early focal brain injury on lateralization of cognitive function. *Current Directions in Psychological Science, 7*, 21–26.

Stiles, J. (2000). Spatial cognitive development following prenatal or perinatal focal brain injury. In H. S. Levin & J. Grafman (Eds.), *Cerebral reorganization of function after brain damage* (pp. 201–217) New York: Oxford University Press.

Stipek, D. (1995). The development of pride and shame in toddlers. In J. P. Tangney & K. W. Fischer (Eds.), *Self-conscious emotions* (pp. 237–252). New York: Guilford.

Stipek, D. J., & Byler, P. (1997). Early childhood education teachers: Do they practice what they preach? *Early Childhood Research Quarterly, 12*, 305–326.

Stipek, D. J., Feiler, R., Daniels, D., & Milburn, S. (1995). Effects of different instructional approaches on young children's achievement and motivation. *Child Development, 66*, 209–223.

Stipek, D. J., Gralinski, J. H., & Kopp, C. B. (1990). Self-concept development in the toddler years. *Developmental Psychology, 26*, 972–977.

Stipek, D. J., & Mac Iver, D. (1989). Developmental change in children's assessment of intellectual competence. *Child Development, 60*, 531–538.

Stoch, M. B., Smythe, P. M., Moodie, A. D., & Bradshaw, D. (1982). Psychosocial outcome and CT findings after growth undernourishment during infancy: A 20-year developmental study. *Developmental Medicine and Child Neurology, 24*, 419–436.

Stocker, C. M., & Dunn, J. (1994). Sibling relationships in childhood and adolescence. In J. C. DeFries, R. Plomin, & D. W. Fulker (Eds.), *Nature and nurture in middle childhood* (pp. 214–232). Cambridge: Blackwell.

Stodolsky, S. S. (1988). *The subject matters*. Chicago: University of Chicago Press.

Stoll, C., Alembik, Y., Dolt, B., & Roth, M. P. (1998). Study of Down syndrome in 238,942 consecutive births. *Annals of Genetics, 41*, 44–51.

Stone, M. R., & Brown, B. B. (1999). Identity claims and projections: Descriptions of self and crowds in secondary school. In J. A. McLellan & M. J. V. Pugh (Eds.), *The role of peer groups in adolescent social identity: Exploring the importance of stability and change* (pp. 7–20). San Francisco: Jossey-Bass.

Stoneman, Z., Brody, G. H., & MacKinnon, C. E. (1986). Same-sex and cross-sex siblings: Activity choices, roles, behavior, and gender stereotypes. *Sex Roles, 15*, 495–511.

Stormshak, E. A., Bierman, K. L., Bruschi, C., Dodge, K. A., & Coie, J. D. (1999). The relation between behavior problems and peer preference in different classroom contexts. *Child Development, 70*, 169–182.

Stormshak, E. A., Bierman, K. L., McMahon, R. J., Lengua, L. J., and the Conduct Problems Prevention Research Group. (2000). Parenting practices and child disruptive behavior problems in early elementary school. *Journal of Clinical Child Psychology, 29*, 17–29.

Strassberg, Z. (1995). Social information processing in compliance situations by mothers of behavior-problem boys. *Child Development, 66*, 376–389.

Strassberg, Z., Dodge, K., Pettit, G. S., & Bates, J. E. (1994). Spanking in the home and children's subsequent aggression toward kindergarten peers. *Development and Psychopathology, 6*, 445–461.

Strauss, R. (1999). Childhood obesity. *Current Problems in Pediatrics, 29*, 5–29.

Strayer, J. (1993). Children's concordant emotions and cognitions in response to observed emotions. *Child Development, 64*, 188–201.

Streissguth, A. (1997). *Fetal alcohol syndrome*. Baltimore: Paul H. Brookes.

Streissguth, A. P., Barr, H. M., Bookstein, F. L., Sampson, P. D., & Olson, H. C. (1999). The long-term neurocognitive consequences of prenatal alcohol exposure: A 14-year study. *Psychological Science, 10*, 186–190.

Streissguth, A. P., Barr, H. M., Sampson, P. D., Darby, B. L., & Martin, D. C. (1989). IQ at age 4 in relation to maternal alcohol use and smoking during pregnancy. *Developmental Psychology, 25*, 3–11.

Streissguth, A. P., Treder, R., Barr, H. M., Shepard, T., Bleyer, W. A., Sampson, P. D., & Martin, D. (1987). Aspirin and acetaminophen use by pregnant women and subsequent child IQ and attention decrements. *Teratology, 35*, 211–219.

Streitmatter, J. L., & Pate, G. S. (1989). Identity status development and cognitive prejudice in early adolescents. *Journal of Early Adolescence, 9*, 142–152.

Strober, M., Freeman, R., Lampert, C., Diamond, J., & Kaye, W. (2000). Controlled family study of anorexia nervosa and bulimia nervosa: Evidence of shared liability and transmission of partial syndromes. *American Journal of Psychiatry, 157*, 393–401.

Stromswold, K. (1995). The acquisition of subject and object questions. *Language Acquisition, 4*, 5–48.

Strouse, D. L. (1999). Adolescent crowd orientations: A social and temporal analysis. In J. A.

McLellan & M. J. V. Pugh (Eds.), *The role of peer groups in adolescent social identity: Exploring the importance of stability and change* (pp. 37–54). San Francisco: Jossey-Bass.

Stryer, B. K., Tofler, I. R., & Lapchick, R. (1998). A developmental overview of child and youth in society. *Child and Adolescent Psychiatric Clinics of North America, 7*, 697–719.

Stunkard, A. J., & Sørenson, T. I. A. (1993). Obesity and socioeconomic status—a complex relation. *New England Journal of Medicine, 329*, 1036–1037.

Stunkard, A. J., Sørenson, T. I. A., Hanis, C., Teasdale, T. W., Chakraborty, R., Schull, W. J., & Schulsinger, F. (1986). An adoption study of human obesity. *New England Journal of Medicine, 314*, 193–198.

Suarez-Orozco, C., & Suarez-Orozco, M. M. (1995). *Transformation: Immigration, family life, and achievement motivation among Latino adolescents*. Stanford, CA: Stanford University Press.

Subbotsky, E. V. (1994). Early rationality and magical thinking in preschoolers: Space and time. *British Journal of Developmental Psychology, 12*, 97–108.

Subrahmanyam, K., & Greenfield, P. M. (1996). Effect of video game practice on spatial skills in girls and boys. In P. M. Greenfield & R. R. Cocking (Eds.), *Interacting with video* (pp. 95–114). Norwood, NJ: Ablex.

Sullivan, H. S. (1953). *The interpersonal theory of psychiatry*. New York: Norton.

Sullivan, S. A., & Birch, L. L. (1990). Pass the sugar, pass the salt: Experience dictates preference. *Developmental Psychology, 26*, 546–551.

Sullivan, S. A., & Birch, L. L. (1994). Infant dietary experience and acceptance of solid foods. *Pediatrics, 93*, 271–277.

Sulzby, E., & Teale, W. (1991). Emergent literacy. In R. Barr, M. L. Kamil, P. B. Mosenthal, & P. D. Pearson (Eds.), *Handbook of reading research* (Vol. 2, pp. 727–757). New York: Longman.

Super, C. M. (1981). Behavioral development in infancy. In R. H. Monroe, R. L. Monroe, & B. B. Whiting (Eds.), *Handbook of cross-cultural human development* (pp. 181–270). New York: Garland.

Super, D. (1980). A life-span, life-space approach to career development. *Journal of Vocational Behavior, 16*, 282–298.

Super, D. (1984). Career and life development. In D. Brown & L. Brooks (Eds.), *Career choice and development* (pp. 192–234). San Francisco: Jossey-Bass.

Sureau, C. (1997). Trials and tribulations of surrogacy: From surrogacy to parenthood. *Human Reproduction, 12,* 410–411.

Svensson, A. (2000). Computers in school: Socially isolating or a tool to promote collaboration. *Journal of Educational Computing Research, 22,* 437–453.

Swanson, J. L., & Fouad, N. A. (1999). Applying theories of person–environment fit to the transition from school to work. *Career Development Quarterly, 47,* 337–347.

Szepkouski, G. M., Gauvain, M., & Carberry, M. (1994). The development of planning skills in children with and without mental retardation. *Journal of Applied Developmental Psychology, 15,* 187–206.

Szkrybalo, J., & Ruble, D. N. (1999). "God made me a girl": Sex-category constancy judgments and explanations revisited. *Developmental Psychology, 35,* 392–402.

Taddio, A., Katz, J., Ilersich, A. L., & Koren, G. (1997). Effect of neonatal circumcision on pain response during subsequent routine vaccination. *Lancet, 349,* 599–603.

Tager-Flusberg, H. (1997). Putting words together: Morphology and syntax in the preschool years. In J. B. Gleason (Ed.), *The development of language* (pp. 162–212). Boston: Allyn and Bacon.

Tager-Flusberg, H. (2000). Putting words together: Morphology and syntax in the preschool years. In J. B. Gleason (Ed.), *The development of language* (4th ed., pp. 159–209). Boston: Allyn and Bacon.

Takahashi, K. (1990). Are the key assumptions of the "Strange Situation" procedure universal? A view from Japanese research. *Human Development, 33,* 23–30.

Tamis-LeMonda, C. S., & Bornstein, M. H. (1989). Habituation and maternal encouragement of attention in infancy as predictors of toddler language, play, and representational competence. *Child Development, 60,* 738–751.

Tamis-LeMonda, C. S., & Bornstein, M. H. (1994). Specificity in mother–toddler language–play relations across the second year. *Developmental Psychology, 30,* 283–292.

Tangney, J. P. (1998). How does guilt differ from shame? In J. Bybee (Ed.), *Guilt and children* (pp. 1–17). San Diego, CA: Academic Press.

Taniguchi, H. (1999). The timing of childbearing and women's wages. *Journal of Marriage and the Family, 61,* 1008–1019.

Tanner, J. M. (1990). *Foetus into man* (2nd ed.). Cambridge, MA: Harvard University Press.

Tanner, J. M., Whitehouse, R. H., Cameron, N., Marshall, W. A., Healey, M. J. R., & Goldstein, H. (1983). *Assessment of skeletal maturity and prediction of adult height (TW2 method)* (2nd ed.). New York: Academic Press.

Tardif, T., Gelman, S. A., & Xu, F. (1999). Putting the "noun bias" in context: A comparison of English and Mandarin. *Child Development, 70,* 620–635.

Taylor, J. H., & Walker, L. J. (1997). Moral climate and the development of moral reasoning: The effects of dyadic discussions between young offenders. *Journal of Moral Education, 26,* 21–43.

Taylor, M. (1996). The development of children's beliefs about the social and biological aspects of gender differences. *Child Development, 67,* 1555–1571.

Taylor, M. (1999). *Imaginary companions and the children who create them.* New York: Oxford University Press.

Taylor, M., & Carlson, S. M. (1997). The relation between individual differences in fantasy and theory of mind. *Child Development, 68,* 436–455.

Taylor, M., Cartwright, B. S., & Carlson, S. M. (1993). A developmental investigation of children's imaginary companions. *Developmental Psychology, 29,* 276–285.

Taylor, M., Esbensen, B. M., & Bennett, R. T. (1994). Children's understanding of knowledge acquisition: The tendency for children to report that they have always known what they have just learned. *Child Development, 65,* 1581–1604.

Taylor, M. C., & Hall, J. A. (1982). Psychological androgyny: Theories, methods, and conclusions. *Psychological Bulletin, 92,* 347–366.

Teele, D. W., Klein, J. O., Chase, C., Menyuk, P., Rosner, B. A., & The Greater Boston Otitis Media Study Group. (1990). Otitis media in infancy and intellectual ability, school achievement, speech, and language at age 7 years. *Journal of Infectious Diseases, 162,* 685–694.

Teikari, J. M., O'Donnell, J., Kaprio, J., & Koskenvuo, M. (1992). Heritability of defects of far vision in young adults—a twin study. *Scandinavian Journal of Social Medicine, 20,* 73–78.

Teller, D. Y. (1998). Spatial and temporal aspects of infant color vision. *Vision Research, 38,* 3275–3282.

Tellings, A. (1999). Psychoanalytical and genetic-structuralistic approaches of moral development: Incompatible views? *Psychoanalytic Review, 86,* 903–914.

Temple, C. M., & Carney, R. A. (1995). Patterns of spatial functioning in Turner's syndrome. *Cortex, 31,* 109–118.

Terestchenko, N. Y., Lyaginskaya, A. M., & Burtzeva, L. I. (1991). Stochastic, nonstochastic effects and some population-genetic characteristics in children of the critical group in period of basic organogenesis. In *The scientific and practical aspects of preservation of health of the people exposed to radiation influence as a result of the accident at the Chernobyl atomic power station* (in Russian) (pp. 73–74). Minsk: Publishing House of Belarussian Committee "Chernobyl Children."

Tertinger, D. A., Greene, B. F., & Lutzker, J. R. (1984). Home safety: Development and validation of one component of an ecobehavioral treatment program for abused and neglected children. *Journal of Applied Behavior Analysis, 17,* 159–174.

Teti, D. M., Gelfand, D. M., Messinger, D. S., & Isabella, R. (1995). Maternal depression and the quality of early attachment: An examination of infants, preschoolers, and their mothers. *Developmental Psychology, 31,* 364–376.

Teti, D. M., & McGourty, S. (1996). Using mothers versus trained observers in assessing children's secure base behavior: Theoretical and methodological considerations. *Child Development, 67,* 597–605.

Teti, D. M., Saken, J. W., Kucera, E., & Corns, K. M. (1996). And baby makes four: Predictors of attachment security among preschool-age firstborns during the transition to siblinghood. *Child Development, 67,* 579–596.

Teyber, E. (1992). *Helping children cope with divorce.* New York: Lexington Books.

Tharp, R. G. (1993). Institutional and social context of educational practice and reform. In E. A. Forman, N. Minick, & C. A. Stone (Eds.), *Contexts for learning* (pp. 269–282). New York: Oxford University Press.

Tharp, R. G. (1994). Intergroup differences among Native Americans in socialization and child cognition: An ethnogenetic analysis. In P. M. Greenfield & R. Cocking (Eds.), *Cross-cultural roots of minority child development* (pp. 87–105). Hillsdale, NJ: Erlbaum.

Tharp, R. G., & Gallimore, R. (1988). *Rousing minds to life: Teaching, learning, and schooling in social context.* Cambridge, England: Cambridge University Press.

Thatcher, R. W., Lyon, G. R., Rumsey, J., & Krasnegor, J. (1996). *Developmental neuroimagining.* San Diego, CA: Academic Press.

Thatcher, R. W., Walker, R. A., & Giudice, S. (1987). Human cerebral hemispheres develop at different rates and ages. *Science, 236,* 1110–1113.

Thelen, E. (1989). The (re)discovery of motor development: Learning new things from an old field. *Developmental Psychology, 25,* 946–949.

Thelen, E. (1994). Three-month-old infants can learn task-specific patterns of inter-limb coordination. *Psychological Science, 5,* 280–285.

Thelen, E., & Adolph, K. E. (1992). Arnold Gesell: The paradox of nature and nurture. *Developmental Psychology, 28,* 368–380.

Thelen, E., Corbetta, D., Kamm, K., Spencer, J. P., Schneider, K., & Zernicke, R. F. (1993). The transition to reaching: Mapping intention and intrinsic dynamics. *Child Development, 64,* 1058–1098.

Thelen, E., Corbetta, D., & Spencer, J. (1996). The development of reaching during the first year: The role of movement speed. *Journal of Experimental Psychology: Human Perception and Performance, 22,* 1059–1076.

Thelen, E., Fisher, D. M., & Ridley-Johnson, R. (1984). The relationship between physical growth and a newborn reflex. *Infant Behavior and Development, 7,* 479–493.

Thelen, E., & Smith, L. B. (1994). *A dynamic systems approach to the development of cognition and action.* Cambridge, MA: MIT Press.

Thelen, E., & Smith, L. B. (1998). Dynamic systems theories. In R. M. Lerner (Ed.), *Handbook of child psychology: Vol. 1. Theoretical models of human development* (5th ed., pp. 563–634). New York: Wiley.

Thelen, E., & Spencer, J. P. (1998). Postural control during reaching in young infants. *Neuroscience and Biobehavioral Reviews, 22,* 507–514.

Thoman, E., & Ingersoll, E. W. (1993). Learning in premature infants. *Developmental Psychology, 29,* 692–700.

Thomas, A., & Chess, S. (1977). *Temperament and development*. New York: Brunner/Mazel.

Thomas, A., Chess, S., & Birch, H. G. (1968). *Temperament and behavior disorders in children*. New York: New York University Press.

Thomas, J. R., & French, K. E. (1985). Gender differences across age in motor performance: A meta-analysis. *Psychological Bulletin, 98*, 260–282.

Thomas, R. M. (2000). *Comparing theories of child development* (5th ed.). Belmont, CA: Wadsworth.

Thompson, P. M., Giedd, J. N., Woods, R. P., MacDonald, D., Evans, A. C., & Toga, A. W. (2000). Growth patterns in the developing brain detected by using continuum mechanical tensor maps. *Nature, 404,* 190–193.

Thompson, R. (1999). Early attachment and later development. In J. Cassidy & P. Shaver (Eds.), *Handbook of attachment: Theory, research, and clinical applications* (pp. 265–286). New York: Guilford.

Thompson, R. A. (1990a). On emotion and self-regulation. In R. A. Thompson (Ed.), *Nebraska Symposia on Motivation* (Vol. 36, pp. 383–483). Lincoln: University of Nebraska Press.

Thompson, R. A. (1990b). Vulnerability in research: A developmental perspective on research risk. *Child Development, 61*, 1–16.

Thompson, R. A. (1994). Emotion regulation: A theme in search of definition. In N. A. Fox (Ed.), The development of emotion regulation. *Monographs of the Society for Research in Child Development, 59* (2–3, Serial No. 240).

Thompson, R. A. (1998). Early sociopersonality development. In N. Eisenberg (Ed.), *Handbook of child psychology: Vol. 3. Social, emotional, and personality development* (5th ed., pp. 25–104). New York: Wiley.

Thompson, R. A., & Limber, S. (1991). "Social anxiety" in infancy: Stranger wariness and separation distress. In H. Leitenberg (Ed.), *Handbook of social and evaluation anxiety* (pp. 85–137). New York: Plenum.

Thompson, R. A., & Nelson, C. A. (2001). Developmental science and the media: Early brain development. *American Psychologist, 56*, 5–15.

Thorndike, R. L., Hagen, E. P., & Sattler, J. M. (1986). *The Stanford-Binet Intelligence Scale.* Chicago: Riverside Publishing.

Thorne, B. (1993). *Gender play: Girls and boys in school.* New Brunswick, NJ: Rutgers University Press.

Tienari, P., Wynne, L. C., Moring, J., & Lahti, I. (1994). The Finnish adoptive family study of schizophrenia: Implications for family research. *British Journal of Psychiatry, 164*, 20–26.

Tietjen, A., & Walker, L. (1985). Moral reasoning and leadership among men in a Papua New Guinea village. *Developmental Psychology, 21*, 982–992.

Tisak, M. S. (1995). Domains of social reasoning and beyond. In R. Vasta (Ed.), *Annals of child development* (Vol. 11, pp. 95–130). London: Jessica Kingsley.

Tizard, B., & Hodges, J. (1978). The effect of early institutional rearing on the development of eight-year-old children. *Journal of Child Psychology and Psychiatry, 19*, 99–118.

Tizard, B., & Rees, J. (1975). The effect of early institutional rearing on the behaviour problems and affectional relationships of four-year-old children. *Journal of Child Psychology and Psychiatry, 16*, 61–73.

Tobias, N. E. (2000). Management of nocturnal enuresis. *Pediatric Advanced Practice Nursing, 35*, 37–60.

Tofler, I. R., Knapp, P. K., & Drell, M. J. (1998). The achievement by proxy spectrum in youth sports: Historical perspective and clinical approach to pressured and high-achieving children and adolescents. *Child and Adolescent Psychiatric Clinics of North America, 7*, 803–820.

Tolson, J. M., & Urberg, K. A. (1993). Similarity between adolescent best friends. *Journal of Adolescent Research, 8*, 274–288.

Tolson, T. F. J., & Wilson, M. N. (1990). The impact of two- and three-generational black family structure on perceived family climate. *Child Development, 61*, 416–428.

Tomasello, M. (1995). Language is not an instinct. *Cognitive Development, 10*, 131–156.

Tomasello, M. (1999). Having intentions, understanding intentions, and understanding communicative intentions. In P. D. Zelazo, J. W. Astington, & J. Wilde (Eds.), *Developing theories of intention: Social understanding and self-control* (pp. 63–75). Mahwah, NJ: Erlbaum.

Tomasello, M. (1999). The human adaptation for culture. *Annual Review of Anthropology, 28*, 509–529.

Tomasello, M. (2000). Do young children have adult syntactic competence? *Cognition, 74*, 209–253.

Tomasello, M., & Akhtar, N. (1995). Two-year-olds use pragmatic cues to differentiate reference to objects and actions. *Cognitive Development, 10*, 201–224.

Tomasello, M., Akhtar, N., Dodson, K., & Rekau, L. (1997). Differential productivity in young children's use of nouns and verbs. *Journal of Child Language, 24*, 373–387.

Tomasello, M., & Brooks, P. (1999). Early syntactic development: A construction grammar approach. In M. Barrett (Ed.), *The development of language* (pp. 161–190). London: UCL Press.

Tomasello, M., Striano, T., & Rochat, P. (1999). Do young children use objects as symbols? *British Journal of Developmental Psychology, 17*, 563–584.

Toner, M. A., & Munro, D. (1996). Peer-social attributions and self-efficacy of peer-rejected preadolescents. *Merrill-Palmer Quarterly, 42*, 339–357.

Tong, S., Caddy, D., & Short, R. V. (1997). Use of dizygotic to monozygotic twinning ratio as a measure of fertility. *Lancet, 349*, 843–845.

Toomela, A. (1999). Drawing development: Stages in the representation of a cube and a cylinder. *Child Development, 70*, 1141–1150.

Torrance, E. P. (1980). *Torrance Tests of Creative Thinking.* New York: Scholastic Testing Service.

Torrance, E. P. (1988). The nature of creativity as manifest in its testing. In R. J. Sternberg (Ed.), *The nature of creativity: Contemporary psychological perspectives* (pp. 43–75). New York: Cambridge University Press.

Touwen, B. C. L. (1984). Primitive reflexes—conceptual or semantic problem? In H. F. R. Prechtl (Ed.), *Continuity of neural functions from prenatal to postnatal life* (Clinics in Developmental Medicine No. 94, pp. 115–125). Philadelphia: Lippincott.

Tower, R. B., Singer, D. G., Singer, J. L., & Biggs, A. (1979). Differential effects of television programming on preschoolers' cognition, imagination, and social play. *American Journal of Orthopsychiatry, 49*, 265–281.

Trasti, N., Vik, T., Jacobson, G., & Bakketeig, L. S. (1999). Smoking in pregnancy and children's mental and motor development at age 1 and 5 years. *Early Human Development, 55*, 137–147.

Treiman, R., Tincoff, R., Rodriguez, K., Mouzaki, A., & Francis, D. J. (1998). The foundations of literacy: Learning the sounds of letters. *Child Development, 69*, 1524–1540.

Tremblay, G. C., & Peterson, L. (1999). Prevention of childhood injury: Clinical and public policy challenges. *Clinical Psychology Review, 19*, 415–434.

Trent, K., & Harlan, S. L. (1994). Teenage mothers in nuclear and extended households. *Journal of Family Issues, 15*, 309–337.

Triandis, H. C. (1995). *Individualism and collectivism.* Boulder, CO: Westview Press.

Triandis, H. C. (1998, May). *Cross-cultural versus cultural psychology: A synthesis?* Colloquium presented at Illinois Wesleyan University, Bloomington, Illinois.

Trickett, P. K., & Putnam, F. W. (1998). Developmental consequences of child sexual abuse. In P. K. Trickett & C. J. Schellenbach (Eds.), *Violence against children in the family and community* (pp. 39–56). Washington, DC: American Psychological Association.

Troiana, R. P., & Flegal, K. M. (1998). Overweight children and adolescents: Description, epidemiology, and demographics. *Pediatrics, 101*, 497–504.

Tronick, E., Morelli, G., & Ivey, P. (1992). The Efe forager infant and toddler's pattern of social relationships: Multiple and simultaneous. *Developmental Psychology, 28*, 568–577.

Tronick, E. Z. (1989). Emotions and emotional communication in infants. *American Psychologist, 44*, 112–119.

Tronick, E. Z., Thomas, R. B., & Daltabuit, M. (1994). The Quechua manta pouch: A caretaking practice for buffering the Peruvian infant against the multiple stressors of high altitude. *Child Development, 65*, 1005–1013.

Tröster, H., & Brambring, M. (1992). Early social-emotional development in blind infants. *Child: Care, Health and Development, 18*, 207–227.

Tröster, H., & Brambring, M. (1993). Early motor development in blind infants. *Journal of Applied Developmental Psychology, 14*, 83–106.

Trounson, A., & Pera, M. (1998). Potential benefits of cell cloning for human medicine. *Reproduction, Fertility, and Development, 10*, 121–125.

Truglio, R. (2000, April). *Research guides "Sesame Street."* Public lecture presented as part of the Consider the Children program, Illinois State University, Normal, IL.

Trusty, J. (1999). Effects of eighth-grade parental involvement on late adolescents' educational expectations. *Journal of Research and Development in Education, 32,* 224–233.

Tsai, L. Y. (1999). Recent neurobiological research in autism. In D. B. Zager (Ed.), *Autism: Identification, education, and treatment* (2nd ed., pp. 63–95). Mahwah, NJ: Erlbaum.

Tuchfarber, B. S., Zins, J. E., & Jason, L. A. (1997). Prevention and control of injuries. In R. Weissberg, T. P. Gullotta, R. L. Hampton, B. A. Ryan, & G. R. Adams (Eds.), *Enhancing children's wellness* (pp. 250–277). Thousand Oaks, CA: Sage.

Tudge, J. R. H. (1992). Processes and consequences of peer collaboration: A Vygotskian analysis. *Child Development, 63,* 1364–1397.

Turiel, E. (1998). The development of morality. In N. Eisenberg (Ed.), *Handbook of child psychology: Vol. 3. Social, emotional, and personality development* (Vol. 3, pp. 863–932). New York: Wiley.

Turkheimer, E., & Gottesman, I. I. (1991). Individual differences and the canalization of human behavior. *Developmental Psychology, 27,* 18–22.

Turner, P. J., & Gervai, J. (1995). A multidimensional study of gender typing in preschool children and their parents: Personality, attitudes, preferences, behavior, and cultural differences. *Developmental Psychology, 31,* 759–772.

Tuss, P., Zimmer, J., & Ho. H-Z. (1995). Causal attributions of underachieving fourth-grade students in China, Japan, and the United States. *Journal of Cross-Cultural Psychology, 26,* 408–425.

Tzuriel, D. (1989). Inferential thinking modifiability in young socially disadvantaged and advantaged children. *International Journal of Dynamic Assessment and Instruction, 1,* 65–80.

Udry, J. R. (1990). Hormonal and social determinants of adolescent sexual initiation. In J. Bancroft & J. M. Reinisch (Eds.), *Adolescence and puberty* (pp. 70–87). New York: Oxford University Press.

Uhari, M., Kontiokari, T., & Niemelä, M. (1998). A novel use of xylitol sugar in preventing acute otitis media. *Pediatrics, 102,* 879–884.

Uhari, M., Mäntysaari, K., & Niemelä, M. (1996). A meta-analytic review of the risk factors for acute otitis media. *Clinical Infectious Diseases, 22,* 1079–1083.

Uhari, M., & Möttönen, M. (1999). An open randomized controlled trial of infection prevention in child day-care centers. *Pediatric Infectious Disease Journal, 18,* 672–677.

Ulrich, B. D., & Ulrich, D. A. (1985). The role of balancing in performance of fundamental motor skills in 3-, 4-, and 5-year-old children. In J. E. Clark & J. H. Humphrey (Eds.), *Motor development* (Vol. 1, pp. 87–98). Princeton, NJ: Princeton Books.

United Nations. (1998). *World population prospects: The 1998 revision* (Vol. 1). New York: Author.

United Nations. (1999). *World social situation in the 1990s.* New York: Author.

U.S. Bureau of the Census. (1997). *Who's minding our preschoolers?* (Current Population Reports, P70-62). Washington, DC: U.S. Government Printing Office.

U.S. Bureau of the Census. (2000). *Statistical abstract of the United States* (120th ed.). Washington, DC: U.S. Government Printing Office.

U.S. Centers for Disease Control. (2000a). *Sexually transmitted disease surveillance, 1999.* Atlanta: Author.

U.S. Centers for Disease Control. (2000b). *Recommended childhood immunization schedule, United States, January–December, 2000.* [On-line] Available: *www.cdc.gov*

U.S. Centers for Disease Control. (2000c). *Six common misconceptions about vaccination.* [On-line]. Available: *www.cdc.gov/nip/publications/6mishome.htm*

U.S. Department of Education. (2000). *Digest of education statistics, 2000.* Washington, DC: U.S. Government Printing Office.

U.S. Department of Education, National Center for Education Statistics. (2000). *Digest of education statistics 1998.* Washington, DC: U.S. Government Printing Office.

U.S. Department of Education. (1998). *Pursuing excellence: A study of U.S. twelfth-grade mathematics and science achievement in international context.* Washington, DC: U.S. Government Printing Office.

U.S. Department of Education. (2000). *Digest of education statistics 1999.* Washington, DC: U.S. Government Printing Office.

U.S. Department of Health and Human Services. (1999a). *Impaired fecundity by age and selected characteristics.* Washington, DC: U.S. Government Printing Office.

U.S. Department of Health and Human Services. (1999b). Knowledge and use of folic acid by women of childbearing age. *Morbidity and Mortality Weekly Report, 48,* 325–327.

U.S. Department of Health and Human Services. (2000a). *The childhood immunization initiative.* [On-line]. Available: *www.hhs.gov/news/press/2000pres/20000706a.html*

U.S. Department of Health and Human Services. (2000b). *Health United States 1997–1998 and injury chartbook.* Washington, DC: U.S. Bureau of the Census.

U.S. Department of Health and Human Services. (2000c). *Health United States 1999–2000 and injury chartbook.* Washington, DC: U.S. Bureau of the Census.

U.S. Department of Health and Human Services. (2000d). *National survey results on drug use from the Monitoring the Future Study. Vol. 1. Secondary school students.* Washington, DC: U.S. Government Printing Office.

U.S. Department of Health and Human Services. (2000e). *Oral health in America: A report of the Surgeon General.* Washington, DC: Author.

U.S. Department of Health and Human Services. (2000f, August 8). *Preventing teenage pregnancy. HHS Fact Sheet.* [On-line] *www.hhs.gov/news/press/*

U.S. Department of Health and Human Services. (2000g). *Promoting better health for young people through physical activity and sports.* Washington, DC: U.S. Government Printing Office.

U.S. Department of Health and Human Services. (2000h). *Vital statistics of the United States, 1997.* Washington, DC: U.S. Government Printing Office.

U.S. Department of Health and Human Services. (2000i). *Vital statistics of the United States, 1998.* Washington, DC: U.S. Government Printing Office.

U.S. Department of Health and Human Services. (2000j, June 9). Youth risk behavior surveillance—United States, 1999. *Morbidity and Mortality Weekly Report, 49* (No. SS–5).

U.S. Department of Justice. (2000). *Crime in the United States.* Washington, DC: U.S. Government Printing Office.

U.S. Department of Labor, Bureau of Labor Statistics. (2000, February). Consumer Price Index. *Monthly Labor Review, 122*(2).

Upchurch, D. M., Aneshensel, C. S., Sucoff, C. A., & Levy-Storms, L. (1999). Neighborhood and family contexts of adolescent sexual activity. *Journal of Marriage and the Family, 61,* 920–933.

Updegraff, K. A., McHale, S. M., & Crouter, A. C. (1996). Gender roles in marriage: What do they mean for girls' and boys' school achievement? *Journal of Youth and Adolescence, 25,* 73–88.

Updegraff, K. A., & Obeidallah, D. A. (1999). Young adolescents' patterns of involvement with siblings and friends. *Social Development, 8,* 52–69.

Uribe, F. M. T., LeVine, R. A., & LeVine, S. E. (1994). Maternal behavior in a Mexican community: The changing environments of children. In P. M. Greenfield & R. R. Cocking (Eds.), *Cross-cultural roots of minority child development* (pp. 41–54). Hillsdale, NJ: Erlbaum.

Usmiani, S., & Daniluk, J. (1997). Mothers and their adolescent daughters: Relationship between self-esteem, gender role identity, and body image. *Journal of Youth and Adolescence, 26,* 45–60.

Valdés, G. (1998). The world outside and inside schools: Language and immigrant children. *Educational Researcher, 27*(6), 4–18.

Valdez, R., Athens, M. A., Thompson, G. H., Bradshaw, G. H., & Stern, M. P. (1994). Birthweight and adult health outcomes in a bi-ethnic population in the U.S.A. *Diabetologia, 37,* 624.

Valdez-Menchaca, M. C., & Whitehurst, G. J. (1992). Accelerating language development through picture book reading: A systematic extension to Mexican day care. *Developmental Psychology, 28,* 1106–1114.

Valian, V. V. (1993). *Parental replies: Linguistic status and didactic role.* Cambridge, MA: MIT Press.

Valian, V. V. (1996). *Parental replies: Linguistic status and didactic role.* Cambridge, MA: MIT Press.

Vance, M. D. (1994, April). *Short stature and psychosocial risks in a nonclinical sample.* Proceedings of the Fourth North Coast Conference of the Society for Pediatric Psychology, Amherst, NY.

Vance, M. L., & Mauras, N. (1999). Growth hormone therapy in adults and children. *Drug Therapy, 341,* 1206–1215.

Vandell, D. L., Dadisman, K., & Gallagher, K. (2000). Another look at the elephant: Child care in the nineties. In R. D. Taylor & M. C. Wang (Eds.), *Resilience across contexts: Family, work, culture, and community* (pp. 91–120). Mahwah, NJ: Erlbaum.

Vandell, D. L., & Hembree, S. E. (1994). Peer social status and friendship: Independent contributors to children's social and academic adjustment. *Merrill-Palmer Quarterly, 40,* 461–477.

Vandell, D. L., & Mueller, E. C. (1995). Peer play and friendships during the first two years. In H. C. Foot, A. J. Chapman, & J. R. Smith (Eds.), *Friendship and social relations in children* (pp. 181–208). New Brunswick, NJ: Transaction.

Vandell, D. L., & Posner, J. K. (1999). Conceptualization and measurement of children's after-school environments. In S. L. Friedman & T. D. Wachs (Eds.), *Measuring environment across the life span* (pp. 167–196). Washington, DC: American Psychological Association.

Vandell, D. L., & Shumow, L. (1999). After-school child care programs. *Future of Children, 9*(2), 64–80.

Vandell, D. L., & Wilson, K. S. (1987). Infants' interactions with mother, sibling, and peer: Contrasts and relations between interaction systems. *Child Development, 58,* 176–186.

Vandell, D. L., Wilson, K. S., & Buchanan, N. R. (1980). Peer interaction in the first year of life: An examination of its structure, content, and sensitivity to toys. *Child Development, 51,* 481–488.

Vandenberg, B. (1998). Real and not real: A vital developmental dichotomy. In O. N. Saracho & B. Spodek (Eds.), *Multiple perspectives on play in early childhood education* (pp. 295–305). Albany: State University of New York Press.

van den Boom, D. C. (1995). Do first-year intervention effects endure? Follow-up during toddlerhood of a sample of Dutch irritable infants. *Child Development, 66,* 1798–1816.

van den Boom, D. C., & Hoeksma, J. B. (1994). The effect of infant irritability on mother–infant interaction: A growth-curve analysis. *Developmental Psychology, 30,* 581–590.

Vanfossen, B., Jones, J., & Spade, J. (1987). Curriculum tracking and status maintenance. *Sociology of Education, 60,* 104–122.

van IJzendoorn, M. H. (1995a). Adult attachment representations, parental responsiveness, and infant attachment: A meta-analysis on the predictive validity of the Adult Attachment Interview. *Psychological Bulletin, 117,* 387–403.

van IJzendoorn, M. H. (1995b). Of the way we are: On temperament, attachment, and the transmission gap: A rejoinder to Fox (1995). *Psychological Bulletin, 117,* 411–415.

van IJzendoorn, M. H., & De Wolff, M. S. (1997). In search of the absent father—meta-analyses of infant–father attachment: A

rejoinder to our discussants. *Child Development, 68,* 604–609.

van IJzendoorn, M. H., Goldberg, S., Kroonenberg, P. M. & Frenkel, O. J. (1992). The relative effects of maternal and child problems on the quality of attachment: A meta-analysis of attachment in clinical samples. *Child Development, 63,* 840–858.

van IJzendoorn, M. H., & Kroonenberg, P. M. (1988). Cross-cultural patterns of attachment: A meta-analysis of the Strange Situation. *Child Development, 59,* 147–156.

van IJzendoorn, M. H., & Sagi, A. (1999). Cross-cultural patterns of attachment. In J. Cassidy & P. R. Shaver (Eds.), *Handbook of attachment: Theory, research, and clinical applications* (pp. 713–734). New York: Guilford.

Varendi, H., Christensson, K., Porter, R. H., & Winberg, J. (1998). Soothing effect of amniotic fluid smell in newborn infants. *Early Human Development, 51,* 47–55.

Vartanian, L. R., & Powlishta, K. K. (1996). A longitudinal examination of the social-cognitive foundations of adolescent egocentrism. *Journal of Early Adolescence, 16,* 157–178.

Vasudev, J., & Hummel, R. C. (1987). Moral stage sequence and principled reasoning in an Indian sample. *Human Development, 30,* 103–118.

Vaughn, B. E., & Bost, K. K. (1999). Attachment and temperament: Redundant, independent, or interacting influences on interpersonal adaptation and personality development? In J. Cassidy & P. Shaver (Eds.), *Handbook of attachment: Theory, research, and clinical applications* (pp. 265–286). New York: Guilford.

Vaughn, B. E., Bradley, C. F., Joffe, L. S., Seifer, R., & Barglow, P. (1987). Maternal characteristics measured prenatally are predictive of ratings of temperamental "difficulty" on the Carey Infant Temperament Questionnaire. *Developmental Psychology, 23,* 152–161.

Vaughn, B. E., Egeland, B. R., Sroufe, L. A., & Waters, E. (1979). Individual differences in infant–mother attachment at twelve and eighteen months: Stability and change in families under stress. *Child Development, 50,* 971–975.

Vaughn, B. E., Kopp, C. B., & Krakow, J. B. (1984). The emergence and consolidation of self-control from eighteen to thirty months of age: Normative trends and individual differences. *Child Development, 55,* 990–1004.

Vaughn, S., & Klingner, J. K. (1998). Students' perceptions of inclusion and resource room settings. *Journal of Special Education, 32,* 79–88.

Ventura, S. J. (1989). Trends and variations in first births to older women in the United States, 1970–86. *Vital and Health Statistics* (Series 21). Hyattsville, MD: U.S. Department of Health and Human Services.

Ventura, S. J., & Freedman, M. A. (2000). Teenage childbearing in the United States, 1960–1997. *American Journal of Preventive Medicine, 19,* 18–25.

Ventura, S. J., Martin, J. A., Curtin, S. C., & Mathews, T. J. (2000). *Births: Final data for 1997: National Vital Statistics Report Supplements.* Washington, DC: U.S. Government Printing Office.

Verba, S., Schlozman, K. L., & Brady, H. E. (1995). *Voice and equality: Civic voluntarism in American politics.* Cambridge, MA: Harvard University Press.

Vergnaud, G. (1996). Education, the best portion of Piaget's heritage. *Swiss Journal of Psychology, 55,* 112–118.

Vernon, P. A. (1993). Intelligence and neural efficiency. In D. K. Detterman (Ed.), *Current topics in human intelligence* (Vol. 3, pp. 171–187). Norwood, NJ: Ablex.

Vernon-Feagans, L., Manlove, E. E., & Volling, B. L. (1996). Otitis media and the social behavior of day-care-attending children. *Child Development, 67,* 1528–1539.

Vinden, P. G. (1996). Junín Quechua children's understanding of mind. *Child Development, 67,* 1707–1716.

Vogel, D. A., Lake, M. A., Evans, S., & Karraker, H. (1991). Children's and adults' sex-stereotyped perceptions of infants. *Sex Roles, 24,* 605–616.

Vogel, L. D. (1998). When children put their fingers in their mouths: Should parents and dentists care? *New York Dental Journal, 64*(2), 48–53.

Vohr, B. R., & Garcia-Coll, C. T. (1988). Follow-up studies of high-risk low-birth-weight infants: Changing trends. In H. E. Fitzgerald, B. M. Lester, & M. W. Yogman (Eds.), *Theory and research in behavioral pediatrics* (pp. 1–65). New York: Plenum.

Volling, B. L., & Belsky, J. (1992). Contribution of mother–child and father–child relationships to the quality of sibling interaction: A longitudinal study. *Child Development, 63,* 1209–1222.

Volling, B. L., & Elins, J. L. (1998). Family relationships and children's

emotional adjustment as correlates of maternal and paternal differential treatment: A replication with toddlers and preschool siblings. *Child Development, 69,* 1640–1656.

Vondra, J. I., Hommerding, K. D., & Shaw, D. S. (1999). Stability and change in infant attachment in a low-income sample. In J. I Vondra & D. Barnett (Eds.), *Atypical attachment in infancy and early childhood among children at developmental risk. Monographs of the Society for Research in Child Development, 64*(3, Serial No. 258), pp. 119–144.

von Hofsten, C., & Rosander, K. (1998). The establishment of gaze control in early infancy. In S. Simion & G. Butterworth (Eds.), *The development of sensory, motor and cognitive capacities in early infancy* (pp. 49–66). Hove, UK: Psychology Press.

Vorhees, C. V. (1986). Principles of behavioral teratology. In E. P. Riley & C. V. Vorhees (Eds.), *Handbook of behavioral teratology* (pp. 23–48). New York: Plenum.

Vorhees, C. V., & Mollnow, E. (1987). Behavioral teratogenesis: Long-term influences on behavior from early exposure to environmental agents. In J. D. Osofsky (Ed.), *Handbook of infant development* (2nd ed., pp. 913–971). New York: Wiley.

Voss, L. D., Mulligan, J., & Betts, P. R. (1998). Short stature at school entry—an index of social deprivation? (The Wessex Growth Study). *Child: Care, Health and Development, 24,* 145–156.

Vostanis, P., Grattan, E., & Cumella, S. (1997). Psychosocial functioning of homeless children. *Journal of the American Academy of Child and Adolescent Psychiatry, 36,* 881–889.

Voyer, D., Voyer, S., & Bryden, M. P. (1995). Magnitude of sex differences in spatial abilities: A meta-analysis and consideration of critical variables. *Psychological Bulletin, 117,* 250–270.

Vurpillot, E. (1968). The development of scanning strategies and their relation to visual differentiation. *Journal of Experimental Psychology, 6,* 632–650.

Vygotsky, L. S. (1978). *Mind in society: The development of higher psychological processes.* Cambridge, MA: Harvard University Press. (Original works published 1930, 1933, and 1935)

Vygotsky, L. S. (1987). Thinking and speech. In R. W. Rieber, A. S. Carton (Eds.), & N. Minick (Trans.), *The collected works of L. S. Vygotsky: Vol. 1. Problems of general psychology* (pp. 37–285).

New York: Plenum. (Original work published 1934)

Wachs, T. D. (1975). Relation of infants' performance on Piagetian scales between twelve and twenty-four months and their Stanford-Binet performance at thirty-one months. *Child Development, 46,* 929–935.

Wachs, T. D. (1995). Relation of mild-to-moderate malnutrition to human development: Correlational studies. *Journal of Nutrition Supplement, 125,* 2245S–2254S.

Wachs, T. D. (1999). The what, why, and how of temperament: A piece of the action. In L. Balter & C. S. Tamis-LeMonda (Eds.), *Child psychology: A handbook of contemporary issues* (pp. 23–44). Philadelphia: Psychology Press.

Wachs, T. D. (2000). *Necessary but not sufficient: The respective roles of single and multiple influences on individual development.* Washington, DC: American Psychological Association.

Wachs, T. D., Bishry, Z., Moussa, W., Yunis, F., McCabe, G., Harrison, G., Swefi, I., Kirksey, A., Galal, O., Jerome, N., & Shaheen, F. (1995). Nutritional intake and context as predictors of cognition and adaptive behavior of Egyptian school-age children. *International Journal of Behavioral Development, 18,* 425–450.

Waddington, C. H. (1957). *The strategy of the genes.* London: Allen & Unwin.

Wagner, B. M., & Phillips, D. A. (1992). Beyond beliefs: Parent and child behaviors and children's perceived academic competence. *Child Development, 63,* 1380–1391.

Wahlsten, D. (1994). The intelligence of heritability. *Canadian Psychology, 35,* 244–259.

Wainryb, C., & Ford, S. (1998). Young children's evaluations of acts based on beliefs different from their own. *Merrill-Palmer Quarterly, 44,* 484–503.

Wainryb, C., Shaw, L. A., & Maianu, C. (1998). Tolerance and intolerance: Children's and adolescents' judgments of dissenting beliefs, speech, persons, and conduct. *Child Development, 69,* 1541–1555.

Wakat, D. K. (1978). Physiological factors of race and sex in sport. In L. K. Bunker & R. J. Rotella (Eds.), *Sport psychology: From theory to practice* (pp. 194–209). Charlotte, VA: University of Virginia. (Proceedings of the 1978 Sport Psychology Institute)

Walberg, H. J. (1986). Synthesis of research on teaching. In M. C. Wittrock (Ed.), *Handbook of research on teaching* (3rd ed., pp. 214–229). New York: Macmillan.

Walco, G. A. (1997). Growing pains. *Developmental and Behavioral Pediatrics, 18,* 107–108.

Walden, T., Lemerise, E., & Smith, M. C. (1999). Friendship and popularity in preschool classrooms. *Early Education & Development, 10,* 351–371.

Waldenström, U. (1999). Experience of labor and birth in 1111 women. *Journal of Psychosomatic Research, 47,* 471–482.

Waldman, I. D., Weinberg, R. A., & Scarr, S. (1994). Racial-group differences in IQ in the Minnesota Transracial Adoption Study: A reply to Levin and Lynn. *Intelligence, 19,* 29–44.

Waldron, N. L., & McLeskey, J. (1998). The effects of an inclusive school program on students with mild and severe learning disabilities. *Exceptional Children, 64,* 395–405.

Wales, R. (1990). Children's pictures. In R. Grieve & M. Hughes (Eds.), *Understanding children* (pp. 140–155). Oxford: Blackwell.

Walker, A., Rosenberg, M., & Balaban-Gil, K. (1999). Neurodevelopmental and neurobehavioral sequelae of selected substances of abuse and psychiatric medications in utero. *Neurological Disorders: Developmental and Behavioral Sequelae, 8,* 845–867.

Walker, D., Greenwood, C., Hart, B., & Carta, J. (1994). Prediction of school outcomes based on early language production and socioeconomic factors. *Child Development, 65,* 606–621.

Walker, L. (1995). Sexism in Kohlberg's moral psychology? In W. M. Kurtines & J. L. Gewirtz (Eds.), *Moral development: An introduction* (pp. 83–107). Boston: Allyn and Bacon.

Walker, L. J. (1989). A longitudinal study of moral reasoning. *Child Development, 60,* 157–166.

Walker, L. J., Pitts, R. C., Hennig, K. H., & Matsuba, M. K. (1995). Reasoning about morality and real-life moral problems. In M. Killen & D. Hart (Eds.), *Morality in everyday life* (pp. 371–407). New York: Cambridge University Press.

Walker, L. J., & Taylor, J. H. (1991a). Family interactions and the development of moral reasoning. *Child Development, 62,* 264–283.

Walker, L. J., & Taylor, J. H. (1991b). Stage transitions in moral reasoning: A longitudinal study of developmental processes. *Developmental Psychology, 27,* 330–337.

Walker-Andrews, A. S. (1997). Infants' perception of expressive behaviors: Differentiation of multimodal information. *Psychological Bulletin, 121,* 437–456.

Wallerstein, J. S., Corbin, S. B., & Lewis, J. M. (1988). Children of divorce: A ten-year study. In E. M. Hetherington & J. Arasteh (Eds.), *Impact of divorce, single parenting, and stepparenting on children* (pp. 198–214). Hillsdale, NJ: Erlbaum.

Wallerstein, J. S., & Kelly, J. B. (1980). *Surviving the break-up: How children and parents cope with divorce.* New York: Basic Books.

Walsh, M. E., & Bibace, R. (1991). Children's conceptions of AIDS: A developmental analysis. *Journal of Pediatric Psychology, 16,* 273–285.

Walton, L., Oliver, C., & Griffin, C. (1999). Divorce mediation: The impact of mediation on the psychological well-being of children and parents. *Journal of Community & Applied Social Psychology, 9,* 35–46.

Wang, Q., Leichtman, M. D., & White, S. H. (1998). Childhood memory and self-description in young Chinese adults: The impact of growing up an only child. *Cognition, 69,* 73–103.

Wangby, M., Bergman, L. R., & Magnesson, D. (1999). Development of adjustment problems in girls: What syndromes emerge? *Child Development, 70,* 678–699.

Wapner, J. J. (1997). Chorionic villus sampling. *Obstetrics and Gynecology Clinics of North America, 24,* 83–110.

Ward, L. M. (1995). Talking about sex: Common themes about sexuality in the prime-time television programs children and adolescents view most. *Journal of Youth and Adolescence, 24,* 595–616.

Wark, G. R., & Krebs, D. L. (1996). Gender and dilemma differences in real-life moral judgment. *Developmental Psychology, 32,* 220–230.

Warren, A. R., & Tate, C. S. (1992). Egocentrism in children's telephone conversations. In R. M. Diaz & L. E. Berk (Eds.), *Private speech: From social interaction to self-regulation* (pp. 245–264). Hillsdale, NJ: Erlbaum.

Warren, D. H. (1994). *Blindness and children: An individual difference approach.* New York: Cambridge University Press.

Wartner, U. G., Grossmann, K., Fremmer-Bombik, E., & Suess, G. (1994). Attachment patterns at age six in south Germany: Predictability from infancy and implications for preschool behavior. *Child Development, 65,* 1014–1027.

Wasserman, G. A., & Miller, L. S. (1998). The prevention of serious and violent juvenile offending. In R. Loeber & D. P. Farrington (Eds.), *Serious and violent juvenile offenders* (pp. 197–247). Thousand Oaks, CA: Sage.

Waters, E., Vaughn, B. E., Posada, G., & Kondo-Ikemura, K. (Eds.). (1995). Caregiving, cultural, and cognitive perspectives on secure-base behavior and working models: New growing points of attachment theory and research. *Monographs of the Society for Research in Child Development, 60* (2–3, Serial No. 244).

Waters, S. M., Treboux, D., Crowell, J., & Albersheim, L. (2000). Attachment security in infancy and early adulthood: A twenty-year longitudinal study. *Child Development, 71,* 684–689.

Watkins, W. E., & Pollitt, E. (1998). Iron deficiency and cognition among school-age children. In S. G. McGregor (Ed.), *Recent advances in research on the effects of health and nutrition on children's development and school achievement in the Third World.* Washington, DC: Pan American Health Organization.

Watson, A. C., Nixon, C. L., Wilson, A., & Capage, L. (1999). Social interaction skills and theory of mind in young children. *Developmental Psychology, 35,* 386–391.

Watson, D. J. (1989). Defining and describing whole language. *Elementary School Journal, 90,* 129–141.

Watson, J. B., & Raynor, R. (1920). Conditioned emotional reactions. *Journal of Experimental Psychology, 3,* 1–14.

Watson, M. (1990). Aspects of self development as reflected in children's role playing. In D. Cicchetti & M. Beeghly (Eds.), *The self in transition: Infancy to childhood* (pp. 281–307). Chicago: University of Chicago Press.

Wattigney, W. A., Srinivasan, S. R., Chen, W., Greenlund, K. J. & Berenson, G. S. (1999). Secular trend of earlier onset of menarche with increasing obesity in black and white girls: The Bogalusa Heart Study. *Ethnicity and Disease, 9,* 181–189.

Waxman, S. R. (1995). Words as invitations to form categories: Evidence from 12- to 13-month-old infants. *Cognitive Psychology, 29,* 254–302.

Waxman, S. R., & Markow, D. B. (1998). Object properties and object kind: Twenty-one-month-old infants' extension of novel adjectives. *Child Development, 69,* 1313–1329.

Waxman, S. R., & Senghas, A. (1992). Relations among word meanings in early lexical development. *Developmental Psychology, 28,* 862–873.

Webb, N. M., Nemer, K. M., & Chizhik, A. W. (1998). Equity issues in collaborative group assessment: Group composition and performance. *American Educational Research Journal, 35,* 607–651.

Wechsler, D. (1989). *Manual for the Wechsler Preschool and Primary Scale of Intelligence–Revised.* New York: Psychological Corporation.

Wechsler, D. (1991). *Manual for the Wechsler Intelligence Test for Children—III.* New York: Psychological Corporation.

Wehren, A., DeLisi, R., & Arnold, M. (1981). The development of noun definition. *Journal of Child Language, 8,* 165–175.

Weikart, D. P. (1998). Changing early childhood development through educational intervention. *Preventive Medicine, 27,* 233–237.

Weinberg, M. K., & Tronick, E. Z. (1994). Beyond the face: An empirical study of infant affective configurations of facial, vocal, gestural, and regulatory behaviors. *Child Development, 65,* 1503–1515.

Weinberg, M. K., & Tronick, E. Z. (1996). Infant affective reactions to the resumption of maternal interaction after the still face. *Child Development, 67,* 905–914.

Weinberg, M. K., Tronick, E. Z., Cohn, J. F., & Olson, K. L. (1999). Gender differences in emotional expressivity and self-regulation during early infancy. *Developmental Psychology, 35,* 175–188.

Weinberg, N. Z., Rahdert, E., Colliver, J. D., & Glantz, M. D. (1998). Adolescent substance abuse: A review of the past 10 years. *Journal of the American Academy of Child and Adolescent Psychiatry, 37,* 252–261.

Weinfield, N. S., Sroufe, L. A., & Egeland, B. (2000). Attachment from infancy to early adulthood in a high-risk sample: Continuity, discontinuity, and their correlates. *Child Development, 71,* 695–702.

Weinstein, R. S., Marshall, H. H., Sharp, L., & Botkin, M. (1987). Pygmalion and the student: Age and classroom differences in children's awareness of teacher expectations. *Child Development, 58,* 1079–1093.

Weisfield, G. (1997). Puberty rites as clues to the nature of human adolescence. *Cross-Cultural Research, 31,* 27–54.

Weisfield, G. E. (1986). Teaching about sex differences in human behavior and the biological approach in general. *Politics and the Life Sciences, 5,* 36–43.

Weisfield, G. E. (1990). Sociobiological patterns of Arab culture. *Ethology and Sociobiology, 11,* 23–49.

Weisner, T. S. (1996). The 5 to 7 transition as an ecocultural project. In A. J. Sameroff & M. M. Haith (Eds.), *The five to seven year shift* (pp. 295–326). Chicago: University of Chicago Press.

Weisner, T. S., & Wilson-Mitchell, J. E. (1990). Nonconventional family life-styles and sex typing in six-year-olds. *Child Development, 61,* 1915–1933.

Weiss, B., Dodge, K. A. Bates, J. E. & Pettit, G. S. (1992). Some consequences of early harsh discipline: Child aggression and a maladaptive social information processing style. *Child Development, 63,* 1321–1335.

Weissberg, R. P., & Greenberg, M. T. (1998). School and community competence-enhancement and prevention programs. In I. E. Sigel & K. A. Renninger (Eds.), *Handbook of child psychology: Vol. 4. Child psychology in practice* (5th ed., 877–954). New York: Wiley.

Weissman, M., Wolk, S., Goldstein, R. B., Moreau, D., Adams, P., & Greenwald, S. (1999). Depressed adolescents grown up. *Journal of the American Medical Association, 281,* 1707–1713.

Weissman, M. M., Warner, V., Wickramaratne, P. K., & Kandel, D. B. (1999). Maternal smoking during pregnancy and psychopathology in offspring followed to adulthood. *Journal of the American Academy of Child and Adolescent Psychiatry, 38,* 892–899.

Wellman, H. M. (1990). *The child's theory of mind.* Cambridge, MA: MIT Press.

Wellman, H. M., & Hickling, A. K. (1994). The mind's "I": Children's conception of the mind as an active agent. *Child Development, 65,* 1564–1580.

Wellman, H. M., Somerville, S. C., & Haake, R. J. (1979). Development of search procedures in real-life spatial environments. *Developmental Psychology, 15,* 530–542.

Wendland-Carro, J., Piccinini, C. A., & Millar, W. S. (1999). The role of an early intervention on enhancing the quality of mother–infant interaction. *Child Development, 70,* 713–721.

Wentzel, K., & Feldman, S. S. (1993). Parental predictors of boys' self-restraint and motivation to achieve at school: A longitudinal study. *Journal of Early Adolescence, 13,* 183–203.

Werker, J. F., Pegg, J. E., & McLeod, P. J. (1994). A cross-language investigation of infant preference for infant-directed communication. *Infant Behavior and Development, 17,* 323–333.

Werker, J. F., & Tees, R. C. (1999). Influences on infant speech processing: Toward a new synthesis. *Annual Review of Psychology, 50,* 509–535.

Werner, E. E. (1989, April). Children of the garden island. *Scientific American, 260*(4), 106–111.

Werner, E. E. (1993). Risk, resilience, and recovery: Perspectives from the Kauai Longitudinal Study. *Development and Psychopathology, 5,* 503–515.

Werner, E. E., & Smith, R. S. (1982). *Vulnerable but invincible: A study of resilient children.* New York: McGraw-Hill.

Werner, E. E., & Smith, R. S. (1992). *Overcoming the odds: High risk children from birth to adulthood.* Ithaca, NY: Cornell University Press.

Wertheim, E. H., Paxton, S. J., Schutz, H. K., & Muir, S. L. (1997). Why do adolescent girls watch their weight? An interview study examining sociocultural pressures to be thin. *Journal of Psychosomatic Research, 42,* 345–355.

Wertsch, J. V., & Tulviste, P. (1992). L. S. Vygotsky and contemporary developmental psychology. *Developmental Psychology, 28,* 548–557.

Wesley, B. D., van den Berg, B. J., & Reece, E. A. (1993). The effect of forceps delivery on cognitive development. *American Journal of Obstetrics and Gynecology, 169,* 1091–1095.

Westen, D., & Gabbard, G. O. (1999). Psychoanalytic approaches to personality. In L. A. Pervin & O. P. John (Eds.), *Handbook of personality: Theory and research* (2nd ed.). New York: Guilford.

Whalen, C. K., Henker, B., Burgess, S., & O'Neil, R. (1995). Young people talk about AIDS: "When you get sick, you stay sick." *Journal of Clinical Child Psychology, 24,* 338–345.

Wheeler, M. D. (1991). Physical changes of puberty. *Endocrinology and Metabolism Clinics of North America, 20,* 1–14.

Wheeler, T., Barker, D. J. P., & O'Brien, P. M. S. (1999). *Fetal programming: Influences on development and disease in later life.* London: RCOG Press.

Whitaker, D. J., & Miller, K. S. (2000). Parent–adolescent discussions about sex and condoms: Impact on peer influences of sexual risk behavior. *Journal of Adolescent Research, 15,* 251–273.

White, B., & Held, R. (1966). Plasticity of sensorimotor development in the human infant. In J. F. Rosenblith & W. Allinsmith (Eds.), *The causes of behavior* (pp. 60–70). Boston: Allyn and Bacon.

White, J. L., Moffitt, T. E., Caspi, A., Bartusch, D. J., Needles, D. J., & Stouthamer-Loeber, M. (1996). Measuring impulsivity and examining its relationship to delinquency. *Journal of Abnormal Psychology, 103,* 192–205.

White, M. A., Wilson, M. E., Elander, G., & Persson, B. (1999). The Swedish family: Transition to parenthood. *Scandinavian Journal of Caring Sciences, 13,* 171–176.

White, S. H. (1992). G. Stanley Hall: From philosophy to developmental psychology. *Developmental Psychology, 28,* 25–34.

Whitehead, J. R., & Corbin, C. B. (1997). Self-esteem in children and youth: The role of sport and physical education. In K. R. Fox (Ed.), *The physical self: From motivation to well-being* (pp. 175–204). Champaign, IL: Human Kinetics.

Whitehurst, G. J., Arnold, D. S., Epstein, J. N., Angell, A. L., Smith, M., & Fischel, J. E. (1994). A picture book reading intervention in day care and home for children from low-income families. *Developmental Psychology, 30,* 679–689.

Whitehurst, G. J., & Lonigan, C. J. (1998). Child development and emergent literacy. *Child Development, 69,* 848–872.

Whitehurst, G. J., & Vasta, R. (1975). Is language acquired through imitation? *Journal of Psycholinguistic Research, 4,* 37–59.

Whiteside, M. F., & Becker, B. J. (2000). Parental factors and the young child's postdivorce adjustment: A meta-analysis with implications for parenting arrangements. *Journal of Family Psychology, 14,* 5–26.

Whiting, B., & Edwards, C. P. (1988a). *Children in different worlds.* Cambridge, MA: Harvard University Press.

Whiting, B., & Edwards, C. P. (1988b). A cross-cultural analysis of sex differences in the behavior of children aged 3 through 11. In G. Handel (Ed.), *Childhood socialization* (pp. 281–297). New York: Aldine de Gruyter.

Whitington, V., & Ward, C. (1999). Intersubjectivity in caregiver–child communication. In L. E. Berk

(Ed.), *Landscapes of development* (pp. 109–120). Belmont, CA: Wadsworth.

Whitney, M. P., & Thoman, E. B. (1994). Sleep in premature and full-term infants from 24-hour home recordings. *Infant Behavior and Development, 17,* 223–234.

Wichstrøm, L. (1999). The emergence of gender difference in depressed mood: The role of intensified gender socialization. *Developmental Psychology, 35,* 232–245.

Wickham, S. (1999, Summer). Homebirth: What are the issues? *Midwifery Today, 50,* 16–18.

Wigfield, A., & Eccles, J. S. (1994). Children's competence beliefs, achievement values, and genderal self-esteem change across elementary and middle school. *Journal of Early Adolescence, 14,* 107–138.

Wigfield, A., Eccles, J. S., Yoon, K. S., Harold, R. D., Arbreton, A. J., Freedman-Doan, C., & Blumenfeld, P. C. (1997). Changes in children's competence beliefs and subjective task values across the elementary school years: A three-year study. *Journal of Educational Psychology, 89,* 451–469.

Wilcox, A. J., & Skjaerven, R. (1992). Birth weight and perinatal mortality: The effect of gestational age. *American Journal of Public Health, 82,* 378–382.

Wilcox, A. J., Weinberg, C. R., & Baird, D. D. (1995). Timing of sexual intercourse in relation to ovulation: Effects on the probability of conception, survival of the pregnancy, and sex of the baby. *New England Journal of Medicine, 333,* 1517–1519.

Willatts, P. (1999). Development of means–end behavior in young infants: Pulling a support to retrieve a distant object. *Developmental Psychology, 35,* 651–667.

Wille, D. E. (1991). Relation of preterm birth with quality of infant–mother attachment at one year. *Infant Behavior and Development, 14,* 227–240.

Williams, B. C., & Kotch, J. B. (1990). Excess injury mortality among children in the United States: Comparison of recent international statistics. *Pediatrics, 86* (6, Pt. 2), 1067–1073.

Williams, E., & Radin, N. (1993). Paternal involvement, maternal employment, and adolescents' academic achievement: An 11-year follow-up. *American Journal of Orthopsychiatry, 63,* 306–312.

Willner, J. P. (1998). Reproductive genetics and today's patient options: Prenatal diagnosis. *Mount Sinai Journal of Medicine, 65,* 173–177.

Wills, T. A., McNamara, G., Vaccaro, D., & Hirky, A. E. (1996). Escalated substance use: A longitudinal grouping analysis from early to middle adolescence. *Journal of Abnormal Psychology, 105,* 166–180.

Wilson, M. N., Greene-Bates, C., McKim, L., Simmons, T. A., Curry-El, J., & Hinton, I. D. (1995). African American family life: The dynamics of interactions, relationships, and roles. In M. N. Wilson (Ed.), *African American family life: Its structural and ecological aspects* (pp. 5–21). San Francisco: Jossey-Bass.

Wilson, R., & Cairns, E. (1988). Sex-role attributes, perceived competence and the development of depression in adolescence. *Journal of Child Psychology and Psychiatry, 29,* 635–650.

Wilson, W. J. (1991). Studying inner-city social dislocations: The challenge of public agenda research. *American Sociological Review, 56,* 1–14.

Windschitl, M. (1998). The WWW and classroom research: What path should we take? *Educational Researcher, 27*(1), 28-33.

Winkleby, M. A., Robinson, T. N., Sundquist, J., & Kraemer, H. C. (1999). Ethnic variation in cardiovascular disease risk factors among children and young adults. *Journal of the American Medical Association, 281,* 1006–1013.

Winner, E. (1986, August). Where pelicans kiss seals. *Psychology Today, 20*(8), 25–35.

Winner, E. (1988). *The point of words: Children's understanding of metaphor and irony.* Cambridge, MA: Harvard University Press.

Winner, E. (1996). *Gifted children: Myths and realities.* New York: Basic Books.

Winner, E. (1997). Exceptionally high intelligence and schooling. *American Psychologist, 52,* 1070–1081.

Winner, E. (2000). The origins and ends of giftedness. *American Psychologist, 55,* 159–169.

Winsler, A., Diaz, R. M., McCarthy, E. M., Atencio, D. J., & Chabay, L. (1999). Mother–child interaction, private speech, and task performance in preschool children with behavior problems. *Journal of Child Psychology and Psychiatry, 40,* 891–904.

Winsler, A., Diaz, R. M., & Montero, I. (1997). The role of private speech in the transition from collaborative to independent task performance in young children. *Early Childhood Research Quarterly, 12,* 59–79.

Wintre, M. G., & Vallance, D. D. (1994). A developmental sequence in the comprehension of emotions: Intensity, multiple emotions, and valence. *Developmental Psychology, 30,* 509–514.

Wiser, A., Maymon, E., Mazor, M., Shoham-Vardi, I., Silberstein, T., Wiznitzer, A., & Katz, M. (1997). Effect of the Yom Kippur fast on parturition. *Harefuah, 132,* 745–748.

Witelson, S. F., & Kigar, D. L. (1988). Anatomical development of the corpus callosum in humans: A review with reference to sex and cognition. In D. L. Molfese & S. J. Segalowitz (Eds.), *Brain lateralization in children* (pp. 35–57). New York: Guilford Press.

Wolchik, S. A., Wilcox, K. L., Tein, J.-Y., & Sandler, I. N. (2000). Maternal acceptance and consistency of discipline as buffers of divorce stressors on children's psychological adjustment problems. *Journal of Abnormal Child Psychology, 28,* 87–102.

Wolfe, D. A. (1999). *Child abuse* (2nd ed.). Thousand Oaks, CA: Sage.

Wolfe, V. V. (1998). Child sexual abuse. In E. J. Mash (Ed.), *Treatment of childhood disorders* (2nd ed., pp. 545–597). New York, NY: Guilford.

Wolfelt, A. D. (1997). Death and grief in the school setting. In T. N. Fairchild (Ed.), *Crisis intervention strategies for school-based helpers* (2nd ed., pp. 199–244). Springfield, IL: Charles C. Thomas.

Wolff, P. H. (1966). The causes, controls and organization of behavior in the neonate. *Psychological Issues, 5*(1, Serial No. 17).

Wolfson, A. R., & Carskadon, M. A. (1998). Sleep schedules and daytime functioning in adolescents. *Child Development, 69,* 875–887.

Wolpe, J., & Plaud, J. J. (1997). Pavlov's contributions to behavior therapy: The obvious and not so obvious. *American Psychologist, 52,* 966–972.

Wood, D. J. (1989). Social interaction as tutoring. In M. H. Bornstein & J. S. Bruner (Eds.), *Interaction in human development* (pp. 59–80). Hillsdale, NJ: Erlbaum.

Woodward, A. L., Markman, E. M., & Fitzsimmons, C. M. (1994). Rapid word learning in 13- and 18-month-olds. *Developmental Psychology, 30,* 553–566.

Woodward, L. J., & Fergusson, D. M. (1999). Childhood peer relationship problems and psychosocial adjustment in late adolescence. *Journal of Abnormal Child Psychology, 27,* e87.

Woodward, L. J., & Fergusson, D. M. (1999). Early conduct problems and later risk of teenage pregnancy in girls. *Development and Psychopathology, 11,* 127–141.

Woolley, J. D. (1997). Thinking about fantasy: Are children fundamentally different thinkers and believers from adults? *Child Development, 68,* 991–1011.

Woolley, J. D., Phelps, K. E., Davis, D. L., & Mandell, D. J. (1999). Where theories of mind meet magic: The development of children's beliefs about wishing. *Child Development, 70,* 571–587.

Wooster, D. M. (1999). Assessment of nonorganic failure to thrive. *Infant-Toddler Intervention, 9,* 353–371.

World Health Organization. (2000). *The World Health Report, 2000.* Geneva: Author.

Wright, J. C., Huston, A. C., Reitz, A. L., & Piemyat, S. (1994). Young children's perceptions of television reality: Determinants and developmental differences. *Developmental Psychology, 30,* 229–239.

Wright, J. W. (Ed.). (1999). *The universal almanac 1999.* Kansas City: Andrews and McMeel.

Wu, M. M., & Edwards, M. H. (1999). The effect of having myopic parents: An analysis of myopia in three generations. *Optometry and Vision Science, 76,* 387–392.

Wurtele, S. K. (1996). Health promotion. In M. C. Roberts (Ed.), *Handbook of pediatric psychology* (2nd ed., pp. 200–216). New York: Guilford.

Wyman, P. A., Cowen, E. L., Work, W. C., Hoyt-Meyers, L., Magnus, K. B., & Fagen, D. B. (1999). Caregiving and developmental factors differentiating young at-risk urban children showing resilient versus stress-affected outcomes: A replication and extension. *Child Development, 70,* 645–659.

Wynn, K. (1998). Psychological foundations of number: Numerical competence in human infants. *Trends in Cognitive Sciences, 2,* 296–303.

Yang, B., Ollendick, T. H., Dong, Q., Xia, Y., & Lin, L. (1995). Only children and children with siblings in the People's Republic of China: Levels of fear, anxiety, and depression. *Child Development, 66,* 1301–1311.

Yang, E. Y., Flake, A. W., & Adzick, N. S. (1999). Prospects for fetal gene therapy. *Seminars in Perinatology, 23,* 524–534.

Yarrow, M. R., Scott, P. M., & Waxler, C. Z. (1973). Learning concern for others. *Developmental Psychology, 8,* 240–260.

Yates, W. R., Cadoret, R. J., & Troughton, E. P. (1999). The Iowa adoption studies: Methods and results. In M. C. LaBuda & E. L. Grigorenko (Eds.), *On the way to individuality: Current methodological issues in behavioral genetics* (pp. 95–125). Commack, NY: Nova Science Publishers.

Yazigi, R. A., Odem, R. R., & Polakoski, K. L. (1991). Demonstration of specific binding of cocaine to human spermatozoa. *Journal of the American Medical Association, 266,* 1956–1959.

Yeates, K. O., Schultz, L. H., & Selman, R. L. (1991). The development of interpersonal negotiation strategies in thought and action: A social-cognitive link to behavioral adjustment and social status. *Merrill-Palmer Quarterly, 37,* 369–405.

Yesalis, C.E., Barsukiewicz, C.K., Kopstein, A.N., & Bahrke, M.S. (1997). Trends in anabolic–androgenic steroid use among adolescents. *Archives of Pediatrics & Adolescent Medicine, 151,* 1197–1206.

Yip, R., Scanlon, K., & Trowbridge, F. (1993). Trends and patterns in height and weight status of low-income U.S. children. *Critical Reviews in Food Science and Nutrition, 33,* 409–421.

Yirmiya, N., Erel, O., Shaked, M., & Solomonica-Levi, D. (1998). Meta-analyses comparing theory of mind abilities of individuals with autism, individuals with mental retardation, and normally developing individuals. *Psychological Bulletin, 124,* 283–307.

Yirmiya, N., Solomonica-Levi, D., & Shulman, C. (1996). The ability to manipulate behavior and to understand manipulation of beliefs: A comparison of individuals with autism, mental retardation, and normal development. *Developmental Psychology, 32,* 62–69.

Yirmiya, N., & Shulman, C. (1996). Seriation, conservation, and theory of mind abilities in individuals with autism, individuals with mental retardation, and normally developing children. *Child Development, 67,* 2045–2059.

Yogman, M. W. (1981). Development of the father–infant relationship. In H. Fitzgerald, B. Lester, & M. W. Yogman (Eds.), *Theory and research in behavioral pediatrics* (Vol. 1, pp. 221–279). New York: Plenum.

Yonas, A., Granrud, E. C., Arterberry, M. E., & Hanson, B. L. (1986). Infants' distance perception from linear perspective and texture gradients. *Infant Behavior and Development, 9,* 247–256.

Yonas, A., & Hartman, B. (1993). Perceiving the affordance of contact in four- and five-month-old infants. *Child Development, 64,* 298–308.

Youngblade, L. M., & Dunn, J. (1995). Individual differences in young children's pretend play with mother and sibling: Links to relationships and understanding of other people's feelings and beliefs. *Child Development, 66,* 1472–1492.

Younger, B. A. (1985). The segregation of items into categories by ten-month-old infants. *Child Development, 56,* 1574–1583.

Youniss, J. (1980). *Parents and peers in social development: A Piagetian-Sullivan perspective.* Chicago: University of Chicago Press.

Youniss, J., McLellan, J. A., & Yates, M. (1997). What we know about engendering civic identity. *American Behavioral Scientist, 40,* 620–631.

Yuill, N., & Pearson, A. (1998). The developmental bases for trait attribution: Children's understanding of traits as causal mechanisms based on desire. *Developmental Psychology, 34,* 574–586.

Yuill, N., & Perner, J. (1988). Intentionality and knowledge in children's judgments of actor's responsibility and recipient's emotional reaction. *Developmental Psychology, 24,* 358–365.

Zabin, L. S., & Hayward, S. C. (1993). *Adolescent sexual behavior and childbearing.* Newbury Park, CA: Sage.

Zahn-Waxler, C., Kochanska, G., Krupnick, J., & McKnew, D. (1990). Patterns of guilt in children of depressed and well mothers. *Developmental Psychology, 26,* 51–59.

Zahn-Waxler, C., & Radke-Yarrow, M. (1990). The origins of empathic concern. *Motivation and Emotion, 14,* 107–130.

Zahn-Waxler, C., Radke-Yarrow, M., & King, R. M. (1979). Child-rearing and children's prosocial initiations toward victims of distress. *Child Development, 50,* 319–330.

Zahn-Waxler, C., Radke-Yarrow, M., Wagner, E., & Chapman, M. (1992). Development of concern for others. *Developmental Psychology, 28,* 126–136.

Zahn-Waxler, C., & Robinson, J. (1995). Empathy and guilt: Early origins of feelings of responsibility. In J. P. Tangney & K. W. Fischer (Eds.), *Self-conscious emotions* (pp. 143–173). New York: Guilford.

Zajonc, R. B., & Mullally, P. R. (1997). Birth order: Reconciling conflicting effects. *American Psychologist, 52,* 685–699.

Zelazo, N. A., Zelazo, P. R., Cohen, K. M., & Zelazo, P. D. (1993). Specificity of practice effects on elementary neuromotor patterns. *Developmental Psychology, 29,* 686–691.

Zelazo, P. R. (1983). The development of walking: New findings on old assumptions. *Journal of Motor Behavior, 2,* 99–137.

Zeldin, A. L. & Pajares, F. (2000). Against the odds: Self-efficacy beliefs of women in mathematical, scientific, and technological careers. *American Educational Research Journal, 37,* 215–246.

Zeskind, P. S., & Barr, R. G. (1997). Acoustic characteristics of naturally occurring cries of infants with "colic." *Child Development, 68,* 394–403.

Zeskind, P. S., & Ramey, C. T. (1978). Fetal malnutrition: An experimental study of its consequences on infant development in two caregiving environments. *Child Development, 49,* 1155–1162.

Zeskind, P. S., & Ramey, C. T. (1981). Preventing intellectual and interactional sequelae of fetal malnutrition: A longitudinal, transactional, and synergistic approach to development. *Child Development, 52,* 213–218.

Zhou, M. & Bankston, C. L. (1998). *Growing up American: How Vietnamese children adapt to life in the United States.* New York: Russell Sage Foundation.

Zigler, E., & Gilman, E. (1998). The legacy of Jean Piaget. In G. A. Kimble & M. Wertheimer (Eds.), *Portraits of pioneers in psychology* (Vol. 3, pp. 145–160). Washington, DC: American Psychological Association.

Zigler, E., & Hall, N. W. (1989). Physical child abuse in America: Past, present, and future. In D. Cicchetti & V. Carlson (Eds.), *Child maltreatment* (pp. 203–253). New York: Cambridge University Press.

Zigler, E., & Styfco, S. J. (1998). Applying findings of developmental psychology to improve early childhood intervention. In S. G. Paris & H. M. Wellman (Eds.), *Global prospects for education: Development, culture, and schooling* (pp. 345–365). Washington, DC: American Psychological Association.

Zigler, E. F., & Finn-Stevenson, M. (1999). Applied developmental psychology. In M. H. Bornstein & M. E. Lamb (Eds.), *Developmental psychology: An advanced textbook* (4th ed., pp. 555–598). Mahwah, NJ: Erlbaum.

Zigler, E. F., & Finn-Stevenson, M. E. (1992). Applied developmental psychology. In M. H. Bornstein & M. E. Lamb (Eds.), *Developmental psychology: An advanced textbook* (2nd ed., pp. 677–729). Hillsdale, NJ: Erlbaum.

Zigler, E. F., & Hall, N. W. (2000). *Child development and social policy: Theory and applications.* New York: McGraw-Hill.

Zill, N., Davies, E., & Daly, M. (1994). *Viewing of Sesame Street by preschool children in the United States and its relationship to school readiness.* Rockville, MD: Westat.

Zill, N., West, J., & Lomax, J. (1997). *The elementary school performance and adjustment of children who enter kindergarten late or repeat kindergarten: Findings from national surveys.* Washington, DC: National Center for Education Statistics.

Zillman, D., Bryant, J., & Huston, A. C. (1994). *Media, family, and children.* Hillsdale, NJ: Erlbaum.

Zimmerman, B. J., Bonner, S., & Kovach, R. (1996). *Developing self-regulated learners: Beyond achievement to self-efficacy.* Washington, DC: American Psychological Association.

Zimmerman, B. J., & Risemberg, R. (1997). Self-regulatory dimensions of academic learning and motivation. In G. D. Phye (Ed.), *Handbook of academic learning: Construction of knowledge* (pp. 105–125). San Diego: Academic Press.

Zimmerman, M. A., & Arunkumar, R. (1994). Resiliency research: Implications for schools and policy. *Social Policy Report of the Society for Research in Child Development, 8*(4).

Zimmerman, M. A., Copeland, L. A., Shope, J. T., & Dielman, T. E. (1997). A longitudinal study of self-esteem: Implications for adolescent development. *Journal of Youth and Adolescence, 26,* 117–141.

Name Index

Subject Index